The Earth and Its Peoples

A Global History

The Earth and Its Peoples

A Global History

Brief Third Edition

Richard W. Bulliet
Columbia University

Pamela Kyle Crossley
Dartmouth College

Daniel R. Headrick
Roosevelt University

Steven W. Hirsch
Tufts University

Lyman L. Johnson
University of North Carolina–Charlotte

David Northrup
Boston College

Houghton Mifflin Company   Boston   New York

Publisher: Charles Hartford
Senior Sponsoring Editor: Nancy Blaine
Assistant Editor: Christina Lembo
Senior Project Editor: Carol Newman
Editorial Assistant: Robert Woo
Senior Art and Design Coordinator: Jill Haber
Senior Composition Buyer: Sarah Ambrose
Senior Photo Editor: Jennifer Meyer Dare
Senior Designer: Henry Rachlin
Manufacturing Coordinator: Renee Ostrowski
Senior Marketing Manager: Sandra McGuire

Cover illustration: Pictures on tilling and weaving, *The Harvest.* One of eight paintings from a set of forty-six, ink and color on silk after Chiao Ping-chên (1726 or later); The Library of Congress, Washington, D. C. © Laurie Platt Winfrey, Inc.

Printed in U.S.A.

Library of Congress Catalog Card Number: 2004114277

ISBN: 0-618-47114-6

1 2 3 4 5 6 7 8 9—VH—09 08 07 06 05

Brief Contents

PART ONE
The Emergence of Human Communities, to 500 B.C.E.   1

1   From the Origins of Agriculture to the First River-Valley Civilizations, 8000–1500 B.C.E.   4

2   New Civilizations in the Eastern and Western Hemispheres, 2200–250 B.C.E.   37

3   The Mediterranean and Middle East, 2000–500 B.C.E.   61

PART TWO
The Formation of New Cultural Communities, 1000 B.C.E.–600 C.E.   91

4   Greece and Iran, 1000–30 B.C.E./ India, 1500 B.C.E.–550 C.E.   94

5   An Age of Empires: Rome and Han China, 753 B.C.E.–330 C.E.   130

6   Networks of Communication and Exchange, 300 B.C.E.–600 C.E.   154

PART THREE
Growth and Interaction of Cultural Communities, 600–1200   177

7   The Rise of Islam, 600–1200   180

8   Christian Europe Emerges, 600–1200   202

9   Central and Eastern Asia, 400–1200   224

10   Peoples and Civilizations of the Americas, 200–1500   244

PART FOUR
Interregional Patterns of Culture and Contact, 1200–1550   267

11   Mongol Eurasia and Its Aftermath, 1200–1500   270

12   Tropical Africa and Asia, 1200–1500   296

13   The Latin West, 1200–1500   316

14   The Maritime Revolution, to 1550   337

PART FIVE
The Globe Encompassed, 1500–1800   361

15   Transformations in Europe, 1500–1750   364

16   The Americas, the Atlantic, and Africa, 1530–1770   387

17   Southwest Asia and the Indian Ocean, 1500–1750   411

18   Northern Eurasia, 1500–1800   432

PART SIX
Revolutions Reshape the World, 1750–1870   457

19   Revolutionary Changes in the Atlantic World, 1750–1850   460

20   The Early Industrial Revolution, 1760–1851   480

21   Africa, India, and the New British Empire, 1750–1870   498

22   Land Empires in the Age of Imperialism, 1800–1870   518

v

PART SEVEN
**Global Dominance and Diversity,
1850–1949**   545

23 The New Power Balance,
     1850–1900 548

24 The New Imperialism,
     1869–1914 569

25 The Crisis of the Imperial Order,
     1900–1929 596

26 The Collapse of the Old Order,
     1929–1949 619

27 Striving for Independence: Africa,
     India, and Latin America,
     1900–1949 641

PART EIGHT
**The Perils and Promises of a Global
Community, 1945 to the Present**   665

28 The Cold War and Decolonization,
     1945–1975 668

29 Crisis, Realignment, and the Dawn of
     the Post–Cold War World,
     1975–1991 689

30 Globalization at the Turn of the
     Millennium 712

Contents

Maps xvii
Environment and Technology xix
Diversity and Dominance xix
Issues in World History xix
Preface xxi
About the Authors xxvii
Note on Spelling and Usage xxix

**PART ONE
The Emergence of Human
Communities,
to 500 B.C.E.**

1

1 From the Origins of Agriculture to the First River-Valley Civilizations, 8000–1500 B.C.E. 4

Before Civilization 5
Food Gathering and Stone Technology 6 • The Agricultural Revolutions 8 • Life in Neolithic Communities 10

Mesopotamia 13
Settled Agriculture in an Unstable Landscape 14 • Cities, Kings, and Trade 15 • Mesopotamian Society 17 • Gods, Priest, and Temples 18 • Technology and Science 19

Egypt 24
The Land of Egypt: "Gift of the Nile" 24 • Divine Kingship 26 • Administration and Communication 27 • The People of Egypt 28 • Belief and Knowledge 29

The Indus Valley Civilization 31
Natural Environment 31 • Material Culture 31 • Transformation of the Indus Valley Civilization 33

Conclusion 34 / Key Terms 35 / Suggested Reading 35 / Notes 36

■ Diversity and Dominance: Violence and Order in the Babylonian New Year's Festival 20

2 New Civilizations in the Eastern and Western Hemispheres, 2200–250 B.C.E. 37

Early China, 2000–221 B.C.E. 38
Geography and Resources 38 • The Shang Period, ca. 1750–1027 B.C.E. 41 • The Zhou Period, 1027–221 B.C.E. 43 • Confucianism, Daoism, and Chinese Society 44

Nubia, 3100 B.C.E.–350 C.E. 45
Early Cultures and Egyptian Domination, 2300–1100 B.C.E. 48 • The Kingdom of Meroë, 800 B.C.E.–350 C.E. 49

Celtic Europe, 1000–50 C.E. 50
The Spread of the Celts 50 • Celtic Society 51 • Belief and Knowledge 52

First Civilizations of the Americas: The Olmec and Chavín, 1200–250 B.C.E. 53
The Mesoamerican Olmec, 1200–400 B.C.E. 53 • Early South American Civilization: Chavín, 900–250 B.C.E. 56

Conclusion 58 / Key Terms 59 / Suggested Reading 59 / Notes 60

■ Diversity and Dominance: Hierarchy and Conduct in the Analects of Confucius 46

3 The Mediterranean and Middle East, 2000–500 B.C.E. 61

The Cosmopolitan Middle East, 1700–1100 B.C.E. 62
Western Asia 64 • New Kingdom Egypt 65 • Commerce and Communication 68

The Aegean World, 2000–1100 B.C.E. 68
Minoan Crete 68 • Mycenaean Greece 70 • The Fall of Late Bronze Age Civilizations 72

The Assyrian Empire, 911–612 B.C.E. 72
God and King 73 • Conquest and Control 73 • Assyrian Society and Culture 75

Israel, 2000–500 B.C.E. 75
Origins, Exodus, and Settlement 76 • Rise of the Monarchy 78 • Fragmentation and Dispersal 79

**Phoenicia and the Mediterranean,
1200–500 B.C.E.** 80
The Phoenician City-States 80 • Expansion into the
Mediterranean 80 • Carthage's Commercial
Empire 82 • War and Religion 84

Failure and Transformation, 750–550 B.C.E. 85
CONCLUSION 86 / KEY TERMS 87 /
SUGGESTED READING 87 / NOTES 88
■ ENVIRONMENT AND TECHNOLOGY:
Ancient Textiles and Dyes 82
ISSUES IN WORLD HISTORY: Animal
Domestication 89

PART TWO
**The Formation of New Cultural
Communities, 1000 B.C.E.–600 C.E.**
91

4   Greece and Iran, 1000–30 B.C.E./
India, 1500 B.C.E.–550 C.E. 94

Ancient Iran 95
Geography and Resources 95 • The Rise of the
Persian Empire 96 • Imperial Organization and
Ideology 98

The Rise of the Greeks 101
Geography and Resources 101 • The Emergence of
the Polis 104 • New Intellectual Currents 106 •
Athens and Sparta 107

The Struggle of Persia and Greece 109
Early Encounters 109 • The Height of Athenian
Power 110 • Inequality in Classical Greece 111 •
Failure of the City-State and Triumph of the
Macedonians 113

The Hellenistic Synthesis 114

Foundations of Indian Civilization 117
The Indian Subcontinent 117 • The Vedic Age,
1500–500 B.C.E. 118 • Challenges to the Old Order:
Jainism and Buddhism 120 • The Rise of
Hinduism 121

Indian Imperial Expansion and Collapse 123
The Mauryan Empire, 324–184 B.C.E. 123 •
Commerce and Culture in an Era of Political
Fragmentation 124 • The Gupta Empire,
320–550 C.E. 125

CONCLUSION 127 / KEY TERMS 128 /
SUGGESTED READING 128 / NOTES 129
■ DIVERSITY AND DOMINANCE: The Persian Idea of
Kingship 102

**5   An Age of Empires: Rome
and Han China,** 753 B.C.E.–
330 C.E. 130

**Rome's Creation of a Mediterranean Empire,
753 B.C.E.–330 C.E.** 131
A Republic of Farmers 131 • Expansion in Italy
and the Mediterranean 135 • The Failure of the
Republic 136 • An Urban Empire 136 • The
Rise of Christianity 138 • Technology and
Transformation 139

**The Origins of Imperial China,
221 B.C.E.–220 C.E.** 141
Resources and Population 142 • Hierarchy,
Obedience, and Belief 142 • The First Chinese
Empire 144 • The Long Reign of the Han 146 •
Technology and Trade 148 • The Decline of the Han
Empire 150

Imperial Parallels 150

CONCLUSION 152 / KEY TERMS 152 /
SUGGESTED READING 152 / NOTES 153
■ ENVIRONMENT AND TECHNOLOGY:
Water Engineering in Rome and China 146

**6   Networks of Communication
and Exchange,** 300 B.C.E.–
600 C.E. 154

The Silk Road 155
Origins and Operations 155

The Sasanid Empire, 224–600 156
The Impact of the Silk Road 159

The Indian Ocean Maritime System 159
Origins of Contact and Trade 161 • The Impact of
Indian Ocean Trade 161

Routes Across the Sahara 165
Early Saharan Cultures 165 • Trade Across the
Sahara 167

Sub-Saharan Africa 167
A Challenging Geography 167 • The Development
of Cultural Unity 168 • African Cultural
Characteristics 168 • The Advent of Iron and the
Bantu Migrations 169

The Spread of Ideas 170
Ideas and Material Evidence 170 • The Spread of
Buddhism 171 • The Spread of Christianity 172

CONCLUSION 173 / KEY TERMS 173 /
SUGGESTED READING 173 / NOTES 174

■ DIVERSITY AND DOMINANCE: The Indian Ocean
   Trading World 162

ISSUES IN WORLD HISTORY: Oral Societies and the
Consequences of Literacy 175

PART THREE
Growth and Interaction of Cultural Communities, 600 –1200

177

7 The Rise of Islam, 600–1200 180

The Origins of Islam 181
The Arabian Peninsula Before Muhammad 181 •
Muhammad in Mecca 182 • The Formation of the
Umma 184

**The Rise and Fall of the Caliphate,
632–1258** 186
The Islamic Conquests, 634–711 186 • The
Umayyad and Early Abbasid Caliphates,
661–850 187 • Political Fragmentation,
850–1050 188 • Assault from Within and Without,
1050–1258 191

Islamic Civilization 193
Law and Dogma 193 • Converts and Cities 194 •
Islam, Women, and Slaves 195 • The Recentering of
Islam 198

CONCLUSION 199 / KEY TERMS 200 /
SUGGESTED READING 200 / NOTES 201

■ DIVERSITY AND DOMINANCE: Beggars, Con Men and
   Singing-girls 196

8 Christian Europe Emerges,
600–1200 202

The Byzantine Empire, 600–1200 203
An Empire Beleaguered 203 • Society and Urban
Life 204 • Cultural Achievements 206

Early Medieval Europe, 600–1000 206
The Time of Insecurity 207 • A Self-Sufficient
Economy 208 • Early Medieval Society in the
West 209

The Western Church 211
Politics and the Church 212 • Monasticism 213

Kievan Russia, 900–1200 215
The Rise of the Kievan State 215 • Society and
Culture 216

Western Europe Revives, 1000–1200 218
The Role of Technology 218 • Cities and the Rebirth
of the Trade 219

The Crusades, 1095–1204 220
The Roots of the Crusades 220 • The Impact of the
Crusades 221

CONCLUSION 222 / KEY TERMS 222 /
SUGGESTED READING 223 / NOTES 223

■ ENVIRONMENT AND TECHNOLOGY:
   Cathedral Organs 214

9 Central and Eastern Asia,
400–1200 224

The Sui and Tang Empires, 581–755 225
Reunification Under the Sui and Tang 225 •
Buddhism and the Tang Empire 225 • To Chang'an
by Land and Sea 227 • Tang Integration 228

**Fractured Power in Central Asia and China,
to 907** 229
Reaction and Repression 229 • The End of the Tang
Empire 231 • The Uighur and Tibetan Empires in
Central Asia 231

The Emergence of East Asia, to 1200 232
The Liao and Jin Challenge 233 • Song
Industries 233 • Economy and Society 236 •
Essential Partners: Korea, Japan, and Vietnam 238

CONCLUSION 242 / KEY TERMS 243 /
SUGGESTED READING 243 / NOTES 243

■ ENVIRONMENT AND TECHNOLOGY:
   Writing in East Asia, 400–1200 240

10   Peoples and Civilizations of the Americas, 200–1500 244

Classic-Era Culture and Society in Mesoamerica, 200–900 245
Teotihuacan 245 • The Maya 246

The Postclassic Period in Mesoamerica, 900–1500 250
The Toltecs 251 • The Aztecs 251

Northern Peoples 254
Southwestern Desert Cultures 254 • Mound Builders: The Adena, Hopewell, and Mississippian Cultures 255

Andean Civilizations, 200–1500 256
Cultural Response to Environmental Challenge 256 • Moche and Chimú 257 • Tiwanaku and Wari 258 • The Inca 259

CONCLUSION 262 / KEY TERMS 263 / SUGGESTED READING 263 / NOTES 263

■ DIVERSITY AND DOMINANCE: Burials as Historical Texts 260

ISSUES IN WORLD HISTORY: Religious Conversion 265

PART FOUR
Interregional Patterns of Culture and Contact, 1200–1550
267

11   Mongol Eurasia and Its Aftermath, 1200–1500 270

The Rise of the Mongols, 1200–1283 271
Nomadism in Central and Inner Asia 271 • The Mongol Conquests, 1215–1283 272 • Overland Trade and the Plague 274

The Mongols and Islam, 1260–1500 276
Mongol Rivalry 276 • Islam and the State 277 • Culture and Science in Islamic Eurasia 277

Regional Responses in Western Eurasia 279
Russia and Rule from Afar 279 • New States in Eastern Europe and Anatolia 281

Mongol Domination in China, 1271–1368 282
The Yuan Empire, 1279–1368 282 • Cultural and Scientific Exchange 284 • The Fall of the Yuan Empire 284

The Early Ming Empire, 1368–1500 285
Ming China on a Mongol Foundation 285 • Technology and Population 287 • The Ming Achievement 289

Centralization and Militarism in East Asia, 1200–1500 289
Korea from the Mongols to the Yi, 1231–1500 289 • Political Transformation in Japan, 1274–1500 290 • The Emergence of Vietnam, 1200–1500 293

CONCLUSION 294 / KEY TERMS 294 / SUGGESTED READING 294 / NOTES 295

■ ENVIRONMENT AND TECHNOLOGY: From Gunpowder to Guns 288

12   Tropical Africa and Asia, 1200–1500 296

Tropical Lands and Peoples 297
The Tropical Environment 297 • Human Ecosystems 298 • Water Systems and Irrigation 299 • Mineral Resources 300

New Islamic Empires 300
Mali in the Western Sudan 300 • The Delhi Sultanate in India 303

Indian Ocean Trade 306
Monsoon Mariners 306 • Africa: The Swahili and Zimbabwe 307 • Arabia: Aden and the Red Sea 309 • India: Gujarat and the Malabar Coast 310 • Southeast Asia: The Rise of Malacca 311

Social and Cultural Change 311
Architecture, Learning, and Religion 311 • Social and Gender Distinctions 312

CONCLUSION 314 / KEY TERMS 314 / SUGGESTED READING 314 / NOTES 315

■ ENVIRONMENT AND TECHNOLOGY: The Indian Ocean Dhow 308

13 The Latin West,
1200–1500 316

Rural Growth and Crisis 317
Peasants, Population, and Plague 317 • Social
Rebellion 320 • Mills and Mines 320

Urban Revival 322
Trading Cities 322 • Civic Life 324 • Gothic
Cathedrals 325

Learning, Literature, and the Renaissance 325
Universities and Scholarship 328 • Humanists and
Printers 329 • Renaissance Artists 330

Political and Military Transformations 331
Monarchs, Nobles, and the Church 331 • The
Hundred Years War 333 • New Monarchies in
France and England 334 • Iberian Unification 334

CONCLUSION 335 / KEY TERMS 335 /
SUGGESTED READING 335 / NOTES 336

◼ DIVERSITY AND DOMINANCE: Persecution and
Protection of Jews, 1272–1349 326

14 The Maritime Revolution,
to 1550 337

Global Maritime Expansion Before 1450 338
The Pacific Ocean 338 • The Indian
Ocean 340 • The Atlantic Ocean 341

Iberian Expansion, 1400–1550 342
Background to Iberian Expansion 342 • Portuguese
Voyages 343 • Spanish Voyages 345

Encounters with Europe, 1450–1550 348
Western Africa 348 • Eastern Africa 352 • Indian
Ocean States 353 • The Americas 354 • Patterns
of Dominance 356

CONCLUSION 357 / KEY TERMS 357 /
SUGGESTED READING 357 / NOTES 358

◼ DIVERSITY AND DOMINANCE: Kongo's Christian
King 350

ISSUES IN WORLD HISTORY: Climate and Population,
to 1500 359

PART FIVE
The Globe Encompassed,
1500–1800
361

15 Transformations in Europe,
1500–1750 364

Culture and Ideas 365
Religious Reformation 365 • Traditional Thinking
and Witch-Hunts 369 • The Scientific
Revolution 370 • The Early Enlightenment 372

Social and Economic Life 372
The Bourgeoisie 373 • Peasants and
Laborers 375 • Women and the Family 377

Political Innovations 378
State Development 379 • Religious Policies 379 •
Monarchies in England and France 380 • Warfare
and Diplomacy 382 • Paying the Piper 383

CONCLUSION 385 / KEY TERMS 385 /
SUGGESTED READING 386 / NOTES 386

◼ ENVIRONMENT AND TECHNOLOGY:
Mapping the World 376

16 The Americas, The Atlantic,
and Africa, 1530–1770 387

Spanish America and Brazil 388
State and Church 388 • Colonial Economies 391 •
Society in Colonial Latin America 392

**English and French Colonies in North
America** 396
The South 396 • New England 397 • Middle
Atlantic Region 398 • French America 398

Plantations in the West Indies 399
Sugar and Slaves 399 • Technology and
Environment 401

Creating the Atlantic Economy 403
Capitalism and Mercantilism 403 • The Great
Circuit and the Middle Passage 404

Africa and the Atlantic 405
The Gold Coast and the Slave Coast 406 • The Bight
of Biafra and Angola 406

The Columbian Exchange 407
Transfers to the Americas 407 • Transfers from the
Americas 408

CONCLUSION 409 / KEY TERMS 410 /
SUGGESTED READING 410 / NOTES 410

▮ DIVERSITY AND DOMINANCE: Race and Ethnicity in
the Spanish Colonies: Negotiating
Hierarchies 394

---

17   Southwest Asia and the
         Indian Ocean, 1500–1750 411

The Ottoman Empire 412
Expansion and Frontiers 412 • Central
Institutions 415 • Crisis of the Military State, 1585–
1650 416 • Economic Change and Growing
Weakness 417

The Safavid Empire 420
Safavid Society and Religion 421 • Isfahan and
Istanbul 421 • Economic Crisis and Political
Collapse 424

The Mughal Empire 424
Political Foundations 425 • Hindus and
Muslims 425 • Central Decay and Regional
Challenges 426

Trade Empires in the Indian Ocean 427
Muslims in the East Indies 427 • Muslims in East
Africa 429 • The Coming of the Dutch 430

CONCLUSION 430 / KEY TERMS 431 /
SUGGESTED READING 431 / NOTES 431

▮ DIVERSITY AND DOMINANCE: Islamic Law and
Ottoman Rule 418

---

18   Northern Eurasia,
         1500–1800 432

Japanese Reunification 433
Civil War and the Invasion of Korea, 1500–1603
433 • The Tokugawa Shogunate, to 1800 434 •
Japan and the Europeans 434 • Elite Decline and
Social Crisis 437

The Later Ming and Early Qing Empires 438
The Ming Empire, 1500–1644 438 • Ming Collapse
and the Rise of the Qing 439 • Trading Companies
and Missionaries 440 • Emperor Kangxi 440 •
Chinese Influences on Europe 443 • Tea and
Diplomacy 444 • Population and Social Stress 445

The Russian Empire 445
The Drive Across Northern Asia 445 • Russian
Society and Politics to 1725 446 • Peter the
Great 449 • Consolidation of the Empire 450

Comparative Perspectives 451
Political Comparisons 451 • Cultural, Social, and
Economic Comparisons 451

CONCLUSION 452 / KEY TERMS 452 /
SUGGESTED READING 453 / NOTES 454

▮ ENVIRONMENT AND TECHNOLOGY:
East Asian Porcelain 436

ISSUES IN WORLD HISTORY: The Little Ice Age 455

PART SIX
Revolutions Reshape the World,
1750–1870
457

---

19   Revolutionary Changes in the
         Atlantic World, 1750–1850 460

**Prelude to Revolution: War and the
Enlightenment** 461

The American Revolution 462
Frontiers and Taxes 462 • The Course of
Revolution 464 • New Republican Institutions 464

The French Revolution 465
French Society and Fiscal Crisis 465 • Protest
Turns to Revolution 466 • Reaction and
Dictatorship 468 • Retrenchment, Reform, and
Revolution 469

Revolution in Haiti and Latin America 469
The Haitian Revolution 469 • Latin American
Revolutions 471 • Mexico 473

**Economic and Social Liberation
Movements** 475
The Abolition of Slavery 475 • Equal Rights for
Women and Blacks 477

CONCLUSION 478 / KEY TERMS 478 /
SUGGESTED READING 478

▮ ENVIRONMENT AND TECHNOLOGY:
Constructing the Port of Buenos Aires,
Argentina 476

20 The Early Industrial Revolution, 1760–1851 480

Causes of the Industrial Revolution 481
Preconditions for Industrialization 481 • Britain's Advantages 482

The Technological Revolution 484
Mass Production and Mechanization 484 • The Iron Industry 486 • The Steam Engine 487 • Railroads 488 • Communication over Wires 489

The Impact of the Industrial Revolution 489
The New Industrial Cities 490 • Rural Environments 490 • Working Conditions 491 • Changes in Society 492

New Economic and Political Ideas 493
Laissez Faire 493 • Positivism and Utopian Socialism 493 • Protests and Reforms 494 • Emigration 494

Industrialization and the Nonindustrial World 495

CONCLUSION 496 / KEY TERMS 497 / SUGGESTED READING 497 / NOTES 497

■ ENVIRONMENT AND TECHNOLOGY:
The Origin of Graphs 484

21 Africa, India, and the New British Empire, 1750–1870 498

Changes and Exchanges in Africa 499
New African States 499 • Modernization in Egypt and Ethiopia 500 • European Penetration 500 • Secondary Empires in Eastern Africa 504

India Under British Rule 504
Company Men 504 • Raj and Rebellion, 1818–1857 506 • Political Reform and Industrial Impact 507 • Rising Indian Nationalism 509

Britain's Eastern Empire 510
Colonies and Commerce 510 • Imperial Policies and Shipping 511 • Colonization of Australia and New Zealand 512 • New Labor Migrations 513

CONCLUSION 516 / KEY TERMS 517 / SUGGESTED READING 517 / NOTES 517

■ ENVIRONMENT AND TECHNOLOGY:
Whaling 514

22 Land Empires in the Age of Imperialism, 1800–1870 518

The Ottoman Empire 519
Egypt and the Napoleonic Example, 1798–1840 519 • Ottoman Reform and the European Model, 1807–1853 520 • The Crimean War and Its Aftermath, 1853–1877 527

The Russian Empire 529
Russia and Europe 529 • Russia and Asia 531 • Cultural Trends 531

The Qing Empire 532
Economic and Social Disorder, 1800–1839 533 • The Opium War and Its Aftermath, 1839–1850 533 • The Taiping Rebellion, 1850–1864 536 • Decentralization at the End of the Qing Empire, 1864–1875 539

CONCLUSION 540 / KEY TERMS 541 / SUGGESTED READING 541

■ DIVERSITY AND DOMINANCE: The French Occupation of Egypt 522

ISSUES IN WORLD HISTORY: State Power, the Census, and the Question of Identity 542

PART SEVEN
Global Dominance and Diversity, 1850–1949
545

23 The New Power Balance, 1850–1900 548

New Technologies and the World Economy 549
The Steel and Chemical Industries 549 • Electricity 549 • Shipping and Telegraph Cables 550 • Railroads 550 • World Trade and Finance 550

Social Transformations 550
Population and Migrations 552 • Urbanization and Social Structures 552 • Labor Movements and Socialist Politics 552 • Working-Class Women and Men 553 • The Victorian Age and Women's "Separate Sphere" 553

Nationalism and the Unification of Germany 557
National Identity Before 1871 557 • The Unification of Germany 558 • Nationalism After 1871 558

The Great Powers of Europe, 1871–1900 560
Germany at the Center of Europe 560 • The Liberal Powers: France and Great Britain 560 • The Conservative Powers: Russia and Austria-Hungary 560

New Great Powers: The United States and Japan 562
The United States, 1865–1900 562 • The Crisis of the Tokugawa Shogunate 563 • The Meiji Restoration and the Modernization of Japan, 1868–1894 564 • The Birth of Japanese Imperialism, 1894–1905 565

CONCLUSION 567 / KEY TERMS 567 / SUGGESTED READING 567

■ DIVERSITY AND DOMINANCE: Marx and Engels on Global Trade and the Bourgeoisie 554

24   The New Imperialism, 1869–1914 569

The New Imperialism: Motives and Methods 570
Political Motives 570 • Cultural Motives 572 • Economic Motives 574 • The Tools of the Imperialists 574 • Colonial Agents and Administration 575

The Scramble for Africa 577
Egypt 577 • Western and Equatorial Africa 579 • Southern Africa 580 • Political and Social Consequences 581 • Cultural Responses 582

Asia and Western Dominance 583
Central Asia 583 • Southeast Asia and Indonesia 583 • Hawaii and the Philippines, 1878–1902 587

Imperialism in Latin America 589
Railroads and the Imperialism of Free Trade 590 • American Expansionism and the Spanish-American War, 1898 591 • American Intervention in the Caribbean and Central America, 1907–1914 591

The World Economy and the Global Environment 592
Expansion of the World Economy 592 • Transformation of the Global Environment 593

CONCLUSION 594 / KEY TERMS 594 / SUGGESTED READING 594 / NOTES 595

■ DIVERSITY AND DOMINANCE: Two Africans Recall the Arrival of the Europeans 584

25   The Crisis of the Imperial Order, 1900–1929 596

Origins of the Crisis in Europe and the Middle East 597
The Ottoman Empire and the Balkans 597 • Nationalism, Alliances, and Military Strategy 597

The "Great War" and the Russian Revolutions 601
Stalemate, 1914–1917 601 • The Home Front and the War Economy 603 • The Ottoman Empire at War 603 • Double Revolution in Russia, 1917 604 • The End of the War in Western Europe, 1917–1918 605

Peace and Dislocation in Europe 605
The Impact of the War 605 • The Peace Treaties 606 • Russian Civil War and the New Economic Policy 606 • An Ephemeral Peace 607

China and Japan: Contrasting Destinies 608
Revolution in China 608 • Japan and World War I 609 • China in the 1920s 609

The New Middle East 610
The Rise of Modern Turkey 610 • Arab Lands and the Question of Palestine 612

Society, Culture, and Technology in the Industrialized World 612
Class and Gender 613 • Revolution in the Sciences 614 • The New Technologies of Modernity 614 • Technology and the Environment 615

CONCLUSION 617 / KEY TERMS 617 / SUGGESTED READING 617

■ ENVIRONMENT AND TECHNOLOGY: Cities Old and New 598

26   The Collapse of the Old Order, 1929–1949 619

Stalin's Revolution 620
Five-Year Plans 620 • Collectivization of Agriculture 620 • Terror and Opportunities 622

The Depression 623
Economic Crisis 623 • Depression in Industrial
Nations 623 • Depression in Nonindustrial
Regions 623

The Rise of Fascism 626
Mussolini's Italy 626 • Hitler's Germany 627 • The
Road to War, 1933–1939 628

East Asia, 1931–1945 629
The Manchurian Incident of 1931 629 • The
Chinese Communists and the Long March 629 •
The Sino-Japanese War, 1937–1945 630

The Second World War 631
The War of Movement 631 • War in Europe and
North Africa 631 • War in Asia and the
Pacific 632 • The End of the War 634 • Chinese
Civil War and Communist Victory 634

The Character of Warfare 635
The War of Science 635 • Bombing Raids 637 • The
Holocaust 637 • The Home Front 638 • War and
the Environment 638

Conclusion 639 / Key Terms 639 /
Suggested Reading 639

■ Diversity and Dominance: Women, Family Values,
and the Russian Revolution 624

27 Striving for Independence:
Africa, India, and Latin
America, 1900–1949 641

Sub-Saharan Africa, 1900–1945 642
Colonial Africa: Economic and Social Changes 642 •
Religious and Political Changes 644

**The Indian Independence Movement,
1905–1947** 646
The Land and the People 646 • British Rule and
Indian Nationalism 647 • Mahatma Gandhi
and Militant Nonviolence 648 • India Moves
Toward Independence 649 • Partition and
Independence 651

The Mexican Revolution, 1910–1940 652
Mexico in 1910 652 • Revolution and Civil War,
1911–1920 654 • The Revolution Institutionalized,
1920–1940 654

Argentina and Brazil, 1900–1949 656
The Transformation of Argentina 657 • Brazil and
Argentina, to 1929 657 • The Depression and the
Vargas Regime in Brazil 658 • Argentina After
1930 659 • Mexico, Argentina, and Brazil: A
Comparison 660

Conclusion 660 / Key Terms 661 /
Suggested Reading 661 / Notes 661

■ Environment and Technology:
Gandhi and Technology 650

Issues in World History: Famines and
Politics 662

PART EIGHT
The Perils and Promises
of a Global Community, 1945
to the Present
665

28 The Cold War and
Decolonization,
1945–1975 668

The Cold War 669
The United Nations 669 • Capitalism and
Communism 670 • West Versus East in Europe and
Korea 672 • U.S. Defeat in Vietnam 673 • The
Race for Nuclear Supremacy 674

Decolonization and Nation Building 675
New Nations in Southern Asia 675 • The Struggle
for Independence in Africa 675 • The Quest for
Economic Freedom in Latin America 678 •
Challenges of Nation Building 679

Beyond a Bipolar World 679
The Third World 679 • Japan and China 683 •
The Middle East 684 • The Emergence of
Environmental Concerns 687

Conclusion 687 / Key Terms 687 /
Suggested Reading 687

■ Diversity and Dominance: Race and the Struggle
for Justice in South Africa 680

29 Crisis, Realignment, and the Dawn of the Post–Cold War World, 1975–1991 689

Postcolonial Crises and Asian Economic Expansion, 1975–1991 690
Revolutions, Repression, and Democratic Reform in Latin America 690 • Islamic Revolutions in Iran and Afghanistan 693 • Asian Transformation 696

The End of the Bipolar World, 1989–1991 699
Crisis in the Soviet Union 699 • The Collapse of the Socialist Bloc 700 • The Persian Gulf War, 1990–1991 702

The Challenge of Population Growth 703
Demographic Transition 703 • The Industrialized Nations 704 • The Developing Nations 705

Unequal Development and the Movement of Peoples 706
The Problem of Growing Inequality 706 • Internal Migration: The Growth of Cities 706 • Global Migration 707

Technological and Environmental Change 708
New Technologies and the World Economy 708 • Conserving and Sharing Resources 709 • Responding to Environmental Threats 709

CONCLUSION 710 / KEY TERMS 710 / SUGGESTED READING 711 / NOTES 711

■ DIVERSITY AND DOMINANCE: The Struggle for Women's Rights in an Era of Global Political and Economic Change 694

30 Globalization at the Turn of the Millennium 712

Global Political Economies 714
The Spread of Democracy 714 • Global Politics 716 • Arms Control and Terrorism 717 • The Global Economy 718 • Managing the Global Economy 720

Trends and Visions 722
A New Age? 722 • Militant Islam 722 • Universal Rights and Values 723 • Women's Rights 725

Global Culture 726
The Media and the Message 727 • The Spread of Pop Culture 729 • The Emerging Global Elite Culture 730 • Enduring Cultural Diversity 731

CONCLUSION 732 / KEY TERMS 732 / SUGGESTED READING 733 / NOTES 733

■ ENVIRONMENT AND TECHNOLOGY: Global Warming 726

GLOSSARY G-1

INDEX I-1

Maps

1.1 River-Valley Civilizations, 3500–
   1500 B.C.E. 12
1.2 Ancient Egypt 24

2.1 China in the Shang and Zhou Periods,
   1750–221 B.C.E. 40
2.2 Olmec and Chavín Civilizations 54

3.1 The Middle East in the Second
   Millennium B.C.E. 65
3.2 Colonization of the Mediterranean 81

4.1 Hellenistic Civilization 115
4.2 Ancient India 118

5.1 The Roman Empire 132
5.2 Han China 143

6.1 Asian Trade and Communication
   Routes 158
6.2 Africa and the Trans-Saharan Trade
   Routes 164

7.1 Rise and Fall of the Abbasid
   Caliphate 189

8.1 Germanic Kingdoms 207
8.2 Kievan Russia and Byzantine Empire in
   the Eleventh Century 217

9.1 The Tang Empire in Inner and Eastern
   Asia, 750 226
9.2 Jin and Southern Song Empires,
   ca. 1200 234

10.1 Major Mesoamerican Civilizations,
   1000 B.C.E.–1519 C.E. 248
10.2 Andean Civilizations, 200 B.C.E.–
   1532 C.E. 256

11.1 The Mongol Domains in Eurasia
   in 1300 275
11.2 The Ming Empire and Its Allies,
   1368–1500 286

12.1 Africa, 1200–1500 302
12.2 South and Southeast Asia,
   1200–1500 304

13.1 Europe in 1453 332

14.1 Exploration and Settlement in the Indian
   and Pacific Oceans Before 1500 340
14.2 European Exploration, 1420–1542 346

15.1 Religious Reformation in Europe 368
15.2 Europe in 1740 384

16.1 Colonial Latin America in the Eighteenth
   Century 390

17.1 Muslim Empires in the Sixteenth and
   Seventeenth Centuries 414
17.2 European Colonization in the Indian
   Ocean to 1750 428

18.1 The Qing Empire, 1644–1783 441
18.2 The Expansion of Russia, 1500–1800 448

19.1 Napoleon's Europe, 1810 470
19.2 Latin America by 1830 474

20.1 The Industrial Revolution in Britain, ca.
   1850 482

21.1 Africa in the Nineteenth Century 502
21.2 India, 1707–1805 505

22.1 The Ottoman and Russian Empires,
   1829–1914 525
22.2 Conflicts in the Qing Empire,
   1839–1870 535

23.1 The Unification of Germany,
   1866–1871 559
23.2 Expansion and Modernization of Japan,
   1868–1918 566

24.1 Africa in 1878 and 1914 578
24.2 Asia in 1914 588

25.1 The First World War in Europe   600
25.2 Territorial Changes in the Middle East After World War I   611

26.1 World War II in Europe and North Africa   633
26.2 World War II in Asia and the Pacific   636

27.1 The Mexican Revolution   655

28.1 Decolonization, 1947–1999   676
28.2 Middle East Oil and the Arab-Israeli Conflict, 1947–1973   685

29.1 The End of Soviet Domination in Eastern Europe   701
29.2 The End of the Soviet Union   702

30.1 Regional Trade Associations, 2004   721

Environment And Technology

Ancient Textiles and Dyes   82
Water Engineering in Rome and China   146
Cathedral Organs   214
Writing in East Asia, 400–1200   240
From Gunpowder to Guns   288
The Indian Ocean Dhow   308
Mapping the World   376
East Asian Porcelain   436

Constructing the Port of Buenos Aires,
  Argentina   476
The Origin of Graphs   484
Whaling   514
Cities Old and New   598
Gandhi and Technology   650
Global Warming   726

Diversity and Dominance

Violence and Order in the Babylonian New
  Year's Festival   20
Hierarchy and Conduct in the Analects of
  Confucius   46
The Persian Idea of Kingship   102
The Indian Ocean Trading World   162
Beggars, Con Men and Singing-girls   196
Burials as Historical Texts   260
Persecution and Protection of Jews,
  1272–1349   326
Kongo's Christian King   350
Race and Ethnicity in the Spanish Colonies:
  Negotiating Hierarchy   394

Islamic Law and Ottoman Rule   418
The French Occupation of Egypt   522
Marx and Engels on Global Trade and the
  Bourgeoisie   554
Two Africans Recall the Arrival of the
  Europeans   584
Women, Family Values, and the Russian
  Revolution   624
Race and the Struggle for Justice in South
  Africa   680
The Struggle for Women's Rights in an Era of
  Global Political and Economic Change   694

Issues in World History

Animal Domestication   89
Oral Societies and the Consequences of
  Literacy   175
Religious Conversion   265
Climate and Population, to 1500   359

The Little Ice Age   455
State Power, the Census, and the Question of
  Identity   542
Famines and Politics   662

Preface

Reaching the point of preparing the third edition of a textbook is particularly gratifying for its authors. The sustained appeal of their writing tells them that they have done something good and useful. But that in turn prompts them to ponder what they can do to make their book still better. Fortunately, feedback from teachers and students provides a regular stream of helpful suggestions. We have tried to respond to the most frequent and constructive of these suggestions in preparing the third edition.

Varying rationales prompt different teachers to prefer the Brief Edition of *The Earth and Its Peoples*. Some feel that a shorter text makes room for more supplementary reading. Some find it more suitable to the students in their particular classrooms. Some find that a reduced number of chapters better fits their academic schedule. Thus the job of revising the Brief Edition to accommodate the changes introduced in the third edition of the comprehensive text is one of balancing change with adherence to the continuing goal of providing a significantly shorter text for those users who prefer this option.

The Brief Edition is produced in two formats: A complete edition covers the entire chronology from prehistory to the present, and a two-volume edition can be used for the two-semester survey. Volume I covers the period from prehistory to 1550 and Volume II covers 1500 to the present. There is a brief introduction to Volume II that orients students to the general political and social climate of the world at 1500.

Our overall goal of *The Earth and Its Peoples* remains unchanged: to produce a textbook that not only speaks for the past, but speaks to today's student and today's teacher. Students and instructors alike should take away from this text a broad vision of human societies beginning as sparse and disconnected communities reacting creatively to local circumstances; experiencing ever more intensive stages of contact, interpenetration, and cultural expansion and amalgamation; and arriving at a twenty-first century world situation in which people increasingly visualize a single global community.

Process, not progress, is the keynote of this book: a steady process of change over time, at first differently experienced in various regions, but eventually interconnecting peoples and traditions from all parts of the globe. Students should come away from this book with a sense that the problems and promises of their world are rooted in a past in which people of every sort, in every part of the world, confronted problems of a similar character and coped with them as best they could. We believe our efforts will help students see where their world has come from and learn thereby something useful for their own lives.

Central Themes

We have subtitled *The Earth and Its Peoples* "A Global History" because the book explores the common challenges and experiences that unite the human past. Although the dispersal of early humans to every liveable environment resulted in a myriad different economic, social, political, and cultural systems, all societies displayed analogous patterns in meeting their needs and exploiting their environments. Our challenge was to select the particular data and episodes that would best illuminate these global patterns of human experience.

To meet this challenge, we adopted two themes to serve as the spinal cord of our history: "technology and the environment," and "diversity and dominance." The former represents the commonplace material bases of all human societies at all times. It grants no special favor to any cultural group even as it embraces subjects of the broadest topical, chronological, and geographical range. The latter expresses the reality that every human society has constructed or inherited structures of domination, whether political, religious, or cultural, but simultaneously recognizes that alternative lifestyles and visions of societal organization continually manifest themselves both within and in dialogue with every structure of domination.

With respect to "technology and the environment," it is vital for students to understand that technology, in the broad sense of experience-based knowledge of the physical world, underlies all human activity. Writing is a technology, but so is oral transmission from generation to generation of lore about medicinal or poisonous plants. The magnetic compass is a navigational technology, but so is a Polynesian mariner's hard-won knowledge of winds, currents, and tides that made possible the settlement of the Pacific islands.

All technological development, moreover, has come about in interaction with environments, both physical and human, and has, in turn, affected those environments. The story of how humanity has changed the face of the globe is an integral part of this central theme.

Yet technology and the environment do not by themselves explain or underlie all important episodes of human change and experience. In keeping with the theme of "diversity and dominance," discussions of politics, culture, and society interweave with our presentation of the material base of human society to reveal additional historical patterns. Thus when narrating the histories of empires, we describe a range of human experiences within and beyond the imperial frontiers without assuming that the imperial institutions are a more fit topic for discussion than the economic and social organization of pastoral nomads or the life patterns of peasant women. And when religious and cultural traditions occupy our narrative, our primary concern is to complement descriptive presentation with commentary on cultural alternatives within the societies in question.

Changes in the Third Edition

This third Brief Edition retains the main structural features of its predecessors, but also incorporates the most important of the changes made in the comprehensive text:

A new primary source feature, "Diversity and Dominance," has replaced the brief "Society and Culture" excerpts of the previous edition. The fea-ture gives students extended documentary selections on which to hone their analytical skills, encouraging them to consider the many forms of dominance that have developed over time and the many ways in which human diversity has continued to express itself regardless of these forms of dominance. The topics covered range from "Hierarchy and Conduct in the Analects of Confucius" (Chapter 2) to "Two Africans Recall the Arrival of the Europeans" (Chapter 24).

"Issues in World History" is a new feature comprised of original essays that appear at the end of Parts One through Seven. As we surveyed the burgeoning field of global history, we became aware of issues of such broad significance that they could not easily be discussed in a chapter concentrating on a specific time and place. We therefore highlight seven of these issues in part-ending essays, addressing topics that range from "Animal Domestication," to "Famines and Politics."

Chapters 2 and 3 have been rethought and reorganized: Chapter 2 now deals with several civilizations that emerged independently in different parts of the world in the second and first millennia B.C.E., while Chapter 3 focuses on the same time period in Western Asia and the Mediterranean, giving greater stress to continuity and interaction in that region.

Chapter 8, on early medieval Europe, has been reorganized so that it opens with Byzantium and then proceeds to western Europe.

We have greatly increased the coverage of Russian history, including an expanded discussion in Chapter 18 and a section in the new Chapter 22, "Land Empires in the Age of Imperialism, 1800–1870."

The history and impact of the Mongols are now covered in a single chapter, Chapter 11, "Mongol Eurasia and Its Aftermath, 1200–1500." This combination allowed us to make more evident the parallels and contrasts between the impact of the Mongols in the west and in the east.

The discussion in Chapter 23 of the modernization of late nineteenth century Japan has been expanded into three sections.

The final chapter, Chapter 30, "Globalization at the Turn of the Millennium," has been entirely rewritten to reflect current developments in global politics, the global economy, and global culture.

The terrorist attacks of September 11 and the responses to them receive special attention.

Organization

The Earth and Its Peoples, Brief Edition uses eight broad chronological divisions to define its conceptual scheme of global historical development. In **Part One: The Emergence of Human Communities, to 500 B.C.E.,** we examine important patterns of human communal organization. Small, dispersed human communities living by foraging spread to most parts of the world over tens of thousands of years. They responded to enormously diverse environmental conditions, at different times and in different ways discovering how to cultivate plants and utilize the products of domestic animals. On the basis of these new modes of sustenance, population grows, permanent towns appear, and political and religious authority, based on collection and control of agricultural surpluses, spreads over extensive areas.

Part Two: The Formation of New Cultural Communities, 1000 B.C.E.–600 C.E., introduces the concept of a "cultural community," in the sense of a coherent pattern of activities and symbols pertaining to a specific human community. While all human communities develop distinctive cultures, including those discussed in Part One, historical development in this stage of global history prolonged and magnified the impact of some cultures more than others. In the geographically contiguous African-Eurasian land mass, the cultures that proved to have the most enduring influence traced their roots to the second and first millennia B.C.E.

Part Three: Growth and Interaction of Cultural Communities, 600–1200, deals with early episodes of technological, social, and cultural exchange and interaction on a continental scale both within and beyond the framework of imperial expansion. These are so different from earlier interactions arising from more limited conquests or extensions of political boundaries that they constitute a distinct era in world history, an era that set the world on the path of increasing global interaction and interdependence that it has been following ever since.

In Part Four: Interregional Patterns of Culture and Contact, 1200–1550, we take a look at the world during three centuries that saw both intensified cultural and commercial contact and increasingly confident self-definition of cultural communities in Europe, Asia, and Africa. The Mongol conquest of a vast empire extending from the Pacific Ocean to eastern Europe greatly stimulated trade and interaction. In the West, strengthened European kingdoms began maritime expansion in the Atlantic, forging direct ties with sub-Saharan Africa and laying the base for expanded global contacts after 1500.

Part Five: The Globe Encompassed, 1500–1800, treats a period dominated by the global effects of European expansion and continued economic growth. European ships took over, expanded, and extended the maritime trade of the Indian Ocean, coastal Africa, and the Asian rim of the Pacific Ocean. This maritime commercial enterprise had its counterpart in European colonial empires in the Americas and a new Atlantic trading system. The contrasting capacities and fortunes of traditional land empires and new maritime empires, along with the exchange of domestic plants and animals between the hemispheres, underline the technological and environmental dimensions of this first era of complete global interaction.

In Part Six: Revolutions Reshape the World, 1750–1870, the word revolution is used in several senses: in the political sense of governmental overthrow, as in France and the Americas; in the metaphorical sense of radical transformative change, as in the Industrial Revolution; and in the broadest sense of a perception of a profound change in circumstances and worldview. Technology and environment lie at the core of these developments. With the rapid ascendancy of the Western belief that science and technology could overcome all challenges, technology became not only an instrument of transformation but also an instrument of domination, to the point of threatening the integrity and autonomy of cultural traditions in nonindustrial lands.

Part Seven: Global Dominance and Diversity, 1850–1949, examines the development of a world arena in which people conceived of events on a global scale. Imperialism, world war, international economic connections, and world-encompassing ideological tendencies, like nationalism and socialism, present the picture of a globe becoming increasingly interconnected. European dominance took on a worldwide dimension, seeming at times to threaten the diversity of human cultural experience with permanent subordination to European values and philosophies, while at other times triggering strong political or cultural resistance. The accelerating pace of technological change deepened other sorts of cleavages as well.

For Part Eight: The Perils and Promises of a Global Community, 1945 to the Present, we decided to divide the last half of the twentieth century into three time periods: 1945 to 1975, 1975 to 1991, and 1991 to the present. Nevertheless, there is a good deal of continuity from chapter to chapter. The challenges of the Cold War and post-colonial nation building dominate the period and involve global economic, technological, and political forces that become increasingly important factors in all aspects of human life. Technology plays a central role in this part both because of its integral role in the growth of a global community and because its many benefits in improving the quality of life seem clouded by real and potential negative impacts on the environment.

Supplements

In keeping with Houghton Mifflin's goal of being your primary source for history, we are proud to announce the History Companion, your new primary source for history technology solutions. The History Companion has three components:

The *Instructor Companion* is an easily searchable CD-ROM that makes hundreds of historical images and maps instantly accessible in Power-Point format. Each image is accompanied by notes that place it in its proper historical context and tips for ways it can be presented in the classroom. This CD is free to instructors with the adoption of this or any Houghton Mifflin history textbook. It also includes our HM Testing program, a computerized version of the Test Items to enable instructors to alter, replace, or add questions, and the Instructor's Resource Manual, both of which have been thoroughly revised by John Reisbord (Ph.D. Northwestern University). You can also access all of these resources, with the exception of the testing material, on the text's Instructor Companion Website. To reach the site, logon to history.college.hmco.com/instructors and select this book.

The *Student Research Companion* is a free Internet-based tool with 100 interactive maps and 500 primary sources. The primary sources include headnotes that provide pertinent background information and questions that students can answer and email to their instructors. To access the site, logon to history.college.hmco.com/students and select this book.

The *Student Study Companion* is a free online study guide that contains ACE self-tests, which feature multiple-choice questions with feedback, an audio pronunciation guide, web-based flashcards, internet exercises, and web links. These study tools will help your students succeed in the classroom. To access the site, logon to history .college.hmco.com/students and select this book.

The Earth and Its Peoples, Brief, 3/e has robust *Blackboard and Web CT* cartridges with all of our instructional and study assets for easy use at institutions using these platforms.

Acknowledgments

As always we are grateful to the following colleagues who took the time to review and comment upon *The Earth and Its Peoples:* Henry Abramson, Florida Atlantic University; Joseph Adams, Walton High School, Cobb County, Georgia; Paul V. Adams, Shippensburg University/University of San Carlos; Siamak Adhami, Saddleback College; William H. Alexander, Norfolk State University; Maria S. Arbelaez, University of Nebraska at Omaha; Monty Armstrong, Cerritos High School, Cerritos, California; William J. Astore, United States Air Force Academy; David G. Atwill, Pennsylvania State University; Lawrence Backlund, Montgomery County Community College; Fritz Blackwell, Washington State University; Corinne Blake, Rowan University; Olwyn M. Blouet, Virginia State University; Eric Bobo, Hinds Community College; Thomas Borstelmann, Cornell University; James Boyden, Tulane University; Byron Cannon, University of Utah; Bruce Castleman, San Diego State University; Craige B. Champion, Syracuse University; David A. Chappell, University of Hawaii; Nancy Clark, California Polytechnic State University at San Luis Obispo; Aaron Cohen, California State University, Sacramento; Eleanor A. Congdon, Youngstown State University; Lee Congdon, James Madison University; James Coolsen, Shippensburg University; Ransom P. Cross, University of Texas at El Paso; Bruce Cruikshank, Hastings College; Philip Daileader, The College of William and Mary; Linda T. Darling, University of Arizona; Susan Deans-Smith, University of Texas at Austin; Gregory C. Ference, Salisbury State University; Alan Fisher, Michigan State University; Donald M. Fisher, Niagara County Community College; Nancy Fitch, California State University, Fullerton; Cathy A. Frierson, University of New Hampshire; Jeffrey S. Gaab, SUNY College at Farmingdale; Rosanna Gatens, Belmont University; Lorne E. Glaim, Pacific Union College; Matthew S. Gordon, Miami University; Steve Gosch, University of Wisconsin at Eau Claire; Kolleen M. Guy, University of Texas at San Antonio; James R. Hansen, Auburn University; Jay Harmon, Catholic High School, Baton Rouge, Louisiana; Randolph C. Head, University of California at Riverside; David Hertzel, Southwestern Oklahoma State University; Catherine Higgs, University of Tennessee; Richard J. Hoffman, San Francisco State University; Amy J. Johnson, Berry College; Catherine M. Jones, North Georgia College and State University; Joy Kammerling, Eastern Illinois University; Carol A. Keller, San Antonio College; Hal Langfur, University of North Carolina, Wilmington; Jonathan Lee, San Antonio College; Miriam R. Levin, Case Western Reserve University; Richard Lewis, St. Cloud State University; James E. Lindsay, Colorado State University; Susan Maneck, Jackson State University; Laurie S. Mannino, Magruder High School, North Potomac, Maryland; Margaret Malamud, New Mexico State University; Dorothea A.L. Martin, Appalachian State University; Charles W. McClellan, Radford University; Andrea McElderry, University of Louisville; Stephen L. McFarland, Auburn University; Randall McGowen, University of Oregon; Margaret McKee, Castilleja School, Palo Alto, California; Mark McLeod, University of Delaware; Gregory McMahon, University of New Hampshire; Stephen S. Michot, Mississippi County Community College; Shawn W. Miller, Brigham Young University; Stephen Morillo, Wabash College; Kalala Joseph Ngalamulume, Central Washington University; Peter A. Ngwafu, Albany State University; Patricia O'Neill, Central Oregon Community College; Chandrika Paul, Shippensburg University; John R. Pavia, Ithaca College; Thomas Earl Porter, North Carolina A&T State University; Diethelm Prowe, Carleton College; Jean H. Quataert, SUNY at Binghamton; Stephen Rapp, Georgia State University; William Reddy, Duke University; Thomas Reeves, Roxbury Community College; Dennis Reinhartz, University of Texas at Arlington; Richard Rice, University of Tennessee at Chattanooga; Michael D. Richards, Sweet Briar College; Jane Scimeca, Brookdale Community College; William Schell, Murray State University; Alyssa Goldstein Sepinwall, California State University at San Marcos; Deborah Shackleton, United States Air Force Academy; Anita Shelton, Eastern Illinois University; Jeffrey M. Shumway, Brigham Young University; Jonathan Skaff, Shippensburg University of Pennsylvania; David R. Smith, California State Polytechnic University at Pomona; Linda Smith, Samford University; Mary Frances Smith, Ohio University; George E. Snow, Shippensburg University; Charlotte D. Staelin, Washington College; Tracy L. Steele, Sam Houston State University; Paul D. Steeves, Stetson University; Robert Shannon Sumner, State University of West Georgia; Yi Sun, University of San Diego; Willard Sunderland, University of Cincinnati; Karen Sundwick, Southern Oregon University; Thaddeus Sunseri, Colorado State University; Sara W. Tucker, Washburn University; David J. Ulbrich, Temple University; John M. VanderLippe, SUNY at New Paltz; Mary A. Watrous-Schlesinger, Washington State University; James A. Wood, North Carolina A&T State University; Eric Van Young, University of California at San Diego; Peter von Sivers, University of Utah; and Alex Zukas, National University, San Diego.

We also want to extend our thanks to Lynda Schaffer for her early conceptual contributions and to the history departments of Shippensburg University, the United States Air Force Academy, and the State University of New York at New Paltz for arranging reviewer conferences that provided crucial feedback for our revisions.

We thank also the many students whose questions and concerns, expressed directly or through their instructors, shaped much of this revision. We continue to welcome all our readers' suggestions, queries, and criticisms. Please contact us at our respective institutions or at this e-mail address: college_history@hmco.com.

About the Authors

Richard W. Bulliet Professor of Middle Eastern History at Columbia University, Richard W. Bulliet received his Ph.D. from Harvard University. He has written scholarly works on a number of topics: the social history of medieval Iran *(The Patricians of Nishapur)*, the historical competition between pack camels and wheeled transport *(The Camel and the Wheel)*, the process of conversion to Islam *(Conversion to Islam in the Medieval Period)*, and the overall course of Islamic social history *(Islam: The View from the Edge)*. He is the editor of the *Columbia History of the Twentieth Century*. He has published four novels, co-edited *The Encyclopedia of the Modern Middle East*, and hosted an educational television series on the Middle East. He was awarded a fellowship by the John Simon Guggenheim Memorial Foundation.

Pamela Kyle Crossley Pamela Kyle Crossley received her Ph.D. in Modern Chinese History from Yale University. She is Professor of History and Rosenwald Research Professor in the Arts and Sciences at Dartmouth College. Her books include *A Translucent Mirror: History and Identity in Qing Imperial Ideology; The Manchus; Orphan Warriors: Three Manchu Generations and the End of the Qing World;* and (with Lynn Hollen Lees and John W. Servos) *Global Society: The World Since 1900.* Her research, which concentrates on the cultural history of China, Inner Asia, and Central Asia, has been supported by the John Simon Guggenheim Memorial Foundation and the National Endowment for the Humanities.

Daniel R. Headrick Daniel R. Headrick received his Ph.D. in History from Princeton University. Professor of History and Social Science at Roosevelt University in Chicago, he is the author of several books on the history of technology, imperialism, and international relations, including *The Tools of Empire: Technology and European Imperialism in the Nineteenth Century; The Tentacles of Progress: Technology Transfer in the Age of Imperialism; The Invisible Weapon: Telecommunications and International Politics;* and *When Information Came of Age: Technologies of Knowledge in the Age of Reason and Revolution, 1700–1850.* His articles have appeared in the *Journal of World History* and the *Journal of Modern History,* and he has been awarded fellowships by the National Endowment for the Humanities, the John Simon Guggenheim Memorial Foundation, and the Alfred P. Sloan Foundation.

Steven W. Hirsch Steven W. Hirsch holds a Ph.D. in Classics from Stanford University and is currently Associate Professor Classics and History at Tufts University. He has received grants from the National Endowment for the Humanities and the Massachusetts Foundation for Humanities and Public Policy. His research and publications include *The Friendship of the Barbarians: Xenophon and the Persian Empire,* as well as articles and reviews in the *Classical Journal,* the *American Journal of Philology,* and the *Journal of Interdisciplinary History.* He is currently working on a comparative study of ancient Mediterranean and Chinese civilizations.

Lyman L. Johnson Professor of History at the University of North Carolina at Charlotte, Lyman L. Johnson earned his Ph.D. in Latin American History from the University of Connecticut. A two-time Senior Fulbright-Hays Lecturer, he also has received fellowships from the Tinker Foundation, the Social Science Research Council, the National Endowment for the Humanities, and the American Philosophical Society. His recent books include *Death, Dismemberment, and Memory; The Faces of Honor* (with Sonya Lipsett-Rivera); *The Problem of Order in Changing Societies; Essays on the Price History of Eighteenth-Century Latin America* (with Enrique Tandeter); and *Colonial Latin America* (with Mark A. Burkholder). He also has published in journals, including the *Hispanic American Historical Review,* the *Journal of Latin American Studies,* the *International Review of Social History, Social History,* and *Desarrollo Económico.* He recently served as president of the Conference on Latin American History.

David Northrup Professor of History at Boston College, David Northrup earned his Ph.D. in African and European History from the University of California at Los Angeles. He earlier taught in Nigeria with the Peace Corps and at Tuskegee Institute. Research supported by the Fulbright-Hays Commission, the National Endowment for the Humanities, and the Social Science Research Council led to publications concerning pre-colonial Nigeria, the Congo (1870–1940), the Atlantic slave trade, and Asian, African, and Pacific Islander indentured labor in the nineteenth century. A contributor to the *Oxford History of the British Empire* and *Blacks in the British Empire,* his latest book is *Africa's Discovery of Europe, 1450–1850.* For 2004 and 2005 he serves as president of the World History Association.

Note on Spelling and Usage

Where necessary for clarity, dates are followed by the letters C.E. or B.C.E. The abbreviation C.E. stands for "Common Era" and is equivalent to A.D. (*anno Domini,* Latin for "in the year of the Lord"). The abbreviation B.C.E stands for "before the Common Era" and means the same as B.C. ("before Christ"). In keeping with our goal of approaching world history without special concentration on one culture or another, we chose these neutral abbreviations as appropriate to our enterprise. Because many readers will be more familiar with English than with metric measurements, however, units of measure are generally given in the English system, with metric equivalents following in parentheses.

In general, Chinese has been romanized according to the *pinyin* method. Exceptions include proper names well established in English (e.g., Canton, Chiang Kai-shek) and a few English words borrowed from Chinese (e.g., kowtow). Spellings of Arabic, Ottoman Turkish, Persian, Mongolian, Manchu, Japanese, and Korean names and terms avoid special diacritical marks for letters that are pronounced only slightly differently in English. An apostrophe is used to indicate when two Chinese syllables are pronounced separately (e.g., Chang'an).

For words transliterated from languages that use the Arabic script—Arabic, Ottoman Turkish, Perisan, Urdu—the apostrophe indicating separately pronounced syllables may represent either of two special consonants, the *hamza* or the *ain.* Because most English-speakers do not hear the distinction between these two, they have not been distinguished in transliteration and are not indicated when they occur at the beginning or end of a word. As with Chinese, some words and commonly used place-names from these languages are given familiar English spellings (e.g., Quran instead of Qur'an, Cairo instead of al-Qahira). Arabic romanization has normally been used for terms relating to Islam, even where the context justifies slightly different Turkish or Persian forms, again for ease of comprehension.

Before 1492 the inhabitants of the Western Hemisphere had no single name for themselves. They had neither a racial consciousness nor a racial identity. Identity was derived from kin groups, language, cultural practices, and political structures. There was no sense that physical similarities created a shared identity. America's original inhabitants had racial consciousness and racial identity imposed on them by conquest and the occupation of their lands by Europeans after 1492. All of the collective terms for these first American peoples are tainted by this history. *Indians, Native Americans, Amerindians, First Peoples, and Indigenous Peoples* are among the terms in common usage. In this book the names of individual cultures and states are used wherever possible. *Amerindian* and other terms that suggest transcultural identity and experience are used most commonly for the period after 1492.

There is an ongoing debate about how best to render Amerindian words in English. It has been common for authors writing in English to follow Mexican usage for Nahuatl and Yucatec Maya words and place-names. In this style, for example, the capital of the Aztec state is spelled Tenochtitlán, and the important late Maya city-state is spelled Chichén Itzá. Although these forms are still common even in the specialist literature, we have chosen to follow the scholarship that sees these accents as unnecessary. The exceptions are modern place-names, such as Mérida and Yucatán, which are accented. A similar problem exists for the spelling of Quechua and Aymara words from the Andean region of South America. Although there is significant disagreement among scholars, we follow the emerging consensus and use the spellings khipu (not quipu), Tiwanaku (not Tiahuanaco), and Wari (not Huari). However, we keep Inca (not Inka) and Cuzco (not Cusco), since these spellings are expected by most of our potential readers and we hope to avoid confusion.

The Earth and Its Peoples

A Global History

PART ONE

The Emergence of Human Communities, to 500 B.C.E.

CHAPTER 1
From the Origins of Agriculture to the First River-Valley Civilizations, 8000–1500 B.C.E.

CHAPTER 2
New Civilizations in the Eastern and Western Hemispheres, 2200–250 B.C.E.

CHAPTER 3
The Mediterranean and Middle East, 2000–500 B.C.E.

Around 10,000 years ago, some human groups in various parts of the world began to cultivate plants, domesticate animals, and make pottery vessels for storage. One consequence of this shift from hunting and gathering to agriculture was the emergence of permanent settlements—at first small villages but eventually larger towns as well.

The earliest complex societies arose in the great river valleys of Asia and Africa, around 3100 B.C.E. in the valley between the Tigris and Euphrates Rivers in Mesopotamia and along the Nile River in Egypt, somewhat later in the valley of the Indus River in Pakistan, and on the floodplain of the Yellow River in China. In these arid regions, agriculture depended on irrigation with river water, and centers of political power arose to organize the massive human labor required to dig and maintain channels to carry water to the fields.

Kings and priests dominated these early societies. Kings controlled the military forces; priests managed the temples and the wealth of the gods. Within the urban centers—in the midst of palaces, temples, fortification walls, and other monumental buildings—lived administrators, soldiers, priests, merchants, craftsmen, and others with specialized skills. The production of surplus food grown on rural estates by a dependent peasantry sustained the activities of these groups. Professional scribes kept administrative and financial records and preserved their civilization's religious and scientific knowledge.

Over time, certain centers extended their influence and came to dominate broad expanses of territory. The rulers of these early empires were motivated primarily by the need to secure access to raw materials, especially tin and copper, from which to make bronze. A similar motive

1

accounts for the development of long-distance trade and diplomatic relations between major powers. Fueling long-distance trade was the desire for bronze, which had both practical and symbolic importance. From bronze, artisans made weapons, tools and utensils, and ritual objects. Ownership of bronze items was a sign of wealth and power. Trade and diplomacy helped spread culture and technology from the core river-valley areas to neighboring regions, such as southern China, Nubia, Syria-Palestine, Anatolia, and the Aegean.

In the Western Hemisphere, different geographical circumstances called forth distinctive patterns of technological and cultural response in the early civilizations of the Olmec in southern Mexico and Chavín in the Andean region of South America. Nevertheless, the challenges of organizing agriculture and trade led to many of the same features of complex societies—social stratification, specialization of labor, urbanization, monumental building, technological development, and artistic achievement.

	8000 B.C.E.	7000 B.C.E.	6000 B.C.E.	5000 B.C.E.
Americas				• 5000 Maize, beans, and squash domestication in Mesoamerica
Europe			• 6000 Farming in southern Europe	
Africa	• 8000 Farming in eastern Sahara			• 5500 Farming in Egypt
Middle East	• 8000 Domestication of plants and animals in Fertile Crescent			• 5000 Irrigation in Mesopotamia
Asia and Oceania			• 6500 Rice cultivation in China	• 5000 Farming in India

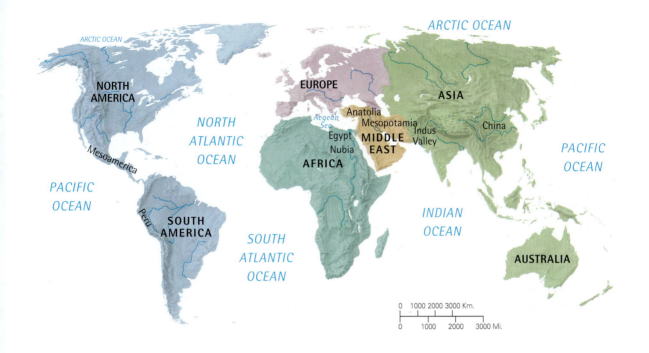

4000 B.C.E.		3000 B.C.E.		2000 B.C.E.		1000 B.C.E.	

- **4000** Maize domestication in Mesoamerica
- **3000** Farming in central Mexico
- **4000** Quinoa and potato domestication in Peru
- **1200** Rise of Olmec civilization in Mesoamerica
- **900** Rise of Chavín civilization in Peru

- **4000** Megaliths
- **3000–1100** Aegean civilization

- **3100** Unification of Egypt
- **2040–1640** Middle Kingdom Egypt
- **2575–2134** Old Kingdom Egypt
- **1532–1070** New Kingdom Egypt
- **2000** Rise of Kush in Nubia

- **3100** Mesopotamian civilization
- **1750** Hammurabi's law code
- **911** Rise of Neo-Assyrian Empire
- Advent of horses in western Asia **2000**
- **1700–1200** Hittites dominant in Anatolia
- **2350** Akkadian kingdom

- Bronze metallurgy in China **2000**
- **1600–1027** Shang kingdom in China
- **2600–1900** Indus Valley civilization
- **1027–221** Zhou kingdom in China

1 From the Origins of Agriculture to the First River-Valley Civilizations, 8000–1500 B.C.E.

CHAPTER OUTLINE

Before Civilization

Mesopotamia

Egypt

The Indus Valley Civilization

DIVERSITY AND DOMINANCE: **Violence and Order in the Babylonian New Year's Festival**

Some 5,000 years ago in Mesopotamia (present-day Iraq), people living in Sumer, the world's first urban civilization, cherished the story of Gilgamesh, superhero king of the city of Uruk. The goddess of creation, it recounted, fashioned the wild man Enkidu°:

> There was virtue in him of the god of war, of Ninurta himself. His body was rough, he had long hair like a woman's; it waved like the hair of Nisaba, the goddess of corn. His body was covered with matted hair like Samuqan's, the god of cattle. He was innocent of mankind; he knew nothing of the cultivated land. Enkidu ate grass in the hills with the gazelle and jostled with the wild beasts at the water-holes; he had joy of the water with the herds of wild game.

When Gilgamesh learns of Enkidu from a hunter, he sends a temple prostitute to tame him. After her seduction causes the wild beasts to shun him, she says:

> Come with me. I will take you to strong-walled Uruk,° to the blessed temple of Ishtar and of Anu, of love and of heaven . . . there all the people are dressed in their gorgeous robes, every day is holiday, the young men and the girls are wonderful to see. How sweet they smell! . . . O Enkidu, you who live life, I will show you Gilgamesh.[1]

She clothes Enkidu and teaches him to eat cooked food, drink beer, and bathe and oil his body. Her words and actions signal the principal traits of civilized life in Sumer, just as the

---

Enkidu (EN-kee-doo)

Uruk (OO-rook)

comparisons of the wild Enkidu to various divinities show Sumer's dependence on grain and livestock.

It has long been said that the first civilizations arose in Mesopotamia and Egypt sometime before 3000 B.C.E. However, since people tend to judge everything by their own viewpoint, it is not safe to accept this without questioning. The Sumerians equated civilization with their own way of life, but other peoples did the same, and lifestyles varied. This, along with the ambiguity of the term *civilization,* makes it difficult to say where civilization began.

Scholars agree that settled agricultural life and certain political, social, economic, and technological traits are indicators of **civilization,** if not of every civilization. These traits include (1) cities as administrative centers, (2) a political system based on defined territory rather than kinship, (3) many people engaged in specialized, non-food-producing activities, (4) status distinctions based largely on accumulation of wealth, (5) monumental building, (6) a system for keeping permanent records, (7) long-distance trade, and (8) sophisticated interest in science and art.

The earliest societies exhibiting these traits appeared in the floodplains of great rivers: the Tigris° and Euphrates° in Iraq, the Indus in Pakistan, the Yellow (Huang He°) in China, and the Nile in Egypt (see Map 1.1). Periodic flooding fertilized the land with silt and provided water for agriculture but also threatened lives and property. To control the floods, the peoples living near the rivers created new technologies and forms of political and social organization.

In this chapter, we describe the origins of domestication among the scattered groups of for-

agers living at the end of the last Ice Age (a long period when glaciers covered much of North America, Europe, and Asia) and the slow development of farming and herding societies. We then trace the rise of complex societies in Mesopotamia, Egypt, and the Indus River Valley from approximately 3500 to 1500 B.C.E. (China, developing slightly later, is discussed in Chapter 2). This story roughly coincides with the origins of writing, allowing us to document aspects of human life not revealed by archaeological evidence alone.

As you read this chapter, ask yourself the following questions:

- How did plant and animal domestication set the scene for the emergence of civilization?

- Why did the earliest civilizations arise in river valleys?

- How did the organization of labor shape political and social structures?

- How did metallurgy, writing, and monumental construction contribute to the power and wealth of elite groups?

- How do religious beliefs reflect interaction with the environment?

BEFORE CIVILIZATION

E vidence of human artistic creativity first came to light in 1940 near Lascaux in southwestern France with the discovery of a vast underground cavern. The cavern walls were covered with paintings of animals, including many that had been extinct for thousands of years. Similar cave paintings have been found in Spain and elsewhere in southern France.

To even the most skeptical person, these artistic troves reveal rich imaginations and sophisticated skills, qualities also apparent in the stone tools and in the evidence of complex social relations uncovered from prehistoric sites. The production of such artworks and tools over wide areas and long periods of time demonstrates that skills and ideas were not

---

Tigris (TIE-gris)   **Euphrates** (you-FRAY-teez)   **Huang He** (hwang huh)

simply individual expressions but were deliberately passed along within societies. These learned patterns of action and expression constitute **culture.** Culture includes material objects, such as dwellings, clothing, tools, and crafts, along with nonmaterial values, beliefs, and languages. Although it is true that some animals also learn new ways, their activities are determined primarily by inherited instincts. Only human communities trace profound cultural developments over time. The development, transmission, and transformation of cultural practices and events are the subject of **history.**

Stone toolmaking, the first recognizable cultural activity, first appeared around 2 million years ago. The **Stone Age,** which lasted from then until around 4,000 years ago, can be a misleading label. Stone tools abound at archaeological sites, but not all tools were of stone. They were made as well of bone, skin, and wood, materials that survive poorly. In addition, this period encompasses many cultures and subperiods. Among the major subdivisions, the **Paleolithic°** (Old Stone Age) lasted until 10,000 years ago, about 3,000 years after the end of the last Ice Age. The **Neolithic°** (New Stone Age), which is associated with the origins of agriculture, followed.

Food Gathering and Stone Technology

Fossilized animal bones bearing the marks of butchering tools testify to the scavenging and hunting activities of Stone Age peoples, but anthropologists do not believe that early humans lived primarily on meat. Modern **foragers** (hunting and food-gathering peoples) in the Kalahari Desert of southern Africa and the Ituri Forest of central Africa derive the bulk of their day-to-day nourishment from wild vegetable foods. They eat meat at feasts. Stone Age peoples probably did the same, even though the tools and equipment for gathering and processing vegetable foods have left few archaeological traces.

Like modern foragers, ancient humans would have used skins and mats woven from leaves for collecting fruits, berries, and wild seeds, and they would have dug up edible roots with wooden sticks. Archaeologists suspect that the doughnut-

Paleolithic (pay-lee-oh-LITH-ik)
Neolithic (nee-oh-LITH-ik)

shaped stones often found at Stone Age sites served as weights to make wooden digging sticks more effective.

Cooking makes both meat and vegetables tastier and easier to digest, something early humans may have discovered inadvertently after wildfires. Humans may have begun setting fires deliberately 1 million to 1.5 million years ago, but proof of cooking does not appear until some 12,500 years ago, when clay cooking pots came into use in East Asia.

Studies of present-day foragers also indicate that Ice Age women probably did most of the gathering and cooking, which they could do while caring for small children. Women past childbearing age would have been the most knowledgeable and productive food gatherers. Men, with stronger arms and shoulders, would have been better suited for hunting, particularly for hunting large animals. Some early cave art suggests male hunting activities.

The same studies, along with archaeological evidence from Ice Age campsites, indicate that early foragers lived in groups that were big enough to defend themselves from predators and divide responsibility for food collection and preparation, but small enough not to exhaust the food resources within walking distance. Even bands of around fifty men, women, and children would have moved regularly to follow migrating animals or collect seasonally ripening plants in different places.

In regions that had severe climates or that lacked natural shelters like caves, people built huts of branches, stones, bones, skins, and leaves as seasonal camps. Animal skins served as clothing, with the earliest evidence of woven cloth appearing about 26,000 years ago. Groups living in the African grasslands and other game-rich areas probably spent only three to five hours a day securing food, clothing, and shelter. This would have left a great deal of time for artistic endeavors, toolmaking, and social life.

The foundations of what later ages called science, art, and religion also date to the Stone Age. Gatherers learned which local plants were edible and when they ripened, as well as which natural substances were effective for medicine, consciousness altering, dyeing, and other purposes. Hunters learned the habits of game animals. People experimented with techniques of using plant and animal materials for clothing, twine, and construction. Knowledge of the environment included

C H R O N O L O G Y

	Mesopotamia	Egypt	Indus Valley
3500 B.C.E.			
3000 B.C.E.	3000–2350 B.C.E. Early Dynastic (Sumerian)	3100–2575 B.C.E. Early Dynastic	
			2600 B.C.E. Beginning of Indus Valley civilization
2500 B.C.E.	2350–2230 B.C.E. Akkadian (Semitic)	2575–2134 B.C.E. Old Kingdom	
	2112–2004 B.C.E. Third Dynasty of Ur (Sumerian)	2134–2040 B.C.E. First Intermediate Period	
2000 B.C.E.	1900–1600 B.C.E. Old Babylonian (Semitic)	2040–1640 B.C.E. Middle Kingdom	1900 B.C.E. End of Indus Valley civilization
		1640–1532 B.C.E. Second Intermediate Period	
1500 B.C.E.	1500–1150 B.C.E. Kassite	1532–1070 B.C.E. New Kingdom	

identifying which minerals made good paints and which stones made good tools. All of these aspects of culture were passed orally from generation to generation.

Early music and dance have left no traces, but visual artwork has survived abundantly. Cave paintings appear as early as 32,000 years ago in Europe and North Africa and somewhat later in other parts of the world. Because many feature food animals like wild oxen, reindeer, and horses, some scholars believe that the art recorded hunting scenes or played a magical and religious role in hunting. A newly discovered cave at Vallon Pont-d'Arc° in southern France, however, features rhinoceros, panthers, bears, owls, and a hyena, which probably were not hunted for food. Other drawings include people dressed in animal skins and smeared with paint and stencils of human hands. Some scholars suspect that other marks in cave paintings and on bones may represent efforts at counting or writing.

Some cave art suggests that Stone Age people had well-developed religions, but without written texts, it is hard to know what they believed. Some graves from about 100,000 years ago contain stone implements, food, clothing, and red-ochre powder, indicating that early people revered their leaders enough to honor them in death and may have believed in an afterlife.

Vallon Pont-d'Arc (vah-LON pon-DAHRK)

The Agricultural Revolutions

Around 10,000 years ago, some human groups began to meet their food needs by raising domesticated plants and animals. Gradually over the next millennium, most people became food producers, although hunting and gathering continued in some places.

The term *Neolithic Revolution,* commonly given to the changeover from food gathering to food producing, can be misleading. *Neolithic* means "new stone," but the new tool designs that accompanied the beginnings of agriculture were not the most important feature of this changeover. Nor was the "revolution" a single event. The changeover occurred at different times in different parts of the world. The term **Agricultural Revolution** is more precise because it emphasizes the central role of food production and signals that the changeover occurred several times. The adoption of agriculture often included the domestication of animals for food.

Food gathering gave way to food production over hundreds of generations. The process may have begun when forager bands, returning year after year to the same seasonal camps, scattered seeds and cleared away weeds to encourage the growth of foods they liked. Such semicultivation could have supplemented food gathering without necessitating permanent settlement. Families choosing to concentrate their energies on food production, however, would have had to settle permanently near their fields.

Specialized stone tools first alerted archaeologists to new food-producing practices: polished or ground stone heads to work the soil, sharp stone chips embedded in bone or wooden handles to cut grasses, and stone mortars to pulverize grain. Early farmers used fire to clear fields of shrubs and trees and discovered that ashes were a natural fertilizer. After the burn-off, farmers used blades and axes to keep the land clear.

Selection of the highest-yielding strains of wild plants led to the development of domesticated varieties over time. As the principal gatherers of wild plant foods, women probably played a major role in this transition to plant cultivation, but the task of clearing fields probably fell to the men.

In the Middle East, the region with the earliest evidence of agriculture, human selection had transformed certain wild grasses into higher-yielding domesticated grains, now known as emmer wheat and barley, by 8000 B.C.E. Farmers there also discovered that alternating the cultivation of grains and pulses (plants yielding edible seeds such as lentils and peas) helped maintain fertility.

Plants domesticated in the Middle East spread to adjacent lands, but agriculture also arose independently in many parts of the world. Exchanges of crops and techniques occurred between regions, but societies that had already turned to farming borrowed new plants, animals, and farming techniques more readily than foraging groups did.

The eastern Sahara, which went through a wet period after 8000 B.C.E., preserves the oldest traces of food production in northern Africa. As in the Middle East, emmer wheat and barley became the principal crops and sheep, goats, and cattle the main domestic animals. When drier conditions returned around 5000 B.C.E., many Saharan farmers moved to the Nile Valley, where the river's annual flood provided water for crops.

In Greece, wheat and barley cultivation, beginning as early as 6000 B.C.E., combined local experiments with Middle Eastern borrowings. Shortly after 4000 B.C.E., farming developed in the light-soiled plains of central Europe and along the Danube River. As forests receded over the next millennium because of climate changes and human clearing efforts, agriculture spread to other parts of Europe.

Early farmers in Europe and elsewhere practiced shifting cultivation, also known as swidden agriculture. After a few growing seasons, farmers left the fields fallow (abandoned to natural vegetation) and cleared new fields nearby. Between 4000 and 3000 B.C.E., for example, communities of forty to sixty people in the Danube Valley supported themselves on about 500 acres (200 hectares) of farmland, cultivating a third or less each year while leaving the rest fallow to regain its fertility. From around 2600 B.C.E., people in central Europe began using ox-drawn wooden plows to till heavier and richer soils.

Although the lands around the Mediterranean seem to have shared a complex of crops and farming techniques, geographical conditions blocked the spread of wheat and barley elsewhere. Rainfall patterns south of the Sahara favored instead locally domesticated grains—sorghums, millets, and (in

Ethiopia) teff. Middle Eastern grains did not grow at all in the humidity of equatorial West Africa; there, yams became an early domestic crop.

Domestic rice originated in southern China, the northern half of Southeast Asia, or northern India, possibly as early as 10,000 B.C.E. but more likely closer to 5000 B.C.E. The warm, wet climate of southern China particularly favored rice. Along with rice, Indian farmers were cultivating hyacinth beans, green grams, and black grams by about 2000 B.C.E.

In the Americas a decline of game animals in the Tehuacán° Valley of Mexico after 8000 B.C.E. increased people's dependence on wild plants. Agriculture based on maize° (corn) developed there about 3000 B.C.E. and gradually spread. At about the same time, the inhabitants of Peru developed a food production pattern based on potatoes and quinoa°, a protein-rich seed grain. People in the more tropical parts of Mesoamerica cultivated tomatoes, peppers, squash, and potatoes. In South America's tropical forests, the root crop manioc became the staple food after 1500 B.C.E. Manioc and maize then spread to the Caribbean islands.

The domestication of animals expanded rapidly during these same millennia. The first domesticated animal, the dog, may have helped hunters track game well before the Neolithic period. Later, animals initially provided meat but eventually supplied milk, wool, and energy as well.

Refuse dumped outside Middle Eastern villages shows a gradual decline in the number of wild gazelle bones after 7000 B.C.E. This probably reflects the depletion of wild game through overhunting by local farmers. Meat eating, however, did not decline. Sheep and goat bones gradually replaced gazelle bones. Possibly wild sheep and goats learned to graze around agricultural villages to take advantage of the suppression of predators by humans. The tamer animals may gradually have accepted human control and thus become a ready supply of food. The bones of tame animals initially differ so little from those of their wild ancestors that the early stages of domestication are hard to date. However, selective breeding for characteristics like a wooly coat and high milk production

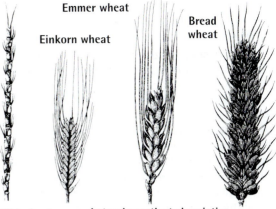

Domestication of Wheat Through selection of the largest seeds of this wild grass, early farmers in the Middle East were able to develop varieties with larger edible kernels. Bread wheat was grown in the Nile Valley by 5000 B.C.E. (From Iris Barn, *Discovering Archaeology*, London: Trewin Copplestone Books, 1981)

eventually yielded distinct breeds of domestic sheep and goats.

Elsewhere, other wild species were evolving domestic forms during the centuries before 3000 B.C.E.: cattle in northern Africa or the Middle East, donkeys in northern Africa, water buffalo in China, humped-back Zebu° cattle in India, horses and two-humped camels in central Asia, one-humped camels in Arabia, chickens in Southeast Asia, and pigs in several places. Like domestic plant species, varieties of domesticated animals spread from one region to another. The Zebu cattle originally domesticated in India, for example, became important in sub-Saharan Africa about 2,000 years ago.

It was a long time after their domestication that cattle and water buffalo became sufficiently tame to be yoked to plows, but once this change occurred, they became essential to the agricultural cycle of grain farmers. In addition, animal droppings provided valuable fertilizer. Wool and milk production also occurred a long time after initial domestication.

In the Americas, domestic llamas provided meat, transport, and wool, while guinea pigs and turkeys provided meat. Dogs assisted hunters and

---

Tehuacán (teh-wah-KAHN) **maize** (mayz) **quinoa** (kee-NOH-uh)

Zebu (ZEE-boo)

also provided meat. Some scholars believe that these were the only domesticated American species, but this cannot be proven. However, domestic species could not have been borrowed from elsewhere because of the geographical isolation of the Americas.

Pastoralism, a way of life dependent on large herds of grazing livestock, came to predominate in arid regions. As the Sahara approached its maximum dryness around 2500 B.C.E., pastoralists replaced farmers who migrated southward (see Chapter 6). Moving herds to new pastures and watering places throughout the year made pastoralists almost as mobile as foragers and discouraged substantial dwellings and the accumulation of bulky possessions. Like modern pastoralists, early cattle keepers probably relied more heavily on milk than on meat, since killing animals diminished the size of their herds. During wet seasons, they may also have engaged in semicultivation or bartered meat and skins for plant foods from nearby farming communities.

Why did the Agricultural Revolutions occur? Some theories assume that growing crops had obvious advantages. Grain, for example, provided both a dietary staple and the makings of beer. Beer drinking appears frequently in ancient Middle Eastern art and can be dated to as early as 3500 B.C.E. Most researchers today, however, believe that climate change drove people to abandon hunting and gathering in favor of pastoralism and agriculture. So great was the global warming that ended the last Ice Age that geologists gave the era since about 11,000 B.C.E. a new name: the **Holocene°**. Scientists have also found evidence that temperate lands were exceptionally warm between 6000 and 2000 B.C.E., when people in many parts of the world adopted agriculture. The precise nature of the climatic crisis probably varied. In the Middle East, shortages of wild food caused by dryness or population growth may have stimulated food production. Elsewhere, a warmer, wetter climate could have turned grasslands into forest and thereby reduced supplies of game and wild grains.

In many drier parts of the world, where wild food remained abundant, agriculture did not arise.

Holocene (HAWL-oh-seen)

The inhabitants of Australia relied exclusively on foraging until recent centuries, as did some peoples on other continents. Amerindians in the arid grasslands from Alaska to the Gulf of Mexico hunted bison, and salmon fishing sustained groups in the Pacific Northwest. Ample supplies of fish, shellfish, and aquatic animals permitted food gatherers east of the Mississippi River to become increasingly sedentary. In the equatorial rain forest and in the southern part of Africa, conditions also favored retention of older ways.

Whatever the causes, the gradual adoption of food production transformed most parts of the world. A hundred thousand years ago, world population, mostly living in the temperate and tropical regions of Africa and Eurasia, did not exceed 2 million. The population may have fallen still lower during the last glacial epoch, between 32,000 and 13,000 years ago. Agriculture supported a gradual population increase, perhaps to 10 million by 5000 B.C.E., and then a mushrooming to between 50 million and 100 million by 1000 B.C.E.[2]

Life in Neolithic Communities

Evidence that an ecological crisis may have triggered the transition to food production has prompted reexamination of the assumption that farmers enjoyed a better life than foragers. Early farmers probably had to work much harder and for much longer periods than food gatherers. Long days spent clearing and cultivating the land yielded meager harvests. Guarding herds from predators, guiding them to fresh pastures, and tending to their needs imposed similar burdens.

Although early farmers commanded a more reliable food supply, their diet contained less variety and nutrition than that of foragers. Skeletons show that Neolithic farmers were shorter on average than earlier foragers. Death from contagious diseases ravaged farming settlements, which were contaminated by human waste, infested by disease-bearing vermin and insects, and inhabited by domesticated animals—especially pigs and cattle—whose diseases could infect people.

However, a dependable supply of food that could be stored between harvests to see people through nonproductive seasons, droughts, and other calamities proved decisive in the long run. Over several millennia, farmers came to outnumber nonfarmers, permanent settlements generated cultural changes, and specialized crafts appeared in fledgling towns.

Some researchers envision violent struggles between farmers and foragers. Others see a more peaceful transition. Violence may well have accompanied land clearance that constrained the foragers' food supplies. And farmers probably fought for control of the best land. In most cases, however, farmers seem to have displaced foragers by gradual infiltration rather than by conquest.

The archaeologist Colin Renfrew maintains that, over a few centuries, farming populations in Europe could have increased by a factor of fifty to one hundred just on the basis of the dependability of their food supply. In his view, as population densities rose, individuals with fields farthest away from their native village formed new settlements, thus contributing to a steady, nonviolent expansion of agriculture consistent with the archaeological record. An expansion by only 12 to 19 miles (20 to 30 kilometers) in a generation could have brought farming to every corner of Europe between 6500 and 3500 B.C.E.[3] Yet it probably happened gradually enough to minimize sharp conflicts with foragers, who would simply have stayed clear of the agricultural frontier or gradually adopted agriculture themselves. Studies that map genetic changes in the population also suggest a gradual spread of agricultural people across Europe from southeast to northwest.[4]

As they did in forager bands, kinship and marriage bound farming communities together. Nuclear family size (parents and their children) may not have risen, but kinship relations traced back over more generations brought distant cousins into a common kin network. This encouraged the holding of land by large kinship units known as lineages° or clans.

Because each person has two parents, four grandparents, eight great-grandparents, and so on, each individual has a bewildering number of ancestors. Some societies trace descent equally through both parents, but most give greater importance to descent through either the mother (matrilineal° societies) or the father (patrilineal° societies).

Some scholars believe that descent through women and perhaps rule by women prevailed in early times. The traditions of Kikuyu° farmers on Mount Kenya in East Africa, for example, relate that women ruled until the Kikuyu men conspired to get all the women pregnant at once and then overthrew them while they were unable to fight back. No specific evidence can prove or disprove legends such as this, but it is important not to confuse tracing descent through women (matrilineality) with rule by women (matriarchy°).

Religiously, kinship led to reverence for departed ancestors. Old persons often received elaborate burials. A plastered skull from Jericho° in the Jordan Valley of modern Israel may be evidence of early ancestor reverence or worship at the dawn of agriculture.

The religions of foragers tended to center on sacred groves, springs, and wild animals. In contrast, the rituals of farmers often centered on the Earth Mother, a deity believed to be the source of new life, and divinities representing fire, wind, and rain. Pastoralists tended to worship the all-powerful (and usually male) Sky God.

Assemblages of **megaliths** (meaning "big stones") seem to relate to religious beliefs. One complex built in the Egyptian desert before 5000 B.C.E. includes stone burial chambers, a calendar circle, and pairs of upright stones that frame the rising sun on the summer solstice. Stonehenge, a famous megalithic site in England constructed about 2000 B.C.E., marked the position of the sun and other celestial bodies at key points in the year. In the Middle East, the Americas, and other parts of the world, giant earth burial mounds may have served similar ritual and symbolic functions.

In some parts of the world, a few Neolithic villages grew into towns, which served as centers of trade and specialized crafts. Two towns in the Middle East, Jericho on the west bank of the Jordan River and Çatal Hüyük° in central Anatolia (modern Turkey), have been extensively excavated (Map 1.1 shows their location). Jericho revealed an elaborate early agricultural settlement. The round mud-brick dwellings characteristic of Jericho around 8000 B.C.E. may have imitated the shape of the tents of

---

lineage (LIN-ee-ij) **matrilineal** (mat-ruh-LIN-ee-uhl) **patrilineal** (pat-ruh-LIN-ee-uhl)

Kikuyu (Ki-KOO-yoo) **matriarchy** (MAY-tree-ahr-key) **Jericho** (JER-ih-koe) **Çatal Hüyük** (cha-TAHL hoo-YOOK)

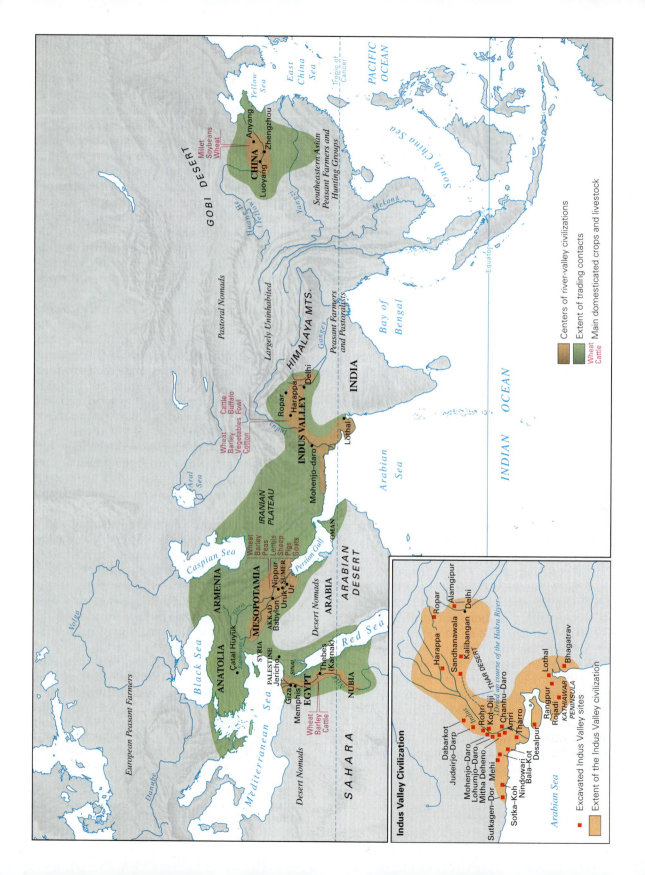

PACIFIC
OCEAN

East
China
Sea

Yellow
Sea

Tropic of Cancer

GOBI DESERT

Millet
Soybeans
Wheat

Anyang
Zhengzhou

CHINA
Luoyang

Huang
(Yellow)

Yangzi

Southeastern Asian
Peasant Farmers and
Hunting Groups

Mekong

South China Sea

Pastoral Nomads

Largely Uninhabited

HIMALAYA MTS.

Ganges

Peasant Farmers
and Pastoralists

INDIA

Bay of
Bengal

Cattle
Buffalo
Fowl

Ropar
Harappa
Delhi

Wheat
Barley
Vegetables
Cotton

INDUS VALLEY

Indus

Mohenjo-daro

Lothal

Arabian
Sea

Aral
Sea

Caspian Sea

IRANIAN
PLATEAU

INDIAN OCEAN

Equator

ARMENIA

Wheat
Barley
Peas
Lentils
Sheep
Pigs
Goats

Nippur
Uruk SUMER
Ur

Persian Gulf

OMAN

Volga

Black Sea

ANATOLIA

Çatal Hüyük

Euphrates

SYRIA

MESOPOTAMIA
AKKAD
Babylon

ARABIA

ARABIAN
DESERT

Desert Nomads

European Peasant Farmers

Mediterranean Sea

PALESTINE
Jericho

SINAI

Giza
Memphis EGYPT

Thebes
(Karnak)

Red Sea

NUBIA

Wheat
Barley
Cattle

Danube

SAHARA

Desert Nomads

Tigris

Centers of river-valley civilizations

Extent of trading contacts

Main domesticated crops and livestock

Wheat
Cattle

Indus Valley Civilization

Ropar
Alamgirpur
Delhi

Harappa
Sandhanawala
Kalibangan

THAR DESERT

Dried-up course of the Hakra River

Dabarkot
Judeirjo-Darp

Rohri
Kot-Diji
Chanhu-Daro
Amri
Tharro

Rangpur
Rojadi

Lothal
Bhagatrav

KATHIAWAR
PENINSULA

Mohenjo-Daro
Lohumjo-Daro
Mitha Deheno

Sutkagen-Dor Mehi
Sotka-Koh
Nindowari
Bala-Kot

Desalpur

Arabian
Sea

■ **Excavated Indus Valley sites**

Extent of the Indus Valley civilization

Map 1.1   River-Valley Civilizations, 3500–1500 B.C.E. The earliest complex societies arose in the floodplains of large rivers: in the fourth millennium B.C.E. in the valley of the Tigris and Euphrates Rivers in Mesopotamia and the Nile River in Egypt, in the third millennium B.C.E. in the valley of the Indus River in Pakistan, and in the second millennium B.C.E. in the valley of the Yellow River in China.

foragers who once had camped near Jericho's natural spring. A millennium later, rectangular rooms with finely plastered walls and floors and wide doorways opened onto central courtyards. Surrounding the 10-acre (4-hectare) settlement, a massive stone wall protected against attacks.

The ruins of Çatal Hüyük, an even larger Neolithic town, date to between 7000 and 5000 B.C.E. and cover 32 acres (13 hectares). Its residents lived in plastered mud-brick rooms with elaborate decorations, but Çatal Hüyük had no wall. Instead, the outer walls of its houses formed a continuous barrier without doors or large windows. Residents entered their houses by climbing down ladders through a hole in the roof.

Long-distance trade at Çatal Hüyük featured obsidian, a hard volcanic rock that artisans chipped, ground, and polished into tools, weapons, mirrors, and ornaments. Other residents made fine pottery, wove baskets and woolen cloth, made stone and shell beads, and worked leather and wood. House sizes varied, but nothing indicates that Çatal Hüyük had a dominant class or a centralized political structure.

Representational art at Çatal Hüyük makes it clear that hunting retained a powerful hold on people's minds. Wall paintings of hunting scenes closely resemble earlier cave paintings. Many depict men and women adorned with leopard skins. Men were buried with weapons rather than with farm tools, and bones from rubbish heaps prove that wild game featured prominently in people's diet.

Yet Çatal Hüyük's economy rested on agriculture. The surrounding fields produced barley and emmer wheat, as well as legumes° and other vegetables. Pigs were kept along with goats and sheep. Nevertheless, foragers' foods, such as acorns and wild grains, had not disappeared.

Çatal Hüyük had one religious shrine for every two houses. At least forty rooms contained shrines with depictions of horned wild bulls, female breasts, goddesses, leopards, and handprints. Rituals involved burning dishes of grain, legumes, and meat but not sacrificing live animals. Statues of plump female deities far outnumber statues of male deities, suggesting that the inhabitants venerated a goddess as their principal deity. The large number of females who were buried elaborately in shrine rooms may have been priestesses of this cult. The site's principal excavator maintains that although male priests existed, "it seems extremely likely that the cult of the goddess was administered mainly by women."[5]

Metalworking became a specialized occupation in the late Neolithic period. At Çatal Hüyük, objects of copper and lead, which occur naturally in fairly pure form, date to about 6400 B.C.E. Silver and gold also appear at early dates in various parts of the world. Because of their rarity and their softness, these metals did not replace stone tools and weapons. The discovery of decorative and ceremonial objects of metal in graves indicates that they became symbols of status and power.

Towns, specialized crafts, and religious shrines forced the farmers to produce extra food for nonfarmers like priests and artisans. The building of permanent houses, walls, and towers, not to mention megalithic monuments, also called for added labor. Stonehenge, for example, took some 30,000 person-hours to build. Whether these tasks were performed freely or coerced is unknown.

MESOPOTAMIA

Because of the unpredictable nature of the Tigris and Euphrates Rivers, the peoples of ancient Mesopotamia saw themselves at the mercy of gods who embodied the forces of nature. The Babylonian Creation Myth (**Babylon** was the most important city in southern Mesopotamia in the second and first millennia B.C.E.) climaxes in a cosmic battle between Marduk, the chief god of Babylon, and Tiamat°, a female figure who personifies

---

legume (LEG-yoom)

Tiamat (TIE-ah-mat)

the salt sea. Marduk cuts up Tiamat and from her body fashions the earth and sky. He then creates the divisions of time, the celestial bodies, rivers, and weather phenomena. From the blood of a defeated rebel god, he creates human beings. Myths of this sort explained to the ancient inhabitants of Mesopotamia the environment in which they were living.

Settled Agriculture in an Unstable Landscape

Mesopotamia means "land between the rivers" in Greek. It reflects the centrality of the Euphrates and Tigris Rivers to the way of life in this region. The plain alongside and between the rivers, which originate in the mountains of eastern Anatolia (modern Turkey) and empty into the Persian Gulf, has gained fertility from the silt deposited by river floods over many millennia.

Today the plain is mostly in Iraq; it gives way to mountains in the north and east: an arc extending from northern Syria through southeastern Anatolia to the Zagros° Mountains that separate the plain from the Iranian Plateau. To the west and southwest lie the Syrian and Arabian Deserts, to the southeast the Persian Gulf. Floods caused by snow melting in the northern mountains can be sudden and violent. They come inconveniently in the spring when crops, planted in winter to avoid the torrid summer temperatures, are ripening. Floods sometimes cause the rivers to change course, abruptly cutting off fields and towns from water and river communication.

Although the first domestication of plants and animals around 8000 B.C.E. occurred nearby, in the "Fertile Crescent" region of northern Syria and southeastern Anatolia, agriculture did not reach Mesopotamia until approximately 5000 B.C.E. "Dry" (unirrigated) farming requires at least 8 inches (20 centimeters) of rain a year. The hot, arid climate of southern Mesopotamia calls for irrigation, the artificial provision of water to crops. Initially, people probably channeled floodwater into nearby fields, but shortly after 3000 B.C.E. they learned to construct canals to supply water as needed and carry it to more distant fields.

Ox-drawn plows, developed by around 4000 B.C.E., cut a furrow in the earth into which carefully measured amounts of seed dropped from an attached funnel. Farmers favored barley as a cereal crop because it could tolerate the Mesopotamian climate and withstand the toxic effects of salt drawn to the surface of the soil by evaporation. Fields stood fallow (unplanted) every other year to replenish the nutrients in the soil. Date palms provided food, fiber, and wood. Garden plots produced vegetables. Reeds growing along the rivers and in the marshy southern delta yielded raw material for mats, baskets, huts, and boats. Fish was a dietary staple. Herds of sheep and goats, which grazed on fallow land or the nearby desert, provided wool, milk, and meat. Donkeys, originally domesticated in northeast Africa, joined cattle as beasts of burden in the third millennium B.C.E., as did camels from Arabia and horses from the mountains in the second millennium B.C.E.

The written record begins with the **Sumerians** and marks the division, by some definitions, between prehistory and history. Archaeological evidence places the Sumerians in southern Mesopotamia at least by 5000 B.C.E. and perhaps even earlier. They created the framework of civilization in Mesopotamia during a long period of dominance in the third millennium B.C.E. Other peoples lived in Mesopotamia as well. As early as 2900 B.C.E., personal names recorded in inscriptions from the more northerly cities reveal a non-Sumerian **Semitic°** language. (*Semitic* refers to a family of languages spoken in parts of western Asia and northern Africa. They include the Hebrew, Aramaic°, and Phoenician° of the ancient world and the Arabic of today.) Possibly the descendants of nomads from the desert west of Mesopotamia, these Semites seem to have lived in peace with the Sumerians, adopting their culture and sometimes achieving positions of wealth and power.

By 2000 B.C.E., the Semitic peoples had become politically dominant. From this time on, Akkadian°, a Semitic language, took precedence over Sumer-

---

Semitic (suh-MIT-ik)   **Aramaic** (ar-uh-MAY-ik)   **Phoenician** (fi-NEE-shuhn)   **Akkadian** (uh-KAY-dee-uhn)

ian, although the Sumerian cultural legacy survived in translation. The Sumerian-Akkadian dictionaries compiled at the time to facilitate translations from Sumerian allow us today to read the language, which has no known relatives. The characteristics and adventures of the Semitic gods also indicate cultural borrowing. This cultural synthesis parallels a biological merging of Sumerians and Semites through intermarriage. Though other ethnic groups, including Kassites° from the eastern mountains and Elamites° and Persians from farther south in Iran, played roles in Mesopotamian history, the Sumerian/Semitic cultural heritage remained fundamentally unaltered until the arrival of Greeks in the late fourth century B.C.E.

Cities, Kings, and Trade

Mesopotamian farmers usually lived in villages. A group of families, totaling a few hundred persons perhaps, could protect one another, work together at key times in the agricultural cycle, and share tools, barns, and threshing floors. Village society also provided companionship and a pool of potential marriage partners.

Occasionally, as a particularly successful village grew, small satellite villages developed nearby and eventually merged with the main village to form an urban center. Cities depended on agriculture and therefore on the villages. Many early Mesopotamian city dwellers went out each day to labor in nearby fields. Other city dwellers, however, depended for food on the surplus food production of the villagers. Some specialized in crafts—for example, pottery, artwork, and weapons, tools, and other objects forged out of metal. Others served the gods or carried out administrative duties. Mesopotamian cities controlled the agricultural land and collected crop surpluses from villages in their vicinity. In return, the city provided rural districts with military protection against bandits and raiders and a market where villagers could acquire manufactured goods produced by urban specialists.

The term **city-state** refers to a self-governing urban center and the agricultural territories it controlled. Stretches of uncultivated land, either desert or swamp, served as buffers between the many small city-states of early Mesopotamia. Nevertheless, disputes over land, water rights, and movable property often sparked hostilities between neighboring cities and the building of protective walls of sun-dried bricks. At other times, cities cooperated, sharing water and allowing traders safe passage through their territories.

Mesopotamians opened new land to agriculture by building and maintaining irrigation networks. Canals brought water from river to field; drainage ditches carried the water back to the river before evaporation could draw harmful salt and minerals to the surface. Weirs (partial dams) raised the water level of the river so that water could flow by gravity into the canals. Dikes along the riverbanks protected against floods. The silt carried by floods clogged the canals, which required frequent dredging. In some places, levers with counterweights lifted buckets of irrigation water out of a river or canal.

Successful operation of such sophisticated irrigation systems depended on leaders compelling or persuading large numbers of people to work together. Other projects called for similar cooperation: harvesting, sheep shearing, building of fortifications and large public buildings, and warfare. Two centers of power, the temple and the palace of the king, have left written records, but details of governmental life remain scanty, as are the hints at some sort of citizens' assembly that may have evolved from traditional village councils.

One or more temples, centrally located, housed each city-state's deity or deities and their associated cults (sets of religious rituals). Temples owned agricultural lands and stored the gifts that worshipers donated. The central location of the temple buildings confirms the importance of cults. Head priests, who controlled each shrine and managed its wealth, played prominent political and economic roles.

In the third millennium B.C.E., Sumerian documents show the emergence of a *lugal*° or "big man"—what we would call a king. An increase in warfare as ever-larger communities quarreled over land, water, and raw materials may have prompted this development, but details are lacking.

Kassite (KAS-ite)   **Elamite** (EE-luh-mite)

lugal (LOO-guhl)

According to one theory, communities chose certain men to lead their armies in time of war, and these individuals found ways to prolong their authority in peacetime and assume judicial and ritual functions. Although the lugal's position was not hereditary, it often passed from a father to a capable son.

The location of the temple in the city's heart and the less prominent siting of the king's palace symbolize the later emergence of royalty. The king's power grew at the expense of the priesthood, however, because the army backed him. The priests and temples retained influence because of their wealth and religious mystique, but they gradually became dependent on the palace. Some Mesopotamian kings claimed divinity, but this concept did not take root. Normally the king portrayed himself as the deity's earthly representative.

By the late third millennium B.C.E., kings assumed responsibility for the upkeep and building of temples and the proper performance of ritual. Other royal responsibilities included maintaining city walls and defenses, extending and repairing irrigation channels, guarding property rights, warding off foreign attacks, and establishing justice.

The *Epic of Gilgamesh* referred to at the beginning of this chapter shows both the ambition of the kings and their value to the community. Gilgamesh, who is probably based on a historical king of Uruk, stirs resentment by demanding sexual favors from new brides, but the community relies on his immense strength, wisdom, and courage. In quest of everlasting glory, Gilgamesh walls the city magnificently, stamping his name on every brick. His journey to the faraway Cedar Mountains reflects the king's role in accessing valuable resources.

A few city-states became powerful enough to dominate their neighbors. Sargon°, ruler of Akkad° around 2350 B.C.E., pioneered in uniting many cities under one king and capital. His title, King of Sumer and Akkad, symbolized this claim to universal dominion. Sargon and the four family members who succeeded him over 120 years secured their power in several ways. They razed the walls of conquered cities and installed governors backed by garrisons of Akkadian troops. They gave soldiers land to ensure their loyalty. Being of Semitic stock, they adapted the cuneiform° system of writing used for Sumerian (discussed later in the chapter) to express their own language. Their administration featured a uniform system of weights and measures and standardized formats for official documents. These measures facilitated assessment and collection of taxes, recruitment of soldiers, and organization of labor projects.

For reasons that remain obscure, the Akkadian state fell around 2230 B.C.E. The Sumerian language and culture revived in the cities of the southern plain under the Third Dynasty of Ur (2112–2004 B.C.E.), a five-king dynasty that maintained itself for a century through campaigns of conquest and prudent marriage alliances. The Akkadian state had controlled more territory, but tighter government control based on a rapidly expanding bureaucracy and obsessive recordkeeping now secured Ur's dominance. Messengers and well-maintained road stations speeded up communications; and an official calendar, standardized weights and measures, and uniform writing practices improved central administration. To protect against nomadic Semitic Amorites° from the northwest, the kings erected a wall 125 miles (201 kilometers) long. Eventually, however, nomad incursions combined with an Elamite attack from the southeast toppled the Third Dynasty of Ur.

The Amorites founded a new city at Babylon, not far from Akkad. Toward the end of a long reign, **Hammurabi°** (r. 1792–1750 B.C.E.) initiated a series of aggressive military campaigns, and Babylon became the capital of what historians have named the "Old Babylonian" state, which eventually stretched beyond Sumer and Akkad into the north and northwest, from 1900 to 1600 B.C.E. Hammurabi's famous Law Code, inscribed on a polished black stone pillar, provided judges with a lengthy set of examples illustrating the principles to be used in deciding cases. Some examples called for severe physical punishments to compensate for crimes. These Amorite notions of justice differed from the monetary penalties prescribed in earlier codes from Ur.

Sargon (SAHR-gone)   **Akkad** (AH-kahd)

cuneiform (kyoo-NEE-uh-form)   **Amorite** (AM-uh-rite)
Hammurabi (HAM-uh-rah-bee)

Conquest gave some Mesopotamian city-states access to vital resources. Trade offered an alternative, and long-distance commerce flourished in most periods. Evidence of seagoing vessels appears as early as the fifth millennium B.C.E. Wood, metals, and stone came from foreign lands in exchange for wool, cloth, barley, and vegetable oil. Cedar forests in Lebanon and Syria yielded wood, Anatolia produced silver, Egypt gold, and the eastern Mediterranean and Oman (on the Arabian peninsula) copper. Tin, which in alloy with copper made bronze, came from Afghanistan (in South-Central Asia), and chlorite, a greenish, easily carved stone, from the Iranian plateau. Jewelers and stone-carvers used black diorite from the Persian Gulf, blue lapis lazuli° from Afghanistan, and reddish carnelian° from Pakistan.

Most merchants worked for the palace or the temple in the third millennium B.C.E. Only these institutions commanded the financial resources and organizational skills needed for acquiring, transporting, and protecting valuable commodities. Merchants exchanged surpluses from the royal or temple farmlands for raw materials and luxury goods. In the second millennium B.C.E., independent merchants and merchant guilds gained increasing influence.

Sources do not reveal whether the most important commercial transactions took place in the area just inside the city gates or in the vicinity of the docks. Wherever they occurred, coined money played no role. Coins—stamped metal pieces of state-guaranteed value—first appeared in the sixth century B.C.E. and did not reach Mesopotamia until several centuries later. For most of Mesopotamian history, items that could not be bartered—traded for one another—had their value calculated in relation to fixed weights of precious metal, primarily silver, or measures of grain.

Mesopotamian Society

Urbanized civilizations foster social division, that is, obvious variation in the status and privileges of different groups according to wealth, social function, and legal and political rights. Urbanization, specialization of function, centralization of power, and the use of written records enabled certain groups to amass unprecedented wealth. Temple leaders and the kings controlled large agricultural estates, and the palace administration collected taxes from subjects. How elite individuals acquired large private landholdings is unknown, since land was rarely put up for sale. In some cases, however, debtors lost their land to creditors, or soldiers and priests received land in return for their services.

The Law Code of Hammurabi in the eighteenth century B.C.E. reflects social divisions that may also have been valid for other places and times, despite inevitable fluctuations. It identifies three classes: (1) the free landowning class—royalty, high-ranking officials, warriors, priests, merchants, and some artisans and shopkeepers; (2) the class of dependent farmers and artisans, whose legal attachment to royal, temple, or private estates made them the primary rural work force; and (3) the class of slaves, primarily employed in domestic service. Penalties prescribed in the Law Code depended on the class of the offender. The lower orders received the most severe punishments. Slaves, many of them prisoners of war from the mountains, and insolvent debtors played a lesser economic role than they would in the later societies of Greece and Rome (see Chapters 4 and 5). Identified by a distinctive hairstyle rather than chains or brands, they would have a barber shave off the telltale mark if they were lucky enough to regain their freedom. Because commodities such as food and oil were distributed to all people in proportion to their age, gender, and task, documents do not always distinguish between slaves or dependent workers and free laborers. In the Old Babylonian period, the class of people who were not dependent on the temple or palace grew, the amount of land and other property in private hands increased, and free laborers became more common.

The daily lives of ordinary Mesopotamians, especially those in villages or on large estates, left few archaeological or literary traces. Peasants built with mud brick and reeds, which quickly disintegrate, and they had few metal possessions. Being illiterate, they left no written record of their lives. It is especially difficult to discover much about the

---

lapis lazuli (LAP-is LAZ-uh-lee)   **carnelian** (kahr-NEEL-yuhn)

experiences of women. Males dominated the position of **scribe**—an administrator or scholar charged by the temple or palace with reading and writing tasks—and, for the most part, their writings reflect elite male activities. Archaeology only partially fills this gap.

Anthropologists theorize that women lost social standing and freedom with the spread of agriculture. In hunting and gathering societies, they believe, women's foraging provided most of the community's food. But in Mesopotamia, food production depended on the heavy physical labor of plowing, harvesting, and digging irrigation channels, jobs usually performed by men. Since food surpluses made larger families possible, bearing and raising children became the primary occupation of many women, leaving them little time to acquire the specialized skills of a scribe or artisan.

Women could own property, maintain control of their dowry, and even engage in trade, but men monopolized political life. Some women worked outside the household in textile factories and breweries or as prostitutes, tavern keepers, bakers, or fortunetellers. Home tasks for nonelite women probably included helping with farming, growing vegetables, cooking, cleaning, fetching water, tending the household fire, and weaving baskets and textiles.

The standing of women seems to have declined further in the second millennium B.C.E., perhaps because of the rise of an urbanized middle class and an increase in private wealth. Husbands gained authority in the household and benefited from marriage and divorce laws. A man normally took just one wife, but he could obtain a second if the first gave him no children. In later Mesopotamian history, kings and rich men had several wives. Marriage alliances arranged between families made women instruments for preserving and enhancing family wealth. Alternatively, a family might decide to avoid a daughter's marriage, with the resulting loss of a dowry, by dedicating her to temple service as "god's bride." Constraints on women's lives that eventually became part of Islamic tradition, such as remaining at home and wearing veils in public, may date back to the second millennium B.C.E. (see Chapter 7).

Gods, Priest, and Temples

The Sumerian gods embodied the forces of nature: Anu the sky, Enlil the air, Enki the water, Utu the sun, and Nanna the moon. The goddess Inanna governed sexual attraction and violence. When the Semitic peoples became dominant, they equated their deities with those of the Sumerians. The Sumerian gods Nanna and Utu, for example, became the Semitic Sin and Shamash, and the goddess Inanna became Ishtar. The Semitic gods took over the myths and many of the rituals of their Sumerian predecessors.

People imagined their gods as anthropomorphic°, that is, like humans in form and conduct. The gods had bodies and senses, sought nourishment from sacrifice, enjoyed the worship and obedience of humanity, and experienced the human emotions of lust, love, hate, anger, and envy. Religious beliefs instilled fear of the gods, who could alter the landscape, and a desire to appease them.

Public, state-organized religion stands out in the archaeological record. Cities built temples and showed devotion to the divinity or divinities who protected the community. All the peoples of Sumer regarded Nippur (see Map 1.1) as a religious center because of its temple to the air god Enlil. As with other temples, they considered it the god's residence and believed the cult statue in its interior shrine embodied his life force. Priests attended this divine image, trying to anticipate and meet its every need in a daily cycle of waking, bathing, dressing, feeding, moving around, entertaining, soothing, and revering. These rituals reflected the message of the Babylonian Creation Myth that humankind existed only to serve the gods. Several thousand priests may have staffed a large temple like that of the god Marduk at Babylon.

Priests passed their office and sacred lore to their sons, and their families lived on rations of food from the deity's estates. The amount an individual received depended on his rank within a complicated hierarchy of status and specialized function. The high priest performed the central acts in the great rituals. Certain priests pleasured the gods with music. Others exorcised evil spirits. Still others interpreted dreams and divined the fu-

---

anthropomorphic (an-thruh-phu-MORE-fik)

ture by examining the organs of sacrificed animals, reading patterns in rising incense smoke, or casting dice.

A high wall surrounded the temple precinct, which contained the shrine of the chief deity; open plazas; chapels for lesser gods; housing, dining facilities, and offices for priests and other temple staff; and buildings for crafts, storage, and other services. The compound focused on the **ziggurat°**, a multistory, mud-brick, pyramid-shaped tower approached by ramps and stairs. Scholars are still debating the ziggurat's function and symbolic meaning.

Scholars similarly debate whether common people had much access to temple buildings and how religious practices and beliefs affected their everyday lives. Individuals placed votive statues in the sanctuaries in the belief that these miniature replicas of themselves could continually seek the deity's favor. The survival of many **amulets** (small charms meant to protect the bearer from evil) and representations of a host of demons suggests widespread belief in magic—the use of special words and rituals to manipulate the forces of nature. They believed, for example, that a demon caused headaches and could be driven out of the ailing body. Lamashtu, the demon who caused miscarriages, could be frightened off if a pregnant woman wore an amulet with the likeness of the hideous but beneficent demon Pazuzu. A god or goddess might also be persuaded to reveal the future in return for a gift or sacrifice.

Elite and common folk came together in great festivals such as the twelve-day New Year's festival held each spring in Babylon as the new grain was beginning to sprout in the fields. In the early days of the festival, in conjunction with rituals of purification and invocations of Marduk, a priest read to the god's image the text of the Babylonian Creation Epic. Many subsequent activities in the temple courtyard and streets reenacted the events of the myth. Following their belief that time moved in a circular path through a cycle of birth, growth, maturity, and death, people hoped through this ritual to persuade the gods to grant a renewal of time and life at winter's end (see Diversity and Dominance: Violence and Order in the Babylonian New Year's Festival).

---

ziggurat (ZIG-uh-rat)

Technology and Science

The term *technology* comes from the Greek word *techne*, meaning "skill" or "specialized knowledge." It normally refers to the tools and processes by which humans manipulate the physical world. However, many scholars also use it more broadly for any specialized knowledge used to transform the natural environment and human society. Ancient Mesopotamian irrigation techniques that expanded agricultural production fit the first definition, priestly belief in their ability to enhance prosperity through prayers and rituals the second.

Writing, which first appeared in Mesopotamia before 3300 B.C.E., partakes more of the second definition than of the first. The earliest inscribed tablets, found in the chief temple at Uruk, date from a time when the temple was the community's most important economic institution. The most plausible current theory maintains that writing originated from a system of tokens used to keep track of property—sheep, cattle, wagon wheels—as wealth accumulated and the volume and complexity of commerce strained people's memories. The shape and number of tokens inserted in clay "envelopes" (balls of clay) indicated the contents of a shipment or storeroom, and pictures of the tokens incised on the outside of the envelope reminded the reader of what was inside.

Eventually people realized that the incised pictures, the first written symbols, provided an adequate record of the transaction and made the tokens inside the envelope redundant. Each early symbol represented a thing, but it could also stand for the sound of the word for that thing when that sound was a syllable of a longer word. For example, the symbols *shu* for "hand" and *mu* for "water" could be combined to form *shumu*, the word for "name."

The usual method of writing involved pressing the point of a sharpened reed into a moist clay tablet. Because the reed made wedge-shaped impressions, the early pictures, which were more or less realistic, evolved into stylized combinations of strokes and wedges, a system known as **cuneiform** (Latin for "wedge-shaped") writing. Mastering cuneiform, which in any particular period involved several hundred signs, compared to the twenty-five or so in an alphabetic system, required years of

DIVERSITY AND DOMINANCE

VIOLENCE AND ORDER IN THE BABYLONIAN NEW YEAR'S FESTIVAL

The twelve-day Babylonian New Year's Festival was one of the grandest and most important religious celebrations in ancient Mesopotamia. Complex rituals, both private and public, were performed in accordance with detailed formulas. Fragmentary Babylonian documents of the third century B.C.E. (fifteen hundred years after Hammurabi) provide most of our information about the festival, but because of the continuity of culture over several millennia, the later Babylonian New Year's Festival is likely to preserve many of the beliefs and practices of earlier epochs.

In the first days of the festival, most of the activity took place in inner chambers of the temple of Marduk, patron deity of Babylon, attended only by ranking members of the priesthood. A particularly interesting ceremony was a ritualized humiliation of the king, followed by a renewal of the institution of divinely sanctioned kingship:

On the fifth day of the month Nisannu . . . they shall bring water for washing the king's hands and then shall accompany him to the temple Esagil. The *urigallu*-priest shall leave the sanctuary and take away the scepter, the circle, and the sword from the king. He shall bring them before the god Bel [Marduk] and place them on a chair. He shall leave the sanctuary and strike the king's cheek. He shall accompany the king into the presence of the god Bel. He shall drag him by the ears and make him bow to the ground. The king shall speak the following only once: "I did not sin, lord of the countries. I was not neglectful of the requirements of your godship. I did not destroy Babylon. The temple Esagil, I did not forget its rites. I did not rain blows on the cheek of a subordinate." . . . [The *urigallu*-priest responds:] "The god Bel will listen to your prayer. He will exalt your kingship. The god Bel will bless you forever. He will destroy your enemy, fell your

adversary." After the *urigallu*-priest says this, the king shall regain his composure. The scepter, circle, and sword shall be restored to the king.

Also in the early days of the festival, in conjunction with rituals of purification and invocations to Marduk, a priest recited the entire text of the Babylonian Creation Epic to the image of the god. After relating the origins of the gods from the mating of two primordial creatures, Tiamat, the female embodiment of the salt sea, and Apsu, the male embodiment of fresh water, the myth tells how Tiamat gathered an army of old gods and monsters to destroy the younger generation of gods.

When her labor of creation was ended, against her children Tiamat began preparations of war . . . all the Anunnaki [the younger gods], the host of gods gathered into that place tongue-tied; they sat with mouths shut for they thought, "What other god can make war on Tiamat? No one else can face her and come back" . . . Lord Marduk exulted, . . . with racing spirits he said to the father of gods, "Creator of the gods who decides their destiny, if I must be your avenger, defeating Tiamat, saving your lives, call the Assembly, give me precedence over all the rest; . . . now and for ever let my word be law; I, not you, will decide the world's nature, the things to come. My decrees shall never be altered, never be annulled, but my creation endures to the ends of the world" . . . He took his route towards the rising sound of Tiamat's rage, and all the gods besides, the fathers of the gods pressed in around him, and the lord approached Tiamat. . . . When Tiamat heard him her wits scattered, she was possessed and shrieked aloud, her legs shook from the crotch down, she gabbled spells, muttered maledictions, while the gods of war sharpened their weapons. . . . The lord shot his net to entangle Tiamat, and the pursuing tumid wind, Imhullu, came from behind and beat in her face. When the mouth gaped open to suck him down he drove Imhullu in, so that the mouth would not shut but wind raged through her belly; her carcass blown up, tumescent. She gaped. And now he shot the arrow that split the belly, that pierced the gut and cut the womb.

Now that the Lord had conquered Tiamat he ended her life, he flung her down and straddled the carcass; the leader was killed, Tiamat was dead her rout was shattered, her band dispersed. . . . The lord rested; he gazed at the huge body, pondering how to use it, what to create from the dead carcass. He split it apart like a cockle-shell; with the upper half he constructed the arc of sky, he pulled down the bar and set a watch on the waters, so they should never escape. . . . He projected positions for the Great Gods conspicuous in the sky, he gave them a starry aspect as constellations; he measured the year, gave it a beginning and an end, and to each month of the twelve three rising stars. . . . Through her ribs he opened gates in the east and west, and gave them strong bolts on the right and left; and high in the belly of Tiamat he set the zenith. He gave the moon the luster of a jewel, he gave him all the night, to mark off days, to watch by night each month the circle of a waxing waning light. . . . When Marduk had sent out the moon, he took the sun and set him to complete the cycle from this one to the next New Year. . . .

Then Marduk considered Tiamat. He skimmed spume from the bitter sea, heaped up the clouds, spindrift of wet and wind and cooling rain, the spittle of Tiamat. With his own hands from the steaming mist he spread the clouds. He pressed hard down the head of water, heaping mountains over it, opening springs to flow: Euphrates and Tigris rose from her eyes, but he closed the nostrils and held back their springhead. He piled huge mountains on her paps and through them drove waterholes to channel the deep sources; and high overhead he arched her tail, locked-in to the wheel of heaven; the pit was under his feet, between was the crotch, the sky's fulcrum. Now the earth had foundations and the sky its mantle. . . . When it was done, when they had made Marduk their king, they pronounced peace and happiness for him, "Over our houses you keep unceasing watch, and all you wish from us, that will be done."

Marduk considered and began to speak to the gods assembled in his presence. This is what he said, "In the former time you inhabited the void above the abyss,

but I have made Earth as the mirror of Heaven, I have consolidated the soil for the foundations, and there I will build my city, my beloved home. A holy precinct shall be established with sacred halls for the presence of the king. When you come up from the deep to join the Synod you will find lodging and sleep by night. When others from heaven descend to the Assembly, you too will find lodging and sleep by night. It shall be BABYLON the home of the gods. The masters of all crafts shall build it according to my plan". . . . Now that Marduk has heard what it is the gods are saying, he is moved with desire to create a work of consummate art. He told Ea the deep thought in his heart.

"Blood to blood
I join,
blood to bone
I form
an original thing,
its name is MAN,
aboriginal man
is mine in making.
"All his occupations
are faithful service . . ."

Ea answered with carefully chosen words, completing the plan for the gods' comfort. He said to Marduk, "Let one of the kindred be taken; only one need die for the new creation. Bring the gods together in the Great Assembly; there let the guilty die, so the rest may live."

Marduk called the Great Gods to the Synod; he presided courteously, he gave instructions and all of them listened with grave attention. The king speaks to the rebel gods, "Declare on your oath if ever before you spoke the truth, who instigated rebellion? Who stirred up Tiamat? Who led the battle? Let the instigator of war be handed over; guilt and retribution are on him, and peace will be yours for ever."

The great Gods answered the Lord of the Universe, the king and counselor of gods, "It was Kingu who instigated rebellion, he stirred up that sea of bitterness and led the battle for her." They declared him guilty, they bound and held him down in front of Ea, they cut his arteries and from his blood they created man; and Ea imposed his servitude. . . .

*M*uch of the subsequent activity of the festival, which took place in the temple courtyard and streets, was a reenactment of the events of the

Creation Myth. The festival occurred at the beginning of spring, when the grain shoots were beginning to emerge, and the essential symbolism of the event concerned the return of natural life to the world. The Babylonians believed that time moved in a circular path and that the natural world had a life cycle consisting of birth, growth, maturity, and death. In winter the cycle drew to a close, and there was no guarantee that it would repeat and that life would return to the world. Babylonians hoped that the New Year's Festival would encourage the gods to grant a renewal of time and life, in essence to recreate the world.

QUESTIONS FOR ANALYSIS

1. According to the Creation Epic, how did the present order of the universe come into being? What does the violent nature of this creation tell us about the Mesopotamian view of the physical world and the gods?

2. How did the symbolism of the events of the New Year's Festival, with its ritual reading and recreation of the story of the Creation Myth, validate such concepts as kingship, the primacy of Babylon, and mankind's relationship to the gods?

3. What is the significance of the distinction between the "private" ceremonies celebrated in the temple precincts and the "public" ceremonies that took place in the streets of the city? What does the festival tell us about the relationship of different social groups to the gods?

Source: Adapted from James B. Pritchard, ed., *Ancient Near Eastern Texts Relating to the Old Testament*, 3d ed. (Princeton, NJ: Princeton University Press, 1969), 332–334. Copyright © 1969 by Princeton University Press. Reprinted by permission of Princeton University Press.

practice. In the "tablet-house" attached to a temple or palace, students learned writing and mathematics under a stern headmaster and endured bullying by older student tutors called "big brothers." The prestige and regular employment that went with their position may have made scribes reluctant to simplify the cuneiform system. In the Old Babylonian period, the growth of private commerce brought an increase in the number of people who could read and write, but literacy remained a rare accomplishment.

Developed originally for the Sumerian language, cuneiform—a system of writing rather than a language—later served to express the Akkadian language of the Mesopotamian Semites as well as other languages of western Asia, such as Hittite, Elamite, and Persian. The remains of the ancient city of Ebla° in northern Syria illustrate the Mesopotamian influence on other parts of western Asia. Ebla's buildings and artifacts follow Mesopotamian models, and thousands of tablets inscribed with cuneiform symbols bear messages in both Sumerian and the local Semitic dialect. The high point of Ebla's wealth and power occurred from 2400 to 2250 B.C.E., roughly contemporary with the Akkadian Empire. Ebla then controlled extensive territory and derived wealth from agriculture, manufacture of woolen cloth, and trade with Mesopotamia and the Mediterranean coast.

Economic concerns predominate in the earliest Sumerian documents, but cuneiform came to have wide-ranging uses beyond the recordkeeping that apparently inspired its invention. Legal acts that had formerly been validated by the recitation of oral formulas and performance of symbolic acts came to be accompanied by written documents marked with the seals of the participants. Cuneiform similarly served political, literary, religious, and scientific purposes.

Other technologies met the challenges of the physical environment. Irrigation, the basis of Mesopotamian agriculture, required the construction and maintenance of canals, weirs, and dikes. Cattle drew carts and sledges in some locations. In the south, where numerous water channels cut up the landscape, boats and barges predominated. In northern Mesopotamia, donkeys served as pack animals for overland caravans in the centuries before the advent of the camel around 1200 B.C.E.

Ebla (EH-bluh)

Mesopotamian Cylinder Seal   Seals indicated the identity of an individual and were impressed into wet clay or wax to "sign" legal documents or to mark ownership of an object. This seal, produced in the period of the Akkadian Empire, depicts Ea (second from right), the god of underground waters, symbolized by the stream with fish emanating from his shoulders; Ishtar, whose attributes of fertility and war are indicated by the date cluster in her hand and the pointed weapons showing above her wings; and the sun-god Shamash, cutting his way out of the mountains with a jagged knife, an evocation of sunrise.   (Courtesy of the Trustees of the British Museum)

To improve on stone tools, the Mesopotamians imported ores containing copper, tin, and arsenic. From these they made bronze, a form of copper alloyed with either tin or arsenic. Craftsmen poured molten bronze into molds shaped like weapons or tools. The cooled metal took a sharper edge than stone, was less likely to break, and was more easily repaired. Yet stone implements remained in use among poor people who could not afford bronze.

Clay, Mesopotamia's most abundant resource, went into the making of mud bricks. Whether dried in the sun or baked in an oven for greater durability, these constituted the main building material. Construction of city walls, temples, and palaces required practical knowledge of architecture and engineering. For example, the reed mats that Mesopotamian builders laid between the mud-brick layers of ziggurats served the same stabilizing purpose as girders in modern high-rise construction. The abundance of good clay also made pottery the most common material for dishes and storage vessels. By

4000 B.C.E., potters had begun to use a revolving platform called a potter's wheel. Spun by hands or feet, the potter's wheel made possible rapid manufacture in precise and complex shapes.

Military technology changed as armies evolved from the early militias called up for short periods to the well-trained and well-paid full-time soldiers of the late third and second millennia B.C.E. In the early second millennium B.C.E., horses appeared in western Asia, and the horse-drawn chariot, a technically complicated device, came into vogue. Infantry found themselves at the mercy of swift chariots carrying a driver and an archer who could easily overtake them. Using increasingly effective siege machinery, Mesopotamian soldiers learned to climb over, undermine, or knock down the walls protecting the cities of their enemies.

In another area where the Mesopotamians sought to gain control of their physical environment, they used a base-60 number system (the origin of the seconds and minutes we use today), in which numbers were expressed as fractions or multiples of 60 (in contrast to our base-10 system). Such advances in mathematics along with careful observation of the skies made the Mesopotamians sophisticated practitioners of astronomy. Mesopotamian priests compiled lists of omens or unusual sightings on earth and in the heavens, together with a record of the events that coincided with them. They consulted these texts at critical times, for they believed that the recurrence of such phenomena could provide clues to future developments. The underlying premise was that the elements of the material universe, from the microcosmic to the macrocosmic, were interconnected in mysterious but undeniable ways.

EGYPT

No other place exhibits the impact of the natural environment on the history and culture of a society better than ancient Egypt. Though located at the intersection of Asia and Africa, Egypt was less a crossroads than an isolated land protected by surrounding barriers of desert and a harborless, marshy seacoast. Whereas Mesopotamia was open to migration or invasion and was dependent on imported resources, Egypt's natural isolation and material self-sufficiency fostered a unique culture that for long periods had relatively little to do with other civilizations.

The Land of Egypt: "Gift of the Nile"

The world's longest river, the Nile flows northward from Lake Victoria and draws water from several large tributaries in the highlands of tropical Africa. Carving a narrow valley between a chain of hills on either side, it terminates at the Mediterranean Sea (see Map 1.2). Though bordered mostly by desert, the banks of the river support lush vegetation. About 100 miles (160 kilometers) from the Mediterranean, the river divides into channels to form a triangular delta. Most of Egypt's population lives on the twisting, green ribbon of land along the river or in the Nile Delta. Bleak deserts of mountains, rocks, and dunes occupy the remaining 90 percent of the country. The ancient Egyptians distin-

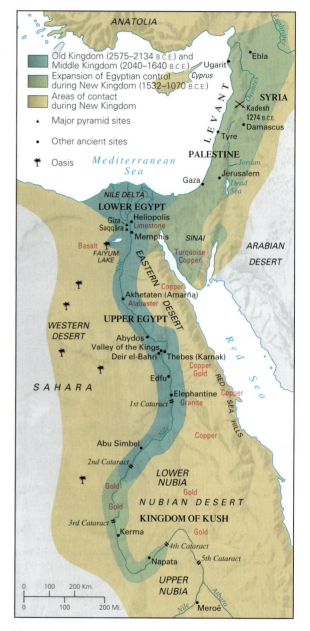

Map 1.2 Ancient Egypt The Nile River, flowing south to north, carved out of the surrounding desert a narrow green valley that became heavily settled in antiquity.

guished between the low-lying, life-sustaining "Black Land" with its dark soil and the elevated, deadly "Red Land" of the desert. The fifth-century

Model of Egyptian River Boat, ca. 1985 B.C.E. This model was buried in the tomb of a Middle Kingdom official, Meketre, who is shown in the cabin being entertained by musicians. The captain stands in front of the cabin, the helmsman on the left steers the boat with the rudder, while the lookout on the right lets out a weighted line to determine the river's depth. The vessel is being rowed downstream (northward); the white post in the middle would support a mast and sail when traveling upstream. (The Metropolitan Museum of Art, Rogers Fund and Edward S. Harkness Gift, 1920 (20.3.1). Photograph © 1992 The Metropolitan Museum of Art.)

B.C.E. Greek traveler Herodotus° called Egypt the "gift of the Nile."

Travel and communication centered on the river, with the most important cities located upstream away from the Mediterranean. Because the river flows from south to north, the Egyptians called the southern part of the country "Upper Egypt" and the northern delta "Lower Egypt." The First Cataract of the Nile, the northernmost of a series of impassable rocks and rapids below Aswan° (about 500 miles [800 kilometers] south of the Mediterranean), formed Egypt's southern boundary in most periods, but Egyptian control sometimes extended farther south into what they called "Kush" (later Nubia, today part of southern Egypt and northern Sudan). The Egyptians also settled certain large oases west of the river, green and habitable "islands" in the midst of the desert.

The hot, sunny climate favored agriculture. Though rain rarely falls south of the delta, the river provided water to irrigation channels that carried water out into the valley and increased the area suitable for planting. In one large depression west of the Nile, drainage techniques reduced the size of Lake Faiyum° and allowed land to be reclaimed for agriculture.

Each September, the river overflowed its banks, spreading water into the bordering valley. Unlike the Mesopotamians, the Egyptians needed no dams or weirs to raise the level of the river and divert water into channels. Moreover, the Nile, unlike the Tigris and Euphrates, flooded at the best time for grain agriculture. When the flood receded and its waters drained back into the river, the land had a fertile new layer of mineral-rich silt, and farmers could easily plant their crops in the moist soil. The Egyptians' many creation myths commonly featured the emergence of a life-supporting mound of earth from a primeval swamp.

The level of the flood's crest determined the abundance of the following harvest. "Nilometers," stone staircases with incised units of height along the river's edge, recorded each flood. Too much

---

Herodotus (he-ROD-uh-tuhs) **Aswan** (AS-wahn)

Faiyum (fie-YOOM)

water washed out the dikes protecting inhabited areas and caused much damage. Too little water left fertile land unirrigated and hence uncultivable, plunging the country into famine. The ebb and flow of successful and failed regimes seems linked to the cycle of floods. Nevertheless, remarkable stability characterized most eras, and Egyptians viewed the universe as an orderly and beneficent place.

Egypt's other natural resources offered further advantages. Papyrus reeds growing in marshy areas yielded fibers that made good sails, ropes, and a kind of paper. The wild animals and birds of the marshes and desert fringe and the abundant river fish attracted hunters and fishermen. Building stone could be quarried and floated downstream from a number of locations in southern Egypt. Clay for mud bricks and pottery could be found almost everywhere. Copper and turquoise deposits in the Sinai desert to the east and gold from Nubia to the south were within reach, and the state organized armed expeditions and forced labor to exploit these resources. Thus, Egypt was substantially more self-sufficient than Mesopotamia.

The farming villages that appeared in Egypt as early as 5500 B.C.E. relied on domesticated plant and animal species that had emerged several millennia earlier in western Asia. Egypt's emergence as a focal point of civilization, however, stemmed at least partially from a gradual change in climate from the fifth to the third millennium B.C.E. Before that time, the Sahara, today the world's largest desert, had a relatively mild and wet climate. Its lakes and grasslands supported a variety of plant and animal species as well as populations of hunter-gatherers (see Chapter 6). As the climate changed and the Sahara began to dry up, displaced groups migrated into the then marshy Nile Valley, where they developed a sedentary way of life.

Divine Kingship

The increasing population called for greater complexity in political organization, including a form of local kingship. Later generations of Egyptians saw the unification of such smaller units into a single state by Menes°, a ruler from the south, as a pivotal event. Scholars question whether this event, dated to around 3100 B.C.E., took place at the hands of a historical or a mythical figure, but many authorities equate Menes with Narmer, a historical ruler who is shown on a decorated slate palette exulting over defeated enemies. Later kings of Egypt bore the title "Ruler of the Two Lands"—Upper and Lower Egypt—and wore two crowns symbolizing the unification of the country. Unlike Mesopotamia, Egypt discovered unity early in its history.

Following the practice of Manetho, an Egyptian priest from the fourth century B.C.E., historians divide Egyptian history into thirty dynasties (sequences of kings from the same family). The rise and fall of dynasties often reflect the dominance of one or another part of the country. Scholars also divide Egyptian history into "Old," "Middle," and "New Kingdoms," each a period of centralized political power and brilliant cultural achievement. "Intermediate Periods" signal political fragmentation and cultural decline. Although experts debate the specific dates, the chronology (on page 7) reflects current opinion.

The Egyptian state centered on the king, often known by the New Kingdom term **pharaoh,** from an Egyptian phrase meaning "palace." From the Old Kingdom on, if not earlier, Egyptians considered the king a god on earth, the incarnation of Horus and the son of the sun-god Re°. In this role he maintained **ma'at°,** the divinely authorized order of the universe. As a link between the people and the gods, his benevolent rule ensured the welfare and prosperity of the country. The Egyptians' conception of a divine king, the source of law and justice, may explain the apparent absence in Egypt of an impersonal code of law comparable to Hammurabi's Code in Mesopotamia.

So much depended on the kings that their deaths evoked elaborate efforts to ensure the well-being of their spirits on their journey to rejoin the gods. Carrying out funerary rites, constructing royal tombs, and sustaining the kings' spirits in the afterlife by perpetual offerings in adjoining funerary chapels demanded massive resources. Flat-topped, rectangular tombs made of mud brick sufficed for the earliest rulers, but around 2630

Menes (MEH-neez)

Re (ray)   ma'at (muh-AHT)

B.C.E., Djoser°, a Third Dynasty king, ordered the construction of a stepped **pyramid**—a series of stone platforms laid one on top of the other—at Saqqara°, near Memphis. Rulers of the Fourth Dynasty filled in the steps of Djoser's tomb to create the smooth-sided, limestone pyramids that most often symbolize ancient Egypt. Between 2550 and 2490 B.C.E., the pharaohs Khufu° and Khefren° erected huge pyramids at Giza, several miles north of Saqqara, the largest stone structures ever built. Khufu's pyramid originally reached a height of 480 feet (146 meters).

Egyptians accomplished this construction with stone tools (bronze was still expensive and rare) and no machinery other than simple levers, pulleys, and rollers. Calculations of the human muscle power needed to build a pyramid within a ruler's lifetime indicate that large numbers of people must have been pressed into service for part of each year, probably during the flood season, when no agricultural work could be done. The Egyptian masses probably considered this demand for labor a kind of religious service that would help ensure prosperity. Most of Egypt's surplus resources went into constructing these artificial mountains of stone. The age of the great pyramids lasted about a century, though construction of pyramids on a smaller scale continued for two millennia.

Administration and Communication

Ruling dynasties usually placed their capitals in the area of their original power base. **Memphis,** near today's Cairo at the apex of the Nile Delta, held this central position during the Old Kingdom; but **Thebes,** far to the south, often supplanted it during the Middle and New Kingdoms (see Map 1.2). A complex bureaucracy kept detailed records of the country's resources. Beginning at the village level and progressing to the district level and finally to the central government based in the capital, bureaucrats kept track of land, labor, products, and people, extracting as taxes a substantial portion—as much as 50 percent—of the annual revenues of the country. This income supported the palace, bureaucracy, and army; paid for building and maintaining temples; and made possible great monuments celebrating the king's grandeur. The government maintained a monopoly over key sectors of the economy and controlled long-distance trade. The urban middle-class traders who increasingly managed the commerce of Mesopotamia had no parallel in Egypt.

A writing system had been developed before the Early Dynastic period, and literacy was the hallmark of the administrative class. **Hieroglyphics°,** the earliest form of this system, featured picture symbols standing for words, syllables, or individual sounds. We can read ancient Egyptian writing today only because of the discovery in the early nineteenth century C.E. of the Rosetta Stone, an inscription from the second century B.C.E. that gave hieroglyphic and Greek versions of the same text.

Hieroglyphic writing was used on monuments and ornamental inscriptions for a long time. By 2500 B.C.E., however, administrators and copyists had developed a cursive script, in which the original pictorial nature of the symbol was less apparent, for their everyday needs. They wrote with ink on a writing material called **papyrus°,** made from the stems of the papyrus reed that grew in the Nile marshes. Papyrus makers laid out the stems in a vertical and horizontal grid pattern, moistened them, and then pounded them with a soft mallet until they adhered into a sheet of writing material. A uniquely Egyptian product, papyrus served scribes throughout the ancient world and was exported in large quantities. The word *paper* comes from Greek and Roman words for papyrus.

Apart from administrative recordkeeping, Egyptian literary compositions included tales of adventure and magic, love poetry, religious hymns, and instruction manuals on technical subjects. Scribes in workshops attached to the temples made copies of traditional texts.

Strong monarchs appointed and promoted officials on the basis of merit and accomplishment, giving them grants of land cultivated by dependent peasants. Low-level officials worked in villages and

---

Djoser (JO-sur) **Saqqara** (suh-KAHR-uh) **Khufu** (KOO-foo) **Khefren** (KEF-ren)

hieroglyphics (high-ruh-GLIF-iks) **papyrus** (puh-PIE-ruhs)

district capitals; high-ranking officials served in the royal capital. During the Old Kingdom, the tombs of officials lay near the monumental tomb of the king so they could serve him in death as they had in life.

Egyptian history exhibits a recurring tension between the centralizing power of the monarchy and the decentralizing tendencies of the bureaucracy. The shift of officials' tombs from the vicinity of the royal tomb to the home districts where they spent much of their time and exercised power more or less independently signaled the breakdown of centralized power in the late Old Kingdom and First Intermediate Period. Inheritance of administrative posts similarly indicated a decline in centralized power. The early monarchs of the Middle Kingdom restored centralized power by reducing the power and prerogatives of the old elite and creating a new middle class of administrators.

The common observation that Egypt was a land of villages without real cities stems from its capitals being primarily extensions of the palace and central administration. Compared to Mesopotamia, a far larger percentage of the Egyptian population lived in farming villages, and Egypt's wealth derived to a higher degree from cultivating the land. The towns and cities that did exist unfortunately lie buried beneath modern urban sites, since Egypt has too little land in its cultivable region to afford abandonment of a large area.

Egypt largely stuck to itself during the Old and Middle Kingdoms, all foreigners being technically regarded as enemies. When necessary, local militia units backed up a small standing army of professional soldiers. Nomadic groups in the eastern and western deserts and Libyans to the northwest posed a nuisance more than a real danger. The king maintained limited contact with other advanced civilizations in the region. Egypt's interests abroad focused on maintaining access to resources rather than on acquiring territory. Trade with the Levant° coast (modern Israel, Lebanon, and Syria) brought in cedar wood in return for grain, papyrus, and gold.

Egypt's strongest interests involved goods from the south. Nubia contained gold mines (in Chapter 2 we examine the rise in Nubia of a civilization influenced by Egypt but also vital, original, and long lasting), and the southern course of the Nile offered access to sub-Saharan Africa. In the Old Kingdom, Egyptian noblemen living at Aswan on the southern border led donkey caravans south in search of gold, incense, and products from tropical Africa such as ivory, ebony, and exotic animals. Forts along the border protected Egypt from attack. In the early second millennium B.C.E., Egyptian forces invaded Nubia and extended the Egyptian border as far as the Third Cataract of the Nile, taking possession of the gold fields.

The People of Egypt

The estimated million to a million and half inhabitants of Egypt included various physical types, ranging from dark-skinned people related to the populations of sub-Saharan Africa to lighter-skinned people akin to the populations of North Africa and western Asia who spoke Berber and Semitic languages, respectively. Though Egypt experienced no migrations or invasions on a scale common in Mesopotamian history, settlers periodically trickled into the Nile Valley and mixed with the local people.

Egypt had less pronounced social divisions than Mesopotamia, where a formal class structure emerged. The king and high-ranking officials enjoyed status, wealth, and power. Below them came lower-level officials, local leaders, priests and other professionals, artisans, and well-to-do farmers. Peasants, at the bottom, constituted the vast majority of the population.

Peasants lived in rural villages and devoted themselves to the seasonally changing tasks of agriculture: plowing, sowing, tending emerging shoots, reaping, threshing, and storing. They maintained irrigation channels, basins, and dikes. Fish and meat from domesticated animals—cattle, sheep, goats, and poultry—supplemented a diet based on wheat or barley, beer, and vegetables. Villages probably shared implements, work animals, and storage facilities and helped one another at peak times in the agricultural cycle and in building projects. Festivals to the local gods and other public celebrations occasionally brought feasting and ceremonies into their lives; labor conscripted for pyramid construction and other state projects

Levant (luh-VANT)

brought hardship. If the burden of taxation or compulsory service proved too great, flight into the desert usually offered the only escape.

This account of village life depends on guesswork and bits and pieces of archaeological and literary evidence. Tomb paintings of the elite sometimes depict the lives of common folk. The artists employed conventions to indicate status: obesity for the rich and comfortable, baldness and deformity for the working classes. Egyptian poets frequently employed metaphors of farming and hunting, and papyrus documents preserved in the hot, dry sands tell of property transactions and legal disputes among ordinary people.

Slavery existed on a limited scale and was of little economic significance. Prisoners of war, condemned criminals, and debtors could be found on country estates or in the households of the king and wealthy families. But humane treatment softened the burden of slavery, as did the possibility of being freed.

Scarceness of sources also clouds the experiences of women. What is known about the lives of elite women derives from the possibly distorted impressions of male artists and scribes. Tomb paintings, rendered with dignity and affection, show women of the royal family and elite classes accompanying their husbands and engaging in domestic activities. Subordination to men is evident. The convention of depicting men with a dark red and women with a yellow flesh tone implies that elite women stayed indoors, away from the searing sun. In the beautiful love poetry of the New Kingdom, lovers address each other in terms of apparent equality and express emotions akin to our own ideal of romantic love. Whether this poetry represents the attitudes prevalent in other periods or among nonelite groups remains unknown.

Legal documents show that Egyptian women could own property, inherit from their parents, and will their property to whomever they wished. Marriage, usually monogamous, arose from a couple's decision to establish a household together rather than through legal or religious ceremony. Either party could dissolve the relationship, and the woman retained rights over her dowry in case of divorce. At certain times, queens and queen-mothers played significant behind-the-scenes roles in the politics of the royal court, and priestesses sometimes supervised the cults of female deities. In general, the limited evidence suggests that women in ancient Egypt enjoyed greater respect and more legal rights and social freedom than women in Mesopotamia and other ancient societies.

Belief and Knowledge

Egyptian religion evoked the landscape of the Nile Valley and the vision of cosmic order that this environment fostered. The sun rose every day into a clear and cloudless sky, and the river flooded on schedule every year, ensuring a bounteous harvest. Recurrent cycles and periodic renewal seemed a part of the natural world. Egyptians imagined the sky to be a great ocean surrounding the inhabited world. The sun-god Re traversed its waters in a boat by day, then returned through the Underworld at night, fighting off the attacks of demonic serpents so that he could be born anew each morning. In one especially popular story, Osiris°, a god who once ruled the land of Egypt, dies at the hand of his jealous brother Seth, who scatters his dismembered remains. Isis, Osiris's sister and wife, finds and reassembles the pieces, while Horus, his son, takes revenge on Seth. Restored to life and installed as king of the Underworld, Osiris represented hope for a new life in a world beyond this one.

The king, represented as Horus and as the son of Re, fit into the pattern of the dead returning to life and the sun-god renewing life. As Egypt's chief priest, he intervened with the gods on behalf of his land and people. When a particular town became the capital of a ruling dynasty, the chief god of that town gained prominence throughout the land. Thus did Ptah° of Memphis, Re of Heliopolis°, and Amon° of Thebes become gods of all Egypt, serving to unify the country and strengthen the monarchy.

Egyptian rulers zealously built new temples, refurbished old ones, and made lavish gifts to the gods, at the same time overseeing construction of their own tombs. Thus, much of the country's wealth went for religious purposes in the ceaseless

---

Osiris (oh-SIGH-ris) **Ptah** (puh-TAH) **Heliopolis** (he-lee-OP-uh-lis) **Amon** (AH-muhn)

effort to win the gods' favor, maintain the continuity of divine kingship, and ensure the renewal of life-giving forces.

Some deities normally appear with animal heads; others always take human form. Few myths about the origins and adventures of the gods have survived, but there must have been a rich oral tradition. Many towns had temples in which locally prominent deities were thought to reside. Such local deities could be viewed as manifestations of the great gods, and gods could merge to form hybrids, such as Amon-Re. Ordinary believers were excluded from cult activities in the inner reaches of the temples, where priests served the daily needs of the deity by attending to his or her statue. Food offered to the image was later distributed to temple staff. As in Mesopotamia, some temples possessed extensive landholdings worked by dependent peasants, and the priests who administered the deity's wealth played an influential role locally and sometimes throughout the land.

During great festivals, the priests paraded a boat-shaped litter carrying the shrouded statue and cult items of the deity around the town. This brought large numbers of people into contact with the deity in an outpouring of devotion and celebration. Little is known about the day-to-day beliefs and practices of the common people, however. At home, family members revered and made small offerings to Bes, the grotesque god of marriage and domestic happiness, to local deities, and to the family's ancestors. They relied on amulets and depictions of demonic figures to ward off evil forces. In later times, Greeks and Romans commented on the Egyptian devotion to magic.

Egyptians believed in the afterlife. They prepared extensively for a safe passage and a comfortable existence once they arrived. Hazards abounded on the soul's journey after death. The Egyptian Book of the Dead, present in many excavated tombs, contained rituals and spells to protect the journeying spirit. The weighing of the deceased's heart (believed to be the source of personality, intellect, and emotion) in the presence of the judges of the Underworld presented the ultimate challenge—the one that determined whether the deceased had led a good life and deserved to reach the blessed destination.

The Egyptian obsession with the afterlife produced concerns about the physical condition of the dead body and a perfection of mummification techniques for preserving it. The idea probably derived from the slow decomposition of bodies buried in hot, dry sand on the edge of the desert, an early practice. The elite classes spent the most on mummification. Specialists removed vital organs for preservation and storage in stone jars laid out around the corpse and filled the body cavities with various packing materials. After immersing the cadaver for long periods in dehydrating and preserving chemicals, they wrapped it in linen. They then placed the **mummy** in one or more decorated wooden caskets with a tomb.

Building tombs at the edge of the desert left the lowlands free for farming. Pictures and samples of food and objects from everyday life accompanied the mummy to provide whatever he or she might need in the next life. Much of what is now known about ancient Egyptian life comes from examining utilitarian and luxury household objects found in tombs. Small figurines called shawabtis° represented the servants whom the deceased might need or the laborers he might send as substitutes if asked to provide compulsory labor. The elite classes ordered chapels attached to their tombs and left endowments to subsidize the daily attendance of a priest and offerings of foodstuffs to sustain their spirits for eternity.

The form of the tomb also reflected wealth and status. Simple pit graves or small mud-brick chambers sufficed for the common people. Members of the privileged classes built larger tombs and covered the walls with pictures and inscriptions. Kings erected pyramids and other grand edifices, employing trickery to hide the sealed chamber containing the body and treasures, as well as curses and other magical precautions to foil tomb robbers. Rarely did they succeed, however. Archaeologists have seldom discovered an undisturbed royal tomb.

The ancient Egyptians explored many areas of knowledge and developed advantageous technologies. They learned about chemistry through developing the mummification process, which also provided opportunities to learn about human anatomy. Egyptian doctors served in royal courts throughout western Asia because of their relatively advanced medical knowledge and techniques.

---

shawabtis (shuh-WAB-tees)

The endless cycle of flooding and irrigation spurred the development of mathematics for determining the dimensions of fields and calculating the quantity of agricultural produce owed to the state. Through careful observation of the stars, they constructed the most accurate calendar in the world, and they knew that when the star Sirius appeared on the horizon shortly before sunrise, the Nile flood surge was imminent.

For pyramids, temple complexes, and other monumental building projects, vast quantities of earth had to be moved and the construction site made level. Large stones had to be quarried, dragged on rollers, floated downstream on barges, lifted into place along ramps of packed earth, carved to the exact size needed, and then made smooth. Long underground passageways connected mortuary temples by the river with tombs near the desert's edge. More practically, several Egyptian kings dredged a canal more than 50 miles (80 kilometers) long to connect the Nile Valley to the Red Sea and expedite the transport of goods.

Besides river barges for transporting building stones, the Nile carried lightweight ships equipped with sails and oars. These sometimes ventured into the Mediterranean and Red Seas. Canals and flooded basins limited the use of carts and sledges, but archaeologists have discovered an 8-mile (13-kilometer) road made of slabs of sandstone and limestone connecting a rock quarry with Faiyum Lake. The oldest known paved road in the world, it dates to the second half of the third millennium B.C.E.

THE INDUS VALLEY CIVILIZATION

Civilization developed almost as early in South Asia as in Mesopotamia and Egypt. Just as each Middle Eastern civilization centered on a great river valley, so civilization in the Indian subcontinent originated on a fertile floodplain. In the valley of the Indus River, settled farming created the agricultural surplus essential to urbanized society.

Natural Environment

A plain of more than 1 million acres (400,000 hectares) stretches between the mountains of western Pakistan and the Thar° Desert to the east in the central portion of the Indus Valley, the province of Sind° in modern Pakistan (see Map 1.1). Silt carried downstream and deposited on the land by the Indus River over many centuries has elevated the riverbed and its banks above the level of the plain. Twice a year, the river overflows and inundates surrounding land as far as 10 miles (16 kilometers) distant. Snowmelt from the Pamir° and Himalaya° Mountains feeds the flood in March and April. In August, seasonal winds called monsoons (see Chapter 4) bring rains from the southwest that feed a second flood. Though extremely dry for the rest of the year, Sind's floods make two crops a year possible. In ancient times, the Hakra° River (sometimes referred to as the Saraswati), which has since dried up, ran parallel to the Indus about 25 miles (40 kilometers) to the east and supplied water to a second cultivable area.

Adjacent regions shared distinctive cultural traits with this core area. In Punjab (literally "five waters"), to the northeast, five rivers converge to feed the main stream of the Indus. Closer to the northern mountains, the Punjab receives more rainfall but less floodwater than Sind. Culturally similar settlements extend from the Punjab as far east as Delhi° in northwest India. Settlement also extended through the Indus delta in southern Sind down into India's hook-shaped Kathiawar° Peninsula, an area of alluvial plains and coastal marshes. The Indus Valley civilization, as scholars labeled this area of cultural homogeneity when they first discovered it eighty years ago, covered an area roughly equivalent to modern France.

Material Culture

Although archaeologists have located several hundred communities that flourished from approximately 2600 to 1900 B.C.E., the remains of two urban sites, known by the modern names **Harappa**

Thar (tahr)   **Sind** (sinned)   **Pamir** (pah-MEER)
Himalaya (him-uh-LAY-uh)   **Hakra** (HAK-ruh)   **Delhi**
(DEL-ee)   **Kathiawar** (kah-tee-uh-WAHR)

and **Mohenjo-Daro°,** best typify the Indus Valley civilization. Unfortunately, the high water table at these sites makes excavation of the earliest levels of settlement nearly impossible.

Scholars once believed that the people who created this civilization spoke Dravidian° languages related to those spoken today in southern India. Invaders from the northwest speaking Indo-European languages, they thought, conquered these people around 1500 B.C.E., causing some of them to migrate to the southeast. Skeletal evidence, however, indicates that the population of the Indus Valley has remained stable from ancient times to the present. Settled agriculture in this region seems to date back to at least 5000 B.C.E. Archaeological investigations have not yet revealed the relations between the Indus Valley civilization and earlier cultural complexes in the Indus Valley and the hilly lands to the west or the forces that gave rise to the urbanization, population increase, and technological advances that occurred in the mid-third millennium B.C.E. Nevertheless, the case for continuity with earlier cultures seems stronger than the case for a sudden transformation due to the arrival of new peoples.

The writing system of the Indus Valley people contained more than four hundred signs to represent syllables and words. Archaeologists have recovered thousands of inscribed seal stones and copper tablets. The inscriptions are so brief, however, that no one has yet deciphered them, though some scholars believe they represent an early Dravidian language.

Harappa, 3.5 miles (5.6 kilometers) in circumference, may have housed a population of 35,000, and Mohenjo-Daro several times that. These cities show marked similarities in planning and construction: high, thick, encircling walls of brick; streets laid out in a rectangular grid; and covered drainpipes to carry away waste. The consistent width of streets and length of city blocks, and the uniformity of the mud bricks used in construction, suggest a strong central authority, located possibly in the citadel—an elevated, enclosed compound containing large buildings. Scholars think the well-ventilated struc-

Mohenjo-Daro (moe-hen-joe-DAHR-oh)   **Dravidian** (druh-VID-ee-uhn)

tures near the citadel stored grain for local use and for export. The presence of barracks may point to some regimentation of skilled artisans.

Though it is presumed that these urban centers controlled the surrounding farmlands, different centers may have served different functions, which might account for their locations. Mohenjo-Daro seems to dominate the great floodplain of the Indus. Harappa, which is nearly 500 miles (805 kilometers) to the north, sits in the zone where farmlands give way to pasturelands. No settlements have been found west of Harappa, which may have served as a gateway for copper, tin, precious stones, and other resources coming from the northwest. Coastal towns to the south engaged in seaborne trade with Sumer and lands around the Persian Gulf, as well as in fishing and gathering highly prized seashells.

Although published accounts of the Indus Valley civilization tend to treat Mohenjo-Daro and Harappa, the most extensively excavated sites, as the norm, most people surely lived in smaller settlements, which exhibit the same artifacts and the same standardization of styles and shapes as the large cities. Some scholars attribute this standardization to extensive exchange of goods within the zone of the Indus Valley civilization rather than to a strong and authoritarian central government.

Metal appears more frequently in Indus Valley sites than in Mesopotamia or Egypt. Tools and other useful objects outweigh in importance the decorative objects—jewelry and the like—so often found in those other regions. Whereas metal goods were largely the possessions of elite groups in the Middle East, in the Indus Valley they belonged to a broad cross-section of the population.

Technologically, the Indus Valley people showed skill in irrigation, used the potter's wheel, and fired bricks to rocky hardness in kilns for use in the foundations of large public buildings (sundried bricks exposed to floodwaters would have dissolved quickly). Smiths worked with various metals—gold, silver, copper, and tin. The varying ratios of tin to copper in their bronze objects suggest awareness of the hardness of different mixtures. They used less tin, a relatively scarce metal, in objects that did not require maximum hardness, like knives, and more tin in things like axes that had to be harder.

Archaeological finds point to widespread trading contacts. Mountain passes through the northwest granted access to the valuable resources of eastern Iran and Afghanistan, as well as to ore deposits in western India. These resources included metals (such as copper and tin), precious stones (lapis lazuli, jade, and turquoise), building stone, and timber. Rivers provided thoroughfares for transporting goods within the zone of Indus Valley culture. The undeciphered writing on the many seal stones, some scholars feel, may represent the names of merchants who stamped their wares.

Inhabitants of the Indus Valley and of Mesopotamia obtained raw materials from some of the same sources. The discovery of Indus Valley seal stones in the Tigris-Euphrates Valley indicates that merchants from the former region may have acted as middlemen in long-distance trade, obtaining raw materials from the northwest and shipping them to the Persian Gulf.

We know little about the political, social, economic, and religious structures of Indus Valley society. Efforts to link artifacts and images to cultural features characteristic of later periods of Indian history (see Chapter 4), including sociopolitical institutions (a system of hereditary occupational groups, the predominant role of priests), architectural forms (bathing tanks like those later found in Hindu temples, private interior courtyards in houses), and religious beliefs and practices (depictions of gods and sacred animals on the seal stones, a cult of the mother-goddess), remain speculative. Further knowledge on these matters awaits additional archaeological finds and deciphering of the Indus Valley script.

Transformation of the Indus Valley Civilization

The Indus Valley cities were abandoned sometime after 1900 B.C.E. Archaeologists once thought that invaders destroyed them, but they now believe this civilization suffered "systems failure"—a breakdown of the fragile interrelationship of political, social, and economic systems that sustained order and prosperity. The precipitating cause may have been one or more natural disasters, such as an earthquake or massive flooding. Gradual ecologi-

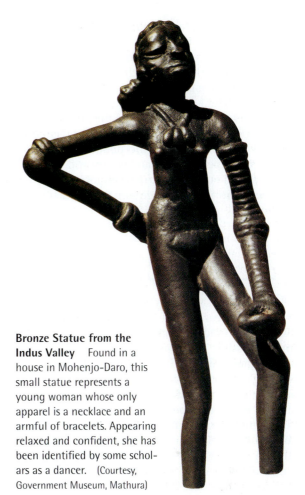

Bronze Statue from the Indus Valley   Found in a house in Mohenjo-Daro, this small statue represents a young woman whose only apparel is a necklace and an armful of bracelets. Appearing relaxed and confident, she has been identified by some scholars as a dancer.   (Courtesy, Government Museum, Mathura)

cal changes may also have played a role as the Hakra river system dried up and salinization (an increase in the amount of plant-inhibiting salt in the soil) and erosion increased.

Towns left dry by a change of riverbed, seaports removed from the coast by silt deposited in deltas, and regions suffering loss of fertile soil would have necessitated the relocation of populations and a change in the livelihood of those who remained. The causes, patterns, and pace of change probably varied, with urbanization persisting longer in some regions than in others. The urban centers eventually succumbed, however, and village-based farming and herding took their place. As the interaction between regions lessened, regional variation replaced the standardization of technology and style of the previous era.

Historians can do little more than speculate about the causes behind the changes and the experiences of the people who lived in the Indus Valley around 1900 B.C.E. Two tendencies bear remembering, however. In most cases like this, the majority of the population adjusts to the new circumstances. But members of the political and social elite, who depend on urban centers and complex political and economic structures, lose the source of their authority and merge with the population as a whole.

CONCLUSION

Tens of thousands of years elapsed between the first appearance of the earliest ancestors of humankind and the agricultural revolutions that made possible the transition to civilization. Domesticated plants and animals contributed to the settling down of wandering groups of foragers and, in time, produced sufficient surplus food to relieve a small minority of people from the labor of tilling fields and watching flocks. Some of these people availed themselves of this opportunity to advance already existing skills—painting, stonework, weaving, building—to higher levels requiring more specialized techniques. Others specialized in warfare, administration, religious ceremonies, and accumulation of knowledge. Thus did humanity pass from the prehistoric era to the era of civilized history.

The first civilizations developed high levels of political centralization, urbanization, and technology because their situations in river valleys too arid to support agriculture through rainfall forced communities to work together on constructing and maintaining canals, dams, weirs, and dikes. Crops harvested from irrigated fields not only fed the farming populations of Mesopotamia, Egypt, and the Indus Valley, but also produced enough surplus to support artisans with specialized expertise in engineering, mathematics, and metallurgy.

Unpredictable and violent floods constantly threatened communities in the Tigris-Euphrates Basin, but the opportune and gradual Nile floods usually brought joy and satisfaction to those in Egypt. Relationships with nature stamped the world-view of both peoples. Mesopotamians tried to appease their harsh deities in order to survive in an unpredictable world. Egyptians trusted in and nurtured the supernatural powers they believed guaranteed orderliness and prosperity.

In both Egypt and Mesopotamia, kingship emerged as the dominant political form. The Egyptian king's divine origins and symbolic association with the forces of renewal made him central to the welfare of the entire country and gave him a religious monopoly, superseding the authority of the temples and priests. Egyptian monarchs lavished much of the country's wealth on their tombs, believing that a proper burial would ensure the continuity of kingship and the attendant blessings that it brought to the land and people. Mesopotamian rulers, who were not normally regarded as divine, built new cities, towering walls, splendid palaces, and religious edifices as lasting testaments to their power.

Both cultures revered a hierarchy of gods, ranging from protective demons and local deities to gods of the state, whose importance rose or fell with the power of the political centers with which they were associated. Cheered by the stability of their environment, Egyptians conceived a positive notion of the gods' designs for humankind. They believed that despite hazards, the righteous spirit could journey to the next world and look forward to a blessed existence. In contrast, terrifying visions of the afterlife torment Gilgamesh, the Mesopotamian hero: disembodied spirits of the dead stumbling around in the darkness of the Underworld for all eternity, eating dust and clay, and slaving for the heartless gods of that realm.

Cultural continuity marked both Egypt and Mesopotamia despite substantial ethnic diversity. Immigrants assimilated to the dominant language, belief system, and lifestyles of the civilization. Culture, not physical appearance, served as the criterion of personal identification. The reduction in freedom and legal privileges for Mesopotamian women in the second millennium B.C.E. may relate to a high degree of urbanization and class stratification. In contrast, Egyptian pictorial documents, love poems, and legal records indicate an attitude of respect and a higher degree of equality for women in the valley of the Nile.

In the second millennium B.C.E., as the societies of Mesopotamia and Egypt consolidated their cultural achievements and entered new phases of political expansion, and as the Indus Valley centers went into irreversible decline, a new and distinctive civilization, based on exploiting the agricultural potential of a floodplain, emerged in the valley of the Yellow River in eastern China. We turn to that area in Chapter 2.

◼ Key Terms

civilization	scribe
culture	ziggurat
history	amulet
Stone Age	cuneiform
Paleolithic	pharaoh
Neolithic	ma'at
foragers	pyramid
Agricultural Revolutions	Memphis
Holocene	Thebes
megalith	hieroglyphics
Babylon	papyrus
Sumerians	mummy
Semitic	Harappa
city-state	Mohenjo-Daro
Hammurabi	

◼ Suggested Reading

Reliable textbooks are Brian Fagan's *People of the Earth: An Introduction to World Prehistory*, 9th ed. (1997), and Robert J. Wenke, *Patterns in Prehistory: Humankind's First Three Million Years*, 4th ed. (1999).

Ann Sieveking, *The Cave Artists* (1979), Mario Ruspoli, *The Cave Art of Lascaux* (1986), and N. K. Sanders, *Prehistoric Art in Europe* (1968) provide overviews of major European sites.

For ideas on the transition to food production, see Jared Diamond, *Guns, Germs, and Steel: The Fates of Human Societies* (1997), and Allen W. Johnson and Timothy Earle, *The Evolution of Human Societies: From Foraging Group to Agrarian State* (1987). Jean-Pierre Mohen, *The World of Megaliths* (1990), analyzes early monumental architecture. James Mellaart, the principal excavator of Çatal Hüyük, discusses his work for the general reader in *Çatal Hüyük: A Neolithic Town in Anatolia* (1967).

Jack M. Sasson, ed., *Civilizations of the Ancient Near East*, 4 vols. (1993), contains up-to-date articles and a bibliography on a wide range of topics. An excellent starting point for geography, chronology, and basic institutions and cultural concepts in ancient western Asia is Michael Roaf, *Cultural Atlas of Mesopotamia and the Ancient Near East* (1990). Amelie Kuhrt, *The Ancient Near East, c. 3000–330 B.C.*, 2 vols. (1995), is the best and most up-to-date introduction to the historical development of western Asia and Egypt, offering a clear and concise historical outline and a balanced presentation of continuing controversies. Other general historical introductions can be found in A. Bernard Knapp, *The History and Culture of Ancient Western Asia and Egypt* (1988); Hans J. Nissen, *The Early History of the Ancient Near East, 9000–2000 B.C.* (1988); H. W. F. Saggs, *Civilization Before Greece and Rome* (1989); and Georges Roux, *Ancient Iraq*, 3d ed. (1992). Joan Oates, *Babylon* (1979), focuses on the most important of all the Mesopotamian cities. J. N. Postgate, *Early Mesopotamia: Society and Economy at the Dawn of History* (1992), offers deep insights into political, social, and economic dynamics. For advanced students, Daniel C. Snell, *Life in the Ancient Near East 3100–322 B.C.E.* (1997), emphasizes social and economic matters. Stephanie Dalley, ed., *The Legacy of Mesopotamia* (1998), explores Mesopotamian interactions with other parts of the ancient world.

David Ferry's *Gilgamesh: A New Rendering in English Verse* (1992) is an attractive translation. The evolving mentality of Mesopotamian religion comes through in Thorkild Jacobsen, *The Treasures of Darkness: A History of Mesopotamian Religion* (1976). Stephanie Dalley, *Myths from Mesopotamia* (1989); Henrietta McCall, *Mesopotamian Myths* (1990); and Jeremy Black and Anthony Green, *Gods, Demons and Symbols of Ancient Mesopotamia* (1992), cover myth, religion, and religious symbolism. Pierre Amiet, *Art of the Ancient Near East* (1980), introduces various arts with good illustrations. Dominique Collon, *First Impressions: Cylinder Seals in the Ancient Near East* (1988), reveals much about art and daily life.

C. B. F. Walker, *Cuneiform* (1987), is a concise guide to the Mesopotamian writing system. James B. Pritchard, *Ancient Near Eastern Texts Relating to the Old Testament*, 3d ed. (1969), contains translated documents and texts from western Asia and Egypt. For women's matters, see Barbara Lesko, "Women of Egypt and the Ancient Near East," in *Becoming Visible: Women in European History*, 2d ed., ed. Renata Bridenthal, Claudia Koonz, and Susan Stuard (1994), and Guity Nashat, "Women in the Ancient Middle East," in *Restoring Women to History* (1988). Harvey Weiss, ed., *Ebla to Damascus: Art and Archaeology of Ancient Syria* (1985), and Giovanni Pettinato, *Ebla: A New Look at History* (1991), discuss Syria's relationship with Mesopotamia.

A lavishly illustrated introduction to ancient Egyptian civilization is David P. Silverman, ed., *Ancient Egypt* (1997). John Baines and Jaromir Malek, *Atlas of Ancient Egypt* (1980), and T. G. H. James, *Ancient Egypt: The Land and Its Legacy* (1988), are organized around the sites of ancient Egypt and provide general introductions. Historical treatments include B. G. Trigger, B. J. Kemp, D. O'Connor, and A. B. Lloyd, *Ancient Egypt: A Social History* (1983); Barry J. Kemp, *Ancient Egypt: Anatomy of a Civilization* (1989); and Nicholas-Cristophe Grimal, *A History of Ancient Egypt* (1992). John Romer, *People of the Nile: Everyday Life in Ancient Egypt* (1982); Miriam Stead, *Egyptian Life* (1986); and Eugen Strouhal, *Life of the Ancient Egyptians* (1992), emphasize social history. For women, see the chapter by Lesko cited above; Barbara Watterson, *Women in Ancient Egypt* (1991); Gay Robins, *Women in Ancient Egypt* (1993); and the articles and museum exhibition catalogue in Anne K. Capel and Glenn E. Markoe, eds., *Mistress of the House, Mistress of Heaven: Women in Ancient Egypt* (1996).

Stephen Quirke, *Ancient Egyptian Religion* (1990), is a highly regarded treatment of a complex subject. George Hart, *Egyptian Myths* (1990), presents evidence for what must have been a thriving oral tradition. Pritchard's collection, cited above, and Miriam Lichtheim, *Ancient Egyptian Literature: A Book of Readings,* Vol. 1, *The Old and Middle Kingdoms* (1973), provide translated texts and documents. William Stevenson Smith, *The Art and Architecture of Ancient Egypt* (1998), and Gay Robins, *The Art of Ancient Egypt* (1997), cover the visual record.

For the Indus Valley civilization, see the brief treatment by Stanley Wolpert, *A New History of India,* 3d ed. (1989). Jonathan Mark Kenoyer, *Ancient Cities of the Indus Valley Civilization* (1998), supersedes the occasionally still useful works of Mortimer Wheeler, *Civilizations of the Indus Valley and Beyond* (1966) and *The Indus Civilization,* 3d ed. (1968). Gregory L. Poschl has edited two collections of articles: *Ancient Cities of the Indus* (1979) and *Harappan Civilization: A Contemporary Perspective* (1982).

■ Notes

1. N. K. Sandars, *The Epic of Gilgamesh* (Baltimore: Penguin Books, 1960), 61–63.
2. Colin McEvedy and Richard Jones, *Atlas of World Population History* (New York: Penguin Books, 1978), 13–15.
3. Colin Renfrew, *Archaeology and Language: The Puzzle of Indo-European Origins* (Cambridge: Cambridge University Press, 1988), 125, 150.
4. Luigi Cavalli-Sforza, L. Luca, Paolo Menozzi, and Alberto Piazza, *The History and Geography of Human Genes* (Princeton, NJ: Princeton University Press, 1994).
5. James Mellaart, *Çatal Hüyük: A Neolithic Town in Anatolia* (New York: McGraw-Hill, 1967), 202.

New Civilizations in the Eastern and Western Hemispheres, 2200–250 B.C.E.

2

CHAPTER OUTLINE

Early China, 2000–221 B.C.E.

Nubia, 3100 B.C.E.–350 C.E.

Celtic Europe, 1000–50 B.C.E.

First Civilizations of the Americas: The Olmec and Chavín, 1200–250 B.C.E.

DIVERSITY AND DOMINANCE: Hierarchy and Conduct in the Analects of Confucius

A round 2200 B.C.E. an Egyptian official named Harkhuf°, who lived at Aswan° on the southern boundary of Egypt, set out on his fourth trek to a place called Yam, far to the south in the land that later came to be called Nubia. He brought gifts from the Egyptian pharaoh for the ruler of Yam, and he returned home with three hundred donkeyloads of incense, ebony, ivory, and other exotic products. Despite the diplomatic fiction of exchanging gifts, we should probably consider Harkhuf a trader; and the prize of this trip was so special that the eight-year-old boy pharaoh, Pepi II, could not contain his excitement. He wrote:

> Come north to the residence at once! Hurry and bring with you this pygmy whom you brought

from the land of the horizon-dwellers live, hale, and healthy, for the dances of the god, to gladden the heart, to delight the heart of king Neferkare [Pepi] who lives forever! When he goes down with you into the ship, get worthy men to be around him on deck, lest he fall into the water! When he lies down at night, get worthy men to lie around him in his tent. Inspect ten times at night! My majesty desires to see this pygmy more than the gifts of the mine-land and of Punt![1]

Some scholars identify Yam with Kerma, later the capital of the kingdom of Nubia, on the upper Nile in modern Sudan. For Egyptians, Nubia was a wild and dangerous place—though pygmies came from further south. But it was developing a more complex political organization that fostered trade with Egypt and tropical regions farther south.

Some of the complex societies examined in

Harkhuf (HAHR-koof)   Aswan (AS- wahn)

this chapter developed in river valleys; others did not. Whereas the Egyptian, Mesopotamian, and Harappan civilizations discussed in the last chapter were originally largely self-sufficient, the civilizations discussed in this chapter and the next were partially shaped by networks of long-distance trade.

In the second millennium B.C.E. a civilization based on irrigation agriculture arose along the valley of the Yellow River and its tributaries in northern China. In the same epoch, in Nubia (southern Egypt and northern Sudan), the first complex society in tropical Africa continued to develop from the roots observed earlier by Harkhuf. The first millennium B.C.E. witnessed the spread of Celtic peoples across much of continental Europe, as well as the flourishing of the earliest complex societies of the Western Hemisphere, the Olmec of Mesoamerica and the Chavín culture on the flanks of the Andes Mountains in South America. These societies had no contact with one another and represent a variety of responses to environmental and historical circumstances. However, as we shall see, they have certain features in common and collectively point to a distinct stage in the development of human societies.

As you read this chapter, ask yourself the following questions:

- How did each of these civilizations develop distinctive political and social institutions, cultural patterns, and technologies in response to environmental challenges?

- How did elite groups dominate the rest of the population?

- In the case of Nubia and the Celts, how did the technological and cultural influences of older centers affect the formation of the new civilizations?

EARLY CHINA, 2000–221 B.C.E.

On the eastern edge of the great Eurasian landmass, Neolithic cultures developed as early as 8000 B.C.E. A more complex civilization evolved in the second millennium B.C.E. Under the Shang and Zhou monarchs, many of the institutions and values of classical Chinese civilization emerged and spread south and west. As elsewhere, the rise of cities, specialization of labor, bureaucratic government, writing, and other advanced technologies depended on intensive agriculture along a great river system—the Yellow River (Huang He°) and its tributaries. Although archaeological finds indicate some movement of goods and ideas from western to eastern Asia, developments in China were largely independent of the complex societies in the Middle East and the Indus Valley.

Geography and Resources

With mountains and deserts to the west and north making overland travel difficult and slow (see Map 2.1), the great river systems of eastern China—the Yellow and the Yangzi° Rivers and their tributaries—provide the main axes of east-west movement. In the eastern river valleys dense populations practiced intensive agriculture; on the steppe lands of Mongolia, the deserts and oases of Xinjiang°, and the high plateau of Tibet sparser populations lived largely by herding. Within the eastern agricultural zone, the north and the south have strikingly different environments. The monsoons that affect India and Southeast Asia (see Chapters 1 and 12) drench southern China with heavy rainfall in the summer, the most beneficial time for agriculture. Rainfall is more erratic and sparse in northern China. As in Mesopotamia and the Indus Valley, where civilizations developed in relatively unfriendly environments, China's early history unfolded in the demanding environment of the northern plains. By the third century C.E., however, the gradual flow of population toward the warmer southern lands caused the political and intellectual center to move south.

Huang He (hwahng-HUH) **Yangzi** (yang-zuh) **Xinjiang** (shin-jyahng)

C H R O N O L O G Y

	China	Nubia	Celtic Europe	Americas
	8000–2000 B.C.E. Neolithic cultures	**4500 B.C.E.** Eary agriculture in Nubia		**3500 B.C.E.** Early agriculture in Mesoamerica and Andes
2500 B.C.E.				**2600 B.C.E.** Rise of Caral
		2200 B.C.E. Harkhuf's expeditions to Yam		
2000 B.C.E.	**2000 B.C.E.** Bronze metallurgy			
	1750–1027 B.C.E. Shang dynasty	**1750 B.C.E.** Rise of kingdom of Kush based on Kerma		
1500 B.C.E.		**1500 B.C.E.** Egyptian conquest of Nubia		
	1027–221 B.C.E. Zhou dynasty			**1200–900 B.C.E.** Rise of Olmec civilization, centered on San Lorenzo
1000 B.C.E.		**1000 B.C.E.** Decline of Egyptian control in Nubia	**1000 B.C.E.** Origin of Celtic culture in central Europe	
				900–600 B.C.E. La Venta, the dominant Olmec center
				900–250 B.C.E. Chavín civilization in the Andes
		750 B.C.E. Rise of kingdom based on Napata		
		712–660 B.C.E. Nubian kings rule Egypt		
	600 B.C.E. Iron metallurgy			**600–400 B.C.E.** Ascendancy of Tres Zapotes and Olmec decline
500 B.C.E.	**531–479 B.C.E.** Confucius		**500 B.C.E.** Celtic elites trade for Mediterranean goods	**500 B.C.E.** Early metallurgy in Andes
			500–300 B.C.E. Migrations across Europe	
		300 B.C.E.–350 C.E. Kingdom of Meroë		

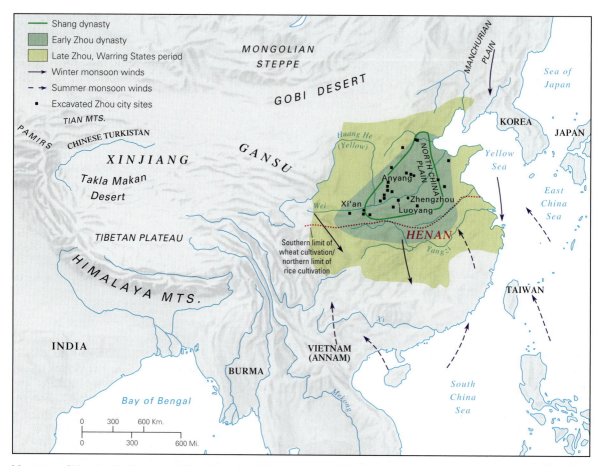

Map 2.1   China in the Shang and Zhou Periods, 1750–221 B.C.E.   The Shang dynasty arose in the second millennium B.C.E. in the floodplain of the Yellow River. Whereas southern China benefits from the monsoon rains, northern China depends on irrigation. As population increased, the Han Chinese migrated from their eastern homeland to other parts of China, carrying their technologies and cultural practices. Other ethnic groups predominated in more outlying regions, and the nomadic peoples of the northwest constantly challenged Chinese authority.

Since prehistoric times, winds blowing from Central Asia had deposited a yellowish-brown dust called **loess°** on the North China Plain, creating an abundance of potentially productive land (this dust suspended in the water gives the Yellow River its distinctive hue and name). The thick soil was extremely fertile and soft enough to be worked with wooden digging sticks. However, in some areas forests had to be cleared; more importantly, recurrent floods on the Yellow River necessitated the construction of earthen dikes and overflow channels. In this land-

scape, agriculture demanded the coordinated efforts of large groups of people. To cope with the periodic droughts, catch basins (reservoirs) were dug to store river water and rainfall. As the population grew, people built retaining walls to partition the hillsides into tiers of flat arable terraces.

The staple crops were millet, a grain indigenous to China, and wheat, originally from the Middle East. Rice required a warmer climate and prospered in the south. The cultivation of rice in the Yangzi River Valley and the south required a great outlay of labor. Rice paddies—the fields where rice is grown—must be absolutely flat and surrounded

loess (less)

by water channels to bring and lead away water according to a precise schedule. Seedlings sprout in a nursery and are transplanted one by one to the paddy, which is then flooded. Flooding eliminates weeds and rival plants and supports microscopic organisms that keep the soil fertile. When the crop is ripe, the paddy is drained; the rice stalks are harvested with a sickle; and the edible kernels are separated out. The reward for this effort is a spectacular yield. Rice can feed more people per cultivated acre than any other grain, which explains why the south eventually became more populous and important than the north.

The Shang Period, 1750–1027 B.C.E.

Archaeologists have identified several Neolithic cultural complexes in China, primarily on the basis of pottery styles and forms of burial. These early populations grew millet, raised pigs and chickens, and used stone tools. They made pottery on a wheel and fired it in high-temperature kilns. They pioneered the production of silk cloth, first raising silkworms on mulberry trees, then carefully unraveling their cocoons to produce silk thread. Lacking building stone, they built walls by hammering soil inside temporary wooden frames until it became hard as cement. By 2000 B.C.E. they had begun to make bronze (roughly a thousand years after bronze-working began in the Middle East).

Chinese legends tell of the ancient dynasty of the Xia, said to have ruled the core region of the Yellow River Valley. Some archaeologists identify the Xia with the Neolithic Longshan cultural complex in the centuries before and after 2000 B.C.E. However, Chinese history proper begins with the rise to power of the Shang clans, which coincides with the earliest Chinese written records.

The **Shang°** originated in the part of the Yellow River Valley that lies in the present-day province of Henan°. After 1750 B.C.E. they extended their control north into Mongolia, west as far as Gansu°, and south to the Yangzi River Valley. The warrior aristocracy that dominated Shang society reveled in warfare, hunting (for recreation and to fine-tune battle skills), exchanging gifts, and feasting.

The king ruled the core area of the Shang state directly. Aristocrats served as generals, ambassadors, and supervisors of public projects. Other members of the royal family and high-ranking nobility governed outlying provinces. The most distant regions were governed by native rulers who swore allegiance to the Shang king. The king was often on the road, traveling to the courts of his subordinates to reinforce their loyalty.

Frequent military campaigns, often against the nomadic peoples who occupied the steppe and desert regions to the north and west, occupied the warrior elite and yielded considerable plunder. (Chinese sources refer to these peoples as "barbarians." Modern readers should be wary of the Chinese claim that they were culturally backward and morally inferior to the Chinese.) Prisoners of war were taken in these campaigns and used as slaves in the Shang capital.

Various cities served as the capital of the Shang kingdom. The last and most important was near modern Anyang° (see Map 2.1). Shang cities were centers of political control and religion. Surrounded by massive walls of pounded earth, they contained palaces, administrative buildings and storehouses, royal tombs, shrines of gods and ancestors, and houses of the nobility. The common people lived in agricultural villages outside these centers. These cities, with a grid plan aligned with the north polar star and gates opening to the cardinal directions, exhibit an ongoing Chinese concern with feng shui,° the spatial orientation of buildings according to a sense of cosmic order.

Writing was key to developing effective administration. Pictograms (pictures representing objects and concepts) and phonetic symbols representing the sounds of syllables were combined to form a complex system of hundreds of signs. Only a small, educated elite had the time to master this system. Despite substantial changes through the ages, the fundamental principles of the Chinese system still endure. As a result, people speaking essentially different languages, such as Mandarin and Cantonese, can read and understand the same text. In contrast, the cuneiform of Mesopotamia and the hieroglyphics of Egypt were eventually replaced by simpler alphabetic scripts.

Shang (shahng)   **Henan** (heh-nahn)   **Gansu** (gahn-soo)

Anyang (ahn-yahng)   **feng shui** (fung shway)

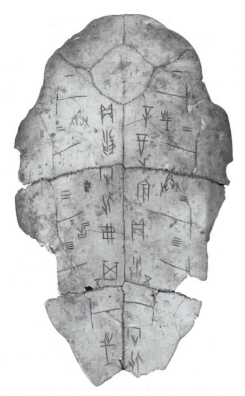

Chinese Divination Shell After inscribing questions on a bone or shell, the diviner applied a red-hot point and interpreted the resulting cracks as a divine response. (Institute of History and Philology, Academia Sinica)

were often inscribed on the back of the shell or bone, the tens of thousands of surviving bones provide a major source of information about Shang life. The rulers asked about the proper performance of ritual, the likely outcome of wars or hunting expeditions, the prospects for rainfall and the harvest, and the meaning of strange occurrences.

Bronze weapons and ritual vessels symbolized authority and nobility. Shang tombs contain many such objects. The relatively modest tomb of one queen yielded 450 bronze articles (ritual vessels, bells, weapons, and mirrors)—remarkable because copper and tin, the principal ingredients of bronze, were not plentiful in northern China. (Also found in the same tomb were numerous objects of jade, bone, ivory, and stone; seven thousand cowrie shells; sixteen sacrificed men, women, and children; and six dogs!)

Bronze Vessel from the Shang Period, 13th–11th Century B.C.E. Vessels such as this large wine jar were used in rituals that allowed members of the Shang ruling class to make contact with their ancestors. Signifying both the source and the proof of the elite's authority, these vessels were often buried in Shang tombs. The complex shapes and elaborate decorations testify to the artisans' skill. (Tokyo National Museum Image: TNM Image)

The Shang ideology of kingship glorified the king as the intermediary between the people and Heaven. Shang religion also revered and made sacrifices to male ancestors, who were believed to be intensely interested in the fortunes of their descendants. Burials of kings also entailed sacrifices, not only of animals but also of humans, including noble officials of the court, women, servants, soldiers, and prisoners of war.

Before taking any action, the Shang rulers used **divination** to determine the will of Heaven. Chief among the tools of divination were oracle bones: tortoiseshells and animal shoulder blades that cracked haphazardly when touched with a hot poker. The cracks were "read" as answers from the spirit world to questions posed by the king. Since the question, the resulting answer, and often the confirmation of the accuracy of the prediction

Finding and mining deposits of copper and tin, transporting the refined metal to the capital, and crafting these beautifully wrought weapons and vessels constituted a major Shang enterprise. Bronzesmiths working in foundries outside the main cities also made chariot fittings and musical instruments. Stylized depictions of real and imaginary animals were a favorite decorative theme.

Far-reaching networks of trade brought to the Shang jade, ivory, and mother of pearl (a hard, shiny substance from the interior of mollusk shells) used for jewelry, carved figurines, and decorative inlays. Some evidence suggests that Shang China may have exchanged goods and ideas with distant Mesopotamia. The horse-drawn chariot, which the Shang adopted from the nomads of the northwest, became a formidable instrument of war.

The Zhou Period, 1027–221 B.C.E.

Shang domination of central and northern China lasted more than six centuries. In the eleventh century B.C.E. the last Shang king was defeated by Wu, the ruler of **Zhou°**, a dependent state in the Wei° River Valley. The Zhou line of kings (ca. 1027–221 B.C.E.) was the longest lasting and most revered of all dynasties in Chinese history. Just as the Semitic peoples in Mesopotamia had adopted and adapted the Sumerian legacy (see Chapter 1), the Zhou preserved the essentials of Shang culture and added new elements of ideology and technology.

To justify their seizure of power to the restive remnants of the Shang clans, the early Zhou monarchs styled themselves "Son of Heaven." Their rule was called the **"Mandate of Heaven."** According to the new theory advanced by their propagandists, the ruler had been chosen by the supreme deity, known as "Heaven," and would retain his backing as long as he served as a wise, principled, and energetic guardian of his people. Prosperity and stability proved divine favor, but royal misbehavior, a fault attributed to the last Shang ruler, could forfeit Heaven's mandate. Corruption, violence, and insurrection were signs of divine displeasure.

The Zhou kings continued some of the Shang rituals, but there was a marked decline in the practice of divination and in extravagant sacrifices and burials. The priestly power of the ruling class, the only ones who had been able to make contact with the spirits of ancestors during the Shang period, faded away. The resulting separation of religion and government made way for the development of important philosophical and mystical systems. The bronze vessels that had been sacred implements in the Shang period now became family treasures.

The early period of Zhou rule, the eleventh through ninth centuries B.C.E., is sometimes called the Western Zhou era because of the location of the capitals in the western part of the kingdom. These centuries saw the development of a sophisticated administrative apparatus. The Zhou built a series of capital cities with pounded-earth foundations and walls. The major buildings all faced south, in keeping with the feng shui principles of harmonious relationship with the terrain, the forces of wind, water, and sunlight, and the invisible energy perceived to be flowing through the natural world. All government officials, including the king, were supposed to be models of morality, fairness, and concern for the welfare of the people.

Like the Shang, the Zhou regime was decentralized. Members and allies of the royal family ruled more than a hundred largely autonomous territories. Elaborate court ceremonials, embellished by music and dance, impressed on observers the glory of Zhou rule and reinforced the bonds of obligation between rulers and ruled.

Around 800 B.C.E. Zhou power began to wane. Ambitious local rulers operated ever more independently and waged war on one another, while nomadic peoples attacked the northwest frontiers (see Map 2.1). In 771 B.C.E. members of the Zhou lineage relocated to a new, more secure, eastern capital near Luoyang°, initiating the five-hundred-year Eastern Zhou era. There they continued to hold the royal title and receive at least nominal homage from local rulers, the real power brokers of the age. Historians conventionally divide this period of political fragmentation, shifting centers of power, and fierce competition among numerous small states into the "Spring and Autumn Period," from 771 to 481 B.C.E., after a collection of chronicles that give annual entries for those two seasons,

---

Zhou (joe)   **Wei** (way)

Luoyang (LWOE-yahng)

and the "Warring States Period," from 480 to the unification of China in 221 B.C.E.

Numerous competing kingdoms meant numerous capital cities, some of which became quite large. To the north, long walls of pounded earth were constructed, the ancestors of the Great Wall of China, to protect the kingdoms from each other and from nomads. Chinese armies adopted the nomad practice of putting fighters on horseback. The northwest nomads also probably were the source of the ironworking skills that led to iron replacing bronze as the primary metal for tools and weapons around 600 B.C.E. Metalworkers in southern China, where copper and tin were scarce, later innovated the forging of steel by removing carbon during the iron-smelting process.

Bureaucracies in many states expanded their functions, composing law codes, collecting taxes directly, imposing monetary standards, and managing large-scale public works projects. Eventually this activity led to a philosophy called **Legalism,** which argued that maintaining the wealth and power of the state justified authoritarian political control. Legalists maintained that human nature is essentially wicked and that people behave properly only if compelled by strict laws and harsh punishments. They believed that every aspect of human society ought to be controlled and personal freedom sacrificed for the good of the state.

Confucianism, Daoism, and Chinese Society

Bureaucratic government superseded aristocratic rule in some of the major Zhou states. To maintain their influence, aristocrats sought a new role as advisers to the rulers. Kongzi (551–479 B.C.E.)—known in the West by the Latin form of his name, **Confucius**—lived through the political flux and social change of this anxious time. Coming from one of the smaller states, he had not been particularly successful in obtaining administrative posts. However, his doctrine of duty and public service, initially aimed at fellow aristocrats, was to become a central influence in Chinese thought (see Diversity and Dominance: Hierarchy and Conduct in the Analects of Confucius).

Many elements in Confucius's teaching had roots in earlier Chinese belief, including folk religion and the rites of the Zhou royal family, such as the veneration of ancestors and elders and worship of the deity Heaven. Confucius drew a parallel between the family and the state. Just as the family is a hierarchy, with the father at its top, sons next, then wives and daughters in order of age, so too the state is a hierarchy, with the ruler at the top, the public officials as the sons, and the common people as the women.

Confucius took a traditional term for the feelings between family members (ren) and expanded it into a universal ideal of benevolence toward all humanity, which he believed was the foundation of moral government. Government exists, he said, to serve the people, and the administrator or ruler gains respect and authority by displaying fairness and integrity. Confucian teachings emphasized benevolence, avoidance of violence, justice, rationalism, loyalty, and dignity.

It is ironic that Confucius, whose ideas were to become so important in Chinese thought, actually had little influence in his own time. His later follower Mencius (Mengzi, 371–289 B.C.E.), who opposed despotism and argued against the authoritarian political ideology of the Legalists, made Confucius's teachings much better known. In the era of the early emperors, Confucianism became the dominant political philosophy and the core of the educational system for government officials (see Chapter 5).

The Warring States Period also saw the rise of the school of thought known as **Daoism°.** According to tradition, Laozi°, the originator of Daoism (believed to have lived in the sixth century B.C.E., though some scholars doubt his existence), sought to stop the warfare of the age by urging humanity to follow the *Dao,* or "path." Daoists accept the world as they find it, avoiding useless struggles and adhering to the "path" of nature. They avoid violence if at all possible and take the minimal action necessary for a task. Rather than fight the current of a stream, a wise man allows the onrushing waters to pass around him. This passivity arises from the Daoist's sense that the world is always changing and lacks any absolute morality or meaning. In the end, Daoists believe, all that matters is the individual's fundamental understanding of the "path."

The original Daoist philosophy was greatly expanded in subsequent centuries to incorporate

---

Daoism (DOW-izm)   **Laozi** (low-zuh)

popular beliefs, magic, and mysticism. Daoism represented an important stream of thought throughout Chinese history. By idealizing individuals who find their own "path" to right conduct, it offered an alternative to the Confucian emphasis on hierarchy and duty and to the Legalist approval of force.

Social organization also changed in this period. The kinship structures of the Shang and early Zhou periods, based on the clan (a relatively large group of related families), gave way to the three-generation family of grandparents, parents, and children as the fundamental social unit. A related development was the emergence of the concept of private property. Land was considered to belong to the men of the family and was divided equally among the sons when the father died.

Little is known about the conditions of life for women in early China. Some scholars believe that women may have acted as shamans, entering into trances to communicate with supernatural forces, making requests on behalf of their communities, and receiving predictions of the future. By the time written records begin to illuminate our knowledge of women's experiences, however, they show women in a subordinate position in the strongly patriarchal family.

Confucian thought codified this male-female hierarchy. Only men could conduct rituals and make offerings to the ancestors, though women could help maintain the household's ancestral shrines. Fathers held authority over the women and children, arranged marriages for their offspring, and could sell the labor of family members. A man was limited to one wife but was permitted additional sexual partners, who had the lower status of concubines. The elite classes used marriage to create political alliances, and it was common for the groom's family to offer a substantial "bride-gift," a proof of the wealth and standing of his family, to the family of the prospective bride. A man whose wife died had a duty to remarry in order to produce male heirs to keep alive the cult of the ancestors.

These differences in male and female activities were explained by the concept of **yin** and **yang,** the complementary nature of male and female roles in the natural order. The male principle (yang) was equated with the sun—active, bright, and shining; the female principle (yin) corresponded to the moon—passive, shaded, and reflective. Female gentleness balanced male toughness, female endurance and need for completion balanced male action and initiative, and female supportiveness balanced male leadership. In its earliest form, the theory considered yin and yang as equal and alternately dominant, like night and day, creating balance in the world. However, as a result of the changing role of women in the Zhou period and the pervasive influence of Confucian ideology, the male principle came to be seen as superior to the female.

The classical Chinese patterns of family, property, and bureaucracy took shape during the long centuries of Zhou rule and the competition among small states. At the end of this period the state of Qin°, whose aggressive and disciplined policies made it the premier power among the warring states, defeated all rivals and unified China (see Chapter 5).

NUBIA, 3100 B.C.E.–350 C.E.

Since the first century the name *Nubia* has been applied to a 1,000-mile (1,600-kilometer) stretch of the Nile Valley lying between Aswan and Khartoum° and straddling the southern part of the modern nation of Egypt and the northern part of Sudan (see Map 1.2). The ancient Egyptians called it Taseti, meaning "Land of the Bow," after the favorite weapon of its warriors. Nubia is the only trade corridor and continuously inhabited stretch of territory connecting sub-Saharan Africa (the lands south of the Sahara Desert) with North Africa. It was richly endowed with natural resources such as gold, copper, and semiprecious stones.

Egypt's quest for Nubian gold helps explain the early rise of a civilization with a complex political organization, social stratification, metallurgy, monumental building, and writing. However, most scholars today have moved away from the traditional view that Nubian civilization derived from Eygpt and emphasize the mutually beneficial interactions between the two lands and the growing evidence that Nubian culture drew on influences from sub-Saharan Africa.

Qin (chin) **Khartoum** (kahr-TOOM)

DIVERSITY AND DOMINANCE

HIERARCHY AND CONDUCT
IN THE ANALECTS OF CONFUCIUS

The Analects are a collection of sayings of Confucius that were probably compiled and written down several generations after he lived, though some elements may have been added even later. They cover a wide range of matters, including ethics, government, education, music, and rituals. Taken as a whole, they are a guide to living a proper, honorable, virtuous, useful, and satisfying life. Although subject to reinterpretation according to the circumstances of the times, Confucian principles have had a great influence on Chinese values and behavior ever since.

Chinese society in Confucius's time was very attuned to distinctions of status. Confucius assumed that hierarchy is innate in the order of the universe and that human society should echo and harmonize with the natural world. Each person has a role to play and must follow prescribed rules of conduct and proper ceremonial behavior to maintain the social order. The following selections illuminate the particular attention paid by Confucius to the important status categories in his society, the proper way for individuals to treat others, and the necessity of hierarchy and inequality.

1:6 Confucius said: "A young man should serve his parents at home and be respectful to elders outside his home. He should be earnest and truthful, loving all, but become intimate with *ren* [an inner capacity, possessed by all human beings, to do good]. After doing this, if he has energy to spare, he can study literature and the arts."

4:18 Confucius said: "When you serve your mother and father it is okay to try to correct them once in a while. But if you see that they are not going to listen to you, keep your respect for them and don't distance yourself from them. Work without complaining."

2:5 Meng Yi Zi asked about the meaning of filial piety. Confucius said, "It means 'not diverging (from your parents).'" Later, when Fan Chi was driving him,

Confucius told Fan Chi, "Meng asked me about the meaning of filial piety, and I told him 'not diverging.'" Fan Chi said, "What did you mean by that?" Confucius said, "When your parents are alive, serve them with propriety; when they die, bury them with propriety, and then worship them with propriety."

1:2 Master You said: "There are few who have developed themselves filially and fraternally who enjoy offending their superiors. Those who do not enjoy offending superiors are never troublemakers. The Superior Man concerns himself with the fundamentals. Once the fundamentals are established, the proper way (*dao*) appears. Are not filial piety and obedience to elders fundamental to the enactment of *ren*?"

1:8 Confucius said: "If the Superior Man is not 'heavy,' then he will not inspire awe in others. If he is not learned, then he will not be on firm ground. He takes loyalty and good faith to be of primary importance, and has no friends who are not of equal (moral) caliber. When he makes a mistake, he doesn't hesitate to correct it."

4:5 Confucius said, "Riches and honors are what all men desire. But if they cannot be attained in accordance with the *dao* they should not be kept. Poverty and low status are what all men hate. But if they cannot be avoided while staying in accordance with the *dao*, you should not avoid them. If a Superior Man departs from *ren*, how can he be worthy of that name? A Superior Man never leaves *ren* for even the time of a single meal. In moments of haste he acts according to it. In times of difficulty or confusion he acts according to it."

15:20 Confucius said: "The Superior Man seeks within himself. The inferior man seeks within others."

16:8 Confucius said: "The Superior Man stands in awe of three things:

(1) He is in awe of the decree of Heaven.

(2) He is in awe of great men.

(3) He is in awe of the words of the sages."

The inferior man does not know the decree of Heaven; takes great men lightly and laughs at the words of the sages."

4:14 Confucius said: "I don't worry about not having a good position; I worry about the means I use to gain position. I don't worry about being unknown; I seek to be known in the right way."

7:15 Confucius said: "I can live with coarse rice to eat, water for drink and my arm as a pillow and still be happy. Wealth and honors that one possesses in the midst of injustice are like floating clouds."

4:17 Confucius said: "When you see a good person, think of becoming like her/him. When you see someone not so good, reflect on your own weak points."

13:6 Confucius said: "When you have gotten your own life straightened out, things will go well without your giving orders. But if your own life isn't straightened out, even if you give orders, no one will follow them."

12:2 Zhonggong asked about the meaning of *ren*. The Master said: "Go out of your home as if you were receiving an important guest. Employ the people as if you were assisting at a great ceremony. What you don't want done to yourself, don't do to others. Live in your town without stirring up resentments, and live in your household without stirring up resentments."

1:5 Confucius said: "If you would govern a state of a thousand chariots (a small-to-middle-size state), you must pay strict attention to business, be true to your word, be economical in expenditure and love the people. You should use them according to the seasons."

2:3 Confucius said: "If you govern the people legalistically and control them by punishment, they will avoid crime, but have no personal sense of shame. If you govern them by means of virtue and control them with propriety, they will gain their own sense of shame, and thus correct themselves."

12:7 Zigong asked about government.

The Master said, "Enough food, enough weapons and the confidence of the people."

Zigong said, "Suppose you had no alternative but to give up one of these three, which one would be let go of first?"

The Master said, "Weapons."

Zigong said, "What if you had to give up one of the remaining two which one would it be?"

The Master said, "Food. From ancient times, death has come to all men, but a people without confidence in its rulers will not stand."

12:19 Ji Kang Zi asked Confucius about government saying: "Suppose I were to kill the unjust, in order to advance the just. Would that be all right?"

Confucius replied: "In doing government, what is the need of killing? If you desire good, the people will be good. The nature of the Superior Man is like the wind, the nature of the inferior man is like the grass. When the wind blows over the grass, it always bends."

2:19 The Duke of Ai asked: "How can I make the people follow me?" Confucius replied: "Advance the upright and set aside the crooked, and the people will follow you. Advance the crooked and set aside the upright, and the people will not follow you."

2:20 Ji Kang Zi asked: "How can I make the people reverent and loyal, so they will work positively for me?" Confucius said, "Approach them with dignity, and they will be reverent. Be filial and compassionate and they will be loyal. Promote the able and teach the incompetent, and they will work positively for you."

QUESTIONS FOR ANALYSIS

1. What are the important social categories and status distinctions in early China? What kinds of behaviors are expected of individuals in particular social categories toward individuals in other categories?

2. How does Confucius explain and justify the inequalities among people? Why is it important for people to behave in appropriate ways toward others?

3. How does the experience of family life prepare an individual to conduct himself or herself properly in the wider spheres of community and state?

4. Which personal qualities and kinds of actions will allow a ruler to govern successfully? Why might Confucius's passionate concern for ethical behavior on the part of officials and rulers arise at a time when the size and power of governments were growing?

Source: From "Hierarchy and Conduct in the Analects of Confucius," translated by Charles Muller, as seen at http://www.human.toyogakuen-u.ac.jp/~acmuller/con-tao/analects.htm.

Early Cultures and Egyptian Domination, 2300–1100 B.C.E.

The central geographical feature of Nubia, as of Egypt, is the Nile River. The Nubian segment of the Nile River flows through a landscape of rocky desert, grassland, and fertile plain. In a torrid climate with minimal rainfall, agriculture depended on river irrigation. Six cataracts, barriers formed by large boulders and rapids, obstructed boat traffic. Boats operating between the cataracts and caravans skirting the river made travel possible.

In the fifth millennium B.C.E. bands of people in northern Nubia made the transition from semi-nomadic hunting and gathering to a settled life based on grain agriculture and cattle herding. The majority of the population came to live in agricultural villages alongside the river. Even before 3000 B.C.E. Egyptian craftsmen were working in ivory and ebony that must have come from tropical Africa by way of Nubia.

As we saw with the journey of Harkhuf at the beginning of this chapter, Nubia enters the Egyptian historical record around 2300 B.C.E. in accounts of trade missions. At that time Aswan, just north of the First Cataract, was the southern limit of Egyptian control. Egyptian noblemen stationed there led donkey caravans south in search of gold, incense, ebony, ivory, slaves, and exotic animals. This was dangerous work, requiring delicate negotiations with local Nubian chiefs to secure protection, but it brought substantial rewards to those who succeeded.

During the Middle Kingdom (ca. 2040–1640 B.C.E.), Egypt adopted a more aggressive stance toward Nubia. Egyptian rulers sought to control the gold mines in the desert east of the Nile and to cut out the Nubian middlemen who drove up the cost of luxury goods from the tropics. A string of mud-brick forts on islands and riverbanks south of the Second Cataract were built to protect Egypt's southern frontier and regulate the flow of commerce. These Egyptian garrisons were sufficiently

Wall Painting of Nubians Arriving in Egypt with Rings and Bags of Gold, 14th Century B.C.E.
This photo decorated the tomb of an Egyptian administrator in Egypt   (Courtesy of the Trustees of the British Museum)

intimidating that relations with the indigenous population of northern Nubia, while intermittent, were generally peaceful.

Farther south, where the Nile makes a great U-shaped turn in a fertile plain (see Map 1.2), a more complex political entity evolved from the chiefdoms of the third millennium B.C.E. The Egyptians gave the name **Kush** to the kingdom whose capital was located at Kerma, one of the earliest urbanized centers in tropical Africa. Beginning around 1750 B.C.E. the kings of Kush marshaled a labor force to build monumental walls and structures of mud brick. Royal burials containing dozens and even hundreds of sacrificed servants and wives, along with sumptuous objects, testify to the wealth and power of the rulers of Kush and suggest a belief in some sort of afterlife in which attendants and possessions would be useful. Kushite craftsmen showed skill in metalworking, whether for weapons or jewelry, and their pottery surpassed anything produced in Egypt.

During the expansionist New Kingdom (ca. 1532–1070 B.C.E.) the Egyptians penetrated more deeply into Nubia (see Chapter 3). They destroyed Kush and its capital and extended their frontier to the Fourth Cataract. A high-ranking Egyptian official called "Overseer of Southern Lands" or "King's Son of Kush" ruled Nubia from a new administrative center at Napata°, near Gebel Barkal°, the "Holy Mountain," believed to be the home of a local god. Egypt exploited the gold mines of Nubia to help buttress their commerce with other lands. Fatalities were high among native workers in the brutal desert climate, and the army had to ward off attacks from desert nomads.

Five hundred years of Egyptian domination in Nubia left many traces. The Egyptian government imposed Egyptian culture on the native population. Children from elite families who were brought to the Egyptian royal court to guarantee the good behavior of their fathers absorbed Egyptian language, culture, and religion, which they later carried home with them. Other Nubians served the Egyptians as archers. The manufactured goods that they brought back to Nubia have been found in their graves. The Nubians built Egyptian-style towns and erected stone temples to Egyptian gods, particularly Amon. The frequent depiction of Amon with the head of a ram may reflect a blending of the chief Egyptian god with a Nubian ram deity.

The Kingdom of Meroë, 800 B.C.E.–350 C.E.

Egypt's weakness after 1200 B.C.E. led to the collapse of its authority in Nubia. In the eighth century B.C.E. a powerful new native kingdom emerged in southern Nubia. Its history can be divided into two parts. During the early period, between the eighth and fourth centuries B.C.E., Napata, the former Egyptian headquarters, was the primary center. During the later period, from the fourth century B.C.E. to the fourth century C.E., the center was farther south, at **Meroë**°, near the Sixth Cataract.

For half a century, from around 712 to 660 B.C.E., the kings of Nubia ruled all of Egypt as the Twenty-fifth Dynasty. They conducted themselves in the age-old manner of Egyptian rulers. Their titles, costumes, and burials followed Egyptian custom. However, they kept their Nubian names and were depicted with physical features suggesting peoples of sub-Saharan Africa. Building on a monumental scale for the first time in centuries and reinvigorating Egyptian art, architecture, and religion, they inaugurated an artistic and cultural renaissance. The Nubian kings resided at Memphis, the Old Kingdom capital, while Thebes, the New Kingdom capital, was the residence of a celibate female member of the king's family who was titled "God's Wife of Amon."

The Nubian dynasty made a disastrous mistake in 701 B.C.E. when it offered help to local rulers in Palestine who were struggling against the Assyrian Empire. The Assyrians retaliated by invading Egypt and driving the Nubian monarchs back to their southern domain by 660 B.C.E. Napata again became the chief royal residence and religious center of the kingdom. However, Egyptian cultural influences remained strong. Court documents continued to be written in Egyptian hieroglyphs, and the mummified remains of the rulers were buried in modestly sized sandstone pyramids along with hundreds of shawabti° figurines.

By the end of the fourth century B.C.E. the center of gravity had shifted south to Meroë, perhaps

---

Napata (nah-PAH-tuh)   **Gebel Barkal** (JEB-uhl BAHR-kahl)

Meroë (MER-oh-ee)   **shawabti** (shuh-WAB-tee)

because Meroë was better situated for agriculture and trade, the economic mainstays of the Nubian kingdom. As a result, sub-Saharan cultural patterns gradually replaced Egyptian ones. Egyptian hieroglyphs gave way to a new set of symbols, still essentially undeciphered, for writing the Meroitic language. People continued to worship Amon as well as Isis, an Egyptian goddess connected to fertility and sexuality, but those deities had to share the stage with Nubian deities like the lion-god Apedemak. Meroitic art combined Egyptian, Greco-Roman, and indigenous traditions.

Women of the royal family played an important role in Meroitic politics, another reflection of the influence of sub-Saharan Africa. The Nubians employed a matrilineal system in which the king was succeeded by the son of his sister. Nubian queens sometimes ruled by themselves and sometimes in partnership with their husbands. Greek, Roman, and biblical sources refer to a queen of Nubia named Candace. Since these sources relate to different times, Candace was probably a title rather than a proper name. At least seven queens ruled between 284 B.C.E. and 115 C.E. They are depicted in scenes reserved for male rulers in Egyptian imagery, smiting enemies in battle and being suckled by the mother-goddess Isis. Roman sources marvel at the fierce resistance put up by a one-eyed warrior-queen.

Meroë was a huge city for its time, more than a square mile in area, and it overlooked fertile grasslands and dominated converging trade routes. Great reservoirs were dug to catch precious rainfall. The city was a major center for iron smelting (after 1000 B.C.E. iron had replaced bronze as the primary metal for tools and weapons). The Temple of Amon was approached by an avenue of stone rams, and the enclosed "Royal City" was filled with palaces, temples, and administrative buildings. In 2002 archaeologists using a magnetometer to detect structures buried in the sand discovered a large palace, and they will soon begin excavation.

Meroë collapsed in the early fourth century C.E. It may have been overrun by nomads from the western desert who had become more mobile because of the arrival of the camel in North Africa. However, Meroë had already been weakened when profitable commerce with the Roman Empire was diverted to the Red Sea and to the rising kingdom of Aksum° in present-day Ethiopia (see Chapter 6).

CELTIC EUROPE, 1000–50 B.C.E.

The southern peninsulas of Europe—present-day Spain, Italy, and Greece—share in the relatively mild climate of all the Mediterranean lands and are separated from "continental" Europe to the north by high mountains (the Pyrenees and Alps). Consequently, the history of southern Europe in antiquity is primarily connected to that of the Middle East, at least until the Roman conquests north of the Alps (see Chapters 3, 4, and 5).

Continental Europe (including the modern nations of France, Germany, Switzerland, Austria, the Czech Republic, Slovakia, Hungary, Poland, and Romania) was more forested but was well suited to agriculture and herding. It contained broad plains with good soil and had a temperate climate with cold winters, warm summers, and ample rainfall. Large, navigable rivers (the Rhone, Rhine, and Danube) facilitated travel and the exploitation of natural resources like timber and metals.

Humans had lived in this part of Europe for many thousands of years, but their lack of a writing system limits our knowledge of the earliest inhabitants. Around 500 B.C.E. Celtic peoples spread across a substantial portion of Europe and, by coming into contact with the literate societies of the Mediterranean, entered the historical record. Information about the early **Celts**° comes from the archaeological record, Greek and Roman authors, and the Celtic oral traditions of Wales and Ireland that were written down during the European Middle Ages.

The Spread of the Celts

The term *Celtic* refers to a branch of the Indo-European family of languages found throughout Europe and in western and southern Asia. Scholars link the Celtic language group to archaeological remains first

---

Aksum (AHK-soom)   **Celts** (kelts)

appearing in parts of present-day Germany, Austria, and the Czech Republic after 1000 B.C.E.. Many early Celts lived in or near hill-forts—lofty natural locations made more defensible by earthwork fortifications. By 500 B.C.E. Celtic elites were trading with Mediterranean societies for crafted goods and wine. This contact may have stimulated the new styles of Celtic manufacture and art that appeared at this time.

These new cultural features coincided with Celtic migrations to many parts of Europe. The motives behind these population movements, their precise timing, and the manner in which they were carried out are not well understood. Celts occupied nearly all of France and much of Britain and Ireland, and they merged with indigenous peoples to create the Celtiberian culture of northern Spain. Other Celtic groups overran northern Italy in the fifth century B.C.E., raided into central Greece, and settled in central Anatolia (modern Turkey). By 300 B.C.E. Celtic peoples were spread across Europe north of the Alps, from present-day Hungary to Spain and Ireland.

These widely diffused Celtic groups shared language and culture, but there was no Celtic "state." They were divided into hundreds of small, loosely organized chiefdoms. Traditional depictions of Celtic society come largely from the observations of Greek and Roman writers. However, current scholarship focuses on the differences as much as the similarities among Celtic peoples. It is unlikely that the ancient Celts ever identified themselves as belonging to anything akin to our modern conception of "Celtic civilization."

The Greeks and Romans remarked particularly on the appearance of male Celts—their burly size, long red hair (which they often made stiff and upright by applying a cementlike solution of lime), shaggy mustaches, and loud, deep voices. Trousers (usually an indication of horse-riding peoples) and twisted gold neck collars were similarly distinctive, but not as unusual as the terrifying warriors who fought naked and collected the skulls of defeated enemies. The surviving accounts describe the Celts as wildly fond of war, courageous, childishly impulsive and emotional, and fond of boasting and exaggeration, yet quick-witted and eager to learn.

Celtic Society

The Roman general Julius Caesar, who conquered Gaul (present-day France) between 58 and 51 B.C.E., penned the greatest source of information about Celtic society. Many Celtic groups in Gaul had once been ruled by kings, but by about 60 B.C.E. they periodically chose public officials, perhaps under Greek and Roman influence. Their society was divided into an elite class of warriors, professional groups of priests and bards (singers of poems about glorious deeds), and commoners. The warriors owned land and flocks of cattle and sheep and monopolized both wealth and power. The common people labored on their land. The Celts built houses (usually round in Britain, rectangular in France) out of wattle and daub—a wooden framework filled in with clay and straw—with thatched straw roofs. Several such houses belonging to related families might be surrounded by a wooden fence for protection.

The warriors of Welsh and Irish legend reflect a stage of political and social development less complex than that of the Celts in Gaul. They raided one another's flocks, reveled in drunken feasts, and engaged in contests of strength and wit. At banquets warriors would fight to the death just to claim the choicest cut of the meat, the "hero's portion."

Druids, the Celtic priests in Gaul and Britain, formed a well-organized fraternity that performed religious, judicial, and educational functions. Trainees spent years memorizing prayers, secret rituals, legal precedents, and other traditions. The priesthood was the one Celtic institution that crossed tribal lines. The Druids sometimes headed off warfare between feuding groups and served as judges in cases involving Celts from different groups. In the first century C.E. the Roman government attempted to stamp out the Druids, probably because of concern that they might serve as a rallying point for Celtic opposition to Roman rule, and also because of their involvement in human sacrifices.

The Celts supported large populations by tilling the heavy but fertile soils of continental Europe, and their metallurgical skills probably surpassed those of the Mediterranean peoples. Celts living on the Atlantic shore of France built sturdy ocean-going boats, and they developed extensive trade networks along Europe's large, navigable rivers. One lucrative commodity was tin, which Celtic traders

The Gundestrup Cauldron
This silver vessel was found in a peat bog in Denmark, but it must have come from elsewhere. It is usually dated to the second or first century B.C.E. On the inside left are Celtic warriors on horse and on foot, with lozenge-shaped shields and long battle-horns. On the inside right is a horned deity, possibly Cernunnos. (The National Museum of Denmark)

from southwest England brought to Greek buyers in southern France. By the first century B.C.E some hill-forts were evolving into urban centers.

Women's lives were focused on child rearing, food production, and some crafts. Their situation was superior to that of women in the Middle East and in the Greek and Roman Mediterranean. Greek and Roman sources depict Celtic women as strong and proud. Welsh and Irish tales portray self-assured women who sit at banquets with their husbands, engage in witty conversation, and provide ingenious solutions to vexing problems. Marriage was a partnership to which both parties contributed property. Each party had the right to inherit the estate if the other died. Celtic women also had greater freedom in their sexual relations than did their southern counterparts.

Tombs of elite women have yielded rich collections of clothing, jewelry, and furniture for use in the next world. Daughters of the elite were married to leading members of other tribes to create alliances. When the Romans invaded Celtic Britain in the first century C.E., they sometimes were opposed by Celtic tribes headed by queens, although some experts see this as an abnormal circumstance created by the Roman invasion itself.

Belief and Knowledge

Historians know the names of more than four hundred Celtic gods and goddesses, mostly associated with particular localities or kinship groups. More widely revered deities included Lug°, the god of light, crafts, and inventions; the horse-goddess Epona°; and the horned god Cernunnos°. "The Mothers," three goddesses depicted together holding symbols of abundance, probably played a part in a fertility cult. Halloween and May Day preserve the ancient Celtic holidays of Samhain° and Beltaine° respectively, which took place at key moments in the agricultural cycle.

The early Celts did not build temples, but instead worshiped wherever they felt the presence of divinity—at springs, groves, and hilltops. At the sources of the Seine and Marne Rivers in France,

---

Lug (loog) **Epona** (eh-POH-nuh) **Cernunnos** (KURN-you-nuhs) **Samhain** (SAH-win) **Beltaine** (BEHL-tayn)

archaeologists have found huge caches of Celtic wooden statues thrown into the water by worshipers.

Wagons filled with extensive grave goods show up in elite burials, suggesting a belief in some sort of afterlife. In Irish and Welsh legends, heroes and gods pass back and forth between the natural and supernatural worlds much more readily than in the mythology of other cultures, and magical occurrences are commonplace. Celtic priests set forth a doctrine of reincarnation—the rebirth of the soul in a new body.

The evolution of Celtic society in Spain, southern Britain, France, and parts of central Europe slowed after the Roman conquests from the second century B.C.E. to the first century C.E. The peoples in these lands largely assimilated Roman ways (see Chapter 5). From the third century C.E. on, Germanic invaders from the east diminished the Celts still further. Only on the western fringes of the European continent—in Brittany (northwest France), Wales, Scotland, and Ireland—did Celtic peoples maintain their language, art, and culture into modern times.

FIRST CIVILIZATIONS OF THE AMERICAS: THE OLMEC AND CHAVÍN, 1200–250 B.C.E.

Humans reached the Western Hemisphere through a series of migrations from Asia. Some scholars believe that the first migrations occurred as early as 35,000 to 25,000 B.C.E., but most accept a later date of 20,000 to 13,000 B.C.E. Although some limited contacts with other cultures—for example, with Polynesians—may have occurred later, the peoples in the Western Hemisphere were virtually isolated from the rest of the world for at least fifteen thousand years. Thus, while technological innovations passed back and forth among the civilizations of Asia, Africa, and Europe, the peoples of the Americas faced the challenges of the natural environment on their own.

As people spread throughout the hemisphere, they encountered environments that ranged from polar extremes, to tropical rain forests, to towering mountain ranges. Mesoamerica (Mexico and northern Central America) and the mountainous Andean region of South America proved conducive to the emergence of complex societies. Well before 1000 B.C.E., plant domestication, technological innovation, and a limited development of trade led to greater social stratification and the beginnings of urbanization in both regions. Cultural elites used their increasing political and religious authority to organize great numbers of laborers. Large-scale irrigation and drainage works, cleared forests, and hillside terracing provided the economic platform for the construction of urban centers. By 1000 B.C.E. the major urban centers of Mesoamerica and the Andes, dominated by monumental structures devoted to religious purposes and elite, had begun to project their political and cultural power over broad territories: they had become civilizations. The cultural legacies of the two most important of these early civilizations, the Olmec of Mesoamerica and the Chavín of the Andes, would persist for more than a thousand years.

The Mesoamerican Olmec, 1200–400 B.C.E.

Mesoamerica is extremely active geologically, experiencing both earthquakes and volcanic eruptions. Mountain ranges break the region into micro-environments, including the temperate climates of the Valley of Mexico and the Guatemalan highlands, the tropical forests of the Peten and Gulf of Mexico coast, the rain forest of the southern Yucatán and Belize, and the drier scrub forest of the northern Yucatán (see Maps 2.2 and 10.1).

Within these ecological niches, specialized technologies made use of a wide variety of indigenous plants, as well as minerals like obsidian, quartz, and jade. But no animals were domesticated. Eventually, contacts across these environmental boundaries led to trade and cultural exchange. Enhanced trade, increasing agricultural productivity, and rising population led, in turn, to urbanization and the gradual appearance of powerful political and religious elites. Yet even though all Mesoamerican civilizations shared fundamental elements of material culture, technology, religious belief and ritual, political organization, art,

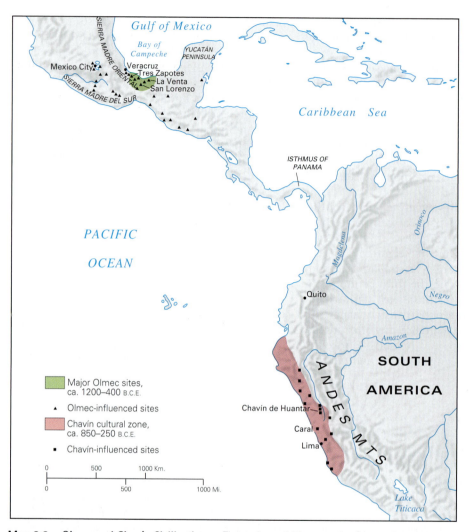

Map 2.2   Olmec and Chavín Civilizations   The regions of Mesoamerica (most of modern Mexico and Central America) and the Andean highlands of South America have hosted impressive civilizations since early times. The civilizations of the Olmec and Chavín were the originating civilizations of these two regions, providing the foundations of architecture, city planning, and religion.

architecture, and sports, the region was never unified politically.

The most influential early Mesoamerican civilization was the **Olmec,** flourishing between 1200 and 400 B.C.E. (see Map 2.2). The center of Olmec civilization was located near the tropical Atlantic coast of what are now the Mexican states of Ver-

acruz and Tabasco. Olmec cultural influence reached as far as the Pacific coast of Central America and the Central Plateau of Mexico.

The earliest settlements in the region depended on rich plant diversity and fishing, but by 3500 B.C.E the staples of the Mesoamerican diet—corn, beans, and squash—had been domesticated.

Recent research indicates that manioc, a calorie-rich root crop, was also grown in the floodplains of the region. The ability of farmers to produce dependable surpluses of these products permitted the first stages of craft specialization and social stratification. As religious and political elites emerged, they used their prestige and authority to organize the population to dig irrigation and drainage canals, develop raised fields in wetlands that could be farmed more intensively, and construct the large-scale religious and civic buildings that became the cultural signature of Olmec civilization.

San Lorenzo and some smaller centers nearby formed the cultural core of the early Olmec civilization (1200–900 B.C.E.). La Venta°, which developed at about the same time, became the most important Olmec center after 900 B.C.E. when San Lorenzo was abandoned or destroyed. Tres Zapotes° was the last dominant center, rising to prominence after La Venta collapsed or was destroyed around 600 B.C.E. (see Map 2.2). Relationships among these centers are unclear. Scholars have found little evidence to suggest that they were either rival city-states or dependent units of a centralized political authority. It appears that each center developed independently to exploit and exchange specialized products like salt, cacao (chocolate beans), potters' clay, and limestone. Each major Olmec center was eventually abandoned, its monuments defaced and buried and its buildings destroyed. Archaeologists interpret these events differently; some see them as evidence of internal upheavals or military defeat by neighboring peoples, and others suggest that they were associated with the death of a ruler.

Large artificial platforms and mounds of packed earth dominated Olmec urban centers and framed the collective ritual and political activities that brought the rural population to the cities at special times in the year. Some of the platforms also served as foundations for elite residences. The Olmec laid out their cities in alignment with the paths of certain stars, reflecting concern for astronomical events. Since these centers had small permanent populations, the scale of construction suggests that the Olmec elite could command the labor of thousands of men and women from the surrounding area for low-skill tasks like moving dirt and stone. Skilled artisans who lived in or near the urban core decorated the buildings with carvings and sculptures. They also produced the exquisite carved jade figurines, necklaces, and ceremonial knives and axes that distinguish Olmec culture. Archaeological evidence points to merchants trading with distant peoples for obsidian, jade, and pottery.

It seems likely that the rise of major urban centers coincided with the appearance of a form of kingship that combined religious and secular roles. Finely crafted objects decorated the households of the elite and distinguished their dress from that of the commoners, who lived in dispersed small structures constructed of sticks and mud. Colossal carved stone heads, some as large as 11 feet (3.4 meters) high, seem to reflect the authority of the rulers and their families. Since each head is unique and suggestive of an individual personality, most archaeologists believe they were carved to memorialize individual rulers. This theory is reinforced by the location of the heads close to the major urban centers, especially San Lorenzo. These remarkable

Olmec Head Giant heads sculpted from basalt are a widely recognized legacy of Olmec culture. Sixteen heads have been found, the largest approximately 11 feet (3.4 meters) tall. Experts in Olmec archaeology believe the heads are portraits of individual rulers, warriors, or ballplayers. (Georg Gerster/Photo Researchers, Inc.)

La Venta (LA BEN-tah)   **Tres Zapotes** (TRACE zah-POE-tace)

stone sculptures are the best-known monuments of Olmec culture.

The organization of collective labor by the Olmec elites benefited the commoners by increasing food production and making it more diverse and reliable. Ceramic products such as utilitarian pots and small figurines as well as small stone carvings associated with religious belief have been found in commoner households. This suggests that at least some advantages gained from urbanization and growing elite power were shared broadly in the society.

The Olmec elite used elaborate religious rituals to control this complex society. Thousands of commoners were drawn from the countryside to attend awe-inspiring ceremonies at the centers. The elevated platforms and mounds with carved stone veneers served as potent backdrops for these rituals. Rulers and their close kin associated themselves with the gods through bloodletting and human sacrifice, evidence of which is found in all the urban centers. The Olmec were polytheistic, and most of their deities had dual (male and female) natures. Human and animal characteristics were also blended. Surviving representations of jaguars, crocodiles, snakes, and sharks suggest that these powerful animals provided the most enduring images used in Olmec religious representation. Humans transforming themselves into these animals constitute a common decorative motif. Rulers were especially associated with the jaguar.

Practical advice about the periodic rains essential to agricultural life came from a class of shamans and healers. They directed the planning of urban centers to reflect astronomical observations and were responsible for developing a form of writing that may have influenced later innovations among the Maya (see Chapter 10). From their close observation of the stars, they produced a calendar that was used to organize ritual life and agriculture. The Olmec were also the likely originators of a ritual ball game that became an enduring part of Mesoamerican ceremonial life.

The discovery of Olmec products and images, such as jade carvings decorated with the jaguar-god, as far away as central Mexico provides evidence that the Olmec exercised cultural influence over a wide area even though they never created an empire. This influence would endure for centuries.

Early South American Civilization: Chavín, 900–250 b.c.e.

Geography played an important role in the development of human society in the Andes. The region's diverse environment—a mountainous core, arid coastal plain, and dense interior jungles—challenged human populations, encouraging the development of specialized regional production as well as complex social institutions and cultural values that facilitated interregional exchanges and shared labor responsibilities. These adaptations to environmental challenge became enduring features of Andean civilization.

The earliest urban centers in the Andean region were villages of a few hundred people built along the coastal plain or in the foothills near the coast. The abundance of fish and mollusks along the coast of Peru provided a dependable supply of food that helped make the development of early cities possible. The coastal populations traded these products along with decorative shells for corn, other foods, and eventually textiles produced in the foothills. The two regions also exchanged ceremonial practices, religious motifs, and aesthetic ideas. Recent discoveries demonstrate that as early as 2600 b.c.e. the vast site called Caral in the Supe Valley had developed many of the characteristics now viewed as the hallmarks of later Andean civilization, including ceremonial plazas, pyramids, elevated platforms and mounds, and extensive irrigation works. The scale of the public works in Caral suggests a population of thousands and a political structure capable of organizing the production and distribution of maritime and agricultural products over a broad area.

Chavín, one of the most impressive of South America's early urban civilizations (see Map 2.2), inherited many of the cultural and economic characteristics of Caral. Its capital, Chavín de Huantar°, was located at 10,300 feet (3,139 meters) in the eastern range of the Andes north of the modern city of Lima. Between 900 and 250 b.c.e., a period roughly coinciding with Olmec civilization in Mesoamerica, Chavín dominated a densely populated region that included large areas of the Peru-

Chavín de Huantar (cha-BEAN day WAHN-tar)

vian coastal plain and Andean foothills. Chavín de Huantar's location at the intersection of trade routes connecting the coast with populous mountain valleys and the tropical lowlands on the eastern flank of the Andes allowed the city's rulers to control trade among these distinct ecological zones and gain an important economic advantage over regional rivals.

Chavín's dominance as a ceremonial and commercial center depended on earlier developments in agriculture and trade, including the introduction of maize cultivation from Mesoamerica. Maize increased the food supplies of the coast and interior foothills, allowing greater levels of urbanization. As Chavín grew, its trade linked the coastal economy with the producers of quinoa (a local grain), potatoes, and llamas in the high mountain valleys and, to a lesser extent, with Amazonian producers of coca (the leaves were chewed, producing a mild narcotic effect) and fruits.

Reciprocal labor obligations that permitted the construction and maintenance of roads, bridges, temples, palaces, and large irrigation and drainage projects, as well as textile production, developed as well. The exact nature of these reciprocal labor obligations at Chavín is unknown. In later times groups of related families who held land communally and claimed descent from a common ancestor organized these labor obligations. Group members thought of each other as brothers and sisters and were obligated to aid each other, providing a model for the organization of labor and the distribution of goods at every level of Andean society.

Llamas were the only domesticated beasts of burden in the Americas, and they played an important role in the integration of the Andean region. They were first domesticated in the mountainous interior of Peru and were crucial to Chavín's development. Llamas provided meat and wool and decreased the labor needed to transport goods. A single driver could control ten to thirty animals, each carrying up to 70 pounds (32 kilograms); a human porter could carry only about 50 pounds (22.5 kilograms). The increased use of llamas to move goods from one ecological zone to another promoted specialization of production and increased trade.

The enormous scale of the capital and the dispersal of Chavín's pottery styles, religious motifs, and architectural forms over a wide area suggest that Chavín imposed some form of political integration and trade dependency on its neighbors that may have relied in part on military force. However, most modern scholars believe that, as in the case of the Olmec civilization, Chavín's influence depended more on the development of an attractive and convincing religious belief system and related rituals. Chavín's most potent religious symbol, a jaguar deity, was dispersed over a broad area, and archaeological evidence suggests that Chavín de Huantar served as a pilgrimage site.

The architectural signature of Chavín was a large complex of multilevel platforms made of packed earth or rubble and faced with cut stone or adobe (sun-dried brick made of clay and straw). Small buildings used for ritual purposes or as elite residences were built on these platforms. Nearly all the buildings were decorated with relief carvings of serpents, condors, jaguars, or humans. The largest building at Chavín de Huantar measured 250 feet (76 meters) on each side and rose to a height of 50 feet (15 meters). About one-third of its interior is hollow, containing narrow galleries and small rooms that may have housed the remains of royal ancestors.

American metallurgy was first developed in the Andean region. The later introduction of metallurgy in Mesoamerica, like the appearance of maize agriculture in the Andes, suggests sustained trade and cultural contacts between the two regions. Archaeological investigations of Chavín de Huantar and smaller centers have revealed remarkable three-dimensional silver, gold, and gold alloy ornaments that represent a clear advance over earlier technologies. Bronze and iron, however, were unknown.

Improvements in both the manufacture and the decoration of textiles are also associated with the rise of Chavín. The quality of these products, which were probably used only by the elite or in religious rituals, added to the reputation and prestige of the culture and aided in the projection of its power and influence. The most common decorative motif in sculpture, pottery, and textiles was a jaguar-man similar in conception to the Olmec symbol. In both civilizations and in many other cultures in the Americas, this powerful predator provided an enduring image of religious authority and a vehicle through which the gods could act in the world of men and women.

Class distinctions also appear to have increased. A class of priests directed religious life. Modern scholars also see evidence that both local chiefs and a more powerful chief or king dominated Chavín's politics. Excavations of graves reveal that superior-quality textiles as well as gold crowns, breastplates, and jewelry distinguished rulers from commoners.

There is no convincing evidence, like defaced buildings or broken images, that the eclipse of Chavín (unlike the Olmec centers) was associated with conquest or rebellion. However, recent investigations have suggested that increased warfare throughout the region around 200 B.C.E. disrupted Chavín's trade and undermined the authority of the governing elite. Regardless of what caused the collapse of this powerful culture, the technologies, material culture, statecraft, architecture, and urban planning associated with Chavín influenced the Andean region for centuries.

CONCLUSION

The civilizations of early China, Nubia, Celtic Europe, the Olmec, and Chavín emerged in very different ecological contexts in widely separated parts of the globe. The patterns of organization, technology, behavior, and belief that they developed were, in large part, responses to the challenges and opportunities of those environments.

In the North China Plain, as in the river-valley civilizations of Mesopotamia and Egypt, the presence of great, flood-prone rivers and the lack of dependable rainfall led to the formation of powerful institutions capable of organizing large numbers of people to dig and maintain irrigation channels and build dikes. An authoritarian central government has been a recurring feature of Chinese history, beginning with the Shang monarchy and warrior elite.

In Nubia, the initial impetus for the formation of a strong state was the need for protection from desert nomads and from the Egyptian rulers who coveted Nubian gold and other resources. Control of these resources and of the trade route between sub-Saharan Africa and the north, as well as the agricultural surplus to feed administrators and specialists in the urban centers, made the rulers of Kush, Napata, and Meroë wealthy and formidable.

The Celtic peoples of continental Europe never developed a strong state. They occupied fertile lands with adequate rainfall for agriculture, grazing territory for flocks, and timber for fuel and construction. Kinship groups dominated by warrior elites and controlling compact territories were the usual form of organization.

Although the ecological zones in Mesoamerica and South America in which the Olmec and Chavín cultures emerged were quite different, both societies created networks that brought together the resources and products of disparate regions. Little is known about the political and social organization of these societies, but archaeological evidence makes clear the existence of ruling elites that gathered wealth and organized labor for the construction of monumental centers.

In most complex societies small groups achieve a level of wealth and prestige that allows them to dominate the majority. It is important to understand how these elite groups maintain and justify their position. Among both the early Chinese and the Celts a warrior aristocracy, with wealth based on land and flocks, controlled significant numbers of human laborers. When the Zhou overthrew the Shang, they curtailed the power of the warrior elite, and over time a new elite of educated government officials evolved. Much less is known about the emergence of elite groups in Nubia and the states of the Olmec and Chavín.

In the Eastern Hemisphere, the production of metal tools, weapons, and luxury and ceremonial implements was vital to the success of elite groups. Bronze metallurgy began at different times—in western Asia around 2500 B.C.E., in East Asia around 2000 B.C.E., in northeastern Africa around 1500 B.C.E. Possession of bronze weapons with hard, sharp edges enabled the warriors of Shang and Zhou China, like the royal armies of Egypt and Mesopotamia, to dominate the peasant masses. In Shang China bronze was also used to craft the vessels that played a vital role in the rituals of contact with the spirits of ancestors.

Throughout history, elites have used religion to bolster their position. The Shang rulers of China were indispensable intermediaries between their kingdom and powerful and protective gods and ancestors. Their Zhou successors developed the concept of the ruler as divine Son of Heaven who ruled in accord with the Mandate of Heaven. The rulers of Nubia, drawing on Egyptian concepts, claimed to be gods on earth. In the Olmec and Chavín zones there is some evidence of religious rituals performed to affirm the position of the ruling class. Human sacrifice was practiced among the Celts and in Shang China, Nubia, and Olmec Mesoamerica.

The construction and use of "urban" centers and monumental spaces and structures for dramatic religious rituals and colorful political events also propagated the ideologies of power. Ceremonies involving impressive pageantry communicated a message of the "superiority" of the elite and the desirability of being associated with them. In early China and the Olmec and Chavín civilizations, the centers appear to have been the sites of palaces, shrines, and the dwellings of the elite.

The comparison of the two hemispheres reveals important differences. Not only did the plant and animal resources differ, but the complex societies of the Western Hemisphere also did not necessarily develop technologies in the same sequence as their Eastern Hemisphere counterparts. The Olmec and Chavín peoples did not possess wheeled vehicles or metal weapons and tools. However, their monumental architecture and artistic expression equaled that of the Eastern Hemisphere. In addition, they created sophisticated political, social, and economic institutions that rivaled those developed in the Eastern Hemisphere in the third and second millennia B.C.E.

■ Key Terms

loess	yin/yang
Shang	Kush
divination	Meroë
Zhou	Celts
Mandate of Heaven	Druids
Legalism	Olmec
Confucius	Chavín
Daoism	llama

■ Suggested Reading

Caroline Blunden and Mark Elvin, *Cultural Atlas of China* (1983), contains general geographic, ethnographic, and historical information about China through the ages, as well as many maps and illustrations. Conrad Schirokauer, *A Brief History of Chinese Civilization* (1991), and John King Fairbank, *China: A New History* (1992), offer useful chapters on early China. Edward L. Shaughnessy and Michael Loewe, eds., *The Cambridge History of Ancient China* (1998), approaches the subject in far greater depth. Nicola Di Cosmo, *Ancient China and Its Enemies: The Rise of Nomadic Power in East Asian History* (2002), sets the development of Chinese civilization in the broader context of interactions with nomadic neighbors. Jessica Rawson, *Ancient China: Art and Archaeology* (1980), Kwang-chih Chang, *The Archaeology of Ancient China*, 4th ed. (1986), and Ronald G. Knapp, *China's Walled Cities* (2000), emphasize archaeological evidence. W. Thomas Chase, *Ancient Chinese Bronze Art: Casting the Precious Sacral Vessel* (1991), contains a brief but useful discussion of the importance of bronzes in ancient China, as well as a detailed discussion of bronze-casting techniques. Robert Temple, *The Genius of China: 3,000 Years of Science, Discovery, and Invention* (1986), explores many aspects of Chinese technology, using a division into general topics such as agriculture, engineering, and medicine. Anne Behnke Kinney, "Women in Ancient China," in *Women's Roles in Ancient Civilizations: A Reference Guide*, ed. Bella Vivante (1999), and Patricia Ebrey, "Women, Marriage, and the Family in Chinese History," in *Heritage of China: Contemporary Perspectives on Chinese Civilization*, ed. Paul S. Ropp (1990), address the very limited evidence for women in early China. Michael Loewe and Carmen Blacker, *Oracles and Divination* (1981), addresses practices in China and other ancient civilizations. Simon Leys, *The Analects of Confucius* (1997), provides a translation of and a commentary on this fundamental text. Benjamin I. Schwartz, *The World of Thought in Ancient China* (1985), is a broad introduction to early Chinese ethical and spiritual concepts.

After a long period of scholarly neglect, with an occasional exception such as Bruce G. Trigger, *Nubia Under the Pharaohs* (1976), the study of ancient Nubia is now receiving considerable attention. David O'Connor, *Ancient Nubia: Egypt's Rival in Africa* (1993); Joyce L. Haynes, *Nubia: Ancient Kingdoms of Africa* (1992); Karl-Heinz Priese, *The Gold of Meroë* (1993); P. L. Shinnie, *Ancient Nubia* (1996); Derek A. Welsby, *The Kingdom of Kush: The Napatan and Meroitic Empires* (1996); and Timothy Kendall, *Kerma and the Kingdom of Kush, 2500–1500 B.C.: The Archaeological Discovery of an Ancient Nubian Empire* (1997), all reflect the new interest of major museums in the art and artifacts of this society. Robert Morkot, "Egypt and Nubia," in *Empires: Perspectives from Archaeology and History,* ed. Susan E. Alcock (2001), examines the political dimension of Egyptian domination, and John H. Taylor, *Egypt and Nubia* (1991), also emphasizes the fruitful interaction of the Egyptian and Nubian cultures.

Simon James, *The World of the Celts* (1993), is a concise, well-illustrated introduction to Celtic civilization. Fuller treatments can be found in Barry W. Cunliffe, *The Ancient Celts* (1997), and Peter Ellis, *The Celtic Empire: The First Millennium of Celtic History, c. 1000 B.C.–51 A.D.* (1990). Miranda J. Green, *The Celtic World* (1995), is a large and comprehensive collection of articles on many aspects of Celtic civilization. Philip Freeman, *War, Women, and Druids: Eyewitness Accounts and Early Reports on the Ancient Celts* (2002), collects the ancient textual evidence. John Haywood, *Atlas of the Celtic World* (2001), is a useful reference. Simon James, *The Atlantic Celts: Ancient People or Modern Invention* (1999), reflects the current scholarly emphasis on articulating the important differences between Celtic groups and deconstructing the modern "myth" of a monolithic Celtic identity. On Celtic religion and mythology, see Bernhard Maier, *Dictionary of Celtic Religion and Culture* (1997); James MacKillop, *Dictionary of Celtic Mythology* (1998); Proinsias Mac Cana, *Celtic Mythology* (1983); Paul R. Lonigan, *The Druids: Priests of the Ancient Celts* (1996); and two books by Miranda Green: *The Gods of the Celts* (1986) and *Celtic Myths* (1993). Peter Ellis, *Celtic Women: Women in Celtic Society and Literature* (1996), collects and evaluates the evidence for women's roles. Celtic art is covered by Ruth

and Vincent Megaw, *Celtic Art: From Its Beginnings to the Book of Kells* (1989), and I. M. Stead, *Celtic Art* (1985). For translations and a brief discussion of Celtic legends, see Patrick K. Ford, *The Mabinogi and Other Medieval Welsh Tales* (1977), and Jeffrey Gantz, *Early Irish Myths and Sagas* (1981).

A number of useful books provide an introduction to the early Americas. In *Prehistory of the Americas* (1987), Stuart Fiedel provides an excellent summary of the early history of the Western Hemisphere. *Early Man in the New World,* ed. Richard Shutler, Jr. (1983), is also a useful general work. *Atlas of Ancient America* (1986), by Michael Coe, Elizabeth P. Benson, and Dean R. Snow, offers a compendium of maps and information. George Kubler, *The Art and Architecture of Ancient America: The Mexican, Maya, and Andean Peoples* (1984), is an essential tool, though dated.

For the Olmecs, see Jacques Soustelle, *The Olmecs: The Oldest Civilization in Mexico* (1984). More reliable is Michael Coe, *The Olmec World* (1996). Richard W. Keatinge, ed., *Peruvian Prehistory* (1988), provides a helpful introduction to the scholarship on Andean societies. The most useful summary of recent research on Chavín is Richard L. Burger, *Chavín and the Origins of Andean Civilization* (1992).

■ Notes

1. Quoted in Miriam Lichtheim, ed., *Ancient Egyptian Literature: A Book of Readings* (Berkeley: University of California Press 1978).

The Mediterranean and Middle East, 2000–500 B.C.E.

3

CHAPTER OUTLINE

The Cosmopolitan Middle East, 1700–1100 B.C.E.

The Aegean World, 2000–1100 B.C.E.

The Assyrian Empire, 911–612 B.C.E.

Israel, 2000–500 B.C.E.

Phoenicia and the Mediterranean, 1200–500 B.C.E.

Failure and Transformation, 750–550 B.C.E.

ENVIRONMENT AND TECHNOLOGY: Ancient Textiles and Dyes

Ancient stories—even those that are not historically accurate—provide valuable insights into how people thought about their origins and identity. One famous story concerned the city of Carthage° in present-day Tunisia, which for centuries dominated the commerce of the western Mediterranean. Tradition held that Dido, a member of the royal family of the Phoenician city-state of Tyre° in southern Lebanon, fled with her supporters to the western Mediterranean after her husband was murdered by her brother, the king of Tyre. Landing on the North African coast, the refugees made friendly contact with local people, who agreed to give them as much land as a cow's hide could cover. By cleverly cutting the hide into narrow strips, they were able to mark out a substantial piece of territory for Kart Khadasht, the "New City" (called Carthago by their Roman enemies). Later, faithful to the memory of her dead husband, Dido committed suicide rather than marry a local chieftain.

This story highlights the spread of cultural patterns from older centers to new regions in the Mediterranean lands and western Asia. Just as Egyptian cultural influences helped transform Nubian society, influences from the older centers in Mesopotamia and Egypt penetrated throughout western Asia and the Mediterranean. Far-flung trade, diplomatic contacts, military conquests, and the relocation of large numbers of people spread knowledge, beliefs, practices, and technologies.

Carthage (KAHR-thuhj)   **Tyre** (tire)

61

By the end of the second millennium B.C.E. many of the societies of the Eastern Hemisphere had entered the **Iron Age.** Iron offered several advantages over bronze. It was a single metal rather than an alloy and thus was simpler to obtain; and there were many sources of iron ore. Once the technology of iron making had been mastered—iron has to be heated to a higher temperature than bronze, and its hardness depends on the amount of carbon added during the forging process—iron tools were found to have harder, sharper edges than bronze tools.

These advantages were not discovered all at once. The Hittites of iron-rich Anatolia had learned to make iron implements by 1500 B.C.E. but did not share their knowledge. Some scholars believe that, in the disrupted period after 1200 B.C.E., blacksmiths from the Hittite core area migrated and spread the technology. Others speculate that metalworkers who could not obtain copper and tin turned to dumps of slag (the byproduct of bronze production) containing iron residue and found that they could create useful objects from it.

The first part of this chapter resumes the story of Mesopotamia and Egypt in the Late Bronze Age, the second millennium B.C.E.: their complex relations with neighboring peoples, the development of a prosperous, "cosmopolitan" network of states in the Middle East, and the period of destruction and decline that set in around 1200 B.C.E. We also look at how the Minoan and Mycenaean civilizations of the Aegean Sea were inspired by the technologies and cultural patterns of the older Middle Eastern centers and prospered from participation in long-distance networks of trade.

Turning to the Early Iron Age, from 1000 to 500 B.C.E., the focus will be on three societies:

the Assyrians of northern Mesopotamia; the Israelites; and the Phoenicians of Lebanon, Syria, and, via their Carthaginian colonies, the western Mediterranean.

As you read this chapter, ask yourself the following questions:

- What environmental, technological, political, and cultural factors led these societies to develop their distinctive institutions and values?

- What new relationships developed between societies, and what were their consequences?

- What were the causes and consequences of large-scale movements of peoples during this era?

- Why were certain cultures destroyed or assimilated while others survived?

THE COSMOPOLITAN MIDDLE EAST, 1700–1100 B.C.E.

Although outside invaders overwhelmed Mesopotamia and Egypt in the seventeenth century B.C.E. (see Chapter 1), the outsiders were eventually either ejected or assimilated, and conditions of stability and prosperity returned. Between 1500 and 1200 B.C.E. large territorial states dominated the Middle East (see Map 3.1). Smaller city-states, kingdoms, and kinship groups fell under their control as they competed for access to commodities and trade routes.

Historians have called the Late Bronze Age a "cosmopolitan" era, meaning a time of widely shared cultures and lifestyles. Diplomatic relations and commercial contacts between states fostered flows of goods and ideas, and elite groups shared similar values and high living standards. The peasants who constituted the majority of the population may have seen some improvement in their standard of living, but they reaped far fewer benefits from the increasing contacts and trade.

C H R O N O L O G Y

	Western Asia	Egypt	Syria-Palestine	Mediterranean
2000 B.C.E.	**2000 B.C.E.** Horses in use	**2040–1640 B.C.E.** Middle Kingdom		**2000 B.C.E.** Rise of Minoan civilization on Crete; early Greeks arrive in Greece
	1700–1200 B.C.E. Hittites dominant in Anatolia	**1640–1532 B.C.E.** Hyksos dominate northern Egypt		**1600 B.C.E.** Rise of Mycenaean civilization in Greece
		1532 B.C.E. Beginning of New Kingdom		
1500 B.C.E.	**1500 B.C.E.** Hittites develop iron metallurgy	**1490 B.C.E.** Queen Hatshepsut dispatches expedition to Punt	**1500 B.C.E.** Early "alphabet" script developed at Ugarit	
	1460 B.C.E. Kassites assume control of southern Mesopotamia	**1353 B.C.E.** Akhenaten launches reforms		**1450 B.C.E.** Destruction of Minoan places in Crete
		1290–1224 B.C.E. Ramessess II reigns	**1250–1200 B.C.E.** Israelite occupation of Canaan	
	1200 B.C.E. Destruction of Hittite kingdom	**1200–1150 B.C.E.** Sea Peoples attack Egypt	**1150 B.C.E.** Philistines settle southern coast of Israel	**1200–1150 B.C.E.** Destruction of Mycenaean centers in Greece
1000 B.C.E.	**1000 B.C.E.** Iron metallurgy begins	**1070 B.C.E.** End of New Kingdom	**1000 B.C.E.** David establishes Jerusalem as Israelite capital	**1000 B.C.E.** Iron metallurgy
			969 B.C.E. Hiram of Tyre comes to power	
			960 B.C.E. Solomon builds First Temple	
			920 B.C.E. Division into two kingdoms of Israel and Judah	
	911 B.C.E. Rise of Neo-Assyrian Empire			**814 B.C.E.** Foundation of Carthage
	744–727 B.C.E. Reforms of Tiglath-pileser		**721 B.C.E.** Assyrian conquest of northern kingdom	
	668–627 B.C.E. Reign of Ashurbanipal		**701 B.C.E.** Assyrian humiliation of Tyre	

(continued)

C H R O N O L O G Y *(continued)*			
	Western Asia	**Egypt**	**Syria-Palestine**	**Mediterranean**

	Western Asia	**Egypt**	**Syria-Palestine**	**Mediterranean**
600 B.C.E.	**626–539 B.C.E.** Neo-Babylonian kingdom **612 B.C.E.** Fall of Assyria	**671 B.C.E.** Assyrian Conquest of Egypt		
500 B.C.E.			**587 B.C.E.** Neo-Babylonian capture of Jerusalem **515 B.C.E.** Deportees from Babylon return to Jerusalem **450 B.C.E.** Completion of Hebrew Bible; Hanno the Phoenician explores West Africa	**550–330 B.C.E.** Rivalry of Carthaginians and Greeks in western Mediterranean

Western Asia

By 1500 B.C.E. Mesopotamia was divided into two distinct political zones: Babylonia in the south and Assyria in the north (see Map 3.1). The city of Babylon had first gained ascendancy under the dynasty of Hammurabi in the eighteenth and seventeenth centuries B.C.E., but Kassite° peoples from the Zagros° Mountains to the east had seized power by 1500 B.C.E. Though Kassite names derive from their native, non-Semitic language, they otherwise embraced Babylonian language and culture and intermarried with the native population. For 350 years, the Kassite lords of Babylonia defended their core area and traded for raw materials, but they did not pursue territorial conquest.

The Assyrians of the north proved more ambitious. As early as the twentieth century B.C.E. the city of Ashur,° the leading urban center on the northern Tigris, anchored a busy trade route across the northern Mesopotamian plain and onto the Anatolian Plateau. Assyrian merchants established settlements outside the walls of important Anatolian cities. They exported textiles and tin, used to make bronze, in exchange for Anatolian silver. In the eigh-

teenth century B.C.E. an Assyrian dynasty briefly controlled the upper Euphrates River near the present-day Syria-Iraq border. The trade routes connecting Mesopotamia to Anatolia and the Syria-Palestine coast were key to the power of this "Old Assyrian" kingdom. After 1400 B.C.E. a resurgent "Middle Assyrian" kingdom again engaged in campaigns of conquest and economic expansion.

Other ambitious states developed around the Mesopotamian heartland, including Elam in southwest Iran and Mitanni° in the broad plain between the upper Euphrates and Tigris Rivers. Most formidable were the **Hittites°,** who became the foremost power in Anatolia from around 1700 to 1200 B.C.E. From their capital at Hattusha°, near present-day Ankara° in central Turkey, they deployed the fearsome new technology of horse-drawn war chariots, which along with their Indo-European language associated them with peoples farther to the north and east. Anatolia's rich deposits of copper, silver, and iron played a major role in Hittite commerce. As mentioned earlier, the Hittites pioneered the use of iron for tools and weapons. They heated the ore un-

---

Kassite (KAS-ite)   **Zagros** (ZAH-groes)   **Ashur** (AH-shoor)

Mitanni (mih-TAH-nee)   **Hittite** (HIT-ite)   **Hattusha** (haht-tush-SHAH)   **Ankara** (ANG-kuh-ruh)

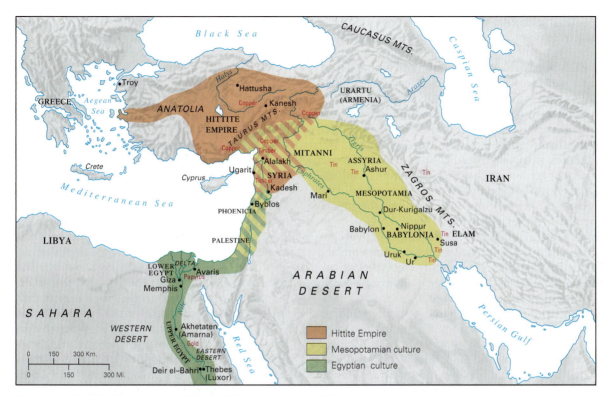

Map 3.1   The Middle East in the Second Millennium B.C.E.   Although warfare was not uncommon, treaties, diplomatic missions, and correspondence in Akkadian cuneiform fostered cooperative relationships between states. All were tied together by extensive networks of exchange centering on the trade in metals, and peripheral regions, such as Nubia and the Aegean Sea, were drawn into the web of commerce.

til it was soft enough to shape, pounded it to remove impurities, and then plunged it into cold water to harden. The Hittites tried to keep knowledge of this process secret because it provided both military and economic advantages.

During the second millennium B.C.E. Mesopotamian political and cultural concepts spread across much of western Asia. Akkadian° became the language of diplomacy and correspondence between governments. The Elamites° and Hittites, among others, adapted the cuneiform system to write their own languages. In the Syrian coastal city of Ugarit° thirty cuneiform symbols were used to write consonant sounds, an early example of the

alphabetic principle and a considerable advance over the hundreds of signs required in conventional cuneiform writing. Mesopotamian myths and artistic tastes were widely imitated.

New Kingdom Egypt

After flourishing for nearly four hundred years (see Chapter 1), the Egyptian Middle Kingdom lost strength in the seventeenth century B.C.E. Egypt entered a period of political fragmentation and economic decline. Around 1640 B.C.E. it came under foreign rule for the first time, at the hands of the Hyksos°, or "Princes of Foreign Lands."

Akkadian (uh-KAY-dee-uhn)   **Elamite** (EE-luh-mite)
Ugarit (OO-guh-reet)

Hyksos (HICK-soes)

Historians are uncertain about who the Hyksos were. Semitic peoples had been migrating from the Syria-Palestine region (sometimes called the Levant: present-day Syria, Lebanon, Jordan, Israel, and the Palestinian territories) into the eastern Nile Delta for centuries. In the chaotic conditions of this time, other peoples may have joined them, establishing control first in the delta and then in the middle of the country. The Hyksos had war chariots and composite bows made of wood and horn for greater range, which gave them an advantage over the Egyptians. Hyksos dominion in Egypt may not have been far different from the Kassite seizure of power in Babylonia. The Hyksos intermarried with Egyptians and assimilated to native ways. They used the Egyptian language and maintained Egyptian institutions and culture. Nevertheless, unlike in Mesopotamia, the Egyptians continued to regard the Hyksos as "foreigners."

As with the formation of the Middle Kingdom five hundred years earlier, the reunification of Egypt under a native dynasty was accomplished by princes from Thebes. After three decades of warfare, Kamose° and Ahmose° expelled the Hyksos from Egypt and inaugurated the New Kingdom, which lasted from about 1532 to 1070 B.C.E.

A century of foreign domination had shattered the isolationist mindset of earlier eras. New Kingdom Egypt was an aggressive and expansionist state, extending its territorial control north into Syria-Palestine and south into Nubia. Timber, gold, copper (bronze metallurgy took hold in Egypt around 1500 B.C.E.), and money in taxes and tribute (payments from the territories it had conquered) were the prizes of this expansion. The occupied territories also provided a buffer zone against foreign attack. In Nubia, Egypt imposed direct control and pressed the native population to adopt Egyptian language and culture (see Chapter 2). In the Syria-Palestine region, in contrast, the Egyptians stationed garrisons at strategically placed forts and supported local rulers willing to collaborate.

The New Kingdom was a period of innovation. Participation in the diplomatic and commercial networks that linked the states of western Asia caused Egyptian soldiers, administrators, diplomats, and merchants to travel widely and learn about exotic fruits and vegetables, new musical instruments, and new technologies, such as an improved potter's wheel and weaver's loom.

At least one woman held the throne of New Kingdom Egypt. When Pharaoh Tuthmosis° II died, his queen, **Hatshepsut°,** served as regent for her young stepson and soon claimed the royal title for herself (r. 1473–1458 B.C.E.). In inscriptions she often used the male pronoun to refer to herself, and drawings and sculptures show her wearing the long beard of the ruler of Egypt.

Around 1490 B.C.E. Hatshepsut sent a naval expedition down the Red Sea to Punt°, an exotic land that historians believe may have been near the coast of eastern Sudan or Eritrea. Hatshepsut was in quest of myrrh°, a reddish-brown resin that the Egyptians burned in religious rites and used in medicines and cosmetics. She hoped to bypass the middlemen who drove up the price exorbitantly and establish direct trade between Punt and Egypt. When the expedition returned with myrrh and various sub-Saharan luxuries—ebony and other rare woods, ivory, live monkeys, panther skins—Hatshepsut celebrated the achievement in words and pictures on the walls of the mortuary temple she built for herself at Deir el-Bahri°. She may have used the success of this expedition to bolster her claim to the throne. After her death, in a reaction that reflected some official opposition to a woman ruler, her image was defaced and her name blotted out wherever it appeared.

Another ruler who departed from traditional ways ascended the throne as Amenhotep° IV. He soon began to refer to himself as **Akhenaten°** (r. 1353–1335 B.C.E.), meaning "beneficial to the Aten°" (the disk of the sun). Changing his name was one way to publicize his belief in Aten as the supreme deity. He closed the temples of other gods, challenging the age-old supremacy of the chief god Amon° and the power and influence of Amon's priests.

Some scholars maintain that Akhenaten pioneered monotheism—the belief in one exclusive god. Akhenaten's goal, however, was more likely a

---

Kamose (KAH-mose)   Ahmose (AH-mose)

Tuthmosis (tuth-MOE-sis)   Hatshepsut (hat-SHEP-soot)
Punt (poont)   myrrh (murr)   Deir el-Bahri (DARE uhl–BAH-ree)   Amenhotep (ah-muhn-HOE-tep)   Akhenaten (ah-ken-AHT-n)   Aten (AHT-n)   Amon (AH-muhn)

The Mortuary Temple of Queen Hatshepsut at Deir el–Bahri, Egypt, ca. 1460 B.C.E.   This beautiful complex of terraces, ramps, and colonnades featured relief sculptures and texts commemorating the famous expedition to Punt.   (Woodfin Camp & Associates)

reassertion of the king's superiority over the priests and a renewal of belief in the king's divinity. Worship of Aten was confined to the royal family: the people of Egypt were pressed to revere the divine ruler.

Akhenaten built a new capital at modern-day Amarna°, halfway between Memphis and Thebes (see Map 3.1). He relocated thousands of Egyptians to construct the site and serve the ruling elite. His artists created a new style that broke with the conventions of earlier art: the king, his wife Nefertiti°, and their daughters were depicted in fluid, natural poses with strangely elongated heads and limbs and swelling abdomens.

Government officials, priests, and others whose privileges and wealth were linked to the tra-

ditional system strongly resented these reforms. After Akhenaten's death the temples were reopened; Amon was reinstated as chief god; the capital returned to Thebes; and the priests regained their influence. The boy-king Tutankhamun° (r. 1333–1323 B.C.E.), one of the immediate successors of Akhenaten and famous solely because his tomb had not been pillaged by tomb robbers when it was found, reveals both in his name (meaning "beautiful in life is Amon") and in his insignificant reign the ultimate failure of Akhenaten's revolution.

In 1323 B.C.E. the general Haremhab seized the throne and established a new dynasty, the Ramessides°. The rulers of this line renewed the policy

Amarna (uh-MAHR-nuh)   **Nefertiti** (nef-uhr-TEE-tee)

Tutankhamun (tuht-uhnk-AH-muhn)   **Ramesside** (RAM-ih-side)

of conquest and expansion that Akhenaten had neglected. **Ramesses° II**—sometimes called Ramesses the Great—ruled for sixty-six years (r. 1290–1224 B.C.E.) and dominated his age. Ramesses looms large in the archaeological record because he undertook monumental building projects all over Egypt. Living into his nineties, he may have fathered more than a hundred children. Since 1990 archaeologists have been excavating a network of more than a hundred corridors and chambers carved deep into a hillside in the Valley of the Kings where many sons of Ramesses were buried.

Commerce and Communication

Early in his reign Ramesses II fought a major battle against the Hittites at Kadesh in northern Syria (1285 B.C.E.). Although Egyptian scribes presented this encounter as a great victory, the lack of territorial gains suggests that it was essentially a draw. In subsequent years Egyptian and Hittite diplomats negotiated a treaty, which was strengthened by Ramesses's marriage to a Hittite princess. At issue was control of Syria-Palestine. The inland cities of Syria-Palestine—such as Mari° on the upper Euphrates and Alalakh° in western Syria—were hubs of international trade. The coastal towns—particularly Ugarit and the Phoenician towns of the Lebanese seaboard—served as transshipment points for trade to and from the lands ringing the Mediterranean Sea.

In the eastern Mediterranean, northeastern Africa, and western Asia in the Late Bronze Age, any state that wanted to project its power needed metal to make tools and weapons. Commerce in metals energized the long-distance trade. We have seen the Assyrian traffic in silver from Anatolia and the Egyptian passion for Nubian gold (see Chapter 2). Copper came from Anatolia and Cyprus, tin from Afghanistan and possibly the British Isles. Both commodities traveled long distances and passed through many hands before reaching their final destinations.

New modes of transportation expedited communications and commerce across great distances and inhospitable landscapes. Horses arrived in western Asia around 2000 B.C.E. First used by nomads in Central Asia, they were brought into Mesopotamia through the Zagros Mountains and reached Egypt by 1600 B.C.E. The speed of the horse contributed to the creation of large states and empires. Soldiers and government agents could cover great distances quickly, and swift, maneuverable horse-drawn chariots became the premier instrument of war. The team of driver and archer could ride forward and unleash a volley of arrows or trample terrified foot soldiers.

Sometime after 1500 B.C.E. in western Asia, but not for another thousand years in Egypt, people began to make common use of camels, though the animal may have been domesticated much earlier in southern Arabia. Their strength made them ideal pack animals, and their ability to go without water made travel across barren terrain possible.

THE AEGEAN WORLD, 2000–1100 B.C.E.

In this era of far-flung trade and communication, the emergence of the Minoan° civilization on the island of Crete and the Mycenaean° civilization of Greece demonstrates the fertilizing influence of older centers on outlying lands and peoples. The landscape of southern Greece and the Aegean islands is rocky and arid, with small plains lying between ranges of hills. The limited arable land was suitable for grains, grapevines, and olive trees. Flocks of sheep and goats grazed the slopes. Sharply indented coastlines, natural harbors, and small islands within sight of one another made the sea the fastest and least costly mode of travel. Lacking metals and timber, Aegean peoples had to import these commodities from abroad. As a result, the rise, success, and eventual fall of the Minoan and Mycenaean societies were closely tied to their relations with other peoples in the region.

Minoan Crete

The first European civilization to have complex political and social structures and advanced tech-

---

Ramesses (RAM-ih-seez)   **Mari** (MAH-ree)   **Alalakh** (UH-luh-luhk)

Minoan (mih-NO-uhn)   **Mycenaean** (my-suh-NEE-uhn)

Fresco from the Aegean Island of Thera, ca. 1650 B.C.E. This picture, originally painted on wet plaster, depicts the arrival of a fleet in a harbor as people watch from the walls of the town. The Minoan civilization of Crete was famous in later legend for its naval power. The fresco reveals the appearance and design of ships in the Bronze Age Aegean. In the seventeenth century B.C.E., the island of Thera was devastated by a massive volcanic explosion, thought by many to be the origin of the myth of Atlantis sinking beneath the sea. (Archaeological Receipts Fund, Athens)

nologies like those found in western Asia and northeastern Africa appeared on the island of Crete by 2000 B.C.E. (see Map 3.1). The **Minoan** civilization featured centralized government, monumental building, bronze metallurgy, writing, and recordkeeping. Archaeologists named this civilization after Greek legends about King Minos, who was said to have ruled a vast naval empire, including the southern Greek mainland, and to have kept the monstrous Minotaur° (half-man, half-bull) beneath his palace in a mazelike labyrinth built by the ingenious inventor Daedalus°. Thus later Greeks recollected a time when Crete was home to many ships and skilled craftsmen.

The ethnicity of the Minoans is uncertain, and their writing has not been deciphered. But their sprawling palace complexes at Cnossus°, Phaistos°, and Mallia° and the distribution of Cretan pottery and other artifacts around the Mediterranean and Middle East testify to widespread trading connections. Egyptian, Syrian, and Mesopotamian influences can be seen in the design of the Minoan palaces, but the absence of identifiable representations of Cretan rulers contrasts sharply with the grandiose depictions of kings in the Middle East and suggests a different conception of authority. Also noteworthy are the absence of fortifications at the

---

Minotaur (MIN-uh-tor   Daedalus (DED-ih-luhs)

Cnossus (NOSS-suhs)   Phaistos (FIE-stuhs)   Mallia (mahl-YAH)

palace sites and the presence of high-quality indoor plumbing.

Statuettes of women with elaborate head-dresses and serpents coiling around their limbs may represent fertility goddesses. Colorful frescoes (paintings done on a moist plaster surface) on palace walls portray groups of women in frilly, layered skirts engaged in conversation or watching rituals or entertainment, as well as young acrobats vaulting over the horns of an onrushing bull, either for sport or as a religious activity. Servants carrying jars and fishermen throwing nets and hooks from their boats suggest a joyful attitude toward work, but this may say more about elite tastes than about the reality of daily toil. Stylized vase painting depicting plants with swaying leaves and playful octopuses with undulating encircling tentacles reflect a delight in nature's beauty.

All the Cretan palaces except Cnossus, along with the houses of the elite and peasants in the countryside, were deliberately destroyed around 1450 B.C.E. Because Mycenaean Greeks took over at Cnossus, most historians regard them as the likely culprits.

Mycenaean Greece

Most historians believe that speakers of an Indo-European language ancestral to Greek migrated into the Greek peninsula around 2000 B.C.E., although some argue for earlier or later dates. Through intermarriage, blending of languages, and melding of cultural practices, the indigenous population and the newcomers created the first Greek culture. For centuries this society remained simple and static. Farmers and shepherds lived in Stone Age conditions, wringing a bare living from the land. Then, sometime around 1600 B.C.E., life changed relatively suddenly.

More than a century ago a German businessman, Heinrich Schliemann°, set out to prove that the *Iliad* and the *Odyssey* were true. These epics attributed to the poet Homer, who probably lived shortly before 700 B.C.E., spoke of Agamemnon°, the king of **Mycenae**° in southern Greece. In 1876 Schliemann stunned the scholarly world by discov-

ering at Mycenae a circle of graves at the base of deep, rectangular shafts. These **shaft graves** contained the bodies of men, women, and children and were filled with gold jewelry and ornaments, weapons, and utensils. Clearly, some people in this society had acquired wealth, authority, and the capacity to mobilize human labor. Subsequent excavation uncovered a large palace complex, massive walls, more shaft graves, and other evidence of a rich and technologically advanced civilization that lasted from around 1600 to 1150 B.C.E.

The sudden appearance of Mycenaean culture in mainland Greece is puzzling. There is no archaeological evidence of Cretan political control of the mainland, but Crete exerted an undeniable cultural influence. The Mycenaeans borrowed the Minoan idea of the palace, centralized economy, and administrative bureaucracy, as well as the Minoan writing system. They adopted Minoan styles and techniques of architecture, pottery making, and fresco and vase painting. But how did they suddenly accumulate power and wealth? Most historians look to the profits from trade and piracy and perhaps also to the pay and booty brought back by mercenaries (soldiers who served for pay in foreign lands).

Excavations at other centers have revealed that Mycenae exemplifies the common pattern: a citadel built on a hilltop and surrounded by high, thick fortifications made of stones so large that later Greeks believed that the legendary giant, one-eyed Cyclopes°, had lifted them into place. The fortified enclosure provided refuge for the community in time of danger and contained the palace and administrative complex. The large central hall with an open hearth and columned porch was surrounded by courtyards, living quarters for the royal family and their retainers, and offices, storerooms, and workshops. Brightly painted scenes of war, the hunt, and daily life, as well as natural motifs, covered the palace walls.

Royal tombs—shaft graves at first; later, stone beehive-shaped structures covered with earthen mounds—were located nearby, as were the large houses of the elite. The peasants lived on the lower slopes and in the plain below.

Over four thousand baked clay tablets written in a script called **Linear B** provide additional infor-

---

Schliemann (SHLEE-muhn)   Agamemnon
(ag-uh-MEM-non)   Mycenae (my-SEE-nee)

Cyclopes (SIGH-kloe-pees)

mation. Like its predecessor, the undeciphered Minoan script called Linear A, Linear B uses pictorial signs to represent syllables, but the language is an early form of Greek. The palace bureaucracy kept track of people, animals, and objects in exhaustive detail. The tablets list everything from the number of chariot wheels in palace storerooms and the rations paid to textile workers to the gifts dedicated to various gods and the ships stationed along the coasts.

The government organized and coordinated grain production and controlled the wool industry. Scribes kept track of flocks in the field, the sheared wool and its allocation to spinners and weavers, and the production, storage, and distribution of textiles.

However, individual people—even kings—receive no mention, leaving us largely in the dark about the political and legal systems, social structures, gender relations, and religious beliefs, not to mention particular historical events.

Evidence for a political organization stretching beyond the city-state is contradictory. In Homer's *Iliad,* Agamemnon, the king of Mycenae, leads a great expedition of Greeks from different regions against the city of Troy in northwest Anatolia. In addition, the Mycenaean centers reflect a remarkable similarity in buildings, tombs, utensils, tools, clothing, and works of art. Some scholars argue that political unity must lay behind this cultural uniformity. The *Iliad,* however, revolves around the difficulties Agamemnon has in asserting control over other leaders. Moreover, the archaeological remains and the Linear B tablets suggest that Mycenae, Pylos°, and other centers wielded power independently.

Long-distance trade was made possible by the seafaring skill of the Minoans and Mycenaeans. Commercial vessels depended primarily on sails, and their crews navigated them during daylight hours to keep the land in sight. Since the ships had little storage area and decking, crews went ashore to eat and sleep every night. The ships' shallow keels enabled the crews to pull them up onto the beach.

Cretan and Greek pottery and crafted goods are found not only in the Aegean but also in other parts of the Mediterranean and Middle East, sometimes in enough quantity and variety to suggest settlements of Aegean peoples. The oldest artifacts are Minoan, but eventually Greek wares replace Cretan goods. This indicates that Cretan merchants pioneered trade routes and then admitted Mycenaean traders, who eventually supplanted them in the fifteenth century B.C.E.

The many Aegean pots found throughout the region must once have contained such products as wine and olive oil. Weapons and other crafted goods may also have been exported, along with slaves and mercenary soldiers. Minoan and Mycenaean vessels may also have carried the trade of other peoples.

As for imports, amber (a yellowish-brown fossil resin used for jewelry) from northern Europe and ivory carved in Syria have been discovered at Aegean sites, and the large population of southwest Greece probably relied on imports of grain. Above all, the Aegean lands needed metals, both the gold prized by rulers and the copper and tin needed to make bronze. Sunken ships carrying copper ingots, most probably from Cyprus, have been found on the floor of the Mediterranean (see Map 3.1). As in early China, metal goods belonged mostly to the elite and may have been symbols of their superior status. Homer's description of bronze tripods piled up in the storerooms of heroes brings to mind the bronze vessels buried in Shang tombs.

In this era, trade and piracy were closely linked. Mycenaeans were tough, warlike, and acquisitive. They traded with those who were strong and took from those who were weak. This may have led to conflict with the Hittite kings of Anatolia in the fourteenth and thirteenth centuries B.C.E. Documents found in the archives at Hattusha, the Hittite capital, refer to the king and land of Ahhijawa°, most likely a Hittite rendering of Achaeans°, the term used most frequently by Homer for the Greeks. The documents indicate that relations were sometimes friendly, sometimes strained, and that the people of Ahhijawa were aggressive and tried to take advantage of Hittite preoccupation or weakness. The *Iliad,* Homer's tale of the Achaeans' ten-year siege and eventual destruction of Troy, a

---

Pylos (PIE-lohs)

Ahhijawa (uh-key-YAW-wuh)   **Achaeans** (uh-KEY-uhns)

city on the fringes of Hittite territory that controlled the sea route between the Mediterranean and Black Seas, should be seen against this backdrop. Archaeology has confirmed a destruction at Troy around 1200 B.C.E.

The Fall of Late Bronze Age Civilizations

For reasons that remain obscure, large numbers of people were on the move around 1200 B.C.E. As migrants swarmed into one region, they displaced other peoples, who then joined the tide of refugees. This process culminated in the destruction of many of the old Middle Eastern and Mediterranean centers. Around 1200 B.C.E. unidentified invaders destroyed Hattusha and the Hittite kingdom. Moving south into Syria, the tide of destruction swept away the great coastal city of Ugarit. Around 1220 B.C.E., Merneptah°, the son and successor of Ramesses II, repulsed an assault on the Nile Delta by people he described as "Libyans and Northerners coming from all lands." About thirty years later Ramesses III checked a major invasion of Palestine by "Sea Peoples," who become known as Philistines and gave their name to the land. Although he claimed a great victory, the Philistines° occupied the coast of Palestine, and Egypt soon withdrew from Syria-Palestine. The Egyptians also lost their foothold in Nubia, opening the way for the emergence of the native kingdom centered in Napata (see Chapter 2).

Among the invaders listed in the Egyptian inscriptions are the Ekwesh°, who could be Achaeans—that is, Greeks. Whether or not the Mycenaeans participated in these or other invasions, their own centers collapsed in the first half of the twelfth century B.C.E. The rulers apparently saw trouble coming; at some sites they undertook more extensive fortifications and measures to ensure water supplies. But their efforts were in vain. Nearly all the palaces were destroyed. The Linear B tablets survive only because they were baked hard in the resulting fires.

Curiously, archaeology reveals no trace of foreign invaders. Yet it is unlikely to be coincidental

that Mycenaean civilization collapsed at roughly the same time as the fall of other regional civilizations. The position of the Mycenaean ruling class may have depended on imports of vital commodities and profits from trade, and they may have suffered from the destruction of trading partners and disruption of routes. Competition for limited resources may have led to internal unrest and, ultimately, political collapse.

The destruction of the palaces ended the domination of the ruling class. The administrative apparatus revealed in the Linear B tablets disappeared, and writing passed out of use along with the palace officials who had utilized it. Archaeological studies indicate the depopulation of some regions of Greece and a flow of people to other regions that escaped destruction. The Greek language persisted, and a thousand years later people were still worshiping gods mentioned in the Linear B tablets. People also continued to make the vessels and implements that they were familiar with, although there was a marked decline in artistic and technical skill in the now impoverished society. Mycenaean cultural uniformity gave way to regional variations in shapes, styles, and techniques, reflecting the increased isolation of different Greek areas. The peoples of the region entered a centuries-long "Dark Age" of poverty, isolation, and loss of knowledge.

THE ASSYRIAN EMPIRE, 911–612 B.C.E.

New centers emerged in the centuries after 1000 B.C.E. The chief force for change was the powerful and aggressive **Neo-Assyrian Empire** (911–612 B.C.E.). Although historians sometimes apply the term *empire* to earlier regional powers, the Assyrians of this era were the first to rule over far-flung lands and diverse peoples.

The Assyrian homeland in northern Mesopotamia differs substantially from the flat expanse of Sumer and Akkad to the south. It is hillier, has a more temperate and rainier climate, and is exposed to raiders from the mountains to the east and north and the arid plain to the west. Peasant farmers, accustomed to defending themselves

---

Merneptah (mehr-NEH-ptuh)   Philistine (FIH-luh-steen)
Ekwesh (ECK-wesh)

against marauders, provided the foot-soldiers for the ceaseless campaigns of the Neo-Assyrian Empire: westward across the steppe and desert as far as the Mediterranean, north into mountainous Urartu° (modern Armenia), east across the Zagros range onto the Iranian Plateau, and south along the Tigris River to Babylonia.

These campaigns followed important trade routes and provided immediate booty and the prospect of tribute and taxes. They also secured access to iron and silver and brought the Assyrians control of international commerce. As noted earlier, Assyria had a long tradition of commercial and political interests in Syria and Anatolia. However, what started out as an aggressive program of self-defense and reassertion of old claims soon became more ambitious. Driven by pride, greed, and religious conviction, the Assyrians defeated the great kingdoms of the day—Elam (southwest Iran), Urartu, Babylon, and Egypt. At its peak their empire stretched from Anatolia, Syria-Palestine, and Egypt in the west, across Armenia and Mesopotamia, and as far as western Iran. Larger in extent than its predecessors, it was founded on the principle of enriching the imperial center at the expense of the subjugated periphery.

God and King

The king was literally and symbolically the center of the Assyrian universe. The land belonged to him, and all the people, even the highest-ranking officials, were his servants. Assyrians believed that the gods chose the king as their earthly representative. Normally the king chose a son as successor, and his choice was confirmed by divine oracles and the Assyrian elite. In the revered ancient city of Ashur the high priest anointed the new king by sprinkling his head with oil and gave him the insignia of kingship: a crown and scepter. The kings were buried in Ashur.

Every day messengers and spies brought the king information from every corner of the empire. He made decisions, appointed officials, and heard complaints. He dictated his correspondence to an army of scribes and received and entertained foreign envoys and high-ranking government figures.

As the country's military leader, the king was responsible for planning campaigns, and he often was away from the capital commanding operations in the field.

Among other responsibilities, the king supervised the state religion, devoting much time to public and private rituals and to temple maintenance. He consulted the gods through elaborate rituals, and all state actions were carried out in the name of Ashur, the chief god. Military victories gave proof of Ashur's superiority over the gods of the conquered peoples.

Relentless government propaganda secured popular support for military campaigns that mostly benefited the king and the nobility. Royal inscriptions posted throughout the empire catalogued military victories, extolled the king, and promised ruthless punishments for those who resisted. Relief sculptures depicting hunts, battles, sieges, executions, and deportations covered the walls of the royal palaces at Kalhu° and Nineveh°. The king loomed over most scenes, larger than anyone else, muscular and fierce, with the appearance of a god. Visitors to the Assyrian court were undoubtedly awed—and intimidated.

Conquest and Control

Superior military organization and technology made the Assyrians' unprecedented conquests possible. At first, armies consisted of soldiers who served in return for grants of land and peasants and slaves contributed by large landowners. Later, King Tiglathpileser° (r. 744–727 B.C.E.) maintained a core of professional soldiers made up of Assyrians and the most warlike subject peoples. At its peak the Assyrian state could mobilize a half-million troops, including light-armed bowmen and slingers, armored spearmen, cavalry equipped with bows or spears, and four-man chariots.

Iron weapons and cavalry gave the Assyrians their edge. However, Assyrian engineers also developed ways of attacking fortified towns. They tunneled under the walls, built movable towers for their archers, and applied battering rams to weak

---

Urartu (ur-RAHR-too)

Kalhu (KAL-oo) **Nineveh** (NIN-uh-vuh) **Tiglathpileser** (TIG-lath-pih-LEE-zuhr)

points. Some of the best-fortified cities of the Middle East—Babylon, Thebes in Egypt, Tyre in Phoenicia, and Susa in Elam—yielded to these tactics. Couriers and signal fires provided long-distance communication, while a network of spies gathered intelligence.

Terror tactics discouraged resistance and rebellion. Civilians were thrown into fires, prisoners were skinned alive, and the severed heads of defeated rulers were hung on city walls, all of which was well publicized. **Mass deportation**—the forcible uprooting and resettling of entire communities—broke the spirit of rebellious peoples. Sumer, Babylon, Urartu, Egypt, and the Hittites had done this before, but the Neo-Assyrian monarchs used it on an unprecedented scale. Surviving documents record the relocation of over 1 million people, and historians estimate that the true figure exceeds 4 million. Deportation also shifted human re-

sources from the periphery to the center, where the deportees worked on royal and noble estates, opened new lands for agriculture, and built palaces and cities. Deportees who were craftsmen and soldiers could be assigned to the Assyrian army.

Faced with an array of peoples with different languages, customs, religions, and political organization, the Assyrians never found a single, enduring method of governing. Control tended to be tight and effective at the center and in lands closest to the core area, and less so farther away. The Assyrian kings waged many campaigns to reimpose control on territories subdued in previous wars.

Assyrian provincial officials oversaw the payment of tribute and taxes, maintained law and order, raised troops, undertook public works, and provisioned armies and administrators passing through their territory. Provincial governors were subject to frequent inspections by royal overseers.

Wall Relief from the Palace of Sennacherib at Nineveh   Against a backdrop of wooded hills representing the landscape of Assyria, workers are hauling a huge stone sculpture from the riverbank to the palace under the watchful eyes of officials and soldiers. They accomplish this task with simple equipment—a lever, a sledge, and thick ropes—and a lot of human muscle power.   (Courtesy of the Trustees of the British Museum)

The elite class was bound to the monarch by oaths of obedience, fear of punishment, and the expectation of land grants or shares of booty and taxes. Skilled professionals—priests, diviners, scribes, doctors, and artisans—were similarly bound.

The Assyrians ruthlessly exploited the wealth and resources of their subjects to fund their military campaigns and administration. Wealth from the periphery flowed to the center, where the king and nobility grew rich. Proud kings expanded the ancestral capital and religious center at Ashur and built magnificent new royal cities encircled by high walls and containing ornate palaces and temples. Dur Sharrukin°, the "Fortress of Sargon," was completed in a mere ten years, thanks to a massive labor force composed of prisoners of war and Assyrian citizens who owed periodic service to the state.

Nevertheless, the Assyrian Empire was not simply parasitic. There is some evidence of royal investment in provincial infrastructure. The cities and merchant classes thrived on expanded long-distance commerce, and some subject populations were surprisingly loyal to their Assyrian rulers.

Assyrian Society and Culture

In the core area people belonged to the same three classes that had existed in Hammurabi's Babylon a millennium before (see Chapter 1): (1) free, landowning citizens, (2) farmers and artisans attached to the estates of the king or other rich landholders, and (3) slaves. Slaves—debtors and prisoners of war—had legal rights and, if sufficiently talented, could rise to positions of influence.

The government normally did not distinguish between native Assyrians and the increasingly large number of immigrants and deportees residing in the Assyrian homeland. All were referred to as "human beings," entitled to the same legal protections and liable for the same labor and military service. Over time the inflow of outsiders changed the ethnic makeup of the core area.

The vast majority of subjects worked on the land. The agricultural surpluses they produced allowed substantial numbers of people—the standing army, government officials, religious experts, merchants, and artisans—to engage in specialized activities.

Most trade took place at the local level, with individual artisans and small workshops producing pottery, tools, and clothing. The state fostered long-distance trade, since imported luxury goods—metals, fine textiles, dyes, gems, and ivory—pleased the elite and brought in substantial customs revenues. Silver was the basic medium of exchange, weighed out for each transaction in a time before the invention of coinage.

Building on earlier Mesopotamian traditions, Assyrian scholars recorded lists of plant and animal names, geographic terms, and astronomical occurrences, and they made original contributions in mathematics and astronomy. Exorcists sought to expel the demons they believed caused disease, but more rational physicians experimented with medicines and surgical treatments.

Some Assyrian temples may have had libraries. At Niveveh the palace of **Ashurbanipal**° (r. 668–627 B.C.E.), one of the last Assyrian kings, yielded more than twenty-five thousand tablets or fragments of tablets, including official documents as well as literary and scientific texts. Some were originals that had been brought to the capital; others were copies made at the king's request.

Ashurbanipal avidly collected the literary and scientific heritage of Mesopotamia, and the "House of Knowledge" referred to in some of the documents may have been an academy of learned men in the imperial center. Much of what we know about Mesopotamian art, literature, and science and earlier Mesopotamian history comes from discoveries at Assyrian sites.

ISRAEL, 2000–500 B.C.E.

On the western edge of the Assyrian Empire lived a people who were destined to play an important role in world history. The history of ancient Israel is marked by two interconnected dramas that played out from around 2000 to 500 B.C.E. First, a loose collection of nomadic kinship groups engaged in herding and caravan traffic became a

---

Dur Sharrukin (DOOR SHAH-roo-keen)

Ashurbanipal (ah-shur-BAH-nee-pahl)

sedentary, agricultural people, developed complex political and social institutions, and became integrated into the commercial and diplomatic networks of the Middle East. Second, these people transformed the austere cult of a desert god into the concept of a single, all-powerful, and all-knowing deity, in the process creating the ethical and intellectual traditions that underlie the beliefs and values of Judaism, Christianity, and Islam.

The land and the people at the heart of this story have borne various names: Canaan, Israel, Palestine; Hebrews, Israelites, Jews. For the sake of consistency, the people are referred to here as Israelites, the land they occupied in antiquity as **Israel.**

Being at a crossroads linking Anatolia, Egypt, Arabia, and Mesopotamia has given Israel an importance in history out of all proportion to its size. Its natural resources are few. The Negev Desert and the vast wasteland of the Sinai° lay to the south. The Mediterranean coastal plain was occupied throughout much of this period by Philistines, who are of uncertain ethnic origin. The center of Israel featured rock-strewn hills. Galilee to the north, with its sea of the same name, was a relatively fertile land of grassy hills and small plains from which the narrow ribbon of the Jordan River flowed down into the Dead Sea, so named because its high salt content is toxic to life.

Origins, Exodus, and Settlement

Information about ancient Israel comes partly from archaeological excavations and documents like the royal annals of Egypt and Assyria. However, the fundamental source is the collection of writings preserved in the **Hebrew Bible** (called the Old Testament by Christians). The Hebrew Bible brings together several collections of materials that originated with different groups, employed distinctive vocabularies, and gave particular interpretations of past events. Traditions about the Israelites' early days were long transmitted orally. Not until the tenth century B.C.E. were they written down in a script borrowed from the Phoenicians. The text that we have today dates from the fifth century B.C.E., with a few later additions, and reflects the point of view of the

priests who controlled the Temple in Jerusalem. Historians disagree about how accurately this document represents Israelite history. In the absence of other written sources, however, it provides a foundation to be used critically and modified in light of archaeological discoveries.

The Hebrew language of the Bible reflects the speech of the Israelites until about 500 B.C.E. It is a Semitic language, most closely related to Phoenician and Aramaic (which later supplanted Hebrew in Israel), more distantly related to Arabic and the Akkadian language of the Assyrians. This linguistic affinity probably parallels the Israelites' ethnic relationship to the neighboring peoples.

Despite some features, the early history of Israel reflects a familiar pattern in the ancient Middle East, a story of nomadic pastoralists who occupied marginal land between the arid desert and settled agricultural areas. Early on, these nomads raided the farms and villages of settled peoples, but eventually they settled down to an agricultural way of life and later developed a unified state.

The Hebrew Bible tells the story of the family of Abraham. Born in the city of Ur in southern Mesopotamia, Abraham rejected the traditional idol worship of his homeland and migrated with his family and livestock across the Syrian Desert. Eventually he arrived in the land of Israel, which, according to the biblical account, had been promised to him and his descendants as part of a "covenant," or pact, with the Israelite god, Yahweh.

These "recollections" of the journey of Abraham (who, if he was a real person, probably lived in the twentieth century B.C.E.) may compress the experiences of generations of pastoralists who migrated from the grazing lands between the upper reaches of the Tigris and Euphrates Rivers to the Mediterranean coastal plain. Following the usual pattern in the region, Abraham, his family, and his companions camped by a permanent water source in the dry season, and then drove herds of sheep, cattle, and donkeys to traditional grazing areas during the rest of the year. The animals provided them with milk, cheese, meat, and cloth.

The early Israelites and the settled peoples of the region were suspicious of one another. This friction between nomadic herders and settled farmers, as well as the Israelites' view of their ancestors as having been nomads, comes through

---

Sinai (SIE-nie)

in the story of the innocent shepherd Abel, who was killed by his farmer brother Cain, and in the story of Sodom° and Gomorrah°, two cities that Yahweh destroyed because of their wickedness.

Abraham's son Isaac and then his grandson Jacob became the leaders of this wandering group of herders. In the next generation the squabbling sons of Jacob's several wives sold their brother Joseph as a slave to passing merchants heading for Egypt. According to the biblical account, through luck and ability Joseph became a high official at Pharaoh's court. Thus he was in a position to help his people when drought struck Israel and forced the Israelites to migrate to Egypt. The sophisticated Egyptians feared and looked down on these rough herders and eventually reduced the Israelites to slaves, putting them to work on the grand building projects of the pharaoh.

Several points need to be made about this version of events. First, the biblical account glosses over the period from 1700 to 1500 B.C.E., when Egypt was dominated by the Hyksos. Since the Hyksos are thought to have been Semitic groups that infiltrated the Nile Delta from the northeast, the Israelite migration to Egypt and later enslavement could have been connected to the Hyksos' rise and fall. Second, although the surviving Egyptian sources do not refer to Israelite slaves, they do complain about *Apiru*°, a derogatory term applied to caravan drivers, outcasts, bandits, and other marginal groups. The word seems to designate a class of people rather than a particular ethnic group, but some scholars believe there may be a connection between the similar-sounding terms *Apiru* and *Hebrew*. Third, the period of alleged Israelite slavery coincided with the era of ambitious building programs launched by several New Kingdom pharaohs.

According to the Hebrew Bible, Moses, an Israelite with connections to the Egyptian royal family, led the Israelites out of captivity. The narrative of their departure, the Exodus, is overlaid with folktale motifs, including the ten plagues that Yahweh inflicted on Egypt to persuade the pharaoh to release the Israelites and the miraculous parting of the waters of the Red Sea that enabled the refugees

to escape. It is possible that oral tradition may have preserved memories of a real emigration from Egypt followed by years of wandering in the wilderness of Sinai.

During their reported forty years in the desert, the Israelites became devoted to a stern and warlike god. According to the Hebrew Bible, Yahweh made a covenant with the Israelites: they would be his "Chosen People" if they promised to worship him exclusively. This pact was confirmed by tablets that Moses brought down from the top of Mount Sinai. Written on the tablets were the Ten Commandments, which set out the basic tenets of Jewish belief and practice. The Commandments prohibited murder, adultery, theft, lying, and envy and demanded respect for parents and rest from work on the Sabbath, the seventh day of the week.

The biblical account tells how Joshua, Moses's successor, led the Israelites from the east side of the Jordan River into the land of Canaan° (modern Israel and the Palestinian territories). They attacked and destroyed Jericho° and other Canaanite° cities. Archaeological evidence confirms the destruction of some Canaanite towns between 1250 and 1200 B.C.E., though not precisely the towns mentioned in the biblical account. Shortly thereafter, lowland sites were resettled and new sites were established in the hills, thanks to the development of cisterns carved into rock to hold rainwater and the construction of terraces for farming. The material culture of the new settlers was cruder but continued Canaanite patterns.

Most scholars doubt that Canaan was conquered by a unified Israelite army. In a time of widespread disruption, movements of peoples, and decline and destruction of cities throughout this region, it is more likely that Israelite migrants took advantage of the disorder and were joined by other loosely organized groups and even refugees from the Canaanite cities.

In a pattern common throughout history, the new coalition of peoples invented a common ancestry. The "Children of Israel," as they called themselves, were divided into twelve tribes supposedly descended from the sons of Jacob and Joseph. Each tribe installed itself in a different part of the

---

Sodom (SOE-duhm) **Gomorrah** (guh-MORE-uh) **Apiru** (uh-PEE-roo)

Canaan (KAY-nuhn) **Jericho** (JEH-rih-koe) **Canaanite** (KAY-nuh-nite)

country. Its chief was primarily responsible for mediating disputes and safeguarding the group. Charismatic figures called "Judges" and famed for their bravery or diplomacy enjoyed a special standing that transcended tribal boundaries. The tribes also shared a shrine in the hill country at Shiloh°, which housed the Ark of the Covenant, a sacred chest containing the tablets that Yahweh had given Moses.

Rise of the Monarchy

The time of troubles that struck the eastern Mediterranean around 1200 B.C.E. also brought the Philistines to Israel. Possibly related to the pre-Greek population of the Aegean Sea region and likely participants in the Sea People's attack on Egypt, the Philistines occupied the coastal plain and fought frequently with the Israelites. The Bible tells of the long-haired strongman Samson, who toppled a Philistine temple, and the shepherd boy David, whose slingshot felled the towering warrior Goliath.

A religious leader named Samuel recognized the need for a stronger central authority to lead the Israelites against the Philistine city-states, and he anointed Saul as the first king of Israel around 1020 B.C.E. When Saul perished in battle, the throne passed to David (r. ca. 1000–960 B.C.E.).

A gifted musician, warrior, and politician, David oversaw Israel's transition from a tribal confederacy to a unified monarchy. He strengthened royal authority by making the captured hill city of Jerusalem, which lay outside tribal boundaries, his capital. Soon after, David brought the Ark to Jerusalem, making the city the religious as well as the political center of the kingdom. A census was taken to facilitate the collection of taxes, and a standing army, with soldiers paid by and loyal to the king, was instituted. These innovations helped David win a string of military victories and expand Israel's borders.

The reign of David's son Solomon (r. ca. 960–920 B.C.E.) marked the high point of the Israelite monarchy. Alliances and trade linked Israel with near and distant lands. Solomon and Hiram, the king of Phoenician Tyre, together commissioned a fleet that sailed into the Red Sea and brought back gold, ivory, jewels, sandalwood, and exotic animals. The story of the visit to Solomon by the queen of Sheba, who brought gold, precious stones, and spices, may be mythical, but it reflects the reality of trade with Saba° in south Arabia (present-day Yemen) or the Horn of Africa (present-day Somalia). Such wealth supported a lavish court life, a sizeable bureaucracy, and an intimidating chariot army that made Israel a regional power. Solomon undertook an ambitious building program employing slaves and the compulsory labor of citizens. To strengthen the link between religious and secular authority, he built the **First Temple** in Jerusalem.

The Temple priests became a powerful and wealthy class, receiving a share of the annual harvest in return for making animal sacrifices to Yahweh. The expansion of Jerusalem, new commercial opportunities, and the increasing prestige of the Temple hierarchy contributed to a growing gap between urban and rural, rich and poor. Fiery prophets, claiming revelation from Yahweh, accused the monarchs and aristocracy of corruption, impiety, and neglect of the poor.

The Israelites lived in extended families, several generations residing together under the authority of the eldest male. Arranged marriages were an important economic as well as social institution. To prove his financial worthiness, the groom gave a substantial gift to the father of the bride. Her entire family participated in the ceremonial weighing of silver or gold. The wife's dowry often included a slave girl who attended her for life.

Male heirs were of paramount importance, and firstborn sons received a double share of the inheritance. If a couple had no son, they could adopt one, or the husband could have a child by the wife's slave attendant. If a man died childless, his brother was expected to marry his widow and father an heir.

Women provided the family with important goods and services and thus were respected and granted relative equality with their husbands. However, they could not inherit property or initiate divorce, and an unfaithful woman could be put to death. Working-class women shared in farming

---

Shiloh (SHIE-loe)

Saba (SUH-buh)

and herding chores in addition to caring for the house and children. Some urban women worked outside the home as cooks, bakers, perfumers, wet nurses (a recent mother hired to provide nourishment to another person's child), prostitutes, and singers of laments at funerals. A few women reached positions of influence, such as Deborah the Judge, who led troops in battle against the Canaanites. Women known collectively as "wise women" appear to have composed sacred texts in poetry and prose. This reality has been obscured, in part by the male bias of the Hebrew Bible, in part because the status of women declined as Israelite society became more urbanized.

Fragmentation and Dispersal

After Solomon's death around 920 B.C.E., resentment over royal demands and the neglect of tribal rights split the monarchy into two kingdoms: Israel in the north, with its capital at Samaria°; and Judah° in the southern territory around Jerusalem. The two were sometimes at war, sometimes allied.

This period saw the final formulation of **monotheism,** the absolute belief in Yahweh as the one and only god. Nevertheless, religious leaders still had to contend with cults professing polytheism (the belief in multiple gods). The rituals of the Canaanite storm-god Baal° and the fertility goddess Astarte° attracted many Israelites. Prophets condemned the adoption of foreign ritual and threatened that Yahweh would punish Israel severely.

The small states of Syria and the two Israelite kingdoms laid aside their rivalries to mount a joint resistance to the Neo-Assyrian Empire, but to no avail. In 721 B.C.E. the Assyrians destroyed the northern kingdom of Israel and deported much of its population to the east. New settlers were brought in from Syria, Babylon, and Iran, changing the area's ethnic, cultural, and religious character. The kingdom of Judah survived for more than a century, sometimes rebelling, sometimes paying tribute to the Assyrians or the Neo-Babylonian

kings (626–539 B.C.E.) that succeeded them. When the Neo-Babylonian monarch Nebuchadnezzar° captured Jerusalem in 587 B.C.E., he destroyed the Temple and deported to Babylon the royal family, the aristocracy, and many skilled workers.

The deportees prospered so well in their new home "by the waters of Babylon" that half a century later most of their descendants refused the offer of the Persian monarch Cyrus (see Chapter 4) to return to their homeland. This was the origin of the **Diaspora°**—a Greek word meaning "dispersion" or "scattering." This dispersion outside the homeland of many Jews—as we may now call these people, since an independent Israel no longer existed—continues to this day. To maintain their religion and culture, the Diaspora communities developed institutions like the synagogue (Greek for "bringing together"), a communal meeting place that served religious, educational, and social functions.

The Babylonian Jews that did make the long trek back to Judah met with a cold reception from the local population. Persevering, they rebuilt the Temple in modest form and drafted the Deuteronomic° Code (*deuteronomic* is Greek for "second set of laws") of law and conduct. The fifth century B.C.E. also saw the compilation of much of the Hebrew Bible in roughly its present form.

Exile and loss of political autonomy sharpened Jewish identity. Jews lived by a rigid set of rules. Dietary restrictions forbade the eating of pork and shellfish and mandated that meat and dairy products not be consumed together. Ritual baths were used to achieve spiritual purity, and women were required to take ritual baths after menstruation. The Jews venerated the Sabbath (Saturday, the seventh day of the week) by refraining from work and from fighting, following the example of Yahweh, who, according to the Bible, rested on the seventh day after creating the world. These strictures and others, including a ban on marrying non-Jews, tended to isolate the Jews from other peoples, but they also fostered a powerful sense of community and the belief that they were protected by a watchful and beneficent deity.

Samaria (suh-MAH-ree-yuh) **Judah** (JOO-duh) **Baal** (BAHL) **Astarte** (uh-STAHR-tee)

Nebuchadnezzar (NAB-oo-kuhd-nez-uhr) **Diaspora** (die-ASS-peh-rah) **Deuteronomic** (doo-tuhr-uh-NAHM-ik)

PHOENICIA AND THE MEDITERRANEAN, 1200–500 B.C.E.

The people who occupied the coast of the Mediterranean north of Israel developed their own distinctive civilization. Historians refer to a major element of the ancient population of Syria-Palestine as **Phoenicians°**, though they referred to themselves as "Can'ani"—Canaanites. Despite the sparse written and archaeological record, enough of their history survives to reveal major transformations.

The Phoenician City-States

Many Canaanite settlements were destroyed during the violent upheavals and mass migrations around 1200 B.C.E. (discussed earlier). Aramaeans°—nomadic pastoralists like the early Israelites—migrated into the interior portions of Syria while Israelites and Philistines gained dominance further south.

By 1100 B.C.E. Canaanite territory had shrunk to a narrow strip of present-day Lebanon between the mountains and the sea. New political forms and seaborne commerce provided the keys to Canaanite survival. Sometime after 1000 B.C.E. the Canaanites encountered the Greeks, who referred to them as *Phoinikes,* or Phoenicians. The term may mean "red men" and refer to the color of their skin, or it may refer to the precious purple dye they extracted from the murex snail (see Environment and Technology: Ancient Textiles and Dyes).

Expansion into the Mediterranean

After 900 B.C.E. Tyre began to turn its attention westward, establishing colonies on Cyprus, a copper-rich island 100 miles (161 kilometers) from the Syrian coast (see Map 3.2). By 700 B.C.E., when Homer mentions seafaring Phoenician merchants in the Aegean Sea, a string of settlements in the western Mediterranean formed a "Phoenician triangle": the North African coast from western Libya to Morocco; the south and southeast coast of Spain, including Gades° (modern Cadiz°) on the Strait of Gibraltar; and the islands of Sardinia, Sicily, and Malta off the coast of Italy (see Map 3.2). The colonists situated many of these new settlements on promontories or off-shore islands in imitation of Tyre.

Overseas settlement provided new sources of trade goods and new trading partners as well as an outlet for excess population. Tyre maintained its autonomy until 701 B.C.E. by paying tribute to the Assyrian kings. In that year it finally fell to an Assyrian army, which stripped it of much of its territory and population, allowing Sidon to become the leading city in Phoenicia.

Phoenician activities in the western Mediterranean often involved conflict with the Greeks, who were also expanding trade and establishing colonies. The focal point of this rivalry was Sicily. Phoenicians occupied the western end of the island, Greeks its eastern and central parts. For centuries Greeks and Phoenicians fought savage wars for control of Sicily. Surviving accounts tell of atrocities, massacres, wholesale enslavements, and mass deportations. The high level of brutality suggests that each side believed its survival to be at stake. Both communities survived, but the Phoenician colony of Carthage in Tunisia, which led the coalition of Phoenician communities in the western Mediterranean, controlled all of Sicily by the mid-third century B.C.E.

Rivers and rocky spurs sliced the Lebanese coastal plain into a series of small city-states, notably Byblos°, Berytus°, Sidon°, and Tyre. Exchange of raw materials (cedar and pine, metals, incense, papyrus), foodstuffs (wine, spices, salted fish), and crafted luxury goods (textiles, carved ivory, glass) brought wealth and influence to the Phoenician city-states.

The Phoenicians also developed an alphabetic system of writing with about two dozen symbols, with each symbol representing a consonant or long vowel. (The Greeks added symbols for short vowel sounds to create the first full alphabet—see Chapter 4.) Little Phoenician writing survives, however, probably because scribes used perishable papyrus.

Phoenician (fi-NEE-shun) **Aramaean** (ah-ruh-MAY-uhn)

Gades (GAH-days) **Cadiz** (kuh-DEEZ) **Byblos** (BIB-loss)
Berytus (buh-RIE-tuhs) **Sidon** (SIE-duhn)

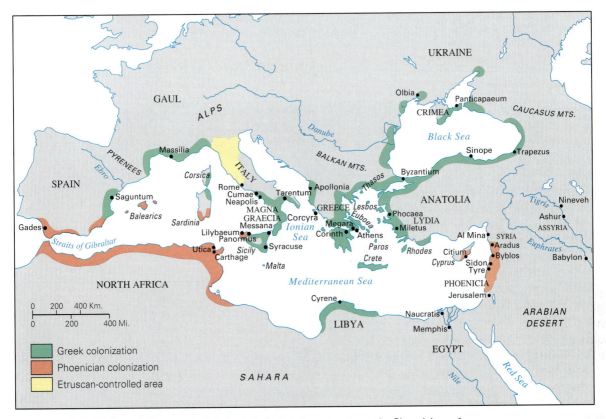

Map 3.2 Colonization of the Mediterranean   In the ninth century B.C.E., the Phoenicians of Lebanon began to explore and colonize parts of the western Mediterranean, including the coast of North Africa, southern and eastern Spain, and the islands of Sicily and Sardinia. The Phoenicians were primarily interested in access to valuable raw materials and trading opportunities.

Before 1000 B.C.E. Byblos was the most important Phoenician city-state. The English word *bible* comes from the Greek *biblion,* meaning "book written on papyrus from Byblos." After 1000 B.C.E. Tyre, in southern Lebanon, surpassed Byblos. According to the Bible, King Hiram, who came to power in 969 B.C.E., formed a close alliance with the Israelite king Solomon and provided Phoenician craftsmen and cedar wood for building the Temple in Jerusalem. In return, Tyre gained access to silver, food, and trade routes to the east and south. In the 800s B.C.E. Tyre took control of nearby Sidon and monopolized the Mediterranean coastal trade.

Located on an offshore island, Tyre was practically impregnable. It had two harbors—one facing north, the other south—that were connected by a canal. The city boasted a large marketplace, a magnificent palace complex with treasury and archives, and temples to the gods Melqart° and Astarte. Some of its thirty thousand or more inhabitants lived in suburbs on the mainland. Its one weakness was its dependence on the mainland for food and fresh water.

Little is known about the internal affairs of Tyre and other Phoenician cities beyond the names of some kings. However, the scant evidence suggests that merchant families dominated the political arena. Faced with Assyrian aggression between the ninth and seventh centuries B.C.E. and Neo-Babylonian and then Persian expansion (see

Melqart (MEL-kahrt)

Throughout human history the production of textiles—cloth for clothing, blankets, carpets, and coverings of various sorts—may have required an expenditure of human labor second only to the amount of work necessary to provide food. Nevertheless, textile production in antiquity has left few traces in the archaeological record. The plant fibers and animal hair used for cloth are organic and quickly decompose except in rare and special circumstances. Some textile remains have been found in the hot, dry conditions of Egypt, the cool, arid Andes of South America, and the peat bogs of northern Europe. But most of our knowledge of ancient textiles depends on the discovery of equipment used in textile production—such as spindles, loom weights, and dyeing vats—and on pictorial representations and descriptions in texts.

Ancient Peruvian Textile The weaving of Chavín was famous for its color and symbolic imagery. Artisans both wove designs into the fabric and used paint or dyes to decorate plain fabric. This early Chavín painted fabric was used in a burial. Notice how the face suggests a jaguar and the headdress includes the image of a serpent. (Private collection)

Chapter 4) a century later, the Phoenician city-states preserved their freedom by playing the great powers off against one another, accepting a subordinate relationship to a distant master only when necessary.

Carthage's Commercial Empire

Thanks to Greek and Roman reports about their wars, historians know more about **Carthage** and the other Phoenician colonies than they do about the Phoenician homeland. For example, the account of the origins of Carthage that began this chapter comes from Roman sources (most famously Virgil's epic poem *The Aeneid*) but probably is based on a Carthaginian original. Archaeological excavation has roughly confirmed the city's traditional foundation date of 814 B.C.E. Situated just outside the present-day city of Tunis, Carthage controlled the middle portion of the Mediterranean where Europe comes closest to Africa. The new settlement grew rapidly and soon dominated other Phoenician colonies in the west.

Occupying a narrow promontory, Carthage

The production of cloth usually has been the work of women for a simple but important reason. Responsibility for child rearing limits women's ability to participate in other activities but does not consume all their time and energy. In many societies textile production has been complementary to child-rearing activities, for it can be done in the home, is relatively safe, does not require great concentration, and can be interrupted without consequence. For many thousands of years cloth production has been one of the great common experiences of women around the globe. The growing and harvesting of plants such as cotton or flax (from which linen is made) and the shearing of wool from sheep and, in the Andes, llamas are outdoor activities, but the subsequent stages of production can be carried out inside the home. The basic methods of textile production did not change much from early antiquity until the late eighteenth century C.E., when the fabrication of textiles was transferred to mills and mass production began.

When textile production has been considered "women's work," most of the output has been for household consumption. One exception was in the early civilizations of Peru, where women weavers developed new raw materials, new techniques, and new decorative motifs around three thousand years ago. They began to use the wool of llamas and alpacas in addition to cotton. Three women worked side by side and passed the weft from hand to hand in order to overcome limitations to the width of woven fabric imposed by the back-strap loom. Women weavers also introduced embroidery, and they decorated garments with new religious motifs, such as the jaguar-god of Chavín. Their high-quality textiles were given as tribute to the elite and were used in trade to acquire luxury goods as well as dyes and metals.

More typically, men dominated commercial production. In ancient Phoenicia, fine textiles with bright, permanent colors became a major export product. These striking colors were produced by dyes derived from several species of snail. Most prized was the red-purple known as Tyrian purple because Tyre was the major source. Persian and Hellenistic kings wore robes dyed this color, and a white toga with a purple border was the sign of a Roman senator.

The production of Tyrian purple was an exceedingly laborious process. The spiny dye-murex snail lives on the sandy Mediterranean bottom at depths ranging from 30 to 500 feet (10 to 150 meters). Nine thousand snails were needed to produce 1 gram (0.035 ounce) of dye. The dye was made from a colorless liquid in the snail's hypobranchial gland. The gland sacs were removed, crushed, soaked with salt, and exposed to sunlight and air for some days; then they were subject to controlled boiling and heating.

Huge mounds of broken shells on the Phoenician coast are testimony to the ancient industry. It is likely that the snail was rendered nearly extinct at many locations, and some scholars have speculated that Phoenician colonization in the Mediterranean may have been motivated in part by the search for new sources of snails.

stretched between Byrsa°, the original hilltop citadel of the community, and a double harbor. The inner harbor could accommodate 220 warships. A watchtower allowed surveillance of the surrounding area, and high walls made it impossible to see in from the outside. The outer commercial harbor was filled with docks for merchant ships and shipyards. In case of attack, a huge iron chain could close off the harbor.

Government offices ringed a large central square where magistrates heard legal cases outdoors. The inner city was a maze of narrow, winding streets, multistory apartment buildings, and sacred enclosures. Farther out lay a sprawling suburban district where the wealthy built spacious villas amid fields and vegetable gardens. This entire urban complex was enclosed by a wall 22 miles (35 kilometers) in length. At the most critical point— the 2.5-mile-wide (4-kilometer-wide) isthmus connecting the promontory to the mainland—the wall was over 40 feet (13 meters) high and 30 feet (10 meters) thick and had high watchtowers.

Byrsa (BURR-suh)

With a population of roughly 400,000, Carthage was one of the largest cities in the world by 500 B.C.E. The population was ethnically diverse, including people of Phoenician stock, indigenous peoples likely to have been the ancestors of modern-day Berbers, and immigrants from other Mediterranean lands and sub-Saharan Africa. Contrary to the story of Dido's reluctance to remarry, Phoenicians intermarried quite readily with other peoples.

Each year two "judges" were elected from upper-class families to serve as heads of state and carry out administrative and judicial functions. The real seat of power was the Senate, where members of the leading merchant families, who sat for life, formulated policy and directed the affairs of the state. An inner circle of thirty or so senators made the crucial decisions. From time to time the leadership convened an Assembly of the citizens to elect public officials or vote on important issues, particularly when the leaders were divided or wanted to stir up popular enthusiasm for some venture.

There is little evidence at Carthage of the kind of social and political unrest that later plagued Greece and Rome (see Chapters 4 and 5). This perception may be due in part to the limited information in existing sources about internal affairs at Carthage. However, a merchant aristocracy (unlike an aristocracy of birth) was not a closed circle, and a climate of economic and social mobility allowed newly successful families and individuals to push their way into the circle of politically influential citizens. The ruling class also made sure that everyone benefited from the riches of empire.

Carthaginian power rested on its navy, which dominated the western Mediterranean for centuries. Phoenician towns provided a chain of friendly ports. The Carthaginian fleet consisted of fast, maneuverable galleys—oared warships. A galley had a sturdy, pointed ram in front that could pierce the hull of an enemy vessel below the water line, while marines (soldiers aboard a ship) fired weapons. Innovations in the placement of benches and oars made room for 30, 50, and eventually as many as 170 rowers.

Carthaginian foreign policy reflected Carthage's economic interests. Protecting the sea-lanes, gaining access to raw materials, and fostering trade mattered most to the dominant merchant class. Foreign merchants were free to sail to Carthage to market their goods, but if they tried to operate on their own, they risked having their ships sunk by the Carthaginian navy. Treaties between Carthage and other states included formal recognition of this maritime commercial monopoly.

The archaeological record provides few clues about the commodities traded. Commerce may have included perishable goods—foodstuffs, textiles, animal skins, slaves—and raw metals such as silver, lead, iron, and tin, whose Carthaginian origin would not be evident. We know that Carthaginian ships carried goods manufactured elsewhere and that products brought to Carthage by foreign traders were reexported.

There is also evidence for trade with sub-Saharan Africa. Hanno°, a Carthaginian captain of the fifth century B.C.E., claimed to have sailed through the Strait of Gibraltar into the Atlantic Ocean and to have explored the West African coast (see Map 3.2). His report includes vivid descriptions of ferocious savages, drums in the night, and rivers of fire. Scholars have had difficulty matching Hanno's topographic descriptions and distances to the geography of West Africa, and some regard his account as outright fiction. Others believe that he misstated distances and exaggerated dangers to keep others from following his route. Other Carthaginians explored the Atlantic coast of Spain and France and secured control of an important source of tin in the "Tin Islands," probably Cornwall in southwestern England.

War and Religion

Carthage did not directly rule a large amount of territory. A belt of fertile land in northeastern Tunisia, owned by Carthaginians but worked by native peasants and imported slaves, provided a secure food supply. Beyond this core area the Carthaginians ruled most of their "empire" indirectly and allowed other Phoenician communities in the western Mediterranean to remain independent. These communities looked to Carthage for military protection and followed its lead in foreign policy. Only Sardinia and southern Spain came under the control of a Carthaginian governor and garrison, presumably to safeguard their resources.

Hanno (HA-noe)

Trade may explain the unusual fact that citizens were not required to serve in the army: they were of more value as traders and sailors. Since the indigenous North African population was not politically or militarily well organized, Carthage had little to fear from enemies close to home. When Carthage was drawn into wars with the Greeks and Romans from the sixth through third centuries B.C.E., it relied on mercenaries from the most warlike peoples in its dominions or from neighboring areas—Numidians from North Africa, Iberians from Spain, Gauls from France, and various Italian peoples. These well-paid mercenaries served under the command of Carthaginian officers.

Another sign that war was not the primary business of the state was the separation of military command from civilian government. Generals were chosen by the Senate and kept in office for as long as they were needed. In contrast, the kings of Assyria and the other major states of the ancient Middle East normally led military campaigns.

Like the deities of Mesopotamia (see Chapter 1), the Carthaginian gods—chiefly Baal Hammon°, a male storm-god, and Tanit°, a female fertility-goddess—were powerful and capricious entities. Roman sources report that members of the Carthaginian elite would sacrifice their own male children to appease the gods in times of crisis. Excavations at Carthage and elsewhere have turned up tophets°—walled enclosures with thousands of small, sealed urns containing the burned bones of children. Although some scholars argue that these were infants born prematurely or taken by childhood illnesses, most maintain that the western Phoenicians practiced child sacrifice on a more or less regular basis. Originally practiced by the upper classes, child sacrifice seems to have become more common and to have involved broader elements of the population after 400 B.C.E.

Plutarch°, a Greek who lived around 100 C.E., long after the demise of Carthage, wrote the following on the basis of earlier sources:

> The Carthaginians are a hard and gloomy people, submissive to their rulers and harsh to their subjects, running to extremes of cowardice in

times of fear and of cruelty in times of anger; they keep obstinately to their decisions, are austere, and care little for amusement or the graces of life.[1]

We should not take the hostile opinions of Greek and Roman sources at face value. Still, it is clear that the Carthaginians were perceived as different and that cultural barriers, leading to misunderstanding and prejudice, played a significant role in ongoing conflicts. The struggle between Carthage and Rome for control of the western Mediterranean was especially protracted and bloody (see Chapter 5).

FAILURE AND TRANSFORMATION, 750–550 B.C.E.

The extension of Assyrian power over the entire Middle East had enormous consequences for all the peoples of this region and caused the stories of Mesopotamia, Israel, and Phoenicia to converge. In 721 B.C.E. the Assyrians destroyed the northern kingdom of Israel, and for over a century the southern kingdom of Judah was exposed to relentless pressure. Assyrian threats spurred the Phoenicians to colonize and exploit the western Mediterranean. Even Egypt, for so long impregnable behind its desert barriers, fell to Assyrian invaders in the mid-seventh century B.C.E. Thebes, its ancient capital, never recovered.

Closer to the Assyrian homeland, the southern plains of Sumer and Akkad, the birthplace of Mesopotamian civilization, were reduced to a protectorate, while Babylon was alternately razed and rebuilt by Assyrian kings. Urartu and Elam, Assyria's great-power rivals, were destroyed.

By 650 B.C.E. Assyria stood unchallenged in western Asia. But the arms race with Urartu, war expenditures, and ever-lengthening borders sapped Assyrian resources. Brutality and exploitation aroused the hatred of conquered peoples. At the same time, changes in the ethnic composition of the army and the population of the homeland reduced popular support for the Assyrian state.

Baal Hammon (BAHL ha-MOHN)   **Tanit** (TAH-nit)
tophet (TOE-fet)   **Plutarch** (PLOO-tawrk)

Two new political entities spearheaded resistance to Assyria. First, Babylonia had been revived by the Neo-Babylonian, or Chaldaean°, dynasty (the Chaldaeans had infiltrated southern Mesopotamia around 1000 B.C.E.). Second, the Medes°, an Iranian people, were extending their kingdom in the Zagros Mountains and Iranian Plateau in the seventh century B.C.E. The two powers launched a series of attacks on the Assyrian homeland that destroyed its chief cities by 612 B.C.E.

The rapidity of the Assyrian fall is stunning. The destruction systematically carried out by the victors led to the depopulation of northern Mesopotamia. Two centuries later, when a corps of Greek mercenaries passed by mounds that concealed the ruins of the Assyrian capitals, the Athenian chronicler Xenophon° had no inkling that their empire had ever existed.

The Medes took over the Assyrian homeland as far as eastern Anatolia, but the campaigns of Kings Nabopolassar° (r. 625–605 B.C.E.) and Nebuchadnezzar (r. 604–562 B.C.E.) gained most of the territory for the **Neo-Babylonian kingdom.** Babylonia underwent a cultural renaissance. The city of Babylon, enlarged and adorned, became the greatest metropolis of the world in the sixth century B.C.E. Old cults were revived, temples rebuilt, festivals resurrected. The related pursuits of mathematics, astronomy, and astrology reached new heights.

CONCLUSION

This chapter traces developments in the Middle East and the Mediterranean from 2000 to 500 B.C.E. The patterns of culture that originated in the river-valley civilizations of Egypt and Mesopotamia persisted into this era. Peoples such as the Amorites, Kassites, and Chaldaeans, who migrated into the Tigris-Euphrates plain, were largely assimilated into the Sumerian-Semitic cultural tradition. Similarly, the Hyksos, who migrated into the Nile Delta and controlled much of Egypt for a time, adopted the ancient ways of Egypt. When the founders of the

New Kingdom finally ended Hyksos domination, they reinstituted the united monarchy and the religious and cultural traditions of earlier eras.

Yet the Middle East was in many important respects a different place after 2000 B.C.E. New centers of political and economic power had emerged—the Elamites in southwest Iran, the Assyrians in northern Mesopotamia, Urartu in present-day Armenia, the Hittites of Anatolia, and the Minoan and Mycenaean peoples of the Aegean Sea. These new centers often borrowed heavily from the technologies and cultural practices of Mesopotamia and Egypt, creating dynamic syntheses of imported and indigenous elements.

The entire Middle East was drawn together by networks of trade and diplomacy. Ultimately, however, the very interdependence of these societies made them vulnerable to the destructions and disorder of the decades around 1200 B.C.E. The entire region slipped into a "Dark Age" of isolation, stagnation, and decline that lasted several centuries.

The early centuries after 1000 B.C.E. saw a resurgence of political organization and international commerce. The Neo-Assyrian Empire, the great power of the time, represented a continuation of the Mesopotamian tradition, though the center of empire moved to the north. Israel and Phoenicia reflected the influence of Mesopotamia and Egypt but also evolved distinctive cultural traditions.

Throughout this era people were on the move, sometimes voluntarily and sometimes under compulsion. The Assyrians deported large numbers of prisoners of war from outlying subject territories to the core area in northern Mesopotamia. The Phoenicians left their overpopulated homeland to establish new settlements in North Africa, Spain, and islands off the coast of Italy. In their new homes the Phoenician colonists tried to duplicate familiar ways of life from the old country. In contrast, the Israelites who settled in Canaan and, at a later time, emigrated to the Diaspora underwent significant political, social, and cultural transformations as they adapted to new circumstances.

Diasporas proved to be fertile sources of innovation and helped preserve culture. The Carthaginian enterprise eventually was cut short by the Romans, but Jews and Greeks survive into our own time. Ironically, the Assyrians, the most powerful of all these societies, suffered the most com-

---

Chaldaean (chal-DEE-uhn)   Mede (MEED)
Mede (MEED)   Xenophon (ZEN-uh-fahn)
Nabopolassar (NAB-oh-poe-lass-uhr)

plete termination of their way of life. Because Assyrians did not settle outside their homeland in significant numbers, when their state was toppled in the late seventh century B.C.E., their culture all but perished.

The Neo-Babylonian kingdom that arose on the ashes of the Neo-Assyrian Empire would be the last revival of the ancient Sumerian and Semitic cultural legacy. The next chapter relates how the destinies of the peoples of the Mediterranean and the Middle East became enmeshed in the new forms of political and social organization emerging from Iran and Greece.

■ Key Terms

Iron Age	mass deportation
Hittites	Ashurbanipal
Hatshepsut	Israel
Akhenaten	Hebrew Bible
Ramesses II	First Temple
Minoan	monotheism
Mycenae	Diaspora
shaft graves	Phoenicians
Linear B	Carthage
Neo-Assyrian Empire	Neo-Babylonian kingdom

■ Suggested Reading

Fundamental for all periods in the ancient Middle East is Jack M. Sasson, ed., *Civilizations of the Ancient Near East*, 4 vols. (1995), containing nearly two hundred articles by contemporary experts and a bibliography on a wide range of topics. John Boardman, I. E. S. Edwards, N. G. L. Hammond, and E. Sollberger, *The Cambridge Ancient History*, 2d ed., vols. 3.1–3.3 (1982–1991), provides extremely detailed historical coverage of the entire Mediterranean and western Asia. Barbara Lesko, ed., *Women's Earliest Records: From Ancient Egypt and Western Asia* (1989), is a collection of papers on the experiences of women in the ancient Middle East.

Many of the books recommended in the Suggested Reading list for Chapter 1 are useful for Mesopotamia, Syria, and Egypt in the Late Bronze Age. In addition, see Miriam Lichtheim, *Ancient Egyptian Literature: A Book of Readings*, vol. 2, *The New Kingdom* (1978); Donald B. Redford, *Egypt, Canaan, and Israel in Ancient Times* (1992), which explores the relations of Egypt with the Syria-Palestine region in this period; Erik Hornung, *Akhenaten and the Religion of Light* (1999), which, while

focusing on the religious innovations, deals with many facets of the reign of Akhenaten; Karol Mysliwiec, *The Twilight of Ancient Egypt: First Millennium B.C.E.* (2000), which traces the story of Egyptian civilization after the New Kingdom; and H. W. F. Saggs, *Babylonians* (1995), which devotes several chapters to this more thinly documented epoch in the history of southern Mesopotamia. The most up-to-date treatment of the Hittites can be found in Trevor Boyce, *The Kingdom of the Hittites* (1998) and *Life and Society in the Hittite World* (2002). Also useful are O. R. Gurney, *The Hittites*, 2d ed., rev. (1990), and J. G. Macqueen, *The Hittites and Their Contemporaries in Asia Minor* (1975).

R. A. Higgins, *The Archaeology of Minoan Crete* (1973) and *Minoan and Mycenaean Art*, new rev. ed. (1997); Rodney Castleden, *Minoans: Life in Bronze Age Crete* (1990); J. Walter Graham, *The Palaces of Crete* (1987); O. Krzyszkowska and L. Nixon, *Minoan Society* (1983); and N. Marinatos, *Minoan Religion* (1993), examine the archaeological evidence for the Minoan civilization. The brief discussion of M. I. Finley, *Early Greece: The Bronze and Archaic Ages* (1970), and the much fuller accounts of Emily Vermeule, *Greece in the Bronze Age* (1972), and J. T. Hooker, *Mycenaean Greece* (1976), are still useful treatments of Mycenaean Greece, based primarily on archaeological evidence. Robert Drews, *The Coming of the Greeks: Indo-European Conquests in the Aegean and the Near East* (1988), examines the evidence for the earliest Greeks. For the Linear B tablets, see John Chadwick, *Linear B and Related Scripts* (1987) and *The Mycenaean World* (1976). J. V. Luce, *Homer and the Heroic Age* (1975), and Carol G. Thomas, *Myth Becomes History: Pre-Classical Greece* (1993), examine the usefulness of the Homeric poems for reconstructing the Greek past. For the disruptions and destructions of the Late Bronze Age in the eastern Mediterranean, see N. K. Sandars, *The Sea Peoples: Warriors of the Ancient Mediterranean* (1978), and Trude Dothan and Moshe Dothan, *People of the Sea: The Search for the Philistines* (1992).

For general history and cultural information about the Neo-Assyrian Empire, Mesopotamia, and western Asia in the first half of the first millennium B.C.E., see Michael Roaf, *Cultural Atlas of Mesopotamia and the Ancient Near East* (1990); Amelie Kuhrt, *The Ancient Near East, c. 3000–300 B.C.* (1995); H. W. F. Saggs, *Civilization Before Greece and Rome* (1989); and A. Bernard Knapp, *The History and Culture of Ancient Western Asia and Egypt* (1988). H. W. F. Saggs, *Babylonians* (1995), has coverage of the fate of the old centers in southern Mesopotamia during this era in which the north attained dominance. Primary texts in translation for Assyria and other parts of western Asia can be found in James B. Pritchard, ed.,

Ancient Near Eastern Texts Relating to the Old Testament, 3d ed. (1969). Jeremy Black and Anthony Green, *Gods, Demons and Symbols of Ancient Mesopotamia: An Illustrated Dictionary* (1992), is valuable for religious concepts, institutions, and mythology. Julian Reade, *Assyrian Sculpture* (1983), provides a succinct introduction to the informative relief sculptures from the Assyrian palaces. J. E. Curtis and J. E. Reade, eds., *Art and Empire: Treasures from Assyria in the British Museum* (1995), relates the art to many facets of Assyrian life. Andre Parrot, *The Arts of Assyria* (1961), provides full coverage of all artistic media.

For general historical introductions to ancient Israel, see Michael Grant, *The History of Israel* (1984); J. Maxwell Miller and John H. Hayes, *A History of Ancient Israel and Judah* (1986); and J. Alberto Soggin, *A History of Israel: From the Beginnings to the Bar Kochba Revolt,* A.D. *135* (1984). Amnon Ben-Tor, *The Archaeology of Ancient Israel* (1991), and Amihai Mazar, *Archaeology of the Land of the Bible, 10,000–586 B.C.E.* (1990), provide overviews of the discoveries of archaeological excavation in Israel. William G. Dever, *What Did the Biblical Writers Know, and When Did They Know It? What Archaeology Can Tell Us About the Reality of Ancient Israel* (2001), and B. J. S. Isserlin, *The Israelites* (2001), both review the archaeological evidence and take moderate positions in the heated debate about the value of the biblical text for reconstructing the history of Israel. Hershel Shanks, *Jerusalem, an Archaeological Biography* (1995), explores the long and colorful history of the city. For social and economic issues, see Shunya Ben-dor, *The Social Structure of Ancient Israel: The Institution of the Family (beit 'ab) from the Settlement to the End of the Monarchy* (1996), and Moses Aberbach, *Labor, Crafts and Commerce in Ancient Israel* (1994). Carol Meyers, *Discovering Eve: Ancient Israelite Women in Context* (1998), carefully sifts through literary and archaeological evidence to reach a balanced assessment of the position of women in the period before the monarchy. Victor H. Matthews, *The Social World of the Hebrew Prophets* (2001), provides social and historical contexts for all the prophets. For the Philistines, see Trude Dothan, *The Philistines and Their Material Culture* (1982).

Glenn Markoe, *Phoenicians* (2000), Sabatino Moscati, *The Phoenicians* (1988), and Gerhard Herm, *The Phoenicians: The Purple Empire of the Ancient World* (1975), are general introductions to the Phoenicians in their homeland. Maria Eugenia Aubet, *The Phoenicians and the West: Politics, Colonies and Trade* (2001), is an insightful investigation of the dynamics of Phoenician expansion into the western Mediterranean. Lionel Casson, *The Ancient Mariners: Seafarers and Sea Fighters of the Mediterranean in Ancient Times,* 2d ed. (1991), 75–79, discusses the design of warships and merchant vessels. For Carthage see Serge Lancel, *Carthage: A History* (1995), and David Soren, Aicha Ben Abed Ben Khader, and Hedi Slim, *Carthage: Uncovering the Mysteries and Splendors of Ancient Tunisia* (1990). Aicha Ben Abed Ben Khader and David Soren, *Carthage: A Mosaic of Ancient Tunisia* (1987), includes articles by American and Tunisian scholars as well as the catalog of a museum exhibition. R. C. C. Law, "North Africa in the Period of Phoenician and Greek Colonization, c. 800 to 323 B.C.," Chapter 2 in *The Cambridge History of Africa,* vol. 2 (1978), places the history of Carthage in an African perspective.

Elizabeth Wayland Barber, *Women's Work: The First 20,000 Years: Women, Cloth, and Society in Early Times* (1994), is an intriguing account of textile manufacture in antiquity, with emphasis on the social implications and primary role of women. I. Irving Ziderman, "Seashells and Ancient Purple Dyeing," *Biblical Archaeologist* 53 (June 1990): 98–101, is a convenient summary of Phoenician purple-dyeing technology.

■ Notes

1. Plutarch, *Moralia,* 799 D, trans. B. H. Warmington, *Carthage* (Harmondsworth, England: Penguin 1960), 163.

Animal Domestication

The earliest domestication of plants and animals took place long before the existence of written records. For this reason, we cannot be sure how and when humans first learned to plant crops and certain animals became tame enough to live among humans. Anthropologists and historians usually link the two processes as part of a Neolithic Revolution, but they were not necessarily connected.

The domestication of plants is much better understood than the domestication of animals. Foraging bands of preagricultural humans gained much of their sustenance from seeds, fruits, and tubers collected from wild plants. Humans may have planted seeds and tubers many times without lasting effect. In a few instances, however, their plantings accidentally included a higher proportion of one naturally occurring variety of a wild species. After repeated planting cycles, this variety, which was rare in the wild, became common. When a new variety suited human needs, usually by having more food value or being easier to grow or process, people stopped collecting the wild types and relied on farming and further developing their new domestic type. In some seemingly wild forest areas of Southeast Asia and Central America, a higher than normal frequency of certain fruit trees indicates that people deliberately planted them sometime in the distant past.

In the case of animals, the question of selection to suit human needs is hard to judge. Archaeologists and anthropologists looking at ancient bones and images interpret changes in hair color, horn shape, and other visible features as indicators of domestication. But these visible changes did not generally serve human purposes. As for the uses that are most commonly associated with domestic animals, some of the most important, such as milking cows, shearing sheep, and harnessing oxen and horses to plows and vehicles, first appeared hundreds and even thousands of years after domestication.

Anthropologists and archaeologists usually assume that animals were domesticated as meat producers, but even this is questionable. Dogs, which became domestic tens of thousands of years before any other species, seem not to have been eaten in most cultures, and cats, which became domestic much later, were eaten even less often.

Cattle, sheep, and goats became domestic around ten thousand years ago in the Middle East and North Africa. Coincidentally, wheat and barley were being domesticated at roughly the same time in the same general area. This is the main reason historians generally conclude that plant and animal domestication are closely related. Yet other major meat animals, such as chickens, which originated as jungle fowl in Southeast Asia, and pigs, which probably became domestic separately in several parts of North Africa, Europe, and Asia, have no agreed-upon association with early plant domestication. Nor is plant domestication connected with the horses and camels that became domestic in western Asia and the donkeys that became domestic in the Sahara region around six thousand years ago. Though the wild forebears of these species were probably eaten, the domestic forms were usually not used for meat.

In the Middle East humans may have originally kept wild sheep, goats, and cattle for food, though wild cattle were large and dangerous and must have been hard to control. It is questionable whether keeping these or other wild animals captive for food would have been more productive, in the earliest stages, than hunting. It is even more questionable whether the humans who kept animals for this purpose had any reason to anticipate that life in captivity would cause them to become domestic.

The human motivations for the domestication of animals can be better assessed after a consideration of the physical changes involved in going from wild to domestic. Genetically transmitted tameness, defined as the ability to live with and accept handling by humans, lies at the core of the domestication process. In separate experiments with wild rats and foxes in the twentieth century, scientists found that wild individuals with strong fight-or-flight tendencies reproduce poorly in captivity. Individual animals with the lowest adrenaline levels have the most offspring in captivity. In the wild, the same low level of excitability would have made these individuals vulnerable to predators and kept their reproduction rate down. Human selection probably reinforced the natural tendency for the least excitable animals to reproduce best in captivity. In other words, humans probably preferred the animals that seemed the tamest, and destroyed those that were most wild. In the rat and fox experiments, after twenty generations or so, the surviving animals were born with much smaller adrenal glands and greatly reduced fight-or-flight reactions. Since adrenaline production normally increases in the transition to adulthood, many of the low-adrenaline animals also retained juvenile characteristics, such as floppy ears and pushed-in snouts, both indicators of domestication. This tendency of certain domestic species to preserve immature characteristics is called *neoteny*.

It is quite probable that animal domestication was not a deliberate process but rather the unanticipated outcome of keeping animals for other purposes. Since a twenty-generation time span for wild cattle and other large quadrupeds would have amounted to several human lifetimes, it is highly unlikely that the people who ended up with domestic cows had any recollection of how the process started. This seems to rule out the possibility that people who had unwittingly domesticated one species would have attempted to repeat the process with other species. Since they probably did not know what they had done to produce genetically transmitted tameness, they would not have known how to duplicate the process.

Historians disagree on this matter. Some assume that domestication was an understood and reproducible process and conclude that through a series of domestication attempts, humans domesticated every species that could be domesticated. This is unlikely. It is probable that more species could be domesticated over time. Twentieth-century efforts to domesticate bison, eland, and elk have not fully succeeded, but they have generally not been maintained for as long as twenty generations. Rats and foxes have more rapid reproduction rates,

and the experiments with them succeeded. In looking at the impact of animal domestication on different parts of the world, it is unwarranted to assume that some regions were luckier than others in being home to species that were ripe for domestication, or that some human societies were cleverer than others in figuring out how to make animals genetically tame.

Rather than being treated as a process once known to early human societies and subsequently forgotten, animal domestication is best studied on a case-by-case basis as an unintended result of other processes. In some instances, sacrifice probably played a key role. Religious traditions of animal sacrifice rarely utilize, and sometimes prohibit, the ritual killing of wild animals. It is reasonable to suppose that the practice of capturing wild animals and holding them for sacrifice sometimes eventually led to the appearance of genetically transmitted tameness as an unplanned result.

Horses and camels were domesticated relatively late, and most likely not for meat consumption. The societies within which these animals first appeared as domestic species already had domestic sheep, goats, and cattle and used oxen to carry loads and pull plows and carts. Horses, camels, and later reindeer may represent successful experiments with substituting one draft animal for another, with genetically transmitted tameness an unexpected consequence of separating animals trained for riding or pulling carts from their wilder kin.

Once human societies had developed the full range of uses of domestic animals—meat, eggs, milk, fiber, labor, transport—the likelihood of domesticating more species diminished. In the absence of concrete knowledge of how domestication had occurred, it was usually easier for people to move domestic livestock to new locations than to attempt to develop new domestic species. Domestic animals accompanied human groups wherever they ventured, and this practice triggered enormous environmental changes as domestic animals, and their human keepers, competed with wild species for food and living space.

PART TWO

The Formation of New Cultural Communities, 1000 B.C.E.–600 C.E.

CHAPTER 4
Greece and Iran, 1000–30 B.C.E. / India, 1500 B.C.E.–550 C.E.

CHAPTER 5
An Age of Empires: Rome and Han China, 753 B.C.E.–330 C.E.

CHAPTER 6
Networks of Communication and Exchange, 300 B.C.E.–600 C.E.

The sixteen centuries from 1000 B.C.E. to 600 C.E. mark a new chapter in the story of humanity. The river-valley civilizations established in the two previous millennia underwent important changes, and the scale of human institutions and activities increased.

The political and social structure of the river-valley centers reflected the importance of irrigation for agriculture. Powerful kings, hereditary priesthoods, dependent laborers, limited availability of metals, and restricted literacy are hallmarks of the complex societies described in Part One. In the first millennium B.C.E., new centers arose, in lands watered by rainfall and worked by a free peasantry, on the shores of the Mediterranean, in Iran, India, and Central and South America. Shaped by the natural environments in which they arose, they developed new patterns of political and social organization and economic activity, and moved in new intellectual, artistic, and spiritual directions, though under the influence of the older centers.

The rulers of the empires of this era took steps intended to control and tax their subjects: they constructed extensive networks of roads and promoted urbanization. As a consequence, communication became more rapid, trade goods were transported over greater distances, and religious ideas, artistic styles, and technologies spread widely. Large cultural zones unified by common traditions emerged. A number of these cultural traditions—Iranian, Hellenistic, Roman—were to exercise substantial influence on subsequent ages. The influence of some—Hindu, Chinese, African, Buddhist—persists into our own time.

The expansion of agriculture and trade and improvements in technology led to population increases, the spread of cities, and the growth of a comfortable middle class. In many parts of the world iron replaced bronze as the preferred metal for weapons, tools, and utensils. People using iron tools cleared extensive forests around the Mediterranean, in India, and in eastern China. Iron weapons gave an advantage to the armies of Greece, Rome, and imperial China. Metal, still an important item of long-distance trade, was available to more people than it had been in the preceding age. Metal coinage, which originated in Anatolia and was subsequently adopted by many peoples, facilitated commercial transactions and the acquisition of wealth along new trade routes crossing the Indian Ocean and Central and Inner Asia.

New systems of writing also developed. Because these systems were more easily and rapidly learned, writing moved out of the control of specialists. Most people remained illiterate, but writing became an increasingly important medium for preserving and transmitting knowledge. The spread of literacy gave birth to new ways of thinking, new genres of literature, and new types of scientific endeavor.

	1000 B.C.E.	800 B.C.E.	600 B.C.E.
Americas	1200–400 Olmec civilization in Mesoamerica		Gold metallurgy in Chavín 500 •
		900–250 Chavín civilization in Peru	
Europe	• 1000 Iron metallurgy	800–500 Archaic period in Greece	Celts spread across Europe 500 •
			Roman Republic 507 •
			477–404 Athenian Empire and democracy
Africa		• 814 Carthage founded	Hanno of Carthage explores West African coast 465 •
	Rise of Nubian kingdom at Napata 800 •	712–660 Nubian domination of Egypt	
Middle East	• 1000 David establishes Jerusalem as capital of Israel	Babylonian conquest of Jerusalem 587 •	522–486 Darius I rules Persian Empire
	911–612 Neo-Assyrian Empire		
Asia and Oceania	• 1000 Aryans settle Ganges Plain	Iron metallurgy in China 600 •	563–483 Life of the Buddha
	1027–221 Zhou kingdom in China		551–479 Life of Confucius

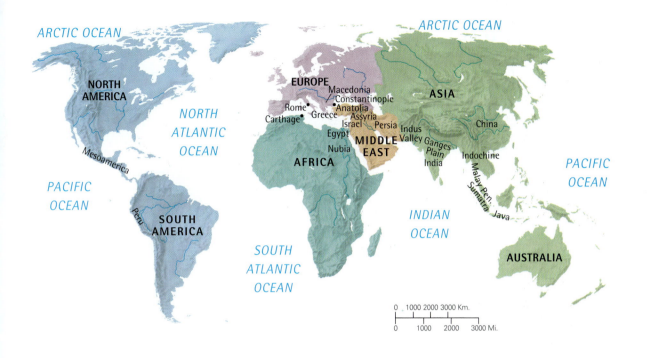

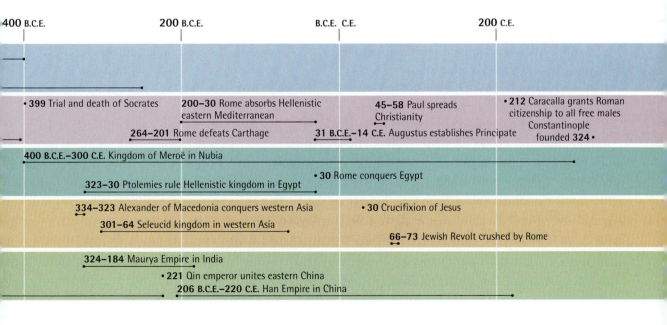

400 B.C.E. 200 B.C.E. B.C.E. C.E. 200 C.E.

• **399** Trial and death of Socrates

200–30 Rome absorbs Hellenistic eastern Mediterranean

45–58 Paul spreads Christianity

• **212** Caracalla grants Roman citizenship to all free males

Constantinople founded **324** •

264–201 Rome defeats Carthage

31 B.C.E.–14 C.E. Augustus establishes Principate

400 B.C.E.–300 C.E. Kingdom of Meroë in Nubia

323–30 Ptolemies rule Hellenistic kingdom in Egypt

• **30** Rome conquers Egypt

334–323 Alexander of Macedonia conquers western Asia

• **30** Crucifixion of Jesus

301–64 Seleucid kingdom in western Asia

66–73 Jewish Revolt crushed by Rome

324–184 Maurya Empire in India

• **221** Qin emperor unites eastern China

206 B.C.E.–220 C.E. Han Empire in China

4 Greece and Iran, 1000–30 B.C.E. / India, 1500 B.C.E.– 550 C.E.

CHAPTER OUTLINE

Ancient Iran

The Rise of the Greeks

The Struggle of Persia and Greece

The Hellenistic Synthesis

Foundations of Indian Civilization

Indian Imperial Expansion and Collapse

DIVERSITY AND DOMINANCE: The Persian Idea of Kingship

The Greek historian Herodotus° (ca. 485–425 B.C.E.) relates that the Persian king Darius° I, whose empire stretched from eastern Europe to northwest India, questioned some Greek and Indian sages. Under what circumstances, he asked the Greeks, would they eat their deceased fathers' bodies? The Greeks, who practiced cremation, recoiled in revulsion. Darius then asked the Indians whether they would ever burn the bodies of their dead parents. This similarly repelled them because they practiced ritual eating of the bodies of the dead. Herodotus argues from this that every group of people regards its own practices as "natural" and superior. This story reminds us that an-

cient sources such as Herodotus's writings are sometimes accurate, as Herodotus is about Greek funerary customs, and sometimes wildly inaccurate, as are his views on Indian rituals.

The story also reminds us that the Persian Empire and the Hellenistic Greek kingdoms that succeeded it brought together peoples and cultural systems from Europe, Africa, and Asia that previously had had little direct contact with one another. This cross-cultural interaction both alarmed and stimulated the peoples involved, in some instances giving rise to new cultural syntheses.

This chapter first recounts the experiences of the Persians and Greeks in the first millennium B.C.E. and then describes the related but strikingly different culture of India. Historians

---

Herodotus (heh-ROD-uh-tuhs)   **Darius** (duh-RIE-us)

94

traditionally consider the rivalry of Greeks and Persians the first act of an age-long drama: the clash of East and West, of fundamentally different ways of life destined to collide. Some regard America's confrontation with hostile states and terrorist organizations in the Islamic world as a contemporary manifestation of this conflict.

Ironically, Greeks and Persians, and many Indian peoples as well, had more in common than they realized. They spoke related languages belonging to the Indo-European family, and they inherited similar cultural traits, forms of social organization, and religious outlooks from their shared past.

As you read this chapter, ask yourself the following questions:

- How did geography, environment, and contacts with other peoples shape the institutions and values of Persians, Greeks, and Indians?

- What brought the Greek city-states and the Persian Empire into conflict, and what determined the outcome of their rivalry?

- How did domination by the Persian Empire and the Greek kingdoms that succeeded it influence—culturally, economically, and politically—the lands and peoples of the eastern Mediterranean and western and southern Asia?

- How did religious traditions with distinctive conceptions of space, time, divinity, and the life cycle shape South Asian culture?

ANCIENT IRAN

Iran, the "land of the Aryans," links western Asia and southern and Central Asia. In the sixth century B.C.E., the Persians of southwest Iran created the largest empire the world had yet seen. Heirs to the legacy of Mesopotamia, they introduced distinctly Iranian elements and developed new forms of political and economic organization.

Scant written evidence from within the Persian Empire forces us to rely on works by Greeks—ignorant outsiders at best, usually hostile, and interested primarily in events affecting themselves. This leaves us largely uninformed about developments in the central and eastern portions of the Persian Empire, though archaeology and close analysis of the few writings from within the empire can supplement and help correct the Greek perspective.

Geography and Resources

The Zagros Mountains bound Iran on the west, the Caucasus° Mountains and Caspian Sea on the northwest and north, the mountains of Afghanistan (ancient Arachosia) and the desert of Baluchistan° (ancient Gedrosia) on the east and southeast, and the Persian Gulf to the southwest. The northeast lies open to attacks or population movements from Central Asia.

Winter rain and snow on the high mountains encircling the country feed streams that flow away from the central plateau into rivers that drain into seas or terminate in interior salt lakes and marshes. Exploiting limited water resources holds the key to survival on the arid interior plateau. Lacking a great river like the Nile, Indus, or Tigris-Euphrates, ancient Iran had a sparse population, most numerous in the moister north and west and decreasing toward the arid south and east. The Great Salt Desert, covering much of eastern Iran and Baluchistan, did not support life. Mountain barriers separated scattered settlements on the narrow plains along the Persian Gulf from the interior plateau.

In the first millennium B.C.E., irrigation made possible an expansion of agriculture from the mountain valleys to the bordering plains. Irrigation specialists laid out underground irrigation channels that prevented evaporation and used gravity to deliver water to the fields. Constructing these channels and the vertical shafts that gave access to them demanded labor cooperation. Local leaders probably supervised the network in each district and expanded it when strong central

Caucasus (KAW-kuh-suhs) **Baluchistan** (buh-loo-chi-STAN)

authorities made possible large-scale labor organization. Royal authority and prosperity went hand in hand. Even so, human survival depended on a delicate ecological balance. A buildup of salt in the soil, a falling water table, or the collapse or silting up of an underground channel sometimes forced the abandonment of settlements.

The mountains yielded copper, tin, iron, gold, and silver, all exploited on a limited scale in antiquity, as well as wood for fuel, construction, and crafts, the hillsides being more heavily wooded than they are now. With little agricultural surplus, export goods consisted largely of minerals and crafted goods such as textiles and metalwork.

The Rise of the Persian Empire

In discussions of ancient history, the term *Iranian* describes a group of peoples speaking related languages and sharing certain cultural characteristics. They lived in a broad area of western and Central Asia comprising not only the modern state of Iran but also Turkmenistan, Uzbekistan, Afghanistan, and Pakistan. One group, the Medes (Mada in Iranian),* instituted a complex political order in northwestern Iran in the late second millennium B.C.E., influenced in part by the ancient centers in Mesopotamia and Urartu (modern Armenia and northeast Turkey). The Medes played a major role in destroying the Assyrian Empire in the late seventh century B.C.E. and extended their control westward across Assyria into Anatolia (modern Turkey). They also projected power southeastward toward the Persian Gulf, a region settled by another Iranian people, the Persians (Parsa).

The Persian rulers, called Achaemenids° because of an ancestor named Achaemenes, cemented relations with the Median court through marriage. **Cyrus** (Kurush), the son of a Persian chieftain and a Median princess, united the Persian tribes and overthrew the Median monarch around 550 B.C.E. The differences between these two peoples being slight—notably in dialect and costume—Cyrus placed both Medes and Persians in positions of responsibility and retained the framework of Median rule. The Greeks could not readily tell the two apart.

Patriarchal family organization among the Medes and Persians, like that among most other Indo-European peoples, gave the male head of the household authority over family members. The warrior class dominated the other two social and occupational classes, the priests and peasants. Noble warriors, the king the most illustrious among them, owned land and took pleasure in hunting, fighting, and gardening. The priests, or magi (*magush*), supervised sacrifices and other rituals. Village-based farmers and shepherds made up the third class.

Over the course of two decades, Cyrus (r. 550–530 B.C.E.) redrew the map of western Asia. In 546 B.C.E., he won a cavalry battle outside Sardis, the capital of Lydia in western Anatolia, reportedly because the smell of his camels caused a panic among his opponents' horses. All Anatolia, including the Greek city-states on the western coast, came under Persian control. In 539 B.C.E., he swept into Mesopotamia, where the Neo-Babylonian dynasty had ruled since the collapse of Assyrian power (see Chapter 3). Cyrus allied with disaffected elements within Babylon, who surrendered the city to him. A skillful propagandist, Cyrus respected the Babylonian priesthood and had his son crowned king in accordance with local tradition.

Cyrus died in 530 B.C.E. while campaigning against nomadic Iranians in the northeast. His son Cambyses° (Kambujiya, r. 530–522 B.C.E.) set his sights on Egypt. Defeating the Egyptians in a series of bloody battles, the Persians sent exploratory expeditions south to Nubia and west to Libya. Greek sources depict Cambyses as a cruel and impious madman, but contemporary Egyptian documents reflect a practical outlook. Like his father, he cultivated local priests and notables and respected their traditions.

When Cambyses died in 522 B.C.E., **Darius I** (Darayavaush) seized the throne, crushing challengers with skill, energy, and ruthlessness. The Medes now played lesser roles; most important posts went to leading Persian nobles. Darius

---

*Familiar Greek names of Iranian groups and individuals are followed by the original Iranian names in parentheses.

Achaemenid (a-KEY-muh-nid)

Cambyses (kam-BIE-sees)

C H R O N O L O G Y

	Greece and the Hellenistic World	Persian Empire	India
1500 B.C.E.			**ca. 1500 B.C.E.** Migration of Indo-European peoples into northwest India
	1150–800 B.C.E. Greece's "Dark Age"		
1000 B.C.E.		**ca 1000 B.C.E.** Persians settle in southwest Iran	**ca. 1000 B.C.E.** Indo-European groups move into the Ganges Plain
800 B.C.E.	**ca. 800 B.C.E.** Resumption of Greek contact with eastern Mediterranean		
	800–480 B.C.E. Greece's Archaic period		
	ca. 750–550 B.C.E. Era of colonization		
	ca. 700 B.C.E. Beginning of hoplite warfare		
600 B.C.E.	**ca. 650–500 B.C.E.** Era of tyrants		
	594 B.C.E. Solon reforms laws at Athens	**550–530 B.C.E.** Reign of Cyrus	
	546–510 B.C.E. Pisistratus and sons control Athens	**530–522 B.C.E.** Reign of Cambyses; conquest of Egypt	
500 B.C.E.		**522–486 B.C.E.** Reign of Darius	**ca. 500 B.C.E.** Siddhartha Gautama founds Buddhism; Mahavira founds Jainism
	490 B.C.E. Athenians check Persians at Marathon	**480–479 B.C.E.** Xerxes' invasion of Greece	
	477 B.C.E. Athens becomes leader of Delian League		
	461–429 B.C.E. Pericles dominant at Athens; Athenian democracy		
	431–404 B.C.E. Peloponnesian War		

(continued)

C H R O N O L O G Y *(continued)*		
Greece and the Hellenistic World	**Persian Empire**	**India**

	Greece and the Hellenistic World	Persian Empire	India
400 B.C.E.	**399 B.C.E.** Trial and execution of Socrates	**387 B.C.E.** King's Peace makes Persia arbiter of Greek affairs	
	338 B.C.E. Philip II of Macedon takes control of Greece	**334–323 B.C.E.** Alexander the Great defeats Persia and creates Empire	**324 B.C.E.** Chandragupta Maurya founds Mauryan Empire
	317 B.C.E. End of democracy in Athens	**323–30 B.C.E.** Hellenistic period	
300 B.C.E.	**ca. 300 B.C.E.** Foundation of the Museum and start of lighthouse construction		**300 B.C.E.** Period of Tamil kingdoms begins
			184 B.C.E. Fall of Mauryan Empire
	200 B.C.E. First Roman intervention in the Hellenistic East		
100 B.C.E.	**30 B.C.E.** Roman annexation of Egypt, the last Hellenistic kingdom		
1 C.E.			
500 C.E.			**320 C.E.** Chandra Gupta establishes Gupta Empire
			550 C.E. Collapse of Gupta Empire
			606–647 C.E. Reign of Harsha Vardhana

(r. 522–486 B.C.E.) extended Persian control eastward to the Indus Valley and westward into Europe, bridging the Danube River and chasing the nomadic Scythians° north of the Black Sea. He erected a string of forts in Thrace (modern-day northeast Greece and Bulgaria). In maritime matters, Darius dispatched a fleet to explore the route

from the Indus Delta to the Red Sea and completed a canal linking the Red Sea with the Nile.

Imperial Organization and Ideology

The empire of Darius I, the largest the world had yet seen, stretched from eastern Europe to Pakistan, from southern Russia to Sudan. It encompassed myriad ethnic groups and every form of

---

Scythian (SITH-ee-uhn)

social and political organization, from nomads to subordinate kingdoms to city-states. Darius created an organizational structure that survived the remaining two centuries of the empire's existence.

He placed each of the empire's twenty provinces under a Persian **satrap°**, or governor, usually a relative or connection by marriage. The satrap's court mirrored the royal court on a smaller scale. Governorships frequently became hereditary, so that satraps' families lived in the province governed by their head, acquired knowledge about local conditions, and formed connections with the local elite. The farther a province was from the empire's center, the more autonomy the satrap had, since slow communications usually made contact with the central administration difficult.

Darius prescribed how much precious metal each province owed annually to the central treasury. The satrap collected and sent it. Some went for necessary expenditures, but most was hoarded. This increasingly took precious metal out of circulation, forcing up the price of gold and silver and making it hard for provinces to meet their quotas. Evidence from Babylonia shows increasing taxes and official corruption, which may have helped cause a gradual economic decline by the fourth century B.C.E.

Royal roads, well maintained and patrolled, connected outlying provinces to the imperial center. Way stations sheltered important travelers and couriers. Garrisons controlled movements at strategic points: mountain passes, river crossings, and important urban centers. The ancient Elamite capital of Susa, in southwest Iran, served as the imperial administrative center. Greeks and others went there with requests and messages for the king. It took at least three months to make the journey to Susa. For Greek ambassadors, the time spent traveling, waiting for an audience, and returning home could take a year or more.

The king lived and traveled with numerous wives and children. Information about the royal women comes from foreign sources and is thus suspect. The Book of Esther in the Hebrew Bible tells how King Ahasuerus° (Xerxes° to the Greeks) picked the Jewish woman Esther as a wife, putting her in a position to save the Jewish people from a plot to massacre them. Greek sources depict royal women as pawns in power struggles—Darius married a daughter of Cyrus, and later the conqueror Alexander the Great married a daughter of the last Persian king—and as intriguers, poisoning rival wives and plotting their sons' paths to the throne.

The king's entourage also included (1) sons of Persian aristocrats, who were educated at court and also served as hostages for their parents' loyalty; (2) noblemen who attended the king when not on other assignments; (3) administrative officers and employees of the treasury, secretariat, and archives; (4) the royal bodyguard; and (5) courtiers and slaves. Long gone were the simple days when the king hunted and caroused with his warrior companions. Inspired by Mesopotamian conceptions of monarchy, the Persian king became an aloof figure of majesty and splendor: "The Great King, King of Kings, King in Persia, King of countries." He referred to everyone, even the Persian nobility, as "my slaves," and anyone who approached him had to bow down before him.

The king owned vast tracts of land throughout the empire, some of which he gave to his supporters. Donations called "bow land," "horse land," and "chariot land" in Babylonian documents obliged the recipient to provide military service. The *paradayadam* (meaning "walled enclosure"—the term has come into English as *paradise*), consisting of gardens or orchards belonging to the king or high nobility, symbolized the prosperity of the king and his servants.

Tradition remembered Darius as issuing the "laws of the King," appointing royal judges throughout the empire, and encouraging the codification of the laws of subject peoples. As master of a decentralized empire, he allowed each people its own traditions and ordinances.

The central administration was based in Elam and Mesopotamia, not in the Persian homeland (present-day Fars). Sometimes, however, the kings returned to **Persepolis** (Parsa), a ceremonial capital in Fars begun by Darius and completed by his son Xerxes (Ahasueras). The palaces, audience halls, treasury buildings, and barracks built on an artificial platform took inspiration from Mesopotamia, where the Assyrian kings had created fortress-cities to advertise their power.

---

satrap (SAY-trap)   Ahasuerus (uh-HAZZ-yoo-ear-uhs)
Xerxes (ZERK-sees)

View of the East Front of the Apadana (Audience Hall) at Persepolis, ca. 500 B.C.E.   To the right lies the Gateway of Xerxes. Persepolis, in the Persian homeland, was built by Darius I and his son Xerxes, and it was used for ceremonies of special importance to the Persian king and people—coronations, royal weddings, funerals, and the New Year's festival. The stone foundations, walls, and stairways of Persepolis are filled with sculpted images of members of the court and embassies bringing gifts, offering a vision of the grandeur and harmony of the Persian Empire.   (Courtesy of the Oriental Institute, University of Chicago)

The Persepolis Treasury and Fortification Texts, inscribed in Elamite cuneiform on baked clay tablets, show government officials distributing food and other goods to workers of various nationalities, some of them prisoners of war working on construction projects, irrigation networks, or royal estates. Women received less than men of equivalent status, but pregnant women and new mothers received more. Skilled workers of either sex received more than the unskilled.

The relief sculptures on the foundations, walls, and stairwells at Persepolis feature representatives of the peoples of the empire—recognizable by distinctive hair styles, beards, dress, hats, and footwear—bringing gifts to the king. These images did not depict a real ceremony but rather advertised the vast extent, abundant resources, and co-operative spirit of the empire. One scene shows erect subjects effortlessly shouldering a giant platform bearing Darius's throne. Similar scenes from the Assyrian empire show the subjects staggering under the weight. Persepolis probably served as a setting for New Year's festivals, coronations, marriages, and funerals. Tombs cut into the cliffs at nearby Naqsh-i Rustam° sheltered the remains of Darius and his successors.

Several dozen inscriptions cut into cliff faces provide perspectives on the imperial ideology (see Diversity and Dominance: The Persian Ideal of Kingship). At Naqsh-i Rustam, for example, Darius claims:

Naqsh-i Rustam (NUHK-shee ROOS-tuhm)

Ahuramazda° [the chief Persian deity], when he saw this earth in commotion, thereafter bestowed it upon me, made me king. . . . By the favor of Ahuramazda I put it down in its place. . . . I am of such a sort that I am a friend to right, I am not a friend to wrong. It is not my desire that the weak man should have wrong done to him by the mighty; nor is that my desire, that the mighty man should have wrong done to him by the weak.[1]

Since the religion of **Zoroastrianism**° recognized Ahuramazda as god, it seems certain that Darius and his successors were Zoroastrians. Questions surround the origins of this religion. Worshipers believe that Zarathushtra (Zoroaster in Greek) wrote hymns called Gathas, the dialect and physical setting of which indicate an origin in eastern Iran. Scholarly guesses place Zarathushtra's life sometime between 1700 and 500 B.C.E. Ahuramazda, "the wise lord," created the world, according to Zarathushtra. Angra Mainyu°, "the hostile spirit," and a host of demons threaten it. In this dualist universe, the struggle between good and evil plays out over 12,000 years. At the end of time, good will prevail, and the world will return to the pure state of creation. In the meantime, humanity participates in this cosmic struggle, and individuals reap rewards or torments in the afterlife according to their actions.

The Persians also drew on pre-Zoroastrian moral and metaphysical concepts. Alive to the beauties of nature, they venerated water, which they kept pure, and fire, which burned continuously at altars. Bodily purity, a matter of intense concern, ceased with death. Zoroastrians exposed corpses to carrion-eating birds and the elements to avoid sullying the earth through burial or fire through cremation. Some earlier gods, such as Mithra, a sun deity and defender of oaths and compacts, retained divine status despite Zarathushtra's focus on one god. The Persians honored promises and telling the truth. Darius's inscriptions castigate evildoers as followers of "the Lie."

Ahuramazda (ah-HOOR-uh-MAZZ-duh)   Zoroastrianism (zo-ro-ASS-tree-uh-niz-uhm)   Angra Mainyu (ANG-ruh MINE-yoo)

Zoroastrianism preached belief in one supreme deity, maintained high ethical standards, and promised salvation. Expanding with the advance of the Persian Empire, it may have influenced Judaism and thus, indirectly, Christianity. God and the devil, heaven and hell, reward and punishment, the Messiah and the end of time: all appear in this belief system. Yet the Islamic conquest of Iran in the seventh century C.E. (see Chapter 7) triggered the faith's decline in Iran. Only tiny communities survive there now. Larger communities, called Parsees, live in South Asia.

THE RISE OF THE GREEKS

The cultural features that emerged in resource-poor Greece in the first millennium B.C.E. depended on access to foreign markets and sources of raw materials. Greek merchants and mercenaries brought home not only raw materials and crafted goods but also ideas. Population pressure, poverty, war, and political crises prompted Greeks to venture throughout the Mediterranean and western Asia, carrying with them their language and culture and exerting influence on other societies. Greek identity and interest in geography, ethnography, and history grew from experience with non-Greek practices and beliefs, as well as a two-century-long rivalry with the Persian Empire.

Geography and Resources

Bounded by the Atlantic, the Alps, the Syrian Desert, and the Sahara, the lands of the Mediterranean climatic zone share seasonal weather patterns and many plants and animals. In summer, a stalled weather front near the entrance of the Mediterranean holds up storms from the Atlantic and allows winds from the Sahara to flow over the region. In winter, the front dissolves, and ocean storms roll in, bringing waves, wind, and cold. Such similarities facilitated migration within the zone, since people did not have to change familiar practices and occupations.

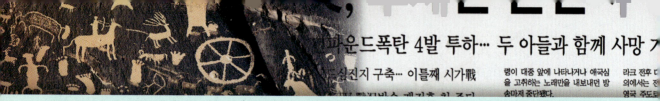

DIVERSITY AND DOMINANCE
THE PERSIAN IDEA OF KINGSHIP

Our most important internal source of information about the Persian Empire is a group of inscriptions commissioned by several kings. The most extensive and informative of these is the inscription that Darius had carved into a cliff face at Behistun (Beh-HISS-toon), high above the road leading from Mesopotamia to northwest Iran through a pass in the Zagros mountain range. It is written in three versions— Old Persian, the language of the ruling people (quite possibly being put into written form for the first time); Elamite, the language native to the ancient kingdom lying between southern Mesopotamia and the Persian homeland and used in Persia for local administrative documents; and Akkadian, the language of Babylonia, widely used for administrative purposes throughout western Asia. The multilingual inscription accompanied a monumental relief representing Darius looming over a line of bound prisoners, the leaders of the many forces he had to defeat in order to secure the throne after the death of Cambyses in 522 B.C.E.

I am Darius, the great king, king of kings, the king of Persia, the king of countries, the son of Hystaspes, the grandson of Arsames, the Achaemenid . . . from antiquity we have been noble; from antiquity has our dynasty been royal . . .

King Darius says: By the grace of Ahuramazda am I king; Ahuramazda has granted me the kingdom.

King Darius says: These are the countries which are subject unto me, and by the grace of Ahuramazda I became king of them: Persia, Elam, Babylonia, Assyria, Arabia, Egypt, the countries by the Sea, Lydia, the Greeks, Media, Armenia, Cappadocia, Parthia, Drangiana, Aria, Chorasmia, Bactria, Sogdiana, Gandara, Scythia, Sattagydia, Arachosia and Maka; twenty-three lands in all.

King Darius says: These are the countries which are subject to me; by the grace of Ahuramazda they be-

came subject to me; they brought tribute unto me. Whatsoever commands have been laid on them by me, by night or by day, have been performed by them.

King Darius says: Within these lands, whosoever was a friend, him have I surely protected; whosoever was hostile, him have I utterly destroyed. By the grace of Ahuramazda these lands have conformed to my decrees; as it was commanded unto them by me, so was it done.

King Darius says: Ahuramazda has granted unto me this empire. Ahuramazda brought me help, until I gained this empire; by the grace of Ahuramazda do I hold this empire.

King Darius says: The following is what was done by me after I became king.

This is followed by a lengthy description of the many battles Darius and his supporters fought against a series of other claimants to power.

King Darius says: This is what I have done. By the grace of Ahuramazda have I always acted. After I became king, I fought nineteen battles in a single year and by the grace of Ahuramazda I overthrew nine kings and I made them captive . . .

King Darius says: As to these provinces which revolted, lies made them revolt, so that they deceived the people. Then Ahuramazda delivered them into my hand; and I did unto them according to my will.

King Darius says: You who shall be king hereafter, protect yourself vigorously from lies; punish the liars well, if thus you shall think, 'May my country be secure!' . . .

King Darius says: On this account Ahuramazda brought me help, and all the other gods, all that there are, because I was not wicked, nor was I a liar, nor was I a tyrant, neither I nor any of my family. I have ruled according to righteousness. Neither to the weak nor to the powerful did I do wrong. Whosoever helped my house, him I favored; he who was hostile, him I destroyed . . .

King Darius says: By the grace of Ahuramazda this is the inscription which I have made. Besides, it was in Aryan script, and it was composed on clay tablets and on parchment. Besides, a sculptured figure of myself I made. Besides, I made my lineage. And it was inscribed and was read off before me. Afterwards this inscription I sent off everywhere among the provinces. The people unitedly worked upon it.

This is an extremely important historical document. For all practical purposes, it is the only version we have of the circumstances by which Darius, who was not a member of the family of Cyrus, took over the Persian throne and established a new dynasty. The account of these events given by the Greek historian Herodotus, for all its additional (and often suspect) detail, is clearly based, however indirectly, on Darius's own account. While scholars have doubted the truthfulness of Darius's claims, the inscription is a resounding example of how the victors often get to impose their version of events on the historical record.

The Behistun inscription is certainly propaganda, but that does not mean that it lacks value. To be effective propaganda must be predicated on the moral values, political principles, and religious beliefs that are familiar and acceptable in a society, and thus it can provide us with a window on those views. The Behistun inscription also allows us to glimpse something of the personality of Darius and how he wished to be perceived.

Another document, found at Persepolis, the magnificent ceremonial center built by Darius and his son Xerxes, expands on the qualities of an exemplary ruler. While it purports to be the words of Xerxes, it is almost an exact copy of an inscription of Darius from nearby Naqsh-i Rustam, where Darius and subsequent kings were buried in monumental tombs carved into the sheer cliff. This shows the continuity of concepts through several reigns.

A great god is Ahuramazda, who created this excellent thing which is seen, who created happiness for man, who set wisdom and capability down upon King Xerxes.

Proclaims Xerxes the King: By the will of Ahuramazda I am of such a sort, I am a friend of the right, of wrong I am not a friend. It is not my wish that the weak should have harm done him by the strong, nor is it my wish that the strong should have harm done him by the weak.

The right, that is my desire. To the man who is a follower of the lie I am no friend. I am not hot-tempered. Whatever befalls me in battle, I hold firmly. I am ruling firmly my own will.

The man who is cooperative, according to his cooperation thus I reward him. Who does harm, him according to the harm I punish. It is not my wish that a man should do harm; nor indeed is it my wish that if he does harm he should not be punished.

What a man says against a man, that does not persuade me, until I hear the sworn statements of both.

What a man does or performs, according to his ability, by that I become satisfied with him, and it is much to my desire, and I am well pleased, and I give much to loyal men.

Of such a sort are my understanding and my judgment: if what has been done by me you see or hear of, both in the palace and in the expeditionary camp, this is my capability over will and understanding.

This indeed my capability: that my body is strong. As a fighter of battles I am a good fighter of battles. When ever with my judgment in a place I determine whether I behold or do not behold an enemy, both with understanding and with judgment, then I think prior to panic, when I see an enemy as when I do not see one.

I am skilled both in hands and in feet. A horseman, I am a good horseman. A bowman, I am a good bowman, both on foot and on horseback. A spearman, I am a good spearman, both on foot and on horseback.

These skills that Ahuramazada set down upon me, and which I am strong enough to bear, by the will of Ahuramazda, what was done by me, with these skills I did, which Ahuramazda set down upon me.

May Ahuramazda protect me and what was done by me.

QUESTIONS FOR ANALYSIS

1. How does Darius justify his assumption of power in the Behistun inscription? What is his relationship to Ahuramazda, the Zoroastrian god, and what role does divinity play in human affairs?

2. How does Darius conceptualize his empire (look at a map and follow the order in which he lists the provinces), and what are the expectations and obligations that he places on his subjects? What does his characterization of his opponents as "followers of the lie" tell us about his view of human nature?

3. According to the document of Xerxes from Persepolis, what qualities (physical, mental, and moral) are desirable in a ruler? What is the Persian concept of justice?

4. To what audiences are Darius and Xerxes directing their messages, and in what media are they being disseminated? Given that Darius himself is, in all likelihood, illiterate, as were most of his subjects, what is the effect of the often repeated phrase: "Darius the King says"?

Sources: Behistun inscription translated by L. W. King and R. C. Thompson, *The Sculptures and Inscription of Darius the Great on the Rock of Behistun in Persia,* London, 1907 (http://www.livius.org/be-bm/behistun03.html); document from Nagsh-i Rustam (http://www.livius.org/x/xerxes/xerxes_texts.htm#daeva)

Greek civilization arose around the Aegean Sea: the Greek mainland, the Aegean islands, and Anatolia's western coast. As we saw in Chapter 3, small plains between low mountain ranges characterize southern Greece, a land with no navigable rivers. The islands dotting the Aegean, inhabited from early times, made sailing from Greece to Ionia (western Anatolia) comparatively easy. From about 1000 B.C.E., Greeks began to settle Ionia, where rivers with broad, fertile plains made for a comfortable life. These coastal Greeks maintained closer contact with Greeks across the Aegean than with the peoples of Anatolia's rugged interior. The sea served as a connector, not a barrier.

Mainland farmers depended on rainfall to water their crops. In the south, limited land, thin topsoil, and sparse rainfall supported only small populations. Farmers planted the plains with barley, which is hardier than wheat, and the edges of the plains with olive trees. Grapevines grew on the terraced lower slopes of the foothills. Sheep and goats grazed the hillsides. Northern Greece, with more rainfall and broader plains, supported herds of cattle and horses. Resources included abundant building stone, including fine marble, but few metal deposits or forests.

The difficulty and expense of overland transport, the availability of good anchorages, and the need to import metals, timber, and grain drew the Greeks to the sea. They obtained timber from the northern Aegean, gold and iron from Anatolia, copper from Cyprus, tin from the western Mediterranean, and grain from the Black Sea, Egypt, and Sicily. Though never comfortable with "the wine-dark sea," as Homer called it, the Greeks relied on it, their small, frail ships hugging the coastline or island hopping where possible.

The Emergence of the Polis

After the destruction of the Mycenaean palace-states (see Chapter 3), Greece lapsed into a "Dark Age" (ca. 1150–800 B.C.E.), a time of depopulation, poverty, and backwardness that has left few archaeological traces. Decline of trade and lack of access to resources lay behind the poverty of the Dark Age. Within Greece, regional distinctiveness in pottery and crafts indicates declining interconnections.

By reestablishing contact between the Aegean and the Middle East, Phoenician traders (see Chapter 3) gave Greek civilization a push that inaugurated the Archaic period of Greek history (ca. 800–480 B.C.E.). Greek ships reappeared in Mediterranean waters looking for raw materials, trade opportunities, and fertile farmland.

Lifelike human and animal figures and imaginative mythical beasts on painted Greek pottery signal new ideas from the east, as does a writing system of Phoenician inspiration. The Phoenicians used twenty-two symbols to represent consonants, leaving most vowel sounds unwritten. The Greek vowels use symbols for Phoenician consonants that do not appear in Greek, thus completing the first true alphabet. Cuneiform or hieroglyphics, systems in which several hundred symbols stood for syllables rather than letters, took years of training and remained the preserve of an elite scribal class. By contrast, the alphabetic symbols made literacy easier to acquire.

Whether first used for economic purposes, as some have argued, or for preserving oral poetry, the Greek alphabet facilitated new forms of literature, law codes, religious dedications, and epitaphs. Yet Greek culture continued to center on storytelling, rituals, and performances. Theatrical drama, philosophical dialogues, and political and courtroom oratory demonstrate the dynamic interaction of speaking and writing.

Population grew rapidly during the Archaic period. Cemeteries around Athens show a five- or sevenfold increase during the eighth century B.C.E. Herding gave way to intensive farming on the previously uncultivated margins of the plains. Increasing population and prosperity stimulated the importation of food and raw materials, a merging of villages into urban centers, and specialization of labor. Freed from farming by rising surpluses, some people developed skills in crafts, commerce, and religion.

The Greek **polis°**, or city-state, ranging in size from a few thousand souls to several hundred thousand in the case of Athens, consisted of an urban center and the surrounding countryside. Typically, a fortified hilltop, the *acropolis* ("top of the city"), offered refuge in emergencies. The town spread around its base. In the open area around government buildings and markets, called an *agora* ("gathering place"), citizens debated the decisions of leaders and organized for war. Walls surrounded the urban center, but population growth prompted construction beyond them. Food came from surrounding farms, though many living within the walls worked nearby fields. Unlike the dependent rural workers of Mesopotamia, Greek farmers enjoyed full citizenship.

Frequent city-state conflicts led, by the early seventh century B.C.E., to a kind of warfare based on **hoplites**—heavily armored infantrymen who fought in close formation. Protected by helmet, breastplate, and leg guards, each hoplite brandished a thrusting spear while guarding his left side and the right side of the hoplite beside him with a round shield, keeping a sword in reserve.

Victory depended on maintaining one's battle line while breaking open the enemy's. The losers suffered most of their casualties while fleeing.

Private citizens, mostly farmers called up for brief periods, rather than professional soldiers served as hoplites. Special training counted less than strength for bearing weapons and armor and courage to stand one's ground. When an army approached, the farmers of the community under attack mustered to defend their land and buildings. The clash of hoplite lines resulted in quick decisions. Battles rarely lasted more than a few hours, with the survivors promptly returning home to their farms.

As population growth strained the agricultural resources of the small plains, many communities sent excess population abroad to establish independent colonies. Sources tell of people chosen by lot to be colonists and forbidden to return on pain of death. Volunteers, however, sought adventure or escape from poverty. Colonists sought the approval of the god Apollo at his sanctuary at Delphi and then departed by sea carrying a fire from the communal hearth of the mother city, a symbol of the kinship and religious ties that would connect the two communities. The "founder," a prominent member of the mother city, chose a hill or other natural refuge, assigned parcels of land, and drafted laws. Sometimes colonists intermarried with local inhabitants; alternatively, they drove them away or reduced them to semiservility.

From the mid-eighth through the mid-sixth centuries B.C.E., colonists spread Greek culture to the northern Aegean area, the Libyan coast of North Africa, and around the Black Sea, with southern Italy and Sicily becoming heavily Greek. Establishing new homes, farms, and communities posed many challenges, but the similarity in climate and ecology helped the Greek settlers transplant their way of life.

Greeks called themselves *Hellenes°* (the Romans later used *Graeci*) to distinguish themselves from *barbaroi* (literally "non-Greek speakers," whence the English word *barbarian*). Interaction with new peoples and exposure to their cultures made the Greeks aware of their unity of language, religion, and lifestyle. It also introduced them to

---

polis (POE-lis)

Hellenes (HELL-leans)

new ideas and technologies. Developments in the colonial world traveled back to the Greek homeland: urban planning, forms of political organization, and new intellectual currents.

Coinage, invented in the early sixth century B.C.E. in Lydia (western Anatolia), spread throughout the Greek world and beyond. Scarcity, durability, divisibility, and ease of use made silver, gold, and copper appropriate for minting into metal pieces of state-guaranteed weight and purity. (Societies in other parts of the world used items with similar qualities, including beads, hard-shelled beans, and cowrie shells.) Coinage made weighing quantities of metal obsolete and fostered quicker trading transactions, better recordkeeping, and easier wealth storage. Trade grew, as did the total wealth of communities, but different weight standards used by different states often confused exchanges of currencies.

Colonization relieved pressures within the Archaic Greek world but did not eliminate political instability. At some point, councils representing the noble families superseded the Dark Age kings depicted in Homer's *Iliad* and *Odyssey*. This aristocracy derived wealth and power from land ownership. The peasants who farmed these lands kept only a portion of their harvest. Debt slaves, people who lost their freedom when they could not repay money or seed borrowed from the lord, also worked the land. Free peasants owned small farms and joined urban-based craftsmen and merchants as part of a "middle class."

Tyrants—individuals who seized power in violation of normal political institutions—gained control of many city-states in the mid-seventh and sixth centuries B.C.E. Often disgruntled aristocrats with middle-class backing, such tyrants appealed to hoplite soldiers, whose numbers increased with growing prosperity and lower prices for weaponry. The tyrants granted these supporters political rights.

Some tyrants passed their positions on to sons, but communities eventually expelled the tyrant families and opted for oligarchy°, where a group of the wealthiest men held power, or **democracy,** where all free, adult males shared power. The absence of a professional military class made this broadening of the political system possible.

The Greeks worshiped several sky-gods—Zeus who sent storms and lightning, Poseidon who controlled the sea and earthquakes—before entering the Greek peninsula at the end of the third millennium B.C.E. The *Iliad* and *Odyssey*, which schoolboys memorized and performers recited, gave personalities to these deities. Homer portrayed them as anthropomorphic°, or humanlike in appearance (though taller, more beautiful, and more powerful, with a supernatural radiance), with humanlike emotions of love, anger, and jealousy. More than anything else, immortality distinguished gods from humans.

State religious ceremonies conferred civic identity. **Sacrifice,** the central ritual, took place at altars in front of temples where the gods were thought to reside. Gifts as humble as a small cake or a cup of wine poured on the ground accompanied prayers for favor and protection. In grander sacrifices, people would kill one or more animals, spray the altar with its blood, and burn parts of its body so that the aroma would ascend to the gods.

Oracles situated at sacred sites responded to human pleas for information, advice, or prediction. At Delphi in central Greece, the most honored site, the god Apollo spoke through his priestess, the Pythia°. The male priests who administered the sanctuary interpreted her obscure utterances. Our dependence on literary texts expressing the values of an educated, urban elite limits our knowledge of fertility cults, which were usually based on female deities and appealed to the agricultural majority of the population.

New Intellectual Currents

Prosperity, new technologies, and social and political development led to innovations in intellectual and artistic outlook, including a growing emphasis on the individual. In early Greek communities, the family enveloped the individual, and land belonged collectively to the family, including ancestors and descendants. Ripped from this communal network and forced to resettle elsewhere, colonists became models of individualism, as did the tyrant who seized power for himself

---

oligarchy (OLL-ih-gahr-key)

anthropomorphic (an-thruh-puh-MORE-fik) Pythia (PITH-ee-uh)

alone. The concept of humanism—a valuing of the uniqueness, talents, and rights of the individual—remains a central tenet of Western civilization.

In the new lyric poetry, short verses deal with personal subjects drawn from the poet's experience. Archilochus°, a soldier and poet living in the first half of the seventh century B.C.E., wrote:

> Some barbarian is waving my shield, since I was obliged to leave that perfectly good piece of equipment behind under a bush. But I got away, so what does it matter? Let the shield go; I can buy another one equally good.[2]

Here Archilochus pokes fun at the heroic ideal that scorned soldiers who ran from the enemy. In challenging traditional values and expressing personal feelings, lyric poets pointed toward the modern Western conception of poetry.

In religion, thinkers now known as pre-Socratic philosophers called into question Homer's representations of the gods. Xenophanes°, living in the sixth century B.C.E., protested:

> But if cattle and horses or lions had hands, or were able to draw with their hands and do the works that men can do, horses would draw the forms of the gods like horses, and cattle like cattle, and they would make their bodies such as they each had themselves.[3]

The term *pre-Socratic* refers to philosophers before Plato, a student of Socrates, who in the later fifth century B.C.E. shifted the focus of philosophy to ethical questions. They rejected traditional explanations of the origins and nature of the world and sought more rational answers: How was the world created? What is it made of? Why does it change? Some postulated that earth, air, fire, and water, the primal elements, combine or dissolve to form the substances found in nature. One taught that microscopic atoms (from a Greek word meaning "indivisible") move through the void of space, colliding randomly and combining in various ways to form the natural world. This intuition coincidentally resembles modern atomic theory. Most pre-Socratics came from Ionia and southern Italy, where Greeks lived close to non-Greeks. Encountering peoples with different ideas may have stimulated some of their thoughts.

Also in Ionia in the sixth century B.C.E., men later referred to as logographers ("writers of prose accounts") gathered information on ethnography (the physical characteristics and cultural practices of a people), Mediterranean geography, the foundation of cities, and the origins of famous families. They called their accumulation of information *historia,* "investigation/research." **Herodotus** (ca. 485–425 B.C.E.), from Halicarnassus in southwest Anatolia, published his *Histories.* Its early parts contain geographic and ethnographic reports, legends, folktales, and marvels. Later parts focus on the Persian-Greek wars of the previous generation. He opens his work as follows:

> I, Herodotus of Halicarnassus, am here setting forth my history, that time may not draw the color from what man has brought into being, nor those great and wonderful deeds, manifested by both Greeks and barbarians, fail of their report, and, together with all this, the reason why they fought one another.[4]

His search for causes reveals the thinking of a true historian. Thus did *historia* begin to narrow and acquire the modern meaning of *history,* with Herodotus gaining the nickname *Father of History.*

Athens and Sparta

Athens and Sparta, the preeminent city-states of the late Archaic and Classical periods, differed in character despite environmental and cultural similarities. The Spartans' ancestors migrated into the Peloponnese°, the southernmost part of Greece, around 1000 B.C.E. Their community resembled others until the seventh century B.C.E., when the population increases and shortage of farmland that affected all communities prompted them to react differently. Instead of sending out colonies, the Spartans invaded the fertile plain of Messenia to the west. The resulting takeover, aided perhaps by hoplite tactics, saw the Messenians reduced to the status of helots°, the most abused and exploited population on the Greek mainland.

Archilochus (ahr-KIL-uh-kuhs) **Xenophanes** (zeh-NOFF-eh-nees)

Peloponnese (PELL-eh-puh-neze) **helot** (HELL-ut)

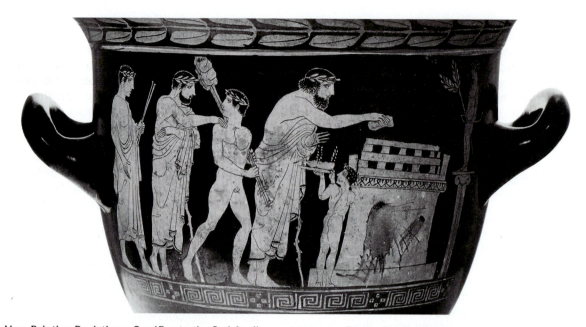

Vase Painting Depicting a Sacrifice to the God Apollo, ca. 440 B.C.E.   For the Greeks, who believed in a multitude of gods who looked and behaved like humans, the central act of worship was the sacrifice, the ritualized offering of a gift. Sacrifice created a relationship between the human worshiper and the deity and raised expectations that the god would bestow favors in return. Here we see a number of male devotees, wearing their finest clothing and garlands in their hair, near a sacred outdoor altar and statue of Apollo. The god is shown at the far right, standing on a pedestal and holding his characteristic bow and laurel branch. The first worshiper offers the god bones wrapped in fat. All of the worshipers will feast on the meat carried by the boy.   (Bildarchiv Preussischer Kultburbesitz/Art Resource, NK)

The Sparta state quickly turned into a military camp, always prepared for a helot uprising. The state divided Messenia and Laconia, the Spartan homeland, into several thousand lots, each assigned to a Spartan citizen. Helots worked the land and turned over part of their harvest to their Spartan masters. Freed from farming, the Spartans devoted their lives to military affairs.

The Spartan army outclassed all others because it did not rely on militias summoned only during crises. The Spartans paid a price, however. Taken from their families and put into barracks at age seven, boys underwent a severe regimen of discipline, beatings, and deprivation. The demands of the state consumed a Spartan male's whole life.

The economic, political, and cultural revival of the Archaic Greek world passed Sparta by: no poets or artists, no precious metals or coinage, no commerce or other activities that could introduce inequality. The fifth-century B.C.E. historian Thucydides°, a native of Athens, remarked that in his day Sparta looked like a large village and that no future observer of the site would be able to guess its power.

Other Greeks admired Spartan courage, commitment, and martial skills but abhorred their arrogance, ignorance, and cruelty. The Spartan Council of Elders and two kings, who commanded in battle, practiced a cautious and isolationist foreign policy. Reluctant to venture far for fear of a helot uprising, they worked for peace through the Peloponnesian League, a system of alliances with their neighbors.

Athens, by comparison, possessed an unusually large and populous territory: the fertile plains

---

Thucydides (thoo-SID-ih-dees)

of Attica with their groves of olive trees. By the fifth century B.C.E., Athens numbered approximately 300,000 people. Villages and a few larger towns dotted the peninsula where the urban center stood beside the sheer-sided Acropolis some 5 miles (8 kilometers) from the sea.

Abundant land lessened the initial stresses of the Archaic period. Nevertheless, in 594 B.C.E., to avoid civil war, the Athenians conferred lawgiving powers on Solon, an aristocrat with ties to the merchant community. He divided the citizens into four classes based on the yield of their farms. The top three classes could hold state offices. The lowest class, with little or no property, held no offices but could participate in meetings of the Assembly. Although a far cry from democracy, this linkage between rights, privileges, and wealth broke the power of a dominant cluster of aristocratic families and favored social and political mobility. By abolishing debt slavery, Solon also guaranteed the freedom of Athenian citizens.

Despite Solon's efforts, in 546 B.C.E. an aristocrat named Pisistratus° seized power. Most Athenians still lived in villages, identified primarily with their district, and accepted the leadership of landlords who lived in sturdy manor houses. So the tyrant Pisistratus turned to the urban population as opposed to the villagers loyal to the landlords. He undertook building projects, including a Temple of Athena on the Acropolis, and instituted or expanded popular urban festivals: the City Dionysia°, later famous for dramatic performances, and the Panathenaea°, a religious procession combined with athletic and poetic competitions.

With Spartan assistance, the Athenians expelled Pisistratus's sons, who had inherited his position. In the 460s and 450s B.C.E., **Pericles**° led a democratic movement to transfer all power to popular organs of government: the Assembly, the Council of 500, and the People's Courts. Henceforward, Athenians of moderate or slender means could hold office and participate in politics. Selected by lot for even the highest positions, officials now received pay for their services so they could afford to leave their other occupations. Some key

offices—managing public money, commanding military forces—were filled by elections that took into account the candidates' abilities.

The Assembly of all citizens held open debates several times a month; anyone could speak to the issues of the day. Members of the Council of 500 took turns presiding and representing the Athenian state. Through effective political organizing, Pericles dominated Athenian politics from 461 B.C.E. until his death in 429 B.C.E.

Athens's economic position paralleled its political evolution. From the time of Pisistratus, Athenian pottery becomes increasingly prominent at archaeological sites around the Mediterranean. These pots often contained olive oil, Athens's chief export, but elegant painted vases were themselves luxury commodities. Trade-related increases in the size and prosperity of the middle class help explain the growth of Athenian democracy.

THE STRUGGLE OF PERSIA AND GREECE

The Persian-Greek wars dominated Greek life in the fifth and fourth centuries B.C.E. Persians probably considered developments farther east more important. Nevertheless, in the end, the encounters profoundly affected the history of the eastern Mediterranean and western Asia.

Early Encounters   Cyrus's conquest of Lydia in 546 B.C.E. led to the subjugation of the Ionian Greek cities. Some groups and individuals collaborated with the Persian government, but in 499 B.C.E. Greeks and other subject peoples on the western frontier staged the Ionian Revolt. The Persians needed five years and massive infusions of troops and resources to stamp out the insurrection.

This failed revolt led to the **Persian Wars**: two Persian attacks on Greece in the early fifth century B.C.E. In 490 B.C.E., Darius dispatched a naval fleet to punish Eretria° and Athens, two mainland Greek

---

Pisistratus (pie-SIS-truh-tuhs)   **Dionysia** (die-uh-NIZ-ee-uh)   **Panathenaea** (pan-ath-uh-NEE-uh)   **Pericles** (PER-eh-kleez)

Eretria (er-EH-tree-uh)

states allied with the Ionian rebels. Disloyal citizens betrayed Eretria to the Persians, who marched the survivors off to exile. In this, as in many other things, the Persians copied their Assyrian predecessors, although they did not boast of mass deportations. Athens would probably have suffered a similar fate if its hoplites had not defeated the lighter-armed Persian troops in a sharp engagement at Marathon, 26 miles (42 kilometers) from Athens.

Xerxes (Khshayarsha, r. 486–465 B.C.E.) succeeded his father in 486 B.C.E. and soon turned his attention to the troublesome Greeks. In 480 B.C.E., he gathered a huge invasion force, including contingents from all over the Persian Empire and a large fleet. Crossing the Hellespont (the narrow strait separating Europe and Asia) and traversing Thrace, the Persian throng descended into central and southern Greece. Xerxes sent messengers ahead demanding of the city-states "earth and water"—tokens of submission.

Many city-states complied. But in southern Greece the Spartans formed an alliance that historians call the Hellenic League. At the pass of Thermopylae° in central Greece, three hundred Spartans and their king fought to the last man to buy time for their fellows to escape. The Persians sacked Athens, but the outnumbered Athenians lured the Persian navy into narrow waters at nearby Salamis°, where, despite their numbers, they could not maneuver. The Persians lost their advantage, and the Athenians administered a devastating defeat. A rout of the Persian army at Plataea the following spring relieved the immediate threat.

Athens's stubborn refusal to submit and the effectiveness of the Athenian navy earned the city great respect. Naval strategies dominated the next phase of the war, which was designed to liberate Greek states still under Persian control. This gave Athens priority over land-based, isolationist Sparta. The Delian League, formed in 477 B.C.E., brought the Greek states together. In less than twenty years, League forces led by Athenian generals swept the Persians from the eastern Mediterranean and freed all Greek communities except those in distant Cyprus.

The Height of Athenian Power

Scholars date the Classical period of Greek history (480–323 B.C.E.) to this defense of the Greek homeland. Ironically, Athens exploited its crucial role in these events to become an imperial power. Some Greek allies contributed money instead of troops, and the Athenians used the money to strengthen their navy. They treated other members of the Delian League as subjects and demanded annual contributions. States attempting to leave the League were brought back by force, stripped of their defenses, and rendered subordinate to Athens.

Athenian naval technology transformed Greek warfare and brought power and wealth to Athens itself. Unlike commercial sailing ships, which over time had developed a stabler and more capacious round-bodied design, military vessels relied on large numbers of rowers. Having little deck room or storage space, these ships hugged the coastline and put ashore nightly to replenish food supplies and let the crew sleep. Fifty-oared ships had dominated naval warfare until the late sixth century B.C.E., when sleek, fast **triremes**° powered by 170 rowers brought an end to crude engagements in which warriors cleared the enemy's decks with spears and arrows before boarding and fighting hand to hand. Approximately 115 by 15 feet (35 by 6 meters) in size, the trireme positioned rowers on three levels with oars of different lengths to avoid interference. The fragile vessels could achieve up to 7 knots in short bursts. Athenian crews, by constant practice, became the best in the eastern Mediterranean. They disabled enemy vessels by sheering off their oars, smashing their hulls below the water line with an iron-tipped prow, or forcing collisions by running around them in ever-tighter circles.

The primacy of the fleet contributed to a democratic system in which each male citizen had, at least in principle, an equal voice. The middle or upper class produced hoplites, who bought their own armor and weapons. Rowers came from the lower classes, but they insisted on full rights as protectors of the community.

Athenian maritime power reached farther than any citizen militia. Victors in Greek wars seldom oc-

---

Thermopylae (thuhr-MOP-uh-lee)   **Salamis** (SAH-lah-miss)   **trireme** (TRY-reem)

cupied enemy lands permanently (the exception being Sparta's takeover of Messenia). Booty with minor adjustments to boundary lines sufficed. But Athens could exert continual domination and readily did so to promote its commerce. Athens's port, Piraeus°, became the most important commercial center in the eastern Mediterranean.

Annual dues from subject states subsidized the increasingly expensive Athenian democracy and paid the construction costs of the Parthenon, a majestic temple to Athena on the Acropolis. The Athenian leader Pericles gained extraordinary popularity by hiring many Athenians to construct and decorate this and other monuments. When political enemies protested Pericles' use of Delian League funds for construction, he replied: "They [Athens's subjects] do not give us a single horse, nor a soldier, nor a ship. All they supply is money. . . . It is no more than fair that after Athens has been equipped with all she needs to carry on the war, she should apply the surplus to public works, which, once completed, will bring her glory for all time."[5]

The proceeds of empire indirectly subsidized the festivals at which the dramatic tragedies of Aeschylus, Sophocles, and Euripides and the comedies of Aristophanes° were performed. The brightest and most creative artists and thinkers flocked to Athens. Traveling teachers called Sophists ("wise men") provided instruction in logic and public speaking to fee-paying pupils. The new discipline of rhetoric—the crafting of attractive and persuasive arguments—gave those with training and quick wits a great advantage in politics and the courts. Greeks became connoisseurs of oratory, eagerly listening for each innovation yet so aware of the power of words that *sophist* came to mean one who uses cleverness to manipulate reality.

These intellectual currents came together in 399 B.C.E. when the philosopher **Socrates** (ca. 470–399 B.C.E.) went on trial charged with corrupting the youth of Athens and not believing in the city's gods. A sculptor by trade, Socrates spent his time conversing with young men who enjoyed hearing him deflate the pretensions of those who thought themselves wise. He wryly commented

Piraeus (pih-RAY-uhs)
Aristophanes (ar-uh-STOFF-uh-neze)

that he knew one more thing than everyone else: that he knew nothing.

At his trial, Socrates easily disposed of the actual charges, because he was a deeply religious man, and the families of the young men he associated with supported him. He argued that the real basis of the prosecution was twofold: (1) blame for attempts by several of his aristocratic students to overthrow the Athenian democracy and (2) blame for the controversial teachings of the Sophists, which many believed undermined morality and religious tradition. In Athenian trials, juries of hundreds of citizens decided guilt and punishment, often spurred by emotion more than legal principles. Convicted by a close vote, Socrates maintained his innocence and said he should be rewarded for his services instead. This led the jury to condemn him to death by drinking hemlock. Socrates' disciples considered him a martyr, and smart young men like Plato withdrew from public life and dedicated themselves to philosophical pursuits.

Socrates himself wrote nothing, preferring to converse with people he met in the street. His disciple Plato (ca. 428–347 B.C.E.) may represent the first truly literate generation. He learned from books and habitually wrote down his thoughts. On the outskirts of Athens, Plato founded the Academy, a school where young men could pursue higher education. Yet even Plato reflected the oral culture of his upbringing by writing dialogues—an oral form—in which his protagonist, Socrates, uses the "Socratic method" of question and answer to reach a deeper understanding of values like justice, excellence, and wisdom. Plato refused to write down the most advanced teachings of the Academy. Higher reality, he believed, appeared only in pale reflection in the sensible world and could be grasped only by "initiates" who had completed the earlier stages.

Inequality in Classical Greece

The Athenian democracy that historically underlies modern traditions of democracy included only a small percentage of Attica's population: true citizens—free adult males of pure Athenian ancestry. Excluding women, children, slaves, and foreigners, this group amounted to 30,000 or 40,000 people out of approximately

300,000. Equally exclusive practices probably existed in less well-known Greek democracies.

Slaves, mostly foreigners, constituted perhaps one-third of the population of Attica in the fifth and fourth centuries B.C.E. The average Athenian family owned one or more. Slaves ran the shop or worked the farm while the master attended meetings of the Assembly or served on a board overseeing the day-to-day activities of the state. As "living pieces of property," slaves did any work, submitted to any sexual acts, and suffered any punishments their owners ordained, though some communities prohibited arbitrarily killing slaves. Overall, Greece saw few of the extremes of cruelty and abuse inflicted on slaves in other places and times.

Farms being small, most slaves performed domestic service rather than field labor, often working with the master or mistress on the same tasks. Daily contact fostered relationships between owners and slaves that made it hard for owners to act inhumanely. Still, Greek thinkers justified slavery by arguing that *barbaroi* (non-Greeks) lacked the capacity to reason and thus were better off under Greek owners. The stigma attached to slavery was so great that most Athenians refused to work as wage laborers because following an employer's orders resembled being his slave.

The position of women varied. Spartan women, who were expected to bear and raise strong children, exercised regularly and enjoyed a level of public visibility and outspokenness that shocked other Greeks. At the opposite extreme, Athenians confined and oppressed women. Ironically, the exploitation of women in Athens reflects the high degree of freedom that Athenian men enjoyed in the democratic state.

Inequality marked Athenian marriages. A man of thirty—reasonably educated, a war veteran, and experienced in business and politics—commonly married, after negotiating with her parents, a teenage woman with no formal education and minimal training in weaving, cooking, and household management. Coming into the home of a husband she hardly knew, the wife had no political rights and limited legal protection. Given the differences in age, social experience, and authority, the relationship between husband and wife resembled that of father and daughter.

The function of marriage was to produce children, preferably male. The ancients were sufficiently ashamed of infanticide—the killing through exposure of unwanted children—to say little about it. But it is likely that more girls than boys were abandoned.

The husband spent his day outdoors attending to work or political responsibilities; he dined with male friends at night. The wife stayed home to cook, clean, raise the children, and supervise the servants. The closest relationship in the family was likely to be between the wife and her slave attendant, a woman of roughly the same age. The servant could be sent on errands. The wife stayed home, except to attend funerals and certain festivals or make discreet visits to female relatives. Greek men claimed that confinement to the home stifled female promiscuity and prevented illegitimate births that could threaten family property and erode regulation of citizenship rights. Athenian law allowed a husband to kill an adulterer caught in the act with his wife.

Without documents written by women, we cannot tell how Athenian women felt about their situation. Women's festivals, such as the Thesmophoria°, provided a rare opportunity for women to get out. During this three-day festival, the women of Athens lived together and managed their own affairs in a great encampment, carrying out mysterious rituals meant to enhance the fertility of the land. Bold and self-assertive women appeared on the Athenian stage: the defiant Antigone° of Sophocles' play, who buried her brother despite the king's prohibition; and the wives in Aristophanes' comedy *Lysistrata*°, who withheld sex from their husbands until the men ended a war. Although imagined by men and probably reflecting a fear of strong women, these characters must partly reflect the playwrights' mothers, sisters, and wives.

To find his intellectual and emotional "equal," men often looked to other men. Bisexuality arose as much from the social structure as from biological inclinations. An older man commonly admired, pursued, and mentored a youth, thus making bisexuality part of the youth's education and initia-

---

Thesmophoria (thes-moe-FOE-ree-uh)   **Antigone** (ar-TIG-uh-nee)   *Lysistrata* (lis-uh-STRAH-tuh)

tion into the adult male community. Though commonplace among the intellectual groups that loom large in the written sources, the frequency of bisexuality and the confinement of women among the Athenian masses remain uncertain.

Failure of the City-State and Triumph of the Macedonians

Athens's rise to empire led in 431 B.C.E. to the outbreak of the **Peloponnesian War,** a struggle for survival between Athenian and Spartan alliances that encompassed most of the Greek world. To insulate themselves from attack by land, in midcentury the Athenians had built three long walls connecting the city with the port of Piraeus and the adjacent shoreline. As long as Athens controlled the sea-lanes and could provision itself, a land-based siege could not starve it into submission.

At the start of the war, Pericles broke precedent by refusing to engage the Spartan-led armies that invaded Attica each year. He knew that the enemy hoplites must soon return to their farms. Thus, instead of culminating in a short, decisive battle, the Peloponnesian War dragged on for nearly three decades, with great loss of life and resources. It sapped the morale of all Greece and ended only with the defeat of Athens in a naval battle in 404 B.C.E. The Persian Empire had bankrolled the construction of ships by the Spartan alliance, so Sparta was able to take the conflict into Athens's own element, the sea.

The victorious Spartans, who had entered the war championing "the freedom of the Greeks," took over Athens's overseas empire until their increasingly high-handed behavior aroused the opposition of other city-states. Indeed, the fourth century B.C.E. was a time of nearly continuous skirmishing among Greek states. The independent polis that lent glory to Greek culture also fostered rivalries and fears among neighbors.

The Persians recouped old losses. By the King's Peace of 387 B.C.E., encompassing most of the war-weary Greek states, all of western Asia, including the Ionian Greek communities, went to Persia. The Persian king guaranteed a status quo that kept the Greeks divided and weak until rebellions in Egypt, Cyprus, and Phoenicia, combined with trouble

from some western satraps, diverted h
from thoughts of another Greek invasio.

Meanwhile, in northern Greece Phili,
336 B.C.E.) was transforming his previou
ward kingdom of Macedonia into a premier military power. (Although southern Greeks long doubted the "Greekness" of the rough and rowdy Macedonians, modern scholarship considers their language and culture Greek at base, though influenced by non-Greek neighbors.) Philip improved the traditional hoplite formation. He increased its striking power and mobility by equipping his soldiers with longer thrusting spears and lighter armor. Using horses bred on Macedonia's broad grassy plains, he experimented with coordinating infantry and cavalry. Finally, his engineers developed new siege weapons, including the first catapults—machines using the power of twisted cords that, when relaxed, hurled arrows or stones great distances.

In 338 B.C.E., Philip defeated a southern coalition and established the Confederacy of Corinth to control the Greek city-states. Appointed military commander of all the Greeks, he planned a campaign against Persia and established a bridgehead on the Asiatic side of the Hellespont. This seems to reflect the advice of Greek thinkers who urged an anti-Persian crusade to unify their quarrelsome countrymen.

An assassin cut short Philip's ambitions in 336 B.C.E. **Alexander** (356–323 B.C.E.), his son, crossed into Asia in 334 B.C.E., vowing revenge for Xerxes' invasion a century and half earlier. He defeated the Persians in three pitched battles—against the western satraps at the Granicus River in northwest Anatolia and against King Darius III (r. 336–330 B.C.E.) himself at Issus in southeast Anatolia and at Gaugamela°, north of Babylon.

Alexander the Great, as he came to be called, maintained the Persian administrative system but replaced Persian officials with Macedonians and Greeks. To control strategic points, he settled wounded and aged ex-soldiers in a series of Greek-style cities, beginning with Alexandria in Egypt. After his victory at Gaugamela (331 B.C.E.), he experimented with leaving cooperative Persian officials in place, also admitting some Persians and other Iranians into his army and court circle.

Gaugamela (GAW-guh-mee-luh)

Adopting elements of Persian dress and court ceremonials, he married several Iranian women who had royal or aristocratic connections and pressed his leading comrades to do the same.

In opting for unexpected policies that the Macedonian nobility fiercely resented, Alexander probably acted from both pragmatic and idealistic motives. His Asian campaign began with visions of glory, booty, and revenge. But the farther east he traveled, the more he saw himself as the legitimate successor of the Persian king (a claim facilitated by the death of Darius III). Alexander may have recognized that he had responsibilities to all the peoples who fell under his control and that controlling so vast an empire would require the cooperation of local leaders. In this, he followed the example of the Achaemenids.

THE HELLENISTIC SYNTHESIS

When he died suddenly in 323 B.C.E. at the age of thirty-two, Alexander had no plans for the succession. A half-century of chaos followed as the most ambitious and ruthless of his generals struggled to succeed him. When the dust cleared, they had broken the empire into three major kingdoms, each ruled by a Macedonian dynasty: the Seleucid°, Ptolemaic°, and Antigonid° kingdoms (see Map 4.1). A rough balance of power prevented any of the three from gaining the upper hand and enabled smaller states to survive by playing off the great powers.

Historians call the epoch following Alexander's conquests the **Hellenistic Age** (323–30 B.C.E.) because large parts of northeastern Africa and western Asia became "Hellenized"—that is, influenced by Greek culture. This era of large kingdoms containing ethnically mixed populations, great cities, powerful rulers, pervasive bureaucracies, and vast disparities in wealth differed profoundly from the Archaic and Classical ages with their small, homogeneous, independent city-states. The Hellenistic world more closely resembled our own in its long-distance trade and communications, new institu-

tions like libraries and universities, new kinds of scholarship and science, and sophisticated tastes in art and literature.

The Seleucids, who ruled the bulk of Alexander's empire, faced the greatest challenges. The Indus Valley and Afghanistan soon split off, and over the course of the third and second centuries B.C.E., Iran fell to the Parthians (see Chapter 6). Mesopotamia, Syria, and parts of Anatolia thus constituted the Seleucid core; the kings ruled from Antioch in Syria. Like the Persians before them, they governed many different ethnic groups organized under various political and social forms. In the farming villages, where most of the population resided, the Seleucids maintained an administration modeled on the Persian system. They also continued Alexander's policy of founding Greek-style cities to serve as administrative centers and attract colonists from Greece. The Seleucids desperately needed Greek soldiers, engineers, and administrators.

The dynasty of the **Ptolemies**° ruled Egypt and sometimes laid claim to Palestine. Since most Egyptians belonged to one ethnic group and lived in villages alongside the Nile, the Ptolemies took over much of the administrative structure of the pharaohs. Vast revenues poured into the royal treasury from rents (the king owned most of the land), taxes, and royal monopolies on olive oil, salt, papyrus, and other key commodities.

The Ptolemies ruled from **Alexandria.** Memphis and Thebes, the capitals of ancient Egypt, had been located upriver. Alexandria, situated near the mouth of the westernmost branch of the Nile, linked Egypt with the Mediterranean world. In the language of the Ptolemaic bureaucracy, Alexandria was technically "beside Egypt" rather than in it, as if to emphasize the gulf between rulers and subjects.

Like the Seleucids, the Ptolemies encouraged Greek immigration. In return for collaboration in the military or civil administration, the immigrants received land and a privileged position in the new society. But the Ptolemies did not plant Greek-style cities throughout the Egyptian countryside and made no effort to force the Greek language or customs on the Egyptian population. So separate was

---

Seleucid (sih-LOO-sid)   Ptolemaic (tawl-uh-MAY-ik)
Antigonid (an-TIG-uh-nid)

Ptolemies (TAWL-uh-meze)

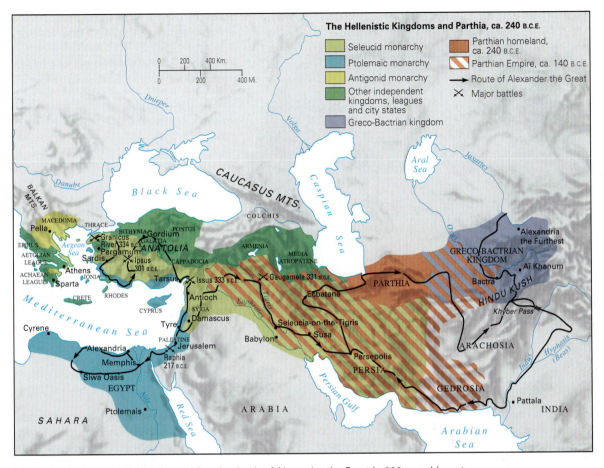

Map 4.1   Hellenistic Civilization   After the death of Alexander the Great in 323 B.C.E., his vast empire soon split apart into a number of large and small political entities. A Macedonian dynasty was established on each continent: the Antigonids ruled the Macedonian homeland and tried with varying success to extend their control over southern Greece; the Ptolemies ruled Egypt; and the Seleucids inherited the majority of Alexander's conquests in Asia, though they lost control of the eastern portions because of the rise of the Parthians of Iran in the second century B.C.E. This period saw Greeks migrating in large numbers from their overcrowded homeland to serve as a privileged class of soldiers and administrators on the new frontiers, where they replicated the lifestyle of the city-state.

the ruling class from the subject population that only the last Ptolemy, Queen Cleopatra (r. 51–30 B.C.E.), bothered to learn the Egyptian language. The advent of new masters brought few changes to the Egyptian peasants. Nevertheless, from the early second century B.C.E., native insurrections in the countryside, though quickly stamped out by government forces and Greek and Hellenized settlers,

indicate growing resentment of Greek exploitation and arrogance.

In Europe, the Antigonid dynasty ruled the Macedonian homeland and parts of northern Greece. Compact and ethnically homogeneous, the Antigonid kingdom experienced little of the hostility that the Seleucid and Ptolemaic rulers faced. Macedonian garrisons gave the Antigonids a

Hellenistic Cameo, Second Century B.C.E.   This sardonyx cameo is an allegory of the prosperity of Ptolemaic Egypt. At left, the bearded river-god Nile holds a horn of plenty while his wife, seated on a sphinx and dressed like the Egyptian goddess Isis, raises a stalk of grain. Their son, at center, carries a seed bag and the shaft of a plow. The Seasons are seated at right. Two wind-gods float overhead. The style is entirely Greek, but the motifs are a blending of Greek and Egyptian elements.   (G. Dagli-Orti/The Art Archive)

toehold in central and southern Greece, and the shadow of Macedonian intervention always threatened the south. The southern states responded by joining confederations, such as the Achaean° League in the Peloponnese, in which the member states maintained local autonomy but pooled resources and military power.

Athens and Sparta stood apart from these confederations. Never abandoning their myth of invincibility, the Spartans made a number of heroic but futile stands against Macedonian armies. Athens, now cherished for the artistic and literary accomplishments of the fifth century B.C.E., pursued a policy of neutrality. The city became a large museum, filled with the relics and memories of a glorious past, as well as a university town that attracted the children of the well-to-do from all over the Mediterranean and western Asia.

Alexandria, the greatest Hellenistic city, with a population of nearly half a million, had at its heart the royal compound, containing the palace and administrative buildings. The magnificent Mausoleum of Alexander enshrined Alexander's body, which the first Ptolemy had stolen during its return to Macedonia for burial. He had hoped that the luster of the great conqueror, who was declared to be a god, would give him legitimacy as a ruler.

The famed Library of Alexandria had several hundred thousand volumes. The Museum, or "House of the Muses" (divinities who presided over the arts and sciences), supported the work of the greatest poets, philosophers, doctors, and scientists. A great lighthouse—a multistory tower with a fiery beacon visible at a distance of 30 miles (48 kilometers)—guided seafarers to two harbors serving the commerce of the Mediterranean, the Red Sea, and the Indian Ocean.

Alexandrian Greeks enjoyed citizenship in a polis, complete with Assembly, Council, and officials overseeing local affairs. They took advantage of Greek-style amenities and institutions: public baths and shaded arcades, theaters featuring revivals of ancient plays, and concert halls for musical

Achaean (uh-KEY-uhn)

performances and demonstrations of oratory. Young men of the privileged classes took classes at gymnasiums where athletics and fitness combined with music and literature in the curriculum. Jews had their own civic corporation, officials, and courts and predominated in two of the five main residential districts. The sights, sounds, and smells of Syria, Anatolia, and the Egyptian countryside lent distinctiveness to other quarters.

In all the Hellenistic states, ambitious members of the indigenous populations learned the Greek language and adopted elements of the Greek lifestyle, because doing so helped them become part of a privileged and wealthy ruling class. Language and customs more than physical traits made a person a Greek. The Hellenistic Age saw a spontaneous synthesis of Greek and indigenous ways. Egyptians migrated to Alexandria, and Greeks and Egyptians intermarried in the villages. Greeks living amid the monuments and descendants of the ancient civilizations of Egypt and western Asia learned the mathematical and astronomical wisdom of Mesopotamia, the mortuary rituals of Egypt, and the attractions of foreign religions. With little official planning or blessing and stemming for the most part from the day-to-day experiences of ordinary people, a great multicultural experiment unfolded as Greek and Middle Eastern cultural traits clashed and merged.

The Hellenistic kingdom farthest removed from Greece and Macedonia flourished in the region of Bactria in northern Afghanistan. Despite being cut off from the other Hellenistic kingdoms by the rise of Parthian power in Persia, Bactria played an important role in transmitting Greek artistic forms to India. We now turn to India as a land of great diversity, many of whose peoples shared with the Greeks and the Iranians a heritage of Indo-European language and culture.

FOUNDATIONS OF INDIAN CIVILIZATION

India is called a *subcontinent* because it is a large—roughly 2,000 miles (3,200 kilometers) in both length and breadth—and physically isolated land-

mass within the continent of Asia. The Himalayas°, the world's highest mountains, form a barrier to the north; the Indian Ocean bounds it on the east, south, and west (see Map 4.2). The one frontier easily accessible to invaders and migrating peoples lies to the northwest. But people using this corridor must cross over the mountain barrier of the Hindu Kush and the Thar° Desert east of the Indus River.

The Indian Subcontinent

This region of the modern states of Pakistan, Nepal, Bhutan, Bangladesh, India, and the adjacent island of Sri Lanka divides into three topographical zones. The mountainous northern zone takes in the heavily forested foothills and high meadows on the edge of the Hindu Kush and Himalaya ranges. Next come the great basins of the Indus and Ganges Rivers. Originating in the mountainous borderlands of Tibet, these rivers flood annually, leaving layers of silt that over time have created large alluvial plains. The Vindhya range and the Deccan°, an arid, rocky plateau reminiscent of the American Southwest, separate northern India from the third zone, the peninsula proper. The tropical coastal strip of Kerala (Malabar) in the west, the Coromandel Coast in the east with its web of rivers descending from the Deccan, the flatlands of Tamil Nadu on the southern tip of the peninsula, and the island of Sri Lanka often have followed paths of political and cultural development separate from those of northern India.

The mountainous northern rim shelters the subcontinent from cold Arctic winds and gives it a subtropical climate. The **monsoon** (seasonal wind) comes annually when the Indian Ocean lags behind the Asian landmass in heating and cooling with the changing seasons. The temperature difference between water and land acts like a bellows, producing a great wind over the ocean. The southwest monsoon begins in June, picks up moisture from the Indian Ocean, and delivers heavy precipitation to the Ganges Basin and the rain-forest belt on India's western coast. The moist, flat Ganges Delta (modern Bengal) favors rice production.

Himalayas (him-uh-LAY-uhs)   **Thar** (tahr)
Deccan (de-KAN)

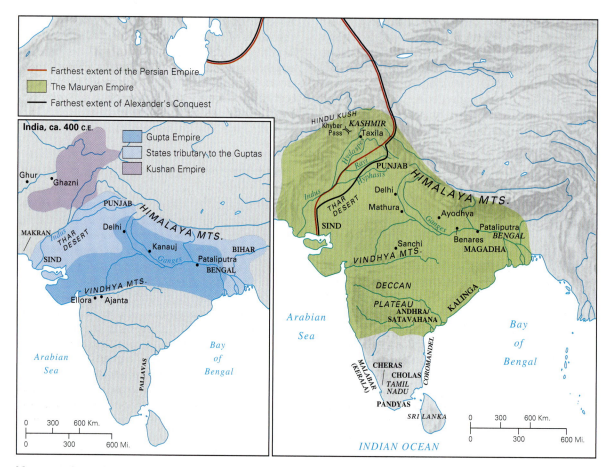

Map 4.2   Ancient India   Mountains and ocean largely separate the Indian subcontinent from the rest of Asia. Migrations and invasions usually came through the Khyber Pass in the northwest. Seaborne commerce with western Asia, Southeast Asia, and East Asia often flourished. Peoples speaking Indo-European languages migrated into the broad valleys of the Indus and Ganges Rivers in the north. Dravidian-speaking peoples remained the dominant population in the south. The diversity of the Indian landscape, the multiplicity of ethnic groups, and the primary identification of people with their class and caste lie behind the division into many small states that has characterized much of Indian political history.

Elsewhere, wheat, barley, and millet predominate. Indus Valley farmers, in contrast, see little precipitation (see Chapter 1) and therefore rely on extensive irrigation.

Indian Ocean mariners learned to ride the monsoon winds across open waters from northeast to southwest in January and to make the return voyage in July. Ships ventured across the Arabian Sea to the Persian Gulf, the southern coast of Arabia, and East Africa, and east across the Bay of Bengal to Indochina and Indonesia (see Chapter 6).

The Vedic Age, 1500–500 B.C.E.

Many features of later Indian civilization surely date back to the Indus Valley civilization of the third and early second millennia B.C.E. (see Chapter 1). Since the writing from that period remains undeciphered, however, the earliest textual knowledge about Indian roots comes from the period 1500 to 500 B.C.E., called the "Vedic Age" after religious texts known as the **Vedas.** Most historians believe that nomads speaking an Indo-European language called Vedic Sanskrit migrated into northwest India at the beginning of the period. Some argue for a much earlier Indo-European presence in this region deriving from the spread of agriculture.

After the collapse of the Indus Valley civilization, the central authority presumed to have organized large-scale irrigation disappeared. The region became home to bands of Vedic-speaking cattle herders who also engaged in farming. As with other Indo-European peoples—Celts, Greeks, Iranians, Romans—patriarchal traditions made the father dominant in the family just as the king ruled the group as a whole. Warriors boasted of their martial skill and courage, relished combat, feasted on beef, and filled their leisure time with chariot racing and gambling.

After 1000 B.C.E., some groups pushed eastward into the Ganges Plain. Iron tools—harder than bronze and able to hold a sharper edge—allowed settlers to fell trees and work the newly cleared land with ox-drawn plows. The fertile plain, watered by the annual monsoon, sustained two or three crops a year. As in Greece at roughly the same time, the use of iron tools must have led to a population increase.

Stories about this era, written down much later but preserved by oral recitation, speak of rivalry and warfare between two peoples: the Aryas, speakers of Vedic Sanskrit and practitioners of the sacrificial religion prescribed in the Vedas, and the Dasas, indigenous speakers of Dravidian languages, whose religion, it is pointedly noted in the Vedas, did not involve sacrifice to or worship of the Vedic gods. Some scholars argue that the real process by which Arya groups became dominant in the north involved the absorption of some Dasas into Arya populations and a merging of elites from both groups. For the most part, however, Aryas pushed the Dasas south into central and southern India, where their descendants still live. Indo-European languages descended from those of the Aryas predominate in northern India today, while Dravidian languages prevail in the south.

The cultural and religious differences between the Aryas and the indigenous peoples contributed to sharp social divisions. A system of ***varnas,*** literally "colors" but usually translated as "castes," indicated something akin to classes. Individuals belonged by birth to one of four classes: *Brahmins,* the group comprising priests and scholars; *Kshatriyas°,* warriors and the king; *Vaishyas°,* all other Aryas; and *Shudras°,* non-Aryas who were servants and slaves of the other three varnas. The designation *Shudra* originally may have signified Dasa. Indeed, the term *dasa* came to mean "slave." Eventually a fifth group emerged: the Untouchables. Excluded from the caste system and shunned by the other castes, they worked in demeaning or polluting trades such as tanning, which involved touching dead animals, and sweeping away ashes after cremations.

According to one creation myth, a primordial man named Purusha allowed himself to be sacrificed. From his mouth sprang the varna of Brahmin priests. From his arms came the Kshatriya warriors; from his thighs the Vaishya merchants, artisans, and peasants; and from his feet the Shudra workers.

Within the broad varna divisions, the population further divided into numerous smaller groups, called ***jatis,*** or castes. Each jati had its proper occupation, duties, and rituals. Members of a given jati lived and married within the group and ate only with fellow jati members. Elaborate rules governed interactions between groups. Members of higher-status groups feared pollution from contacting lower-caste individuals and had to undergo rituals of purification to remove any taint.

The caste system became connected to a belief in reincarnation. The Brahmin priests taught that every living creature had an immortal essence: the *atman,* or "self." Separated from the body at death, the atman returned in the body of an insect, an animal, or a human depending on the **karma,** or deeds, of the atman in its previous incarnations. People of exemplary goodness returned in a higher caste. Those who misbehaved fell to a lower caste or even a lower life form. The underlying message ran: You are where you deserve to be, and the only way

---

Kshatriya (kshuh-TREE-yuh)   **Vaishya** (VIESH-yuh)
Shudra (SHOOD-ra)

to improve your lot in the next incarnation is to accept your current station and its attendant duties.

Many of the Vedic deities, mostly male, were associated with the heavens. Indra, like Zeus a god of war and master of the thunderbolt, commanded the greatest devotion and represented the chieftains who led their warriors into battle. Agni, the fire god, consumed the sacrifice and bridged the spheres of gods and humans. Vedic religion centered on sacrifice, the dedication to a god of a valued possession, often a living creature. The offerings invigorated the gods and thereby sustained their creative powers and promoted stability in the world.

Brahmin priests alone knew the rituals and prayers. The Rig Veda, a collection of more than a thousand poetic hymns to various deities, and the Brahmanas, detailed prose descriptions and explanations of ritual procedures, all in the Sanskrit language of the Arya upper classes, passed orally from one generation of priests to the next. The Brahmins may have opposed the introduction of writing. This would explain why this technology did not spread in India until the Gupta period (320–550 C.E.). The priests' "knowledge" (the term *veda* means just that) earned them rewards for officiating at sacrifices and gave them social and political power as the intermediaries between gods and humans.

As elsewhere in the ancient world, the lives of Indian women left few traces. Limited evidence indicates that in the Vedic period women studied sacred lore, composed religious hymns, and participated in sacrifices. They could own property and usually did not marry until their middle or late teens. A number of strong and resourceful women appear in the Mahabharata epic. In the Ramayana epic, on the other hand, we see the familiar motif of the hero Rama rescuing his wife Sita after she has been abducted.

The internal divisions of Indian society, the complex hierarchy of groups, and the claims of some to superior virtue and purity provided each individual with a clear identity and role and offered the benefits of group solidarity and support. Sometimes groups even upgraded their status within the system, which was not entirely static and provided mechanisms for releasing social tensions. Many of these features persisted into modern times.

Challenges to the Old Order: Jainism and Buddhism

After 700 B.C.E., reactions against Brahmin power and privilege emerged. People who objected to the rigid social hierarchy could always retreat to the forest, which, despite extensive clearing for agriculture, covered much of ancient India. Never far away, these wild places symbolized freedom from societal constraints.

Individuals who wandered in the forest sometimes attracted followers. Questioning priestly power and the necessity of sacrifices, they offered alternate paths to salvation: individual pursuit of insight into the nature of the self and the universe through physical and mental discipline (*yoga*), which included dietary restrictions, and meditation. They taught that by distancing oneself from desire for the things of this world, one could achieve **moksha,** or liberation, "a deep, dreamless sleep" that released one from endless reincarnations through union with the divine force of the universe. The Upanishads, which continue the explanations of ritual begun in the Brahmanas, also reflect this questioning of Vedic ritualism.

Jainism° and Buddhism challenged not only Vedic ritualism, but the authority of the Vedic priests themselves. Jainism took its name from the teacher Mahavira (540–468 B.C.E.), known to his followers as Jina, "the Conqueror." Mahavira respected the life force so much that he commanded strict nonviolence. Jains wore masks to avoid inadvertently inhaling small insects and before sitting down brushed off the seat. Some practiced extreme asceticism by practicing nudity and eventually starving themselves to death. Less zealous Jains engaged in commerce in cities, since agricultural work inevitably involved killing.

Buddhism, a far more successful movement, stemmed from the life of Siddhartha Gautama (563–483 B.C.E.), known as the **Buddha,** "the Enlightened One," about whom myriad legends have arisen. From a Kshatriya family in what is now Nepal, he enjoyed the princely lifestyle that was his birthright until he experienced a change of heart and gave up family and privilege to become a wandering ascetic. After six years, he decided that asceticism was no more likely to produce spiritual

---

Jainism (JINE-iz-uhm)

insight than his earlier luxurious life, so he opted for a "Middle Path." Sitting under a tree in a deer park near Benares on the Ganges River, he gained a sudden and profound insight, which he set forth as "Four Noble Truths": (1) life is suffering, (2) suffering arises from desire, (3) the solution to suffering lies in curbing desire, and (4) desire can be curbed if a person follows the "Eightfold Path" of right views, aspirations, speech, conduct, livelihood, effort, mindfulness, and meditation. Rising up, the Buddha preached his First Sermon, a central text of Buddhism, and set into motion the "Wheel of the Law." He soon attracted followers, some of whom took vows of celibacy, nonviolence, and poverty.

At first, Buddhism centered on the individual. It denied the usefulness of the gods to a person seeking enlightenment. What mattered was living moderately to minimize desire and suffering, and searching for spiritual truth through self-discipline and meditation. One should seek *nirvana,* literally "snuffing out the flame," a release from the cycle of reincarnations and enjoyment of perpetual tranquility. The Upanishadic tradition emphasized the eternal survival of the atman, the "self" or nonmaterial essence of the individual. Buddhism, on the other hand, regarded the individual as a composite of features such as breath and wind, but without a soul.

At his death, Buddha left no final instructions, urging his disciples to "be their own lamp." His followers spread his philosophy throughout India and into Central, Southeast, and East Asia. Its wide appeal subverted its individualistic and atheistic underpinnings. Buddhist monasteries with hierarchies of monks and nuns came into being. Worshipers erected *stupas* (large earthen mounds symbolizing the universe) over relics of the cremated founder and other holy men and walked around them in a clockwise direction. Believers began to worship the Buddha himself as a god. Many Buddhists also revered *bodhisattvas*°, men and women who had achieved enlightenment and were on the threshold of nirvana but chose rebirth into mortal bodies to help others along the path to salvation.

Early representations show the Buddha only indirectly, through symbols such as his footprints, begging bowl, or the tree under which he achieved enlightenment, as if to emphasize his achievement of a state of nonexistence. From the second century C.E., however, statues of the Buddha and bodhisattvas proliferated, sculpted in styles that showed the influence of the Greek settlements established in Bactria (northern Afghanistan) by Alexander the Great. A schism emerged within Buddhism. Devotees of **Mahayana**° ("Great Vehicle") **Buddhism** embraced the popular new features. Practitioners of **Theravada**° ("Teachings of the Elders") **Buddhism** followed most of the original teachings of the founder.

The Rise of Hinduism

Challenged by the new religious movements, Vedic religion evolved by the fourth century C.E. into **Hinduism,** the dominant religion in South Asia today. (The term *Hinduism* originated with Islamic invaders in the eleventh century C.E. as a label for the diverse practices they encountered: "what the Indians do.") Though based on the Vedic religion of northern India, Hinduism incorporated Dravidian cultural elements from the south, such as intense devotion to a deity and the prominence of goddesses.

Brahmin priests survived the transition with their social status and influence intact, but sacrifice lost its central place. Opportunities for individual worshipers to have direct contact with deities increased. Hinduism emphasized the worshiper's personal devotion to a particular deity, usually Vishnu or Shiva, or Devi ("the Goddess"). The goddess is of Dravidian origin, and her incorporation into the cult shows how Arya and indigenous cultures fused to form Hindu civilization. Vishnu, who has a clear Aryan pedigree, remains more popular in northern India, and Shiva is dominant in the south. These deities appear in many guises, bear various cult names, and give rise to a complex symbolism of stories, companion animals, birds, and objects.

Vishnu, the preserver, benevolently helps his devotees in time of need. Hindus believe that whenever demonic forces threaten the cosmic order, an *avatara,* or incarnation of Vishnu, appears

---

bodhisattva (boe-dih-SUT-vuh)

Mahayana (mah-huh-YAH-nuh) **Theravada** (there-eh-VAH-duh)

Hindu Temple at Khajuraho   This sandstone temple of the Hindu deity Shiva, representing the celestial mountain of the gods, was erected at Khajuraho, in central India, around 1000 C.E., but it reflects the architectural symbolism of Hindu temples developed in the Gupta period. Worshipers made their way through several rooms to the image of the deity, which was located in the inner-most "womb-chamber" directly beneath the tallest tower.   (Jean-Louis Nou/akg-images)

on earth. His avatars include the legendary hero Rama, the cowherd god Krishna, and the Buddha (a clear attempt to co-opt the rival religion's founder). Shiva, who lives in ascetic isolation on Mount Kailasa in the Himalayas, represents a cyclical process of creation and destruction that is symbolized in statues showing him dancing. Devi can manifest herself as a full-bodied mother goddess representing fertility and procreation, as Shiva's loving wife, Parvati, or as the frightening deity who, under the name Kali or Durga, lets loose violence and destruction.

The multiplicity of gods (330 million according to one tradition), sects, and local practices within Hinduism reflects the ethnic, linguistic, and cultural diversity of India. Yet within this variety, there is unity. A worshiper's devotion to one god or goddess does not entail denial of the other main deities or the host of lesser divinities and spirits. Ulti-mately, all are manifestations of a single divine force pervading the universe. This underlying unity appears in the way various manifestations of Devi represent different female potentials, in composite statues—half Shiva, half Vishnu—signifying complementary aspects of one cosmic principle, and in sacred texts like the Bhagavad-Gita in which the warrior Arjuna sees the god Krishna in his true aspect after thinking that he was merely his chariot driver:

> It was a multiform, wondrous vision,
> with countless mouths and eyes
> and celestial ornaments.
> Everywhere was boundless divinity
> containing all astonishing things,
> wearing divine garlands and garments,
> anointed with divine perfume.
> If the light of a thousand suns
> were to rise in the sky at once,

it would be like the light
of that great spirit.
Arjuna saw all the universe
in its many ways and parts,
standing as one in the body
of the god of gods.[6]

Hindus may approach god and obtain divine favor through special knowledge of sacred truths, mental and physical discipline, or extraordinary devotion to the deity. Worship centers on temples, which range from humble shrines to richly decorated stone edifices built under royal patronage. Statues beckon the deity to take up temporary residence within the image and be available to eager worshipers. *Puja,* or service to the deity, can include bathing, clothing, or feeding the statue. Glimpsing the divine image conveys potent blessings.

Sacred places where a worshiper can directly sense and benefit from divine power dot the Indian subcontinent. Mystery and sanctity surround certain mountains, caves, trees, plants, and rocks. *Tirthayatra,* the term for a pilgrimage site, means "journey to a river crossing," illustrating the association of Hindu sacred places with flowing water. The Ganges River is especially sacred. Millions of worshipers travel each year to bathe and receive the restorative and purifying power of its waters. Pilgrimage to shrines fosters contact and exchange of ideas among people from different parts of India, helping to create a broad Hindu identity and the concept of India as a single civilization.

Religious duties depend on social standing and gender as well as stage of life. Young men from the three highest classes (Brahmin, Kshatriya, and Vaishya) undergo ritual rebirth through the ceremony of the sacred thread, marking attainment of manhood and readiness to receive religious knowledge. The life cycle then passes through four stages: (1) student of the sacred texts, (2) married householder with children and material goods, (3) forest dweller meditating on the meaning of existence after the birth of his grandchildren, and (4) wandering ascetic awaiting death. The person living such a life fulfills first his duties to society and then his duties to himself, leaving him disconnected from the world and prepared for moksha (liberation).

Hinduism responded to the needs of people for personal deities with whom they could establish direct connections. The austerity of early Buddhism, its denial of the importance of gods, and its demand that individuals find their own path to enlightenment may have required too much of ordinary people. What eventually made Mahayana Buddhism popular—gods, saints, and myths—also made it more easily absorbed into the social and cultural fabric of Hinduism.

INDIAN IMPERIAL EXPANSION AND COLLAPSE

Political unity has rarely lasted in India. The varied terrain—mountains, foothills, plains, forests, steppes, deserts—favors different forms of organization and economic activity. Peoples occupying topographically diverse zones may also differ in language and cultural practices. Caste and family have generated the strongest feeling of personal identity, allegiance to a higher political authority being a secondary concern.

Nevertheless, two empires arose in the Ganges Plain: the Mauryan Empire of the fourth to second centuries B.C.E. and the Gupta Empire of the fourth to sixth centuries C.E.

The Mauryan Empire, 324–184 B.C.E.

Among the many kinship groups and independent states that dotted the north Indian landscape, the kingdom of Magadha, in the modern Indian state of Bihar, began to play an influential role around 600 B.C.E. thanks to wealth based on agriculture, iron mines, and strategic location astride the trade routes of the eastern Ganges Basin. In the late fourth century B.C.E., Chandragupta Maurya°, a man of Vaishya or Shudra origins, took control of Magadha and founded the **Mauryan Empire.** Greek tradition claimed that Alexander the Great met an Indian native named "Sandracottus," an

Maurya (MORE-yuh)

apparent corruption of "Chandragupta," when his armies reached the Punjab (northern Pakistan) in 326 B.C.E., implying that he might have served as a role model for the new ruler.

Greek rule in the Punjab collapsed after Alexander's death, allowing Chandragupta (r. 324–301 B.C.E.) and his successors Bindusara (r. 301–269 B.C.E.) and Ashoka (r. 269–232 B.C.E.) to extend Mauryan control over the entire subcontinent except for its southern tip.

Tradition holds that Kautilya, a crafty elderly Brahmin, guided Chandragupta and wrote a treatise on government, the *Arthashastra*. Although recent studies have shown that the existing form of the *Arthashastra* dates only to the third century C.E., its core may well go back to Kautilya. This pragmatic guide to political success advocates the so-called *mandala* (circle) theory of foreign policy: "My enemy's enemy is my friend." It also lists schemes for enforcing and increasing tax collection and prescribes the use of spies to keep watch on one's subjects.

A quarter of all agricultural output went in taxes to support the Mauryan government. Relatives and associates of the king governed districts based on ethnic boundaries. The imperial army—with infantry, cavalry, chariot, and elephant divisions—secured central authority, which also controlled mining, shipbuilding, and arms making. Standard coinage fostered support for the government and promoted trade.

The Mauryan kings ruled from Pataliputra (modern Patna), where five tributaries join the Ganges. Descriptions by foreign visitors testify to the international connections of the Indian monarchs. Surrounded by a timber wall and moat, the city extended along the river for 8 miles (13 kilometers). Six governing committees oversaw manufacturing, trade, sales, taxes, the welfare of foreigners, and the registration of births and deaths.

Ashoka, Chandragupta's grandson, began his reign by extending the boundaries of the empire. After killing, wounding, or deporting thousands of people during his conquest of Kalinga (modern Orissa, a coastal region southeast of Magadha), remorse overcame him and he converted to Buddhism, thereafter preaching nonviolence, morality, moderation, and religious tolerance in both government and private life.

Ashoka publicized this program through edicts inscribed on great rocks and polished sandstone, the earliest decipherable Indian texts:

> For . . . many hundreds of years the sacrificial slaughter of animals, violence toward creatures, unfilial conduct toward kinsmen, improper conduct toward Brahmins and ascetics [have increased]. Now with the practice of morality by King [Ashoka], the sound of war drums has become the call to morality. . . . You [government officials] are appointed to rule over thousands of human beings in the expectation that you will win the affection of all men. All men are my children. Just as I desire that my children will fare well and be happy in this world and the next, I desire the same for all men. . . . King [Ashoka] . . . desires that there should be the growth of the essential spirit of morality or holiness among all sects. . . . There should not be glorification of one's own sect and denunciation of the sect of others for little or no reason. For all the sects are worthy of reverence for one reason or another.[7]

Despite his commitment to employ peaceful means whenever possible, Ashoka reminded potential transgressors that "the king, remorseful as he is, has the strength to punish the wrongdoers who do not repent."

Commerce and Culture in an Era of Political Fragmentation

The Mauryan Empire prospered for a time after Ashoka's death in 232 B.C.E. Then, weakened by dynastic disputes, it collapsed under attacks from the northwest in 184 B.C.E. Five hundred years passed before another state succeeded in extending control over northern India. Despite the political fragmentation, however, economic, cultural, and intellectual development continued. The roads and towns of the Mauryans fostered commerce within the subcontinent, while land and sea routes linked India to China, Southeast Asia, Central Asia, the Middle East, East Africa, and the lands of the Mediterranean. Guilds of merchants and artisans regulated the lives of their members and had an important voice in local affairs. They patronized culture and endowed religious sects, particularly Buddhism and Jainism, with temples and monuments.

During the last centuries B.C.E. and the first centuries C.E., the greatest Indian epics, the Ramayana and the Mahabharata, based on centuries-old oral predecessors, achieved their final form. They place the events they describe in the distant past, but their proud kings, beautiful queens, family wars, heroic conduct, and chivalric values seem to reflect the late Vedic period, when Aryan warrior societies moved onto the Ganges Plain.

The Ramayana relates the exploits of Rama, a heroic prince who came to be considered an incarnation of Vishnu. When the chief of the demons kidnaps his wife, Sita, he destroys the demons with the help of his brother and a troop of monkeys. The vast **Mahabharata**—eight times the length of the *Iliad* and *Odyssey* combined—tells how two sets of cousins, the Pandavas and Kauravas, quarreled over succession to the throne and fought a cataclysmic battle at Kurukshetra. The battle is so destructive on both sides that Yudhishthira, the eldest of the Pandava brothers and their leader, accepts the fruits of victory only reluctantly because the battle losses were so great.

The **Bhagavad-Gita** is a self-contained (and perhaps originally separate) episode set in the battle. The hero Arjuna shrinks from fighting his kinsmen until his charioteer, the god Krishna, tutors him on the necessity of fulfilling his duty as a warrior. Death means nothing in a universe of endless reincarnation. The Bhagavad-Gita resolves the tension in Indian civilization between duty to society and duty to one's soul. Dutiful action taken without regard for personal benefit serves society and may earn release from the cycle of rebirths.

Science and technology flourished in this era as well. Indian doctors applied herbal remedies and served in the courts of western and southern Asia. In linguistics, Panini (late fourth century B.C.E.) undertook a detailed analysis of Sanskrit word forms and grammar. This led to the standardization of Sanskrit, which arrested its natural development and turned it into a formal, literary language. Prakrits—popular dialects—emerged to become the ancestors of the modern languages of northern and central India.

Historians of southern India consider the period from the third century B.C.E. to the third century C.E., dominated by three often feuding **Tamil kingdoms**—the Cholas, Pandyas, and Cheras—a "classical" period for Tamil art and literature. Patronized by the Pandya kings and guided by an academy of five hundred authors, Tamil writers composed grammatical treatises, collections of ethical proverbs, epics, and short poems about love, war, wealth, and the beauty of nature while performers excelled in music, dance, and drama.

The Gupta Empire, 320–550 C.E.

Like its Mauryan predecessor, the **Gupta Empire** grew from the kingdom of Magadha and had its capital at Pataliputra. Its founder called himself Chandra Gupta (r. 320–335 C.E.), borrowing the name of the Mauryan founder. Though they never controlled as much land as the Mauryans, the Gupta monarchs took the title "Great King of Kings."

Trade, agriculture, and iron mining brought prosperity to the Guptas as they had to the Mauryans, and the kings followed similar methods of taxation and administration. In addition to a 25 percent tax on agriculture, users of the irrigation network paid fees, and some commodities were subject to special taxes. The state maintained monopolies over mining and salt production, exploited state-owned farmlands, and required subjects to work a specified number of days on maintaining roads, wells, and irrigation works.

The Gupta administration and intelligence network were smaller and less pervasive than those of the Mauryans. A powerful army maintained tight control of the empire's core, but provincial governors had a freer hand, which they sometimes used to exploit the populace. Governorships often passed from father to son within high-ranking military or administrative families. The most distant areas, controlled by kinship groups or subordinate kings, made annual donations of tribute. Garrisons stationed at frontier points kept trade routes open and ensured the collection of customs duties.

A constant round of solemn rituals, dramatic ceremonies, and cultural events in Pataliputra demonstrated to visitors from remote areas the benefits of belonging to the empire. Modern historians call such a regime a **theater-state.** Ruler and subjects in the Gupta theater-state had an

Wall Painting from the Caves at Ajanta, Fifth or Sixth Century C.E.   During and after the Gupta period, natural caves in the Deccan were turned into complexes of shrines decorated with sculpture and painting. This painting depicts one of the earlier lives of the Buddha, a king named Mahajanaka who lost and regained his kingdom, here listening to his queen, Sivali. While representing scenes from the earlier lives of the Buddha, the artists also give us a glimpse of life at the royal court in their own times.   (Benoy K. Behl)

economic relationship. The former accumulated luxury goods and profits from trade and redistributed them to dependents through gifts and other means. Subordinate princes gained prestige by emulating the center and maintained close ties through visits, gifts, and marriages with the Gupta family. Gupta patronage also supported the Indian mathematicians, who invented the concept of zero and developed the so-called Arabic numerals and place-value notation.

The moist climate of the Ganges Plain does not favor the preservation of buildings and artifacts, so archaeology has little to say about the Gupta era. However, a Chinese Buddhist monk named Faxian°,

who made a pilgrimage to the homeland of his faith around 400 C.E., penned a description of the Gupta kingdom:

> The cities and towns of this country are the greatest of all in the Middle Kingdom. The inhabitants are rich and prosperous, and vie with one another in the practice of benevolence and righteousness. . . . The heads of the Vaishya families in them establish in the cities houses for dispensing charity and medicines. All the poor and destitute in the country, orphans, widowers, and childless men, maimed people and cripples, and all who are diseased, go to those houses, and are provided with every kind of help.[8]

At this time, the civil disabilities of women, which had always existed as custom, hardened into

---

Faxian (fah-shee-en)

law with the emergence of law books like *The Laws of Manu*. Indian women lost the right to own or inherit property, and girls married at increasingly early ages, sometimes at six or seven. The husband could thus ensure his wife's virginity, and, by bringing her up in his own household, he could train her to suit his purposes. As in Confucian China, a woman owed obedience to her father, then her husband, and finally her sons (see Chapter 2). In certain parts of India, a practice called *sati*° required a widow to cremate herself on her husband's funeral pyre. Widows who refused to follow this custom could not remarry and suffered social rejection.

Entry into a Jainist or Buddhist religious community offered some women an escape from male control. Women from powerful families and courtesans trained in poetry and music, as well as sexual technique, sometimes enjoyed high social standing and gave money for Buddhist stupas and other shrines.

The Gupta monarchs sought sanctity through reviving Vedic practices. The influence of Brahmin priests gained renewed prominence. Yet the kings also patronized Buddhist and Jain endeavors. Buddhist monasteries with hundreds, even thousands, of monks and nuns flourished in the cities. Northern India drew Buddhist pilgrims from Southeast and East Asia to the birthplace of their faith.

The classic form of the Hindu temple, evolved during the Gupta era, symbolizes the sacred mountain or palace where the gods reside. Sitting atop a raised platform surmounted by high towers, it mirrored the order of the universe. From an exterior courtyard, worshipers approached the central shrine containing the statue of the deity. In rich temples, painted or sculpted gods and mythical events covered the walls. Frescoes and statues also adorned cave temples carved into cliffs.

The vibrant commerce of the period of fragmentation continued under the Guptas. Coins served as the medium of exchange, and artisan guilds influenced the economic, political, and religious life of towns. The Guptas sought control of the ports on the Arabian Sea but saw trade with the weakening Roman Empire decline. Trade with Southeast and East Asia increased, however. Merchants from eastern and southern India voyaged to the Malay° Peninsula and the islands of Indonesia to exchange cotton cloth, ivory, metalwork, and exotic animals for Chinese silk or Indonesian spices. The overland Silk Road from China brought further trade but was vulnerable to disruption by Central Asian nomads (see Chapter 6).

The Gupta Empire collapsed around 550 C.E. under the pressure of nomadic invaders from the northwest. In the early seventh century, Harsha Vardhana (r. 606–647), the ruler of the region around Delhi, briefly restored imperial power. An account of his reign by a courtier named Bana shows him to be a fervent Buddhist, poet, patron of artists, and dynamic warrior. After Harsha's death, northern India reverted to political fragmentation and remained divided until the Muslim invasions of the eleventh and twelfth centuries (see Chapter 12).

CONCLUSION

Greece, Iran, and India represent three ways in which societies with shared Indo-European linguistic and religious roots adapted to different geographical environments and indigenous cultures. Although scholars can easily trace resemblances among gods, customs, and philosophical outlooks in these areas, the peoples themselves had no sense of kinship with one another. Only briefly, under Alexander the Great, did they come into direct contact in meaningful ways, and the resulting Hellenistic culture touched all three regions.

While some technologies, such as coinage, took hold in all areas, and trade flourished, both overland and across the Mediterranean Sea and Indian Ocean, local circumstances dictated political and social formations. The ancient cultural centers of Egypt and Mesopotamia influenced the Greeks and the Persians, while India saw a synthesis of the cultures and social systems of the Aryan peoples and their Dravidian precursors.

In comparing the histories of these regions, the question arises of the degree to which different states and societies follow similar paths because of shared heritages, as opposed to responding similarly but independently to analogous challenges.

sati (suh-TEE)

Malay (muh-LAY)

We will explore this subject in the next chapter through a comparison of Rome and China under the Han dynasty.

■ Key Terms

Cyrus	Alexandria
Darius I	monsoon
satrap	Vedas
Persepolis	*varnas*
Zoroastrianism	*jatis*
polis	karma
hoplite	*moksha*
tyrant	Buddha
democracy	Mahayana Buddhism
sacrifice	Theravada Buddhism
Herodotus	Hinduism
Pericles	Mauryan Empire
Persian Wars	Ashoka
triremes	Mahabharata
Socrates	Bhagavad-Gita
Peloponnesian War	Tamil kingdoms
Alexander	Gupta Empire
Hellenistic Age	theater-state
Ptolemies	

■ Suggested Reading

The most up-to-date treatment of ancient Persia is Pierre Briant, *From Cyrus to Alexander: A History of the Persian Empire* (2002). Also useful is J. M. Cook, *The Persian Empire* (1983). Josef Wiesehofer, *Ancient Persia: From 550 B.C. to 650 A.D.* (1996); Richard N. Frye, *The History of Ancient Iran* (1984); and volume 2 of *The Cambridge History of Iran,* ed. Ilya Gershevitch (1985), give the interpretations of Iranian specialists and include good bibliographies. John Curtis, *Ancient Persia* (1989), emphasizes the archaeological record. Maria Brosius, *Women in Ancient Persia, 559–331 B.C.* (1996), draws together scattered evidence. Vesta Sarkhosh Curtis, *Persian Myths* (1993), concisely introduces Iranian myths and legends, with illustrations.

The Cambridge Ancient History, 3d ed., vols. 3–7 (1970–), treats the history of this period fully. Sarah B. Pomeroy, Stanley M. Burstein, Walter Donlan, and Jennifer Tolbert Roberts, *Ancient Greece: A Political, Social, and Cultural History* (1999), offers a fine one-volume treatment. Frank J. Frost, *Greek Society,* 3d ed. (1987), covers social history. Peter Levi, *Atlas of the Greek World* (1980), contains maps and pictures. For essays by contemporary experts on every aspect of Greco-Roman civilization with up-to-date bibliographies, see Michael Grant and Rachel Kitzinger, eds., *Civilization of the Ancient Mediterranean* (1987).

Consult Michael Crawford and David Whitehead, eds., *Archaic and Classical Greece: A Selection of Ancient Sources in Translation* (1983), for translated documents. David G. Rice and John E. Stambaugh, eds., *Sources for the Study of Greek Religion* (1979); Mary R. Lefkowitz and Maureen B. Fant, eds., *Women's Life in Greece and Rome: A Source Book in Translation* (1982); Thomas Wiedemann, ed., *Greek and Roman Slavery* (1981); and Michael Gagarin and Paul Woodruff, *Early Greek Political Thought from Homer to the Sophists* (1995), are specialized collections.

Victor Davis Hanson, *The Other Greeks: The Family Farm and the Agrarian Roots of Western Civilization* (1995); Eric A. Havelock, *The Muse Learns to Write: Reflections on Orality and Literacy from Antiquity to the Present* (1986); Elaine Fantham, Helene Peet Foley, Natalie Boymel Kampen, Sarah B. Pomeroy, and H. Alan Shapiro, *Women in the Classical World* (1994); Cynthia Patterson, *The Family in Greek History* (1998); Yvon Garlan, *Slavery in Ancient Greece* (1988); Walter Burkert, *Greek Religion* (1985); Victor Davis Hanson, *The Western Way of War: Infantry Battle in Classical Greece* (1989); Lionel Casson, *The Ancient Mariners: Seafarers and Sea Fighters of the Mediterranean in Ancient Times,* 2d ed. (1991); Michail Yu Treister, *The Role of Metals in Ancient Greek History* (1996); Joint Association of Classical Teachers, *The World of Athens: An Introduction to Classical Athenian Culture* (1984); N. G. L. Hammond, *The Macedonian State: The Origins, Institutions and History* (1989); Joseph Roisman, ed., *Alexander the Great: Ancient and Modern Perspectives* (1995); and William R. Biers, *The Archaeology of Greece: An Introduction* (1990) explore specific aspects of Greek culture and society. For the Hellenistic world, see F. W. Walbank, *The Hellenistic World,* rev. ed. (1993), and Michael Grant, *From Alexander to Cleopatra: The Hellenistic World* (1982).

Karl J. Schmidt, *An Atlas and Survey of South Asian History* (1995), provides a good starting point with maps and facing text illustrating diverse features of Indian civilization. Concise histories include Stanley Wolpert, *A New History of India,* 3d ed. (1989), and Romila Thapar, *A History of India,* vol. 1 (1966). D. D. Kosambi, *Ancient India: A History of Its Culture and Civilization* (1965), and Paul Masson-Oursel, *Ancient India and Indian Civilization* (1998), offer fuller presentations.

Translations of primary texts with an emphasis on religion take up Ainslie T. Embree's *Sources of Indian Tradition,* vol. 1, 2d ed. (1988). Barbara Stoler Miller, *The Bhagavad-Gita: Krishna's Counsel in Time of War* (1986), is a readable translation. R. K. Narayan's *The Mahab-*

harata: A Shortened Modern Prose Version of the Indian Epic (1978) abbreviates this huge epic. For a classic Sanskrit text on state building, see T. N. Ramaswamy, *Essentials of Indian Statecraft: Kautilya's Arthasastra for Contemporary Readers* (1962). Romila Thapar, *Asoka and the Decline of the Mauryas* (1963), covers the most important Mauryan king.

David R. Kinsley, *Hinduism: A Cultural Perspective* (1982), and David G. Mandelbaum, *Society in India*, 2 vols. (1970), provide insights into religion and social status. Jacob Pandian, *The Making of India and Indian Tradition* (1995), gives attention to southern India in analyzing the diversity of contemporary India. Stephanie W. Jamison, *Sacrificed Wife/Sacrificer's Wife: Women, Ritual, and Hospitality in Ancient India* (1996), deals with the roles of early Indian women. Stella Kramrisch, *The Hindu Temple*, 2 vols. (1946), and Surinder M. Bhardwaj, *Hindu Places of Pilgrimage in India: A Study in Cultural Geography* (1973), examine elements of Hindu worship.

For special topics, see Georges Ifrah, *From One to Zero: A Universal History of Numbers* (1985); Jean W. Sedlar, *India and the Greek World: A Study in the Transmission of Culture* (1980); and Liu Hsin-ju, *Ancient India and Ancient China: Trade and Religious Exchanges, A.D. 1–600* (1994).

■ Notes

1. Quoted in Roland G. Kent, *Old Persian: Grammar, Texts, Lexicon,* 2d ed. (New Haven, CT: American Oriental Society, 1953), 138, 140.
2. Richmond Lattimore, *Greek Lyrics,* 2d ed. (Chicago: University of Chicago Press, 1960), 2.
3. G. S. Kirk and J. E. Raven, *The Presocratic Philosophers: A Critical History with a Selection of Texts* (Cambridge, England: Cambridge University Press, 1957), 169.
4. Herodotus, *The History,* trans. David Grene (Chicago: University of Chicago Press, 1988), 33. (Herodotus 1.1)
5. Plutarch, *Pericles* 12, trans. Ian Scott-Kilvert, *The Rise and Fall of Athens: Nine Greek Lives by Plutarch* (Harmondsworth: Penguin Books, 1960), 178.
6. Barbara Stoller Miller, *The Bhagavad-Gita: Krishna's Counsel in Time of War* (New York: Bantam, 1986), 98–99.
7. B. G. Gokhale, *Asoka Maurya* (New York: Twayne, 1966), 152–153, 156–157, 160.
8. James Legge, *The Travels of Fa-hien: Fa-hien's Record of Buddhistic Kingdoms* (New Delhi: Oriental Publishers, 1971), 77–79.

5 An Age of Empires: Rome and Han China, 753 B.C.E.–330 C.E.

CHAPTER OUTLINE

Rome's Creation of a Mediterranean Empire, 753 B.C.E.–330 C.E.

The Origins of Imperial China, 221 B.C.E.–220 C.E.

Imperial Parallels

ENVIRONMENT AND TECHNOLOGY: Water Engineering in Rome and China

According to Chinese sources, in the year 166 C.E., a group of travelers identifying themselves as delegates from Andun, the king of distant Da Qin, arrived at the court of the Chinese emperor Huan, one of the Han rulers. Andun was Marcus Aurelius Antoninus, the emperor of Rome.

These first known "Romans" to reach China probably hailed from one of Rome's eastern provinces, perhaps Egypt or Syria, and may have stretched the truth in claiming to be representatives of the Roman emperor. The Chinese officials had had no direct contact with the Roman Empire, however, and so the travelers, probably merchants hoping to trade for highly prized Chinese silk, easily got away with the imposture.

Direct or regular contact between the empires never developed, but the episode reveals that in the early centuries C.E. Rome and China dimly recognized each other's existence across the far-flung trading networks that spanned the Eastern Hemisphere. Both states, moreover, emerged from the last centuries B.C.E. and the first centuries C.E. as a new kind of empire, both qualitatively and quantitatively.

The Roman Empire encompassed the lands surrounding the Mediterranean Sea and substantial portions of inland Europe and the Middle East. The Han Empire, named for China's ruling family, stretched from the Pacific Ocean to the oases of Central Asia. The largest empires the world had yet seen, they nevertheless managed to centralize control, achieve unprecedented stability and longevity, and assert dominance over the many cultures and peoples within their borders.

Since neither empire influenced the other, what caused them to arise and flourish at the same time? Some stress supposedly common factors, such as climate change or challenges from Central Asian nomads, but no theory has won the general support of scholars.

As you read this chapter, ask yourself the following questions:

- How did the Roman and Han Empires come into being?

- What fostered their stability or instability?

- What benefits and liabilities did they confer on rulers and subjects?

ROME'S CREATION OF A MEDITERRANEAN EMPIRE, 753 B.C.E.–330 C.E.

The boot-shaped Italian peninsula, with the large island of Sicily, constitutes a bridge almost linking Europe and Africa (see Map 5.1). Rome too lay at a crossroads, being situated at the midpoint of the peninsula, about 15 miles (24 kilometers) from its western coast, where a north-south road intersected an east-west river route. The Tiber River on one side and a double ring of seven hills on the other afforded natural protection to the site.

The Apennine Mountains form Italy's spine, separating the eastern and western coastal plains, and the arc of the Alps shields it on the north. Navigable rivers and passes through the Apennines, and even through the snowcapped Alps, eased travel by merchants and armies. The Mediterranean climate afforded a long growing season and favorable conditions for a wide variety of crops. Hillside forests, today largely gone, provided timber for construction and fuel. Iron and other metals came from the region of Etruria in the northwest.

Although hills account for 75 percent of Italy's land area, the coastal plains and river valleys provide arable land, with fertile volcanic soil capable of supporting a much larger population than that of Greece. While expanding within Italy, the Roman state effectively tapped these human resources.

A Republic of Farmers

According to legend, Romulus, cast adrift on the Tiber River as a baby and nursed by a she-wolf, founded Rome in 753 B.C.E. Archaeological research, however, has revealed occupation on the Palatine Hill, one of the city's seven hills, dating to 1000 B.C.E. Several hilltop communities merged shortly before 600 B.C.E., forming an urban nucleus made possible by the draining of a swamp on the site of the future Roman Forum (civic center).

The Latin speech and cultural patterns of the inhabitants of the site resembled those of most of the other peoples of the peninsula. However, tradition remembered Etruscan immigrants arriving in the seventh century B.C.E. and being taken in; Rome came to pride itself on offering hospitality to exiles and outcasts.

Agriculture anchored the economy of early Rome, and land constituted wealth. Landownership brought social status and political privilege while buttressing fundamental values. Most early Romans cultivated their own small plots of land, but a few families managed to acquire large tracts of land. The heads of these wealthy families served in the Senate, a "Council of Elders" that dominated the politics of the Roman state. Their families constituted the senatorial class.

Tradition maintains that seven kings ruled Rome between 753 and 507 B.C.E., Romulus being the first and the tyrannical Tarquinius Superbus the last. In 507 B.C.E., members of the senatorial class, led by Brutus "the Liberator," deposed Tarquinius Superbus and instituted a *res publica,* a "public possession," or republic.

Far from being a democracy, the **Roman Republic,** which lasted from 507 to 31 B.C.E., vested power in several assemblies. Male citizens could attend their sessions, but the votes of the wealthy counted for more than the votes of the poor. The hierarchy of state officials, elected for one year, culminated in two consuls, who presided over the Senate and other assemblies and commanded the army on campaigns.

Technically an advisory council, first to the kings and later to the annually changing Republican officials, the **Roman Senate** increasingly made policy and governed. Senators nominated their sons for public offices and filled senatorial vacancies with

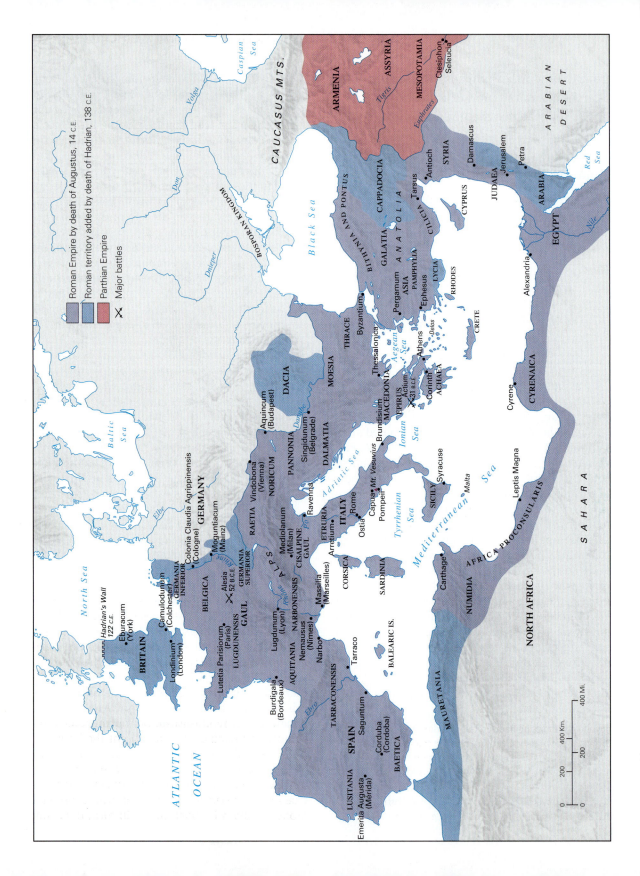

Roman Empire by death of Augustus, 14 C.E.

Roman territory added by death of Hadrian, 138 C.E.

Parthian Empire

X Major battles

CASPIAN Sea

CAUCASUS MTS.

Volga

Don

Dnieper

BOSPORAN KINGDOM

ARMENIA

ASSYRIA

MESOPOTAMIA

Ctesiphon
Seleucia

Tigris

Euphrates

Damascus

Antioch
SYRIA
Jerusalem
JUDAEA
Petra
ARABIA

ARABIAN DESERT

Red Sea

Nile

EGYPT

Alexandria

CYPRUS

CILICIA
Tarsus

CAPPADOCIA

GALATIA

BITHYNIA AND PONTUS

ANATOLIA

Pergamum
ASIA
Ephesus
LYCIA
RHODES
PAMPHYLIA

Black Sea

Byzantium

THRACE

MOESIA

DACIA

Thessalonica

MACEDONIA

EPIRUS
Actium
31 B.C.E.

ACHAEA
Corinth
Athens
Delos

Aegean Sea

CRETE

CYRENAICA

Cyrene

Baltic Sea

North Sea

Hadrian's Wall
122 C.E.

Eburacum
(York)

BRITAIN

Camulodunum
(Colchester)

Londinium
(London)

ATLANTIC OCEAN

Elbe

GERMANY

Colonia Claudia Agrippinensis
(Cologne)

GERMANIA
INFERIOR

Moguntiacum
(Mainz)

GERMANIA
SUPERIOR

RAETIA

BELGICA

Rhine

Alesia
52 B.C.E.

GAUL

Lutetia Parisiorum
(Paris)

LUGDUNENSIS

Lugdunum
(Lyon)

AQUITANIA

NARBONENSIS

Nemausus
(Nîmes)

Narbo

Massilia
(Marseilles)

Burdigala
(Bordeaux)

Rhône

TARRACONENSIS

Tarraco

Saguntum

SPAIN

Corduba
(Cordoba)

BAETICA

LUSITANIA

Emerita Augusta
(Mérida)

Ebro

BALEARIC IS.

CORSICA

SARDINIA

Vindobona
(Vienna)

NORICUM

PANNONIA

Aquincum
(Budapest)

Danube

Singidunum
(Belgrade)

DALMATIA

Mediolanum
(Milan)

CISALPINE
GAUL.

ALPS

Po

Ravenna

ETRURIA

Arretium

ITALY

Rome

Ostia

Capua

Pompeii

Mt. Vesuvius

Adriatic Sea

Brundisium

Ionian Sea

Tyrrhenian Sea

SICILY

Syracuse

Malta

Carthage

NUMIDIA

MAURETANIA

NORTH AFRICA

AFRICA PROCONSULARIS

Leptis Magna

Mediterranean Sea

SAHARA

400 Mi.

400 Km.

200

200

0

0

CHRONOLOGY

	Rome	China
	1000 B.C.E. First settlement on site of Rome	
500 B.C.E.	**507 B.C.E.** Establishment of the Republic	
		480–221 B.C.E. Warring States Period
300 B.C.E.		
	264–202 B.C.E. Wars against Carthage guarantee Roman control of western Mediterranean	**221 B.C.E.** Qin emperor unites eastern China
200 B.C.E.	**200–146 B.C.E.** Wars against Hellenistic kingdoms lead to control of eastern Mediterranean	**206 B.C.E.** Han dynasty succeeds Qin
100 B.C.E.		**140–87 B.C.E.** Emperor Wu expands the Han Empire
	88–31 B.C.E. Civil wars and failure of the Republic	
	31 B.C.E.–14 C.E. Augustus establishes the Principate	**23 C.E.** Han capital transferred from Chang'an to Luoyang
50 C.E.	**45–58 C.E.** Paul spreads Christianity in the eastern Mediterranean	
200 C.E.	**235–284 C.E.** Third-century crisis	**220 C.E.** Fall of Han Empire
300 C.E.	**324 C.E.** Constantine moves capital to Constantinople	

former officials. This self-perpetuating body, whose members served for life, brought together wealth, influence, and political and military experience.

Map 5.1   The Roman Empire   The Roman Empire came to encompass all the lands surrounding the Mediterranean Sea, as well as parts of continental Europe. When Augustus died in 14 C.E., he left instructions to his successors not to expand beyond the limits he had set, but Claudius invaded southern Britain in the mid-first century and the soldier-emperor Trajan added Romania early in the second century. Deserts and seas provided solid natural boundaries, but the long and vulnerable river border in central and eastern Europe would eventually prove expensive to defend and vulnerable to invasion by Germanic and Central Asian peoples.

Roman families consisted of several generations as well as domestic slaves. The oldest living male, the *paterfamilias,* exercised absolute authority over every family member. This *auctoritas,* enjoyed by important male members of the society as a whole, enabled a man to inspire and demand obedience from his inferiors.

Complex ties of obligation, such as the **patron/client relationship,** bound together individuals and families. *Clients* sought the help and protection of *patrons,* men of wealth and influence. A senator might have dozens or even hundreds of clients, to whom he provided legal advice and representation, physical protection, and monetary loans in tough times. In turn, the client

Statue of a Roman Carrying Busts of His Ancestors, First Century B.C.E. Roman society was extremely conscious of status, and the status of an elite Roman family was determined in large part by the public achievements of ancestors and living members. A visitor to a Roman home found portraits of distinguished ancestors in the entry hall, along with labels listing the offices they held. Portrait heads were carried in funeral processions. (Alinari/Art Resource, NY)

followed his patron out to battle, supported him in the political arena, worked on his land, and even contributed to his daughter's dowry. Throngs of

clients awaited their patrons in the morning and accompanied them to the Forum for the day's business. Especially large retinues brought great prestige. Middle-class clients of the aristocracy might be patrons to poorer men. Rome thus accepted and institutionalized inequality and made of it a system of mutual benefits and obligations.

Roman women played no public role and hence appear infrequently in sources. Nearly all information pertains to those in the upper classes. In early Rome, a woman never ceased to be a child in the eyes of the law. She started out under the absolute authority of her paterfamilias. When she married, she came under the jurisdiction of the paterfamilias of her husband's family. Unable to own property or represent herself in legal proceedings, she had to depend on a male guardian to advocate her interests.

Despite the limitations, Roman women seem less constrained than their Greek counterparts (see Chapter 4). Over time, they gained greater personal protection and economic freedom. Some took advantage of a form of marriage that left a woman under the jurisdiction of her father and independent after his death. Many stories involve strong women who greatly influenced their husbands or sons and thereby helped shape Roman history. Roman poets expressed love for women who appeared educated and outspoken, and the careers of the early emperors abound with tales of self-assured and assertive queen-mothers and consorts.

Like other Italian peoples, Romans believed in invisible, shapeless forces known as *numina*. Vesta, the living, pulsating energy of fire, dwelled in the hearth. Janus guarded the door. The Penates watched over food stored in the cupboard. Other deities resided in hills, caves, grottoes, and springs. Small offerings of cakes and liquids supplicated the favor of these spirits. Certain gods operated in larger spheres—for example, Jupiter, the god of the sky, and Mars, initially a god of agriculture as well as war.

The Romans strove to maintain the *pax deorum* ("peace of the gods"), a covenant between the gods and the Roman state. Boards of priests drawn from the aristocracy performed sacrifices and other rituals to win the gods' favor. In return, the Roman state counted on the gods for success in its undertakings. When the Romans encountered the Greeks of southern Italy they equated their major deities with gods from the Greek pantheon, such as Zeus (Jupiter) and Ares (Mars), and took over the myths attached to them.

Expansion in Italy and the Mediterranean

The fledgling Roman Republic of 500 B.C.E. did not stand out among the city-states of Latium, a region of central Italy. Three and a half centuries later, Rome commanded a huge empire encompassing virtually all the Mediterranean lands. Expansion began slowly but picked up momentum, peaking in the third and second centuries B.C.E.

Some scholars ascribe Rome's success to the greed and aggressiveness of a people fond of war. Others observe that the structure of the Roman state encouraged recourse to war, because the two consuls had only one year in office in which to gain military glory. The Romans invariably claimed they were only defending themselves. Possibly fear drove the Romans to expand their territory: each new conquest became vulnerable, necessitating ever more buffers against attack.

Ongoing friction between the pastoral hill peoples of the Apennines, who depended on herding, and the farmers of the coastal plains sparked Rome's conquest of Italy. In the fifth century B.C.E., Rome achieved leadership within a league of central Italian cities organized for defense against the hill peoples. In the fourth century B.C.E., the Romans occasionally defended the wealthy and sophisticated cities of Campania, the region on the Bay of Naples possessing the richest farmland in the peninsula. By 290 B.C.E., after three wars with the peoples of Samnium in central Italy, the Romans had extended their "protection" over nearly the entire peninsula.

The Romans consolidated their hold over Italy by granting the political, legal, and economic privileges of citizenship to conquered populations. In this, they contrasted with the Greeks, who did not share citizenship with outsiders (see Chapter 4). The Romans co-opted the most influential elements within the conquered communities and made Rome's interests their interests. Rome demanded that its Italian subjects provide soldiers. A seemingly inexhaustible reservoir of manpower bolstered military success. Rome could endure higher casualties than the enemy and prevail by sheer numbers.

Between 264 and 202 B.C.E., Rome fought two protracted wars against the Carthaginians, those energetic descendants of the Phoenicians who had settled in Tunisia and dominated the commerce of the western Mediterranean (see Chapter 3). The Roman state emerged as the master of the western Mediterranean and acquired its first overseas provinces in Sicily, Sardinia, and Spain (see Map 5.1). Between 200 and 146 B.C.E., a series of wars pitted the Roman state against the major Hellenistic kingdoms in the eastern Mediterranean (see Chapter 4). Reluctant to occupy such distant territories, the Romans withdrew their troops at the conclusion of several wars. But when the settlements they imposed failed to take root, a frustrated Roman government took over direct administration of these turbulent lands. The conquest of the Celtic peoples of Gaul (modern France; see Chapter 2) by Rome's most brilliant general, Gaius Julius Caesar, between 59 and 51 B.C.E., led to the first territorial acquisitions in Europe's heartland.

The Romans resisted extending to distant provinces the governing system and privileges of citizenship they employed in Italy. Indigenous elite groups willing to collaborate with Rome enjoyed considerable autonomy, including responsibility for local administration and tax collection. Every year a senator, usually someone who had held high office, served as governor in each province. Accompanied by a surprisingly small retinue of friends and relations who served as advisers and deputies, the governor defended the province against outside attack and internal disruption, oversaw the collection of taxes, and judged legal cases.

Over time, this system proved inadequate. Officials chosen through political connections often lacked competence, and the one-year period of service gave them little time to gain experience. A few governors extorted huge sums of money from the provincial populace. Rome still depended on the institutions and attitudes of a city-state to govern an ever-growing empire.

The Failure of the Republic

The frequent wars and territorial expansion of the third and second centuries B.C.E. set off changes in the Italian landscape. Peasant farmers spent long periods of time away from home on military service, while most of the wealth generated by conquest and empire ended up helping the upper classes purchase Italian land. Investors easily acquired the property of absent soldier-farmers by purchase, deception, or intimidation. The small self-sufficient farms of the Italian countryside, whose peasant owners provided the backbone of the Roman legions (units of 6,000 soldiers), gave way to *latifundia*, literally "broad estates," or ranches.

The new owners had ample space to graze herds of cattle or grow grapes for wine in the place of less profitable wheat. Thus, much of Italy, especially in the cities, became dependent on expensive imported grain. Meanwhile, cheap slave labor provided by war prisoners made it hard for peasants who had lost their farms to find work in the countryside. They moved to Rome and other cities, but found no work there either and ended up living in poverty. The growing urban masses, idle and prone to riot, would play a major role in the political struggles of the late Republic.

The decline of peasant farmers in Italy produced a shortage of men who owned the minimum amount of property required for military service. During a war that the Romans fought in North Africa at the end of the second century B.C.E., Gaius Marius—a "new man" as the Romans labeled politically active individuals from outside the traditional ruling class—achieved political prominence by enlisting in the legions poor, propertyless men to whom he promised farms upon retirement from military service. These grateful troops helped Marius get elected to an unprecedented (and illegal) six consulships.

Between 88 and 31 B.C.E., several ambitious individuals—Sulla, Pompey, Julius Caesar, Mark Antony, and Octavian—commanded armies that were more loyal to them than to the state. Their use of Roman troops to increase their personal power led to civil wars between military factions. The generals who seized Rome on several occasions executed their political opponents and exercised dictatorial control.

Julius Caesar's grandnephew and heir, Octavian (63 B.C.E.–14 C.E.), eliminated all rivals by 31 B.C.E. and set about refashioning the Roman system of government while retaining the offices, honors, and social prerogatives of the senatorial class. A dictator in fact, he never called himself king or emperor, claiming merely to be *princeps,* "first among equals," hence the term **Roman Principate** for the period following the Roman Republic. **Augustus,** a title Octavian received from the Senate, implied prosperity and piety and became the name by which he is known to posterity. Augustus's ruthlessness, patience, and intuitive grasp of psychology enabled him to manipulate each group in society. When he died in 14 C.E., after forty-five years of carefully veiled rule, scarcely anyone could remember the Republic. During his reign, the empire expanded into Egypt and parts of the Middle East and central Europe, leaving only the southern half of Britain and modern Romania to be added later.

So popular was Augustus that four members of his family succeeded to the position of "emperor" (as we call it) despite serious personal and political shortcomings. After the mid–first century C.E., other families obtained the post. In theory, the Senate affirmed the early emperors; in reality, the armies chose them. By the second century C.E., the so-called Good Emperors instituted a new mechanism of succession: each designated as his successor a mature man of proven ability whom he adopted as his son and with whom he shared offices and privileges.

Augustus had allied himself with the **equites,** the class of well-to-do Italian merchants and landowners second in wealth and social status only to the senatorial class. These competent and self-assured individuals became the core of a new civil service. At last Rome had an administrative bureaucracy capable of managing a large empire with considerable honesty, consistency, and efficiency.

An Urban Empire

Calling the Roman Empire of the first three centuries C.E. an "urban" empire does not mean that most people lived in cities and towns. Perhaps 80 percent of the empire's 50 to 60 million people lived in agricultural villages or on isolated farms.

The network of towns and cities served as administrative centers, however, with corresponding benefits for the urban populace.

Numerous towns had several thousand inhabitants. A handful of major cities—Alexandria in Egypt, Antioch in Syria, and Carthage—had populations of several hundred thousand. Rome itself had approximately a million residents. The largest cities put huge strains on the government's technical ability to provide food and water and remove sewage.

At Rome, the upper classes lived in elegant hillside townhouses. The house centered around an *atrium,* a rectangular courtyard with an open skylight in the ceiling to let in light and rainwater for drinking and washing. A dining room for dinner and drinking parties, an interior garden, a kitchen, and perhaps a private bath surrounded the atrium with bedrooms on an upper level. Pebble mosaics on the floors and frescoes of mythological scenes or outdoor vistas on the walls and ceilings gave a sense of openness in the absence of windows. The typical aristocrat also owned a number of villas in the countryside as retreats from the pressures of city life.

The poor inhabited crowded slums in the low-lying parts of the city. Damp, dark, and smelly, with few furnishings, their wooden tenements suffered from frequent fires. Fortunately, Romans could spend the day outdoors for much of the year.

Other cities and towns, including the ramshackle settlements that sprang up beside frontier forts, mirrored the capital city in political organization, physical layout, and appearance. A town council and two annually elected officials drawn from prosperous members of the community maintained law and order and collected both urban and rural taxes. In return for the privilege of running local affairs and in appreciation of the state's protection of their wealth and position, this "municipal aristocracy" served Rome loyally. In striving to imitate Roman senators, they lavishly endowed their cities and towns, which had little revenue of their own, with attractive elements of Roman urban life: a forum, government buildings, temples, gardens, baths, theaters, amphitheaters, and games and public entertainments of all sorts. These amenities made the situation of the urban poor superior to that of the rural poor. Poor people in a city could pass time at the baths, seek refuge from the elements under the colonnades, and attend the games.

Hard work and drudgery marked life in the countryside, relieved only by occasional festive days and the everyday pleasures of sex, family, and social exchange. Rural people had to fend for themselves in dealing with bandits, wild animals, and other hazards. People outside urban centers had little direct contact with the government beyond an occasional run-in with bullying soldiers and the dreaded arrival of the tax collector.

The concentration of ownership reversed temporarily during the civil wars that ended the Republic; it resumed under the emperors. But the end of new conquests reduced the number of slaves and forced landowners to find new labor. Landlords turned to tenant farmers, whom they allowed to live on and cultivate plots of land in return for a portion of their crop. The landowners themselves still lived in cities and hired foremen to manage their estates. Thus, wealth based on rural productivity became concentrated in the cities.

Some urban dwellers became rich from manufacture and trade. The ***pax romana*** ("Roman peace"), the safety and stability guaranteed by Roman might, favored commerce. Grain, meat, and vegetables usually could be exchanged only locally because transportation was costly and many products spoiled quickly. The city of Rome, however, depended on grain shipments from Sicily and Egypt to feed its huge population. Special naval squadrons performed this task.

Some exporters dealt in glass, metalwork, delicate pottery, and other fine manufactures. The centers of production, first located in Italy, moved into the provinces as knowledge of the necessary skills spread. Roman armies on the frontiers provided a large market, and their presence promoted the prosperity of border provinces. Other merchants traded in luxury items from beyond the empire's boundaries, especially Chinese silks, Indian spices, and Arabian incense. The tax revenues of rich provinces like Gaul (France) and Egypt flowed to Rome to support the emperor and the central government, and to the frontier provinces to subsidize the armies.

Romanization, the spread of the Latin language and Roman way of life, proved an enduring consequence of empire among the diverse peoples in the western provinces. Hellenism dominated the eastern Mediterranean (see Chapter 4). Portuguese,

Spanish, French, Italian, and Romanian evolved from the Latin language, proving that the language of the conquerors spread among the common people as well as the elite. However, in frontier areas along the Rhine and Danube Rivers, where Roman control was tenuous and migrations by Germanic peoples were changing the ethnic balance by the third century C.E., Latin made only limited headway.

The Roman government did not force Romanization. The inhabitants of the provinces themselves chose Latin and adopted cultural practices like wearing the *toga* (the traditional cloak worn by Roman male citizens). Making this choice brought advantages, as do learning English and wearing a suit and tie today in some developing nations. Latin facilitated dealings with the administration and helped merchants get contracts to supply the military. Many also must have been drawn by the aura of success surrounding the language and culture of a people who had created so vast an empire.

As towns sprang up and acquired the Roman urban amenities, they attracted ambitious members of the indigenous populations. The empire gradually and reluctantly extended Roman citizenship, with its attendant privileges, legal protections, and certain tax exemptions, to people living outside Italy. Completing a twenty-six-year term of service in the native military units that backed up the Roman legions earned soldiers citizenship that could pass to their descendants. Emperors granted citizenship to individuals or entire communities as rewards for service. Then in 212 C.E. the emperor Caracalla granted citizenship to all free, adult, male inhabitants of the empire.

The gradual extension of citizenship mirrored the empire's transformation from an Italian dominion over the Mediterranean lands into a commonwealth of peoples. As early as the first century C.E., some of the leading literary and intellectual figures came from the provinces. By the second century, even the emperors hailed from Spain, Gaul, and North Africa.

The Rise of Christianity

The Jewish homeland of Judaea (see Chapter 3), roughly equivalent to present-day Israel, came under direct Roman rule in 6 C.E. Over the next half-century, Roman governors insensitive to the Jewish belief in one god managed to increase tensions. Various kinds of opposition to Roman rule sprang up. Many Jews anticipated the arrival of the Messiah, the "Anointed One," presumed to be a military leader who would liberate the Jewish people and drive the Romans out.

It is in this context that we must see the career of **Jesus,** a young carpenter from the Galilee region in northern Israel. In place of what he considered excessive concern with money and power among Jewish leaders and perfunctory religious observance by mainstream Jews, Jesus prescribed a return to the personal faith and spirituality of an earlier age. He eventually attracted the attention of the Jewish authorities in Jerusalem, who regarded popular reformers as potential troublemakers. They turned him over to the Roman governor, Pontius Pilate. Jesus was imprisoned, condemned, and executed by crucifixion, a punishment usually reserved for common criminals. His followers, the Apostles, subsequently sought to spread his teachings and their belief that he had been resurrected (returned from death to life) among their fellow Jews.

Paul, a Jew from the Greek city of Tarsus in southern Anatolia, converted to the new creed and between 45 and 58 C.E. devoted himself to spreading the word. Traveling throughout Syria-Palestine, Anatolia, and Greece, he found most Jews unwilling to accept his claim that Jesus was the Messiah and had ushered in a new age. Frustrated, Paul redirected his efforts toward non-Jews (sometimes called "gentiles") who were also experiencing a spiritual hunger. He set up a string of Christian (from the Greek term *christos,* meaning "anointed one," given to Jesus by his followers) communities in the eastern Mediterranean.

Paul's career exemplifies the cosmopolitan nature of the Roman Empire in this era. Speaking both Greek and Aramaic, he moved comfortably between the Greco-Roman and Jewish worlds. He used Roman roads, depended on the peace guaranteed by Roman arms, called on his Roman citizenship to protect him from local authorities, and moved from city to city in his quest for converts.

In 66 C.E., tensions in Roman Judaea erupted in a revolt that lasted until 73. The Jerusalem-based Christian community, which focused on converting Jews, fell victim to the Roman reconquest. This cleared the field for Paul's non-Jewish converts, and Christianity began to diverge more and more from its Jewish roots.

The sect grew slowly but steadily. Many early converts came from disenfranchised groups: women, slaves, and the urban poor. They hoped to receive a respect not accorded them in the larger society and to obtain positions of responsibility when the early Christian communities elected their leaders. However, as the religious movement grew and prospered, it developed a hierarchy of priests and bishops and engaged in bitter disputes over theological doctrine (see Chapter 8).

As monotheists forbidden to worship other gods, early Christians met persecution from Roman officials who took their refusal to worship the emperor as a sign of disloyalty. Nevertheless, despite mob attacks and occasional government attempts at suppression, or perhaps because of them, the Christian movement continued to attract converts. By the late third century C.E., adherents to Christianity were a sizeable minority within the empire and included many educated and prosperous people holding local and imperial posts.

By the Greek Classical period, a number of "mystery" cults had gained popularity by claiming to provide secret information about the nature of life and death and promising a blessed afterlife to their adherents. In the Hellenistic and Roman periods, belief systems making similar promises arose in the eastern Mediterranean and spread throughout the Greco-Roman lands, presumably responding to a spiritual and intellectual hunger not satisfied by paganism. These included the cults of the mother-goddess Cybele in Anatolia, the Egyptian goddess Isis, and the Iranian sun-god Mithra. As we shall see shortly, the ultimate victory of Christianity over these rivals arose from historical circumstances as much as from spiritual appeal.

Technology and Transformation

The ease and safety of travel brought by Roman arms and engineering helped the early Christians spread their faith. Surviving remnants of roads, fortification walls, aqueducts, and buildings testify to the Romans' engineering expertise. Some of the best engineers served with the army, building bridges, siege works, and siege weapons. In peacetime, soldiers often worked on construction projects. **Aqueducts**—long elevated or underground conduits—used gravity to carry water from a source to an urban center. The Romans pioneered the use of arches, which allow the even distribution of great weights without thick supporting walls. The invention of concrete—a mixture of lime powder, sand, and water that could be poured into molds—enabled the construction of vast vaulted and domed interior spaces, in contrast to the rectilinear post-and-lintel designs employed by the Greeks and Egyptians.

Defending borders that stretched for thousands of miles posed a great administrative challenge. In a document released after his death, Augustus advised against expanding the empire because the costs of administration and defense would exceed any increase in revenues. His successors' reorganization and redeployment of the Roman army reflect the shift from an offensive to a defensive strategy. Mountains, deserts, and seas protected the empire at most points. But the lengthy Rhine/Danube frontier in Germany and central Europe was vulnerable and thus was guarded by forts whose relatively small garrisons were not always up to the task of repelling raiders. On more desolate frontiers in Britain and North Africa, the Romans built long walls to keep out the peoples who lived beyond.

Most of Rome's neighbors lacked sufficient technology and military organization to pose a serious threat. The one exception lay on the eastern frontier, where the Parthian kingdom controlled the lands that are today Iran and Iraq. Rome and Parthia fought exhaustingly for centuries, with neither side gaining significant territory.

The Roman state prospered for two and a half centuries after Augustus stabilized the political situation and instituted a program of reforms. In the third century C.E., cracks in the edifice became visible. Historians call the period from 235 to 284 C.E. the **third-century crisis,** a time when political, military, and economic problems nearly destroyed the empire. A frequent change of rulers marked the crisis. Twenty or more men claimed the office of emperor during this period. Most reigned for only a few months or years before being overthrown by a rival or killed by their own troops. Germanic peoples on the Rhine/Danube frontier took advantage of the disorders to raid deep into the empire. For

Roman Aqueduct near Tarragona, Spain   How to provide an adequate supply of water was a problem posed by the growth of Roman towns and cities. Aqueducts channeled water from a source, sometimes many miles away, to an urban complex, using only the force of gravity. To bring an aqueduct from high ground into the city, Roman engineers designed long, continuous rows of arches that maintained a steady downhill slope. Roman troops were often used in such large-scale construction projects. Scholars sometimes can roughly estimate the population of an ancient city by calculating the amount of water that was available to it.   (Robert Frerck/Woodfin Camp & Associates)

the first time in centuries, Roman cities built protective walls. Some regions, feeling a lack of imperial protection, turned to anyone who promised to put their interests first.

Political and military emergencies devastated the empire's economy. Buying the loyalty of the army and paying to defend the increasingly permeable frontiers drained the treasury. The resultant demands for more tax revenues from the provinces, as well as the interruption of commerce by fighting, eroded urban prosperity. Shortsighted emperors, desperate for cash, secretly reduced the amount of precious metal in Roman coins and

pocketed the excess. But the public quickly caught on, and the devalued coinage became less and less acceptable in the marketplace. Indeed, the empire reverted to a barter economy, which curtailed large-scale and long-distance commerce even more.

The municipal aristocracy, once the empire's most vital and public-spirited class, suffered heavily. As town councilors, its members had to make up any shortfall in taxes owed to the state. As the decline in trade eroded their wealth, which often derived from manufacture and commerce, many evaded their civic duties and even went into hiding.

Population shifted out of the cities and into the countryside. Many people sought employment and protection from raiders *and* government officials on the estates of wealthy and powerful country landowners. This process laid the foundation for the social and economic structures of the European Middle Ages—a period of roughly seven hundred years in which wealthy rural lords dominated a peasant population tied to the land (see Chapter 8).

Just when things looked bleakest, one man pulled the empire back from the brink. Diocletian, like several other emperors, hailed from one of the eastern European provinces most vulnerable to invasion. Of humble origins, he rose through the ranks of the army and gained power in 284. He was so successful that he ruled for over twenty years and died in bed.

To halt inflation (the process by which prices rise as money becomes worth less), Diocletian issued an edict specifying the maximum prices for various commodities and services. To ensure an adequate labor supply in vital services, he froze people in their professions and made them train their sons to succeed them. This unprecedented regulation of prices and vocations had unforeseen consequences. A "black market" arose among buyers and sellers who chose to ignore the price controls. More broadly, many imperial citizens began to see the government as an oppressive entity that no longer deserved their loyalty.

When Diocletian resigned in 305, the old divisiveness reemerged as various claimants battled for the throne. By 324, a general named **Constantine** (r. 306–337) had reunited the empire under his sole rule. In 312, Constantine won a key battle at the Milvian Bridge over the Tiber River near Rome. He later claimed that before this battle, he had seen in the sky a cross (the sign of the Christian God) superimposed on the sun. Believing that the Christian God had helped him achieve the victory, Constantine converted to Christianity. Throughout his reign, he supported the Christian church, although he tolerated other beliefs as well. Historians disagree about whether Constantine's conversion resulted from spiritual motives or from a pragmatic desire to unify the empire under a single religion. Regardless of the reason, large numbers of people now converted, because they saw that Christians had advantages over non-Christians in seeking offices and favors.

Constantine also transferred the capital in 324 from Rome to Byzantium, an ancient Greek city on the Bosporus° strait leading from the Mediterranean into the Black Sea. Renamed Constantinople° ("City of Constantine"), it represented a concentration of attention on the threatened imperial borders in eastern Europe (see Map 5.1). The cities and middle classes of the eastern provinces had better withstood the third-century crisis than those in the west. In addition, more educated people and more Christians lived in the east (see Chapter 8).

Some see the conversion of Constantine and the transfer of the imperial capital as events marking the end of Roman history. But many of the important changes that culminated during Constantine's reign had their roots in the previous two centuries, and the Roman Empire as a whole survived for at least another century. Moreover, the eastern, or Byzantine, portion of it (discussed in Chapter 8) survived Constantine by more than a thousand years. Nevertheless, the Roman Empire of the fourth century differed fundamentally from what had existed before, a fact that justifies seeing Constantine's reign as the beginning of a new epoch in the West.

THE ORIGINS OF IMPERIAL CHINA, 221 B.C.E.–220 C.E.

A fragmentation seemingly dictated by geography characterized the early history of China (see Chapter 2). The Shang (ca. 1750–1027 B.C.E.) and Zhou (1027–221 B.C.E.) wielded authority over a relatively compact zone in northeastern China. The last few centuries of nominal Zhou rule—the Warring States Period—saw rivalry among a group of small states, a situation reminiscent of the contemporary Greek city-states (see Chapter 4). As in Greece, competition and conflict fostered many elements of a national culture.

In the second half of the third century B.C.E. the Qin° state in the Wei° Valley conquered its rivals and created China's first empire (221–206 B.C.E.).

Bosporus (BAHS-puhr-uhs)   **Constantinople** (cahn-stan-tih-NO-pul)   **Qin** (chin)   **Wei** (way)

But it barely survived the death of its founder, Shi Huangdi. Power passed to a new dynasty, the Han, which ruled China from 206 B.C.E. to 220 C.E. (see Map 5.2). The imperial tradition of political and cultural unity thus begun lasted into the twentieth century and still has meaning for China today.

Resources and Population

An imperial state controlling lands of great diversity in topography, climate, plant and animal life, and human population faced greater obstacles to long-distance communications and a uniform way of life than did the Roman Empire. Rome's territories were roughly similar in climate and agriculture, and Rome benefited from an internal sea—the Mediterranean— that facilitated rapid and inexpensive transport. What resources, technologies, institutions, and values made the Chinese empire possible?

Agriculture produced the wealth and taxes that supported the institutions of imperial China. The main tax, a percentage of the annual harvest, funded government activities ranging from the luxurious lifestyle of the royal court to the military garrisons on the frontiers. The imperial capitals, first Chang'an° and later Luoyang°, housed large populations that had to be fed. As intensive agriculture spread in the Yangzi River Valley, the need to transport southern crops to the north spurred the construction of canals to connect the Yangzi with the Yellow River. The government also stored surplus grain during prosperous times for sale at reasonable prices during shortages.

To assess its labor resources, the government periodically conducted a census. Results survive for the years 2 C.E. and 140 C.E. The earlier survey indicates approximately 12 million households and 60 million people; the later, not quite 10 million households and 49 million people. Then as now, the vast majority of the population lived in the eastern river valley regions that supported intensive agriculture. The early demographic center in the Yellow River Valley and North China Plain had begun to shift south to the Yangzi River Valley by early Han times.

In the intervals between seasonal agricultural tasks, able-bodied men donated one month of la-

Chang'an (chahng-ahn)   **Luoyang** (LWOE-yahng)

bor to public building projects—palaces, temples, fortifications, and roads—or to transporting goods, excavating and maintaining canals, cultivating imperial estates, or mining. The state also required two years of military service. On the frontiers, conscripted young Chinese men built walls and forts, kept an eye on barbarian neighbors, fought when necessary, and grew crops to support themselves. Registers of land and households enabled imperial officials to keep track of money and services due. Like the Romans, the Chinese governments depended on a large population of free peasants to contribute taxes and services to the state.

Throughout the Han period, the Han Chinese gradually expanded into the territory of other ethnic groups. Population growth in the core regions and a shortage of good land spurred the pioneers onward. Sometimes the government organized new settlements—at militarily strategic sites, for example, and on the frontiers. Neighboring kingdoms also invited Chinese settlers so they could exploit their skills and learn their technologies.

Han people preferred regions suitable to the agriculture they had practiced in the eastern river valleys. On the northern frontier, they pushed back nomadic populations. They also expanded into the tropical forests of southern China and settled in the western oases. Places not suitable for their preferred kind of agriculture, particularly the steppe and deserts, did not attract them.

Hierarchy, Obedience, and Belief

The Han Chinese brought with them their social organization, values, language, and other cultural practices. The Chinese family, the basic social unit, included not only the living generations but also the previous generations—the ancestors. The Chinese believed their ancestors maintained an ongoing interest in the fortunes of the family and therefore consulted, appeased, and venerated their ancestors to maintain their favor. Viewed as a living, self-renewing organism, the family required sons to perpetuate itself and ensure the immortality offered by the ancestor cult.

The doctrine of Confucius (Kongzi), which had its origins in the sixth century B.C.E. (see Chapter 2), became a fundamental source of values in

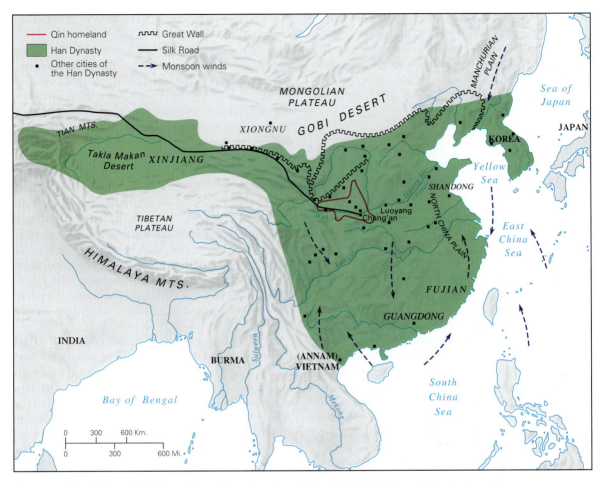

Map 5.2   Han China   The Qin and Han rulers of northeast China extended their control over all of eastern China and extensive territories to the west. A series of walls in the north and northwest, built to check the incursions of nomadic peoples from the steppes, were joined together to form the ancestor of the present-day Great Wall of China. An extensive network of roads connecting towns, cities, and frontier forts promoted rapid communication and facilitated trade. The Silk Road carried China's most treasured product to Central, South, and West Asia and the Mediterranean lands.

the imperial period. Confucianism considered hierarchy a natural social phenomenon and assigned tasks and rules of conduct to each person. Absolute authority rested with the father, who presided over the rituals that linked living family members to the ancestors. People saw themselves as having responsibilities within the domestic hierarchy according to gender, age, and family relationship rather than as individual agents. The same concepts operated in society as a whole. Peasants, soldiers, administrators, and rulers all contributed distinctively to the welfare of society. Confucianism optimistically maintained that education, imitation of role models, and self-improvement could guide people to the right path. Because the state mirrored the family, the basic family values of loyalty, obedience to authority, respect for elders and ancestors, and concern for honor and appropriate conduct carried over into relations between individuals and the state.

Contemporary written sources say little about the experiences of women. Confucian ethics stressed the impropriety of women participating in public life. Traditional wisdom about the appropriate female conduct appears in a story of the mother of the Confucian philosopher Mencius (Mengzi):

> A woman's duties are to cook the five grains, heat the wine, look after her parents-in-law, make clothes, and that is all! . . . [She] has no ambition to manage affairs outside the house. . . . She must follow the "three submissions." When she is young, she must submit to her parents. After her marriage, she must submit to her husband. When she is widowed, she must submit to her son.[1]

This ideal, perpetuated by males of the upper classes who composed most of the surviving texts, placed women under considerable pressure to conform. Women of the lower classes, less affected by Confucian ways of thinking, may have been less constrained than their more "privileged" counterparts.

After her parents arranged her marriage, a young bride went to live with her husband's family, who saw her as a stranger until she proved herself. Ability and force of personality (as well as the capacity to produce sons) could make a difference, but dissension between the wife and her mother-in-law and sisters-in-law grew out of their competition for influence with husbands, sons, and brothers and for a larger share of the economic resources held in common by the family.

Like the early Romans, the Chinese believed that divinity resided within nature rather than outside and above it. They worshiped and tried to appease the forces of nature. The state maintained shrines to the lords of rain and winds, as well as to certain great rivers and high mountains. Gathering at mounds or altars dedicated to local earth spirits, people sacrificed sheep and pigs and beat drums to promote fertility. Unusual natural phenomena like eclipses or heavy rains prompted them to tie a red cord around the sacred spot, symbolically restraining the deity. A belief that supernatural forces, bringing good and evil fortune, flowed through the landscape led experts in *feng shui*, "earth divination," to determine the most favorable location and orientation for buildings and

graves. The faithful adapted their lives to the complex rhythms of nature.

Some people sought to cheat death by taking life-enhancing drugs or building ostentatious tombs, flanked by towers or covered by mounds of earth, and filling them with what they believed they would need for a blessed afterlife. The objects in these tombs provide a wealth of knowledge about Han society.

The First Chinese Empire

As mentioned, in the second half of the third century B.C.E., the state of the **Qin** suddenly burst forth and took over the other "warring states" one by one. By 221 B.C.E., the first emperor had united the northern plain and the Yangzi River Valley under one rule, marking the creation of China and the inauguration of the imperial age. The name "China" may derive from "Qin."

The Qin ruler, entitled **Shi Huangdi** ("First Emperor"), and his adviser Li Si were able and ruthless men who exploited the exhaustion resulting from centuries of interstate rivalry. The Qin homeland in the valley of the Wei, a tributary of the Yellow River, provided a large pool of sturdy peasants to serve in the army but was less urbanized and commercialized than the kingdoms farther east. Mobilizing manpower for irrigation and flood-control works had strengthened the authority of the Qin king at the expense of the nobles and taught his administrators organizational skills.

Shi Huangdi and Li Si created a totalitarian structure that subordinated the individual to the needs of the state. They cracked down on Confucianism, regarding its demands for benevolent and nonviolent conduct from rulers as a check on the absolute power they sought. They favored instead a philosophy known as Legalism (see Chapter 2). Its major proponent, Li Si himself, considered the will of the ruler supreme. Discipline and obedience maintained through the rigid application of rewards and punishments defined the lives of his subjects.

The new regime sought to eliminate the landowning aristocracy of the conquered states and the system supporting their wealth and power. It abolished primogeniture—the eldest son's inher-

Terracotta Soldiers from the Tomb of Shi Huangdi, "First Emperor" of China   Thousands of these life-size, baked-clay figures, each with distinctive features, have been unearthed. This buried model army reflects the power and totalitarian rule of the Qin Empire.   (© 1995 Dennis Cox / ChinaStock)

itance of a family's lands—because it allowed a few individuals to accumulate vast estates. Estates now had to be broken up and passed on to several heirs.

Slaves and peasant serfs, who owed the landlord a substantial portion of their harvest, worked the lands of the aristocracy. The Qin abolished slavery and established a free peasantry who owed taxes and labor, as well as military service, to the state.

During the Warring States Period, the small states had emphasized their independence through differing symbolic practices. For example, each state had its own forms of music, with different scales, systems of notation, and instruments. The Qin imposed standard weights, measures, and coinage, a uniform law code, a common sys-

tem of writing, and even regulations governing the axle length of carts so as to standardize road and street widths.

Thousands of miles of roads, comparable in scale to the roads of the Roman Empire, connected the parts of the empire and helped move Qin armies quickly. The Qin also built canals to connect the northern and southern river systems. The 20-mile-long (32.2-kilometer-long) Magic Canal (see Environment and Technology: Water Engineering in Rome and China), which ingeniously linked two rivers that flowed in opposite directions with strong currents, is still in use. The frontier walls of the old states were gradually combined into a continuous barricade, the precursor of the Great Wall, to protect cultivated lands from raids by

ENVIRONMENT + TECHNOLOGY

Water Engineering in Rome and China

People needed water to drink; it was vital for agriculture; and it provided a rapid and economical means for transporting people and goods. Some of the most impressive technological achievements of ancient Rome and China involved hydraulic (water) engineering.

Roman cities, with their large populations, required abundant and reliable sources of water. One way to obtain it was to build aqueducts—stone channels to bring water from distant lakes and streams to the cities. The water flowing in these conduits was moved only by the force of gravity. Surveyors measured the land's elevation and plotted a course that very gradually moved downhill.

Some conduits were elevated atop walls or bridges, which made it difficult for unauthorized parties to tap the water line for their own use. Portions of some aqueducts were built underground. Still-standing aboveground segments indicate that the Roman aqueducts were well-built structures made of large cut stones closely fitted and held together by a cement-like mortar. Construction of the aqueducts was labor-intensive, and often both design and construction were carried out by military personnel. This was one of the ways in which the Roman government could keep large numbers of soldiers busy in peacetime.

Sections of aqueduct that crossed rivers presented the same construction challenges as bridges. Roman engineers lowered prefabricated wooden cofferdams—large, hollow cylinders—into the riverbed and pumped out the water so workers could descend and construct cement piers to support the arched segments of the bridge and the water channel itself. This technique is still used for construction in water.

When an aqueduct reached the outskirts of a city, the water flowed into a reservoir, where it was stored. Pipes connected the reservoir to different parts of the city. Even within the city, gravity provided the motive force until the water reached the public fountains used by the poor and the private storage tanks of individuals wealthy enough to have plumbing in their houses.

In ancient China, rivers running generally in an east-west direction were the main thoroughfares. The earliest development of complex societies centered on the Yellow River Valley, but by the beginning of the Qin Empire the Yangzi River Valley and regions farther south were

northern nomads. Shi Huangdi's financial exploitation and demands for forced labor led, after his death in 210 B.C.E., to rebellions that ended the dynasty.

The Long Reign of the Han

When the dust cleared, Liu Bang, possibly a peasant by background, had outlasted his rivals and established a new dynasty, the **Han** (206 B.C.E.–220 C.E.). Rejecting the excesses and mistakes of the Qin, he restored the institutions of a venerable past. Yet the Han administration retained much of the structure and Legalist ideology put in place by the Qin, though with less fanatical zeal. A form of Confucianism revised to address the circumstances of a large, centralized political entity tempered the Legalist methods. This Confucianism emphasized the benevolence of government and the appropriateness of particular rituals and behaviors in a manifestly hierarchical society. The Han administration became the standard for later ages, and the Chinese people today refer to themselves ethnically as Han.

After eighty years of imperial consolidation, Emperor Wu (r. 140–87 B.C.E.) launched a period of military expansion, south into Fujian, Guangdong, and present-day north Vietnam and north into Manchuria and present-day North Korea. Han armies went west, to inner Mongolia and Xinjiang°, to secure the lucrative Silk Road (see Chapter 6). However, controlling the newly acquired

Xinjiang (SHIN-jyahng)

The Magic Canal Engineers of Shi Huangdi, "First Emperor" of China, exploited the contours of the landscape to connect the river systems of northern and southern China. (From Robert Temple, *The Genius of China* [1986]. Photographer: Robert Temple)

becoming increasingly important to China's political and economic vitality. In this era the Chinese began to build canals connecting the northern and southern zones, at first for military purposes but eventually for transporting commercial goods as well. In later periods, with the acquisition of more advanced engineering skills, an extensive network of canals was built, including the 1,100-mile-long (1,771-kilometer-long) Grand Canal.

One of the earliest efforts was the construction of the Magic Canal. A Chinese historian tells us that the Qin emperor Shi Huangdi ordered his engineers to join two rivers by a 20-mile-long (32.2-kilometer-long) canal so that he could more easily supply his armies of conquest in the south. Construction of the canal posed a difficult engineering challenge, because the rivers Hsiang and Li, though coming within 3 miles (4.8 kilometers) of one another, flowed in opposite directions and with a strong current.

The engineers took advantage of a low point in the chain of hills between the rivers to maintain a relatively level grade. The final element of the solution was to build a snout-shaped mound to divide the waters of the Hsiang, funneling part of that river into an artificial channel. Several spillways further reduced the volume of water flowing into the canal, which was 15 feet wide and 3 feet deep (about 4.5 meters wide and 1 meter deep). The joining of the two rivers completed a network of waterways that permitted continuous inland water transport of goods between the latitudes of Beijing and Guangzhou (Canton), a distance of 1,250 miles (2,012 kilometers). Modifications were made in later centuries, but the Magic Canal is still in use.

territories proved expensive, so Wu's successors curtailed further expansion.

The Han Empire endured, with a brief interruption between 9 and 23 C.E., for more than four hundred years. **Chang'an,** in the Wei Valley, an ancient seat of power from which the Zhou and Qin dynasties had emerged, served as the capital from 202 B.C.E. to 8 C.E.—the period of the Early, or Western, Han. From 23 to 220 C.E., the Later, or Eastern, Han established its base in the more centrally located Luoyang.

A wall of pounded earth and brick 15 miles (24 kilometers) in circumference surrounded Chang'an, which had a population of 246,000 in 2 C.E. Contemporaries described it as a bustling place, filled with courtiers, officials, soldiers, merchants, craftsmen, and foreign visitors. Broad thoroughfares running north and south intersected others running east and west. High walls protected and restricted access to the imperial palaces, administrative offices, barracks, and storehouses. Temples and marketplaces were scattered about the civic center. Chang'an became a model of urban planning, its main features being imitated throughout the Han Empire.

Living in multistory houses, wearing fine silks, and traveling about the capital in ornate horse-drawn carriages, well-to-do officials and merchants devoted their leisure time to art and literature, occult religious practices, elegant banquets, and various entertainments: music and dance, juggling and acrobatics, dog and horse races, cock and tiger fights. In contrast, the common people inhabited a sprawling warren of alleys, living in dwellings packed "as closely as the teeth of a comb," as one poet put it.

As in the Zhou monarchy (see Chapter 2), people thought the emperor, the "Son of Heaven," enjoyed the Mandate of Heaven. He stood at the center of government and society like a father wielding authority in a family and linking the living generations with the ancestors. He brought the support of powerful imperial ancestors and guaranteed the harmonious interaction of heaven and earth. More than his Roman counterpart, he was regarded as a divinity on earth. His word was law. Failure to govern well, however, could lose him the backing of Heaven. Given their belief that events in Heaven, the natural world, and human society corresponded, his subjects might regard floods, droughts, and earthquakes as both the consequences and symptoms of ethical failure and mismanagement. Successful revolutions thus proved to many that Heaven had withdrawn its support from an unworthy ruler.

Secluded within the palace compound, surrounded by his many wives and children, servants, courtiers, and officials, the emperor presided over an unceasing round of pomp and ritual emphasizing the worship of Heaven and imperial ancestors, as well as the practical business of government. When the emperor died, his chief widow chose his heir from the male members of the ruling clan, thus making the royal compound a hive of intrigue.

A prime minister, a civil service director, and nine ministers charged with military, economic, legal, and religious responsibilities ran the central government. As in imperial Rome, the Han depended on local officials for the day-to-day administration of the vast empire. Local people collected taxes and dispatched revenues to the central government, oversaw conscription for the army and labor projects, provided local protection, and settled disputes. The remote central government rarely impinged on the lives of most citizens, who normally contacted only local officials. Who, then, were the local officials?

The Han period saw the rise of a class that scholars call the **gentry.** To weaken the rural aristocrats, the Qin and Han emperors allied themselves with the class next in wealth below them. These moderately prosperous landowners, usually men with education and valued expertise, resembled the Roman equites favored by Augustus and his successors. The local officials who came from this class became a privileged and respected group within Chinese society and made the government more efficient and responsive.

The new gentry class, with imperial support, adopted a version of Confucianism that provided a system for training officials to be intellectually capable and morally worthy of their roles and set forth a code of conduct for measuring their performance. Chinese tradition speaks of an imperial university, located outside Chang'an and said to have thirty thousand students, as well as provincial centers of learning. (Some scholars doubt that such a complex institution existed this early.)

From these centers, students entered government service, receiving distinctive emblems and privileges, including preferential legal treatment and exemption from military service, as they advanced in rank. In theory, young men from any class could rise in the state hierarchy. In practice, sons of the gentry had an advantage, because they received better training in the Confucian classics. Gradually, the gentry became a new aristocracy of sorts, banding together in cliques and family alliances that worked to advance the careers of group members.

Daoism, which originated in the Warring States Period (see Chapter 2), took deeper root among the common people in the Han period. With its emphasis on the *Dao,* or "path," of nature, its valuing of harmony with the cycles and patterns of the natural world, and its search for enlightenment through solitary contemplation and physical and mental discipline rather than education, Daoism called into question age-old beliefs and values and rejected the hierarchy, rules, and rituals of Confucianism. It urged passive acceptance of the disorder of the world, denial of ambition, contentment with simple pleasures, and trust in one's own instincts.

Technology and Trade

Chinese tradition seems to recognize the importance of technology for the success and spread of Chinese civilization. It credits the legendary first five emperors with the introduction of major new technologies.

The advent of bronze tools around 1500 B.C.E. helped open land for agriculture on the North

Han-Era (First Century B.C.E.) Stone Rubbing of a Horse-Drawn Carriage The "trace harness," a strap running across the horse's chest, was a Chinese invention that allowed horses to pull far heavier loads than were possible with the constricting throat harness used in Europe. In the Han period, officials, professionals, and soldiers who served the regime enjoyed a lifestyle made pleasant by fine clothing, comfortable transportation, servants, and delightful pastimes, but at the same time they were guided by a Confucian emphasis on duty, honesty, and appropriate behavior. (From Wu family shrine, Jiaxiang, Shantung. From *Chin-shih-so* [Jinshisuo])

China Plain. A millennium later, iron arrived. The Qin took full advantage of iron technology. Chinese metalworkers used more advanced techniques than those elsewhere in the hemisphere. Whereas Roman blacksmiths produced wrought-iron tools and weapons by hammering heated iron, the Chinese mastered the technique of liquefying iron and pouring it into molds. The resulting cast-iron and steel tools and weapons had a higher carbon content and were harder and more durable.

In the succeeding centuries, crossbows and cavalry helped the Chinese military to beat off the attacks of nomads. The watermill, which harnessed the power of running water to turn a grindstone, appeared in China long before it did in Europe. Horse collar and breast strap harnessing that did not constrict the animal's neck allowed horses in China to pull heavier loads than European horses could.

The Han rulers continued the Qin road-building program. Besides using the roads to move troops and supplies, the government created a network of official couriers using horses, boats, and even footpaths, and it provided food and shelter at relay stations. Canal construction also continued, and river navigation improved.

The population growth and increasing trade that resulted gave rise to local market centers. Some of these became county seats from which imperial officials operated. Estimates of the proportion of the population living in Han towns and cities range from 10 percent, a number roughly comparable to Europe, to 30 percent.

Silk dominated China's export trade. Silk cocoons are secreted onto the leaves of mulberry trees by silkworms. The Chinese understood this and kept it a closely guarded secret, which gave them a monopoly on the manufacture of silk. Carried through the Central Asian oases to the Middle East, India, and the Mediterranean, and passing through the hands of middlemen who added their own fees to the price, this beautiful textile may have increased in value a hundred-fold by the end of its journey. Controlling the Silk Road and its profits justified periodic military campaigns into Central Asia and the installation there of garrisons and Chinese colonies.

The Decline of the Han Empire

For the Han, as for the Romans, maintaining frontier security, particularly in the north and northwest, posed a serious challenge. In the end, non-Chinese peoples raiding across the frontier or moving into imperial territory proved a major factor in bringing the empire down.

The different ways of life of farmers, who usually accepted Han rule, and herders, who preferred their own kings, gave rise to insulting stereotypes on both sides. The settled Chinese thought of nomads as "barbarians"—rough, uncivilized people—a viewpoint much like that of the Romans who looked down on the Germanic peoples on their frontiers.

Often, the closeness of herding and farming populations led to commercial exchange. The nomads sought agricultural products and crafted goods, while the settled peoples bought horses and other herd animals and animal products. Sometimes, however, nomad raiders seized what they wanted from farming settlements. Tough and warlike because of their way of life, mounted nomads struck swiftly and as swiftly disappeared.

Although nomadic groups tended to be small and inclined to fight one another, circumstances and a charismatic leader could bring them together from time to time. In the Han period, the **Xiongnu°**, a great confederacy of Turkic peoples, threatened the empire, though they were usually contained on the frontier by cavalry forces created to match the nomads' mobility. This strategy made access to good horses and pastureland a state priority. Other strategies included maintaining garrisons and colonies of soldier-farmers on the frontier, settling compliant nomads within the borders to serve as a buffer, bribing nomad chiefs to promote disunity, and paying protection money. The "tributary system," in which nomad rulers accepted Chinese supremacy and exchanged tribute payments for marriages to Chinese princesses, receptions at court, and imperial gifts worth more than the tribute, often worked well.

Yet military vigilance burdened Han finances and made the economic troubles of later Han times worse. Despite measures to suppress the aristocracy and turn land over to a free peasantry,

by the end of the first century B.C.E. nobles and successful merchants again acquired control of huge estates, and many peasants sought their protection against the exactions of the imperial government. This trend spread over the next two centuries. As strongmen largely independent of imperial control emerged, the central government lost tax revenues and manpower. Military conscription broke down, forcing the government to hire more and more foreign soldiers and officers. These served for pay, but their loyalty was weak.

The Han regime fell in 220 C.E. for several reasons: factional intrigues within the ruling clan, official corruption and inefficiency, uprisings of desperate and hungry peasants, the spread of banditry, unsuccessful reform movements, attacks by nomads, and the ambitions of rural warlords. China entered a period of political fragmentation and economic and cultural regression that lasted until the rise of the Sui° and Tang° dynasties in the late sixth and early seventh centuries C.E., a story that we take up in Chapter 9.

IMPERIAL PARALLELS

The similarities between the Han and Roman Empires begin with the family, comprising in both cultures the living generations who obeyed an all-powerful patriarch. Strong loyalties and obligations bound the family members. Obedience, respect for superiors, piety, and a strong sense of duty and honor—family values that individuals carried into the wider social and political world—created a pervasive social cohesion.

Agriculture provided the fundamental economic activity and source of wealth for both. Government revenues derived primarily from taxes on the annual harvest. Both empires depended on a free peasantry for military service and compulsory labor. Conflicts over landownership and land use prompted political and social turmoil in both territories. Autocratic rulers secured their positions by seizing some of the aristocrats' lands and reallocating them to small farmers (while keeping extensive

---

Xiongnu (SHE-OONG-noo)

Sui (sway)   **Tang** (tahng)

tracts for themselves). They pretended that these revolutionary changes simply restored venerable institutions. The later reversal of this process, as wealthy noblemen once again acquired estates and turned peasants into tenant farmers, signaled the erosion of state authority.

Spreading from ethnically homogeneous cores, both empires encompassed diverse ecosystems, populations, and ways of life, and the cultural unity they fostered has persisted, at least in part, to the present day. The skills of Roman and Chinese farmers produced high yields that led to population growth. This pressure caused Italian and Han settlers to move from the core areas into new regions, bringing along their languages, beliefs, customs, and technologies. Many people in the conquered lands adopted the culture of the rulers to attach themselves to a "winning cause."

In order to administer far-flung territories in an era when a man on horseback provided the fastest communication, the central governments delegated considerable autonomy to local officials. These elites identified their own interests with those of the state they served. Thus developed a kind of civil service, staffed by educated and capable members of a prosperous middle class.

Roads built for moving troops became the highways of commerce and the thoroughfares by which imperial culture spread. A network of cities and towns provided each empire with local administrative centers while fostering commerce and radiating imperial culture into the surrounding countryside.

Cities and towns modeled themselves on the capital cities—Rome and Chang'an. Travelers could find in outlying regions the same types of buildings and urban amenities that they knew from the capital, though on a smaller scale. People living in urban centers enjoyed the advantages of empire most. The majority of the population, however, resided in the countryside.

The Roman and Han Empires faced similar defense problems: long borders far from the capital and aggressive neighbors. The staggering cost of building walls and maintaining frontier forts and garrisons eventually eroded economic prosperity. Rough neighbors acquired the skills that had given the empires an initial advantage and thereby closed the technology gap. Increasingly beholden to the military, governments demanded more taxes and

services from the hard-pressed civilians. This cost them the loyalty of many people, some of whom sought protection on the estates of powerful landowners. Eventually, borders were overrun and the central governments collapsed. Ironically, the new immigrants who took control respected the imperial culture so deeply that they maintained it to the best of their abilities.

The respective ends of the two empires had different long-term consequences, however. The Chinese imperial model revived in subsequent eras, but the lands of the Roman Empire never again achieved such unification. Several interrelated factors help to account for the different outcomes.

First, these cultures assessed the obligations of the individual to the state differently. In China, the individual was deeply embedded in the larger social group. Family hierarchy, unquestioning obedience, and solemn rituals of deference to elders and ancestors served as the model for society and the state. Respect for authority still remains a deep-seated habit. Qin Legalism made the word of the emperor law, and Confucianism sanctified hierarchy and governed the conduct of professionals and public officials. Although the Roman family had its own hierarchy and traditions of obedience, the family did not serve as the model for society and state. Rome also lacked a philosophy like Confucianism that could perpetuate its political organization and social code.

Economic and social mobility, which enable some people to rise dramatically in wealth and status, tend to enhance the significance of the individual. Ancient China presented few opportunities for individuals to improve their economic status. The government frequently disparaged and constrained the merchant class. The more important role of commerce in the Roman Empire, and the resulting economic mobility, heightened Roman awareness of individual rights.

Although Roman emperors tried to create an ideology to bolster their position, persistent Republican traditions and ambiguities about the imperial office deliberately cultivated by Augustus hampered this effort. Consequently, the dynastic principle remained weak, the cult of the emperor lacked spiritual content, and the army or the Senate chose the emperors. This contrasts sharply with the Chinese belief in the emperor as the Son of Heaven with privileged access to the power of the royal ancestors. Thus, Rome's fall left to later ages no compelling basis for reviving the position of emperor or imperial territorial claims.

Finally, weight must be given to new belief systems that took root in each empire. In insisting on monotheism and one doctrine of truth, Christianity negated the emperor's pretensions to divinity and would not compromise with pagan beliefs. Christianity's spread, and the collapse of the western half of the empire in the fifth century C.E. (see Chapter 8), constituted an irreversible break with the past. In contrast, Buddhism, which came to China in the early centuries C.E. and flourished in the post-Han era (see Chapter 9), accommodated traditional Chinese values and beliefs more easily.

CONCLUSION

Both the Roman Empire and the first Chinese empire arose from relatively small states. Discipline and military toughness enabled them to subdue other small quarreling neighbors. Ultimately, they unified widespread territories under strong central governments.

The Qin Empire could emerge during the reign of a single ruler because many elements of unification were already present. The Shang and Zhou states had controlled large core areas in the North China Plain. The "First Emperor" drew on the preexisting concept of the Mandate of Heaven, which claimed divine backing for the ruler as the Son of Heaven, and the Legalist ideology justified authoritarian measures. Although resistance to the harshness of the new order soon brought down the Qin dynasty, its Han successors moderated and built on Qin institutions to create a durable imperial regime.

The early Roman state enjoyed no similar precedents. The Roman Empire grew more slowly, with solutions evolving by trial and error. The Republican form of government, appropriate for an Italian city-state, proved inadequate to the demands of empire, and Rome's military success led to social and economic disruption and acute political conflict. Out of this crisis emerged the institutions of the Principate, which persevered for several centuries. Even so, the Roman emperors never developed an effective ideology of rule.

In both empires, professional armies maintained order and defended the frontiers. Educated civil servants kept records and collected taxes to support the military and government. Roads, cities, standardized systems of money and measurement, and widely understood languages facilitated travel, commerce, and communication. The culture of the imperial center spread, and this shared culture, as well as shared self-interest, bonded local elites to the empire's ruling class.

For long periods, these stabilizing forces, bringing peace, prosperity, and improved standards of living, outweighed the weaknesses inherent in the two systems. Over time, however, the costs of defending lengthy frontiers drained imperial treasuries and increased taxation. As hard-pressed subjects sought the protection of rural landowners, cities shrank, commerce declined, and the central government found fewer ways of compelling tax payment and fewer recruits for the army.

In the end, both empires succumbed to external pressures and internal divisions. In China, however, the imperial tradition and the class structure and value system that maintained it lived on (see Chapters 2 and 9). In Europe, North Africa, and the Middle East, the Roman Empire passed into history. In the next chapter, we will look at some of the forces leading these areas in different directions.

◾ Key Terms

Roman Republic	aqueducts
Roman Senate	third-century crisis
patron/client relationship	Constantine
Roman Principate	Qin
Augustus	Shi Huangdi
equites	Han
pax romana	Chang'an
Romanization	gentry
Jesus	Xiongnu
Paul	

◾ Suggested Reading

Tim Cornell and John Matthews, *Atlas of the Roman World* (1982), offers a general introduction, pictures, and maps. Michael Grant and Rachel Kitzinger, eds., *Civilization of the Ancient Mediterranean*, 3 vols. (1988), contains essays with bibliographies by specialists on different aspects of the Greek and Roman worlds. Michael Grant, *History of Rome* (1978), is a good survey. Naphtali Lewis and Meyer Reinhold, eds., *Roman Civilization,* 2 vols. (1951), contains ancient sources in translation.

For Roman institutions, attitudes, and values, see J. A. Crook, *Law and Life of Rome: 90 B.C.–A.D. 212* (1967). Michael Crawford, *The Roman Republic,* 2d ed. (1993), and Chester G. Starr, *The Roman Empire, 27 B.C.–A.D. 476: A Study in Survival* (1982), discuss the state during the Republic and Principate. Fergus Millar, *The Emperor in the Roman World (31 B.C.–A.D. 337)* (1977), studies the position of the princeps. Barbara Levick, *The Government of the Roman Empire: A Sourcebook* (2000), presents original texts in translation.

For Roman military matters, see W. V. Harris, *War and Imperialism in Republican Rome* (1979), and Stephen L. Dyson, *The Creation of the Roman Frontier* (1985). For military technology, see M. C. Bishop, *Roman Military Equipment: From the Punic Wars to the Fall of Rome* (1993). David Macaulay, *City: A Story of Roman Planning and Construction* (1974), and K. D. White, *Greek and Roman Technology* (1984), reveal the wonders of Roman engineering. For urban life, see John E. Stambaugh, *The Ancient Roman City* (1988).

Kevin Greene, *The Archaeology of the Roman Economy* (1986), deals with social and economic history. Suzanne Dickson, *The Roman Family* (1992), Lionel Casson, *Everyday Life in Ancient Rome* (1998), and U. E. Paoli, *Rome: Its People, Life and Customs* (1983), look at social life. Jo-Ann Shelton, ed., *As the Romans Did: A Sourcebook in Roman Social History* (1998), offers translated sources. Elaine Fantham, Helene Peet Foley, Natalie Boymel Kampen, Sarah B. Pomeroy, and H. Alan Shapiro, *Women in the Classical World: Image and Text* (1994), provides an up-to-date discussion. Mary R. Lefkowitz and Maureen B. Fant, eds., *Women's Life in Greece and Rome: A Source Book in Translation* (1982), and Thomas Wiedemann, ed., *Greek and Roman Slavery* (1981), offer translated sources on these topics.

John Boardman, Jasper Griffin, and Oswyn Murray, eds., *The Roman World* (1988), contains chapters on Roman intellectual and literary achievements. Ronald Mellor, ed., *The Historians of Ancient Rome* (1998), provides context for reading historical sources. Michael von Albrecht, *History of Roman Literature: From Livius Andronicus to Boethius: With Special Regard to Its Influence on World Literature* (1997), and Nancy H. Ramage and Andrew Ramage, *The Cambridge Illustrated History of Roman Art* (1991), survey Roman creativity. Robert Turcan, *The Gods of Ancient Rome: Religion in Everyday Life from Archaic to Imperial Times* (2000), and R. M. Ogilvie, *The Romans and Their Gods in the Age of Augustus* (1969), introduce public

and private religion. Joseph F. Kelly, *The World of the Early Christians* (1997), W. H. C. Frend, *The Rise of Christianity* (1984), and R. A. Markus, *Christianity in the Roman World* (1974), investigate Christian matters, and Michael Grant, *The Jews in the Roman World* (1973) and Erich S. Gruen, *Diaspora: Jews Amidst Greeks and Romans* (2002), explore the complicated situation of Jews in the Roman Empire.

For the geography and demography of China, see the well-illustrated *Cultural Atlas of China* (1983), by Caroline Blunden and Mark Elvin. Basic surveys include Jacques Gernet, *A History of Chinese Civilization* (1982), and John K. Fairbank, *China: A New History* (1992). For greater depth on the ancient period, see Edward L. Shaughnessy and Michael Loewe, eds., *The Cambridge History of Ancient China* (1998); Denis Twitchett and Michael Loewe, eds., *The Cambridge History of China,* vol. 1, *The Ch'in and Han Empires, 221 B.C.–A.D. 220* (1986); Michele Pirazzoli-t'Serstevens, *The Han Dynasty* (1982); and Kwang-chih Chang, *The Archaeology of Ancient China,* 4th ed. (1986). W. de Bary, W. Chan, and B. Watson, eds., have assembled sources in translation in *Sources of Chinese Tradition* (1960). Sima Qian, *Historical Records* (1994), translated by Raymond Dawson, provides a readable selection of varied material pertaining to the Qin dynasty compiled by the premier historian of the Han period.

For social history, see Michael Loewe, *Everyday Life in Early Imperial China During the Han Period, 202 B.C.–A.D. 220* (1988), and Barbara N. Ramusack and Sharon L. Sievers, eds., *Restoring Women to History. Women in Asia* (1999). For economic history and foreign relations, see Hsin-ju Liu, *Ancient India and Ancient China: Trade and Religious Exchanges, A.D. 1–600* (1994), and Ying-shih Yu, *Trade and Expansion in Han China* (1967). For scientific and technological achievements, see Robert Temple, *The Genius of China: 3,000 Years of Science, Discovery, and Invention* (1986).

Benjamin I. Schwartz addresses intellectual history in *The World of Thought in Ancient China* (1985). Spiritual matters are taken up by Laurence G. Thompson, *Chinese Religion: An Introduction,* 3d ed. (1979). For art, see Michael Sullivan, *A Short History of Chinese Art,* rev. ed. (1970), and Jessica Rawson, *Ancient China: Art and Archaeology* (1980).

For a stimulating comparison of the Roman and Han Empires that emphasizes their differences, see the first chapter of S. A. M. Adshead, *China in World History,* 2d ed. (1995).

■ Notes

1. Patricia Buckley Ebrey, ed., *Chinese Civilization and Society: A Sourcebook* (New York: Free Press, 1981), 33–34.

6 Networks of Communication and Exchange, 300 B.C.E.–600 C.E.

CHAPTER OUTLINE

The Silk Road

The Sasanid Empire, 224–600

The Indian Ocean Maritime System

Routes Across the Sahara

Sub-Saharan Africa

The Spread of Ideas

DIVERSITY AND DOMINANCE The Indian Ocean Trading World

Inspired by the tradition of the Silk Road, a Chinese poet named Po Zhuyi° nostalgically wrote:

> Iranian whirling girl, Iranian whirling girl—
> Her heart answers to the strings,
> Her hands answer to the drums.
> At the sound of the strings and drums, she raises her arms,
> Like whirling snowflakes tossed about, she turns in her twirling dance.
> Iranian whirling girl,
> You came from Sogdiana°.
> In vain did you labor to come east more than ten thousand tricents.
> For in the central plains there were already some who could do the Iranian whirl,
> And in a contest of wonderful abilities, you would not be their equal.[1]

The western part of Central Asia, the region around Samarkand° and Bukhara° known in the eighth century C.E. as Sogdiana, was 2,500 miles (4,000 kilometers) from the Chinese capital of Chang'an°. Caravans took more than four months to trek across the mostly unsettled deserts, mountains, and grasslands.

The Silk Road connecting China and the Middle East across Central Asia fostered the exchange of agricultural goods, manufactured products, and ideas. Musicians and dancing girls traveled, too—as did camel pullers, merchants, monks, and pilgrims. The Silk Road was not just a means of bringing peoples and parts of the world into contact; it was a social system.

Po Zhuyi (boh joo-yee)   **Sogdiana** (sog-dee-A-nuh)

Samarkand (SAM-mar-kand)   **Bukhara** (boo-CAR-ruh)
Chang'an (chahng-ahn)

With every expansion of territory, the growing wealth of temples, kings, and emperors enticed traders to venture ever farther afield for precious goods. For the most part, the customers were wealthy elites. But the new products, agricultural and industrial processes, and foreign ideas and customs these long-distance traders brought with them sometimes affected an entire society.

Travelers and traders seldom owned much land or wielded political power. Socially isolated (sometimes by law) and secretive because any talk about markets, products, routes, and travel conditions could help their competitors, they nevertheless contributed more to drawing the world together than did all but a few kings and emperors.

This chapter examines the social systems and historical impact of exchange networks that developed between 300 B.C.E. and 600 C.E. in Europe, Asia, and Africa. The Silk Road and the Indian Ocean maritime system illustrate the nature of long-distance trade in this era.

Trading networks were not the only medium for the spread of new ideas, products, and customs. This chapter compares developments along trade routes with folk migration by looking at the beginnings of contact across the Sahara and the simultaneous spread of Bantu-speaking peoples within sub-Saharan Africa. Chapter 5 discussed a third pattern of cultural contact and exchange, that taking place with the beginning of Christian missionary activity in the Roman Empire. This chapter further explores the process by examining the spread of Buddhism in Asia and Christianity in Africa and Asia.

As you read this chapter, ask yourself the following questions:

- What role does technology play in long-distance trade?

- How does geography affect trade patterns?

- How do human groups affect communication between regions?

- Why do some goods and ideas travel more easily than others?

- How do the three modes of cultural contact and exchange—long-distance trade, folk migration, and religious missionary activity—affect patterns of dominance and diversity?

THE SILK ROAD

Archaeology and linguistic studies show that the peoples of Central Asia engaged in long-distance movement and exchange from at least 1500 B.C.E. In Roman times Europeans became captivated by the idea of a trade route linking the lands of the Mediterranean with China by way of Mesopotamia, Iran, and Central Asia. The **Silk Road,** as it came to be called in modern times, experienced several periods of heavy use (see Map 6.1). The first began around 100 B.C.E.

Origins and Operations

The Seleucid kings who succeeded to the eastern parts of Alexander the Great's empire in the third century B.C.E. focused their energies on Mesopotamia and Syria. This allowed an Iranian nomadic leader to establish an independent kingdom in northeastern Iran. The **Parthians,** a people originally from east of the Caspian Sea, had become a major force by 247 B.C.E. They left few written sources, and recurring wars with Greeks and Romans to the west prevented travelers from the Mediterranean region from gaining firm knowledge of their kingdom. It seems likely, however, that their being located on the threshold of Central Asia and sharing customs with steppe nomads farther to the east helped foster the Silk Road.

In 128 B.C.E. a Chinese general named Zhang Jian° made his first exploratory journey across the deserts and mountains of Inner Asia on behalf of

Zhang Jian (jahng jee-en)

Iranian Musicians from Silk Road This three-color glazed pottery figurine, 23 inches (58.4 centimeters) high, comes from a northern Chinese tomb of the Tang era (sixth to ninth centuries C.E.). The musicians playing Iranian instruments confirm the migration of Iranian culture across the Silk Road. At the same time, dishes decorated by the Chinese three-color glaze technique were in vogue in northern Iran. (The National Museum of Chinese History)

mately led eighteen expeditions, as the originator of overland trade with the western lands, and they credited him with personally introducing a whole garden of new plants and trees to China.

Long-distance travel suited the people of the steppes more than the Chinese. The populations of Ferghana and neighboring regions included many nomads who followed their herds. Their migrations had little to do with trade, but they provided pack animals and controlled transit across their lands. The trading demands that brought the Silk Road into being were Chinese eagerness for western products, especially horses, and on the western end, the organized Parthian state, which had captured the flourishing markets of Mesopotamia from the Seleucids.

By 100 B.C.E., Greeks could buy Chinese silk from Parthian traders in Mesopotamian border entrepôts. Yet caravans also bought and sold goods along the way in prosperous Central Asian cities like Samarkand and Bukhara. These cities grew and flourished, often under the rule of local princes.

General Zhang definitely seems to have brought two plants to China: alfalfa and wine grapes. The former provided the best fodder for horses. In addition, Chinese farmers adopted pistachios, walnuts, pomegranates, sesame, coriander, spinach, and other new crops. Chinese artisans and physicians made good use of other trade products, such as jasmine oil, oak galls (used in tanning animal hides, dyeing, and making ink), sal ammoniac (for medicines), copper oxides, zinc, and precious stones.

Traders going west from China carried new fruits such as peaches and apricots, which the Romans mistakenly attributed to other eastern lands, calling them Persian plums and Armenia plums, respectively. They also carried cinnamon, ginger, and other spices that could not be grown in the West.

THE SASANID EMPIRE, 224–600

The rise of the **Sasanid Empire** in Iran brought a continuation of the rivalry between Rome and the Parthians along the Euphrates frontier and an intensification of trade along the Silk Road; but

Emperor Wu of the Han dynasty. After crossing the broad and desolate Tarim Basin north of Tibet, he reached the fertile valley of Ferghana° and for the first time encountered westward-flowing rivers. There he found horse breeders whose animals far outclassed any horses he had seen. Later Chinese historians looked on General Zhang, who ulti-

---

Ferghana (fer-GAH-nuh)

C H R O N O L O G Y			
	Silk Road	**Indian Ocean Trade**	**Saharan Trade**
500 B.C.E.	**247 B.C.E.** Parthian rule begins in Iran **128 B.C.E.** General Zhang Jian reaches Ferghana **100 B.C.E.–300 C.E.** Kushans rule northern Afghanistan and Sogdiana		**500 B.C.E.–ca. 1000 C.E.** Bantu migrations **ca. 200 B.C.E.** Camel nomads in southern Sahara
1 C.E.	**1st cent. C.E.** First evidence of the stirrup	**1st cent. C.E.** *Periplus of the Erythaean Sea;* Indonesian migration to Madagascar	**46 B.C.E.** First mention of camels in northern Sahara
300 C.E.	**ca. 400** Buddhist pilgrim Faxian travels Silk Road		**ca. 300** Beginning of camel nomadism in northern Sahara

otherwise it differed greatly from its Parthian predecessor. Ardashir, a descendant of an ancestor named Sasan, defeated the Parthians around 224. Unlike the Parthians, who originated as nomads in northeastern Iran, the Sasanids came from the southwest, the same region that earlier gave rise to the Achaemenids (see Chapter 4).

In contrast to the sparse material remains of the Parthian period, Sasanid silver work and silk fabrics testify to the sumptuous and sedentary lifestyle of the warrior elite. Cities in Iran were small walled communities that served more as military strongpoints protecting long-distance trade than as centers of population and production.

The Silk Road now brought many new crops to Mesopotamia. Sasanid farmers pioneered in planting cotton, sugar cane, rice, citrus trees, eggplants, and other crops adopted from India and China. Although the acreage devoted to new crops increased slowly, these products became important consumption and trade items in later centuries.

The Sasanids established their Zoroastrian faith (see Chapter 4), which the Parthians had not particularly stressed, as a state religion similar to Christianity in the Byzantine Empire (see Chapter 5). The proclamation of Christianity and Zoroastrianism as official faiths marked the fresh emergence of religion as an instrument of politics both within and between the empires. This politicization of religion greatly affected the culture of the Silk Road.

Both Zoroastrianism and Christianity practiced intolerance. A late-third-century inscription in Iran boasts of the persecutions of Christians, Jews, and Buddhists carried out by the Zoroastrian high priest. Yet sizeable Christian and Jewish communities remained, especially in Mesopotamia. Similarly, from the fourth century onward, councils of Christian bishops declared many theological beliefs heretical—so unacceptable that they were un-Christian.

Christians became pawns in the political rivalry with the Byzantines and were sometimes persecuted, sometimes patronized, by the Sasanid kings. In 431 a council of bishops called by the Byzantine emperor declared the Nestorian Christians heretics for overemphasizing the humanness of Christ. The Nestorians believed that a human nature and a divine nature coexisted in Jesus and that Mary was not the mother of God, as many other Christians maintained, but the mother of the human Jesus. After the bishops' ruling, the Nestorians sought refuge under the Sasanid shah and engaged in missionary activities along the Silk Road.

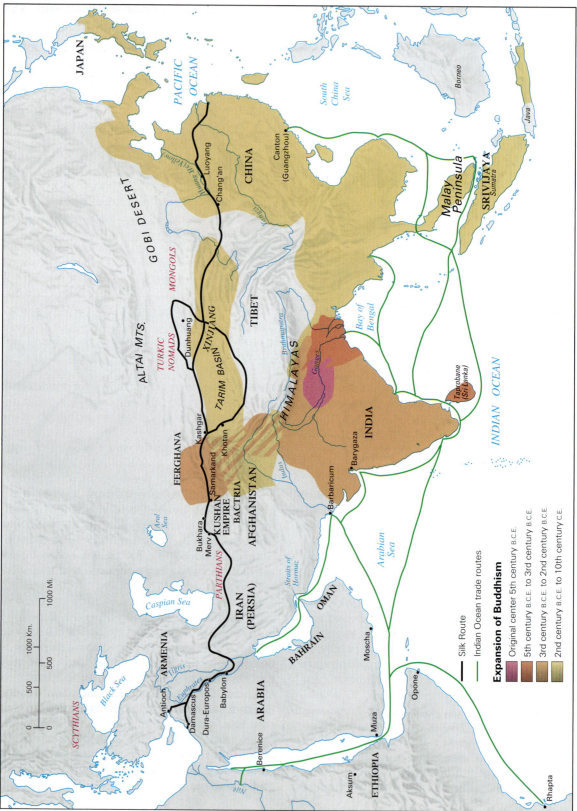

JAPAN

PACIFIC
OCEAN

Borneo

South
China
Sea

GOBI DESERT

ALTAI MTS.

MONGOLS

CHINA

Canton
(Guangzhou)

Luoyang

Chang'an

Huang He (Yellow)

Java

Sumatra

SRIVIJAYA

Malay
Peninsula

TURKIC
NOMADS

Dunhuang

XINJIANG

TIBET

TARIM BASIN

HIMALAYAS

Brahmaputra

Bay of
Bengal

Ganges

INDIAN OCEAN

Kashgar

Khotan

Indus

INDIA

Barygaza

Taprobane
(Sri Lanka)

FERGHANA

Samarkand

BACTRIA

AFGHANISTAN

Bukhara

Merv

KUSHAN
EMPIRE

Barbaricum

Aral
Sea

PARTHIANS

Straits of
Hormuz

Arabian
Sea

Caspian Sea

IRAN
(PERSIA)

OMAN

BAHRAIN

Moscha

ARMENIA

Tigris

Euphrates

Black Sea

SCYTHIANS

Antioch

Babylon

Damascus

Dura-Europos

ARABIA

Berenice

Muza

Opone

ETHIOPIA

Aksum

Nile

Rhapta

1000 Mi.

1000 Km.

500

500

0

0

Silk Route

Indian Ocean trade routes

Expansion of Buddhism

Original center 5th century B.C.E.

5th century B.C.E. to 3rd century B.C.E.

3rd century B.C.E. to 2nd century B.C.E.

2nd century B.C.E. to 10th century C.E.

A parallel episode within Zoroastrianism transpired in the third century. A preacher named Mani founded a new religion in Mesopotamia: Manichaeism. He preached a dualist faith—a struggle between Good and Evil—theologically derived from Zoroastrianism. Although at first Mani enjoyed the favor of the shah, he and many of his followers were martyred in 276. His religion survived and spread widely, particularly along the Silk Road. Nestorian missionaries thus competed with Manichaean missionaries for converts in Central Asia.

The Impact of the Silk Road

As trade became a more important part of Central Asian life, the Iranian-speaking peoples increasingly settled in trading cities and surrounding farm villages. By the sixth century C.E., nomads originally from the Altai Mountains farther east had spread across the steppes and become the dominant pastoral group. These peoples spoke Turkic languages unrelated to the Iranian tongues. The nomads continued to live in the round, portable felt huts called yurts that can still occasionally be seen in Central Asia, but prosperous individuals, both Turks and Iranians, built stately homes decorated with brightly colored wall paintings. The paintings show people wearing Chinese silks and Iranian brocades and riding on richly outfitted horses and camels. They also indicate an avid interest in Buddhism (see below), which competed with Nestorian Christianity, Manichaeism, and Zoroastrianism in a lively and inquiring intellectual milieu.

Missionary influences exemplify the impact of foreign customs and beliefs on the peoples along the Silk Road. Military technology affords an example of the opposite phenomenon, steppe customs radiating into foreign lands. Chariot warfare and the use of mounted bowmen originated in Central Asia and spread eastward and westward through military campaigns and folk migrations that began in the second millennium B.C.E. and recurred throughout the period of the Silk Road.

Evidence of the **stirrup,** one of the most important inventions, comes first from the Kushan people who ruled northern Afghanistan in approximately the first century C.E. At first a solid bar, then a loop of leather to support the rider's big toe, and finally a device of leather and metal or wood supporting the instep, the stirrup gave riders far greater stability in the saddle—which itself was in all likelihood an earlier Central Asian invention.

Using stirrups, a mounted warrior could supplement his bow and arrow with a long lance and charge his enemy at a gallop without fear that the impact of his attack would push him off his mount. Far to the west, the stirrup made possible the armored knights who dominated the battlefields of Europe (see Chapter 8), and it contributed to the superiority of the Tang cavalry in China (see Chapter 9).

THE INDIAN OCEAN MARITIME SYSTEM

A multilingual, multiethnic society of seafarers established the **Indian Ocean Maritime System,** a trade network across the Indian Ocean and the South China Sea. These people left few records and seldom played a visible part in the rise and fall of kingdoms and empires, but they forged increasingly strong economic and social ties between the coastal lands of East Africa, southern Arabia, the Persian Gulf, India, Southeast Asia, and southern China.

This trade took place in three distinct regions: (1) In the South China Sea, Chinese and Malays (including Indonesians) dominated trade. (2) From the east coast of India to the islands of Southeast Asia, Indians and Malays were the main traders. (3) From the west coast of India to the Persian Gulf and the east coast of Africa, merchants and sailors were predominantly Persians and Arabs. However, Chinese and Malay sailors could and did voyage to East Africa, and Arab and Persian traders reached southern China.

Map 6.1 Asian Trade and Communication Routes The overland Silk Road was vulnerable to political disruption, but it was much shorter than the maritime route from the South China Sea to the Red Sea, and ships were more expensive than pack animals. Moreover, China's political centers were in the north.

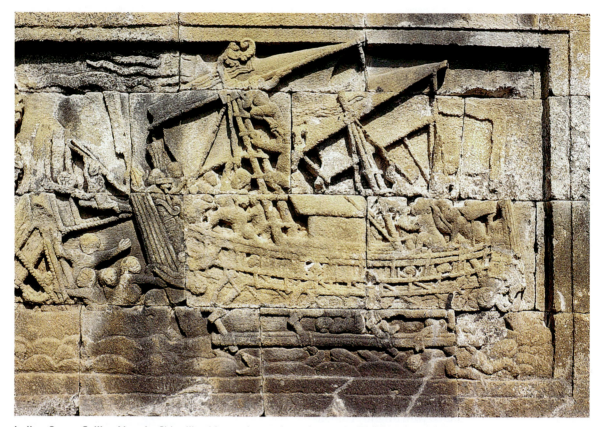

Indian Ocean Sailing Vessel Ships like this one, in a rock carving on the Buddhist temple of Borobodur in Java, probably carried colonists from Indonesia to Madagascar. (Allan Eaton/Ancient Art & Architecture)

From the time of Herodotus in the fifth century B.C.E., Greek writers regaled their readers with stories of marvelous voyages down the Red Sea into the Indian Ocean and around Africa from the west. Most often, they attributed such trips to the Phoenicians, the most fearless of Mediterranean seafarers. Occasionally a Greek appears. One such was Hippalus, a Greek ship's pilot who was said to have discovered the seasonal monsoon winds that facilitate sailing across the Indian Ocean (see Diversity and Dominance: The Indian Ocean Trading World).

Of course, the regular, seasonal alternation of steady winds could not have remained unnoticed for thousands of years, waiting for an alert Greek to happen along. The great voyages and discoveries made before written records became common

should surely be attributed to the peoples who lived around the Indian Ocean rather than to interlopers from the Mediterranean Sea. The story of Hippalus resembles the Chinese story of General Zhang Jian, whose role in opening trade with Central Asia overshadows the anonymous contributions made by the indigenous peoples. The Chinese may indeed have learned from General Zhang and the Greeks from Hippalus, but other people played important roles anonymously.

Mediterranean sailors of the time of Alexander used square sails and long banks of oars to maneuver among the sea's many islands and small harbors. Indian Ocean vessels relied on roughly triangular lateen sails and normally did without oars in running before the wind on long ocean stretches. Mediterranean shipbuilders nailed their vessels together. The planks of Indian Ocean ships were pierced, tied together with palm fiber, and caulked with bitumen. Mediterranean sailors rarely ventured out of sight of land. Indian Ocean sailors, thanks to the monsoon winds, could cover long reaches entirely at sea.

These technological differences prove that the world of the Indian Ocean developed differently from the world of the Mediterranean Sea, where the Phoenicians and Greeks established colonies that maintained contact with their home cities (see Chapters 3 and 4). The traders of the Indian Ocean, where distances were greater and contacts less frequent, seldom retained political ties with their homelands. The colonies they established were sometimes socially distinctive but rarely independent of the local political powers.

Origins of Contact and Trade

By 2000 B.C.E. Sumerian records indicate regular trade between Mesopotamia, the islands of the Persian Gulf, Oman, and the Indus Valley. However, this early trading contact broke off, and later Mesopotamian trade references mention East Africa more often than India.

A similarly early chapter in Indian Ocean history concerns migrations from Southeast Asia to Madagascar, the world's fourth largest island, situated off the southeastern coast of Africa. About two thousand years ago, people from one of the many Indonesian islands of Southeast Asia established themselves in that forested, mountainous land 6,000 miles (9,500 kilometers) from home. They could not possibly have carried enough supplies for a direct voyage across the Indian Ocean, so their route must have touched the coasts of India and southern Arabia. No physical remains of their journeys have been discovered, however.

Apparently, the sailing canoes of these people plied the seas along the increasingly familiar route for several hundred years. Settlers farmed the new land and entered into relations with Africans who found their way across the 250-mile-wide (400-kilometer-wide) Mozambique° Channel around the fifth century C.E. Descendants of the seafarers preserved the language of their homeland and some

Mozambique (moe-zam-BEEK)

of its culture, such as the cultivation of bananas, yams, and other native Southeast Asian plants. These food crops spread to mainland Africa. But the memory of their distant origins gradually faded, not to be recovered until modern times, when scholars established the linguistic link between the two lands.

The Impact of Indian Ocean Trade

The demand for products from the coastal lands inspired mariners to persist in their long ocean voyages. Africa produced exotic animals, wood, and ivory. Since ivory also came from India, Mesopotamia, and North Africa, the extent of African ivory exports cannot be determined. The highlands of northern Somalia and southern Arabia grew the scrubby trees whose aromatic resins were valued as frankincense and myrrh. Pearls abounded in the Persian Gulf, and evidence of ancient copper mines has been found in Oman in southeastern Arabia. India shipped spices and manufactured goods, and more spices came from Southeast Asia, along with manufactured items, particularly pottery, obtained in trade with China. In sum, the Indian Ocean trading region had a great variety of highly valued products. Given the long distances and the comparative lack of islands, however, the volume of trade there was undoubtedly much lower than in the Mediterranean Sea.

Furthermore, the culture of the Indian Ocean ports was often isolated from the hinterlands, particularly in the west. The coasts of the Arabian peninsula, the African side of the Red Sea, southern Iran, and northern India (today's Pakistan) were mostly barren desert. Ports in all these areas tended to be small, and many suffered from meager supplies of fresh water. Farther south in India, the monsoon provided ample water, but steep mountains cut off the coastal plain from the interior of the country. Thus few ports between Zanzibar and Sri Lanka had substantial inland populations within easy reach. The head of the Persian Gulf was one exception: ship-borne trade was possible from the port of Apologus (later called Ubulla, the precursor of modern Basra) as far north as Babylon and, from the eighth century C.E., nearby Baghdad.

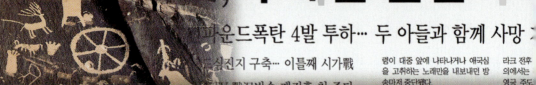

DIVERSITY AND DOMINANCE

THE INDIAN OCEAN TRADING WORLD

*T*he most revealing description of ancient trade in the Indian Ocean and of the diversity and economic forces shaping the Indian Ocean trading system, *The Periplus of the Erythraean Sea, a sailing itinerary (periplus in Greek), was composed in the first century C.E. by an unknown Greco-Egyptian merchant. It highlights the diversity of peoples and products from the Red Sea to the Bay of Bengal and illustrates the comparative absence of a dominating political force in the Indian Ocean trading system. Historians believe that the descriptions of market towns were based on firsthand experience. Information on more remote regions was probably hearsay (see Map 6.1).*

Of the designated ports on the Erythraean Sea [Indian Ocean], and the market-towns around it, the first is the Egyptian port of Mussel Harbor. To those sailing down from that place, on the right hand . . . there is Berenice. The harbors of both are at the boundary of Egypt. . . .

On the right-hand coast next below Berenice is the country of the Berbers. Along the shore are the Fish-Eaters, living in scattered caves in the narrow valleys. Further inland are the Berbers, and beyond them the Wild-flesh-Eaters and Calf-Eaters, each tribe governed by its chief; and behind them, further inland, in the country towards the west, there lies a city called Meroe.

Below the Calf-Eaters there is a little market-town on the shore . . . called Ptolemais of the Hunts, from which the hunters started for the interior under the dynasty of the Ptolemies. . . . But the place has no harbor and is reached only by small boats. . . .

Beyond this place, the coast trending toward the south, there is the Market and Cape of Spices, an abrupt promontory, at the very end of the Berber coast toward the east. . . . A sign of an approaching storm . . . is that the deep water becomes more turbid and changes its color. When this happens they all run to a large promontory called Tabae, which offers safe shelter. . . .

Beyond Tabae [lies] . . . another market-town called Opone . . . [I]n it the greatest quantity of cinnamon is produced . . . and slaves of the better sort, which are brought to Egypt in increasing numbers. . . .

[Ships also come] from the places across this sea, from . . . Barygaza, bringing to these . . . market-towns the products of their own places; wheat, rice, clarified butter, sesame oil, cotton cloth . . . and honey from the reed called sacchari [sugar cane]. Some make the voyage especially to these market-towns, and others exchange their cargoes while sailing along the coast. This country is not subject to a King, but each market-town is ruled by its separate chief.

Beyond Opone, the shore trending more toward the south . . . this coast [the Somali region of Azania, or East Africa] is destitute of harbors . . . until the Pyralax islands [Zanzibar]. . . . [A] little to the south of south-west . . . is the island Menuthias [Madagascar], about three hundred stadia from the mainland, low and wooded, in which there are rivers and many kinds of birds and the mountain-tortoise. . . . In this place there are sewed boats, and canoes hollowed from single logs. . . .

Two days' sail beyond, there lies the very last market-town of the continent of Azania, which is called Rhapta [Dar es-Salaam]; which has its name from the sewed boats (*rhapton ploiarion*) . . . ; in which there is ivory in great quantity, and tortoise-shell. Along this coast live men of piratical habits, very great in stature, and under separate chiefs for each place. [One] chief governs it under some ancient right that subjects it to the sovereignty of the state that is become first in Arabia. And the people of Muza [Mocha in Yemen] now hold it under his authority, and send thither many large ships; using Arab captains and agents, who are familiar with the natives and intermarry with them, and who know the whole coast and understand the language. . . .

And these markets of Azania are the very last of the continent that stretches down on the right hand from Berenice; for beyond these places the unexplored ocean curves around toward the west, and running along by the regions to the south of Aethiopia and Libya and Africa, it mingles with the western sea. . . .

Beyond the harbor of Moscha [Musqat in Oman] . . . a mountain range runs along the shore; at the end of which, in a row, lie seven islands. . . . Beyond these there is a barbarous region which is no longer of the same Kingdom, but now belongs to Persia. . . .

[T]here follows not far beyond, the mouth of the Persian Gulf, where there is much diving for the pearl-mussel. . . . At the upper end of this Gulf there is a market-town designated by law called Apologus, situated near . . . the River Euphrates.

Sailing [southeast] through the mouth of the Gulf, after a six-days' course there is another market-town of Persia called Ommana. . . . [L]arge vessels are regularly sent from Barygaza, loaded with copper and sandalwood and timbers of teakwood and logs of black-wood and ebony. . . .

Beyond this region . . . there follows the coast district of Scythia, which lies above toward the north; the whole marshy; from which flows down the river Sinthus [Indus], the greatest of all the rivers that flow into the Erythraean Sea, bringing down an enormous volume of water. . . . This river has seven mouths, very shallow and marshy, so that they are not navigable, except the one in the middle; at which by the shore, is the market-town, Barbaricum. . . . [I]nland behind it is the metropolis of Scythia . . . it is subject to Parthian princes who are constantly driving each other out. . . .

The country inland from Barygaza is inhabited by numerous tribes. . . . Above these is the very warlike nation of the Bactrians, who are under their own king. And Alexander, setting out from these parts, penetrated to the Ganges. . . . [T]o the present day ancient drachmae are current in Barygaza, coming from this country, bearing inscriptions in Greek letters, and the devices of those who reigned after Alexander. . . .

Inland from this place and to the east, is the city called Ozene [Ujjain]. . . . [F]rom this place are brought down all things needed for the welfare of the country about Barygaza, and many things for our trade: agate and carnelian, Indian muslins. . . .

There are imported into this market-town, wine, Italian preferred, also Laodicean and Arabian; copper, tin, and lead; coral and topaz; thin clothing and inferior sorts of all kinds . . . gold and silver coin, on which there is a profit when exchanged for the money of the country. . . . And for the King there are brought into those places very costly vessels of silver, singing boys, beautiful maidens for the harem, fine wines, thin clothing of the finest weaves, and the choicest ointments. There are exported from these places [spices], ivory, agate and carnelian . . . cotton cloth of all kinds, silk cloth. . . .

Beyond Barygaza the adjoining coast extends in a straight line from north to south. . . . The inland country back from the coast toward the east comprises many desert regions and great mountains; and all kinds of wild beasts—leopards, tigers, elephants, enormous serpents, hyenas, and baboons of many sorts; and many populous nations, as far as the Ganges. . . .

This whole voyage as above described . . . they used to make in small vessels, sailing close around the shores of the gulfs; and Hippalus was the pilot who by observing the location of the ports and the conditions of the sea, first discovered how to lay his course straight across the ocean. . . .

About the following region, the course trending toward the east, lying out at sea toward the west is the island Palaesimundu, called by the ancients Taprobane [Sri Lanka]. . . . It produces pearls, transparent stones, muslins, and tortoise-shell. . . .

Beyond this, the course trending toward the north, there are many barbarous tribes, among whom are the Cirrhadae, a race of men with flattened noses, very savage; another tribe, the Bargysi; and the Horse-faces and the Long-faces, who are said to be cannibals.

After these, the course turns toward the east again, and sailing with the ocean to the right and the shore remaining beyond to the left, Ganges comes into view. . . . And just opposite this river there is an island in the ocean, the last part of the inhabited world toward the east, under the rising sun itself; it is called Chryse; and it has the best tortoise-shell of all the places on the Erythraean Sea.

QUESTIONS FOR ANALYSIS

1. Of what importance were political organization and ethnicity to a traveling merchant?

2. How might a manual like this have been used?

3. To what extent can the observations of a Greco-Egyptian merchant be taken as evidence for understanding how merchants from other lands saw the trade in the Indian Ocean?

Source: Excerpts from W. H. Schoff (tr. & ed.), The Periplus of the Erythraean Sea: Travel and Trade in the Indian Ocean by a Merchant of the First Century (London, Bombay & Calcutta, 1912).

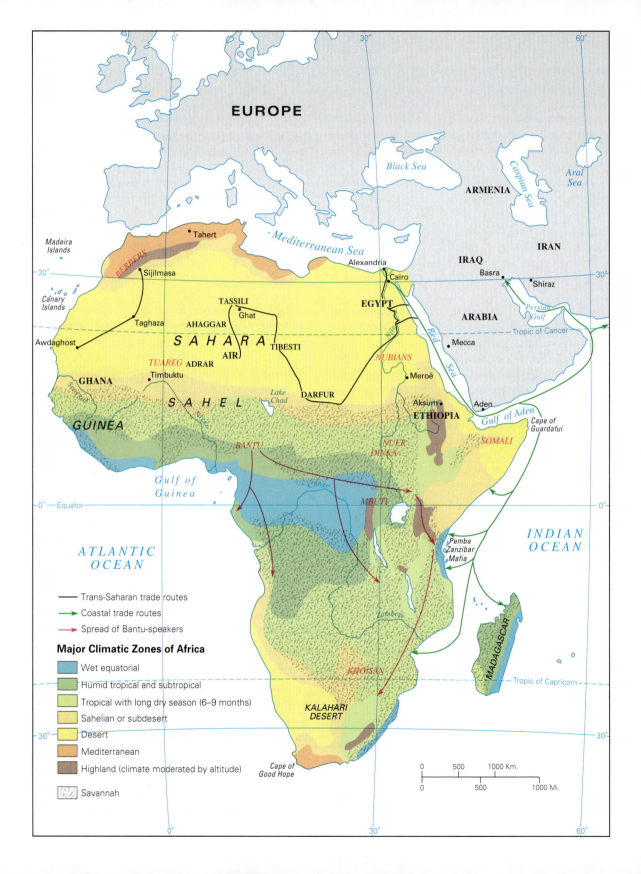

EUROPE

Madeira
Islands

Black Sea

Caspian Sea

Aral
Sea

ARMENIA

Mediterranean Sea

IRAN

30°

Tahert

BERBERS

Sijilmasa

Alexandria

Cairo

IRAQ

Basra

30°

Shiraz

Canary
Islands

Taghaza

TASSILI

Ghat

EGYPT

ARABIA

Persian
Gulf

Awdaghost

AHAGGAR

S A H A R A

AIR

TIBESTI

Tropic of Cancer

Mecca

Red Sea

TUAREG ADRAR

NUBIANS

GHANA

Timbuktu

Meroë

Senegal

S A H E L

Lake
Chad

DARFUR

Aksum

Aden

GUINEA

ETHIOPIA

Gulf of Aden

Cape of
Guardafui

BANTU

NUER
DINKA

SOMALI

Gulf of
Guinea

Congo

MBUTI

0° — Equator

0°

INDIAN
OCEAN

ATLANTIC
OCEAN

Pemba
Zanzibar
Mafia

Zambezi

MADAGASCAR

Trans-Saharan trade routes

Coastal trade routes

Spread of Bantu-speakers

Major Climatic Zones of Africa

Wet equatorial

Humid tropical and subtropical

Tropical with long dry season (6–9 months)

Sahelian or subdesert

Desert

Mediterranean

Highland (climate moderated by altitude)

Savannah

KHOISAN

Tropic of Capricorn

30°

KALAHARI
DESERT

30°

Cape of
Good Hope

0   500   1000 Km.

0   500   1000 Mi.

0°

30°

60°

Map 6.2 Africa and the Trans-Saharan Trade Routes
The Sahara and the surrounding oceans isolated most of Africa from foreign contact before 1000 C.E. The Nile Valley, a few trading points on the east coast, and limited trans-desert trade provided exceptions to this rule; but the dominant forms of sub-Saharan African culture originated far to the west, north of the Gulf of Guinea.

By contrast, eastern India, the Malay Peninsula, and Indonesia afforded more hospitable and densely populated shores with easier access to inland populations. Though the fishers, sailors, and traders of the western Indian Ocean system supplied a long series of kingdoms and empires, none of these consumer societies became primarily maritime in orientation, as the Greeks and Phoenicians did in the Mediterranean. In the east, in contrast, seaborne trade and influence seem to have been important even to the earliest states of Southeast Asia.

In coastal areas throughout the Indian Ocean system, small groups of seafarers sometimes had a significant social impact despite their usual lack of political power. Women seldom accompanied the men on long sea voyages, so sailors and merchants often married local women in port cities. The families thus established were bilingual and bicultural. As in many other situations in world history, women played a crucial though not well-documented role as mediators between cultures. Not only did they raise their children to be more cosmopolitan than children from inland regions, but they also introduced the men to customs and attitudes that they carried with them when they returned to sea. As a consequence, the designation of specific seafarers as Persian, Arab, Indian, or Malay often conceals mixed heritages and a rich cultural diversity.

ROUTES ACROSS THE SAHARA

The windswept Sahara, a desert stretching from the Red Sea to the Atlantic Ocean and broken only by the Nile River, isolates sub-Saharan Africa from the Mediterranean world (see Map 6.2). The current dryness of the Sahara dates only to about 2500 B.C.E. The period of drying out that preceded that date lasted twenty-five centuries and encompassed several cultural changes. During that time, travel between a slowly shrinking number of grassy areas was comparatively easy. However, by 300 B.C.E., scarcity of water was restricting travel to a few difficult routes initially known only to desert nomads. Trade over **trans-Saharan caravan routes,** at first only a trickle, eventually expanded into a significant stream.

Early Saharan Cultures

Sprawling sand dunes, sandy plains, and vast expanses of exposed rock make up most of the great desert. Stark and rugged mountain and highland areas separate its northern and southern portions. The cliffs and caves of these highlands, the last spots where water and grassland could be found as the climate changed, preserve rock paintings and engravings that constitute the primary evidence for early Saharan history.

Though dating is difficult, what appear to be the earliest images, left by hunters in much wetter times, include elephants, giraffes, rhinoceros, crocodiles, and other animals that have long been extinct in the region. Overlaps in the artwork indicate that the hunting societies were gradually joined by new cultures based on cattle breeding and well adapted to the sparse grazing that remained. Domestic cattle may have originated in western Asia or in North Africa. They certainly reached the Sahara before it became completely dry. The beautiful paintings of cattle and scenes of daily life seen in the Saharan rock art depict pastoral societies that bear little similarity to any in western Asia. The people seem physically akin to today's West Africans, and the customs depicted, such as dancing and wearing masks, as well as the breeds of cattle, particularly those with piebald coloring (splotches of black and white), strongly suggest later societies to the south of the Sahara. These factors support the hypothesis that some southern cultural patterns originated in the Sahara.

Overlaps in artwork also show that horse herders succeeded the cattle herders. The rock art changes dramatically in style, from the superb

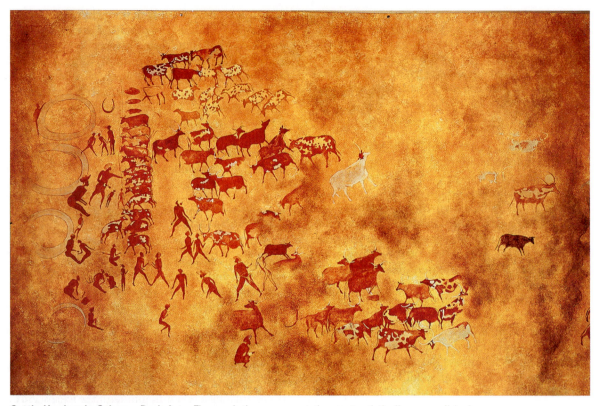

Cattle Herders in Saharan Rock Art   These paintings represent the most artistically accomplished type of Saharan art. Herding societies of modern times living in the Sahel region south of the Sahara strongly resemble the society depicted here.   (Henri Lhote)

realism of the cattle pictures to sketchier images that are often strongly geometric. Moreover, the horses are frequently shown drawing light chariots. According to the most common theory, intrepid charioteers from the Mediterranean shore drove their flimsy vehicles across the desert and established societies in the few remaining grassy areas of the central Saharan highlands. Some scholars suggest possible chariot routes that refugees from the collapse of the Mycenaean and Minoan civilizations of Greece and Crete (see Chapter 3) might have followed deep into the desert around the twelfth century B.C.E. However, no archaeological evidence of actual chariot use in the Sahara has been discovered, and it is difficult to imagine large numbers of refugees from the politically chaotic

Mediterranean region driving chariots into a waterless, trackless desert in search of a new homeland somewhere to the south.

As with the cattle herders, therefore, the identity of the Saharan horse breeders and the source of their passion for drawing chariots remain a mystery. Only with the coming of the camel is it possible to make firm connections with the Saharan nomads of today through the depiction of objects and geometric patterns still used by the veiled, blue-robed Tuareg° people of the highlands in southern Algeria, Niger, and Mali.

Some historians maintain that the Romans inaugurated an important trans-Saharan trade, but

---

Tuareg (TWAH-reg)

they lack firm archaeological evidence. More plausibly, Saharan trade relates to the spread of camel domestication. Supporting evidence comes from rock art, where overlaps of images imply that camel riders in desert costume constitute the latest Saharan population. The camel-oriented images are decidedly the crudest to be found in the region.

The first mention of camels in North Africa comes in a Latin text of 46 B.C.E. Since the native camels of Africa probably died out before the era of domestication, the domestic animals probably reached the Sahara from Arabia, probably by way of Egypt in the first millennium B.C.E. They could have been adopted by peoples farther and farther to the west, from one central Saharan highland to the next, only much later spreading northward and coming to the attention of the Romans. Camel herding made it easier for people to move away from the Saharan highlands and roam the deep desert.

Trade Across the Sahara

Linkage between two different trading systems, one in the south, the other in the north, developed slowly. Southern traders concentrated on supplying salt from large deposits in the southern desert to the peoples of sub-Saharan Africa. Traders from the equatorial forest zone brought forest products, such as kola nuts (a condiment and source of caffeine) and edible palm oil, to trading centers near the desert's southern fringe. Each received the products they needed in their homelands from the other, or from the farming peoples of the **Sahel°**—literally "the coast" in Arabic, the southern borderlands of the Sahara (see Map 6.2). Middlemen who were native to the Sahel played an important role in this trade, but precise historical details are lacking.

In the north, Roman colonists supplied Italy with agricultural products, primarily wheat and olives. Surviving mosaic pavements depicting scenes from daily life show that people living on the farms and in the towns of the interior consumed Roman manufactured goods and shared Roman styles. This northern pattern began to

change only in the third century C.E. with the decline of the Roman Empire, the abandonment of many Roman farms, the growth of nomadism, and a lessening of trade across the Mediterranean.

SUB-SAHARAN AFRICA

The Indian Ocean network and later trade across the Sahara provided **sub-Saharan Africa,** the portion of Africa south of the Sahara, with a few external contacts. The most important African network of cultural exchange from 300 B.C.E. to 1100 C.E., however, arose within the region and took the form of folk migration. These migrations and exchanges put in place enduring characteristics of African culture.

A Challenging Geography

Many geographic obstacles impede access to and movement within sub-Saharan Africa (see Map 6.2). The Sahara, the Atlantic and Indian Oceans, and the Red Sea form the boundaries of the region. With the exception of the Nile, a ribbon of green traversing the Sahara from south to north, the major river systems empty into oceans: the Senegal, Niger, and Zaire° Rivers empty into the Atlantic, and the Zambezi River empties into the Mozambique Channel of the Indian Ocean. Rapids limit the use of these rivers for navigation.

Stretching over 50 degrees of latitude, sub-Saharan Africa encompasses dramatically different environments. A 4,000-mile (6,500-kilometer) trek from the southern edge of the Sahara to the Cape of Good Hope would take a traveler from the flat, semiarid **steppes** of the Sahel region to tropical **savanna** covered by long grasses and scattered forest, and then to **tropical rain forest** on the lower Niger and in the Zaire Basin. The rain forest gives way to another broad expanse of savanna, followed by more steppe and desert, and finally by a region of temperate highlands at the southern extremity, located as far south of the equator as Greece and

---

Sahel (SAH-hel)

Zaire (zah-EER)

Sicily are to its north. East-west travel is comparatively easy in the steppe and savanna regions—a caravan from Senegal to the Red Sea would have traversed a distance comparable to that of the Silk Road—but difficult in the equatorial rain-forest belt and across the mountains and deep rift valleys that abut the rain forest to the east and separate East from West Africa.

The Development of Cultural Unity

Cultural heritages shared by the educated elites within each region—heritages that some anthropologists call **"great traditions"**—typically include a written language, common legal and belief systems, ethical codes, and other intellectual attitudes. They loom large in written records as traditions that rise above the diversity of local customs and beliefs commonly distinguished as **"small traditions."**

By the year 1 C.E. sub-Saharan Africa had become a distinct cultural region, though one not shaped by imperial conquest or characterized by a shared elite culture, a "great tradition." The cultural unity of sub-Saharan Africa rested on similar characteristics shared to varying degrees by many popular cultures, or "small traditions." These had developed during the region's long period of isolation from the rest of the world and had been refined, renewed, and interwoven by repeated episodes of migration and social interaction. Historians know little about this complex prehistory. Thus, to a greater degree than in other regions, they call on anthropological descriptions, oral history, and comparatively late records of various "small traditions" to reconstruct the broad outlines of cultural formation.

Sub-Saharan Africa's cultural unity is less immediately apparent than its diversity. By one estimate, Africa is home to two thousand distinct languages, many corresponding to social and belief systems endowed with distinctive rituals and cosmologies. There are likewise numerous food production systems, ranging from hunting and gathering—very differently carried out by the Mbuti° Pygmies of the equatorial rain forest and the Khoisan° peoples of the southwestern deserts—to

Mbuti (m-BOO-tee)   **Khoisan** (KOI-sahn)

the cultivation of bananas, yams, and other root crops in forest clearings and of sorghum and other grains in the savanna lands. Pastoral societies, particularly those depending on cattle, display somewhat less diversity across the Sahel and savanna belt from Senegal to Kenya.

Sub-Saharan Africa covered a larger and more diverse area than any other cultural region of the first millennium C.E. and had a lower overall population density. Thus societies and polities had ample room to form and reform, and a substantial amount of space separated different groups. The contacts that did occur did not last long enough to produce rigid cultural uniformity.

In addition, for centuries external conquerors could not penetrate the region's natural barriers and impose a uniform culture. The Egyptians occupied Nubia, and some traces of Egyptian influence appear in Saharan rock art farther west, but the Nile cataracts and the vast swampland in the Nile's upper reaches blocked movement farther south. The Romans sent expeditions against pastoral peoples living in the Libyan Sahara but could not incorporate them into the Roman world. Not until the nineteenth century did outsiders gain control of the continent and begin the process of establishing an elite culture—that of European imperialism.

African Cultural Characterisitics

European travelers who got to know the sub-Saharan region well in the nineteenth and twentieth centuries observed broad commonalities underlying African life and culture. In agriculture, the common technique was cultivation by hoe and digging stick. Musically, different groups of Africans played many instruments, especially types of drums, but common features, particularly in rhythm, gave African music as a whole a distinctive character. Music played an important role in social rituals, as did dancing and wearing masks, which often showed great artistry in their design.

African kingdoms varied, but kingship displayed common features, most notably the ritual isolation of the king himself. Fixed social categories—age groupings, kinship divisions, distinct gender roles and relations, and occupational groupings—also show resemblances from one region to another, even in societies too small to organize themselves into kingdoms. Though not hierarchical, these categories played a role similar to the divisions between noble, commoner, and slave prevalent where kings ruled. Such indications of underlying cultural unity have led modern observers to identify a common African quality throughout most of the region, even though most sub-Saharan Africans themselves did not perceive it. An eminent Belgian anthropologist, Jacques Maquet, has called this quality "Africanity."

Some historians hypothesize that this cultural unity emanated from the peoples who once occupied the southern Sahara. In Paleolithic times, periods of dryness alternated with periods of wetness as the Ice Age that locked up much of the world's fresh water in glaciers and icecaps came and went. When European glaciers receded with the waning of the Ice Age, a storm belt brought increased wetness to the Saharan region. Rushing rivers scoured deep canyons. Now filled with fine sand, those canyons are easily visible on flights over the southern parts of the desert. As the glaciers receded farther, the storm belt moved northward to Europe, and dryness set in after 5000 B.C.E. As a consequence, runs the hypothesis, the region's population migrated southward, becoming increasingly concentrated in the Sahel, which may have been the initial incubation center for Pan-African cultural patterns.

Increasing dryness and the resulting difficulty in supporting the population would have driven some people out of this core into more sparsely settled lands to the east, west, and south. In a parallel development farther to the east, migration away from the growing aridity of the desert seems to have contributed to the settling of the Nile Valley and the emergence of the Old Kingdom of Egypt (see Chapter 1).

The Advent of Iron and the Bantu Migrations

Archaeology confirms that agriculture had become common between the equator and the Sahara by the early second millennium B.C.E. It then spread southward, displacing hunting and gathering as a way of life. Moreover, botanical evidence indicates that banana trees, probably introduced to southeastern Africa from Southeast Asia, made their way north and west, retracing in the opposite direction the presumed migration routes of the first agriculturists.

Archaeology has also uncovered traces of copper mining in the Sahara from the early first millennium B.C.E. Copper appears in the Niger Valley somewhat later and in the Central African copper belt after 400 C.E. Most important of all, iron smelting began in northern sub-Saharan Africa in the early first millennium C.E. and spread southward from there.

Many historians believe that the secret of smelting iron, which requires very high temperatures, was discovered only once, by the Hittites of Anatolia (modern Turkey) around 1500 B.C.E. (see Chapter 3). If that is the case, it is hard to explain how iron smelting reached sub-Saharan Africa. The earliest evidence of ironworking from the kingdom of Meroë, situated on the upper Nile and in cultural contact with Egypt, is no earlier than the evidence from West Africa (northern Nigeria). Even less plausible than the Nile Valley as a route of technological diffusion is the idea of a spread southward from Phoenician settlements in North Africa, since archaeological evidence has failed to substantiate the vague Greek and Latin accounts of Phoenician excursions to the south.

A more plausible scenario focuses on Africans' discovering for themselves how to smelt iron. Some historians suggest that they might have done so while firing pottery in kilns. No firm evidence exists to prove or disprove this theory.

Linguistic analysis provides the strongest evidence of extensive contacts among sub-Saharan Africans in the first millennium C.E.—and offers suggestions about the spread of iron. More than three hundred languages spoken south of the equator belong to the branch of the Niger-Congo family known as **Bantu,** after the word meaning "people" in most of the languages.

The distribution of the Bantu languages both north and south of the equator is consistent with a divergence beginning in the first millennium B.C.E. By comparing core words common to most of the languages, linguists have drawn some conclusions about the original Bantu-speakers, whom they call "proto-Bantu." These people engaged in fishing, using canoes, nets, lines, and hooks. They lived in permanent villages on the edge of the rain forest, where they grew yams and grains and harvested wild palm nuts from which they pressed oil. They possessed domesticated goats, dogs, and perhaps other animals. They made pottery and cloth. Linguists surmise that the proto-Bantu homeland was near the modern boundary of Nigeria and Cameroon.

Because the presumed home of the proto-Bantu lies near the known sites of early iron smelting, migration by Bantu-speakers seems a likely mechanism for the southward spread of iron. The migrants probably used iron axes and hoes to hack out forest clearings and plant crops. According to this scenario, their actions would have established an economic basis for new societies capable of sustaining much denser populations than could earlier societies dependent on hunting and gathering alone. Thus the period from 500 B.C.E. to 1000 C.E. saw a massive transfer of Bantu traditions and practices southward, eastward, and westward and their transformation, through intermingling with preexisting societies, into Pan-African traditions and practices.

THE SPREAD OF IDEAS

Ideas, like social customs, religious attitudes, and artistic styles, can spread along trade routes and through folk migrations. In both cases, documenting the dissemination of ideas, particularly in preliterate societies, poses a difficult historical problem.

Ideas and Material Evidence

Historians know about some ideas only through the survival of written sources. Other ideas do not depend on writing but are inherent in material objects studied by archaeologists and anthropologists. Customs surrounding the eating of pork are a case in point. Scholars disagree about whether pigs became domestic in only one place, from which the practice of pig keeping spread elsewhere, or whether several peoples hit on the same idea at different times and in different places.

Southeast Asia was an important early center of pig domestication. Anthropological studies tell us that the eating of pork became highly ritualized in this area and that it was sometimes allowed only on ceremonial occasions. On the other side of the Indian Ocean, wild swine were common in the Nile swamps of ancient Egypt. There, too, pigs took on a sacred role, being associated with the evil god Set, and eating them was prohibited. The biblical prohibition on the Israelites' eating pork, echoed later by the Muslims, probably came from Egypt in the second millennium B.C.E.

In a third locale in eastern Iran, an archaeological site dating from the third millennium B.C.E. provides evidence of another religious taboo relating to pork. Although the area around the site was swampy and home to many wild pigs, not a single pig bone has been found. Yet small pig figurines seem to have been used as symbolic religious offerings, and the later Iranian religion associates the boar with an important god.

What accounts for the apparent connection between domestic pigs and religion in these far-flung areas? There is no way of knowing. It has been hypothesized that pigs were first domesticated in Southeast Asia by people who had no herd animals—sheep, goats, cattle, or horses—and who relied on fish for most of their animal protein. The pig therefore became a special animal to them. The practice of pig herding, along with religious beliefs and rituals associated with the consumption of pork, could conceivably have spread from Southeast Asia along the maritime routes of the Indian Ocean, eventually reaching Iran and Egypt. But no evidence survives to support this hypothesis. In this case, therefore, material evidence can only hint at the spread of religious ideas, leaving the door open for other explanations.

A more certain example of objects' indicating the spread of an idea is the practice of hammering a carved die onto a piece of precious metal and using the resulting coin as a medium of exchange. From its origin in the Lydian kingdom in Anatolia in the first millennium B.C.E. (see Chapter 4), the idea of trading by means of struck coinage spread rapidly to Europe, North Africa, and India. Was the low-value copper coinage of China, made by pouring molten metal into a mold, also inspired by this practice from far away? It may have been, but it might also derive from indigenous Chinese metal-working. There is no way to be sure.

The Spread of Buddhism

While material objects associated with religious beliefs and rituals are important indicators of the spread of spiritual ideas, written sources deal with the spread of today's major religions. Buddhism grew to become, with Christianity and Islam (see Chapter 7), one of the most popular and widespread religions in the world. In all three cases, the religious ideas spread without dependency on a single ethnic or kinship group.

King Ashoka, the Mauryan ruler of India, and Kanishka, the greatest king of the Kushans of northern Afghanistan, promoted Buddhism between the third century B.C.E. and the second century C.E. However, monks, missionaries, and pilgrims who crisscrossed India, followed the Silk Road, or took ships on the Indian Ocean brought the Buddha's teachings to Southeast Asia, China, Korea, and ultimately Japan (see Map 6.1).

The Chinese pilgrim Faxian° (died between 418 and 423 C.E.) left a written account of his travels. Faxian began his trip in the company of a Chinese envoy to an unspecified ruler or people in Central Asia. After traveling from one Buddhist site to another across Afghanistan and India, he reached Sri Lanka, a Buddhist land, where he lived for two years. He then embarked for China on a merchant ship with two hundred men aboard. A storm drove the ship to Java, which he chose not to describe since it was Hindu rather than Buddhist. After five months ashore, Faxian finally reached China on another ship.

Less reliable accounts make reference to missionaries traveling to Syria, Egypt, and Macedonia, as well as to Southeast Asia. One of Ashoka's sons allegedly led a band of missionaries to Sri Lanka. Later, his sister brought a company of nuns there, along with a branch of the sacred Bo tree under which the Buddha had received enlightenment. At the same time, there are reports of other monks traveling to Burma, Thailand, and Sumatra. Ashoka's missionaries may also have reached Tibet by way of trade routes across the Himalayas.

Faxian (fah-shee-en)

The different lands that received the story and teachings of the Buddha preserved or adapted them in different ways. Theravada Buddhism, "Teachings of the Elder," was centered in Sri Lanka. Holding closely to the Buddha's earliest teachings, it maintained that the goal of religion, available only to monks, is *nirvana*, the total absence of suffering

Statue of a Bodhisattva at Bamian This is one of two monumental Buddhist sculptures near the top of a high mountain pass connecting Kabul, Afghanistan, with the northern parts of the country. Carved into the side of a cliff in the sixth or seventh century C.E., the sculptures were surrounded by cave dwellings of monks and rock sanctuaries, some dating to the first century B.C.E. This statue and the one alongside it were blown to pieces by the intolerant Taliban regime in Afghanistan in 2001. (Ian Griffiths/Robert Harding Picture Library)

and the end of the cycle of rebirth (see Chapter 4). This teaching contrasted with Mahayana, or "Great Vehicle" Buddhism, which stressed the goal of becoming a *bodhisattva*, a person who attains nirvana but chooses to remain in human company to help and guide others.

The Spread of Christianity

The post-Roman development of Christianity in Europe is discussed in Chapter 8. The Christian faith enjoyed an earlier spread in Asia and Africa before its confrontation with Islam (described in Chapter 7). Jerusalem in Palestine, Antioch in Syria, and Alexandria in Egypt became centers of Christian authority soon after the crucifixion, but the spread of Christianity to Armenia and Ethiopia illustrates the connections between religion, trade, and imperial politics.

Situated in eastern Anatolia (modern Turkey), **Armenia** served recurrently as a battleground between Iranian states to the south and east and Mediterranean states to the west. Each imperial power wanted to control this region so close to the frontier where Silk Road traders met their Mediterranean counterparts. In Parthian times, Armenia's kings favored Zoroastrianism. The invention of an Armenian alphabet in the early fifth century opened the way to a wider spread of Christianity. The Iranians did not give up domination easily, but within a century the Armenian Apostolic Church had become the center of Armenian cultural life.

Far to the south Christians similarly sought to outflank Iran. The Christian emperors in Constantinople (see Chapter 5) sent missionaries along the Red Sea trade route to seek converts in Yemen and **Ethiopia.** In the fourth century C.E. a Syrian philosopher traveling with two young relatives sailed to India. On the way back the ship docked at a Red Sea port occupied by Ethiopians from the prosperous kingdom of Aksum. Being then at odds with the Romans, the Ethiopians killed everyone on board except the two boys, Aedisius—who later narrated this story—and Frumentius. Impressed by their learning, the king made the former his cupbearer and the latter his treasurer and secretary.

When the king died, his wife urged Frumentius to govern Aksum on her behalf and that of her

Stele of Aksum   This 70-foot (21-meter) stone is the tallest remnant of a field of stelae, or standing stones, marking the tombs of Aksumite kings. The carvings of doors, windows, and beam ends imitate common features of Aksumite architecture, suggesting that each stele symbolized a multistory royal palace. The largest stelae date from the fourth century C.E.   (J. Allan Cash)

infant son, Ezana. As regent, Frumentius sought out Roman Christians among the merchants who visited the country and helped them establish

Christian communities. When he became king, Ezana, who may have become a Christian, permitted Aedisius and Frumentius to return to Syria. The patriarch of Alexandria, on learning about the progress of Christianity in Aksum, elevated Frumentius to the rank of bishop, though he had not previously been a clergyman, and sent him back to Ethiopia as the first leader of its church.

The spread of Christianity into Nubia, the land south of Egypt along the Nile River, proceeded from Ethiopia rather than Egypt. Politically and economically, Ethiopia became a power at the western end of the Indian Ocean trading system, occasionally even extending its influence across the Red Sea and asserting itself in Yemen (see Map 6.2).

CONCLUSION

Exchange facilitated by the early long-distance trading systems differed in many ways from the ebb and flow of culture, language, and custom that folk migrations brought about. Transportable goods and livestock and ideas about new technologies and agricultural products sometimes worked great changes on the landscape and in people's lives. But nothing resembling the Africanity observed south of the Sahara can be attributed to the societies involved in the Silk Road, Indian Ocean, or trans-Saharan exchanges. Few people were directly involved in these complex social systems of travel and trade compared with the populations with whom they were brought into contact, and their lifestyles as pastoral nomads or seafarers isolated them still more. Communities of traders contributed to this isolation by their reluctance to share knowledge with people who might become commercial competitors.

The Bantu, however, if current theories are correct, spread far and wide in sub-Saharan Africa with the deliberate intent of settling and implanting a lifestyle based on iron implements and agriculture. The metallurgical skills and agricultural techniques they brought with them permitted much denser habitation and helped ensure that the languages of the immigrants would supplant those of their hunting and gathering predecessors. Where

the trading systems encouraged diversity by introducing new products and ideas, the Bantu migrations brought a degree of cultural dominance that strongly affected later African history.

An apparent exception to the generalization that trading systems have less impact than folk migrations on patterns of dominance lies in the intangible area of ideas. Christianity and Buddhism both spread along trade routes, at least to some degree. Each instance of spread, however, gave rise to new forms of cultural diversity even as overall doctrinal unity made these religions dominant. As "great traditions," the new faiths based on conversion linked priests, monks, nuns, and religious scholars across vast distances. However, these same religions merged with myriad "small traditions" to provide for the social and spiritual needs of peoples living in many lands under widely varying circumstances.

■ Key Terms

Silk Road	steppes
Parthians	savanna
Sasanid Empire	tropical rain forest
stirrup	"great traditions"
Indian Ocean Maritime System	"small traditions"
trans-Saharan caravan routes	Bantu
Sahel	Armenia
sub-Saharan Africa	Ethiopia

■ Suggested Reading

For broad and suggestive overviews on cross-cultural exchange, see Philip D. Curtin, *Cross-Cultural Trade in World History* (1985), and C. G. F. Simkin, *The Traditional Trade of Asia* (1968).

Readable overviews of the Silk Road include Luce Boulnois, *The Silk Road* (1966), and Irene M. Franck and David M. Brownstone, *The Silk Road: A History* (1986). For products traded across Central Asia based on an eighth-century Japanese collection, see Ryoichi Hayashi, *The Silk Road and the Shoso-in* (1975). Xinru Liu, *Silk and Religion* (1996), covers one specific product. Owen Lattimore gives a first-person account of traveling by camel caravan in *The Desert Road to Turkestan* (1928). More generally on Central Asia, see Denis Sinor, *Inner Asia, History-Civilization-Languages: A Syllabus* (1987), and Karl Jettmar, *Art of the Steppes*, rev. ed. (1967). Richard

Foltz, *Religions of the Silk Road* (1999), is an excellent brief introduction.

For a readable but sketchy historical overview, see August Toussaint, *History of the Indian Ocean* (1966). Alan Villiers recounts what it was like to sail dhows between East Africa and the Persian Gulf in *Sons of Sinbad* (1940).

On a more scholarly plane, see K. N. Chaudhuri's *Trade and Civilization in the Indian Ocean: An Economic History from the Rise of Islam to 1750* (1985). Archaeologist Pierre Vérin treats the special problem of Madagascar in *The History of Civilisation in North Madagascar* (1986). For Rome and India, see E. H. Warmington's *The Commerce Between the Roman Empire and India* (1974); J. Innes Miller's *The Spice Trade of the Roman Empire, 29 B.C. to A.D. 641* (1969); and Vimala Begley and Richard Daniel De Puma's edited collection of articles, *Rome and India: The Ancient Sea Trade* (1991), along with the primary source *The Periplus Maris Erythraei: Text with Introduction, Translation, and Commentary* (1989), edited and translated by Lionel Casson. George F. Hourani's brief *Arab Seafaring in the Indian Ocean in Ancient and Early Medieval Times* (1975) covers materials in Arabic sources.

Nicholas Tarling, ed., *The Cambridge History of Southeast Asia*, vol. 1 (1992); D. R. Sardesai, *Southeast Asia: Past and Present*, 3d ed. (1994); and Milton E. Osborne, *Southeast Asia: An Introductory History* (1995), provide general accounts of Southeast Asian history. Lynda Shaffer, *Maritime Southeast Asia to 1500* (1996), focuses on the world historical context. Also useful is Kenneth R. Hall, *Maritime Trade and State Development in Early Southeast Asia* (1985).

On art, see Maud Girard-Geslan et al., *Art of Southeast Asia* (1998), and Daigoro Chihara, *Hindu-Buddhist Architecture in Southeast Asia* (1996).

Richard W. Bulliet's *The Camel and the Wheel* (1975) deals with camel use in the Middle East, along the Silk Road, and in North Africa and the Sahara. For a well-illustrated account of Saharan rock art, see Henri Lhote, *The Search for the Tassili Frescoes: The Story of the Prehistoric Rock-Paintings of the Sahara* (1959).

J. F. A. Ajayi and Michael Crowder, *A History of West Africa*, vol. 1 (1976), and G. Mokhtar, ed., *General History of Africa II: Ancient Civilizations of Africa* (1981), include many articles by numerous authors; the latter work specifically treats ironworking and the Bantu migrations. On African cultural unity, see Jacques Maquet, *Africanity: The Cultural Unity of Black Africa* (1972).

Of special importance on Christianity in Asia and Africa is Garth Fowden, *Empire to Commonwealth: Consequences of Monotheism in Late Antiquity* (1993). For specific topics treated in this chapter, see Stuart Munro-Hay, *Aksum: An African Civilisation of Late Antiquity* (1991); Xinru Liu, *Ancient India and Ancient China: Trade and Religious Exchanges, A.D. 1–600* (1998); Rolf A. Stein, *Tibetan Civilization* (1972); and Tilak Hettiarachchy, *History of Kingship in Ceylon up to the Fourth Century A.D.* (1972). *The Travels of Fahsien (399–414 A.D.), or, Record of the Buddhistic Kingdoms*, trans. H. A. Giles (1923; reprint, 1981) recounts the experiences of a Chinese pilgrim.

■ Notes

1. Victor H. Mair, ed., *The Columbia Anthology of Traditional Chinese Literature* (New York: Columbia University Press, 1994), 485; translated by Victor H. Mair.

Oral Societies and the Consequences of Literacy

The availability of written documents is one of the key factors historians use to divide human prehistory from history. When we can read what the people of the past thought and said about their lives, we can begin to understand their cultures, institutions, values, and beliefs in ways that are not possible based only on the material remains unearthed by archaeologists.

There are profound differences between nonliterate and literate societies. However, literacy and nonliteracy are not absolute alternatives. Personal literacy ranges from illiteracy through many shades of partial literacy (the ability to write one's name or to read simple texts with difficulty) to the fluent ability to read that is possessed by anyone reading this textbook. And there are degrees of societal literacy, ranging from nonliteracy through so-called craft literacy—in which a small specialized elite uses writing for limited purposes, such as administrative record-keeping—and a spectrum of conditions in which more and more people use writing for more and more purposes, up to the near-universal literacy and the use of writing for innumerable purposes that is the norm in the developed world in our times.

The vast majority of human beings of the last five to six thousand years living in societies that possessed the technology of writing were not themselves literate. If most people in a society rely on the spoken word and memory, that culture is essentially "oral" even if some members know how to write. The differences between oral and literate cultures are immense, affecting not only the kinds of knowledge that are valued and the forms in which information is preserved, but the very use of language, the categories for conceptualizing the world, and ultimately the hard-wiring of the individual human brain (now recognized by neuroscientists to be strongly influenced by individual experience and mental activity).

Ancient Greece of the Archaic and Classical periods (ca. 800–323 B.C.E.) offers a particularly instructive case study because we can observe the process by which writing was introduced into an oral society as well as the far-reaching consequences. The Greeks of the Dark Age and early Archaic Period lived in a purely oral society; all knowledge was preserved in human memory and passed on by telling it to others. The *Iliad* and the *Odyssey* (ca. 700 B.C.E.), Homer's epic poems, reflect this state of affairs. Scholars recognize that the creator of these poems was an oral poet, almost certainly not literate, who had heard and memorized the poems of predecessors and retold them his own way. The poems are treasuries of information that this society regarded as useful—events of the past; the conduct expected of warriors, kings, noblewomen, and servants; how to perform a sacrifice, build a raft, put on armor, and entertain guests; and much more.

Embedding this information in a story and using the colorful language, fixed phrases, and predictable rhythm of poetry made it easier for poet and audience to remember vast amounts of material. The early Greek poets, drawing on their strong memories, skill with words, and talent for dramatic performance, developed highly specialized techniques to assist them in memorizing and presenting their tales. They played a vital role in the preservation and transmission of information and thus enjoyed a relatively high social standing and comfortable standard of living. Analogous groups can be found in many other oral cultures of the past, including the bards of medieval Celtic lands, Norse *skalds*, west African *griots*, and the tribal historians of Native American peoples.

Nevertheless, human memory, however cleverly trained and well-practiced, can only do so much. Oral societies must be extremely selective about what information to preserve in the limited storage medium of human memory, and they are slow to give up old information to make way for new.

Sometime in the eighth century B.C.E. the Greeks borrowed the system of writing used by the Phoenicians of Lebanon and, in adapting it to their language, created the first purely alphabetic writing, employing several dozen symbols to express the sounds of speech. The Greek alphabet, although relatively simple to learn as compared to the large and cumbersome sets of symbols in such craft-literacy systems as cuneiform, hieroglyphics, or Linear B, was probably known at first only to a small number of people and used for restricted purposes. Scholars believe that it may have taken three or four centuries for knowledge of reading and writing to spread to large numbers of Greeks and for the written word to became the primary storage medium for the accumulated knowledge of Greek civilization. Throughout that time Greece was still primarily an oral society, even though some Greeks, mostly highly educated members of the upper classes, were beginning to write down poems, scientific speculations, stories about the past, philosophic musings, and the laws of their communities.

It is no accident that some of the most important intellectual and artistic achievements of the Greeks, including early science, history, drama, and rhetoric, developed in the period when oral and literate ways existed side-by-side. Scholars have persuasively argued that writing, by opening up a virtually limitless capacity to store information, released the human mind from the hard discipline of memorization and ended the need to be so painfully selective about what was preserved. This made previously unimaginable innovation and experimentation possible. We can observe changes in the Greek language as it developed a vocabulary full of abstract nouns, accompanied by increasing complex sentence structure now that the reader had time to go back over the text.

Nevertheless, all the developments associated with literacy were shaped by the deeply rooted oral habits of Greek culture. It is often said that Plato (ca. 429–347 B.C.E.) and his contemporaries of the later Classical period may have been the first generation of Greeks who learned much of what they knew from books. Even so, Plato was a disciple of the philosopher Socrates, who wrote nothing, and Plato employed the oral form of the dialogue, a dramatized sequence of questions and answers, to convey his ideas in written form.

The transition from orality to literacy met stiff resistance in some quarters. Groups whose position in the oral culture was based on the special knowledge only they possessed—members of the elite who judged disputes, priests who knew the time-honored formulas and rituals for appeasing the gods, oral poets who preserved and performed the stories of a heroic past—resented the conse-

quences of literacy. They did what they could to inflame the common people's suspicions of the impiety of literate men who sought scientific explanations for phenomena, such as lightning and eclipses, that had traditionally been attributed to the will and action of the gods. They attacked the so-called Sophists, or "wise men," who charged fees to teach what they claimed were the skills necessary for success, accusing them of subverting traditional morals and corrupting the young.

Other societies, ancient and modern, offer parallel examples of these processes. Oral "specialists" in antiquity, including the Brahmin priests of India and the Celtic Druids, preserved in memory valuable religious information about how to win the favor of the gods. These groups jealously guarded their knowledge because it was the basis of their livelihood and social standing. They resisted committing it to writing even after that technology was available, in their determination to select and to maintain control over those who received it from them. The ways in which oral authorities feel threatened by writing and resist it can be seen in the following quotation from a twentieth century C.E. "griot," an oral rememberer and teller of the past in Mali in West Africa:

We griots are depositories of the knowledge of the past . . . Other peoples use writing to record the past, but this invention has killed the faculty of memory among them. They do not feel the past anymore, for writing lacks the warmth of the human voice. With them everybody thinks he knows, whereas learning should be a secret . . . What paltry learning is that which is congealed in dumb books! . . . For generations we have passed on the history of kings from father to son. The narrative was passed on to me without alteration, for I received it free from all untruth.[1]

This point of view is hard for us to grasp, living as we do in an intensely literate society in which the written word is often felt to be more authoritative and objective than the spoken word. It is important, in striving to understand societies of the past, not to superimpose our assumptions on them, and to appreciate the complex interplay of oral and literate patterns in many of them.

■ Notes

1. D. T. Niane, *Sundiata: An Epic of Old Mali.* (Harlow U.K.: Longman, 1986), 41.

PART THREE

Growth and Interaction of Cultural Communities, 600–1200

CHAPTER 7
The Rise of Islam, 600–1200

CHAPTER 8
Christian Europe Emerges, 600–1200

CHAPTER 9
Central and Eastern Asia, 400–1200

CHAPTER 10
Peoples and Civilizations of the Americas, 200–1500

The six centuries from 600 to 1200 witnessed a consolidation of cultural communities, as previously separated religious, ethnic, and linguistic traditions became incorporated into larger cultural units. In Europe and the Middle East the defining feature was religion—Catholic or Orthodox Christianity, or Islam. In East Asia, the political and social teachings of Confucianism guided the creation of new states and societies. In the Americas, ethnic ties shaped the cultures of new communities.

In the 600s and early 700s, the Arabs of the Arabian peninsula conquered an empire that stretched from Spain to India. The unified empire they established proved short-lived, but it provided a framework for implanting the Muslim faith and accompanying cultural values, including a vibrant urban-based style of life. Simultaneously the expansion of the Tang Empire spread Chinese culture and technologies throughout Inner and East Asia, while introducing Buddhism and Inner Asian cultural practices into China.

In Europe, missionaries labored to convert the Celtic, Germanic, and Slavic peoples to Christianity. Christian beliefs became enmeshed in new political and social structures. In western Europe, this produced a struggle between royal and church authority. In the eastern Mediterranean, religious and imperial authority came together in the Byzantine Empire, although many eastern Christians lost their imperial connection when Egypt, Syria, and North Africa fell to Arab armies. In Kievan Russia, the Byzantine imperial tradition produced a look-alike offshoot that split the Slavic peoples between Catholics (e.g., Poland) and Orthodox (e.g., Russia). Competition between Islam and Christianity climaxed in the Crusades, which also opened contacts between western Europe and lands to the east after centuries of isolation.

The development of a significant level of trade across the Sahara desert brought sub-Saharan Africa into contact with some of these developments. The Muslim principalities in North Africa that pioneered the trade also began the long process of converting sub-Saharan African peoples to Islam.

By the end of the period, the major cultural regions in Europe, North Africa, and Asia had come into a substantial degree of contact. The knowledge that increasingly circulated about distant lands contributed to the first era of world-encompassing political and economic development after 1200.

Unexplored seas still separated the Eastern and Western Hemispheres. The European voyagers who would find their way across the Atlantic Ocean in the ensuing period would encounter developed urban and agricultural civilizations in the Andes, the Yucatán lowlands, and the central plateau of Mexico as well as less intensely developed areas of settled agricultural life in parts of North America.

	300 B.C.E.	B.C.E. C.E.	300 C.E.
Americas	• **300** Migrants from Mesoamerica bring irrigation farming to Arizona	• **100** Teotihuacan founded	**250–900** Classic period of Maya civilizatio **200–700** Moche culture in coastal Peru
Europe			Council of Nicaea **325** • Reign of Roman emperor Diocletian **284–305** — Fall of Roman Empire in West **476** •
Africa	Bananas and yams reach Africa from Southeast Asia **ca. 100** • **500 B.C.E.–1000 C.E.** Bantu migrations	First Christian bishop in Ethiopia **ca. 330** •	
Middle East	• **300** Petra flourishes as caravan city in Jordan **248 B.C.E–226 C.E** Kingdom of Parthia in Iran		• **276** Prophet Mani martyred **226–650** Sasanid Empire in Iraq and Iran
Asia and Oceania	• **128** Chinese general Zhang Jian explores Silk Road **206 B.C.E–220 C.E** Han Empire in China	• **ca. 100** Stirrup developed in Afghanistan	**200–400** Rice introduced to Japan from Korea

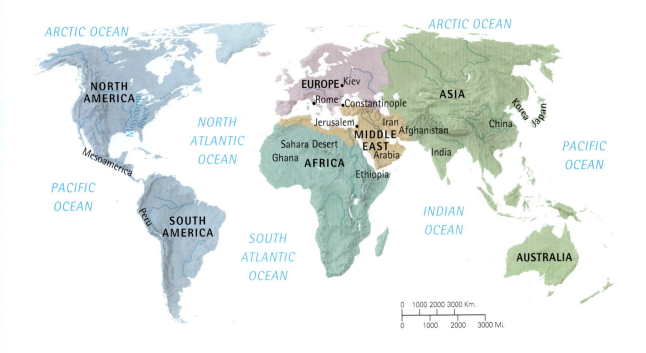

ARCTIC OCEAN

ARCTIC OCEAN

NORTH
AMERICA

NORTH
ATLANTIC
OCEAN

EUROPE •Kiev

•Rome •Constantinople

ASIA

Korea Japan

Jerusalem •Iran Afghanistan China

MIDDLE EAST

PACIFIC
OCEAN

Sahara Desert
Ghana AFRICA

Arabia India

Mississippi River

Mesoamerica

Ethiopia

PACIFIC
OCEAN

Peru

SOUTH
AMERICA

SOUTH
ATLANTIC
OCEAN

INDIAN
OCEAN

AUSTRALIA

0 1000 2000 3000 Km.

0 1000 2000 3000 Mi.

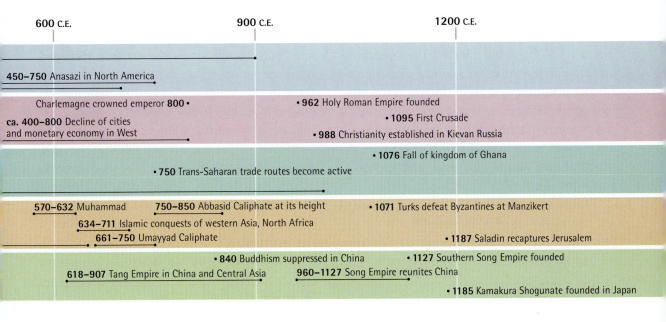

600 C.E.

900 C.E.

1200 C.E.

450–750 Anasazi in North America

Charlemagne crowned emperor **800** •

• 962 Holy Roman Empire founded

ca. 400–800 Decline of cities
and monetary economy in West

• 1095 First Crusade

• 988 Christianity established in Kievan Russia

• 1076 Fall of kingdom of Ghana

• 750 Trans-Saharan trade routes become active

570–632 Muhammad

750–850 Abbasid Caliphate at its height

• 1071 Turks defeat Byzantines at Manzikert

634–711 Islamic conquests of western Asia, North Africa

661–750 Umayyad Caliphate

• 1187 Saladin recaptures Jerusalem

• 840 Buddhism suppressed in China

• 1127 Southern Song Empire founded

618–907 Tang Empire in China and Central Asia

960–1127 Song Empire reunites China

• 1185 Kamakura Shogunate founded in Japan

7

The Rise of Islam, 600–1200

CHAPTER OUTLINE

The Origins of Islam

The Rise and Fall of the Caliphate, 632–1258

Islamic Civilization

DIVERSITY AND DOMINANCE: Beggars, Con Men, and Singing-girls

The story is told that in the early days of Islam, at the time of the Prophet Muhammad's last pilgrimage to Mecca in 630, a dispute over distribution of booty arose between his daughter's husband, Ali, who was also Muhammad's first cousin, and some troops Ali commanded. Muhammad quelled the grumbling and later on the same journey, at a place named Ghadir al-Khumm°, drew his followers together, took Ali's hand, and declared: "Am I not nearer to the believers than their own selves? Whomever I am nearest to, so likewise is Ali. O God, be the friend of him who is his friend, and the foe of him who is his foe."

Written narratives of Muhammad's praise of Ali, like all stories of Muhammad's life, date to well over a century after the event. By that time, Ali had served as leader of Muhammad's community for a brief time and had then been defeated in a civil war and assassinated. Subsequently, his son Husayn, along with his family, died in a hopelessly lopsided battle while trying to claim leadership as the Prophet's grandson.

Out of these events grew a division in the Islamic community: some believers, called **Shi'ites°,** from the Arabic term *Shi'at Ali* ("Party of Ali"), thought that religious leadership rightfully belonged to Ali and his descendants; others, eventually called **Sunnis°,** followers of the sunna, or "tradition" of the community, felt that the community should choose its leaders more broadly. Sunnis and Shi'ites agreed that Muhammad commended Ali at Ghadir al-Khumm. But the Sunnis considered his remarks to relate only to the distribution of the booty, and the Shi'ites understood them to be Muhammad's formal and

Ghadir al-Khumm (ga-DEER al-KUM)

Shi'ite (SHE-ite)   Sunni (SUN-nee)

public declaration of Ali's special and elevated position, and hence of his right to rule.

Shi'ite rulers rarely achieved power, but those who ruled from Cairo between 969 and 1171 made the commemoration of Ghadir al-Khumm a major festival. At the beginning of every year, Shi'ites everywhere also engaged in public mourning over the deaths of Husayn and his family. Sunni rulers, in contrast, sometimes ordered that Ali be cursed in public prayers.

Muhammad's Arab followers conquered an enormous territory in the seventh century. In the name of Islam, they created an empire that encompassed many peoples speaking many languages and worshiping in many ways. The empire's immediate forerunners, the realms of the Byzantine emperors (see Chapter 5) and Iran's Sasanid° shahs (see Chapter 6), closely linked religion with imperial politics.

Although urbanism, science, manufacturing, trade, and architecture flourished in the lands of Islam while medieval Europe was enduring hardship and economic contraction, religion shaped both societies. Just as the medieval Christian calendar revolved around Easter and Christmas, Islamic fasts, pilgrimages, and political religious observances like Ghadir al-Khumm marked the yearly cycle in the lands of Muhammad's followers.

As you read this chapter, ask yourself the following questions:

- How did the Arab conquests grow out of the career of Muhammad?
- Why did the caliphate break up?
- How did Muslim societies differ from region to region?
- What was the relationship between urbanization and the development of Islamic culture?

Sasanid (suh-SAH-nid)

THE ORIGINS OF ISLAM

The Arabs of 600 C.E. lived exclusively in the Arabian peninsula and on the desert fringes of Syria, Jordan, and Iraq. Along their Euphrates frontier, the Sasanids subsidized nomadic Arab chieftains to protect their empire from invasion. The Byzantines did the same with Arabs on their Jordanian frontier. Arab pastoralists farther to the south remained isolated and independent, seldom engaging the attention of the shahs and emperors. It was in these interior Arabian lands that the religion of Islam took form.

The Arabian Peninsula Before Muhammad

Throughout history more people living on the Arabian peninsula have subsisted as farmers or sailors than as pastoral nomads. Farming villages support the comparatively dense population of Yemen, where the highlands receive abundant rainfall during the spring monsoon. Small inlets along the southern coast favored fishing and trading communities. However, the enormous sea of sand known as the "Empty Quarter" isolated many southern regions from the Arabian interior. In the seventh century, most people in southern Arabia knew more about Africa, India, and the Persian Gulf (see Chapter 6, Diversity and Dominance: The Indian Ocean Trading World) than about the forbidding interior and the scattered camel- and sheep-herding nomads who lived there.

Exceptions to this pattern mostly involved caravan trading. Nomads derived income from providing camels, guides, and safe passage to merchants wanting to transport northward the primary product of the south: the aromatic resins frankincense and myrrh that were burned in religious rituals. Return caravans brought manufactured products from Mesopotamia and the Mediterranean.

Nomad dominance of the caravan trade received a boost from the invention of militarily efficient camel saddles. This contributed to the rise of Arab-dominated caravan cities and to Arab pastoralists becoming the primary suppliers of animal power throughout the region. By 600 C.E., wheeled vehicles—mostly ox carts and horse-drawn chariots—had all but disappeared from the Middle East, replaced by pack camels and donkeys.

Arabs who accompanied the caravans became familiar with the cultures and lifestyles of the Sasanid and Byzantine Empires, and many of those who pastured their herds on the imperial frontiers adopted one form or another of Christianity. Even in the interior deserts, Semitic polytheism, with its worship of natural forces and celestial bodies, began to encounter more sophisticated religions.

Mecca, a late-blooming caravan city, lies in a barren mountain valley halfway between Yemen and Syria and a short way inland from the Red Sea coast of Arabia. A nomadic kin group known as the Quraysh° settled in Mecca in the fifth century and assumed control of trade. Mecca rapidly achieved a measure of prosperity, partly because it was too far from Byzantine Syria, Sasanid Iraq, and Ethiopian-controlled Yemen for them to attack it.

A cubical shrine called the Ka'ba°, containing idols, a holy well called Zamzam, and a sacred precinct surrounding the two wherein killing was prohibited contributed to the emergence of Mecca as a pilgrimage site. Some Meccans associated the shrine with stories known to Jews and Christians. They regarded Abraham (Ibrahim in Arabic) as the builder of the Ka'ba, and they identified a site outside Mecca as the location where God asked Abraham to sacrifice his son. The son was not Isaac (Ishaq in Arabic), the son of Sarah, but Ishmael (Isma'il in Arabic), the son of Hagar, cited in the Bible as the forefather of the Arabs.

Muhammad in Mecca

Born in Mecca in 570, **Muhammad** grew up an orphan in the house of his uncle. He engaged in trade and married a Quraysh widow named Khadija°, whose caravan interests he superintended. Their son died in childhood, but several daughters survived. Around 610 Muhammad began meditating at night in the mountainous terrain around Mecca. During one night vigil, known to later tradition as the "Night of Power and Excellence," a being whom Muhammad later understood to be the angel Gabriel (Jibra'il in Arabic) spoke to him:

> Proclaim! In the name of your Lord who created.
> Created man from a clot of congealed blood.
> Proclaim! And your Lord is the Most Bountiful.
> He who has taught by the pen.
> Taught man that which he knew not.[1]

For three years he shared this and subsequent revelations only with close friends and family members. This period culminated in Muhammad's conviction that he was hearing the words of God (Allah° in Arabic). Khadija, his uncle's son Ali, his friend Abu Bakr°, and others close to him shared this conviction. The revelations continued until Muhammad's death in 632.

Like most people of the time, including Christians and Jews, the Arabs believed in unseen spirits: gods, desert spirits called *jinns*, demonic *shaitans*, and others. They further believed that certain individuals had contact with the spirit world, notably seers and poets, who were thought to be possessed by jinns. Therefore, when Muhammad began to recite his rhymed revelations in public, many people believed he was inspired by an unseen spirit, even if it was not, as Muhammad asserted, the one true god.

Muhammad's earliest revelations called on people to witness that one god had created the universe and everything in it, including themselves. At the end of time, their souls would be judged, their sins balanced against their good deeds. The blameless would go to paradise; the sinful would taste hellfire:

> By the night as it conceals the light;
> By the day as it appears in glory;
> By the mystery of the creation of male and female;
> Verily, the ends ye strive for are diverse.
> So he who gives in charity and fears God,
> And in all sincerity testifies to the best,
> We will indeed make smooth for him the path to Bliss.
> But he who is a greedy miser and thinks himself self-sufficient,
> And gives the lie to the best,
> We will indeed make smooth for him the path to misery.[2]

Quraysh (koo-RYYSH)   Ka'ba (KAH-buh)   Khadija (kah-DEE-juh)

Allah (AH-luh)   Abu Bakr (ah-boo BAK-uhr)

C H R O N O L O G Y

	The Arab Lands	Iran and Central Asia
600	**570–632** Life of the Prophet Muhammad	
	634 Conquests of Iraq and Syria commence	
	639–642 Conquest of Egypt by Arabs	
	656–661 Ali caliph; first civil war	
	661–750 Umayyad Caliphate rules from Damascus	
700	**711** Berbers and Arabs invade Spain from North Africa	**711** Arabs capture Sind in India
		747 Abbasid revolt begins in Khurasan
	750 Beginning of Abbasid Caliphate	
	755 Umayyad state established in Spain	
	776–809 Caliphate of Harun al-Rashid	
800	**835–892** Abbasid capital moved from Baghdad to Samarra	
		875 Independent Samanid state founded in Bukhara
900	**909** Fatimids seize North Africa, found Shi'ite caliphate	
	929 Abd al-Rahman III declares himself caliph in Cordoba	
	945 Shi'ite Buyids take control in Baghdad	**945** Buyids from northern Iran take control of Abbasid Caliphate
	969 Fatimids conquer Egypt	
1000		**1036** Beginning of Turkish Seljuk rule in Khurasan
	1055 Seljuk Turks take control in Baghdad	
	1099 First Crusade captures Jerusalem	
1100	**1171** Fall of Fatimid Egypt	
	1187 Saladin recaptures Jerusalem	
1200	**1250** Mamluks control Egypt	
	1258 Mongols sack Baghdad and end Abbasid Caliphate	
	1260 Mamluks defeat Mongols at Ain Jalut	

Sasanid Silver Vase   The Sasanid aristocracy, based in the countryside, invested part of its wealth in silver plates and vessels. The image is of the fertility goddess Anahita, a deity acceptable to the Zoroastrian faith. One inscription in Pahlavi (a Middle Persian language) gives the weight, 116.9 grams in modern terms, while another in Sogdian, a language common along the Silk Road, gives the owner's name, Mithrak.   (The State Heritage Museum, St Petersburg)

The revelation called all people to submit to God and accept Muhammad as the last of his messengers. Doing so made one a **muslim,** meaning one who makes "submission," **Islam,** to the will of God.

Because earlier messengers mentioned in the revelations included Noah, Moses, and Jesus, Muhammad's hearers felt that his message resembled the Judaism and Christianity they were already somewhat familiar with. Yet his revelations charged the Jews and Christians with being negligent in preserving God's revealed word. Thus, even though they identified Abraham/Ibrahim, whom

Muslims consider the first Muslim, as the builder of the Ka'ba, which superseded Jerusalem as the focus of Muslim prayer in 624, Muhammad's followers considered his revelation more perfect than the Bible because it had not gone through an editing process.

Some scholars maintain that Muhammad's revelations appealed especially to people distressed over wealth replacing kinship as the most important aspect of social relations. They see a message of social reform in verses criticizing taking pride in money and neglecting obligations to orphans and other powerless people. Other scholars, along with most Muslims, put less emphasis on a social message and stress the power and beauty of Muhammad's revelations. Forceful rhetoric and poetic vision, coming in the Muslim view directly from God, go far to explain Muhammad's early success.

The Formation of the Umma

Mecca's leaders feared that accepting Muhammad as the sole agent of the one true God would threaten their power and prosperity. They pressured his kin to disavow him and persecuted the weakest of his followers. Stymied by this hostility, Muhammad and his followers fled Mecca in 622 to take up residence in the agricultural community of **Medina** 215 miles (346 kilometers) to the north. This hijra° marks the beginning of the Muslim calendar.

Prior to the hijra, Medinan representatives had met with Muhammad and agreed to accept and protect him and his followers because they saw him as an inspired leader who could calm their perpetual feuding. Together, the Meccan migrants and major groups in Medina bound themselves into a single **umma**°, a community defined solely by acceptance of Islam and of Muhammad as the "Messenger of God," his most common title. Partly because three Jewish kin groups chose to retain their own faith, the direction of prayer was changed from Jerusalem toward the Ka'ba in Mecca, now thought of as the "House of God."

Having left their Meccan kin groups, the immigrants in Medina felt vulnerable, and during the last decade of his life, Muhammad took active re-

hijra (HIJ-ruh)   **umma** (UM-muh)

The Origins of Islam **185**

sponsibility for his umma. Fresh revelations provided a framework for regulating social and legal affairs and stirred the Muslims to fight against the still-unbelieving city of Mecca. At various points during the war, Muhammad charged the Jewish kin groups, whom he had initially hoped would recognize him as God's messenger, with disloyalty, and he finally expelled or eliminated them. The sporadic war, largely conducted by raiding and negotiating with desert nomads, sapped Mecca's strength and convinced many Meccans that God favored Muhammad. In 630 Mecca surrendered, and Muhammad and his followers made the pilgrimage to the Ka'ba unhindered.

Muhammad did not return to Mecca again but stayed in Medina, which had grown into a bustling city-state. Delegations from all over Arabia came to meet him, and he sent emissaries back with them to teach about Islam and collect their alms. Muhammad's mission to bring God's message to humanity had brought him unchallenged control of a state that was coming to dominate the Arabian peninsula. But the supremacy of the Medinan state, unlike preceding short-lived nomadic kingdoms, depended not on kinship but on a common faith in a single god.

In 632, after a brief illness, Muhammad died. Within twenty-four hours a group of Medinan leaders, along with three of Muhammad's close friends, determined that Abu Bakr, one of the earliest believers and the father of Muhammad's favorite wife A'isha°, should succeed him. They called him the *khalifa°,* or "successor," the English version of which is *caliph.* But calling Abu Bakr a successor did not clarify his powers. Everyone knew that neither Abu Bakr nor anyone else could receive revelations, and they likewise knew that Muhammad's revelations made no provision for succession or for any government purpose beyond maintaining the umma.

Abu Bakr continued and confirmed Muhammad's religious practices, notably the so-called Five Pillars of Islam: (1) avowal that there is only one god and Muhammad is his messenger, (2) prayer five times a day, (3) fasting during the lunar month of Ramadan, (4) paying alms, and (5) making the pilgrimage to Mecca at least once during one's life-

time. He also reestablished and expanded Muslim authority over Arabia's nomadic and settled communities. After Muhammad's death, some had abandoned their allegiance to Medina or followed various would-be prophets. Muslim armies fought hard to confirm the authority of the newborn **caliphate.** In the process, some fighting spilled over into non-Arab areas in Iraq.

Abu Bakr ordered those who had acted as secretaries for Muhammad to organize the Prophet's revelations into a book. Hitherto written haphazardly on pieces of leather or bone, the verses of revelation became a single document gathered into chapters. This resulting book, which Muslims believe acquired its final form around the year 650, was called the **Quran°,** or the Recitation. Muslims regard it not as the words of Muhammad but as the unalterable word of God. As such, it compares not so much to the Bible, a book written by many hands over many centuries, as to the person of Jesus Christ, whom Christians consider a human manifestation of God.

Though united in its acceptance of God's will, the umma soon disagreed over the succession to the caliphate. The first civil war in Islam followed the assassination by rebels of the third caliph, Uthman°, in 656. His assassins nominated Ali, Muhammad's first cousin and the husband of his daughter Fatima, to succeed Uthman. Ali had been passed over three times previously, even though many people considered him to be the Prophet's natural heir. As mentioned previously, Ali and his supporters felt that Muhammad had indicated as much at Ghadir al-Khumm.

When Ali accepted the nomination to be caliph, two of Muhammad's close companions and his favorite wife A'isha challenged him. Ali defeated them in the Battle of the Camel (656), so called because the fighting raged around the camel on which A'isha was seated in an enclosed woman's saddle.

After the battle, the governor of Syria, Mu'awiya°, a kinsman of the slain Uthman from the Umayya clan of the Quraysh, renewed the challenge. Inconclusive battle gave way to arbitration. The arbitrators decided that Uthman, whom his

---

A'isha (AH-ee-shah)   **khalifa** (kah-LEE-fuh)

Quran (kuh-RAHN)   **Uthman** (ooth-MAHN)   **Mu'awiya** (moo-AH-we-yuh)

assassins considered corrupt, had not deserved death and that Ali had erred in accepting the nomination. Ali rejected the arbitrators' findings, but before he could resume fighting, one of his own supporters killed him for agreeing to the arbitration. Mu'awiya then offered Ali's son Hasan a dignified retirement and thus emerged as caliph in 661.

Mu'awiya chose his own son, Yazid, to succeed him, thereby instituting the **Umayyad° Caliphate.** When Hasan's brother Husayn revolted in 680 to reestablish the right of Ali's family to rule, Yazid ordered Husayn and his family killed. Sympathy for Husayn's martyrdom helped transform Shi'ism from a political movement into a religious sect.

Several variations in Shi'ite belief developed, but Shi'ites have always agreed that Ali was the rightful successor to Muhammad and that God's choice as Imam, leader of the Muslim community, has always been one or another of Ali's descendants. They see the office of caliph as more secular than religious. Because the Shi'ites seldom held power, their religious feelings came to focus on outpourings of sympathy for Husayn and other martyrs and on messianic dreams that one of their Imams would someday triumph.

Those Muslims who supported the first three caliphs gradually came to be called "People of Tradition and Community"—in Arabic, *Ahl al-Sunna wa'l-Jama'a,* Sunnis for short. Sunnis consider the caliphs to be Imams. As for Ali's followers who had abhorred his acceptance of arbitration, they evolved into small and rebellious Kharijite sects (from *kharaja,* meaning "to secede or rebel") claiming righteousness for themselves alone. These three divisions of Islam, the last now quite minor, still survive.

THE RISE AND FALL OF THE CALIPHATE, 632–1258

The Islamic caliphate built on the conquests the Arabs carried out after Muhammad's death gave birth to a dynamic and creative religious society. By the late 800s, however, one piece

after another of this huge realm broke away. Yet the idea of a caliphate, however unrealistic it became, remained a touchstone of Sunni belief in the unity of the umma.

Sunni Islam never gave a single person the power to define true belief, expel heretics, and discipline clergy. Thus, unlike Christian popes and patriarchs, the caliphs had little basis for reestablishing their universal authority once they lost political and military power.

The Islamic Conquests, 634–711

Arab conquests outside Arabia began under the second caliph, Umar (r. 634–644), possibly prompted by earlier forays into Iraq. Arab armies wrenched Syria (636) and Egypt (639–642) away from the Byzantine Empire and defeated the last Sasanid shah, Yazdigird III (r. 632–651). After a decade-long lull, expansion began again. Tunisia fell and became the governing center from which was organized, in 711, the conquest of Spain by an Arab-led army mostly composed of Berbers from North Africa. In the same year, Sind—the southern Indus Valley and westernmost region of India—succumbed to invaders from Iraq. The Muslim dominion remained roughly stable for the next three centuries. In the eleventh century, conquest began anew in India, Anatolia, and sub-Saharan Africa. Islam also expanded peacefully by trade in these and other areas both before and after the year 1000.

The close Meccan companions of the Prophet, men of political and economic sophistication inspired by his charisma, guided the conquests. The social structure and hardy nature of Arab society lent itself to flexible military operations; and the authority of Medina, reconfirmed during the caliphate of Abu Bakr, ensured obedience.

The decision made during Umar's caliphate to prohibit Arabs from assuming ownership of conquered territory proved important. Umar tied army service, with its regular pay and windfalls of booty, to residence in large military camps—two in Iraq (Kufa and Basra), one in Egypt (Fustat), and one in Tunisia (Qairawan). East of Iraq, Arabs settled around small garrison towns at strategic locations and in one large garrison at Marv in present-day Turkmenistan. Down to the early eighth century, this policy kept the

Umayyad (oo-MY-ad)

armies together and ready for action and preserved life in the countryside, where some three-fourths of the population lived, virtually unchanged. Only a tiny proportion of the Syrian, Egyptian, and Iraqi populations understood the Arabic language.

The million or so Arabs who participated in the conquests over several generations constituted a small, self-isolated ruling minority living on the taxes paid by a vastly larger non-Arab, non-Muslim subject population. The Arabs had little material incentive to encourage conversion, and there is no evidence of coherent missionary efforts to spread Islam during the conquest period.

The Umayyad and Early Abbasid Caliphates, 661–850

The Umayyad caliphs presided over an ethnically defined Arab realm rather than a religious empire. Ruling from Damascus, their armies consisted almost entirely of Muslim Arabs. They adopted and adapted the administrative practices of their Sasanid and Byzantine predecessors, as had the caliphs who preceded them. Only gradually did they replace non-Muslim secretaries and tax officials with Muslims and introduce Arabic as the language of government. The introduction of distinctively Muslim silver and gold coins early in the eighth century symbolized the new order. From that time on, silver dirhams and gold dinars bearing Arabic religious phrases circulated in monetary exchanges from Morocco to the frontiers of China.

The Umayyad dynasty fell in 750 after a decade of growing unrest. Converts to Islam, by that date no more than 10 percent of the indigenous population, were still numerically significant because of the comparatively small number of Arab warriors, and they resented not achieving equal status with the Arabs. In Iraq and elsewhere, Arabs envied the Syrian Arab influence in caliphal affairs, and pious Muslims looked askance at the secular and even irreligious behavior of the caliphs. In addition, Shi'ites and Kharijites attacked the Umayyad family's legitimacy as rulers, launching a number of rebellions.

In 750 one such rebellion, in the region of Khurasan° in what is today northeastern Iran,

overthrew the last Umayyad caliph, though one family member escaped to Spain and founded an Umayyad principality there in 755. Many Shi'ites supported the rebellion, thinking they were fighting for the family of Ali. As it turned out, the family of Abbas, one of Muhammad's uncles, controlled the secret organization that coordinated the revolt. Upon victory they established the **Abbasid° Caliphate.** Some of the Abbasid caliphs who ruled after 750 befriended their relatives in Ali's family, and one even flirted with transferring the caliphate to them. The Abbasid family, however, held on to the caliphate until 1258, when Mongol invaders killed the last of them in Baghdad (see Chapter 11).

At its outset the Abbasid dynasty made a fine show of leadership and concern for Islam. Theology and religious law became preoccupations at court and among a growing community of scholars, along with interpretating the Quran, collecting the sayings of the Prophet, and compiling Arabic grammar. (In recent years, some western scholars have maintained that the Quran, the sayings of the Prophet, and the biography of the Prophet were all composed around this time to provide a legendary base for the regime. This reinterpretation of Islamic origins has not been generally accepted either in the scholarly community or among Muslims.) Some caliphs sponsored ambitious projects to translate great works of Greek, Persian, and Indian thought into Arabic.

With its roots among the semi-Persianized Arabs of Khurasan, the new dynasty gradually adopted the ceremonies and customs of the Sasanid shahs. Government grew increasingly complex in Baghdad, the newly built capital city on the Tigris River. As more non-Arabs converted to Islam, the ruling elite became more cosmopolitan. Greek, Iranian, Central Asian, and African cultural currents met in the capital and gave rise to an abundance of literary works, a process facilitated by the introduction of papermaking from China. Arab poets neglected the traditional odes extolling life in the desert and wrote instead wine songs (despite Islam's prohibition of alcohol) or poems in praise of their patrons.

The translation of Aristotle into Arabic, the founding of the main currents of theology and law,

---

Khurasan (kor-uh-SAHN)   **Abbasid** (ah-BASS-id)

and the splendor of the Abbasid court—reflected in stories of *The Arabian Nights* set in the time of the caliph Harun al-Rashid° (r. 776–809)—in some respects warrant calling the early Abbasid period a "golden age." Yet the refinement of Baghdad culture only slowly made its way into the provinces. Egypt remained predominantly Christian and Coptic-speaking in the early Abbasid period. Iran never adopted Arabic as a spoken tongue. Most of Berber-speaking North Africa rebelled and freed itself of direct caliphal rule after 740.

Gradual conversion to Islam among the conquered population accelerated in the second quarter of the ninth century. Social discrimination against non-Arab converts gradually faded, and the Arabs themselves—at least those living in cosmopolitan urban settings—lost their previously strong attachment to kinship and ethnic identity.

Political Fragmentation, 850–1050

Abbasid decline became evident in the second half of the ninth century as the conversion to Islam accelerated (see Map 7.1). No government ruling so vast an empire could hold power easily. Caravans traveled only 20 miles (32 kilometers) a day, and the couriers of the caliphal post system usually did not exceed 100 miles (160 kilometers) a day. News of frontier revolts took weeks to reach Baghdad. Military responses might take months. Administrators struggled to centralize tax payments, often made in grain or other produce rather than cash, and to ensure that provincial governors forwarded the proper amounts to Baghdad.

During the first two Islamic centuries, revolts against Muslim rule had been a concern. The Muslim umma had therefore clung together, despite the long distances. But with the growing conversion of the population to Islam, fears that Islamic dominion might be overthrown faded. Once they became the overwhelming majority, Muslims realized that a highly centralized empire did not necessarily serve the interests of all the people.

By the middle of the ninth century, revolts targeting Arab or Muslim domination gave way to movements within the Islamic community concentrating on seizure of territory and formation of principalities. None of the states carved out of the Abbasid Caliphate after that time repudiated or even threatened Islam. They did, however, cut the flow of tax revenues to Baghdad, thereby increasing local prosperity.

Increasingly starved for funds by breakaway provinces and by an unexplained fall in revenues from Iraq itself, the caliphate experienced a crisis in the late ninth century. Distrusting generals and troops from outlying areas, the caliphs purchased Turkic slaves, **mamluks**°, from Central Asia and established them as a standing army. Well trained and hardy, the Turks proved an effective but expensive military force. When the government could not pay them, the mamluks took it on themselves to seat and unseat caliphs, a process made easier by the construction of a new capital at Samarra, north of Baghdad on the Tigris River.

The Turks dominated Samarra without interference from an unruly Baghdad populace that regarded them as rude and highhanded. However, the money and effort that went into the huge city, which was occupied only from 835 to 892, further sapped the caliphs' financial strength and deflected labor from more productive pursuits.

In 945, after several attempts to find a strongman to reform government administration and restore military power, the Abbasid Caliphate fell under the control of rude mountain warriors from the province of Daylam in northern Iran. Led by the Shi'ite Buyid° family, they conquered western Iran as well as Iraq. Each Buyid commander ruled his own principality. After almost two centuries of glory, the sun began to set on Baghdad. The Abbasid caliph remained, but the Buyid princes controlled him. Being Shi'ites, the Buyids had no special reverence for the Sunni caliph. According to their particular Shi'ite sect, the twelfth and last divinely appointed Imam had disappeared around 873 and would return as a messiah only at the end of the world. Thus they had no Shi'ite Imam to defer to and retained the caliph only to help control their predominantly Sunni subjects.

Dynamic growth in outlying provinces paralleled the caliphate's gradual loss of temporal power.

Harun al-Rashid (hah-ROON al–rah-SHEED)

mamluk (MAM-luke) **Buyid** (BOO-yid)

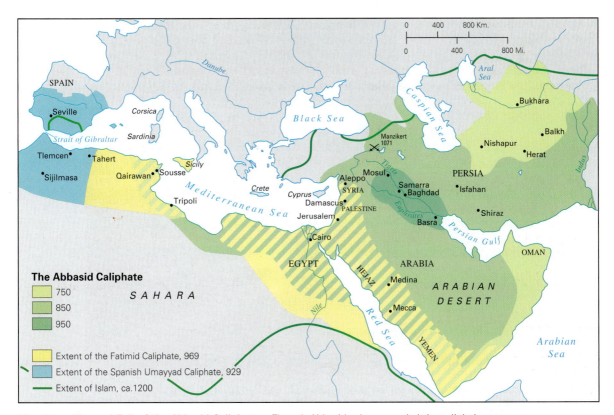

Map 7.1   Rise and Fall of the Abbasid Caliphate   Though Abbasid rulers occupied the caliphal seat in Iraq from 750 to 1258, when Mongol armies destroyed Baghdad, real political power waned sharply and steadily after 850. The rival caliphates of the Fatimids (909–1171) and Spanish Umayyads (929–976) were comparatively short-lived.

In the east in 875, the dynasty of the Samanids°, one of several Iranian families to achieve independence, established a glittering court in Bukhara, a major city on the Silk Road (see Map 7.1). Samanid princes patronized literature and learning, but the language they favored was Persian written in Arabic letters. For the first time, a non-Arabic literature rose to challenge the eminence of Arabic within the Islamic world.

In the west, the Berber revolts against Arab rule led to the appearance after 740 of the city-states of Sijilmasa° and Tahert° on the northern fringe of the Sahara. The Kharijite beliefs of these states' rulers interfered with their east-west over-land trade and led them to develop the first regular trade across the Sahara desert. Once traders looked to the desert, they discovered that Berber speakers in the southern Sahara were already carrying salt from the desert into the Sahel region. The northern traders discovered that they could trade salt for gold by providing the southern nomads, who controlled the salt sources but had little use for gold, with more useful products, such as copper and manufactured goods. Sijilmasa and Tahert became wealthy cities, the former minting gold coins that circulated as far away as Egypt and Syria.

The earliest known sub-Saharan beneficiary of the new exchange system was the kingdom of **Ghana°**. It first appears in an Arabic text of the late

---

Samanid (sah-MAN-id)   **Sijilmasa** (sih-jil-MAS-suh)
Tahert (TAH-hert)

Ghana (GAH-nuh)

Mosque of Ibn Tulun is Fustat Completed in 877, this mosque symbolized Egypt becoming for the first time a quasi-independent province under its governor. The kiosk in the center of the courtyard contains fountains for washing before prayer. Before its restoration in the thirteenth century, the mosque had a spiral minaret and a door to an adjoining governor's palace. (Ellen Rooney/Robert Harding Picture Library)

eighth century as the "land of gold." Few details survive about the early years of this realm, which was established by the Soninke° people and covered parts of Mali, Mauritania, and Senegal, but it prospered until 1076, when it was conquered by nomads from the desert. It was one of the first lands outside the orbit of the caliphate to experience a gradual and peaceful conversion to Islam.

The North African city-states lost their independence after the Fatimid° dynasty, whose members claimed (perhaps falsely) to be Shi'ite Imams descended from Ali, established itself in Tunisia in 909. After consolidating their hold on northwest Africa, the Fatimids culminated their rise to power by conquering Egypt in 969. Claiming the title of caliph in a direct challenge to the Abbasids, the Fa-

timid rulers governed from a palace complex outside the old conquest-era garrison city of Fustat°. They named the complex Cairo. For the first time Egypt became a major cultural, intellectual, and political center of Islam. The abundance of Fatimid gold coinage, now channeled to Egypt from West Africa, made the Fatimids an economic power in the Mediterranean.

Cut off from the rest of the Islamic world by the Strait of Gibraltar and, from 740 onward, by independent city-states in Morocco and Algeria, Umayyad Spain developed a distinctive Islamic culture blending Roman, Germanic, and Jewish traditions with those of the Arabs and Berbers. Historians disagree on how rapidly and completely the Spanish population converted to Islam. If we assume

Soninke (soh-NIN-kay) **Fatimid** (FAT-uh-mid)

Fustat (fuss-TAHT)

a process similar to that in the eastern regions, it seems likely that the most rapid surge in Islamization occurred in the middle of the tenth century.

As in the east, governing cities symbolized the Islamic presence in al-Andalus, as the Muslims called their Iberian territories. Cordoba, Seville, Toledo, and other cities grew substantially, becoming much larger and richer than contemporary cities in neighboring France. Converts to Islam and their descendants, unconverted Arabic-speaking Christians, and Jews joined with the comparatively few descendants of Arab settlers to create new architectural and literary styles. In the countryside, where the Berbers preferred to settle, a fusion of preexisting agricultural technologies with new crops, notably citrus fruits, and irrigation techniques from the east gave Spain the most diverse and sophisticated agricultural economy in Europe.

The rulers of al-Andalus took the title *caliph* only in 929, when Abd al-Rahman° III (r. 912–961) did so in response to a similar declaration by the newly established (909) Fatimid ruler in Tunisia. By the century's end, however, this caliphate encountered challenges from breakaway movements that eventually splintered al-Andalus into a number of small states. Political decay did not impede cultural growth. Some of the greatest writers and thinkers in Jewish history worked in Muslim Spain in the eleventh and twelfth centuries, sometimes writing in Arabic, sometimes in Hebrew. Judah Halevi (1075–1141) composed exquisite poetry and explored questions of religious philosophy. Maimonides (1135–1204) made a major compilation of Judaic law and expounded on Aristotelian philosophy. At the same time, Islamic thought in Spain attained its loftiest peaks in Ibn Hazm's (994–1064) treatises on love and other subjects, the Aristotelian philosophical writings of Ibn Rushd° (1126–1198, known in Latin as Averroës°) and Ibn Tufayl° (d. 1185), and the mystic speculations of Ibn al-Arabi° (1165–1240). Christians, too, shared in the intellectual and cultural dynamism of al-Andalus. Translations from Arabic to Latin made during this period had a profound effect on the later intellectual development of western Europe (see Chapter 8).

The Samanids, Fatimids, and Spanish Umayyads, three of many regional principalities, represent the political diversity and awakening of local awareness that coincided with Abbasid decline. Yet drawing and redrawing political boundaries did not result in the rigid division of the Islamic world into kingdoms. Religious and cultural developments, particularly the rise in cities of a social group of religious scholars known as the **ulama**°— Arabic for "people with (religious) knowledge"— worked against any permanent division of the Islamic umma.

Assault from Within and Without, 1050–1258

The role played by Turkish mamluks in the decline of Abbasid power established an enduring stereotype of the Turk as a ferocious, unsophisticated warrior. This image gained strength in the 1030s when the Seljuk° family established a Turkish Muslim state based on nomadic power. Taking the Arabic title *Sultan*, meaning "power," and the revived Persian title *Shahan-shah*, or King of Kings, the Seljuk ruler Tughril° Beg created a kingdom that stretched from northern Afghanistan to Baghdad, which he occupied in 1055. After a century under the thumb of the Shi'ite Buyids, the Abbasid caliph breathed easier under the slightly lighter thumb of the Sunni Turks. The Seljuks pressed on into Syria and Anatolia, administering a lethal blow to Byzantine power at the Battle of Manzikert° in 1071. The Byzantine army fell back on Constantinople, leaving Anatolia open to Turkish occupation.

Under Turkish rule, cities shrank as pastoralists overran their agricultural hinterlands. Irrigation works suffered from lack of maintenance in the unsettled countryside. Tax revenues fell. Twelfth-century Seljuk princes contesting for power fought over cities, but few Turks participated in urban cultural and religious life. The gulf between a religiously based urban society and the culture and personnel of the government deepened. When factional riots broke out between Sunnis and Shi'ites, or between rival schools of Sunni law,

---

Abd al-Rahman (AHB-d al-ruh-MAHN)   **Ibn Rushd** (IB-uhn RUSHED)   **Averroës** (uh-VERR-oh-eez)   **Ibn Tufayl** (IB-uhn too-FILE)   **Ibn al-Arabi** (IB-uhn ahl-AH-rah-bee)

ulama (oo-leh-MAH)   **Seljuk** (sel-JOOK)   **Tughril** (TUUG-ruhl)   **Manzikert** (MANZ-ih-kuhrt)

rulers generally remained aloof, even as destruction and loss of life mounted. Similarly, when princes fought for the title *sultan*, religious leaders advised citizens to remain neutral.

By the early twelfth century, unrepaired damage from floods, fires, and civil disorder had reduced old Baghdad on the west side of the Tigris to ruins. The withering of Baghdad reflected a broader environmental problem: the collapse of the canal system on which agriculture in the Tigris and Euphrates Valley depended. For millennia a center of world civilization, Mesopotamia underwent substantial population loss and never again regained its geographical importance.

The Turks alone cannot be blamed for the demographic and economic misfortunes of Iran and Iraq. Too-robust urbanization had strained food resources, and political fragmentation had dissipated revenues. The growing practice of using land grants to pay soldiers and courtiers also played a role. When absentee grant holders used agents to collect taxes, the agents tended to gouge villagers and to take little interest in improving production, all of which weakened the agricultural base of the economy.

The Seljuk Empire was beset by internal quarrels when the first crusading armies of Christians reached the Holy Land. The First Crusade captured Jerusalem in 1099 (see Chapter 8). Though charged with the stuff of romance, the Crusades had little lasting impact on the Islamic lands. The four crusader principalities of Edessa, Antioch, Tripoli, and Jerusalem simply became pawns in the shifting pattern of politics already in place. Newly arrived knights eagerly attacked the Muslim enemy, whom they called "Saracens°"; but veteran crusaders recognized that practicing diplomacy and seeking partners of convenience among rival Muslim princes offered a sounder strategy.

The Muslims finally unified to face the European enemy in the mid-twelfth century. Nur al-Din ibn Zangi° established a strong state based in Damascus and sent an army to terminate the Fatimid Caliphate in Egypt. A nephew of the Kurdish commander of that expedition, Salah-al-Din, known in the West as Saladin, took advantage of

Nur al-Din's timely death to seize power and unify Egypt and Syria. The Fatimid dynasty fell in 1171. In 1187 Saladin recaptured Jerusalem from the Europeans.

Saladin's descendants fought off subsequent Crusades. After one such battle, however, in 1250, Turkish mamluk troops seized control of the government in Cairo, ending Saladin's dynasty. In 1260 these mamluks rode east to confront a new invading force. At the Battle of Ain Jalut° (Spring of Goliath) in Syria, they met and defeated an army of Mongols from Central Asia (see Chapter 11), thus stemming an invasion that had begun several decades before and legitimizing their claim to dominion over Egypt and Syria.

A succession of slave-soldier sultans, whose reigns come to be termed "the Mamluk period," ruled Egypt and Syria until 1517. Fear of new Mongol attacks receded after 1300, but by then the new ruling system had become fixed. Young Turkish or Circassian slaves, the latter from the eastern end of the Black Sea, were imported from non-Muslim lands, raised in military training barracks, and converted to Islam. Owing loyalty to the Mamluk officers who purchased them, they formed a military ruling class that was socially disconnected from the Arabic-speaking native population.

The Mongol invasions, especially their destruction of the Abbasid Caliphate in Baghdad in 1258, shocked the world of Islam. The Mamluk sultan placed a relative of the last Baghdad caliph on a caliphal throne in Cairo, but the Egyptian Abbasids were never more than puppets serving Mamluk interests. In the Muslim lands from Iraq eastward, non-Muslim rule lasted for much of the thirteenth century. Although the Mongols left few ethnic or linguistic traces in these lands, their initial destruction of cities and slaughter of civilian populations, their diversion of Silk Road trade from the traditional route terminating in Baghdad to more northerly routes ending at ports on the Black Sea, and their casual disregard, even after their conversion to Islam, of Muslim religious life and urban culture hastened currents of change already under way.

Saracen (SAR-uh-suhn)   **Nur al-Din ibn Zangi** (NOOR-al-DEEN ib-uhn ZAN-gee)

Ain Jalut (ine jah-LOOT)

ISLAMIC CIVILIZATION

Though increasingly unsettled in its political dimension and subject to economic disruptions caused by war, the ever-expanding Islamic world underwent a fruitful evolution in law, social structure, and religious expression. Religious conversion and urbanization reinforced each other to create a distinct Islamic civilization. The immense geographical and human diversity of the Muslim lands allowed many "small traditions" to coexist with the developing "great tradition" of Islam.

Law and Dogma

The Shari'a, the law of Islam, provides the foundation of Islamic civilization. Yet aside from certain Quranic verses conveying specific divine ordinances—most pertaining to personal and family matters—Islam had no legal system in the time of Muhammad. Arab custom and the Prophet's own authority offered the only guidance. After Muhammad died, the umma tried to follow his example. This became harder and harder to do, however, as those who knew Muhammad best passed away and many Arabs found themselves living in far-off lands. Non-Arab converts to Islam, who at first tried to follow Arab customs they had little familiarity with, had an even harder time.

Islam slowly developed laws to govern social and religious life. The full sense of Islamic civilization, however, goes well beyond the basic Five Pillars mentioned earlier. Some Muslim thinkers felt that the reasoned consideration of a mature man offered the best resolution of issues not covered by Quranic revelation. Others argued for the sunna, or tradition, of the Prophet as the best guide. To

Scholarly Life in Medieval Islam   Books being scarce and expensive, teachers dictated to their students, as shown on the right. Notice that the student is writing on a single sheet of paper while the scholar in the center holds an entire book. On the left, an author presents his work to a wealthy patron.   (Bibliothèque nationale de France)

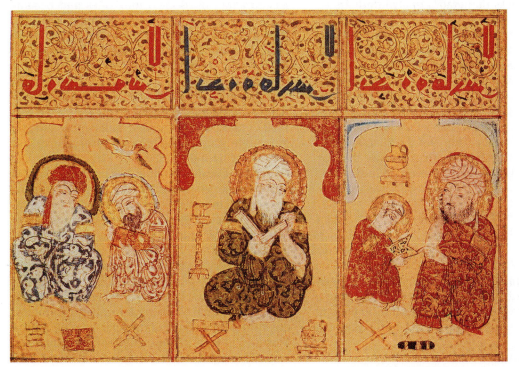

understand that sunna they collected and studied thousands of reports, called **hadith°**, purporting to convey the precise words or deeds of Muhammad. It became customary to precede each hadith with a chain of oral authorities leading back to the person who had direct acquaintance with the Prophet.

Many hadith dealt with ritual matters, such as how to wash before prayer. Others provided answers to legal questions not covered by Quranic revelation or suggested principles for deciding such matters. By the eleventh century most legal thinkers had accepted the idea that Muhammad's personal behavior provided the best role model, and that the hadith constituted the most authoritative basis for law after the Quran itself.

Yet the hadith posed a problem because the tens of thousands of anecdotes included both genuine and invented reports, the latter sometimes politically motivated, as well as stories derived from non-Muslim religious traditions. Only a specialist could hope to separate a sound from a weak tradition. As the hadith grew in importance, so did the branch of learning devoted to their analysis. Scholars discarded thousands for having faulty chains of authority. The most reliable they collected into books that gradually achieved authoritative status. Sunnis placed six books in this category; Shi'ites, four.

As it gradually evolved, the Shari'a embodied a vision of an umma in which all subscribed to the same moral values and political and ethnic distinctions lost importance. Every Muslim ruler was expected to abide by and enforce the religious law. In practice, this expectation often lost out in the hurly-burly of political life. But the Shari'a proved an important basis for an urban lifestyle that varied surprisingly little from Morocco to India.

Converts and Cities

Conversion to Islam, more the outcome of people's learning about the new rulers' religion than an escape from the tax on non-Muslims, as some scholars have suggested, helped spur urbanization. Conversion did not require extensive knowledge of the faith. To become a Muslim, a person simply stated, in the presence

of a Muslim: "There is no God but God, and Muhammad is the Messenger of God."

Few converts spoke Arabic, and fewer could read the Quran. Many converts knew no more of the Quran than the verses they memorized for daily prayers. Muhammad had established no priesthood to define and spread the faith. Thus new converts, whether Arab or non-Arab, faced the problem of finding out for themselves what Islam was about and how they should act as Muslims. This meant spending time with Muslims, learning their language, and imitating their practices.

In many areas, conversion involved migrating to an Arab governing center. The alternative, converting to Islam but remaining in one's home community, was difficult because religion had become the main component of social identity in Byzantine and Sasanid times. Converts to Islam thus encountered discrimination if they stayed in their Christian, Jewish, or Zoroastrian communities. Migration both averted discrimination and took advantage of the economic opportunities opened up by tax revenues flowing into the Arab governing centers.

The Arab military settlements of Kufa and Basra in Iraq blossomed into cities and became important centers for Muslim cultural activities. As conversion rapidly spread in the mid-ninth century, urbanization accelerated in other regions, most visibly in Iran, where most cities previously had been quite small. Nishapur in the northeast grew from fewer than 10,000 pre-Islamic inhabitants to between 100,000 and 200,000 by the year 1000. Other Iranian cities experienced similar growth. In Iraq, Baghdad and Mosul joined Kufa and Basra as major cities. In Syria, Aleppo and Damascus flourished under Muslim rule. Fustat in Egypt developed into Cairo, one of the largest and greatest Islamic cities. The primarily Christian patriarchal cities of Jerusalem, Antioch, and Alexandria, not being Muslim governing centers, shrank and stagnated.

Conversion-related migration meant that cities became heavily Muslim before the countryside did. This reinforced the urban orientation deriving from the fact that Muhammad and his first followers came from the commercial city of Mecca. Mosques in large cities served both as ritual centers and as places for learning and social activities.

Islam colored all aspects of urban social life (see Diversity and Dominance: Beggars, Con Men, and Singing-girls). Initially the new Muslims imitated Arab dress and customs and emulated people they regarded as particularly pious. In the absence of a central religious authority, local variations developed in the way people practiced Islam and in the hadith they attributed to the Prophet. This gave the rapidly growing religion the flexibility to accommodate many different social situations.

By the tenth century, urban growth was affecting the countryside by expanding the consumer market. Citrus fruits, rice, and sugar cane, introduced by the Sasanids, increased in acreage and spread to new areas. Cotton became a major crop in Iran and elsewhere and stimulated textile production. Irrigation works expanded. Abundant coinage facilitated a flourishing intercity and long-distance trade that provided regular links between isolated districts and integrated the pastoral nomads, who provided pack animals, into the region's economy. Trade encouraged the manufacture of cloth, metal goods, and pottery.

Science and technology also flourished. Building on Hellenistic traditions and their own observations and experience, Muslim doctors and astronomers developed skills and theories far in advance of their European counterparts. Working in Egypt in the eleventh century, the mathematician and physicist Ibn al-Haytham° wrote more than a hundred works. Among other things, he determined that the Milky Way lies far beyond earth's atmosphere, proved that light travels from a seen object to the eye and not the reverse, and explained why the sun and moon appear larger on the horizon than overhead.

Islam, Women, and Slaves

Women seldom traveled. Those living in rural areas worked in the fields and tended animals. Urban women, particularly members of the elite, lived in seclusion and did not leave their homes without covering themselves. Seclusion of women and veiling in public already existed in Byzantine and Sasanid times. Through interpretation of specific verses from the Quran,

Ibn al-Haytham (IB-uhn al–HY-tham)

these practices now became fixtures of Muslim social life. Although women sometimes became literate and studied with relatives, they did so away from the gaze of unrelated men. Although women played influential roles within the family, public roles were generally barred. Only slave women could perform before unrelated men as musicians and dancers. A man could have sexual relations with as many slave concubines as he pleased, in addition to marrying as many as four wives.

Islamic law granted women greater status than did Christian or Jewish law. Muslim women inherited property and retained it in marriage. They had a right to remarry, and they received a cash payment upon divorce. Although a man could divorce his wife without stating a cause, a woman could initiate divorce under specified conditions. Women could practice birth control. They could testify in court, although their testimony counted as half that of a man. They could go on pilgrimage. Nevertheless, a misogynistic tone sometimes appears in Islamic writings. One saying attributed to the Prophet observed: "I was raised up to heaven and saw that most of its denizens were poor people; I was raised into the hellfire and saw that most of its denizens were women."[3]

In the absence of writings by women from this period, the status of women must be deduced from the writings of men. Two episodes involving the Prophet's wife A'isha, the daughter of Abu Bakr, demonstrate how Muslim men appraised women in society. As a fourteen-year-old she had become separated from a caravan and rejoined it only after traveling through the night with a man who found her alone in the desert. Gossips accused her of being untrue to the Prophet, but a revelation from God proved her innocence. The second event was her participation in the Battle of the Camel, fought to derail Ali's caliphate. These two episodes came to epitomize what Muslim men feared most about women: sexual infidelity and meddling in politics.

The earliest literature dealing with A'isha stresses her position as Muhammad's favorite and her role as a prolific transmitter of hadith. In time, however, his first wife, Khadija, and his daughter, Ali's wife Fatima, surpassed A'isha as ideal women. Both appear as model wives and mothers with no suspicion of sexual irregularity or political manipulation.

운드폭탄 4발 투하… 두 아들과 함께 사망
실진지 구축… 이튿날 시가戰
령이 대중 앞에 나타나거나 애국심
을 고취하는 노래만을 내보내던 방
송마저 중단됐다.
라크 전후
의에서는
영국 주도

DIVERSITY AND DOMINANCE

BEGGARS, CON MEN, AND SINGING-GIRLS

Though rulers, warriors, and religious scholars dominate the traditional narratives, the society that developed over the early centuries of Islam was remarkably diverse. Beggars, tricksters, and street performers belonged to a single loose fraternity: the Banu Sasan, or Tribe of Sasan. Tales of their tricks and exploits amused staid, pious Muslims, who often encountered them in cities and on their scholarly travels. The tenth-century poet Abu Dulaf al-Khazraji, who lived in Iran, studied the jargon of the Banu Sasan and their way of life and composed a long poem in which he cast himself as one of the group. However, he added a commentary to each verse to explain the jargon words that his sophisticated court audience would have found unfamiliar.

We are the beggars' brotherhood, and no one can deny us our lofty pride . . .

And of our number is the feigned madman and mad woman, with metal charms strung from their necks.

And the ones with ornaments drooping from their ears, and with collars of leather or brass round their necks . . .

And the one who simulates a festering internal wound, and the people with false bandages round their heads and sickly, jaundiced faces.

And the one who slashes himself, alleging that he has been mutilated by assailants, or the one who darkens his skin artificially pretending that he has been beaten up and wounded . . .

And the one who practices as a manipulator and quack dentist, or who escapes from chains wound round his body, or the one who uses almost invisible silk thread mysteriously to draw off rings . . .

And of our number are those who claim to be refugees from the Byzantine frontier regions, those who go round begging on pretext of having left behind captive families . . .

And the one who feigns an internal discharge, or who showers the passers-by with his urine, or who farts in the mosque and makes a nuisance of himself, thus wheedling money out of people . . .

And of our number are the ones who purvey objects of veneration made from clay, and those who have their beards smeared with red dye.

And the one who brings up secret writing by immersing it in what looks like water, and the one who similarly brings up the writing by exposing it to burning embers.

One of the greatest masters of Arabic prose, Jahiz (776– 869), was a famously ugly man—his name means "Pop-eyed"—of Abyssinian family origin. Spending part of his life in his native Basra, in southern Iraq, and part in Baghdad, the Abbasid capital, he wrote voluminously on subjects ranging from theology to zoology to miserliness. These excerpts come from his book devoted to the business of training slave girls as musicians, a lucrative practice of suspect morality but great popularity among men of wealth. He pretends that he is not the author, but merely writing down the views of the owners of singing-girls.

Now I will describe for you the definition of the passion of love, so that you may understand what exactly it is. It is a malady which smites the spirit, and affects the body as well by contagion: just as physical weakness impairs the spirit and low spirits in a man make him emaciated . . . The stronger the constituent causes of the malady are, the more inveterate it is, and the slower to clear up . . .

Passion for singing-girls is dangerous, in view of their manifold excellences and the satisfaction one's soul finds in them. . . . The singing-girl is hardly ever sincere in her passion, or wholehearted in her affection. For both by training and by innate instinct her nature is to set up snares and traps for the victims, in order that they may fall into her toils. As soon as the observer notices her, she exchanges provocative glances with him, gives him playful smiles, dallies with him in verses set to music, falls in with his suggestions, is eager to drink when he drinks, expresses her fervent desire for him to stay a long while, her yearning for his prompt return, and her sorrow at his departure. Then when she perceives that her sorcery has worked on him and that he has become entangled in the net, she redoubles the wiles she had used at first, and leads him to suppose that she is more in love than he is . . .

An accomplished singing-girl has a repertoire of upwards of four thousands songs, each of them two to four verses long, so that the total amount . . . comes to ten thousand verses, in which there is not one mention of God (except by inadvertence). . . . They are all founded on references to fornication, pimping, passion, yearning, desire, and lust. . . .

Among the advantages enjoyed by each man among us [i.e., speaking as a keeper of singing-girls] is that other men seek him out eagerly in his abode, just as one eagerly seeks out caliphs and great folk; is visited without having the trouble of visiting; receives gifts and is not compelled to give; has presents made to him and none required from him. . . .

The owner of singing-girls . . . takes the substance and gives the appearance, gets the real thing and gives the shadow, and sells the gusty wind for solid ore and pieces of silver and gold. Between the suitors and what they desire lies the thorniest of obstacles. For the owner, were he not to abstain from granting the dupe his desire for motives of purity and decency, would at any rate do so out of sharp-wittedness and wiliness, and to safeguard his trade and defend the sanctity of his estate. For when the lover once possesses himself of the beloved, nine-tenths of his ardour disappear, and his liberality and contributions [to the owner] diminish on the same scale.

If he were not a past-master in this splendid and noble profession, why is it that he abandons jealous surveillance of the girls (though choosing his spies well), accepts the room rent, pretends to doze off before supper, takes no notice of winkings, is indulgent to a kiss, ignores signs [passing between the pair of lovers], turns a blind eye to the exchange of billets-doux, affects to forget all about the girl on the day of the visit, does not scold her for retiring to a private

place, does not pry into her secrets or cross-examine her about how she passed the night, and does not bother to lock the doors and draw close the curtains? He reckons up each victim's income separately, and knows how much money he is good for; just as the trader sorts out his various kinds of merchandise and prices them according to their value . . . When he has an influential customer, he takes advantage of his influence and makes requests from him; if the customer is rich but not influential, he borrows money from him without interest. If he is a person connected with the authorities, such a one can be used as a shield against the unfriendly attentions of the police; and when such a one comes on a visit, drums and hautbois [i.e., double-reed pipes] are sounded.

*B*oth of these passages fall into the category of Arabic literature known as adab, or belles-lettres. The purpose of adab was to entertain and instruct through a succession of short anecdotes, verses, and expository discussions. It attracted the finest writers of the Abbasid era and affords one of the richest sources for looking at everyday life, always keeping in mind that the intended readers were a restricted class of educated men, including merchants, court and government officials, and even men of religion.

QUESTIONS FOR ANALYSIS

1. What do the authors' portrayals of beggars, con men, singing-girls, and keepers of singing-girls indicate about the diversity of life in the city?

2. Taken together, what do these passages indicate about the conventional portrayal of religious laws and moral teachings dominating everyday life?

3. In the discussion of singing-girls, what do you see as the importance of the practices of veiling and seclusion among urban, free-born, Muslim women?

4. In evaluating these as historical sources, is it necessary to take the tastes of the intended audience into account?

Sources: First selection excerpts from Clifford Edmund Bosworth, *The Mediaeval Islamic Underworld: The Banu Sasan in Arabic Society and Literature* (Leiden: E. I. Brill, 1976), 191–199. Copyright © 1976. With kind permission of Koninklijke Brill N.V. Leiden, the Netherlands. Second selection excerpts from Jahiz, *The Epistle on Singing-Girls*, tr. and ed. A. F. L. Beeston (Warminster: Aris and Phillips, 1980), 28–37. Reprinted with permission of Oxbow Books, Ltd.

Women Playing Chess in Muslim Spain As shown in this thirteenth-century miniature, women in their own quarters, without men present, wore whatever clothes and jewels they liked. Notice the henna decorating the hands of the woman in the middle. The woman on the left, probably a slave, plays an oud. (Institute Amatller d'Art Hispanic. © Patrimonio Nacional, Madrid)

As the seclusion of women became common-place in urban Muslim society, some writers extolled homosexual relationships, partly because a male lover could appear in public or go on a journey. Although Islam deplored homosexuality, one ruler wrote a book advising his son to follow moderation in all things and thus share his affections equally between men and women. Another ruler and his slave-boy became models of perfect love in the verses of mystic poets.

Islam allowed slavery but forbade Muslims from enslaving other Muslims or so-called People of the Book—Jews, Christians, and Zoroastrians, who revered holy books respected by the Muslims. Being enslaved as a prisoner of war constituted an exception. Later centuries saw a constant flow of slaves into Islamic territory from Africa and Central Asia. A hereditary slave society, however, did not develop. Usually slaves converted to Islam, and many masters then freed them as an act of piety. The offspring of slave women and Muslim men were born free.

The Recentering of Islam

Early Islam centered on the caliphate, the political expression of the unity of the umma. No formal organization or hierarchy, however, directed the process of conversion. Thus there emerged a multitude of local Islamic communities so disconnected from each other that numerous competing interpretations of the developing religion arose. Inevitably, the centrality of the caliphate diminished (see Map 7.1). The appearance of rival caliphates in Tunisia and Cordoba accentuated the problem of decentralization.

The rise of the ulama as community leaders did not prevent growing fragmentation because the ulama themselves divided into contentious factions. During the twelfth century factionalism began to abate, and new socioreligious institutions emerged to provide the umma with a different sort of religious center. These new developments stemmed in part from an exodus of religious scholars from Iran in response to economic and political disintegration during the late eleventh and twelfth centuries. The flow of Iranians to the Arab lands and to newly conquered territories in India and Anatolia increased after the Mongol invasion.

Fully versed in Arabic as well as their native Persian, immigrant scholars were warmly received. They brought with them a view of religion developed in Iran's urban centers. A type of religious college, the *madrasa*°, gained sudden popularity outside Iran, where madrasas had been known since the tenth century. Scores of madrasas, many founded by local rulers, appeared throughout the Islamic world.

Iranians also contributed to the growth of mystic groups known as *Sufi* brotherhoods in the twelfth and thirteenth centuries. The doctrines and rituals of certain Sufis spread from city to city, giving rise to the first geographically extensive Islamic religious organizations. Sufi doctrines varied, but a quest for a sense of union with God through rituals and training was a common denominator. Sufism had begun in early Islamic times and had doubtless benefited from the ideas and beliefs of people from religions with mystic traditions who converted to Islam.

The early Sufis had been saintly individuals given to ecstatic and poetic utterances and wonderworking. They attracted disciples but did not try to organize them. The growth of brotherhoods, a less ecstatic form of Sufism, set a tone for society in general. It soon became common for most Muslim men, particularly in the cities, to belong to at least one brotherhood.

A sense of the social climate the Sufi brotherhoods fostered can be gained from a twelfth-century manual:

> Every limb has its own special ethics. . . . The ethics of the tongue. The tongue should always be busy in reciting God's names (*dhikr*) and in saying good things of the brethren, praying for them,

and giving them counsel. . . . The ethics of hearing. One should not listen to indecencies and slander. . . . The ethics of sight. One should lower one's eyes in order not to see forbidden things.[4]

Special dispensations allowed people who merely wanted to emulate the Sufis and enjoy their company to follow less demanding rules:

> It is allowed by way of dispensation to possess an estate or to rely on a regular income. The Sufis' rule in this matter is that one should not use all of it for himself, but should dedicate this to public charities and should take from it only enough for one year for himself and his family. . . .
>
> There is a dispensation allowing one to be occupied in business; this dispensation is granted to him who has to support a family. But this should not keep him away from the regular performance of prayers. . . .
>
> There is a dispensation allowing one to watch all kinds of amusement. This is, however, limited by the rule: What you are forbidden from doing, you are also forbidden from watching.[5]

Some Sufi brotherhoods spread in the countryside. Local shrines and pilgrimages to the tombs of Muhammad's descendants and saintly Sufis became popular. The end of the Abbasid Caliphate enhanced the religious centrality of Mecca, which eventually became an important center of madrasa education, and gave renewed importance to the annual pilgrimage.

CONCLUSION

The inspiration of Muhammad's teachings and the leadership his close followers provided after his death helped unite the Arabs and guide their conquests. But the formation of Islamic society was a more gradual affair. The caliphate was the culmination of a transformation, begun in Byzantine and Sasanid times, from ethnically and religiously diverse societies held together by the power and grandeur of kings to a unified realm based on religious identity. The concept of the umma, as set forth in the Quran, united Muslims in a universal community embracing enormous diversity of

madrasa (MAH-dras-uh)

language and social custom. Though Muslim communities adapted to local "small traditions," by the twelfth century a religious scholar could travel throughout the Islamic world and blend easily into the local Muslim community.

By the ninth century, the forces of conversion and urbanization fostered social and religious experimentation in urban settings. But from the eleventh century onward, political disruption and the spread of pastoral nomadism slowed this early economic and technological dynamism. The Muslim community then turned to new religious institutions, such as the madrasas and Sufi brotherhoods, to create the flexible and durable community structures that carried Islam into new regions and protected ordinary believers from capricious political rule.

■ Key Terms

Shi'ites	caliphate
Sunnis	Quran
Mecca	Umayyad Caliphate
Muhammad	Abbasid Caliphate
muslim	mamluks
Islam	Ghana
Medina	ulama
umma	hadith

■ Suggested Reading

Ira M. Lapidus, *A History of Islamic Societies* (1988), focuses on social developments and includes the histories of Islam in India, Southeast Asia, sub-Saharan Africa, and other parts of the world. Marshall G. S. Hodgson, *The Venture of Islam*, 3 vols. (1974), critiques traditional ways of studying the Islamic Middle East while offering an alternative interpretation. Bernard Lewis's *The Middle East: A Brief History of the Last 2,000 Years* (1995) provides a lively narration from the time of Christ.

For an up-to-date shorter survey, see Jonathan Berkey, *The Formation of Islam: Religion and Society in the Near East, 600–1800* (2002). Richard W. Bulliet, *Islam: The View from the Edge* (1993), offers, in brief form, an approach that concentrates on the lives of converts to Islam and local religious notables.

Muslims regard the Quran as untranslatable because they consider the Arabic in which it is couched to be inseparable from God's message. Most "interpretations" in English adhere reasonably closely to the Arabic text.

Martin Lings, *Muhammad: His Life Based on the Earliest Sources,* rev. ed. (1991), offers a readable biography reflecting Muslim viewpoints. Standard Western treatments include W. Montgomery Watt's *Muhammad at Mecca* (1953) and *Muhammad at Medina* (1956; reprint, 1981); and the one-volume summary: *Muhammad, Prophet and Statesman* (1974). Michael A. Cook, *Muhammad* (1983), intelligently discusses historiographical problems and source difficulties. Karen Armstrong's *Muhammad: A Biography of the Prophet* (1993) achieves a sympathetic balance.

For information on the new school of thought that rejects the traditional accounts of Muhammad's life and of the origins of the Quran, see Patricia Crone and Michael Cook, *Hagarism* (1977), Patricia Crone, *Meccan Trade and the Rise of Islam* (1987), and Fred Donner, *Narratives of Islamic Origins* (1998).

Wilfred Madelung's *The Succession to Muhammad: A Study of the Early Caliphate* (1997) gives an interpretation unusually sympathetic to Shi'ite viewpoints. G. R. Hawting, *The First Dynasty of Islam: The Umayyad Caliphate, A.D. 661–750* (1987), offers a more conventional and easily readable history of a crucial century.

Western historians have debated the beginnings of the Abbasid Caliphate. Moshe Sharon, *Black Banners from the East: The Establishment of the 'Abbasid State—Incubation of a Revolt* (1983), and Jacob Lassner, *Islamic Revolution and Historical Memory: An Inquiry into the Art of Abbasid Apologetics* (1987), give differing accounts based on newly utilized sources. For a broader history that puts the first three centuries of Abbasid rule into the context of the earlier periods, see Hugh N. Kennedy, *The Prophet and the Age of the Caliphates: The Islamic Near East from the Sixth to the Eleventh Century* (1986). Harold Bowen, *The Life and Times of Ali ibn Isa "The Good Vizier"* (1928; reprint, 1975), supplements Kennedy's narrative superbly with a detailed study of corrupt caliphal politics in the tumultuous early tenth century.

Articles in Michael Gervers and Ramzi Jibran Bikhazi, eds., *Conversion and Continuity: Indigenous Christian Communities in Islamic Lands, Eighth to Eighteenth Centuries* (1990), detail Christian responses to Islam. For a Zoroastrian perspective see Jamsheed K. Choksy, *Conflict and Cooperation: Zoroastrian Subalterns and Muslim Elites in Medieval Iranian Society* (1997). Jacob Lassner summarizes S. D. Goitein's definitive multivolume study of the Jews of medieval Egypt in *A Mediterranean Society: An Abridgement in One Volume* (1999). On the process of conversion, see the work in quantitative history of Richard W. Bulliet, *Conversion to Islam in the Medieval Period* (1979).

With the fragmentation of the Abbasid Caliphate beginning in the ninth century, studies of separate areas become more useful than general histories. Richard N. Frye, *The Golden Age of Persia: The Arabs in the East* (1975), skillfully evokes the complicated world of early Islamic Iran and the survival and revival of Persian national identity. Thomas F. Glick, *Islamic and Christian Spain in the Early Middle Ages* (1979) and *From Muslim Fortress to Christian Castle: Social and Cultural Change in Medieval Spain* (1995), questions standard ideas about Christians and Muslims in Spain from a geographical and technological standpoint. For North Africa, Charles-André Julien, *History of North Africa: Tunisia, Algeria, Morocco, from the Arab Conquest to 1830* (1970), summarizes a literature primarily written in French. This same French historiographical tradition is challenged and revised by Abdallah Laroui, *The History of the Maghrib: An Interpretive Essay* (1977). For a detailed primary source, see the English translation of the most important chronicle of early Islamic history, *The History of al-Tabari*, published in thirty-eight volumes under the general editorship of Ehsan Yarshater.

Roy P. Mottahedeh, *Loyalty and Leadership in an Early Islamic Society* (1980); Richard W. Bulliet, *The Patricians of Nishapur* (1972); and Ira Marvin Lapidus, *Muslim Cities in the Later Middle Ages* (1984), discuss social history in tenth-century Iran, eleventh-century Iran, and fourteenth-century Syria, respectively. Jonathan Berkey, *The Transmission of Knowledge in Medieval Cairo: A Social History of Islamic Education* (1992), and Michael Chamberlain, *Knowledge and Social Practice in Medieval Damascus, 1190–1350* (1994), put forward competing assessments of education and the ulama. For urban geography see Paul Wheatley, *The Places Where Men Pray Together* (2001).

Ahmad Y. al-Hassan and Donald R. Hill, *Islamic Technology: An Illustrated History* (1986), introduce a little-studied field. For a more crafts-oriented look, see Hans E. Wulff, *The Traditional Crafts of Persia: Their Development, Technology, and Influence on Eastern and Western Civilizations* (1966). Jonathan Bloom's *Paper Before Print* (2001) details the great impact of papermaking in many cultural areas.

Denise Spellberg, *Politics, Gender, and the Islamic Past: The Legacy of A'isha bint Abi Bakr* (1994), provides pathbreaking guidance on women's history. Basim Musallam, *Sex and Society in Islamic Civilization* (1983), treats the social, medical, and legal history of birth control. On race and slavery, see Bernard Lewis, *Race and Slavery in the Middle East: A Historical Enquiry* (1992).

Among the numerous introductory books on Islam as a religion, a reliable starting point is David Waines, *An Introduction to Islam* (1995). For more advanced work, Fazlur Rahman, *Islam*, 2d ed. (1979), skillfully discusses some of the subject's difficulties. Islamic law is well covered in Noel J. Coulson, *A History of Islamic Law* (1979). For Sufism see Annemarie Schimmel, *Mystical Dimensions of Islam* (1975).

Two religious texts available in translation are Abu Hamid al-Ghazali, *The Faith and Practice of al-Ghazali*, trans. W. Montgomery Watt (1967; reprint, 1982), and Abu al-Najib al-Suhrawardi, *A Sufi Rule for Novices*, trans. Menahem Milson (1975).

For detailed and abundant maps, see William C. Brice, ed., *An Historical Atlas of Islam* (1981). The most complete reference work for people working in Islamic studies is *The Encyclopedia of Islam*, new ed. (Leiden: E. J. Brill, 1960–), now available in CD-ROM format. For encyclopedia-type articles on pre-Islamic topics, see G.W. Bowersock, Peter Brown, and Oleg Grabar, *Late Antiquity: A Guide to the Postclassical World* (1999). On Iran, see the excellent but still unfinished *Encyclopedia Iranica*, edited by Ehsan Yarshater.

◼ Notes

1. Quran. Sura 96, verses 1–5.
2. Quran. Sura 92, verses 1–10.
3. Richard W. Bulliet, *Islam: The View from the Edge* (New York: Columbia University Press, 1994), 87.
4. Abu Najib al-Suhrawardi, *A Sufi Rule for Novices*, trans. Menahem Milson (Cambridge, MA: Harvard University Press, 1975), 45–58.
5. Ibid., 73–82.

8 Christian Europe Emerges, 600–1200

CHAPTER OUTLINE

The Byzantine Empire, 600–1200

Early Medieval Europe, 600–1000

The Western Church

Kievan Russia, 900–1200

Western Europe Revives, 1000–1200

The Crusades, 1095–1204

ENVIRONMENT AND TECHNOLOGY: Cathedral Organs

Christmas Day in 800 found Charles, king of the Franks, in Rome instead of at his palace at Aachen in northwestern Germany. At six-foot-three, Charles towered over the average man of his time, and his royal career had been equally gargantuan. Crowned king in his mid-twenties in 768, he had crisscrossed Europe for three decades, waging war on Muslim invaders from Spain, Avar° invaders from Hungary, and a number of German princes.

Charles had subdued many enemies and had become protector of the papacy. So not all historians believe the eyewitness report of his secretary and biographer that Charles was sur-

prised when, as the king rose from his prayers, Pope Leo III placed a new crown on his head. "Life and victory to Charles the August, crowned by God the great and pacific Emperor of the Romans," proclaimed the pope.[1] Then, amid the cheers of the crowd, he humbly knelt before the new emperor.

Charlemagne° (from Latin *Carolus magnus,* "Charles the Great") was the first in western Europe to bear the title *emperor* in over three hundred years. Rome's decline and Charlemagne's rise marked a shift of focus for Europe—away from the Mediterranean and toward the north and west. German custom and Christian piety

---

Avar (ah-vahr)

Charlemagne (SHAHR-leh-mane)

transformed the Roman heritage to create a new civilization. Irish monks preaching in Latin became important intellectual influences in some parts of Europe, while the memory of Greek and Roman philosophy faded. Urban life continued the decline that had begun in the later days of the Roman Empire. Historians originally called this era **"medieval,"** literally "middle age," because it comes between the era of Greco-Roman civilization and the intellectual, artistic, and economic changes of the Renaissance in the fourteenth century; but research has uncovered many aspects of medieval culture that are as rich and creative as those that came earlier and later.

Charlemagne was not the only ruler in Europe to claim the title emperor. Another emperor held sway in the Greek-speaking east, where Rome's political and legal heritage continued. The Eastern Roman Empire was often called the **Byzantine Empire** after the seventh century, and it was known to the Muslims as Rum. Western Europeans lived amid the ruins of empire, while the Byzantines maintained and reinterpreted Roman traditions. The authority of the Byzantine emperors blended with the influence of the Christian church to form a cultural synthesis that helped shape the emerging kingdom of **Kievan Russia.** Byzantium's centuries-long conflict with Islam helped spur the crusading passion that overtook western Europe in the eleventh century.

The comparison between western and eastern Europe appears paradoxical. Byzantium inherited a robust and self-confident late Roman society and economy, while western Europe could not achieve political unity and suffered severe economic decline. Yet by 1200 western Europe was showing renewed vitality and flexing its military muscles, while Byzantium was showing signs of decline and military weakness. As we ex-

plore the causes and consequences of these different historical paths, we must remember that the emergence of Christian Europe included both developments.

As you read this chapter, ask yourself the following questions:

- What role did Christianity play in reshaping European society in east and west?

- How did the Roman heritage differently affect the east and the west?

- How can one compare Kievan Russia's resemblances to western Europe and to the Byzantine Empire?

- How did Mediterranean trade and the Crusades help revive western Europe?

THE BYZANTINE EMPIRE, 600–1200

The Byzantine emperors established Christianity as their official religion (see Chapter 5). They also represented a continuation of Roman imperial rule and tradition that was largely absent in the kingdoms that succeeded Rome in the west. Byzantium inherited imperial law intact; only provincial forms of Roman law survived in the west. Combining the imperial role with political oversight over the Christian church, the emperors made a comfortable transition into the role of all-powerful Christian monarchs. The Byzantine drama, however, played on a steadily shrinking stage. Territorial losses and almost constant military pressure from north and south deprived the empire of long periods of peace.

An Empire Beleaguered Having a single ruler endowed with supreme legal and religious authority prevented the breakup of the Eastern Empire into petty principalities, but a series of territorial losses sapped the empire's strength. Between 634 and 650, Arab armies destroyed the Sasanid Empire and captured Byzantine Egypt, Syria, and Tunisia (see Chapter 7). Islam posed a religious as well as a political challenge. By the end of the twelfth century, some two-thirds of the Christians in these former Byzantine territories had adopted the Muslim faith.

The loss of such populous and prosperous provinces shook the empire and reduced its power. Although it had largely recovered and reorganized militarily by the tenth century, it never regained the lost lands. Though Crusaders from western Europe established short-lived Christian principalities at the eastern end of the Mediterranean Sea in the eleventh century, the Byzantines found them almost as hostile as the Muslims (see the section below on the Crusades). Eventually the empire succumbed to Muslim conquest in 1453.

The later Byzantine emperors faced new enemies in the north and south. Following the wave of Germanic migrations (see Chapter 5), Slavic and Turkic peoples appeared on the northern frontiers as part of centuries-long and poorly understood population migrations in Eurasian steppe lands. Other Turks led by the Seljuk family became the primary foe in the south (see Chapter 7).

At the same time, relations with the popes and princes of western Europe steadily worsened. In the mid-ninth century the patriarchs of Constantinople had challenged the territorial jurisdiction of the popes of Rome and some of the practices of the Latin Church. These arguments worsened over time and in 1054 culminated in a formal **schism°** between the Latin Church and the Orthodox Church—a break that has been only partially mended.

Society and Urban Life

Imperial authority and urban prosperity in the eastern provinces of the Late Roman Empire initially sheltered Byzantium from many of the economic reverses and population losses suffered by western Europe. However, the two regions shared a common demographic crisis during a sixth-century epidemic of bubonic plague known as "the plague of Justinian," named after the

emperor who ruled from 527 to 565. A similar though gradual and less pronounced social transformation set in around the seventh century, possibly sparked by further epidemics and the loss of Egypt and Syria to the Muslims. Narrative histories tell us little, but popular narratives of saints' lives show a transition from stories about educated saints hailing from cities to stories about saints who originated as peasants. In many areas, barter replaced money transactions; some cities declined in population and wealth; and the traditional class of local urban notables nearly disappeared.

As the urban elite class shrank, the importance of high-ranking aristocrats at the imperial court and of rural landowners increased. Power organized by family began to rival power from class-based officeholding. By the end of the eleventh century, a family-based military aristocracy had emerged. Of Byzantine emperor Alexius Comnenus° (r. 1081–1118) it was said: "He considered himself not a ruler, but a lord, conceiving and calling the empire his own house."[2] The situation of women changed, too. Although earlier Roman family life was centered on a legally all-powerful father, women had enjoyed comparative freedom in public. After the seventh century women increasingly found themselves confined to the home. Some sources indicate that when they went out, they concealed their faces behind veils. The only men they socialized with were family members. Paradoxically, however, from 1028 to 1056 women ruled the Byzantine Empire alongside their husbands. These social changes and the apparent increase in the seclusion of women resemble simultaneous developments in neighboring Islamic countries, but historians have not uncovered any firm linkage between them.

Economically, the Byzantine emperors continued the Late Roman inclination to set prices, organize grain shipments to the capital, and monopolize trade in luxury goods like Tyrian purple cloth. Such government intervention may have slowed technological development and economic innovation. So long as merchants and pilgrims hastened to Constantinople from all points of the compass, aristocrats could buy rare and costly goods. Just as the provisioning and physical im-

---

schism (SKIZ-uhm)

Alexius Comnenus (uh-LEX-see-uhs kom-NAY-nuhs)

CHRONOLOGY

	Western Europe	Eastern Europe
600		**634–650** Muslims conquer Byzantine provinces of Syria, Egypt, and Tunisia
	711 Muslim conquest of Spain	
	732 Battle of Tours	
800	**800** Coronation of Charlemagne	
	843 Treaty of Verdun divides Carolingian Empire among Charlemagne's grandsons	**882** Varangians take control of Kiev
	910 Monastery of Cluny founded	
	962 Beginning of Holy Roman Empire	**980** Vladimir becomes grand prince of Kievan Russia
1000	**1054** Formal schism between Latin and Orthodox Churches	
	1066 Normans under William the Conqueror invade England	
	1076–1078 Climax of investiture controversy	**1081–1118** Alexius Comnenus rules Byzantine Empire, calls for western military aid against Muslims
	1095 Pope Urban II preaches First Crusade	
1200		**1204** Western knights sack Constantinople in Fourth Crusade

provement of Rome overshadowed the development of other cities at the height of the Roman Empire, so other Byzantine cities suffered from the intense focus on Constantinople. In the countryside, Byzantine farmers continued to use slow oxcarts and light scratch plows, which were efficient for many, but not all, soil types, long after farmers in western Europe had begun to adopt more efficient techniques (see below).

Because Byzantium's Roman inheritance remained so much more intact than western Europe's, few people recognized the slow deterioration. Gradually, however, pilgrims and visitors from the west saw the reality beyond the awe-inspiring,

incense-filled domes of cathedrals and beneath the glitter and silken garments of the royal court. An eleventh-century French visitor wrote:

> The city itself [Constantinople] is squalid and fetid and in many places harmed by permanent darkness, for the wealthy overshadow the streets with buildings and leave these dirty, dark places to the poor and to travelers; there murders and robberies and other crimes which love the darkness are committed. Moreover, since people live lawlessly in this city, which has as many lords as rich men and almost as many thieves as poor men, a criminal knows neither fear nor shame, because crime is

Byzantine Church from a Twelfth-Century Manuscript
The upper portion shows the church façade and domes.
The lower portion shows the interior with a mosaic of
Christ enthroned at the altar end. (Bibliothèque nationale
de France)

Cultural Achievements

Though the greatest Byzantine architectural monument, Constantinople's Hagia Sophia° ("Sacred Wisdom") cathedral, dates to the reign of Justinian, artistic creativity continually manifested itself in the design and ornamentation of other churches and monasteries. Byzantine religious art, featuring stiff but arresting images of holy figures against gold backgrounds, strongly influenced painting in western Europe down to the thirteenth century, and Byzantine musical traditions strongly affected the chanting employed in medieval Latin churches.

Another important Byzantine achievement dates to the empire's long period of political decline. In the ninth century brothers named Cyril and Methodius embarked on a highly successful mission to the Slavs of Moravia (part of the modern Czech Republic). They preached in the local language, and their followers perfected a writing system, called Cyrillic°, that came to be used by Slavic Christians adhering to the Orthodox—that is, Byzantine—rite. Their careers also mark the beginning of a competition between the Greek and Latin forms of Christianity for the allegiance of the Slavs. The use today of the Cyrillic alphabet among the Russians and other Slavic peoples of Orthodox Christian faith, and of the Roman alphabet among the Poles, Czechs, and Croatians, testifies to this competition (see the section below on Kievan Russia).

not punished by law and never entirely comes to light. In every respect she exceeds moderation; for, just as she surpasses other cities in wealth, so too, does she surpass them in vice.[3]

A Byzantine contemporary, Anna Comnena, the brilliant daughter of Emperor Alexius Comnenus, expressed the view from the other side. She scornfully described a prominent churchman and philosopher who happened to be from Italy: "Italos . . . was unable with his barbaric, stupid temperament to grasp the profound truths of philosophy; even in the act of learning he utterly rejected the teacher's guiding hand, and full of temerity and barbaric folly, [believed] even before study that he excelled all others."[4]

EARLY MEDIEVAL EUROPE, 600–1000

The disappearance of the imperial legal framework that had persisted to the final days of the Western Roman Empire (see Chapter 5) and the rise of various kings, nobles, and chieftains changed the legal and political landscape of western Europe. In region after region, the family-based traditions of the Germanic peoples, which often fit local conditions better than previous practices, supplanted the edicts of the Roman emperors.

Hagia Sophia (AH-yah SOH-fee-uh)   **Cyrillic** (sih-RIL-ik)

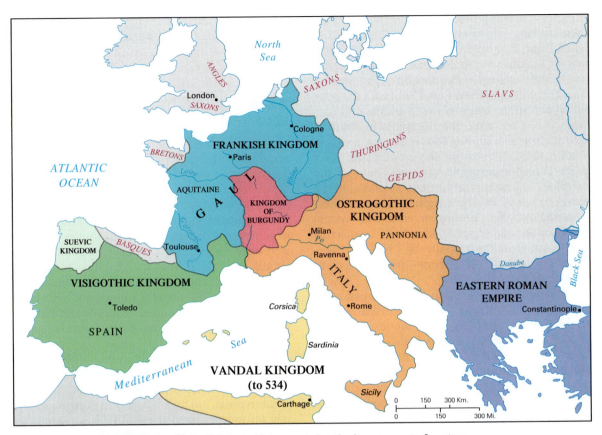

Map 8.1   Germanic Kingdoms   Though German kings asserted authority over most of western Europe, German-speaking peoples were most numerous east of the Rhine River. In most other areas, Celtic languages, for example, Breton on this map, or languages derived from Latin predominated. Though the Germanic Anglo-Saxon tongue increasingly supplanted Welsh and Scottish in Britain, the absolute number of Germanic settlers seems to have been fairly limited.

Fear and physical insecurity led communities to seek the protection of local strongmen. In places where looters and pillagers might appear at any moment, a local lord with a castle at which peasants could take refuge counted for more than a distant king. Dependency of weak people on strong people became a hallmark of the post-Roman period in western Europe.

The Time of Insecurity

In 711 a frontier raiding party of Arabs and Berbers, acting under the authority of the Umayyad caliph in Syria, crossed the Strait of Gibraltar and overturned the kingdom of the Visigoths in Spain (see Chapter 7). The disunited Europeans could not stop them from consolidating their hold on the Iberian Peninsula. After pushing the remaining Christian chieftains into the northern mountains, the Muslims moved on to France. They occupied much of the southern coast and penetrated as far north as Tours, less than 150 miles (240 kilometers) from the English Channel, before Charlemagne's grandfather, Charles Martel, stopped their most advanced raiding party in 732.

Military effectiveness was the key element in the rise of the Carolingian° family (from Latin *Carolus*,

Carolingian (kah-roe-LIN-gee-uhn)

"Charles"), first as protectors of the Frankish kings, then as kings themselves under Charlemagne's father Pepin (r. 751–768), and finally, under Charlemagne, as emperors. At the peak of Charlemagne's power, the Carolingian Empire encompassed all of Gaul and parts of Germany and Italy, with the pope ruling part of the latter. When Charlemagne's son, Louis the Pious, died, the Germanic tradition of splitting property among sons led to the Treaty of Verdun (843), which split the empire into three parts. French-speaking in the west (France) and middle (Burgundy), and German-speaking in the east (Germany), the three regions never reunited. Nevertheless, the Carolingian economic system based on landed wealth and a brief intellectual revival sponsored personally by Charlemagne—though he himself was illiterate—provided a common heritage.

A new threat to western Europe appeared in 793, when the Vikings, sea raiders from Scandinavia, attacked and plundered a monastery on the English coast, the first of hundreds of such raids. Local sources from France, the British Isles, and Muslim Spain attest to widespread dread of Viking warriors descending from multi-oared, dragon-prowed boats to pillage monasteries, villages, and towns. Viking shipbuilders made versatile vessels that could brave the stormy North Atlantic and also maneuver up rivers to attack inland towns. As we shall see, in the ninth century raiders from Denmark and Norway harried the British and French coasts while Varangians° (Swedes) pursued raiding and trading interests, and eventually the building of kingdoms, along the rivers of eastern Europe and Russia. Although many Viking raiders sought booty and slaves, in the 800s and 900s Viking captains organized the settlement of Iceland, Greenland, and, around the year 1000, Vinland on the northern tip of Newfoundland.

Vikings long settled on lands they had seized in Normandy (in northwestern France) organized the most important and ambitious expeditions in terms of numbers of men and horses and long-lasting impact. William the Conqueror, the duke of Normandy, invaded England in 1066 and brought Anglo-Saxon domination of the island to an end. Other Normans (from "north men") attacked Mus-

Varangians (va-RAN-gee-anz)

lim Sicily in the 1060s and, after thirty years of fighting, permanently severed it from the Muslim world.

A Self-Sufficient Economy

Archaeology and records kept by Christian monasteries and convents reveal a profound economic transformation that accompanied the new Germanic political order. The new rulers cared little for the urban-based civilization of the Romans, which accordingly shrank in importance. Though the pace of change differed from region to region, most cities lost population, in some cases becoming villages. Roman roads fell into disuse and disrepair. Small thatched houses sprang up beside abandoned villas, and public buildings made of marble became dilapidated in the absence of the laborers, money, and civic leadership needed to maintain them. Paying for purchases in coin largely gave way to bartering goods and services.

Trade across the Mediterranean did not entirely stop after the Muslim conquests; occasional shipments from Egypt and Syria continued to reach western ports. But most of western Europe came to rely on meager local resources. These resources, moreover, underwent redistribution.

Roman centralization had channeled the wealth and production of the empire to the capital, which in turn radiated Roman cultural styles and tastes to the provinces. As Roman governors were replaced by Germanic territorial lords, who found the riches of their own culture more appealing than those of Rome, local self-sufficiency became more important. The decline of literacy and other aspects of Roman life made room for the growth of Germanic cultural traditions.

The diet in the northern countries featured beer, lard or butter, and bread made of barley, rye, or wheat, all supplemented by pork from herds of swine fed on forest acorns and beechnuts, and by game from the same forests. Nobles ate better than peasants, but even the peasant diet was reasonably balanced. The Roman diet based on wheat, wine, and olive oil persisted in the south. The average western European of the ninth century was probably better nourished than his or her descendants three hundred years later, when population was increasing and the nobility monopolized the resources of the forests.

In both north and south, self-sufficient farming estates known as **manors** became the primary centers of agricultural production. Fear of attack led many common farmers in the most vulnerable regions to give their lands to large landowners in return for political and physical protection. The warfare and instability of the post-Roman centuries made unprotected country houses especially vulnerable to pillaging. Isolated by poor communications and lack of organized government, landowners depended on their own resources for survival. Many became warriors or maintained a force of armed men. Others swore allegiance to landowners who had armed forces to protect them.

A well-appointed manor possessed fields, gardens, grazing lands, fishponds, a mill, a church, workshops for making farm and household implements, and a village where the farmers dependent on the lord of the manor lived. Depending on local conditions, protection ranged from a ditch and wooden stockade to a stone wall surrounding a fortified keep (a stone building). Fortification tended to increase until the twelfth century, when stronger monarchies made it less necessary.

Manor life reflected personal status. Nobles and their families exercised almost unlimited power over the **serfs**—agricultural workers who belonged to the manor, tilled its fields, and owed other dues and obligations. Serfs could not leave the manor where they were born and attach themselves to another lord. Most peasants in England, France, and western Germany were unfree serfs in the tenth and eleventh centuries. In Bordeaux°, Saxony, and a few other regions, free peasantry survived based on the egalitarian social structure of the Germanic peoples during their period of migration. Outright slavery, the mainstay of the Roman economy (see Chapter 5), diminished as more and more peasants became serfs in return for a lord's protection. At the same time, the enslavement of prisoners to serve as laborers became less important as an object of warfare.

Early Medieval Society in the West

Europe's reversion to a self-sufficient economy limited the freedom and potential for personal achievement of most people, but an emerging class of nobles reaped great benefits. During the Germanic migrations and later among the Vikings of Scandinavia, men regularly answered the call to arms issued by war chiefs, to whom they swore allegiance. All warriors shared in the booty gained from raiding. As settlement enhanced the importance of agricultural tasks, laying down the plow and picking up the sword at the chieftain's call became harder.

Those who, out of loyalty or desire for adventure, continued to join the war parties included a growing number of horsemen. Mounted warriors became the central force of the Carolingian army. At first, fighting from horseback did not make a person either a nobleman or a landowner. By the tenth century, however, nearly constant warfare to protect land rights or support the claims of a lord brought about a gradual transformation in the status of the mounted warrior, which led, at different rates in different areas, to landholding becoming almost inseparable from military service.

In trying to understand long-standing traditions of landholding and obligation, lawyers in the sixteenth century and later simplified thousands of individual agreements into a neat system they called "feudalism," from Latin *feodum*, meaning a land awarded for military service. It became common to refer to medieval Europe as a "feudal society" in which kings and lords gave land to "vassals" in return for sworn military support. By analyzing original records, more recent historians have discovered this to be an oversimplification. Relations between landholders and serfs and between lords and vassals differed too much from one place to another, and from one time to another, to fit together in anything resembling a system.

The German foes of the Roman legions had equipped themselves with helmets, shields, and swords, spears, or throwing axes. Some rode horses, but most fought on foot. Before the invention of the stirrup by Central Asian pastoralists in approximately the first century C.E., horsemen had gripped their mounts with their legs and fought with bows and arrows, throwing javelins, stabbing

---

Bordeaux (bore-DOE)

Noblewoman Directing Construction of a Church   This picture of Berthe, wife of Girat de Rouis-sillion, acting as mistress of the works comes from a tenth-century manuscript that shows a scene from the ninth century. Wheelbarrows rarely appear in medieval building scenes.   (Copyright Brussels, Royal Library of Belgium)

spears, and swords. Stirrups allowed a rider to stand in the saddle and absorb the impact when his lance struck an enemy at full gallop. This type of warfare required grain-fed horses that were larger and heavier than the small, grass-fed animals of the Central Asian nomads, though smaller and lighter than the draft horses bred in later times for hauling heavy loads. Thus agricultural Europe rather than the grassy steppes produced the charges of armored knights that came to dominate the battlefield.

By the eleventh century, the knight, called by different terms in different places, had emerged as the central figure in medieval warfare. He wore an open-faced helmet and a long linen shirt, or hauberk°, studded with small metal disks. A cen-

tury later, knightly equipment commonly included a visored helmet that covered the head and neck and a hauberk of chain mail.

Each increase in armor for knight and horse entailed a greater financial outlay. Since land was the basis of wealth, a knight needed financial support from land revenues. Accordingly, kings began to reward armed service with grants of land from their own property. Lesser nobles with extensive properties built their own military retinues the same way.

A grant of land in return for a pledge to provide military service was often called a **fief.** At first, kings granted fiefs to their noble followers, known as **vassals,** on a temporary basis. By the tenth century, most fiefs could be inherited as long as the specified military service continued to be provided. Though patterns varied greatly, the associa-

---

hauberk (HAW-berk)

tion of landholding with military service made the medieval society of western Europe quite different from the contemporary city-based societies of the Islamic world.

Kings and lords might be able to command the service of their vassals for only part of the year. Vassals could hold land from several different lords and owe loyalty to each one. Moreover, the allegiance that a vassal owed to one lord could entail military service to that lord's master in time of need.

A "typical" medieval realm—actual practices varied between and within realms—consisted of lands directly owned by a king or a count and administered by his royal officers. The king's or count's major vassals held and administered other lands, often the greater portion, in return for military service. These vassals, in turn, granted land to their own vassals.

The lord of a manor provided governance and justice, direct royal government being quite limited. The king had few financial resources and seldom exercised legal jurisdiction at a local level. Members of the clergy, as well as the extensive agricultural lands owned by monasteries and nunneries, fell under the jurisdiction of the church, which further limited the reach and authority of the monarch.

Noblewomen became enmeshed in this tangle of obligations as heiresses and as candidates for marriage. A man who married the widow or daughter of a lord with no sons could gain control of that lord's property. Marriage alliances affected entire kingdoms. Noble daughters and sons had little say in marriage matters; issues of land, power, and military service took precedence. Noblemen guarded the women in their families as closely as their other valuables.

Nevertheless, women could own land. A noblewoman sometimes administered her husband's estates when he was away at war. Nonnoble women usually worked alongside their menfolk, performing agricultural tasks such as raking and stacking hay, shearing sheep, and picking vegetables. As artisans, women spun, wove, and sewed clothing. The Bayeux° Tapestry, a piece of embroidery 230 feet (70 meters) long and 20 inches (51 centimeters) wide depicting William the Conqueror's invasion of England in 1066, was designed and executed entirely by women, though historians do not agree on who those women were.

THE WESTERN CHURCH

Just as the Christian populations in eastern Europe followed the religious guidance of the patriarch of Constantinople appointed by the Byzantine emperor, so the pope commanded similar authority over church affairs in western Europe. And just as missionaries in the east spread Christianity among the Slavs, so missionaries in the west added territory to Christendom with forays into the British Isles and the lands of the Germans. Throughout the period covered by this chapter, Christian society was emerging and changing in both areas.

In the west Roman nobles lost control of the **papacy**—the office of the pope—and it became a more powerful international office after the tenth century. Councils of bishops—which normally set rules, called canons, to regulate the priests and laypeople (men and women who were not members of the clergy) under their jurisdiction—became increasingly responsive to papal direction.

Nevertheless, regional disagreements over church regulations, shortages of educated and trained clergy, difficult communications, political disorder, and the general insecurity of the period posed formidable obstacles to unifying church standards and practices. Clerics in some parts of western Europe were still issuing prohibitions against the worship of rivers, trees, and mountains as late as the eleventh century. Church problems included lingering polytheism, lax enforcement of prohibitions against marriage of clergy, nepotism (giving preferment to one's close kin), and simony (selling ecclesiastical appointments, often to people who were not members of the clergy). The persistence of the papacy in asserting its legal jurisdiction over clergy, combating polytheism and heretical beliefs, and calling on secular rulers to recognize the pope's authority, including unpopular rulings like a ban on first-cousin marriage, constituted a rare force for unity and order in a time of disunity and chaos.

Bayeux (bay-YUH)

Politics and the Church

In politically fragmented western Europe, the pope needed allies. Like his son, Charlemagne's father Pepin was a strong supporter of the papacy. The relationship between kings and popes was tense, however, since both thought of themselves as ultimate authorities. In 962 the pope crowned the first "Holy Roman Emperor" (Charlemagne never held this full title). This designation of a secular political authority as the guardian of general Christian interests proved more apparent then real. Essentially a loose confederation of German princes who named one of their own to the highest office, the **Holy Roman Empire** had little influence west of the Rhine River.

Although the pope crowned the early Holy Roman Emperors, this did not signify political superiority. The law of the church (known as canon law because each law was called a canon) gave the pope exclusive legal jurisdiction over all clergy and church property wherever located. But bishops who held land as vassals owed military support or other services and dues to kings and princes. The secular rulers argued that they should have the power to appoint those bishops because that was the only way to guarantee fulfillment of their duties as vassals. The popes disagreed.

In the eleventh century, this conflict over the control of ecclesiastical appointments came to a head. Hildebrand°, an Italian monk, capped a career of reorganizing church finances when the cardinals (a group of senior bishops) meeting in Rome selected him to be Pope Gregory VII in 1073. His personal notion of the papacy (preserved among his letters) represented an extreme position, stating among other claims, that

§ The pope can be judged by no one;
§ The Roman church has never erred and never will err till the end of time;
§ The pope alone can depose and restore bishops;
§ He alone can call general councils and authorize canon law;
§ He can depose emperors;
§ He can absolve subjects from their allegiance;
§ All princes should kiss his feet.[5]

Such claims antagonized lords and monarchs, who had become accustomed to *investing*—that is, conferring a ring and a staff as symbols of authority on bishops and abbots in their domains. Historians apply the term **investiture controversy** to the medieval struggle between the church and the lay lords to control ecclesiastical appointments; the term also refers to the broader conflict of popes versus emperors and kings. When Holy Roman Emperor Henry IV defied Gregory's reforms, Gregory excommunicated him in 1076, thereby cutting him off from church rituals. Stung by the resulting decline in his influence, Henry stood barefoot in the snow for three days outside a castle in northern Italy waiting for Gregory, a guest there, to receive him. Henry's formal act of penance induced Gregory to forgive him and restore him to the church; but the reconciliation, an apparent victory for the pope, did not last. In 1078 Gregory declared Henry deposed. The emperor then forced Gregory to flee from Rome to Salerno, where he died two years later.

The struggle between the popes and the emperors continued until 1122, when a compromise was reached at Worms, a town in Germany. In the Concordat of Worms, Emperor Henry V renounced his right to choose bishops and abbots or bestow spiritual symbols upon them. In return, Pope Calixtus II permitted the emperor to invest papally appointed bishops and abbots with any lay rights or obligations before their spiritual consecration. Such compromises did not fully solve the problem, but they reduced tensions between the two sides.

Assertions of royal authority triggered other conflicts as well. Though barely twenty when he became king of England in 1154, Henry II, a great-grandson of William the Conqueror, instituted reforms designed to strengthen the power of the Crown and weaken the nobility. He appointed traveling justices to enforce his laws and made juries, a holdover from traditional Germanic law, into powerful legal instruments. He also established the principle that criminal acts violated the "king's peace" and should be tried and punished in accordance with charges brought by the Crown instead of in response to charges brought by victims.

Henry had a harder time controlling the church. His closest friend and chancellor, or chief administrator, Thomas à Becket (ca. 1118–1170), lived the

---

Hildebrand (HILL-de-brand)

grand and luxurious life of a courtier. In 1162 Henry persuaded Becket to become a priest and assume the position of archbishop of Canterbury, the highest church office in England. Becket agreed but cautioned that from then on he would act solely in the interest of the church if it came into conflict with the Crown. When Henry sought to try clerics accused of crimes in royal instead of ecclesiastical courts, Archbishop Thomas, now leading an austere and pious life, resisted.

In 1170 four of Henry's knights, knowing that the king desired Becket's death, murdered the archbishop in Canterbury Cathedral. Their crime backfired, and an outpouring of sympathy caused Canterbury to become a major pilgrimage center. In 1173 the pope declared the martyred Becket a saint. Henry allowed himself to be publicly whipped twice in penance for the crime, but his authority had been badly damaged.

Henry II's conflict with Thomas à Becket, like the Concordat of Worms, yielded no clear victor. The problem of competing legal traditions made political life in western Europe more complicated than in Byzantium or the lands of Islam (see Chapter 7). Feudal law, rooted in Germanic custom, gave supreme power to the king. Canon law, based on Roman precedent, visualized a single hierarchical legal institution with jurisdiction over all of Western Christendom. In the eleventh century Roman civil law, contained in the *Corpus Juris Civilis,* added a third tradition.

Monasticism

Monasticism featured prominently in the religious life of almost all medieval Christian lands. The origins of group monasticism lay in the eastern lands of the Roman Empire. Pre-Christian practices such as celibacy, continual devotion to prayer, and living apart from society (alone or in small groups) came together in Christian form in Egypt.

The most important form of monasticism in western Europe, however, involved groups of monks or nuns living together in organized communities. The person most responsible for introducing this originally Egyptian practice in the Latin west was Benedict of Nursia (ca. 480–547) in Italy. Benedict began his pious career as a hermit in a cave but eventually organized several monasteries, each headed by an abbot. In the seventh century monasteries based on his model spread far beyond Italy. The Rule Benedict wrote to govern the monks' behavior envisions a balanced life of devotion and work, along with obligations of celibacy, poverty, and obedience to the abbot. Those who lived by this or other monastic rules became *regular clergy,* in contrast to *secular clergy,* priests who lived in society instead of in seclusion and did not follow a formal code of regulations. The Rule of Benedict was the starting point for most forms of western European monastic life and remains in force today in Benedictine monasteries.

Though monks and nuns, women who lived by monastic rules in convents, made up a small percentage of the total population, their secluded way of life reinforced the separation of religious affairs from ordinary politics and economics. Monasteries followed Jesus' axiom to "render unto Caesar what is Caesar's and unto God what is God's" better than the many town-based bishops who behaved like lords.

Monasteries preserved literacy and learning in the early medieval period, although some rulers, like Charlemagne, encouraged scholarship at court. Many illiterate lay nobles interested themselves only in warfare and hunting. Monks (but seldom nuns) saw copying manuscripts and even writing books as a religious calling. Monastic scribes preserved many ancient Latin works that would otherwise have disappeared. The survival of Greek works depended more on Byzantine and Muslim scribes in the east.

Monasteries and convents served other functions as well (see Environment and Technology: Cathedral Organs). A few planted Christianity in new lands, as Irish monks did in parts of Germany. Most serviced the needs of travelers, organized agricultural production on their lands, and took in infants abandoned by their parents. Convents provided refuge for widows and other women who lacked male protection in the harsh medieval world or who desired a spiritual life. These religious houses presented problems of oversight to the church, however. A bishop might have authority over an abbot or abbess (head of a convent), but he could not exercise constant vigilance over what went on behind monastery walls.

Cathedral Organs

The Christian church directly encouraged musical development. Pope Gregory I (d. 604) is traditionally credited with making a standard collection of chants then in use. Later, a special school in Rome trained choir directors who were sent out to teach the chants in cathedrals and monasteries. Organ accompaniment, initially in the form of long, sustained bass notes, came into common use by the end of the seventh century. The organ worked by directing a current of air to a set of pipes of different lengths that could be opened or closed at one end. Each pipe sounded a tone as long as the air was flowing past its open end.

A monk named Wulstan (d. 963) described the organ installed in Winchester Cathedral in England:

Twice six bellows above are ranged in a row, and fourteen lie below. These, by alternate blasts, supply an immense quantity of wind, and are worked by 70 strong men, laboring with their arms, covered with perspiration, each inciting his companions to drive the wind up with all his strength, that the full-bosomed box may speak with its 400 pipes, which the hand of the organist governs. Some when closed he opens, others when open he closes, as the individual nature of the varied sound requires. Two brethren of concordant spirit sit at the instrument . . . Like thunder their tones batter the ear, so that it may receive no sound but that alone. To such an amount does it reverberate, echoing in every direction, that everyone stops with his hand his gaping ears, being in no wise able to draw near and bear the sound, which so many combinations produce.

A century later huge levers or keys came into use for opening and closing the pipes. Each was several inches in width, one or two inches thick, and up to three feet in length. So much muscle was required to operate the keys that organists were called "organ pounders." Over time, organs became smaller and capable of playing magnificent music.

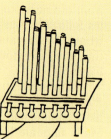

Cathedral Organ   Note the unhappy faces on the men assigned the dreary and noisy job of pumping the bellows for an organ. Note also the ping-pong paddle shaped keys that are more appropriate to pounding with a fist than pressing with a finger.   (St. John's College Library, Cambridge Manuscript, B.18)

Source: Alexander Russell, "Organ," *The International Cyclopedia of Music and Musicians,* ed. Oscar Thompson (New York: Dodd, Mead, 1943), 1315.

The failure of some abbots to maintain monastic discipline led to the growth of a reform movement centered on the Benedictine abbey of Cluny° in eastern France. Founded in 910 by William the Pious, the first duke of Aquitaine, who completely freed it of lay authority, Cluny gained similar freedom from the local bishop a century later. Its abbots pursued a vigorous campaign, eventually in alliance with reforming popes like Gregory VII, to improve monastic discipline and administration. A magnificent new abbey church symbolized Cluny's claims to eminence. With later additions, it became the largest church in the world.

At the peak of Cluny's influence, nearly a thousand Benedictine abbeys and priories (lower-level monastic houses) in various countries accepted the authority of its abbot. The Benedictine Rule had presumed that each monastery would be independent; the Cluniac reformers stipulated that every abbot and every prior (head of a priory) be appointed by the abbot of Cluny and have personal experience of the religious life of Cluny. Monastic reform gained new impetus in the second half of the twelfth century with the rapid rise of the Cistercian order, which emphasized a life of asceticism and poverty. These movements set the pattern for the monasteries, cathedral clergy, and preaching friars that would dominate ecclesiastical life in the thirteenth century.

KIEVAN RUSSIA, 900–1200

Though Latin and Orthodox Christendom followed different paths in later centuries, which had a more promising future was not apparent in 900. The Poles and other Slavic peoples living in the north eventually accepted the Christianity of Rome as taught by German priests and missionaries. The Serbs and other southern Slavs took their faith from Constantinople.

The conversion of Kievan Russia, farther to the east, shows how economics, politics, and religious life were closely intertwined. The choice of orthodoxy over Catholicism had important consequences for later European history.

The Rise of the Kievan State

The territory between the Black and Caspian Seas in the south and the Baltic and White Seas in the north divides into a series of east-west zones. Frozen tundra in the far north gives way to a cold forest zone, then to a more temperate forest, then to a mix of forest and steppe grasslands, and finally to grassland only. Several navigable rivers, including the Volga, the Dnieper°, and the Don, run from north to south across these zones.

Early historical sources reflect repeated linguistic and territorial changes, seemingly under pressure from poorly understood population migrations. Most of the Germanic peoples, along with some Iranian and west Slavic peoples, migrated into eastern Europe from Ukraine and Russia in Roman times. The peoples who remained behind spoke eastern Slavic languages, except in the far north and south: Finns and related peoples lived in the former region, Turkic-speakers in the latter.

Forest dwellers, farmers, and steppe nomads complemented each other economically. Nomads traded animals for the farmers' grain; and honey, wax, and furs from the forest became important exchange items. Traders could travel east and west by steppe caravan (see Chapters 6 and 11), or they could use boats on the rivers to move north and south.

Hoards containing thousands of Byzantine and Islamic coins buried in Poland and on islands in the Baltic Sea where fairs were held attest to the trading activity of Varangians (Swedish Vikings) who sailed across the Baltic and down Russia's rivers. They exchanged forest products and slaves for manufactured goods and coins, which they may have used as jewelry rather than as money, at markets controlled by the Khazar Turks. The powerful Khazar kingdom centered around the mouth of the Volga River.

Historians debate the early meaning of the word *Rus* (from which *Russia* is derived), but at some point it came to refer to Slavic-speaking peoples ruled by Varangians. Unlike western European lords, the Varangian princes and their *druzhina* (military retainers) lived in cities, while the Slavs farmed. The princes occupied themselves with trade and fending off enemies. The Rus of the city

---

Cluny (KLOO-nee)

Dnieper (d-NYEP-er)

of Kiev°, which was taken over by Varangians in 882, controlled trade on the Dnieper River and dealt more with Byzantium than with the Muslim world because the Dnieper flows into the Black Sea. The Rus of Novgorod° played the same role on the Volga. The semilegendary account of the Kievan Rus conversion to Christianity must be seen against this background.

In 980 Vladimir° I, a ruler of Novgorod who had fallen from power, returned from exile to Kiev with a band of Varangians and made himself the grand prince of Kievan Russia (see Map 8.2). Though his grandmother Olga had been a Christian, Vladimir built a temple on Kiev's heights and placed there the statues of the six gods his Slavic subjects worshiped. The earliest Russian chronicle reports that Vladimir and his advisers decided against Islam as the official religion because of its ban on alcohol, rejected Judaism (the religion to which the Khazars had converted) because they thought that a truly powerful god would not have let the ancient Jewish kingdom be destroyed, and even spoke with German emissaries advocating Latin Christianity. Why Vladimir chose Orthodox Christianity over the Latin version is not precisely known. The magnificence of Constantinople seems to have been a consideration. After visiting Byzantine churches, his agents reported: "We knew not whether we were in heaven or on earth, for on earth there is no such splendor of [sic] such beauty, and we are at a loss how to describe it. We know only that God dwells there among men, and their service is finer than the ceremonies of other nations."[6]

After choosing a reluctant bride from the Byzantine imperial family, Vladimir converted to Orthodox Christianity, probably in 988, and opened his lands to Orthodox clerics and missionaries. The patriarch of Constantinople appointed a metropolitan (chief bishop) at Kiev to govern ecclesiastical affairs. Churches arose in Kiev, one of them on the ruins of Vladimir's earlier hilltop temple. Writing was introduced, using the Cyrillic alphabet devised earlier for the western Slavs. This extension of Orthodox Christendom northward provided a barrier against the eastward expansion of Latin Christianity. Kiev became firmly oriented toward trade

Kiev (KEE-yev)   Novgorod (NOHV-goh-rod)   Vladimir (VLAD-ih-mir)

Map 8.2   Kievan Russia and the Byzantine Empire in the Eleventh Century   By the mid-eleventh century, the princes of Kievan Russia had brought all the eastern Slavs under their rule. The loss of Egypt, Syria, and Tunisia to Arab invaders in the seventh to eighth century had turned Byzantium from a far-flung empire into a fairly compact state. From then on the Byzantine rulers looked to the Balkans and Kievan Russia as the primary arena for extending their political and religious influence.

with Byzantium and turned its back on the Muslim world, though the Volga trade continued through Novgorod.

Struggles within the ruling family and with other enemies, most notably the steppe peoples of the south, marked the later political history of Kievan Russia. But down to the time of the Mongols in the thirteenth century (see Chapter 11), the state remained and served as an instrument for the Christianization of the eastern Slavs.

Society and Culture

In Kievan Russia political power derived from trade rather than from landholding, so the manorial agricultural system of western Europe never developed. Farmers practiced shifting cultivation of their own lands. They would burn a section of forest, then lightly scratch the ash-strewn surface with a plow. When fertility waned, they would move to another section of forest. Poor land and a short growing season in the most northerly latitudes made food scarce. Living on their own estates, the druzhina evolved from infantry into cavalry and focused their efforts more on horse breeding than on agriculture.

Large cities like Kiev and Novgorod may have reached thirty thousand or fifty thousand people—roughly the size of contemporary London or Paris, but far smaller than Constantinople or major Muslim metropolises like Baghdad and Nishapur. Many cities amounted to little more than fortified trading posts. Yet they served as centers for the development of crafts, some, such as glassmaking, based on skills imported from Byzantium. Artisans enjoyed higher status in society than peasant farmers. Construction relied on wood from the forests, although

URAL MTS.

FINNS

Novgorod

Suzdal

VOLGA
BULGARS

Volga

ESTS

Moscow

Baltic Sea

W. Dvina

Smolensk

KIEVAN
RUSSIA

LITHUANIANS

PRUSSIANS

Minsk

KHAZARS

Volga

POLAND

Chernigov

Kiev

Cracow

Dnieper

PECHENEGS

Don

Caspian
Sea

CARPATHIAN MOUNTAINS

HUNGARY

Kaffa

Cherson

CAUCASUS MTS

Danube

Black Sea

Adriatic Sea

Sinope

Trebizond

Adrianople

BYZANTINE

Bari

Constantinople

Nicaea

Ancyra

Brindisi

EMPIRE

Aegean
Sea

Athens

Antioch

Crete

Cyprus

Mediterranean Sea

| 0 | | 250 | | 500 Km. |
| 0 | | 250 | | 500 Mi. |

Christianity brought the building of stone cathedrals and churches on the Byzantine model.

Christianity penetrated the general population slowly. Several polytheist uprisings occurred in the eleventh century, particularly in times of famine. Passive resistance led some groups to reject Christian burial and persist in cremating the dead and keeping the bones of the deceased in urns. Women continued to use polytheist designs on their clothing and bracelets, and as late as the twelfth century they were still turning to polytheist priests for charms to cure sick children. Traditional Slavic marriage practices involving casual and polygamous relations particularly scandalized the clergy.

Christianity eventually triumphed, and its success led to increasing church engagement in political and economic affairs. In the twelfth century, Christian clergy became involved in government administration, some of them collecting fees and taxes related to trade. Direct and indirect revenue from trade provided the rulers with the money they needed to pay their soldiers. The rule of law also spread as Kievan Russia experienced its peak of culture and prosperity in the century before the Mongol invasion of 1237.

WESTERN EUROPE REVIVES, 1000–1200

Between 1000 and 1200 western Europe slowly emerged from nearly seven centuries of subsistence economy—in which most people who worked on the land could meet only their basic needs for food, clothing, and shelter. Population and agricultural production climbed, and a growing food surplus found its way to town markets, speeding the return of a money-based economy and providing support for larger numbers of craftspeople, construction workers, and traders.

Historians have attributed western Europe's revival to population growth spurred by new technologies and to the appearance in Italy and Flanders, on the coast of the North Sea, of self-governing cities devoted primarily to seaborne trade. For monarchs, the changes facilitated improvements in central administration, greater control over vassals, and consolidation of realms on the way to becoming stronger kingdoms.

The Role of Technology

A lack of concrete evidence confirming the spread of technological innovations frustrates efforts to relate the exact course of Europe's revival to technological change. Nevertheless, most historians agree that technology played a significant role in the near doubling of the population of western Europe between 1000 and 1200. The population of England seems to have risen from 1.1 million in 1086 to 1.9 million in 1200, and the population of the territory of modern France seems to have risen from 5.2 million to 9.2 million over the same period.

Examples that illustrate the difficulty of drawing historical conclusions from scattered evidence of technological change were a new type of plow and the use of efficient draft harnesses for pulling wagons. The Roman plow, which farmers in southern Europe and Byzantium continued to use, scratched shallow grooves, as was appropriate for loose, dry Mediterranean soils. The new plow cut deep into the soil with a knifelike blade, while a curved board mounted behind the blade lifted the cut layer and turned it over. This made it possible to farm the heavy, wet clays of the northern river valleys. Pulling the new plow took more energy, which could mean harnessing several teams of oxen or horses.

Horses plowed faster than oxen but were more delicate. Iron horseshoes, which were widely adopted in this period, helped protect their feet, but like the plow itself, they added to the farmer's expenses. Roman horse harnesses, inefficiently modeled on the yoke used for oxen, put such pressure on the animal's neck that a horse pulling a heavy load risked strangulation. A mystery surrounds the adoption of more efficient designs. The **horse collar,** which moves the point of traction from the animal's throat to its shoulders, first appeared around 800 in a miniature painting, and it is shown clearly as a harness for plow horses in the Bayeux Tapestry, embroidered after 1066. The breast-strap harness, which is not as well adapted for the heaviest work but was preferred in southern Europe, seems to have appeared around 500. In both cases, linguists have tried to trace key technical terms to Chinese or Turko-Mongol words and have argued for technological diffusion across Eurasia. Yet third-century Roman farmers in Tunisia and Libya used both types of harness to hitch horses and camels to plows and carts. This technology, which is still employed in Tunisia, appears clearly on Roman bas-reliefs and lamps; but there is no more evidence of its movement northward into Europe than there is of similar harnessing moving across Asia. Thus the question of where efficient harnessing came from and whether it began in 500 or in 800, or was known even earlier but not extensively used, cannot be easily resolved.

Hinging on this problem is the question of when and why landowners in northern Europe began to use teams of horses to pull plows through moist, fertile river-valley soils that were too heavy for teams of oxen. Stronger and faster than oxen, horses increased productivity by reducing the time needed for plowing, but they cost more to feed and equip. Thus, it is difficult to say that one technology was always better: although agricultural surpluses did grow and better plowing did play a role in this growth, areas that continued to use oxen and even old-style plows seem to have shared in the general population growth of the period.

Cities and the Rebirth of the Trade

Independent cities governed and defended by communes appeared first in Italy and Flanders and then elsewhere. Communes were groups of leading citizens who banded together to defend their cities and demand the privilege of self-government from their lay or ecclesiastical lord. Lords who granted such privileges benefited from the commune's economic dynamism. Lacking extensive farmlands, these cities turned to manufacturing and trade, which they encouraged through the laws they enacted. Laws making serfs free once they came into the city, for example, attracted many workers from the countryside. Cities in Italy that had shrunk within walls built by the Romans now pressed against those walls, forcing the construction of new ones. Pisa built a new wall in 1000 and ex-

panded it in 1156. Other twelfth-century cities that built new walls include Florence, Brescia°, Pavia, and Siena°.

Settlers on a group of islands at the northern end of the Adriatic Sea that had been largely uninhabited in Roman times organized themselves into the city of Venice. In the eleventh century it became the dominant sea power in the Adriatic. Venice competed with Pisa and Genoa, its rivals on the western side of Italy, for leadership in the trade with Muslim ports in North Africa and the eastern Mediterranean. A somewhat later merchant's list mentions trade in some three thousand "spices" (including dyestuffs, textile fibers, and raw materials), some of them products of Muslim lands and some coming via the Silk Road or the Indian Ocean trading system (see Chapter 6). Among them were eleven types of alum (for dyeing), eleven types of wax, eight types of cotton, four types of indigo, five types of ginger, four types of paper, and fifteen types of sugar, along with cloves, caraway, tamarind, and fresh oranges. By the time of the Crusades (see below), maritime commerce throughout the Mediterranean had come to depend heavily on ships from Genoa, Venice, and Pisa.

Ghent, Bruges°, and Ypres° in Flanders rivaled the Italian cities in prosperity, trade, and industry. Enjoying comparable independence based on privileges granted by the counts of Flanders, these cities centralized the fishing and wool trades of the North Sea region. Around 1200 raw wool from England began to be woven into woolen cloth for a very large market.

More abundant coinage also signaled the upturn in economic activity. In the ninth and tenth centuries most gold coins had come from Muslim lands and the Byzantine Empire. Being worth too much for most trading purposes, they seldom reached Germany, France, and England. The widely imitated Carolingian silver penny sufficed. With the economic revival of the twelfth century, minting of silver coins began in Scandinavia, Poland, and other outlying regions. In the following century the reinvigoration of Mediterranean trade made possible a new and abundant gold coinage.

Brescia (BREH-shee-uh)   **Siena** (see-EN-uh)   **Bruges** (broozh)   **Ypres** (EEP-r)

THE CRUSADES, 1095–1204

Western European revival coincided with and contributed to the **Crusades,** a series of religiously inspired Christian military campaigns against Muslims in the eastern Mediterranean that dominated the politics of Europe from 1095 to 1204 (see Chapter 7). Four great expeditions, the last redirected against the Byzantines and resulting in the Latin capture of Constantinople, constituted the region's largest military undertakings since the fall of Rome. As a result of the Crusades, noble courts and burgeoning cities in western Europe consumed more goods from the east. This set the stage for the later adoption of ideas, artistic styles, and industrial processes from Byzantium and the lands of Islam.

The Roots of the Crusades

Several social and economic currents of the eleventh century contributed to the Crusades. First, reforming leaders of the Latin Church, seeking to soften the warlike tone of society, popularized the Truce of God. This movement limited fighting between Christian lords by specifying times of truce, such as during Lent (the forty days before Easter) and on Sundays. Many knights welcomed a religiously approved alternative to fighting other Christians. Second, ambitious rulers, like the Norman chieftains who invaded England and Sicily, were looking for new lands to conquer. Nobles, particularly younger sons in areas where the oldest son inherited everything, were hungry for land and titles to maintain their status. Third, Italian merchants wanted to increase trade in the eastern Mediterranean and acquire trading posts in Muslim territory. However, without the rivalry between popes and kings already discussed, and without the desire of the church to demonstrate political authority over western Christendom, the Crusades might never have occurred.

Several factors focused attention on the Holy Land, which had been under Muslim rule for four centuries. **Pilgrimages** played an important role in European religious life. In western Europe, pilgrims traveled under royal protection, with a few in their number actually being tramps, thieves, beggars, peddlers, and merchants for whom pilgrimage was a safe way of traveling. Genuinely pious pilgrims often journeyed to visit the old churches and sacred relics preserved in Rome or Constantinople. The most intrepid went to Jerusalem, Antioch, and other cities under Muslim control to fulfill a vow or to atone for a sin.

Knights who followed a popular pilgrimage route across northern Spain to pray at the shrine of Santiago de Compostela learned of the expanding efforts of Christian kings to dislodge the Muslims. The Umayyad Caliphate in al-Andalus had broken up in the eleventh century, leaving its smaller successor states prey to Christian attacks from the north (see Chapter 7). This was the beginning of a movement of reconquest that culminated in 1492 with the surrender of the last Muslim kingdom. The word *crusade,* taken from Latin *crux* for "cross," was first used in Spain. Stories also circulated of the war conducted by seafaring Normans against the Muslims in Sicily, whom they finally defeated in the 1090s after thirty years of fighting.

The tales of pilgrims returning from Palestine further induced both churchmen and nobles to consider the Muslims a proper target for Christian militancy. Muslim rulers, who had controlled Jerusalem, Antioch, and Alexandria since the seventh century, generally tolerated and protected Christian pilgrims. But after 1071, when a Seljuk army defeated the Byzantine emperor at the Battle of Manzikert (see Chapter 7), Turkish nomads spread throughout the region, and security along the pilgrimage route through Anatolia, already none too good, deteriorated further. The decline of Byzantine power threatened ancient centers of Christianity, such as Ephesus in Anatolia, previously under imperial control.

Despite the theological differences between the Orthodox and Roman churches, the Byzantine emperor Alexius Comnenus asked the pope and western European rulers to help him confront the Muslim threat and reconquer what the Christians termed the Holy Land, the early centers of Christianity in Palestine and Syria. Pope Urban II responded at the Council of Clermont in 1095. He addressed a huge crowd of people gathered in a field and called on them, as Christians, to stop fighting one another and go to the Holy Land to fight Muslims.

"God wills it!" exclaimed voices in the crowd. People cut cloth into crosses and sewed them on their shirts to symbolize their willingness to march on Jerusalem. Thus began the holy war now known as the "First Crusade." People at the time more often used the word *peregrinatio*, "pilgrimage." Urban promised to free crusaders who had committed sins from their normal penance, or acts of atonement, the usual reward for peaceful pilgrims to Jerusalem.

The First Crusade captured Jerusalem in 1099 and established four crusader principalities, the most important being the Latin Kingdom of Jerusalem. The next two expeditions strove with diminishing success to protect these gains. Muslim forces retook Jerusalem in 1187. By the time of the Fourth Crusade in 1204, the original religious ardor had so diminished that the commanders agreed, at the urging of the Venetians, to sack Constantinople first to help pay the cost of transporting the army by ship.

The Impact of the Crusades

Exposure to Muslim culture in Spain, Sicily, and the crusader principalities established in the Holy Land made many Europeans aware of things lacking in their own lives. Borrowings from Muslim society occurred gradually and are not always easy to date, but Europeans eventually learned how to manufacture pasta, paper, refined sugar, colored glass, and many other items that had formerly been imported. Arabic translations of and commentaries on Greek philosophical and scientific works, and equally important original works by Arabs and Iranians, provided a vital stimulus to European thought.

Some works were brought directly into the Latin world through the conquests of Sicily, parts of Spain and the Holy Land, and Constantinople (for Greek texts). Others were rendered into Latin by translators who worked in parts of Spain that continued under Muslim rule. Generations passed before all these works were studied and understood, but they eventually transformed the intellectual world of the western Europeans, who previously had had little familiarity with Greek writings. The works of Aristotle and the Muslim commentaries on them were of particular impor-

Armored Knights in Battle   This painting from around 1135 shows the armament of knights at the time of the Crusades. Chain mail, a helmet, and a shield carried on the left side protect the rider. The lance carried under the arm and the sword are the primary weapons. Notice that riders about to make contact with lances have their legs straight and braced in the stirrups, whereas riders with swords and in flight have bent legs.   (Pierpont Morgan Library/Art Resource, NY)

tance to theologians, but Muslim writers like Avicenna (980–1037) were of parallel importance in medicine.

Changes affecting the lifestyle of the nobles took place more quickly. Eleanor of Aquitaine (1122?–1204), one of the most influential women of the crusading era, accompanied her husband, King Louis VII of France, on the Second Crusade (1147–1149). The court life of her uncle Raymond, ruler of the crusader principality of Antioch, particularly appealed to her. After her return to France, a lack of male offspring led to an annulment of her marriage with Louis, and she married Henry of Anjou in 1151. He inherited the throne of England as Henry II three years later. Eleanor's sons Richard Lion-Heart, famed in romance as the chivalrous foe of Saladin during the Third Crusade (1189–1192), and John rebelled against their father but eventually succeeded him as kings of England.

In Aquitaine, a powerful duchy in southern France, Eleanor maintained her own court for a time. The poet-singers called troubadours who enjoyed her favor made her court a center for new music based on the idea of "courtly love," an idealization of feminine beauty and grace that influenced later European ideas of romance. Thousands of troubadour melodies survive in manuscripts, and some show the influence of the poetry styles then current in Muslim Spain. The favorite troubadour instrument, moreover, was the lute, a guitar-like instrument with a bulging shape whose design and name (Arabic *al-ud*) come from Muslim Spain. In centuries to come the lute would become the mainstay of Renaissance music in Italy.

CONCLUSION

The legacy of Roman rule affected eastern and western Europe in different ways. Byzantium inherited the grandeur, pomp, and legal supremacy of the imperial office and merged it with leadership of the Christian church. Byzantium guarded its shrinking frontiers against foreign invasion but gradually contracted around Constantinople, its imperial capital, as more and more territory was lost. By contrast, no Roman core survived in the west. The Germanic peoples overwhelmed the legions guarding the frontiers and established kingdoms based on their own traditions. The law of the king and the law of the church did not echo each other. Yet memories of Roman grandeur and territorial unity resurfaced with the idea of a Holy Roman Empire, however unworkable that empire proved to be.

The competition between the Orthodox and Catholic forms of Christianity complicated the role of religion in the emergence of medieval European society and culture. The Byzantine Empire, constructed on a Roman political and legal heritage that had largely passed away in the west, was generally more prosperous than the Germanic kingdoms of western Europe, and its arts and culture were initially more sophisticated. Furthermore, Byzantine society became deeply Christian well before a comparable degree of Christianization had been reached in western Europe. Yet despite their success in transmitting their version of Christianity and imperial rule to Kievan Russia, and in the process erecting a barrier between the Orthodox Russians and the Catholic Slavs to their west, the Byzantines failed to demonstrate the dynamism and ferment that characterized both the Europeans to their west and the Muslims to their south. Byzantine armies played only a supporting role in the Crusades, and the emperors lost their capital and their power, at least temporarily, to western crusaders in 1204.

Technology and commerce deepened the political and religious gulf between the two Christian zones. Changes in military techniques in western Europe increased battlefield effectiveness, while new agricultural technologies led to population increases that revitalized urban life and contributed to the crusading movement by making the nobility hunger for new lands. At the same time, the need to import food for growing urban populations contributed to the growth of maritime commerce in the Mediterranean and North Seas. Culture and manufacturing benefited greatly from the increased pace of communication and exchange. Lacking parallel developments of a similar scale, the Byzantine Empire steadily lost the dynamism of its early centuries and by the end of the period had clearly fallen behind western Europe in prosperity and cultural innovation.

■ Key Terms

Charlemagne	**vassal**
medieval	**papacy**
Byzantine Empire	**Holy Roman Empire**
Kievan Russia	**investiture controversy**
schism	**monasticism**
manor	**horse collar**
serf	**Crusades**
fief	**pilgrimage**

■ Suggested Reading

Standard Byzantine histories include Dimitri Obolensky, *The Byzantine Commonwealth* (1971), and Warren Treadgold, *A History of Byzantine State and Society* (1997). Cyril Mango's *Byzantium: The Empire of New Rome* (1980) emphasizes cultural matters. For later Byzantine history see A. P. Kazhdan and Ann Wharton Epstein in *Change in Byzantine Culture in the Eleventh and Twelfth Centuries* (1985), which stresses social and economic issues, and D. M. Nicol, *Byzantium and Venice* (1988).

Roger Collins's *Early Medieval Europe, 300–1000* (1991) surveys institutional and political developments, and Robert Merrill Bartlett, *The Making of Europe* (1994), emphasizes frontiers. For the later part of the period see Susan Reynolds, *Kingdoms and Communities in Western Europe, 900–1300*, 2d ed. (1997). Jacques Le Goff, *Medieval Civilization, 400–1500* (1989), stresses questions of social structure. Among many books on religious matters, see Richard W. Southern, *Western Society and the Church in the Middle Ages* (1970), and Richard Fletcher, *The Barbarian Conversion* (1997). Susan Reynolds makes the case for avoiding the term *feudalism* in *Fiefs and Vassals* (1994).

More specialized economic and technological studies begin with the classic Lynn White, Jr., *Medieval Technology and Social Change* (1962). See also Michael McCormick, *Origins of the European Economy: Communications and Commerce, AD 300–900* (2002); C. M. Cipolla, *Money, Prices and Civilization in the Mediterranean World, Fifth to Seventeenth Century* (1956); and Georges Duby, *Rural Economy and Country Life in the Medieval West* (1990), which includes translated documents. J. C. Russell, *The Control of Late Ancient and Medieval Population* (1985), analyzes demographic history and the problems of data.

On France, see the numerous works of Rosamond McKitterick, including *The Frankish Kingdoms Under the Carolingians, 751– 987* (1983). On England, see Peter Hunter Blair, *An Introduction to Anglo-Saxon England* (1977), and Christopher Brooke, *The Saxon and Norman Kings*, 3d ed. (2001). On Italy, see Chris Wickham, *Early Medieval Italy: Central Power and Local Society, 400–1000* (1981), and Edward Burman, *Emperor to Emperor: Italy Before the Renaissance* (1991). On Germany and the Holy Roman Empire, see Timothy Reuter, *Germany in the Early Middle Ages, c. 800–1056* (1991). On Spain, see J. F. O'Callaghan, *A History of Medieval Spain* (1975), and R. Collins, *Early Medieval Spain: Unity and Diversity 400–1000* (1983). On Viking Scandinavia, see John Haywood's illustrated *Encyclopaedia of the Viking Age* (2000).

Amy Keller's popularly written *Eleanor of Aquitaine and the Four Kings* (1950) tells the story of an extraordinary woman. Dhuoda, *Handbook for William: A Carolingian Woman's Counsel for Her Son*, trans. Carol Neel (1991), offers a firsthand look at a Carolingian noblewoman. More general works include Margaret Wade's *A Small Sound of the Trumpet: Women in Medieval Life* (1986) and Bonnie S. Anderson and Judith P. Zinsser's *A History of Their Own: Women in Europe from Prehistory to the Present* (1989). In the area of religion, Caroline Bynum's *Jesus as Mother: Studies in the Spirituality of the High Middle Ages* (1982) illustrates new views about women.

On Kievan Russia, see Janet Martin, *Medieval Russia, 980–1584* (1995); Simon Franklin and Jonathan Shepard, *The Emergence of Rus: 750–1200* (1996); and Thomas S. Noonan, *The Islamic World, Russia and the Vikings, 750–900: The Numismatic Evidence* (1998).

Jonathan Riley-Smith, *The Crusades: A Short History* (1987), is a standard work. He has also a more colorful version in *The Oxford Illustrated History of the Crusades* (1995). For other views see Jonathan Phillips, *The Crusades, 1095–1197* (2002), and Norman Housley, *Crusading and Warfare in Medieval and Renaissance Europe* (2001). For a masterful account with a Byzantine viewpoint, see Steven Runciman, *A History of the Crusades*, 3 vols. (1987). For accounts from the Muslim side, see Carole Hillenbrand, *The Crusades: Islamic Perspectives* (1999).

Henri Pirenne, *Medieval Cities: Their Origins and the Revival of Trade* (1952), and Robert S. Lopez, *The Commercial Revolution of the Middle Ages, 950–1350* (1971), masterfully discuss the revival of trade. Lopez and Irving W. Raymond compile and translate primary documents in *Medieval Trade in the Mediterranean World: Illustrative Documents with Introductions and Notes* (1990).

■ Notes

1. Lewis G. M. Thorpe, *Two Lives of Charlemagne* (Harmondsworth, England: Penguin, 1969).
2. A. P. Kazhdan and Ann Wharton Epstein, *Change in Byzantine Culture in the Eleventh and Twelfth Centuries* (Berkeley: University of California Press, 1985), 71.
3. Ibid., 248.
4. Ibid., 255.
5. R. W. Southern, *Western Society and the Church in the Middle Ages* (Harmondsworth, England: Penguin, 1970), 102.
6. S. A. Zenkovsky, ed., *Medieval Russia's Epics, Chronicles, and Tales* (New York: New American Library, 1974), 67.

9 Central and Eastern Asia, 400–1200

CHAPTER OUTLINE

The Sui and Tang Empires, 581–755

Fractured Power in Central Asia and China, to 907

The Emergence of East Asia, to 1200

ENVIRONMENT AND TECHNOLOGY: Writing in East Asia, 400–1200

In the warfare that resulted from Han disintegration in 220 C.E. and the subsequent competition among the small kingdoms that divided its territory, infectious diseases spread from one army to another and among the civilian population. The scholar Ge Hong° (281–361 C.E.) described epidemics—probably smallpox—and the circumstances of their spread: "Because the epidemic was introduced . . . when Chinese armies attacked the barbarians . . . it was given the name of 'Barbarian pox.'"[1] As refugees fled south of the Yellow River, they carried the deadly infection with them.

Remarkable discoveries and inventions accompanied the social dislocation and disease of the third to sixth centuries. Ge Hong, a Daoist and alchemist, sought the elixir of life (a formula for immortality). Although alchemists failed in this quest, their investigations increased knowledge of physiology and permitted the refinement and use of stimulants such as ephedrine. Daoists also made advances in metallurgy, pharmacology, and mathematics. Ge Hong himself passed on knowledge of hallucinogenic drugs, the prevention of rabies, and magnetism, among other things.

With China's reunification in the late sixth century, the new knowledge spread over recentralized networks of trade, travel, and education. Under the Sui° and then the Tang° rulers, scientific and cultural influences spread throughout Central Asia and East Asia.

Many of the smaller empires that followed the fall of the Tang Empire in 907 preserved and added to the cultural, scientific, and political heritage of the Tang. Song° China excelled in science, mathe-

---

Ge Hong (guh hoong)

Sui (sway)   **Tang** (tahng)   **Song** (soong)

matics, and engineering, Korea in printing and textiles, Japan in metallurgy and ceramics. This specialization and diversification of knowledge fostered new technologies, economic growth, and brilliant achievements in philosophy and the arts.

As you read, ask yourself the following questions:

- On what were new relationships among East Asian societies based after the fall of the Tang?

- Why does Buddhism play different political roles in Tang China, Tibet, Korea, and Japan after the ninth century?

- What accounts for the scientific and economic advancement of Song China?

THE SUI AND TANG EMPIRES, 581–755

The brief Sui Empire and its long-lived successor, the Tang, sprang from the political diversity of the period of disunion. The fall of the Han Empire left a power vacuum in which many small kingdoms explored various political styles. Some favored the Chinese style, with an emperor, a bureaucracy using the Chinese language exclusively, and a Confucian state philosophy (see Chapter 2). Others reflected Tibetan, Turkic, or other regional cultures and depended on Buddhism to legitimate their rule.

Reunification Under the Sui and Tang

In less than forty years, the Sui rulers reunified China. They reestablished Confucianism as the governing philosophy and passed it on to the Tang. But Buddhism exerted a strong political influence too, and other religious and philosophical beliefs, including Daoism, Nestorian Christianity, and Islam, became popular.

The Sui rulers called their new capital Chang'an° in honor of the old Han capital nearby in the Wei°

River Valley (modern Shaanxi province). To facilitate communication and trade with growing population centers to the south, they built the 1,100-mile **Grand Canal** linking the Yellow River with the Yangzi° River. The Sui also improved the Great Wall, constructed irrigation systems in the increasingly populated Yangzi River Valley, and waged war against Korea and Vietnam.

Such intense military expansion and public works required levels of organization and resources—people, livestock, wood, iron, staple crops—that the Sui could not sustain. Overextension weakened Sui authority and prompted the transition to the Tang.

In 618, the powerful Li family ended Sui rule and created the **Tang Empire** (Map 9.1). The Tang expanded primarily westward into Central Asia under the brilliant emperor **Li Shimin°** (r. 627–649). They avoided overcentralization by allowing local nobles, gentry, officials, and religious establishments to exercise significant power.

As descendants of both the Turkic elites that built small states in northern China after the Han and Chinese officials and settlers intermarried with the Turks, the Tang emperors and nobility appreciated Central Asian culture as well as Chinese traditions. In warfare, for instance, the Tang combined Chinese weapons—the crossbow and armored infantrymen—with Central Asian expertise in horsemanship and the use of iron stirrups. From about 650 to about 750, this combination made the Tang armies the most formidable in the world.

Buddhism and the Tang Empire

The Central Asian heritage of the Tang rulers showed in their political use of Buddhism, a religion that charged kings and emperors with the spiritual function of bringing humankind into the Buddhist realm. Protecting spirits were to help the ruler govern and prevent harm from coming to his people. State cults based on Buddhism flourished in Central Asia and north China after the fall of the Han.

In Central and East Asia, Mahayana°, or "Great Vehicle," Buddhism predominated. Mahayana

Chang'an (chahng-ahn)   Wei (way)

Yangzi (yahng-zeh)   Li Shimin (lee shir-meen)
Mahayana (mah-HAH-YAH-nah)

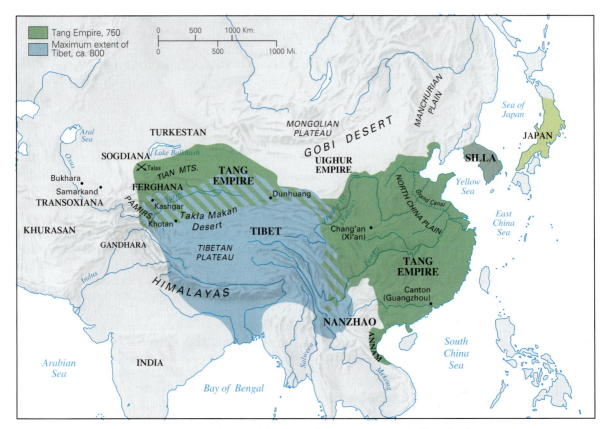

Map 9.1   The Tang Empire in Inner and Eastern Asia, 750   For over a century the Tang Empire controlled China and a very large part of Inner Asia. The defeat of Tang armies in 751 by a force of Arabs, Turks, and Tibetans at the Talas River in present-day Kirgizstan ended Tang westward expansion. To the east the Tang dominated Annam, and Japan and the Silla kingdom in Korea were leading tributary states of the Tang.

fostered faith in enlightened beings—bodhisattvas—who postpone nirvana (see Chapter 4) to help others achieve enlightenment. This permitted the absorption of local gods and goddesses into Mahayana sainthood. Mahayana also encouraged translating Buddhist scripture into local languages, and it accepted religious practices not based on written texts. The tremendous reach of Mahayana views, which proved so adaptable to different societies and classes of people, invigorated travel, language learning, and cultural exchange.

Early Tang princes competing for political influence enlisted monastic leaders to pray for them, preach on their behalf, counsel aristocrats to support them, and—perhaps most important—

contribute monastic wealth to their war chests. In return, the monasteries received tax exemptions, land privileges, and gifts.

As the Tang Empire expanded westward, contacts with Central Asia and India increased, and so did the complexity of Buddhist influence throughout China. Chang'an, the Tang capital, became the center of a continent-wide system of communication. Central Asians, Tibetans, Vietnamese, Japanese, and Koreans regularly visited the capital and took away with them the most recent ideas and styles. Thus, the Mahayana network connecting Central Asia and China intersected with a vigorous commercial world where material goods and cultural influences mixed. Regional variety coexisted

C H R O N O L O G Y

	Central Asia	China	Northeast Asia	Japan
200		**220–589** China disunited		
	552 Turkic Empire founded	**581–618** Sui dynasty rules		
600		**618** Tang Empire founded		
		627–649 Li Shimin reign		**645–655** Taika era
		690–705 Wu Zhao reign	**668** Silla victory in Korea	
	744 Uighur Empire founded			**710–784** Nara as capital
	751 Battle of Talas River	**755–763** An Lushan rebellion		**752** "Eye-opening" ceremony
800				**794–1185** Heian era
	ca. 850 Buddhist political power secured in Tibet	**840** Suppression of Buddhism		
		879–881 Huang Chao rebellion		
		907 End of Tang	**907** Liao Empire founded	
			918 Koryo founded	
		938 Liao capital at Beijing		**ca. 950–1180** Fujiwara influence
		960 Song Empire founded		**ca. 1000** *The Tale of Genji*
1000		**1127–1279** Southern Song period	**1125** Jin Empire founded	**1185** Kamakura Shogunate founded

with shared knowledge of Buddhism, Confucianism, and other philosophies and written Chinese with regional commitments to other languages and writing systems. Textiles reflected Persian, Korean, and Vietnamese styles, and influences from every part of Asia appeared in sports, music, and painting. Many historians characterize the Tang Empire as "cosmopolitan" because of its breadth and diversity.

To Chang'an by Land and Sea

Well-maintained roads and water transport, including the Grand Canal, connected Chang'an, the capital and hub of Tang communications, to the coastal towns of south China, most importantly Canton (Guangzhou°).

Guangzhou (gwahng-jo)

Chang'an became the center of what is often called the **tributary system,** dating from Han times, by which independent countries acknowledged the Chinese emperor's supremacy by sending regular embassies to the capital to pay tribute (see Chapter 5).

During the Tang period, Chang'an had something over a million people, a minority of whom lived in the central city. Most people lived in the suburbs that extended beyond the main gates. Many dwelled in towns that had special responsibilities like maintaining the imperial tombs or operating the imperial resort, where aristocrats relaxed in sunken tile tubs while the steamy waters of the natural springs swirled around them.

Special compounds in Chang'an, including living accommodations and general stores, serviced foreign merchants, students, and ambassadors. Restaurants, inns, temples, mosques, and street stalls along the main streets kept busy every evening. At curfew, generally between eight and ten o'clock, commoners returned to their neighborhoods, which were enclosed by brick walls and wooden gates that guards locked until dawn to control crime.

Of the many routes converging on Chang'an, the Grand Canal commanded special importance with its own army patrols, boat design, canal towns, and maintenance budget. It contributed to the economic and cultural development of eastern China. After the Tang, Chinese rulers established capitals farther to the east largely because of the economic and political effects of the Grand Canal.

The Tang consolidated Chinese control of the southern coastal region, thus increasing access to the Indian Ocean and helping Islamic and Jewish influences to spread. The uncle of Muhammad is credited with erecting the Red Mosque at Canton in the mid-seventh century. By the end of the Tang period, West Asians in Chang'an probably numbered over 100,000.

Chinese seamen excelled in compass design and the design of very large oceangoing vessels. The government built grain transport vessels for the Chinese coastal cities and the Grand Canal. Commercial ships, built to sail from south China to the Philippines and Southeast Asia, carried twice as much as contemporary Byzantine and Abbasid vessels.

The sea route between West Asia and Canton also brought **bubonic plague** to East Asia in the fifth century. References to plague in Canton and south China date to the early 600s. The pestilence found a hospitable environment in parts of southwestern China and lingered there long after its disappearance in West Asia and Europe. The disease followed trade and embassy routes to Korea, Japan, and Tibet, where initial outbreaks followed the establishment of diplomatic ties in the seventh century. Unlike their contemporaries in Europe and West Asia, city dwellers in East Asia learned to control its spread through sanitation measures, but the disease persisted in isolated rural areas.

Tang Integration

Influences from Central Asia and the Islamic world introduced lively new animal motifs to ceramics, painting, and silk designs. Life-size sculpture also became common. In north China, clothing styles changed. Working people switched from robes to the pants favored by horse-riding Turks from Central Asia. Inexpensive cotton, imported from Central Asia, gradually replaced hemp in clothes worn by commoners. The Tang court promoted polo playing, a Central Asian pastime, and followed the Central Asian tradition of allowing noblewomen to compete. Various stringed instruments reached China across the Silk Road, along with Central Asian folk melodies. Grape wine, tea, sugar, and spices transformed the Chinese diet.

Such changes reflected new economic and trade relationships with South Asia, West Asia, and northeastern Africa. Silk had dominated the caravan trade across Central Asia in Han times. Now China's monopoly on silk disappeared as several centers in West Asia learned to compete. However, western Asia lost its monopoly in cotton: by the end of the Tang, China had begun to produce its own. This process of import substitution—the domestic production and sale of previously imported goods— also affected tea and sugar.

By about the year 1000, the magnitude of exports from Tang territories, facilitated by China's excellent transportation systems, dwarfed the burgeoning trade between Europe, West Asia, and South Asia. Anecdotal accounts claimed that ships

Tang Women at Polo   The Tang Empire, like the Sui, was strongly influenced by Inner Asian as well as Chinese traditions. As in many Inner Asian cultures, women in Tang China were likely to exercise greater influence in the management of property, in the arts, and in politics than women in Chinese society at later times. They were not excluded from public view, and noblewomen could even compete at polo. The game, widely known in various forms in Central and Inner Asia from a very early date, combined the Tang love of riding, military arts, and festive spectacles. (The Nelson-Atkins Museum of Art, Kansas City, Missouri)

FRACTURED POWER IN CENTRAL ASIA AND CHINA, TO 907

Between 600 and 750, the Uighurs° (a Turkic group in Inner Asia) and Tibetans built states to rival the Tang Empire, reaching some degree of political accommodation by the end of the period. However, by the mid-800s, all three empires were experiencing political decay and military decline. The problems of one aggravated those of the others, since governmental collapse allowed soldiers, criminals, and freebooters to roam without hindrance into neighboring territories.

Centralization and integration being deepest in Tang territory, the impact fell most heavily there. Nothing remained of Tang power but pretense by the early 800s. In the provinces, military governors suppressed the rebellion of the general An Lushan°, which raged from 755 to 763, and then seized power for themselves. Farmers felt helpless before local bosses with private armies. Eunuchs controlled Chang'an and the Tang court and publicly executed bureaucrats who opposed them.

The nomads of Central Asia survived the social disorder and agricultural losses best. The caravan cities, which had prospered from overland trade, had as much to lose as China itself, but the economies of Central Asia and East Asia proved resilient. The strongest backlashes were cultural, particularly in China, where disillusionment with Central Asian neighbors and social anxieties fueled a powerful reaction against "foreign" cultures.

carrying Chinese exports outnumbered those laden with South Asian, West Asian, European, or African goods by a hundred to one. Regardless of the exact figures, Tang exports unbalanced the commerce of both Central Asia and the Indian Ocean.

China remained the source of superior silks. Tang factories created more and more complex styles, partly to counter foreign competition. China became the sole supplier of porcelain—a fine, durable ceramic made from a special clay—to West Asia. As travel across Central Asia, Southeast Asia, and the Indian Ocean increased, the economies of ports and oases involved in the trade—even distant ones—became increasingly commercialized, creating special needs for new instruments of credit and finance.

Reaction and Repression

After two centuries of widespread Buddhist influence, members of the imperial family began to distrust the monasteries and blame the Buddhist clergy for political upheavals. In 840 (a year of disintegration on many fronts), the government moved to crush the monasteries. The Tang elites strongly reasserted

Uighur (WEE-ger)   **An Lushan** (ahn loo-shahn)

Buddhist Cave Painting at Dunhuang   Hundreds of caves dating to the period when Buddhism enjoyed popularity and government favor in China survive in Gansu province, which was beyond the reach of the Tang rulers when they turned against Buddhism. This cave, dated to the year 538/9, contains elaborate wall decorations narrating the life of the Buddha and depicting scenes from the Western Paradise, where devotees of the Pure Land sect of Buddhism hoped to be reborn.   (NHK International, Inc.)

Confucian ideology instead, particularly the rationalist "neo-Confucian" school.

Even Chinese gentry living in safe and prosperous localities associated Buddhism with social ills. People who worried about "barbarians" ruining their society pointed to Buddhism as evidence of the foreign evil since it had such strong roots in Central Asia and Tibet. They claimed that eradicating Buddhist influence would restore the ancient values of hierarchy and social harmony. Because Buddhism shunned earthly ties, monks and nuns severed relations with the secular world in search of enlightenment. They paid no taxes, served in no army, deprived their families of advantageous marriage alliances, and denied descendants to their ancestors. The Confucian elites saw all this as threatening to the family and to the family estates that underlay the Tang economic and political structure.

Wealthy believers gave the monasteries large tracts of land. In addition, the tax exemption of monasteries allowed them to purchase land and precious objects and employ large numbers of poor people to work as artisans, field hands, cooks, housekeepers, and guards. Some eventually converted to Buddhism and took up the monastic life; others came as beggars and then began to study the religion. By the ninth century, hundreds of thousands of people had entered monasteries and nunneries.

The Tang elites saw Buddhism as undermining the Confucian idea of the family as the model for the state as well as women's roles in politics. Wu Zhao°, a woman who had married into the imperial family, seized control of the government in 690,

Wu Zhao (woo jow)

declared herself emperor, and reigned until 705. She based her legitimacy on the claim of being a bodhisattva, and she favored Buddhists and Daoists over Confucianists.

Later Confucian writers expressed contempt for Emperor Wu and other powerful women, such as the concubine Yang Guifei°. Bo Zhuyi°, in his poem "Everlasting Remorse," lamented the influence of women at the Tang court, which had caused "the hearts of fathers and mothers everywhere not to value the birth of boys, but the birth of girls."[2] Confucian elites heaped every possible charge on prominent women who offended them, blaming Yang Guifei for the An Lushan rebellion and accusing Emperor Wu of grotesque tortures and murders, including tossing the dismembered but still living bodies of enemies into wine vats and cauldrons.

Serious historians dismiss the stories about Wu Zhao as stereotypical characterizations of "evil" rulers. In fact, she seems to have ruled effectively and was not deposed until extreme old age (eighty-plus in 705) incapacitated her. Nevertheless, since Confucian historians commonly describe unorthodox rulers and all powerful women as evil, the true facts about Wu will never be known.

The dissolution of the monasteries caused an incalculable loss in cultural artifacts. Some sculptures and grottoes survived in defaced form. Wooden temples and facades sheltering great stone carvings burned to the ground. Monasteries became legal again in later times, but Buddhism never recovered the social, political, and cultural influence of early Tang times.

Despite the continuing prosperity, political disintegration and the elite's sense of cultural decay created an unsettled environment that encouraged aspiring dictators. A disgruntled member of the gentry, Huang Chao, led the most devastating uprising between 879 and 881. Despite imposing ruthless and violent control over the villages it controlled, the revolt attracted hundreds of thousands of poor farmers and tenants who could not protect themselves from local bosses, sought escape from oppressive landlords or taxes, or simply did not know what else to do in the deepening chaos. The new hatred of "barbarians" spurred the rebels to murder thousands of foreign residents in Canton and Peking.

Local bosses finally wiped out the rebels using the same violent tactics, but Tang society did not find peace. Refugees, the urban homeless, and migrant workers became permanent fixtures. Residents of northern China fled to the southern frontiers as groups from Central Asia moved into the north.

The smaller states that succeeded the Tang Empire in 907 each controlled considerable territory, and some of them had lasting historical influence. But none could integrate the economic and cultural interests of vastly disparate territories or transmit goods and knowledge across huge distances. East Asia fragmented and lost its communication with Europe and the Islamic world. Important artistic styles, technical advances, and philosophical developments emerged in East Asia, but the brilliant cosmopolitanism of the Tang disappeared for centuries.

The End of the Tang Empire

The Tang order succumbed to the very forces that were essential to its creation and maintenance. The campaigns of expansion in the seventh century left the empire dependent on local military commanders and a complex tax collection system. The battle of Talas River halted the drive westward across Central Asia. Such reverses led to military demoralization and underfunding. Suppressing the An Lushan rebellion a few years later gave provincial military governors new powers and independence.

Yang Guifei (yahng gway-fay)   **Bo Zhuyi** (baw joo-ee)

The Uighur and Tibetan Empires in Central Asia

The original homeland of the Turks lay in the northern part of modern Mongolia. After the fall of the Han Empire, Turkic peoples began moving south and west through Mongolia, and then on to Central Asia, on the long migration that eventually brought them to Anatolia (modern Turkey). Various Turkic groups controlled Central Asia during the period of fragmentation between the Han and Tang Empires, but in 552 a unified Turkic Empire arose, only to split internally a century later. This fissure helped the Tang Empire under Li Shimin to establish control over Central Asia. Yet within a century, a new Turkic group, the **Uighurs,** had taken much of Central Asia.

Under the Uighurs, caravan cities like Bukhara, Samarkand, and Tashkent (see Map 9.1) displayed a literate culture with strong ties to both the Islamic world and China. The Uighurs excelled as merchants and as scribes able to transact business in many languages. They adapted the Sogdians' (people to the west in Central Asia) syllabic script, which was related to the Syriac script used in West Asia, to writing Turkic. This made possible several innovations in Uighur government, such as changing from a tax paid in kind (with products or services) to a money tax and, later, the minting of coins. Their flourishing urban culture embraced the Buddhist classics, religious art derived from northern India, and a mixture of East Asian and Islamic styles.

Unified Uighur power collapsed after half a century, leaving only Tibet as a Central Asian rival to the Tang. A large, stable empire critically positioned where China, Southeast Asia, South Asia, and Central Asia meet, Tibet experienced a variety of cultural influences. In the seventh century, Chinese Buddhists on pilgrimage to India advanced contacts between India and Tibet. The Tibetans derived their alphabet from India, as well as a variety of artistic and architectural styles. Mathematics, astronomy, divination, the cultivation of grains, and the use of millstones came from India and China, knowledge of Islam and the monarchical traditions of Iran and Rome from Central Asia and the Middle East. The Tibetan royal family favored Greek medicine transmitted through Iran.

Under Li Shimin, cautious friendliness prevailed between the empires. A Tang princess, called Kongjo by the Tibetans, came to Tibet to marry the Tibetan king and thereby forge an alliance in 634. She brought with her Mahayana Buddhism, which combined with the native religion to create a local religious style. Tibet sent ambassadors to join Koreans, Japanese, and other peoples as students in the Tang imperial capital.

Regular contact and Buddhist influences consolidated the Tang-Tibet relationship for a time. The Tibetan kings encouraged Buddhist religious establishments and prided themselves on being cultural intermediaries between India and China.

Tibet also excelled at war. Horses and armor, borrowed from the Turks, raised Tibetan forces to a level that startled even the Tang. By the late 600s, the Tang emperor and the Tibetan king were rivals for religious leadership and political dominance in Central Asia, and Tibetan power reached into what are now Qinghai°, Sichuan°, and Xinjiang° provinces in China. Tensions grew, and peace returned only after the Tang defeat on the Talas River in 751.

Yet political differences remained. Although a new king in Tibet decided to follow the Tang lead and eradicate the political and social influence of the monasteries in the 800s, monks assassinated him, and control of the Tibetan royal family passed into the hands of religious leaders. In ensuing years, monastic domination isolated Tibet from surrounding regions.

THE EMERGENCE OF EAST ASIA, TO 1200

In the aftermath of the Tang, new states emerged and competed to inherit its legacy. The Liao° Empire of the Khitan° people established their rule in the north, at what is now Beijing°, immediately after the overthrow of the last Tang emperor. Soon after, the Minyak people (closely related to the Tibetans) established a large empire in western China and called themselves "Tangguts°" to show their connection with the former empire. In 960, the **Song Empire** arose in central China.

While these empires competed, the earlier relationship between East Asia and Central Asia ended. Sea connections among East Asia, West Asia, and Southeast Asia continued, however, and the Song developed advanced seafaring and sailing technologies. The Song elite, like their late Tang predecessors, rejected "barbaric" or "foreign" influences while struggling under enormous military demands. Meanwhile, Korea and Japan strengthened political and cultural ties with China, and some South-

Qinghai (CHING-hie)   **Sichuan** (SUH-chwahn)   **Xinjiang** (shin-jee-yahng)   **Liao** (lee-OW)   **Khitan** (kee-tan)   **Beijing** (bay-jeeng)   **Tanggut** (TAHNG-gut)

east Asian states, relieved of any Tang military threat, entered into friendly relations with the Song court. The allied societies of East Asia formed a Confucian region actively exchanging goods, resources, and knowledge.

The Liao and Jin Challenge

The Liao and other northern empires included many nomads. Their rulers acknowledged the economic and social differences between peoples and made no attempt to create a single elite culture. They encouraged Chinese elites to use their own language, study their own classics, and see the emperor through Confucian eyes, and they encouraged other peoples to use their own languages and see the emperor as a champion of Buddhism or as a nomadic leader. As a consequence, Buddhism far outweighed Confucianism in the northern states, where rulers depended on their roles as bodhisattvas or as Buddhist kings to legitimate power.

The Liao Empire of the Kitan people ruled an expanse from Siberia to Central Asia and thus connected China with societies to the north and west. Variations on the Kitan name became the name for China in these distant regions: "Kitai" for the Mongols, "Khitai" for the Russians, and "Cathay" for those, like the contemporaries of Marco Polo, who reached China from Europe.

Liao rule lasted from 907 to 1125. Relics of the Liao period can today be seen in Beijing, one of its capitals. In ceramics, painting, horsemanship, religion, and some forms of architecture, Liao made a lasting contribution to Asian civilization.

Superb horsemen and archers, the Kitans adapted siege machines from China and Central Asia and challenged the Song. In 1005, the Song agreed to a truce that included enormous annual payments in cash and silk to the Liao to forestall further war. Liao and Song worked out an efficient and sophisticated diplomatic system. But the economically burdensome relations with the Liao eventually led the Song into a secret alliance with the Jurchens of northeastern Asia, also chafing under Liao rule. In 1125 the Jurchens destroyed the Liao capital in Mongolia, proclaimed their own empire—the Jin—and turned against the Song (Map 9.2).

The Jurchens grew grains, tended livestock, and hunted and fished. They had learned the Kitan military arts and political organization and became formidable enemies of the Song Empire, mounting an all-out campaign in 1127. They laid siege to the Song capital, Kaifeng°, and captured the Song emperor. Within a few years the Song withdrew south of the Yellow River, leaving central as well as northern China in Jurchen control. The Song also made annual payments to the Jin Empire to avoid open warfare. Historians generally refer to this period as the "Southern Song" (1127–1279).

Song Industries

China in this period did not have access to the Tang's far-flung networks of communication. Many of the advances in technology, medicine, astronomy, and mathematics for which the Song is famous derived from information that had come to China in Tang times, sometimes from very distant places. The Song had the motivation and resources to adapt Tang information and technology to meet practical, sometimes urgent, requirements, particularly in warfare and colonization and in the development of new methods for managing economic and social changes.

The arts of measurement and observation absorbed Chinese scholars, as they did the Indian and West Asian mathematicians and astronomers who had migrated to the Tang Empire, bringing their knowledge with them. Song mathematicians innovated the use of fractions, first employing them to describe the phases of the moon. From lunar observations, Song astronomers constructed a precise calendar and alone among the world's astronomers noted the explosion of the Crab Nebula in 1054. Chinese scholars used their work in astronomy and mathematics to make significant contributions to timekeeping and the development of the compass.

In 1088, the engineer Su Song constructed a gigantic mechanical celestial clock. Escapement mechanisms for controlling the revolving wheels in water-powered clocks had appeared under the Tang, as had the application of water wheels to weaving and threshing. But this knowledge had not

Kaifeng (kie-fuhng)

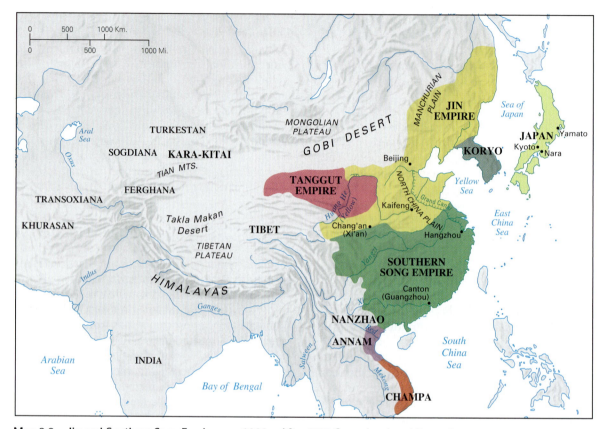

Map 9.2   Jin and Southern Song Empires, ca. 1200   After 1127, Song abandoned its northern territories to Jin. The Southern Song continued the policy of annual payments—to Jin rather than Liao—and maintained high military preparedness to prevent further invasions.

been widely applied. Su Song adapted the escapement and water wheel to his clock, which featured the first known chain-drive mechanism. The clock told the time of day and the day of the month, and it indicated the movement of the moon and certain stars and planets across the night sky. An observation deck and a mechanically rotated armillary sphere crowned the 80-foot (24-meter) structure. The clock exemplified the Song ability to integrate observational astronomy, applied mathematics, and engineering.

Familiarity with celestial coordinates, particularly the Pole Star, refined the design of compasses. Long known in China, the magnetic compass shrank in size in Song times, and it gained a fixed stem and sometimes even a small protective case with a glass covering for the needle. These changes

made the compass suitable for seafaring, a use first attested in 1090. The Chinese compass and the Greek astrolabe, introduced later, improved navigation throughout Southeast Asia and the Indian Ocean.

Development of the seaworthy compass coincided with new techniques in building **junks.** A stern-mounted rudder improved the steering of the large ships in uneasy seas, and watertight bulkheads helped keep them afloat in emergencies. The merchants of the Persian Gulf quickly adopted these features.

Military pressure from the Liao and Jin Empires helped feed the technological explosion. Although less than half the size of the Tang Empire, the Song fielded an army four times as large—about 1.25 million men (roughly the size of the

Su Song's Astronomical Clock This gigantic clock built at Kaifeng between 1088 and 1092 combined mathematics, astronomy, and calendar-making with skillful engineering. The team overseen by Su Song placed an armillary sphere on the observation platform and linked it with chains to the water-driven central mechanism shown in the cutaway view. The water wheel also rotated the buddha statues in the multistory pagoda the spectators are looking at. Other devices displayed the time of the day, the month, and the year. (Courtesy, Joseph Needham, Science and Civilization in China)

present-day army of the United States of America). Song commanders were educated especially for the task, examined on military subjects, and paid regular salaries.

Because of the military importance of iron and steel, the Song and their northern rivals fought over the iron ore and coal regions of north China. The volume of Song mining and iron production, which again became a government monopoly in the eleventh century, soared. By the end of that century, cast-iron production reached about 125,000 tons (113,700 metric tons), putting it on a par with the output of eighteenth-century Britain. Engineers became skilled at high-temperature metallurgy. They produced steel weapons of unprecedented strength through the use of enormous bellows, often driven by water wheels, to superheat the molten ore. Im-

pervious to fire or concussion, iron buttressed Song defensive works, featured in mass-produced body armor (in small, medium, and large sizes), and provided the material of bridges and small buildings. Mass production techniques in use in China for nearly two thousand years for bronze and ceramics were adapted to iron casting and assembly.

To counter cavalry assaults, the Song experimented with **gunpowder,** which they used to propel a cluster of flaming arrows. During the wars against the Jurchens in the 1100s, the Song introduced a new and terrifying weapon. Shells launched from Song fortifications exploded in the midst of the enemy, blowing out shards of iron and dismembering men and horses. But the short range of the shells limited them to defensive uses, and they made no major impact on the overall conduct of war.

Economy and Society

Despite the continuous military threats and the vigor of Song responses, Song elite culture idealized civil pursuits. Socially, the civil man outranked the military man. Private academies, designed to train students for the official examinations and develop intellectual interests, became influential in culture and politics. The neo-Confucianism of the late Tang period became more sophisticated, more idealistic, and much more pervasive during the Song era. But popular Buddhist sects persisted, and elites elaborated on and adopted some Tang era folk practices derived from India and Tibet. The best known, Chan Buddhism (in Japan known as **Zen,** in Korea as Son), asserted that mental discipline alone could win salvation.

Meditation offered scholars relief from preparation for civil service examinations, the examination system dating from the Tang period. Dramatically different from the Han policy of hiring and promoting on the basis of recommendations, Song-style examinations persisted for nearly a thousand years. A large bureaucracy oversaw their design and administration. Test questions, which changed each time the examinations were given, often related to economic management or foreign policy.

The examinations had social implications, for hereditary class distinctions meant less than they had in Tang times. The new system recruited the most talented men, both prestigious and humble in origin, for government service. Men from wealthy families, however, succeeded most often. The tests required memorization of classics believed to date from the time of Confucius. Preparation consumed so much time that peasant boys, who worked in the fields, could rarely compete.

Success in the examinations brought good marriage prospects, the chance for a high salary, and enormous prestige. Failure could bankrupt a family and ruin a man socially and psychologically. This put great pressure on candidates, who spent days at a time in tiny, dim, airless examination cells, attempting to produce—in beautiful calligraphy—their answers to questions.

Changes in printing, from woodblock to an early form of movable type, allowed cheaper printing of many kinds of informative books and test materials. The Song government realized that the examination system indoctrinated millions of ambitious young men—many times the number who eventually would pass the tests. The advancement of printing thus aided the ideological goals of the government and the personal goals of the candidates. Mass production of authorized preparation books appeared by the year 1000. Although a man had to be literate to buy even the cheap preparation books, and basic education was still not common, access to the examinations for people of limited means did increase, and a moderate number of candidates entered the bureaucracy without noble, gentry, or elite backgrounds.

Printing changed country life as well, as printed texts offered advice on planting and irrigation techniques, harvesting, tree cultivation, threshing, and weaving. Landlords frequently gathered their tenants and workers to show them illustrated texts and explain their meaning. This dissemination of knowledge, along with new technologies, furthered the development of new agricultural land south of the Yangzi River. Iron agricultural implements such as plows and rakes, first used in the Tang, were adapted to wet-rice cultivation as the population moved south. Landowners and village leaders learned from books how to fight the mosquitoes that carried malaria. Control of the disease allowed more immigration by northerners and a sharp increase in population.

The profitability of farming stimulated the production of books on the subject. Commercial agriculture interested the sons of the gentry. Still a frontier for Chinese settlers under the Tang, the south saw an increasing concentration of landownership in the hands of a few wealthy families who claimed extensive tracts in advance of later colonists. In the settlement process, the indigenous inhabitants of the region, related to the modern populations of Malaysia, Thailand, and Laos, retreated into the mountains or southward toward Vietnam.

During the 1100s, the total population of the Chinese territories, spurred by prosperity, rose above 100 million. An increasing proportion lived in large towns and cities, though the leading Song cities had under a million inhabitants apiece. This still put them among the largest cities in the world.

In the Song capitals, multistory wooden apartment houses and narrow streets—sometimes only 4 or 5 feet (1.2 to 1.5 meters) wide and clogged by peddlers or families spending time outdoors—created a crush that demanded expertise in waste management, water supply, and firefighting. Controlling urban rodent and insect infestations improved health and usually kept the bubonic plague isolated to a few rural areas.

In Hangzhou°, in particular, engineers channeled the currents of the nearby river to produce a steady flow of water and air through the city, flushing away waste and disease. Turkic, Arab, and European travelers, sensitive to urban crowding in their own societies, expressed amazement at the way Hangzhou sheltered its densely packed population from danger, while restaurants, parks, bookstores, wine shops, tea houses, and theaters gave beauty and pleasure to the inhabitants.

The idea of credit, originating in the robust long-distance trade of the Tang period, spread widely under the Song. Intercity or interregional credit—what the Song called "flying money"—depended on the acceptance of guarantees that the paper could be redeemed for coinage at another location. The public accepted the practice because credit networks tended to be managed by families, so that usually brothers and cousins were honoring each other's certificates.

"Flying money" certificates differed from government-issued paper money, which the Song pioneered. In some years, military expenditures consumed 80 percent of the government budget. The state responded to this financial pressure by distributing paper money. But this made inflation so severe that, by the beginning of the 1100s, paper money traded for only 1 percent of its face value. Eventually, the government withdrew the paper money and instead imposed new taxes, sold monopolies, and offered financial incentives to merchants.

Rapid economic growth undermined the government monopolies and strict regulation that had become traditional. Hard-pressed for the revenue needed to maintain the army, canals, roads, waterworks, and other state functions, the government sold some functions, such as tax collection, to privateers, who made their profit by collecting the maximum amount and sending an agreed-on smaller amount to the government. This meant ex-

orbitant rates for services and much heavier tax burdens on the common people. But economic privatization also created opportunities for individuals with capital to engage in businesses that previously had been state monopolies.

Now, merchants and artisans as well as gentry and officials could make fortunes. Urban life reflected the elite's growing taste for fine fabrics, porcelain, exotic foods, large houses, and exquisite paintings and books. With land no longer the only source of wealth, the traditional social hierarchy common to an agricultural economy weakened, while cities, commerce, consumption, and the use of money and credit boomed. Because the government and traditional elites did not control much of the new commercial and industrial activities, historians often describe Song China as "modern."

For women, the Song era initiated a long period of cultural subordination, legal disenfranchisement, and social restriction. This fit with the backlash against Buddhism and revival of Confucianism that began under the Tang and intensified under the Song. It also related closely to the economic and status concerns of the gentry and the rising merchant classes.

Merchants spent long periods away from home, and many maintained more than one household. Frequently, they depended on wives to manage their homes and even their businesses in their absence. As women took on responsibility for the management of their husbands' property, they steadily lost the right to control property of their own. Laws changed in the Song period. A woman's property automatically passed to her husband, and women could not remarry if their husbands divorced them or died.

Absolute subordination of women to men proved compatible with Confucianism, and it became fashionable to educate girls just enough to read simple versions of Confucian philosophy, edited to emphasize the lowly role of women. Modest education made these young women more marketable as companions for the sons of other gentry or noble families and more desirable as mothers to the sons of aspiring families. Only occasionally did women of extremely high station and unusual personal determination, such as the poet Li Qingzhao (1083–1141), manage to acquire extensive education and freedom to pursue the literary arts.

Hangzhou (hahng-jo)

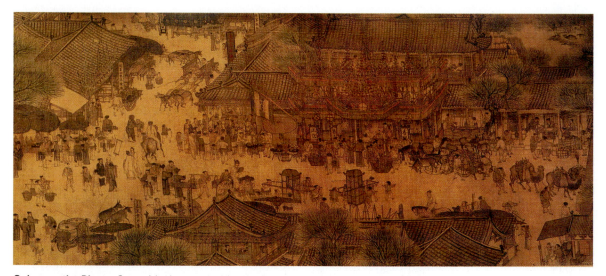

Going up the River   Song cities hummed with commercial and industrial activity, much of it concentrated on the rivers and canals linking the capital, Kaifeng, to the provinces. This detail from *Going Upriver at the Qingming [Spring] Festival* shows a tiny portion of the scroll painting's panorama. Painted by Zhang Zeduan sometime before 1125, its depiction of daily life makes it an important source of information on working people. Before open shop fronts and tea houses, a camel caravan departs, donkey carts are unloaded, a scholar rides loftily (if gingerly) on horseback, and women of wealth go by in closed sedan chairs.   (The Palace Museum, Beijing)

Female footbinding, first in evidence among slave dancers at the Tang court but not widespread before the Song, forced the toes under and toward the heel, so that the bones eventually broke and the woman could not walk on her own. In noble and gentry families, footbinding began when girls were between ages five and seven. In less wealthy families, girls worked until they were older, so footbinding began only in a girl's teens.

Many literate men condemned the maiming of innocent girls and the general uselessness of footbinding. Nevertheless, bound feet became a status symbol. By 1200, a woman with unbound feet had become undesirable in elite circles, and mothers of elite status, or aspiring to it, almost without exception bound their daughters' feet. They knew that girls with unbound feet faced rejection by society, prospective husbands, and ultimately their own families. Footbinding did not occur among working women and the native peoples of the south. Women in these classes and cultures enjoyed considerably more economic independence than did elite women.

Essential Partners: Korea, Japan, and Vietnam

Korea, Japan, and Vietnam, like Song China, depended overwhelmingly on agriculture. The cultivation of rice, an increasingly widespread crop, fit well with Confucian social ideas. Tending the young rice plants, irrigating the rice paddies, and managing the harvest required coordination among many village and kin groups and rewarded hierarchy, obedience, and self-discipline. Confucianism also justified using agricultural profits to support the education, safety, and comfort of the literate elite.

Political ideologies in Korea, Japan, and Vietnam varied somewhat from the Song, which asserted Confucian predominance over all other philosophies, particularly Buddhism. These three East Asian neighbors had first centralized power under a ruling house in the early Tang period, and their state ideologies continued to resemble that of the early Tang, when Buddhism and Confucianism were compatible.

Government service in Korea, Japan, and Vietnam did not rest on an elaborate examination and never called for the esoteric knowledge of Confucian texts. Landowning and agriculture remained the major sources of income and did not face challenges from huge cities or the rise of a large merchant class.

Nevertheless, men in Korea, Japan, and Vietnam prized literacy in classical Chinese and a good knowledge of Confucian texts. Popular education and indoctrination by the elite increasingly instilled the Confucian emphasis on hierarchy and harmony into the minds of ordinary people. Since Han times, Confucianism had spread through East Asia with the spread of the Chinese writing system. The elite in every country learned to read Chinese and the Confucian classics, and the Chinese characters contributed to locally invented writing systems (see Environment and Technology: Writing in East Asia, 400–1200).

Those developments came too slow for the East Asian societies to record their earliest histories. Our first knowledge of Korea, Japan, and Vietnam comes from early Chinese officials and travelers. When the Qin Empire established its first colony in Korea in the third century B.C.E., Chinese bureaucrats began documenting Korean history. Han writers noted the horse breeding, strong hereditary elites, and **shamanism** (belief in the ability of certain individuals to contact the ancestors and the invisible spirit world) of Korea's small kingdoms. But Korea quickly absorbed Confucianism and Buddhism, both of which it transmitted to Japan.

Korea's hereditary elites remained strong and in the early 500s made inherited status—the "bone ranks"—permanent in Silla°, the leading Korean state. In 668, with Tang encouragement, Silla conquered its neighbors and took control of much of the Korean peninsula. But Silla proved unable to maintain its position without Tang support. After the fall of the Tang in the early 900s, the ruling house of **Koryo°,** from which the modern name "Korea" derives, united the peninsula. At constant threat from the Liao and then the Jin, Koryo pursued amicable relations with Song China. The Koryo kings supported Buddhism and made superb printed editions of Buddhist texts.

Woodblock printing exemplifies the technological exchanges that Korea enjoyed with China.

The Players   Women, often enslaved, entertained at Chinese courts from early times. Tang art often depicts women with slender figures, but Tang taste also admired more robust physiques. Song women, usually pale with willowy figures, appear as here with bound feet. The practice appeared in Tang times but was not widespread until the Song, when the image of weak, housebound women unable to work became a status symbol and pushed aside the earlier enthusiasm for healthy women who participated in family businesses.   (The Palace Museum, Beijing)

The oldest surviving woodblock print in Chinese characters comes from Korea in the mid-700s. Commonly used during the Tang period, woodblock printing was time-consuming work; skilled artisans carved hundreds of characters to produce a single printed page. Koreans developed their own advances in printing. By Song times, Korean experiments with **movable type** reached China, where further improvements led to metal or porcelain type from which texts could be cheaply printed.

Japan's earliest history, like Korea's, comes from Chinese records. The first description, dating from the fourth century, tells of an island at the eastern edge of the world, divided into hundreds of small countries and ruled over by a shamaness named Himiko or Pimiko. This account shows the Japanese terrain, mountainous with small pockets

---

Silla (SILL-ah or SHILL-ah)   **Koryo** (KAW-ree-oh)

Writing in East Asia, 400–1200

An ideographic writing system that originated in China became a communications tool throughout East Asia. Variations on this system, based more on depictions of meanings than representations of sound, spread widely by the time of the Sui and Tang Empires. Many East Asian peoples adapted ideographic techniques to writing languages unrelated to Chinese in grammar or sound.

The Vietnamese, Koreans, and Japanese often simplified Chinese characters and associated them with the sounds of local languages. For instance, the Chinese character *an,* meaning "peace" (Fig. 1), was pronounced "an" in Japanese and was familiar as a Chinese character to Confucian scholars in Japan's Heian (hay-ahn) period. However, nonscholars simplified the character and used it to write the Japanese sound "a" (Fig. 2). A set of more than thirty of these syllabic symbols adapted from Chinese characters could represent the inflected forms of any Japanese word. Murasaki Shikibu used such a syllabic system when she wrote *The Tale of Genji.*

In Vietnam and later in northern Asia, phonetic and ideographic elements combined in new ways. The apparent circles in some *chu nom* writing from Vietnam (Fig. 3) derive from the Chinese character for "mouth" and indicate a primary sound association for the word. The Kitans, who spoke a language related to Mongolian, developed an ideographic system of their own, inspired by Chinese characters. The Chinese character *wang* (Fig. 4), meaning "king, prince, ruler," was changed to represent the Khitan word for "emperor" by adding an upward stroke representing a "superior" ruler (Fig. 5). Because the system was ideographic, we do not know the pronunciation of this Khitan word. The Khitan character for "God" or "Heaven" adds a top stroke representing the "supreme" ruler or power to the character meaning "ruler" (Fig. 6). Though inspired by Chinese characters, Khitan writings could not be read by anyone who was not specifically educated in them.

The Khitans developed another system to represent the sounds and grammar of their language. They used small, simplified elements arranged within an imaginary frame to indicate the sounds in any word. This idea might have come from the phonetic script used by the Uighurs. Here (Fig. 7) we see the word for horse in a Khitan inscription. Fitting sound elements within a frame also occurred later in *hangul,* the Korean phonetic system introduced in the 1400s. Here (Fig. 8) we see the two words making up the country name "Korea."

The Chinese writing system served the needs of the Chinese elite well. But peoples speaking unrelated languages continually experimented with the Chinese invention to produce new ways of expressing themselves. Some of the resulting sound-based writing systems remain in common use; others are still being deciphered.

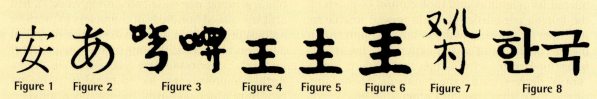

Figure 1   Figure 2   Figure 3   Figure 4   Figure 5   Figure 6   Figure 7   Figure 8

and stretches of land suitable for agriculture, as influencing the social and political structures of the early period. The unification of central Japan came in the fourth or fifth century C.E. How it occurred remains a question, but horse-riding warriors from Korea may have united the small countries of Japan under a central government at Yamato, on the central plain of Honshu island.

In the mid-600s, the rulers based at Yamato implemented the Taika° and other reforms, giving the Yamato regime key features of Tang government, known through embassies to Chang'an: a legal code, an official variety of Confucianism, and a strong state interest in Buddhism. Within a century, a complex system of law stipulated a centralized government, and a massive history in the Confucian style appeared. The Japanese mastered Chinese building techniques so well that Nara° and Kyoto, Japan's early capitals, provide invaluable evidence of the wooden architecture that vanished from China. During the eighth century, Japan in some ways surpassed China in Buddhist studies. In 752, dignitaries from all over Mahayana Buddhist Asia gathered at the enormous Todaiji temple, near Nara, to celebrate the "eye-opening" of the "Great Buddha" statue.

All things Chinese did not come to Japan, however. Although the Japanese adopted Chinese building styles and some street plans, constant warfare did not plague central Japan in the seventh and eighth centuries as it did China, so Japanese cities were built without walls. Also, the Confucian Mandate of Heaven, which justified dynastic changes, played no role in legitimating Japanese government. The *tenno*—often called "emperor" in English—belonged to a family believed to have ruled Japan since the beginning of known history. The dynasty never changed. The royal family endured because the emperors seldom wielded political power. A prime minister and the leaders of the native religion, in later times called Shinto—the "way of the gods"—exercised real control.

In 794, the central government moved to Kyoto, usually called by its ancient name, Heian. Legally centralized government lasted there until 1185, although power became decentralized toward the end. Members of the Fujiwara° family, an ancient family of priests, bureaucrats, and warriors, controlled power and protected the emperor. The Fujiwara elevated men of Confucian learning over the generally illiterate warriors. Noblemen of the Fujiwara period read the Chinese classics, appreciated painting and poetry, and refined their sense of wardrobe and interior decoration.

Pursuit of an aesthetic way of life prompted the Fujiwara nobles to entrust responsibility for local government, policing, and tax collection to their warriors. Though often of humble origins, a small number of warriors had achieved wealth and power by the late 1000s. By the mid-1100s, the nobility had lost control, and civil war between rival warrior clans engulfed the capital.

A literary epic, the *Tale of the Heike,* later celebrated a new elite culture based on military values. The standing of the Fujiwara family fell as nobles and the emperor hurried to accommodate the new warlords. The new warrior class (in later times called *samurai*) eventually absorbed some of the Fujiwara aristocratic values, but the age of the civil elite had ended. In 1185, the **Kamakura° Shogunate,** the first of three decentralized military regimes, established itself in eastern Honshu, far from the old religious and political center at Kyoto.

Vietnam had had contact with empires based in China since the third century B.C.E., but not until Tang times did the relationship become close enough for economic and cultural assimilation. The rice-based agriculture of Vietnam made the region well suited for integration with southern China. As in southern China, the wet climate and hilly terrain of Vietnam demanded expertise in irrigation.

The ancestors of the Vietnamese may have preceded the Chinese in using draft animals in farming, working with metal, and making certain kinds of pots. But in Tang and Song times, the elites of "Annam°"—as the Chinese called early Vietnam—adopted Confucian bureaucratic training, Mahayana Buddhism, and other Chinese cultural traits. Annamese elites continued to rule in the Tang style after that dynasty's fall. Annam assumed the name Dai Viet° in 936 and maintained good relations with Song China as an independent country.

Taika (TIE-kah)   **Nara** (NAH-rah)   **Fujiwara** (foo-jee-WAH-rah)

Kamakura (kah-mah-KOO-rah)   **Annam** (ahn-nahm)
Dai Viet (die vee-yet)

Champa, located largely in what is now southern Vietnam, rivaled the Dai Viet state. The cultures of India and Malaya strongly influenced Champa through the networks of trade and communication that encompassed the Indian Ocean. Although hostile to one another during the period of Tang domination in the north, Champa and Dai Viet both cooperated with the Song, the former as a voluntary tributary state. **Champa rice** (originally from India), a fast-maturing variety, came to the Song from Champa as a tribute gift and contributed to the advancement and specialization of Song agriculture.

All the East Asian societies shared a Confucian interest in hierarchy, but practices relating to gender differed. Footbinding did not spread. In Korea, strong family alliances that functioned like political and economic organizations allowed women a role in negotiating and disposing of property. Before Confucianism, Annamese women enjoyed higher status than women in China, perhaps because of the need for both women and men to participate in wet-rice cultivation. Women in south and southeastern China may have enjoyed similar high status before the growth of northern Chinese influence. The Trung sisters of Vietnam, who lived in the second century C.E. and led local farmers in resistance against the Han Empire, still serve as national symbols in Vietnam and as local heroes in southern China. They recall a time when women played visible and active roles in community and political life.

All the East Asian neighbors believed in limited education for women, as Confucianism prescribed. The hero of a Japanese novel, *The Tale of Genji*, written around the year 1000 by the noblewoman Murasaki Shikibu, accurately and ironically remarks: "Women should have a general knowledge of several subjects, but it gives a bad impression if they show themselves to be attached to a particular branch of learning."[3] Fujiwara noblewomen lived in near-total isolation, generally spending their leisure time studying Buddhism. To communicate with their families or among themselves, they depended on writing. The simplified syllabic script that they used represented the Japanese language in its fully inflected form (the Chinese classical script used by Fujiwara men could not do so). Loneliness, free time, and a ready instrument for expression produced an outpouring of poetry, diaries, and storytelling by women of the Fujiwara era. Their best-known achievement, however, remains Murasaki's portrait of Fujiwara court culture.

CONCLUSION

The Tang Empire put into place a solid system of travel, trade, and communications that allowed cultural and economic influences to move quickly from Central Asia to Japan. Diversity within the empire produced great wealth and new ideas. But tensions among rival groups weakened the political structure and led to great violence and misery.

The post-Tang fragmentation permitted regional cultures to emerge. They experimented with and often improved on Tang military, architectural, and scientific technologies. In northern and Central Asia, these refinements included state ideologies based on Buddhism, bureaucratic practices based on Chinese traditions, and military techniques combining nomadic horsemanship and strategies with Chinese armaments and weapons. In Song China, the spread of Tang technological knowledge resulted in the privatization of commerce, major advances in technology and industry, increased productivity in agriculture, and deeper exploration of ideas relating to time, cosmology, and mathematics. China, however, was not self-reliant. Like its East Asian neighbors Korea, Japan, and Vietnam, it was enriched by the sharing of technological advances.

The brilliant achievements of the Song period came from mutually reinforcing developments in economy and technology. Avoiding the Tang's distortion of trade relations and inhibition of innovation and competition, the Song economy, though much smaller than its predecessor, showed great productivity, circulating goods and money throughout East Asia and stimulating the economies of neighbors. All of the East Asian societies made advances in agricultural technology and productivity. All raised their literacy rates after the improvement of printing. In terms of industrial specialization, Song China dominated military technology and engineering, Japan developed advanced techniques in steel making, and Korea excelled in textiles and agriculture. In the long run, Song China could not maintain the equilibrium necessary to sustain its own prosperity and that of the region. Constant military challenges from the north eventually overwhelmed Song finances, and the need for steel from Japan caused a drain of copper coinage.

The potential of any of the East Asian societies to adjust their mutual relationships and deepen their involvement in Pacific trade will never be known. In the thirteenth century, the societies of continental eastern Asia were destroyed—and the region was united again—by the forces of the Mongol Empire.

■ Key Terms

Grand Canal	**gunpowder**
Tang Empire	**Zen**
Li Shimin	**shamanism**
tributary system	**Koryo**
bubonic plague	**movable type**
Uighurs	**Kamakura Shogunate**
Song Empire	**Champa rice**
junks	

■ Suggested Reading

René Grousset's *The Empire of the Steppes: A History of Central Asia* (1988) is a classic text that can be profitably supplemented by Denis Sinor, ed., *The Cambridge History of Early Inner Asia* (1990). On the transport technologies of Central Asia, see Richard Bulliet, *The Camel and the Wheel* (1975). Francesca Bray, *The Rice Economies: Technology and Development in Asian Societies* (1994), furnishes an important discussion of comparative economy, technology, and society.

Arthur Wright, *The Sui Dynasty* (1978), offers a readable narrative of sixth-century China. For a variety of enduring essays, see Arthur F. Wright and David Twitchett, eds., *Perspectives on the T'ang* (1973). On Tang contacts with other cultures, see Edward Schaeffer, *The Golden Peaches of Samarkand* (1963), *The Vermilion Bird* (1967), and *Pacing the Void* (1977). Christopher I. Beckwith, *The Tibetan Empire in Central Asia* (1987), and Rolf Stein, *Tibetan Civilization* (1972), introduce medieval Tibet. On the Uighurs, see Colin MacKarras, *The Uighur Empire* (1968).

Karl Wittfogel and Chia-sheng Feng, *History of Chinese Society: Liao* (1949), is a classic text on the post-Tang empires of Central and northern Asia, which are poorly covered in English. On the Jurchen Jin, see Jin-sheng Tao, *The Jurchens in Twelfth Century China* (1976); on the Tangguts, see Ruth Dunnell, *The State of High and White: Buddhism and the State in Eleventh-Century Xia* (1996).

Joseph Needham's monumental work covering Song technology is introduced in his *Science in Traditional China* (1981). Mark Elvin, *The Pattern of the Chinese Past* (1973), presents a classic thesis on Song advancement (and Ming backwardness). Joel Mokyr, *The Lever of Riches* (1990), puts China in comparative context. On the poet Li Qingzhao, see Hu Pin-ch'ing, *Li Ch'ing-chao* (1966). For neo-Confucianism and Buddhism, see W. T. de Bary, W-T. Chan, and B. Watson, comps., *Sources of Chinese Tradition*, vol. 1 (1964). On social and economic history, see Miyazaki Ichisada, *China's Examination Hell* (1971); Richard von Glahn, *The Land of Streams and Grottoes* (1987); and Patricia Ebery, *The Inner Quarters: Marriage and the Lives of Chinese Women in the Sung Period* (1993).

For Korean history, see Andrew C. Nahm, *Introduction to Korean History and Culture* (1993), and Ki-Baik Kim, *A New History of Korea* (1984). Paul H. Varley, *Japanese Culture* (1984), introduces Japanese history well. David John Lu, *Sources of Japanese History*, vol. 1 (1974), and R. Tsunoda, W. T. de Bary, and D. Keene, comps., *Sources of Japanese Tradition*, vol. 1 (1964), contain translated sources. Ivan Morris, *The World of the Shining Prince: Court Life in Ancient Japan* (1979), describes the literature and culture of Fujiwara Japan. For Vietnam, see Keith Weller Taylor, *The Birth of Vietnam* (1983).

■ Notes

1. The edited quotation is from William H. McNeill, *Plagues and Peoples* (Garden City, NY: Anchor Press, 1976), 118. McNeill, following his translator, mistakes Ge Hong as "Ho Kung" (pinyin romanization "He Gong").
2. Quoted in David Lattimore, "Allusion in T'ang Poetry," in *Perspectives on the T'ang*, ed. Arthur F. Wright and David Twitchett (New Haven, CT: Yale University Press, 1973), 436.
3. Quoted in Ivan Morris, *The World of the Shining Prince: Court Life in Ancient Japan* (New York: Penguin Books, 1979), 221–222.

10 Peoples and Civilizations of the Americas, 200–1500

CHAPTER OUTLINE

Classic-Era Culture and Society in Mesoamerica, 200–900

The Postclassic Period in Mesoamerica, 900–1500

Northern Peoples

Andean Civilizations, 200–1500

DIVERSITY AND DOMINANCE: Burials as Historical Texts

In late August 682 c.e., the Maya° princess Lady Wac-Chanil-Ahau° walked down the steep steps from her family's residence and mounted a sedan chair decorated with rich textiles and animal skins. As they left the urban center of Dos Pilas°, her military escort spread through the fields and woods to prevent an ambush. Her destination was the Maya city of Naranjo°, where she was to marry a powerful nobleman and thereby reestablish the royal dynasty that had fallen when Caracol defeated Naranjo. Lady Wac-Chanil-Ahau's passage to Naranjo symbolized her father's quest for a military alliance to resist Caracol.

Smoking Squirrel, the son of Lady Wac-Chanil-Ahau, ascended the throne of Naranjo as a five-year-old in 693 c.e. During his long reign,

he proved a careful diplomat, formidable warrior, and prodigious builder. He expanded and beautified his capital and, mindful of his mother's Dos Pilas lineage, erected numerous stelae (carved stone monuments) that celebrated her life.[1]

Warfare and dynastic crisis, caused by population increase and scarcity of resources, convulsed the world of Wac-Chanil-Ahau. Caracol's defeat of the city-states of Tikal and Naranjo undermined long-standing commercial and political relations in southern Mesoamerica. The dynasty created by the heirs of Lady Wac-Chanil-Ahau eventually challenged Caracol. Yet despite a shared culture and religion, the Maya city-states remained divided by dynastic ambition and competition for resources.

The Amerindian[2] hereditary elites organized their societies to meet these challenges, even as their ambitions ignited new conflicts. No single

---

Maya (MY-ah) **Wac-Chanil-Ahau** (wac-cha-NEEL-ah-HOW) **Dos Pilas** (dohs PEE-las) **Naranjo** (na-ROHN-hoe)

set of political institutions or technologies worked in every environment, so American cultures varied widely. Productive and diversified agriculture and cities that rivaled the Chinese and Roman capitals in size and beauty developed in Mesoamerica (Mexico and northern Central America) and the Andean region of South America. In the rest of the hemisphere, indigenous peoples maintained a wide variety of settlement patterns, political forms, and cultural traditions based on combinations of hunting and agriculture.

As you read this chapter, ask yourself the following questions:

- What environmental differences influenced the Mesoamerican, Andean, and northern peoples?

- What technologies developed to meet environmental challenges?

- What similarities and differences marked the civilizations of Mesoamerica and the Andean region?

- How did religious belief and practice affect political life?

CLASSIC-ERA CULTURE AND SOCIETY IN MESOAMERICA, 200–900

Between 200 and 900 C.E., the peoples of Mesoamerica created a civilization based on similarities in material culture, religious beliefs and practices, and social structures, despite differences in language and the absence of regional political integration. Building on the achievements of the Olmecs and others (see Chapter 2), the peoples then living in Central America and south and central Mexico developed new political institutions, made great strides in astronomy and mathematics, and improved agricultural productivity. During the

classic period, population grew, a greater variety of products were traded over longer distances, social hierarchies became more complex, and great cities served as governing and religious centers.

The platforms and pyramids devoted to religious functions that still dominated the cities featured more impressive and diversified architecture. Large full-time urban populations, divided into classes, served hereditary political and religious elites who also controlled the nearby towns and countryside.

The agricultural foundation of Mesoamerican civilization had been developed centuries earlier. The major agricultural technologies—irrigation, wetland drainage, and hillside terracing—preceded the cities built after 200 C.E. by more than a thousand years. What made the achievements of the classic era possible was the extended reach and power of religious and political leaders. The impressive architecture and great size of Teotihuacan° and the great Maya cities illustrate both Mesoamerican aesthetic achievements and the development of powerful political institutions.

Teotihuacan

At the height of its power, from 450 to 600 C.E., **Teotihuacan** (100 B.C.E.–750 C.E.), located about 30 miles (48 kilometers) northeast of modern Mexico City (see Map 10.1), housed between 125,000 and 200,000 inhabitants. The largest city in the Americas, it outshone all but a few contemporary European and Asian cities.

Enormous pyramids dedicated to the sun and moon and more than twenty smaller temples devoted to other gods flanked a central avenue. Among the man-gods worshiped, Quetzalcoatl°, the feathered serpent, was considered the originator of agriculture and the arts. Like the Olmecs, people of Teotihuacan practiced human sacrifice as a sacred duty toward the gods and a necessity for the well-being of human society. The excavation of the temple of Quetzalcoatl uncovered scores of sacrificial victims.

The urban population had grown rapidly from the forced relocation of villagers in the region. More

---

Teotihuacan (teh-o-tee-WAH-kahn)   **Quetzalcoatl** (kate-zahl-CO-ah-tal)

than two-thirds of the city's residents continued to farm, walking from their city homes to the fields. The elite used the city's growing labor resources to expand agriculture, draining swamps, building irrigation works, and cutting terraces into hillsides. They also expanded **chinampas°**, sometimes called "floating gardens." These narrow artificial islands, anchored by trees and created by heaping lake muck and waste material on beds of reeds, permitted year-round agriculture because the subsurface irrigation resisted frost and thus helped greatly to sustain the region's growing population.

The housing of commoners changed as the population grew. Apartment-like stone buildings housed, among other people, the craftsmen who produced goods for export. Teotihuacan pottery has turned up throughout central Mexico and even in the Maya region of Guatemala. More than 2 percent of the urban population crafted similarly widespread obsidian tools and weapons.

The city's role as a religious center signified divine approval of the increasingly prosperous elite. Members of this elite controlled the state bureaucracy, tax collection, and commerce. Their diet and style of dress reflected their prestige, and they lived in separate aristocratic compounds. Temple and palace murals confirm the central position and great prestige of the priestly class. Pilgrims came to Teotihuacan from as far away as Oaxaca and Veracruz. Some became permanent residents.

Unlike other classic-period societies, the people of Teotihuacan did not have a single ruler. The deeds of the rulers do not feature in public art, nor were they represented by statues as in other Mesoamerican civilizations. Some scholars see alliances of elite families or weak kings dominated by powerful families as Teotihuacan's governing authority.

Historians debate the role of the military at Teotihuacan. The absence of walls or other defensive structures before 500 C.E. suggests relative peace during its early development. However, archaeology indicates that the city created a powerful military to protect long-distance trade and compel peasants to hand over their surplus production. The discovery of representations of soldiers in typical Teotihuacan dress in the Maya region of Guatemala may indicate that the military were used to

expand trade. Unlike later postclassic civilizations, however, Teotihuacan was not an imperial state controlled by a military elite.

Although the reason for the burning of the main buildings of Teotihuacan about 650 C.E. remains a mystery, evidence of weakness appears as early as 500 C.E., when the urban population declined to about forty thousand and the city began to build defensive walls. These fortifications and pictorial evidence from murals point to violent decades toward the end. Indications of conflict within the ruling elite and of mismanagement of resources have challenged earlier theories of conquest by a rival city nearby or by nomadic peoples from the north. Class conflict and the breakdown of public order may explain the destruction of the most important temples in the city center, the defacing of religious images, and the burning of elite palaces. Regardless of the causes, the eclipse of Teotihuacan reverberated throughout Mexico and into Central America.

The Maya

Contemporary with Teotihuacan, the **Maya** developed a civilization in the region that today includes Guatemala, Honduras, Belize, and southern Mexico (see Map 10.1). The difficulties of a tropical climate and fragile soils make the cultural and architectural achievements of the Maya all the more remarkable. Although they shared a single culture, they never unified politically. Instead, rival kingdoms led by hereditary rulers competed for regional dominance.

Today, Maya farmers prepare their fields by cutting down small trees and brush and burning the dead vegetation to fertilize the land. This swidden agriculture produces high yields for a few years, but it exhausts the soil's nutrients, eventually forcing a move to fresh land. The high population levels of the Maya classic period (250–900 C.E.) required more intensive forms of agriculture. Maya living near the major urban centers achieved high agricultural yields by draining swamps and building elevated fields. They used irrigation in areas with long dry seasons, and they terraced hillsides in the cooler highlands. Nearly every household planted a garden to provide condiments and fruits. The Maya also practiced forest management, favoring the growth of useful trees and shrubs and

chinampas (chee-NAM-pahs)

C H R O N O L O G Y

	Mesoamerica	Northern Peoples	Andes
100	100 Teotihuacan founded 250 Maya early classic period begins	100–400 Hopewell culture in Ohio River Valley	200–700 Moche culture of Peruvian coast
400			500–1000 Tiwanaku and Wari control Peruvian highlands
700	ca. 750 Teotihuacan destroyed 800–900 Maya centers abandoned, end of classic period 968 Toltec capital of Tula founded	700 Anasazi and Mississippian cultures begin	
1000	1156 Tula destroyed	1050–1250 Cahokia reaches peak power 1150 Collapse of Anasazi centers begins 1200 Anasazi culture declines	1200 Chimú begins military expansion
1300	1325 Aztec capital Tenochtitlan founded		1438 Inca expansion begins 1465 Inca conquer Chimú
1500	1502 Moctezuma II crowned Aztec ruler	1500 Mississippian culture declines	1500–1525 Inca conquer Ecuador

promoting the conservation of deer and other animals hunted for food.

During the classic period, city-states proliferated, the most powerful controlling groups of smaller dependent cities. Religious temples and rituals linked the power of kings to the gods. Unlike earlier sites, these cities had dense central precincts dominated by monumental architecture that was commonly aligned with the movements of the sun and Venus. High pyramids and elaborately decorated palaces, often built on high ground or constructed mounds, surrounded open plazas, an awesome prospect for the masses drawn in for religious and political rituals.

Bas-reliefs and bright paint covered nearly all public buildings. Common motifs included religious allegories, the genealogies of rulers, and important historical events. Carved altars and stone

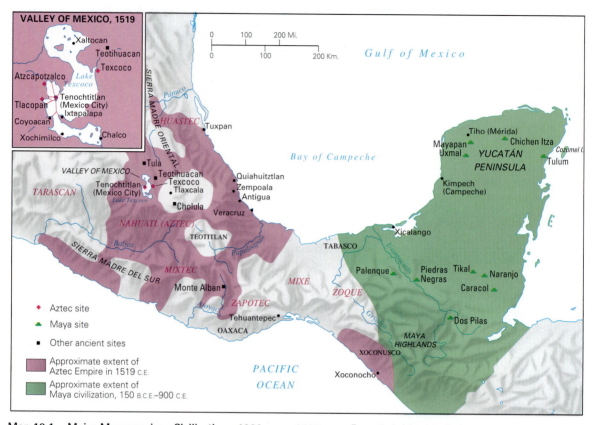

Map 10.1   Major Mesoamerican Civilizations, 1000 B.C.E.–1519 C.E.   From their island capital of Tenochtitlan, the Aztecs militarily and commercially dominated a large region. Aztec achievements were built on the legacy of earlier civilizations such as the Olmecs and Maya.

monoliths arose near major temples. Masses of men and women aided only by levers and stone tools cut and carried construction materials and lifted them into place.

The Maya cosmos consisted of three layers connected along a vertical axis that traced the course of the sun. The earthly arena of human existence came between the heavens, conceptualized as a sky-monster, and a dark underworld. A sacred tree rose through the layers, its roots in the underworld and its branches in the heavens. The temple precincts of Maya cities physically represented this cosmology: the pyramids as sacred mountains reaching to the heavens, their doorways as portals to the underworld.

Rulers and other members of the elite decorated their bodies with paint and tattoos and wore

elaborate costumes of textiles, animal skins, and feathers to project both secular power and divine sanction. Kings communicated directly with the supernatural residents of the other worlds and with deified royal ancestors through bloodletting rituals and hallucinogenic trances. Scenes of rulers drawing blood from lips, ears, and penises are common in frescoes and on painted pottery.

Warfare in particular was infused with religious meaning and elaborate ritual. Scenes of battle and the torture and sacrifice of captives appear frequently. Days of fasting, sacred ritual, and purification rites preceded battle. The king, his kinsmen, and other ranking nobles fought personally, with the goal of taking captives. Elite captives nearly always became sacrificial victims; commoners usually became slaves.

The Great Plaza at Tikal   Still visible in the ruins of Tikal, in modern Guatemala, are the impressive architectural and artistic achievements of the classic-era Maya. Maya centers provided a dramatic setting for the rituals that dominated public life. Construction of Tikal began before 150 B.C.E.; the city was abandoned about 900 C.E. A ball court and residences for the elite were part of the Great Plaza.   (Martha Cooper/Peter Arnold, Inc.)

Two women are known to have ruled Maya kingdoms, though women from ruling lineages also played other political and religious roles. The consorts of male rulers participated in bloodletting rituals and in other public ceremonies. Their noble blood helped legitimate their husbands' rule. Though generally patrilineal (tracing descent in the male line), some male rulers traced their lineages bilaterally (in both the male and the female lines). Like Lady Wac-Chanil-Ahau's son Smoking Squirrel, some rulers emphasized the female line if it held higher status. As for women of the lower classes, scholars believe that they played a central role in the household economy, maintaining garden plots, weaving, and managing family life.

Building on Olmec precedents, the Maya advanced the development of the calendar, mathematics, and writing. The complexity of their calendric system, with each day marked by three separate dating systems, reflects their interest in time and the cosmos. One calendar, shared by other Mesoamerican peoples, tracked the ritual cycle (260 days divided into 13 months of 20 days), another the solar calendar (365 days divided into 18 months of 20 days, plus 5 "unfavorable days" at the end of the year). The concurrence of these two calendars every 52 years was considered especially ominous. Alone among Mesoamerican peoples, the Maya also maintained a continuous "long count" calendar, which began at a fixed date in the

Maya Scribe Maya scribes used a complex writing system to record religious concepts and memorialize the actions of their kings. This picture of a scribe was painted on a ceramic plate. (Justin Kerr)

past that scholars have identified as 3114 B.C.E., a date probably associated with creation.

Their system of mathematics, which underlay the calendar, incorporated the concept of the zero and place value, but it had limited notational signs. Maya writing used hieroglyphs that signified whole words or concepts as well as phonetic cues or syllables. Aspects of public life, religious belief, and the biographies of rulers and their ancestors were recorded in deerskin and bark-paper books, on pottery, and on the stone columns and monumental buildings of the urban centers.

Abandonment or destruction befell many of the major urban centers between 800 and 900 C.E., although a small number survived for centuries. In some areas, decades of urban population decline and increased warfare preceded the collapse. Some experts maintain that the destruction of Teotihuacan after 650 C.E. disrupted trade, thus undermining the legitimacy of Maya rulers who used trade

goods in rituals. Others suggest that population pressure led to environmental degradation and declining agricultural productivity. This, in turn, might have caused social conflict and warfare as desperate elites sought additional agricultural land through conquest. Epidemic disease and pestilence may have contributed as well.

The Postclassic Period in Mesoamerica, 900–1500

The collapse of Teotihuacan and many of the major Maya centers occurred over more than a century and a half, making the division between classic and postclassic periods somewhat arbitrary. In fact, some important classic-period civilizations survived unscathed; and essential cultural characteristics in religious belief and practice, architecture, urban planning, and social organization carried over to the postclassic.

Important differences exist nevertheless. The population of Mesoamerica apparently expanded during the postclassic period, causing an intensification of agricultural practices and increased warfare. The governing elites of the major postclassic states—the Toltecs and the Aztecs—increased the size of their armies and developing political institutions that facilitated control of large and culturally diverse territories gained through conquest.

The Toltecs

Scholars speculate that the **Toltecs°**, little known before their arrival in central Mexico, originated as a satellite population protecting the northern frontier of Teotihuacan from nomad raids. After migrating south, they created an important postclassic civilization on the cultural legacy of Teotihuacan. Memories of their military achievements and the violent imagery of their political and religious rituals dominated the Mesoamerican imagination in the late postclassic period. In the fourteenth century, the Aztecs and their contemporaries erroneously believed that the Toltecs created nearly all of Mesoamerica's cultural monuments. One Aztec source declared:

> In truth [the Toltecs] invented all the precious and marvelous things. . . . All that now exists was their discovery. . . . And these Toltecs were very wise; they were thinkers, for they originated the year count, the day count. All their discoveries formed the book for interpreting dreams. . . .
> And so wise were they [that] they understood the stars which were in the heavens.[3]

Actually, the most important Toltec innovations came in politics and war. The Toltecs created the first conquest state as they extended their political influence from north of modern Mexico City to Central America. Established about 968 c.e., Tula°, the Toltec capital, followed the grand style (see Map 10.1). Its public architecture featured colonnaded patios and numerous temples. Though never as large as Teotihuacan, Tula dominated central Mexico. Nearly all its public buildings and temples carried representations of warriors and scenes suggesting human sacrifice, reflecting an increasingly warlike and violent world view.

Two chieftains or kings apparently ruled the Toltec state together, a system that may eventually have sapped Toltec power and opened Tula to destruction. Sometime after 1000 c.e., a struggle between elite groups identified with rival religious cults undermined the Toltec state. According to later Aztec legends, Topiltzin°—one of the two rulers and a priest of the cult of Quetzalcoatl—and his followers bitterly accepted exile in the east, "the land of the rising sun." These legendary events coincided with growing Toltec influence among the Maya of the Yucatán Peninsula. One text relates the following:

> Thereupon he [Topiltzin] looked toward Tula, and then wept. . . . And when he had done these things . . . he went to reach the seacoast. Then he fashioned a raft of serpents. When he had arranged the raft, he placed himself as if it were his boat. Then he set off across the sea.[4]

Toltec decline set in after the exile of Topiltzin, and around 1156 c.e. northern invaders overcame Tula itself. This destruction triggered a centuries-long process of cultural and political assimilation to produce a new political order based on the Toltec heritage. Like Semitic peoples of the third millennium b.c.e. interacting with Sumerian culture (see Chapter 1), the new Mesoamerican elites came in part from the invading cultures. The Aztecs of the Valley of Mexico became the most important of these late postclassic peoples.

The Aztecs

The Mexica°, more commonly known as the **Aztecs**, pushed into central Mexico from the north after Tula's fall. Originally based on clans, they began to adopt the political and social practices of predecessors who had developed both agriculture and cities. Serving first as serfs and mercenaries for more powerful neighbors, the Aztecs gained strength and relocated to some small islands near the shore of Lake Texcoco. They began to build

---

Toltec (TOLL-tek)   **Tula** (TOO-la

Topiltzin (tow-PEELT-zeen)   **Mexica** (meh-SHE-ca)

Costumes of Aztec Warriors   In Mesoamerican warfare individual warriors sought to gain prestige and improve their status by taking captives. This illustration from the sixteenth-century Codex Mendoza was drawn by an Amerindian artist. It shows the Aztecs' use of distinctive costumes to acknowledge the prowess of warriors. These costumes indicate the taking of two (top left) to six captives (bottom center). The individual on the bottom right shown without a weapon was a military leader. As was common in Mesoamerican illustrations of military conflict, the captives, held by their hair, are shown kneeling before the victors.   (The Bodleian Library, University of Oxford, Selder. A.I. fol. 64r)

their twin capitals, **Tenochtitlan°** and Tlatelolco (together the foundation for modern Mexico City), around 1325 C.E.

The increased economic independence and greater political security they gained by seizing control of additional agricultural land along the lakeshore eased the introduction of a monarchical system similar to that of more powerful neighboring states. Clans persisted down to the Spanish conquest, but power increasingly flowed to hereditary aristocrats and monarchs, though the latter had neither absolute power nor succession based on primogeniture. A council of powerful aristocrats selected new rulers from male members of the ruling lineage. Once selected, the ruler renegotiated the submission of tribute-paying dependencies and demonstrated his divine mandate by new conquests. War took on religious meaning, providing the ruler with legitimacy and increasing the prestige of successful warriors.

As kinship-based clans lost influence, social divisions sharpened. Conquest allowed the warrior

Tenochtitlan (teh-noch-TIT-lan)

elite to seize land and peasant labor as spoils of war (see Map 10.1). The royal family and highest-ranking aristocrats came to own extensive estates cultivated by slaves and landless commoners. The lower classes received some rewards from imperial expansion but lost most of their influence over decisions. Hereditary nobles monopolized the highest social ranks, although some commoners gained status through success on the battlefield or by entering the priesthood.

Urban space in Tenochtitlan and Tlatelolco continued to recognize the clans, whose members maintained a common ritual life and accepted responsibilities like caring for the sick and elderly. Clan members also fought as military units. However, their control over common agricultural land and fishing and hunting rights declined. By 1500 C.E., great inequalities in wealth and privilege characterized Aztec society.

Elaborate ceremonies distinguished kings and aristocrats from commoners. One Spaniard who witnessed the conquest of the Aztec Empire remembered his first meeting with the Aztec ruler Moctezuma° II (r. 1502–1520): "Many great lords walked before the great Montezuma [Moctezuma II], sweeping the ground on which he was to tread and laying down cloaks so that his feet should not touch the earth. Not one of these chieftains dared look him in the face."[5]

Commoners lived in small dwellings and ate a limited diet of staples. Nobles lived in well-constructed two-story houses and dined on meat and other dishes flavored by condiments and expensive imports like chocolate brought from Maya country to the south. Rich dress and jewelry also set apart the elite, who practiced polygamy while the commoners were monogamous.

The Aztec state fed an urban population of approximately 150,000 by efficiently organizing the clans and additional laborers sent by defeated peoples to expand agricultural land. Land reclamation centered on a dike more than 5½ miles (9 kilometers) long by 23 feet (7 meters) wide that separated the freshwater and saltwater parts of Lake Texcoco. The dike, whose construction consumed 4 million person-days, made possible greater irrigation and more chinampas. Aztec chinampas

contributed maize, fruits, and vegetables to the markets of Tenochtitlan. The imposition of a **tribute system** on conquered peoples helped relieve the capital's population pressure. Unlike Tang China, where tribute had a largely symbolic character (see Chapter 9), one-quarter of Tenochtitlan food requirements came from maize, beans, and other foods sent by nearby political dependencies. The Aztecs also demanded cotton cloth, military equipment, luxury goods like jade and feathers, and sacrificial victims.

A specialized class of merchants controlled long-distance trade. In the absence of draft animals and wheeled vehicles, lightweight and valuable products like gold, jewels, feathered garments, cacao, and animal skins dominated this commerce. Merchants also provided political and military intelligence. Operating beyond the reach of Aztec military power, merchant expeditions carried arms and often used them. Although some merchants became wealthy and powerful, none could enter the ranks of the high nobility.

Mesoamerican commerce took place without money or credit, but cacao, quills filled with gold, and cotton cloth provided standard units of value in barter transactions. Aztec expansion integrated producers and consumers in the central Mexican economy so that the markets of Tenochtitlan and Tlatelolco offered goods from as far away as Central America and what is now the southwestern border of the United States. Hernán Cortés (1485–1547), the Spanish adventurer who conquered the Aztecs, admired the abundance of the Aztec marketplace:

> One square in particular is twice as big as that of Salamanca and completely surrounded by arcades where there are daily more than sixty thousand folk buying and selling. Every kind of merchandise such as may be met with in every land is for sale. . . . There is nothing to be found in all the land which is not sold in these markets, for over and above what I have mentioned there are so many and such various things that on account of their very number . . . I cannot detail them.[6]

The combined population of Tenochtitlan and Tlatelolco and the cities and hamlets of the surrounding lakeshore totaled approximately 500,000 by 1500 C.E. In the island capital, canals and streets

---

Moctezuma (mock-teh-ZU-ma)

intersected at right angles. Three causeways connected the city to the lakeshore.

Religious rituals dominated public life. The Aztecs worshiped numerous gods, most of them having both male and female natures. As the Aztec state grew in power and wealth, the cult of Huitzilopochtli°, the southern hummingbird, grew in importance. Although originally associated with war, Huitzilopochtli eventually symbolized the sun, which was worshiped as a divinity throughout Mesoamerica. To bring the sun's warmth to the world, Huitzilopochtli required a daily diet of human hearts. Twin temples devoted to Huitzilopochtli and Tlaloc, the rain god—the two symbolizing war and agriculture as the bases of the Aztec system—dominated Tenochtitlan.

Sacrificial victims included preferably war captives but also criminals, slaves, and people provided as tribute by dependent regions. The Aztecs and other societies of the late postclassic period transformed the Mesoamerican tradition of human sacrifice by increasing its scale. The numbers sacrificed reached into the thousands every year. Some scholars have emphasized the politically intimidating nature of this rising tide, noting that sacrifices took place before large crowds that included leaders from enemy and subject states, as well as the masses of Aztec society.

NORTHERN PEOPLES

By the end of the classic period in Mesoamerica, around 900 C.E., improved agricultural productivity and population growth had fostered settled life and complex social and political structures in the southwestern desert region and along the Ohio and Mississippi River Valleys of what is now the United States. In the Ohio Valley, Amerindian peoples who lived by hunting and gathering and harvesting locally domesticated seed crops developed large villages with monumental earthworks.

Growing populations cultivating maize, a staple introduced from Mesoamerica, undertook large-scale irrigation projects in the southwestern desert and the eastern river valleys. However, the two re-

gions evolved different political traditions. The Anasazi° and their neighbors in the southwest maintained a relatively egalitarian social structure and retained collective forms of political organization based on kinship and age. The mound builders of the eastern river valleys evolved more hierarchical political institutions: a hereditary chief wielded both secular and religious authority over his political center and subordinate groups of small towns.

Southwestern Desert Cultures

Immigrants from Mexico brought irrigation agriculture to Arizona around 300 B.C.E. With two harvests per year, the population grew, and settled village life soon appeared. The Hohokam of the Salt and Gila River Valleys show the strongest Mexican influence, with platform mounds and ball courts similar to those of Mesoamerica. Hohokam pottery, clay figurines, cast copper bells, and turquoise mosaics also reflect Mexican influence. By 1000 C.E., the Hohokam had constructed an elaborate irrigation system that included one canal more than 18 miles (30 kilometers) in length. Hohokam agricultural and ceramic technology gradually spread, but it was the Anasazi to the north who left the most vivid legacy.

Archaeologists use **Anasazi,** a Navajo word meaning "ancient ones," to identify a number of dispersed though similar desert cultures located in the Four Corners region of Arizona, New Mexico, Colorado, and Utah. Between 500 and 750 C.E. the early Anasazi lived in large villages and grew maize, beans, and squash. Their cultural life centered on underground buildings called kivas, which they may have used for weaving cotton and making pottery with geometric patterns. After 900 C.E., they began to construct large multistory residential and ritual centers.

Chaco Canyon in northwestern New Mexico sheltered one of the largest communities: eight large towns in the canyon itself and four more on surrounding mesas, suggesting a regional population of approximately fifteen thousand. Many smaller villages were located nearby. Each town contained hundreds of rooms arranged in tiers around a central plaza. At Pueblo Bonito, the largest town, a four-story block of residences and

---

Huitzilopochtli (wheat-zeel-oh-POSHT-lee)

Anasazi (ah-nah-SAH-zee)

storage spaces contained more than 650 rooms. Pueblo Bonito had thirty-eight kivas, including a great kiva more than 65 feet (19 meters) in diameter. Social life and craft activities took place in small, open plazas or common rooms. Hunting, trade, and maintenance of irrigation works often drew men away from the village. Besides preparing food and caring for children, women shared in agricultural tasks and many crafts. The practice of modern Pueblos, cultural descendants of the Anasazi, suggests that houses and furnishings may have belonged to women formed into extended families with their mothers and sisters.

Pueblo Bonito and its nearest neighbors exerted some kind of political or religious dominance over a large region. The Chaco Canyon culture may have originated as a colonial appendage of Mesoamerica, but archaeological evidence is scarce. Merchants from Chaco provided Toltec-period peoples in northern Mexico with turquoise in exchange for shell jewelry, copper bells, macaws, and trumpets. But these exchanges occurred late in Chaco's development. More important signs of Mesoamerican influence, such as pyramid-shaped mounds, ball courts, and class distinctions signaled by burials or residences, do not appear at Chaco. Instead, it appears that the Chaco Canyon culture developed from earlier societies in the region.

Drought probably forced the abandonment of Chaco Canyon in the twelfth century. Nevertheless, the Anasazi continued in the Four Corners region for more than a century. Anasazi settlements on the Colorado Plateau and in Arizona used large natural caves high above valley floors. Such hard-to-reach locations suggest increased warfare, probably provoked by population pressure on limited arable land. The Pueblo peoples of the Rio Grande Valley and Arizona still live in multistory villages and worship in kivas.

Mound Builders: The Adena, Hopewell, and Mississippian Cultures

The Adena people of the Ohio River Valley, who lived from hunting and gathering supplemented by harvests of locally domesticated seed crops, constructed large villages with monumental earthworks from about 500 B.C.E. Most Adena mounds contained burials with contents indicative of a hierarchical society. The elite owned rare and valuable goods such as mica from North Carolina and copper from the Great Lakes region.

Around 100 C.E., the Adena culture blended into a successor culture now called Hopewell, also centered in the Ohio River Valley but spreading as far as Wisconsin, New York, Louisiana, and Florida. Hopewell people shared the sustenance patterns of the Adena but had a political system based on **chiefdoms**—territories with as many as ten thousand people ruled by a chief, a hereditary leader with both religious and secular responsibilities. Chiefs organized rituals of feasting and gift giving that established bonds among diverse kinship groups and guaranteed access to specialized crops and craft goods. They also managed long-distance trade, which provided luxury goods and additional food supplies.

The largest Hopewell towns in the Ohio River Valley served as ceremonial and political centers and had several thousand inhabitants. Large mounds housing elite burials and serving as platforms for temples and the chief's residence dominated these centers. Elite burial vaults containing valuable goods like river pearls and copper jewelry sometimes entomb women and retainers apparently sacrificed to accompany a dead chief into the afterlife. The abandonment of major Hopewell sites around 400 C.E. has no clear environmental or political explanation.

Hopewell technology and mound building continued in smaller centers linked to the development of Mississippian culture (700–1500 C.E.). Maize, beans, and squash suggest to some a Mississippian cultural link to Mesoamerica, but these plants and related technologies probably arrived by way of intervening cultures.

The urbanized Mississippian chiefdoms resulted from the accumulated effects of small increases in agricultural productivity, the adoption of the bow and arrow, and the expansion of trade networks. The largest towns shared a common urban plan based on a central plaza surrounded by large platform mounds. People bartered essential commodities, such as flint used for weapons and tools, in these centers.

The Mississippian culture culminated in the great urban site of Cahokia, located near East St.

Louis, Illinois. North America's largest mound, a terraced structure 100 feet (30 meters) high and 1,037 by 790 feet (316 by 241 meters) at the base, stands at its center, an area of elite housing and temples ringed by areas where commoners lived. At its height in about 1200 C.E., Cahokia had a population of about thirty thousand—as large as the great Maya city Tikal.

Cahokia controlled surrounding agricultural lands and a number of secondary towns ruled by subchiefs. One burial containing more than fifty young women and retainers sacrificed to accompany a ruler after death suggests the exalted position of Cahokia's chiefs. Nothing links the decline and eventual abandonment of Cahokia (1250 C.E.) to military defeat or civil war, although climate changes and population pressures may have undermined its vitality. After the decline of Cahokia, smaller Mississippian centers flourished in the southeast until the arrival of Europeans.

ANDEAN CIVILIZATIONS, 200–1500

Much of the Andean region's mountainous zone seems too high for agriculture and human habitation, and the arid plain of its Pacific coastland poses difficult challenges to cultivation. To the east of the Andes Mountains, the hot, humid Amazon headwaters also would seem to discourage the organization of complex societies. Yet the Amerindian peoples of the region developed some of the most socially complex and politically advanced societies of the Western Hemisphere (see Map 10.2).

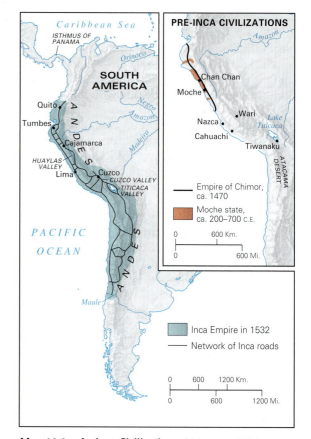

Map 10.2 Andean Civilizations, 200 B.C.E.–1532 C.E. In response to environmental challenges posed by an arid coastal plain and high interior mountain ranges, Andean peoples made complex social and technological adaptations. Irrigation systems, the domestication of the llama, metallurgy, and shared labor obligations helped provide a firm economic foundation for powerful, centralized states. In 1532 the Inca Empire's vast territory stretched from modern Chile in the south to Colombia in the north.

Cultural Response to Environmental Challenge

People living in the high mountain valleys and on the dry coastal plain overcame the environmental challenges through effective organization of labor using a recordkeeping system more limited than those of Mesoamerica. A system of knotted colored cords, **khipus°**, helped administrators record population counts and tribute obligations. Large-scale drainage and irrigation works and the terracing of hillsides to control erosion and provide additional farmland increased agricultural production. People worked collectively on road building, urban construction, and even textile production.

The clan, or **ayllu°**, provided the foundation for Andean achievement. Members of an ayllu

khipus (KEY-pooz)

ayllu (aye-YOU)

claiming descent from a common ancestor, though not necessarily related in fact, held land communally. Ayllu members thought of each other as brothers and sisters with obligations to help each other in tasks beyond the ability of a single household. These reciprocal obligations provided the model for the organization of labor and the distribution of goods at every level of Andean society. Just as individuals and families provided labor to kinsmen, members of an ayllu provided labor and goods to their hereditary chief.

When territorial states ruled by hereditary aristocracies and kings developed after 1000 B.C.E., these obligations grew in scale. The **mit'a**° required ayllu members to work the fields and care for the herds of llamas and alpacas owned by religious establishments, the royal court, and the aristocracy. Each allyu met a yearly quota of workers for specific tasks. Mit'a laborers built and maintained roads, bridges, temples, palaces, and large irrigation and drainage projects. They produced textiles and goods essential to ritual life, such as beer made from maize and coca (dried leaves chewed as a stimulant and now also a source of cocaine).

Jobs divided along gender lines, but the work of men and women was interdependent. Men hunted and served as soldiers and administrators. Women had responsibilities in textile production, agriculture, and the home. One early Spanish commentator remarked:

> [Women] did not just perform domestic tasks, but also [labored] in the fields, in the cultivation of their lands, in building houses, and carrying burdens. . . . And more than once I heard that while women were carrying these burdens, they would feel labor pains, and giving birth, they would go to a place where there was water and wash the baby and themselves. Putting the baby on top of the load they were carrying, they would then continue walking as before they gave birth.[7]

Because the region's mountain ranges created a multitude of small ecological areas with specialized resources, each community sought to control a variety of environments to gain access to essential goods. Coastal regions produced maize, fish, and cotton. Mountain valleys contributed quinoa (the local grain), potatoes, and other tubers. Higher elevations contributed the wool and meat of llamas and alpacas. The Amazonian region provided coca and fruits. Colonists sent to exploit these ecological niches remained linked to their original region and ayllu by marriage and ritual. Historians commonly refer to this system of controlled exchange across ecological boundaries as vertical integration, or verticality.

Both Mesoamerica and the Andes region developed integrated political and economic systems long before 1500. However, the unique environmental challenges of the Andean region led to distinctive highland and coastal cultures. Here, more than in Mesoamerica, geography influenced regional cultural integration and state formation.

Moche and Chimú

Around 200 C.E., some four centuries after the collapse of Chavín (see Chapter 2), the **Moche**° achieved dominance of the north coastal region of Peru. They did not establish a centralized state, but they did deploy military forces, and major urban centers like Cerro Blanco near the modern Peruvian city of Trujillo (see Map 10.2) established hegemony over smaller towns and villages.

The Moche cultivated maize, quinoa, beans, manioc, and sweet potatoes with the aid of massive irrigation works. At higher elevations, they produced coca, used ritually. Complex networks of canals and aqueducts connecting fields with water sources as far away as 75 miles (121 kilometers) depended on mit'a labor imposed on Moche commoners and subject peoples. Large herds of alpacas and llamas transported goods across difficult terrain. Their wool, along with cotton, provided raw material textile production, and their meat was an important dietary element.

Murals and decorated ceramics show Moche society to be stratified and theocratic. Labor organization helped to promote class divisions. Wealth and power, along with political control, lay with the priests and military leaders, a situation reinforced by military conquest of neighboring regions. The elite literally lived above the commoners, having

---

mit'a (MEET-ah)

Moche (MO-che)

their residences on large platforms at Moche ceremonial centers. Their rich clothing, including tall headdresses, confirmed their divine status and set them further apart from commoners. Gold and gold alloy jewelry signified social position: gold plates suspended from the noses concealed the lower portion of the faces, and large gold plugs decorated the ears (see Diversity and Dominance: Burials as Historical Texts).

One tomb of a warrior-priest buried from the Lambeyeque Valley contained a treasure that included gold, silver, and copper jewelry; textiles; feather ornaments; and shells. Two women and three men accompanied him in death. Each retainer had one foot amputated to ensure continued subservience and dependence in the afterlife.

Commoners lived by subsistence farming and labored for their ayllu and the elite. Agriculture, the care of llama herds, and the household economy involved both men and women. They lived in one-room buildings clustered in the outlying areas of cities and in surrounding agricultural zones.

Moche textiles, ceramics, and metallurgy give evidence of numerous skilled artisans. As in Chavín, women played a major role in textile production; even elite women devoted time to weaving. Moche craftsmen produced highly individualized portrait vases, ceramics decorated with line drawings representing myths and rituals, and vessels depicting explicit sexual acts. Their metalwork included gold and silver objects devoted to religious and decorative functions or to elite adornment, as well as heavy copper and copper alloy tools for agricultural and military purposes.

The archaeological record shows that the rapid decline of the major centers coincided with a succession of natural disasters in the sixth century and the rise of a new military power in the Andean highlands. When an earthquake altered the course of the Moche River, major flooding caused serious damage, and a thirty-year period of drought expanded the area of coastal sand dunes, which then blew over cultivated fields, overwhelming the irrigation system. As the land dried, periodic heavy rains caused erosion, which further damaged the economy. Religious and political leaders whose privileges stemmed from a presumed ability to control natural forces through rituals lost credibility. Despite massive efforts to maintain irrigation

and the construction of new urban centers in less vulnerable valleys to the north, Moche civilization never recovered. In the eighth century, a new military power, the **Wari°**, put pressure on trade routes linking the coastal region with the highlands and thus contributed to the disappearance of the Moche.

At the end of the Moche period, the **Chimú°** developed a more powerful coastal civilization centered on Chan Chan, a capital built around 800 C.E. near the earlier Moche cultural center. Chimú expanded aggressively after 1200 C.E. and at the apex of its power controlled 625 miles (1,000 kilometers) of the Peruvian coast.

Within Chan Chan was a series of walled compounds, each one containing a burial pyramid. Scholars believe that each Chimú ruler built his own walled compound in Chan Chan and was buried there beneath a pyramid. Sacrifices and rich grave goods accompanied each royal burial. As with the Moche, Chimú's rulers separated themselves from the masses and demonstrated divine favor through consumption of rare and beautiful textiles, ceramics, and precious metals. The Chimú dynasty may have practiced split inheritance, the goods and lands of the deceased ruler going to secondary heirs or for religious sacrifices. The heir who inherited the throne therefore had to construct his own residence compound and undertake new conquests to fund his household. After the Inca conquered the northern coast in 1465, they borrowed from the rituals and court customs of Chimú.

Tiwanaku and Wari

After 500 C.E., two powerful civilizations developed in the Andean highlands. At nearly 13,000 feet (3,962 meters) on the high, treeless plain near Lake Titicaca in modern Bolivia stand the ruins of **Tiwanaku°** (see Map 10.2). Initial occupation may have occurred as early as 400 B.C.E., but significant urbanization began only after 200 C.E. Modern excavations provide the outline of vast drainage projects that reclaimed nearly 200,000 acres (8,000 hectares) of rich lakeside marshes for

---

Wari (WAH-ree   **Chimú** (chee-MOO)
Tiwanaku (tee-wah-NA-coo)

agriculture. This system of raised fields and ditches permitted intensive cultivation similar to that achieved through chinampas in Mesoamerica. Fish and llamas added protein to a diet largely dependent on potatoes and grains. Llamas also serviced long-distance trade that brought in corn, coca, tropical fruits, and medicinal plants.

Tiwanaku's construction featured high-quality stone masonry. An organized work force—probably thousands of laborers over a period of years—moved large stones and quarried blocks many miles to construct a terraced pyramid, walled enclosures, and a reservoir. With copper alloy tools their only metallic resource, Tiwanaku's artisans cut stone so precisely that little mortar was needed to fit the blocks. They also produced gigantic human statuary; the largest example, a stern figure with a military bearing, was cut from a single stone 24 feet (7 meters) high.

Evidence of daily life is scarce, but Tiwanaku clearly had a stratified society ruled by a hereditary elite. Most women and men devoted their time to agriculture and the care of llamas, though construction and pottery required specialized artisans. Tiwanaku ceramics found in distant places suggest a specialized merchant class as well.

Many scholars portray Tiwanaku as the capital of a vast empire, a precursor to the later Inca state. The elite certainly controlled a large, disciplined labor force in the surrounding region, and conquests and the establishment of colonies provided the highland capital with products from ecologically distinct zones. Tiwanaku influence also extended eastward to the jungles and southward to the coastal regions and oases of the Atacama Desert in Chile. But archaeological evidence suggests that, in comparison with contemporary Teotihuacan in central Mexico, Tiwanaku had a relatively small full-time population of around thirty thousand, and it served as a ceremonial and political center for a large regional population more than as a metropolis.

The contemporary site of Wari about 450 miles (751 kilometers) to the northwest, near the modern Peruvian city of Ayacucho, had cultural and technological links, but the exact relationship remains unclear. Wari may have begun as a dependency of Tiwanaku, or they may have been joint capitals of a single empire. Each had a unique cultural signature.

Wari exceeded Tiwanaku in size, measuring nearly 4 square miles (10 square kilometers). A massive wall surrounded the city center, which included a large temple and numerous multifamily housing blocks. Housing for commoners sprawled across a suburban zone. Unlike most other urban centers in the Andes, Wari had no central planning.

The small scale of its monumental architecture and the near absence of cut stone masonry in public and private buildings distinguish Wari from Tiwanaku. Wari ceramic style also differs, the difference enabling experts to trace Wari's expansion, at a time of increasing warfare throughout the Andes, to the coastal area earlier controlled by the Moche and to the northern highlands. Wari roads maintained communications with remote fortified dependencies. Perhaps as a consequence of military conflict, both Tiwanaku and Wari declined to insignificance by about 1000 C.E.

The Inca

In little more than one hundred years, the **Inca** developed a vast imperial state, which they called "Land of Four Corners." By 1525, the empire had a population of more than 6 million inhabitants and stretched from the Maule River in Chile to northern Ecuador, from the Pacific coast across the Andes to the upper Amazon and, in the south, into Argentina (see Map 10.2). In the early fifteenth century, the Inca competed for power locally in the southern highlands, an area of limited significance after the collapse of Wari. Centered in the valley of Cuzco, the Inca were initially organized as a chiefdom based on reciprocal gift giving and the redistribution of food and textiles. Strong leaders consolidated political authority in the 1430s and undertook a campaign of military expansion.

The Inca state incorporated traditional Andean social customs and economic practices. Tiwanaku had used colonists to provide resources from ecologically distinct zones. The Inca built on this by using their large, professional military to conquer distant territories and by increasing the scale of forced exchanges.

Like earlier highland civilizations, the Inca were pastoralists, their prosperity and military strength depending on vast herds of llamas and alpacas. Both men and women cared for these herds—the women

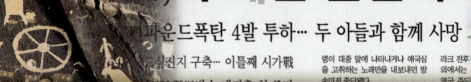

DIVERSITY AND DOMINANCE

BURIALS AS HISTORICAL TEXTS

Efforts to reveal the history of the Americas before the arrival of Europeans depend on the work of archaeologists. The burials of rulers and other members of elites can be viewed as historical texts that describe how textiles, precious metals, beautifully decorated ceramics, and other commodities were used to reinforce the political and cultural power of ruling lineages. In public, members of the elite were always surrounded by the most desirable and rarest products as well as by elaborate rituals and ceremonies. The effect was to create an aura of godlike power. The material elements of political and cultural power were integrated into the experience of death and burial as members of the elite were sent into the afterlife.

The first photograph is of an excavated Moche tomb in Sipán, Peru. The Moche (100 C.E.–ca. 700 C.E.) were one of the most important of the pre-Inca civilizations of the Andean region. They were masters of metallurgy, ceramics, and textiles. The excavations at Sipán revealed a "warrior/priest" buried with an amazing array of gold ornaments, jewels, textiles, and ceramics. He was also buried with two women, perhaps wives or concubines, two male servants, and a warrior. The warrior, one woman, and one man are missing feet, as if this deformation would guarantee their continued faithfulness to the deceased ruler.

The second photograph shows the excavation of a classic-era (250 C.E.–ca. 900 C.E.) Maya burial at Rio Azul in Guatemala. Here a member of the elite was laid out on a carved wooden platform and cotton mattress; his body was painted with decorations. He was covered in beautifully woven textiles and surrounded by valuable goods. Among the discoveries were a necklace of individual stones carved in the shape of heads, perhaps a symbol of his prowess in battle, and high-quality ceramics, some filled with foods consumed by the elite, like cacao. As with the Moche warrior/priest, the careful preparation of the burial chamber had required the work of numerous artisans and laborers. In death, as in life, these early American civilizations acknowledged the high status, political power, and religious authority of their elites.

QUESTIONS FOR ANALYSIS

1. If these burials are texts, what are stories?
2. Are there any visible differences in the two burials?
3. What questions might historians ask of these burials that cannot be answered?
4. Are modern burials texts in similar ways to these ancient practices?

weaving woolen cloth, the men driving animals in long-distance trade. This pastoral background led the Inca to believe that the gods and their ruler shared the obligations of the shepherd to his flock, an idea reminiscent of the Old Testament image conveyed by the lines, "The Lord is my Shepherd."

Cuzco, the imperial capital, and the provincial cities, the royal court, the imperial armies, and the state's religious cults all rested on the efforts of mit'a laborers. The mit'a system also provided the bare necessities for the old, weak, and ill of Inca society. Each ayllu contributed approximately one-seventh of its adult male population to meet these collective obligations. These draft laborers served as soldiers, construction workers, craftsmen, and runners to carry messages along post roads. They also drained swamps, terraced mountainsides, filled in valley floors, built and maintained irrigation works, and built storage facilities and roads. Inca laborers constructed 13,000 miles (20,930

Burials Reveal Ancient Civilizations (Left) Buried around 300 C.E., this Moche warrior-priest was buried amid rich tribute at Sipán in Peru. Also buried were the bodies of retainers or kinsmen, probably sacrificed to accompany this powerful man. The body lies with the head on the right and the feet on the left. (Right) Similarly, the burial of a member of the Maya elite at Rio Azul in northern Guatemala indicates the care taken to surround the powerful with fine ceramics, jewelry and other valuable goods. (*left*: Heinze Plenge/NGS Image Collection; *right*: George Mobley/NGS Image Collection)

kilometers) of road, facilitating military troop movements, administration, and trade.

Imperial administration incorporated existing political structures and established elite groups. The hereditary chiefs of ayllus carried out administrative and judicial functions. As the Inca expanded, they generally left local rulers in place. This risked rebellion, but the Inca controlled these risks through a thinly veiled system of hostage taking and the use of military garrisons. Rulers of de-

feated regions sent their heirs to live at the Inca court in Cuzco, and representations of important local gods were brought to Cuzco to join the imperial pantheon.

Conquests magnified the authority of the Inca ruler and led to the creation of an imperial bureaucracy drawn from his kinsmen. The royal family claimed descent from the sun, the primary Inca god. Members of the royal family lived in palaces maintained by armies of servants. Political and religious rituals dominated the lives of the ruler and his family and helped legitimize their authority. Each new ruler began his reign with conquest because extending imperial boundaries by warfare constituted an imperial duty.

At the height of Inca power in 1530, Cuzco had a population of fewer than thirty thousand, a fifth that of Tenochtitlan at the same time. Nevertheless, Cuzco contains impressive buildings constructed of carefully cut stones fitted together without mortar. Laid out in the shape of a giant puma (a mountain lion), the city's center contained the palaces each ruler built on ascending the throne, as well as the major temples. The Temple of the Sun had an interior lined with sheets of gold and a patio decorated with golden representations of llamas and corn. The ruler made every effort to awe and intimidate visitors and residents with a nearly continuous series of rituals, feasts, and sacrifices. Sacrifices of textiles, animals, and other goods sent as tribute dominated the city's calendar. The destruction of these valuable commodities and a small number of human sacrifices conveyed an impression of splendor and sumptuous abundance that appeared to validate the ruler's descent from the sun.

We know that astronomical observation occupied the priestly class, as in Mesoamerica, but the Inca calendar is unknown. Non-oral communication involved the khipus borrowed from earlier Andean civilizations. Inca weaving and metallurgy, building on earlier regional developments, excelled that of Mesoamerica. Inca craftsmen produced tools and weapons of copper and bronze along with decorative objects of gold and silver. Inca women produced textiles of extraordinary beauty from cotton and llama and alpaca wool.

The Inca did not introduce new technologies, but they increased economic output and added to the region's prosperity. Ruling large populations in environmentally distinct regions allowed the Inca to multiply exchanges between ecological niches. But imperial economic and political expansion reduced equality and diminished local autonomy. The imperial elite lived in richly decorated palaces in Cuzco and other urban centers, increasingly cut off from the masses. The royal court held members of the provincial nobility at arm's length, and commoners faced execution if they looked directly at the ruler's face.

After only a century of regional dominance, the Inca Empire faced a crisis in 1525. The death of the Inca ruler Huayna Capac at the conclusion of the conquest of Ecuador initiated a bloody struggle for the throne. Powerful factions coalesced around two sons whose rivalry compelled both the military and the Inca elite to choose sides. The resulting civil war weakened imperial institutions and ignited the resentments of conquered peoples spread over more than 3,000 miles (4,830 kilometers) of mountainous terrain. On the eve of the arrival of Europeans, this violent conflict undermined the institutions and economy of Andean civilization.

CONCLUSION

The indigenous societies of the Western Hemisphere developed unique technologies and cultural forms in mountainous regions, tropical rain forests, deserts, woodlands, and arctic regions. In Mesoamerica, North America, and the Andean region, the natural environment powerfully influenced cultural development. The Maya of southern Mexico developed agricultural technologies that compensated for the tropical cycle of heavy rains followed by long dry periods. On the Peruvian coast, the Moche used systems of trade and mutual labor obligation to meet the challenge of an arid climate and mountainous terrain. The mound builders of North America expanded agricultural production by using the floodplains of the Ohio and Mississippi Rivers. Across the Americas, hunting and gathering peoples and urbanized agricultural societies alike developed religious and aesthetic traditions, suitable technologies, and effective social institutions in response to local conditions. These cultural traditions proved very durable.

The Aztec and Inca Empires culminated a long developmental process that began before 1000 B.C.E. Each empire controlled extensive and diverse territories with ethnically and environmentally diverse populations that numbered in the millions. The capital cities of Tenochtitlan and Cuzco displayed some of the finest achievements of Amerindian technology, art, and architecture. Both states grew through conquest and depended on the tribute of subject peoples. In both traditions, religion met spiritual needs while also organizing collective life and legitimizing the authority of powerful hereditary rulers.

Yet the empires differed significantly. Elementary markets developed in Mesoamerica to distribute specialized regional production, although the forced payment of goods as tribute remained important. In the Andes, allocation of goods involved reciprocal labor obligations and managed exchange relationships. The Aztecs forced defeated peoples to provide food, textiles, and sacrificial captives as tribute, but they left local hereditary elites in place. The Incas created a more centralized administrative structure managed by a trained bureaucracy.

As the Western Hemisphere's long isolation drew to a close in the late fifteenth century, powerful neighbors or internal revolts shook both empires. In earlier periods, similar challenges had contributed to the decline of great civilizations in both Mesoamerica and the Andean region. Long periods of adjustment and the creation of new institutions followed the collapse of powers such as the Toltecs in Mesoamerica and the Tiwanaku in the Andes. The arrival of Europeans would transform this cycle of crisis and adjustment, and the future of Amerindian peoples would become linked to the cultures of the Old World.

◼ Key Terms

Teotihuacan	khipu
chinampas	ayllu
Maya	mit'a
Toltecs	Moche
Aztecs	Wari
Tenochtitlan	Chimú
tribute system	Tiwanaku
Anasazi	Inca
chiefdoms	

◼ Suggested Reading

In *Prehistory of the Americas* (1987), Stuart Fiedel summarizes the early history of the Western Hemisphere. Alvin M. Josephy, Jr., in *The Indian Heritage of America* (1968), also provides a good introduction. *Canada's First Nations* (1992), by Olive Patricia Dickason, traces Canada's Amerindian peoples to the modern era. *Early*

Man in the New World, edited by Richard Shutler, Jr. (1983), complements these works. *Atlas of Ancient America* (1986), by Michael Coe, Elizabeth P. Benson, and Dean R. Snow, contains useful maps and information. George Kubler, *The Art and Architecture of Ancient America* (1962), is valuable though dated.

Eric Wolf provides an enduring synthesis of Mesoamerican history in *Sons of the Shaking Earth* (1959). For recent research on Teotihuacan, see Esther Pasztori, *Teotihuacan* (1997). Linda Schele and David Freidel summarize recent research on the classic-period Maya in *A Forest of Kings* (1990). The best summary of Aztec history is Nigel Davies, *The Aztec Empire: The Toltec Resurgence* (1987). Jacques Soustelle, *Daily Life of the Aztecs*, translated by Patrick O'Brian (1961), is a good introduction. Though controversial, Inga Clendinnen's *Aztecs* (1991) makes an important contribution.

Chaco and Hohokam (1991), edited by Patricia L. Crown and W. James Judge, summarizes research issues. Robert Silverberg, *Mound Builders of Ancient America* (1968), supplies a good introduction.

For an introduction to early Andean societies, see Karen Olsen Bruhns, *Ancient South America* (1994). For the Moche, see Garth Bawden, *The Moche* (1996). *The History of the Incas* (1970), by Alfred Metraux, offers a dated but useful summary. The best recent synthesis is María Rostworowski de Diez Canseco, *History of the Inca Realm*, trans. Harry B. Iceland (1999). John Murra, *The Economic Organization of the Inca State* (1980), and Irene Silverblatt, *Moon, Sun, and Witches: Gender Ideologies and Class in Inca and Colonial Peru* (1987), offer challenging views of pre-Columbian Peru. Frederick Katz, *The Ancient Civilizations of the Americas* (1972), offers a useful comparative perspective.

◼ Notes

1. This summary follows closely the narrative offered by Linda Schele and David Freidel in *A Forest of Kings: The Untold Story of the Ancient Maya* (New York: Morrow, 1990), 182–186.

2. Before 1492, the inhabitants of the Western Hemisphere had no single name for themselves, no sense that physical similarities created a shared identity. Identity derived from kin groups, language, cultural practices, and political structures. Conquest and the occupation by Europeans after 1492 imposed on America's original inhabitants a racial consciousness and racial identity. All collective terms for these first American peoples reflect this history. *Indians, Native Americans, Amerindians, First Peoples,* and *Indigenous*

Peoples find common usage. This book uses the names of individual cultures and states wherever possible. It tries to reserve *Amerindian* and other terms that suggest transcultural identity and experience for the period after 1492.

3. From the Florentine Codex, quoted in Inga Clendinnen, *Aztecs* (Cambridge: Cambridge University Press, 1991), 213.

4. Quoted in Nigel Davies, *The Toltec Heritage: From the Fall of Tula to the Rise of Tenochtitlán* (Norman: University of Oklahoma Press, 1980), 3.

5. Bernal Díaz del Castillo, *The Conquest of New Spain*, trans. J. M. Cohen (London: Penguin Books, 1963), 217.

6. Hernando Cortés, *Five Letters, 1519–1526,* trans. J. Bayard Morris (New York: Norton, 1991), 87.

7. Quoted in Irene Silverblatt, *Moon, Sun, and Witches: Gender Ideologies and Class in Inca and Colonial Peru* (Princeton, NJ: Princeton University Press, 1987), 10.

Religious Conversion

*R**eligious conversion* has two meanings that often get confused. The term can refer to the inner transformation an individual may feel on joining a new religious community or becoming revitalized in his or her religious belief. Conversions of this sort are often sudden and deeply emotional. In historical terms, they may be important when they transform the lives of prominent individuals.

In its other meaning, *religious conversion* refers to a change in the religious identity of an entire population, or a large portion of a population. This generally occurs slowly and is hard to trace in historical documents. As a result, historians have sometimes used superficial indicators to trace the spread of a religion. Doing so can result in misleading conclusions, such as considering the spread of the Islamic faith to be the result of forced conversion by Arab conquerors, or taking the routes traveled by Christian or Buddhist missionaries as evidence that the

people they encountered adopted their spiritual message, or assuming that a king or chieftain's adherence to a new religion immediately resulted in a religious change among subjects or followers.

In addition to being difficult to document, religious conversion in the broad societal sense has followed different patterns according to changing circumstances of time and place. Historians have devised several models to explain the different conversion patterns. According to one model, religious labels in a society change quickly, through mass baptism, for example, but devotional practices remain largely the same. Evidence for this can be found in the continuation of old religious customs among people who identify themselves as belonging to a new religion. Another model sees religious change as primarily a function of economic benefit or escape from persecution. Taking this approach makes it difficult to explain the endurance of

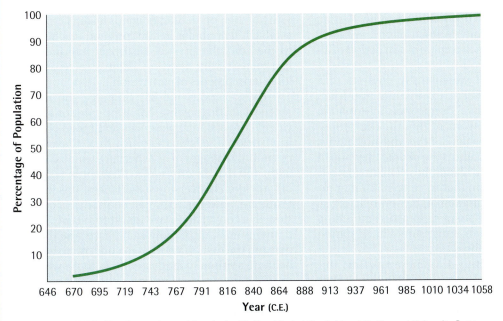

Source: Richard W. Bulliet, *Conversion to Islam in the Medieval Period,* Cambridge, MA: Harvard University Press, 1979, 23. Copyright ©1979 by the President and Fellows of Harvard College.

certain religious communities in the face of hardship and discrimination. Nevertheless, most historians pay attention to economic advantage in their assessments of mass conversion. A third model associates a society's religious conversion with its desire to adopt a more sophisticated way of life, by shifting, for example, from a religion that does not use written texts to one that does.

One final conceptual approach to explaining the process of mass religious change draws on the quantitative models of innovation diffusion that were originally developed to analyze the spread of new technologies in the twentieth century. According to this approach, new ideas, whether in the material or religious realm, depend on the spread of information. A few early adopters—missionaries, pilgrims, or conquerors, perhaps—spread word of the new faith to the people they come in contact with, some of whom follow their example and convert. Those converts in turn spread the word to others, and a chain reaction picks up speed in what might be called a bandwagon effect. The period of bandwagon conversion tapers off when the number of people who have not yet been offered an opportunity to convert diminishes. The entire process can be graphed as a *logistic* or S-shaped curve. Figure 1, the graph of conversion to Islam in Iran based on changes from Persian (non-Islamic) to Arabic (Islamic) names in family genealogies, shows such a curve over a period of almost four centuries.

In societies that were largely illiterate, like those in which Buddhism, Christianity, and Islam slowly achieved spiritual dominance, information spread primarily by word of mouth. The proponents of the new religious views did not always speak the same language as the people they hoped to bring into the faith. Under these circumstances, significant conversion, that is, conversion that involved some understanding of the new religion, as opposed to forced baptism or imposed mouthing of a profession of faith, must surely have started with fairly small numbers.

Language was crucial. Chinese pilgrims undertook lengthy travels to visit early Buddhist sites in India. There they acquired Sanskrit texts, which they translated into Chinese. These translations became the core texts of Chinese Buddhism. In early Christendom, the presence of bilingual (Greek-Aramaic) Jewish communities in the eastern parts of the Roman Empire facilitated the early spread of the religion beyond its Aramaic-speaking homeland. By contrast, Arabic, the language of Islam, was spoken only in the Arabian peninsula and the desert borderlands that extended northwards from Arabia between Syria, Jordan, and Iraq. This initial impediment to the spread of knowledge about Islam dissolved only when intermarriage with non-Muslim, non-Arab women, many of them taken captive and distributed as booty during the conquests, produced bilingual offspring. Bilingual preachers of the Christian faith were similarly needed in the Celtic, Germanic, and Slavic language areas of western and eastern Europe.

This slow process of information diffusion, which varied from region to region, made changing demands on religious leaders and institutions. When a faith was professed primarily by a ruler, his army, and his dependents, religious leaders gave the highest priority to servicing the needs of the ruling minority and perhaps discrediting, denigrating, or exterminating the practices of the majority. Once a few centuries had passed and the new faith had become the religion of the great majority of the population, religious leaders turned to establishing popular institutions and reaching out to the common people. Historical interpretation can benefit from knowing where a society is in a long-term process of conversion.

These various models reinforce the importance of distinguishing between emotional individual conversion experiences and broad changes in a society's religious identity. New converts are commonly thought of as especially zealous in their faith, and that description is often apt in instances of individual conversion experiences. It is less appropriate, however, to broader episodes of conversion. In a conversion wave that starts slowly, builds momentum in the bandwagon phase, and then tapers off, the first individuals to convert are likely to be more spiritually motivated than those who join the movement toward its end. Religious growth depends as much on making the faith attractive to late converts as to ecstatic early converts.

PART FOUR

Interregional Patterns of Culture and Contact, 1200–1550

CHAPTER 11
Mongol Eurasia and Its Aftermath, 1200–1500

CHAPTER 12
Tropical Africa and Asia, 1200–1500

CHAPTER 13
The Latin West, 1200–1500

CHAPTER 14
The Maritime Revolution, to 1550

In Eurasia, overland trade along the Silk Road, which had begun before the Roman and Han empires, reached its peak during the era of the Mongol empires. Beginning in 1206 with the rise of Genghis Khan, the Mongols tied Europe, the Middle East, Russia, and East Asia together with threads of conquest and trade centered on Central and Inner Asia. For over a century and a half, some communities thrived on the continental connections that the Mongols fostered, while others groaned under the tax burdens and physical devastation of Mongol rule. But whether for good or ill, Mongol power was based on the skills, strategies, and technologies of the overland trade and life on the steppes.

The impact of the Mongols was also felt by societies that escaped conquest. In Eastern Europe, the Mediterranean coastal areas of the Middle East, Southeast Asia, and Japan, fear of

Mongol attack stimulated societies to organize more intensively in their own defense, accelerating processes of urbanization, technological development, and political centralization that in many cases were already underway.

By 1500, Mongol dominance was past, and new powers had emerged. A new Chinese empire, the Ming, was expanding its influence in Southeast Asia. The Ottomans had captured Constantinople and overthrown the Byzantine Empire. And the Christian monarchs who had defeated the Muslims in Spain and Portugal were laying the foundations of new overseas empires. With the fall of the Mongol Empire, Central and Inner Asia were no longer at the center of Eurasian trade.

As the overland trade of Eurasia faded, merchants, soldiers, and explorers took to the seas. The most spectacular of the early state-sponsored long-distance ocean voyages were undertaken by the Chinese admiral Zheng He. The 1300s and 1400s also saw African exploration of the Atlantic and Polynesian colonization of the central and eastern Pacific. By 1500 the navigator Christopher Columbus, sailing for Spain, had reached the Americas; within twenty-five years a Portuguese ship would sail all the way around the world. New sailing technologies and a sounder knowledge of the size of the globe and the contours of its shorelines made sub-Saharan Africa, the Indian Ocean, Asia, Europe, and finally the Americas more accessible to each other than ever before.

The great overland routes of Eurasia had generated massive wealth in East Asia and a growing hunger for commerce in Europe. These factors animated the development of the sea trade, too. Exposure to the achievements, wealth, and resources of societies in the Americas, sub-Saharan Africa, and Asia enticed the emerging European monarchies to pursue further exploration and control of the seas.

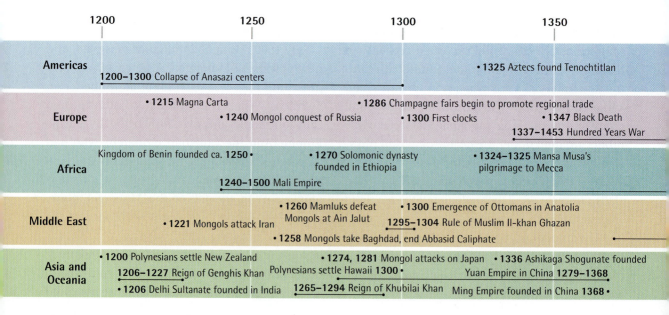

1200 · 1250 · 1300 · 1350

Americas
1200–1300 Collapse of Anasazi centers
• 1325 Aztecs found Tenochtitlan

Europe
• 1215 Magna Carta
• 1240 Mongol conquest of Russia
• 1286 Champagne fairs begin to promote regional trade
• 1300 First clocks
• 1347 Black Death
1337–1453 Hundred Years War

Africa
Kingdom of Benin founded ca. 1250 •
• 1270 Solomonic dynasty founded in Ethiopia
• 1324–1325 Mansa Musa's pilgrimage to Mecca
1240–1500 Mali Empire

Middle East
• 1221 Mongols attack Iran
• 1260 Mamluks defeat Mongols at Ain Jalut
• 1300 Emergence of Ottomans in Anatolia
1295–1304 Rule of Muslim Il-khan Ghazan
• 1258 Mongols take Baghdad, end Abbasid Caliphate

Asia and Oceania
• 1200 Polynesians settle New Zealand
1206–1227 Reign of Genghis Khan
• 1206 Delhi Sultanate founded in India
• 1274, 1281 Mongol attacks on Japan
Polynesians settle Hawaii 1300 •
1265–1294 Reign of Khubilai Khan
• 1336 Ashikaga Shogunate founded
Yuan Empire in China 1279–1368
Ming Empire founded in China 1368 •

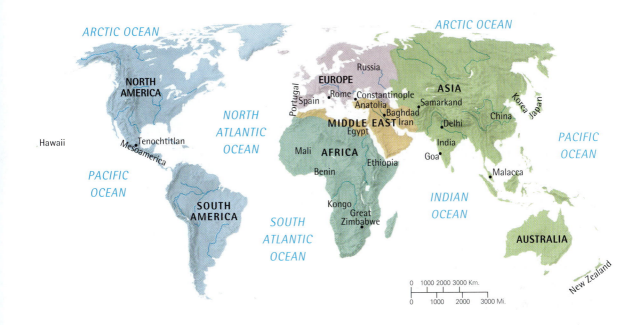

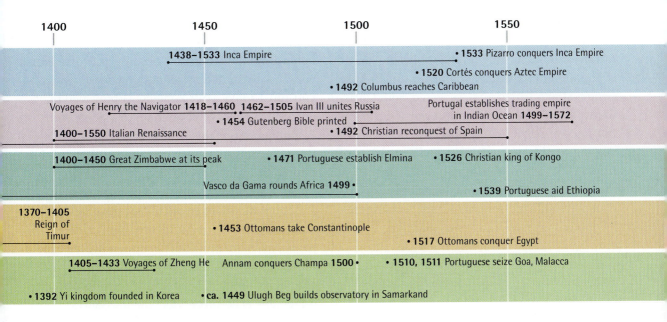

1400	1450	1500	1550

1438–1533 Inca Empire
• **1533** Pizarro conquers Inca Empire
• **1520** Cortés conquers Aztec Empire
• **1492** Columbus reaches Caribbean

Voyages of Henry the Navigator **1418–1460** **1462–1505** Ivan III unites Russia Portugal establishes trading empire in Indian Ocean **1499–1572**
• **1454** Gutenberg Bible printed
1400–1550 Italian Renaissance • **1492** Christian reconquest of Spain

1400–1450 Great Zimbabwe at its peak • **1471** Portuguese establish Elmina • **1526** Christian king of Kongo
Vasco da Gama rounds Africa **1499** •
• **1539** Portuguese aid Ethiopia

1370–1405 Reign of Timur
• **1453** Ottomans take Constantinople
• **1517** Ottomans conquer Egypt

1405–1433 Voyages of Zheng He Annam conquers Champa **1500** • • **1510, 1511** Portuguese seize Goa, Malacca
• **1392** Yi kingdom founded in Korea • **ca. 1449** Ulugh Beg builds observatory in Samarkand

11 Mongol Eurasia and Its Aftermath, 1200–1500

CHAPTER OUTLINE

The Rise of the Mongols, 1200–1283

The Mongols and Islam, 1260–1500

Regional Responses in Western Eurasia

Mongol Domination in China, 1271–1368

The Early Ming Empire, 1368–1500

Centralization and Militarism in East Asia, 1200–1500

ENVIRONMENT AND TECHNOLOGY: From Gunpowder to Guns

When Temüjin° was a boy, a rival group murdered his father. Temüjin's mother tried to shelter him, but she could not find a safe haven. At fifteen Temüjin sought refuge with the leader of the Keraits°, a warring confederation whose people spoke Turkic and respected both Christianity and Buddhism. Temüjin learned the importance of religious tolerance, the necessity of dealing harshly with enemies, and the variety of Inner Asia's cultural and economic traditions.

In 1206 the **Mongols** and their allies acknowledged Temüjin as **Genghis Khan°**, or supreme leader. His advisers spoke many languages and belonged to different religions. His deathbed speech, which cannot be literally true even though a contemporary recorded it, captures the strategy behind Mongol success: "If you want to retain your possessions and conquer your enemies, you must make your subjects submit willingly and unite your diverse energies to a single end."[1] By implementing this strategy, Genghis Khan became the most famous conqueror in history, initiating an expansion of Mongol dominion that by 1250 stretched from Poland to northern China.

Scholars today stress the positive developments that transpired under Mongol rule. European and Asian sources of the time, however, vilify the Mongols as agents of death, suffering, and conflagration, a still-common viewpoint based on reliable accounts of horrible massacres.

Temüjin (TEM-uh-jin)   **Keraits** (keh-rates)   **Genghis Khan** (GENG-iz KAHN)

The tremendous extent of the Mongol Empire promoted the movement of people and ideas from one end of Eurasia to the other. Trade routes improved, markets expanded, and the demand for products grew. Trade on the Silk Road, which had declined with the fall of the Tang Empire (see Chapter 9), revived.

Between 1218 and about 1350 in western Eurasia and down to 1368 in China, the Mongols focused on specific economic and strategic interests, usually permitting local cultures to survive and develop. In some regions, local reactions to Mongol domination sowed seeds of regional and ethnic identity that blossomed in the period of Mongol decline. Regions as widely separated as Russia, Iran, China, Korea, and Japan benefited from the Mongol stimulation of economic and cultural exchange and also found in their opposition to the Mongols new bases for political consolidation and affirmation of cultural difference.

As you read this chapter, ask yourself the following questions:

- What accounts for the magnitude and speed of the Mongol conquests?

- What benefits resulted from the integration of Eurasia in the Mongol Empire?

- How did the effect of Mongol rule on Russia and the lands of Islam differ from its effect on East Asia?

- In what ways did the Ming Empire continue or discontinue Mongol practices?

THE RISE OF THE MONGOLS, 1200–1283

The Mongol Empire owed much of its success to the cultural institutions and political traditions of the Eurasian steppes (prairies) and deserts. The pastoral way of life known as **nomadism** gives rise to imperial expansion only occasionally, and historians disagree about what triggers these episodes. In the case of the Mongols, a precise assessment of the personal contributions of Genghis Khan and his successors remains uncertain.

Nomadism in Central and Inner Asia

The steppe nomads are described as superb riders, herdsmen, and hunters as early as the Greek writer Herodotus in the sixth century B.C.E. Tradition maintains that the Mongols put their infants on goats to accustom them to riding. Moving regularly with flocks and herds required firm decision making, and the independence of individual Mongols made this decision making public, with many voices being heard. A council with representatives from powerful families ratified the decisions of the leader, the *khan*. People who disagreed could strike off on their own. Even during military campaigns, warriors moved with their families and possessions.

Menial work fell to slaves, who were either war captives or who accepted slavery to escape starvation. Weak groups gained protection from strong groups by providing them with slaves, livestock, weapons, silk, or cash. More powerful groups, such as Genghis Khan's extended family and descendants, lived almost entirely off tribute, so they spent less time and fewer resources on herding and more on tribute-generating warfare.

Marriages, which often served to combine resources and solidify intergroup alliances, were arranged in childhood—in Temüjin's case, at age eight—and children thus became pawns of diplomacy. Women from prestigious families could wield power in negotiation and management, though they ran the risk of assassination or execution just like men.

Different faiths, most commonly Buddhism, Christianity, or Islam, could be found in the same family. Yet traditional shamanism, in which special individuals visited and influenced the supernatural world, appealed to everyone. Whatever their faith, the Mongols believed in world rulership by a khan who, with his shamans, could communicate with an ultimate god, represented as Sky or Heaven. This universal ruler transcended particular cultures and dominated them all.

The Mongols were familiar with farming and used agricultural products, but their ideal was self-sufficiency. Since their wanderings with their herds normally took them far from arable land, they relied heavily on meat and milk and made their clothing from felt, leather, and furs. Women oversaw the breeding of livestock and the preparation of furs.

The Mongols acquired iron through trade with settled areas, and they crafted it into bridles, stirrups, cart fittings, and weapons. As early as the 600s the Turks, a related pastoral people, had large ironworking stations south of the Altai Mountains in western Mongolia. Neighboring agricultural states tried to limit the export of iron but never succeeded. Indeed, Central Asians developed improved techniques of iron forging, which the agricultural regions then adopted. The Mongols revered iron and the secrets of ironworking. *Temüjin* means "blacksmith," and several of his prominent followers were the sons of blacksmiths.

Steppe nomads situated near settled areas traded wool, leather, and horses for wood, cotton, silk, vegetables, grain, and tea. Some nomadic groups even used migrants from agricultural regions to establish villages at strategic points. The steppe frontiers east of the Caspian Sea and in northern China thus became economically and culturally diverse. Yet nomads and farmers often came into conflict, sometimes to the point of full-scale invasions in which the nomads' warrior skills usually brought at least temporary victory.

The Mongol Conquests, 1215–1283

Shortly after his acclamation in 1206, Genghis initiated two decades of Mongol aggression designed to win tribute from the kingdoms of Eurasia. By 1209 he had forced the Tanggut rulers of northwest China to submit, and in 1215 he captured the Jin capital of Yanjing, today known as Beijing. He turned westward in 1219 with an invasion of Khwarezm, a state east of the Caspian Sea that included much of Iran. Most of Iran had fallen by 1221, after which Genghis left the command of most campaigns to subordinate generals.

After Genghis Khan's death in 1227, his son Ögödei° became the Great Khan and continued the assault on China. He destroyed the Tanggut and then the Jin and put their territories under Mongol governors. By 1234 the Mongols controlled most of northern China and were threatening the Southern Song (see Chapter 9). In 1236 Genghis's grandson Batu° (d. 1255) attacked Russian territories, took control of all the towns along the Volga° River, and within five years conquered Kievan Russia, Moscow, Poland, and Hungary. Europe would have suffered graver damage had not the death of Ögödei in 1241 compelled the Mongol forces to suspend their campaign. With Genghis's grandson Güyük° installed as the new Great Khan, the conquests resumed. In the Middle East they sacked Baghdad in 1258 and executed the last Abbasid caliph (see Chapter 7).

Although Genghis Khan's original objective may have been tribute, the success of the Mongol conquests created a new historical situation. Ögödei unquestionably sought territorial rule, but after his death in 1241 family unity began to unravel. The Great Khans originally ruled a united empire from their capital at Karakorum°. The khans of the Golden Horde in Russia and the Jagadai domains in Central Asia, as well as the Il-khans in Iran, held subordinate positions (see Map 11.1). When Khubilai° declared himself Great Khan in 1265, however, the descendants of Genghis's son Jagadai (d. 1242) and other branches of the family refused to accept him. After Karakorum was destroyed in the ensuing fighting, Khubilai transferred his court to the old Jin capital that is now Beijing. In 1271 he declared himself founder of the **Yuan Empire**.

Jagadai's descendants continued to dominate Central Asia and enjoyed close relations with the Turkic-speaking nomads of that region. This, plus a continuing hatred of Khubilai, contributed to strengthening Central Asia as an independent Mongol center and to the spread of Islam there.

After the Yuan destroyed the Southern Song (see Chapter 9) in 1279, Mongol troops crossed

Ögödei (ERG-uh-day) **Batu** (BAH-too) **Volga** (VOHL-gah) **Güyük** (gi-yik) **Karakorum** (kah-rah-KOR-um) **Khubilai** (KOO-bih-lie)

C H R O N O L O G Y

	Mongolia and China	Central Asia and Middle East	Russia	Korea, Japan, and Southeast Asia
1200	**1206** Temüjin chosen Genghis Khan of the Mongols	**1219–1221** First Mongol attacks in Iran	**1221–1123** First Mongol attacks on Russia	
	1227 Death of Genghis Khan			
	1227–1241 Reign of Great Khan Ögödei			
	1234 Mongols conquer northern China		**1240** Mongols sack Kiev	
			1242 Alexander Nevskii defeats Teutonic Knights	
		1250 Mamluk regime controls Egypt and Syria		
		1258 Mongols sack Baghdad and kill the caliph		**1258** Mongols conquer Koryo rulers in Korea
		1260 Mamluks defeat Il-khans at Ain Jalut	**1260** War between Il-khans and Golden Horde	
	1271 Founding of Yuan Empire			
	1279 Mongol conquest of Southern Song			**1274, 1281** Mongols attack Japan
				1283 Yuan invades Annam
		1295 Il-khan Ghazan converts to Islam		**1293** Yuan attacks Java
1300				**1333–1338** End of Kamakura Shogunate in Japan, beginning of Ashikaga
		1349 End of Il-khan rule	**1346** Plague outbreak at Kaffa	
		ca. 1350 Egypt infected by plague		
	1368 Ming Empire founded			*(continued)*

C H R O N O L O G Y *(continued)*

	Mongolia and China	Central Asia and Middle East	Russia	Korea, Japan, and Southeast Asia
1400	**1403–1424** Reign of Yongle **1405–1433** Voyages of Zheng He	**1370–1405** Reign of Timur **1402** Timur defeats Ottoman sultan **1453** Ottomans capture Constantinople	**1462–1505** Ivan III establishes authority as tsar. Moscow emerges as major political center	**1392** Founding of Yi kingdom in Korea **1471–1500** Annam conquers Champa

south of the Red River and attacked Annam—now northern Vietnam. They occupied Hanoi three times and then withdrew after arranging for the payment of tribute. In 1283 Khubilai's forces invaded Champa in what is now southern Vietnam and made it a tribute nation as well. A plan to invade Java by sea failed, as did two invasions of Japan in 1274 and 1281.

In tactical terms, the Mongols did not usually outnumber their enemies, but like all steppe nomads they displayed extraordinary abilities on horseback and utilized superior bows. The Central Asian bow, made strong by laminated layers of wood, leather, and bone, could shoot one-third farther (and was significantly more difficult to pull) than the bows used by their enemies in the settled lands.

Mounted Mongol archers rarely expended all of the five dozen or more arrows they carried in their quivers. As the battle opened, they shot arrows from a distance to decimate enemy marksmen. Then they galloped against the enemy's infantry to fight with sword, lance, javelin, and mace. The Mongol cavalry met its match only at the Battle of Ain Jalut°, where it confronted Turkic-speaking Mamluk forces whose war techniques came from the same traditions (see Chapter 7).

To penetrate fortifications, the Mongols fired flaming arrows and hurled enormous projectiles—sometimes flaming—from catapults. The first Mongol catapults, built on Chinese models, transported easily but had short range and poor accuracy. During western campaigns in Central Asia, the Mongols encountered a catapult design that was half again as powerful as the Chinese model. They used this improved weapon against the cities of Iran and Iraq.

Cities that resisted Mongol attack faced siege and annihilation. Surrender was the only option. The slaughter the Mongols inflicted on Balkh° (in present-day northern Afghanistan) and other cities spread terror and caused other cities to surrender. Each conquered area helped swell the "Mongol" armies. In campaigns in the Middle East a few Mongol officers commanded armies of recently recruited Turks and Iranians.

Overland Trade and the Plague

Commercial integration under Mongol rule affected both the eastern and western wings of the empire. Like earlier nomad elites, Mongol nobles had the exclusive right

---

Ain Jalut (ine jah-LOOT)

Balkh (bahlk)

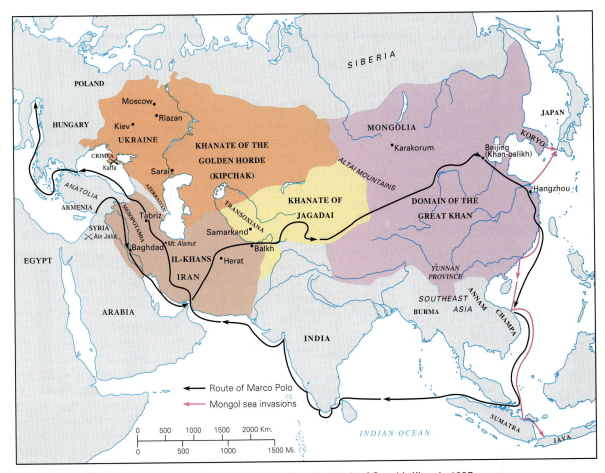

Map 11.1   The Mongol Domains in Eurasia in 1300   After the death of Genghis Khan in 1227, his empire was divided among his sons and grandsons. Son Ögödei succeeded Genghis as Great Khan. Grandson Khubilai expanded the domain of the Great Khan into southern China by 1279. Grandson Hülegü was the first Il-khan in the Middle East. Grandson Batu founded the Khanate of the Golden Horde in southern Russia. Son Jagadai ruled the Jagadai Khanate in Central Asia.

to wear silk, almost all of which came from China. Trade brought new styles and huge quantities of silk westward, not just for clothing but also for wall hangings and furnishings. Abundant silk fed the luxury trade in the Middle East and Europe, and artistic motifs from Japan and Tibet reached as far as England and Morocco. Porcelain, another eastern luxury, became important in trade and strongly influenced later tastes in the Islamic world.

Traders from all over Eurasia enjoyed the benefits of Mongol control. Merchants encountered ambassadors, scholars, and missionaries over the

long routes to the Mongol courts. Some of the resulting travel literature, like the account of the Venetian Marco Polo° (1254–1324), freely mixed the fantastic with the factual. Stories of fantastic wealth stimulated a European ambition to find easier routes to Asia.

Exchange also held great dangers. In southwestern China **bubonic plague** had festered in Yunnan° province since the early Tang period. In the mid-thirteenth century Mongol troops established

Marco Polo (mar-koe POE-loe)   **Yunnan** (YOON-nahn)

a garrison in Yunnan whose military and supply traffic provided the means for flea-infested rats to spread the disease. Marmots and other desert rodents along the caravan routes became infected and passed the disease to dogs and people in oasis towns. The plague incapacitated the Mongol army during their assault on the city of Kaffa° in Crimea° in 1346. They withdrew, but the plague remained. From Kaffa rats infected by fleas reached Europe and Egypt by ship (see Chapter 13).

Typhus, influenza, and smallpox traveled with the plague. The combination of these and other diseases created what is called the "great pandemic" of 1347–1352 and spread devastation far in excess of what the Mongols inflicted in war. Peace and trade, not conquest, ended up taking the greatest toll in lives.

THE MONGOLS AND ISLAM, 1260–1500

From the perspective of Mongol imperial history, the issue of which branches of the family espoused Islam and which did not mostly concerns their political rivalries. From the standpoint of the history of Islam, however, recovery from the political, religious, and physical devastation that culminated in the destruction of the Abbasid caliphate in Baghdad in 1258 attests to the vitality of the faith and the ability of Muslims to overcome adversity. Within fifty years of its darkest hour, Islam had reemerged as a potent ideological and political force.

Mongol Rivalry

By 1260 the **Il-khan°** state, established by Genghis's grandson Hülegü, controlled Iran, Azerbaijan, Mesopotamia, and parts of Armenia. North of the Caspian Sea the Mongols who had conquered southern Russia established the capital of their Khanate of the **Golden Horde** (also called the Kipchak° Khanate) at Sarai° on the Volga River.

Like the Il-khans, they ruled an indigenous Muslim population, mostly Turkic-speaking.

Some members of the Mongol imperial family had professed Islam before the Mongol assault on the Middle East, and Turkic Muslims had served the family in various capacities. Hülegü himself, though a Buddhist, had a trusted Shi'ite adviser and granted privileges to the Shi'ites. As a whole, however, the Mongols under Hülegü's command came only slowly to Islam.

The passage of time did little to reconcile Islamic doctrines with Mongol ways. Muslims abhorred the Mongols' worship of Buddhist and shamanist idols. Furthermore, Mongol law specified slaughtering animals without spilling blood, which involved opening the chest and stopping the heart. This horrified Muslims, who were forbidden to consume blood and slaughtered animals by slitting their throats and draining the blood.

Islam became a point of inter-Mongol tension when Batu's successor as leader of the Golden Horde declared himself a Muslim. He swore to avenge the murder of the Abbasid caliph and laid claim to the Caucasus—the mountains between the Black and Caspian Seas—which the Il-khans also claimed.

Some European leaders believed that if they helped the non-Muslim Il-khans repel the Golden Horde from the Caucasus, the Il-khans would help them relieve Muslim pressure on the crusader principalities in Syria, Lebanon, and Palestine (see Chapter 7). This resulted in a brief correspondence between the Il-khan court and Pope Nicholas IV (r. 1288–1292) and a diplomatic mission that sent two Christian Turks to western Europe as Il-khan ambassadors in the late 1200s. Many Christian crusaders enlisted in the Il-khan effort, but the pope later excommunicated some for doing so.

The Golden Horde responded by seeking an alliance with the Muslim Mamluks in Egypt (see Chapter 7) against both the crusaders and the Il-khans. These complicated efforts effectively extended the life of the crusader principalities; the Mamluks did not finish ejecting the crusaders until the fifteenth century.

Before the Europeans' diplomatic efforts could produce a formal alliance, however, a new Il-khan ruler, Ghazan° (1271–1304), declared himself a

---

Kaffa (KAH-fah)   **Crimea** (cry-MEE-ah)   **Il-khan** (IL-con)
Kipchak (KIP-chahk)   **Sarai** (sah-RYE)

Ghazan (haz-ZAHN)

Muslim in 1295. Conflicting indications of Sunni and Shi'ite affiliation on such things as coins indicate that the Il-khans did not pay too much attention to theological matters. Nor is it clear whether the many Muslim Turkic nomads who served alongside the Mongols in the army were Shi'ite or Sunni.

Islam and the State

Like the Turks before them, the Il-khans gradually came to appreciate the traditional urban culture of the Muslim territories they ruled. Though nomads continued to serve in their armies, the Il-khans used tax farming, a fiscal method developed earlier in the Middle East, to extract maximum wealth from their domain. The government sold tax-collecting contracts to small partnerships, mostly consisting of merchants who might also finance caravans, small industries, or military expeditions. Whoever offered to collect the most revenue for the government won the contracts. They could use whatever methods they chose and could keep anything over the contracted amount.

Contracting tax collection initially lowered administrative costs; but over the long term, the extortions of the tax farmers drove many landowners into debt and servitude. Agricultural productivity declined, making it hard to procure supplies for the soldiers. So the government resorted to taking land to grow its own grain. Like land held by religious trusts, this land paid no taxes. Thus the tax base shrank even as the demands of the army and the Mongol nobility continued to grow.

Ghazan faced many economic problems. Citing the humane values of Islam, he promised to reduce taxes, but the need for revenues kept the decrease from being permanent. He also witnessed the failure of a predecessor's experiment with the Chinese practice of using paper money. Having no previous exposure to paper money, the Il-khan's subjects responded negatively, and the economy sank into a depression that lasted beyond the end of the Il-khan state in 1349. High taxes caused popular unrest and resentment. Mongol nobles competed among themselves for the decreasing revenues, and fighting among Mongol factions destabilized the government.

In the mid-fourteenth century Mongols from the Golden Horde moved through the Caucasus into the western regions of the Il-khan Empire and then into the Il-khan's central territory, Azerbaijan, briefly occupying its major cities. At the same time a new power was emerging to the east, in the Central Asian Khanate of Jagadai (see Map 11.1). The leader **Timur°,** known to Europeans as Tamerlane, skillfully maneuvered himself into command of the Jagadai forces and launched campaigns into western Eurasia, apparently seeing himself as a new Genghis Khan. By ethnic background he was a Turk with only an in-law relationship to the family of the Mongol conqueror. This prevented him from assuming the title *khan,* but not from sacking the Muslim sultanate of Delhi in northern India in 1398 or defeating the sultan of the rising Ottoman Empire in Anatolia in 1402. By that time he had subdued much of the Middle East, and he was reportedly preparing to march on China when he died in 1405. Timur's descendants could not hold the empire together, but they laid the groundwork for the establishment in India of a Muslim Mongol-Turkic regime, the Mughals, in the sixteenth century.

Culture and Science in Islamic Eurasia

The Il-khans of Iran and Timurids (descendants of Timur) of Central Asia presided over a brilliant cultural flowering in Iran, Afghanistan, and Central Asia based on the sharing of artistic trends, administrative practices, and political ideas between Iran and China, the dominant urban civilizations at opposite ends of the Silk Road. The dominant cultural tendencies of the Il-khan and Timurid periods are Muslim, however. Although Timur died before he could reunite Iran and China, his forcible concentration of Middle Eastern scholars, artists, and craftsmen in his capital, Samarkand, fostered cultural advancement under his descendants.

The historian Juvaini° (d. 1283), who recorded Genghis Khan's deathbed speech, came from the city of Balkh, which the Mongols had devastated in 1221. His family switched their allegiance to the Mongols, and both Juvaini and his older brother assumed high government posts. The Il-khan

Timur (TEE-moor)   **Juvaini** (joo-VINE-nee)

Hülegü, seeking to immortalize and justify the Mongol conquest of the Middle East, enthusiastically supported Juvaini's writing. This resulted in the first comprehensive narrative of the rise of the Mongols under Genghis Khan.

Juvaini combined a florid style with historical objectivity, often criticizing the Mongols. This approach served as an inspiration to **Rashid al-Din°**, Ghazan's prime minister, when he attempted the first history of the world. Rashid al-Din's work included the earliest known general history of Europe, derived from conversations with European monks, and a detailed description of China based on information from an important Chinese Muslim official stationed in Iran. The miniature paintings that accompanied some copies of Rashid al-Din's work included depictions of European and Chinese people and events and reflected the artistic traditions of both cultures. The Chinese techniques of composition helped inaugurate the greatest period of Islamic miniature painting under the Timurids.

Rashid al-Din traveled widely and collaborated with administrators from other parts of the far-flung Mongol dominions. His idea that government should be in accord with the moral principles of the majority of the population buttressed Ghazan's adherence to Islam. Administratively, however, Ghazan did not restrict himself to Muslim precedents but employed financial and monetary techniques that roughly resembled those used in Russia and China.

Under the Timurids, the tradition of the Il-khan historians continued. After conquering Damascus, Timur himself met there with the greatest historian of the age, Ibn Khaldun° (1332–1406), a Tunisian. In a scene reminiscent of Ghazan's answering Rashid al-Din's questions on the history of the Mongols, Timur and Ibn Khaldun exchanged historical, philosophical, and geographical viewpoints. Like Genghis, Timur saw himself as a world conqueror. At their capitals of Samarkand and Herat (in western Afghanistan), later Timurid rulers sponsored historical writing in both Persian and Turkish.

A Shi'ite scholar named **Nasir al-Din Tusi°** represents the beginning of Mongol interest in the scientific traditions of the Muslim lands. Nasir al-Din may have joined the entourage of Hülegü during a campaign in 1256 against the Assassins, a Shi'ite religious sect derived from the Fatimid dynasty in Egypt and at odds with his more mainstream Shi'ite views (see Chapter 7). Nasir al-Din wrote on history, poetry, ethics, and religion, but he made his most outstanding contributions in mathematics and cosmology. Following Omar Khayyam° (1038?–1131), a poet and mathematician of the Seljuk° period, he laid new foundations for algebra and trigonometry. Some followers working at an observatory built for Nasir al-Din at Maragheh°, near the Il-khan capital of Tabriz, used the new mathematical techniques to reach a better understanding of the orbits of the celestial bodies. The mathematical tables and geometric models of lunar motion devised by one of his students somehow became known to Nicholas Copernicus (1473–1543), a Polish monk and astronomer. Copernicus adopted this lunar model as his own, virtually without revision. He then proposed the model of lunar movement developed under the Il-khans as the proper model for planetary movement as well—but with the planets circling the sun.

Observational astronomy and calendar making had engaged the interest of earlier Central Asian rulers, particularly the Uighurs° and the Seljuks. Under the Il-khans, the astronomers of Maragheh excelled in predicting lunar and solar eclipses. Astrolabes, armillary spheres, three-dimensional quadrants, and other instruments acquired new precision.

The remarkably accurate eclipse predictions and tables prepared by Il-khan and Timurid astronomers reached the hostile Mamluk lands in Arabic translation. Byzantine monks took them to Constantinople and translated them into Greek, Christian scholars working in Muslim Spain translated them into Latin, and in India the sultan of Delhi ordered them translated into Sanskrit. The Great Khan Khubilai (see below) summoned a team of Iranians to Beijing to build an observatory for him. Timur's grandson Ulugh Beg° (1394–1449), whose avocation was astronomy, constructed a

---

Rashid al-Din (ra-SHEED ad-DEEN)   **Ibn Khaldun** (ee-bin hal-DOON)   **Nasir al-Din Tusi** (nah-SEER ad-DEEN TOO-si)

Omar Khayyam (oh-mar kie-YAM)   **Seljuk** (SEL-jook) **Maragheh** (mah-RAH-gah)   **Uighur** (WEE-ger)   **Ulugh Beg** (oo-loog bek)

Astronomy and Engineering   Observational astronomy went hand in hand not only with mathematics and calendrical science but also with engineering as the construction of platforms, instruments for celestial measurement, and armillary spheres became more sophisticated. This manual in Persian, completed in the 1500s but illustrating activities of the Il-khan period, illustrates the use of a plumb line with an enormous armillary sphere.   (Istanbul University Library)

great observatory in Samarkand and actively participated in compiling observational tables that were later translated into Latin and used by European astronomers.

A further advance made under Ulugh Beg came from the mathematician Ghiyas al-Din Jamshid al-Kashi°, who noted that Chinese astronomers had

Ghiyas al-Din Jamshid al-Kashi (gee-YASS ad-DIN jam-SHEED al-KAH-shee)

long used one ten-thousandth of a day as a unit in calculating the occurrence of a new moon. This seems to have inspired him to employ decimal notation, by which quantities less than one could be represented by a marker to show place. Al-Kashi's proposed value for pi (π) was far more precise than any previously calculated. This innovation arrived in Europe by way of Constantinople, where a Greek translation of al-Kashi's work appeared in the fifteenth century.

REGIONAL RESPONSES IN WESTERN EURASIA

Safe, reliable overland trade throughout Eurasia benefited Mongol ruling centers and commercial cities along the length of the Silk Road. But the countryside, ravaged by conquest, sporadic violence, and heavy taxes, suffered terribly. As Mongol control weakened, regional forces in Russia, eastern Europe, and Anatolia reasserted themselves. All were influenced by Mongol predecessors, and all had to respond to the social and economic changes of the Mongol era. Sometimes this meant collaborating with the Mongols. At other times it meant using local ethnic or religious traditions to resist or roll back Mongol influence.

Russia and Rule from Afar

The Golden Horde established by Genghis's grandson Batu after his defeat of a combined Russian and Kipchak (a Turkic people) army in 1223 started as a unified state but gradually lost its unity as some districts crystallized into smaller khanates. The White Horde, for instance, came to rule much of southeastern Russia in the fifteenth century, and the Crimean khanate on the northern shore of the Black Sea succumbed to Russian invasion only in 1783.

Trade routes east and west across the steppe and north and south along the rivers of Russia and Ukraine° conferred importance on certain trading entrepôts (places where goods are stored

Ukraine (you-CRANE)

or deposited and from which they are distributed), as they had under Kievan Russia (see Chapter 8). The Mongols of the Golden Horde settled at (Old) Sarai, just north of where the Volga flows into the Caspian Sea (see Map 11.1). They ruled their Russian domains to the north and east from afar. To facilitate their control, they granted privileges to the Orthodox Church, which then helped reconcile the Russian people to their distant masters.

The politics of language played a role in subsequent history. Old Church Slavonic, an ecclesiastical language, revived; but Russian steadily acquired greater importance and eventually became the dominant written language. Russian scholars shunned Byzantine Greek, previously the main written tongue, even after the Golden Horde permitted renewed contacts with Constantinople. The Golden Horde enlisted Russian princes to act as their agents, primarily as tax collectors and census takers.

The flow of silver and gold into Mongol hands starved the local economy of precious metal. Like the Il-khans, the khans of the Golden Horde attempted to introduce paper money as a response to the currency shortage. The unsuccessful experiment left such a vivid memory that the Russian word for money (*denga*°) comes from the Mongolian word for the stamp (*tamga*°) used to create paper currency. In fact, commerce depended more on direct exchange of goods than on currency transactions.

Alexander Nevskii° (ca. 1220–1263), the prince of Novgorod, persuaded some fellow princes to submit to the Mongols. In return, the Mongols favored both Novgorod and the emerging town of Moscow, ruled by Alexander's son Daniel. As these towns eclipsed devastated Kiev as political, cultural, and economic centers, they drew people northward to open new agricultural land far from the Mongol steppe lands. Decentralization continued in the 1300s, with Moscow only very gradually becoming Russia's dominant political center.

Historians debate the Mongol impact on Russia. Some stress the destructiveness of the Mongol conquests. Bubonic plague became endemic among rodents in the Crimea. Ukraine, a fertile and well-populated region in the late Kievan period (1000–1230), suffered severe population loss from Mongol armies raiding villages to collect taxes. The domination of the khans, these historians argue, isolated Russia and parts of eastern Europe from developments to the west, burdening the area with the "Mongol yoke" of a sluggish economy and a dormant culture.

Others point out that Kiev declined economically well before the Mongols struck. The Kievan princes had already ceased to mint coins. Yet the Russian territories regularly paid the heavy Mongol

Transformation of the Kremlin Like other northern Europeans, the Russians preferred to build in wood, which was easy to handle and comfortable to live in. But they fortified important political centers with stone ramparts. In the 1300s, the city of Moscow emerged as a new capital, and its old wooden palace, the Kremlin, was gradually transformed into a stone structure. (Novosti)

---

denga (DENG-ah) **tamga** (TAHM-gah) **Nevskii** (nih-EFF-skee)

taxes in silver, indicating both economic surpluses and an ability to convert goods into cash. The burdensome taxes stemmed less from the Mongols than from their tax collectors, Russian princes who often exempted their own lands and shifted the load to the peasants.

As for Russia's cultural isolation, skeptics observe that before the Mongol invasion, the powerful and constructive role played by the Orthodox Church oriented Russia primarily toward Byzantium (see Chapter 8). This situation discouraged but did not eliminate contacts with western Europe, which probably would have become stronger after the fall of Constantinople to the Ottomans in 1453 regardless of Mongol influence.

The traditional structure of local government survived Mongol rule, as did the Russian princely families, who continued to battle among themselves for dominance. The Mongols merely added a new player to those struggles.

Ivan° III, the prince of Moscow (r. 1462–1505), established himself as an autocratic ruler in the late 1400s. Before Ivan, the title *tsar* (from *caesar*), of Byzantine origin, applied only to foreign rulers, whether the emperors of Byzantium or the Turkic khans of the steppe. Ivan's use of the title, which began early in his reign, probably represents an effort to establish a basis for legitimate rule with the decline of the Golden Horde and the disappearance of the Byzantine Empire.

New States in Eastern Europe and Anatolia

Anatolia and parts of Europe responded dynamically to the Mongol challenges. Raised in Sicily, the Holy Roman Emperor Frederick II (r. 1212–1250) appreciated Muslim culture and did not recoil from negotiating with Muslims. When the pope threatened to excommunicate him unless he waged a crusade, Frederick nominally regained Jerusalem through a flimsy treaty with the Mamluk sultan in Egypt. Dissatisfied, the pope continued to quarrel with the emperor, leaving Hungary, Poland, and Lithuania to deal with the Mongol onslaught on their own. Many princes capitulated and went to (Old) Sarai to offer their submission to Batu.

However, the Teutonic° Knights resisted. These German-speaking warriors were dedicated to Christianizing the Slavic and Kipchak populations of northern Europe and to colonizing their territories with thousands of German settlers. To protect Slav territory from German expansion, Alexander Nevskii joined the Mongols in fighting the Teutonic Knights and their Finnish allies. The latter suffered a catastrophe in 1242, when many broke through an icy northern lake and drowned. This destroyed the power of the Knights, and the northern Crusades virtually ceased.

The "Mongol" armies encountered by the Europeans consisted mostly of Turks, Chinese, Iranians, a few Europeans, and at least one Englishman, who went to crusade in the Middle East but joined the Mongols and served in Hungary. But most commanders were Mongol.

Initial wild theories describing the Mongols as coming from Hell or from the caves where Alexander the Great confined the monsters of antiquity gradually yielded to a more sophisticated understanding as European embassies to Mongol courts returned with more reliable intelligence. In some quarters terror gave way to awe. Europeans learned about diplomatic passports, coal mining, movable type, high-temperature metallurgy, higher mathematics, gunpowder, and, in the fourteenth century, the casting and use of bronze cannon. Yet with the outbreak of bubonic plague in the late 1340s (see Chapter 13), the memory of Mongol terror helped ignite religious speculation that God might again be punishing the Christians.

In the fourteenth century several regions, most notably Lithuania°, escaped the Mongol grip. When Russia fell to the Mongols, Lithuania had experienced an unprecedented centralization and military strengthening. Like Alexander Nevskii, the Lithuanian leaders maintained their independence by cooperating with the Mongols. In the late 1300s Lithuania capitalized on its privileged position to dominate Poland and ended the Teutonic Knights' hope of regaining power.

In the Balkans independent kingdoms separated themselves from the chaos of the Byzantine Empire and thrived amidst the political uncertainties of the Mongol period. The Serbian king Stephen

---

Ivan (ee-VAHN)

Teutonic (two-TOHN-ik)   **Lithuania** (lith-oo-WAY-nee-ah)

Dushan (ca. 1308–1355) proved the most effective leader. Seizing power from his father in 1331, he took advantage of Byzantine weakness to turn the archbishop of Serbia into an independent patriarch. In 1346 the patriarch crowned him "tsar and autocrat of the Serbs, Greeks, Bulgarians, and Albanians," a title that fairly represents the wide extent of his rule. As in the case of Timur, however, his kingdom declined after his death in 1355 and disappeared entirely after a defeat by the Ottomans at the battle of Kosovo in 1389.

The Turkic nomads whose descendants established the **Ottoman Empire** came to Anatolia in the same wave of Turkic migrations as the Seljuks (see Chapter 7). They escaped the main Mongol thrust because the Il-khans were centered in Iran and preoccupied with quarrels with the Golden Horde. Though Il-khan influence was strong in eastern Anatolia, a number of small Turkic principalities emerged in the west. The Ottoman principality was situated in the northwest, close to the Sea of Marmara. This not only put them in a position to cross into Europe and take part in the dynastic struggles of the declining Byzantine state, but it also attracted Muslim religious warriors who wished to do battle with Christians on the frontiers. Though the Ottoman sultan suffered defeat at the hands of Timur in 1402, this was only a temporary setback. In 1453 Sultan Mehmet II captured Constantinople and brought the Byzantine Empire to an end.

The Ottoman sultans, like the rulers of Russia, Lithuania, and Serbia, seized the political opportunity that arose with the decay of Mongol power. The powerful states they created put strong emphasis on religious and linguistic identity, factors that the Mongols themselves did not stress. As we shall see, Mongol rule stimulated similar reactions in the lands of East and Southeast Asia.

MONGOL DOMINATION IN
CHINA, 1271–1368

After the Mongols conquered northern China in the 1230s, Great Khan Ögödei told a newly recruited Confucian adviser that he planned to turn the heavily populated North China Plain into a pasture for livestock. The adviser reacted calmly but argued that taxing the cities and villages would bring greater wealth. The Great Khan agreed, but he imposed the oppressive tax-farming system in use in the Il-khan Empire, rather than the fixed-rate method traditional to China.

The Chinese suffered under this system during the early years, but Mongol rule under the Yuan Empire, established by Genghis Khan's grandson Khubilai in 1271, also brought benefits: secure trade routes; exchange of experts between eastern and western Eurasia; and transmission of information, ideas, and skills.

The Yuan Empire, 1271–1368

Just as the Il-khans in Iran and the Golden Horde in Russia came to accept many aspects of Muslim and Christian culture, so the Mongols in China sought to construct a fruitful synthesis of the Mongol and Chinese traditions. **Khubilai Khan** gave his oldest son a Chinese name and had Confucianists participate in the boy's education. In public announcements and the crafting of laws, he took Confucian conventions into consideration. Buddhist and Daoist leaders who visited the Great Khan came away believing that they had all but convinced him of their beliefs.

Buddhist priests from Tibet called **lamas°** became popular with some Mongol rulers. Their idea of a militant universal ruler bringing the whole world under control of the Buddha and thus pushing it nearer to salvation mirrored an ancient Inner Asian idea of universal rulership.

Beijing, the Yuan capital, became the center of cultural and economic life. Whereas Karakorum had been geographically remote, Beijing served as the eastern terminus of caravan routes that began near Tabriz, the Il-khan capital, and (Old) Sarai, the Golden Horde capital. A horseback courier system utilizing hundreds of stations maintained close communications along routes that were generally safe for travelers. Ambassadors and merchants arriving in Beijing found a city that was much more Chinese in character than Karakorum had been.

Called Great Capital (Dadu) or City of the Khan (khan-balikh°, Marco Polo's "Cambaluc"), Khubi-

---

lama (LAH-mah)   **khan-balikh** (kahn-BAL-ik)

lai's capital included the Forbidden City, a closed imperial complex with wide streets and a network of linked lakes and artificial islands. In summer, Khubilai practiced riding and shooting at a palace and park in Inner Mongolia. This was Shangdu°, the "Xanadu°" with its "stately pleasure dome" celebrated by the English poet Samuel Taylor Coleridge.

What we think of today as "China" had been divided into three separate states before the Mongols unified the country (see Chapter 9). The Tanggut and Jin Empires controlled the north, the Southern Song most of the area south of the Yellow River. These states had different languages, writing systems, forms of government, and elite cultures. The Great Khans destroyed all three and encouraged the restoration or preservation of many features of Chinese government and society, thereby reuniting China in what proved to be a permanent fashion.

By law, Mongols had the highest social ranking. Below them came Central Asians and Middle Easterners, then northern Chinese, and finally southern Chinese. This apparent racial ranking also reflected a hierarchy of functions, the Mongols being the empire's warriors, the Central Asians and Middle Easterners its census takers and tax collectors. The northern Chinese outranked the southern Chinese because they had come under Mongol control almost two generations earlier.

Though Khubilai included some "Confucians" (under the Yuan, a formal and hereditary status) in government, their position compared poorly with pre-Mongol times. The Confucians criticized the favoring of merchants, many of whom were from the Middle East or Central Asia, and physicians. They regarded doctors as mere technicians, or even heretical practitioners of Daoist mysticism. The Yuan encouraged medicine and began the long process of integrating Chinese medical and herbal knowledge with approaches derived from Greco-Roman and Muslim sources.

Like the Il-khans in the Middle East, the Yuan rulers stressed census taking and tax collecting. Persian, Arab, and Uighur administrators staffed the offices of taxation and finance, and Muslim scholars worked at calendar-making and astronomy. The Mongols organized all of China into provinces. Central appointment of provincial gov-

ernors, tax collectors, and garrison commanders marked a radical change by systematizing government control in all parts of the country.

The scarcity of documents and the hostility of later Chinese writers make examination of the Yuan economy difficult. Many cities seem to have prospered: in north China by being on the caravan routes; in the interior by being on the Grand Canal; and along the coast by participation in maritime grain shipments from south China. The reintegration of East Asia (though not Japan) with the overland Eurasian trade, which had lapsed with the fall of the Tang (see Chapter 9), stimulated the urban economies.

With merchants a privileged group, life in the cities changed. So few government posts were open to the old Chinese elite that families that had previously spent fortunes on educating sons for government service sought other opportunities. Many gentry families chose commerce. Corporations—investor groups that behaved as single commercial and legal units and shared the risk of doing business—handled most economic activities, starting with financing caravans and expanding into tax farming and lending money to the Mongol aristocracy. Central Asians and Middle Easterners headed most corporations in China in the early Yuan period; but as Chinese bought shares, most corporations acquired mixed membership, or even complete Chinese ownership.

The agricultural base, damaged by war, overtaxation, and the passage of armies, could not satisfy the financial needs of the Mongol aristocracy. Following earlier precedent, the imperial government issued paper money to make up the shortfall. But the massive scale of the Yuan experiment led people to doubt the value of the notes, which were unsecured. Copper coinage partially offset the failure of the paper currency. During the Song, exports of copper to Japan, where the metal was scarce, had caused a severe shortage in China, leading to a rise in value of copper in relation to silver. By cutting off trade with Japan, the Mongols intentionally or unintentionally stabilized the value of copper coins.

Many gentry families moved from their traditional homes in the countryside to engage in urban commerce as city life began to cater to the tastes of merchants instead of scholars. Specialized shops selling clothing, grape wine, furniture, and

---

Shangdu (shahng-DOO)   **Xanadu** (ZAH-nah-doo)

religiously butchered meats became common. Tea-houses offered sing-song girls, drum singers, operas, and other entertainments previously considered coarse. Writers published works in the style of everyday speech. And the increasing influence of the northern, Mongolian-influenced Chinese language, often called Mandarin in the West, resulted in lasting linguistic change.

Cottage industries linked to the urban economies dotted the countryside, where 90 percent of the people lived. Some villages cultivated mulberry trees and cotton using dams, water wheels, and irrigation systems patterned in part on Middle Eastern models. Treatises on planting, harvesting, threshing, and butchering were published. One technological innovator, Huang Dao Po°, brought knowledge of cotton growing, spinning, and weaving from her native Hainan Island to the fertile Yangzi Delta.

Yet on the whole, the countryside did poorly during the Yuan period. After the initial conquests, the Mongol princes evicted many farmers and subjected the rest to brutal tax collection. By the time the Yuan shifted to lighter taxes and encouragement of farming at the end of the 1200s, it was too late. Servitude or homelessness had overtaken many farmers. Neglect of dams and dikes caused disastrous flooding, particularly on the Yellow River.

According to Song records from before the Mongol conquest and the Ming census taken after their overthrow—each, of course, subject to inaccuracy or exaggeration—China's population may have shrunk by 40 percent during eighty years of Mongol rule, with many localities in northern China losing up to five-sixths of their inhabitants. Scholars have suggested several causes: prolonged warfare, rural distress causing people to resort to female infanticide, a southward flight of refugees, and flooding on the Yellow River. The last helps explain why losses in the north exceeded those in the south and why the population along the Yangzi River markedly increased. Bubonic plague and its attendant diseases contributed as well, though cities seem to have managed outbreaks of disease better than rural areas as the epidemic moved from south to north in the 1300s.

Cultural and Scientific Exchange

While Chinese silks and porcelains affected elite tastes at the western end of the Silk Road, Il-khan engineering, astronomy, and mathematics reached China and Korea. Just as Chinese painters taught Iranian artists appealing new ways of drawing clouds, rocks, and trees, Muslims from the Middle East oversaw most of the weapons manufacture and engineering projects for Khubilai's armies. Similarly, the Il-khans imported scholars and texts that helped them understand Chinese technological advances, including stabilized sighting tubes for precisely noting the positions of astronomical objects, mechanically driven armillary spheres that showed how the sun, moon, and planets moved in relation to one another, and new techniques for measuring the movement of the moon. And Khubilai brought Iranians to Beijing to construct an observatory and an institute for astronomical studies similar to the Il-khans' facility at Maragheh.

The Fall of the Yuan Empire

In the 1340s strife broke out among the Mongol princes. Within twenty years farmer rebellions and inter-Mongol feuds engulfed the land. Amidst the chaos, a charismatic Chinese leader, Zhu Yuanzhang°, mounted a campaign that destroyed the Yuan Empire and brought China under control of his new empire, the Ming, in 1368. Many Mongols—as well as the Muslims, Jews, and Christians who had come with them—remained in China. Most of their descendants took Chinese names and became part of the diverse cultural world of China.

Many other Mongols, however, had never moved out of their home territories in Mongolia. Now they welcomed back refugees from the Yuan collapse. Though Turkic peoples were becoming predominant in the steppe regions in the west, including territories still ruled by descendants of Genghis Khan, Mongols continued to predominate in Inner Asia, the steppe regions bordering on Mongolia. Some Mongol groups adopted Islam; others favored Tibetan Buddhism. But religious af-

---

Huang Dao Po (hwahng DOW poh)

Zhu Yuanzhang (JOO yuwen-JAHNG)

filiation proved less important than Mongol identity in fostering a renewed sense of unity.

The Ming thus fell short of dominating all the Mongols. The Mongols of Inner Asia paid tribute to the extent that doing so facilitated their trade. Other Mongols, however, remained a continuing threat on the northern Ming frontier.

THE EARLY MING EMPIRE, 1368–1500

Historians of China, like historians of Russia and Iran, divide over the overall impact of the Mongol era. Since the **Ming Empire** reestablished many practices that are seen as purely Chinese, they receive praise from people who ascribe central importance to Chinese traditions. On the other hand, historians who look upon the Mongol era as a pivotal historical moment when communication across the vast interior of Eurasia served to bring east and west together sometimes see the inward-looking Ming as less dynamic and productive than the Yuan.

Ming China on a Mongol Foundation

Zhu Yuanzhang, a former monk, soldier, and bandit, had watched his parents and other family members die of famine and disease, conditions he blamed on Mongol misrule. During the Yuan Empire's chaotic last decades, he vanquished rival rebels and assumed imperial power under the name Hongwu (r. 1368–1398).

Hongwu moved the capital to Nanjing° ("southern capital") on the Yangzi River, turning away from the Mongol's Beijing ("northern capital"; see Map 11.2). Though Zhu Yuanzhang the rebel had espoused a radical Buddhist belief in a coming age of salvation, once in power he used Confucianism to depict the emperor as the champion of civilization and virtue.

Hongwu choked off relations with Central Asia and the Middle East and imposed strict limits on imports and foreign visitors. Silver replaced paper money for tax payments and commerce. These practices, illustrative of an anti-Mongol ideology, proved as economically unhealthy as some of the Yuan economic policies and did not last. Eventually, the Ming government came to resemble the Yuan. Ming rulers retained the provincial structure and continued to observe the hereditary professional categories of the Yuan period. Muslims made calendars and astronomical calculations at a new observatory at Nanjing, a replica of Khubilai's at Beijing. The Mongol calendar continued in use.

Continuities with the Yuan became more evident after an imperial prince seized power through a coup d'état to rule as the emperor **Yongle°** (r. 1403–1424). He returned the capital to Beijing, enlarging and improving Khubilai's Forbidden City, which now acquired its present features: moats, orange-red outer walls, golden roofs, and marble bridges. Yongle intended this combination fortress, religious site, bureaucratic center, and imperial residential park to overshadow Nanjing, and it survives today as China's most imposing traditional architectural complex.

Yongle also restored commercial links with the Middle East. Because hostile Mongols still controlled much of the caravan route, Yongle explored maritime connections. In Southeast Asia, Annam became a Ming province as the early emperors continued the Mongol program of aggression. This focus on the southern frontier helped inspire the naval expeditions of the trusted imperial eunuch **Zheng He°** from 1405 to 1433.

A Muslim whose father and grandfather had made the pilgrimage to Mecca, Zheng He had a good knowledge of the Middle East; and his religion eased relations with the states of the Indian subcontinent, where he directed his first three voyages. Subsequent expeditions reached Hormuz on the Persian Gulf, sailed the southern coast of Arabia and the Horn of Africa (modern Somalia), and possibly reached as far south as the Strait of Madagascar.

On early voyages he visited long-established Chinese merchant communities in Southeast Asia in order to cement their allegiance to the Ming

---

Nanjing (nahn-JING)

Yongle (yoong-LAW)   **Zheng He** (JEHNG HUH)

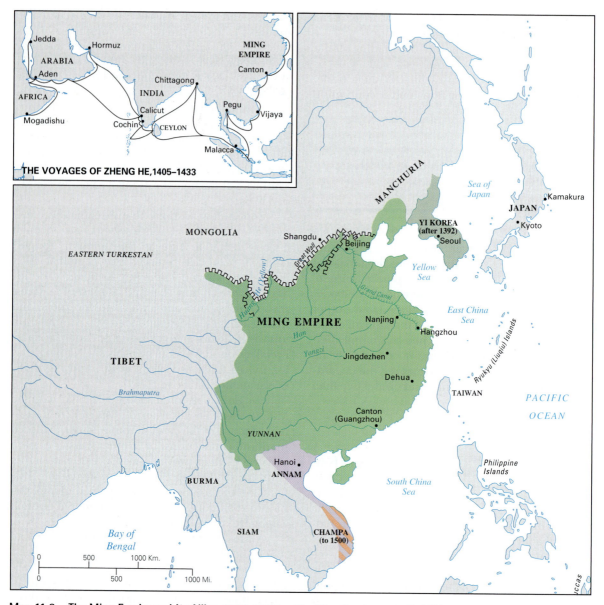

THE VOYAGES OF ZHENG HE, 1405–1433

Map 11.2   The Ming Empire and Its Allies, 1368–1500   The Ming Empire controlled China but had a hostile relationship with peoples in Mongolia and Inner Asia who had been under the rule of the Mongol Yuan emperors. Mongol attempts at conquest by sea were continued by the Ming mariner Zheng He. Between 1405 and 1433 he sailed to Southeast Asia and then beyond, to India, the Persian Gulf, and East Africa.

Empire and to collect taxes. When a community on the island of Sumatra resisted, he slaughtered the men to set an example. The expeditions added some fifty new tributary states to the Ming im-

perial universe, but trade did not increase as dramatically. Sporadic embassies reached Beijing from rulers in India, the Middle East, Africa, and Southeast Asia. During one visit the ruler of

Brunei° died and received a grand burial at the Chinese capital. The expeditions stopped in the 1430s after the deaths of Yongle and Zheng He.

Having demonstrated such abilities at long-distance navigation, why did the Chinese not develop seafaring for commercial and military gain? Contemporaries considered the voyages a personal project of Yongle, an upstart ruler who had always sought to prove his worthiness. Building the Forbidden City in Beijing and sponsoring gigantic encyclopedia projects might be taken to reflect a similar motivation. Yongle may also have been emulating Khubilai Khan, who had sent enormous fleets against Japan and Southeast Asia. This would fit with the rumor spread by Yongle's political enemies that he was actually a Mongol.

A less speculative approach to the question starts with the fact that the new commercial opportunities fell short of expectations, despite bringing foreign nations into the Ming orbit. In the meantime, Japanese coastal piracy intensified, and Mongol threats in the north and west grew. The human and financial demands of fortifying the north, redesigning and strengthening Beijing, and outfitting military expeditions against the Mongols ultimately took priority over the quest for maritime empire.

Technology and Population

Although innovation continued under the Ming, advances were less frequent and less significant than under the Song, particularly in agriculture. Agricultural production peaked around the mid-1400s and remained level for more than a century.

Because the Ming government limited mining, partly to reinforce the value of metal coins and partly to tax the industry, copper, iron, and steel became too expensive for some people, especially farmers, who needed metals for farm implements. With peace came a decline in techniques for making high-quality bronze and steel, which were especially used for weapons. As a result, Japan quickly surpassed China in the production of extremely high-quality steel swords.

Brunei (broo-NIE)

After the death of Emperor Yongle in 1424, shipbuilding also declined, and few advances occurred in printing, timekeeping, and agricultural technology. New weaving techniques did appear, but technological development in this field had peaked by 1500.

Reactivation of the examination system as a way of recruiting government officials (see Chapter 9) drew large numbers of ambitious men into a renewed study of the Confucian classics. This reduced the vitality of commerce, where they had previously been employed, just as population increase was creating a labor surplus. Records indicating a growth from 60 million at the end of the Yuan period in 1368 to nearly 100 million by 1400 may not be entirely reliable, but rapid population growth encouraged the production of staples—wheat, millet, and barley in the north and rice in the south—at the expense of commercial crops such as cotton that had stimulated many technological innovations under the Song. Staple crops yielded lower profits, which further discouraged capital improvements. New foods, such as sweet potatoes, became available but were little adopted. Population growth in southern and central China caused deforestation and raised the price of wood.

The Mongols that the Ming confronted in the north fought on horseback with simple weapons. The Ming fought back with arrows, scattershot mortars, and explosive canisters. They even used a few cannon, which they knew about from contacts with the Middle East and later with Europeans (see Environment and Technology: From Gunpowder to Guns). Fearing that technological secrets would get into enemy hands, the government censored the chapters on gunpowder and guns in early Ming encyclopedias. Shipyards and ports shut down to avoid contact with Japanese pirates and to prevent Chinese from migrating to Southeast Asia.

A technology gap with Korea and Japan opened up nevertheless. When superior steel was needed, supplies came from Japan. Korea moved ahead of China in the design and production of firearms and ships, in printing techniques, and in the sciences of weather prediction and calendar-making. The desire to tap the wealthy Ming market spurred some of these advances.

From Gunpowder to Guns

Long before the invention of guns, gunpowder was used in China and Korea to excavate mines, build canals, and channel irrigation. Alchemists in China used related formulas to make noxious gas pellets to paralyze enemies and expel evil spirits. A more realistic benefit was eliminating disease-carrying insects, a critical aid to the colonization of malarial regions in China and Southeast Asia. The Mongol Empire staged fireworks displays on ceremonial occasions, delighting European visitors to Karakorum who saw them for the first time.

Anecdotal evidence in Chinese records gives credit for the introduction of gunpowder to a Sogdian Buddhist monk of the 500s. The monk described the wondrous alchemical transformation of elements produced by a combination of charcoal and saltpeter. In this connection he also mentioned sulfur. The distillation of naphtha, a light, flammable derivative of oil or coal, seems also to have been first developed in Central Asia, the earliest evidence coming from the Gandhara region (in modern Pakistan).

By the eleventh century, the Chinese had developed flamethrowers powered by burning naphtha, sulfur, or gunpowder in a long tube. These weapons intimidated and injured foot soldiers and horses and also set fire to thatched roofs in hostile villages and, occasionally, the rigging of enemy ships.

In their long struggle against the Mongols, the Song learned to enrich saltpeter to increase the amount of nitrate in gunpowder. This produced forceful explosions rather than jets of fire. Launched from catapults, gunpowder-filled canisters could rupture fortifications and inflict mass casualties. Explosives hurled from a distance could sink or burn ships.

The Song also experimented with firing projectiles from metal gun barrels. The earliest gun barrels were broad and squat and were transported on special wagons to their emplacements. The mouths of the barrels projected saltpeter mixed with scattershot minerals. The Chinese and then the Koreans adapted gunpowder to shooting masses of arrows—sometimes flaming—at enemy fortifications.

In 1280 weapons makers of the Yuan Empire produced the first device featuring a projectile that completely filled the mouth of the cannon and thus concentrated the explosive force. The Yuan used cast bronze for the barrel and iron for the cannonball. The new weapon shot farther and more accurately, and was much more destructive, than the earlier Song devices.

Knowledge of the cannon and cannonball moved westward across Eurasia. By the end of the thirteenth century cannon were being produced in the Middle East. By 1327 small, squat cannon called "bombards" were being used in Europe.

Launching Flaming Arrows Song soldiers used gunpowder to launch flaming arrows. (British Library)

The Ming Achievement

In the late 1300s and the 1400s the wealth and consumerism of the early Ming stimulated high achievement in literature, the decorative arts, and painting. The Yuan period interest in plain writing had produced some of the world's earliest novels. This type of literature flourished under the Ming. *Water Margin,* which originated in the raucous drum-song performances loosely related to Chinese opera, features dashing Chinese bandits who struggle against Mongol rule, much as Robin Hood and his merry men resisted Norman rule in England. Many authors had a hand in the final print version.

Luo Guanzhong°, one of the authors of *Water Margin,* is also credited with *Romance of the Three Kingdoms,* based on a much older series of stories that in some ways resemble the Arthurian legends. It describes the attempts of an upright but doomed war leader and his followers to restore the Han Empire of ancient times and resist the power of the cynical but brilliant villain. *Romance of the Three Kingdoms* and *Water Margin* expressed much of the militant but joyous pro-China sentiment of the early Ming era and remain among the most appreciated Chinese fictional works.

Probably the best-known product of Ming technological advance was porcelain. The imperial ceramic works at Jingdezhen° experimented with new production techniques and new ways of organizing and rationalizing workers. "Ming ware," a blue-on-white style developed in the 1400s from Indian, Central Asian, and Middle Eastern motifs, became especially prized around the world. Other Ming goods in high demand included furniture, lacquered screens, and silk, all eagerly transported by Chinese and foreign merchants throughout Southeast Asia and the Pacific, India, the Middle East, and East Africa.

CENTRALIZATION AND MILITARISM IN EAST ASIA, 1200–1500

Korea, Japan, and Annam, the other major states of East Asia, were all affected by confrontation with the Mongols, but with differing results. Japan and Annam escaped Mongol conquest but changed in response to the Mongol threat, becoming more effective and expansive regimes with enhanced commitments to independence.

As for Korea, just as the Ming stressed Chinese traditions and identity in the aftermath of Yuan rule, so Mongol domination contributed to revitalized interest in Korea's own language and history. The Mongols conquered Korea after a difficult war, and though Korea suffered socially and economically under Mongol rule, members of the elite associated closely with the Yuan Empire. After the fall of the Yuan, merchants continued the international connections established in the Mongol period, while Korean armies consolidated a new kingdom and fended off pirates.

Korea from the Mongols to the Yi, 1231–1500

In their effort to establish control over all of China, the Mongols searched for coastal areas from which to launch naval expeditions and choke off the sea trade of their adversaries. Korea offered such possibilities. When the Mongols attacked in 1231, the leader of a prominent Korean family assumed the role of military commander and protector of the king (not unlike the shoguns of Japan). His defensive war, which lasted over twenty years, left a ravaged countryside, exhausted armies, and burned treasures, including the renowned nine-story pagoda at Hwangnyong-sa° and the wooden printing blocks of the Tripitaka°, a ninth-century masterpiece of printing art. The commander's underlings killed him in 1258. Soon afterward the

---

Luo Guanzhong (LAW GWAHB-JOONG)   **Jingdezhen** (JING-deh-JUHN)

Hwangnyong-sa (hwahng-NEEYAHNG-sah)   **Tripitaka** (tri-PIH-tah-kah)

Koryo° king surrendered to the Mongols and became a subject monarch by linking his family to the Great Khan by marriage.

By the mid-1300s the Koryo kings were of mostly Mongol descent and favored Mongol dress, customs, and language. Many lived in Beijing. The kings, their families, and their entourages often traveled between China and Korea, thus exposing Korea to the philosophical and artistic styles of Yuan China: neo-Confucianism, Chan Buddhism (called Soøn in Korea), and celadon (light green) ceramics.

Mongol control was a stimulus after centuries of comparative isolation. Cotton began to be grown in southern Korea; gunpowder came into use; and the art of calendar-making stimulated astronomical observation and mathematics. Celestial clocks built for the royal observatory at Seoul reflected Central Asian and Islamic influences more than Chinese. Avenues of advancement opened for Korean scholars willing to learn Mongolian, landowners willing to open their lands to falconry and grazing, and merchants servicing the new royal exchanges with Beijing. These developments contributed to the rise of a new landed and educated class.

When the Yuan Empire fell in 1368, the Koryo ruling family remained loyal to the Mongols and had to be forced to recognize the new Ming Empire. In 1392 the **Yi**° established a new kingdom with a capital in Seoul and sought to reestablish a local identity. Like Russia and China after the Mongols, the Yi regime publicly rejected the period of Mongol domination. Yet the Yi government continued to employ Mongol-style land surveys, taxation in kind, and military garrison techniques.

Like the Ming emperors, the Yi kings revived the study of the Confucian classics, an activity that required knowledge of Chinese and showed the dedication of the state to learning. This revival may have led to a key technological breakthrough in printing technology.

Koreans had begun using Chinese woodblock printing in the 700s. This technology worked well in China, where a large number of buyers wanted copies of a comparatively small number of texts. But in Korea, the comparatively few literate men had interests in a wide range of texts. Movable wooden or ceramic type appeared in Korea in the early thir-

teenth century and may have been invented there. But the texts were frequently inaccurate and difficult to read. In the 1400s Yi printers, working directly with the king, developed a reliable device to anchor the pieces of type to the printing plate: they replaced the old beeswax adhesive with solid copper frames. This improved the legibility of the printed page, and high-volume, accurate production became possible. Combined with the phonetic han'gul° writing system, this printing technology laid the foundation for a high literacy rate in Korea.

Yi publications told readers how to produce and use fertilizer, transplant rice seedlings, and engineer reservoirs. Building on Eurasian knowledge imported by the Mongols and introduced under the Koryo, Yi scholars developed a meteorological science of their own. They invented or redesigned instruments to measure wind speed and rainfall and perfected a calendar based on minute comparisons of the Chinese and Islamic systems.

In agriculture, farmers expanded the cultivation of cash crops, the reverse of what was happening in Ming China. Cotton, the primary crop, enjoyed such high value that the state accepted it for tax payments. The Yi army used cotton uniforms, and cotton became the favored fabric of the Korean elite. With cotton gins and spinning wheels powered by water, Korea advanced more rapidly than China in mechanization and began to export considerable amounts of cotton to China and Japan.

Although both the Yuan and the Ming withheld the formula for gunpowder from the Korean government, Korean officials acquired the information by subterfuge. By the later 1300s they had mounted cannon on ships that patrolled against pirates and used gunpowder-driven arrow launchers against enemy personnel and the rigging of enemy ships. Combined with skills in armoring ships, these techniques made the small Yi navy a formidable defense force.

Political Transformation in Japan, 1274–1500

Having secured Korea, the Mongols looked toward Japan, a target they could easily reach from Korea and a possible base for controlling China's southern coast. Their first thirty-thousand-man invasion force

---

Koryo (KAW-ree-oh) [36]   **Yi** (YEE)

han'gul (HAHN-goor)

Movable Type   The improvement of cast bronze tiles, each showing a single character, eliminated the need to cast or carve whole pages. Individual tiles—the ones shown are Korean—could be moved from page frame to page frame and gave an even and pleasing appearance. All parts of East Asia eventually adopted this form of printing for cheap, popular books. In the mid-1400s Korea also experimented with a fully phonetic form of writing, which in combination with movable type allowed Koreans unprecedented levels of literacy and access to printed works.   (Courtesy, Yushin Yoo)

in 1274 included Mongol cavalry and archers and sailors from Korea and northeastern Asia. Its weaponry included light catapults and incendiary and explosive projectiles of Chinese manufacture. The Mongol forces landed successfully and decimated the Japanese cavalry, but a great storm on Hakata° Bay on the north side of Kyushu° Island prevented the establishment of a beachhead and forced the Mongols to sail back to Korea.

The invasion deeply impressed Japan's leaders and hastened social and political changes that were already under way. Under the Kamakura° Shogunate established in 1185—another powerful

family actually exercised control—the shogun, or military leader, distributed land and privileges to his followers. In return they paid him tribute and supplied him with soldiers. This stable, but decentralized, system depended on balancing the power of regional warlords. Lords in the north and east of Japan's main island were remote from those in the south and west. Beyond devotion to the emperor and the shogun, little united them until the terrifying Mongol threat materialized.

After the return of his fleet, Khubilai sent envoys to Japan demanding submission. Japanese leaders executed them and prepared for war. The shogun took steps to centralize his military government. The effect was to increase the influence of warlords from the south and west of Honshu

---

Hakata (HAH-kah-tah)   **Kyushu** (KYOO-shoo)
Kamakura (kah-mah-KOO-rah)

Defending Japan   Japanese warriors board Mongol warships with swords to prevent the landing of the invasion force in 1281.   (Imperial Household Agency/International Society for Educational Information, Japan)

(Japan's main island) and from the island of Kyushu, because this was where invasion seemed most likely, and they were the local commanders acting under the shogun's orders.

Military planners studied Mongol tactics and retrained and outfitted Japanese warriors for defense against advanced weaponry. Farm laborers drafted from all over the country constructed defensive fortifications at Hakata and other points along the Honshu and Kyushu coasts. This effort demanded, for the first time, a national system to move resources toward western points rather than toward the imperial or shogunal centers to the east.

The Mongols attacked in 1281. They brought 140,000 warriors, including many non-Mongols, as well as thousands of horses, in hundreds of ships. However, the wall the Japanese had built to cut off Hakata Bay from the mainland deprived the Mongol forces of a reliable landing point. Japanese swordsmen rowed out and boarded the Mongol ships lingering offshore. Their superb steel swords shocked the invaders. After a prolonged standoff, a typhoon struck and sank perhaps half of the Mongol ships. The remainder sailed away, never again to harass Japan. The Japanese gave thanks to the "wind of the Gods"—**_kamikaze_**°—for driving away the Mongols.

Nevertheless, the Mongol threat continued to influence Japanese development. Prior to his death in 1294, Khubilai had in mind a third invasion. His successors did not carry through with it, but the shoguns did not know that the Mongols had given up the idea of conquering Japan. They rebuilt coastal defenses well into the fourteenth century, helping to consolidate the social position of Japan's warrior elite and stimulating the development of a national infrastructure for trade and communication. But the

kamikaze (KUM-i-kuh-zee)

Kamakura Shogunate, based on regionally collected and regionally dispersed revenues, suffered financial strain in trying to pay for centralized road and defense systems.

Between 1333 and 1338 the emperor Go-Daigo broke the centuries-old tradition of imperial seclusion and aloofness from government and tried to reclaim power from the shoguns. This ignited a civil war that destroyed the Kamakura system. In 1338, with the Mongol threat waning, the **Ashikaga° Shogunate** took control at the imperial center of Kyoto.

Provincial warlords enjoyed renewed independence. Around their imposing castles, they sponsored the development of market towns, religious institutions, and schools. The application of technologies imported in earlier periods, including water wheels, improved plows, and Champa rice, increased agricultural productivity. Growing wealth and relative peace stimulated artistic creativity, mostly reflecting Zen Buddhist beliefs held by the warrior elite. In the simple elegance of architecture and gardens, in the contemplative landscapes of artists, and in the eerie, stylized performances of the No theater, the aesthetic code of Zen became established in the Ashikaga era.

Despite the technological advancement, artistic productivity, and rapid urbanization of this period, competition among warlords and their followers led to regional wars. By the later 1400s these conflicts resulted in the near destruction of the warlords. The great Onin War in 1477 left Kyoto devastated and the Ashikaga Shogunate a central government in name only. Ambitious but low-ranking warriors, some with links to trade with the continent, began to scramble for control of the provinces.

After the fall of the Yuan in 1368 Japan resumed overseas trade, exporting raw materials and swords, as well as folding fans, invented in Japan during the period of isolation. Japan's primary imports from China were books and porcelain. The volatile political environment in Japan gave rise to partnerships between warlords and local merchants. All worked to strengthen their own towns and treasuries through overseas commerce or, sometimes, through piracy.

Ashikaga (ah-shee-KAH-gah)

The Emergence of Vietnam, 1200–1500

Before the first Mongol attack in 1257, the states of Annam (northern Vietnam) and Champa (southern Vietnam) had clashed frequently. Annam (once called Dai Viet) looked toward China and had once been subject to the Tang. Chinese political ideas, social philosophies, dress, religion, and language heavily influenced its official culture. Champa related more closely to the trading networks of the Indian Ocean; its official culture was strongly influenced by Indian religion, language, architecture, and dress.

Champa's relationship with China depended in part on how close its enemy Annam was to China at any particular time. During the Song period Annam was neither formally subject to China nor particularly threatening to Champa militarily, so Champa inaugurated a trade and tribute relationship with China that spread fast-ripening Champa rice throughout East Asia.

The Mongols exacted tribute from both Annam and Champa until the fall of the Yuan Empire in 1368. Mongol political and military ambitions were mostly focused elsewhere, however, which minimized their impact on politics and culture. The two Vietnamese kingdoms soon resumed their warfare. When Annam moved its army to reinforce its southern border, Ming troops occupied the capital, Hanoi, and installed a puppet government. Almost thirty years elapsed before Annam regained independence and resumed a tributary status. By then the Ming were turning to meet Mongol challenges to their north. In a series of ruthless campaigns, Annam terminated Champa's independence, and by 1500 the ancestor of the modern state of Vietnam, still called Annam, had been born.

The new state still relied on Confucian bureaucratic government and an examination system, but some practices differed from those in China. The Vietnamese legal code, for example, preserved group landowning and decision making within the villages, as well as women's property rights. Both developments probably had roots in an early rural culture based on the growing of rice in wet paddies; by this time the Annamese considered them distinctive features of their own culture.

CONCLUSION

Despite their brutality and devastation, the Mongol conquests brought a degree of unity to the lands between China and Europe that had never before been known. Nomadic mobility and expertise in military technology contributed to communication across vast spaces and initially, at least, an often-callous disregard for the welfare of farmers, as manifested in oppressive tax policies. By contrast, trade received active Mongol stimulation through the protection of routes and encouragement of industrial production.

The Mongols ruled with an unprecedented openness, employing talented people irrespective of their linguistic, ethnic, or religious affiliations. As a consequence, the period of comparative Mongol unity, which lasted less than a century, saw a remarkable exchange of ideas, techniques, and products across the breadth of Eurasia. Chinese gunpowder spurred the development of Ottoman and European cannon; Muslim astronomers introduced new instruments and mathematical techniques to Chinese observatories.

However, rule over dozens of restive peoples could not endure. Where Mongol military enterprise reached its limit of expansion, it stimulated local aspirations for independence. Division and hostility among branches of Genghis Khan's family—between the Yuan in China and the Jagadai in Central Asia or between the Golden Horde in Russia and the Il-khans in Iran—provided opportunities for achieving these aspirations. The Russians gained freedom from Mongol domination in western Eurasia, and the general political disruption and uncertainty of the Mongol era assisted the emergence of the Lithuanian, Serbian, and Ottoman states.

In the east, China, Korea, and Annam similarly found renewed political identity in the aftermath of Mongol rule, while Japan fought off two Mongol invasions and transformed its internal political and cultural identity in the process. In every case, the reality or threat of Mongol attack and domination encouraged centralization of government, improvement of military techniques, and renewed stress on local cultural identity. Thus, in retrospect, despite its traditional association with death and destruction, the Mongol period appears as a watershed establishing new connections between widespread parts of Eurasia and leading to the development of strong, assertive, and culturally creative regional states.

■ Key Terms

Mongols	tsar
Genghis Khan	Ottoman Empire
nomadism	Khubilai Khan
Yuan Empire	lama
bubonic plague	Beijing
Il-khan	Ming Empire
Golden Horde	Yongle
Timur	Zheng He
Rashid al-Din	Yi
Nasir al-Din Tusi	*kamikaze*
Alexander Nevskii	Ashikaga Shogunate

■ Suggested Reading

David Morgan's *The Mongols* (1986) affords an accessible introduction to the Mongol Empire. Morgan and Reuven Amitai-Preiss have also edited a valuable collection of essays, *The Mongol Empire and Its Legacy* (2000). Thomas T. Allsen has written more specialized studies: *Mongol Imperialism: The Policies of the Grand Qan Möngke in China, Russia, and the Islamic Lands, 1251–1259* (1987); *Commodity and Exchange in the Mongol Empire: A Cultural History of Islamic Textiles* (2002); and *Culture and Conquest in Mongol Eurasia* (2001). Larry Moses and Stephen A. Halkovic, Jr., *Introduction to Mongolian History and Culture* (1985), links early and modern Mongol history and culture. Tim Severin, *In Search of Chinggis Khan* (1992), revisits the paths of Genghis's conquests.

William H. McNeill's *Plagues and Peoples* (1976) outlines the demographic effects of the Mongol conquests, and Joel Mokyr discusses their technological impact in *The Lever of Riches: Technological Creativity and Economic Progress* (1990). Connections between commercial development in Europe and Eurasian trade routes of the Mongol era within a broad theoretical framework inform Janet L. Abu-Lughod's *Before European Hegemony: The World System A.D. 1250–1350* (1989).

The only "primary" document relating to Genghis Khan, *Secret History of the Mongols*, has been reconstructed in Mongolian from Chinese script and has been variously produced in scholarly editions by Igor de Rachewilz and Francis Woodman Cleaves, among others. Paul Kahn produced a readable prose English paraphrase of the work in 1984. Biographies of Genghis Khan include Leo de Hartog, *Genghis Khan, Conqueror of the World* (1989); Michel Hoang, *Genghis Khan*, trans. Ingrid Canfield (1991); and Paul Ratchnevsky, *Genghis Khan: His Life and Legacy*, trans. and ed. Thomas Nivison Haining (1992), which is most detailed on Genghis's childhood and youth.

On Central Asia after the conquests, see S. A. M. Adshead, *Central Asia in World History* (1993). The most recent scholarly study of Timur is Beatrice Manz, *The Rise and Rule of Tamerlane* (1989).

David Christian, *A History of Russia, Central Asia, and Mongolia* (1998), and Charles Halperin, *Russia and the Golden Horde: The Mongol Impact on Medieval Russian History* (1987), provide one-volume accounts of the Mongols in Russia. A more detailed study is John Lister Illingworth Fennell, *The Crisis of Medieval Russia, 1200–1304* (1983). See also Donald Ostrowski, *Muscovy and the Mongols: Cross-Cultural Influences on the Steppe Frontier* (1998). Religion forms the topic of Devin DeWeese, *Islamization and Native Religion in the Golden Horde* (1994). *The Cambridge History of Iran*, vol. 5, *The Saljuq and Mongol Periods*, ed. J. A. Boyle (1968), and vol. 6, *The Timurid and Safavid Periods*, ed. Peter Jackson and Laurence Lockhart (reprint, 2001), contain detailed scholarly articles covering the period in Iran and Central Asia.

Translations from the great historians of the Il-khan period include Juvaini, 'Ala al-Din 'Ata Malek, *The History of the World-Conqueror*, trans. John Andrew Boyle (1958), and Rashid al-Din, *The Successors of Genghis Khan*, trans. John Andrew Boyle (1971). The greatest traveler of the time was Ibn Battuta; see C. Defremery and B. R. Sanguinetti, eds., *The Travels of Ibn Battuta*, A.D. *1325–1354*, translated with revisions and notes from the Arabic text by H. A. R. Gibb (1994), and Ross E. Dunn, *The Adventures of Ibn Battuta, a Muslim Traveler of the 14th Century* (1986).

On Europe's Mongol encounter, see James Chambers, *The Devil's Horsemen: The Mongol Invasion of Europe* (1979). Christopher Dawson, ed., *Mission to Asia* (1955; reprinted 1981), assembles some of the best-known European travel accounts. See also Marco Polo, *The Travels of Marco Polo* (many editions), and the controversial skeptical appraisal of his account in Frances Wood, *Did Marco Polo Really Go to China?* (1995). Morris Rossabi's *Visitor from Xanadu* (1992) deals with the European travels of Rabban Sauma, a Christian Turk.

For China under the Mongols, see Morris Rossabi's *Khubilai Khan: His Life and Times* (1988). On the Mongol im-pact on economy and technology in Yuan and Ming China, see Mark Elvin, *The Pattern of the Chinese Past* (1973); and Joseph Needham, *Science in Traditional China* (1981). Also see the important interpretation of Ming economic achievement in Andre Gunder Frank, *Re-ORIENT: Global Economy in the Asian Age* (1998).

The Cambridge History of China, vol. 8, *The Ming Dynasty 1368–1644*, part 2, ed. Denis Twitchett and Frederick W. Mote (1998), provides scholarly essays about a little studied period. See also Albert Chan, *The Glory and Fall of the Ming Dynasty* (1982), and Edward L. Farmer, *Early Ming Government: The Evolution of Dual Capitals* (1976).

On early Ming literature, see Lo Kuan-chung, *Three Kingdoms: A Historical Novel Attributed to Luo Guanzhong*, translated and annotated by Moss Roberts (1991); Pearl Buck's translation of *Water Margin*, entitled *All Men Are Brothers*, 2 vols. (1933), and a later translation by J. H. Jackson, *Water Margin, Written by Shih Nai-an* (1937); and Shelley HsŸeh-lun Chang, *History and Legend: Ideas and Images in the Ming Historical Novels* (1990).

Joseph R. Levenson, ed., *European Expansion and the Counter-Example of Asia, 1300–1600* (1967), recounts the Zheng He expeditions. Philip Snow's *The Star Raft* (1988) contains more recent scholarship, and Louise Levathes, *When China Ruled the Seas* (1993), makes for lively reading.

For a general history of Korea in this period, see Andrew C. Nahm, *Introduction to Korean History and Culture* (1993); Ki-Baik Lee, *A New History of Korea* (1984); and William E. Henthorn, *Korea: The Mongol Invasions* (1963). On a more specialized topic, see Joseph Needham et al., *The Hall of Heavenly Records: Korean Astronomical Instruments and Clocks, 1380–1780* (1986).

For a collection of up-to-date scholarly essays on Japan, see Kozo Yamamura, ed., *The Cambridge History of Japan*, vol. 3, *Medieval Japan* (1990). See also John W. Hall and Toyoda Takeshi, eds., *Japan in the Muromachi Age* (1977); H. Paul Varley, trans., *The Onin War: History of Its Origins and Background with a Selective Translation of the Chronicle of Onin* (1967); Yamada Nakaba, *Ghenko, the Mongol Invasion of Japan*, with an Introduction by Lord Armstrong (1916); and the novel *Fûtô* by Inoue Yasushi, translated by James T. Araki as *Wind and Waves* (1989).

◼ Notes

1. Quotation adapted from Desmond Martin, *Chingis Khan and His Conquest of North China* (Baltimore: The John Hopkins Press, 1950), 303.

12 Tropical Africa and Asia, 1200–1500

CHAPTER OUTLINE

Tropical Lands and Peoples

New Islamic Empires

Indian Ocean Trade

Social and Cultural Change

ENVIRONMENT AND TECHNOLOGY: The Indian Ocean Dhow

Sultan Abu Bakr° customarily offered hospitality to distinguished visitors to his city of Mogadishu, an Indian Ocean port on the northeast coast of Africa. In 1331, he provided food and lodging for Muhammad ibn Abdullah **Ibn Battuta°** (1304–1369), a young Muslim scholar from Morocco who had set out to explore the Islamic world. With a pilgrimage to Mecca and travel throughout the Middle East behind him, Ibn Battuta was touring the trading cities of the Red Sea and East Africa. Subsequent travels took him to Central Asia and India, China and Southeast Asia, Muslim Spain, and sub-Saharan West Africa. Recounting some 75,000 miles (120,000 kilometers) of travel over twenty-nine years, Ibn Battuta's journal provides invaluable information on these lands.

Hospitality being considered a noble virtue among Muslims, regardless of physical and cultural differences, the reception at Mogadishu mirrored that at other cities. Ibn Battuta noted that Sultan Abu Bakr had skin darker than his own and spoke a different native language (Somali), but as brothers in faith, they prayed together at Friday services, where the sultan greeted his foreign guest in Arabic, the common language of the Islamic world: "You are heartily welcome, and you have honored our land and given us pleasure." When Sultan Abu Bakr and his jurists heard and decided cases after the mosque service, they used the religious law familiar in all Muslim lands.

Islam aside, the most basic links among the diverse peoples of Africa and southern Asia

---

Abu Bakr (a-BOO BAK-uhr)   Ibn Battuta (IB-uhn ba-TOO-tuh)

derived from the tropical environment itself. A network of overland and maritime routes joined their lands (see Chapter 6), providing avenues for the spread of beliefs and technologies, as well as goods. Ibn Battuta sailed with merchants down the coast of East Africa and joined trading caravans across the Sahara to West Africa. His path to India followed overland trade routes, and a merchant ship carried him on to China.

As you read this chapter, ask yourself the following questions:

- How did environmental differences shape cultural differences in tropical Africa and Asia?

- How did cultural and ecological differences promote trade in specialized goods from one place to another?

- How did trade and other contacts promote state growth and the spread of Islam?

TROPICAL LANDS AND PEOPLES

To obtain food, the people who inhabited the tropical regions of Africa and Asia used methods that generations of experimentation had proved successful, whether at the desert's edge, in grasslands, or in tropical rain forests. Much of their success lay in learning how to blend human activities with the natural order, but their ability to modify the environment to suit their needs appeared in irrigation works and mining.

The Tropical Environment   Because of the angle of earth's axis, the sun's rays warm the **tropics** year-round. The equator marks the center of the tropical zone, and the Tropic of Cancer and Tropic of Capricorn mark its outer limits. Africa lies almost entirely within the tropics, as do southern Arabia, most of India, and all of the Southeast Asian mainland and islands.

Lacking the hot and cold seasons of temperate lands, the rainy and dry seasons of the Afro-Asian tropics derive from wind patterns across the surrounding oceans. Winds from a permanent high-pressure air mass over the South Atlantic deliver heavy rainfall to the western coast of Africa during much of the year. However, in December and January, large high-pressure zones over northern Africa and Arabia produce a southward movement of dry air that limits the inland penetration of the moist ocean winds.

In the lands around the Indian Ocean, the rainy and dry seasons reflect the influence of alternating winds known as **monsoons.** A gigantic high-pressure zone over the Himalaya° Mountains that peaks from December to March produces southern Asia's dry season through a strong southward air movement (the northeast monsoon) in the western Indian Ocean. Between April and August, a low-pressure zone over India creates a northward movement of air from across the ocean (the southwest monsoon) that brings southern Asia the heavy rains of its wet season.

Areas with the heaviest rainfall—the broad belt along the equator in coastal West Africa and west-central Africa, parts of coastal India, and Southeast Asia—have dense rain forests. Lighter rains produce other forest patterns. The English word *jungle* comes from an Indian word for the tangled undergrowth in the forests that once covered most of India.

Some other parts of the tropics rarely see rain at all. The world's largest desert, the Sahara, stretches across northern Africa and continues eastward across Arabia, southern Iran and Pakistan, and northwest India. Another desert occupies southwestern Africa. Most of tropical India and Africa falls between the deserts and rain forests and experiences moderate rainy seasons. These lands range from fairly wet woodlands to the much drier grasslands characteristic of much of East Africa.

Altitude produces other climatic variations. Thin atmospheres at high altitudes hold less heat than atmospheres at lower elevations. Snow covers some of the volcanic mountains of eastern Africa all or part of the year. The snowcapped Himalayas

---

Himalaya (him-uh-LAY-uh)

that form India's northern frontier rise so high that they block cold air from moving south and thus give northern India a more tropical climate than its latitude would suggest. The plateaus of inland Africa and the Deccan° Plateau of central India also enjoy cooler temperatures than the coastal plains.

Human Ecosystems

Thinkers in temperate lands once imagined surviving in the tropics to be simply a matter of picking wild fruit off trees. A careful observer touring the tropics in 1200 would have noticed, however, many differences in societies deriving from their particular ecosystems—that is, from how human groups used the plants, animals, and other resources of their physical environments.

Domesticated plants and animals had become commonplace long before 1200, but people in some environments continued to rely primarily on hunting, fishing, and gathering. For Pygmy° hunters in the dense forests of Central Africa, small size permitted pursuit of prey through dense undergrowth. Hunting also prevailed in the upper altitudes of the Himalayas and in some desert environments. A Portuguese expedition led by Vasco da Gama visited the arid coast of southwestern Africa in 1497 and saw there a healthy group of people feeding themselves on "the flesh of seals, whales, and gazelles, and the roots of wild plants." Fishing, which was common along all the major lakes and rivers as well as in the oceans, might be combined with farming. The ocean fishermen of East Africa, Southeast Asia, and coastal India had boating skills that often led to engagement in ocean trade.

Herding provided sustenance in areas too arid for agriculture. Pastoralists consumed milk from their herds and traded hides and meat to farmers in return for grain and vegetables. The world's largest concentration of pastoralists inhabited the arid and semiarid lands of northeastern Africa and Arabia. Like Ibn Battuta's host at Mogadishu, some Somalis lived in towns, but most grazed goats and camels in the desert hinterland of the Horn of Africa. The western Sahara sustained herds of sheep and camels belonging to the Tuareg°, whose

intimate knowledge of the desert made them invaluable as guides to caravans, such as the one Ibn Battuta joined on the two-month journey across the desert. Along the Sahara's southern edge the cattle-herding Fulani° people gradually extended their range during this period. By 1500, they had spread throughout the western and central Sudan. A few weeks after encountering the hunter-gatherers of southwest Africa, Vasco da Gama's expedition bartered for meat with a pastoral people possessing fat cattle and sheep.

The density of agricultural populations reflected the adequacy of rainfall and soils. South and Southeast Asia were generally wetter than tropical Africa, making intensive cultivation possible. High yields supported dense populations. In 1200, over 100 million people lived in South and Southeast Asia, more than four-fifths of them on the fertile Indian mainland. Though a little less than the population of China, this was triple the number of people living in all of Africa and nearly double the number in Europe.

India's lush vegetation led one Middle Eastern writer to call it "the most agreeable abode on earth. Its delightful plains resemble the garden of Paradise."[1] Rice cultivation dominated in the fertile Ganges plain of northeast India, mainland Southeast Asia, and southern China. In drier areas, farmers grew grains—wheat, sorghum, and millet, and legumes such as peas and beans whose ripening cycles matched the pattern of the rainy and dry seasons. Tubers and tree crops characterized farming in rain-forest clearings.

The spread of farming, including the movement to Africa of Asian crops like yams, cocoyams, and bananas, did not necessarily change the natural environment. In most of sub-Saharan Africa and much of Southeast Asia, extensive rather than intensive cultivation prevailed. Instead of enriching fields with manure and vegetable compost so they could be cultivated year after year, farmers abandoned fields when the natural fertility of the soil fell and cleared new fields. Ashes from the brush, grasses, and tree limbs they cut down and burned boosted the new fields' fertility. Shifting to new land every few years made efficient use of labor in areas with comparatively poor soils.

Deccan (de-KAN)   **Pygmy** (PIG-mee)   **Tuareg** (TWAH-reg)   **Fulani** (foo-LAH-nee)

C H R O N O L O G Y

	Tropical Africa	Tropical Asia
1200		1206 Delhi Sultanate founded in India
	1230s Mali Empire founded	
	1270 Solomonic dynasty in Ethiopia founded	
		1298 Delhi Sultanate annexes Gujarat
1300		
	1324–1325 Mansa Musa's pilgrimage to Mecca	
		1398 Timur sacks Delhi; Delhi Sultanate declines
1400	1400s Great Zimbabwe at its peak	
	1433 Tuareg retake Timbuktu; Mali declines	
1500		1500 Port of Malacca at its peak

Water Systems and Irrigation

Though the inland delta of the Niger River received naturally fertilizing annual floods and could grow rice for sale to the trading cities along the Niger bend, many tropical farmers had to move the water to their crops. Conserving some of the monsoon rainfall for use during the dry season helped in Vietnam, Java, Malaya, and Burma, which had terraced hillsides with special water-control systems for growing rice. North and south India also had water-storage dams and irrigation canals. In this time period, villagers in southeast India built stone and earthen dams across rivers to store water for gradual release through elaborate irrigation canals. Extended over many generations, these canals irrigated a wide area.

As had been true since the days of the first river-valley civilizations (see Chapter 1), governments built and controlled the largest irrigation systems. The **Delhi° Sultanate** (1206–1526) in northern India acquired extensive new water-control systems. Ibn Battuta admired a large reservoir constructed in

the first quarter of the thirteenth century that supplied the city of Delhi with water. Farmers planted sugar cane, cucumbers, and melons along the reservoir's rim as the water level fell during the dry season. In the fourteenth century, the Delhi sultan built in the Ganges plain a network of irrigation canals that remained unsurpassed until the nineteenth century. Such systems made it possible to grow crops throughout the year.

Since the tenth century, the Indian Ocean island of Ceylon (modern Sri Lanka°) had been home to the world's greatest concentration of irrigation reservoirs and canals. These facilities supported the large population of the Sinhalese° kingdom in arid northern Ceylon. In Southeast Asia, another impressive system of reservoirs and canals served Cambodia's capital city, Angkor°.

Between 1250 and 1400, however, the irrigation complex in Ceylon fell into ruin when invaders from south India disrupted the Sinhalese government. As a result, malaria spread by mosquitoes breeding in the irrigation canals ravaged the population. In the

Delhi (DEL-ee)

Sri Lanka (sree LAHNG-kuh)   Sinhalese (sin-huh-LEEZ)
Angkor (ANG-kor)

fifteenth century, the great Cambodian system fell into ruin when the government that maintained it collapsed. Neither system was ever rebuilt.

The vulnerability of complex irrigation systems built by powerful governments contrasts with village-based irrigation systems. Invasion and natural calamity might damage the latter, but they usually bounced back because they depended on local initiative and simpler technologies.

| Mineral Resources | The most productive metal trade in the tropics, ironworking, provided the |

hoes, axes, and knives farmers used to clear and cultivate their fields. Between 1200 and 1500, the rain forests of coastal West Africa and Southeast Asia opened up for farming. Iron also supplied spear and arrow points, needles, and nails. Indian metalsmiths became known for forging strong and beautiful swords. In Africa, many people attributed magical powers to iron smelters and blacksmiths.

Copper and its alloys had special importance in the Copperbelt of southeastern Africa during the fourteenth and fifteenth centuries. Smelters cast the metal into large X-shaped ingots (metal castings). Local coppersmiths worked these into wire and decorative objects. In the western Sudan, Ibn Battuta described a mining town that produced two sizes of copper bars that served as currency in place of coins. Some coppersmiths in West Africa cast copper and brass (an alloy of copper and zinc) statues and heads that now rank as masterpieces of world art. They utilized the "lost-wax" method, in which molten metal melts a thin layer of wax sandwiched between clay forms, replacing the "lost" wax with hard metal.

African gold moved in quantity across the Sahara and into the Indian Ocean and Red Sea trades. Some came from streambeds along the upper Niger River and farther south in modern Ghana°. In the hills south of the Zambezi° River (in modern Zimbabwe°), archaeologists have discovered thousands of mineshafts, dating from 1200, that were sunk up to 100 feet (30 meters) into the ground to get at gold ores. Although panning for gold remained important in the streams descending from the mountains of northern India, the gold and silver mines in India seem to have been exhausted by this period. Thus, Indians imported from Southeast Asia and Africa considerable quantities of gold for jewelry and temple decoration.

The labors and skills of ordinary people—farmers, fishermen, herders, metalworkers, and others—made possible the rise of powerful states and commercial systems. Caravans could not have crossed the Sahara without desert dwellers serving as guides. The seafaring skills of coastal fishermen underlay the trade of the Indian Ocean. Farmers produced the taxes that supported the city-based empires of Delhi and Mali.

NEW ISLAMIC EMPIRES

The empires of Mali in West Africa and Delhi in northern India, the largest and richest tropical states of the period between 1200 and 1500, both utilized administrative and military systems introduced from the Islamic heartland. Yet **Mali,** an indigenous African dynasty that had earlier adopted Islam through the peaceful influence of Muslim merchants and scholars, differed in many ways from the Delhi Sultanate founded and ruled by invading Turkish and Afghan Muslims. The wealth of Mali depended on trans-Saharan trade, but long-distance trade played only a minor role in Delhi.

| Mali in the Western Sudan | Muslim rule beginning in the seventh century (see Chapter 7) greatly stimu- |

lated increased trade along the routes that crossed the Sahara. In the centuries that followed, the faith of Muhammad gradually spread to the lands south of the desert, which the Arabs called the *bilad al-sudan*°, "land of the blacks."

Muslim Berbers invading out of the desert in 1076 caused the collapse of Ghana, the empire that preceded Mali in the western Sudan (see Chapter 7), but their conquest did little to spread Islam. To the east, the Muslim attacks that destroyed the

---

Ghana (GAH-nuh) **Zambezi** (zam-BEE-zee) **Zimbabwe** (zim-BAHB-way)

bilad al-sudan (bih-LAD uhs-soo-DAN)

Christian Nubian kingdoms on the upper Nile in the late thirteenth century opened that area to Muslim influences, but Christian Ethiopia successfully withstood Muslim advances. Instead, Islam's spread south of the Sahara usually followed a pattern of gradual and peaceful conversion. The expansion of commercial contacts in the western Sudan and on the East African coast greatly promoted the conversion process. Most Africans found meaning and benefit in the teachings of Islam and found it suited their interests. Takrur° in the far western Sudan became the first sub-Saharan African state to adopt the new faith around 1030.

Shortly after 1200, Takrur expanded under King Sumanguru° only to suffer a major defeat some thirty years later at the hands of Sundiata°, the upstart leader of the Malinke° people. Though both leaders professed Islam, Malinke legends recall their battles as clashes between powerful magicians, suggesting how much old and new beliefs mingled. Sumanguru could reportedly appear and disappear at will, assume dozens of shapes, and catch arrows in midflight. Sundiata defeated Sumanguru's much larger forces through superior military maneuvers and by successfully wounding his adversary with a special arrow that robbed him of his magical powers. This victory was followed by others that created Sundiata's Mali Empire (see Map 12.1).

Mali, the empire that grew from Sundiata's victories, depended on a well-developed agricultural base and control of the regional and trans-Saharan trade routes, as had Ghana before it. Mali, however, controlled a greater area than Ghana, including not only the core trading area of the upper Niger but the gold fields of the Niger headwaters to the southwest as well. Moreover, its rulers fostered the spread of Islam among the empire's political and trading elites. Control of the gold and copper trades and contacts with North African Muslim traders gave Mali unprecedented prosperity.

Under the ruler **Mansa Kankan Musa°** (r. 1312–1337), the empire's reputation for wealth spread far and wide. Mansa Musa's pilgrimage to Mecca in 1324–1325 fulfilled his personal duty as a Muslim and at the same time put on display his exceptional

wealth. He traveled with a large entourage. Besides his senior wife and five hundred of her ladies in waiting and their slaves, one account says there were also sixty thousand porters and a vast caravan of camels carrying supplies and provisions. For purchases and gifts, he brought along eighty packages of gold, each weighing 122 ounces (3.8 kilograms). In addition, five hundred slaves each carried a golden staff. Mansa Musa dispersed so many gifts when he passed through Cairo that the value of gold was depressed for years.

On his return from this pilgrimage, Mansa Musa built new mosques and opened Quran schools in the cities along the Niger bend. Ibn Battuta, who visited Mali from 1352 to 1354 during the reign of Mansa Musa's successor, Mansa Suleiman° (r. 1341–1360), lauded the Malians for their faithful recitation of prayers and their zeal in teaching children the Quran. He also reported that "complete and general safety" prevailed in the vast territories ruled by Suleiman and that foreign travelers had no reason to fear being robbed or having their goods confiscated if they died.

Two centuries after its founding, Mali began to disintegrate. Mansa Suleiman's successors could not prevent rebellions breaking out among the diverse peoples subjected to Malinke rule. Other groups attacked from without. The desert Tuareg retook their city of Timbuktu° in 1433. By 1500, the rulers of Mali had dominion over little more than the Malinke heartland.

The cities of the upper Niger survived Mali's collapse, but some trade and intellectual life moved east to the central Sudan. Shortly after 1450, the rulers of several Hausa city-states officially adopted Islam. These states took on importance as manufacturing and trading centers, becoming famous for cotton textiles and leatherworking. The central Sudanic state of Kanem-Bornu° also expanded in the late fifteenth century from the ancient kingdom of Kanem, whose rulers had accepted Islam in about 1085. At its peak around 1250, Kanem had absorbed the state of Bornu south and west of Lake Chad and gained control of routes crossing the central Sahara. As Kanem-Bornu's armies conquered new territories, they also spread the rule of Islam.

Takrur (TAHK-roor)   Sumanguru (soo-muhn-GOO-roo)
Sundiata (soon-JAH-tuh)   Malinke (muh-LING-kay)
Mansa Kankan Musa (MAHN-suh KAHN-kahn MOO-suh)

Mansa Suleiman (MAHN-suh SOO-lay-mahn)   Timbuktu
(tim-buk-TOO)   Kanem-Bornu (KAH-nuhm-BOR-noo)

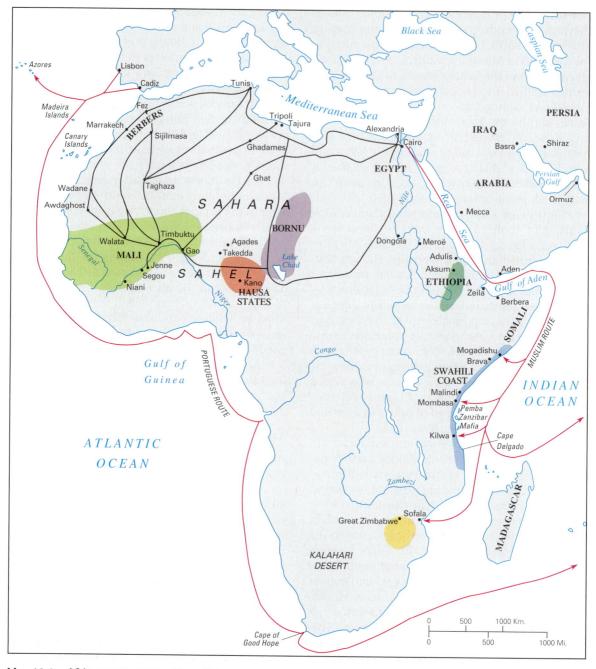

Map 12.1   Africa, 1200–1500   Many African states had beneficial links to the trade that crossed the Sahara and the Indian Ocean. Before 1500, sub-Saharan Africa's external ties were primarily with the Islamic world.

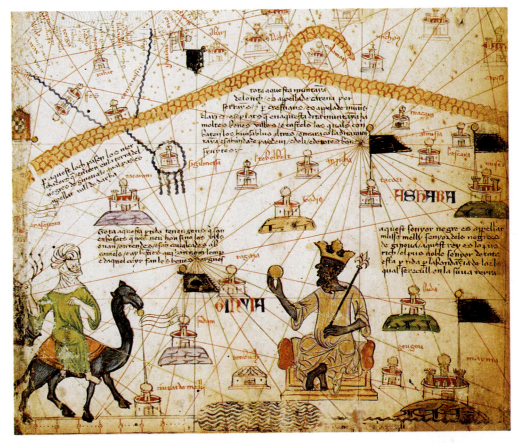

Map of the Western Sudan (1375)   A Jewish geographer on the Mediterranean island of Majorca drew this lavish map in 1375, incorporating all that was known in Europe about the rest of the world. This portion of the Catalan Atlas shows a North African trader approaching the king of Mali, who holds a gold nugget in one hand and a golden scepter in the other. A caption identifies the black ruler as Mansa Musa, "the richest and noblest king in all the land."   (Bibliothèque Nationale de France)

The Delhi Sultanate in India

Having long ago lost the defensive unity of the Gupta Empire (see Chapter 4), the divided states of northwest India fell prey to raids by Afghan warlords beginning in the early eleventh century. In the last decades of the twelfth century, a Turkish dynasty armed with powerful crossbows captured the northern Indian cities of Lahore and Delhi. One partisan Muslim chronicler wrote: "The city [Delhi] and its vicinity was freed from idols and idol-worship, and in the sanctuaries of the images of the [Hindu] Gods, mosques were raised by the worshippers of one God."[2] Turkish adventurers from Central Asia flocked to join the invading armies, overwhelming the small Indian states, which were often at war with one another.

Between 1206 and 1236, the Muslim invaders extended their rule over the Hindu princes and chiefs in much of northern India. Sultan Iltutmish° (r. 1211–1236) consolidated the conquest in a series of military expeditions that made his realm the largest in India (see Map 12.2). He also secured official recognition of the Delhi Sultanate as a Muslim state by the caliph of Baghdad. Although

Iltutmish (il-TOOT-mish)

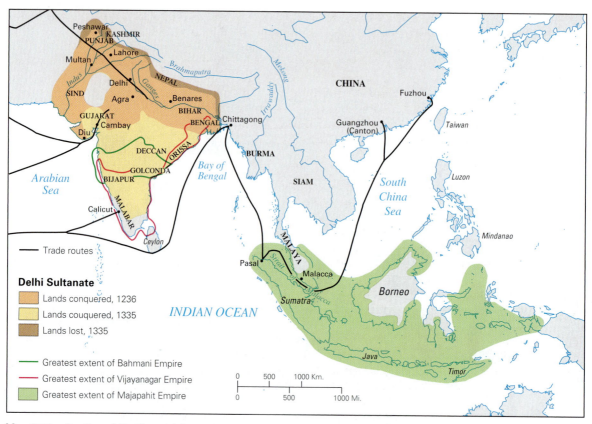

Map 12.2 South and Southeast Asia, 1200–1500 The rise of new empires and the expansion of maritime trade reshaped the lives of many tropical Asians.

pillaging continued, especially on the frontiers, the incorporation of north India into the Islamic world marked the beginning of the invaders' transformation from brutal conquerors to somewhat more benign rulers. Muslim commanders extended protection to the conquered, freeing them from persecution in return for payment of a special tax. Yet Hindus never forgot the intolerance and destruction of their first contacts with the invaders.

Iltutmish astonished his ministers by passing over his weak and pleasure-seeking sons and designating as his heir his beloved and talented daughter Raziya°. When they questioned the unprecedented idea of a woman ruling a Muslim state, he said, "My sons are devoted to the pleasures of youth: no one of them is qualified to be king. . . . There is no one

more competent to guide the State than my daughter." Her brother—who delighted in riding his elephant through the bazaar, showering the crowds with coins—ruled ineptly for seven months before the ministers relented and put Raziya on the throne.

A chronicler who knew her explained why this able ruler lasted less than four years (r. 1236–1240):

Sultan Raziya was a great monarch. She was wise, just, and generous, a benefactor to her kingdom, a dispenser of justice, the protector of her subjects, and the leader of her armies. She was endowed with all the qualities befitting a king, but that she was not born of the right sex, and so in the estimation of men all these virtues were worthless. May God have mercy upon her![3]

Raziya (rah-ZEE-uh)

Doing her best to prove herself a proper king, Raziya dressed like a man and led her troops atop an elephant. In the end, however, the Turkish chiefs imprisoned her; she escaped, but she was killed by a robber soon after.

After a half-century of stagnation and rebellion, the ruthless but efficient policies of Sultan Ala-ud-din Khalji° (r. 1296–1316) increased his control over the empire's outlying provinces. Successful frontier raids and high taxes kept his treasury full, wage and price controls in Delhi kept down the cost of maintaining a large army, and a network of spies stifled intrigue. When a Mongol threat from Central Asia eased, Ala-ud-din's forces extended the sultanate's southern flank, seizing the rich trading state of **Gujarat**° in 1298, and then drove southward, briefly seizing the southern tip of the Indian peninsula.

When Ibn Battuta visited Delhi, Sultan Muhammad ibn Tughluq° (r. 1325–1351) received him in his celebrated Hall of a Thousand Pillars. The world traveler praised the sultan's piety and generosity, but he also recounted his cruelties. The sultan enlarged the sultanate to its greatest extent at the expense of the independent Indian states but balanced his aggressive policy with religious toleration. He even attended Hindu religious festivals. However, his successor, Firuz Shah° (r. 1351–1388), alienated powerful Hindus by taxing the Brahmins, preferring to cultivate good relations with the Muslim elite. Muslim chroniclers praised him for constructing forty mosques, thirty colleges, and a hundred hospitals.

A small minority in a giant land, the Turkish rulers relied on terror to keep their subjects submissive, on harsh military reprisals to put down rebellion, and on pillage and high taxes to sustain the ruling elite in luxury and power. Though little different from most other large states of this time (including Mali) in being more a burden than a benefit to most of its subjects, the sultanate never lost the disadvantage of foreign origins and alien religious identity. Nevertheless, over time, the sultans did incorporate some Hindus into their administrations, and some members of the ruling elite also married women from prominent Hindu families, though the brides had to become Muslim.

Personal and religious rivalries within the Muslim elite, along with Hindu discontent, threatened the Delhi Sultanate whenever it showed weakness and finally hastened its end. In the mid-fourteenth century, Muslim nobles challenged the suttan's dominion and established the independent Bahmani° kingdom (1347–1482) on the Deccan Plateau. Defending against the southward push of Bahmani armies, the Hindu states of south India united to form the Vijayanagar° Empire (1336–1565), which at its height controlled the rich trading ports on both coasts of south India and held Ceylon as a tributary state.

The elites of Vijayanagar and the Bahmani state turned a blind eye to religious differences when doing so favored their interests. Bahmani rulers sought to balance Muslim domination with the practical policies of incorporating the Hindu leaders into the government, marrying Hindu wives, and appointing Brahmins to high offices. Vijayanagar rulers hired Muslim horsemen and archers to strengthen their military forces and formed an alliance with the Muslim-ruled state of Gujarat.

By 1351, when all of south India had cast off Delhi's rule, much of north India rose in rebellion. In the east, Bengal broke away from the sultanate in 1338, becoming a center of the mystical Sufi tradition of Islam (see Chapter 7). In the west, Gujarat regained its independence by 1390. The weakening of Delhi's central authority tempted fresh Mongol interest in the area. In 1398, the Turko-Mongol leader Timur (see Chapter 11) captured the city of Delhi. When his armies withdrew the next year with vast quantities of loot and tens of thousands of captives, the largest city in southern Asia lay empty and in ruins. The Delhi Sultanate never recovered.

For all its shortcomings, the Delhi Sultanate triggered the development of centralized political authority in India. Prime ministers and provincial governors serving under the sultans established a bureaucracy, improved food production, promoted trade, and put in circulation a common currency. Despite the many conflicts that Muslim

---

Ala-ud-din Khalji (uh-LAH-uh-DEEN KAL-jee)   **Gujarat** (goo-juh-RAHT)   **Tughluq** (toog-LOOK)   **Firuz Shah** (fuh-ROOZ shah)

Bahmani (bah MAHN-ee)   **Vijayanagar** (vee-juh-yah-NAH-gar)

Meenakshi Temple, Madurai, India Some 15,000 pilgrims a day visit the large Hindu temple of Meenakshi (the fish-eyed goddess) in the ancient holy city of Madurai in India's southeastern province of Tamil Nadu. The temple complex dates from at least 1000 C.E., although the elaborately painted statues of these gopuram (gate towers) have been rebuilt and restored many times. The largest gopura rises 150 feet (46 meters) above the ground.   (Jean Louis Nou/ akg-images)

conquest and rule provoked, Islam gradually acquired a permanent place in South Asia.

INDIAN OCEAN TRADE

The maritime network that stretched across the Indian Ocean from the Islamic heartlands of Iran and Arabia to Southeast Asia connected with routes reaching into Europe, Africa, and China. The Indian Ocean routes also facilitated the spread of Islam.

Monsoon Mariners

Between 1200 and 1500, the volume of trade in the Indian Ocean increased, stimulated by and contributing to the prosperity of Islamic and Mongol empires in Asia,

cities in Europe, and new kingdoms in Africa and Southeast Asia. The demand for luxuries—precious metals and jewels, rare spices, fine textiles, and other manufactures—rose. Larger ships made shipments of bulk cargoes of ordinary cotton textiles, pepper, food grains (rice, wheat, barley), timber, horses, and other goods profitable. When the collapse of the Mongol Empire in the fourteenth century disrupted overland routes across Central Asia, the Indian Ocean assumed greater strategic importance in tying together the peoples of Eurasia and Africa.

Some goods were transported from one end of this trading network to the other, but few ships or crews made a complete circuit. Instead, the Indian Ocean trade divided into two legs: from the Middle East across the Arabian Sea to India and from India across the Bay of Bengal to Southeast Asia (see Map 12.2).

Shipyards in ports on the Malabar Coast (southwestern India) built large numbers of **dhows°,** the characteristic cargo and passenger ships of the Arabian Sea. They grew from an average capacity of 100 tons in 1200 to 400 tons in 1500. On a typical expedition, a dhow might sail west from India to Arabia and Africa on the northeast monsoon winds (December to March) and return on the southwest monsoons (April to August). Small dhows kept the coast in sight. Relying on the stars to guide them, skilled pilots steered large vessels by the quicker route straight across the water. A large dhow could sail from the Red Sea to mainland Southeast Asia in two to four months, but few did so. Eastbound cargoes and passengers from dhows reaching India were likely to be transferred to junks, which dominated the eastern half of the Indian Ocean and the South China Sea (see Environment and Technology: The Indian Ocean Dhow).

The largest, most technologically advanced, and most seaworthy vessels of this time, junks first appeared in China and spread with Chinese influence. Enormous nails held together hulls of heavy spruce or fir planks, in contrast with dhows, whose planks were sewn together with palm fiber. Below the deck, watertight compartments minimized flooding in case of damage to the ship's hull. According to Ibn Battuta, the largest junks had twelve sails made of bamboo and carried a crew of a thousand men, including four hundred soldiers. A large junk might accommodate a hundred passenger cabins and a cargo of over 1,000 tons. Junks dominated China's foreign shipping to Southeast Asia and India, but the Chinese did not control all of the junks that plied these waters. During the fifteenth century, similar vessels came out of shipyards in Bengal and Southeast Asia to be sailed by local crews.

Decentralized and cooperative commercial interests, rather than political authorities, connected the several regions that participated in the Indian Ocean trade. The **Swahili° Coast** supplied gold from inland areas of eastern Africa. Ports around the Arabian peninsula supplied horses and goods from the northern parts of the Middle East, the Mediterranean, and eastern Europe. Merchants in the cities of coastal India received goods from east and west, sold some locally, passed others along, and added Indian goods to the trade. The Strait of Malacca°, between the eastern end of the Indian Ocean and the South China Sea, provided a meeting point for trade from Southeast Asia, China, and the Indian Ocean. In each region, certain ports functioned as giant emporia, consolidating goods from smaller ports and inland areas for transport across the seas.

Africa: The Swahili Coast and Zimbabwe

Trade expanded steadily along the East African coast from about 1250, giving rise to between thirty and forty separate city-states by 1500. After 1200, masonry buildings as much as four stories high replaced mud and thatch dwellings, and archaeological findings include imported glass beads, Chinese porcelain, and other exotic goods. Coastal and island peoples shared a common culture and a language built on African grammar and vocabulary but enriched with many Arabic and Persian terms and written in Arabic script. In time, these people became known as "Swahili," from the Arabic name *sawahil° al-sudan,* meaning "shores of the blacks."

Sometime after Ibn Battuta's visit to Mogadishu in 1331, the more southerly city of Kilwa surpassed it as the Swahili Coast's most important commercial center (see Map 12.1). Ibn Battuta declared Kilwa "one of the most beautiful and well-constructed towns in the world." He noted its inhabitants' dark skins and Muslim piety, and he praised their ruler for the traditional Muslim virtues of humility and generosity.

What attracted the Arab and Iranian merchants whom oral traditions associate with the Swahili Coast's commercial expansion? By the late fifteenth century, Kilwa was annually exporting a ton of gold mined by inland Africans much farther south. Much of it came from or passed through a powerful state on the plateau south of the Zambezi River. At its peak in about 1400, its capital city, now known as **Great Zimbabwe,** occupied 193 acres (78 hectares) and had some eighteen thousand inhabitants.

Between about 1250 and 1450, local African craftsmen built stone structures for Great Zimbabwe's rulers, priests, and wealthy citizens. The

---

dhow (dow)   **Swahili** (swah-HEE-lee)

Malacca (meh-LAK-eh)   *sawahil* (suh-WAH-hil)

The Indian Ocean Dhow

The sailing vessels that crossed the Indian Ocean shared the diversity of that trading area. The name by which we know them, *dhow*, comes from the Swahili language of the East African coast. The planks of teak from which their hulls were constructed were hewn from the tropical forests of south India and Southeast Asia. Their pilots, who navigated by stars at night, used the ancient technique that Arabs had used to find their way across the desert. Some pilots used a magnetic compass, which originated in China.

Dhows came in various sizes and designs, but all shared two distinctive features. The first was hull construction. The hulls of dhows consisted of planks that were sewn together, not nailed. Cord made of fiber from the husk of coconuts or other materials was passed through rows of holes drilled in the planks. Because cord is weaker than nails, outsiders considered this shipbuilding technique strange. Marco Polo fancifully suggested that it indicated sailors' fear that large ocean magnets would pull any nails out of their ships. More probable explanations are that pliant sewn hulls were cheaper to build than rigid nailed hulls and were less likely to be damaged if the ships ran aground on coral reefs.

The second distinctive feature of dhows was their triangular (lateen) sails made of palm leaves or cotton. The sails were suspended from tall masts and could be turned to catch the wind.

The sewn hull and lateen sails were technologies developed centuries earlier, but two innovations were made between 1200 and 1500. First, a rudder positioned at the stern (rear end) of the ship replaced the large side oar that formerly had controlled steering. Second, shipbuilders increased the size of dhows to accommodate bulkier cargoes.

Dhow This modern model shows the vessel's main features. (National Maritime Museum, London)

largest structure, an enclosure the size and shape of a large football stadium with walls of unmortared stone 17 feet (5 meters) thick and 32 feet (10 meters) high, served as the king's court. A large conical stone tower was among the many buildings inside the walls.

As in Mali, mixed farming and cattle herding provided the economic basis of the Great Zimbabwe state, but long-distance trade brought added wealth. Trade began regionally with copper ingots from the upper Zambezi Valley, salt, and local manufactures. Gold exports to the coast expanded in the fourteenth and fifteenth centuries and brought Zimbabwe to its peak. However, histo-

Royal Enclosure, Great Zimbabwe Inside these oval stone walls the rulers of the trading state of Great Zimbabwe lived. Forced to enter the enclosure through a narrow corridor between two high walls, visitors were meant to be awestruck. (Courtesy of the Department of Information, Rhodesia)

rians suspect that the city's residents depleted nearby forests for firewood while their cattle overgrazed surrounding grasslands. The resulting ecological crisis hastened the empire's decline in the fifteenth century.

Arabia: Aden and the Red Sea

The city of **Aden**° near the southwestern tip of the Arabian peninsula had a double advantage in the Indian Ocean trade. Monsoon winds brought enough rainfall to supply drinking water to a large population and grow grain for export, and its location made it a convenient stopover for trade with India, the Persian Gulf, East Africa, and Egypt. Aden's merchants dealt in cotton cloth and beads from India; spices from Southeast Asia; horses from Arabia and Ethiopia; pearls from the Red Sea; manufactured luxuries from Cairo; slaves, gold, and ivory from Ethiopia; and grain, opium, and dyes from Aden's own hinterland.

After visiting Mecca in 1331, Ibn Battuta sailed down the Red Sea to Aden, probably wedged in among bales of trade goods. His comments on the wealth of Aden's leading merchants include a story about the slave of one merchant who bought a ram for the fabulous sum of 400 dinars in order to keep

Aden (AY-den

the slave of another merchant from buying it. Instead of punishing the slave for extravagance, the master freed him as a reward for outdoing his rival. Ninety years later, a Chinese Muslim visitor, Ma Huan, found "the country . . . rich, and the people numerous," living in stone residences several stories high.

Common commercial interests generally promoted good relations among the different religions and cultures of this region. For example, in the mid-thirteenth century, a wealthy Jew from Aden named Yosef settled in Christian Ethiopia, where he acted as an adviser. South Arabia had been trading with neighboring parts of Africa since before the times of King Solomon of Israel. The dynasty that ruled Ethiopia after 1270 claimed descent from Solomon and from the South Arabian princess Sheba. Solomonic Ethiopia's consolidation accompanied a great increase in trade through the Red Sea port of Zeila°, including slaves, amber, and animal pelts, which went to Aden and on to other destinations.

Friction sometimes arose, however. In the fourteenth century, the Sunni Muslim king of Yemen sent materials for building a large mosque in Zeila, but the local Somalis (who were Shi'ite Muslims) threw the stones into the sea. This resulted in a yearlong embargo of Zeila ships in Aden. In the late fifteenth century, Ethiopia's territorial expansion and efforts to increase control over the trade provoked conflicts with Muslims who ruled the coastal states of the Red Sea.

India: Gujarat and the Malabar Coast

The state of Gujarat in western India prospered from the expanding trade of the Arabian Sea and the rise of the Delhi Sultanate. Blessed with a rich agricultural hinterland and a long coastline, Gujarat attracted new trade after the Mongol destruction of Baghdad in 1258 disrupted the northern land routes. After the initial violence of its forced incorporation into the Delhi Sultanate in 1298, Gujarat prospered from increased trade with Delhi's ruling class, despite occasional military crackdowns. Independent again after 1390, the Muslim rulers of Gujarat extended their control over neighboring Hindu states and regained their preeminent position in the Indian Ocean trade.

Gujaratis exported cotton textiles and indigo to the Middle East and Europe, in return for gold and silver. They also shipped cotton cloth, carnelian beads, and foodstuffs to the Swahili Coast in exchange for ebony, slaves, ivory, and gold. During the fifteenth century, traders expanded eastward to the Strait of Malacca. These Gujarati merchants helped spread the Islamic faith among East Indian traders, some of whom even imported specially carved gravestones from Gujarat.

Unlike Kilwa and Aden, Gujarat manufactured goods for trade. According to the thirteenth-century Venetian traveler Marco Polo, Gujarat's leatherworkers dressed enough skins in a year to fill several ships to Arabia and other places. They made sleeping mats for export to the Middle East "in red and blue leather, exquisitely inlaid with figures of birds and beasts, and skillfully embroidered with gold and silver wire," as well as leather cushions embroidered in gold. Later observers compared the Gujarati city of Cambay with cities in Flanders and northern Italy (see Chapter 13) in the scale, artisanry, and diversity of its textile industries. Cotton, linen, and silk cloth, along with carpets and quilts, found a large market in Europe, Africa, the Middle East, and Southeast Asia. Cambay also produced polished gemstones, gold jewelry, carved ivory, stone beads, and both natural and artificial pearls. At the height of its prosperity in the fifteenth century, its well-laid-out streets and open places boasted fine stone houses with tiled roofs. Although Muslim residents controlled most Gujarati overseas trade, its Hindu merchant caste profited so much from related commercial activities that their wealth and luxurious lives became the envy of other Indians.

More southerly cities on the Malabar Coast duplicated Gujarat's success. Calicut° and other coastal cities prospered from locally made cotton textiles and locally grown grains and spices, and served as clearing-houses for the long-distance trade of the Indian Ocean. The Zamorin° (ruler) of Calicut presided over a loose federation of its Hindu rulers that united the coastal region. As in

---

Zeila (ZEYE-luh)

Calicut (KAL-ih-cut)   **Zamorin** (ZAH-much-ruhn)

eastern Africa and Arabia, rulers generally tolerated religious and ethnic groups who contributed to commercial profits. Most trading activity lay in the hands of Muslims, many originally from Iran and Arabia, who intermarried with local Indian Muslims. Jewish merchants also operated from Malabar's trading cities.

Southeast Asia: The Rise of Malacca

At the eastern end of the Indian Ocean, the Strait of Malacca between the Malay Peninsula and the island of Sumatra provided the principal passage into the South China Sea (see Map 12.2). As trade increased in the fourteenth and fifteenth centuries, this commercial choke point became the site of political rivalry. The mainland kingdom of Siam controlled most of the upper Malay Peninsula, while the Java-based kingdom of Majapahit° extended its dominion over the lower Malay Peninsula and much of Sumatra. Majapahit, however, could not suppress a nest of Chinese pirates based at the Sumatran city of Palembang° who preyed on ships sailing through the strait. In 1407, a fleet sent from China smashed the pirates' power and took their chief back home for trial.

Majapahit, weakened by internal struggles, could not take advantage of China's intervention, making the chief beneficiary the newer port of **Malacca** (or Melaka), which dominated the narrowest part of the strait. Under a prince from Palembang, Malacca had grown from an obscure fishing village into an important port through a series of astute alliances. Nominally subject to the king of Siam, Malacca also secured an alliance with China that was sealed by the visit of the imperial fleet in 1407. The conversion of an early ruler from Hinduism to Islam helped promote trade with Muslim merchants from Gujarat and elsewhere. Merchants also appreciated Malacca's security and low taxes.

Malacca served not just as a meeting point but also as an emporium for Southeast Asian products: rubies and musk from Burma, tin from Malaya, gold from Sumatra, cloves and nutmeg from the Moluccas (or Spice Islands, as Europeans later dubbed them). Shortly after 1500, when Malacca was at its height, one resident counted eighty-four languages spoken among the merchants gathered there, who came from as far away as Turkey, Ethiopia, and the Swahili Coast. Four officials administered the foreign merchant communities: one for the Gujaratis, one for other Indians and Burmese, one for Southeast Asians, and one for the Chinese and Japanese. Malacca's wealth and its cosmopolitan residents set the standard for luxury in Malaya for centuries to come.

SOCIAL AND CULTURAL CHANGE

State growth, commercial expansion, and the spread of Islam between 1200 and 1500 led to many changes in the social and cultural life of tropical peoples. The political and commercial elites grew in size and power, as did the number of slaves they owned. The spread of Muslim practices and beliefs affected social and cultural life—witness words of Arabic origin like *Sahara, Sudan, Swahili,* and *monsoon*—yet local traditions remained important.

Architecture, Learning, and Religion

Social and cultural changes typically affected cities more than rural areas. As Ibn Battuta and other travelers observed, wealthy merchants and ruling elites spent lavishly on mansions, palaces, and places of worship. Most places of worship surviving from this period blend older traditions and new influences. African Muslims produced Middle Eastern mosque designs in local building materials: sunbaked clay and wood in the western Sudan and coral stone on the Swahili Coast. Hindu temple architecture influenced mosque designs in Gujarat, which sometimes incorporated pieces of older structures. The congregational mosque at Cambay, built in 1325 with the traditional Islamic courtyard, cloisters, and porches, utilized pillars, porches, and arches taken from sacked Hindu and Jain° temples. The congregational mosque erected at the Gujarati capital of Ahmadabad° in 1423 had the open courtyard typical of

---

Majapahit (mah-jah-PAH-hit)   **Palembang** (pah-lem-BONG)

Jain (jine)   **Ahmadabad** (AH-muhd-ah-bahd)

mosques everywhere, but the surrounding verandas incorporated many typical Gujarati details and architectural conventions.

In Africa, King Lalibela° of Ethiopia constructed his capital, Lalibela, during the first third of the thirteenth century and ordered eleven churches to be carved out of solid rock, each commemorating a sacred Christian site in Jerusalem. These structures carried on an old Ethiopian tradition of rock sculpture, though on a far grander scale.

Mosques, churches, and temples were centers of education as well as prayer. Muslims promoted literacy among their sons (and sometimes their daughters) so that they could read sacred texts. Ibn Battuta reported seeing several boys in Mali wearing chains until they completed memorizing passages of the Quran. Literacy and Islam spread together in sub-Saharan Africa, where Christian Ethiopia had previously been the only literate society. In time, scholars adapted the Arabic alphabet to write local languages.

Islam affected literacy less in India, which had a long literate heritage. Arabic served primarily for religious purposes, while Persian became the language of high culture used at court. Eventually **Urdu**° arose, a Persian-influenced literary form of Hindi written in Arabic characters. Muslims also introduced papermaking in India.

Advanced Muslim scholars studied Islamic law, theology, and administration, as well as works on mathematics, medicine, science, and philosophy, partly derived from ancient Greek writings. In sixteenth-century **Timbuktu** (see Map 12.1), over 150 schools taught the Quran while leading clerics taught advanced classes in mosques or homes. Books imported from North Africa brought high prices. Al-Hajj Ahmed, a scholar who died in Timbuktu in 1536, possessed some seven hundred volumes, an unusually large library for that time. In Southeast Asia, Malacca became a center of Islamic learning from which scholars spread Islam throughout the region. Other important centers of learning developed in Muslim India, particularly in Delhi, the capital.

Even in lands seized by conquest, Muslim rulers seldom required conversion. Example and

persuasion by merchants and Sufis proved more effective. Many Muslims worked hard to persuade others of Islam's superiority. Muslim domination of long-distance trade assisted the adoption of Islam. Commercial transactions could take place across religious boundaries, but the common code of morality and law that Islam provided encouraged trust and drew many local merchants to Islam. From the major trading centers along the Swahili Coast, in the Sudan, in coastal India, and in Southeast Asia, Islam's influence spread along regional trade routes.

Marriage also played a role. Single Muslim men traveling to and settling in tropical Africa and Asia often married local women. Their children grew up in the Islamic faith. Some wealthy men had dozens of children from up to four wives and additional slave concubines. Servants and slaves in such households normally professed Islam.

In India, Muslim invasions eliminated the last strongholds of long-declining Buddhism, including, in 1196, the great Buddhist center of study at Nalanda° in Bihar°. Its manuscripts were burned and thousands of monks killed or driven into exile in Nepal and Tibet. With Buddhism reduced to a minor faith in the land of its birth, Islam emerged as India's second most important religion. Hinduism still prevailed in 1500, but Islam displaced Hinduism in most of maritime Southeast Asia.

Islam also spread among rural peoples, such as the pastoral Fulani of West Africa and Somali of northeastern Africa and various pastoralists in northwest India. In Bengal, Muslim religious figures oversaw the conversion of jungle into farmland and thereby gained many converts.

The spread of Islam did not mean simply the replacement of one set of beliefs by another. Islam adapted to the cultures of the regions it penetrated, developing African, Indian, and Indonesian varieties.

Social and Gender Distinctions

A growth in slavery accompanied the rising prosperity of the elites. Military campaigns in India, according to Islamic sources, reduced hundreds of thousands of Hindu

---

Lalibela (LAH-lee-BEL-uh)   Urdu (ER-doo)

Nalanda (nuh-LAN-duh)   Bihar (bee-HAHR)

"infidels" to slavery. Delhi overflowed with slaves. Sultan Ala ud-Din owned 50,000 and Firuz Shah 180,000, including 12,000 skilled artisans. Sultan Tughluq sent 100 male slaves and 100 female slaves as a gift to the emperor of China in return for a similar gift.

Mali and Bornu sent slaves across the Sahara to North Africa, including beautiful maidens and eunuchs (castrated males). The expanding Ethiopian Empire regularly sent captives for sale to Aden traders at Zeila. According to modern estimates, Saharan and Red Sea traders sold about 2.5 million enslaved Africans between 1200 and 1500. African slaves from the Swahili Coast played conspicuous roles in the navies, armies, and administrations of some Indian states, especially in the fifteenth century. A few African slaves even reached China, where a source from about 1225 says rich families preferred gatekeepers with bodies "black as lacquer."

With "free" labor abundant and cheap, few slaves worked as farmers. In some places, hereditary castes of slaves dominated certain trades and military units. Indeed, the earliest rulers of the Delhi Sultanate rose from military slavery. A slave general in the western Sudan named Askia Muhammad seized control of the Songhai Empire (Mali's successor) in 1493. Less fortunate slaves, like the men and women who mined copper in Mali, did hard menial work.

Wealthy households used many slave servants. Eunuchs guarded the harems of wealthy Muslims, but women predominated as household slaves, serving also as entertainers and concubines. Some rich men aspired to having a concubine from every part of the world. One of Firuz Shah's nobles reportedly had two thousand harem slaves, including women from Turkey and China.

Sultan Ala ud-Din's campaigns against Gujarat at the end of the thirteenth century yielded a booty of twenty thousand maidens in addition to innumerable younger children of both sexes. The supply of captives became so great that the lowest grade of horse sold for five times as much as an ordinary female slave, although beautiful young virgins commanded far higher prices.

Hindu legal digests and commentaries suggest that the position of Hindu women may have improved somewhat compared to earlier periods. The

ancient practice of sati°—that is, of an upper-caste widow throwing herself on her husband's funeral pyre—remained a meritorious act strongly approved by social custom. But Ibn Battuta makes it clear that sati was strictly optional. Since the Hindu commentaries devote considerable attention to the rights of widows without sons to inherit their husbands' estates, one may even conclude that sati was exceptional.

Indian parents still gave their daughters in marriage before the age of puberty, but consummation of the marriage took place only when the young woman was ready. Wives faced far stricter rules of fidelity and chastity than their husbands and could be abandoned for any serious breach. But other offenses against law and custom usually brought lighter penalties than for men. A woman's male master—father, husband, or owner—determined her status. Women seldom played active roles in commerce, administration, or religion.

Besides child rearing, women involved themselves with food preparation and, when not prohibited by religious restrictions, brewing. In many parts of Africa, women commonly made beer from grains or bananas. These mildly alcoholic beverages played an important part in male rituals of hospitality and relaxation.

Throughout tropical Africa and Asia, women did much of the farm work. They also toted home heavy loads of food, firewood, and water balanced on their heads. Other common female activities included making clay pots for cooking and storage and making clothing. In India, the spinning wheel, introduced by the Muslim invaders, greatly reduced the cost of making thread for weaving. Women typically spun at home, leaving weaving to men. In West Africa, women often sold agricultural products, pottery, and other craftwork in the markets.

Adopting Islam did not necessarily mean accepting the social customs of the Arab world. In Mali's capital, Ibn Battuta was appalled that Muslim women both free and slave did not completely cover their bodies and veil their faces when appearing in public. He considered their nakedness an offense to women's (and men's) modesty. In another part of Mali, he berated a Muslim merchant from Morocco for permitting his wife to sit on a couch and chat with

sati (suh-TEE)

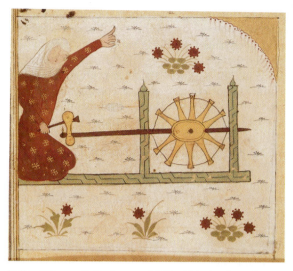

Indian Woman Spinning, ca. 1500   This drawing of a Muslim woman by an Indian artist shows the influence of Persian styles. The spinning of cotton fiber into thread—women's work—was made much easier by the spinning wheel, which the Muslim invaders introduced. Men then wove the threads into the cotton textiles for which India was celebrated.   (British Library, Oriental and Indian Office Library, Or 3299, f. 151)

her male friend. The husband replied, "The association of women with men is agreeable to us and part of good manners, to which no suspicion attaches." Ibn Battuta refused to visit the merchant again.

CONCLUSION

Tropical Africa and Asia contained 40 percent of the world's population and over a quarter of its habitable land. Between 1200 and 1500, commercial, political, and cultural currents drew the region's peoples closer together. The Indian Ocean became the world's most important and richest trading area. The Delhi Sultanate brought the greatest political unity to India since the decline of the Guptas. Mali extended the political and trading role pioneered by Ghana in the western Sudan. Trade and empire followed closely the enlargement of Islam's presence and the accompanying diversification of Islamic customs.

Yet many social and cultural practices remained stable. Most tropical Africans and Asians never ventured far outside the rural communities where their families had lived for generations. Their lives followed the pattern of the seasons, the cycle of religious rituals and festivals, and the stages from childhood to elder status. Most people engaged in farming, herding, and fishing. Village communities proved remarkably hardy. They might be ravaged by natural disaster or pillaged by advancing armies, but over time most recovered. Empires and kingdoms rose and fell, but the villages endured.

In comparison, social, political, and environmental changes taking place in the Latin West, described in the next chapter, had great implications for tropical peoples after 1500.

■ Key Terms

Ibn Battuta	dhows
tropics	Swahili Coast
monsoons	Great Zimbabwe
Delhi Sultanate	Aden
Mali	Malacca
Mansa Kankan Musa	Urdu
Gujarat	Timbuktu

■ Suggested Reading

Patricia Risso, *Merchants and Faith: Muslim Commerce and Culture in the Indian Ocean* (1995), briefly introduces the Indian Ocean trading system. Janet Abu-Lughod, *Before European Hegemony: The World System, A.D. 1250–1350* (1989), provides a more extensive and speculative view that may usefully be read with K. N. Chaudhuri, *Asia Before Europe: Economy and Civilization of the Indian Ocean from the Rise of Islam to 1750* (1991). For Islam's influences in tropical Asia and Africa, see Ira Lapidus, *A History of Islamic Societies*, 2d ed. (2002), part 2, and for commercial relations, Philip D. Curtin, *Cross-Cultural Trade in World History* (1984).

Greater detail on Southeast Asia is contained in Nicholas Tarling, ed., *The Cambridge History of Southeast Asia*, vol. 1 (1992); John F. Cady, *Southeast Asia: Its Historical Development* (1964); and G. Coedes, *The Indianized States of Southeast Asia*, ed. Walter F. Vella (1968). R. C. Majumdar, ed., *The History and Culture of the Indian People*, vol. 4, *The Delhi Sultanate*, 2d ed. (1967), covers India at length. Stanley Wolpert, *A New History of India*, 6th ed. (1999), offers a briefer account, and David Ludden, *A Peasant History of South India* (1985), approaches it from an intriguing perspective. For advanced topics, see Tapan Raychaudhuri and Irfan Habib, eds., *The Cambridge Economic History of India,* vol. 1, *c. 1200–c. 1750* (1982).

A great deal of new scholarship on Africa in this period is summarized in chapters 6 and 7 of Christopher Ehret's *The Civilizations of Africa: A History to 1800* (2002). See also Graham Connah's *African Civilizations: Precolonial Cities and States in Tropical Africa: An Archaeological Perspective* (1987), which covers Africa in general. For studies of greater depth, see D. T. Niane, ed., *UNESCO General History of Africa,* vol. 4, *Africa from the Twelfth to the Sixteenth Century* (1984), and Roland Oliver, ed., *The Cambridge History of Africa,* vol. 3, *c. 1050 to c. 1600* (1977).

Salim Kidwai, "Sultans, Eunuchs and Domestics: New Forms of Bondage in Medieval India," in *Chains of Servitude: Bondage and Slavery in India,* edited by Utsa Patnaik and Manjari Dingwaney (1985), and the first two chapters of Paul E. Lovejoy, *Transformations in Slavery: A History of Slavery in Africa*, 2d ed. (2000), give good treatments of slavery and the slave trade.

Along with H. A. R. Gibb's three-volume translation of *The Travels of Ibn Battuta,* A.D. *1325–1354* (1958–1971), see Ross E. Dunn, *The Adventures of Ibn Battuta: A Muslim of the Fourteenth Century* (1986). For annotated selections, see Said Hamdun and Noèl King, *Ibn Battuta in Black Africa* (1995).

The most accessible survey of Indian Ocean sea travel is George F. Hourani, *Arab Seafaring,* expanded ed. (1995). For a Muslim Chinese traveler's observations, see Ma Huan, *Ying-yai Sheng-lan, "The Overall Survey of the Ocean's Shore" [1433],* translated and edited by J. V. G. Mills (1970). Another valuable contemporary account is G. R. Tibbetts, *Arab Navigation in the Indian Ocean Before the Coming of the Portuguese, Being a Translation of the Kitab al-Fawa'id . . . of Ahmad b. Majidal-Najdi* (1981).

■ Notes

1. Tarikh-i-Wassaf, in Henry M. Elliot, *The History of India as Told by Its Own Historians,* ed. John Dowson (London: Trübner and Co., 1869–1871), 2:28.
2. Hasan Nizami, Taju-l Ma-asir, in ibid., 2:219.
3. Minhaju-s Siraj, Tabakat-i Nasiri, in ibid., 2:332–333.

13 The Latin West, 1200–1500

CHAPTER OUTLINE

Rural Growth and Crisis

Urban Revival

Learning, Literature, and the Renaissance

Political and Military Transformations

DIVERSITY AND DOMINANCE: Persecution and Protection of Jews, 1272–1349

In the summer of 1454, a year after the Ottoman Turks captured the Greek Christian city of Constantinople, Aeneas Sylvius Piccolomini°, destined in four years to become pope, expressed doubts as to whether anyone could persuade the rulers of Christian Europe to take up arms together against the Muslims: "Christendom has no head whom all will obey—neither the pope nor the emperor receives his due." The Christian states thought more of fighting each other. French and English armies had been battling for over a century. The German emperor presided over dozens of states but did not really control them. The numerous kingdoms and principalities of Spain and Italy could

not unite. With only slight exaggeration, Aeneas Sylvius moaned, "Every city has its own king, and there are as many princes as there are households." He attributed this lack of unity to European preoccupation with personal welfare and material gain. Both pessimism about human nature and materialism had increased during the previous century, after a devastating plague had carried off a third of western Europe's population.

Yet despite all these divisions, disasters, and wars, historians now see the period from 1200 to 1500 (Europe's Later Middle Ages) as a time of unusual progress. Prosperous cities adorned with splendid architecture, institutions of higher learning, and cultural achievements counterbalanced the avarice and greed that Aeneas Sylvius lamented. Frequent wars caused havoc

---

Aeneas Sylvius Piccolomini (uh-NEE-uhs SIL-vee-uhs pee-kuh-lo-MEE-nee)

and destruction, but they also promoted the development of military technology and more unified monarchies.

Although their Muslim and Byzantine neighbors commonly called western Europeans "Franks," they ordinarily referred to themselves as "Latins," underscoring their allegiance to Roman Catholicism and the Latin language used in its rituals. Some common elements promoted the **Latin West's** vigorous revival: competition, the pursuit of success, and the effective use of borrowed technology and learning.

As you read this chapter, ask yourself the following questions:

- How well did western Europeans deal with their natural environment?

- How did warfare help rulers in the Latin West acquire the skills, weapons, and determination to challenge other parts of the world?

- How did technology promote excellence in business, learning, and architecture in the Latin West?

- How much did the region's achievements depend on its own people and how much on things borrowed from Muslim and Byzantine neighbors?

RURAL GROWTH AND CRISIS

Between 1200 and 1500, the Latin West brought more land under cultivation using new farming techniques and made greater use of machinery and mechanical forms of energy. Yet for the nine out of ten people who lived in the countryside, hard labor brought meager returns, and famine, epidemics, and war struck often. After the devastation of the Black Death between 1347 and 1351, social changes speeded up by peasant revolts released many persons from serfdom and brought some improvements to rural life.

Peasants, Population, and Plague

In 1200, most western Europeans lived as serfs tilling the soil on large estates owned by the nobility and the church (see Chapter 8). They owed their lord both a share of their harvests and numerous labor services. As a consequence of the inefficiency of farming practices and their obligations to landowners, peasants received meager returns for their hard work. Even with numerous religious holidays, peasants labored some 54 hours a week in their fields, more than half the time in support of the local nobility. Each noble household typically lived from the labor of fifteen to thirty peasant families. The standard of life in the lord's stone castle or manor house contrasted sharply with the peasant's one-room thatched cottage containing little furniture and no luxuries.

Scenes of rural life show both men and women at work in the fields, but equality of labor did not mean equality in decision making at home. In the peasant's hut as elsewhere in medieval Europe, women were subordinate to men. The influential theologian Thomas Aquinas° (1225–1274) spoke for his age when he argued that although both men and women were created in God's image, there was a sense in which "the image of God is found in man, and not in woman: for man is the beginning and end of woman; as God is the beginning and end of every creature."[1]

Rural poverty resulted from rapid population growth as well as inefficient farming methods and social inequality. In 1200, China's population may have exceeded Europe's by two to one; by 1300, the population of each was about 80 million. China's population fell because of the Mongol conquest (see Chapter 11), while Europe's more than doubled between 1100 and 1445. Some historians believe the reviving economy stimulated the increase. Others argue that severe epidemics were few, and warmer-than-usual temperatures reduced mortality from starvation and exposure.

More people required more productive farming and new agricultural settlements. One widespread new technique, the **three-field system,** replaced the custom of leaving half the land fallow

Aquinas (uh-KWY-nuhs)

Rural French Peasants Many scenes of peasant life in winter are visible in this small painting by the Flemish Limbourg brothers from the 1410s. Above the snow-covered beehives one man chops firewood, while another drives a donkey loaded with firewood to a little village. At the lower right a woman, blowing on her frozen fingers, heads past the huddled sheep and hungry birds to join other women warming themselves in the cottage (whose outer wall the artists have cut away). (Musée Conde, Chantilly, France/Art Resource, NY)

(uncultivated) every year to regain its fertility. Farmers grew crops on two-thirds of their land each year and planted the third field in oats. The oats restored nitrogen to the depleted soil and produced feed for plow horses. In much of Europe, however, farmers continued to let half of their land lie fallow and use oxen (less efficient but cheaper than horses) to pull their plows.

Population growth also encouraged new agricultural settlements. In the twelfth and thirteenth centuries, large numbers of Germans migrated into the fertile lands east of the Elbe River and into the eastern Baltic states. Knights belonging to Latin Christian religious orders slaughtered or drove away native inhabitants who had not yet adopted Christianity. During the thirteenth century, the Order of Teutonic Knights conquered, resettled, and administered a vast area along the Baltic that later became Prussia (see Map 13.1). Other Latin Christians founded new settlements on lands conquered from the Muslims and Byzantines in southern Europe and on Celtic lands in the British Isles.

Draining swamps and clearing forests also brought new land under cultivation. But as population continued to rise, some people had to farm lands that had poor soils or were vulnerable to flooding, frost, or drought. Average crop yields fell accordingly after 1250, and more people lived at the edge of starvation. According to one historian, "By 1300, almost every child born in western Europe faced the probability of extreme hunger at least once or twice during his expected 30 to 35 years of life."[2] One unusually cold spell produced the Great Famine of 1315–1317, which affected much of Europe.

The **Black Death** reversed the population growth. This terrible plague originated in China and spread across Central Asia with the Mongol armies (see Chapter 11). In 1346, the Mongols attacked the city of Kaffa° on the Black Sea; a year later, Genoese° traders in Kaffa carried the disease to Italy and southern France. For two years, the Black Death spread across Europe, in some places carrying off two-thirds of the population. Average losses in western Europe amounted to one in three.

Victims developed boils the size of eggs in their groins and armpits, black blotches on their skin, foul body odors, and severe pain. In most cases, death came within a few days. Town officials closed their gates to people from infected areas and burned the victims' possessions. Such measures helped to spare some communities but could not halt the advance of the disease. Bubonic plague, the primary form of the Black Death, spreads from person to person and through the bites of fleas infesting the fur of certain rats. Although medieval doctors did not associate the disease with rats, eliminating the rats that thrived on urban refuse would have been difficult.

The plague left a psychological mark, bringing home to people how sudden and unexpected death could be. Some people became more religious, giv-

Kaffa (KAH-fah)   **Genoese** (JEN-oh-eez)

C H R O N O L O G Y

	Technology and Environment	Culture	Politics and Society
1200	**1200s** Use of crossbows widespread; windmills in increased use		**1200s** Champagne fairs flourish **1204** Fourth Crusade launched
		1210s Religious orders founded; Teutonic Knights, Franciscans, Dominicans	**1215** Magna Carta issued
		1225–1274 Thomas Aquinas, monk and philosopher	
		1265–1321 Dante Alighieri, poet	
		ca. 1267–1337 Giotto, painter	
1300		**1300–1500** Rise of universities	
		1304–1374 Francesco Petrarch, humanist writer	
	1315–1317 Great Famine	**1313–1375** Giovanni Boccaccio, humanist writer	
		ca. 1340–1400 Geoffrey Chaucer, poet	**1337** Start of Hundred Years War
	1347–1351 Black Death		
	ca. 1350 Growing deforestation	**1389–1464** Cosimo de' Medici, banker	**1381** Wat Tyler's Rebellion
		ca. 1390–1441 Jan van Eyck, painter	
1400	**1400s** Large cannon in use in warfare; hand-held firearms become prominent		**1415** Portuguese take Ceuta **1431** Joan of Art burned as witch
	ca. 1450 First printing with movable type in the West	**1449–1492** Lorenzo de' Medici, art patron	
		1452–1519 Leonardo da Vinci, artist	**1453** End of Hundred Years War; Turks take Constantinople
	1454 Gutenberg Bible printed		

(continued)

	Technology and Environment	Culture	Politics and Society
		ca. 1466–1536 Erasmus of Rotterdam, humanist	1469 Marriage of Ferdinand of Aragon and Isabella of Castile
		1472–1564 Michelangelo, artist	
		1492 Explusion of Jews from Spain	1492 Fall of Muslim state of Granada

ing money to the church or hitting themselves with iron-tipped whips to atone for their sins. Others chose reckless enjoyment, spending their money on fancy clothes, feasts, and drinking. Whatever their mood, most people soon resumed their daily routines.

Periodic returns of plague made recovery from population losses slow and uneven. Europe's population in 1400 equaled that in 1200. Not until after 1500 did it rise above its preplague level.

Social Rebellion

In addition to its demographic and psychological effects, the Black Death triggered social changes in western Europe. Skilled and manual laborers who survived demanded higher pay for their services. At first, authorities tried to freeze wages at the old levels. Seeing this as a plot by the rich, peasants rose up against wealthy nobles and churchmen. During a widespread revolt in France in 1358, known as the Jacquerie, peasants looted castles and killed dozens of persons. In a large revolt led by Wat Tyler in 1381, English peasants invaded London, calling for an end to serfdom and obligations to landowners. Demonstrators murdered the archbishop of Canterbury and many royal officials. Authorities put down these rebellions with even greater bloodshed and cruelty, but they could not stave off the higher wages and other social changes the rebels demanded.

Serfdom practically disappeared in western Europe as peasants bought their freedom or ran away. Many free persons earning higher wages saved their money and bought land. Some English landowners who could no longer afford to hire enough field-workers began pasturing sheep for their wool. Others grew crops that required less care or made greater use of draft animals and laborsaving tools. Because the plague had not killed wild and domesticated animals, survivors had abundant meat and leather for shoes. Thus, the welfare of the rural masses generally improved after the Black Death, though the gap between rich and poor remained wide.

In urban areas, employers raised wages to attract workers. Guilds (see below) shortened the period of apprenticeship. Competition within crafts also became more common. Although the overall economy shrank with the decline in population, per capita production actually rose.

Mills and Mines

Mining, metalworking, and the use of mechanical energy expanded so greatly in the centuries before 1500 that some historians speak of an "industrial revolution" in medieval Europe. That may be too strong a term, but the landscape fairly bristled with mechanical devices. Mills powered by water or wind ground grain, sawed logs, crushed olives, tanned leather, and made paper.

Watermills on the Seine River in Paris Sacks of grain were brought to these mills under the bridge called the Grand Pont to be ground into flour. The water wheels were turned by the river flowing under them. Gears translated the vertical motion of the wheels into the horizontal motion of the millstones. (Bibliothèque Nationale de France)

In 1086, 5,600 watermills flanked England's many rivers. After 1200, mills spread rapidly across the western European mainland. By the early fourteenth century, entrepreneurs had crammed 68 watermills into a one-mile section of the Seine° River in Paris. Less efficient **water wheels** depended on the flow of a river passing beneath them. Greater efficiency came from channeling water to fall over the top of the wheel so that gravity added force to the water's flow. Dams ensured a steady flow of water throughout the year. Some watermills in France and England even harnessed the power of ocean tides.

Windmills multiplied in comparatively dry lands like Spain and in northern Europe, where ice made water wheels useless in winter. Designs for watermills dated back to Roman times, and the Islamic world, which inherited Hellenistic technologies, knew both water wheels and windmills. But people in the medieval Latin West used these devices on a much larger scale than did people elsewhere.

Owners invested heavily in building mills, but since nature furnished the energy to run them for free, they returned great profits. Individuals or monasteries constructed some mills, but most were built by groups of investors. Rich millers often aroused the jealousy of their neighbors. In his *Canterbury Tales,* the English poet Geoffrey Chaucer (c. 1340–1400) captured their unsavory reputation

by portraying a miller as "a master-hand at stealing grain" by pushing down on the balance scale with his thumb.[3]

Waterpower aided the great expansion of iron making. Water powered the stamping mills that broke up the iron, the trip hammers that pounded it, and the bellows (first documented in the West in 1323) that raised temperatures to the point where the iron was liquid enough to be poured into molds. Blast furnaces producing high-quality iron are documented from 1380. Finished products ranged from armor to nails, from horseshoes to hoes.

Demand stimulated iron mining in many parts of Europe. In addition, new silver, lead, and copper mines in Austria and Hungary supplied metal for coins, church bells, cannons, and statues. Techniques of deep mining developed in Central Europe spread west in the latter part of the fifteenth century. A building boom stimulated stone quarrying in France during the eleventh, twelfth, and thirteenth centuries.

Industrial growth changed the landscape. Towns grew outward and new ones were founded, dams and canals changed the flow of rivers, and quarries and mines scarred the hillsides. Urban tanneries (factories that cured and processed leather), the runoff from slaughterhouses, and human waste polluted streams. England's Parliament enacted the first recorded antipollution law in 1388, but enforcement proved difficult.

Seine (sen)

Deforestation accelerated. Trees provided timber for buildings and ships. Tanneries stripped bark to make acid for tanning leather. Many forests gave way to farmland. The glass and iron industries used great quantities of charcoal, made by controlled burning of oak or other hardwood, to produce the high temperatures required. A single iron furnace could consume all the trees within five-eighths of a mile (1 kilometer) in just forty days. Consequently, the later Middle Ages saw the end of many of western Europe's once-dense forests, except in places where powerful landowners established hunting preserves.

URBAN REVIVAL

In the tenth century, no town in the Latin West could compete in size, wealth, or comfort with the cities of Byzantium and Islam. Yet by the later Middle Ages, the Mediterranean, Baltic, and Atlantic coasts boasted wealthy port cities, as did some major rivers draining into these seas. Some Byzantine and Muslim cities still exceeded those of the West in size, but not in commercial, cultural, and administrative dynamism, as marked by impressive new churches, guild halls, and residences.

Trading Cities

Most urban growth after 1200 resulted from manufacturing and trade, both between cities and their hinterlands and over long distances. Northern Italy particularly benefited from maritime trade with the port cities of the eastern Mediterranean and, through them, the markets of the Indian Ocean and East Asia. In northern Europe, commercial cities in the county of Flanders (roughly today's Belgium) and around the Baltic Sea profited from regional networks and from overland and sea routes to the Mediterranean.

A Venetian-inspired assault in 1204 against the city of Constantinople, misleadingly named the "Fourth Crusade," temporarily eliminated Byzantine control of the passage between the Mediterranean and the Black Sea and thereby allowed Venice to seize Crete and expand its trading colonies around the Black Sea. Another boon to

Italian trade came from the westward expansion of the Mongol Empire, which opened trade routes from the Mediterranean to China (see Chapter 11).

A young merchant named Marco Polo set out from Venice in 1271 and reached the Mongol court in China after a long trek across Central Asia. He served the emperor Khubilai Khan for many years as an ambassador and governor of a Chinese province. Some scholars question Marco's later account of these adventures and a treacherous return voyage through the Indian Ocean that returned him to Venice in 1295, after an absence of twenty-four years. Similar reports of the riches of the East came from other European travelers.

When Mongol decline interrupted the caravan trade in the fourteenth century, Venetian merchants purchased eastern silks and spices brought by other middlemen to Constantinople, Damascus, and Cairo. Three times a year, Venice dispatched convoys of two or three galleys, with sixty oarsmen each, capable of bringing back 2,000 tons of goods. Other merchants explored new overland or sea routes.

The sea trade of Genoa on northern Italy's west coast probably equaled that of Venice. Genoese merchants established colonies in the western and eastern Mediterranean and around the Black Sea. In northern Europe, an association of trading cities known as the **Hanseatic° League** traded extensively in the Baltic, including the coasts of Prussia, newly conquered by German knights. Their merchants ranged eastward to Novgorod in Russia and westward across the North Sea to London.

In the late thirteenth century, Genoese galleys from the Mediterranean and Hanseatic ships from the Baltic were converging on the trading and manufacturing cities in Flanders. Artisans in the Flemish towns of Bruges°, Ghent°, and Ypres° transformed raw wool from England into a fine cloth that was softer and smoother than the coarse "homespuns" from simple village looms. Dyed in vivid hues, these Flemish textiles appealed to wealthy Europeans, who also appreciated fine textiles from Asia.

Along the overland route connecting Flanders and northern Italy, important trading fairs developed in the Champagne° region of Burgundy.

Hanseatic (han-see-AT-ik) **Bruges** (broozh) **Ghent** (gent [hard *g* as in *get*]) **Ypres** (EE-pruh) **Champagne** (sham-PAIN)

Flemish Weavers, Ypres   The spread of textile weaving gave employment to many people in the Netherlands. The city of Ypres in Flanders (now northern Belgium) was an important textile center in the thirteenth century. This drawing from a fourteenth-century manuscript shows a man and a woman weaving cloth on a horizontal loom, while a child makes thread on a spinning wheel. (Stedelijke Openbare Bibliotheek, Ypres)

The Champagne fairs began as regional markets, exchanging manufactured goods, livestock, and farm produce once or twice a year. When the king of France gained control of Champagne at the end of the twelfth century, royal guarantees of safe conduct to merchants turned these markets into international fairs that were important for currency exchange and other financial transactions as well. A century later, fifteen Italian cities had permanent consulates in Champagne to represent the interests of their citizens. During the fourteenth century, the large volume of trade made it cheaper to ship Flemish woolens to Italy by sea than to pack them overland on animal backs. Champagne's fairs consequently lost some international trade, but they remained important as regional markets.

In the late thirteenth century, the English monarchy raised taxes on exports of raw wool, making cloth manufacture in England more profitable than in Flanders. Flemish specialists crossed the English Channel and introduced the spinning wheel and other devices to England. Annual raw wool exports fell from 35,000 sacks of wool at the beginning of the fourteenth century to 8,000 in the mid-fifteenth century, while English wool cloth production rose from 4,000 pieces just before 1350 to 54,000 a century later.

Florence also replaced Flemish imports with its own woolens industry financed by local banking families. In 1338, Florence manufactured 80,000 pieces of cloth, while importing only 10,000. These changes in the textile industry show how competition promoted the spread of manufacturing and encouraged new specialties.

The growing textile industries used the power of wind and water channeled through gears, pulleys, and belts to drive all sorts of machinery. Flemish mills cleaned and thickened woven cloth by beating it in water, a process known as fulling. Other mills produced paper, starting in southern Europe in the thirteenth century. Unlike the Chinese and Muslim papermakers, who had pursued the craft for centuries, the Europeans introduced machines to do the heavy work.

In the fifteenth century, Venice surpassed its European rivals in the volume of its trade in the Mediterranean as well as across the Alps into central Europe. Its craftspeople manufactured luxury goods once obtainable only from eastern sources, notably silk and cotton textiles, glassware and mirrors, jewelry, and paper. Exports of Italian and northern European woolens to the eastern Mediterranean also rose. In the space of a few centuries, western European cities had used the eastern trade to increase their prosperity and then reduce their dependence on eastern goods.

Civic Life

Most northern Italian and German cities were independent states, much like the port cities of the Indian Ocean Basin (see Chapter 12). Other European cities held royal charters exempting them from the authority of local nobles. Their autonomy enabled them to adapt to changing market conditions more quickly than cities controlled by imperial authorities, as in China and the Islamic world. Since anyone who lived in a chartered city for over a year could claim freedom, urban life promoted social mobility.

Europe's Jews mostly lived in cities. Spain had the largest communities because of the tolerance of earlier Muslim rulers. Commercial cities elsewhere welcomed Jews with manufacturing and business skills. Despite official protection by certain Christian princes and kings, Jews endured violent religious persecutions or expulsions in times of crisis, such as during the Black Death (see Diversity and Dominance: Persecution and Protection of Jews, 1272–1349). In 1492, the Spanish monarchs expelled all Jews in the name of religious and eth-

nic purity. Only the papal city of Rome left its Jews undisturbed throughout the centuries before 1500.

Within most towns and cities, powerful associations known as guilds dominated civic life. **Guilds** brought together craft specialists, such as silversmiths, or merchants working in a particular trade, to regulate business practices and set prices. Guilds also trained apprentices and promoted members' interests with the city government. By denying membership to outsiders and Jews, guilds protected the interests of families that already belonged. Guilds also perpetuated male dominance of most skilled jobs.

Nevertheless, in a few places, women could join guilds either on their own or as the wives, widows, or daughters of male guild members. Large numbers of poor women also toiled in nonguild jobs in urban textile industries and in the food and beverage trades, generally receiving lower wages than men.

Some women advanced socially through marriage to wealthy men. One of Chaucer's *Canterbury Tales* concerns a woman from Bath, a city in southern England, who became wealthy by marrying a succession of old men for their money (and then two other husbands for love), "aside from other company in youth." She was also a skilled weaver, Chaucer says: "In making cloth she showed so great a bent, / She bettered those of Ypres and of Ghent."

By the fifteenth century, a new class of wealthy merchant-bankers was operating on a vast scale and specializing in money changing and loans and making investments on behalf of other parties. Merchants great and small used their services. They also handled the financial transactions of ecclesiastical and secular officials and arranged for the transmission to the pope of funds known as Peter's pence, a collection taken up annually in every church in the Latin West. Princes and kings supported their wars and lavish courts with credit. Some merchant-bankers even developed their own news services, gathering information on any topic that could affect business.

Florentine financiers invented checking accounts, organized private shareholding companies (the forerunners of modern corporations), and improved bookkeeping techniques. In the fifteenth century, the Medici° family of Florence operated

---

Medici (MED-ih-chee)

banks in Italy, Flanders, and London. Medicis also controlled the government of Florence and commissioned art works. The Fuggers° of Augsburg, who had ten times the Medici bank's lending capital, topped Europe's banking fraternity by 1500. Beginning as cloth merchants under Jacob "the Rich" (1459–1525), the family's many activities included the trade in Hungarian copper, essential for casting cannon.

Since Latin Christians generally considered charging interest (usury) sinful, Jews predominated in money lending. Christian bankers devised ways to profit from loans indirectly in order to get around the condemnation of usury. Some borrowers repaid loans in a different currency at a rate of exchange favorable to the lender. Others added to their repayment a "gift" in thanks to the lender. For example, in 1501, church officials agreed to repay a Fugger loan of 6,000 gold ducats in five months along with a "gift" of 400 ducats, amounting to an effective interest rate of 16 percent a year. In fact, the return was less since the church failed to repay the loan on time.

Yet most residents of western European cities lived in poverty and squalor rather than wealth. European cities generally lacked civic amenities, such as public baths and water supply systems, that had existed in the cities of Western antiquity and still survived in cities of the Islamic Middle East.

Gothic Cathedrals Master builders and associated craftsmen counted among the skilled people in greatest demand. Though cities competed with one another in the magnificence of their guild halls, town halls, and other structures, **Gothic cathedrals,** first appearing about 1140 in France, cost the most and brought the greatest prestige. The pointed, or Gothic, arch, replacing the older round, or Roman, arch proved a hallmark of the new design. External (flying) buttresses stabilizing the high, thin stone columns below the arches constituted another distinctive feature. This method of construction enabled master builders to push the Gothic cathedrals to great heights and fill the outside walls with giant windows depicting religious scenes in brilliantly colored stained glass. During the next four

Fuggers (FOOG-uhrz)

centuries, interior heights soared ever higher, towers and spires pierced the heavens, and walls became dazzling curtains of stained glass.

The men who designed and built the cathedrals had little or no formal education and limited understanding of the mathematical principles of modern civil engineering. Master masons sometimes miscalculated, causing parts of some overly ambitious cathedrals to collapse. The record-high choir vault of Beauvais Cathedral, for instance—154 feet (47 meters) in height—came tumbling down in 1284. But as builders gained experience and invented novel solutions to their problems, success rose from the rubble of their mistakes. The cathedral spire in Strasbourg reached 466 feet (142 meters) into the air—as high as a forty-story building. Such heights were unsurpassed until the twentieth century.

LEARNING, LITERATURE, AND THE RENAISSANCE

Throughout the Middle Ages, people in the Latin West lived amid reminders of the achievements of the Romans. They wrote and worshiped in a version of their language, traveled their roads, and obeyed some of their laws. The vestments and robes of popes, kings, and emperors followed the designs of Roman officials. Yet the learning of Greco-Roman antiquity virtually disappeared with the rise of the biblical world described in the Hebrew and Christian scriptures.

A small revival of learning associated with the court of Charlemagne in the ninth century was followed by a larger renaissance (rebirth) in the twelfth century. Cities became centers of intellectual and artistic life. The universities established across the Latin West after 1200 contributed to this cultural revival. In the mid-fourteenth century, the pace of intellectual and artistic life quickened in what is often called the **Renaissance,** which began in northern Italy and later spread to northern Europe. Some Italian authors saw the Italian Renaissance as a sharp break with an age of darkness. Others see this era as the high noon of a day that had been dawning for several centuries.

파운드폭탄 4발 투하··· 두 아들과 함께 사망

실진지 구축··· 이틀째 시가戰

령이 대중 앞에 나타나거나 애국심
을 고취하는 노래만을 내보내던 방
송마저 중단됐다.

라크 전후
의에서는
영국 주5

DIVERSITY AND DOMINANCE

PERSECUTION AND PROTECTION OF JEWS, 1272–1349

Because they did not belong to the dominant Latin Christian faith, Jews suffered from periodic discrimination and persecution. For the most part, religious and secular authorities tried to curb such anti-Semitism. Jews, after all, were useful citizens who worshipped the same God as their Christian neighbors. Still it was hard to know where to draw the line between justifiable and unjustifiable discrimination. The famous reviser of Catholic theology, St. Thomas Aquinas, made one such distinction in his Summa Theologica *with regard to attempts at forced conversion.*

Now, the practice of the Church never held that the children of Jews should be baptized against the will of their parents. . . . Therefore, it seems dangerous to bring forward this new view, that contrary to the previously established custom of the Church, the children of Jews should be baptized against the will of their parents.

There are two reasons for this position. One stems from danger to faith. For, if children without the use of reason were to receive baptism, then after reaching maturity they could easily be persuaded by their parents to relinquish what they had received in ignorance. This would tend to do harm to the faith.

The second reason is that it is opposed to natural justice . . . it [is] a matter of natural right that a son, before he has the use of reason, is under the care of his father. Hence, it would be against natural justice for the boy, before he has the use of reason, to be removed from the care of his parents, or for anything to be arranged for him against the will of his parents.

The "new view" Aquinas opposed was much in the air, for in 1272 Pope Gregory X issued a decree condemning forced baptism. The pope's decree reviews the history of papal protection given to the Jews, starting with a quotation from Pope Gregory I dating from 598, and decrees two new protections of Jews' legal rights.

Even as it is not allowed to the Jews in their assemblies presumptuously to undertake for themselves more than that which is permitted them by law, even so they ought not to suffer any disadvantage in those [privileges] which have been granted them.

Although they prefer to persist in their stubbornness rather than to recognize the words of their prophets and the mysteries of the Scriptures, and thus to arrive at a knowledge of Christian faith and salvation; nevertheless, inasmuch as they have made an appeal for our protection and help, we therefore admit their petition and offer them the shield of our protection through the clemency of Christian piety. In so doing we follow in the footsteps of our predecessors of happy memory, the popes of Rome—Calixtus, Eugene, Alexander, Clement, Celestine, Innocent, and Honorius.

We decree moreover that no Christian shall compel them or any one of their group to come to baptism unwillingly. But if any one of them shall take refuge of his own accord with Christians, because of conviction, then, after his intention will have been made manifest, he shall be made a Christian without any intrigue. For indeed that person who is known to come to Christian baptism not freely, but unwillingly, is not believed to possess the Christian faith.

Moreover, no Christian shall presume to seize, imprison, wound, torture, mutilate, kill, or inflict violence on them; furthermore no one shall presume, except by judicial action of the authorities of the country, to change the good customs in the land where they live for the purpose of taking their money or goods from them or from others.

In addition, no one shall disturb them in any way during the celebration of their festivals, whether by day or by night, with clubs or stones or anything else. Also no one shall exact any compulsory service of them unless it be that which they have been accustomed to render in previous times.

Inasmuch as the Jews are not able to bear witness against the Christians, we decree furthermore that the testimony of Christians against Jews shall not be valid unless there is among these Christians some Jew who is there for the purpose of offering testimony.

Since it occasionally happens that some Christians lose their Christian children, the Jews are accused by their enemies of secretly carrying off and killing these same Christian children, and of making sacrifices of the heart and blood of these very children. It happens, too, that the parents of these children, or some other Christian enemies of these Jews, secretly hide these very children in order that they may be able to injure these Jews, and in order that they may be able to extort from them a certain amount of money by redeeming them from their straits.

And most falsely do these Christians claim that the Jews have secretly and furtively carried away these children and killed them, and that the Jews offer sacrifice from the heart and the blood of these children, since their law in this matter precisely and expressly forbids Jews to sacrifice, eat, or drink the blood, or eat the flesh of animals having claws. This has been demonstrated many times at our court by Jews converted to the Christian faith: nevertheless very many Jews are often seized and detained unjustly because of this.

We decree, therefore, that Christians need not be obeyed against Jews in such a case or situation of this type, and we order that Jews seized under such a silly pretext be freed from imprisonment, and that they shall not be arrested henceforth on such a miserable pretext, unless—which we do not believe—they be caught in the commission of the crime. We decree that no Christian shall stir up anything against them, but that they should be maintained in that status and position in which they were from the time of our predecessors, from antiquity till now.

We decree, in order to stop the wickedness and avarice of bad men, that no one shall dare to devastate or to destroy a cemetery of the Jews or to dig up human bodies for the sake of getting money [by holding them for ransom]. Moreover, if anyone, after having known the content of this decree, should—which we hope will not happen—attempt audaciously to act contrary to it, then let him suffer punishment in his rank and position, or let him be punished by the penalty of excommunication, unless he makes amends for his boldness by proper recompense. Moreover, we wish that only those Jews who have not attempted to contrive anything toward the destruction of the Christian faith be fortified by the support of such protection. . . .

Despite such decrees violence against Jews might burst out when fears and emotions were running high. This selection is from the official chronicles of the upper-Rhineland towns.

In the year 1349 there occurred the greatest epidemic that ever happened. Death went from one end of the earth to the other, on that side and this side of the [Mediterranean] sea, and it was greater among the Saracens [Muslims] than among the Christians. In some lands everyone died so that no one was left. Ships were also found on the sea laden with wares; the crew had all died and no one guided the ship. The Bishop of Marseilles and priests and monks and more than half of all the people there died with them. In other kingdoms and cities so many people perished that it would be horrible to describe. The pope at Avignon stopped all sessions of court, locked himself in a room, allowed no one to approach him and had a fire burning before him all the time. And from what this epidemic came, all wise teachers and physicians could only say that it was the God's will. And the plague was now here, so it was in other places, and lasted more than a whole year. This epidemic also came to Strasbourg in the summer of the above mentioned year, and it is estimated about sixteen thousand people died.

In the matter of this plague the Jews throughout the world were reviled and accused in all lands of having caused it through the poison which they are said to have put into the water and the wells—that is what they were accused of—and for this reason the Jews were burnt all the way from the Mediterranean into Germany, but not in Avignon, for the pope protected them there.

Nevertheless they tortured a number of Jews in Berne and Zofingen who admitted they had put poison into many wells, and they found the poison in the wells. Thereupon they burnt the Jews in many towns and wrote of this affair to Strasbourg, Freibourg, and Basel in order that they too should burn their Jews. . . . The deputies of the city of Strasbourg were asked what they were going to do with their Jews. They answered and said that they knew no evil of them. Then . . . there was a great indignation and clamor against the deputies from Strasbourg. So finally the Bishop and the lords and the Imperial Cities agreed to do away with the Jews. The result was that they were burnt in many cities, and wherever they were expelled they were caught by the peasants and stabbed to death or drowned. . . .

On Saturday—that was St. Valentine's Day—they burnt the Jews on a wooden platform in their cemetery. There were about two thousand people of them. Those who wanted to baptize themselves were spared. Many small children were taken out of the fire and baptized against the will of their fathers and mothers. And everything that was owed to the Jews was cancelled, and the Jews had to surrender all pledges and notes that they had taken for debts. The council, however, took the cash that the Jews possessed and divided it among the working-men proportionately. The money was indeed the thing that killed the Jews. If they had been poor and if the feudal lords had not been in debt to them, they would not have been burnt.

QUESTIONS FOR ANALYSIS

1. Why do Aquinas and Pope Gregory oppose prejudicial actions against Jews?

2. Why did prejudice increase at the time of the Black Death?

3. What factors account for the differences between the views of Christian leaders and the Christian masses?

Source: First selection reprinted with permission of Pocket Books, an imprint of Simon & Schuster Adult Publishing Group, from *The Pocket Aquinas,* edited with translations by Vernon J. Bourke. Copyright © 1960 by Washington Square Press. Copyright renewed © 1988 by Simon & Schuster Adult Publishing Group. Second and third selections from Jacob R. Marcus, ed., *The Jew in the Medieval World: A Source Book, 315–1791* (Cincinnati: Union of American Hebrew Congregations, 1938), 152–154, 45–47. Reprinted with permission of the Hebrew Union College Press, Cincinnati.

Universities and Scholarship

Before 1100, Byzantine and Islamic scholarship generally surpassed scholarship in Latin Europe. When Latin Christians wrested southern Italy from the Byzantines and Sicily and Toledo from the Muslims in the eleventh century, they acquired many manuscripts of Greek and Arabic works. These included works by Plato and Aristotle° and Greek treatises on medicine, mathematics, and geography, as well as scientific and philosophical writings by Muslim writers. Latin translations of the Iranian philosopher Ibn Sina° (980–1037), known in the West as Avicenna°, had great influence because of their sophisticated blend of Aristotelian and Islamic philosophy. Jewish scholars contributed significantly to the translation and explication of Arabic and other manuscripts.

The thirteenth century saw the foundation of two new religious orders, the Dominicans and the Franciscans, some of whose most talented members taught in the independent colleges that arose after 1200. Some scholars believe that the colleges established in Paris and Oxford patterned themselves on similarly endowed places of study then spreading in the Islamic world—*madrasas,* which provided subsidized housing for poor students and paid the salaries of their teachers. The Latin West, however, innovated the idea of **universities,** degree-granting corporations specializing in multidisciplinary research and advanced teaching.

Between 1300 and 1500, sixty universities joined the twenty established before that time. Students banded together to start some of them; guilds of professors founded others. Teaching guilds, like the guilds overseeing manufacturing and commerce, set standards for the profession, trained apprentices and masters, and defended their professional interests.

Universities set the curriculum for each discipline and instituted final examinations for degrees. Students who passed the exams that ended their apprenticeship received a "license" to teach. Students who completed longer training and defended a masterwork of scholarship became "masters" and "doctors." The University of Paris gradually absorbed the city's various colleges, but the colleges of Oxford and Cambridge remained independent, self-governing organizations.

Since all universities used Latin, students and masters could move freely across political and linguistic lines, seeking the courses they wanted and

Aristotle (AR-ih-stah-tahl) Ibn Sina (IB-uhn SEE-nah)
Avicenna (av-uh-SEN-uh)

the most interesting professors. Some universities offered specialized training. Legal training centered on Bologna°; Montpellier and Salerno focused on medicine; Paris and Oxford excelled in theology.

The prominence of theology stemmed from many students aspiring to ecclesiastical careers, but scholars also saw theology as "queen of the sciences"—the central discipline encompassing all knowledge. Hence, thirteenth-century theologians sought to synthesize the rediscovered philosophical works of Aristotle and the commentaries of Avicenna with the Bible's revealed truth. These efforts to synthesize reason and faith were known as **scholasticism°**.

Thomas Aquinas, a brilliant Dominican priest who taught theology at the University of Paris, wrote the most notable scholastic work, the *Summa Theologica°*, between 1267 and 1273. Although his exposition of Christian belief organized on Aristotelian principles came to be accepted as a masterly demonstration of the reasonableness of Christianity, scholasticism upset many traditional thinkers. Some church authorities tried to ban Aristotle from the curriculum. In addition, rivalry between the leading Dominican and Franciscan theological scholars continued over the next two centuries. However, the considerable freedom of medieval universities from both secular and religious authorities enabled the new ideas to prevail over the fears of church administrators.

Humanists and Printers

Dante Alighieri° (1265–1321) completed a long, elegant poem, the *Divine Comedy*, shortly before his death. This supreme expression of medieval preoccupations tells the allegorical story of Dante's journey through the nine circles of Hell and the seven terraces of Purgatory, followed by his entry into Paradise. The Roman poet Virgil guides him through Hell and Purgatory; Beatrice, a woman he had loved from afar since childhood and whose death inspired the poem, guides him to Paradise.

The *Divine Comedy* foreshadows the literary fashions of the later Italian Renaissance. Like Dante, later Italian writers made use of Greco-Roman classical themes and mythology and sometimes courted a broader audience by writing not in Latin but in their local language (Dante used the vernacular spoken in Tuscany°).

The poet Geoffrey Chaucer, many of whose works show the influence of Dante, wrote in vernacular English. The *Canterbury Tales*, a lengthy poem written in the last dozen years of his life, contains often humorous and earthy tales told by fictional pilgrims on their way to the shrine of Thomas à Becket in Canterbury (see Chapter 8). They present a vivid cross-section of medieval people and attitudes.

Dante influenced a literary movement of the **humanists** that began in his native Florence in the mid-fourteenth century. The term refers to their interest in grammar, rhetoric, poetry, history, and moral philosophy (ethics)—subjects known collectively as the humanities, an ancient discipline. With the brash exaggeration characteristic of new intellectual fashions, humanist writers like the poet Francesco Petrarch° (1304–1374) and the poet and storyteller Giovanni Boccaccio° (1313–1375) proclaimed a revival of the classical Greco-Roman tradition they felt had for centuries lain buried under the rubble of the Middle Ages.

This idea of a rebirth of learning dismisses too readily the monastic and university scholars who for centuries had been recovering all sorts of Greco-Roman learning, as well as writers like Dante (whom the humanists revered), who anticipated humanist interests by a generation. Yet the humanists had a great impact as educators, advisers, and reformers. Their greatest influence came in reforming secondary education. They introduced a curriculum centered on the languages and literature of Greco-Roman antiquity, which they felt provided intellectual discipline, moral lessons, and refined tastes. This curriculum dominated European secondary schools well into the twentieth century. The universities felt the humanist influence less, mostly after 1500. Theology, law, medicine, and branches of philosophy other than ethics remained prominent in university education during this period.

Bologna (buh-LOHN-yuh)   **scholasticism** (skoh-LAS-tih-sizm)   *Summa Theologica* (SOOM-uh thee-uh-LOH-jih-kuh)   **Dante Alighieri** (DAHN-tay ah-lee-GYEH-ree)

Tuscany (TUS-kuh-nee)   **Francesco Petrarch** (fran-CHES-koh PAY-trahrk)   **Giovanni Boccaccio** (jo-VAH-nee boh-KAH-chee-oh)

Many humanists tried to duplicate the elegance of classical Latin and (to a lesser extent) Greek, which they revered as the pinnacle of learning, beauty, and wisdom. Boccaccio gained fame with his vernacular writings, which resemble Dante's, and especially for the *Decameron,* an earthy work that has much in common with Chaucer's boisterous tales. Under Petrarch's influence, however, Boccaccio turned to writing in classical Latin.

As humanist scholars mastered Latin and Greek, they turned their language skills to restoring the original texts of Greco-Roman writers and of the Bible. By comparing different manuscripts, they eliminated errors introduced by generations of copyists. To aid in this task, Pope Nicholas V (r. 1447–1455) created the Vatican Library, buying scrolls of Greco-Roman writings and paying to have accurate copies and translations made. Working independently, the Dutch scholar Erasmus° of Rotterdam (ca. 1466–1536) produced a critical edition of the New Testament in Greek. Erasmus corrected many errors and mistranslations in the Latin text that had been in general use throughout the Middle Ages. Later, this humanist priest and theologian wrote—in classical Latin—influential moral guides, including the *Enchiridion militis christiani* (*The Manual of the Christian Knight,* 1503) and *The Education of a Christian Prince* (1515).

The influence of the humanists grew as the new technology of printing made their critical editions of ancient texts, literary works, and moral guides more available. The Chinese and the Arabs used carved wood blocks for printing, and block-printed playing cards circulated in Europe before 1450, but after that date three European improvements revolutionized printing: (1) movable pieces of type consisting of individual letters, (2) new ink suitable for printing on paper, and (3) the **printing press,** a mechanical device that pressed inked type onto sheets of paper.

Johann Gutenberg° (ca. 1394–1468) of Mainz led the way. The Gutenberg Bible of 1454, the first book in the West printed from movable type, exhibited a beauty and craftsmanship that bore witness to the printer's years of experimentation. Humanists worked closely with the printers, who spread the new techniques to Italy and France. Erasmus did editing and proofreading for the Italian scholar-printer Aldo Manuzio (1449–1515) in Venice. Manuzio's press published many critical editions of classical Latin and Greek texts.

By 1500, at least 10 million printed volumes flowed from presses in 238 European towns, launching a revolution that affected students, scholars, and a growing literate population. These readers consumed unorthodox political and religious tracts along with ancient texts.

Renaissance Artists

Although the artists of the fourteenth and fifteenth centuries continued to depict biblical subjects, the Greco-Roman revival led some, especially in Italy, to portray ancient deities and myths. Another popular trend involved scenes of daily life.

Neither theme was entirely new, however. Renaissance art, like Renaissance scholarship, owed a debt to earlier generations. Italian painters of the fifteenth century credited the Florentine painter Giotto° (ca. 1267–1337) with single-handedly reviving the "lost art of painting." In religious scenes, Giotto replaced the stiff, staring figures of the Byzantine style, which were intended to overawe viewers, with more natural and human portraits with whose emotions of grief and love viewers could identify. Rather than floating on backgrounds of gold leaf, his saints inhabit earthly landscapes.

North of the Alps, the Flemish painter Jan van Eyck° (ca. 1390–1441) mixed his pigments with linseed oil in place of the egg yolk of earlier centuries. Oil paints dried more slowly and gave pictures a superior luster. Italian painters quickly copied van Eyck's technique, though his own masterfully realistic paintings on religious and domestic themes remained distinctive.

Leonardo da Vinci° (1452–1519) used oil paints for his *Mona Lisa.* Renaissance artists like Leonardo worked in many media, including bronze sculptures and frescos (painting on wet plaster) like *The Last Supper.* His notebooks contain imaginative designs for airplanes, submarines, and tanks. Leonardo's

---

Erasmus (uh-RAZ-muhs) **Johann Gutenberg** (yoh-HAHN GOO-ten-burg)

Giotto (JAW-toh) **Jan van Eyck** (yahn vahn-IKE)
Leonardo da Vinci (lay-own-AHR-doh dah-VIN-chee)

A French Printshop, 1537   A workman operates the "press," quite literally a screw device that presses the paper to the inked type. Other employees examine the printed sheets, each of which holds four pages. When folded, the sheets make a book.   (Giraudon/Art Resource, NY)

younger contemporary Michelangelo° (1472–1564) painted frescoes of biblical scenes on the ceiling of the Sistine Chapel in the Vatican, sculpted statues of David and Moses, and designed the dome for a new Saint Peter's Basilica in Rome.

The patronage of wealthy and educated merchants and prelates underlay the artistic blossoming in the cities of northern Italy and Flanders. The Florentine banker Cosimo de' Medici (1389–1464) and his grandson Lorenzo (1449–1492), known as "the Magnificent," spent immense sums on paintings, sculpture, and public buildings. In Rome, the papacy° launched a building program that culminated in the construction of the new Saint Peter's Basilica and a residence for the pope.

These scholarly and artistic achievements exemplify the innovation and striving for excellence

Michelangelo (my-kuhl-AN-juh-low)   papacy (PAY-puh-see)

of the Late Middle Ages. The new literary themes and artistic styles of this period had lasting influence on Western culture. But the innovations in the organization of universities, in printing, and in oil painting had wider implications, for they were later adopted by cultures all over the world.

POLITICAL AND MILITARY TRANSFORMATIONS

Stronger and more unified states and armies developed in western Europe in parallel with the economic and cultural revivals (see Map 13.1). Through the prolonged struggle of the Hundred Years War, French and English monarchs forged closer ties with the nobility, the church, and the merchants. Crusades against Muslim states brought consolidation to Spain and Portugal. In Italy and Germany, however, political power remained in the hands of small states and loose alliances.

Monarchs, Nobles, and the Church

Thirteenth-century states continued early medieval state structures (see Chapter 8). Hereditary monarchs topped the political pyramid, but modest treasuries and the rights of nobles and the church limited their powers. Powerful noblemen who controlled vast estates had an important voice in matters of state. The church guarded closely its traditional rights and independence. Towns, too, had acquired rights and privileges. Towns in Flanders, the Hanseatic League, and Italy approached independence from royal interference.

In theory the ruler's noble vassals owed military service in time of war. In practice, vassals sought to limit the monarch's power.

In the year 1200, knights still formed the backbone of western European armies, but changes in weaponry brought this into question. Improved crossbows could shoot metal-tipped arrows with enough force to pierce helmets and light body armor. Professional crossbowmen, hired for wages, became increasingly common and much feared. Indeed, a church council in 1139 outlawed the crossbow—ineffectively—as being too deadly for

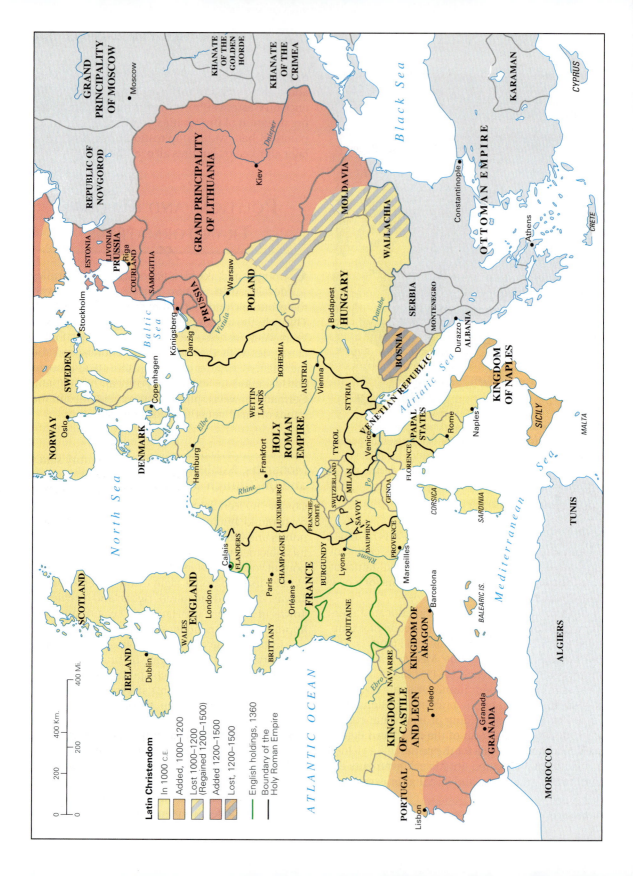

GRAND
PRINCIPALITY
OF MOSCOW

• Moscow

KHANATE
OF THE
GOLDEN
HORDE

KHANATE
OF THE
CRIMEA

KARAMAN

CYPRUS

REPUBLIC OF NOVGOROD

Black Sea

GRAND PRINCIPALITY
OF LITHUANIA

Dnieper

Kiev •

MOLDAVIA

OTTOMAN EMPIRE

ESTONIA

LIVONIA
Riga •
PRUSSIA
COURLAND
SAMOGITIA

Stockholm •

*Baltic
Sea*

Königsberg •
Danzig •

WALLACHIA

Constantinople •

Athens •

CRETE

SWEDEN

Warsaw •

POLAND

SERBIA

MONTENEGRO

Budapest •

HUNGARY

Danube

BOSNIA

Ob

KINGDOM
OF NAPLES

NORWAY
Oslo •

DENMARK
Copenhagen •

BOHEMIA

WETTIN
LANDS

AUSTRIA
Vienna •

STYRIA

ALBANIA
Durazzo •

VENETIAN REPUBLIC

Adriatic Sea

Rome •

SICILY

MALTA

Hamburg •

Frankfort •

HOLY
ROMAN
EMPIRE

Elbe

TYROL

SWITZERLAND

MILAN

A L P S

Venice •

PAPAL
STATES

FLORENCE

Naples •

North Sea

Rhine

LUXEMBURG

FRANCHE-
COMTÉ

SAVOY

GENOA

CORSICA

SARDINIA

Po

DAUPHINY

*Mediterranean
Sea*

TUNIS

Calais •
FLANDERS

Paris •

CHAMPAGNE

BURGUNDY

Lyons •

Rhône

PROVENCE

Marseilles •

SCOTLAND

WALES

ENGLAND
London •

BRITTANY

FRANCE

Orleans •

AQUITAINE

Barcelona •

BALEARIC IS.

ALGIERS

IRELAND
Dublin •

NAVARRE

KINGDOM OF
ARAGON

ATLANTIC OCEAN

Ebro

KINGDOM
OF CASTILE
AND LEON

Toledo •

Granada •
GRANADA

MOROCCO

PORTUGAL
Lisbon •

Latin Christendom

In 1000 c.e.

Added, 1000–1200

Lost 1000–1200
(Regained 1200–1500)

Added 1200–1500

Lost, 1200–1500

English holdings, 1360

Boundary of the
Holy Roman Empire

400 Mi.

400 Km.

200

200

0

0

Map 13.1   Europe in 1453   This year marked the end of the Hundred Years War between France and England and the fall of the Byzantine capital city of Constantinople to the Ottoman Turks. Muslim advances into southeastern Europe were offset by the Latin Christian reconquests of Islamic holdings in southern Italy and the Iberian Peninsula and by the conversion of Lithuania.

use against Christians. The arrival in Europe of firearms based on the Chinese invention of gunpowder (see Chapter 11) further transformed the medieval army.

The church also resisted royal control. In 1302, the outraged Pope Boniface VIII (r. 1294–1303) asserted that divine law made the papacy superior to "every human creature," including monarchs. Issuing his own claim of superiority, King Philip "the Fair" of France (r. 1285–1314) sent an army to arrest the pope, a chastisement that hastened Pope Boniface's death. Philip then engineered the election of a French pope, who established a new papal residence at Avignon° in southern France in 1309.

A succession of French-dominated popes residing in Avignon improved church discipline but at the price of compromising their neutrality in the eyes of other rulers. The **Great Western Schism** between 1378 and 1415 saw rival papal claimants at Avignon and Rome vying for Christian loyalties. The papacy eventually regained its independence and returned to Rome, but the long crisis broke the pope's ability to challenge the rising power of monarchs like Philip, who had used the dispute to persuade his nobles to grant him a new tax.

The English monarchy wielded more centralized power as a result of consolidation that took place after the Norman conquest of 1066. The Anglo-Norman kings also extended their realm by assaults on their Celtic neighbors. Between 1200 and 1400, they incorporated Wales and reasserted control over most of Ireland. Nevertheless, under King John (r. 1199–1216), royal power suffered a severe setback. Forced to acknowledge the pope as his overlord in 1213, he lost his bid to reassert claims to Aquitaine in southern France the following year and then yielded to his nobles by signing the Magna Carta in 1215. This "Great Charter" affirmed that monarchs were

Avignon (ah-vee-NYON)

subject to established law, confirmed the independence of the church and the city of London, and guaranteed the nobles' hereditary rights.

The Hundred Years War

The conflict between the king of France and his vassals known as the **Hundred Years War** (1337–1453) affords a key example of the transformation in politics and war. These vassals included the kings of England (for lands that belonged to their Norman ancestors), the counts of prosperous and independent-minded Flanders, and the dukes of Brittany and Burgundy. In typical fashion, the conflict grew out of a marriage alliance.

Marriage between Princess Isabella of France and King Edward II of England (r. 1307–1327) should have ensured the king's loyalty, as a vassal, to the French monarchy. However, when the next generation of the French ruling house produced no other sons, Isabella's son, King Edward III of England (r. 1327–1377), laid claim to the French throne in 1337. French courts instead awarded the throne to a more distant (and more French) cousin. Edward decided to fight for his rights.

The new military technology shaped the conflict. Early in the war, hired Italian crossbowmen reinforced the French cavalry, but the English longbow proved superior. Adopted from the Welsh, the 6-foot (1.8-meter) longbow could shoot farther and more rapidly than the crossbow. Its arrows could not pierce armor, but concentrated volleys found gaps in the knights' defenses or struck their less-protected horses. Heavier and more encompassing armor provided a defense but limited a knight's movements. Once pulled off his steed by a foot soldier armed with a pike (hooked pole), he could not get up.

Later in the Hundred Years War, firearms gained prominence. The first cannons scared the horses with smoke and noise but did little damage. As they grew larger, however, they proved effective in battering the walls of castles and towns. The first artillery use against the French, at the Battle of Agincourt (1415), gave the English an important victory.

Faced with a young French peasant woman called Joan of Arc, subsequent English gains stalled. Acting, she believed, on God's instructions, she put on armor and rallied the French troops to defeat the English in 1429. Shortly afterward, she fell into

English hands; she was tried by English churchmen and burned at the stake as a witch in 1431.

In the final battles, French cannon demolished the walls of once-secure castles held by the English and their allies. The truce that ended the struggle in 1453 left the French monarchy in firm control.

New Monarchies in France and England

The war proved a watershed in the rise of **new monarchies** in France and England, centralized states with fixed "national" boundaries and stronger representative institutions. English monarchs after 1453 consolidated control over territory within the British Isles, though the Scots defended their independence. The French monarchs also turned to consolidating control over powerful noble families, especially those headed by women. Mary of Burgundy (1457–1482) was forced to surrender most of her family's vast holdings to the king. Then in 1491, Anne of Brittany's forced marriage to the king led to the eventual incorporation of her duchy° into France.

Military technology undermined the nobility. Smaller, more mobile cannon developed in the late fifteenth century pounded castle walls. Improvements in hand-held firearms, able by the late fifteenth century to pierce the heaviest armor, ended the domination of the armored knight. Armies now depended less on knights and more on bowmen, pikemen, musketeers, and artillerymen.

The new monarchies needed a way to finance their full-time armies. Some nobles agreed to money payments in place of military service and to additional taxes in time of war. For example, in 1439 and 1445, Charles VII of France (r. 1422–1461) successfully levied a new tax on his vassals' land. This not only paid the costs of the war with England but also provided the monarchy a financial base for the next 350 years.

Merchants' taxes also provided revenues. Taxes on the English wool trade, begun by King Edward III, paid most of the costs of the Hundred Years War. Some rulers taxed Jewish merchants or extorted large contributions from wealthy towns. Individual merchants sometimes curried royal favor with loans.

The fifteenth-century French merchant Jacques Coeur° gained many social and financial benefits for himself and his family by lending money to French courtiers, but his debtors accused him of murder and had his fortune confiscated.

The church provided a third source of revenue through voluntary contributions to support a war. English and French monarchs won the right to appoint important church officials in their realms in the fifteenth century. They subsequently used state power to enforce religious orthodoxy more vigorously than the popes had been able to do. But reformers complained that the church's spiritual mission became subordinate to political and economic concerns.

The shift in power to the monarchs and away from the nobility and the church did not deprive nobles of their social position and roles as government officials and military officers. Moreover, the kings of England and France in 1500 had to deal with representative institutions that had not existed in 1200. The English Parliament proved a permanent check on royal power: the House of Lords contained the great nobles and church officials; the House of Commons represented the towns and the leading citizens of the counties. In France, the Estates General, a similar but less effective representative body, represented the church, the nobles, and the towns.

Iberian Unification

Spain and Portugal's **reconquest of Iberia** from Muslim rule expanded the boundaries of Latin Christianity. The knights who pushed the borders of their kingdoms southward furthered both Christianity and their own interests. The spoils of victory included irrigated farmland, rich cities, and ports on the Mediterranean Sea and Atlantic Ocean. Serving God, growing rich, and living off the labor of others became a way of life for the Iberian nobility.

The reconquest proceeded over several centuries. Toledo fell and became a Christian outpost in 1085. English crusaders bound for the Holy Land helped take Lisbon in 1147. It displaced the older city of Oporto (meaning "the port"), from which Portugal took its name, as both capital and the kingdom's

---

duchy (DUTCH-ee)

Coeur (cur)

leading city. A Christian victory in 1212 broke the back of Muslim power; the reconquest accelerated. Within decades, Portuguese and Castilian forces captured the prosperous cities of Cordova (1236) and Seville (1248) and drove the Muslims from the southwestern region known as Algarve° ("the west" in Arabic). Only the small kingdom of Granada hugging the Mediterranean coast remained in Muslim hands.

By incorporating Algarve in 1249, Portugal attained its modern territorial limits. After a pause to colonize, Christianize, and consolidate this land, Portugal took the crusade to North Africa. In 1415, Portuguese knights seized the port of Ceuta° in Morocco, where they learned more about the Saharan caravan trade in gold and slaves (see Chapter 14). During the next few decades, Portuguese mariners sailed down the Atlantic coast of Africa seeking rumored African Christian allies and access to this trade (see Chapter 14).

Elsewhere in Iberia, the reconquest continued. Spain came into being when the marriage of Princess Isabella of Castile and Prince Ferdinand of Aragon in 1469 led to the union of their kingdoms when they inherited their respective thrones a decade later. Their conquest of Granada in 1492 secured the final piece of Muslim territory for the new kingdom.

Ferdinand and Isabella sponsored the first voyage of Christopher Columbus in 1492 (see Chapter 14). In a third momentous event of that year, the monarchs manifested their crusading mentality by ordering all Jews expelled from their kingdoms. Attempts to convert or expel the remaining Muslims led to a revolt at the end of 1499 that lasted until 1501. The Spanish rulers expelled the last Muslims in 1502. Portugal expelled the Jews in 1496, including 100,000 refugees from Spain.

CONCLUSION

Ecologically, the peoples of Latin Europe harnessed the power of wind and water and mined and refined their mineral wealth at the cost of localized pollution and deforestation. However, inability to improve food production and distribution in response to population growth created a demographic crisis that climaxed with the Black Death that devastated Europe in the mid-fourteenth century.

Politically, basic features of the modern European state began to emerge. Frequent wars caused kingdoms of moderate size to develop exceptional military strength. The ruling class saw economic strength as the twin of political power and promoted the welfare of cities specializing in trade, manufacturing, and finance, the profits of which they taxed.

Culturally, autonomous universities and printing supported the advance of knowledge. Art and architecture reached unsurpassed peaks in the Renaissance. Late medieval society displayed a fundamental fascination with tools and techniques. New inventions and improved versions of old ones underlay the new dynamism in commerce, warfare, industry, and navigation.

Ironically, many of the tools that the Latin West would use to challenge Eastern supremacy—printing, firearms, and navigational devices—originally came from the East. However, western European success depended as much on strong motives for expansion. From the eleventh century onward, population pressure, religious zeal, economic enterprise, and intellectual curiosity drove an expansion of territory and resources that took the crusaders to the Holy Land, merchants to the eastern Mediterranean and Black Seas, the English into Wales and Ireland, German settlers across the Elbe River, and Iberian Christians into the Muslim south. The early voyages into the Atlantic, discussed in the next chapter, extended these activities.

■ Key Terms

Latin West	universities
three-field system	scholasticism
Black Death	humanists (Renaissance)
water wheel	printing press
Hanseatic League	Great Western Schism
guilds	Hundred Years War
Gothic cathedrals	new monarchies
Renaissance (European)	reconquest of Iberia

■ Suggested Reading

Robert Fossier, ed., *The Cambridge Illustrated History of the Middle Ages,* vol. 3, *1250–1520* (1986), provides a fine

---

Algarve (ahl-GAHRV)   **Ceuta** (say-OO-tuh)

guide to the Latin West. Denys Hay, *Europe in the Fourteenth and Fifteenth Centuries,* 2d ed. (1989), is comprehensive and up-to-date. For economic matters, see Robert S. Lopez, *The Commercial Revolution of the Middle Ages, 950–1350* (1976), and Harry A. Miskimin, *The Economy of Early Renaissance Europe, 1300–1460* (1975).

James Bruce Ross and Mary Martin McLaughlin, eds., *The Portable Medieval Reader* (1977) and *The Portable Renaissance Reader* (1977), provide excerpts from primary sources. *The Notebooks of Leonardo da Vinci,* edited by Pamela Taylor (1960), show this versatile genius at work.

For technological change, see Arnold Pacey, *The Maze of Ingenuity: Ideas and Idealism in the Development of Technology* (1974); Jean Gimpel, *The Medieval Machine: The Industrial Revolution of the Middle Ages* (1977); and William H. McNeill, *The Pursuit of Power: Technology, Armed Force, and Society Since A.D. 1000* (1982). On the environment, see Roland Bechmann, *Trees and Man: The Forest in the Middle Ages* (1990).

Olef Pedersen, *The First Universities: Studium Generale and the Origins of University Education in Europe* (1998), and Johan Huizinga, *The Waning of the Middle Ages* (1924), discuss intellectual currents. For the Renaissance, see Lisa Jardine, *Worldly Goods: A New History of the Renaissance* (1996), and John R. Hale, *The Civilization of Europe in the Renaissance* (1995).

Georges Duby, *Rural Economy and Country Life in the Medieval West* (1990), covers social history in the earlier centuries. George Huppert, *After the Black Death: A Social History of Early Modern Europe* (1986), takes the analysis past 1500. Eileen Power, *Medieval People,* new ed. (1997), and Frances Gies and Joseph Gies, *Women in the Middle Ages* (1978), highlight individual lives. Mary Erler and Maryanne Kowaleski, eds., *Women and Power in the Middle Ages* (1988), contains more systematic essays. Vita Sackville-West, *Saint Joan of Arc* (1926; reprint, 1991), introduces this extraordinary person.

Christopher Alland, *The Hundred Years War: England and France at War, ca. 1300–ca. 1450* (1988), covers key events. Joseph F. O'Callaghan, *A History of Medieval Spain* (1975), provides good one-volume coverage. Jocelyn N. Hillgarth, *The Spanish Kingdoms,* 2 vols. (1976, 1978), offers more detail. For a popular account, see Barbara W. Tuchman, *A Distant Mirror: The Calamitous Fourteenth Century* (1978). Norman Cantor, *In the Wake of the Plague: The Black Death and the World It Made* (2001), supplies a thorough introduction.

On the Latin West's expansion, see Robert Bartlett, *The Making of Europe: Conquest, Colonization, and Cultural Change* (1993); J. R. S. Phillips, *The Medieval Expansion of Europe,* new ed. (1998); and P. E. Russell, *Portugal, Spain and the African Atlantic, 1343–1492* (1998).

Francis C. Oakley, *The Western Church in the Later Middle Ages* (1985), summarizes modern scholarship. Kenneth R. Stow, *Alienated Minority: The Jews of Medieval Latin Europe* (1992), provides a survey through the fourteenth century. On the Latin West's external ties, see Khalil I. Semaan, ed., *Islam and the Medieval West: Aspects of Intercultural Relations* (1980).

■ Notes

1. Quoted in Marina Warner, *Alone of All Her Sex: The Myth and Cult of the Virgin Mary* (New York: Random House, 1983), 179.
2. Harry Miskimin, *The Economy of the Early Renaissance, 1300–1460* (Englewood Cliffs, NJ: Prentice Hall, 1969), 26–27.
3. Quotations here and later in the chapter are from Geoffrey Chaucer, *The Canterbury Tales,* trans. Nevill Coghill (New York: Penguin Books, 1952), 25, 29, 32.

The Maritime Revolution, to 1550

CHAPTER OUTLINE
Global Maritime Expansion Before 1450
Iberian Expansion, 1400–1550
Encounters with Europe, 1450–1550
DIVERSITY AND DOMINANCE: Kongo's Christian King

In 1511, the young Ferdinand Magellan sailed from Europe around the southern tip of Africa and eastward across the Indian Ocean as a member of the first Portuguese expedition to explore the East Indies (maritime Southeast Asia). Eight years later, in the service of Spain, he headed an expedition that sought to reach the East Indies by sailing westward from Europe. By the middle of 1521, Magellan's expedition had sailed across the Atlantic, rounded the southern tip of South America, and crossed the Pacific Ocean—but at a high price.

One of the five ships wrecked on a reef; the captain of another deserted and sailed back to Spain. The passage across the Pacific took much longer than anticipated. Dozens of sailors died of starvation and disease. In the Philippines, Magellan himself was killed on April 27, 1521, while aiding a local king who had prom-

ised to become a Christian. Magellan's successor met the same fate a few days later.

The expedition's survivors consolidated their resources by burning the least seaworthy of their remaining three ships and transferring the men and supplies to the smaller *Victoria,* which continued westward across the Indian Ocean, around Africa, and back to Europe. Magellan's flagship, the *Trinidad,* tried unsuccessfully to recross the Pacific to Central America. However, the *Victoria*'s return to Spain on September 8, 1522, confirmed Europe's ability and determination to master the oceans. The Portuguese crown had backed a century of daring and dangerous voyages to open routes to Africa, Brazil, and the Indian Ocean. Since 1492, Spain had opened contacts with the American continents. Now the broad Pacific Ocean had been crossed.

Before 1500, powerful states and the rich trading networks of Asia had led the way in overland and maritime expansion. The Iberians set out on their voyages of exploration to reach Eastern markets, and their success began a new era in which the West gradually became the world's center of power, wealth, and innovation.

As you read this chapter, ask yourself the following questions:

- Why did Portugal and Spain undertake voyages of exploration?

- Why do the voyages of Magellan and other Iberians mark a turning point in world history?

- What were the consequences for the different peoples of the world of the contacts resulting from these voyages?

GLOBAL MARITIME EXPANSION BEFORE 1450

By 1450, mariners had discovered and settled most of the islands of the Pacific, the Atlantic, and the Indian Oceans, and a great trading system united the peoples around the Indian Ocean. But we know of no individual crossing the Pacific in either direction. Even the narrower Atlantic formed a barrier that kept the peoples of the Americas, Europe, and Africa in ignorance of each other's existence. The inhabitants of Australia were also completely cut off from contact with the rest of humanity. All this was about to change.

The Pacific Ocean   The vast distances that Polynesian peoples voyaged out of sight of land across the Pacific Ocean are one of the most impressive feats in maritime history before 1450 (see Map 14.1). Though they left no written records, over several thousand years mariners from the Malay° Peninsula of Southeast Asia explored and settled the island

chains of the East Indies and continued on to New Guinea and the smaller islands of Melanesia°. Beginning sometime before the Common Era (C.E.), a wave of expansion from the area of Fiji brought the first humans to the islands of the central Pacific known as Polynesia. Their sailing canoes reached the easternmost Marquesas° Islands about 400 C.E.; Easter Island, 2,200 miles (3,540 kilometers) off the coast of South America, a century later; and the Hawaiian Islands by 500 C.E. Settlement in New Zealand began about 1200. Between 1100 and 1300, new voyages northward from Tahiti brought more Polynesian settlers to Hawaii.

Historians have puzzled over how the Polynesians reached the eastern Pacific islands without compasses to plot their way, particularly in view of the difficulties Magellan's flagship encountered sailing eastward across the Pacific. In 1947, explorer Thor Heyerdahl° argued that Easter Island and Hawaii were settled from the Americas and sought to prove his theory by sailing his balsawood raft *Kon Tiki* westward from Peru.

Although some Amerindian voyagers did use ocean currents to travel northward from Peru to Mexico between 300 and 900 C.E., there is now considerable evidence that planned expansion by Polynesian mariners accomplished the settlement of the islands of the eastern Pacific. The languages of the islanders relate closely to the languages of the western Pacific and ultimately to those of Malaya. In addition, accidental voyages could not have brought sufficient numbers of men and women for founding a new colony along with all the plants and domesticated animals common to other Polynesian islands.

In 1976, a Polynesian crew led by anthropologist Ben Finney used traditional navigational methods to sail the *Hokulea,* a 62-foot-long (19-meter-long) double canoe, from Hawaii south to Tahiti. Patterned after old oceangoing canoes, some of which measured 120 feet (35 meters) long, it used inverted triangular sails and was steered by paddles (not by a rudder). The *Hokulea*'s crew navigated using only their observation of the currents, stars, and evidence of land.

Melanesia (mel-uh-NEE-zhuh)   **Marquesas** (mar-KAY-suhs)   **Heyerdahl** (HIGH-uhr-dahl)

Malay (May-LAY)

C H R O N O L O G Y

	Pacific Ocean	Atlantic Ocean	Indian Ocean
Pre-1400	**400–1300** Polynesian settlement of Pacific Islands	**700–1200** Viking voyages **1300s** Settlement of Madeira, Azores, Canaries **Early 1300s** Mali voyages	
1400 to 1500		**1418–1460** Voyages of Henry the Navigator **1440s** Slaves from West Africa **1482** Portuguese at Gold Coast and Kongo **1486** Portuguese at Benin **1492** Columbus reaches Caribbean **1493** Columbus returns to Caribbean (second voyage) **1493–1502** Spanish conquer Hispaniola **1498** Columbus reaches mainland of South America (third voyage) **1500** Cabral reaches Brazil	**1405–1433** Voyages of Zheng He **1498** Vasco da Gama reaches India
1500 to 1550	**1519–1522** Magellan expedition	**1513** Ponce de Léon explores Florida **1519–1520** Cortés conquers Aztec Empire **1532–1533** Pizarro conquers Inca Empire	**1505** Portuguese bombard Swahili Coast cities **1510** Portuguese take Goa **1511** Portuguese take Malacca **1515** Portuguese take Hormuz **1535** Portuguese take Diu **1538** Portuguese defeat Ottoman fleet **1539** Portuguese aid Ethiopia

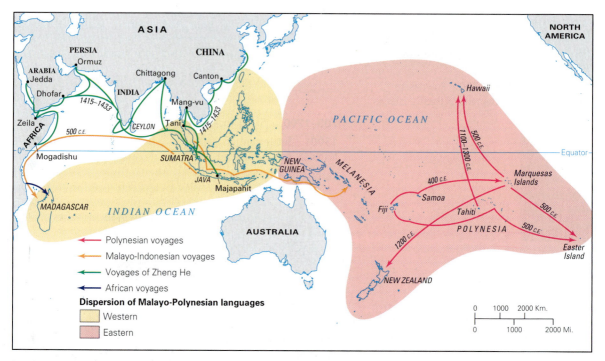

Map 14.1 Exploration and Settlement in the Indian and Pacific Oceans Before 1500 Over many centuries, mariners originating in Southeast Asia gradually colonized the islands of the Pacific and Indian Oceans. The Chinese voyages led by Zheng He in the fifteenth century were lavish official expeditions.

The Indian Ocean

While Polynesian mariners settled the Pacific islands, other Malayo-Indonesians sailed westward across the Indian Ocean and colonized the large island of Madagascar off the southeastern coast of Africa. These voyages continued through the fifteenth century. To this day, the inhabitants of Madagascar speak Malayo-Polynesian languages. However, part of the island's population is descended from Africans who crossed the 600 miles (1,000 kilometers) from the mainland to Madagascar, most likely in the centuries just before 1500.

The rise of Islam gave Indian Ocean trade an important boost. The great Muslim cities of the Middle East provided a demand for valuable commodities, and networks of Muslim traders tied the region together. The Indian Ocean traders operated largely independent of the empires and states that they served, but in East Asia, China's early Ming emperors took an active interest in these

wealthy ports of trade, sending Admiral **Zheng He**° on a series of expeditions.

The first Ming fleet in 1405 consisted of sixty-two specially built "treasure ships," large Chinese junks each about 300 feet long by 150 feet wide (90 by 45 meters). Most of the one hundred smaller accompanying vessels exceeded in size the flagship in which Columbus later sailed across the Atlantic. Each treasure ship had nine masts, twelve sails, many decks, and a carrying capacity of 3,000 tons (six times the capacity of Columbus's entire fleet). One expedition carried over 27,000 individuals, including infantry and cavalry troops. Although the ships carried small cannon, highly accurate crossbows dominated most Chinese sea battles.

One Chinese-Arabic interpreter kept a journal recording the customs, dress, and beliefs of the people visited, along with the trade, towns, and ani-

Zheng He (jung huh)

Polynesian Canoes   Pacific Ocean mariners sailing canoes such as these, shown in an eighteenth-century painting, made epic voyages of exploration and settlement. A large platform connects two canoes at the left, providing more room for the members of the expedition, and a sail supplements the paddlers.   ("Tereoboo, King of Owyhee, bringing presents to Captain Cook," D. L. Ref. p. xx 2f. 35. Courtesy, The Dixson Library, State Library of New South Wales)

mals of their countries. Among his observations were these: exotic animals such as the black panther of Malaya and the tapir of Sumatra; beliefs in legendary "corpse-headed barbarians" whose heads left their bodies at night and caused infants to die; the division of coastal Indians into five classes, which correspond to the four Hindu varnas and a separate Muslim class; and the fact that traders in the Indian port of Calicut° could perform error-free calculations by counting on their fingers and toes rather than using the Chinese abacus. After his return, the interpreter went on tour in China, telling of these exotic places and "how far the majestic virtue of [China's] imperial dynasty extended."[1]

Interest in new contacts was not confined to the Chinese side. In 1415–1416, at least three trading cities on the Swahili° Coast of East Africa sent delegations to China. Although no record of African and Chinese reactions to one another survives, China's lavish gifts to local rulers stimulated the Swahili market for silk and porcelain.

The Atlantic Ocean

The Vikings, northern European raiders and pirates, used their small, open ships to attack coastal European settlements for several centuries. They also discovered and settled one island after another in the North Atlantic. Like the Polynesians, the Vikings had neither maps nor navigational devices. They found their way using their knowledge of the heavens and the seas.

Calicut (KAL-ih-kut)

Swahili (swah-HEE-lee)

The Vikings first settled Iceland in 770. From there, some moved on to Greenland in 982, and one group sighted North America in 986. Fifteen years later, Leif Ericsson established a short-lived Viking settlement on the island of Newfoundland, which he called Vinland. When the climate turned colder after 1200, the northern settlements in Greenland went into decline. Vinland became a mysterious place mentioned in Norse sagas.

Some southern Europeans also explored the Atlantic. In 1291, two Vivaldo brothers from Genoa set out to sail around Africa to India. They were never heard of again. Other Genoese and Portuguese expeditions into the Atlantic in the fourteenth century discovered (and settled) the islands of Madeira°, the Azores°, and the Canaries.

Mention also occurs of African voyages of exploration in the Atlantic. The Syrian geographer al-Umari (1301–1349) relates that when Mansa Kankan Musa°, the ruler of the West African empire of Mali, passed through Egypt on his lavish pilgrimage to Mecca in 1324, he told of voyages to cross the Atlantic undertaken by his predecessor, Mansa Muhammad. Muhammad had sent out four hundred vessels with men and supplies, telling them, "Do not return until you have reached the other side of the ocean or if you have exhausted your food or water." After a long time, one canoe returned, reporting the others had been swept away by a "violent current in the middle of the sea." Muhammad himself then set out at the head of a second, even larger, expedition, from which no one returned.

On the other side of the Atlantic, Amerindian voyagers from South America colonized the West Indies. By the year 1000, Amerindians known as the **Arawak**° had moved from the small islands of the Lesser Antilles (Barbados, Martinique, Guadaloupe) into the Greater Antilles (Cuba, Hispaniola, Jamaica, and Puerto Rico), as well as into the Bahamas. Another people, the Carib, followed their route. By the late fifteenth century, they had overrun most Arawak settlements in the Lesser Antilles and were raiding parts of the Greater Antilles. From the West Indies, Arawak and Carib also undertook voyages to the North American mainland.

Madeira (muh-DEER-uh)   Azores (A-zorz)   **Mansa Kankan Musa** (MAHN-suh KAHN-kahn MOO-suh)   **Arawak** (AR-uh-wahk)

IBERIAN EXPANSION, 1400–1550

The preceding survey shows that maritime exploration occurred in many parts of the world before 1450. The sea voyages sponsored by the Iberian kingdoms of Portugal and Spain attract special interest because they began a maritime revolution that profoundly altered the course of world history. The Portuguese and Spanish expeditions ended the isolation of the Americas and increased global interaction. The influence in world affairs of the Iberians and other Europeans who followed them overseas rose steadily after 1500.

Iberian overseas expansion arose from two related phenomena. First, Iberian rulers had strong economic, religious, and political motives to expand their contacts and increase their dominance. Second, improvements in maritime and military technologies gave them the means to master treacherous and unfamiliar ocean environments, seize control of existing maritime trade routes, and conquer new lands.

Background to Iberian Expansion

In many ways, these voyages continued four trends evident in the Latin West from about the year 1000: (1) the revival of urban life and trade, (2) a struggle with Islamic powers for dominance of the Mediterranean that mixed religious motives with the desire for trade with distant lands, (3) growing intellectual curiosity about the outside world, and (4) a peculiarly European alliance between merchants and rulers.

The city-states of northern Italy took the lead in all of these developments. By 1450, they had well-established trade links to northern Europe, the Indian Ocean, and the Black Sea, and their merchant princes had sponsored an intellectual and artistic Renaissance. But the Italian states did not take the lead in exploring the Atlantic, even after the expansion of the Ottoman Empire in the fourteenth and fifteenth centuries disrupted their trade to the East, because Venice and Genoa preferred to continue the lucrative alliances with Muslims that had given their merchants privileged positions and because Mediterranean ships were ill suited to the more violent weather of the Atlantic. However, many individual Italians played leading roles in Atlantic exploration.

By contrast, the Iberian kingdoms had engaged in anti-Muslim warfare since the eighth century, when Muslim forces overran most of the peninsula. By about 1250, the Iberian kingdoms of Portugal, Castile, and Aragon had conquered all the Muslim lands in Iberia except the southern kingdom of Granada, which finally fell to the united kingdom of Castile and Aragon in 1492. These territories gradually amalgamated to form Spain, sixteenth-century Europe's most powerful state.

Christian militancy continued to drive Portugal and Spain in their overseas ventures. But the Iberian rulers and their adventurous subjects also sought material returns. Their small share of the Mediterranean trade made them more willing than the Italians to take risks to find new routes to Africa and Asia through the Atlantic. Moreover, both kingdoms participated in the shipbuilding changes and the gunpowder revolution under way in Atlantic Europe. Though not centers of Renaissance learning, both states had exceptional rulers who appreciated new geographical knowledge.

Portuguese Voyages

When the Muslim government of Morocco in northwestern Africa weakened in the fifteenth century, the Portuguese went on the attack, beginning with the city of Ceuta° in 1415. This assault combined aspects of a religious crusade, a plundering expedition, and a military tournament in which young Portuguese knights displayed their bravery. Despite the capture of several more ports along Morocco's Atlantic coast, the Portuguese could not push inland and gain access to the gold trade they learned about, so they sought more direct contact with the gold producers by sailing down the African coast.

Young Prince Henry (1394–1460), third son of the king of Portugal, led the attack on Ceuta. Because he devoted the rest of his life to promoting exploration, he is known as **Henry the Navigator.** His official biographer emphasized his desire to convert Africans to Christianity, make contact with Christian rulers believed to exist in Africa, and launch joint crusades with them against the Ottomans. Profit also figured in his dreams. His initial explorations focused on Africa. His ships established permanent contact with the islands of Madeira in 1418 and the Azores in 1439. Only later did reaching India become a goal.

"The Navigator" himself never ventured farther from home than North Africa. Instead, he founded a sort of research institute at Sagres° for studying navigation and collecting information about new lands. His staff drew on the pioneering efforts of Italian merchants, especially the Genoese, who had learned some of the secrets of the trans-Saharan trade, and of fourteenth-century Jewish cartographers who used information from Arab and European sources to produce remarkably accurate sea charts and maps of distant places. They also studied and improved navigational instruments that had come into Europe from China and the Islamic world: the magnetic compass, first developed in China, and the astrolabe, an instrument of Arab or Greek invention that enabled mariners to determine their latitude by measuring the position of the sun or the stars.

The Portuguese developed a new type of long-distance sailing vessel, the **caravel°.** The many-oared galleys of the Mediterranean could not carry enough food and water for long ocean voyages. The three-masted ships of the North Atlantic, powered by square sails, could not sail at much of an angle against the wind. The caravel, which was only one-fifth the size of the largest European ships and the large Chinese junks, could enter shallow coastal waters and explore upriver, yet it had the strength to weather ocean storms. When equipped with lateen sails, caravels had great maneuverability and could sail deeply into the wind; when sporting square Atlantic sails, they had great speed. The addition of small cannon made them good fighting ships as well. The caravels' economy, speed, agility, and power justified a contemporary's claim that they were "the best ships that sailed the seas."[2]

Pioneering captains had to overcome crews' fears that the South Atlantic waters were boiling hot and contained ocean currents that would prevent

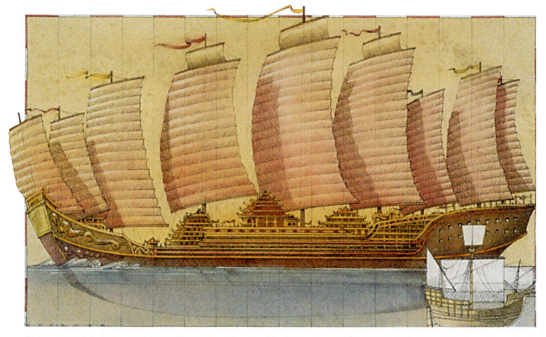

Chinese Junk   This modern drawing shows how much larger one of Zheng He's ships was than one of Vasco da Gama's vessels. Watertight interior bulkheads made junks the most seaworthy large ships of the fifteenth century. Sails made of pleated bamboo matting hung from the junk's masts, and a stern rudder provided steering. European ships of exploration, though smaller, were faster and more maneuverable.   (Dugald Stermer)

their ever returning home. It took Prince Henry from 1420 to 1434 to coax an expedition to venture beyond southern Morocco in northwest Africa (see Map 14.2). The next stretch of coast, 800 miles (1,300 kilometers) of desert, offered little of interest to the explorers. Finally in 1444, the mariners reached the Senegal River and the populous, well-watered lands below the Sahara beginning at what they named Cape Verde (Green Cape) because of its vegetation.

In the years that followed, Henry's explorers learned how to return speedily to Portugal. Instead of battling the prevailing northeast trade winds and currents back up the coast, they discovered that by sailing northwest into the Atlantic to the latitude of the Azores, ships could pick up prevailing westerly winds that would blow them back to Portugal. The knowledge that ocean winds tend to form large circular patterns helped explorers discover many other ocean routes.

To pay for the research, ships, and expeditions,

Prince Henry drew partly on the income of the Order of Christ, a military religious order of which he was the governor. The Order of Christ had been founded to inherit the Portuguese properties and the crusading tradition of the Order of Knights Templar, which had disbanded in 1314. The Order of Christ received the exclusive right to promote Christianity in all the lands that were discovered, and the Portuguese emblazoned their ships' sails with the crusaders' red cross.

The first financial returns came from selling into slavery Africans captured in raids on the northwest coast of Africa and the Canary Islands during the 1440s. The Portuguese had captured or purchased eighty thousand Africans by the end of the century. However, gold quickly became more important than slavery. By 1457, enough African gold was coming back to Portugal for the kingdom to issue a new gold coin called the *cruzado* (crusade), another reminder of how deeply the Portuguese entwined religious and secular motives.

By the time Prince Henry died in 1460, his explorers had established a base of operations in the uninhabited Cape Verde Islands and explored 600 miles (950 kilometers) of coast beyond Cape Verde, as far as what they named Sierra Leone° (Lion Mountain). From there, they knew the coast of Africa curved sharply toward the east. After spending four decades covering the 1,500 miles (2,400 kilometers) from Lisbon to Sierra Leone, Portuguese explorers traveled the remaining 4,000 miles (6,400 kilometers) to the continent's southern tip in only three decades.

Royal sponsorship continued, but private commercial participation sped the progress. In 1469, a Lisbon merchant named Fernão Gomes purchased from the Crown the privilege of exploring 350 miles (550 kilometers) of new coast a year for five years and a monopoly on any resulting trade. Gomes discovered the uninhabited island of São Tomé° on the equator; in the next century, it became a major source of sugar produced with African slave labor. He also explored what later Europeans called the **Gold Coast,** which became the headquarters of Portugal's West African trade.

The expectation of finding a passage around Africa to the Indian Ocean spurred the final thrust down the African coast. **Bartolomeu Dias** rounded the southern tip of Africa (in 1488) and entered the Indian Ocean. In 1497–1498, **Vasco da Gama** led a Portuguese expedition around Africa to India. In 1500, ships in an expedition under Pedro Alvares Cabral°, while swinging wide to the west in the South Atlantic to catch the winds that would sweep them around southern Africa and on to India, came on the eastern coast of South America, laying the basis for Portugal's later claim to Brazil.

Spanish Voyages

Spain's early discoveries owed more to haste and blind luck than to careful planning. Only in the last decade of the fifteenth century did the Spanish monarchs turn their attention from reconquest and organization of previously Muslim territories to overseas exploration. By this time, the Portuguese had already found their route to the Indian Ocean.

Sierra Leone (see-ER-uh lee-OWN)   São Tomé (sow toh-MAY)   Cabral (kah-BRAHL)

The leader of their overseas mission would be **Christopher Columbus** (1451–1506), a Genoese mariner. His three voyages between 1492 and 1498 would reveal the existence of vast and unexpected lands across the Atlantic. But this momentous discovery fell disappointingly short of Columbus's intention of finding a new route to the Indian Ocean even shorter than that of the Portuguese.

As a younger man, Columbus had gained considerable experience while participating in Portuguese explorations along the African coast, but he dreamed of a shorter way to the riches of the East. By his reckoning (based on a serious misreading of a ninth-century Arab authority), a mere 2,400 nautical miles (4,450 kilometers) separated the Canary Islands from Japan. The actual distance was five times greater.

Portuguese authorities twice rejected his plan to reach the East by sailing west, first in 1485 following a careful study and again in 1488 after Dias had established the feasibility of the African route. Columbus received more sympathy, but initially no support, from Queen Isabella of Castile. A Castilian commission appointed by Isabella studied the proposal for four years and concluded that a westward sea route to the Indies rested on questionable geographical assumptions. Nevertheless, Columbus's persistence finally won over the queen and her husband, King Ferdinand of Aragon. In 1492, elated perhaps by finally expelling the Muslims from Granada, they agreed to fund a modest expedition.

Columbus recorded in his log that the *Santa María*, the *Santa Clara* (nicknamed the *Niña*), and a vessel now known only by its nickname, the *Pinta*, with a mostly Spanish crew of ninety men "departed Friday the third day of August of the year 1492," toward "the regions of India." Their mission, the royal contract stated, was "to discover and acquire certain islands and mainland in the Ocean Sea." Columbus carried letters of introduction from the Spanish sovereigns to Eastern rulers, including one to the "Grand Khan" (meaning the Chinese emperor). An Arabic-speaking Jewish convert to Christianity had the job of communicating with the peoples of eastern Asia.

Unfavorable headwinds had discouraged other attempts to explore the Atlantic west of the Azores. But on earlier voyages along the African coast,

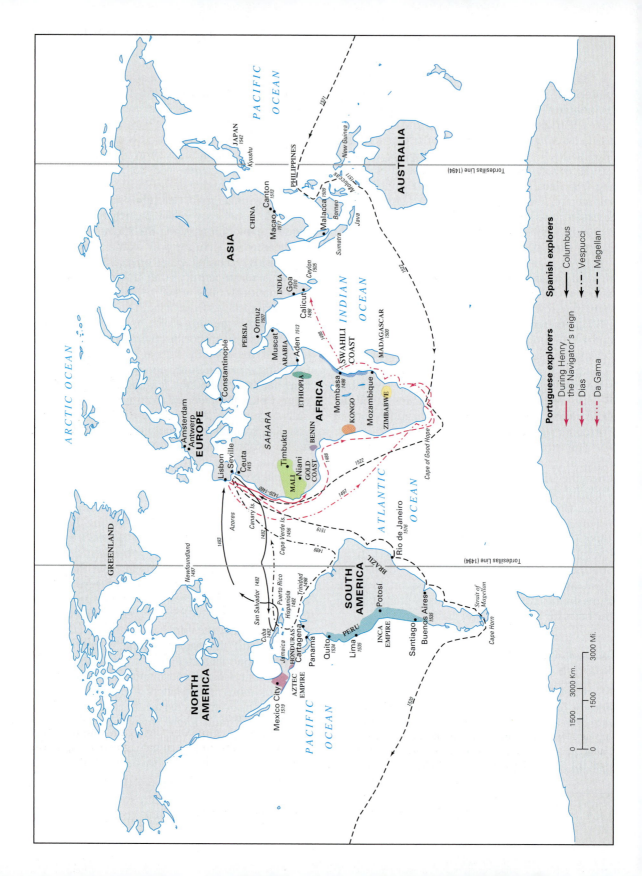

ARCTIC OCEAN

PACIFIC OCEAN

GREENLAND

NORTH AMERICA

EUROPE

ASIA

AUSTRALIA

Amsterdam
Antwerp
Constantinople
Lisbon
Seville
Ceuta *1415*

JAPAN *1542*
Kyushu

CHINA
Canton *1513*
Macao *1517*

PHILIPPINES
1521

New Guinea

Molucca *1511*
Borneo
Malacca *1509*
Java
Sumatra

INDIA
Goa *1510*
Calicut *1498*
Ceylon *1505*

PERSIA
Ormuz *1507*
Muscat
ARABIA
Aden *1513*

ETHIOPIA
BENIN
SAHARA
Timbuktu
MALI
Niani
GOLD COAST *1488*
AFRICA
Mombasa *1498*
KONGO
Mozambique
ZIMBABWE
SWAHILI COAST

MADAGASCAR *1500*

INDIAN OCEAN

1498
Cape of Good Hope
1497
1488
1522
1420–1400

ATLANTIC OCEAN

Tordesillas Line (1494)

Azores
Canary Is.
Cape Verde Is. *1456*

Newfoundland *1497*
1493
San Salvador *1492*
Cuba *1492*
Puerto Rico
Hispaniola *1492*
Trinidad
Jamaica
HONDURAS
Cartagena
Panama
AZTEC EMPIRE
Mexico City *1519*

SOUTH AMERICA
BRAZIL
Rio de Janeiro *1516*
Quito *1534*
Lima *1535*
PERU
Potosí
INCA EMPIRE
Santiago
Buenos Aires *1536*
Strait of Magellan
Cape Horn

Tordesillas Line (1494)

1499
1519
1497
1522
1520

PACIFIC OCEAN

Portuguese explorers

During Henry
the Navigator's reign
Dias
Da Gama

Spanish explorers

Columbus
Vespucci
Magellan

0   1500   3000 Km.
0   1500   3000 Mi.

Columbus Prepares to Cross the Atlantic, 1492   This later representation shows Columbus with the ships, soldiers, priests, and seamen that were part of Spain's enterprise.   (G. Dagli Orti/The Art Archive)

Columbus had learned about winds blowing westward at the latitude of the Canaries. After reaching the Canaries, he replaced the *Niña*'s lateen sails with square sails, for he knew that from then on, speed would be more important than maneuverability since his supplies would last for only a fixed number of days.

In October, the expedition encountered the islands of the Caribbean. Columbus called the in-

Map 14.2   European Exploration, 1420–1542   Portuguese and Spanish explorers showed the possibility and practicality of intercontinental maritime trade. Before 1540 European trade with Africa and Asia was much more important than that with the Americas, but after the Spanish conquest of the Aztec and Inca Empires transatlantic trade began to increase. Notice the Tordesillas line, which in theory separated the Spanish and Portuguese spheres of activity.

habitants "Indians" because he believed he had reached the East Indies. A second voyage in 1493 did nothing to change his mind. On a third voyage in 1498, two months after Vasco da Gama reached India, Columbus sighted the mainland of South America, which he insisted was part of Asia. But by then, other Europeans had become convinced that his discoveries were of lands previously unknown to the Old World (Europe, Asia, and Africa). Amerigo Vespucci's explorations, first on behalf of Spain and then for Portugal, led mapmakers to name the new continents "America," after him.

To prevent disputes about exploiting these new lands and spreading Christianity among their peoples, Spain and Portugal agreed to split the world between them. Modifying an earlier papal proposal, the Treaty of Tordesillas°, negotiated

Tordesillas (tor-duh-SEE-yuhs)

by the pope in 1494, drew an imaginary north-south line down the middle of the Atlantic Ocean. Lands east of the line in Africa and southern Asia could be claimed by Portugal; lands to the west in the Americas belonged to Spain. Cabral's discovery of Brazil, however, gave Portugal a valid claim to the part of South America that bulged east of the line.

But if the Tordesillas line were extended around the earth, where would Spain's and Portugal's spheres of influence divide in the East? Given European ignorance of the earth's true size in 1494, no one knew whether the Moluccas°, the source of the valuable spices of the East Indies, belonged to Portugal or Spain. The missing information concerned the size of the Pacific Ocean, which a Spanish adventurer named Vasco Núñez de Balboa° had spotted in 1513 when he crossed the isthmus (a narrow neck of land) of Panama from the east. The 1519 expedition of **Ferdinand Magellan** (ca. 1480–1521) sought to complete Columbus's interrupted westward voyage by sailing around the Americas and across the Pacific. The Moluccas turned out to lie well within Portugal's sphere, as Spain formally acknowledged in 1529.

Magellan's voyage laid the basis for Spanish colonization of the Philippine Islands after 1564. It also gave Magellan credit, despite his death, for being the first person to encircle the globe, for a decade earlier, he had sailed from Europe to the East Indies on an expedition sponsored by his native Portugal.

Columbus and those who followed in his path laid the basis for the colonial empires of Spain and other European nations. In turn, these empires promoted, among the four Atlantic continents, a new trading network whose importance rivaled and eventually surpassed that of the Indian Ocean. Of more immediate importance, Portugal's entry into the Indian Ocean led quickly to a major European presence and profit. Both the eastward and the westward voyages of exploration marked a tremendous expansion of Europe's role in world history.

ENCOUNTERS WITH EUROPE, 1450–1550

The ways in which Africans, Asians, and Amerindians perceived their European visitors and interacted with them influenced their future relations. Some welcomed the Europeans as potential allies; others viewed them as rivals or enemies. In general, Africans and Asians readily recognized the benefits and dangers of European contact. However, the long isolation of the Amerindians added to the strangeness of their encounter with the Spanish and made them more vulnerable to the unfamiliar diseases the Spanish inadvertently introduced.

Western Africa

Many Africans welcomed trade with the Portuguese, which gave them new markets for their exports and access to imports cheaper than those coming by caravan across the Sahara. Miners in the hinterland of the Gold Coast, which the Portuguese first visited in 1471, had long sold their gold to merchants from trading cities along the southern edge of the Sahara for transshipment to North Africa. Recognizing the possibility of more favorable trading terms, coastal Africans negotiated with the royal representative of Portugal, who arrived in 1482 seeking permission to erect a trading fort.

The Portuguese noble in charge and his officers (likely including the young Christopher Columbus, who had entered Portuguese service in 1476) strove to make a proper impression. They dressed in their best clothes, erected a fancy reception platform, celebrated a Catholic Mass, and signaled the start of negotiations with trumpets, tambourines, and drums. The African king, Caramansa, staged his entrance with equal ceremony, arriving with a large retinue of attendants and musicians. Through an African interpreter, the two leaders exchanged flowery speeches pledging goodwill and mutual benefit. Caramansa then gave permission for a small trading fort, assured, he said, by the appearance of these royal delegates that they were honorable persons, unlike the "few, foul, and vile" Portuguese visitors of the previous decade.

Moluccas (muh-LOO-kuhz)   **Balboa** (bal-BOH-uh)

Neither side made a show of force, but Cara-mansa warned that if the Portuguese failed to be peaceful and honest traders, he and his people would move away and deprive their post of food and trade. Trade at the post of Saint George of the Mine (later called Elmina) enriched both sides. The Portuguese crown was soon purchasing gold amounting to one-tenth of the world's production at the time. In return, Africans received shiploads of goods brought by the Portuguese from Asia, Europe, and other parts of Africa.

Early contacts involved a mixture of commercial, military, and religious interests. Some African rulers quickly saw the value of European firearms. Coastal rulers also proved willing to test the value of Christian practices, which the Portuguese eagerly promoted. The rulers of Benin and Kongo, the largest coastal kingdoms, invited Portuguese missionaries and soldiers to accompany them into battle to test the Christians' religion along with their muskets (see Diversity and Dominance: Kongo's Christian King).

The kingdom of Benin in the Niger Delta, near the peak of its power after a century of aggressive expansion, had a large capital city, also known as Benin. Its *oba* (king) responded to a Portuguese visit in 1486 by sending an ambassador to Portugal to learn more about their homeland. Then he established a royal monopoly on Portuguese trade, selling pepper and ivory tusks (to be taken back to Portugal) as well as stone beads, textiles, and prisoners of war (to be resold at Elmina). In return, Portuguese merchants provided Benin with copper and brass, fine textiles, glass beads, and a horse for the king's royal procession. In the early sixteenth century, as the demand for slaves for the Portuguese sugar plantations on the nearby island of São Tomé grew, the oba first raised the price of slaves and then imposed restrictions on their sale.

Efforts to spread Catholicism ultimately failed. Early kings showed some interest, but after 1538, the rulers declined to receive further missionaries. They also closed the market in male slaves for the rest of the sixteenth century. Both steps illustrate their power to control how much interaction they wanted.

Farther south, on the lower Congo River, the *manikongo*° (king) of Kongo also sent delegates to

Afro–Portuguese Ivory A skilled ivory carver from the kingdom of Benin probably made this saltcellar. Intended for a European market, it depicts a Portuguese ship on the cover and Portuguese nobles around the base. However European the subject, the craftsmanship is typical of Benin. (Courtesy of the Trustees of the British Museum)

Portugal, established a royal monopoly on trade, and expressed interest in missionary teachings. But here the royal family made Catholicism the kingdom's official faith. Lacking ivory and pepper, Kongo sold more and more slaves to acquire the goods brought by the Portuguese and to pay missionary expenses.

Soon the royal trade monopoly broke down. In 1526, the Christian manikongo, Afonso I (r. 1506–ca. 1540), wrote to his royal "brother," the king of Portugal, begging for his help in stopping the slave trade

---

manikongo (mah-NEE-KONG-goh)

운드폭탄 4발 투하… 두 아들과 함께 사망
싶진지 구축… 이틀째 시가戰
령이 대중 앞에 나타나거나 애국심
을 고취하는 노래만을 내보내던 방
송마저 중단됐다.

라크 전후
의에서는
영국 주도

DIVERSITY AND DOMINANCE

KONGO'S CHRISTIAN KING

The new overseas voyages brought conquest to some and opportunities for fruitful borrowings and exchanges to others. The decision of the ruler of the kingdom of Kongo to adopt Christianity in 1491 added cultural diversity to Kongolese society and in some ways strengthened the hand of the king. From then on Kongolese rulers sought to introduce Christian beliefs and rituals while at the same time Africanizing Christianity to make it more intelligible to their subjects. In addition, the kings of Kongo sought a variety of more secular aid from Portugal, including schools and medicine. Trade with the Portuguese introduced new social and political tensions, especially in the case of the export trade in slaves for the Portuguese sugar plantations on the island of São Tomé to the north.

Two letters sent to King João (zhwao) III of Portugal in 1526 illustrate how King Afonso of Kongo saw his kingdom's new relationship with Portugal and the problems that resulted from it. (Afonso adopted that name when he was baptized as a young prince.) After the death of his father in 1506, Afonso successfully claimed the throne and ruled until 1542. His son Henrique became the first Catholic bishop of the Kongo in 1521.

These letters were written in Portuguese and penned by the king's secretary João Teixera (tay-SHER-uh), a Kongo Christian, who, like Afonso, had been educated by Portuguese missionaries.

6 July 1526

To the very powerful and excellent prince Dom João, our brother:

On the 20th of June just past, we received word that a trading ship from your highness had just come to our port of Sonyo. We were greatly pleased by that arrival for it had been many days since a ship had come to our kingdom, for by it we would get news of your highness, which many times we had desired to know, . . . and likewise as there was a great and dire need for wine and flour for the holy sacrament; and of this we had had no great hope for we have the same need frequently. And that, sir, arises from the great negligence of your highness's officials toward us and toward shipping us those things. . . .

Sir, your highness should know how our kingdom is being lost in so many ways that we will need to provide the needed cure, since this is caused by the excessive license given by your agents and officials to the men and merchants who come to this kingdom to set up shops with goods and many things which have been prohibited by us, and which they spread throughout our kingdoms and domains in such abundance that many of our vassals, whose submission we could once rely on, now act independently so as to get the things in greater abundance than we ourselves; whom we had formerly held content and submissive and under our vassalage and jurisdiction, so it is doing a great harm not only to the service of God, but also to the security and peace of our kingdoms and state.

And we cannot reckon how great the damage is, since every day the mentioned merchants are taking our people, sons of the land and the sons of our noblemen and vassals and our relatives, because the thieves and men of bad conscience grab them so as to have the things and wares of this kingdom that they crave; they grab them and bring them to be sold. In such a manner, sir, has been the corruption and deprivation that our land is becoming completely depopulated, and your highness should not deem this good nor in your service. And to avoid this we need from these kingdoms [of yours] no more than priests and a few people to teach in schools, and no other goods except wine and flour for the holy sacrament, which is why we beg of your highness to help and assist us in this matter. Order your agents to send here neither merchants nor wares, because it is our will that in these kingdoms there should not be any dealing in slaves nor outlet for them, for the reasons stated above. Again we beg your highness's agreement, since otherwise we cannot cure such manifest harm. May Our Lord in His mercy have your highness always under His protection and may you always do the things of His holy service. I kiss your hands many times.

From our city of Kongo. . . .

The King, Dom Afonso

18 October 1526

Very high and very powerful prince King of Portugal, our brother,

Sir, your highness has been so good as to promise us that anything we need we should ask for in our letters, and that everything will be provided. And so that there may be peace and health of our kingdoms, by God's will, in our lifetime. And as there are among us old folks and people who have lived for many days, many and different diseases happen so often that we are pushed to the ultimate extremes. And the same happens to our children, relatives, and people, because this country lacks physicians and surgeons who might know the proper cures for such diseases, as well as pharmacies and drugs to make them better. And for this reason many of those who had been already confirmed and instructed in the things of the holy faith of Our Lord Jesus Christ perish and die. And the rest of the people for the most part cure themselves with herbs and sticks and other ancient methods, so that they live putting all their faith in these herbs and ceremonies, and die believing that they are saved; and this serves God poorly.

And to avoid such a great error, I think, and inconvenience, since it is from God and from your highness that all the good and the drugs and medicines have come to us for our salvation, we ask your merciful highness to send us two physicians and two pharmacists and one surgeon, so that they may come with their pharmacies and neces-

sary things to be in our kingdoms, for we have extreme need of each and every one of them. We will be very good and merciful to them, since sent by your highness, their work and coming should be for good. We ask your highness as a great favor to do this for us, because besides being good in itself it is in the service of God as we have said above.

Moreover, sir, in our kingdoms there is another great inconvenience which is of little service to God, and this is that many of our people, out of great desire for the wares and things of your kingdoms, which are brought here by your people, and in order to satisfy their disordered appetite, seize many of our people, freed and exempt men. And many times noblemen and the sons of noblemen, and our relatives are stolen, and they take them to be sold to the white men who are in our kingdoms and take them hidden or by night, so that they are not recognized. And as soon as they are taken by the white men, they are immediately ironed and branded with fire. And when they are carried off to be embarked, if they are caught by our guards, the whites allege that they have bought them and cannot say from whom, so that it is our duty to do justice and to restore to the free their freedom. And so they went away offended.

And to avoid such a great evil we passed a law so that every white man living in our kingdoms and wanting to purchase slaves by whatever means should first inform three of our noblemen and officials of our court on whom we rely in this matter, namely Dom Pedro Manipunzo and Dom Manuel Manissaba, our head bailiff, and Gonçalo Pires, our chief supplier, who should investigate if the said slaves are captives or free men, and, if cleared with them, there will be no further doubt nor embargo and they can be taken and embarked. And if they reach the opposite conclusion, they will lose the aforementioned slaves. Whatever favor and license we give them [the white men] for the sake of your highness in this case is because we know that it is in your service too that these slaves are taken from our kingdom; otherwise we should not consent to this for the reasons stated above that we make known completely to your highness so that no one could say the contrary, as they said in many other cases to your highness, so that the care and remembrance that we and this kingdom have should not be withdrawn. . . .

We kiss your hands of your highness many times.

From our city of Kongo, the 18th day of October,

The King, Dom Afonso

QUESTIONS FOR ANALYSIS

1. What sorts of things does King Afonso desire from the Portuguese?
2. What is he willing and unwilling to do in return?
3. What problem with his own people has the slave trade created, and what has King Afonso done about it?
4. Does King Afonso see himself as an equal to King João or his subordinate? Do you agree with that analysis?

Source: From António Brásio, ed., *Monumenta Missionaria Africana: Africa Ocidental (1471–1531)* (Lisbon: Agência Geral do Ultramar, 1952), I:468, 470–471, 488–491. Translated by David Northrup.

because unauthorized Kongolese were kidnapping and selling people, even members of good families. Afonso's appeal that contacts be limited to "some priests and a few people to teach in the schools, and no other goods except wine and flour for the holy sacrament" received no reply. After 1540, the major part of the slave trade from this part of Africa moved farther south.

Eastern Africa

As Vasco da Gama sailed up the eastern coast of Africa in 1498, most rulers of the coastal trading states received him coolly. Visitors who painted crusader crosses on their sails raised their suspicions. The ruler of Malindi, however, saw in the Portuguese an ally who could help him expand Malindi's trade, and he provided da Gama with a pilot to guide him to India. The suspicions of most rulers came to fruition seven years later when a Portuguese war fleet bombarded and looted most of the coastal cities in the name of Christ and commerce. It spared Malindi.

Christian Ethiopia also saw benefits in allying with the Portuguese. In the fourteenth and fifteenth centuries, Ethiopian conflicts with Muslim states along the Red Sea increased. After the Ottoman Turks conquered Egypt and launched a fleet in the Indian Ocean to counter the Portuguese in 1517, the warlord of the Muslim state of Adal attacked Ethiopia. A decisive victory in 1529 put the Christian kingdom in jeopardy, making Portuguese support a crucial matter.

For decades, delegations from Portugal and Ethiopia had talked of a Christian alliance. Queen Helena of Ethiopia, who acted as regent for her young sons after her husband's death in 1478, sent a letter in 1509 to "our very dear and well-beloved brother," the king of Portugal, along with a gift of two tiny crucifixes said to be made of wood from the cross on which Christ was crucified. She proposed to combine her land army and Portugal's fleet against the Turks. At her death in 1522, no alliance had come into being, but the worsening situation brought renewed Ethiopian appeals.

Finally, a small Portuguese force commanded by Vasco da Gama's son Christopher reached Ethiopia in 1539. With Portuguese help, another queen rallied the desperate Ethiopians. Muslim foes captured Christopher da Gama and tortured him to death but lost heart when their leader fell in battle. Portuguese aid helped save the Ethiopian kingdom from extinction, but Ethiopia's refusal to transfer their Christian affiliation from the patriarch of Alexandria to the pope prevented a permanent alliance.

As these examples illustrate, African encounters with the Portuguese before 1550 varied considerably. Africans and Portuguese might become royal brothers, bitter opponents, or partners in a mutually profitable trade, but Europeans were still a minor presence in most of Africa in 1550. The

Indian Ocean trade by then was occupying most of their attention.

Indian Ocean States

Vasco da Gama's arrival on the Malabar Coast of India in May 1498 did not impress the citizens of Calicut. The Chinese fleets of gigantic junks that had called at Calicut sixty-five years earlier dwarfed his four small ships, which were no larger than many of the dhows° already filling the harbor. The *samorin* (ruler) of Calicut and his Muslim officials showed mild interest, but the gifts da Gama brought evoked derisive laughter: twelve pieces of striped cloth, four scarlet hoods, six hats, and six wash basins. When da Gama defended his gifts as those of an explorer, not a merchant, the samorin cut him short, asking whether he had come to discover men or stones: "If he had come to discover men, as he said, why had he brought nothing?"

Coastal rulers soon discovered that the Portuguese had no intention of remaining poor competitors in the Indian Ocean trade. Upon da Gama's return to Portugal in 1499, the jubilant King Manuel styled himself "Lord of the Conquest, Navigation, and Commerce of Ethiopia, Arabia, Persia, and India." Previously, the Indian Ocean had been an open sea, used by merchants (and pirates) of all the surrounding coasts. Now the Portuguese crown intended to make it Portugal's sea, which others might use only on Portuguese terms.

Portugal's hope of controlling the Indian Ocean stemmed from the superiority of its ships and weapons over the smaller and lightly armed merchant dhows. In 1505, the Portuguese fleet of 81 ships and some 7,000 men bombarded Swahili Coast cities. Goa, on the west coast of India, fell to a well-armed fleet in 1510, becoming the base from which the Portuguese menaced the trading cities of Gujarat° to the north and Calicut and other Malabar Coast cities to the south. The port of Hormuz, controlling the entry to the Persian Gulf, fell in 1515. Aden, at the entrance to the Red Sea, preserved its independence, but the capture of the Gujarati port of Diu in 1535 consolidated Portuguese dominance of the western Indian Ocean.

Farther east, the independent city of Malacca° on the strait separating the Malay Peninsula and Sumatra became the focus of their attention. During the fifteenth century, Malacca had become the main entrepôt° (a place where goods are stored or deposited and from which they are distributed) for the trade from China, Japan, India, the Southeast Asian mainland, and the Moluccas. The city's 100,000 residents spoke eighty-four different languages, according to a Portuguese source, and included merchants from Cairo, Ethiopia, and the Swahili Coast. Many non-Muslim residents supported letting the Portuguese join this cosmopolitan trading community, perhaps to offset the growing solidarity of Muslim traders. In 1511, however, the Portuguese seized Malacca with a force of a thousand fighting men, including three hundred recruited in southern India.

On the China coast, local officials and merchants persuaded the imperial government to allow the Portuguese to establish a trading post at Macao° in 1557. Subsequently, Portuguese ships nearly monopolized trade between China and Japan.

Control of the major port cities enabled the Portuguese to enforce their demands that all spices be carried in Portuguese ships, as well as all goods on the major ocean routes such as between Goa and Macao. The Portuguese also tried to control and tax other Indian Ocean trade. Merchant ships entering and leaving their ports had to carry a Portuguese passport and pay customs duties. Portuguese patrols seized vessels that did not comply, confiscated their cargoes, and either killed the captain and crew or sentenced them to forced labor.

Reactions to this power grab varied. Like the emperors of China, the Mughal° emperors of India largely ignored Portugal's maritime intrusions. The Ottomans confronted the Christian intruders more aggressively. They supported Egypt's defensive efforts from 1501 to 1509 and then sent their own fleet into the Indian Ocean in 1538. However, Ottoman galleys proved no match for the faster, better-armed Portuguese vessels in the open ocean. They retained their advantage only in the Red Sea and Persian Gulf, where they controlled many ports.

---

dhow (dow)   Gujarat (goo-juh-RAHT)

Malacca (muh-LAH-kuh)   **entrepôt** (ON-truh-poh)
Macao (muh-COW)   **Mughal** (MOO-gahl)

Smaller trading states could not challenge the Portuguese. Mutual rivalry kept them from forming a common front. Some cooperated with the Portuguese to safeguard their prosperity and security. Others engaged in evasion and resistance.

When the merchants of Calicut put up sustained resistance, the Portuguese embargoed all trade with Aden, Calicut's principal trading partner, and centered their trade on the port of Cochin, which had once been a dependency of Calicut. Some Calicut merchants evaded their patrols, but Calicut's importance shrank as Cochin gradually became the major pepper-exporting port on the Malabar Coast.

Farther north, Gujarat initially resisted Portuguese attempts at monopoly and in 1509 joined Egypt's futile effort to sweep the Portuguese from the Arabian Sea. But in 1535, with his state weakened by Mughal attacks, the ruler allowed the Portuguese to build a fort at Diu in return for their support. Once established, the Portuguese gradually extended their control. By midcentury, they were licensing and taxing all Gujarati ships. Even after the Mughals took control of Gujarat in 1572, the Mughal emperor, Akbar, permitted the Portuguese to continue their maritime monopoly in return for allowing one pilgrim ship a year to sail to Mecca without paying a fee.

The Portuguese never gained complete control of the Indian Ocean trade, but their domination of key ports and trade routes brought them considerable profit in the form of spices and other luxury goods. The Portuguese broke the trading monopoly of Venice and Genoa by selling pepper for less than what they charged for shipments obtained through Egyptian middlemen.

The Americas

In the Americas, the Spanish established a vast territorial empire, in contrast to the trading empire of the Portuguese. The Spanish kingdoms drew on somewhat greater resources, but the Spanish and Portuguese monarchies had similar motives for expansion and used identical ships and weapons. The isolation of the Amerindian peoples provided a key difference. The first European settlers in the Caribbean resorted to conquest and plunder rather than trade. They later extended this practice to the more powerful Amerindian kingdoms on the American mainland. After 1518, deadly epidemics among the Amerindians weakened their ability to resist.

The Arawak whom Columbus first encountered on Hispaniola (modern Haiti and the Dominican Republic) in the Greater Antilles and the Bahamas to the north cultivated maize (corn), cassava (a tuber), sweet potatoes, and hot peppers, as well as cotton and tobacco. They mined and worked gold, but they did not trade gold, nor did they have iron. They extended a cautious welcome to Columbus but told him exaggerated stories about gold in other places to persuade him to move on.

Columbus brought with him several hundred settlers from southern Iberia, as well as missionaries, on his second trip to Hispaniola in 1493. The settlers stole gold ornaments, confiscated food, and raped women, provoking the Hispaniola Arawak to war in 1495. With the advantage of horses and body armor, the Spaniards slaughtered tens of thousands of Arawak and forced the survivors to pay a heavy tax in gold, spun cotton, and food. Whoever failed to meet the quotas faced forced labor. Meanwhile, the cattle, pigs, and goats introduced by the settlers devoured the Arawak's food crops, causing deaths from famine and disease. A governor appointed by the Spanish crown in 1502 forced the Arawak on Hispaniola to become laborers under the control of Spanish settlers.

The actions of the Spanish in the Antilles reflected Spanish behavior during the wars against the Muslims in the previous centuries. They sought to serve God by defeating, controlling, and converting nonbelievers and to become rich in the process. Individual **conquistadors**° (conquerors) extended that pattern around the Caribbean. Some raided the Bahamas for gold and labor as both grew scarce on Hispaniola. Arawak from the Bahamas served as slaves on Hispaniola. Juan Ponce de León (1460–1521), a veteran of the conquest of Muslim Spain and the seizure of Hispaniola, conquered the island of Borinquen (Puerto Rico) in 1508 and in 1513 explored southeastern Florida.

An ambitious and ruthless nobleman, **Hernán Cortés**° (1485–1547), led the most audacious expedition to the mainland. Cortés left Cuba in 1519 with six hundred fighting men and most of the is-

conquistador (kon-KEY-stuh-dor) **Cortés** (kor-TEZ)

land's weapons to assault the Mexican mainland in search of slaves and trade. Learning of the rich Aztec Empire in central Mexico, Cortés expanded on the American mainland the exploitation and conquest carried out in the Greater Antilles.

Many of the Amerindians whom the Aztecs had subjugated during the previous century resented the tribute, forced labor, and the large-scale human sacrifices to Aztec gods their rulers imposed on them. Consequently, some gave the Spanish their support as allies against the Aztecs. Like the Caribbean people, the mainland Amerindians had no precedent by which to judge these strangers. Later accounts suggest that some believed Cortés to be the legendary ruler Quetzalcoatl°, whose return to earth had been prophesied, and treated him with great deference.

Another consequence of millennia of isolation proved even more fatal: the lack of acquired immunity to Old World diseases. Smallpox, the most deadly of the early epidemics, appeared for the first time on the island of Hispaniola late in 1518. An infected member of the Cortés expedition then transmitted smallpox to Mexico in 1519, where it spread with deadly efficiency.

The Aztec emperor **Moctezuma°** II (r. 1502–1520) sent messengers to greet Cortés and determine whether he was god or man, friend or foe. Cortés advanced steadily toward the capital, Tenochtitlan°, overcoming Aztec opposition with cavalry charges and steel swords and gaining the support of discontented tributary peoples. When the Spaniards drew near, the emperor went out in a great procession, dressed in all his finery, to welcome Cortés with gifts and flower garlands.

Despite Cortés's initial promise of friendship, Moctezuma quickly found himself a prisoner in his own palace. The Spaniards looted his treasury, melting down its gold. Soon full-scale battle broke out. The Aztecs and their supporters briefly gained the upper hand. They destroyed half the Spanish force and four thousand of their Amerindian allies, sacrificing fifty-three Spanish prisoners and four horses to their gods and displaying their severed heads in rows on pikes. Reinforcements from Cuba enabled Cortés to regain the advantage. Smallpox,

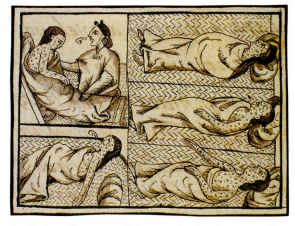

Death from Smallpox This Aztec drawing shows a healer attending smallpox victims. The little puffs coming from their mouths represent speech.   (Biblioteca Medicea Laurenziana. Photo: MicroFoto, Florence)

which weakened and killed more of the city's defenders than died in the fighting, also assisted his capture of Tenochtitlan in 1520. One source remembered that the disease "spread over the people as a great destruction."

After the capital fell, the conquistadors took over other parts of Mexico. Then some Spaniards began eyeing the Inca Empire, stretching nearly 3,000 miles (5,000 kilometers) south from the equator and containing half of the population in South America. The Inca had conquered the inhabitants of the Andes Mountains and the Pacific coast of South America during the previous century, and their rule was not fully accepted by the subjugated peoples.

The Inca rulers administered a well-organized empire with highly productive agriculture, exquisite stone cities (such as the capital, Cuzco), and rich gold and silver mines. The power of the Inca emperor rested on the belief that he was descended from the Sun God and on an efficient system of roads and messengers that kept him informed about major events. Yet at the end of the 1520s, before the Spanish had even been heard of, smallpox claimed countless lives, perhaps including the Inca emperor in 1530.

An even more devastating threat loomed: **Francisco Pizarro°** (ca. 1478–1541) and his motley band

---

Quetzalcoatl (ket-zahl-COH-ah-tal) **Moctezuma** (mock-teh-ZOO-ma) **Tenochtitlan** (teh-noch-TIT-lan)

Pizarro (pih-ZAHR-oh)

of 180 men, 37 horses, and 2 cannon. With limited education and some military experience, Pizarro had come to the Americas in 1502 at the age of twenty-five to seek his fortune. He had participated in the conquest of Hispaniola and in Balboa's expedition across the isthmus of Panama. By 1520 a wealthy landowner and official in Panama, he nevertheless gambled his fortune on exploring the Pacific coast to a point south of the equator, where he learned of the riches of the Inca. With a license from the king of Spain, he set out from Panama in 1531 to conquer them.

In November 1532, Pizarro arranged to meet the new Inca emperor, **Atahualpa**° (r. 1531–1533), near the Andean city of Cajamarca°. With supreme boldness and brutality, Pizarro's small band grabbed Atahualpa from a rich litter borne by eighty nobles as it passed through an enclosed courtyard. Though surrounded by an Inca army of at least 40,000, the Spaniards used their cannon to create confusion while their swords sliced the emperor's lightly armed retainers and servants to pieces.

Noting the glee with which the Spaniards seized gold, silver, and emeralds, the captive Atahualpa offered them what he thought would satisfy even the greediest among them in exchange for his freedom: a roomful of gold and silver. But after receiving 13,400 pounds (6,000 kilograms) of gold and 26,000 pounds (12,000 kilograms) of silver, the Spaniards gave Atahualpa a choice: being burned at the stake as a heathen or being strangled after a Christian baptism. He chose the latter. His death and the Spanish occupation broke the unity of the Inca Empire.

In 1533, the Spaniards took Cuzco and from there set out to conquer and loot the rest of the empire. The defeat of a final rebellion in 1536 spelled the end of Inca rule. Five years later, Pizarro himself met a violent death at the hands of Spanish rivals, but the conquest of the mainland continued. Incited by the fabulous wealth of the Aztecs and Inca, conquistadors extended Spanish conquest and exploration in South and North America, dreaming of new treasuries to loot.

Atahualpa (ah-tuh-WAHL-puh)   Cajamarca (kah-hah-MAHR-kah)

Patterns of Dominance

Within fifty years of Columbus's first landing, the Spanish had located and occupied the major population centers of the Americas and penetrated many of the more thinly populated areas. Why did the peoples of the Americas suffer a fate so different from that of peoples in Africa and Asia? Why were the Spanish able to erect a vast land empire in the Americas so quickly?

First, unfamiliar illnesses devastated the Caribbean islands and then the mainland. Contemporaries estimated that between 25 and 50 percent of those infected with smallpox died. Repeated epidemics inhibited the Amerindians' ability to regain control. Estimates of the size of the population before Columbus's arrival, based on sparse evidence, vary widely. Yet historians agree that the Amerindian population fell sharply during the sixteenth century. The Americas became a "widowed land," open to resettlement from across the Atlantic.

A second factor was Spain's superior military technology. Steel swords, protective armor, and horses gave the Spaniards an advantage over their Amerindian opponents. Though few in number, muskets and cannon provided a psychological edge. However, the Spanish conquests depended heavily on large numbers of Amerindian allies armed with indigenous weapons. The most decisive military advantage may have been the no-holds-barred fighting techniques the Spaniards had developed during their wars at home.

The third factor in Spain's conquest was the precedent established by the reconquest of Granada in 1492: forced labor, forced conversion, and the incorporation of conquered lands into a new empire.

The same three factors help explain the different outcomes elsewhere. Centuries of contacts before 1500 meant that Europeans, Africans, and Asians shared the same Old World diseases. Only very isolated peoples in Africa and Asia suffered a demographic calamity. The Iberians enjoyed a military advantage at sea, but on land they had no decisive advantage against more numerous indigenous armies. Everywhere, Iberian religious zeal went hand in hand with a desire for riches. In Iberia and America, conquest itself brought wealth. But in

Africa and Asia, existing trading networks made wealth dependent on commercial domination rather than conquest.

CONCLUSION

H istorians consider the century between 1450 and 1550 a turning point in world history. Some assign names: the "Vasco da Gama epoch," the "Columbian era," the "age of Magellan," or simply the "modern period." During those years, European explorers opened new long-distance trade routes across the world's oceans, for the first time establishing regular contact among all the continents. By 1550, those who followed them had broadened trading contacts with sub-Saharan Africa, gained mastery of the Indian Ocean trade routes, and conquered a land empire in the Americas.

What gave this maritime revolution unprecedented importance had more to do with what happened after 1550 than with what happened earlier. European overseas empires would endure longer than the Mongols' and would continue to expand for three and a half centuries. Unlike the Chinese, the Europeans did not turn their backs on the world after an initial burst of exploration. Not content with dominating the Indian Ocean, Europeans opened in the Atlantic a maritime network of comparable wealth. They also established regular trade across the Pacific. The maritime expansion begun between 1450 and 1550 marked the beginning of an age of growing global interaction.

■ Key Terms

Zheng He	Christopher Columbus
Arawak	Ferdinand Magellan
Henry the Navigator	conquistadors
caravel	Hernán Cortés
Gold Goast	Moctezuma
Bartolomeu Dias	Francisco Pizarro
Vasco da Gama	Atahualpa

■ Suggested Reading

The selections edited by Joseph R. Levenson, *European Expansion and the Counter Example of Asia, 1300–1600*

(1967), describe Chinese expansion and Western impressions of China. Janet Abu-Lughod, *Before European Hegemony: The World System, A.D. 1250–1350* (1989), affords a speculative reassessment of the Mongols and the Indian Ocean trade in creating the modern world system; she summarizes her thesis in the American Historical Association (AHA) booklet *The World System in the Thirteenth Century: Dead-End or Precursor?* (1993).

The Chinese account of Zheng He's voyages is Ma Huan, *Ying-yai Sheng-lan: "The Overall Survey of the Ocean's Shores"* [1433], edited and translated by J. V. G. Mills (1970). On Polynesian expansion, see Jesse D. Jennings, ed., *The Prehistory of Polynesia* (1979). In it, the chapter "Voyaging," by Ben R. Finney, encapsulates his *Voyage of Rediscovery: A Cultural Odyssey Through Polynesia* (1994). Felipe Fernandez-Armesto, *Before Columbus: Exploration and Colonization from the Mediterranean to the Atlantic, 1229–1492* (1987), summarizes the medieval background to European intercontinental voyages. Tim Severin, *The Brendan Voyage* (2000), vividly recounts a modern retracing of even earlier Irish voyages.

For the technologies of European expansion, see Carlo M. Cipolla, *Guns, Sails, and Empires: Technological Innovation and the Early Phases of European Expansion, 1400–1700* (1965; reprint, 1985), or the more advanced study by Roger C. Smith, *Vanguard of Empire: Ships of Exploration in the Age of Columbus* (1993).

Surveys of European explorations based on contemporary records include Boies Penrose, *Travel and Discovery in the Age of the Renaissance, 1420–1620* (1952); J. H. Parry, *The Age of Reconnaissance: Discovery, Exploration, and Settlement, 1450–1650* (1963); and G. V. Scammell, *The World Encompassed: The First European Maritime Empires, c. 800–1650* (1981).

C. R. Boxer, *The Portuguese Seaborne Empire, 1415–1825* (1969), gives a general account, with more detail to be found in Bailey W. Diffie and George D. Winius, *Foundations of the Portuguese Empire, 1415–1580* (1977); A. J. R. Russell-Wood, *The Portuguese Empire: A World on the Move* (1998); and Luc Cuyvers, *Into the Rising Sun: The Journey of Vasco da Gama and the Discovery of the Modern World* (1998). John William Blake, ed., *Europeans in West Africa, 1450–1560* (1942), excerpts contemporary Portuguese, Castilian, and English sources. Elaine Sanceau, *The Life of Prester John: A Chronicle of Portuguese Exploration* (1941), covers Portuguese relations with Ethiopia. *The Summa Oriental of Tomé Pires: An Account of the East, from the Red Sea to Japan, Written in Malacca and India in 1512–1515*, translated by Armando Cortesão (1944), provides a firsthand account of the Portuguese in the Indian Ocean.

For Spanish expansion, see J. H. Parry, *The Spanish Seaborne Empire* (1967). Samuel Eliot Morison's excellent *Admiral of the Ocean Sea: A Life of Christopher Columbus* (1942) is available in an abridged version as *Christopher Columbus, Mariner* (1955). Tzvetan Todorov, *The Conquest of America,* translated by Richard Howard (1985), focuses on Spanish shortcomings. Marvin Lunenfeld, ed., *1492: Discovery, Invasion, Encounter* (1991), critically examines contemporary sources and interpretations. William D. Phillips and Carla Rhan Phillips, *The Worlds of Christopher Columbus* (1992), looks at the subject in terms of modern concerns. Peggy K. Liss, *Isabel the Queen: Life and Times* (1992), affords a sympathetic account. James Lockhart's *Men of Cajamarca: A Social and Biographical Study of the First Conquerors of Peru* (1972) contains biographies of Pizarro's men. A firsthand account of Magellan's expedition is Antonio Pigafetta, *Magellan's Voyage: A Narrative Account of the First Circumnavigation,* available in a two-volume edition (1969) that includes a facsimile reprint of the manuscript.

J. H. Elliott, *The Old World and the New, 1492–1650* (1970), describes the transatlantic encounters of Europe and the Americas. Alfred W. Crosby, *The Columbian Voyages, the Columbian Exchange, and Their Historians* (1987), available as an American Historical Association booklet, surveys the first encounters and their long-term consequences. Mark A. Burkholder and Lyman L. Johnson, *Colonial Latin America,* 2d ed. (1994), give a balanced account of the Spanish conquest.

David Northrup, *Africa's Discovery of Europe, 1450–1850* (2002), and John Thornton, *Africa and Africans in the Making of the Atlantic World, 1400–1800,* 2d ed. (1998), examine encounters with Europeans, Africa in the Atlantic economy, and African impact in the New World. *The Broken Spears: The Aztec Account of the Conquest of Mexico,* edited by Miguel Leon-Portilla (1962), presents Amerindian chronicles, as does Nathan Wachtel, *The Vision of the Vanquished: The Spanish Conquest of Peru Through Indian Eyes* (1977). Anthony Reid, *Southeast Asia in the Age of Commerce, 1450–1680,* 2 vols. (1988, 1993), deals with that region.

■ Notes

1. Ma Huan, *Ying-yai Sheng-lan: "The Overall Survey of the Ocean's Shores,"* ed. Feng Ch'eng-Chün, trans. J. V. G. Mills (Cambridge, England: Cambridge University Press, 1970), 180.
2. Alvise da Cadamosto in *The Voyages of Cadamosto and Other Documents,* ed. and trans. G. R. Crone (London: Hakluyt Society, 1937), 2.

Climate and Population, to 1500

During the millennia before 1500 human populations expanded in three momentous surges. The first occurred after 50,000 B.C.E. when humans emigrated from their African homeland to all of the inhabitable continents. After that, the global population remained steady for several millennia. During the second expansion, between about 5000 and 500 B.C.E., population rose from about 5 million to 100 million as agricultural societies spread around the world (see Figure 1). Again population growth then slowed for several centuries before a third surge took world population to over 350 million by 1200 C.E. (see Figure 2).

For a long time historians tended to attribute these population surges to cultural and technological advances. Indeed, a great many changes in culture and technology are associated with adaptation to different climates and food supplies in the first surge and with the domestication of plants and animals in the second. However, historians have not found a cultural or technological change to explain the third surge, nor can they explain why creativity would have stagnated for long periods between the surges. Something else must have been at work.

Recently historians have begun to pay more attention to the impact of long-term variations in global climate. By examining ice cores drilled out of glaciers, scientists have been able to compile records of thousands of years of climate change. The comparative width of tree rings from ancient forests has provided additional data on periods of favorable and unfavorable growth. Such evidence shows that cycles of population growth and stagnation followed changes in global climate.

Historians now believe that global temperatures were above normal for extended periods from the late 1100s to the late 1200s C.E. In the temperate lands where most of the world's people lived, above-normal temperatures meant a longer growing season, more bountiful harvests, and thus a more adequate and reliable food supply. The ways in which societies responded to the medieval warm period are as important as the climate change, but it is unlikely that human agency alone would have produced the medieval surge. One notable response was that of the Vikings, who increased the size and range of their settlements in the North Atlantic, although their raids also caused death and destruction.

Some of the complexities involved in the interaction of human agency, climate, and other natural factors are also evident in the demographic changes that followed the medieval warm period. During the 1200s the Mongol invasions caused death and disruption of agriculture across Eurasia. China's population, which had been over 100 million in 1200, declined by a third or more by 1300. The Mongol invasions did not cause harm west of Russia, but climate changes in the 1300s resulted in population losses in Europe. Unusually heavy rains caused crop failures and a prolonged famine in northern Europe from 1315 to 1319.

The freer movement of merchants within the Mongol empire also facilitated the spread of disease across Eurasia, culminating in the great pandemic known as the Black Death in Europe. The demographic recovery underway in China was reversed. The even larger population losses in Europe may have been affected by the decrease in global temperatures to their lowest point in many millennia between 1350 and 1375. Improving economic conditions enabled population to recover more rapidly in Europe after 1400 than in China, where the conditions of rural life remained harsh.

Because many other historical circumstances interact with changing weather patterns, historians have a long way to go in deciphering the role of climate in history. Nevertheless, it is a factor that can no longer be ignored.

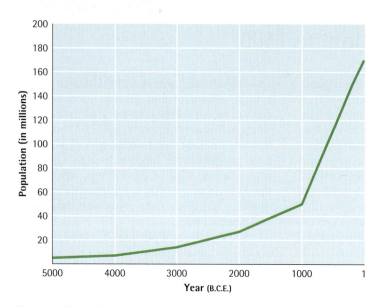

Figure 1 World Population, 5000–1 B.C.E.

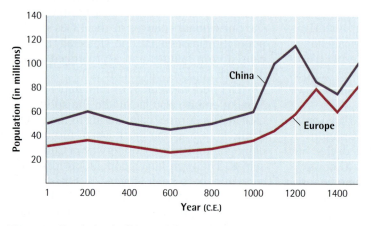

Figure 2 Population in China and Europe, 1–1500 C.E.

PART FIVE

The Globe Encompassed, 1500–1800

CHAPTER 15
Transformations in Europe, 1500–1750

CHAPTER 16
The Americas, the Atlantic, and Africa, 1530–1770

CHAPTER 17
Southwest Asia and the Indian Ocean, 1500–1750

CHAPTER 18
Northern Eurasia, 1500–1800

The decades between 1500 and 1800 witnessed a tremendous expansion of commercial, cultural, and biological exchanges around the world. New long-distance sea routes linked Europe with sub-Saharan Africa and the existing maritime networks of the Indian Ocean and East Asia. Spanish and Portuguese voyages ended the isolation of the Americas and created new webs of exchange in the Atlantic and Pacific. Overland expansion of Muslim, Russian, and Chinese empires also increased global interaction.

These expanding contacts had major demographic and cultural consequences. In the Americas, European diseases devastated the Amerindian population, facilitating the establishment of large Spanish, Portuguese, French, and British empires. Europeans introduced enslaved Africans to relieve the labor shortage. Immigrant Africans and Europeans brought new languages, religious practices, music, and forms of personal adornment.

In Asia and Africa, by contrast, the most important changes owed more to internal forces than to European actions. The Portuguese seized control of some important trading ports and networks in the Indian Ocean and pioneered new contacts with China and Japan. In time, the Dutch, French, and English expanded these profitable connections, but in 1750 Europeans were still primarily a maritime force. Asians and Africans generally retained control of their lands and participated freely in overseas trade.

The Islamic world saw the expansion of the Ottoman Empire in the Middle East and the establishment of the Safavid Empire in Iran and the Mughal Empire in South Asia. In northern Eurasia, Russia and China acquired vast new territories and populations, while a new national government in Japan promoted economic development and stemmed foreign influence.

Ecological change was rapid in areas of rising population and economic activity. Forests were cut down to meet the increasing need for farmland, timber, and fuel. Population growth in parts of Eurasia placed great strain on the environment. On a more positive note, domesticated animals and crops from the Old World transformed agriculture in the Americas, while Amerindian foods such as the potato became staples of the diet of the Old World.

New goods, new wealth, and new tastes from overseas transformed Europe in this period. Global and regional trade promoted urban growth, but conflict was also rife. States spent heavily on warfare in Europe and abroad. The printing press spread new religious and scientific ideas, and challenges to established values and institutions.

By 1750 the balance of power in the world had begun to shift from the East to the West. The Ottoman, Mughal, and Chinese empires had declined in relative strength compared to the much smaller but technologically more sophisticated states of northwestern Europe.

	1500	**1550**	**1600**	**1650**
Americas	• 1500 Portuguese discover Brazil Viceroyalty of Mexico 1535 •	• 1540 Viceroyalty of Peru • 1545 Silver discovered at Potosi, Bolivia	Brazil is world's main source of sugar 1600 •	Dutch bring sugar and slavery to West Indies 1640s • 1607–1640 England and France found colonies	English take Jamaica 1660 •
Europe	1500–1600 Spain's golden century • 1519 Protestant Reformation begins Catholic Reformation begins 1545 •	English defeat Spanish Armada 1588 • • 1550 Scientific Revolution begins	1618–1648 Thirty Years War 1600–1700 Netherlands' golden century
Africa	• 1505 Portuguese begin assault on Swahili cities		• 1591 Morocco conquers Songhai Empire	
Middle East	1520–1566 Reign of Ottoman sultan Suleiman the Magnificent	• 1571 Ottoman defeat at Lepanto 1588–1629 Reign of Safavid shah Abbas the Great	• 1622 Iranians expel Portuguese from Hormuz
Asia and Oceania	Reign of Mughal emperor Akbar 1556–1605 • 1526 Mughal Empire founded in India Russia conquers Sibir Khanate 1582 •	"Closing" of Japan 1639 • • 1603 Tokugawa Shogunate founded in Japan	• 1644 Qing Empire begins in China

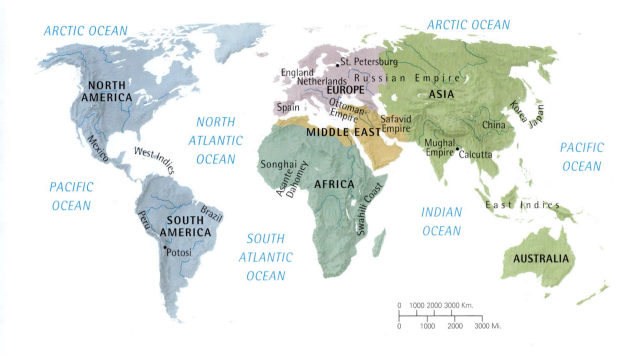

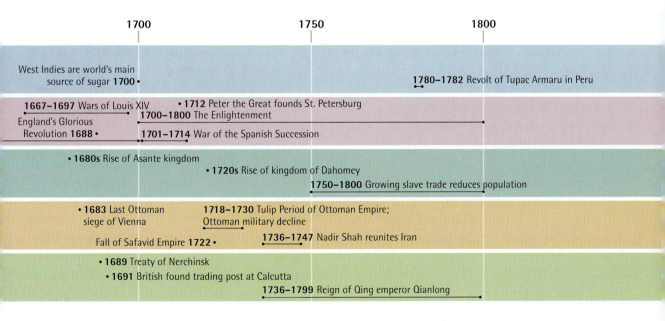

1700	1750	1800

West Indies are world's main source of sugar **1700** •

1780–1782 Revolt of Tupac Armaru in Peru

1667–1697 Wars of Louis XIV

• **1712** Peter the Great founds St. Petersburg

England's Glorious Revolution **1688** •

1700–1800 The Enlightenment

1701–1714 War of the Spanish Succession

• **1680s** Rise of Asante kingdom

• **1720s** Rise of kingdom of Dahomey

1750–1800 Growing slave trade reduces population

• **1683** Last Ottoman siege of Vienna

1718–1730 Tulip Period of Ottoman Empire; Ottoman military decline

Fall of Safavid Empire **1722** •

1736–1747 Nadir Shah reunites Iran

• **1689** Treaty of Nerchinsk

• **1691** British found trading post at Calcutta

1736–1799 Reign of Qing emperor Qianlong

15 Transformations in Europe, 1500–1750

CHAPTER OUTLINE

Culture and Ideas

Social and Economic Life

Political Innovations

Environment and Technology: Mapping the World

As he neared the end of his life in 1575, the French scholar and humanist Loys Le Roy° reflected on the times in which he lived. It was, he believed, a golden age for Europe, and he ticked off the names of more than 130 scholars and translators, writers and poets, artists and sculptors, and explorers and philosophers whose work over the preceding two centuries had restored the standards of ancient learning. Later ages would call this scholarly and artistic revival the European **Renaissance**.

In addition, Le Roy enumerated a series of technological innovations that he believed had also transformed his age: printing, the marine compass, and cannonry. He put printing first because its rapid spread across Europe had done so much to communicate the literary and

scholarly revival. The marine compass had made possible the sea voyages that now connected Europe directly to Africa and Asia and had led to the discovery and conquest of the Americas.

Le Roy gave third place to firearms because they had transformed warfare. Cannon and more recently devised hand-held weapons had swept before them all older military instruments. His enthusiasm for this transformation was dampened by the demonstrated capacity of firearms to cause devastation and ruin. Among the other evils of his age Le Roy enumerated syphilis and the spread of religious heresies and sects.

Reading Loys Le Roy's analysis more than four centuries later, one is struck not only by the acuity of his judgment and the beauty and clarity of his prose, but also by the astonishing geo-

Loys Le Roy (lwa-EES le-RWAH)

graphical and historical range of his understanding. He credits both ancient and modern Greeks and Italians for their cultural contributions, the Germans for their role in perfecting printing and cannonry, and the Spanish for their overseas voyages. But his frame of reference is not confined to Europe. He cites the mathematical skills of ancient Egyptians; the military conquests of Mongols, Turks, and Persians (Iranians); Arabs' contributions to science and medicine; and China's contributions to the development of printing.

The global framework of Le Roy's analysis led him to conclude that he was living at a turning point in world history. For long centuries, he argued, the military might of the Mongols and Turks had threatened the peoples of Europe, and Safavid Iran and Mamluk Egypt had surpassed any European land in riches. Now the West was in the ascendancy. Europeans' military might equaled that of their Middle Eastern neighbors. They were amassing new wealth from Asian trade and American silver. Most of all, the explosion of learning and knowledge had given Europe intellectual equality and perhaps superiority. Le Roy noted perceptively that while printing presses were in use all across Europe, the Islamic world had closed itself off from the benefits of this new technology, refusing to allow presses to be set up and even forbidding the printing of Arabic works about their lands in Europe.

As you read this chapter, ask yourself these questions:

- How perceptive was Loys Le Roy about his own age and its place in world history?

- How much did learning, printing, and firearms define early modern Europe?

- Would someone from a lower social station in Europe share Le Roy's optimism about this era?

CULTURE AND IDEAS

One place to observe the conflict and continuity of early modern Europe is in the world of ideas. Theological controversies broke the religious unity of the Latin Church and contributed to violent wars. A huge witch scare showed the power of Christian beliefs about the Devil and of traditional folklore about malevolent powers. The influence of classical ideas from Greco-Roman antiquity increased among better-educated people, but some thinkers challenged the authority of the ancients. Their new models of the motion of the planets encouraged others to challenge traditional social and political systems, with important implications for the period after 1750. Each of these events had its own causes, but the technology of the printing press enhanced the impact of all.

Religious Reformation

In 1500 the **papacy,** the central government of Latin Christianity, was simultaneously gaining stature and suffering from corruption and dissent. Larger donations and tax receipts let popes fund ambitious construction projects in Rome, their capital city. During the sixteenth century Rome gained fifty-four new churches and other buildings, which showcased the artistic Renaissance then under way. However, the church's wealth and power also attracted ambitious men, including some whose personal lives became the source of scandal.

The jewel of the building projects was the new Saint Peter's Basilica in Rome. The unprecedented size and splendor of this church were intended to glorify God and enhance the standing of the papacy. Such a project required refined tastes and vast sums of money.

The skillful overseer of the design and financing of the new Saint Peter's was Pope Leo X (r. 1513–1521), a member of the wealthy Medici° family of Florence, famous for its patronage of the arts. Pope Leo's artistic taste was superb and his personal life free from scandal, but he was more a man of action than a spiritual leader. One

Medici (MED-ih-chee)

technique that he used to raise funds for the basilica was to authorize an **indulgence**—a forgiveness of the punishment due for past sins, granted by church authorities as a reward for a pious act such as making a pilgrimage, saying a particular prayer, or making a donation to a religious cause.

A young professor of sacred scripture, Martin Luther (1483–1546), objected to the way the new indulgence was preached. As the result of a powerful religious experience, Luther had forsaken money and marriage for a monastic life of prayer, self-denial, and study. He found personal consolation in a passage in Saint Paul's Epistle to the Romans stating that salvation came not from "doing certain things" but from religious faith. That passage also led Luther to object to the way the indulgence preachers appeared to emphasize giving money more than the faith behind the act. He wrote to Pope Leo, asking him to stop this abuse, and challenged the preachers to a debate on the theology of indulgences.

This theological dispute escalated into a contest between two strong-minded men. Largely ignoring Luther's theological objections, Pope Leo regarded his letter as a challenge to papal power and moved to silence him. During a debate in 1519, a papal representative led Luther into open disagreement with some church doctrines, for which the papacy condemned him. Unable to reform the church from within, Luther burned the papal bull (document) of condemnation, rejecting the pope's authority and beginning the movement known as the **Protestant Reformation.**

Accusing those whom he called "Romanists" (Roman Catholics) of relying on "good works," Luther insisted that the only way to salvation was through faith in Jesus Christ. He further declared that Christian belief must be based on the word of God in the Bible and on Christian tradition, not on the authority of the pope, as Catholics held. Eventually his conclusions led him to abandon his monastic prayers and penances and to marry a former nun.

Today Roman Catholics and Lutherans have resolved many of their theological differences, but in the sixteenth century stubbornness on both sides made reconciliation impossible. Moreover, Luther's use of the printing press to promote his ideas won him the support of powerful Germans, who responded to his nationalist portrayal of the dispute as an effort of an Italian pope to beautify his city with German funds.

Inspired by Luther's denunciation of church corruption, leaders elsewhere called for a return to authentic Christian practices and beliefs. John Calvin (1509–1564), a Frenchman who turned from the study of law to theology after experiencing a religious conversion, became a highly influential Protestant leader. As a young man, Calvin published *The Institutes of the Christian Religion,* a masterful synthesis of Christian teachings, in 1535. Calvin's teaching differed from that of Roman Catholics and Lutherans in two respects. First, while agreeing with Luther's emphasis on faith over works, Calvin denied that even human faith could merit salvation. Salvation, said Calvin, was a gift God gave to those He "predestined" for salvation. Second, Calvin went farther than Luther in curtailing the power of a clerical hierarchy and in simplifying religious rituals. Calvinist congregations elected their own governing committees and in time created regional and national synods (councils) to regulate doctrinal issues. Calvinists also displayed simplicity in dress, life, and worship. In an age of ornate garments, they wore simple black clothes, avoided ostentatious living, and worshiped in churches devoid of statues, most musical instruments, stained-glass windows, incense, and vestments.

The Reformers appealed to genuine religious sentiments, but political circumstances (discussed below) and the social agendas that motivated people to join them contributed to their successes and failures. Lutheranism appealed most strongly to German speakers and linguistically related Scandinavians. Peasants and urban laborers sometimes defied their masters by adopting a different faith. Protestants were no more inclined than Roman Catholics to question male dominance in the church and the family, but most Protestants rejected the tradition of celibate priests and nuns and advocated Christian marriage for all adults.

Shaken by the Protestant Reformers' appeal, the Catholic Church undertook its own reforms. A council that met at the city of Trent, in northern Italy, in three sessions between 1545 and 1563 painstakingly distinguished proper Catholic doctrines from Protestant "errors." The council also

C H R O N O L O G Y

	Politics and Culture	Environment and Technology	Warfare
1500	**1500s** Spain's golden century	**Mid-1500s** Increasing land drainage in Holland	**1526–1571** Ottoman wars
	1519 Protestant Reformation begins		**1546–1555** German Wars of Religion
	1540s Scientific Revolution begins		**1562–1589** French Wars of Religion
	1545 Catholic Reformation begins		**1566–1648** Netherlands Revolt
	Late 1500s Witch-hunts increase	**1590s** Dutch develop fly-boats; Little Ice Age begins	
1600	**1600s** Holland's golden century	**1600s** Depletion of forests growing	
		1609 Galileo's astronomical telescope	
			1618–1648 Thirty Years War
			1642–1648 English Civil War
			1652–1678 Anglo-Dutch Wars
			1667–1697 Wars of Louis XIV
		1682 Canal du Midi completed	**1683–1697** Ottoman wars
1700	**1700s** The Enlightenment begins		**1700–1721** Great Northern War
			1701–1714 War of the Spanish Succession
		1750 English mine nearly 5 million tons of coal a year	
		1755 Lisbon earthquake	

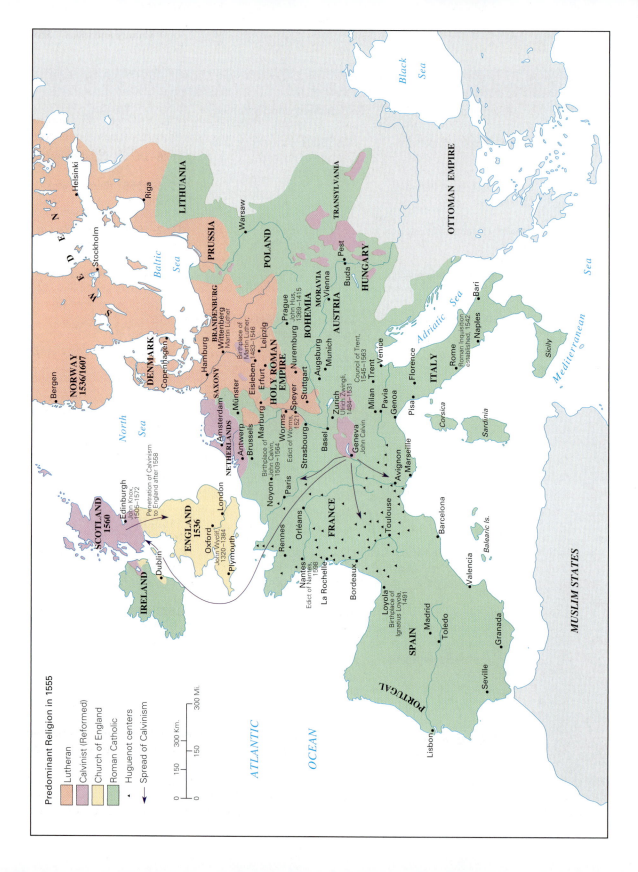

Predominant Religion in 1555

Lutheran

Calvinist (Reformed)

Church of England

Roman Catholic

▾ Huguenot centers

→ Spread of Calvinism

| 0 | 150 | 300 Km. |
| 0 | 150 | 300 Mi. |

ATLANTIC

OCEAN

North Sea

Baltic Sea

Black Sea

Adriatic Sea

Mediterranean Sea

SWEDEN

NORWAY 1536/1607

Bergen

Helsinki

Stockholm

Riga

LITHUANIA

Warsaw

PRUSSIA

POLAND

TRANSYLVANIA

OTTOMAN EMPIRE

DENMARK

Copenhagen

Hamburg

BRANDENBURG

SAXONY

Wittenberg
Birthplace of Martin Luther, Martin Luther

Eisleben, 1483–1546

Erfurt

Leipzig

Prague
John Hus, 1369–1415

BOHEMIA

MORAVIA

Buda

Pest

Vienna

AUSTRIA

HUNGARY

Bari

NETHERLANDS

Amsterdam

Münster

Antwerp

Brussels

Marburg

HOLY ROMAN EMPIRE

Nuremburg

Augsburg

Munich

Speyer

Worms

Birthplace of John Calvin, 1509–1564

Noyon

Edict of Worms, 1521

Strasbourg

Basel

Zurich
Ulrich Zwingli, 1484–1531

Geneva
John Calvin

Council of Trent, 1545–1563

Trent

Venice

Milan

Pavia

Genoa

Florence

Pisa

ITALY

Rome
Roman Inquisition established, 1542

Naples

Sicily

Corsica

Sardinia

Stuttgart

Paris

Avignon

Marseille

FRANCE

Orléans

Rennes

Nantes
Edict of Nantes, 1598

La Rochelle

Bordeaux

Toulouse

Barcelona

Valencia

Balearic Is.

SCOTLAND 1560

Edinburgh
John Knox, 1505–1572

Penetration of Calvinism to England after 1558

ENGLAND 1536

Oxford
John Wyclif, 1320–1384

London

Plymouth

IRELAND

Dublin

Loyola
Birthplace of Ignatius Loyola, 1491

Madrid

Toledo

Granada

SPAIN

Seville

PORTUGAL

Lisbon

MUSLIM STATES

reaffirmed the supremacy of the pope and called for a number of reforms, including requiring each bishop to reside in his diocese and each diocese to have a theological seminary to train priests. Also important to this **Catholic Reformation** were the activities of a new religious order—the Society of Jesus, or "Jesuits," that Ignatius of Loyola (1491–1556), a Spanish nobleman, founded in 1540. Well-educated Jesuits helped win back some adherents by their teaching and preaching (see Map 15.1). Other Jesuits became missionaries overseas (see Chapters 16 and 18).

Given the complexity of the issues and the intensity of the emotions that the Protestant Reformation stirred, it is not surprising that violence often flared up. Both sides persecuted and sometimes executed those of differing views. Bitter "wars of religion," fought over a mixture of religious and secular issues, continued in parts of western Europe until 1648.

Traditional Thinking and Witch-Hunts

Religious differences among Protestants and between them and Catholics continued to generate animosity long after the first generation of reformers, but from a global perspective European Christians still had much in common both in their theology and in the local folk customs and pre-Christian beliefs that remained powerful everywhere in Europe. The widespread **witch-hunts** that Protestants and Catholics undertook in early modern Europe are a dramatic illustration of those common beliefs.

Prevailing European ideas about the natural world blended two distinct traditions: the folklore about magic and forest spirits passed down orally from pre-Christian times, and the teachings of the Bible heard by all in church and read by growing numbers in vernacular translations. In the minds of most people, Christian teachings about miracles, saints, and devils mixed with folklore.

Like people in other parts of the world, most early modern Europeans believed that natural events could have supernatural causes. When crops failed or domestic animals died unexpectedly, many people blamed unseen spirits. People also attributed human triumphs and tragedies to supernatural causes. When an earthquake destroyed much of Lisbon, Portugal's capital city, in November 1755, for example, both educated and uneducated people saw the event as a punishment sent by God. A Jesuit charged it "scandalous to pretend that the earthquake was just a natural event." An English Protestant leader agreed, comparing Lisbon's fate with that of Sodom, the biblical city that God destroyed because of the sinfulness of its citizens.

The extraordinary fear of the power of witches that swept across northern Europe in the late sixteenth and seventeenth centuries grew out of these beliefs. It is estimated that secular and church authorities tried over a hundred thousand people—some three-fourths of them women—for practicing witchcraft. Some were acquitted; some recanted; but more than half were executed—most in Protestant lands. Torture and badgering questions persuaded many accused witches to confess to casting spells and to describe in vivid detail their encounters with the Devil and their attendance at nighttime assemblies of witches.

The trial records make it clear that both the accusers and the accused believed that it was possible for angry and jealous individuals to use evil magic and the power of the Devil to attack people and domestic animals or to cause crops to wither in the fields. Researchers think that at least some of those accused may really have tried to use witchcraft to harm their enemies. However, it was the Reformation's focus on the Devil—the enemy of God—as the source of evil that made such malevolence so serious a crime and that helped revive older fears of witchcraft.

Modern historians also argue that many accusations against widows and independent-minded women drew on the widespread distrust of women not directly under the control of fathers or husbands. The fact that such women had important roles in tending animals and the sick and in childbirth also made them suspects if death occurred.

Map 15.1 Religious Reformation in Europe   The Reformation brought greater religious freedom but also led to religious conflict and persecution. In many places the Reformation accelerated the trend toward state control of religion and added religious differences to the motives for wars among Europeans.

Death to Witches   This woodcut from 1574 depicts three women convicted of witchcraft being burned alive in Baden, Switzerland. The well-dressed townsmen look on stolidly.   (Zentralbibliothek Zurich)

In parts of the world where belief in witchcraft is still strong, witch-hunts arise at times of social stress, and people who are marginalized by poverty and by the suspicions of others often relish the celebrity that public confession brings. "Confessing" may even bring release from the guilt the accused feel for wishing evil on their neighbors.

No single reason can explain the witchcraft hysteria in early modern Europe, but, for both the accusers and the accused, there are plausible connections between the witch-hunts and rising social tensions, rural poverty, and environmental strains. Far from being a bizarre aberration, witch-hunts reflected the larger social climate of early modern Europe.

The Scientific Revolution

Among the educated, the Bible and the writings of Greco-Roman antiquity, many of them newly discovered by Renaissance scholars, were more trusted guides to the natural world than was folklore. The greatest authority on physics was Aristotle, a Greek philosopher who taught that everything on earth was reducible to four elements. The surface of the earth was composed of the two heavy elements, earth and water. The atmosphere was made up of two lighter elements, air and fire, which floated above the ground. Higher still were the sun, moon, planets, and stars, which, according to Aristotelian physics, were so light and pure that they floated in crystalline spheres. This theory accorded perfectly with the commonsense perception that all heavenly bodies revolved around the earth.

The ideas of the ancient Greek mathematician Pythagoras supported this view. Pythagoreans attributed to mystical properties the ability of simple mathematical equations to describe physical objects. They attached special significance to the simplest (to them perfect) geometrical shapes: the circle (a point rotated around another point) and the sphere (a circle rotated on its axis). They believed that celestial objects were perfect spheres orbiting the earth in perfectly circular orbits.

In the sixteenth century, however, careful observations and mathematical calculations, many of them made by astronomers in the Muslim world and translated into Latin, led some imaginative European investigators to challenge these traditional views. These pioneers of the **Scientific Revolution** took issue with the efforts of earlier astronomers and mathematicians to fit their observations of the heavens into the prevailing theories of circular orbits. Rejecting the accumulation of ingenious theories and eighty hypothetical spheres used to explain some seemingly irregular movements, a Polish monk and mathematician named Nicholas Copernicus (1473–1543), possibly building on the theories of Muslim astronomers, came up with a mathematically simpler solution: switching the center of the different orbits from the earth to the sun, which would reduce the number of spheres that were needed.

Copernicus did not challenge the idea that the sun, moon, and planets were light, perfect spheres or that they moved in circular orbits. But his placement of the sun, not the earth, at the center of things began a revolution in understanding the structure of the heavens and the place of humans in the universe. To escape the anticipated controversies, Copernicus delayed the publication of his heliocentric (sun-centered) theory until the end of his life.

Other astronomers, including the Danish Tycho Brahe (1546–1601) and his German assistant Johannes Kepler (1571–1630), strengthened and improved on Copernicus's model, showing that planets actually move in elliptical, not circular orbits. The most brilliant of the Copernicans was the Italian Galileo Galilei° (1564–1642). In 1609 Galileo built a telescope through which he took a closer look at the heavens. Able to magnify distant objects thirty times beyond the power of the naked eye, Galileo saw that heavenly bodies were not the perfectly smooth spheres of the Aristotelians. The moon, he reported in *The Starry Messenger* (1610), had mountains and valleys; the sun had spots; other planets had their own moons. In other words, the earth was not alone in being heavy and changeable.

At first, the Copernican universe found more critics than supporters because it so directly challenged not just popular ideas but also the intellectual synthesis of classical and biblical authorities. How, demanded Aristotle's defenders, could the heavy earth move without producing vibrations that would shake the planet apart? Is the Bible wrong, asked the theologians, when the Book of Joshua says that, by God's command, "the sun [not the earth] stood still . . . for about a whole day" to give the ancient Israelites victory in their conquest of Palestine? If Aristotle's physics was wrong, worried other traditionalists, would not the theological synthesis built on other parts of his philosophy be open to question?

Intellectual and religious leaders encouraged political authorities to suppress the new ideas. Most Protestant leaders, following the lead of Martin Luther, condemned the heliocentric universe as contrary to the Bible. Catholic authorities waited longer to act. After all, both Copernicus and Galileo were Roman Catholics. Copernicus had dedicated his book to the pope, and in 1582 another pope, Gregory XIII, had used the latest astronomical findings to issue a new and more accurate calendar (still used today). Galileo ingeniously argued that the conflict between scripture and sci-

ence was only apparent: the word of God revealed in the Bible was expressed in the imperfect language of ordinary people, but in nature God's truth was revealed more perfectly in a language that could be learned by careful observation and scientific reasoning.

Unfortunately, Galileo also ridiculed those who were slow to accept his findings, charging that Copernican ideas were "mocked and hooted at by an infinite multitude . . . of fools." Smarting under Galileo's stinging sarcasm, some Jesuits and other critics got his ideas condemned by the Roman Inquisition in 1616, which put *The Starry Messenger* on the Index of Forbidden Books and prohibited Galileo from publishing further on the subject. (In 1992 the Catholic Church officially retracted its condemnation of Galileo.)

Despite official opposition, printed books spread the new scientific ideas among scholars across Europe. In England, Robert Boyle (1627–1691) used experimental methods and a trial-and-error approach to examine the inner workings of chemistry. Through the Royal Society, chartered in London in 1662 to promote knowledge of the natural world, Boyle and others became enthusiastic missionaries of mechanical science and fierce opponents of the Aristotelians.

Meanwhile, English mathematician Isaac Newton (1642–1727) was carrying Galileo's demonstration that the heavens and earth share a common physics to its logical conclusion. Newton formulated a set of mathematical laws that all physical objects obeyed. It was the force of gravity—not angels—that governed the elliptical orbits of heavenly bodies. It was gravitation (and the resistance of air) that caused cannonballs to fall back to earth. From 1703 until his death Newton served as president of the Royal Society, using his prestige to promote the new science that came to bear his name.

As the condemnation of Galileo demonstrates, in 1700 most religious and intellectual leaders viewed the new science with suspicion or outright hostility because of the challenge it posed to established ways of thought. Yet the principal pioneers of the Scientific Revolution were convinced that scientific discoveries and revealed religion were not in conflict. At the peak of his fame Newton promoted a series of lectures devoted to proving the validity of Christianity. However, by showing that

---

Galileo Galilei (gal-uh-LAY-oh gal-uh-LAY-ee)

the Aristotelians and biblical writers held ideas about the natural world that were naive and unfactual, these pioneers opened the door to others who used reason to challenge a broader range of unquestioned traditions and superstitions. The world of ideas was forever changed.

The Early Enlightenment

The advances in scientific thought inspired a few brave souls to question the reasonableness of everything from agricultural methods to laws, religion, and social hierarchies. The belief that human reason could discover scientific laws governing social behavior, parallel to those governing physical properties, energized a movement known as the **Enlightenment.** Like the Scientific Revolution, this movement was the work of a few "enlightened" individuals, who often faced bitter opposition from the political, intellectual, and religious establishment. Leading Enlightenment thinkers became accustomed to having their books burned or banned and spent long periods in exile to escape being imprisoned.

Influences besides the Scientific Revolution affected the Enlightenment. The partisan bickering and bloodshed of the Reformation had led some people to doubt the superiority of any theological position and to recommend toleration of all religions. The killing of suspected witches also shocked many thoughtful people. The leading French thinker Voltaire (1694–1778) declared: "No opinion is worth burning your neighbor for."

Accounts of cultures in other parts of the world also raised questions about the presumed superiority of European political institutions, moral standards, and religious beliefs. Reports of Amerindian life, though romanticized, led some to conclude that those whom they had called savages were in many ways nobler than European Christians. Matteo Ricci, a Jesuit missionary to China whose journals made a strong impression in Europe, contrasted the lack of territorial ambition of the Chinese with the constant warfare in the West and attributed the difference to the fact that China was wisely ruled by educated men whom he called "Philosophers."

Although many circumstances shaped "enlightened" thinking, the new scientific methods and discoveries provided the clearest model for changing European society. Voltaire posed the issues in these terms: "it would be very peculiar that all nature, all the planets, should obey eternal laws" but a human being, "in contempt of these laws, could act as he pleased solely according to his caprice." The English poet Alexander Pope (1688–1774) made a similar point in verse: "Nature and Nature's laws lay hidden in night;/God said, 'Let Newton be' and all was light."

The Enlightenment was more a frame of mind than a coherent movement. By 1750 its proponents were clearer about what they disliked than about what new institutions should be created. Some thought society could be made to function with the mechanical orderliness of planets spinning in their orbits. Nearly all were optimistic that—at least in the long run—human beliefs and institutions could be improved. This belief in progress would help foster political and social revolutions after 1750, as Chapter 19 recounts.

Despite the enthusiasm the Enlightenment aroused in some circles, it was decidedly unpopular with many absolutist rulers and with most clergymen. Europe in 1750 was neither enlightened nor scientific. It was a place where political and religious divisions, growing literacy, and the printing press made possible the survival of the new ideas that profoundly changed life in future centuries.

SOCIAL AND ECONOMIC LIFE

From a distance European society seemed quite rigid. At the top of the social pyramid a small number of noble families monopolized high offices in the church, government, and military and enjoyed many special privileges, including exemption from taxation. Merchants and professionals, who had acquired wealth but no legal privileges, ranked well below them. At the base of the pyramid, the masses, mostly rural peasants and landless laborers, served everyone above them. The subordination of women to men seemed equally rigid.

However, even contemporaries knew that this model was too simple. A study of English society in 1688, for example, distinguished twenty-five different social categories and pointed up the shocking inequality among them. It argued that less than half the population contributed to increasing the wealth of the kingdom, while the rest—the majority—were too poor and unskilled to make any substantial contribution.

Some social mobility did occur, particularly in the middle. The principal engine of social change was the economy, and the places where social change occurred most readily were the cities. A secondary means of change was education—for those who could get it.

The Bourgeoisie

Europe's growing cities were the products of a changing economy. In 1500 Paris was the only northern European city with over 100,000 inhabitants. By 1700 both Paris and London had populations over 500,000, and twenty other European cities contained over 60,000 people.

The wealth of the cities came from manufacturing and finance, but especially from trade, both within Europe and overseas. The French called the urban class that dominated these activities the **bourgeoisie°** (burghers, town dwellers). Members of the bourgeoisie poured much of their profit back into their businesses or into new ventures. Even so, they had enough money to live comfortably in large houses with many servants. In the seventeenth and eighteenth centuries wealthier urban classes could buy exotic luxuries imported from the far corners of the earth—Caribbean and Brazilian sugar and rum, Mexican chocolate, Virginia tobacco, North American furs, East Indian cotton textiles and spices, and Chinese tea.

The Netherlands showed great bourgeois enterprise in the seventeenth century. A wide variety of goods flowed from factories and workshops of the many Dutch cities and towns. The highly successful textile industry concentrated on weaving and printing of cloth, leaving the spinning of thread to low-paid workers elsewhere. Along with fine woolens and linens the Dutch made cheaper textiles for mass markets. Other factories in Holland refined West Indian sugar, brewed beer from Baltic grain, processed Virginia tobacco, and made imitations of Chinese ceramics (see Environment

bourgeoisie (boor-zwah-ZEE)

and Technology: East Asian Porcelain in Chapter 18). Free from the censorship imposed in neighboring countries, Holland's printers published books in many languages, including manuals with the latest advances in machinery, metallurgy, agriculture, and other technical areas. For a small province barely above sea level, lacking timber and other natural resources, this was a remarkable achievement.

Burgeoning from a fishing village to a metropolis of some 200,000 by 1700, Amsterdam was Holland's largest city and Europe's major port. The bourgeoisie there and in other cities developed huge commercial fleets that dominated sea trade in Europe and overseas. Dutch ships carried over 80 percent of the trade between Spain and northern Europe, even while Spain and the Netherlands were at war. By one estimate, the Dutch conducted more than half of all the oceangoing commercial shipping in the world in the seventeenth century (for details see Chapters 17 and 18).

Amsterdam also served as Europe's financial center. Seventeenth-century Dutch banks had such a reputation for security that wealthy individuals and governments from all over western Europe entrusted them with their money. The banks in turn invested these funds in real estate, loaned money to factory owners and governments, and provided capital for business operations overseas.

Maritime expansion led to new designs for merchant ships. In this, too, the Dutch played a dominant role, using timber imported from northern Europe to build their own vast fleets as well as ships for export. Especially successful was the fluit, or "flyboat," a large-capacity cargo ship developed in the 1590s. It was inexpensive to build and required only a small crew. Another successful type of merchant ship, the heavily armed "East Indiaman," helped the Dutch establish their supremacy in the Indian Ocean. The Dutch also excelled at mapmaking (see Environment and Technology: Mapping the World).

Like merchants in the Islamic world, Europe's merchants relied on family and ethnic networks. Many northern European cities contained merchant colonies from Venice, Florence, Genoa, and other Italian cities. In Amsterdam and Hamburg lived Jewish merchants who had fled religious persecution in Iberia. Other Jewish communities

Port of Amsterdam   Ships, barges, and boats of all types are visible in this busy seventeenth-century scene. The large building in the center is the Admiralty House, the headquarters of the Dutch East India Company.   (Mansell TimeLife Pictures/Getty Images)

expanded out of eastern Europe into the German states, especially after the Thirty Years War. Armenian merchants from Iran were moving into the Mediterranean and became important in Russia in the seventeenth century.

The bourgeoisie sought mutually beneficial alliances with European monarchs, who welcomed economic growth as a means of increasing state revenues. The Dutch government pioneered chartering **joint-stock companies.** The Dutch East India Company received a monopoly over trade to the East Indies, as did the Dutch West India Company for the New World. France and England chartered companies of their own. The companies sold shares to individuals to fund their overseas enterprises, thus spreading the risks (and profits) among many investors (see Chapter 16). Investors bought and sold shares in specialized markets called **stock exchanges,** an Italian innovation transferred to the cities of northwestern Europe in the sixteenth century. The greatest stock market in the seventeenth and eighteenth centuries was the Amsterdam Exchange, founded in 1530. Large insurance companies also emerged in this period, and insuring long voyages against loss became a standard practice after 1700.

Governments also undertook large projects to improve water transport. The Dutch built numerous canals for transport and to drain the lowlands for agriculture. Other governments also financed canals, which included elaborate systems of locks to raise barges up over hills. One of the most important was the 150-mile (240-kilometer) Canal du Midi in France, built by the French government between 1661 and 1682 to link the Atlantic and the Mediterranean. By the seventeenth century rulers sought the talents of successful businessmen as administrators. Jean Baptiste Colbert° (1619–1683), Louis XIV's able minister of finance, was a notable example.

Some members of the bourgeoisie in England and France used their wealth to raise their social status. By retiring from their businesses and buying country estates, they could become members of the **gentry.** These landowners affected the lifestyle of the old aristocracy. The gentry loaned money to impoverished peasants and to members of the nobility and in time increased their ownership of land. Some families sought aristocratic husbands for their daughters. The old nobility found such

Colbert (kohl-BEAR)

alliances attractive because of the large dowries that the bourgeoisie provided. In France a family could gain the exemption from taxation by living in gentility for three generations or, more quickly, by purchasing a title from the king.

Peasants and Laborers

At the other end of society things were bad, but they had been worse. Serfdom, which bound men and women to land owned by a local lord, had been in deep decline since the great plague of the mid-fourteenth century. In western Europe the institution did not return even though competition for work exerted a downward pressure on wages as the population recovered. In eastern Europe, however, the development of large estates raising grain for the cities led to the rise of serfdom for the first time. Slavery, which had briefly expanded in southern Europe around 1500 as the result of the Atlantic slave trade from sub-Saharan Africa, declined. After 1600, Europeans shipped nearly all African slaves to the Americas.

There is much truth in the argument that western Europe continued to depend on unfree labor but kept it at a distance rather than at home. In any event, legal freedom did little to make a peasant's life safer and more secure. The techniques and efficiency of European agriculture had improved little since 1300. As a result, bad years brought famine; good ones provided only small surpluses. Indeed, the condition of the average person in western Europe may have worsened between 1500 and 1750 as the result of prolonged warfare, environmental problems, and varying economic conditions. In addition, Europeans felt the adverse effects of a century of relatively cool weather that began in the 1590s. During this **Little Ice Age** average temperatures fell only a few degrees, but the effects were startling (see Issues in World History: The Little Ice Age).

By 1700 high-yielding new crops from the Americas were helping the rural poor avoid starvation. Once grown only as hedges against famine, potatoes and maize (corn) became staples for the rural poor in the eighteenth century. Potatoes sustained life in northeastern and central Europe and in Ireland, and poor peasants in Italy subsisted on maize. Ironically, all of these lands were major exporters of wheat, which the agricultural laborers could not afford to eat. Instead, the grain was put on carts, barges, and ships and carried to the cities of western Europe. Other fleets brought wine from southern to northern Europe. Parisians downed 100,000 barrels of wine a year at the end of the seventeenth century. Some of the grain was made into beer, which the poor drank because it was cheaper than wine. In 1750 Parisian breweries brewed 23 million quarts (22 million liters) of beer for local consumption.

Some rural men worked as miners, lumberjacks, and charcoal makers. The expanding iron industry in England provided work for all three, but the high consumption of wood fuel for this and other purposes caused serious **deforestation.** One early-seventeenth-century observer lamented: "within man's memory, it was held impossible to have any want of wood in England. But . . . at present, through the great consuming of wood . . . and the neglect of planting of woods, there is a great scarcity of wood throughout the whole kingdom."[1] The managers of the hundreds of ironworks in England tried to meet the shortages by importing timber and charcoal from more heavily forested Scandinavian countries and Russia. Eventually, the high price of wood and charcoal encouraged smelters to use coal as an alternative fuel. England's coal mining increased twelvefold, from 210,000 tons in 1550 to 2,500,000 tons in 1700. Starting in 1709, coke—coal refined to remove impurities—gradually replaced charcoal in the smelting of iron. These new demands drove English coal production to nearly 5 million tons a year by 1750.

France was much more forested than England, but increasing deforestation there prompted Colbert to predict that "France will perish for lack of wood." By the late eighteenth century deforestation had become an issue even in Sweden and Russia, where iron production had become a major industry. New laws in France and England designed to protect the forests were largely inspired by fears of shortages for naval vessels, whose keels required high-quality timbers of exceptional size and particular curvature. Although wood consumption remained high, rising prices encouraged some individuals to plant trees for future harvest. Everywhere in Europe the rural poor felt the depletion of the forests most strongly, since for centuries they

Mapping the World

In 1602 in China the Jesuit missionary Matteo Ricci printed an elaborate map of the world. Working from maps produced in Europe and incorporating the latest knowledge gathered by European maritime explorers, Ricci introduced two changes to make the map more appealing to his Chinese hosts. He labeled it in Chinese characters, and he split his map down the middle of the Atlantic so that China lay in the center. This version pleased Chinese elite, who considered China the "Middle Kingdom" surrounded by lesser states. A copy of Ricci's map in six large panels adorned the emperor's Beijing palace.

The stunningly beautiful maps and globes of sixteenth-century Europe were the most complete, detailed, and useful representations of the earth that any society had ever produced. The best mapmaker of the century was Gerhard Kremer, who is remembered as Mercator (the merchant) because his maps were so useful to European ocean traders. By incorporating the latest discoveries and scientific measurements, Merca-

tor could depict the outlines of the major continents in painstaking detail, even if their interiors were still largely unknown to outsiders.

To represent the spherical globe on a flat map, Mercator drew the lines of longitude as parallel lines. Because such lines actually meet at the poles, Mercator's projection greatly exaggerated the size of every landmass and body of water distant from the equator. However, Mercator's rendering offered a very practical advantage: sailors could plot their course by drawing a straight line between their point of departure and their destination. Because of this useful feature, the Mercator projection of the world remained in common use until quite recently. To some extent, its popularity came from the exaggerated size this projection gave to Europe. Like the Chinese, Europeans liked to think of themselves as at the center of things. Europeans also understood their true geographical position better than people in any other part of the world.

---

had depended on woodlands for wild nuts and berries, free firewood and building materials, and wild game.

Modest improvements in food production in some places were overwhelmed by population growth. Rural women had long supplemented household incomes by spinning yarn. From the mid-1600s rising wages in towns led textile manufacturers to farm more and more weaving out to rural areas with high underemployment. This provided men and women with enough to survive on, but the piecework paid very little for long hours of tedious labor.

Throughout this period, many rural poor migrated to the towns and cities in hopes of better jobs, but only some were successful. Even in the prosperous Dutch towns, half of the population lived in acute poverty. Authorities estimated that

those permanent city residents who were too poor to tax, the "deserving poor," made up 10 to 20 percent of the population. That calculation did not include the large numbers of "unworthy poor"— recent migrants from impoverished rural areas, peddlers traveling from place to place, and beggars (many with horrible deformities and sores) who tried to survive on charity. Desperation forced many young women into prostitution. There were also many criminals, usually organized in gangs, ranging from youthful pickpockets to highway robbers.

The pervasive poverty of rural and urban Europe shocked those who were not hardened to it. In about 1580 the mayor of the French city of Bordeaux° asked a group of visiting Amerindian chiefs what impressed them most about European cities.

Bordeaux (bor-DOH)

Dutch World Map, 1641   It is easy to see why the Chinese would not have liked to see their empire at the far right edge of this widely printed map. Besides the distortions caused by the Mercator projection, geographical ignorance exaggerates the size of North America and Antarctica. (Courtesy of the Trustees of the British Museum)

The chiefs are said to have expressed astonishment at the disparity between the fat, well-fed people and the poor, half-starved men and women in rags. Why, the visitors wondered, did the poor not grab the rich by the throat or set fire to their homes?[2]

In fact, misery provoked many rebellions in early modern Europe. For example, in 1525 peasant rebels in the Alps attacked both nobles and clergy as representatives of the privileged and landowning classes. They had no love for merchants either, whom they denounced for lending at interest and charging high prices. Rebellions multiplied as rural conditions worsened. In southwestern France alone some 450 uprisings occurred between 1590 and 1715, many of them set off by food shortages and tax increases. The exemption of the wealthy from taxation was a frequent source of complaint. A rebellion in southern France in 1670

began when a mob of townswomen attacked the tax collector. It quickly spread to the country, where peasant leaders cried, "Death to the people's oppressors!" Authorities dealt severely with such revolts and executed or maimed their leaders.

Women and the Family

Women's status and work were closely tied to those of their husbands and families. In rare instances, a woman in a royal family might inherit a throne (see Table 15.1 for examples) in the absence of a male heir, but such exceptions do not negate the rule that women everywhere ranked below men. Nevertheless, class and wealth defined a woman's position in life more than gender. A wife or daughter in a rich family, for example, had a much better life than any poor man.

377

Occasionally, a single woman might be secure and respected, as in the case of women from good families heading convents of nuns in Catholic countries. But unmarried women and widows fared poorly compared to their married sisters.

Men and women in early modern Europe most often chose their own spouses. Ironically, privileged families were more inclined to control marriage plans than poor ones. Royal and noble families carefully plotted their children's marriages to further the family's status. Bourgeois parents were less likely to force their children into arranged marriages. Nevertheless, nearly all found spouses within their social class, sometimes to buttress business connections.

Europeans also married late. The children of craftspeople and the poor had to delay marriage until they could afford to live on their own. Young men served long apprenticeships to learn trades. Young women worked helping their parents, or as domestic servants, or in some other capacity to save money for their dowry: the money and household goods—the amount varied by social class—that enabled a young couple to begin marriage independent of their parents. The typical groom in western and central Europe could not hope to marry before his late twenties. His bride would be a few years younger. Marriage also came late in bourgeois families, in part to allow young men to complete their education.

The late age of marriage held down the birthrate and thus limited family size. Even so, about one in ten urban babies was born to an unmarried woman, often a servant. Such newborns were generally left on the doorsteps of churches, convents, or rich homes. Many perished. Public brothels also went with delayed marriage. They provided a place for young men to satisfy their desires at the expense of unfortunate young women, often newly arrived from impoverished villages. Nevertheless, rape was a common occurrence, especially assaults by gangs of young men. Some historians believe these crimes reflect the envy poor young men had of older men's easier access to women.

Bourgeois parents focused on giving their children the education and training necessary for success. They promoted the establishment of municipal schools where they could learn Latin and perhaps Greek. Then they sent their sons abroad to learn modern languages or to a university to earn a law degree. Legal training helped them conduct business and was necessary for obtaining a judgeship or treasury position. Daughters were less likely to be groomed for business careers, but wives often helped their husbands as bookkeepers and sometimes inherited businesses.

The fact that most schools, like most guilds and professions, barred females explains why women were not prominent in the cultural movements of the period. Yet from a global perspective, women in early modern Europe were more prominent in the creation of high culture than were women in most other parts of the world. Recent research has identified successful women who were painters, musicians, and writers. Indeed, the spread of learning, the stress on religious reading, and the growth of business may have made Europe the leading area of the world in female literacy. Nevertheless, illiteracy was widespread for both sexes, and only women in wealthier families might have a good education. From the late 1600s some wealthy French women ran intellectual gatherings in their homes. Others were prominent letter writers. Galileo's daughter, Maria Celeste Galilei, carried on a detailed correspondence with her father from behind the walls of her convent, which she had vowed never to leave.

POLITICAL INNOVATIONS

The monarchs of early modern Europe occupied the apex of the social order, arbitrated intellectual and religious conflicts, and greatly influenced economic life. Thus an overview of political life incorporates all the developments so far described in this chapter. In addition, royal political agendas introduced new elements of conflict and change.

Though no unified European empire emerged, a higher degree of political centralization was achieved in separate kingdoms. The frequent civil and international conflicts of this era sometimes promoted cooperation and often encouraged innovation. Leadership and success passed from Spain to the Netherlands and then to England and France.

State Development

Political diversity characterized Europe. City-states and principalities abounded, either independently or bound into loose federations, of which the **Holy Roman Empire** of the German heartland was the most notable example. In western Europe the strong monarchies that had emerged earlier were acquiring national identities, but some rulers dreamed of a European empire comparable to that of Rome or some Asian realm.

In 1519 electors of the Holy Roman Empire chose Charles V (r. 1519–1556) as emperor. Like his predecessors for three generations, Charles belonged to the powerful **Habsburg°** family of Austria, but he had recently inherited the Spanish thrones of Castile and Aragon. With the vast resources of these lands behind him, Charles hoped to centralize his imperial power and lead a Christian coalition to halt the advance into southeastern Europe of the Ottoman Empire, which already controlled most of the Middle East and North Africa.

Stout defense and bad weather eventually halted the Ottomans at the gates of Vienna in 1529, but Charles's efforts to forge his several possessions into Europe's strongest state failed as Ottoman attacks continued on and off until 1697. King Francis I of France, who had lost to Charles in the election for Holy Roman Emperor, openly supported the Muslim Turks to weaken his rival. In addition, some of the Holy Roman Empire's many member states used Luther's religious Reformation to frustrate Charles's efforts to curb their autonomy. Swayed partly by Luther's appeals to German national sentiment, many German princes opposed Charles's defense of Catholic doctrine in the imperial Diet (assembly).

After decades of bitter squabbles turned to open warfare in 1546 (the German Wars of Religion), Charles V finally gave up his efforts at unification, abdicated control of his various possessions to different heirs, and retired to a monastery. By the Peace of Augsburg (1555), he recognized the princes' right to choose either Catholicism or Lutheranism as their state religion, and he allowed them to keep the church lands they had seized before 1552. The triumph of religious diversity that derailed Charles's plan for centralizing authority in central Europe postponed German political unification for three centuries.

Meanwhile, the rulers of Spain, France, and England were building more effective programs of political centralization and religious unity. The most successful rulers reduced the autonomy of the church and the nobility, while making them part of a unified national structure headed by the monarch. Getting control of the church in the sixteenth century was a stormy process, but the outcome was clear. Bringing the nobles and other powerful interests into a centralized political system took longer and led to more diverse outcomes.

Religious Policies

The rulers of Spain and France successfully defended the Catholic tradition against Protestant challenges. Adopting the techniques of his predecessors for suppressing Jews and Muslims, King Philip II of Spain used an ecclesiastical court, the Spanish Inquisition, to bring into line those who resisted his authority. Suspected Protestants, as well as critics of the king, found themselves accused of heresy, an offense punishable by death. Even those who were acquitted of the charge learned not to oppose the king again.

In France the Calvinist opponents of the Valois rulers gained the military advantage in the French Wars of Religion (1562–1598), but in the interest of forging lasting unity, their leader Prince Henry of Navarre then embraced the Catholic faith of the majority of his subjects. The Bourbon king who followed him, Henry IV, his son King Louis XIII, and his grandson King Louis XIV were as supportive of the Catholic Church as their counterparts in Spain. In 1685 Louis XIV even revoked the Edict of Nantes°, by which his grandfather had granted the Protestants religious freedom in 1598.

In England King Henry VIII initially defended the papacy against Lutheran criticism. But when the pope refused to annul his marriage to Catherine of Aragon, who had not produced a male heir, Henry challenged the papacy's authority by ordering the English archbishop of Canterbury to annul the marriage in 1533. The breach with Rome was sealed

---

Habsburg (HABZ-berg)

Nantes (nahnt)

Table 15.1   Rulers in Early Modern Western Europe

Spain	France	England/Great Britain
Habsburg Dynasty	**Valois Dynasty**	**Tudor Dynasty**
Charles I (1516–1556) (Holy Roman Emperor Charles V)	Francis I (1515–1547)	Henry VIII (1509–1547)
Philip II (1556–1598)	Henry II (1547–1559)	Edward VI (1547–1553)
	Francis II (1559–1560)	Mary I (1553–1558)
	Charles IX (1560–1574)	Elizabeth I (1558–1603)
	Henry III (1574–1589)	
	Bourbon Dynasty	**Stuart Dynasty**
Philip III (1598–1621)	Henry IV (1589–1610)[a]	James I (1603–1625)
Philip IV (1621–1665)	Louis XIII (1610–1643)	Charles I (1625–1649)[a, b]
Charles II (1665–1700)	Louis XIV (1643–1715)	(Puritan Republic, 1649–1660)
		Charles II (1660–1685)
		James II (1685–1688)[b]
		William III (1689–1702) and Mary II (1689–1694)
Bourbon Dynasty		Anne (1702–1714)
Philip V (1700–1746)		**Hanoverian Dynasty**
	Louis XV (1715–1774)	George I (1714–1727)
Ferdinand VI (1746–1759)		George II (1727–1760)

[a]Died a violent death.   [b]Was overthrown.

the next year when Parliament made the English monarch head of the Church of England.

Like many Protestant rulers, Henry disbanded monasteries and convents and seized their lands. He gave some lands to his powerful allies and sold others to pay for his new navy. Yet the attitudes toward ritual and theology of the new Anglican Church remained too close to those of Roman Catholicism to satisfy English Puritans (Calvinists who wanted to "purify" the Anglican Church of Catholic practices and beliefs). In 1603 the first Stuart king, James I, dismissed a Puritan petition to eliminate bishops with the statement "No bishops, no king"—a reminder of the essential role of the church in supporting royal power.

Monarchies in England and France

Over the course of the seventeenth century, the rulers of England and France contested with their leading subjects over the limits of royal authority. Religion was never absent in these struggles, but the different constitutional outcomes they produced were more significant in the long run.

To evade any check on his power, King Charles I of England (see Table 15.1) ruled for eleven years without summoning Parliament, his kingdom's representative body. Lacking Parliament's consent to new taxes, he raised funds by coercing "loans" from wealthy subjects and applying existing tax laws more broadly. Then in 1640 a rebellion in Scotland forced him to summon a Parliament to approve new taxes to pay for an army. Noblemen and churchmen sat in the House of Lords. Representatives from the towns and counties sat in the House of Commons. Before it would authorize new taxes, Parliament insisted on strict guarantees that the king would never again ignore the body's traditional rights. These King Charles refused to grant. When he ordered the arrest of his leading critics in the House of Commons in 1642, he plunged the kingdom into the **English Civil War.**

Versailles, 1722   This painting by P.-D. Martin shows the east expanse of buildings and court-yards that make up the palace complex built by King Louis XIV.   (Giraudon/Art Resource, NY)

Even after defeat on the battlefield, Charles refused to compromise. In 1649 a "Rump" Parliament (one purged of his supporters) ordered him executed and replaced the monarchy with a republic under Oliver Cromwell, a Puritan general. Cromwell expanded England's presence overseas and imposed firm control over Ireland and Scotland, but he was as unwilling as the Stuart kings to share power with Parliament. After his death Parliament restored the Stuart line, making it unclear, for a time, which side had won the war.

King James II clarified matters when he refused to respect Parliament's rights and had his heir baptized a Roman Catholic. Parliament responded by forcing James into exile in the bloodless coup known as "the Glorious Revolution of 1688." The Bill of Rights of 1689 specified that Parliament had to be called frequently and had to consent to changes in laws and to the raising of an army in peacetime. Another law reaffirmed the official status of the Church of England but extended religious toleration to the Puritans.

A similar struggle in France produced a different outcome. There the Estates General represented the traditional rights of the clergy, the nobility, and the towns (that is, the bourgeoisie). The Estates General was able to assert its rights during the sixteenth-century French Wars of Religion, when the monarchy was weak. But thereafter the Bourbon monarchs generally ruled without having to call it into session. They avoided financial crises by more efficient tax collection and by selling appointments to high government offices. In justification they claimed that the monarch had absolute authority to rule in God's name.

Louis XIV's gigantic new palace at **Versailles°** symbolized the monarch's triumph over the nobility, clergy, and towns. Capable of housing ten thousand people and surrounded by elaborately landscaped grounds and parks, the palace was a sort of theme park of royal absolutism. Elaborate ceremonies and banquets centered on the king deterred the nobles who lived at Versailles from plotting rebellion. According to one of them, the duke of Saint-Simon°, "no one was so clever in devising petty distractions" as the king.

Though the balance of powers in the English model would be widely admired in later times, most European rulers admired and imitated the centralized powers and absolutist claims of the French until well after 1750. Some even built imitations of Versailles. The English model exerted its influence more slowly. In his *Second Treatise of Civil Government* (1690), the English political philosopher John Locke (1632–1704) disputed monarchial claims to absolute authority by divine right. Rather, he argued, rulers derived their authority from the consent of the governed and, like everyone else, were subject to the law. If monarchs overstepped the law, citizens had not only the right but also the duty to rebel. The later consequences of this idea are considered in Chapter 19.

Warfare and Diplomacy

In addition to the bitter civil wars that pounded the Holy Roman Empire, France, and England, European states engaged in numerous international conflicts. Warfare was almost constant in early modern Europe (see the Chronology at the beginning of the chapter). The worst of the international conflicts, the Thirty Years War (1618–1648), caused long-lasting depopulation and economic decline in much of the Holy Roman Empire.

The wars also produced dramatic improvements in weaponry and war-making skills, causing European armed forces to become the most powerful in the world. The numbers of men in arms increased steadily. French forces, for example, grew from about 150,000 in 1630 to 400,000 by the early eighteenth century. Even smaller European states built up impressive armies. Sweden, with under a million people, had one of the best-armed military forces in seventeenth-century Europe. Prussia, a country with fewer than 2 million inhabitants in 1700, had a strong army that made it one of Europe's major powers.

Larger armies required more effective command structures. In the words of a modern historian, European armies "evolved . . . the equivalent of a central nervous system, capable of activating technologically differentiated claws and teeth."[3] New signaling techniques improved control of battlefield maneuvers. Frequent marching drills trained troops to obey orders instantly and gave them a close sense of comradeship. Since battles between evenly matched armies often ended in stalemates that prolonged the wars, victory increasingly depended on naval superiority.

England alone did without a peacetime standing army, but England's rise as a sea power had begun under King Henry VIII, who spent heavily on ships and promoted a domestic iron-smelting industry to supply cannon. The Royal Navy also copied innovative ship designs from the Dutch in the second half of the seventeenth century. By the early eighteenth century the Royal Navy surpassed the rival French fleet in numbers. By then, England had merged with Scotland to become Great Britain, annexed Ireland, and built a North American empire.

Although France was Europe's most powerful state, Louis XIV's efforts to expand were increasingly frustrated by coalitions of the other great powers. In a series of eighteenth-century wars beginning with the War of the Spanish Succession (1701–1714), the combination of Britain's naval strength and the land armies of its Austrian and Prussian allies blocked French ambitions and prevented the Bourbons from uniting the thrones of France and Spain.

This defeat of the French monarchy's empire-building efforts illustrated the principle of **balance of power** in international relations: the major European states formed temporary alliances to prevent any one state from becoming too powerful. Russia emerged as a major power in Europe after its modernized armies defeated Sweden in the Great Northern War (1700–1721). During the next two centuries, though adhering to four differ-

---

Versailles (vuhr-SIGH)   **Saint-Simon** (san see-MON)

ent branches of Christianity, the great powers of Europe—Catholic France, Anglican Britain, Catholic Austria, Lutheran Prussia, and Orthodox Russia (see Map 15.2)—maintained an effective balance of power by shifting their alliances for geopolitical rather than religious reasons. These pragmatic alliances were the first successful efforts at international peacekeeping.

Paying the Piper

To pay the heavy military costs of their wars, European rulers had to increase their revenues. The most successful of them after 1600 promoted mutually beneficial alliances with the rising commercial elite. Both sides understood that trade thrived where government taxation and regulation were not excessive, where courts enforced contracts and collected debts, and where military power stood ready to protect overseas expansion.

Spain, sixteenth-century Europe's mightiest state, illustrates how the financial drains of an aggressive military policy and the failure to promote economic development could lead to decline. Expensive wars against the Ottomans, northern European Protestants, and rebellious Dutch subjects caused the treasury to default on its debts four times during the reign of King Philip II. Moreover, the Spanish rulers' concerns for religious uniformity and traditional aristocratic privilege further undermined the country's economy. In the name of religious uniformity they expelled Jewish merchants, persecuted Protestant dissenters, and forced tens of thousands of farmers and artisans into exile because of their Muslim ancestry. In the name of aristocratic privilege the 3 percent of the population that controlled 97 percent of the land in 1600 was exempt from taxation, while high sales taxes discouraged manufacturing.

For a time, vast imports of silver and gold bullion from Spain's American colonies filled the government treasury. These bullion shipments also contributed to severe inflation (rising prices), not just in Spain but also to a lesser degree throughout the rest of Europe. A Spanish saying captured the problem: American silver was like rain on the roof—it poured down and washed away. Huge debts for foreign wars drained bullion from Spain to its creditors. More wealth flowed out to purchase manufactured goods and even food in the seventeenth century.

The rise of the Netherlands as an economic power stemmed from opposite policies. The Spanish crown had acquired these resource-poor but commercially successful provinces as part of Charles V's inheritance. But King Philip II's decision to impose Spain's ruinously heavy sales tax and enforce Catholic orthodoxy drove the Dutch to revolt in 1566 and again in 1572. If successful, those measures would have discouraged business and driven away the Calvinists, Jews, and other key contributors to Dutch prosperity. The Dutch fought with skill and ingenuity, raising and training an army and a navy that were among the most effective in Europe. By 1609 Spain was forced to agree to a truce that recognized the autonomy of the northern part of the Netherlands. In 1648, after eight decades of warfare, the independence of these seven United Provinces of the Free Netherlands (their full name) became final.

Rather than being ruined by the long war, the United Netherlands emerged as the dominant commercial power in Europe and the world's greatest trading nation. This economic success owed much to a decentralized government. During the long struggle against Spain, the provinces united around the prince of Orange, their sovereign, who served as commander-in-chief of the armed forces. But in economic matters each province was free to pursue its own interests. The maritime province of Holland grew rich by favoring commercial interests.

After 1650 the Dutch faced growing competition from the English, who were developing their own close association of business with government. In a series of wars (1652–1678) England used its naval might to break Dutch dominance in overseas trade and to extend its own colonial empire. With government support, the English merchant fleet doubled between 1660 and 1700, and foreign trade rose by 50 percent. As a result, state revenue from customs duties tripled. During the eighteenth century Britain's trading position strengthened still more.

The debts run up by the Anglo-Dutch Wars helped persuade the English monarchy to greatly enlarge the government's role in managing the economy. The outcome has been called a "financial revolution." The government increased revenues

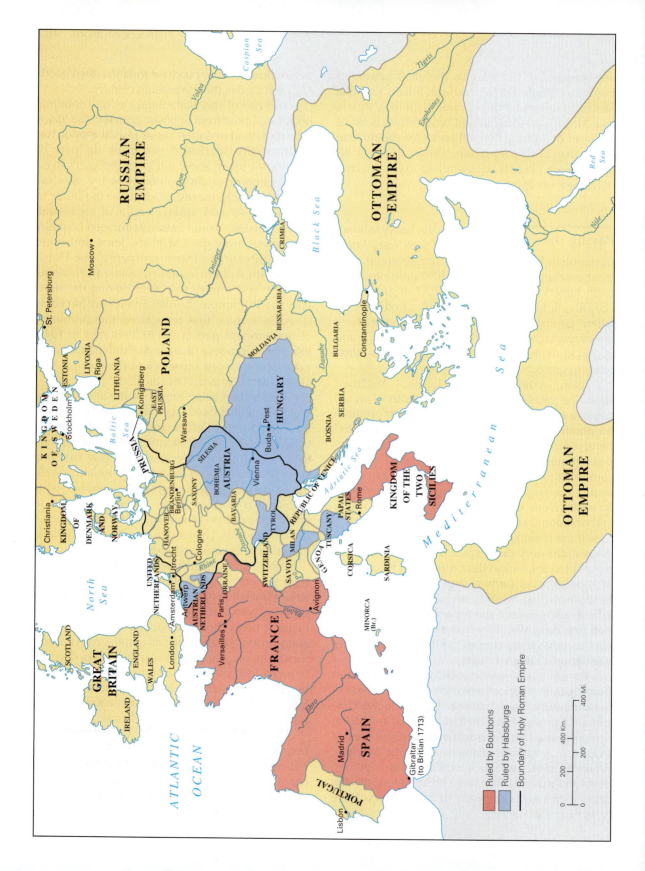

RUSSIAN EMPIRE

OTTOMAN EMPIRE

OTTOMAN EMPIRE

Caspian Sea

Tigris

Volga

Euphrates

Red Sea

Don

Nile

Black Sea

Moscow

St. Petersburg

CRIMEA

Dnieper

BESSARABIA

MOLDAVIA

Constantinople

Riga

LIVONIA

ESTONIA

LITHUANIA

Baltic Sea

Stockholm

KINGDOM OF SWEDEN

POLAND

Warsaw

Königsberg

EAST PRUSSIA

PRUSSIA

BULGARIA

SERBIA

BOSNIA

HUNGARY

Buda Pest

Vienna

SILESIA

AUSTRIA

BOHEMIA

Danube

Adriatic Sea

REPUBLIC OF VENICE

TYROL

Christiania

KINGDOM OF DENMARK AND NORWAY

BRANDENBURG

Berlin

SAXONY

BAVARIA

HANOVER

Cologne

Rhine

Danube

SWITZERLAND

MILAN

SAVOY

GENOA

TUSCANY

PAPAL STATES

Rome

KINGDOM OF THE TWO SICILIES

Mediterranean Sea

UNITED NETHERLANDS

Utrecht

Amsterdam

Antwerp

AUSTRIAN NETHERLANDS

LORRAINE

Paris

Versailles

FRANCE

Rhône

Po

CORSICA

SARDINIA

MINORCA (Br.)

North Sea

SCOTLAND

GREAT BRITAIN

ENGLAND

WALES

London

IRELAND

ATLANTIC OCEAN

Ebro

SPAIN

Madrid

Gibraltar (to Britian 1713)

PORTUGAL

Lisbon

Avignon

Ruled by Bourbons
Ruled by Habsburgs
—— Boundary of Holy Roman Empire

400 Mi.

400 Km.

200

200

0

0

Map 15.2   Europe in 1740   By the middle of the eighteenth century the great powers of Europe were France, the Austrian Empire, Great Britain, Prussia, and Russia. Spain, the Holy Roman Empire, and the Ottoman Empire were far weaker in 1740 than they had been two centuries earlier.

by taxing the formerly exempt landed estates of the aristocrats and by collecting taxes directly. Previously, private individuals known as tax farmers had advanced the government a fixed sum of money; in return they could keep whatever money they were able to collect from taxpayers. England also followed the Dutch lead in creating a central bank, from which the government was able to obtain long-term loans at low rates.

Under the leadership of Colbert, the French too experienced economic development. He streamlined tax collection, promoted French manufacturing and shipping by imposing taxes on foreign goods, and improved inland transportation. Yet the power of the wealthy aristocrats kept the French government from following England's lead in taxing wealthy landowners, collecting taxes directly, and securing low-cost loans. Nor did France succeed in managing its debt as efficiently as England. (The role of governments in promoting overseas trade is further discussed in Chapter 16.)

CONCLUSION

European historians have used the word *revolution* to describe many different changes taking place in Europe between 1500 and 1750. The expansion of trade has been called a commercial revolution, the reform of state spending a financial revolution, and the changes in weapons and warfare a military revolution. We have also encountered a scientific revolution and the religious revolution of the Reformation.

These important changes in government, economy, society, and thought were parts of a dynamic process that began in the Late Middle Ages and led to even bigger industrial and political revolutions before the eighteenth century was over. Yet the years from 1500 to 1750 were not simply—perhaps not even primarily—an age of progress for Europe. For many, the ferocious competition of European armies, merchants, and ideas was a wrenching experience. The growth of powerful states exacted a terrible price in death, destruction, and misery. The Reformation brought greater individual choice in religion but widespread religious persecution as well. The expanding economy benefited members of the emerging merchant elite and their political allies, but most Europeans became worse off as prices rose faster than wages. New scientific and enlightened ideas ignited controversies long before they yielded any tangible benefits.

The historical significance of this period of European history is clearer when viewed in a global context. What stands out are the powerful and efficient European armies, economies, and governments, which larger states elsewhere in the world feared, envied, and sometimes imitated. From a global perspective, the balance of political and economic power was shifting slowly, but inexorably, in the Europeans' favor. In 1500 the Ottomans threatened Europe. By 1750, as the remaining chapters of Part Five detail, Europeans had brought the world's seas and a growing portion of its lands and peoples under their control. No single group of Europeans accomplished this. The Dutch eclipsed the pioneering Portuguese and Spanish; then the English and French bested the Dutch. Competition, too, was a factor in European success.

Other changes in Europe during this period had no great overseas significance at the time. The new ideas of the Scientific Revolution and the Enlightenment were still of minor importance. Their full effects in furthering global European dominion were felt after 1750, as Parts Six and Seven explore.

■ Key Terms

Renaissance (European)
papacy
indulgence
Protestant Reformation
Catholic Reformation
witch-hunt
Scientific Revolution
Enlightenment
bourgeoisie
joint-stock company

stock exchange
gentry
Little Ice Age
deforestation
Holy Roman Empire
Habsburg
English Civil War
Versailles
balance of power

■ Suggested Reading

Overviews of this period include Euan Cameron, ed., *Early Modern Europe* (1999); H. G. Koenigsberger, *Early Modern Europe: Fifteen Hundred to Seventeen Eighty-Nine* (1987); and Joseph Bergin, *The Short Oxford History of Europe: The Seventeenth Century* (2001). Global perspectives can be found in Fernand Braudel, *Civilization and Capitalism, 15th–18th Century,* trans. Siân Reynolds, 3 vols. (1979), and Immanuel Wallerstein, *The Modern World-System,* vol. 2, *Mercantilism and the Consolidation of the European World-Economy, 1600–1750* (1980).

Technological and environmental changes are the focus of Geoffrey Parker, *Military Revolution: Military Innovation and the Rise of the West, 1500–1800,* 2d ed. (1996); William H. McNeill, *The Pursuit of Power: Technology, Armed Force, and Society Since* A.D. *1000* (1982); Robert Greenhalgh Albion, *Forests and Sea Power: The Timber Problem of the Royal Navy, 1652–1862* (1965); Emmanuel Le Roy Ladurie, *Times of Feast, Times of Famine: A History of Climate Since the Year 1000,* trans. Barbara Bray (1971); and Brian Fagan, *The Little Ice Age: How Climate Made History, 1300–1850* (1988). Robert C. Allen, *Enclosure and the Yeoman: The Agricultural Development of the South Midlands, 1450–1850* (1992), focuses on England.

Steven Stapin, *The Scientific Revolution* (1998), and Hugh Kearney, *Science and Change, 1500–1700* (1971), are accessible introductions. Thomas S. Kuhn, *The Structure of Scientific Revolution,* 3d ed. (1996), and A. R. Hall, *The Scientific Revolution, 1500–1800: The Formation of the Modern Scientific Attitude,* 2d ed. (1962), are classic studies. Carolyn Merchant, *The Death of Nature: Women, Ecology and the Scientific Revolution* (1980), tries to combine several broad perspectives. *The Sciences in Enlightened Europe,* ed. W. Clark, J. Golinski, and S. Schaffer (1999), examines particular topics in a sophisticated way. Dorinda Outram, *The Enlightenment* (1995), provides a recent summary of research.

Excellent introductions to social and economic life are George Huppert, *After the Black Death: A Social History of Early Modern Europe* (1986), and Carlo M. Cipolla, *Before the Industrial Revolution: European Society and Economy, 1000–1700,* 2d ed. (1980). Peter Burke, *Popular Culture in Early Modern Europe* (1978), offers a broad treatment of nonelite perspectives, as does Robert Jütte, *Poverty and Deviance in Early Modern Europe* (1994). For more economic detail, see Robert S. DuPlessis, *Transitions to Capitalism in Early Modern Europe* (1997); Myron P. Gutmann, *Toward the Modern Economy: Early Industry in Europe, 1500–1800* (1988); and Carlo M. Cipolla, ed., *The Fontana Economic History of Europe,* vol. 2, *The Sixteenth and Seventeenth Centuries* (1974).

Topics of women's history are examined by Merry Wiesner, *Women and Gender in Early Modern Europe,* 2d ed. (2000); Bonie S. Anderson and Judith Zinsser, *A History of Their Own: Women in Europe,* vol. 2, rev. ed. (2000); and Monica Chojnacka and Merry E. Wiesner-Hanks, *Ages of Woman, Ages of Man* (2002). An excellent place to begin examining the complex subject of witchcraft is Brian Levack, *The Witch-Hunt in Early Modern Europe,* 2d ed. (1995); other up-to-date perspectives can be found in J. Barry, M. Hester, and G. Roberts, eds., *Witchcraft in Early Modern Europe: Studies in Culture and Belief* (1998), and Carlo Ginzburg, *The Night Battles: Witchcraft and Agrarian Cults in the Sixteenth and Seventeenth Centuries,* trans. John and Anne Tedechi (1983).

Good single-country surveys are J. A. Sharpe, *Early Modern England: A Social History,* 2d ed. (1997); Emmanuel Le Roy Ladurie, *The Royal French State, 1460–1610* (1994) and *The Ancien Régime: A History of France, 1610–1774* (1998); Jonathan Israel, *The Dutch Republic: Its Rise, Greatness and Fall, 1477–1806* (1995); and James Casey, *Early Modern Spain: A Social History* (1999).

■ Notes

1. Quoted by Carlo M. Cipolla, "Introduction," *The Fontana Economic History of Europe,* vol. 2, *The Sixteenth and Seventeenth Centuries* (Glasgow: Collins/Fontana Books, 1974), 11–12.

2. Michel de Montaigne, *Essais* (1588), ch. 31, "Des Cannibales."

3. William H. McNeill, *The Pursuit of Power: Technology, Armed Force, and Society Since* A.D. *1000* (Chicago: University of Chicago Press, 1982), 124.

The Americas, the Atlantic, and Africa, 1530–1770   16

CHAPTER OUTLINE

Spanish America and Brazil

English and French Colonies in North America

Plantations in the West Indies

Creating the Atlantic Economy

Africa and the Atlantic

The Columbian Exchange

DIVERSITY AND DOMINANCE: Race and Ethnicity in the Spanish Colonies: Negotiating Hierarchy

Because of their long isolation from other continents, the peoples of the New World lacked immunity to diseases introduced from the Old World. Smallpox arrived in the Caribbean in 1518, killing most of the native peoples there. In short order, smallpox killed 50 percent or more of the Amerindian population of Mexico and Central America. The disease then spread to North and South America with equally devastating effects. Other diseases added to the toll: measles in the 1530s, followed by diphtheria, typhus, influenza, and perhaps pulmonary plague. Between 1520 and 1521, influenza in combination with other ailments attacked the Cakchiquel of Guatemala. Their chronicle recalls:

Great was the stench of the dead. After our fathers and grandfathers succumbed, half the people fled to the fields. The dogs and vultures devoured the bodies. . . . So it was that we became orphans, oh my sons! . . . We were born to die![1]

By the mid-seventeenth century, malaria and yellow fever were also present in tropical regions.

The development of English and French colonies in North America in the seventeenth century led to similar patterns of contagion and mortality. In 1616 and 1617, epidemics nearly exterminated many of New England's indigenous groups. French fur traders transmitted measles, smallpox, and other diseases as far as Hudson Bay and the Great Lakes.

387

Although there is very little evidence that Europeans consciously used disease as a tool of empire, the deadly results of contact clearly undermined the ability of native peoples to resist European settlement. Europeans and their African slaves occupied these depopulated lands. The Americas were transformed biologically and culturally. They were subjected to Europeans' political and economic demands.

The colonies of the Americas were crucial pieces of a new **Atlantic system.** This network of trading links moved people and cultures as well as goods and wealth around the Atlantic. The Atlantic system also affected Africa, but less severely than the Americas. Despite the loss of millions of people to the slave trade, Africa did not suffer such severe population loss as the Americas. Most important, Africans remained in control of their lands.

Amerindians, Europeans, and Africans all contributed to the creation of new cultures in the Americas. The societies that arose reflected each colony's mix of native peoples, its connections to the slave trade, and the policies of its European rulers.

As you read this chapter, ask yourself the following questions:

- How different and how similar were the colonial societies and economies of the Americas?

- Why did forced labor and slavery become so important in many New World colonies?

- How did participation in the Atlantic system affect Europe, Africa, and the Americas?

SPANISH AMERICA AND BRAZIL

The frontiers of conquest and settlement expanded rapidly. Within one hundred years of Columbus's first voyage to the Western Hemisphere, the Spanish Empire in America included most of the islands of the Caribbean, Mexico, the American Southwest, Central America, the Caribbean and Pacific coasts of South America, the Andean highlands, and the vast plains of the Río de la Plata region (a region that includes the modern nations of Argentina, Uruguay, and Paraguay). Portuguese settlement in the New World developed more slowly. But before the end of the sixteenth century, Portugal occupied most of the Brazilian coast.

Early settlers from Spain and Portugal sought to create colonial societies based on the institutions and customs of their homelands. They viewed society as a vertical arrangement of estates (classes of society), as uniformly Catholic, and as an arrangement of patriarchal extended-family networks. Despite the imposition of foreign institutions and the massive loss of life caused by epidemics, indigenous peoples still exercised a powerful influence on the development of colonial societies. Aztec and Inca elite families sought to protect their traditional privileges and rights through marriage or less formal alliances with the Spanish settlers. They also often used colonial courts to defend their claims to land. Nearly everywhere, Amerindian religious beliefs and practices survived beneath the surface of an imposed Christianity. Amerindian languages, cuisine, medical practices, and agricultural techniques also survived the conquest and influenced the development of Latin American culture.

The African slave trade added a third cultural stream to colonial Latin American society. By the end of the colonial era, Africans and their descendants were living throughout Latin America, enriching colonial societies with their traditional agricultural practices, music, religious beliefs, cuisine, and social customs.

State and Church   The Spanish crown moved quickly to curb the independent power of the conquistadors and establish royal authority over both the defeated native populations and the rising tide of European settlers. Created in 1524, the **Council of the Indies** in Spain supervised all government, ecclesiastical, and commercial activity in the Spanish colonies. Political and economic power was concentrated in Mexico City, capital of the Viceroyalty of New Spain

C H R O N O L O G Y

	Latin America	North America	West Indies	Atlantic
1500	**1518** Smallpox arrives in Caribbean **1535** Creation of Viceroyalty of New Spain **1540s** Creation of Viceroyalty of Peru **1542** New Laws outlaw Amerindian enslavement **1545** Silver discovered at Potosí, Bolivia	**1524–1554** French explore Newfoundland and Gulf of St. Lawrence	**ca. 1500** Spanish settlers introduce sugar-cane cultivation	**1530** Amsterdam Exchange opens
1600	**By 1620** African slaves the majority of Brazilian plantation workers	**1607** Jamestown founded **1608** Quebec founded **1620** Plymouth founded **1660** Slavery in Virginia begins to grow rapidly **1664** English take New York from Dutch **1699** Louisiana founded	**1620s and 1630s** English and French colonies in Caribbean **1640s** Dutch bring sugar plantation system from Brazil **1655** English take Jamaica **1670s** French occupy western half of Hispaniola	**1621** Dutch West India Company chartered **1660s** English Navigation Acts **1672** Royal African Company chartered **1698** French *Exclusif*
1700		**1756–1763** French and Indian War	**1700** West Indies surpass Brazil in sugar production	**1700–1830** Slave trade at its peak

(created in 1535), and in Lima, capital of the Viceroyalty of Peru (created in the 1540s). Each viceroyalty was divided into a number of judicial and administrative districts. Until the seventeenth century, almost all of the officials appointed to high positions in Spain's colonial bureaucracy were born in Spain. Later, local-born members of the colonial elite gained many offices.

In the sixteenth century, Portugal concentrated its resources and energies on Asia and Africa, because early settlers found neither mineral wealth nor rich native empires in Brazil. Finally, the king appointed a governor-general in 1549 and designated Salvador, in the northern province of Bahia, Brazil's capital. In 1720, the first viceroy of Brazil was named (see Map 16.1).

Just as these colonial bureaucracies imposed Iberian economic and political institutions, the Catholic Church became the primary agent for the introduction and transmission of Christian belief and European culture in South America. Spain and Portugal justified their American conquests by assuming an obligation to convert native populations to Christianity. In Mexico alone, hundreds of thousands of conversions and baptisms were achieved within a few years of the conquest.

The Catholic clergy sought to win over the Amerindians by first converting native elites. But these efforts were abandoned when church authorities discovered that many converts were secretly observing old beliefs and rituals. In the 1560s, Spanish clergy resorted to torture, executions, and the destruction of native manuscripts to eradicate traditional beliefs and rituals among the Maya. Repelled by these events, the church hierarchy ended both the violent repression of native religious practice and efforts to recruit an Amerindian clergy.

Despite its failures, the Catholic clergy did provide native peoples with some protections against

Map 16.1 Colonial Latin America in the Eighteenth Century   Spain and Portugal controlled most of the Western Hemisphere in the eighteenth century. In the sixteenth century they had created new administrative jurisdictions—viceroyalties—to defend their respective colonies against European rivals. Taxes assessed on colonial products helped pay for this extension of governmental authority.

the abuse and exploitation of Spanish settlers. The priest **Bartolomé de Las Casas** (1474–1566), who served as the most important advocate for native peoples, wrote a number of books that detailed their mistreatment by the Spanish. His most important achievement was the enactment of the New Laws of 1542, which outlawed the enslavement of Amerindians and limited other forms of forced labor.

Despite the disapproval of most European clergy and settlers, Amerindians blended Catholic Christian beliefs with important elements of traditional native cosmology and ritual. Most commonly, indigenous beliefs and rituals came to be embedded in the celebration of saints' days or Catholic rituals associated with the Virgin Mary, illustrating the cultural borrowing and innovation that contributed to a distinct and original Latin American culture.

After 1600, the Catholic Church redirected most of its resources from the countryside to growing colonial cities and towns with large European populations. One important outcome of this altered mission was the founding of universities and secondary schools, which stimulated urban intellectual life.

Colonial Economies

The silver mines of Peru and Mexico and the sugar plantations of Brazil dominated the colonial economy and fueled the early development of European capitalism. Profits produced in these economic centers also promoted the growth of colonial cities, concentrated scarce investment capital and labor resources, and stimulated the development of livestock raising and agriculture in neighboring rural areas. Dependence on mineral and agricultural exports was an enduring theme in Latin America.

Although millions of pesos of gold were mined in Latin America, silver mines generated more wealth and exercised greater economic influence. In 1545, the single richest silver deposit in the Americas was discovered at **Potosí°**, in what is now Bolivia, and until 1680 the silver production of Bolivia and Peru dominated the Spanish colonial economy.

Silver mining also greatly altered the environment. Within a short time, wasteful use of forest

Potosí (poh-toh-SEE)

resources for fuel destroyed forests near the mining centers. Faced with rising fuel costs, miners developed an efficient method of chemical extraction that relied on mixing mercury with the silver ore. But mercury is a poison, and its use contaminated the environment and sickened the Amerindian work force.

From the time of Columbus, indigenous populations had been compelled to provide labor for European settlers in the Americas. Until the 1540s in Spanish colonies, Amerindian peoples were divided among the settlers and were forced to provide them with labor or with textiles, food, or other goods. This form of forced labor was called the **encomienda°**. The discovery of silver in Peru led to a new form of compulsory labor called the mita°. Under this system, one-seventh of the adult male Amerindians were compelled to work for six months each year in mines or on farms or in textile factories. The most dangerous working conditions existed in the silver mines.

In the Spanish mita, few Amerindian workers could survive on their wages. Wives and children were commonly forced to join the work force to help meet expenses. Even those who remained behind in the village were forced to send food and cash to support mita workers.

The Portuguese, who had developed sugar plantations that depended on slave labor on the Atlantic islands of Madeira, the Azores, the Cape Verdes, and São Tomé, transferred this profitable form of agriculture to Brazil. By the seventeenth century, sugar dominated the Brazilian economy. At first, the Portuguese enslaved Amerindian men as field hands, but sugar planters eventually came to rely more on African slaves, who were more resistant to disease. Imports of African slaves rose from an average of 2,000 per year in the late sixteenth century to approximately 7,000 per year a century later, far outstripping the immigration of free Portuguese settlers.

The mining centers of Latin America exercised global economic influence. American silver increased the European money supply, promoting commercial expansion. Large amounts of silver also flowed across the Pacific, where it was exchanged for Asian spices, silks, and pottery. In the Americas, the rich mines stimulated urban population growth, as well as commercial links with agricultural and textile producers.

The sugar plantations of Brazil played a similar role in integrating the economy of the South Atlantic region. At the end of the seventeenth century, the discovery of gold in Brazil helped overcome this large region's currency shortage and promoted further economic integration.

Both Spain and Portugal attempted to control the trade of their American colonies, but the combination of monopoly commerce and convoy shipping slowed the flow of European goods to the colonies and kept prices high. Frustrated by these restraints, colonial populations established illegal commercial relations with the English, French, and Dutch. By the middle of the seventeenth century, a majority of European imports were arriving in Latin America illegally.

Society in Colonial Latin America

With the exception of a few early viceroys, few members of Spain's great noble families came to the New World. *Hidalgos°*—lesser nobles—were well represented, as were Spanish merchants, artisans, miners, priests, and lawyers. Small numbers of criminals, beggars, and prostitutes also found their way to the colonies. Spanish settlers, however, were always a tiny minority in a colonial society numerically dominated by Amerindians and rapidly growing populations of Africans, **creoles** (whites born in America to European parents), and people of mixed ancestry (see Diversity and Dominance: Race and Ethnicity in the Spanish Colonies).

Conquistadors and early settlers who received from the Crown grants of labor and tribute goods (encomienda) from Amerindian communities as rewards for service to Spain dominated colonial society in early Spanish America. These *encomenderos* sought to create a hereditary social and political class comparable to the nobles of Europe. But their systematic abuse of Amerindian communities and the catastrophic loss of Amerindian life during the epidemics of the sixteenth century undermined their position, as did the growing power

---

encomienda (in-co-mee-EN-dah)   *mita* (MEE-tah)

hidalgos (ee-DAHL-goes)

of colonial viceroys, judges, and bishops appointed by the king.

By the end of the sixteenth century, the elite of Spanish America included both European immigrants and creoles. Europeans dominated the highest levels of the church and government, as well as commerce. Creoles commonly controlled colonial agriculture and mining. Although tensions between Spaniards and creoles were inevitable, most elite families had members from both groups.

Before the Europeans arrived in the Americas, the native peoples were members of a large number of distinct cultural and linguistic groups. Cultural diversity and class distinctions were present even in the highly centralized Aztec and Inca Empires. The loss of life provoked by the European conquest undermined this rich social and cultural complexity, and the imposition of Catholic Christianity further eroded ethnic boundaries among native peoples. Colonial administrators and settlers broadly applied the racial label *Indian,* which facilitated the imposition of special taxes and labor obligations while erasing long-standing class and ethnic differences.

Indigenous Amerindian elites survived only briefly in the Spanish colonies and Brazil. Some of the conquistadors and early settlers married or established less formal relations with elite Amerindian women, but fewer of these alliances occurred after European women began to arrive. Some descendants of the powerful Amerindian families prospered in the colonial period as ranchers, muleteers, and merchants; many others lived in the same materially deprived conditions as Amerindian commoners.

Thousands of blacks participated in the conquest and settlement of Spanish America, and the opening of a direct slave trade with Africa added millions more. Settlers' views of African slaves' cultural differences as signs of inferiority ultimately served as a justification for slavery. By 1600, anyone with black ancestry was barred from positions in church, government, and many skilled crafts. Even so, African languages, religious beliefs, and marriage customs mixed with European (and in some cases Amerindian) languages and beliefs to forge distinct local cultures. The rapid growth of an American-born slave population accelerated this process of cultural change.

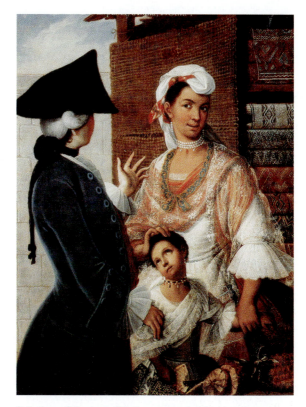

Painting of Castas   This is an example of a common genre of colonial Spanish American painting. In the eighteenth century there was increased interest in ethnic mixing, and wealthy colonials as well as some Europeans commissioned sets of paintings that showed mixed families. The paintings commonly also indicated what the artist believed was an appropriate class setting. In this painting a richly dressed Spaniard is depicted with his Amerindian wife dressed in European clothing. Notice that the painter has the mestiza daughter look to her European father for guidance.   (Private Collection. Photographer: Camilo Garza/Fotocam, Monterrey, Mexico)

African slaves became skilled artisans, musicians, servants, artists, cowboys, and even soldiers. However, the vast majority worked in agriculture. To escape harsh discipline, brutal punishments, and backbreaking labor, many slaves rebelled or ran away. Communities of runaways (called *quilombos*° in Brazil and *palenques*° in Spanish colonies) were common. The largest quilombo was Palmares, where thousands of slaves defended

---

quilombos (ley-LOM-bos)   *palenques* (pah-LEN-kays)

파운드폭탄 4발 투하… 두 아들과 함께 사망
삼진지 구축… 이틀째 시가戰

령이 대중 앞에 나타나거나 애국심
을 고취하는 노래만을 내보내던 방
송마저 중단됐다.

라크 전후
외에서는
영국 주도

DIVERSITY AND DOMINANCE

RACE AND ETHNICITY IN THE SPANISH COLONIES: NEGOTIATING HIERARCHY

*M*any European visitors to colonial Latin America were interested in the mixing of Europeans, Amerindians, and Africans in the colonies. Many also commented on the treatment of slaves. The passages that follow allow us to examine two colonial societies.

The first selection was written by two young Spanish naval officers and scientists, Jorge Juan and Antonio de Ulloa, who arrived in the colonies in 1735 as members of a scientific expedition. They visited the major cities of the Pacific coast of South America and traveled across some of the most difficult terrain in the hemisphere. In addition to their scientific chores, they described architecture, local customs, and the social order. In this section they describe the ethnic mix in Quito, now the capital of Ecuador.

The second selection was published in Lima under the pseudonym Concolorcorvo around 1776. We now know that the author was Alonso Carrío de la Vandera. Born in Spain, he traveled to the colonies as a young man. He served in many minor bureaucratic positions, one of which was the inspection of the postal route between Buenos Aires and Lima. Carrío turned his long and often uncomfortable trip into an insightful, and sometimes highly critical, examination of colonial society. The selection that follows describes Córdoba, Argentina.

Juan and Ulloa and Carrío seem perplexed by colonial efforts to create and enforce a racial taxonomy that stipulated and named every possible mixture of European, Amerindian, and African, noting the vanity and social presumptions of the dominant white population. We are fortunate to have these contemporary descriptions of the diversity of colonial society, but it is important to remember that these authors were clearly rooted in their time and confident in the superiority of Europe. Although they noted many of the abuses of Amerindian, mixed, and African populations while puncturing the pretensions of the colonial elites, they were also quick to assume the inferiority of the nonwhite population.

Quito

This city is very populous, and has, among its inhabitants, some families of high rank and distinction; though their number is but small considering its extent, the poorer class bearing here too great a proportion. The former are the descendants either of the original conquerors, or of presidents, auditors, or other persons of character [high rank], who at different times came over from Spain invested with some lucrative post, and have still preserved their luster, both of wealth and descent, by intermarriages, without intermixing with meaner families though famous for their riches. The commonalty may be divided into four classes; Spaniards or Whites, Mestizos, Indians or Natives, and Negroes, with their progeny. These last are not proportionally so numerous as in the other parts of the Indies; occasioned by it being something inconvenient to bring Negroes to Quito, and the different kinds of agriculture being generally performed by Indians.

The name of Spaniard here has a different meaning from that of Chapitone [sic] or European, as properly signifying a person descended from a Spaniard without a mixture of blood. Many Mestizos, from the advantage of a fresh complexion, appear to be Spaniards more than those who are so in reality; and from only this fortuitous advantage are accounted as such. The Whites, according to this construction of the word, may be considered as one sixth part of the inhabitants.

The Mestizos are the descendants of Spaniards and Indians, and are to be considered here in the same different degrees between the Negroes and Whites, as before at Carthagena [sic]; but with this difference, that at Quito the degrees of Mestizos are not carried so far back; for, even in the second or third generations, when they acquire the European color, they are considered as Spaniards. The complexion of the Mestizos is swarthy and reddish, but not of that red common in the fair Mulattos. This is the first degree, or the immediate issue of a Spaniard and Indian. Some are, however, equally tawny with the Indians themselves, though they are distinguished from them by their beards: while others, on the contrary, have so fine a complexion that they might pass for Whites, were it not for some signs which betray them, when viewed attentively. Among these, the most remarkable is the lowness of the forehead, which often leaves but a small space between their hair and eye-brows; at the same time the hair grows remarkably forward on the temples, extending to the lower part of the ear. Besides, the hair itself is harsh, lank, coarse, and very black; their nose very small, thin, and has a little rising on the middle, from whence it forms a small curve, terminating in a point, bending towards the upper lip. These marks, besides some dark spots on the body, are so constant and invariable, as to make it very difficult to conceal the fallacy of their complexion. The Mestizos may be reckoned a third part of the inhabitants.

The next class is the Indians, who form about another third; and the others, who are about one sixth, are the Castes [mixed]. These four classes, according to the most authentic accounts taken from the parish register, amount to between 50 and 60,000 persons, of all ages, sexes, and ranks. If among these classes the Spaniards, as is natural to think, are the most eminent for riches, rank, and power, it must at the same time be owned, however melancholy the truth may appear, they are in proportion the most poor, miserable and distressed; for they refuse to apply themselves to any mechanic business, considering it as a disgrace to that quality they so highly value themselves upon, which consists in not being black, brown, or of a copper color. The Mestizos, whose pride is regulated by prudence, readily apply themselves to arts and trades, but chose those of the greatest repute, as painting, sculpture, and the like, leaving the meaner sort to the Indians.

Córdoba

There was not a person who would give me even an estimate of the number of residents comprising this city, because neither the secular nor the ecclesiastical council has a register, and I know not how these colonists prove the ancient and distinguished nobility of which they boast; it may be that each family has its genealogical history in reserve. In my computation, there must be within the city and its limited common lands around 500 to 600 residents, but in the principal houses there are a very large number of slaves, most of them Creoles [native born] of all conceivable classes, because in this city and in all of Tucumán there is no leniency about granting freedom to any of them. They are easily supported since the principal aliment, meat, is of such moderate price, and there is a custom of dressing them only in ordinary cloth which is made at home by the slaves themselves, shoes being very rare. They aid their masters in many profitable ways and under this system do not think of freedom, thus exposing themselves to a sorrowful end, as is happening in Lima.

As I was passing through Córdoba, they were selling 2,000 Negroes, all Creoles from Temporalidades [property confiscated from the Jesuit order in 1767], from just the two farms of the [Jesuit] colleges of this city. I have seen the lists, for each one has its own, and they proceed by families numbering from two to eleven, all pure Negroes and Creoles back to the fourth generation, because the priests used to sell all of those born with a mixture of Spanish, mulatto, or Indian blood. Among this multitude of Negroes were many musicians and many of other crafts; they proceeded with the sale by families. I was assured that the nuns of Santa Teresa alone had a group of 300 slaves of both sexes, to whom they give their just ration of meat and dress in the coarse cloth which they make, while these good nuns content themselves with what is left from other ministrations. The number attached to other religious establishments is much smaller, but there is a private home which has 30 or 40, the majority of whom are engaged in various gainful activities. The result is a large number of excellent washerwomen whose accomplishments are valued so highly that they never mend their outer skirts in order that the whiteness of their undergarments may be seen. They do the laundry in the river, in water up to the waist, saying vaingloriously that she who is not soaked cannot wash well. They make ponchos [hand-woven capes], rugs, sashes,

(continued)

and sundries, and especially decorated leather cases which the men sell for 8 reales each, because the hides have no outlet due to the great distance to the port; the same thing happens on the banks of the Tercero and Cuarto rivers, where they are sold at 2 reales and frequently for less.

The principal men of the city wear very expensive clothes, but this is not true of the women, who are an exception in both Americas and even in the entire world, because they dress decorously in clothing of little cost. They are very tenacious in preserving the customs of their ancestors. They do not permit slaves, or even freedmen who have a mixture of Negro blood, to wear any cloth other than that made in this country, which is quite coarse. I was told recently that a certain bedecked mulatto [woman] who appeared in Córdoba was sent word by the ladies of the city that she should dress according to her station, but since she paid no attention to this reproach, they endured her negligence until one of the ladies, summoning her to her home under some other pretext, had the servants undress her, whip her, burn her finery before her eyes, and dress her in the clothes befitting her class; despite the fact that the [victim] was not lacking in persons to defend her, she disappeared lest the tragedy be repeated.

QUESTIONS FOR ANALYSIS

1. What do the authors of these selections seem to think about the white elites of the colonies? Are there similarities in the ways that Juan and Ulloa and Carrío describe the mixed population of Quito and the slave population of Córdoba?

2. Are there differences in the way that the authors characterize the relationship between color and class?

3. What does the humiliation of the mixed-race woman in Córdoba tell us about ideas of race and class in the Spanish colony?

Sources: Jorge Juan and Antonio de Ulloa, *A Voyage to South America,* The John Adams translation (abridged), Introduction by Irving A. Leonard (New York: Alfred A. Knopf, 1964), 135–137, copyright © 1964 by Alfred A. Knopf, Inc. Used by permission of Alfred A. Knopf, a division of Random House, Inc.; Concolorcorvo, *El Lazarillo, A Guide for Inexperienced Travelers between Buenos Aires and Lima,* 1773, translated by Walter D. Kline (Bloomington: Indiana University Press, 1965), 78–80. Used with permission of Indiana University Press.

themselves against Brazilian authorities for sixty years until they were finally overrun in 1694.

ENGLISH AND FRENCH COLONIES IN NORTH AMERICA

The North American colonial empires of England and France and the colonies of Spain and Portugal had many characteristics in common. The governments of England and France hoped to find easily extracted forms of wealth or great indigenous empires like those of the Aztecs or Inca. Like the Spanish and Portuguese, English and French settlers responded to native peoples with a mixture of diplomacy and violence. African slaves proved crucial to the development of all four colonial economies.

There were also important differences. The English and French colonies were founded nearly a century after Cortés's conquest of Mexico and initial Portuguese settlement in Brazil. Distracted by ventures elsewhere, neither England nor France imitated the large and expensive colonial bureaucracies that Spain and Portugal established. Instead, private companies and individual proprietors pioneered the development of English and French colonies. This practice led to greater regional variety in economic activity, political institutions and culture, and social structure than was evident in Latin American colonies.

The South

London investors, organized as the privately funded Virginia Company, got off to a rocky start. Nearly 80 percent of the settlers at Jamestown in 1607 and 1608 soon died of disease or Amerindian attacks. After the English crown dissolved the Virginia Company in 1624 because of its mismanagement, colonists pushed deeper into the interior, developing a sustainable economy based on furs, timber, and, increasingly, tobacco. The profits from tobacco soon attracted new immigrants and new capital. Along the shoreline of Chesapeake Bay and the rivers that fed it, settlers spread out, developing plantations and farms.

Indentured servants eventually accounted for approximately 80 percent of all English immigrants to the Chesapeake Bay region. Young men and women unable to pay for their transportation to the New World accepted indentures (contracts) that bound them to a term ranging from four to seven years of labor in return for passage, a small parcel of land, and some tools and clothes. During the seventeenth century, approximately fifteen hundred indentured servants, mostly male, arrived each year. As life expectancy in the colony improved, planters began to purchase more slaves. They calculated that greater profits could be secured by paying the higher initial cost of slaves owned for life than by purchasing the contracts of indentured servants bound for short periods of time. As a result, Virginia's slave population grew rapidly, from 950 in 1660 to 120,000 by 1756.

Ironically, this dramatic increase in the colony's slave population occurred along with the expansion in colonial liberties and political rights. At first, colonial government had been administered by a Crown-appointed governor and his council, as well as by representatives of towns meeting together as the **House of Burgesses.** When these representatives began to meet alone as a deliberative body, they initiated a form of democratic representation that distinguished the English colonies of North America from the colonies of other European powers. The intertwined evolution of freedom and slavery gave England's southern colonies a unique and conflicted political character.

Colonial South Carolina was the most hierarchical society in British North America. Planters controlled the economy and political life. The richest maintained households in both the countryside and Charleston, the largest city in the southern colonies. Small farmers, cattlemen, artisans, merchants, and fur traders held an intermediate but clearly subordinate social position. African slaves were present from the founding of Charleston. They were instrumental in introducing irrigated rice agriculture and in developing indigo (a plant that produced a blue dye) plantations. Native peoples remained influential participants in colonial society through commercial contacts and alliances, but they were increasingly marginalized.

New England

New England was colonized by two separate groups of Protestant dissenters. The **Pilgrims** established the colony of Plymouth on the coast of present-day Massachusetts in 1620. Although nearly half of the settlers died during the first winter, the colony survived. In 1691, Plymouth was absorbed into the larger Massachusetts Bay Colony of the **Puritans.** The Puritan leaders had received a royal charter to finance the Massachusetts Bay Colony. By 1643, more than 20,000 Puritans had settled in the Bay Colony.

Unlike in the southern colonies, most newcomers to Massachusetts arrived with their families. A normal gender balance and a healthy climate resulted in a rapid natural increase in population. Massachusetts also was more homogeneous and less hierarchical than the southern colonies.

Political institutions evolved out of the terms of the royal charter. A governor was elected, along with a council of magistrates drawn from the board of directors of the Massachusetts Bay Company. Disagreements between this council and elected representatives of the towns led, by 1650, to the creation of a lower legislative house that selected its own speaker and began to develop procedures and rules similar to those of the House of Commons in England.

Economically, Massachusetts differed dramatically from the southern colonies. Agriculture met basic needs, but poor soils and harsh climate offered no opportunity to develop cash crops like tobacco or rice. To pay for imported tools, textiles, and other essentials, the colonists began to provide commercial and shipping services to the southern colonies, the smaller Caribbean islands, Africa, and Europe.

In contrast to Latin America's heavily capitalized monopolies, New England merchants' success rested on market intelligence, flexibility, and streamlined organization. With 16,000 inhabitants in 1740, Boston was the largest city in British North America.

Middle Atlantic Region

The rapid economic development and remarkable cultural diversity of the Middle Atlantic colonies added to the success of English-speaking North America. The **Iroquois Confederacy,** an alliance of several native peoples, established treaties and trading relationships with the Dutch. When confronted by an English military expedition in 1664, the Dutch surrendered their colony of New Netherland without a fight. Renamed New York, the colony's success was guaranteed in large measure by the development of New York City as a commercial and shipping center. Located at the mouth of the Hudson River, the city played an essential role in connecting the region's grain farmers to the booming markets of the Caribbean and southern Europe. By the early eighteenth century, New York Colony had a diverse population that included (in addition to English colonists) Dutch, German, and Swedish settlers, as well as a large slave community.

Pennsylvania began as a proprietary colony in 1682 and as a refuge for Quakers, a persecuted religious minority. The founder, William Penn, quickly lost control of the colony's political life, but the colony enjoyed remarkable success. By 1700, Pennsylvania had a population of more than 21,000, and Philadelphia, its capital, soon passed Boston to become the largest city in the British colonies. Healthy climate, excellent land, and relatively peaceful relations with native peoples attracted free workers, including a large number of German families. As a result, Pennsylvania's economic expansion in the late seventeenth century occurred without reproducing South Carolina's hierarchical and repressive social order. By the early eighteenth century, however, the prosperous city of Philadelphia included a large population of black slaves, servants, and skilled tradesmen.

French America

French settlement patterns more closely resembled those of Spain and Portugal than of England. The French were committed to missionary activity among Amerindian peoples and emphasized extracting resources—in this case, furs.

Coming to Canada after spending years in the West Indies, Samuel de Champlain founded the

Canadian Fur Trader   The fur trade provided the economic foundation of early Canadian settlement. The trade depended on a mix of native and European skills and resources. Fur traders were cultural intermediaries. They transmitted European technologies and products like firearms and machine-made textiles to native peoples and native technologies and products like canoes and furs to European settlements. Many were the sons of native women, and nearly all were fluent in native languages. (National Archives of Canada)

colony of **New France** at Quebec°, on the banks of the St. Lawrence River, in 1608. The European market for fur, especially beaver, fueled French settlement. Young Frenchmen were sent to live among native peoples to master their languages and customs. These men and their children by native women organized the fur trade and led French expansion to the west and south. Amerindians ac-

Quebec (kwuh-BEC)

tively participated in this trade because they came to depend on the goods they received in exchange for furs: firearms, metal tools and utensils, textiles, and alcohol.

The Iroquois Confederacy responded to the increased military strength of France's Algonkian allies by forging commercial and military links with Dutch and later English settlements in the Hudson River Valley. Well armed by the Dutch and English, the Iroquois Confederacy nearly eradicated the Huron in 1649 and inflicted a series of humiliating defeats on the French. At the high point of their power in the early 1680s, Iroquois hunters and military forces gained control of much of the Great Lakes region and the Ohio River Valley. A large French military expedition and a relentless attack focused on Iroquois villages and agriculture finally checked Iroquois power in 1701.

Use of firearms in hunting and warfare moved west and south, reaching indigenous plains cultures that previously had adopted the horse introduced by the Spanish. This intersection of horse and gun frontiers in the early eighteenth century dramatically increased the military power and hunting efficiency of the Sioux, Comanche, Cheyenne, and other indigenous peoples and slowed the pace of European settlement in North America.

In French Canada, the Jesuits led the effort to convert native peoples to Christianity. Building on earlier evangelical efforts in Brazil and Paraguay, French Catholic missionaries mastered native languages, created boarding schools for young boys and girls, and set up model agricultural communities for converted Amerindians. The Jesuits' greatest successes coincided with a destructive wave of epidemics and renewed warfare among native peoples in the 1630s. Nevertheless, local cultures persisted.

Although the fur trade flourished, settlers were few. Founded at about the same time, Virginia had twenty times as many European residents as Canada by 1627. Canada's small settler population and the fur trade's dependence on Amerindians allowed indigenous peoples to retain greater independence and more control over their encounters with new religious, technological, and market realities.

The French aggressively expanded. Louisiana, founded in 1699, depended on the fur trade with Amerindians. France's North American colonies were threatened by a series of wars with England and the neighboring English colonies. The "French and Indian War" (also known as the Seven Years War, 1756–1763) proved to be the final contest for the North American empire. England committed a larger military force to the struggle and, despite early defeats, took the French capital of Quebec in 1759. The peace agreement forced France to yield Canada to the English and cede Louisiana to Spain. The French then concentrated their efforts on their sugar-producing colonies in the Caribbean.

PLANTATIONS IN THE WEST INDIES

The West Indies was the first place in the Americas that Columbus reached and the first part of the Americas where native populations collapsed. It took a long time to repopulate these islands from abroad and forge new economic links between them and other parts of the Atlantic. But after 1650, sugar plantations, African slaves, and European capital made these islands a major center of the Atlantic economy.

Spanish settlers had introduced sugar-cane cultivation into the West Indies shortly after 1500, but these colonies soon fell into neglect as attention shifted to colonizing the American mainland. In the 1620s and 1630s, the West Indies revived as a focus of colonization, this time by English and French settlers interested in growing tobacco and other crops. The islands' value mushroomed after the Dutch reintroduced sugar cultivation from Brazil in the 1640s and supplied the African slaves and European capital necessary to create a new economy.

Sugar and Slaves   The English colony of Barbados illustrates the dramatic transformation that sugar brought to the seventeenth-century Caribbean. In 1640, Barbados's economy depended largely on tobacco, mostly grown by European settlers, both free and indentured. By the 1680s, sugar had become the colony's principal crop, and enslaved Africans were three

Market in Rio de Janeiro In many of the cities of colonial Latin America female slaves and black free women dominated retail markets. In this scene from late colonial Brazil, Afro-Brazilian women sell a variety of foods and crafts. (Sir Henry Chamberlain, Views and Costumes of the City and Neighborhoods of Rio de Janeiro, London, 1822)

times as numerous as Europeans. Exporting up to 15,000 tons of sugar a year, Barbados had become the wealthiest and most populous of England's American colonies. By 1700, the West Indies had surpassed Brazil as the world's principal source of sugar.

The expansion of sugar plantations in the West Indies required a sharp increase in the volume of the slave trade from Africa. During the first half of the seventeenth century, about 10,000 slaves a year had arrived from Africa, most destined for Brazil and the mainland Spanish colonies. In the second half of the century, the trade averaged 20,000 slaves a year. More than half were intended for the English, French, and Dutch West Indies and most of the rest for Brazil. A century later, the volume of the Atlantic slave trade was three times larger.

What produced this shift in favor of African slaves? Recent scholarship has cast doubt on the once-common assertion that Africans were more suited than Europeans to field labor; in fact, both died in large numbers in the American tropics. The West Indian historian Eric Williams has also refuted the idea that the rise of African slave labor was primarily motivated by prejudice. Citing the West Indian colonies' prior use of enslaved Amerindians and indentured Europeans, along with European convicts and prisoners of war, he argued, "Slavery was not born of racism: rather, racism was the consequence of slavery."[2] Williams suggested the shift was due to the lower cost of African labor.

Yet slaves were far from cheap. Cash-short tobacco planters in the seventeenth century preferred indentured Europeans because they cost half as much as African slaves. Poor European men and women were willing to work for little to get to the Americas, where they could acquire their own land cheaply at the end of their term of service. However, as the cultivation of sugar spread after 1750, rich speculators drove the price of land in the West Indies up so high that end-of-term indentured servants could not afford to buy it. As a result, poor Europeans chose to indenture themselves in the mainland North American colonies, where cheap land was still available. Rather than raise wages to attract European laborers, Caribbean sugar planters switched to slaves.

Rising sugar prices helped the West Indian sugar planters afford the higher cost of African slaves. The planters could rely on the Dutch and other traders to supply them with enough new slaves to meet the demands of the expanding plantations. Rising demand drove slave prices up steadily during the eighteenth century. These high labor costs were one more factor favoring large plantations over smaller operations.

To find more land for sugar plantations, France and England founded new Caribbean colonies. In 1655, the English had wrested the island of Jamaica from the Spanish (see Map 16.1). The French seized the western half of the large Spanish island of Hispaniola in the 1670s. During the eighteenth century, this new French colony of Saint Domingue° (present-day Haiti) became the greatest producer of sugar in the Atlantic world, while Jamaica surpassed Barbados as England's most important sugar colony.

Technology and Environment

What made the sugar plantation a complex investment was that it had to be a factory as well as a farm. Freshly cut canes needed to be crushed within a few hours to extract the sugary sap. Thus, for maximum efficiency, each plantation needed its own expensive crushing and processing equipment.

At the heart of the sugar works was the mill where canes were crushed between sets of heavy rollers. From the mill, lead-lined wooden troughs carried the cane juice to a series of large copper kettles in the boiling shed, where the excess water boiled off, leaving a thick syrup. Workers poured the syrup into conical molds in the drying shed.

Saint Domingue (san doh-MANGH)

The sugar crystals that formed in the molds were packed in wooden barrels for shipment to Europe.

To make their operation more efficient and profitable, investors gradually increased the size of the typical West Indian plantation from around 100 acres (40 hectares) in the seventeenth century to at least twice that size in the eighteenth century. A plantation became a huge investment. One source estimated that a planter had to invest nearly £20,000 ($100,000) to acquire a Jamaican plantation of 600 acres (240 hectares) in 1774: a third for land, a quarter for equipment, and £8,000 for 200 slaves. Jamaica specialized so heavily in sugar production that the island had to import most of its food. Saint Domingue was more diverse in its economy.

In some ways, the mature sugar plantation was environmentally responsible. The crushing mill was powered by water, wind, or animal power, not fossil fuels. The boilers were largely fueled by burning the crushed canes, and the fields were fertilized by cattle manure. In two respects, however, the plantation was very damaging to the environment: soil exhaustion and deforestation.

Instead of rotating sugar with other crops to restore the nutrients naturally, planters found it more profitable to clear new lands when yields declined too much in the old fields. When land close to the sea was exhausted, planters moved on to new islands. Many of the English who first settled Jamaica were from Barbados, and the pioneer planters on Saint Domingue came from older French sugar colonies. In the second half of the eighteenth century, Jamaican sugar production began to fall behind that of Saint Domingue, which still had access to virgin land. Thus, the plantations of this period were not a stable form of agriculture but one that gradually laid waste to the landscape.

Deforestation, the second form of environmental damage, continued a trend begun in the sixteenth century. By the end of the eighteenth century, only land in the interior of the islands retained dense forests.

The most tragic and dramatic transformation in the West Indies occurred in the human population. During the eighteenth century, West Indian plantation colonies were the world's most polarized societies. On most islands, 90 percent or more of the inhabitants became slaves. A small number of very rich men owned most of the slaves and most of the land as well. Between the slaves and the masters might be found only a few others: a few estate managers and government officials and, in the French islands, some small farmers, both white and black. The profitability of a Caribbean plantation depended on extracting as much work as possible from the slaves through the use of force and the threat of force.

On a typical Jamaican plantation, about 80 percent of the slaves actively engaged in productive tasks; the only exceptions were infants, the seriously ill, and the very old. Slave labor was organized by age, sex, and ability. About 70 percent of the able-bodied slaves worked in the fields, generally in one of three labor gangs. Women formed the majority of the field laborers, even in the great gang. A little over half of the adult males were employed in nongang work, tending the livestock or serving as blacksmiths and carpenters. The most important artisan slave was the head boiler, who oversaw the delicate process of reducing the cane sap to crystallized sugar and molasses.

Skilled slaves received rewards of food and clothing or time off for good work, but the most common reason for working hard was to escape punishment. A slave gang was headed by a privileged male slave, appropriately called the **driver,** whose job was to ensure that the gang completed its work. Production quotas were high, and slaves toiled in the fields from sunup to sunset, except for meal breaks. Those who fell behind because of fatigue or illness soon felt the sting of the whip. Openly rebellious slaves who refused to work, disobeyed orders, or tried to escape were punished with flogging, confinement in irons, or mutilation.

The harsh conditions of plantation life played a major role in shortening slaves' lives, but the greatest killer was disease. The very young were carried off by dysentery caused by contaminated food and water. Slaves newly arrived from Africa went through a period of adjustment to the new environment known as **seasoning,** during which one-third on average died of unfamiliar diseases. Slaves also suffered from diseases they brought with them, including malaria. On one plantation, for example, more than half of the slaves incapacitated by illness had yaws, a painful and debilitating skin disease common in Africa.

Such high mortality greatly added to the volume of the Atlantic slave trade, since plantations had to purchase new slaves every year or two to replace those who had died. The additional imports of slaves to permit the expansion of the sugar plantations meant that the majority of slaves on most West Indian plantations were African-born. As a result, African religious beliefs, patterns of speech, styles of dress and adornment, and music were prominent parts of West Indian life.

Given the harsh conditions of their lives, it is not surprising that slaves in the West Indies often sought to regain the freedom into which most had been born. Individual slaves often ran away, hoping to elude the men and dogs who would track them. Sometimes large groups of plantation slaves rose in rebellion against their bondage and abuse. For example, a large rebellion in Jamaica in 1760 was led by a slave named Tacky, who had been a chief on the Gold Coast of Africa. One night, his followers broke into a fort and armed themselves. Joined by slaves from nearby plantations, they stormed several plantations, setting them on fire and killing the planter families. Tacky died in the fighting that followed, and three other rebel leaders stoically endured cruel deaths by torture that were meant to deter others from rebellion.

Because they believed rebellions were usually led by slaves with the strongest African heritage, European planters tried to curtail African cultural traditions. They required slaves to learn the colonial language and discouraged the use of African languages by deliberately mixing slaves from different parts of Africa. In French and Portuguese colonies, slaves were encouraged to adopt Catholic religious practices, though African deities and beliefs also survived. In the British West Indies, where only Quaker slave owners encouraged Christianity among their slaves before 1800, African herbal medicine remained strong, as did African beliefs concerning nature spirits and witchcraft.

As in Latin America, slavery also provoked flight. In the Caribbean, runaways were known as **maroons.** Maroon communities were especially numerous in the mountainous interiors of Jamaica and Hispaniola, as well as in the island parts of the Guianas°. The Jamaican maroons, after withstand-

---

Guianas (guy-AHN-uhs)

ing several attacks by the colony's militia, signed a treaty in 1739 that recognized their independence in return for their cooperation in stopping new runaways and suppressing slave revolts. Similar treaties with the large maroon population in the Dutch colony of Surinam (Dutch Guiana) recognized their possession of large inland regions.

CREATING THE ATLANTIC ECONOMY

The West Indian plantation colonies were at once archaic in their cruel system of slavery and oddly modern in their specialization in a single product. Besides the plantation system itself, three other elements went into the creation of the new Atlantic economy: new economic institutions, new partnerships between private investors and governments in Europe, and new working relationships between European and African merchants. The new trading system is a prime example of how European capitalist relationships were reshaping the world.

Capitalism and Mercantilism

The Spanish and Portuguese voyages of exploration in the fifteenth and sixteenth centuries were government ventures, and both countries tried to keep their overseas trade and colonies royal monopolies. Monopoly control, however, proved both expensive and inefficient. The success of the Atlantic economy in the seventeenth and eighteenth centuries owed much to private enterprise, which made trading venues more efficient and profitable.

Two European innovations, capitalism and mercantilism, enabled private investors to fund the rapid growth of the Atlantic economy. **Capitalism** was a system of large financial institutions—banks, stock exchanges, and chartered trading companies—that enabled wealthy investors to reduce risks and increase profits. Early capitalism was buttressed by **mercantilism,** policies adopted by European states to promote their citizens' overseas trade and defend it, by armed force when necessary.

Chartered companies were one of the first examples of mercantilist capitalism. A charter issued by the government of the Netherlands in 1602 gave the Dutch East India Company a legal monopoly over all Dutch trade in the Indian Ocean. This privilege encouraged private investors to buy shares in the company. They were amply rewarded when the Dutch East India Company captured control of the long-distance trade routes in the Indian Ocean from the Portuguese (see Chapter 17). A sister firm, the **Dutch West India Company,** was chartered in 1621 to engage in the Atlantic trade and to seize sugar-producing areas in Brazil and African slaving ports from the Portuguese.

Such successes inspired other governments to set up their own chartered companies. In 1672, a royal charter placed all English trade with West Africa in the hands of the new **Royal African Company,** which established its headquarters at Cape Coast Castle, just east of Elmina on the Gold Coast. The French government chartered East India and West India companies to reduce French colonies' dependence on Dutch and English traders.

French and English governments also used military force in pursuit of commercial dominance, especially to break the trading advantage of the Dutch in the Americas. Restrictions on Dutch access to French and English colonies provoked a series of wars with the Netherlands between 1652 and 1678, during which the larger English and French navies defeated the Dutch and drove the Dutch West India Company into bankruptcy.

With Dutch competition in the Atlantic reduced, the French and English governments moved to revoke the monopoly privileges of their chartered companies. England opened trade in Africa to any English subject in 1698 on the grounds that ending monopolies would be "highly beneficial and advantageous to this kingdom." It was hoped that such competition would also cut the cost of slaves to West Indian planters, though the demand for slaves soon drove the prices up again.

Such new mercantilist policies fostered competition among a nation's own citizens, while using high tariffs and restrictions to exclude foreigners. In the 1660s, England had passed a series of Navigation Acts that confined trade with its colonies to English ships and cargoes. The French called their mercantilist legislation, first codified in 1698, the

Exclusif°, highlighting its exclusionary intentions. Other mercantilist laws defended manufacturing and processing interests in Europe against competition from colonies, imposing prohibitively high taxes on any manufactured goods and refined sugar imported from the colonies.

As a result of such mercantilist measures, the Atlantic became Britain, France, and Portugal's most important overseas trading area in the eighteenth century. Britain's imports from its West Indian colonies in this period accounted for over one-fifth of the value of total British imports. The French West Indian colonies played an even larger role in France's overseas trade. Only the Dutch, closed out of much of the American trade, found Asian trade of greater value. Profits from the Atlantic economy, in turn, promoted further economic expansion and increased the revenues of European governments.

The Great Circuit and the Middle Passage

At the heart of the Atlantic system was a great clockwise network of trade routes known as the **Great Circuit.** It began in Europe, ran south to Africa, turned west across the Atlantic Ocean to the Americas, and then swept back to Europe. Like Asian sailors in the Indian Ocean, Atlantic mariners depended on the prevailing winds and currents to propel their ships. What drove the ships as much as the winds and currents was the desire for the profits that each leg of the circuit was expected to produce.

The first leg, from Europe to Africa, carried European manufactures—notably metal bars, hardware, and guns—as well as great quantities of cotton textiles brought from India. Some of these goods were traded for West African gold, timber, and other products, which were taken back to Europe. More goods went to purchase slaves, who were transported across the Atlantic to the plantation colonies in the part of the Great Circuit known as the **Middle Passage.** On the third leg, plantation goods from the colonies returned to Europe. Each leg of the circuit carried goods from where they were abundant and relatively cheap to where they were scarce and therefore more valuable. Thus, in theory, each leg of the Great Circuit could earn

much more than its costs, and a ship that completed all three legs could return a handsome profit to its owners. In practice, shipwrecks, deaths, piracy, and other risks could turn profit into loss.

The three-sided Great Circuit is only the simplest model of Atlantic trade. Many other trading voyages supplemented the basic circuit. Cargo ships made long voyages from Europe to the Indian Ocean, passed southward through the Atlantic with quantities of African gold and American silver, and returned with the cotton textiles necessary to the African trade. Other sea routes brought to the West Indies manufactured goods from Europe or foodstuffs and lumber from New England.

European interests dominated the Atlantic system. The manufacturers who supplied the trade goods and the investors who provided the capital were all based in Europe, as were the principal consumers of the plantation products. Before the seventeenth century, sugar had been rare and fairly expensive in western Europe. By 1700, annual consumption of sugar in England had risen to about 4 pounds (nearly 2 kilograms) per person. Rising western European prosperity and declining sugar prices promoted additional consumption, starting with the upper classes and working its way down the social ladder. People spooned sugar into popular new beverages imported from overseas—tea, coffee, and chocolate—to overcome the beverages' natural bitterness. By 1750, annual sugar consumption in Britain had doubled, and it doubled again to about 18 pounds (8 kilograms) per person by the early nineteenth century.

The flow of sugar to Europe depended on another key component of the Atlantic trading system: the flow of slaves from Africa. The rising volume of the Middle Passage also measures the Atlantic system's expansion. During the first 150 years after the European discovery of the Americas, some 800,000 Africans had begun the journey across the Atlantic. During the boom in sugar production between 1650 and 1800, the slave trade amounted to nearly 7.5 million. Of the survivors, over half landed in the West Indies and nearly a third in Brazil. Plantations in North America imported another 5 percent, and the rest went to other parts of Spanish America.

In these peak decades, the transportation of slaves from Africa was a highly specialized trade.

Exclusif (ek-skloo-SEEF)

Most slaves were carried in ships that had been specially built or modified for the slave trade by the construction between the ships' decks of additional platforms on which the human cargo was packed as tightly as possible.

Seventeenth-century mercantilist policies placed much of the Atlantic slave trade in the hands of chartered companies. During their existence, the Dutch West India Company and the English Royal African Company each carried about 100,000 slaves across the Atlantic. In the eighteenth century, private English traders from Liverpool and Bristol controlled about 40 percent of the slave trade. The French, operating out of Nantes and Bordeaux, handled about half as much, and the Dutch hung on to only 6 percent. The Portuguese, supplying Brazil and other places, had nearly 30 percent of the Atlantic slave trade, in contrast to the 3 percent carried in North American ships.

To make a profit, European slave traders had to buy slaves in Africa for less than the cost of the goods they traded in return. Then they had to deliver as many healthy slaves as possible across the Atlantic for resale in the plantation colonies. The treacherous voyage to the Americas lasted from six to ten weeks. Some ships completed it with all of their slaves alive, but large, even catastrophic losses of life were common. On average between 1650 and 1800, about one slave in every six perished during the Middle Passage.

Some deaths resulted from the efforts of the captives to escape. To inhibit such attempts, African men were confined below deck during most of the voyage, and special netting was installed around the outside of the ship. Some slaves fell into deep psychological depression, known to contemporaries as "fixed melancholy," from which many perished. Others refused to eat, so forced feeding was used to keep slaves alive. When opportunities presented themselves (nearness to land, illness among the crew), some cargoes of enslaved Africans tried to overpower their captors. Such "mutinies" were rarely successful and were put down with brutality that occasioned further losses of life.

Other deaths during the Middle Passage were due to the ill treatment slaves received. Although it was in the interests of the captain and crew to deliver their slave cargo in good condition, whippings, beatings, and even executions were used to

maintain order and force the captives to take nourishment. Moreover, the dangers and brutalities of the slave trade were so notorious that many ordinary seamen shunned such work. As a consequence, cruel and brutal characters abounded among the officers and crews on slave ships.

Although examples of unspeakable cruelties are common in the records, most deaths in the Middle Passage were the result of disease rather than abuse, just as on plantations. Dysentery spread by contaminated food and water caused many deaths. Others died of contagious diseases such as smallpox, carried by persons whose infections were not detected during the medical examinations of slaves prior to boarding. Such maladies spread quickly in the crowded and unsanitary confines of the ships, claiming the lives of many slaves already physically weakened and mentally traumatized by their ordeals.

Crew members who were in close contact with the slaves were equally exposed to the epidemics and regularly suffered heavy losses. Moreover, sailors often fell victim to tropical diseases, such as malaria, to which Africans had acquired resistance. It is a measure of the callousness of the age, as well as the cheapness of European labor, that over the course of a Great Circuit voyage the proportion of crew deaths could be as high as the slave deaths on the Middle Passage.

AFRICA AND THE ATLANTIC

The Atlantic system took a terrible toll in African lives both during the Middle Passage and under the harsh conditions of plantation slavery. Many other Africans died while being marched to African coastal ports for sale overseas. The overall effects on Africa of these losses and of other aspects of the slave trade have been the subject of considerable historical debate. It is clear that the trade's impact depended on the intensity and terms of different African regions' involvement.

Any assessment of the Atlantic system's effects in Africa must also take into consideration the fact that some Africans profited from the trade by capturing and selling slaves. They chained the slaves together or bound them to forked sticks for the march to the coast, then bartered them to the European slavers for trade goods. The effects on the enslaver were different from the effects on the enslaved.

The Gold Coast and the Slave Coast

The transition to slave trading was not sudden. Even as slaves were becoming Atlantic Africa's most valuable export, nonslave goods remained a significant part of the total trade. For example, during its eight decades of operation from 1672 to 1752, the English Royal African Company made 40 percent of its profits from dealings in gold, ivory, and forest products. In some parts of West Africa, such nonslave exports remained predominant even at the peak of the trade.

African merchants were very discriminating about what merchandise they received in return for slaves or other goods. A European ship that arrived with goods of low quality or unsuited to local tastes found it hard to purchase a cargo at a profitable price. Africans' greatest demands were for textiles, hardware, and guns. Of the goods the Royal African Company traded in West Africa in the 1680s, over 60 percent were Indian and European textiles and 30 percent hardware and weaponry. Beads and other jewelry formed 3 percent. The rest consisted of cowrie shells, which were used as money. In the eighteenth century, tobacco and rum from the Americas became welcome imports.

Both Europeans and Africans naturally attempted to drive the best bargain for themselves and sometimes engaged in deceitful practices. The strength of the African bargaining position, however, may be inferred from the fact that as the demand for slaves rose, so too did their price in Africa. In the course of the eighteenth century, the goods needed to purchase a slave on the Gold Coast doubled and in some places tripled or quadrupled.

African governments on the Gold Coast and the Slave Coast just east of it made Europeans observe African trading customs and prevented them from taking control of African territory. Rivalry among European nations, each of which established its own trading "castles" along the Gold Coast, also reduced Europeans' bargaining strength.

How did African kings and merchants obtain slaves for sale? Most accounts agree that prisoners taken in war were the greatest source of slaves for the Atlantic trade, but it is difficult to say how often capturing slaves for export was the main cause of warfare. An early-nineteenth-century king of Asante stated, "I cannot make war to catch slaves in the bush, like a thief. My ancestors never did so. But if I fight a king, and kill him when he is insolent, then certainly I must have his gold, and his slaves, and his people are mine too. Do not the white kings act like this?"[3] English rulers had indeed sentenced seventeenth-century Scottish and Irish prisoners to forced labor in the West Indies.

The Bight of Biafra and Angola

In the eighteenth century, the slave trade expanded eastward to the Bight (bay) of Biafra. In contrast to the Gold and Slave Coasts, where strong kingdoms predominated, the densely populated interior of the Bight of Biafra contained no large states. Even so, the powerful merchant princes of the coastal ports made European traders give them rich presents. Because of the absence of sizeable states, there were no large-scale wars and consequently few prisoners of war. Instead, kidnapping was the major means of getting slaves.

As the volume of the Atlantic trade along the Bight of Biafra expanded in the late eighteenth century, some inland markets evolved into giant fairs, with different sections specializing in slaves and imported goods. An English ship's doctor reported that in the 1780s slaves were "bought by the black traders at fairs, which are held for that purpose, at a distance of upwards of two hundred miles from the sea coast." He reported seeing from twelve hundred to fifteen hundred enslaved men and women arriving at the coast from a single fair.[4]

Angola, south of the Congo estuary, was the greatest source of slaves for the Atlantic trade. This was also the one place along the Atlantic coast where a single European nation, Portugal, controlled a significant amount of territory. Portuguese residents of the main coastal ports served as middlemen between caravans that arrived from the far interior and ships from Brazil.

Many of the slaves sold at Angolan markets were prisoners of war captured by expanding African states. As elsewhere in Africa, such prisoners seem to have been a byproduct of African wars rather than the purpose for which the wars were fought.

Recent research has linked other enslavement with environmental crises in the hinterland of Angola. During the eighteenth century, these southern grasslands periodically suffered severe droughts, which drove famished refugees to areas with more plentiful water. In return for food and water, powerful African leaders gained control of many refugees and sold into the Atlantic trade the men, who were more likely than the women and children to escape or challenge the ruler's authority. The most successful of these inland Angolan leaders became heads of powerful new states that stabilized areas devastated by war and drought and repopulated them with the refugees and prisoners they retained. The slave frontier then moved farther inland. This cruel system worked to the benefit of a few African rulers and merchants at the expense of the many thousands of Africans who were sent to death or perpetual bondage in the Americas.

It is impossible to assess with precision the complex effects of the goods received in sub-Saharan Africa from these trades. Africans were very particular about what they received, so it is unlikely that they could have been consistently cheated. Some researchers have suggested that imports of textiles and metals undermined African weavers and metalworkers, but most economic historians calculate that, on a per capita basis, the volume of these imports was too small to have idled many African artisans. Imports supplemented rather than replaced local production. The goods received in sub-Saharan Africa were intended for consumption and thus did not develop the economy. Likewise, the sugar, tea, and chocolate Europeans consumed did little to promote economic development in Europe. However, both African and European merchants profited from trading these consumer goods. Because they directed the whole Atlantic system, Europeans gained far more wealth than Africans did.

Historians disagree in their assessment of how deeply European capitalism dominated Africa before 1800, but Europeans clearly had much less political and economic impact in Africa than in the West Indies or in other parts of the Americas. Still, it is significant that Western capitalism was expanding rapidly in the seventeenth century, while the Ottoman Empire, the dominant state of the Middle East, was entering a period of economic and political decline (see Chapter 17). The tide of influence in Africa was thus running in the Europeans' direction.

THE COLUMBIAN EXCHANGE

The term **Columbian Exchange** refers to the transfer of peoples, animals, plants, diseases, and technology between the New and Old Worlds that European trade in the Atlantic opened up. We have already seen how Old World diseases devastated Amerindian peoples and led to the resettlement of the Americas by Europeans and Africans. In addition, the domesticated livestock and major agricultural crops of the Old World spread over much of the Americas, and Amerindians' staple crops enriched the agricultures of Europe and Africa. This vast exchange of plants and animals radically altered diets and lifestyles around the Atlantic.

Transfers to the Americas

Within a century of Columbus's first voyage, new settlers in the Americas were growing all the staples of southern European agriculture—wheat, olives, grapes, and garden vegetables—along with African and Asian crops such as rice, bananas, coconuts, breadfruit, and sugar cane. Native peoples remained loyal to their traditional staples but added many Old World plants to their diet. Citrus fruits, melons, figs, and sugar, as well as onions, radishes, and salad greens, all found a place in Amerindian cuisine.

By the eighteenth century, nearly all of the domesticated animals and cultivated plants in the Caribbean were ones that Europeans had introduced. The Spanish had brought cattle, pigs, and horses, all of which multiplied rapidly. They had also introduced new plants. Of these, bananas and plantain from the Canary Islands were a valuable addition to the food supply, and sugar and rice formed the basis of plantation agriculture, along with native tobacco. Other food crops arrived with the slaves from Africa, including okra, black-eyed peas, yams, grains such as millet and sorghum, and mangoes. Many of these new animals and plants were useful additions to the islands, but they crowded out indigenous species. The central importance of sugar cane in transforming Brazil and the Caribbean has already been noted.

The introduction of European livestock to the mainland had a dramatic impact. Faced with few natural predators, cattle, pigs, horses, and sheep, as well as pests like rats and rabbits, multiplied rapidly in the open spaces of the Americas. On the vast plains of present-day southern Brazil, Uruguay, and Argentina, herds of wild cattle and horses exceeded 50 million by 1700. Large herds of both animals also appeared in northern Mexico and what became the Southwest of the United States.

Where Old World livestock spread most rapidly, environmental changes were most dramatic. Marauding livestock often had a destructive impact on Amerindian agriculturists. But on the plains of South America, northern Mexico, and Texas, cattle provided indigenous peoples with abundant supplies of meat and hides. In the present-day south-western United States, the Navajo became sheep-herders and expert weavers of woolen cloth. Individual Amerindians became muleteers, cowboys, and sheepherders.

No animal had a more striking effect on the cultures of native peoples than the horse, which increased the efficiency of hunters and the military capacity of warriors on the plains. The horse permitted the Apache, Sioux, Blackfoot, Comanche, Assiniboine, and others to hunt the vast herds of buffalo in North America more efficiently.

Transfers from the Americas

In return, the Americas offered the Old World an abundance of useful plants. The New World staples of maize and potatoes revolutionized agriculture and diet in parts of Europe, because they provided more calories per acre than any of the Old World staples except rice. Beans, squash, tomatoes, sweet potatoes, peanuts,

Tobacco Factory Machinery in Colonial Mexico City   The tobacco factory in eighteenth-century Mexico City used a horse-driven mechanical shredder to produce snuff and cigarette tobacco. (Archivo General de la Nacion, Buenos Aires)

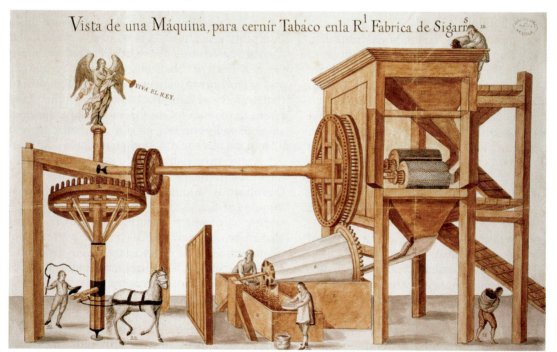

chilis, and chocolate also gained widespread acceptance in Europe and other parts of the Old World. The New World also provided the Old with plants that provided dyes, medicines, and tobacco.

Maize and cassava (a Brazilian plant cultivated for its edible roots) moved across the Atlantic to Africa. Cassava became the most important New World food in Africa. Truly a marvel, cassava had the highest yield of calories per acre of any staple food and thrived even in poor soils and during droughts. Both the leaves and the root could be eaten. Ground into meal, the root could be made into a bread that would keep for up to six months, or it could be fermented into a beverage.

Cassava and maize were probably introduced accidentally into Africa by Portuguese ships from Brazil that discarded leftover supplies after reaching Angola. It did not take long for local Africans to recognize the food value of these new crops, especially in drought-prone areas. By the eighteenth century, Central African rulers hundreds of miles from the Angolan coast were actively promoting the cultivation of maize and cassava on their royal estates in order to provide a more secure food supply. Some historians believe that in the inland areas these Amerindian food crops provided the nutritional base for a population increase that partially offset losses due to the Atlantic slave trade.

CONCLUSION

The New World colonial empires of Spain, Portugal, France, and England had many characteristics in common. All subjugated Amerindian peoples and introduced large numbers of enslaved Africans. Within all four empires, forests were cut down, virgin soils were turned with the plow, and Old World animals and plants were introduced. Colonists in all four applied the technologies of the Old World to the resources of the New, producing wealth and exploiting the commercial possibilities of the emerging Atlantic market. Yet each of the New World empires also reflected the distinctive cultural and institutional heritages of its colonizing power.

Mineral wealth allowed Spain to develop the most centralized empire. Political and economic power was concentrated in the great capital cities of Mexico City and Lima. Portugal and France pursued similar objectives in their colonies. However, neither Brazil's agricultural economy nor France's Canadian fur trade produced the financial resources that made possible the centralized control achieved by Spain. Nevertheless, all three of these Catholic powers were able to impose and enforce significant levels of religious and cultural uniformity.

Greater cultural and religious diversity characterized British North America. Thus, colonists there were better able to respond to changing economic and political circumstances. Most important, the British colonies attracted many more European immigrants than did the other New World colonies.

The new Atlantic trading system had great importance and momentous implications for world history. In the first phase of their expansion, Europeans had conquered and colonized the Americas and captured major Indian Ocean trade routes. The development of the Atlantic system showed Europeans' ability to move beyond the conquest and capture of existing systems to create a major new trading system that could transform a region almost beyond recognition.

The West Indies felt the transforming power of capitalism more profoundly than did any other place outside Europe in this period. The establishment of sugar plantation societies was not just a matter of replacing native vegetation with alien plants and native peoples with Europeans and Africans. More fundamentally, it made these once-isolated islands part of a dynamic trading system controlled from Europe. To be sure, the Caribbean was not the only place affected. Parts of northern Brazil were touched as deeply by the sugar revolution, and other parts of the Americas were yielding to the power of European colonization and capitalism.

Historians have seen the Atlantic system as a model of the kind of highly interactive economy that became global in later centuries. For that reason, the Atlantic system was a milestone in a much larger historical process, but not a monument to be admired. Its transformations were destructive as well as creative, producing victims as well as victors. Yet one cannot ignore that the system's awesome power came from its ability to create wealth. As the next chapter describes, southern Asia and the Indian Ocean Basin were also beginning to feel the effects of Europeans' rising power.

■ Key Terms

Atlantic system	driver
Council of the Indies	seasoning
Bartolomé de Las Casas	maroon
Potosí	capitalism
encomienda	mercantilism
creole	chartered companies
indentured servants	Dutch West India Company
House of Burgesses	Royal African Company
Pilgrims	Great Circuit
Puritans	Middle Passage
Iroquois Confederacy	Columbian Exchange
New France	

■ Suggested Reading

Alfred W. Crosby, Jr., is justifiably the best-known student of the Columbian Exchange. See his *The Columbian Exchange: Biological and Cultural Consequences of 1492* (1972) and *Ecological Imperialism* (1986). William H. McNeill, *Plagues and People* (1976), puts the discussion of the American exchange in a world history context. Elinor G. K. Melville, *A Plague of Sheep: Environmental Consequences of the Spanish Conquest of Mexico* (1994), is the most important recent contribution to this field.

Colonial Latin America, 4th ed. (2001), by Mark A. Burkholder and Lyman L. Johnson, provides a good introduction to colonial Latin American history. *Early Latin America* (1983) by James Lockhart and Stuart B. Schwartz and *Spain and Portugal in the New World, 1492–1700* (1984) by Lyle N. McAlister are both useful introductions as well.

Among the useful general studies of the British colonies are Charles M. Andrews, *The Colonial Period of American History: The Settlements*, 3 vols. (1934–1937); David Hackett Fischer, *Albion's Seed: Four British Folkways in America* (1989); and Gary B. Nash, *Red, White, and Black: The Peoples of Early America*, 2d ed. (1982). For slavery,

see David Brion Davis, *The Problem of Slavery in Western Culture* (1966).

On French North America, William J. Eccles, *France in America*, rev. ed. (1990), is an excellent overview; see also his *The Canadian Frontier, 1534–1760* (1969).

The global context of early modern capitalism is examined by Immanuel Wallerstein, *The Modern World-System*, 3 vols. (1974–1989), and by Fernand Braudel, *Civilization and Capitalism, 15th–18th Century*, 3 vols. (1982–1984). The best general introductions to the Atlantic system are Philip D. Curtin, *The Rise and Fall of the Plantation Complex* (1990), Herbert S. Klein, *The Atlantic Slave Trade* (1999), and David Ellis, *The Rise of African Slavery in the Americas* (2000). A useful collection of primary and secondary sources is David Northrup, ed., *The Atlantic Slave Trade*, 2d ed. (2001).

The cultural connections among African communities on both sides of the Atlantic are explored by John Thornton, *Africa and Africans in the Making of the Atlantic World, 1400–1800*, 2d ed. (1998). Herbert S. Klein's *African Slavery in Latin America and the Caribbean* (1986) is an exceptionally fine synthesis of research on New World slavery, including North American slave systems. For recent research on slavery and the African, Atlantic, and Muslim slave trades with Africa, see Paul Lovejoy, *Transformations in Slavery: A History of Slavery in Africa*, 2d ed. (2000).

■ Notes

1. Quoted in Alfred W. Crosby, Jr., *The Columbian Exchange: Biological and Cultural Consequences of 1492* (Westport, CT: Greenwood, 1972), 58.
2. Eric Williams, *Capitalism and Slavery* (Charlotte: University of North Carolina Press, 1944), 7.
3. King Osei Bonsu, quoted in David Northrup, ed., *The Atlantic Slave Trade*, 2d ed. (Boston: Houghton Mifflin, 2001), 176.
4. Alexander Falconbridge, *Account of the Slave Trade on the Coast of Africa* (London: J. Phillips, 1788), 12.

Southwest Asia and the Indian Ocean, 1500–1750

17

CHAPTER OUTLINE

The Ottoman Empire
The Safavid Empire
The Mughal Empire
Trade Empires in the Indian Ocean
DIVERSITY AND DOMINANCE: Islamic Law and Ottoman Rule

Anthony Jenkinson, merchant-adventurer for the Muscovy Company, founded in 1555 to develop trade with Russia, was the first Englishman to set foot in Iran. Eight years after the first English ship dropped anchor at Archangel on the White Sea in Russia's frigid north, Jenkinson made his way through Russia, down the Volga River, and across the Caspian Sea. The local ruler he met when he disembarked in 1561 in northwestern Iran was an object of wonder:

> richly appareled with long garments of silk, and cloth of gold, embroidered with pearls of stone; upon his head was a *tolipane* [headdress shaped like a tulip] with a sharp end pointing upwards half a yard long, of rich cloth of gold, wrapped about with a piece of India silk of twenty yards long, wrought in gold richly enameled, and set

with precious stones; his earrings had pendants of gold a handful long, with two rubies of great value, set in the ends thereof.

Moving on to Qazvin°, Iran's capital, Jenkinson met the shah. After presenting a letter from Queen Elizabeth in Latin, English, Hebrew, and Italian but finding no one capable of reading it, he managed nevertheless to propose trade between England and Iran. The shah rejected the idea, since diverting Iranian silk from the markets of the Ottoman sultans, with whom he was negotiating a truce after a half-century of intermittent war, would have been undiplomatic.

Qazvin (kaz-VEEN)

411

Though Central Asia's bazaars were only meagerly supplied with goods, as Jenkinson and later merchants discovered, the idea of bypassing the Ottomans in the eastern Mediterranean and trading directly with Iran through Russia remained tempting. By the same token, the Ottomans were tempted by the idea of outflanking Safavid Iran. In 1569, an Ottoman army tried unsuccessfully to dig a 40-mile (64-kilometer) canal between the Don River, which opened into the Black Sea, and the Volga, which flowed into the Caspian. Their objective was to enable Ottoman ships to reach the Caspian and attack Iran from the north.

The Ottomans' foe was Russia, then ruled by Tsar Ivan IV (r. 1533–1584), known as Ivan the Terrible or Awesome. Ivan transformed his principality from a second-rate power into the sultan's primary competitor in Central Asia. In the river-crossed steppe, where Turkic nomads had long enjoyed uncontested sway, Slavic Christian Cossacks from the region of the Don and Dnieper Rivers used armed wagon trains and river craft fitted with small cannon to push southward and establish a Russian presence.

A contest for trade with or control of Central Asia was natural after the centrality conferred on the region by three centuries of Mongol and Turkic conquest, highlighted by the campaigns of Genghis Khan and Timur. But, as we shall see, changes in the organization of trade were sapping the vitality of the Silk Road. Wealth and power were shifting to European seaborne empires linking the Atlantic with the Indian Ocean. Though the Ottomans were a formidable naval power in the Mediterranean, neither they nor the Safavid shahs in Iran nor the Mughal emperors of India deployed more than a token navy in the southern seas.

As you read this chapter, ask yourself the following questions:

- What were the advantages and disadvantages of a land as opposed to a maritime empire?

- What role did religion play in political alliances and rivalries and in the formation of states?

- How did trading patterns change between 1500 and 1750?

THE OTTOMAN EMPIRE

The most long-lived of the post-Mongol Muslim empires was the **Ottoman Empire,** founded around 1300 (see Map 17.1). By extending Islamic conquests into eastern Europe, starting in the late fourteenth century, and by taking Syria and Egypt from the Mamluk rulers in the early sixteenth, the Ottomans seemed to recreate the might of the original Islamic caliphate, the empire established by the Muslim Arab conquests in the seventh century. However, the empire was actually more like the new centralized monarchies of France and Spain (see Chapter 15) than any medieval model.

Enduring more than five centuries, until 1922, the Ottoman Empire survived several periods of wrenching change, some caused by internal problems, others by the growing power of European adversaries. These periods of change reveal the problems faced by huge land-based empires around the world.

Expansion and Frontiers

Established around 1300, the Ottoman Empire grew from a tiny state in northwestern Anatolia because of three factors: (1) the shrewdness of its founder, Osman (from which the name *Ottoman* comes), and his descendants, (2) control of a strategic link between Europe and Asia on the Dardanelles strait, and (3) the creation of an army that took advantage of the traditional skills of the Turkish cavalryman and the new military possibilities presented by gunpowder.

At first, Ottoman armies concentrated on Christian enemies in Greece and the Balkans, in 1389 conquering a strong Serbian kingdom at the Battle of

C H R O N O L O G Y

	Ottoman Empire	Safavid Empire	Mughal Empire
1500	**1516–1517** Selim I conquers Egypt and Syria	**1502–1524** Shah Ismail establishes Safavid rule in Iran	
	1520–1566 Reign of Suleiman the Magnificent; peak of Ottoman Empire		**1526** Babur defeats last sultan of Delhi
	1529 First Ottoman siege of Vienna		**1556–1605** Akbar rules in Agra; peak of Mughal Empire
	1571 Ottoman naval defeat at Lepanto	**1587–1629** Reign of Shah Abbas the Great; peak of Safavid Empire	
1600	**1610** End of Anatolian revolts		
1700			**1658–1707** Aurangzeb imposes conservative Islamic regime
		1722 Afghan invaders topple last Safavid shah	
	1730 Janissary revolt		
	1730 Janissary revolt begins period of Ottoman conservatism	**1736–1747** Nadir Shah temporarily reunites Iran; invades India (1739)	
			1739 Iranians under Nadir Shah sack Delhi

Kosovo°. Much of southeastern Europe and Anatolia was under the control of the sultans by 1402. In 1453, Sultan Mehmed II, "the Conqueror," laid siege to Constantinople. His forces used enormous cannon to bash in the city's walls, dragged warships over a

high hill from the Bosporus strait to the city's inner harbor to get around its sea defenses, and finally penetrated the city's land walls through a series of direct infantry assaults. The fall of Constantinople—henceforth commonly known as Istanbul—brought to an end over eleven hundred years of Byzantine rule and made the Ottomans seem invincible.

Kosovo (KO-so-vo)

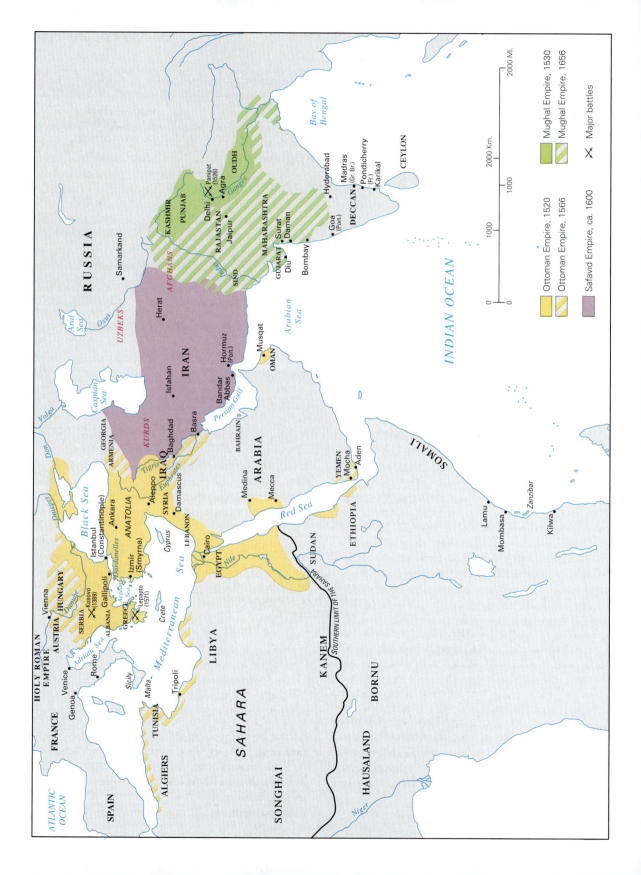

RUSSIA

•Samarkand

UZBEKS

Oxus

Aral
Sea

Volga

Caspian
Sea

GEORGIA

ARMENIA

KURDS

AFGHANS

Herat•

IRAN

Isfahan•

Bandar
Abbas•

Hormuz
(Port.)

Musqat•

OMAN

*Arabian
Sea*

INDIAN OCEAN

KASHMIR

PUNJAB

Panipat
(1526)

Delhi✕ *Ganges* Agra

RAJASTAN Jaipur•

SIND

Indus

OUDH

MAHARASHTRA

GUJARAT Surat• Daman•

Diu• Bombay•

Goa•
(Port.)

DECCAN

Hyderabad•

Madras
(Gr. Br.)

Pondicherry
(Fr.)

Karikal•

CEYLON

*Bay of
Bengal*

2000 Mi.

2000 Km.

1000

1000

0   0

Mughal Empire, 1530   Mughal Empire, 1656

Ottoman Empire, 1520   Ottoman Empire, 1566

Safavid Empire, ca. 1600

✕ Major battles

Don

Dnieper

Black Sea

Istanbul
(Constantinople)

Ankara•

ANATOLIA

Izmir
(Smyrna)•

GREECE

Dardanelles

*Aegean
Sea*

Cyprus

Baghdad•

Basra•

IRAQ

Tigris *Euphrates*

Aleppo•

SYRIA Damascus•

LEBANON

Cairo•

EGYPT

Nile

BAHRAIN•

ARABIA

Medina•

Mecca•

Red Sea

SUDAN

SOUTHERN LIMIT OF THE SAHARA

ETHIOPIA

YEMEN
Mocha•
Aden•

SOMALI

Lamu•

Mombasa•

Zanzibar

Kilwa•

Vienna•

HOLY ROMAN
EMPIRE

AUSTRIA

HUNGARY

Danube

Kosovo (1389)✕

SERBIA

ALBANIA

Lepanto
(1571)✕

FRANCE

Venice•

Genoa•

Rome•

Sicily

Malta

Adriatic Sea

Crete

*Mediterranean
Sea*

Tripoli•

SPAIN

ALGIERS

TUNISIA

LIBYA

SAHARA

SONGHAI

KANEM

BORNU

HAUSALAND

Niger

*ATLANTIC
OCEAN*

Map 17.1   Muslim Empires in the Sixteenth and Seventeenth Centuries   Iran, a Shi'ite state flanked by Sunni Ottomans on the west and Sunni Mughals on the east, had the least exposure to European influences. Ottoman expansion across the southern Mediterranean Sea intensified European fears of Islam. The areas of strongest Mughal control dictated that Islam's spread into Southeast Asia would be heavily influenced by merchants and religious figures from Gujarat instead of from eastern India.

Selim° I, "the Inexorable," conquered Egypt and Syria in 1516 and 1517, making the Red Sea the Ottomans' southern frontier. His son, **Suleiman° the Magnificent** (r. 1520–1566), presided over the greatest Ottoman assault on Christian Europe. Suleiman seemed unstoppable: he conquered Belgrade in 1521, expelled the Knights of the Hospital of St. John from the island of Rhodes the following year, and laid siege to Vienna in 1529. Vienna was saved by the need to retreat before the onset of winter more than by military action. In later centuries, Ottoman historians looked back on the reign of Suleiman as the period when the imperial system worked to perfection, and they spoke of it as the golden age of Ottoman greatness.

While Ottoman armies pressed deeper and deeper into eastern Europe, the sultans also sought to control the Mediterranean. Between 1453 and 1502, the Ottomans fought the opening rounds of a two-century war with Venice, the most powerful of Italy's commercial city-states. The initial fighting left Venice in control of its lucrative islands for another century. But it also left Venice a reduced military power compelled to pay tribute to the Ottomans.

It never occurred to the Ottomans that a sea empire held together by flimsy ships could truly rival a great land empire fielding an army of a hundred thousand men. In the early sixteenth century, merchants from southern India and Sumatra sent emissaries to Istanbul requesting naval support against the Portuguese. The Ottomans responded vigorously to Portuguese threats close to their territories, such as at Aden at the southern entrance to the Red Sea, but their efforts farther afield were insufficient to stifle growing Portuguese domination.

Eastern luxury products still flowed to Ottoman markets. Portuguese power was territorially limited to fortified coastal points, such as Hormuz at the entrance to the Persian Gulf, Goa in western India, and Malacca in Malaya. Why commit major resources to subduing an enemy whose main threat was a demand that merchant vessels, mostly belonging to non-Ottoman Muslims, buy protection from Portuguese attack? The Ottomans did send a small naval force to Indonesia, but they never formulated a consistent or aggressive policy with regard to political and economic developments in the Indian Ocean.

Central Institutions

By the 1520s, the Ottoman Empire was the most powerful and best-organized state in either Europe or the Islamic world. Its military was balanced between cavalry archers, primarily Turks, and **Janissaries°**, Christian prisoners of war induced to serve as military slaves.

Slave soldiery had a long history in Islamic lands, but the conquest of Christian territories in the Balkans in the late fourteenth century gave the Ottomans access to a new military resource. Converted to Islam, these "new troops," called *yeni cheri* in Turkish and *Janissaries* in English, gave the Ottomans unusual military flexibility. Since horseback riding and bowmanship were not part of their cultural backgrounds, they readily accepted the idea of fighting on foot and learning to use guns, which at that time were still too heavy and awkward for a horseman to load and fire. The Janissaries lived in barracks and trained all year round.

The process of selection for Janissary training changed early in the fifteenth century. The new system imposed a regular levy of male children on Christian villages in the Balkans and occasionally elsewhere. Recruited children were placed with Turkish families to learn their language and then were sent to the sultan's palace in Istanbul for an education that included instruction in Islam, military training, and, for the most talented, what we might call liberal arts. This regime, sophisticated for its time, produced not only the Janissary soldiers

---

Selim (seh-LEEM)   **Suleiman** (SOO-lay-man)

Janissaries (JAN-nih-say-rees)

but also, from among the chosen few who received special training, senior military commanders and heads of government departments up to the rank of grand vizier.

The cavalrymen were supported by land grants and administered most rural areas in Anatolia and the Balkans. They maintained order, collected taxes, and reported for each summer's campaign with their horses, retainers, and supplies, all paid for from the taxes they collected. When not campaigning, they stayed at home.

A galley-equipped navy was manned by Greek, Turkish, Algerian, and Tunisian sailors, usually under the command of an admiral from one of the North African ports. The balance of the Ottoman land forces brought success to Ottoman arms in recurrent wars with the Safavids, who were much slower to adopt firearms, and in the inexorable conquest of the Balkans. Expansion by sea was less dramatic. A major expedition against Malta in the western Mediterranean failed in 1565. Combined Christian forces also achieved a massive naval victory at the Battle of Lepanto, off Greece, in 1571. But the Ottomans' resources were so extensive that in a year's time they had replaced all of the galleys sunk in that battle.

The Ottoman Empire became cosmopolitan in character. The sophisticated court language, Osmanli° (the Turkish form of *Ottoman*), shared basic grammar and vocabulary with Turkish, but Arabic and Persian elements made it distinct from the language spoken by Anatolia's nomads and villagers. Everyone who served in the military or the bureaucracy and conversed in Osmanli was considered to belong to the *askeri°*, or "military," class. Members of this class were exempt from taxes and owed their well-being to the sultan.

The Ottomans saw the sultan as providing justice for his "flock of sheep" (*raya°*) and the military protecting them. In return, the raya paid the taxes that supported both the sultan and the military. In reality, the sultan's government remained comparatively isolated from the lives of most subjects. As Islam gradually became the majority religion in Balkan regions, Islamic law (the Shari'a°) conditioned urban institutions and social life. Local cus-

Ottoman Glassmakers on Parade   Celebrations of the circumcisions of the sultan's sons featured parades organized by the craft guilds of Istanbul. This float features glassmaking, a common craft in Islamic realms. The most elaborate glasswork included oil lamps for mosques and colored glass for the small stained-glass windows below mosque domes.   (Topkapi Saray Museum)

toms prevailed among non-Muslims and in many rural areas; and non-Muslims looked to their own religious leaders for guidance in family and spiritual matters (see Diversity and Dominance: Islamic Law and Ottoman Rule).

Crisis of the Military State, 1585–1650

As military technology evolved, cannon and lighter-weight firearms played an ever-larger role on the battlefield. Accordingly, the size of the Janissary corps—and its cost to the government—grew steadily, and the role of the Turkish cavalry diminished. To pay the Janissaries, the sultan started reducing the number of landholding cavalrymen. Revenues previously spent on their living expenses and military equipment went directly into the imperial treasury. Inflation caused by a flood of cheap silver from the New World bankrupted many of the remaining landholders restricted by law to collecting a fixed amount of taxes. Their land was returned

Osmanli (os-MAHN-lee)   *askeri* (AS-keh-ree)
raya (RAH-yah)   **Shari'a** (sha-REE-ah)

to the state. Displaced cavalrymen, armed and un-happy, became a restive element in rural Anatolia.

This complicated situation resulted in revolts that devastated Anatolia between 1590 and 1610. Former landholding cavalrymen, short-term sol-diers released at the end of the campaign season, peasants overburdened by emergency taxes, and even impoverished students of religion formed bands of marauders. Anatolia experienced the worst of the rebellions and suffered greatly from emigration and the loss of agricultural production. But an increase in banditry, made worse by the government's inability to stem the spread of mus-kets among the general public, beset other parts of the empire as well.

In the meantime, the Janissaries took advan-tage of their growing influence to gain relief from prohibitions on their marrying and engaging in business. Janissaries who involved themselves in commerce lessened the burden on the state bud-get, and married Janissaries who enrolled sons or relatives in the corps made it possible in the sev-enteenth century for the government to save state funds by abolishing forced recruitment. These sav-ings, however, were more than offset by the in-crease in the total number of Janissaries and in their steady deterioration as a military force, which necessitated the hiring of more and more supple-mental troops.

Economic Change and Growing Weakness

A very different Ottoman Empire emerged from this crisis. The sultan once had led armies. Now he mostly resided in his palace and had little experience of the real world, and the affairs of government were overseen more and more by the chief administra-tors—the grand viziers.

The Janissaries took advantage of their in-creased power to make membership in their corps hereditary. Their involvement in crafts and trading took a toll on their military skills, but they contin-ued to be a powerful faction in urban politics. Land grants in return for military service also disap-peared. Tax farming arose in their place. Tax farm-ers paid specific taxes, such as customs duties, in advance in return for the privilege of collecting a greater amount from the actual taxpayers.

Rural administration, already disrupted by the rebellions, suffered from the transition to tax farms. The former military landholders had kept order on their lands in order to maintain their incomes. Tax farmers were less likely to live on the land. The imperial government therefore faced greater ad-ministrative burdens and came to rely heavily on powerful provincial governors or on wealthy men who purchased lifelong tax collection rights and behaved more or less like private landowners.

Rural disorder and decline in administrative control sometimes opened the way for new eco-nomic opportunities. The Aegean port of Izmir° (an-cient Smyrna) was able to transform itself between 1580 and 1650 from a small Muslim Turkish town into a multiethnic, multireligious, multilinguistic en-trepôt because of the Ottoman government's inability to control trade and the slowly growing dominance of European traders in the Indian Ocean. Local farm-ers who previously had grown grain for subsistence shifted their plantings more and more to cotton and other cash crops sought by European traders at Izmir. After its introduction in the 1590s, tobacco quickly became popular in the Ottoman Empire de-spite government prohibitions. In this way, the agri-cultural economy of western Anatolia, the Balkans, and the Mediterranean coast—the Ottoman lands most accessible to Europe—became enmeshed in the seventeenth century in a growing European commercial network.

The Ottoman Empire lacked both the wealth and the inclination to match European economic advances. Overland trade from the east dwindled as political disorder in Safavid Iran cut deeply into Iranian silk production. Coffee, an Arabian prod-uct that rose from obscurity in the fifteenth cen-tury to become the rage first in the Ottoman Empire and then in Europe, was grown in the high-lands of Yemen and exported by way of Egypt. By 1770, however, Muslim merchants trading in the Yemeni port of Mocha° (literally "the coffee place") were charged 15 percent in duties and fees. But Eu-ropean traders, benefiting from long-standing trade agreements with the Ottoman Empire, paid little more than 3 percent. Such trade agreements led to European domination of Ottoman import and export trade by sea.

Izmir (IZ-meer)   **Mocha** (MOH-kuh)

DIVERSITY AND DOMINANCE

ISLAMIC LAW AND OTTOMAN RULE

*E*bu's-Su'ud was the mufti of Istanbul from 1545 to 1574, serving under the sultans Suleiman the Magnificent (1520–1566) and his son Selim II (1566–1574). Originally one of many city-based religious scholars giving opinions on matters of law, the mufti of Istanbul by Ebu's-Su'ud's time had become the top religious official in the empire and the personal adviser to the sultan on religious and legal matters. The position would later acquire the title Shaikh al-Islam.

Historians debate the degree of independence these muftis had. Since the ruler, as a Muslim, was subject to the Shari'a, the mufti could theoretically veto his policies. On important matters, however, the mufti more often seemed to come up with the answer that best suited the sultan who appointed him. This bias is not apparent in more mundane areas of the law.

The collection of Ebu's-Su'ud's fatwas, or legal opinions, from which the examples below are drawn shows the range of matters that came to his attention. They are also an excellent source for understanding the problems of his time, the relationship between Islamic law and imperial governance, and the means by which the state asserted its dominance over the common people. Some opinions respond directly to questions posed by the sultan. Others are hypothetical, using the names Zeyd, 'Amr, and Hind the way police today use John Doe and Jane Doe. While qadis, or Islamic judges, made findings of fact in specific cases on trial, muftis issued only opinions on matters of law. A qadi as well as a plaintiff or defendant might ask a question of a mufti. Later jurists consulted collections of fatwas for precedents, but the fatwas had no permanent binding power.

On the Plan of Selim II to Attack the Venetians in Crete in 1570

A land was previously in the realm of Islam. After a while, the abject infidels overran it, destroyed the colleges and mosques, and left them vacant. They filled the pulpits and the galleries with the tokens of infidelity and error, intending to insult the religion of Islam with all kinds of vile deeds, and by spreading their ugly acts to all corners of the earth.

His Excellency the Sultan, the Refuge of Religion, has, as zeal for Islam requires, determined to take the aforementioned land from the possession of the shameful infidels and to annex it to the realm of Islam.

When peace was previously concluded with the other lands in the possession of the said infidels, the aforenamed land was included. An explanation is sought as to whether, in accordance with the Pure shari'a, this is an impediment to the Sultan's determining to break the treaty.

Answer: There is no possibility that it could ever be an impediment. For the Sultan of the People of Islam (may God glorify his victories) to make peace with the infidels is legal only when there is a benefit to all Muslims. When there is no benefit, peace is never legal. When a benefit has been seen, and it is then observed to be more beneficial to break it, then to break it becomes absolutely obligatory and binding.

His Excellency [Muhammad] the Apostle of God (may God bless him and give him peace) made a ten-year truce with the Meccan infidels in the sixth year of the Hegira. His Excellency 'Ali (may God ennoble his face) wrote a document that was corroborated and confirmed. Then, in the following year, it was considered more beneficial to break it and, in the eighth year of the Hegira, [the Prophet] attacked [the Meccans], and conquered Mecca the Mighty.

On War Against the Shi'ite Muslim Safavids of Iran

Is it licit according to the shari'a to fight the followers of the Safavids? Is the person who kills them a holy warrior, and the person who dies at their hands a martyr?

Answer: Yes, it is a great holy war and a glorious martyrdom.

Assuming that it is licit to fight them, is this simply because of their rebellion and enmity against the [Ottoman] Sultan of the People of Islam, because they drew the sword against the troops of Islam, or what?

Answer: They are both rebels and, from many points of view, infidels.

Can the children of Safavid subjects captured in the Nakhichevan campaign be enslaved?

Answer: No.

The followers of the Safavids are killed by order of the Sultan. If it turns out that some of the prisoners, young and old, are [Christian] Armenian[s], are they set free?

Answer: Yes. So long as the Armenians have not joined the Safavid troops in attacking and fighting against the troops of Islam, it is illegal to take them prisoner.

On the Holy Land

Are all the Arab realms Holy Land, or does it have specific boundaries, and what is the difference between the Holy Land and other lands?

Answer: Syria is certainly called the Holy Land. Jerusalem, Aleppo and its surroundings, and Damascus belong to it.

On Land Grants

What lands are private property, and what lands are held by feudal tenure [i.e., assignment in exchange for military service]?

Answer: Plots of land within towns are private property. Their owners may sell them, donate them or convert them to trust. When [the owner] dies, [the land] passes to all the heirs. Lands held by feudal tenure are cultivated lands around villages, whose occupants bear the burden of their services and pay a portion of their [produce in tax]. They cannot sell the land, donate it or convert it to trust. When they die, if they have sons, these have the use [of the land]. Otherwise, the cavalryman gives [it to someone else] by tapu [title deed].

On the Consumption of Coffee

Zeyd drinks coffee to aid concentration or digestion. Is this licit?

Answer: How can anyone consume this reprehensible [substance], which dissolute men drink when engaged in games and debauchery?

The Sultan, the Refuge of Religion, has on many occasions banned coffee-houses. However, a group of ruffians take no notice, but keep coffee-houses for a living. In order to draw the crowds, they take on unbearded apprentices, and have ready instruments of entertainment and play, such as chess and backgammon. The city's rakes, rogues and vagabond boys gather there to consume opium and hashish. On top of this, they drink coffee and, when they are high, engage in games and false sciences, and neglect the prescribed prayers. In law, what should happen to a judge who is able to prevent the said coffee-sellers and drinkers, but does not do so?

Answer: Those who perpetrate these ugly deeds should be prevented and deterred by severe chastisement and long imprisonment. Judges who neglect to deter them should be dismissed.

On Matters of Theft

How are thieves to be "carefully examined"?

Answer: His Excellency 'Ali (may God ennoble his face) appointed Imam Shuraih as judge. It so happened that, at that time, several people took a Muslim's son to another district. The boy disappeared and, when the people came back, the missing boy's father brought them before Judge Shuraih. [When he brought] a claim [against them on account of the loss of his son], they denied it, saying: "No harm came to him from us." Judge Shuraih thought deeply and was perplexed.

When the man told his tale to His Excellency 'Ali, [the latter] summoned Judge Shuraih and questioned him. When Shuraih said; "Nothing came to light by the shari'a," ['Ali] summoned all the people who had taken the man's son, separated them from one another, and questioned them separately. For each of their stopping

(continued)

places, he asked: "What was the boy wearing in that place? What did you eat? And where did he disappear?" In short, he made each of them give a detailed account, and when their words contradicted each other, each of their statements was written down separately. Then he brought them all together, and when the contradictions became apparent, they were no longer able to deny [their guilt] and confessed to what had happened.

This kind of ingenuity is a requirement of the case.

[This fatwa appears to justify investigation of crimes by the state instead of by the qadi. Judging from court records, which contain very few criminal cases, it seems likely that in practice, many criminal cases were dealt with outside the jurisdiction of the qadi's court.]

Zeyd takes 'Amr's donkey without his knowledge and sells it. Is he a thief?

Answer: His hand is not cut off.

Zeyd mounts 'Amr's horse as a courier and loses it. Is compensation necessary?

Answer: Yes.

In which case: What if Zeyd has a Sultanic decree [authorising him] to take horses for courier service?

Answer: Compensation is required in any case. He was not commanded to lose [the horse]. Even if he were commanded, it is the person who loses it who is liable.

On Homicides

Zeyd enters Hind's house and tries to have intercourse forcibly. Since Hind can repel him by no other means, she strikes and wounds him with an axe. If Zeyd dies of the wound, is Hind liable for anything?

Answer: She has performed an act of Holy War.

QUESTIONS FOR ANALYSIS

1. What do these fatwas indicate with regard to the balance between practical legal reasoning and religious dictates?

2. How much was the Ottoman government constrained by the Shari'a?

3. What can be learned about day-to-day life from materials of this sort?

Source: Excerpts from Colin Imber, *Ebu's-Su'ud: The Islamic Legal Tradition* (Stanford, CA: University Press, 1997), 84–88, 93–94, 223–226, 250, 257. Copyright © 1997 Colin Imber, originating publisher Edinburg University Press. Used with permission of Stanford University Press, www.sup.org.

To most people, the downward course of imperial power was not evident, much less the reasons behind it. Far from seeing Europe as the enemy that eventually would dismantle the weakening Ottoman Empire, the Istanbul elite experimented with European clothing and furniture styles and purchased printed books from the empire's first (and short-lived) press.

In 1730, however, a conservative Janissary revolt with strong religious overtones toppled Sultan Ahmed III. The rebellion confirmed the perceptions of a few that the Ottoman Empire was facing severe difficulties. But decay at the center spelled benefit elsewhere. In the provinces, ambitious and competent governors, wealthy landholders, urban notables, and nomad chieftains were well placed to take advantage of the central government's weakness.

By the middle of the eighteenth century, groups of Mamluks had regained a dominant position in

Egypt, and Janissary commanders had become virtually independent rulers in Baghdad. Although no region declared full independence, the sultan's power was slipping away to the advantage of a broad array of lower officials and upstart chieftains in all parts of the empire, and the Ottoman economy was reorienting itself toward Europe.

THE SAFAVID EMPIRE

The **Safavid Empire** of Iran (see Map 17.1) resembled its long-time Ottoman foe in many ways: it initially relied militarily on cavalry paid through land grants; its population spoke several different languages; and it was oriented inward away from the sea. It also had distinct qualities that to this day set Iran off from its neighbors: it derived part of its legitimacy from the pre-Islamic dynasties of ancient Iran, and it adopted the Shi'ite form of Islam.

Safavid Society and Religion

The ultimate victor in a complicated struggle for power among Turkish chieftains west of the Ottoman Empire was Ismail°, a boy of Kurdish, Iranian, and Greek ancestry. In 1502, at the age of sixteen, Ismail proclaimed himself shah of Iran and declared that from that time forward his realm would be devoted to **Shi'ite** Islam, which revered the family of Muhammad's son-in-law Ali. Although Ismail's reasons for compelling Iran's conversion to Shi'ism are unknown, the effect of this radical act was to create a deep chasm between Iran and its neighbors, all of which were Sunni. Iran became a truly separate country for the first time since its incorporation into the Islamic caliphate in the seventh century.

The imposition of Shi'ite belief made the split permanent, but differences between Iran and its neighbors had long been in the making. Persian, written in the Arabic script from the tenth century onward, had emerged as the second language of Islam. Iranian scholars and writers normally read Arabic as well as Persian and sprinkled their writings with Arabic phrases, but their Arab counterparts were much less inclined to learn Persian. After the Mongols destroyed Baghdad, the capital of the Islamic caliphate, in 1258, Iran developed largely on its own, having more extensive contacts with India—where Muslim rulers favored the Persian language—than with the Arabs.

In the post-Mongol period, artistic styles in the East also went their own way. Painted and molded tiles and tile mosaics, often in vivid turquoise blue, became the standard exterior decoration of mosques in Iran but never were used in Syria and Egypt. Persian poets raised verse to peaks of perfection that had no reflection in Arabic poetry, generally considered to be in a state of decline.

To be sure, Islam itself provided a tradition of belief, learning, and law that crossed ethnic and linguistic borders, but Shah Ismail's imposition of Shi'ism set Iran significantly apart. Shi'ite doctrine says that all temporal rulers, regardless of title, are temporary stand-ins for the **"Hidden Imam":** the twelfth descendant of Ali, the prophet Muhammad's cousin and son-in-law who disappeared as a child in the ninth century. Some Shi'ite scholars concluded that the faithful should calmly accept the world as it was and wait quietly for the Hidden Imam's return. Others maintained that they themselves should play a stronger role in political affairs because they were best qualified to know the Hidden Imam's wishes. These two positions, which still play a role in Iranian Shi'ism, tended to enhance the self-image of religious scholars as independent of imperial authority and stood in the way of their becoming subordinate government functionaries, as happened in the Ottoman Empire.

Shi'ism also affected the psychological life of the people. Annual commemoration of the martyrdom of Imam Husayn (d. 680), Ali's son and the third Imam, regularized an emotional outpouring with no parallel in Sunni lands. Day after day for two weeks, preachers recited the woeful tale to crowds of weeping believers, and elaborate street processions, often organized by craft guilds, paraded chanting and self-flagellating men past crowds of reverent onlookers. Of course, Shi'ites elsewhere observed rites of mourning for Imam Husayn, but the impact of these rites was especially great in Iran, where 90 percent of the population was Shi'ite. Over time, the subjects of the Safavid shahs came to feel more than ever a people apart.

Isfahan and Istanbul

Outwardly, the Ottoman capital of Istanbul looked quite different from Isfahan°, which became Iran's capital in 1598 by decree of **Shah Abbas I** (r. 1587–1629). Built on seven hills on the south side of the narrow Golden Horn inlet, Istanbul boasted a skyline punctuated by the gray stone domes and thin, pointed minarets of the great imperial mosques. The mosques surrounding the royal plaza in Isfahan, in contrast, had unobtrusive minarets and brightly tiled domes that rose to gentle peaks. High walls surrounded the sultan's palace in Istanbul. Shah Abbas in Isfahan focused his capital on the giant royal plaza, which

Safavid Shah with Attendants and Musicians   This painting by Ali-Quli Jubbadar, a European convert to Islam working for the Safavid armory, reflects Western influences. Notice the use of light and shadow to model faces and the costume of the attendant to the shah's right. The shah's water-pipe indicates the spread of tobacco, a New World crop, to the Middle East.   (Courtesy of Oriental Institute, Academy of Sciences, Leningrad. Reproduced from Album of Persian and Indian Miniatures [Moscow, 1962], ill. no. 98)

was large enough for his army to play polo, and he used an airy palace overlooking the plaza to receive dignitaries and review his troops.

The harbor of Istanbul, the primary Ottoman seaport, teemed with sailing ships and smaller craft, many of them belonging to a colony of European merchants perched on a hilltop on the north side of the Golden Horn. Isfahan, far from the sea, was only occasionally visited by Europeans. Most of its trade was in the hands of Jews, Hindus, and especially a colony of Armenian Christians brought in by Shah Abbas.

Beneath these superficial differences, the two capitals had much in common. Wheeled vehicles were scarce in hilly Istanbul and nonexistent in Isfahan. Both cities were built for walking and, aside from the royal plaza in Isfahan, lacked the open spaces common in contemporary European cities. Streets were narrow and irregular. Houses crowded against each other in dead-end lanes. Residents enjoyed their privacy in interior courtyards. Arti-

sans and merchants organized themselves into guilds that had strong social and religious as well as economic bonds. The shops of each guild adjoined each other in the markets.

Women were seldom seen in public, even in Istanbul's mazelike covered market or in Isfahan's long, serpentine bazaar. At home, the women's quarters—called *anderun°*, or "interior," in Iran and *harem*, or "forbidden area," in Istanbul—were separate from the public rooms where the men of the family received visitors. In both areas, low cushions, charcoal braziers for warmth, carpets, and small tables constituted most of the furnishings.

The private side of family life has left few traces, but it is apparent that women's society—consisting of wives, children, female servants, and sometimes one or more eunuchs—was not entirely cut off from the outside world. Ottoman court records reveal that women, using male agents,

anderun (an-deh-ROON)

Aya Sofya Mosque in Istanbul Originally a Byzantine cathedral, Aya Sofya (in Greek, Hagia Sophia) was transformed into a mosque after 1453, and four minarets were added. It then became a model for subsequent Ottoman mosques. To the right behind it is the Bosporus strait dividing Europe and Asia, to the left the Golden Horn inlet separating the old city of Istanbul from the newer parts. The gate to the Ottoman sultan's palace is to the right of the mosque. The pointed tower to the left of the dome is part of the palace. (Robert Frerck/Woodfin Camp & Associates)

were very active in the urban real estate market. Often they were selling inherited shares of their father's estate, but some both bought and sold real estate on a regular basis and even established religious endowments for pious purposes. The fact that Islamic law, unlike some European codes, permitted a wife to retain her property after marriage gave some women a stake in the general economy and a degree of independence from their spouses. Women also appeared in other types of court cases, where they often testified for themselves, for Islamic courts did not recognize the role of attorney. Although comparable Safavid court records do not survive, historians assume that a parallel situation prevailed in Iran.

European travelers commented on the veiling of women outside the home, but the norm for both sexes was complete coverage of arms, legs, and hair. Miniature paintings indicate that ordinary female garb consisted of a long, ample dress with a scarf or long shawl pulled tight over the forehead to conceal the hair. Lightweight trousers, either close-fitting or baggy, were often worn under the dress. This mode of dress was not far different from that of men. Poor men wore light trousers, a long shirt, a jacket, and a hat or turban. Wealthier men wore over their trousers ankle-length caftans, often closely fitted around the chest. Public life was almost entirely the domain of men. Poetry and art, both somewhat more elegantly developed in Isfahan than in Istanbul, were as likely to extol the charms of beardless boys as pretty women. Despite religious disapproval of homosexuality, attachments to adolescent boys were neither unusual nor hidden. Women who appeared in public—aside from non-Muslims, the aged, and the very poor—were likely to be slaves. Miniature paintings frequently depict female dancers, musicians, and even acrobats in attitudes and costumes that range from decorous to decidedly erotic.

Despite social similarities, the overall flavors of Isfahan and Istanbul were not the same. Isfahan had its prosperous Armenian quarter across the river from the city's center, but it was not a truly cosmopolitan capital, just as the peoples of the Safavid realm were not remarkably diverse. Like other rulers of extensive land empires, Shah Abbas located his capital toward the center of his domain within comparatively easy reach of any threatened frontier. Istanbul, in contrast, was a great seaport and a crossroads located on the straits separating the sultan's European and Asian possessions. People of all sorts lived or spent time in Istanbul: Venetians, Genoese, Arabs, Turks, Greeks, Armenians, Albanians, Serbs, Jews, Bulgarians, and more. In this respect, Istanbul conveyed the cosmopolitan character of major seaports from London to Canton (Guangzhou) and belied the fact that its prosperity rested on the vast reach of the sultan's territories rather than on the voyages of its merchants.

Economic Crisis and Political Collapse

The silk fabrics of northern Iran were the mainstay of the Safavid Empire's foreign trade. However, the manufacture that eventually became most powerfully associated with Iran was the deep-pile carpet made by knotting colored yarns around stretched warp threads. Different cities produced distinctive carpet designs. Women and girls did much of the actual knotting work.

Overall, Iran's manufacturing sector was neither large nor notably productive. Most of the shah's subjects, whether Iranians, Turks, Kurds, or Arabs, lived by subsistence farming or herding. Neither area of activity recorded significant technological advances during the Safavid period.

The Safavids, like the Ottomans, had difficulty finding the money to pay troops armed with firearms. This crisis occurred somewhat later in Iran because of its greater distance from Europe. By the end of the sixteenth century, it was evident that a more systematic adoption of cannon and firearms in the Safavid Empire would be needed to hold off the Ottomans and the Uzbeks° (Turkish rulers who had succeeded the Timurids on Iran's Central Asian frontier; see Map 17.1). Like

the Ottoman cavalry a century earlier, the warriors furnished by the nomad leaders were not inclined to trade in their bows for firearms. Shah Abbas responded by establishing a slave corps of year-round soldiers and arming them with guns. The Christian converts to Islam who initially provided the manpower for the new corps were mostly captives taken in raids on Georgia in the Caucasus°.

In the late sixteenth century, the inflation caused by cheap silver spread into Iran; then overland trade through Safavid territory declined because of mismanagement of the silk monopoly after Shah Abbas's death in 1629. As a result, the country faced the unsolvable problem of finding money to pay the army and bureaucracy. Trying to unseat the nomads from their lands to regain control of taxes was more difficult and more disruptive militarily than the piecemeal dismantlement of the land-grant system in the Ottoman Empire. The nomads were still a cohesive military force, and pressure from the center simply caused them to withdraw to their mountain pastures until the pressure subsided. By 1722, the government had become so weak and commanded so little support from the nomadic groups that an army of marauding Afghans was able to capture Isfahan and effectively end Safavid rule.

THE MUGHAL EMPIRE

What distinguished the Indian empire of the Mughal° sultans from the empires of the Ottomans and Safavids was the fact that India was a land of Hindus ruled by a Muslim minority. Muslim dominion in India was the result of repeated military campaigns from the early eleventh century onward, and the Mughals had to contend with the Hindus' long-standing resentment of the destruction of their culture by Muslims. Thus, the challenge facing the Mughals was not just conquering and organizing a large territorial state but also finding a formula for Hindu-Muslim coexistence.

Uzbeks (UHZ-bex)

Caucasus (CAW-kuh-suhs)   **Mughal** (MOH-guhl)

Political Foundations

Babur° (1483–1530), the founder of the **Mughal Empire,** was a Muslim descendant of both Timur and Genghis Khan (*Mughal* is Persian for "Mongol"). Invading from Central Asia, Babur defeated the last Muslim sultan of Delhi° in 1526. Babur's grandson **Akbar** (r. 1556–1605), a brilliant but mercurial man, established the central administration of the expanding state. Under him and his three successors—the last of whom died in 1707—all but the southern tip of India fell under Mughal rule, administered first from Agra and then from Delhi.

Akbar granted land revenues to military officers and government officials in return for their service. Ranks, called *mansabs*°, some high and some low, entitled their holders to revenue assignments. As in the other Islamic empires, revenue grants were not considered hereditary, and the central government kept careful track of their issuance.

With a population of 100 million, a thriving trading economy based on cotton cloth, and a generally efficient administration, India under Akbar was probably the most prosperous empire of the sixteenth century. He and his successors faced few external threats and experienced generally peaceful conditions in their northern Indian heartland.

Foreign trade boomed at the port of Surat in the northwest, which also served as an embarkation point for pilgrims on their way to Mecca. Like the Safavids, the Mughals had no navy or merchant ships. The government saw the Europeans—after Akbar's time, primarily Dutch and English, the Portuguese having lost most of their Indian ports—less as enemies than as shipmasters whose naval support could be procured as needed in return for trading privileges.

Elephants Breaking Bridge of Boats   This illustration of an incident in the life of Akbar illustrates the ability of Mughal miniature painters to depict unconventional action scenes. Because the flow of rivers in India and the Middle East varied greatly from dry season to wet season, boat bridges were much more common than permanent constructions.   (Victoria and Albert Museum, London/Bridgeman Art Library)

Hindus and Muslims

The Mughal state inherited traditions of unified imperial rule from both the Islamic caliphate and the more recent examples of Genghis Khan and Timur. Those traditions did not necessarily mean religious intolerance. Seventy percent of the *mansabdars*° (officials holding land revenues) appointed under Akbar were Muslim soldiers born outside India, but 15 percent were Hindus. Most of the Hindu appointees were warriors from the north called **Rajputs**°, one of whom rose to be a powerful revenue minister.

Babur (BAH-bur)   **Delhi** (DEL-ee)   *mansabs* (MAN-sabz)   *mansabdars* (man-sab-DAHRZ)   **Rajputs** (RAHJ-putz)

Akbar, the most illustrious ruler of his dynasty, differed from his Ottoman and Safavid counterparts—Suleiman the Magnificent and Shah Abbas the Great—in his striving for social harmony and not just for more territory and revenue. His marriage to a Rajput princess signaled his desire for reconciliation and even intermarriage between Muslims and Hindus. The birth of a son in 1569 ensured that future rulers would have both Muslim and Hindu ancestry.

Akbar ruled that in legal disputes between two Hindus, decisions would be made according to village custom or Hindu law as interpreted by local Hindu scholars. Shari'a law was in force for Muslims. Akbar made himself the legal court of last resort, creating an appeals process not usually present in Islamic jurisprudence.

Akbar also made himself the center of a new "Divine Faith" incorporating Muslim, Hindu, Zoroastrian, Sikh°, and Christian beliefs. He was strongly attracted by Sufi ideas, which permeated the religious rituals he instituted at his court. To promote serious consideration of his religious principles, he oversaw, from a catwalk high above the audience, debates among scholars of all religions assembled in his octagonal private audience chamber. When courtiers uttered the Muslim exclamation "Allahu Akbar"—"God is great"—they also understood it in its second grammatical meaning: "God is Akbar."

Akbar's religious views did not survive him, but the court culture he fostered, reflecting a mixture of Muslim and Hindu traditions, flourished until his zealous great-grandson Aurangzeb° (r. 1658–1707) reinstituted many restrictions on Hindus. Mughal and Rajput miniature paintings reveled in precise portraits of political figures and depictions of scantily clad women, even though they brought frowns to the faces of pious Muslims, who deplored the representation of human beings. Most of the leading painters were Hindus. In addition to the florid style of Persian verse favored at court, a new taste developed for poetry and prose in the popular language of the Delhi region. The modern descendant of this language is called *Urdu* in Pakistan and *Hindi* in India.

Central Decay and Regional Challenges

Mughal power did not long survive Aurangzeb's death in 1707. Some historians consider the land-grant system a central element in the rapid decline of imperial authority, but other factors were at play as well. Aurangzeb's additions to Mughal territory in southern India were not all well integrated into the imperial structure, and strong regional powers arose to challenge Mughal military supremacy. A climax came in 1739 when Nadir Shah, a warlord who had seized power in Iran after the fall of the Safavids, invaded the Mughal capital and carried off to Iran the "peacock throne," the priceless jewel-encrusted symbol of Mughal grandeur. Another throne was found for the later Mughals to sit on; but their empire, which survived in name to 1857, was finished.

In 1723, Nizam al-Mulk°, the powerful vizier of the Mughal sultan, gave up on the central government and established his own nearly independent state at Hyderabad in the eastern Deccan. Other officials bearing the title *nawab*° became similarly independent in Bengal and Oudh° in the northeast, as did the Marathas in the center. In the northwest, simultaneous Iranian and Mughal weakness allowed the Afghans to establish an independent kingdom.

Some of these regional powers, and the smaller princely states that arose on former Mughal territory, were prosperous and benefited from the removal of the sultan's heavy hand. Linguistic and religious communities, freed from the religious intolerance instituted during the reign of Aurangzeb, similarly enjoyed greater opportunity for political expression. However, this disintegration of central power favored the intrusion of European adventurers.

Joseph François Dupleix° took over the presidency of the French stronghold of Pondicherry° in 1741 and began a new phase of European involvement in India. He captured the English trading center of Madras and used his small contingent of European and European-trained Indian troops to

---

Sikh (sick)   Aurangzeb (ow-rang-ZEB)

Nizam al-Mulk (nee-ZAHM al-MULK)   *nawab* (NAH-wab)
Oudh (OW-ad)   Dupleix (doo-PLAY)   Pondicherry (pon-dih-CHER-ree)

become a power broker in southern India. Though offered the title *nawab,* Dupleix preferred to operate behind the scenes, using Indian princes as puppets. His career ended in 1754 when he was called home. Deeply involved in wars in Europe, the French government was unwilling to pursue further adventures in India. Dupleix's departure opened the way for the British, whose ventures in India are described in Chapter 21.

TRADE EMPIRES IN THE INDIAN OCEAN

Although the Ottomans, Safavids, and Mughals did not seriously contest the growth of Portuguese and then Dutch, English, and French maritime power, the majority of non-European shipbuilders, captains, sailors, and traders were Muslim. Groups of Armenian, Jewish, and Hindu traders were also active, but they remained almost as aloof from the Europeans as the Muslims did. The presence in every port of Muslims following the same legal traditions and practicing their faith in similar ways cemented the Muslims' trading network. Islam, from its very outset in the life and preachings of Muhammad (570–632), was always congenial to trade and traders. Unlike Hinduism, it was a proselytizing religion, a factor that encouraged the growth of coastal Muslim communities as local non-Muslims were drawn into Muslim commercial activities, were converted, and intermarried with Muslims from abroad.

Although European missionaries, particularly the Jesuits, tried to extend Christianity into Asia and Africa (see Chapters 14 and 18), most Europeans, the Portuguese excepted, were less inclined than the Muslims were to treat local converts or the offspring of mixed marriages as full members of their communities. As a consequence, Islam spread extensively into East Africa and Southeast Asia during precisely the time of rapid European commercial expansion. Even without the support of the Muslim land empires, Islam became a source of resistance to growing European domination.

Muslims in the East Indies

Historians disagree about the chronology and manner of Islam's spread in Southeast Asia. Arab traders were well known in southern China as early as the eighth century, so Muslims probably reached the East Indies at a similarly early date. Nevertheless, the dominance of Indian cultural influences in the area for several centuries thereafter indicates that early Muslim visitors had little impact on local beliefs. Clearer indications of conversion and the formation of Muslim communities date from roughly the fourteenth century. The strongest overseas linkage is to the port of Cambay in India (see Map 17.2) rather than to the Arab world. Islam took root first in port cities and in some royal courts and spread inland slowly, possibly transmitted by itinerant Sufis.

Although appeals to the Ottoman sultan for support against the Europeans ultimately proved of little use, Islam as a political ideology strengthened resistance to Portuguese, Spanish, and Dutch intruders. When the Spaniards conquered the Philippines during the decades following the establishment of their first fort in 1565, they encountered Muslims on the southern island of Mindanao° and the nearby Sulu archipelago. They called them "Moros," the Spanish term for their old enemies, the Muslims of North Africa. In the ensuing Moro wars, the Spaniards portrayed the Moros as greedy pirates who raided non-Muslim territories for slaves. In fact, they were political, religious, and commercial competitors whose perseverance enabled them to establish the Sulu Empire based in the southern Philippines, one of the strongest states in Southeast Asia from 1768 to 1848.

Other local kingdoms that looked on Islam as a force to counter the aggressive Christianity of the Europeans included the actively proselytizing Brunei° Sultanate in northern Borneo and the **Acheh° Sultanate** in northern Sumatra. At its peak in the early seventeenth century, Acheh succeeded Malacca as the main center of Islamic expansion in Southeast Asia. It prospered from trade in pepper and cotton cloth from Gujarat in India. Acheh declined after the Dutch seized Malacca from Portugal in 1641.

Mindanao (min-duh-NOW)   **Brunei** (BROO-nie)   **Acheh** (AH-cheh)

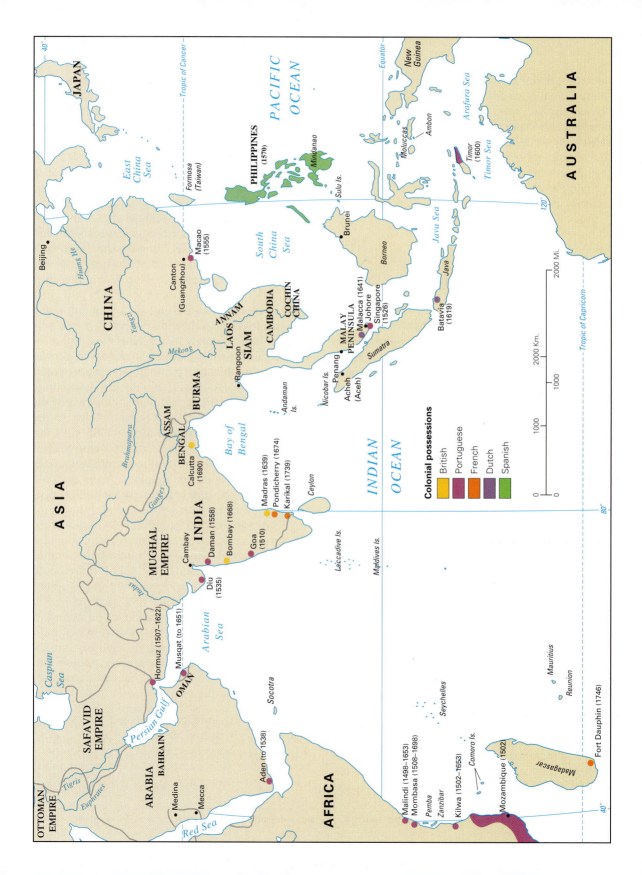

Map 17.2 European Colonization in the Indian Ocean to 1750 Since Portuguese explorers were the first Europeans to reach India by rounding Africa, Portugal gained a strong foothold in both areas. Rival Spain was barred from colonizing the region by the Treaty of Tordesillas in 1494, which limited Spanish efforts to lands west of a line drawn through the mid-Atlantic Ocean. The line carried around the globe provided justification of Spanish colonization in the Philippines. French, British, and Dutch colonies date from after 1600, when joint-stock companies provided a new stimulus for overseas commerce.

How well Islam was understood in these Muslim kingdoms is open to question. In Acheh, for example, a series of women ruled between 1641 and 1699. This practice came to an end when local Muslim scholars obtained a ruling from scholars in Mecca and Medina that Islam did not approve of female rulers. This ruling became a turning point after which scholarly understandings of Islam gained greater prominence in the East Indies.

Historians have theorized that the first propagators of Islam in Southeast Asia were merchants, Sufi preachers, or both. The scholarly vision of Islam, however, took root in the sixteenth century by way of pilgrims returning from years of study in Mecca and Medina. Islam was the primary force in the dissemination of writing in the region. Some of the returning pilgrims wrote in Arabic, others in Malay or Javanese. As Islam continued to spread, *adat*, a form of Islam rooted in pre-Muslim religious and social practices, retained its preeminence in rural areas over practices centered on the Shari'a, the religious law. But the royal courts in the port cities began to heed the views of the pilgrim teachers, as in their condemnation of female rulers. Though different in many ways, both varieties of Islam provided believers with a firm basis of identification in the face of the growing European presence. Christian missionaries gained most of their converts in regions that had not yet converted to Islam, such as the northern Philippines.

Muslims in East Africa

The East African ports that the Portuguese began to visit in the fifteenth century were governed by Muslim rulers but were not linked politically (see Map 17.2). People living in

the millet and rice lands of the Swahili Coast—from the Arabic *sawahil°* meaning "coasts"—had little contact with those in the dry hinterlands. Throughout this period, the East African lakes region and the highlands of Kenya witnessed unprecedented migration and relocation of peoples because of drought conditions that persisted from the late sixteenth through most of the seventeenth century.

Cooperation among the trading ports of Kilwa, Mombasa, and Malindi was hindered by the thick bush country that separated the cultivated tracts of coastal land and by the fact that the ports competed with one another in the export of ivory; ambergris° (a whale byproduct used in perfumes); and forest products such as beeswax, copal tree resin, and wood (Kilwa also exported gold). In the eighteenth century, slave trading, primarily to Arabian ports but also to India, increased in importance. Because Europeans—the only peoples who kept consistent records of slave-trading activities—played a minor role in this slave trade, few records have survived to indicate its extent. Perhaps the best estimate is that 2.1 million slaves were exported between 1500 and 1890, a little over 12.5 percent of the total traffic in African slaves during that period (see Chapter 16).

The Portuguese conquered all of the coastal ports from Mozambique northward except Malindi, with whose ruler Portugal cooperated. A Portuguese description of the ruler indicates some of the cloth and metal goods that Malindi imported, as well as some local manufactures:

> The King wore a robe of damask trimmed with green satin and a rich [cap]. He was seated on two cushioned chairs of bronze, beneath a rough sunshade of crimson satin attached to a pole. An old man, who attended him as a page, carried a short sword in a silver sheath. There were many players on [horns], and two trumpets of ivory richly carved and of the size of a man, which were blown through a hole in the side, and made sweet harmony with the [horns].[1]

Initially, the Portuguese favored the port of Malindi, which caused the decline of Kilwa and Mombasa. Repeatedly plagued by local rebellion, Portuguese power suffered severe blows when the Arabs of **Oman** in southeastern Arabia captured

sawahil (suh-WAH-hil) **ambergris** (AM-ber-grees)

their south Arabian stronghold at Musqat (1650) and then went on in support of African resistance to seize Mombasa (1698), which had become the Portuguese capital in East Africa. The Portuguese briefly retook Mombasa but lost control permanently in 1729. From then on, the Portuguese had to content themselves with Mozambique in Africa and a few remaining ports in India (Goa) and farther east (Macao and Timor).

The Omanis created a maritime empire of their own, but one that worked in greater cooperation with the African populations. The Bantu language of the coast, broadened by the absorption of Arabic, Persian, and Portuguese loan words, developed into **Swahili°,** which was spoken throughout the region. Arabs and other Muslims who settled in the region intermarried with local families, giving rise to a mixed population that played an important role in developing a distinctive Swahili culture.

Islam also spread in the southern Sudan in this period, particularly in the dry areas away from the Nile River. This growth coincided with a waning of Ethiopian power as a result of Portugal's stifling of trade in the Red Sea. Yet no significant contact developed between the emerging Muslim Swahili culture and that of the Muslims in the Sudan, to the north.

The Coming of the Dutch

The Dutch played a major role in driving the Portuguese from their possessions in the East Indies. They were better organized than the Portuguese through the Dutch East India Company (see Chapter 16). Just as the Portuguese had tried to dominate the trade in spices, so the Dutch concentrated at first on the spice-producing islands of Southeast Asia. The Portuguese had seized Malacca, a strategic town on the narrow strait at the end of the Malay Peninsula, from a local Malay ruler in 1511. The Dutch took it away from them in 1641, leaving Portugal little foothold in the East Indies except the islands of Ambon° and Timor (see Map 17.2).

Although the United Netherlands was one of the least autocratic countries of Europe, the governors-general appointed by the Dutch East India Company deployed almost unlimited powers in their efforts to maintain their trade monopoly. They could even order the execution of their own employees for "smuggling"—that is, trading on their own. Under strong governors-general, the Dutch fought a series of wars against Acheh and other local kingdoms on Sumatra and Java. In 1628 and 1629, their new capital at **Batavia,** now the city of Jakarta on Java, was besieged by a fleet of fifty ships belonging to the sultan of Mataram°, a Javanese kingdom. The Dutch held out with difficulty and eventually prevailed when the sultan was unable to get effective help from the English.

Suppressing local rulers, however, was not enough to control the spice trade once other European countries adopted Dutch methods, became more knowledgeable about where goods might be acquired, and started to send more ships to Southeast Asia. In the course of the eighteenth century, therefore, the Dutch gradually turned from being a middleman for Southeast Asian producers and European buyers to being a producer of crops in areas they controlled, notably in Java. Javanese teak forests yielded high-quality lumber, and coffee, transplanted from Yemen, grew well in the hilly regions of western Java. In this new phase of colonial export production, Batavia developed from being the headquarters town of a far-flung enterprise to being the administrative capital of a conquered land.

Beyond the East Indies, the Dutch utilized their discovery of a band of powerful eastward-blowing winds (called the "Roaring Forties" because they blow throughout the year between 40 and 50 degrees south latitude) to reach Australia in 1606. In 1642 and 1643, Abel Tasman became the first European to set foot on Tasmania and New Zealand and to sail around Australia, signaling European involvement in that region.

CONCLUSION

It is no coincidence that the Mughal, Safavid, and Ottoman Empires declined simultaneously in the seventeenth and eighteenth centuries. The complex changes in military technology and in the world economy that were under way in smaller Eu-

---

Swahili (swah-HEE-lee) **Ambon** (am-BOHN)

Mataram (MAH-ah-ram)

ropean countries either passed them by or affected them adversely. Despite their efforts on conquering more and more land, these land-based empires faced increasing difficulty in maintaining traditional military forces paid through land grants.

The opposite was true for seafaring countries intent on turning trade networks into maritime empires. Improvements in ship design, navigation accuracy, and the use of cannon gave an ever-increasing edge to European powers competing with local seafaring peoples. In contrast to the age-old Asian tradition that imperial wealth came from control of broad expanses of agricultural land, European countries promoted joint-stock companies and luxuriated in the prosperity gained from their ever-increasing control of Indian Ocean commerce.

That a major shift in world economic and political alignments was well under way by the late seventeenth century was scarcely perceivable in those parts of Asia and Africa ruled by the Ottoman and Mughal sultans and the Safavid shahs. They relied mostly on land taxes, usually indirectly collected via holders of land grants or tax farmers, rather than on customs duties or control of markets to fill the government coffers. With ever-increasing military expenditures, these taxes fell short of the rulers' needs. Oblivious to the fundamental problem of the entire economic system, imperial courtiers pursued their luxurious ways, poetry and the arts continued to flourish, and the quality of manufacturing and craft production remained generally high. Eighteenth-century European observers marveled no less at the riches and industry of these eastern lands than at the fundamental weakness of their political and military systems.

■ Key Terms

Ottoman Empire	Akbar
Suleiman the Magnificent	*mansabs*
Janissaries	Rajputs
Safavid Empire	Acheh Sultanate
Shi'ite	Oman
Hidden Imam	Swahili
Shah Abbas I	Batavia
Mughal Empire	

■ Suggested Reading

The best comprehensive and comparative account of the post-Mongol Islamic land empires, with an emphasis on social history, is Ira Lapidus, *A History of Islamic Societies* (1988). For a brief, general introduction to the relations between the Muslim land empires and the development of Indian Ocean trade, see Patricia Risso, *Merchants and Faith: Muslim Commerce and Culture in the Indian Ocean* (1995).

On the Ottoman Empire in its prime, see Colin Imber, *The Ottoman Empire, 1300–1650* (2002). Daniel Goffman, *The Ottoman Empire and the Early Modern Europe* (2002), compares the Ottomans with contemporary European kingdoms. Jason Goodwin, *Lords of the Horizons: A History of the Ottoman Empire* (1999), offers a more readable and journalistic account.

The most comprehensive treatment of the history of Safavid Iran is in the articles in Peter Jackson and Laurence Lockhart, eds., *The Cambridge History of Iran*, vol. 6, *The Timurid and Safavid Periods* (1986). For the artistic side of Safavid history, abundantly illustrated, see Anthony Welch, *Shah Abbas and the Arts of Isfahan* (1973).

A highly readable work that situates the Mughal Empire within the overall history of the subcontinent is Stanley Wolpert, *A New History of India*, 6th ed. (1999). For a broad treatment of the entire development of Islamic society in India with emphasis on the Mughal period, see S. M. Ikram, *History of Muslim Civilization in India and Pakistan* (1989). Wheeler Thackston has made a lively translation of Babur's autobiography in *The Baburnama: Memoirs of Babur, Prince and Emperor* (1996). For a comprehensive history of the Mughals, see John F. Richards, *The Mughal Empire* (1993).

For a brief introduction to the relations between the Muslim land empires and the development of Indian Ocean trade, see Patricis Risso, *Merchants and Faith: Muslim Commerce in the Indian Ocean* (1995).

■ Notes

1. Esmond Bradley Martin and Chryssee Perry Martin, *Cargoes of the East: The Ports, Trade and Culture of the Arabian Seas and Western Indian Ocean* (London: Elm Tree Books, 1978), 17.

18

Northern Eurasia, 1500–1800

CHAPTER OUTLINE

Japanese Reunification

The Later Ming and Early Qing Empires

The Russian Empire

Comparative Perspectives

ENVIRONMENT AND TECHNOLOGY: East Asian Porcelain

Li Zicheng° was an apprentice ironworker in a barren northern Chinese province. His dreams for the future were dashed when, in a desperate effort to save money, the Hanli emperor ordered the elimination of Li's job and those of many other government employees. The savings went to fund more troops to defend the capital city of Beijing° against attacks by **Manchu** armies from Manchuria in the northeast. By 1630 Li Zicheng had found work as a soldier, but he and his fellow soldiers mutinied when the government failed to provide them with needed supplies. A natural leader, Li soon headed a group of several thousand Chinese rebels. In 1635 he and other rebel leaders were strong enough to control much of north central China.

Wedged between the armies of the Manchu pressing from the north and the rebels to the southwest, the Ming government grew ever weaker. Taking advantage of the weakness, Li Zicheng's forces began to move toward Beijing. Along the way they captured towns and conscripted young men into their army. The rebels also won popular support with promises to end the abuses of the Ming and restore peace and prosperity. In April 1644 Li's armies were able to take over Beijing without a fight. The last Ming emperor hanged himself in the palace garden, bringing to an end the dynasty that had ruled China since 1368.

The rebels' success was short-lived. Believing there was more to fear from uneducated, violent men like Li, the Ming general Wu Sangui joined forces with the Manchu. Wu may have been influenced by the fact that Li had captured

Li Zicheng (lee ZUH-cheng)   **Beijing** (bay-JING))

one of the general's favorite concubines and taken her for himself. Together Wu and the Manchu retook Beijing in June. Li's forces scattered, and a year later he was dead, either a suicide or beaten to death by peasants whose food he tried to steal.[1]

Meanwhile, the Manchu were making it clear that they intended to be the new masters of China. They installed their young sovereign as the new emperor and over the next two decades hunted down the last of the Ming loyalists and heirs to the throne.

China was not the only state in northern Eurasia facing uprisings from within and foreign threats. In the period from 1500 to 1800 Japan and Russia experienced turbulence as they underwent massive political change and economic growth. Besides challenges from nearby neighbors, the three also faced new contacts and challenges from the commercially and militarily powerful European states.

As you read this chapter, ask yourself the following questions:

- How did Japan, China, and Russia respond to internal social, economic, and political pressures?

- How did China and Russia deal with military challenges from their immediate neighbors?

- How did Japan, China, and Russia differ in the ways they reacted to western European commercial and cultural contacts?

JAPANESE REUNIFICATION

Like China and Russia in the centuries between 1500 and 1800, Japan experienced three major changes: internal and external military conflicts, political growth and strengthening, and expanded commercial and cultural contacts. Along with its culturally homogenous population and natural boundaries, Japan's smaller size made the process of political unification shorter than in the great empires of China and Russia. Japan also differed in its responses to new contacts with western Europeans.

Civil War and the Invasion of Korea, 1500–1603

In the twelfth century different parts of Japan had fallen under the rule of warlords known as *daimyo*° (see Chapter 11). Each daimyo had a castle town, a small bureaucracy, and a band of warriors, the *samurai*°. Daimyo pledged a loose allegiance to the Japanese emperor residing in the capital city of Kyoto° and to the shogun, the hereditary chief of the emperor's government and armies. But neither figure held significant political power.

Warfare among the different daimyo was common, and in the late 1500s it culminated in a prolonged civil war. The warlord to emerge from the war was Hideyoshi°. In 1592, buoyed with his success in Japan, the supremely confident Hideyoshi invaded the Asian mainland with 160,000 men. His apparent intention was not just to conquer the Korean peninsula but also to make himself emperor of China.

The Korean and Japanese languages are closely related, but the dominant influence on Korean culture had long been China, to which Korean rulers generally paid tribute. In many ways the Yi dynasty that ruled Korea from 1392 to 1910 was a model Confucian state. Although Korea had developed its own system of writing in 1443 and made extensive use of printing with movable type from the fifteenth century on, most printing continued to use Chinese characters.

Against Hideyoshi's invaders the Koreans employed all the technological and military skill for which the Yi period was renowned. Ingenious covered warships, or "turtle boats," intercepted a portion of the Japanese fleet. The mentally unstable Hideyoshi countered with brutal punitive measures as his armies advanced through the Korean peninsula and into the Chinese province of Manchuria. However, after Hideyoshi's death in 1598, the other Japanese military leaders withdrew their

---

daimyo (DIE-mee-oh)   *samurai* (SAH-moo-rye)   **Kyoto** (KYOH-toh)   **Hideyoshi** (HEE-duh-YOH-shee)

forces, and the Japanese government made peace in 1606.

The invasion devastated Korea. In the turmoil after the Japanese withdrawal, the Korean *yangban* (nobility) were able to lay claim to so much tax-paying land that royal revenues may have fallen by two-thirds. China, however, suffered even more dire consequences. The battles in Manchuria weakened Chinese garrisons there, permitting Manchu opposition to consolidate. Manchu forces invaded Korea in the 1620s and eventually compelled the Yi to become a tributary state. As already related, the Manchus would be in possession of Beijing, China's capital, by 1644.

The Tokugawa Shogunate, to 1800

After Hideyoshi's demise, Tokugawa Ieyasu° (1543–1616) asserted his domination over other daimyo and in 1603 established a new military government known as the **Tokugawa Shogunate.** The shoguns created a new administrative capital at Edo° (now Tokyo). Trade along the well-maintained road between Edo and the imperial capital of Kyoto promoted the development of the Japanese economy and the formation of other trading centers (see Map 18.1).

Although the Tokugawa Shogunate gave Japan more political unity than the islands had seen in centuries, the regionally based daimyo still had a great deal of power and autonomy. Ieyasu and his successors worked hard to keep the political system from disintegrating; nevertheless, economic integration was more a feature of Tokugawa Japan than political centralization. Because shoguns required the daimyo to visit Edo frequently, good roads and maritime transport linked the city to the castle towns on three of Japan's four main islands. Commercial traffic developed along these routes. The shogun paid the lords in rice, and the lords paid their followers in rice. Recipients converted much of this rice into cash, a practice that led to the development of rice exchanges at Edo and at Osaka°, where merchants speculated in rice prices. By the late seventeenth century Edo was one of the largest cities in the world, with nearly a million inhabitants.

The domestic peace of the Tokugawa era forced the warrior class to adapt itself to the growing bureaucratic needs of the state. As the samurai became better educated and more attuned to the tastes of the civil elite, they became important customers for merchants dealing in silks, *sake*° (rice wine), fans, porcelain, lacquer ware, books, and money-lending. The state attempted—unsuccessfully—to curb the independence of the merchants when the economic well-being of the samurai was threatened by low rice prices or high interest rates.

The 1600s and 1700s were centuries of high achievement in artisanship, and Japanese skills in steel making, pottery, and lacquer ware were joined by excellence in the production and decoration of porcelain (see Environment and Technology: East Asian Porcelain), thanks in no small part to Korean experts brought back to Japan after the invasion of 1592. In the early 1600s manufacturers and merchants amassed enormous family fortunes. Several of the most important industrial and financial enterprises—for instance, the Mitsui° companies—had their origins in sake breweries of the early Tokugawa period and then branched out into manufacturing, finance, and transport.

Wealthy merchants weakened the Tokugawa policy of controlling commerce by cultivating close alliances with their regional daimyo and, if possible, with the shogun himself. By the end of the 1700s the merchant families of Tokugawa Japan held the key to future modernization and the development of heavy industry.

Japan and the Europeans

Direct contacts with Europeans presented Japan with new opportunities and problems. Within thirty years of the arrival of the first Portuguese in 1543, the daimyo were fighting with Western-style firearms, copied and improved upon by Japanese armorers.

The Japanese welcomed but closely regulated traders from Portugal, Spain, the Netherlands, and England. Aside from the brief boom in porcelain exports in the seventeenth century, few Japanese

---

Tokugawa Ieyasu (TOH-koo-GAH-wah ee-ay-YAH-soo)
Edo (ED-oh) **Osaka** (OH-sah-kah)

sake (SAH-kay) **Mitsui** (MIT-soo-ee)

CHRONOLOGY

	Korea and Japan	China and Central Asia	Russia
1500	**1543** First Portuguese contacts	**1517** Portuguese embassy to China	**1547** Ivan IV adopts title of tsar
	1592 Japanese invasion of Korea		**1582** Russians conquer Khanate of Sibir
1600		**1601** Matteo Ricci allowed to reside in Beijing	
	1603 Tokugawa Shogunate formed		**1613–1645** Rule of Mikhail, the first Romanov tsar
	1633–1639 Edicts close down trade with Europe	**1644** Qing conquest of Beijing	**1649** Subordination of serfs complete
		1662–1722 Rule of Emperor Kangxi	
		1689 Treaty of Nerchinsk with Russia	**1689–1725** Rule of Peter the Great
		1691 Qing control of Inner Mongolia	
1700	**1702** Trial of the Forty-Seven Ronin		**1712** St. Petersburg becomes Russia's capital
		1736–1796 Rule of Emperor Qianlong	**1762–1796** Rule of Catherine the Great
	1792 Russian ships first spotted off the coast of Japan		**1799** Alaska becomes a Russian colony

East Asian Porcelain

By the 1400s artisans in China, Korea, and Japan were all producing high-quality pottery with lustrous surface glazes. The best quality, intended for the homes of the wealthy and powerful, was made of pure white clay and covered with a hard translucent glaze. Artisans often added intricate decorations in cobalt blue and other colors. Cheaper pottery found a huge market in East Asia.

Such pottery was also exported to Southeast Asia, the Indian Ocean, and the Middle East. Little found its way to Europe before 1600, but imports soared once the Dutch established trading bases in East Asia. Europeans called the high-quality ware "porcelain." Blue and white designs were especially popular.

One of the great centers of Chinese production was at the large artisan factory at Jingdezhen (JING-deh-JUHN). No sooner had the Dutch tapped into this source than the civil wars and Manchu conquests disrupted production in the middle 1600s. Desperate for a substitute source, the Dutch turned to porcelain from Japanese producers at Arita and Imari, near Nagasaki. Despite Japan's restriction of European trade, the Dutch East India Company transported some 190,000 pieces of Japanese ceramic ware to the Netherlands between 1653 and 1682.

In addition to a wide range of Asian designs, Chinese and Japanese artisans made all sorts of porcelain for the European market. These included purely decorative pottery birds, vases, and pots as well as utilitarian vessels and dishes intended for table use. The serving dish illustrated here came from dinnerware sets the Japanese made especially for the Dutch East India Company. The VOC logo at the center represents the first letters of the company's name in Dutch. It is surrounded by Asian design motifs.

After the return of peace in China, the VOC imported tens of thousands of Chinese porcelain pieces a year. The Chinese artisans sometimes produced imitations of Japanese designs that had become popular in Europe. Meanwhile, the Dutch were experimenting with making their own imitations of East Asian porcelain, right down to the Asian motifs and colors that had become so fashionable in Europe.

Japanese Export Porcelain   Part of a larger set made for the Dutch East India Company.   (Photograph courtesy Peabody Essex Museum, #83830)

goods went to Europe, and not much from Europe found a market in Japan. The Japanese sold the Dutch copper and silver, which the Dutch exchanged in China for silks that they then resold in Japan. The Japanese, of course, had their own trade with China.

Portuguese and Spanish merchant ships also brought Catholic missionaries. One of the first, Francis Xavier, went to India in the mid-sixteenth century looking for converts and later traveled throughout Southeast and East Asia. He spent two years in Japan and died in 1552, hoping to gain entry to China.

Japanese responses to Xavier and other Jesuits (members of the Catholic religious order the Society of Jesus) were decidedly mixed. Many ordinary Japanese found the new faith deeply meaningful, but the Japanese elite more often opposed it as disruptive and foreign. By 1580 more than 100,000 Japanese had become Christians, and one daimyo gave Jesuit missionaries the port city of Nagasaki°. In 1613 Date Masamune°, the fierce and independent daimyo of northern Honshu°, sent his own embassy to the Vatican, by way of the Philippines (where there were significant communities of Japanese merchants and pirates) and Mexico City. Some daimyo converts ordered their subjects to become Christians as well.

By the early seventeenth century there were some 300,000 Japanese Christians and even some Japanese priests. However, suspicions about the intentions of the Europeans and their well-armed ships turned the new shogunate in Edo into a center of hostility toward Christianity. A decree issued in 1614 banned Christianity and charged its adherents with seeking to overthrow true doctrine, change the government, and seize the country. Some missionaries left Japan; others worked underground. The government began persecutions in earnest in 1617, and the beheadings, crucifixions, and forced recantations over the next several decades destroyed almost the entire Christian community.

To keep Christianity from resurfacing, a series of decrees issued between 1633 and 1639 sharply curtailed trade with Europe. Europeans who entered illegally faced the death penalty. Japanese subjects were required to produce certificates from Buddhist temples attesting to their religious orthodoxy and loyalty to the regime.

The exclusion of Europe was not total. A few Dutch were permitted to reside on a small artificial island in Nagasaki's harbor, and a few Japanese were licensed to supply their needs. What these intermediaries learned about European weapons technology, shipbuilding, mathematics and astronomy, anatomy and medicine, and geography was termed "Dutch studies."

Tokugawa restrictions on the number of Chinese ships that could trade in Japan were harder to enforce. Regional lords in northern and southern Japan not only pursued overseas trade and piracy but also claimed dominion over islands between Japan and Korea and southward toward Taiwan, including present-day Okinawa. Despite such evasions, the new shogunate unquestionably achieved substantial success in exercising its authority.

Elite Decline and Social Crisis

During the 1700s population growth put a great strain on the well-developed lands of central Japan. In more remote provinces, where the lords promoted new settlements and agricultural expansion, the rate of economic growth was significantly greater.

Also troubling the Tokugawa government in the 1700s was the shogunate's inability to stabilize rice prices and halt the economic decline of the samurai. The Tokugawa government realized that the rice brokers could manipulate rice prices and interest rates to enrich themselves at the expense of the samurai, who had to convert their rice allotments into cash. Early Tokugawa laws designed to regulate interest and prices were later supplemented by laws requiring moneylenders to forgive samurai debts. But these laws were not always enforced. By the early 1700s many lords and samurai were dependent on the willingness of merchants to provide credit.

The legitimacy of the Tokugawa shoguns rested on their ability to reward and protect the interests of the lords and samurai who had supported their rise to power. Moreover, the Tokugawa government, like the governments of China, Korea, and Vietnam, accepted the Confucian idea that agriculture should be the basis of state wealth and that merchants, who were considered morally weak, should occupy lowly positions in society. Tokugawa decentralization, however, not only failed to hinder but actually stimulated the growth of commercial activities. From the founding of the Tokugawa Shogunate in 1603 until 1800, the economy grew faster than the population. Household amenities and cultural resources that in China appeared only in the cities were common in the Japanese countryside. Despite official disapproval, merchants enjoyed relative freedom and influence in eighteenth-century Japan. They produced a vivid

---

Nagasaki (NAH-guh-SAHK-kee)   **Date Masamune** (DAH-tay mah-suh-MOO-nay)   **Honshu** (HOHN-shoo)

Woodblock Print of the "Forty-Seven Ronin" Story
The saga of the forty-seven ronin and the avenging of their fallen leader has fascinated the Japanese public since the event occurred in 1702. This watercolor from the Tokugawa period shows the leaders of the group pausing on the snowy banks of the Sumida River in Edo (Tokyo) before storming their enemy's residence.   (Private Collection)

culture of their own, fostering the development of *kabuki* theater, colorful woodblock prints and silk-screened fabrics, and restaurants.

The "Forty-Seven Ronin°" incident of 1701–1703 exemplified the ideological and social crisis of Japan's transformation from a military to a civil society. A senior minister provoked a young daimyo into drawing his sword at the shogun's court. For this offense the young lord was sentenced to commit *seppuku°*, the ritual suicide of the samurai. His own followers then became *ronin,* "masterless samurai," obliged by the traditional code of the warrior to avenge their deceased master. They broke into the house of the senior minister and

killed him and others in his household. Then they withdrew to a temple in Edo and notified the shogun of what they had done out of loyalty to their lord and to avenge his death.

A legal debate ensued. To deny the righteousness of the ronin would be to deny samurai values. But to approve their actions would create social chaos, undermine laws against murder, and deny the shogunal government the right to try cases of samurai violence. The shogun ruled that the ronin had to die but would be permitted to die honorably by committing seppuku. Traditional samurai values had to surrender to the supremacy of law. The purity of purpose of the ronin is still celebrated in Japan, but since then Japanese writers, historians, and teachers have recognized that the self-sacrifice of the ronin for the sake of upholding civil law was necessary.

THE LATER MING AND EARLY QING EMPIRES

Like Japan, China after 1500 experienced civil and foreign wars, an important change in government, and new trading and cultural relations with Europe and its neighbors. The internal and external forces at work in China were different and operated on a much larger scale, but they led in similar directions. By 1800 China had a greatly enhanced empire, an expanding economy, and growing doubts about the importance of European trade and Christianity.

The Ming Empire, 1500–1644

The economic and cultural achievements of the early **Ming Empire** (see Chapter 11) continued during the 1500s. But this productive period was followed by many decades of political weakness, warfare, and rural woes until a new dynasty, the Qing° from Manchuria, guided China back to peace and prosperity.

The Europeans whose ships began to seek out new contacts with China in the early sixteenth cen-

---

ronin (ROH-neen)   *seppuku* (SEP-poo-koo)

Qing (ching)

tury left many accounts of their impressions. They were astonished at Ming China's imperial power, exquisite manufactures, and vast population. European merchants bought such large quantities of the high-grade blue-on-white porcelain commonly used by China's upper classes that in English all fine dishes became known simply as "china."

The growing integration of China into the world economy stimulated rapid growth in the silk, cotton, and porcelain industries. Agricultural regions that supplied raw materials to these industries and food for the expanding urban populations also prospered. In exchange for Chinese exports, tens of thousands of tons of silver from Japan and Latin America flooded into China in the century before 1640. The influx of silver led many Chinese to substitute payments in silver for land taxes, labor obligations, and other kinds of dues.

Ming cities had long been culturally and commercially vibrant. Many large landowners and absentee landlords lived in town, as did officials, artists, and rich merchants who had purchased ranks or prepared their sons for the examinations. The elite classes had created a brilliant culture in which novels, operas, poetry, porcelain, and painting were all closely interwoven. Small businesses catering to the urban elites prospered through printing, tailoring, running restaurants, or selling paper, ink, ink-stones, and writing brushes. The imperial government operated factories for the production of ceramics and silks. Enormous government complexes at Jingdezhen and elsewhere invented assembly-line techniques and produced large quantities of high-quality ceramics for sale in China and abroad.

Despite these achievements, serious problems developed that left the Ming Empire economically and politically exhausted. There is evidence that the climate changes known as the Little Ice Age in seventeenth-century Europe affected the climate in China as well (see Issues in World History: The Little Ice Age). Annual temperatures dropped, reached a low point about 1645, and remained low until the early 1700s. The resulting agricultural distress and famine fueled large uprisings that speeded the end of the Ming Empire. The devastation caused by these uprisings and the spread of epidemic disease resulted in steep declines in local populations.

The rapid urban growth and business speculation that were part of the burgeoning of the trading economy also produced problems. Some provinces suffered from price inflation caused by the flood of silver. In contrast to the growing involvement of European governments in promoting economic growth, the Ming government pursued some policies that hindered growth. Despite the fact that experiments with paper currency had failed as far back as the 1350s, Ming governments persisted in issuing new paper money and copper coinage, even after abundant supplies of silver had won the approval of the markets. Corruption was also a serious government problem. By the end of the Ming period the imperial factories were plagued by disorder and inefficiency. The situation became so bad during the late sixteenth and seventeenth centuries that workers held strikes with increasing frequency. During a labor protest at Jingdezhen in 1601, workers threw themselves into the kilns to protest working conditions.

Yet the urban and industrial sectors of later Ming society fared much better than the agricultural sector, which failed to maintain the strong growth of early Ming times. Despite knowledge of new African and American crops gained from European traders, farmers were slow to change their ways. Neither the rice-growing regions in southern China nor the wheat-growing regions in northern China experienced a meaningful increase in productivity under the later Ming. After 1500 economic depression in the countryside, combined with recurring epidemics in central and southern China, kept rural population growth in check.

Ming Collapse and the Rise of the Qing

Although these environmental, economic, and administrative problems existed, the primary reasons for the fall of the Ming Empire were internal rebellion and rising Manchu power on the frontier. Insecure boundaries had been a recurrent peril. The Ming had long been under pressure from the powerful Mongol federations of the north and west. In the late 1500s large numbers of Mongols were unified by their devotion to the Dalai Lama°,

Dalai Lama (DAH-lie LAH-mah)

or universal teacher, of Tibetan Buddhism, whom they regarded as their spiritual leader. Building on this spiritual unity, a brilliant leader named Galdan restored Mongolia as a regional military power around 1600. The Manchus, an agricultural people who controlled the region north of Korea, grew stronger in the northeast.

In the southwest, native peoples repeatedly resisted the immigration of Chinese farmers. Pirates based in Okinawa and Taiwan, many of them Japanese, frequently looted the southeast coast. Ming military resources, concentrated against the Mongols and the Manchus in the north, could not be deployed to defend the coasts. As a result, many southern Chinese migrated to Southeast Asia to profit from the sea-trading networks of the Indian Ocean.

The Japanese invasion of 1592 to 1598 (see section on Japan) prompted the Ming to seek the assistance of Manchu troops that they were then unable to restrain. With the rebel leader Li Zicheng in possession of Beijing (see the beginning of this chapter) and the emperor dead by his own hand, a Ming general joined forces with the Manchu leaders in the summer of 1644. Instead of restoring the Ming, however, the Manchus claimed China for their own and began a forty-year conquest of the rest of the Ming territories, as well as Taiwan and parts of Mongolia and Central Asia (see Map 18.1).

A Manchu family headed the new **Qing Empire,** and Manchu generals commanded the military forces. But Manchus made up a very small portion of the population. The overwhelming majority of Qing officials, soldiers, merchants, and farmers were ethnic Chinese. Like other successful invaders of China, the Qing soon adopted Chinese institutions and policies.

Trading Companies and Missionaries

For European merchants, the China trade was second in importance only to the spice trade of southern Asia. China's vast population and manufacturing skills drew a steady stream of ships from western Europe, but enthusiasm for the trade developed only slowly at the imperial court.

A Portuguese ship reached China at the end of 1513 but was not permitted to trade. A formal Portuguese embassy in 1517 got bogged down in Chi-nese protocol and procrastination, and China expelled the Portuguese in 1522. Finally, in 1557 the Portuguese gained the right to trade from a base in Macao° on the southern coast. Spain's Asian trade was conducted from Manila in the Philippines, which also linked with South America across the Pacific. For a time, the Spanish and the Dutch both maintained trading outposts on the island of Taiwan, but in 1662 they were forced to concede control to the Qing, who for the first time incorporated Taiwan into China.

By then, the Dutch East India Company (VOC) had displaced the Portuguese as the major European trader in the Indian Ocean and was establishing itself as the main European trader in East Asia. VOC representatives courted official favor in China by acknowledging the moral superiority of the emperor. They performed the ritual kowtow (in which the visitor knocked his head on the floor while crawling toward the throne) to the Ming emperor.

Catholic missionaries accompanied the Portuguese and Spanish merchants to China, just as they did to Japan. While the Franciscans and Dominicans pursued the conversion efforts at the bottom of society that had worked so well in Japan, the Jesuits focused on China's intellectual and political elite. In this they were far more successful than they had been in Japan—at least until the eighteenth century.

The outstanding Jesuit of late Ming China, Matteo Ricci° (1552–1610), became expert in the Chinese language and an accomplished scholar of the Confucian classics. Under Ricci's leadership, the Jesuits sought to adapt Catholic Christianity to Chinese cultural traditions while enhancing their status by introducing the Chinese to the latest science and technology from Europe. From 1601 Ricci was allowed to reside in Beijing on an imperial stipend as a Western scholar. Later Jesuits headed the office of astronomy that issued the official calendar.

Emperor Kangxi

The seventeenth and eighteenth centuries—particularly the reigns of the **Kangxi**° (r. 1662–1722) and Qianlong° (r. 1736–1796) emperors—were a pe-

Macao (muh-KOW)   **Matteo Ricci** (mah-TAY-oh REE-chee)
Kangxi (KAHNG-shee)   **Qianlong** (chee-YEN-loong)

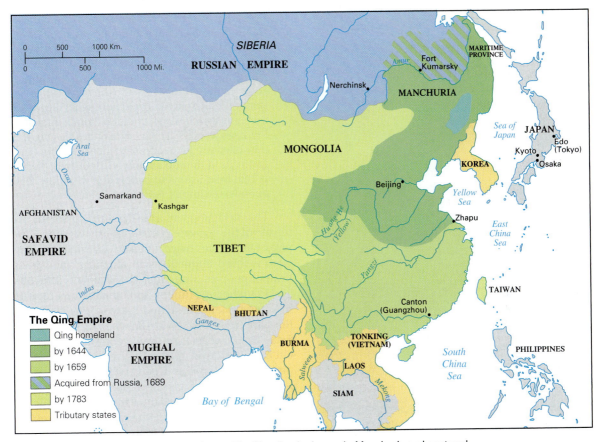

Map 18.1 The Qing Empire, 1644–1783   The Qing Empire began in Manchuria and captured north China in 1644. Between 1644 and 1783 the Qing conquered all the former Ming territories and added Taiwan, the lower Amur River Basin, Inner Mongolia, eastern Turkestan, and Tibet. The resulting state was more than twice the size of the Ming Empire.

riod of great economic, military, and cultural achievement in China. To foster economic and demographic recovery, the early Qing emperors repaired the roads and waterworks, lowered transit taxes, mandated comparatively low rents and interest rates, and established economic incentives for resettling areas devastated by peasant rebellions. Foreign trade was encouraged. Vietnam, Burma, and Nepal sent regular embassies to the Qing tribute court and carried the latest Chinese fashions back home. Overland routes of communication from Korea to Central Asia revived, and through its conquests the Qing Empire gained access to the superior horses of Afghanistan.

The Manchu aristocrats who led the conquest of Beijing and north China dominated the first Qing emperor and served as regents for his young son, who was declared emperor in 1662. This child-emperor, Kangxi, sparred politically with the regents until 1669, when he executed the chief regent and thereby gained real control of the government. He was then sixteen and an intellectual prodigy who had mastered classical Chinese, Manchu, and Mongolian at an early age and memorized the Chinese classics. His reign, lasting until his death in 1722, was marked not only by imperial expansion but also by great stability.

In the north, the Qing rulers especially feared

Emperor Kangxi In a portrait from about 1690, the young Manchu ruler is portrayed as a refined scholar in the Confucian tradition. He was a scholar and had great intellectual curiosity, but this portrait would not suggest that he was also capable of leading troops in battle. (The Palace Museum, Beijing)

an alliance between Galdan's Mongol state and the expanding Russian presence along the **Amur° River.** In the 1680s Qing forces attacked the wooden forts built by hardy Russian scouts on the river's northern bank. Neither empire sent large forces into the Amur territories, so the contest was partly a struggle for the goodwill of the local Evenk and Dagur peoples. The Qing emperor emphasized the importance of treading lightly in the struggle and well understood the principles of espionage:

Amur (AH-moor)

Upon reaching the lands of the Evenks and the Dagurs you will send to announce that you have come to hunt deer. Meanwhile, keep a careful record of the distance and go, while hunting, along the northern bank of the Amur until you come by the shortest route to the town of Russian settlement at Albazin. Thoroughly reconnoiter its location and situation. I don't think the Russians will take a chance on attacking you. If they offer you food, accept it and show your gratitude. If they do attack you, don't fight back. In that case, lead your people and withdraw into our own territories. For I have a plan of my own.[2]

That delicacy gives a false impression of the intensity of the struggle between these two great empires. Qing forces twice attacked Albazin. The Qing were worried about Russian alliances with other frontier peoples, while Russia wished to protect its access to the furs, timber, and metals concentrated in Siberia, Manchuria, and Yakutsk. The Qing and Russians were also rivals for control of northern Asia's Pacific coast. Continued conflict would benefit neither side. In 1689 the Qing and Russian Empires negotiated the Treaty of Nerchinsk, using Jesuit missionaries as interpreters. The treaty fixed the border along the Amur River and regulated trade across it. Although this was a thinly settled area, the treaty proved important since the frontier it demarcated has long endured.

The next step was to settle the Mongolian frontier. Kangxi personally led troops in the great campaigns that defeated Galdan and brought Inner Mongolia under Qing control by 1691.

Kangxi was distinguished by his openness to new ideas and technologies from different regions. Unlike the rulers of Japan, who drove Christian missionaries out, he welcomed Jesuit advisers, discussed scientific and philosophical issues with them, and put them in important offices. Jesuits helped create maps in the European style as practical guides to newly conquered regions and as symbols of Qing dominance. Kangxi considered introducing the European calendar, but protests from the Confucian elite caused him to drop the plan. When he fell ill with malaria in the 1690s, Jesuit medical expertise (in this case, the use of quinine) aided his recovery. Kangxi also ordered the creation of illustrated books in Manchu detailing European anatomical and pharmaceutical knowledge.

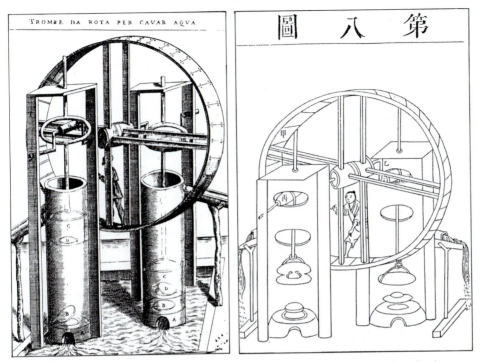

From the Jesuit Library at Beijing   Jesuits such as Matteo Ricci were willing to share books on technology and science with Chinese scholars. But without firsthand experience it was impossible for Chinese translators to convey how the devices actually worked. Here, a man walking in a wheel drives a shaft that changes the pressure inside two pumps. In the Chinese translation of the drawing, the mechanisms were all lost.   (Left: From Zonca, *Trombe da Rota per Cavar Aqua* [1607]. Right: "Diagram Number Eight" from *Qi tushuo* [*Illustrations on Energy*] [1627]. Both courtesy of Joseph Needham, *Science and Civilization in China*, vol. 4)

To gain converts among the Chinese elite, the Jesuits made important compromises in their religious teaching. The most important was their toleration of Confucian ancestor worship. The matter caused great controversy between the Jesuits and their Catholic rivals in China, the Franciscans and Dominicans, and also between the Jesuits and the pope. In 1690 the disagreement reached a high pitch. Kangxi wrote to Rome supporting the Jesuit position. Further disagreement with a papal legate to China led Kangxi to order the expulsion of all missionaries who refused to sign a certificate accepting his position. Most of the Jesuits signed, but relations with the imperial court were irreparably harmed. The Jesuit presence in China declined in the eighteenth century, and later Qing emperors persecuted Christians rather than naming them to high offices.

Chinese Influences on Europe

The exchange of information between the Qing and the Europeans that Kangxi had fostered was never one-way. When the Jesuits informed the Qing court on matters of anatomy, for instance, the Qing were able to demonstrate an early form of inoculation, called "variolation," that had been used to stem the spread of smallpox after the Qing conquest of Beijing. The technique helped inspire the development of other vaccines later in Europe.

Similarly, Jesuit writings about the intellectual and cultural achievements of China excited admiration in Europe. The wealthy and the aspiring middle classes of Europe demanded Chinese things—or things that looked to Europeans as if they could be Chinese. Silk, porcelain, and tea were avidly sought, along with cloisonné jewelry, lacquered and jeweled room dividers, painted fans, and carved jade and ivory (which originated in Africa and was finished in China). One of the most striking Chinese influences was wallpaper—an adaptation of the Chinese practice of covering walls with enormous loose-hanging watercolors or calligraphy scrolls. By the mid-1700s special workshops throughout China were producing wallpaper and other consumer items according to the specifications of European merchants. The items were shipped to Canton for export to Europe.

In political philosophy, too, the Europeans felt they had something to learn. In the late 1770s poems supposedly written by Emperor Qianlong were translated into French and disseminated in European intellectual circles. These works depicted the Qing emperors as benevolent despots who campaigned against superstition and ignorance, curbed the excesses of the aristocracy, and patronized science and the arts. European intellectuals who were questioning their own political systems found the image of a practical, secular, compassionate ruler intriguing. The French thinker Voltaire proclaimed the Qing emperors model philosopher-kings and advocated such rulership as a protection against the growth of aristocratic privilege.

Tea and Diplomacy

To maintain strict control over trade, facilitate tax collection, and suppress piracy, the Qing permitted only one market point for each foreign sector. Thus Europeans were permitted to trade only at Canton.

This system worked well enough for European traders until the late 1700s, when Britain became worried about its massive trade deficit with China. From bases in India and Singapore, British traders moved eastward to China and eventually displaced the Dutch as China's leading European trading partner. The directors of the East India Company (EIC) believed that China's technological achievements and gigantic potential markets could produce limitless profit. By the early 1700s the EIC dominated European trading in Canton.

Tea from China had spread overland on Eurasian routes in medieval and early modern times to become a prized import in Russia, Central Asia, and the Middle East, all of which know it by its northern Chinese name, cha—as do the Portuguese. Other western Europeans acquired tea from the sea routes and thus know it by its name in the Fujian province of coastal China and Taiwan: te. In much of Europe, tea competed with chocolate and coffee as a fashionable drink by the mid-1600s.

Great fortunes were being made in the tea trade, but the English had not found a comparable product to sell to China. They believed that China was a vast unexploited market, with hundreds of millions of potential consumers of lamp oil made from whale blubber, cotton grown in India or the American South, or guns manufactured in London or Connecticut. Particularly after the loss of the thirteen American colonies, Britain feared that its markets would diminish, and the EIC and other British merchants concluded that the Qing trade system—the "Canton system," as the British called it—stood in the way of opening new commercial paths.

A massive trade deficit constituted another British worry. Because the Qing Empire rarely bought anything from Britain, British silver poured into China to pay for tea and other imports. The Qing government, whose revenues were declining in the later 1700s while its expenses rose, needed the silver and was not inclined to loosen restrictions on imported foreign goods. To make matters worse, the East India Company had managed its worldwide holdings badly, and as it teetered on bankruptcy, its attempts to manipulate Parliament became increasingly intrusive. In 1792 the British government dispatched Lord George Macartney, a well-connected peer with practical experience in Russia and India, to China. Including scientists, artists, and translators as well as guards and diplomats, the **Macartney mission** showed Britain's great interest in the Qing Empire as well as the EIC's desire to revise the trade system.

China was not familiar with the European system of ambassadors, and Macartney struggled to portray himself in Chinese terms as a "tribute emissary" come to salute the Qianlong emperor's eightieth birthday. However, he steadfastly refused to perform the kowtow, though he did agree to bow on one knee as he would to his own monarch, King George III. The Qianlong emperor received

Macartney courteously in September 1793 but refused to alter the Canton trading system, open new ports of trade, or allow the British to establish a permanent mission in Beijing. Qianlong sent a letter to King George explaining that China had no need to increase its foreign trade, had no use for Britain's ingenious devices and manufacturers, and set no value on closer diplomatic ties.

Dutch, French, and Russian embassies soon attempted to achieve what Macartney had failed to do. When they also failed, European frustration with the Qing mounted. The great European admiration for China faded. Political solutions seemed impossible because the Qing court would not communicate with foreign envoys or observe the simplest rules of the diplomatic system familiar to Europeans. In Macartney's view, China was like a venerable old warship, well maintained and splendid to look at, but obsolete and no longer up to the task.

Population and Social Stress

The Chinese who escorted Macartney and his entourage in 1792–1793 took them through China's prosperous cities and productive farmland. The visitors did not see evidence of the economic and environmental decline that had set in during the last decades of the 1700s. Population growth had intensified demand for rice and wheat, as well as for growing new crops like corn and sweet potatoes, and for more thorough exploitation of land already in use.

In the peaceful decades of Qing rule, China grew to three times its size in 1500. If one accepts an estimate of some 350 million in the late 1700s, China had twice the population of all of Europe. Despite the efficiency of Chinese agriculture and the gradual adoption of New World crops, population growth led to social and environmental problems. More people meant less farmland per person. Increased demand for building materials and firewood reduced woodlands. Deforestation, in turn, accelerated wind and water erosion and increased flooding. Dams and dikes were not maintained, and silted-up river channels were not dredged. By the end of the eighteenth century parts of the thousand-year-old Grand Canal linking the rivers of north and south

China were nearly unusable, and the towns that bordered it were starved for commerce.

The result was misery in many parts of interior China. Some districts responded by increasing production of tea, cotton, and silk, crops that were tied to the export market. Some peasants sought seasonal jobs in better-off agricultural areas or worked in low-status jobs as barge pullers, charcoal burners, or night soil carriers. Many drifted to the cities to make their way by begging, prostitution, or theft. In central and southwestern China, where floods had impoverished many farmers, rebellions became endemic. Indigenous peoples concentrated in the less fertile lands in the south and in the northern and western borderlands of the empire often joined in revolts.

The Qing government was not up to controlling its vast empire. It was twice the size of the Ming geographically, but it employed about the same number of officials. The government's dependence on working alliances with local elites had led to widespread corruption and shrinking government revenues. As was the case with other empires, the Qing's spectacular rise had ended, and decline had set in.

THE RUSSIAN EMPIRE

From modest beginnings in 1500, Russia expanded rapidly during the next three centuries to create an empire that stretched from eastern Europe across northern Asia and into North America. Russia also became one of the major powers of Europe by 1750, with armies capable of mounting challenges to its Asian and European neighbors.

The Drive Across Northern Asia

During the centuries just before 1500, the history of the Russians had been dominated by steppe nomads (see Chapter 11). The Mongol Khanate of the Golden Horde ruled the Russians and their neighbors from the 1240s until 1480.

Under the Golden Horde Moscow became the most important Russian city and the center of political power. Moscow lay in the forest zone that stretched across Eurasia north of the treeless steppe (plains) favored by Mongol horsemen. The princes of **Muscovy°,** the territory surrounding the city of Moscow, led the movement against the Golden Horde and ruthlessly annexed the territories of the neighboring Russian state of Novgorod in 1478.

Once free from Mongol domination, the princes of Moscovy set out on conquests that in time made them masters of all the Golden Horde territories and then of a far greater empire. Prince Ivan IV (r. 1533–1584) pushed the conquests south and east at the expense of the Khanates of Kazan and Astrakhan (see Map 18.2).

At the end of the sixteenth century, Russians ruled the largest state in Europe and large territories on the Asian side of the **Ural Mountains** as well. Since 1547 the Russian ruler used the title **tsar°** (from the Roman imperial title *caesar*), the term Russians had used for the rulers of the Mongol Empire. The Russian church promoted the idea of Moscow as the "third Rome," successor to the Roman Empire's second capital, Constantinople, which had fallen to the Ottoman Turks in 1453. But such foreign titles did not disguise a very Russian pattern of expansion.

Russian claims to greatness were also exaggerated: in 1600 the empire was poor, backward, and landlocked. Only the northern city of Arkhangelsk was connected by water to the rest of the world—when its harbor was not frozen. The Turkic-speaking Crimean peoples to the south were powerful enough to sack Moscow in 1571. Beyond them, the still vigorous Ottoman Empire controlled the shores of the Black Sea, while the Safavid rulers of Iran dominated the trade routes of southern Central Asia. The powerful kingdoms of Sweden and Poland-Lithuania to the west turned back Russian forces seeking access to ports on the Baltic Sea.

A path of less resistance lay to the east across **Siberia,** and it had much to recommend it. Many Russians felt more at home in the forested north than on the open steppes; and the thinly inhabited region abounded in valuable resources, most notably the soft, dense fur that forest animals grew to survive the long winter cold. Like their counter-

parts in Canada (see Chapter 16), hardy Russian pioneers in Siberia made a living from animal pelts. The merchants from western Europe and other lands who came to buy these furs in Moscow provided the tsars with revenue and access to European technology.

Early Russian exploration of Siberia was not the work of the state but of the Strogonovs, a wealthy Russian trading family. The small bands of hunting and fishing peoples who inhabited this cold and desolate region had no way of resisting the armed adventurers the Strogonovs hired. Using rifles, their troops attacked and destroyed the only political power in the region, the Khanate of Sibir, in 1582. Rivers provided the best routes for moving through the dense forests and enabled Russian fur trappers to reach the Pacific during the seventeenth century. Soon they crossed over into Alaska. Russian political control followed at a much slower pace. In the seventeenth century Siberia was a frontier zone with widely scattered forts, not a province under full control. The Russians had to placate rebellious leaders of the native Siberian peoples with gifts and acknowledge their rights and authority. Beginning in the early seventeenth century the tsar also used Siberia as a penal colony for criminals and political prisoners.

In the 1640s Russian settlers began to move into the valley of the Amur River east of Mongolia in order to grow grain. As seen already, by the time the Qing were in a position to confront the Russian presence, the worrisome threat of Galdan's Mongol military power had arisen. The Russians, who shared a concern about the Mongols, were pleased to work out a frontier agreement with China. The 1689 Treaty of Nerchinsk recognized Russian claims west of Mongolia but required the Russians to withdraw their settlements farther east. Moreover, the negotiations signaled China's recognition of Russia as an important and powerful neighbor.

Russian Society and Politics to 1725

Russian expansion involved demographic changes as well as new relations between the tsar and the elite classes. A third transformation affected the freedom and mobility of the Russian peasantry.

Muscovy (MUSS-koe-vee)   **tsar** (zahr)

As the empire expanded, it incorporated people with different languages, religious beliefs, and ethnic identities. Language differences were not hard to overcome, but religious and other cultural differences often caused tensions, especially when differences were manipulated for political purposes. Orthodox missionaries made great efforts to Christianize the peoples of Siberia in much the same way that Catholic missionaries did in Canada. But among the relatively more populous steppe peoples, Islam won out over Christianity as the dominant religion. More fundamental than language, ethnicity, or religion were the differences in how people made their living. Russians tended to live as farmers, hunters, builders, scribes, or merchants, while those newly incorporated into the empire were mostly herders, caravan workers, and soldiers.

As people mixed, individual and group identities became complex. Even among Russian speakers who were members of the Russian Orthodox Church there was wide diversity of identity. The **Cossacks** are a revealing example. The name probably came from a Turkic word for a warrior or mercenary soldier and referred to bands of people living on the steppes between Moscovy and the Caspian and Black Seas. In practice, Cossacks became highly diverse in their origins and beliefs. What mattered was that they belonged to close-knit bands, were superb riders and fighters, and were feared by both the villagers and the legal authorities. Cossacks made temporary allegiances with many rulers but were most loyal to their bands and to whoever was currently paying for their military services.

Cossacks constituted the majority of the soldiers and early settlers employed by the Strogonovs to penetrate Siberia. Most historians believe that Cossacks founded all the major towns of Russian Siberia. They also manned the Russian camps on the Amur River. The Cossacks west of the Urals performed distinctive service for Russia in defending against Swedish and Ottoman incursions, but they also resisted any efforts to undermine their own political autonomy. Those in the rich and populous lands of the Ukraine, for example, rebelled when the tsar agreed to a division of their lands with Poland-Lithuania in 1667.

In the early seventeenth century Swedish and Polish forces briefly occupied Moscow on separate occasions. In the midst of this "Time of Troubles" the old line of Muscovite rulers was finally deposed, and the Russian aristocracy—the boyars°—allowed one of their own, Mikhail Romanov°, to become tsar (r. 1613–1645). The early Romanov rulers saw a close connection between the consolidation of their own authority and successful competition with neighboring powers. They tended to represent conflicts between Slavic Russians and Turkic peoples of Central Asia as being between Christians and "infidels" or between the civilized and the "barbaric." Despite this rhetoric, it is important to understand that these cultural groups were defined less by blood ties than by the way in which they lived.

The political and economic transformations of the Russian Empire had serious repercussions for the peasants who tilled the land in European Russia. As centralized power rose, the freedom of the peasants fell. The process was longer and more complex than the rise of slavery in the Americas. The Moscovy rulers and early tsars rewarded their loyal nobles with grants of land that included obligations of the local peasants to work for these lords. Law and custom permitted peasants to change masters during a two-week period each year, which encouraged lords to treat their peasants well; but the rising commercialization of agriculture also raised the value of these labor obligations.

Long periods of civil and foreign warfare in the late sixteenth and early seventeenth centuries caused such disruption that many peasants fled to the Cossacks or across the Urals. Some who couldn't flee sold themselves into slavery to ensure a steady supply of food. When peace returned, landlords sought to recover these runaway peasants and bind them more firmly to their land. A law change in 1649 completed the transformation of peasants into **serfs** by eliminating the period when they could change masters and decreeing that runaways could be forced to return to their masters no matter how many years had elapsed.

Like slavery, serfdom was a hereditary status. In theory the serf was tied to a piece of land, not owned by a master. In practice, the difference

---

boyar (BOY-ar)   **Romanov** (ROH-man-off or roh-MAN-off)

The Russian Empire

- Russia in 1533
- Added by 1598
- Added by 1721
- Added by 1796
- ■ Fort

PACIFIC
OCEAN

BRITISH NORTH AMERICA
(CANADA)

Novo Arkhangelsk
(Sitka)
TLINGIT

Border set in 1826

RUSSIAN
AMERICA
(ALASKA)

ALEUTS

INUIT

50°

Bering Strait

60°

Bering
Sea

70°

INUIT

INUIT

GREENLAND

ARCTIC
OCEAN

100° 120° 140°
160°
180°
160°
140°
120°
100°

60°
40°
20°
20°
40° 60° 80°
80°

CHUKCHI

KORYAKS

Kolyma

Petropavlovsk
ALEUTS
Kamchatka
Peninsula

Sea of
Okhotsk

Zashiversk

Okhotsk

Sakalin

Yana

Arctic Circle

70°

Novaya Zemlya

Kara
Sea

S
I
B
E
R
I
A

Khatanga

Lena

Olenek

Zhigansk

EVENKI

Yakutsk

Vilyuy

YAKUTS

LAMUTS

Aldan

Barents
Sea

Lower Tunguska

EVENKI

Amur

MANCHURIA

SWEDEN

Obdorsk

SAMOYEDS

Arkhangelsk

OSTYAKS

URAL MOUNTAINS

FINLAND

OSTYAKS

Upper Tunguska

TUNGUSY

Yenisey

Nerchinsk

St. Petersburg

Surgut

Kem

Bratsk

Krasnoyarsk

Irkutsk

Baltic
Sea

Novgorod

Verkhoturye

TARTARS

Ob

Riga

Tula

Tobol

Ishim

Omsk

Biysk

MONGOLIA

PRUSSIA

Moscow

Smolensk

Nizhni
Novgorod

Kama

Tula

Irtysh

POLAND

Kiev

Samara

UKRAINIANS

Saratov

COSSACKS

Ural

Q I N G
E M P I R E

AUSTRIA

Dnieper

COSSACKS

Volga

KAZAKS

OTTOMAN EMPIRE

Black Sea

Dniester

GEORGIA

Aral
Sea

Caspian
Sea

TIBET

BHUTAN

AFGHANISTAN

NEPAL

BURMA

IRAN

I N D I A

Map 18.2   The Expansion of Russia, 1500–1800
Sweden and Poland initially blocked Russian expansion in Europe, while the Ottoman Empire blocked the southwest. In the sixteenth century, Russia began to expand east, toward Siberia and the Pacific Ocean. By the end of the rule of Catherine the Great in 1796, Russia encompassed all of northern and northeastern Eurasia.

between serfdom and slavery narrowed as the laws regulating selfdom became stricter. By 1723 all Russian slaves were transformed into serfs. In the Russian census of 1795, serfs made up over half the population and were under the control of landowners, who made up only 2 percent, similar to the size of the slave-owning class in the Caribbean.

Peter the Great

The greatest of the Romanovs was Tsar **Peter the Great** (r. 1689–1725), who reduced Russia's isolation and increased the empire's size and power. Tsar Peter is remembered for his efforts to turn Russia away from its Asian cultural connections and toward what he deemed the advanced civilization of the West. In fact, he accelerated trends under way for some time. When he ascended the throne, there were already hundreds of foreign merchants in Moscow. Military officers from western Europe had already trained a major part of the army in new weapons and techniques, and Italian builders had already influenced church and palace architecture. It was on this substantial base that Peter erected a more rapid transformation of Russia.

Peter matured quickly both physically and mentally. In his youth the government was in the hands of his half-sister Sophia, who was regent on behalf of him and her sickly brother Ivan. Living on an estate near the foreigners' quarter outside Moscow, Peter learned what he could of life outside Russia and busied himself gaining practical skills in blacksmithing, carpentry, shipbuilding, and the arts of war. He organized his own military drill unit among other young men. When Princess Sophia tried to take complete control of the government in 1689, Peter rallied enough support to send her to a monastery, secure the abdication of Ivan, and take charge of Russia. He was still in his teens.

Peter concerned himself with Russia's expansion and modernization. To secure a warm-water

Peter the Great   This portrait from his time as a student in Holland in 1697 shows Peter as ruggedly masculine and practical, quite unlike most royal portraits of the day that posed rulers in foppish elegance and haughty majesty. Peter was a popular military leader as well as an autocratic ruler. (Collection, Countess Bobrinskoy/Michael Holford)

port on the Black Sea, he constructed a small but formidable navy that could blockade Ottoman ports. Describing his wars with the Ottoman Empire as a new crusade to liberate Constantinople from the Muslim sultans, Peter also saw himself as the legal protector of Orthodox Christians living under Ottoman rule. Peter's forces seized the port of Azov in 1696, but the fortress was lost again in 1713, and Russian expansion southward was blocked for the rest of Peter's reign.

In the winter of 1697–1698, after his Black Sea campaign, Peter traveled in disguise across Europe to discover how western European societies were becoming so powerful and wealthy. The young tsar paid special attention to ships and weapons, even working for a time as a ship's carpenter in the Netherlands. With great insight, he perceived that western European success owed as much to trade and toleration as to technology. Trade generated the money to spend on weapons, while toleration attracted talented persons fleeing persecution. Upon his return to Russia, Peter resolved to expand and reform his vast and backward empire.

In the long and costly Great Northern War (1700–1721), his modernized armies broke Swedish control of the Baltic Sea, making possible more direct contacts between Russia and Europe. Peter's victory forced the European powers to recognize Russia as a major power for the first time.

On land captured from Sweden at the eastern end of the Baltic, Peter built St. Petersburg, a new city that was to be his window on the West. In 1712 the city became Russia's capital. To demonstrate Russia's new sophistication, Peter ordered architects to build St. Petersburg's houses and public buildings in the baroque style then fashionable in France.

Peter also pushed the Russian elite to imitate western European fashions. He personally shaved off his noblemen's long beards to conform to Western styles and ordered them to wear Western clothing. To end the traditional seclusion of upper-class Russian women, Peter required officials, military officers, and merchants to bring their wives to the social gatherings he organized in the capital. He also directed the nobles to educate their children.

Another of Peter's strategies was to reorganize Russian government along the lines of the powerful German state of Prussia. To break the power of the boyars he sharply reduced their traditional roles in government and the army. The old boyar council of Moscow was replaced by a group of advisers in St. Petersburg whom the tsar appointed. Members of the traditional nobility continued to serve as generals and admirals, but officers in Peter's modern, professional army and navy were promoted according to merit, not birth.

The goal of Peter's westernization strategy was to strengthen the Russian state and increase the power of the tsar. A decree of 1716 proclaimed that the tsar "is not obliged to answer to anyone in the world for his doings, but possesses power and authority over his kingdom and land, to rule them at his will and pleasure as a Christian ruler." Under this expansive definition of his role, Peter brought the Russian Orthodox Church more firmly under state control, built factories and iron and copper foundries to provide munitions and supplies for the military, and increased the burdens of taxes and forced labor on the serfs. Peter was an absolutist ruler of the sort then common in western Europe, and he had no more intention of improving the conditions of the serfs, on whose labors the production of basic foodstuffs depended, than did the European slave owners of the Americas.

Consolidation of the Empire

Russia's eastward expansion also continued under Peter the Great and his successors. The frontier settlement with China and Qianlong's quashing of Inner Mongolia in 1689 freed Russians to concentrate on the northern Pacific. The Pacific northeast was colonized, and in 1741 an expedition led by Captain Vitus Bering crossed the strait (later named for him) into North America. In 1799 a Russian company of merchants received a monopoly over the Alaskan fur trade, and its agents were soon active along the entire northwestern coast of North America.

Far more important than these immense territories in the cold and thinly populated north were the populous agricultural lands to the west acquired during the reign of Catherine the Great (r. 1762–1796). A successful war with the Ottoman Empire gave Russia control of the north shore of the Black Sea by 1783. As a result of three successive partitions of the once powerful kingdom of Poland between 1772 and 1795, Russia's frontiers advanced 600 miles (nearly 1,000 kilometers) to the west (see Map 18.2). When Catherine died, the Russian Empire extended from Poland in the west to Alaska in the east, from the Barents Sea in the north to the Black Sea in the south.

Catherine also made important additions to Peter's policies of promoting industry and building a canal system to improve trade. Besides furs, the Russians had also become major exporters of gold, iron, and timber. Catherine implemented administrative reforms and showed a special talent for diplomacy. Through her promotion of the ideas of the Enlightenment, she expanded Peter's policies of westernizing the Russian elite.

COMPARATIVE PERSPECTIVES

Considered separately, the histories of Japan, China, and Russia overlap very little. Contacts with each other were far less important than forces within each state. However, when examined comparatively, these separate histories reveal similarities and differences that help explain the global dynamics and larger historical patterns of this period.

Political Comparisons

China and Russia exemplify the phenomenal flourishing of Eurasian empires between 1500 and 1800. Already a vast empire under the Ming, China doubled in size under the Qing, mostly through westward expansion into less densely populated areas. As for Russia, the addition of rich and well-populated lands to the west and south and far larger but less populous lands to the east transformed a modestly sized principality into the world's largest land empire. Russia and China were land based, just like the Ottoman, Safavid, and Mughal Empires (see Chapter 17), with the strengths and problems of administrative control and tax collection that size entailed.

Although western Europe is often seen as particularly imperialist in the centuries after 1500, only Spain's empire merits comparison with Russia's. By contrast, the new seaborne trading empires of the Portuguese, Dutch, French, and English had much less territory, far tighter administration, and a much more global sweep.

Japan was different. Though nominally headed by an emperor, Japan's size and ethnic homogeneity do not support calling it an empire in the same breath with China and Russia. Tokugawa Japan was similar in size and population to France, the most powerful state of western Europe, but its political system was much more decentralized. Japan's efforts to add colonies on the East Asian mainland had failed.

China had once led the world in military innovation (including the first uses of gunpowder), but the modern "gunpowder revolution" of the fifteenth and sixteenth centuries was centered in the Ottoman Empire and western European states. Although the centuries after 1500 were full of successful military operations, Chinese armies continued to depend on superior numbers and tactics for their success, rather than on new technology.

The military forces of Japan and Russia underwent more innovative changes than those of China, in part through Western contacts. In the course of its sixteenth-century wars of unification, Japan produced its own gunpowder revolution but thereafter lacked the motivation and the means to stay abreast of the world's most advanced military technology. By the eighteenth century Russia had made greater progress in catching up with its European neighbors, but its armies still relied more on their size than on the sophistication of their weapons.

Naval power provides the greatest military contrast among the three. Eighteenth-century Russia constructed modern fleets of warships in the Baltic and the Black Seas, but neither China nor Japan developed navies commensurate with their size and coastlines. China's defenses against pirates and other sea invaders were left to its maritime provinces, whose small war junks were armed with only a half-dozen cannon. Japan's naval capacity was similarly decentralized. In 1792, when Russian ships exploring the North Pacific turned toward the Japanese coast, the local daimyo used his own forces to chase them away. All Japanese daimyo understood that they would be on their own if foreign incursions increased.

Cultural, Social, and Economic Comparisons

The expansion of China and Russia incorporated not just new lands but also diverse new peoples. Both empires pursued policies that tolerated diversity along with policies to promote cultural assimilation. In contrast, Japan remained more culturally homogeneous, and the government reacted with great intolerance to the growing influence of converts to Christianity.

Chinese society had long been diverse, and its geographical, occupational, linguistic, and religious differences grew as the Qing expanded. China had also long used Confucian models, imperial customs, and a common system of writing to transcend such differences. These techniques were most effective in assimilating elites. It is striking how quickly and thoroughly the Manchu conquerors adopted Chinese imperial ways of thinking and acting as well as of dressing, speaking, and writing.

Kangxi's reign is a notable example of how receptive the Chinese elite could be to new ideas. Yet the Jesuits' success owed much to their portraying themselves as supporters of Confucian values and learning. Although Chinese converts to Catholicism were instrumental in introducing European techniques of crop production and engineering, influential members of China's government were highly suspicious of the loyalties of these converts, persecuted them, and eventually moved to prohibit or severely limit missionary activity.

Russia likewise approached its new peoples with a mixture of pragmatic tolerance and a propensity for seeing Russian ways and beliefs as superior. Religion was a particular sore point. With the support of the tsars, Russian Orthodox missionaries encouraged conversion of Siberian peoples. In the new lands of eastern Europe, Orthodoxy was a common bond for some new subjects, but the Roman Catholic Poles, incorporated in the late 1700s, would soon suffer greatly for their divergent beliefs and practices. The Russian language was strongly promoted. Russia was also notable for its absorption of new ideas and styles from western Europe, especially under the leadership of its eighteenth-century rulers. Even among the elite, however, these influences often overlay Russian cultural traditions in a very superficial way.

Forced labor remained common in the Russian and Chinese Empires. Serfdom grew more brutal and widespread in Russia in the seventeenth and eighteenth centuries, although the expansion of the frontier eastward across Siberia also opened an escape route for many peasants and serfs. Some Chinese peasants also improved their lot by moving to new territories, but population growth increased overall misery in the eighteenth century. China was also notable for the size of its popular insurrections, especially the one that toppled the Ming.

In striking contrast to the rising importance of elite merchants in the West, private merchants in China and Japan occupied precarious positions. Confucian thought ranked merchants below peasants in their contributions to society. In Japan maritime traders were also sometimes pirates, though Chinese and even European sea trade was not much different. Governments conducted diplomatic and strategic missions but had no interest in encouraging overseas voyages or colonies. Instead both Japan and China moved to restrict overseas trade. In the end, commercial contacts were far more important to Europe than to East Asia.

CONCLUSION

As the world has grown more interconnected, it has become increasingly difficult to sort out the degree to which major historical changes were due to forces within a society or to outside forces acting upon it. The histories of Japan, China, and Russia between 1500 and 1800 reveal how internal forces operated separately from external ones and the degree to which they were intertwined.

The formation of the Tokugawa Shogunate in Japan is a clear example of a society changing from within. The decisions of government to suppress Christianity and sharply curtail commercial and intellectual contacts with distant Europe illustrate how easily even the most decentralized of the three states could control its dealings with outsiders.

China's history illustrates a more complex interplay of internal and external forces, notably in the details of the final days of the Ming dynasty, which involved a Japanese invasion through Korea, a rebellion from within, and a conquering army from Manchuria.. The Qing's settlement of the Amur frontier with Russia illustrates how diplomacy and compromise could serve mutual interests. Finally, the Chinese added new European customers to already extensive internal and external markets and developed both positive and problematic cultural relations with the Jesuits and some other Europeans. From a Chinese perspective, European contacts could be useful but were neither essential nor of great importance.

The internal and external factors in Russia's history are the hardest to sort out. Especially problematic is assessing the rising importance of the West in light of Russia's growing trade in that direction, Russia's emergence as a European Great Power, and the stated policies of both Peter the Great and Catherine the Great to westernize their people. Clearly, Western influences were very important, but just as clearly their importance can easily be exaggerated. The impetus for Muscovy's expansion came out of its own history and domination by the Mongols. Trade with western Europe was not the center of the Russian economy. Tsar Peter was more interested in Western technology than in the full range of Western culture. The Russian church was quite hostile to the Catholics and Protestants to their west, whom it regarded as heretics. Peter the Great banned the Jesuits from Russia, considering them a subversive and backward influence.

Looking at each country separately and from within, the influence of western Europeans seems clearly inferior to a host of internal and regional influences. Yet when one looks at what happened in Japan, China, and Russia in the decades after 1800, it is hard to avoid the conclusion that their relationship with the West was a common factor that, when combined with unresolved internal problems, would have a tremendous impact on the course of their history. Qianlong might tell Macartney and the British that he had no use for expanded contacts, but the sentiment was not mutual. As the next part details, after the increasingly powerful Western societies got over dealing with their own internal problems, they would be back, and they would be impossible to dismiss or resist.

■ Key Terms

Manchu	Macartney mission
daimyo	Muscovy
samurai	Ural Mountains
Tokugawa Shogunate	tsar
Ming Empire	Siberia
Qing Empire	Cossacks
Kangxi	serfs
Amur River	Peter the Great

■ Suggested Reading

A fascinating place to begin is with John E. Wills, Jr., *1688: A Global History* (2001), Part III, "Three Worlds Apart: Russia, China, and Japan."

On Japan in this period, see Andrew Gordon, *A Modern History of Japan: From Tokugawa Times to the Present* (2003); *The Cambridge History of Japan*, vol. 4, *Early Modern Japan*, ed. John Whitney Hall (1991); Chie Nakane and Shinzaburo Oishi, *Tokugawa Japan: The Social and Economic Antecedents of Modern Japan*, trans. Conrad Totman (1990); and Tessa Morris-Suzuki, *The Technological Transformation of Japan from the Seventeenth to the Twenty-First Century* (1994). Mary Elizabeth Berry, *Hideyoshi* (1982), is an account of the reunification of Japan at the end of the sixteenth century and the invasion of Korea. See also Michael Cooper, ed., *They Came to Japan: An Anthology of European Reports on Japan, 1543–1640* (1965).

For China during the transition from the Ming to Qing periods, see Jonathan D. Spence, *The Search for Modern China* (1990); James W. Tong, *Disorder Under Heaven: Collective Violence in the Ming Dynasty* (1991); Frederic Wakeman, *The Great Enterprise* (1985); and Lynn Struve, *Voices from the Ming-Qing Cataclysm: In Tiger's Jaws* (1993). The latest work on the late Ming is summarized in *The Cambridge History of China*, vol. 8, *The Ming Dynasty, 1368–1644*, Part 2 (1998). On the history of the Manchu and of the Qing Empire, see Evelyn Sakakida Rawski, *The Last Emperors* (1999), and Pamela Kyle Crossley, *The Manchus* (1997).

On Chinese society generally in this period, see two classic (though slightly dated) works by Ping-ti Ho, *The Ladder of Success in Imperial China: Aspects of Social Mobility, 1368–1911* (1962), and *Studies in the Population of China 1368–1953* (1959); and see the general study by Susan Naquin and Evelyn S. Rawski, *Chinese Society in the Eighteenth Century* (1987). On the two greatest of the Qing emperors and their times, see Jonathan D. Spence, *Emperor of China; Self Portrait of K'ang Hsi, 1654–1722* (1974). For a more scholarly treatment, see Lawrence D. Kessler, *K'ang-hsi and the Consolidation of Ch'ing Rule, 1661–1684* (1976); Jonathan D. Spence, *Ts'ao Yin and the K'ang-hsi Emperor: Bondservant and Master* (1966); and Harold Kahn, *Monarchy in the Emperor's Eyes: Image and Reality in the Ch'ien-lung Reign* (1971).

On the Qing trade systems, see John E. Wills, *Embassies and Illusions: Dutch and Portuguese Envoys to K'ang-hsi, 1666–1687* (1984), and Craig Clunas, *Chinese Export Art and Design* (1987). There is a great deal published on the Macartney mission, much of it originating in the diaries and memoirs of the participants. See the exhaustively detailed Alain Peyrefitte, *The Immobile Empire*, trans. Jon Rothschild (1992). For a more theoretical discussion, see James L. Hevia, *Cherishing Men from Afar: Qing Guest Ritual and the Macartney Embassy of 1793* (1995).

On early modern Russian history, see Robert O. Crummey, *Aristocrats and Servitors: The Boyar Elite in Russia, 1613–1689* (1983), and Andreas Kappeler, *The Russian Empire: A Multiethnic History* (2001). Western perceptions of Russia are examined in Marshall T. Poe, *"A People Born to Slavery": Russia in Early Modern European Ethnography* (2000), and Lloyd E. Berry and Robert O. Crummey, ed., *Rude and Barbarous Kingdom: Russia in the Accounts of Sixteenth-Century English Voyagers* (1968). Among the best-known recent books on Tsar Peter are Matthew Smith Anderson, *Peter the Great*, 2d ed. (1995); Robert K. Massie, *Peter the Great: His Life and World* (1980); and Lindsey Hughes, *Russia in the Age of Peter the Great: 1682–1725* (1998). For Russian naval development and Russian influence in the Pacific and in America, see Glynn Barratt, *Russia in Pacific Waters, 1715–1825: A Survey of the Origins of Russia's Naval Presence in the North and South Pacific* (1981), and Howard I. Kushner, *Conflict on the Northwest Coast: American-Russian Rivalry in the Pacific Northwest, 1790–1867* (1975).

For Jesuits in East Asia in the sixteenth and seventeenth centuries, see Michael Cooper, S. J., *Rodrigues the Interpreter: An Early Jesuit in Japan and China* (1974); David E. Mungello, *Curious Land: Jesuit Accommodation and the Origins of Sinology* (1985); and Jonathan D. Spence, *The Memory Palace of Matteo Ricci* (1984). Still useful are C. R. Boxer, *The Christian Century in Japan, 1549–1650* (1951),

and Cornelius Wessels, *Early Jesuit Travellers in Central Asia, 1603–1721* (1924). On European images of and interactions with China connected to the Jesuits, see the relevant portions of Jonathan D. Spence, *The Chan's Great Continent: China in Western Minds* (1998); Joanna Waley-Cohen, *The Sextants of Beijing: Global Currents in Chinese History* (1999); and David E. Mungello, *The Great Encounter of China and the West, 1500–1800* (1999).

On the East India companies, see John E. Wills, *Pepper, Guns, and Parleys: The Dutch East India Company and China, 1662–1681* (1974); Dianne Lewis, *Jan Compagnie in the Straits of Malacca, 1641–1795* (1995); and John Keay, *The Honourable Company: A History of the English East India Company* (1991). On the development of global commerce in tea, coffee, and cocoa, see the relevant chapters in Roy Porter and Mikulås Teich, *Drugs and Narcotics in History* (1995).

■ Notes

1. Adapted from Jonathan D. Spence, *The Search for Modern China* (New York: W. W. Norton, 1990), 21–25.
2. Adapted from G. V. Melikhov, "Manzhou Penetration into the Basin of the Upper Amur in the 1680s," in S. L. Tikhvinshii, ed., *Manzhou Rule in China* (Moscow: Progress Publishers, 1983).

The Little Ice Age

A giant volcanic eruption in the Peruvian Andes in 1600 affected the weather in many parts of the world for several years. When volcanic ash from the eruption of Mount Huanyaputina (hoo-AHN-yah-poo-TEE-nuh) shot into the upper atmosphere and spread around the world, it screened out sunlight. As a result, the summer of 1601 was the coldest in two hundred years in the northern hemisphere.

Archaeologist Brian Fagan has pointed out that Mount Huanyaputina's chilling effects were a spectacular event in a much longer pattern of climate change that has been called the Little Ice Age.[1] Although global climate had been cooling since the late 1200s, in the northern temperate regions the 1590s had been exceptionally cold. Temperatures remained cooler than normal throughout the seventeenth century.

The most detailed information on the Little Ice Age comes from Europe. Glaciers in the Alps grew much larger. Trade became difficult when rivers and canals that had once been navigable in winter froze solid from bank to bank. In the coldest years, the growing season in some places was as much as two months shorter than normal. Unexpectedly late frosts withered the tender shoots of newly planted crops in spring. Wheat and barley ripened more slowly during cooler summers and were often damaged by early fall frosts.

People could survive a smaller-than-average harvest in one year by drawing on food reserves, but when cold weather damaged crops in two or more successive years, the consequences were devastating. Deaths due to malnutrition and cold increased sharply when summer temperatures in northern Europe registered 2.7°F (1.5°C) lower than average in 1674 and 1675 and again in 1694 and 1695. The cold spell of 1694 and 1695 caused a famine in Finland that carried off a quarter to a third of the population.

At the time people had no idea what was causing the unusual cold of the Little Ice Age. Advances in climate history make it clear that the cause was not a single terrestrial event such as the eruption of Mount Huanyaputina. Nor was the Little Ice Age the product of human actions, unlike some climate changes such as today's global warming.

Ultimately, the earth's weather is governed by the sun. In the seventeenth century astronomers in Europe reported seeing fewer sunspots, dark spots on the sun's surface that are indicative of solar activity and thus the sun's warming power. Diminished activity in the sun was primarily responsible for the Little Ice Age.

If the sun was the root cause, the effects of global cooling should not have been confined to northern Europe. Although contemporary accounts are much scarcer in other parts of the world, there is evidence of climate changes around the world in this period. Observations of sunspots in China, Korea, and Japan drop to zero between 1639 and 1700. China experienced unusually cool weather in the seventeenth century, but the warfare and disruption accompanying the fall of the Ming and the rise of the Qing probably were much more to blame for the famines and rural distress of that period.

By itself, a relatively slight decrease in average annual temperature would not have a serious effect on human life outside the northern temperate areas. However, evidence suggests that there was also a significant rise in humidity in this period in other parts of the world. Ice cores drilled into ancient glaciers in the Arctic and Antarctic show increased snowfall. Information compiled by historian James L. A. Webb, Jr., shows that lands south of the Sahara received more rainfall between 1550 and 1750 than they had during the previous era.[2] Increased rainfall would have been favorable for pastoral people, whose herds found new pasture in what had once been desert, and for the farmers farther south whose crops got more rain.

In the eighteenth century the sun's activity began to return to normal. Rising temperatures led to milder winters and better harvests in northern Eurasia. Falling rainfall allowed the Sahara to advance southward, forcing the agricultural frontier to retreat.

■ Notes

1. Brian Fagan, *The Littlest Ice Age: How Climate Made History, 1300–1850* (New York: Basic Books, 2000).
2. James L. A. Webb, Jr., *Desert Frontier: Ecological Change Along the Western Sahel, 1600–1850* (Madison: University of Wisconsin Press, 1995).

PART SIX

Revolutions Reshape the World, 1750–1870

CHAPTER 19
Revolutionary Changes in the Atlantic World,
1750–1850

CHAPTER 20
The Early Industrial Revolution, 1760–1851

CHAPTER 21
Africa, India, and the New British Empire,
1750–1870

CHAPTER 22
Land Empires in the Age of Imperialism,
1800–1870

Between 1750 and 1870, nearly every part of the world experienced dramatic political, economic, and social change. The beginnings of industrialization, the American and French Revolutions, and the revolutions for independence in Latin America transformed political and economic life in Europe and the Americas. European nations expanded into Africa, Asia, and the Middle East while Russia and the United States acquired vast new territories.

The American, French, and Latin American revolutions unleashed the forces of nationalism and social reform. The Industrial Revolution introduced new technologies and work patterns making industrial societies wealthier, mightier, and more fluid socially. The practical benefits of science and technology pushed Western intellectual life to become more secular. Reformers led efforts to abolish the Atlantic slave trade and, later, slavery itself in the Western Hemisphere. Expanded voting rights and improvement in the status of women gained support in Europe and the Americas.

European empires in the Western Hemisphere were largely dismantled by 1825. But the Industrial Revolution led to a new wave of imperialist expansion. France conquered Algeria, while Great Britain expanded its colonial rule in India and established new colonies in Australia and New Zealand.

European economic influence expanded throughout Africa, cementing the region's connection to the Atlantic economy. Some African states were invigorated by this era of intensified cultural exchange, creating new institutions and developing new products for export. The Ottoman Empire and the Qing Empire also responded to Western expansionism. Both empires met this challenge by implementing reform programs while adopting elements of Western technology and organization. The Qing Empire survived the period of European expansion, but a series of military defeats and a prolonged civil war severely weakened the authority of the central government. Russia lagged behind Western Europe in transforming its economy and political institutions, but military failures and internal reform pressures spurred modernization efforts, including the abolition of serfdom.

Some of the nations of Asia, Africa, and Latin America resisted foreign intrusions by reforming and strengthening their own institutions, forms of production, and military technologies. Others pushed for more radical change, adopting Western commercial policies, industrial technologies, and government institutions. But after 1870, all these states would face even more aggressive Western imperialism, which few of them would be able to resist.

	1750	1775	1800	
Americas	1754–1763 French and Indian War	U.S. Declaration of Independence **1776** •	• **1789** U.S. Constitution implemented • **1791** Slaves revolt in Haiti	**1809–1825** Wars for independence in Spanish America
Europe	• **ca. 1750** Industrial Revolution begins in Britain 1756–1763 Seven Years War		**1789–1799** French Revolution **1799–1815** Rule of Napoleon in France	**1814–1815** Congress of Vienna
Africa	1750–1800 Growing slave trade reduces population		Britain takes Cape Colony **1795** •	Sokoto Caliphate founded **1809** • Shaka founds Zulu kingdom **1818** •
Middle East		1769–1772 High point of restored Mamluk influence in Egypt	**1789–1807** Reign of Ottoman sultan Selim III • **1798** Napoleon invades Egypt Muhammad Ali founds dynasty in Egypt **1805** •	
Asia and Oceania	• **1755** Qing conquest of Turkestan East India Company rule of Bengal begins **1765** •	1769–1778 Captain Cook's exploration of Australia, New Zealand	White Lotus Rebellion in China **1796–1804**	East India Company creates Bombay presidency **1818** •

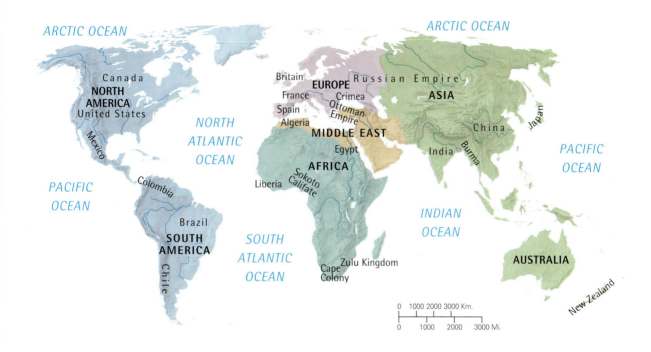

ARCTIC OCEAN

ARCTIC OCEAN

Canada

NORTH
AMERICA
United States

Mexico

NORTH
ATLANTIC
OCEAN

Colombia

Brazil

PACIFIC
OCEAN

SOUTH
AMERICA

Chile

SOUTH
ATLANTIC
OCEAN

Britain

EUROPE

France

Spain

Algeria

Liberia

AFRICA

Sokoto
Califate

Cape
Colony

Zulu Kingdom

Russian Empire

Crimea

Ottoman
Empire

MIDDLE EAST

Egypt

ASIA

China

Japan

India

Burma

PACIFIC
OCEAN

INDIAN
OCEAN

AUSTRALIA

New Zealand

0   1000 2000 3000 Km.

0   1000   2000   3000 Mi.

1825	1850	1875

• **1822** Independence of Brazil

• **1830** Revolutions of 1830   **1852–1870** Rule of Napoleon III in France

Abolition of slavery in   • **1848** Revolutions of 1848
British Empire **1834** •   Crimean War **1853–1856**   • **1861** Russia abolishes serfdom

• **1821** Republic of Liberia founded

1836–1839 Afrikaners' Great Trek

• **1826** Ottoman ruler Mahmud II dissolves Janissary corps

                                                    • **1869** Suez Canal opens

        • **1839** Ottoman ruler Abdul Mejid launches Tanzimat reforms

• **1826** East India Company annexes Assam,   **1850–1864** Taiping Rebellion in China
  northern Burma   **1839–1842** Opium War   **1857–1858** Sepoy Rebellion in India
    1829–1864 Russia completes conquest of Central Asia

19 Revolutionary Changes in the Atlantic World, 1750–1850

CHAPTER OUTLINE

Prelude to Revolution: War and the Enlightenment

The American Revolution

The French Revolution

Revolution in Haiti and Latin America

Economic and Social Liberation Movements

ENVIRONMENT AND TECHNOLOGY: Constructing the Port of Buenos Aires, Argentina

On the evening of August 14, 1791, more than two hundred slaves and black freedmen met in secret in the plantation district of northern Saint Domingue° (present-day Haiti) to set the date for an armed uprising against local slave owners. Although the delegates agreed to delay the attack for a week, violence began almost immediately. During the following decade, the Haitian rebels abolished slavery, defeated military forces from Britain and France, and gained independence.

News and rumors about revolutionary events in France that had spread through the island incited the slave community and divided the island's white population between royalists (supporters of France's King Louis XVI) and re-publicans (supporters of democracy). The free mixed-race population initially gained some political rights from the French Assembly but was then forced to rebel when the slave-owning elite reacted violently.

Among those planning the insurrection was Toussaint L'Ouverture°, a black freedman. This remarkable revolutionary organized the rebels into a potent military force, negotiated with the island's royalist and republican factions, and, with representatives of Great Britain and France, wrote his nation's first constitution. Throughout the Western Hemisphere, Toussaint became a towering symbol of resistance to oppression for slaves and a fiend in the eyes of slave owners.

Saint Domingue (san doe-MANG)

Toussaint L'Ouverture (too-SAN loo-ver-CHORE)

The Haitian slave rebellion was an important episode in the long and painful political and cultural transformation of the modern Western world. Economic expansion and the growth of trade were creating unprecedented wealth. Intellectuals were questioning the traditional place of monarchy and slavery in society. An emerging class of merchants, professionals, and manufacturers began to press for a larger political role, and economies were increasingly opened to competition.

Imperial powers resisted the loss of colonies, and monarchs and nobles struggled to retain their ancient privileges. Revolutionary steps forward were often matched by reactionary steps backward. The liberal and nationalist ideals of the eighteenth-century revolutionary movements were only imperfectly realized in Europe and the Americas in the nineteenth century.

As you read this chapter, ask yourself the following questions:

- How did imperial wars among European powers provoke revolution?

- How did revolution in one country help to incite revolution elsewhere?

- Why were the revolutions in France and Haiti more violent than the American Revolution?

- How were political revolts linked to the abolition of slavery?

PRELUDE TO REVOLUTION: WAR AND THE ENLIGHTENMENT

In large measure, the cost of wars fought among Europe's major powers over colonies and trade precipitated the revolutionary era that began in 1775 with the American Revolution. The struggle of Britain, France, and Spain for political preeminence in western Europe and overseas produced many violent conflicts during the eighteenth century. In the Seven Years War (1756–1763), known as the French and Indian War in America, Britain gained dominance in North America and in India. All parties suffered from the enormous costs of these conflicts.

However, new Western ideas and political environments now made people much more critical of any effort to extend the power of a monarch or impose new taxes, and they also raised questions about the rights of individuals. As Chapter 15 recounted, the **Enlightenment** applied the methods and questions of the Scientific Revolution to the study of human society. Some thinkers challenged long-established religious and political institutions. They argued that if scientists could understand the laws of nature, then surely similar forms of disciplined investigation might reveal laws of human nature. Others wondered whether society and government might be better regulated and more productive if guided by reason rather than by hereditary rulers and the church.

These new perspectives and the intellectual optimism that fed them were to help guide the English political philosopher John Locke (1632–1704). Locke argued in 1690 that governments were created to protect life, liberty, and property and that the people had a right to rebel when a monarch violated these natural rights. In *The Social Contract*, published in 1762, the French-Swiss intellectual Jean-Jacques Rousseau° (1712–1778) asserted that the will of the people was sacred and that the legitimacy of the monarch depended on the consent of the people. Although both men believed that government rested on the will of the people rather than divine will, Locke emphasized the importance of individual rights, and Rousseau envisioned the people acting collectively because of their shared historical experience.

The Enlightenment is commonly associated with hostility toward monarchy, but Voltaire, one of the Enlightenment's most critical intellects, believed that Europe's monarchs were likely agents

---

Jean-Jacques Rousseau (zhahn-zhock roo-SOE)

of political and economic reform, and he wrote favorably of China's Qing° emperors. Indeed, some sympathetic members of the nobility and reforming monarchs in Spain, Russia, Austria, and Prussia actively sponsored and promoted the dissemination of new ideas, providing patronage for many intellectuals. They recognized that elements of the Enlightenment critique of the *ancien régime*° buttressed their own efforts to expand royal authority at the expense of religious institutions, the nobility, and regional autonomy. Monarchs also understood that the era's passion for science and technology held the potential of fattening national treasuries and improving economic performance.

The Western Hemisphere shared in the debates of Europe. In colonial societies where political rights were even more limited than in Europe, the idea that government authority ultimately rested on the consent of the governed was potentially explosive. The efforts of ordinary men and women to resist the growth of government power and the imposition of new cultural forms provide an important political undercurrent to much of the revolutionary agitation and conflict from 1750 to 1850. But spontaneous popular uprisings gained revolutionary potential only when they coincided with ideological divisions and conflicts within the governing class itself.

THE AMERICAN REVOLUTION

After defeating the French in the French and Indian War, the British government faced two related problems in its North American colonies. One was the likelihood of armed conflict with Amerindian peoples as settlers quickly pushed west of the Appalachian Mountains and across the Ohio River. Already burdened with war debts, Britain desperately wanted to avoid additional expenditures for frontier defense. The other problem was how to get the colonists to shoulder more of the costs of imperial defense and colonial administration. Every effort to impose new taxes or prevent the settlement of the trans-Appalachian frontier provoked angry protests in the colonies. The con-

frontational and impolitic way in which a succession of weak British governments responded made the situation politically explosive.

Frontiers and Taxes

The British Proclamation of 1763, which sought to establish an effective western limit for settlement, threw into question the claims of thousands of already established farmers without effectively protecting Amerindian land. The Quebec Act of 1774 annexed disputed lands to the province of Quebec, thus denying eastern colonies the authority to distribute lands claimed as a result of original charters. Colonists saw the Quebec Act as punitive and tyrannical, and Amerindian peoples received no relief from the continuous assault on their land.

New commercial regulations that increased the cost of foreign molasses and endangered New England's profitable trade with Spanish and French Caribbean sugar colonies provoked widespread boycotts of British goods. The Stamp Act of 1765, which imposed a tax on all legal documents, newspapers, pamphlets, and other types of printed material, led to violent protest and more effective boycotts. Parliament imposed new taxes and duties soon after repealing the Stamp Act in 1766, even sending British troops to quell urban riots. Unable to control the streets of Boston, British authorities reacted by threatening traditional liberties, dissolving the colonial legislature of Massachusetts, and dispatching a warship and two regiments of soldiers to reestablish control. Support for a complete break with Britain grew when a British force fired on an angry Boston crowd on March 5, 1770, killing five civilians. This "Boston Massacre," which seemed to expose the naked force on which colonial rule rested, radicalized public opinion throughout the colonies.

Parliament attempted to calm public opinion by repealing some of the taxes and duties, then stumbled into another crisis by granting the British East India Company a monopoly for importing tea to the colonies, which raised anew the constitutional issue of Parliament's right to tax the colonies. It also offended wealthy colonial merchants, who were excluded from this profitable commerce. The crisis came to a head in the already politically overheated port of Boston when tea worth £10,000 was

---

Qing (ching)   *ancien régime* (ahn-see-EN ray-ZHEEM)

C H R O N O L O G Y

	The Americas	Europe
1750	**1756–1763** French and Indian War	**1756–1763** Seven Years War
1775	**1770** Boston Massacre	
	1776 American Declaration of Independence	
	1783 Treaty of Paris ends American Revolution	
		1789 Storming of Bastille begins French Revolution
	1791 Slaves revolt in Saint Domingue (Haiti)	
		1793–1794 Reign of Terror in France
		1795–1799 The Directory rules France
	1798 Toussaint L'Ouverture defeats British in Haiti	**1799** Napoleon overthrows the Directory
1800	**1804** Haitians defeat French invasion and declare independence	**1804** Napoleon crowns himself emperor
	1808 Portuguese royal family arrives in Brazil	
	1808–1809 Revolutions for independence begin in Spanish South America	
		1814 Napoleon abdicates; Congress of Vienna opens
1825	**1822** Brazil gains independence	**1830** Greece gains independence; revolution in France
1850	**1848** Women's Rights Convention in Seneca Falls, New York	**1848** Revolutions in France, Austria, Germany, Hungary, and Italy
	1861–1865 American Civil War	
1875	**1865** End of slavery in United States	
	1886 End of slavery in Cuba	
	1888 End of slavery in Brazil	

The Tarring and Feathering of a British Official, 1774
This illustration from a British periodical shows the unfortunate John Malcomb, commissioner of customs at Boston. By the mid-1770s British periodicals were focusing public opinion on mob violence and the breakdown of public order in the colonies. British critics of colonial political protests viewed the demand for liberty as little more than an excuse for mob violence. (The Granger Collection, New York)

assumed the powers of government, creating a currency and organizing an army. **George Washington** (1732–1799), a Virginia planter who had served in the French and Indian War, was named commander. On July 4, 1776, Congress approved the Declaration of Independence, the document that proved to be the most enduring statement of the revolutionary era's ideology:

> We hold these truths to be self evident: That all men are created equal; that they are endowed by their creator with certain unalienable rights; that among these are life, liberty and the pursuit of happiness; that, to secure these rights, governments are instituted among men, deriving their just powers from the consent of the governed.

This affirmation of popular sovereignty and individual rights influenced the language of revolution and popular protest around the world.

To shore up British authority, Great Britain sent more than 400 ships, 50,000 soldiers, and 30,000 German mercenaries. But this military commitment proved futile. Although British forces won most of the battles, Washington slowly built a competent Continental army and civilian support networks that provided supplies and financial resources. In the final decisive battle, fought at Yorktown, Virginia, an American army, supported by French soldiers, besieged a British army led by General Charles Cornwallis. With escape cut off by a French fleet, Cornwallis surrendered to Washington as the British military band played "The World Turned Upside-Down."

dumped into the harbor by protesters disguised as Amerindians.

The Course of the Revolution

As the crisis mounted, patriots created new governing bodies, effectively deposed many British governors and other officials, passed laws, appointed judges, and even took control of colonial militias. Simultaneously, radical leaders organized crowds to intimidate loyalists—people who were pro-British—and to enforce the boycott of British goods.

Events were propelling the colonies toward revolution. Elected representatives, meeting in Philadelphia as the Continental Congress in 1775,

New Republican Institutions

Ignoring the British example of an unwritten constitution, representatives in each of the newly independent states drafted formal charters and submitted the results to voters for ratification. Europeans were fascinated by these written constitutions and by their formal ratification by the people. Here was the social contract of Locke and Rousseau made manifest. The state constitutions also placed severe limits on executive authority but granted legislatures greater powers than in colonial times. Many states also inserted in their constitutions a bill of rights to provide further protection against government tyranny.

An effective constitution for the new national government was developed more slowly and hesitantly. The Articles of Confederation—the first constitution of the United States—were not accepted by all the states until 1781. With the coming of peace in 1783, there was an effort to fashion a new constitution.

Debate at the **Constitutional Convention,** which began meeting in May 1787, focused on several issues: representation, electoral procedures, executive powers, and the relationship between the federal government and the states. The final compromise provided for a two-house legislature: the lower house (the House of Representatives) to be elected directly by voters and the upper house (the Senate) to be elected by state legislatures. The chief executive—the president—was to be elected indirectly by "electors" selected by ballot in the states (each state had a number of electors equal to the number of its representatives and senators).

Although the U.S. Constitution created the most democratic government of the era, only a minority of the adult population was given full rights. Southern leaders were able to protect the institution of slavery by counting three-fifths of the slave population in the calculations that determined their states' congressional representatives. Although women had led prewar boycotts and had organized relief and charitable organizations during the war, they were denied political rights in the new republic.

THE FRENCH REVOLUTION

The French Revolution confronted the entrenched privileges of an established church, monarchy, and aristocracy more directly than the American Revolution did. It also expanded mass participation in political life and radicalized the democratic tradition. But in the end, the passions unleashed in France by revolutionary events could not be sustained.

French Society and Fiscal Crisis

French society was divided into three groups. The clergy, the First Estate, numbered about 130,000 in a nation of 28 million. The Catholic Church owned about 10 percent of the nation's land and extracted substantial amounts of wealth from the economy in the form of tithes and ecclesiastical fees. Despite its substantial wealth, the church was exempted from nearly all taxes.

The 300,000 members of the nobility, the Second Estate, controlled about 30 percent of the land and retained ancient rights on much of the rest. Nobles held the vast majority of high administrative, judicial, military, and church positions. Though traditionally barred from some types of commercial activity, nobles were important participants in wholesale trade, banking, manufacturing, and mining.

The Third Estate included everyone else. There were three times as many members of the bourgeoisie° in 1774, when Louis XVI took the throne, as there had been in 1715, at the end of Louis XIV's reign. Peasants accounted for 80 percent of the French population. They owned some property and lived decently when crops were good and prices stable. By 1780, poor harvests had decreased their incomes.

The nation's poor were a large, growing, and troublesome sector. Urban streets swarmed with beggars and prostitutes. Unable to afford decent housing, obtain steady employment, or protect their children, the poor periodically erupted in violent protest and rage. In the countryside, violence was often the reaction to increased dues and fees. In towns and cities, an increase in the price of bread often provided the spark.

These explosive episodes, however, were not revolutionary in character. The remedies sought were conventional and immediate rather than structural and long term. That was to change when the Crown tried to solve its fiscal crisis by imposing new taxes on the nobility and on other groups that in the past had enjoyed exemptions. But this effort failed in the face of widespread protest and the refusal of the Parlement of Paris, a court of appeal that heard appeals from local courts throughout France, to register the new tax. In 1768, frustrated authorities exiled the members of that Parlement and pushed through a series of unpopular fiscal measures. Despite the worsening fiscal crisis, the

bourgeoisie (boor-zwah-ZEE)

French took on the heavy burden of supporting the American Revolution, delaying collapse by borrowing enormous sums. By the end of the war with Britain, more than half of France's national budget was required to service the debt alone. In 1787, the desperate king called an Assembly of Notables to approve a radical and comprehensive reform of the economy and fiscal policy. Although the members of this assembly were selected by the king's advisers from the high nobility, the judiciary, and the clergy, they proved unwilling to act as a rubber stamp for the proposed reforms or new taxes. Instead, these representatives of France's most privileged classes sought to protect their interests by questioning the competence of the king and his ministers to supervise the nation's affairs, thus creating the conditions for political revolution.

Protest Turns to Revolution

Unable to extract needed tax concessions from the notables, King Louis XVI was forced to call the **Estates General,** the French national legislature, which had not met since 1614. Traditionally, the three estates met separately, and a positive vote by two of the three was required for action. Tradition, however, was quickly overturned when the Third Estate refused to conduct business until the king ordered the other two estates to sit with it in a single body. During a six-week period of stalemate, many parish priests deserted the First Estate to meet with them.

When this expanded Third Estate declared itself the **National Assembly,** the king and his advisers recognized that the reformers intended to force them to accept a constitutional monarchy. Louis's agenda for fiscal reform was being displaced by the central ideas of the era: the people were sovereign, and the legitimacy of political institutions and individual rulers ultimately depended on their carrying out the people's will. Louis prepared for a confrontation with the National Assembly by moving military forces to Versailles. But before he could act, the people of Paris intervened.

A succession of bad harvests beginning in 1785 had propelled bread prices upward throughout France and provoked an economic depression. By the time the Estates General met, nearly a third of the Parisian work force was unemployed. Hunger and anger marched hand in hand through working-class neighborhoods.

When the people of Paris heard that the king was massing troops to arrest their representatives, crowds of common people began to seize arms and mobilize. On July 14, 1789, a crowd searching for military supplies attacked the Bastille°, a medieval fortress used as a prison. The futile defense of the Bastille cost ninety-eight lives before its garrison surrendered. Enraged, the attackers hacked the commander to death and then paraded through the city with his head and that of Paris's chief magistrate stuck on pikes.

These events coincided with uprisings in the country. Peasants sacked manor houses and destroyed documents that recorded their traditional obligations. They refused to pay taxes and dues to landowners and seized common lands. Forced to recognize the fury raging through rural areas, the National Assembly voted to end traditional obligations and to reform the tax system. Having forced acceptance of their narrow agenda, the peasants ceased their revolt.

These popular uprisings strengthened the hand of the National Assembly in its dealings with the king. One manifestation of this altered relationship was passage of the **Declaration of the Rights of Man.** The French declaration, however, was more sweeping in its language than the American Declaration of Independence. Among the enumerated natural rights were "liberty, property, security, and resistance to oppression." The Declaration of the Rights of Man also guaranteed free expression of ideas, equality before the law, and representative government.

While delegates debated political issues in Versailles, the economic crisis worsened in Paris. Because the working women of Paris faced high food prices every day as they struggled to feed their families, their anger had a hard edge. On October 5, market women organized a crowd of thousands to march the 12 miles (19 kilometers) to Versailles°. Once there, they forced their way into the National Assembly to demand action from the frightened representatives: "The point is that we want bread." The crowd then entered the royal apartments, killed some of the king's guards, and searched for Queen

---

Bastille (bass-TEEL)   **Versailles** (vuhr-SIGH)

Parisians Storm the Bastille   This depiction of the storming of the Bastille on July 14, 1789, was painted by an artist who witnessed the epochal event, still celebrated by the French as a national holiday.   (Photos12.com-ARJ)

Marie Antoinette°, whom they loathed as a symbol of extravagance. Eventually, the crowd demanded that the royal family return to Paris. Preceded by the heads of two aristocrats carried on pikes and hauling away the palace's supply of flour, the triumphant crowd escorted the royal family to Paris.

The National Assembly achieved a radically restructured French society in the next two years. It passed a new constitution that dramatically limited monarchical power and abolished the nobility as a hereditary class. Economic reforms swept away monopolies and trade barriers within France. The Legislative Assembly created by the new constitution seized church lands to use as collateral for a new paper currency, and priests, who were to be

elected, were put on the state payroll. When the government tried to force priests to take a loyalty oath, however, many Catholics joined a growing counterrevolutionary movement.

At first, many European monarchs had welcomed the weakening of the French king, but by 1791 Austria and Prussia threatened to intervene in support of the monarchy. The Legislative Assembly responded by declaring war. Although the war went badly at first for French forces, people across France responded patriotically to foreign invasions, forming huge new volunteer armies and mobilizing national resources to meet the challenge. By the end of 1792, French armies had gained the upper hand everywhere.

In this period of national crisis and foreign threat, the French Revolution entered its most

Antoinette (ann-twah-NET)

radical phase. A failed effort by the king and queen to escape from Paris and find foreign allies cost the king any remaining popular support. As foreign armies crossed into France, his behavior was increasingly viewed as treasonous. In August 1792, the Legislative Assembly suspended the king, ordered his imprisonment, and called for the formation of a new National Convention to be elected by the vote of all men. Swept along by popular passion, the newly elected National Convention convicted Louis XVI of treason, sentencing him to death and proclaiming France a republic.

The guillotine ended the king's life in January 1793. Invented in the spirit of the era as a more humane way to execute the condemned, this machine was to become the bloody symbol of the revolution. During the period of repression called the Reign of Terror (1793–1794), approximately 40,000 people were executed or died in prison. This radical phase ended in July 1794 when the Terror's leaders were executed by guillotine.

Reaction and Dictatorship

Purged of the radicals, the National Convention—the new legislative assembly of the French republic—began to undo the radical reforms. It removed many of the emergency economic controls that had been holding down prices and protecting the working class. When the Paris working class rose in protest in 1795, the Convention approved the use of overwhelming military force. The Convention also permitted the Catholic Church to regain much of its former influence, but it would not return the church's confiscated wealth. Finally, it ratified a more conservative constitution, which protected property, established a voting process that reduced the power of the masses, and created a new executive authority, the Directory. Once installed in power, however, the Directory proved unable to end the foreign wars or solve domestic economic problems.

After losing the election of 1797, the Directory suspended the results. The republican phase of the Revolution was clearly dead. Legitimacy was now based on coercive power rather than on elections. Two years later, **Napoleon Bonaparte** (1769–1821), a brilliant young general in the French army, seized

power. Just as the American and French Revolutions had been the start of the modern democratic tradition, the military intervention that brought Napoleon to power in 1799 marked the advent of another modern form of government: popular authoritarianism.

In contrast to the National Convention, Napoleon proved capable of realizing France's dream of dominating Europe and providing effective protection for persons and property at home. Negotiations with the Catholic Church led to the Concordat of 1801, which gave French Catholics the right to practice their religion freely. Napoleon's Civil Code of 1804 asserted two basic principles inherited from the moderate first stage of the French Revolution: equality in law and protection of property. Even some members of the nobility became supporters after Napoleon declared himself emperor and France an empire in 1804.

While providing personal security, the Napoleonic system denied or restricted many individual rights. Women were denied basic political rights. Free speech and free expression were limited. Criticism of the government, viewed as subversive, was proscribed, and most opposition newspapers disappeared.

Ultimately, the Napoleonic system depended on the success of French arms and French diplomacy (see Map 19.1). From Napoleon's assumption of power until his fall, no single European state could defeat the French military. Austria and Prussia were forced to become allies of France. Only Britain, protected by its powerful navy, remained able to thwart Napoleon's plans to dominate Europe. In June 1812, Napoleon made the fateful decision to invade Russia with the largest army ever assembled in Europe, approximately 600,000 men. Five weeks after occupying Moscow, he was forced to retreat. The brutal Russian winter and attacks by Russian forces destroyed his army. A broken and battered fragment of 30,000 men returned home to France.

After the debacle in Russia, Austria and Prussia deserted Napoleon and entered an alliance with Britain and Russia. Unable to defend Paris, Napoleon was forced to abdicate the French throne in April 1814. The allies exiled Napoleon to the island of Elba off the coast of Italy and restored the French monarchy.

Retrenchment, Reform, and Revolution

The French Revolution and Napoleon's imperial ambitions had threatened the survival of the European old order. Ancient monarchies had been overturned and long-established political institutions tossed aside. The very existence of the nobility and church had been put at risk. Under the leadership of the Austrian foreign minister, Prince Klemens von Metternich° (1773–1859), Britain, Russia, Austria, and Prussia, along with representatives of other nations, worked together in Vienna to create a comprehensive peace settlement that they hoped would safeguard the conservative order. Because the participants in the **Congress of Vienna** believed that a strong and stable France was the best guarantee of future peace, the French monarchy was reestablished. Metternich sought to offset French strength with a balance of power.

Despite the power of the conservative monarchs, popular support for national self-determination and democratic reform grew throughout Europe. In 1821, Greek patriots launched a movement for independence from Ottoman control. In 1830, Russia, France, and Great Britain forced the Ottoman Empire to recognize Greek independence. That same year, the people of Paris rose up and forced King Charles X to abdicate. His successor, Louis Philippe° (r. 1830–1848), reestablished the constitution and extended voting privileges.

Despite limited political reform, conservatives continued to hold the upper hand in Europe. Finally, in 1848, the desire for democratic reform and national self-determination and the frustrations of urban workers led to upheavals across Europe. The **Revolutions of 1848** began in Paris, where members of the middle class and workers united to overthrow the regime of Louis Philippe and create the Second French Republic. Adult men were given voting rights, slavery was abolished in French colonies, the death penalty was ended, and a ten-hour workday was legislated for Paris. But Parisian workers' demand for programs to reduce unemployment and lower prices provoked conflicts with the middle class, which wanted to protect property rights. Desiring the reestablishment of order, the French elected Louis Napoleon, nephew of the former emperor, president in December 1848. Three years later, he overturned the constitution as a result of popular plebiscite and, after ruling briefly as dictator, became Emperor Napoleon III. He remained in power until 1871.

Despite their heroism on the barricades of Vienna, Rome, and Berlin, the revolutionaries of 1848 also failed to gain either their nationalist or their republican objectives. Metternich, the symbol of reaction, fled Vienna in disguise, but little lasting change occurred. Monarchs retained the support not only of aristocrats but also of professional militaries, largely recruited from among peasants who had little sympathy for urban workers.

REVOLUTION IN HAITI AND LATIN AMERICA

In the Americas, the revolutionary ideology of the American and French Revolutions was spreading and taking hold. On the island of Hispaniola, a revolution ended slavery and French rule in Saint Domingue. The same economic and political forces that had undermined British rule in the colonies that became the United States were present in Spanish America and Brazil.

The Haitian Revolution

The French colony of Saint Domingue produced two-thirds of France's tropical imports and generated nearly one-third of all French foreign trade. This impressive wealth depended on a brutal slave regime. Saint Domingue's harsh punishments and high mortality were notorious throughout the Caribbean.

In 1789, when news of the calling of France's Estates General arrived on the island, wealthy white planters sent a delegation to Paris charged with seeking more home rule and greater economic freedom. The **_gens de couleur_**° also sent representatives. Mostly small planters or urban merchants, these free mixed-race delegates focused on ending

---

Metternich (MET-uhr-nik)   **Louis Philippe** (loo-EE fee-LEEP)

gens de couleur (zhahn deh koo-LUHR)

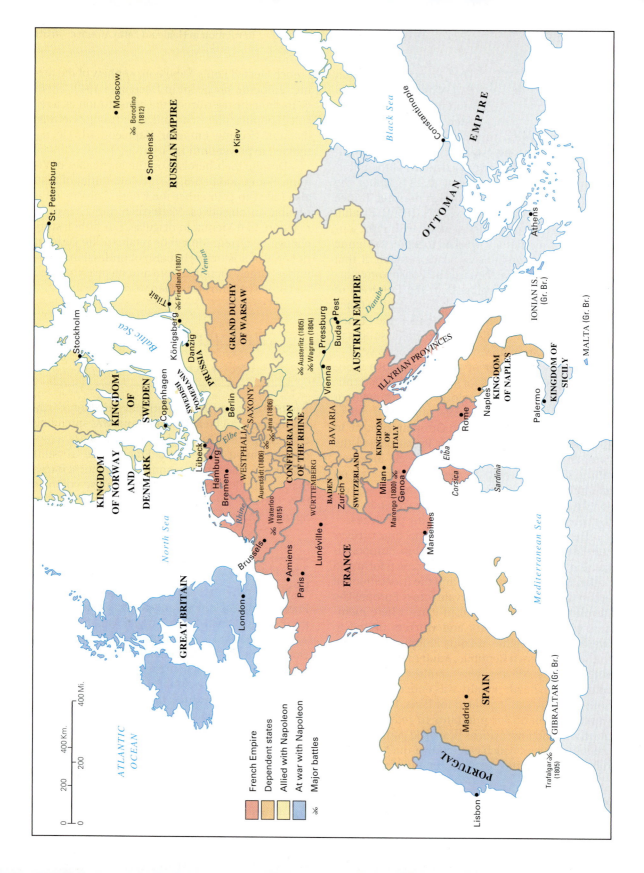

RUSSIAN EMPIRE

Moscow

Borodino (1812)

Smolensk

Kiev

St. Petersburg

Black Sea

Constantinople

OTTOMAN EMPIRE

Athens

IONIAN IS. (Gr. Br.)

MALTA (Gr. Br.)

Stockholm

Baltic Sea

Neman

Friedland (1807)

Tilsit

Königsberg

Danzig

GRAND DUCHY OF WARSAW

Pressburg

Buda

Pest

Austerlitz (1805)

Wagram (1809)

Vienna

Danube

AUSTRIAN EMPIRE

ILLYRIAN PROVINCES

KINGDOM OF NAPLES

KINGDOM OF SICILY

KINGDOM OF NORWAY AND DENMARK

KINGDOM OF SWEDEN

SWEDISH POMERANIA

PRUSSIA

Copenhagen

Berlin

WESTPHALIA

SAXONY

CONFEDERATION OF THE RHINE

BAVARIA

Jena (1806)

Elbe

Lübeck

Hamburg

Bremen

Auerstädt (1806)

Rhine

WÜRTTEMBERG

BADEN

SWITZERLAND

KINGDOM OF ITALY

Milan

Marengo (1800)

Genoa

Rome

Naples

Palermo

Elba

Corsica

Sardinia

North Sea

GREAT BRITAIN

London

Brussels

Waterloo (1815)

Amiens

Paris

Lunéville

FRANCE

Zurich

Marseilles

Mediterranean Sea

SPAIN

Madrid

PORTUGAL

Lisbon

GIBRALTAR (Gr. Br.)

Trafalgar (1805)

ATLANTIC OCEAN

400 Mi.

400 Km.

200

200

0

0

French Empire

Dependent states

Allied with Napoleon

At war with Napoleon

Major battles

Map 19.1   Napoleon's Europe, 1810   By 1810 Great Britain was the only remaining European power at war with Napoleon. Because of the loss of the French fleet at the Battle of Trafalgar in 1805, Napoleon was unable to threaten Britain with invasion, and Britain was able to actively assist the resistance movements in Spain and Portugal, thereby helping weaken French power.

race discrimination and political inequality. They did not seek freedom for slaves, because the most prosperous gens de couleur were slave owners themselves.

The political turmoil in France weakened colonial authority, permitting rich planters, poor whites, gens de couleur, and slaves to pursue their narrow interests, in an increasingly bitter and confrontational struggle. By 1791, whites and the gens de couleur were engaged in open warfare. This breach between the two groups of slave owners gave the slaves an opening. Their rebellion began on the plantations of the north and spread throughout the colony. Plantations were destroyed, masters and overseers killed, and crops burned.

The rebellious slaves eventually gained the upper hand under the military leadership of **Toussaint L'Ouverture,** a former domestic slave. Politically strengthened in 1794 when the radical National Convention in Paris abolished slavery in all French possessions, Toussaint overcame his rivals in Saint Domingue, defeated a British expeditionary force in 1798, and then led an invasion of neighboring Santo Domingo, freeing the slaves there. Toussaint continued to assert his loyalty to France but gave the French government no effective role in local affairs.

In 1802, Napoleon sent a large military force to Saint Domingue to reestablish both French authority and slavery. At first, the French forces were successful. Toussaint was captured and sent to France, where he died in prison. Eventually, however, French losses to yellow fever and the resistance of the revolutionaries turned the tide. Few slave women had taken up arms during the early stages of the Haitian Revolution, but now they joined the armed resistance. In 1804, the free republic of Haiti joined the United States as the second independent nation in the Western Hemisphere. But independence and emancipation were achieved at a terrible price. Tens of thousands had died, and the economy was destroyed.

Latin American Revolutions

The great works of the Enlightenment as well as revolutionary documents like the Declaration of Independence and the Declaration of the Rights of Man circulated widely in Latin America. But it was Napoleon's decision to invade Portugal (1807) and Spain (1808), not revolutionary ideas, that ignited Latin America's struggle for independence.

In 1808, the royal family of Portugal fled to Brazil and maintained court there for over a decade. In Spain, in contrast, Napoleon forced King Ferdinand VII to abdicate and placed his own brother, Joseph Bonaparte, on the throne. When Spanish patriots fighting against the French created a new political body, the Junta° Central, and claimed the right to exercise the king's powers over Spain's colonies, a vocal minority of powerful colonists objected. In late 1808 and 1809, popular movements overthrew Spanish colonial officials in Venezuela, Mexico, and Bolivia and created local juntas. In each case, Spanish officials' harsh repression gave rise to a greater sense of a separate American nationality. By 1810, Spanish colonial authorities were facing a new round of revolutions more clearly focused on the achievement of independence.

In Caracas (the capital city of modern Venezuela), a revolutionary junta led by creoles (colonial-born whites) declared independence in 1811. Its leaders were large landowners who espoused popular sovereignty and representative democracy, defended slavery, and opposed full citizenship for the black and mixed-race majority. The junta's narrow agenda spurred loyalists in the colonial administration and church hierarchy to rally thousands of free blacks and slaves to defend the Spanish Empire. **Simón Bolívar°** (1783–1830) became the preeminent leader of the independence movement in Spanish South America.

Between 1813 and 1817, military advantage

Junta (HUN-tah)   **Simón Bolívar** (see-MOAN bow-LEE-varh)

Haiti's Former Slaves Defend Their Freedom In this representation, a veteran army sent by Napoleon to reassert French control in Haiti battles with Haitian forces in a tropical forest. The combination of Haitian resistance and yellow fever defeated the French invasion. (Bettmann/Corbis)

shifted back and forth between the patriots and loyalists, but by 1820, momentum swung irreversibly to the patriots. After liberating present-day Venezuela, Colombia, Ecuador, Peru, and Bolivia, Bolívar's army defeated the last Spanish armies in 1824. But Bolívar's attempt to draw the former Spanish colonies into a formal confederation failed (see Map 19.2).

Buenos Aires (the capital city of modern Argentina) was the second important center of revolutionary activity in Spanish South America (see Environment and Technology: Constructing the Port of Buenos Aires, Argentina). In the south, a coalition of militia commanders, merchants, and ranchers declared independence as the United Provinces of the Río de la Plata in 1816. Patriot leaders in Buenos Aires at first sought to retain control over the old Viceroyalty of Río de la Plata, but a separatist movement defeated these ambitions. A mixed force of Chileans and Argentines, led by José de San

Martín° (1778–1850), liberated Chile in 1820. Simón Bolívar overcame final Spanish resistance in Peru in 1824.

The arrival of the Portuguese royal family in Brazil in 1808 had helped to maintain the loyalty of the colonial elite and to stimulate the local economy. But when King John VI returned to Portugal in 1821, Brazilians began to reevaluate Brazil's relationship with Portugal and to talk openly of independence.

Unwilling to return to Portugal and committed to maintaining his family's hold on Brazil, King John's son Pedro aligned himself with the rising tide of independence sentiment. In 1822, he declared Brazilian independence. Unlike its neighbors, which became constitutional republics, Brazil gained independence as a constitutional monarchy with Pedro I, heir to the throne of Portugal, as

José de San Martín (hoe-SAY deh san mar-TEEN)

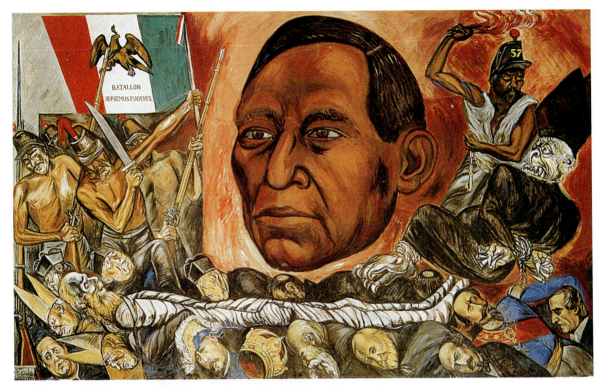

The Revolutionary Tradition in Mexico   This 1948 mural by José Clemente Orozco commemorates the Mexican struggle to restore its republican tradition after France intervened—using collection of overdue debts as a pretext—and enthroned the Austrian archduke Maximilian as emperor of Mexico. Maximilian reigned from 1864 to 1867, when he was overthrown and executed by a popular movement led by Benito Juarez, shown in the center of the painting. Orozco depicts Maximilian's bandage-swathed body being borne by the Catholic clergy, military commanders, and foreign interlopers who constituted the conservative opposition to Juarez's republicanism.   (Muséo Nacional de Historia/CENIDIAP-INBA)

emperor. The monarchy lasted until 1889, when it was overthrown by republicans.

Mexico

In 1810, Mexico was Spain's richest and most populous colony. But the sharp distinctions among its creole, native, and Spanish populations made it ripe for revolution. The first stage of the revolution against Spain occurred in central Mexico, where wealthy ranchers and farmers had aggressively forced many Amerindian communities from their traditional agricultural lands. By the time news of Napoleon's invasion of Spain reached the region,

crop failures and epidemics had further afflicted the poor.

On September 16, 1810, **Miguel Hidalgo y Costilla°,** parish priest of the small town of Dolores, rang the church bells, attracting thousands. In a fiery speech, he urged the crowd to rise up against the oppression of Spanish officials. Tens of thousands of the rural and urban poor joined his movement. They lacked military discipline and adequate weapons but knew who their oppressors were. At first sympathetic to Hidalgo's objectives, wealthy

---

Miguel Hidalgo y Costilla (mee-GEHL ee-DAHL-go ee cos-TEA-ah)

Map 19.2   **Latin America by 1830**   By 1830 patriot forces had overturned the Spanish and Portuguese Empires of the Western Hemisphere. Regional conflicts, local wars, and foreign interventions challenged the survival of many of these new nations following independence.

Mexicans eventually turned against Hidalgo, who was captured, tried, and executed in 1811.

Although insurgents continued to wage war against Spanish forces, colonial rule seemed secure in 1820. However, news of the military revolt in Spain unsettled the conservative groups and church officials who had defended Spanish rule against Hidalgo and José Morelos, who continued the revolution after Hidalgo's execution. In 1821, Colonel Agustín de Iturbide° and other loyalist commanders forged an alliance with remaining insurgents and declared Mexico's independence. The conservative origins of Mexico's transition to independence were highlighted by the decision to create a monarchial form of government and crown Iturbide as emperor. In early 1823, however, the army overthrew Iturbide and Mexico became a republic.

ECONOMIC AND SOCIAL LIBERATION MOVEMENTS

During the nineteenth century, the newly independent nations of the Western Hemisphere struggled to realize the Enlightenment ideals of freedom and individual liberty. The persistence of slavery and women's inequality raised troubling questions about these ideals. By century's end, reform movements in many of the hemisphere's nations had made significant progress, but much remained to be done.

The Abolition of Slavery

In both the United States and Latin America, strong antislavery sentiments were expressed during the struggles for independence. In nearly all the new nations of the Western Hemisphere, revolutionary leaders asserted universal ideals of freedom and citizenship that contrasted sharply with the reality of slavery. Men and women who wanted to outlaw slavery were called **abolitionists.** Despite their efforts, slavery survived in much of the hemisphere until the 1850s. In regions where the export of plantation products was most important—such as the United States, Brazil, and Cuba—the abolition of slavery was achieved with great difficulty.

In the United States, some northern states had abolished slavery after the Revolution, and Congress banned the importation of new slaves in 1808. But this progress was stalled by the profitable expansion of cotton agriculture after the War of 1812. In Spanish America, tens of thousands of slaves gained freedom by joining revolutionary armies during the wars for independence. After independence, most Spanish American republics prohibited the slave trade. Counteracting that trend was the growing international demand for sugar and coffee, products traditionally produced on plantations by slaves. As prices rose for plantation products in the first half of the nineteenth century, Brazil and Cuba (a Spanish colony until 1899) increased their imports of slaves.

During the long struggle to end slavery in the United States, American abolitionists argued that slavery offended both morality and the universal rights asserted in the Declaration of Independence. Two groups denied full rights of citizenship under the Constitution, women and free African-Americans, played important roles in the abolition of slavery. Women served on the executive committee of the American Anti-Slavery Society and produced some of the most effective propaganda against slavery. Many women abolitionists advocated female suffrage as well. Frederick Douglass, a former slave, became one of the most effective abolitionist speakers and writers. More radical black leaders saw civil war or slave insurrection as necessary for ending slavery.

During the Civil War, pressure for emancipation rose as tens of thousands of black freemen and escaped slaves joined the Union army. Hundreds of thousands of other slaves fled their masters' plantations and farms for the protection of advancing northern armies. In 1863, in the midst of

---

Agustín de Iturbide (ah-goos-TEEN deh ee-tur-BEE-deh)

Constructing the Port of Buenos Aires, Argentina

Located on the banks of the Río de la Plata, Buenos Aires had been a major commercial center and port since the late eighteenth century. But Buenos Aires was not a natural harbor. Because of the shallowness of the river, the largest oceangoing ships were forced to anchor hundreds of yards offshore while goods and passengers were unloaded by small boats or by specially built ox carts with huge wheels. Smaller vessels docked at a river port to the city's south.

By the 1880s the Argentine economy was being transformed by the growing demands of European consumers for meat and grain. As exports surged and land values exploded, the wages of Argentines rose, and the nation became a favored destination for European immigrants. Argentina was becoming the wealthiest nation in Latin America.

The nation's political and economic elites decided that future growth required the modernization and expansion of port facilities. Two competing plans were debated. The first emphasized the incremental expansion and dredging of the river port. This plan was supported by local engineers and political groups suspicious of foreign economic interests. The second, and ultimately successful, plan involved dredging a port and deep-water channel from the low mud flats near the city center. This plan was more expensive and relied on British engineering firms, British banks, and British technology. It was supported by Argentine economic interests most closely tied to the European export trade and by national political leaders who believed progress and prosperity required the imitation of European models. Already the British were the nation's primary creditors as well as leaders in the development of the nation's railroads, streetcar lines, and gas works in Buenos Aires.

The photograph shows the construction of Puerto Madero, the new port of Buenos Aires, in the 1890s. The work force was almost entirely recruited from recent immigrants. The engineering staff was dominated by British experts. Most of the profits were culled by the local elite through real estate deals and commissions associated with construction. Puerto Madero, named after its local promoter, was opened in stages beginning in 1890. Cost overruns and corruption

the Civil War, President Lincoln began the abolition of slavery by issuing the Emancipation Proclamation, which ended slavery in rebel states not occupied by the Union army. Final abolition was accomplished in 1865, by the Thirteenth Amendment to the Constitution.

After Britain ended its participation in the slave trade in 1807, it negotiated treaties with Spain, Brazil, and other importers of slaves to eliminate the slave trade to the Americas. But enforcement proved difficult. For example, Brazil, despite its treaty of 1830, illegally imported over a half-million more African slaves before the British navy finally forced compliance in the 1850s. The Brazilian parliament passed legislation abolishing slavery in 1888.

Slavery lasted longest in Cuba. Despite strong British pressure, the Spanish colony continued to import large numbers of African slaves until the 1860s. More important, however, was the growth of support for abolition in these colonies. Both Cuba and Puerto Rico had larger white and free colored populations than did the Caribbean colonies of Britain and France. As a result, there was less fear in Cuba and Puerto Rico that abolition would lead to the political ascendancy of former slaves (as had occurred in Haiti). In Puerto Rico, where slaves numbered approximately thirty thousand, local reformers sought and gained the abolition of slavery in 1873. Eventually, during a decade-long war to defeat forces seeking the independence of Cuba, the Spanish government moved

Excavation of Port of Buenos Aires, Argentina Relying on foreign capital and engineering, the government of Argentina improved the port to facilitate the nation's rapidly expanding export economy. (Courtesy, Hack Hoffenburg, South American Resources)

lion tons. But the project was poorly designed, and "improvements" were still being made in the 1920s.

Why had the government of Argentina chosen the costliest and most difficult design? Argentine politicians were seduced by the idea of modernity; they chose the most complex and technologically sophisticated solution to the port problem. And they believed that British engineering and British capital were guarantees of modernity. The new port facilities did facilitate a boom in exports and imports, and the huge public works budget did provide incomes for thousands of laborers. However, debts, design flaws, and the increased influence of foreign capital in Argentina left a legacy of problems that Argentina would be forced to

stretched out completion to 1898. By 1910 arrivals and departures reached thirty thousand ships and 18 million tons.

deal with in the future. (See the discussion of Juan Perón in Chapter 27.)

Equal Rights for Women and Blacks

The abolition of slavery in the Western Hemisphere did not end racial discrimination or provide full political rights for every citizen. Not only blacks but also women suffered political and economic discrimination during the nineteenth century.

In 1848, a group of women angered by their exclusion from an international antislavery meeting issued a call for a meeting to discuss women's rights. The **Women's Rights Convention** at Seneca Falls, New York, issued a statement that said in part, "We hold these truths to be self-evident: that all men and women are equal." While moderates focused on the issues of greater economic independence and full legal rights, increasing numbers of women demanded the right to vote. Others lobbied to provide better conditions for women working outside the home, especially in textile factories.

Progress toward equality between men and women was equally slow in Canada and Latin America. Canada's first women doctors received their training in the United States because no woman was able to receive a medical degree in Canada until 1895. Argentina and Uruguay were among the first Latin American nations to provide public education for women. Both nations introduced coeducation in the 1870s. Chilean women

477

gained access to some careers in medicine and law in the 1870s. In Brazil, where many women were active in the abolitionist movement, four women graduated in medicine by 1882. Throughout the hemisphere, more rapid progress was achieved in lower-status careers that threatened male economic power less directly, and by the end of the century, women dominated elementary school teaching throughout the Western Hemisphere.

From Canada to Argentina and Chile, the majority of working-class women had no direct involvement in these reform movements, but in their daily lives, they succeeded in transforming gender relations. By the end of the nineteenth century, large numbers of poor women worked outside the home on farms, in markets, and, increasingly, in factories.

Throughout the hemisphere, there was little progress toward eliminating racial discrimination. Blacks were denied the vote throughout the southern United States and subjected to the indignity of segregation. Racial discrimination against men and women of African descent was also common in Latin America, though seldom spelled out in legal codes. Latin Americans tended to view racial identity across a continuum of physical characteristics rather than in the narrow terms of black and white that defined race relations in the United States.

CONCLUSION

The revolutions of the late eighteenth century hastened the transformation of Western society. Royal governments attempting to impose new taxes to pay war debts collided with ideas of elections and representative institutions. French officers who took part in the American Revolution helped ignite the French Revolution. Black freemen from Haiti traveled to France to seek their rights and returned to spread revolutionary passions. Napoleon's invasion of Portugal and Spain then helped initiate the movement toward independence in Latin America. The promises of universal citizenship were only partially achieved.

Each revolution had its own character. The revolutions in France and Haiti were more violent and destructive than the mainland American revo-

lutions. In many places, monarchy, multinational empires, and the established church contested with liberal and nationalist sentiments well into the nineteenth century. Only a minority gained full political rights. Democratic institutions often failed, and slavery endured in the Americas past the mid-1800s.

■ Key Terms

Enlightenment

George Washington

Constitutional Convention

Estates General

National Assembly

Declaration of the Rights of Man

Napoleon Bonaparte

Congress of Vienna

Revolutions of 1848

gens de couleur

Toussaint L'Ouverture

Simón Bolívar

Miguel Hidalgo y Costilla

abolitionists

Women's Rights Convention

■ Suggested Reading

Eric Hobsbawm's *The Age of Revolution* (1962) provides a clear analysis of the class issues that appeared during this era. The American Revolution has received a great amount of attention from scholars. Colin Bonwick, *The American Revolution* (1991), and Edward Countryman, *The American Revolution* (1985), provide excellent introductions.

François Furet, *Interpreting the French Revolution* (1981), breaks with interpretations that emphasize class and ideological interpretations. Georges Lefebve, *The Coming of the French Revolution*, trans. R. R. Palmer (1947), presents the classic class-based analysis. George Rudé, *The Crowd in History: Popular Disturbances in France and England* (1981), remains the best introduction to the role of mass protest in the period. The recently published *The Women of Paris and Their French Revolution* (1998) by Dominique Godineau; Felix Markham, *Napoleon* (1963); and Robert B. Holtman, *The Napoleonic Revolution* (1967), provide reliable summaries of the period. For a brief survey of the revolutions of 1830 and 1848, see Arthur J. May, *The Age of Metternich, 1814–48*, rev. ed. (1963).

The classic study of the Haitian Revolution is C. L. R. James, *The Black Jacobins*, 2d ed. (1963). For the independence era in Latin America, see John Lynch, *The Spanish American Revolutions, 1808–1826*, 2d ed. (1986); Jay Kinsbruner, *Independence in Spanish America* (1994); and A. J. R. Russell-Wood, ed., *From Colony to Nation: Essays on the Independence of Brazil* (1976).

On the issue of slavery, see David Brion Davis, *Slavery and Human Progress* (1984); George M. Frederickson, *The Black Image in the White Mind: The Debate on Afro-American Character and Destiny, 1817–1914* (1971); and Benjamin Quarles, *Black Abolitionists* (1969). For abolition in Latin America and the Caribbean, see Rebecca Scott, *Slave Emancipation in Cuba: The Transition to Free Labor, 1860–1899* (1985); Robert Conrad, *The Destruction of Brazilian Slavery, 1850–1888* (1973); and William A. Green, *British Slave Emancipation: The Sugar Colonies and the Great Experiment, 1830–1865* (1976).

For the women's rights movement, see Ellen Carol DuBois, *Feminism and Suffrage: The Emergence of an Independent Women's Movement in America, 1848–1869* (1999).

20 The Early Industrial Revolution, 1760–1851

CHAPTER OUTLINE

Causes of the Industrial Revolution
The Technological Revolution
The Impact of the Industrial Revolution
New Economic and Political Ideas
Industrialization and the Nonindustrial World
ENVIRONMENT AND TECHNOLOGY: The Origin of Graphs

From 1765 until the 1790s a small group of men calling themselves the Lunar Society met once a month in Birmingham, England. They gathered on nights when the moon was full so they could find their way home in the dark. Among them were the pottery manufacturer Josiah Wedgwood, the engine designer James Watt, the chemist Joseph Priestley, the iron manufacturer Matthew Boulton, and the naturalist Erasmus Darwin. They did not leave a record of what they discussed, but the fact that businessmen, craftsmen, and scientists had interests in common was something new in the history of the world. Though members of very different professions, they were willing to exchange ideas and discoveries in an atmosphere of experimentation and innovation. They invited experts in industry, science, and engineering to speak at their meetings so that they could obtain the latest information in their fields.

By focusing on the practical application of knowledge, groups like the Lunar Society laid the groundwork for the economic and social transformations that historians call the **Industrial Revolution.** This revolution involved dramatic innovations in manufacturing, mining, transportation, and communications and equally rapid changes in society and commerce. New relationships between social groups created an environment that was conducive to technical innovation and economic growth. New technologies and new social and economic arrangements allowed the industrializing countries—first Britain, then western Europe and the United

States—to unleash massive increases in production and productivity, exploit the world's natural resources as never before, and transform the environment and human life in unprecedented ways.

The distribution of power and wealth generated by the Industrial Revolution was very uneven, for industrialization widened the gap between rich and poor. The people who owned and controlled the innovations amassed wealth and power over nature and over other people. Some of them lived lives of spectacular luxury. Workers, including children, worked long hours in dangerous factories and lived crowded together in unsanitary tenements.

The effect of the Industrial Revolution around the world was also very uneven. The first countries to industrialize grew rich and powerful. In Egypt and India, the economic and military power of the European countries stifled the tentative beginnings of industrialization. Regions that had little or no industry were easily taken advantage of. The disparity between the industrial and the developing countries that exists today has its origins in the early nineteenth century.

As you read this chapter, ask yourself the following questions:

- What caused the Industrial Revolution?

- What were the key innovations that increased productivity and drove industrialization?

- What was the impact of these changes on the society and environment of the industrializing countries?

- How did the Industrial Revolution affect the relations between the industrialized and the nonindustrialized parts of the world?

CAUSES OF THE INDUSTRIAL REVOLUTION

What caused the Industrial Revolution, and why did it begin in England in the late eighteenth century? The basic preconditions of this momentous event seem to have been population growth, an agricultural revolution, the expansion of trade, and an openness to innovation.

Preconditions for Industrialization

The population of Europe rose in the eighteenth century—slowly at first, faster after 1780, then even faster in the early nineteenth century. The population of England and Wales rose unusually fast—from 5.5 million in 1688 to 18 million by 1851. Industrialization and the population boom reinforced each other. A high birthrate meant a large percentage of children, which explains both the vitality of the British people in that period and the widespread use of child labor.

This population explosion and urbanization could only have taken place alongside an **agricultural revolution** that provided food for city dwellers and forced poorer peasants off the land. Long before the eighteenth century, the introduction and acceptance of the potato and maize from the Americas had increased food supplies in Europe. In the cool and humid regions of Europe, from Ireland to Russia, potatoes yielded two or three times more food per acre than grain. Maize (American corn) was grown across Europe from southwestern France to the Balkans.

During the seventeenth century, rich English landowners began draining marshes, improving the soil, and introducing crop rotation using turnips, legumes, and clover that did not deplete the soil and could be fed to cattle. Additional manure from improved breeds of livestock fertilized the soil for other crops. Some also "enclosed" land—that is, consolidated their holdings, including commons that in the past had been open to all. This "enclosure movement" also turned tenants and sharecroppers into landless farm laborers.

Many moved to the cities to seek work; others became homeless migrants and vagrants; still others emigrated.

The growth of the population and food supply was accompanied by the growth of trade. Most of it was local, but a growing share consisted of imports from other parts of the world like tea and sugar and simple goods that even middle-class people could afford, such as cotton textiles, iron hardware, and pottery.

Trade was accompanied by a growing interest in technology and innovation among educated people throughout Europe and eastern North America. They read descriptions of new techniques and inventions in many publications, and some experimented on their own.

Britain's Advantages

These changes were widespread, but Britain in the eighteenth century had the fastest-growing population, food supply, and overseas trade. The British also put inventions into practice more quickly than other people. (see Environment and Technology: The Origin of Graphs). In the eighteenth century, Britain became the world's leading exporter of tools, guns, hardware, and other craft goods. Its mining and metal industries employed engineers willing to experiment with new ideas. It had the largest merchant marine and produced more ships, naval supplies, and navigation instruments than other countries.

Moreover, Britain had a more fluid society than the rest of Europe. Political power was not as centralized as on the European continent, and the government employed fewer bureaucrats and officials. Class lines eased as members of the gentry, and even some aristocrats, married into merchant families. Intermarriage among the families of petty merchants, yeoman farmers, and town craftsmen was common.

At a time when transportation by land was very costly, Great Britain had good water transportation, thanks to its indented coastline, navigable rivers, and growing network of canals (see Map 20.1). It had a unified internal market, with none of the duties and tolls that goods had to pay every few miles in France. This encouraged specialization and trade. More people there were involved in production for export and in trade and finance than in any other major country. It had financial and insurance institutions able to support growing business enterprises and a patent system that offered inventors the hope of rich rewards.

By 1830, the political climate in western Europe was as favorable to business as Britain's had been a half-century earlier. Industrialization first took hold in Belgium and northern France, as their businessmen visited Britain to observe the changes and to spy out industrial secrets. In spite of British laws forbidding the emigration of skilled workers and

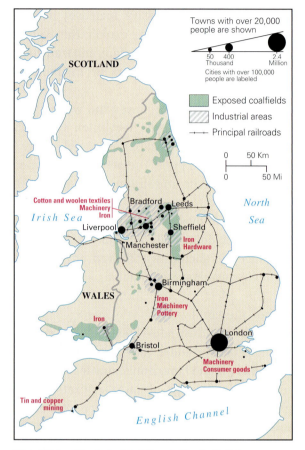

Map 20.1 The Industrial Revolution in Britain, ca. 1850 The first industries arose in northern and western England. These regions had abundant coal and iron-ore deposits for the iron industry and moist climate and fast-flowing rivers for the cotton textile industry.

C H R O N O L O G Y

	Technology	Economy, Society, and Politics
1750		
	1759 Josiah Wedgwood opens pottery factory	
	1764 Spinning jenny	
	1769 Richard Arkwright's water frame; James Watt patents steam engine	
		1776 Adam Smith's *Wealth of Nations*
		1776–1783 American Revolution
	1779 First iron bridge	
	1785 Boulton and Watt sell steam engines; Samuel Crompton's mule	
		1789–1799 French Revolution
	1793 Eli Whitney's cotton gin	
1800	**1800** Alessandro Volta's battery	
		1804–1815 Napoleonic Wars
	1807 Robert Fulton's *North River*	
	1820s Construction of Erie Canal	**1820s** U.S. cotton industry begins
		1833 Factory Act in Britain
		1834 Robert Owen's Grand National Consolidated Trade Union
	1837 Wheatstone and Cooke's telegraph	
	1838 First ships steam across the Atlantic	
	1840 *Nemesis* sails to China	
	1843 Samuel Morse's Baltimore-to-Washington telegraph	
		1847–1848 Irish famine
		1848 Collapse of chartist movement; revolutions in Europe
1850	**1851** Crystal palace opens in London	

the export of textile machinery, many slipped through, setting up machines, training workers in the new methods, and even starting their own businesses. European governments created technical schools; eliminated internal tariff barriers, tolls, and other hindrances to trade; and encouraged the formation of joint-stock companies and banks to channel private savings into industrial investments.

The Origin of Graphs

Not all technologies involve hardware. There are also information technologies, such as graphs, the visual representation of numerical tables. We see graphs so often in textbooks, magazines, and newspapers that we take them for granted. But they too have a history.

Scientists in France and England created the first graphs in the seventeenth century to illustrate natural phenomena. Some represented tables of data, such as the movements of stars and atmospheric pressure. Until the late eighteenth century few people outside of scientific circles knew or cared about such graphs. This changed with the growing public interest in economic data, population statistics, and other secular subjects that were so much a part of the Enlightenment.

The first person to publish graphs of interest to the general public was William Playfair (1729–1823), an Englishman who started his career as a draftsman for

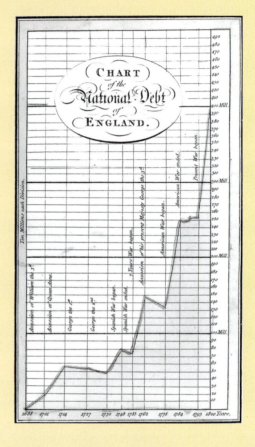

Line Graph of National Debt of England, 1803 This graph by William Playfair is designed to shock the viewer by showing the national debt of Britain skyrocketing out of control, especially during the country's many wars. (British Library)

On the European continent, as in Britain, cotton was the first industry to industrialize.

THE TECHNOLOGICAL REVOLUTION

Five revolutionary innovations spurred industrialization: (1) mass production through the division of labor, (2) new machines and mechanization, (3) a great increase in the supply of iron, (4) the steam engine and the changes it made possible in industry and transportation, and (5) the electric telegraph.

Mass Production and Mechanization

The pottery industry offers a good example of **mass production,** the making of many identical items by breaking the process into simple repetitive tasks. **Josiah Wedgwood** opened a pottery

the engine-manufacturing firm of Boulton and Watt. In 1786 he published *The Commercial and Political Atlas*, a book that was widely read and went though several editions. All but one of the forty-four graphs in it were line graphs with the vertical axis showing economic data and the horizontal axis representing time. Playfair explained to skeptical readers how a line could represent money:

> This method has struck several persons as being fallacious, because geometrical measurement has not any relation to money or to time; yet here it is made to represent both. The most familiar and simple answer to this objection is by giving an example. Suppose the money received by a man in trade were all in guineas, and that every evening he made a single pile of all the guineas received during the day, each pile would represent a day, and its height would be proportioned to the receipts of that day; so that by this plain operation, time, proportion, *and* amount would all be physically combined.
>
> Lineal arithmetic then, it may be averred, is nothing more than those piles of guineas represented on paper, and on a small scale, in which an inch (suppose) represents the thickness of five millions of guineas, as in geography it does the breadth of a river, or any other extent of country.

As for why it was necessary to show economic data in the form of a graph, Playfair explained:

> Men of high rank, or active business, can only pay attention to general outlines; nor is attention to particulars of use, any further than they give a general information; it is hoped that, with the Assistance of these Charts, such information will be got, without the fatigue and trouble of studying the particulars of which it is composed.

Today, graphs are an indispensable means of conveying information in business and finance, in the sciences, and in government. We need graphs because they give us information quickly and efficiently, "without the fatigue and trouble of studying the particulars."

Source: William Playfair, *The Commercial and Political Atlas*, 3rd ed. (London: J. Wallis, 1801), ix, xiv–xv.

business in 1759 that was able to produce porcelain cheaply, by means of the **division of labor.** He subdivided the work into highly specialized and repetitive tasks, such as unloading the clay, mixing it, pressing flat pieces, dipping the pieces in glaze, putting handles on cups, packing kilns, and carrying things from one part of his plant to another. He substituted the use of molds for the potter's wheel wherever possible, a change that not only saved labor but also created identical plates and bowls that could be stacked. These radical departures from the age-old methods of craftsmanship allowed Wedgwood to lower the cost of his products while improving their quality. As a result, his factory grew far larger than his competitors' factories and employed several hundred workers. His own salesmen traveled throughout England touting his goods.

Wedgwood was also interested in new technologies. He invested in toll roads and canals so that clay could be shipped economically from southwestern England to his factories in the Midlands. In 1782, to mix clay and grind flint, he purchased one of the first steam engines to be used in industry. Wedgwood's interest in applying technology to manufacturing was connected with his member-ship in the Birmingham Lunar Society, a group of manufacturers, scientists, and inventors who met to exchange ideas and discoveries. They were part of the atmosphere of experimentation and innovation that characterized late-eighteenth-century England. Similar societies throughout Britain were creating a vogue for science and giving the word *progress* a new meaning: "change for the better."

The cotton industry, the largest industry in this period, illustrates the role of **mechanization,** the use of machines to do work previously done by hand. The cotton plant did not grow in Europe, but the cloth was so much cooler, softer, and cleaner than wool that wealthy Europeans developed a liking for this costly import. When the powerful English woolen industry persuaded Parliament to forbid the import of cotton cloth into England, it stimulated attempts to import cotton fiber and make the cloth locally. Here was an opportunity for enterprising inventors to reduce costs with labor-saving machinery.

Beginning in the 1760s, a series of inventions—the spinning jenny, the water frame, and the mule—revolutionized the spinning of cotton thread and allowed British industry to undersell high-quality handmade cotton cloth from India. British cotton output increased tenfold between 1770 and 1790.

When the boom in thread production and the soaring demand for cloth created bottlenecks in weaving, inventors in England rose to the chal-lenge with power looms, carding machines, chlo-rine bleach, and cylindrical printing presses. By the 1830s, large English textile mills powered by steam engines were turning raw cotton into printed cloth. This was a far cry from the cottage industries of the previous century.

Mechanization offered two advantages: (1) pro-ductivity for the manufacturer and (2) price for the consumer. Whereas in India it took 500 hours to spin a pound of cotton, the improved mule of 1830 required only 80 minutes. Cotton mills needed very few skilled workers, and managers often hired children to tend the spinning machines. Mecha-nization and cheap labor allowed the price of cloth to fall by 90 percent from 1782 to 1812, and it kept on dropping.

The industrialization of Britain made cotton into America's most valuable crop. In 1793, the American Eli Whitney patented his cotton gin, a simple device that separated the bolls from the fiber and made the growing of short-staple cotton economical. This invention permitted the spread of cotton farming into Georgia, then into Alabama, Mississippi, and Louisiana, and finally as far west as Texas. By the late 1850s, the southern states were producing a million tons of cotton a year, five-sixths of the world's total.

With the help of British craftsmen who intro-duced jennies, mules, and power looms, Ameri-cans developed a cotton industry in the 1820s. By 1840, the United States had 1,200 cotton mills, two-thirds of them in New England, powered by water rather than steam.

The Iron Industry

Iron making also was transformed during the Industrial Revolution. Iron had been in use for thousands of years for tools, swords and other weapons, and household items such as knives, pots, hinges, and locks. Wherever it was produced, however, deforestation eventually drove up the cost of charcoal (used for smelting) and restricted output. Furthermore, iron had to be repeatedly heated and hammered to drive out impurities, a difficult and costly process. Then in 1709, Abraham Darby discovered that coke (coal from which the impurities have been cooked out) could be used in place of charcoal. The resulting metal was of lower quality than charcoal iron but much cheaper to produce, for coal was plentiful. Just as importantly, in 1784 Henry Cort found a way to remove some of the impurities in coke-iron by puddling—stirring the molten iron with long rods. Cort's process made it possible to turn high-sulfur English coal into coke to produce wrought iron (a soft and mal-leable form of iron) very cheaply. By 1790 four-fifths of Britain's iron was made with coke, while other countries were still using charcoal. Coke-iron was cheaper and less destructive of forests, and it allowed a great expansion in the size of individual blast furnaces, substantially reducing the cost of iron. There seemed almost no limit to the quantity of iron that could be produced with coke. Britain's iron production began rising fast, from 17,000 tons in 1740 to 3 million tons in 1844, as much as in the rest of the world put together.

In turn, there seemed no limit to the amount of iron that an industrializing society would purchase or to the novel applications for this cheap and useful material. In 1779 the iron manufacturer Abraham Darby III (grandson of the first Abraham Darby) built a bridge of iron across the Severn River. In 1851 Londoners marveled at the **Crystal Palace,** a huge greenhouse made entirely of iron and glass and large enough to enclose the tallest trees.

The availability of cheap iron made the mass production of objects such as guns, hardware, and tools appealing. However, fitting together the parts of these products required a great deal of labor. To reduce labor costs, manufacturers turned to the idea of interchangeable parts. This idea originated in the eighteenth century when French army officers attempted, without success, to persuade gun makers to produce precisely identical parts. Craftsmen continued to use traditional methods to make parts that had to be filed to fit together with other parts. By the mid-nineteenth century, however, interchangeable-parts procedures had been adopted in the manufacture of firearms, farm equipment, and sewing machines. At the Crystal Palace exhibition of 1851, Europeans called it the "American system of manufactures." In the next hundred years the use of machinery to mass-produce consumer items was to become the hallmark of American industry.

The Steam Engine

The first machine to transform fossil fuel into mechanical energy was the **steam engine.** Although the mechanization of manufacturing was very important, the steam engine was what set the Industrial Revolution apart from all previous periods of growth and innovation.

Before the eighteenth century, many activities had been limited by the lack of energy. For example, deep mines filled with water faster than horses could pump it out. Scientists understood the concept of atmospheric pressure and had created experimental devices to turn heat into motion, but they had not found a way to put those devices to practical use. Then, between 1702 and 1712 Thomas Newcomen developed the first practical steam engine, a crude but effective device. One engine could pump water out of a mine as fast as four horses and could run day and night without getting tired.

The Newcomen engine's voracious appetite for fuel mattered little in coal mines, where fuel was cheap, but it made the engine too costly for other uses. In 1764 **James Watt,** an instrument maker at Glasgow University in Scotland, was asked to repair the university's model Newcomen engine. Watt realized that the engine wasted fuel because the cylinder had to be alternately heated and cooled. He developed a separate condenser—a vessel into which the steam was allowed to escape after it had done work, leaving the cylinder always hot and the condenser always cold. Watt patented his idea in 1769. He enlisted the help of the iron manufacturer Matthew Boulton to turn his invention into a commercial product. Their first engines were sold to pump water out of copper and tin mines, where fuel was too costly for Newcomen engines. In 1781 Watt invented the sun-and-planet gear, which turned the back-and-forth action of the piston into rotary motion. This allowed steam engines to power machinery in flour and cotton mills, pottery factories, and other industries.

Watt's steam engine was the most celebrated invention of the eighteenth century. Because there seemed almost no limit to the amount of coal in the ground, steam-generated energy seemed an inexhaustible source of power, and steam engines could be used where animal, wind, and water power were lacking.

Inspired by the success of Watt's engine, inventors in France in 1783, in the United States in 1787, and in England in 1788 put steam engines on boats. The need to travel great distances explains why the first commercially successful steamboat was Robert Fulton's *North River,* which steamed between New York City and Albany in 1807. Soon steamboats were launched on other American rivers. In the 1820s the Erie Canal linked the Atlantic seaboard with the Great Lakes and opened Ohio, Indiana, and Illinois to European settlement. Steamboats proliferated west of the Appalachian Mountains; by 1830 some three hundred plied the Mississippi and its tributaries. To counter the competition from New York State, Pennsylvania built a thousand miles of canals by 1840. The United States was fast becoming a nation that moved by water.

Pit Head of a Coal Mine This is a small coal mine. In the center of this picture stands a Newcomen engine used to pump water. The work of hauling coal out of the mine was still done by horses and mules. The smoke coming out of the smokestack is a trademark of the early industrial era. (National Museums and Galleries on Merseyside, Walker Art Gallery [WAG 659])

Oceangoing steam-powered ships were much more difficult to build than riverboats, for the first steam engines used so much coal that no ship could carry more than a few days' supply. The *Savannah,* which crossed the Atlantic in 1819, was a sailing ship with an auxiliary steam engine that was used for only ninety hours of its twenty-nine-day trip. However, engineers soon developed more efficient engines, and in 1838 two steamers, the *Great Western* and the *Sirius,* crossed the Atlantic on steam power alone.

Railroads

On land as on water, the problem was not imagining uses for steam-powered vehicles but building ones that worked, for steam engines were too heavy and weak to pull any weight. After Watt's patent expired in 1800, inventors experimented with lighter, more powerful high-pressure engines and in the early 1800s built several steam-powered vehicles able to travel on roads or rails. Between 1830 and 1850, a railroad-building mania swept Britain. The first lines linked towns and mines with

the nearest harbor or waterway. As passenger traffic soared, entrepreneurs built lines between the major cities and then to small towns as well. Railroads were far cheaper, faster, and more comfortable than stagecoaches, and millions of people got in the habit of traveling.

In the United States, entrepreneurs built railroads as fast and cheaply as possible. By the 1840s, 6,000 miles (10,000 kilometers) of track radiated westward from Boston, New York, Philadelphia, and Baltimore. The boom of the 1840s was dwarfed by the mania of the 1850s, when 21,000 miles (34,000 kilometers) of new track were laid, much of it westward across the Appalachians to Memphis, St. Louis, and Chicago. The trip from New York to Chicago, which once took three weeks by boat and on horseback, could be made in forty-eight hours. The railroads opened up the Midwest, turning the vast prairie into wheat fields and pasture for cattle to feed the industrial cities of the eastern United States.

Railways triggered the industrialization of Europe. Belgium, independent since 1830, quickly copied the British. State-planned and -supervised

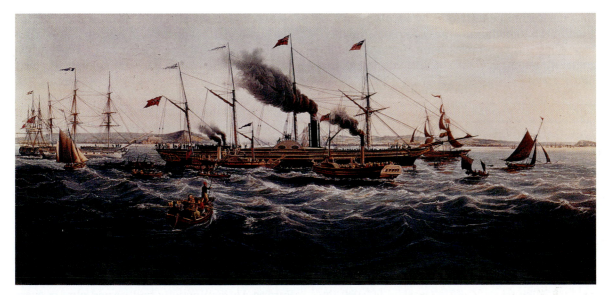

Transatlantic Steamship Race   In 1838, two ships equipped with steam engines, the *Sirius* and the *Great Western*, steamed from England to New York. Although the *Sirius* left a few days earlier, the *Great Western*—shown here arriving in New York harbor—almost caught up with it, arriving just four hours after the *Sirius*. This race inaugurated regular transatlantic steamship service.   (Courtesy of the Mariners' Museum, Newport News, VA)

railroad construction in the mid-1840s in France and Prussia not only satisfied the long-standing need for transportation, but also stimulated the iron, machinery, and construction industries. In the 1850s and 1860s, the states of Germany also experienced an industrial boom.

Communication over Wires

The advent of railroads coincided with the development of the **electric telegraph.** After the Italian scientist Alessandro Volta invented the battery in 1800, making it possible to produce an electric current, many inventors tried to apply electricity to communication. The first practical telegraphy systems were developed almost simultaneously in England and America. In England, Wheatstone and Cooke introduced a five-needle telegraph in 1837; it remained in use until the early twentieth century. That same year, the American Samuel Morse introduced a code of dots and dashes that could be transmitted with a single wire; in 1843, he erected a line between Washington and Baltimore.

By the late 1840s, telegraph wires were being strung throughout the eastern United States and western Europe. In 1851, the first submarine telegraph cable was laid across the English Channel from England to France; it was the beginning of a network that eventually enclosed the entire globe. The world was rapidly shrinking, to the applause of Europeans and Americans, for whom speed was a clear measure of progress. No longer were communications limited to the speed by which a ship could sail or a horse could gallop.

THE IMPACT OF THE INDUSTRIAL REVOLUTION

Although inventions were the most visible aspect of the Industrial Revolution, many other changes in society, politics, and the economy took place. Early changes—smoky cities, slum neighborhoods, polluted water, child labor in mines and textile mills—were being alleviated by the mid-nineteenth century. But by then national or even international problems were replacing these local ones: business cycles, labor conflicts, and the transformation of entire regions into industrial landscapes.

New Industrial Cities

The most dramatic environmental changes brought about by industrialization occurred in the towns. Never before had towns grown so fast. London, one of the largest cities in Europe in 1700 with 500,000 inhabitants, grew to 959,000 by 1800 and to 2,363,000 by 1850, by then the largest city in the world. Smaller towns grew even faster. Manchester's population increased eightfold in a century. Liverpool grew sixfold in the first sixty years of the nineteenth century. New York City, already 100,000 strong in 1815, reached 600,000 (including Brooklyn) in 1850. In some areas, towns merged and formed megalopolises, such as Greater London, the English Midlands, central Belgium, and the Ruhr district of Germany.

People who prospered greatly from industrialization poured their new wealth into fine new homes, churches, museums, and theaters. Yet by all accounts, the industrial cities grew much too fast. As poor migrants streamed in from the countryside, developers built cheap, shoddy row houses for them to rent. These tenements were dangerously overcrowded. Often, several families had to live in one small room. Town dwellers recently arrived from the country brought country ways with them. People threw their sewage and trash out the windows to be washed down the gutters in the streets. The poor kept pigs and chickens, the rich kept horses, and pedestrians stepped into the street at their own risk. Air pollution from burning coal got steadily worse. People drank water drawn from wells and rivers contaminated by sewage and industrial runoff. The River Irwell, which ran through Manchester, was, in the words of one visitor, "considerably less a river than a flood of liquid manure."[1] To the long list of preindustrial urban diseases such as smallpox, dysentery, and tuberculosis, industrialization added new ailments. Rickets, a bone disease caused by lack of sunshine, became endemic in dark and smoky industrial cities. Steamships brought cholera from India, causing great epidemics that struck the poor neighborhoods especially hard. In the 1850s, when the average life expectancy in England was forty years, it was only twenty-four years in Manchester, and around seventeen years in Manchester's poorest neighborhoods, because of the high infant mortality. Shocking reports of slum life led to municipal reforms, such as garbage removal, water and sewage systems, and parks and schools. These measures began to alleviate the ills of urban life after the mid-nineteenth century.

Rural Environments

Long before the Industrial Revolution began, practically no wilderness areas were left in Britain and very few in western Europe. Human activity had turned almost every exploitable piece of land into fields, pastures, or towns. The most serious problem was deforestation. People cut timber to build ships and houses, to heat homes, and to manufacture bricks, iron, glass, beer, bread, and many other items.

Americans transformed their environment even faster than Europeans did. Settlers viewed forests not as a valuable resource but as a hindrance to development. In their haste to "open up the West," pioneers felled trees and burned them, built houses and abandoned them when they moved on. The cultivation of cotton was especially harmful. Planters cut down forests, grew cotton for a few years until it depleted the soil, and then moved west, abandoning the land to scrub pines. The American idea of nature as an obstacle to be overcome and dominated persisted long after the entire continent was occupied.

To contemporaries, the new transportation systems brought the most obvious changes in rural life. Governments and private trusts built numerous roads. Canal building boomed in Britain, France, and the Low Countries in the late eighteenth century. Canals were marvels of construction, with deep cuts, tunnels, and even aqueducts that carried barges over rivers. They also were a sort of school where engineers learned skills they were able to apply to the next great transportation system: the railroads. They laid track across rolling country by

Overcrowded London   The French artist Gustave Doré depicted the tenements of industrial London where workers and their families lived. This drawing shows crowded and unsanitary row houses, each one room wide with tiny back yards, and a train steaming across a viaduct overhead.   (New York Public Library/Art Resource, NY)

cutting deeply into hillsides and erecting daringly long bridges of stone and iron across valleys. Soon, clanking trains pulled by puffing, smoke-belching locomotives were invading long-isolated districts.

Thus, in the century after industrialization began, the landscape of industrializing countries was transformed more rapidly than ever before. But the ecological changes, like the technological and economic changes that caused them, were only beginning.

Working Conditions

Most industrial jobs were unskilled, repetitive, and boring. Factory work did not vary with the seasons or the time of day but began and ended by the clock. Workdays were long, there were few breaks, and foremen watched constantly. Workers who performed one simple task over and over had little sense of achievement or connection to the final product. Industrial accidents were common and could ruin a family.

Unlike even the poorest preindustrial farmer or artisan, factory workers had no control over their tools, jobs, or working hours.

Women workers were concentrated in textile mills, partly because of ancient traditions, partly because textile work required less strength than metalworking, construction, or hauling. On average, women earned one-third to one-half as much as men. Young unmarried women worked to support themselves or to save for marriage. Married women took factory jobs when their husbands were unable to support the family. Mothers of infants faced a hard choice: whether to leave their babies with wet nurses at great expense and danger or to bring them to the factory and keep them quiet with opiates. Rather than working together as family units, husbands and wives increasingly worked in different places.

Factory work was never the main occupation of working women. Most young women who sought paid employment in the early years of industrialization became domestic servants in spite of the low pay, drudgery, and risk of sexual abuse. Other women with small children tried hard to find work they could do at home, such as laundry, sewing, embroidery, millinery, or taking in lodgers.

Even with both parents working, poor families found it hard to make ends meet. As in preindustrial societies, parents thought children should contribute to their upkeep as soon as they were able to. The first generation of workers brought their children with them to the factories and mines as early as age five or six; they had little choice, since there were no public schools or day-care centers. Employers encouraged the practice and even hired orphans. They preferred children because they were cheaper and more docile than adults and were better able to tie broken threads or crawl under machines to sweep the dust. Mine operators used children to pull coal carts along the low passageways from the coal face to the mine shaft. In the mid-nineteenth century, when the British government began restricting child labor, mill owners increasingly recruited Irish immigrants.

American industry began on a somewhat different note than the British. When Francis Cabot Lowell built a cotton mill in Massachusetts, he deliberately hired the unmarried daughters of New England farmers, promising decent wages and housing in dormitories under careful moral supervision. Other manufacturers eager to combine profits with morality followed his example. But soon the profit motive won out, and manufacturers imposed longer hours, harsher working conditions, and lower wages. When the young women went on strike, the factory owners replaced them with Irish immigrant women willing to accept lower pay and worse conditions.

The rising demand for cotton and the abolition of the African slave trade in the United States in 1808 caused an increase in the price of slaves. As the "Cotton Kingdom" expanded, the number of slaves rose through natural increase, from 700,000 in the 1790s to 3,200,000 slaves by 1850. Similarly, Europe and North America's surging demand for tea and coffee prolonged slavery on sugar plantations in the West Indies and caused it to spread to the coffee-growing regions of southern Brazil. Slavery was part and parcel of the Industrial Revolution, just as much as child labor in Britain, the clothes that people wore, and the beverages they drank.

Changes in Society

Industrialization accentuated the polarization of society and disparities of income. In Britain, the worst-off were those who clung to an obsolete skill or craft, such as handloom weavers in a time of power looms. Even by working more hours, they could not escape destitution.

The wages and standard of living of factory workers did not decline steadily like those of handloom weavers; they fluctuated wildly with the cycles of economic growth and contraction. During the war years 1792 to 1815, the poor suffered hardship when the price of food rose faster than wages. Then, in the 1820s, real wages and public health began to improve, as industrial production grew at over 3 percent a year, pulling the rest of the economy along. Prices fell so that even the poor could afford comfortable, washable cotton clothes.

Overall, the benefits of industrialization—cheaper food, clothing, and utensils—did not improve workers' standard of living until the 1850s. The real beneficiaries of the early Industrial Revolution were the entrepreneurs whose money came from manufacturing. Most were the sons of middling shopkeepers, craftsmen, or farmers who had a little capital to start a cotton-spinning or machine-building business. Many tried and some succeeded, largely by plowing their profits back into the business. A generation later, in the nineteenth century, some newly rich industrialists bought their way into high society. With industrialization also came a "cult of domesticity" that removed middle-class women from contact with the business world and left them responsible for the home, the servants, the education of children, and the family's social life.

NEW ECONOMIC AND POLITICAL IDEAS

Changes as profound as the Industrial Revolution could not occur without political ferment and ideological conflict. So many other momentous events took place during those years—the American Revolution (1776–1783), the French Revolution (1789–1799), the Napoleonic Wars (1804–1815), the reactions and revolts that periodically swept over Europe after 1815—that we cannot neatly separate out the consequences of industrialization from the rest. But it is clear that the Industrial Revolution strengthened the ideas of laissez faire° and socialism and sparked workers' protests.

Laissez Faire

The most celebrated exponent of **laissez faire** ("let them do") was Adam Smith (1723–1790), a Scottish economist. In *The Wealth of Nations* (1776), Smith argued that if individuals were allowed to seek their personal gain, the effect, as though guided by an "invisible hand," would be to increase the general welfare. Except to protect private property, the government should refrain from interfering in business; it should even allow duty-free trade with foreign countries.

Although it was true that governments at the

time were incompetent at regulating their national economies, it was becoming obvious that industrialization was not improving the general welfare but was for some causing great misery. Other thinkers blamed the workers' plight on the population boom, which outstripped the food supply and led to falling wages. The workers' poverty, they claimed, was as much a result of "natural law" as the wealth of successful businessmen, and the only way the working class could avoid mass famine was to delay marriage and practice self-restraint and sexual abstinence.

Laissez faire provided an ideological justification for a special kind of capitalism: banks, stock markets, and chartered companies allowed investors to obtain profits with reasonable risks but with much less government control and interference than in the past. But not everyone accepted the grim conclusions of the "dismal science," as economics was then known. Jeremy Bentham (1748–1832) believed that it was possible to maximize "the greatest happiness of the greatest number," if only a Parliament of enlightened reformers would study the social problems of the day and pass appropriate legislation; his philosophy became known as utilitarianism.

Positivism and Utopian Socialism

Some French social thinkers, moved by sincere concern for the poor, offered a more radically new vision of a just civilization. Espousing a philosophy called **positivism,** the count of Saint-Simon (1760–1825) argued that the scientific method could solve social as well as technical problems. He recommended that the poor, guided by scientists and artists, form workers' communities under the protection of benevolent business leaders. These ideas found no following among workers, but they attracted the enthusiastic support of bankers and entrepreneurs, who were inspired by visions of railroads, canals, and other symbols of progress and invested their money accordingly.

Meanwhile, the **utopian° socialism** of Charles Fourier (1768–1837), who loathed capitalists, imagined an ideal society in which groups of sixteen

---

laissez faire (lay-say fair)

utopian (you-TOE-pee-uhn)

hundred workers would live in dormitories and work together on the land and in workshops where music, wine, and pastries would soften the hardships of labor. For this idea, critics called him "utopian"—a dreamer.

The person who came closest to creating a utopian community was the Englishman Robert Owen (1771–1858), a successful cotton manufacturer who believed that industry could provide prosperity for all. Conscience-stricken by the appalling plight of the workers, Owen took over the management of New Lanark, a mill town south of Glasgow. He improved the housing and added schools, a church, and other amenities. He also testified before Parliament against child labor and for government inspection of working conditions, thereby angering his fellow industrialists.

Protests and Reforms

Workers benefited little from the ideas of these middle-class philosophers. Instead, they resisted the harsh working conditions in their own ways. They changed jobs frequently and were often absent, especially on Mondays. Periodically, workers rioted or went on strike. Such acts of resistance did nothing, however, to change the nature of industrial work. Not until workers learned to act together could they hope to have much influence.

Gradually, they formed benevolent societies and organizations to demand universal male suffrage and shorter workdays. In 1834, Robert Owen organized the Grand National Consolidated Trade Union to lobby for an eight-hour workday; it gained half a million members but failed a few months later in the face of government prosecution of trade union activities. The Chartist movement had more success, gathering petitions by the thousands to present to Parliament. Although Chartism collapsed in 1848, it left a legacy of labor organizing. Eventually, mass movements persuaded political leaders to look into the abuses of industrial life, despite the prevailing laissez-faire philosophy.

In the 1820s and 1830s, the British Parliament began investigating conditions in the factories and mines. The Factory Act of 1833 prohibited the employment of children under age nine in textile mills and limited the working hours of children between the ages of nine and eighteen. The Mines Act of 1842 prohibited the employment of all women and of boys under age ten underground. Several decades passed before the government appointed enough inspectors to enforce the new laws.

The British learned to seek reform through accommodation. On the European continent, in contrast, the revolutions of 1848 (see Chapter 19) revealed widespread discontent with repressive governments but failed to soften the hardships of industrialization.

Emigration

Another response to growing population, rural crises, and business cycles was emigration. Many poor Irish emigrated to England in search of work in construction and factories. After the potato crop failed in Ireland in 1847–1848, one-quarter of the Irish population died in the resulting famine, and another quarter emigrated to England and America. On the European continent, the negative effects of economic downturns were tempered by the existence of small family farms to which urban workers could return when they were laid off, but vast numbers still left Europe in search of better opportunities in the Western Hemisphere.

The United States received approximately 600,000 European immigrants in the 1830s, 1.5 million in the 1840s, and then 2.5 million per decade until 1880. In the 1890s, an astonishing total of 5.2 million immigrants arrived. European immigration to Latin America also increased dramatically after 1880. Immigrants from Europe faced prejudice and discrimination from those who believed they threatened the well-being of native-born workers by accepting low wages, and they threatened national culture by resisting assimilation.

Asian immigration to the Western Hemisphere also increased after 1850. Between 1849 and 1875, approximately 570,000 Chinese immigrants arrived in the Americas, half in the United States. India also contributed more than a half-million immigrants to the Caribbean region. Asians faced more obstacles to immigration than did Europeans and were often victims of violence and more extreme forms of discrimination in the New World.

Despite discrimination, most immigrants were also motivated to assimilate. Many intellectuals and political leaders wondered if the evolving mix of culturally diverse populations could sustain a common citizenship. As a result, efforts were directed toward compelling immigrants to assimilate. They learned the language spoken in their adopted countries as fast as possible in order to improve their earning capacity.

Union movements and electoral politics in the hemisphere also felt the influence of new arrivals who aggressively sought to influence government and improve working conditions. Immigrants also introduced new languages, foods, and customs. Mutual benevolent societies and less formal ethnic associations pooled resources to help immigrants open businesses, aid the immigration of their relatives, or bury their family members, sometimes worsening the fears of the native-born that immigration posed a threat to national culture. They also established links with political movements, sometimes exchanging votes for favors.

Industrialization and the Nonindustrial World

The spread of the Industrial Revolution in the early nineteenth century transformed the relations of western Europe and North America with the rest of the world. For most of the world, trade with the industrial countries meant exporting raw materials, not locally made handicraft products. However, new machines helped England defeat and humiliate China, and in Egypt and India cheap industrial imports, backed by the power of Great Britain, delayed industrialization for a century or more. In these three cases, we can discern the outlines of the Western domination that has characterized the history of the world since the late nineteenth century.

In January 1840 a shipyard in Britain launched a radically new ship. The *Nemesis* had an iron hull, a flat bottom that allowed it to navigate in shallow waters, and a steam engine to power it upriver and against the wind. The ship was heavily armed. In November it arrived off the coast of China. Though ships from Europe had been sailing to China for three hundred years, the *Nemesis* was the first steam-powered iron gunboat seen in Asian waters. A Chinese observer noted: "Iron is employed to make it strong. The hull is painted black, weaver's shuttle fashion. On each side is a wheel, which by the use of coal fire is made to revolve as fast as a running horse. . . . At the vessel's head is a Marine God, and at the head, stern, and sides are cannon, which give it a terrific appearance. Steam vessels are a wonderful invention of foreigners, and are calculated to offer delight to many."[2]

Instead of offering delight, the *Nemesis* and other steam-powered warships that soon joined it steamed up the Chinese rivers, bombarded forts and cities, and transported troops and supplies from place to place along the coast and up rivers far more quickly than Chinese soldiers could move on foot. With this new weapon, Britain, a small island nation half a world away, was able to defeat the largest and most populated country in the world (see Chapter 22).

Egypt, strongly influenced by European ideas since the French invasion of 1798, began to industrialize in the early nineteenth century. The driving force was its ruler, Muhammad Ali (1769–1849), a man who was to play a major role in the history of not only Egypt but also the Middle East and East Africa (see Chapter 21). He wanted to build up the Egyptian economy and military in order to become less dependent on the Ottoman sultan, his nominal overlord. To do so, he imported advisers and technicians from Europe and built cotton mills, foundries, shipyards, weapons factories, and other industrial enterprises. To pay for all this, he made the peasants grow wheat and cotton, which the government bought at a low price and exported at a profit. He also imposed high tariffs on imported goods to force the pace of industrialization.

Muhammad Ali's efforts fell afoul of the British, who did not want a powerful country threatening to interrupt the flow of travelers and mail across Egypt, the shortest route between Europe and India. When Egypt went to war against the Ottoman Empire in 1839, Britain intervened and forced Muhammad Ali to eliminate all import duties in the name of free trade. Unprotected, Egypt's fledgling industries could not compete with the flood of cheap British products. Thereafter, Egypt exported raw cotton, imported manufactured goods, and became, in effect, an economic dependency of Britain.

Steam Tractor in India   Power machinery was introduced into India because of the abundance of skilled low-cost labor. In this scene, a steam tractor fords a shallow stream to the delight of onlookers. The towerlike construction on the right is probably a pier for a railroad bridge.   (Billie Love Historical Society)

Until the late eighteenth century, India had been the world's largest producer and exporter of cotton textiles, handmade by skilled spinners and weavers. The British East India Company took over large parts of India just as the Industrial Revolution was beginning in Britain (see Chapter 21). It allowed cheap British factory-made yarn and cloth to flood the Indian market duty-free, putting spinners and later handloom weavers out of work. Unlike Britain, India had no factories to which displaced handicraft workers could turn for work. Most of them became landless peasants, eking out a precarious living.

Like other tropical regions, India became an exporter of raw materials and an importer of British industrial goods. To hasten the process, British entrepreneurs and colonial officials introduced railroads into the subcontinent. The construction of India's railroad network began in the mid-1850s, along with coal mining to fuel the locomotives and the installation of telegraph lines to connect the major cities.

Some Indian entrepreneurs saw opportunities in the atmosphere of change that the British created. In 1854 the Bombay merchant Cowasjee Nanabhoy Davar imported an engineer, four skilled workers, and several textile machines from Britain and started India's first textile mill. This was the beginning of India's mechanized cotton industry. But despite many gifted entrepreneurs, India's industrialization proceeded at a snail's pace, for the government was in British hands and the British did nothing to encourage Indian industry.

The cases of Egypt, India, and China show how the demands of Western nations and the military advantage that industrialization gave them led them to interfere in the internal affairs of nonindustrial societies. As we shall see in Chapter 21, this was the start of a new age of Western dominance.

CONCLUSION

The great change we call the Industrial Revolution began in Great Britain, a society that was open to innovation, commercial enterprise, and the cross-fertilization of science, technology, and business. New machines and processes in the cotton and iron industries were instrumental in launching the Industrial Revolution, but what made industrialization an ongoing phenomenon was a new source of energy, the steam engine.

In the period from 1760 to 1851 the new technologies of the Industrial Revolution greatly increased humans' power over nature. Goods could be manufactured in vast quantities at low cost. People and messages could travel at unprecedented speeds. Most important, humans gained access to the energy stored in coal and used it to power machinery and propel ships and trains faster than vehicles had ever traveled before. With their newfound power, humans turned woodland into farmland, dug canals and laid tracks, bridged rivers and cut through mountains, and covered the countryside with towns and cities.

The ability to command nature, far from benefiting everyone, increased the disparities between individuals and societies. Industrialization brought forth entrepreneurs—whether in the mills of England or on plantations in the American South—

with enormous power over their employees or slaves, a power that they found easy and profitable to abuse. Some people acquired great wealth; others lived in poverty and squalor. While middle-class women were restricted to caring for their homes and children, many working-class women had to leave home to earn wages in factories or as domestic servants. These changes in work and family life provoked intense debates among intellectuals. Some defended the disparities in the name of laissez faire; others criticized the injustices the industrialization brought. Society was slow to bring these abuses under control.

By the 1850s the Industrial Revolution had spread from Britain to western Europe and the United States, and its impact was being felt around the world. To make a product that was sold on every continent, the British cotton industry used African slaves, American land, British machines, and Irish workers. As we shall see in Chapter 24, this was the start of a new age of Western dominance.

■ Key Terms

Industrial Revolution	Crystal Palace
agricultural revolution (eighteenth century)	steam engine
	James Watt
mass production	electric telegraph
Josiah Wedgwood	laissez faire
division of labor	positivism
mechanization	utopian socialism

■ Suggested Reading

General works on the history of technology give pride of place to industrialization. For an optimistic overview, see Joel Mokyr, *The Lever of Riches: Technological Creativity and Economic Progress* (1990). Other important recent works include James McClellan III and Harold Dorn, *Science and Technology in World History* (1999); David Landes, *The Wealth and Poverty of Nations* (1998); and Ian Inkster, *Technology and Industrialization: Historical Case Studies and International Perspectives* (1998).

There is a rich literature on the British industrial revolution, beginning with T. S. Ashton's classic *The Industrial Revolution, 1760–1830,* published in 1948 and often reprinted.

The impact of industrialization on workers is the theme of E. P. Thompson's classic work, *The Making of the English Working Class* (1963), but see also E. R. Pike, *"Hard Times": Human Documents of the Industrial Revolution* (1966). The role of women is most ably revealed in Lynn Y. Weiner, *From Working Girl to Working Mother: The Female Labor Force in the United States, 1820–1980* (1985), and in Louise Tilly and Joan Scott, *Women, Work, and Family* (1978).

European industrialization is the subject of J. Goodman and K. Honeyman, *Gainful Pursuits: The Making of Industrial Europe: 1600–1914* (1988); John Harris, *Industrial Espionage and Technology Transfer: Britain and France in the Eighteenth Century* (1998); and David Landes, *The Unbound Prometheus: Technological Change and Industrial Development in Western Europe from 1750 to the Present* (1972). On the beginnings of American industrialization, see David Jeremy, *Artisans, Entrepreneurs and Machines: Essays on the Early Anglo-American Textile Industry, 1770–1840* (1998).

An excellent history of immigration is Walter Nagent, *Crossings: The Great Transatlantic Migrations, 1870–1914* (1992).

On the environmental impact of industrialization, see Richard Wilkinson, *Poverty and Progress: An Ecological Perspective on Economic Development* (1973), and Richard Tucker and John Richards, *Global Deforestation in the Nineteenth-Century World Economy* (1983).

The first book to treat industrialization as a global phenomenon is Peter Stearns, *The Industrial Revolution in World History* (1993); see also Louise Tilly's important article "Connections," *American Historical Review* (February 1994).

■ Notes

1. Quoted in Lewis Mumford, *The City in History* (New York: Harcourt Brace, 1961), 460.
2. *Nautilus Magazine* 12 (1843): 346.

21

Africa, India, and the New British Empire, 1750–1870

CHAPTER OUTLINE

Changes and Exchanges in Africa

India Under British Rule

Britain's Eastern Empire

ENVIRONMENT AND TECHNOLOGY: Whaling

In 1782, Tipu Sultan inherited the throne of Mysore°, which his father had made the most powerful state in south India. The ambitious and talented new ruler also inherited a healthy distrust of the British East India Company's territorial ambitions. Before the company could invade Mysore, Tipu Sultan launched his own attack in 1785. He then sent an embassy to France in 1788 seeking an alliance against Britain. Neither of these ventures was immediately successful.

Not until a decade later did the French agree to a loose alliance with Tipu Sultan to challenge Britain's colonial and commercial supremacy in the Indian Ocean. General Napoleon Bonaparte invaded Egypt in 1798 to threaten British trade routes to India and hoped to use the alliance

Mysore (MY-sore)

with Tipu Sultan to drive the British out of India. The French invasion of Egypt went well enough at first, but a British naval blockade and the ravages of disease crippled the French force. When the French withdrew, another military adventurer, Muhammad Ali, commander of the Ottoman army in Egypt, took advantage of the situation to revitalize Egypt and expand its rule.

Meanwhile, Tipu's alliance with France did not protect him from the East India Company, whose military victory in 1792 deprived him of most of his seacoast. Tipu lost his life in 1799 while defending his capital against another British assault. Mysore was divided between the British and their Indian allies.

As these events illustrate, talented local leaders and European powers were both vying to expand their influence in South Asia and Africa between 1750 and 1870. Midway through that period, it was by no means clear who would gain the upper hand. Britain and France were as likely to fight each other as they were to fight any Asian or African state. In 1800, the two nations were engaged in their third major war for overseas supremacy since 1750. By 1870, however, Britain had gained a decisive advantage over France and had established commercial dominance in trade in Africa, the Indian Ocean, and East Asia. Moreover, Britain created a new colonial empire in the East.

As you read this chapter, ask yourself the following questions:

- Why were the British able to gain decisive advantages in distant lands?

- Why were Asians and Africans so divided, some choosing to cooperate with the Europeans while others resisted their advances?

- How important an advantage were Britain's weapons, ships, and economic motives?

- How much of the outcome was the result of advance planning, and how much was due to particular individuals or to chance?

CHANGES AND EXCHANGES IN AFRICA

During the century before 1870, Africa underwent dynamic political changes and a great expansion of foreign trade. Indigenous African leaders as well as Middle Eastern and European imperialists built powerful new states or expanded old ones. As the continent's external slave trades to the Americas and to Islamic lands died slowly under British pressure, trade in goods such as palm oil, ivory, timber, and gold grew sharply. In return, Africans imported large quantities of machine-made textiles and firearms. These complex changes are best understood by looking at African regions separately.

New African States

Internal forces produced clusters of new states in two parts of sub-Saharan Africa in the early nineteenth century (see Map 21.1). In the fertile coastlands of southeastern Africa (in modern South Africa), a serious drought at the beginning of the nineteenth century led to conflict for grazing and farming lands among the small, independent chiefdoms of the region. An upstart named Shaka emerged in 1818 as head of a new **Zulu** kingdom, whose military discipline and courage soon made them the most powerful and most feared fighters in southern Africa. Shaka's regiments raided his African neighbors, seized their

Zulu in Battle Dress, 1838   Elaborate costumes helped impress opponents with the Zulu's strength. Shown here are long-handled spears and thick leather shields. The stabbing spear is not shown.   (Killie Campbell Africana Library. Photo: Jane Taylor/Sonia Halliday Photographs)

cattle, and captured their women and children. To protect themselves from the Zulu, some neighboring Africans created their own states.

Although Shaka ruled for little more than a decade, he successfully instilled a new national identity into his newly conquered subjects. He grouped all the young people into regiments that lived together and were taught Zulu customs and fighting methods. At public festivals, regiments of young men and women paraded, danced, and pledged their loyalty to Shaka.

Meanwhile, Islamic reform movements were creating another powerful state in the savannas of West Africa. The reformers followed a classic Muslim pattern: a *jihad* (holy war) added new lands, spreading Islamic beliefs and laws among conquered people. The largest reform movement was led by Usuman dan Fodio° (1745–1817), whose armed supporters conquered and combined the older Hausa states into a new empire ruled by a caliph (sultan) in the city of Sokoto. The **Sokoto Caliphate** (1809–1906) was the largest state in West Africa since the fall of Songhai in the sixteenth century (see Chapter 12).

In addition to being a center of Islamic learning and reform, the Sokoto Caliphate became a center of slavery. Many captured in the wars were enslaved and put to work in the empire or sold away across the Sahara or the Atlantic.

Modernization in Egypt and Ethiopia

In northeastern Africa, the ancient African states of Egypt and Ethiopia were undergoing a period of growth and **modernization.** Napoleon's invasion of Egypt ended in 1801, but the shock of this display of European strength and Egyptian weakness prompted **Muhammad Ali,** who eliminated his rivals and ruled Egypt from 1805 to 1848, to begin political, social, and economic reforms in that country.

As we saw in the last chapter, Muhammad Ali's central aim was to strengthen Egypt militarily by making use of European experts and technology. Despite the shattering of his imperial dreams by the British after 1839, by the end of Muhammad Ali's reign in 1848, modernization was well rooted in Egypt. The trade with Europe had expanded by almost 600 percent, and a new class of educated Egyptians had begun to replace the old ruling aristocracy.

Ali's grandson Ismail° (r. 1863–1879) placed even more emphasis on Westernizing Egypt. "My country is no longer in Africa," Ismail declared, "it is in Europe."[1] A huge increase in cotton exports during the American Civil War helped finance a network of new irrigation canals, 800 miles (1,300 kilometers) of railroads, a modern postal service, and dazzling changes in the capital city of Cairo.

State building and reform also were under way in the ancient Christian kingdom of Ethiopia. Beginning in the 1840s, Ethiopian rulers purchased modern weapons from European sources and created strong armies loyal to the ruler. Emperor Téwodros° II (r. 1833–1868) and his successor, Yohannes° IV (r. 1872–1889), brought back under imperial rule large areas of ancient Ethiopia. When King Menelik of Shoa succeeded Yohannes as emperor in 1889, the merger of their separate realms created the modern boundaries of Ethiopia.

European Penetration

France's long and difficult war to conquer the North African country of Algeria from 1830 to 1847 was a rare example of European use of force in Africa before 1870. More typical was the peaceful penetration of European explorers, missionaries, and traders.

Small expeditions of adventurous explorers, using their own funds or financed by private geographical societies, were seeking to uncover the mysteries of inner Africa that had eluded earlier Europeans. Many of the explorers sought to map the course of Africa's great rivers: the Niger, the Nile, and the Congo.

In contrast to these heavily financed expeditions with hundreds of African porters, the Scottish missionary David Livingstone (1813–1873) organized modest treks through southern and Central Africa to scout out locations for Christian missions. His several expeditions in southern and equatorial Africa

---

Usuman dan Fodio (OO-soo-mahn dahn FOH-dee-oh)

Ismail (is-MAH-eel)   **Téwodros** (tay-WOH-druhs)
Yohannes (yoh-HAHN-nehs)

C H R O N O L O G Y

	Africa	India	Empire
1750		**1756** Black Hole of Calcutta	**1763** End of Seven Years War
		1765 East India Company (EIC) rule of Bengal begins	**1769–1778** Captain James Cook explores New Zealand and eastern Australia
	1795 Britain seizes Cape Colony from Dutch	**1795** Britain seizes Ceylon from the Dutch	**1795** End of Dutch East India Company
	1798 Napoleon invades Egypt	**1799** EIC defeats Mysore	
1800	**1805** Muhammad Ali seizes Egypt		
	1807–1808 Britain outlaws slave trade and takes over Sierra Leone		**1808** Britain outlaws slave trade
	1809 Sokoto Caliphate founded		
	1818 Shaka founds Zulu kingdom	**1818** EIC creates Bombay Presidency	
	1821 Foundation of Republic of Liberia; Egypt takes control of Sudan	**1826** EIC annexes Assam and northern Burma	
	1830–1847 Algerians resist French takeover	**1828** Brahmo Samaj founded	
	1834 Britain abolishes slavery		**1834** Britain abolishes slavery
	1840 Omani sultan moves capital to Zanzibar		
1850		**1857–1858** Sepoy Rebellion leads to end of EIC rule and Mughal rule	
	1867 End of Atlantic slave trade		**1867** End of Atlantic slave trade
		1877 Queen Victoria becomes empress of India	**1877** Victoria becomes Empress of India
		1885 First Indian National Congress	
	1889 Menelik unites modern Ethiopia		

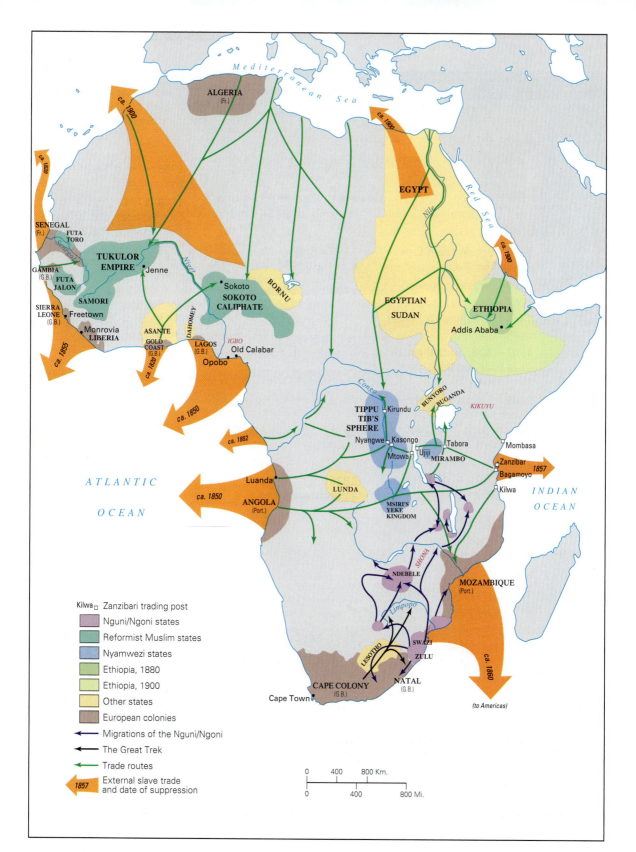

Mediterranean Sea

ALGERIA
(Fr.)

ca. 1900

EGYPT

Red Sea

ca. 1900

ca. 1820

SENEGAL
(Fr.)

FUTA
TORO

Senegal

TUKULOR
EMPIRE

Jenne

Niger

Sokoto

SOKOTO
CALIPHATE

BORNU

Nile

EGYPTIAN
SUDAN

ca. 1900

ETHIOPIA

Addis Ababa

GAMBIA
(G.B.)

FUTA
JALON

SIERRA
LEONE
(G.B.)

Freetown

Monrovia

LIBERIA

SAMORI

ca. 1855

ASANTE
GOLD
COAST
(G.B.)

DAHOMEY

LAGOS
(G.B.)

Opobo

IGBO

Old Calabar

ca. 1820

ca. 1850

ca. 1862

Congo

TIPPU
TIB'S
SPHERE

Kirundu

BUNYORO

BUGANDA

KIKUYU

Nyangwe

Kasongo

Mtowa

Ujiji

Tabora

MIRAMBO

Mombasa

ATLANTIC

OCEAN

Luanda

ca. 1850

ANGOLA
(Port.)

LUNDA

MSIRI'S
YEKE
KINGDOM

Zanzibar

Bagamoyo

1857

Kilwa

INDIAN

OCEAN

SHONA

NDEBELE

MOZAMBIQUE
(Port.)

Limpopo

ca. 1860

Kilwa □ Zanzibari trading post

Nguni/Ngoni states

Reformist Muslim states

Nyamwezi states

Ethiopia, 1880

Ethiopia, 1900

Other states

European colonies

Migrations of the Nguni/Ngoni

The Great Trek

Trade routes

1857 External slave trade
and date of suppression

SWAZI

ZULU

LESOTHO

CAPE COLONY
(G.B.)

Cape Town

NATAL
(G.B.)

(to Americas)

0   400   800 Km.

0   400   800 Mi.

made him a celebrity. In 1871, he was met by the Welsh-American journalist Henry Morton Stanley (1841–1904) on a publicity-motivated search for the "lost" missionary doctor. On an expedition from 1874 to 1877, Stanley descended the Congo River to its mouth.

The most significant European influence in Africa between 1750 and 1870 was commercial. No sooner was the mouth of the Niger River discovered in 1830 than eager entrepreneurs began to send expeditions up the river to scout out its potential for trade. The value of trade between Africa and the other Atlantic continents more than doubled between the 1730s and the 1780s, then doubled again by 1870.[2] Before about 1825, the slave trade accounted for most of that increase, but thereafter African exports of vegetable oils, gold, ivory, and other goods drove overseas trade to new heights.

As Chapter 19 recounted, the successful revolutions in the United States, France, Saint Domingue, and Latin America helped turn Western opinion against the slave trade and slavery. Once the world's greatest slave traders, the British became the most aggressive abolitionists. During the half-century after 1815, Britain spent some $60 million (£12 million) in its efforts to end the slave trade through naval patrols, a sum equal to the profits British slave traders had made in the fifty years before the trade was banned in 1807. Although British patrols captured 1,635 slave ships and liberated over 160,000 enslaved Africans, continued demand for slaves in Cuba and Brazil kept the trade going until 1867.

The demand for slaves in the Americas claimed the lives and endangered the safety of untold numbers of Africans, but the exchanges satisfied other Africans' desires for cloth, metals, and other goods. To continue their access to those imports after slavery was outlawed, Africans expanded their **"legitimate" trade** (exports other than slaves). The most successful of the new exports from West Africa was palm oil, a vegetable oil used by British manufacturers for soap, candles, and lubricants. From the mid-1830s, the trading states of the Niger Delta emerged as the premier exporters of palm oil. Coastal Africans there grew rich and used their wealth to buy large numbers of male slaves to paddle the giant dugout canoes that transported palm oil from inland markets along the narrow delta creeks to the trading ports.

Another effect of the suppression of the slave trade was the spread of Western cultural influences in West Africa. To serve as a base for their anti–slave trade naval squadron, in 1808 the British had taken over the small colony of Sierra Leone°. Over the next several years, 130,000 men, women, and children taken from "captured" vessels were liberated in Sierra Leone. Christian missionaries helped settle these impoverished and dispirited **recaptives** in and around Freetown, the capital. In time, the mission churches and schools made many willing converts among such men and women.

Sierra Leone's schools also produced a number of distinguished graduates. For example, Samuel Adjai Crowther (1808–1891), freed as a youth from a slave ship in 1821 by the British squadron, became the first Anglican bishop in West Africa in 1864, administering a pioneering diocese along the lower Niger River. James Africanus Horton (1835–1882), the son of a slave liberated in Sierra Leone, became a doctor and the author of many studies of West Africa.

Other Western cultural influences came from people of African birth or descent returning to their ancestral homeland in this era. In 1821, to the south of Sierra Leone, free black Americans began a settlement that grew into the Republic of Liberia, a place of liberty at a time when slavery was legal and flourishing in the United States. Free blacks from Brazil and Cuba chartered ships to return to their West African homelands, bringing with them Roman Catholicism, architectural motifs, and clothing fashions from the New World. Although the number of Africans exposed to Western culture in 1870 was still small, this influence grew rapidly.

Map 21.1 Africa in the Nineteenth Century Expanding internal and overseas trade drew much of Africa into global networks, but foreign colonies in 1870 were largely confined to Algeria and southern Africa. Growing trade, Islamic reform movements, and other internal forces created important new states throughout the continent.

Sierra Leone (see-ER-uh lee-OWN)

Secondary Empires in Eastern Africa

When British patrols hampered the slave trade in West Africa, slavers moved southward and then around the tip of southern Africa to eastern Africa. There the Atlantic slave trade joined an existing trade in slaves to the Islamic world that also was expanding. Two-thirds of the 1.2 million slaves exported from eastern Africa in the nineteenth century went to markets in North Africa and the Middle East; the other third went to European plantations in the Americas and the Indian Ocean.

Slavery within eastern Africa also grew between 1800 and 1873, as Arab and Swahili owners purchased some 700,000 slaves from inland eastern Africa to do the labor-intensive work of harvesting cloves on plantations on Zanzibar Island and the neighboring coast. These territories belonged to the sultan of Oman, an Arabian kingdom on the Persian Gulf. The sultan moved his court to Zanzibar in 1840. Zanzibar also was an important market for ivory, most of which was shipped to India, where much of it was carved into decorative objects for middle-class Europeans.

Caravans led by African and Arab merchants brought ivory from hundreds of miles inland. Some of these merchants created large personal empires by using capital they had borrowed from Indian bankers and modern firearms they had bought from Europeans and Americans. These modern rifles felled countless elephants for their ivory tusks and inflicted widespread devastation and misery on the inland people.

One can blame the Zanzibari traders for the pillage and havoc in the once-peaceful center of Africa. However, the circle of responsibility was still broader. Europeans supplied the weapons used by the invaders and were major consumers of ivory and cloves. For this reason, histories have referred to the states carved out of eastern Africa as "secondary empires," in contrast to the empire that Britain was establishing directly. At the same time, Britain was working to bring the Indian Ocean slave trade to an end in eastern Africa. British officials pressured the sultan of Oman into halting the Indian Ocean slave trade from Zanzibar in 1857 and ending the import of slaves into Zanzibar in 1873.

INDIA UNDER BRITISH RULE

The people of South Asia felt the impact of European commercial, cultural, and colonial expansion more immediately and profoundly than did the people of Africa. While Europeans were laying claim to only small parts of Africa between 1750 and 1870, nearly all of India (with three times the population of all of Africa) came under Britain's direct or indirect rule. After the founding of the East India Company in 1600, it took British interests 250 years to commandeer the colonies and trade of the Dutch, fight off French and Indian challenges, and pick up the pieces of the decaying Mughal° Empire. By 1763 the French were stymied, in 1795 the Dutch company was dissolved, and in 1858 the last Mughal emperor was dethroned, leaving the vast subcontinent in British hands.

Company Men

As Mughal power weakened in the eighteenth century, British, Dutch, and French companies expanded into India (see Map 21.2). Such far-flung European trading companies were speculative and risky ventures. Their success depended on hard-drinking and ambitious young "Company Men," who used hard bargaining, and hard fighting when necessary, to persuade Indian rulers to allow them to establish trading posts at strategic points along the coast. To protect their fortified warehouses from attack by other Europeans or by native states, the companies hired and trained Indian troops known as sepoys°. In divided India, these private armies came to hold the balance of power.

In 1691, the East India Company (EIC) had convinced the nawab° (the term used for Mughal governors) of the large state of Bengal in northeast India to let the company establish a fortified outpost at the fishing port of Calcutta. A new nawab, pressing claims for additional tribute from the prospering port, overran the fort in 1756 and imprisoned a group of EIC men in a cell so small that many died of suffocation. To avenge their deaths in this "Black Hole of Calcutta," a large EIC force from Madras overthrew the nawab. The weak Mughal

---

Mughal (MOO-guhl)   **sepoy** (SEE-poy)   **nawab** (NAH-wab)

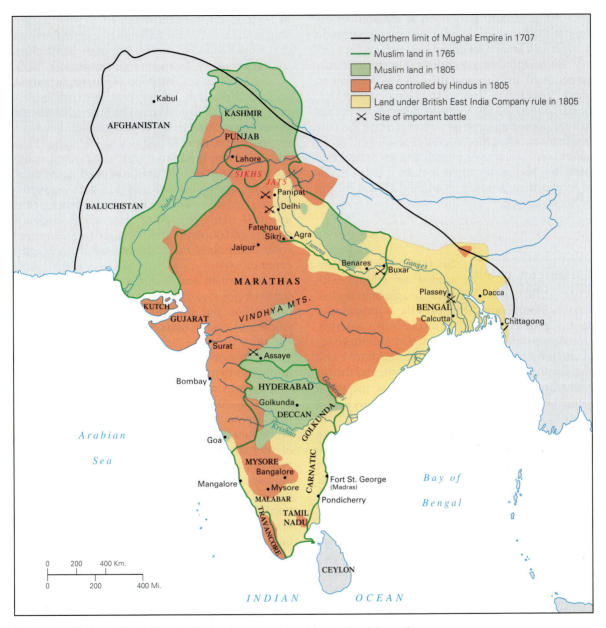

Map 21.2   India, 1707–1805   As Mughal power weakened during the eighteenth century, other Indian states and the British East India Company expanded their territories.

emperor was persuaded to acknowledge the EIC's right to rule Bengal in 1765. Fed by the tax revenues of Bengal as well as by profits from trade, the EIC was on its way. Calcutta grew into a city of 250,000 by 1788.

In southern India, EIC forces secured victory for the British Indian candidate for nawab of Arcot during the Seven Years War, thereby gaining an advantage over French traders who had supported the loser. The defeat of Tipu Sultan of Mysore at the end of the century (described at the start of the chapter) secured south India for the company and prevented a French resurgence.

Along with Calcutta and Madras, the third major center of British power in India was Bombay, on the western coast. There, after a long conflict with Indian rulers, the EIC gained a decisive advantage in 1818, annexing large territories to form the core of what was called the "Bombay Presidency." Some states were taken over completely, as Bengal had been, but very many others remained in the hands of local princes who accepted the political control of the company.

Raj and Rebellion, 1818–1857

In 1818, the EIC controlled an empire with more people than in all of western Europe and fifty times the population of the colonies the British had lost in North America. One thrust of **British raj** (reign) was to remake India on a British model through administrative and social reform, economic development, and the introduction of new technology. But at the same time, the Company Men—like the Mughals before them—had to temper their interference with Indian social and religious customs lest they provoke rebellion or lose the support of their Indian princely allies. For this reason and because of the complexity of the task of ruling such a vast empire, there were many inconsistencies in Britain's policies toward India.

The main policy was to create a powerful and efficient system of government. British rule before 1850 relied heavily on military power—170 sepoy regiments and 16 European regiments. Another policy was to disarm approximately 2 million warriors who had served India's many states and turn them to civilian tasks, mostly cultivation. A third policy gave freer rein to Christian missionaries eager to convert and uplift India's masses. Few converts were made, but the missionaries kept up steady pressure for social reforms.

Another key British policy was to turn India's complex and overlapping patterns of landholding into private property. In Bengal, this reform worked to the advantage of large landowners, but

in Mysore, the peasantry gained. Private ownership made it easier for the state to collect the taxes that were needed to pay for the costs of administration, the army, and economic reform.

Such policies of "Westernization, Anglicization, and modernization," as they have been called, were only one side of British rule. The other side was the bolstering of "traditions"—both real and newly invented. In the name of tradition, the Indian princes who ruled nearly half of British India were permitted by their British overlords to expand their power, splendor, and tenure well beyond what their predecessors had ever had. The British rulers themselves invented many "traditions"—including elaborate parades and displays—half borrowed from European royal pomp, half freely improvised from Mughal ceremonies.

The British and Indian elites danced sometimes in close partnership, sometimes in apparent opposition. But the ordinary people of India—women of every status, members of subordinate Hindu castes, the "untouchables" and "tribals" outside the caste system, and the poor generally—found less benefit in the British reforms and much new oppression in the new taxes and "traditions."

The transformation of British India's economy was also doubled-edged. On the one hand, British raj created many new jobs as a result of the growth of internal and external trade and the expansion of agricultural production, such as in opium in Bengal (largely for export to China), coffee in Ceylon (an island off the tip of India), and tea in Assam (a state in northeastern India). On the other hand, competition from cheap cotton goods produced in Britain's industrial mills drove many Indians out of the handicraft textile industry. In the eighteenth century, India had been the world's greatest exporter of cotton textiles; in the nineteenth century, India increasingly shipped raw cotton fiber to Britain.

Even the beneficial economic changes introduced under British rule were disruptive, and there were no safety nets for the needy. Thus, local rebellions by displaced ruling elites, disgruntled religious traditionalists, and the economically dispossessed were almost constant during the first half of the nineteenth century. The greatest concern was over the continuing loyalty of Indian sepoys in the EIC's army.

Discontent was growing among Indian soldiers. In the early decades of EIC rule, most sepoys came from Bengal, one of the first states the company had annexed. The Bengali sepoys resented the active recruitment of other ethnic groups into the army after 1848, such as Sikhs° from Punjab and Gurkhas from Nepal. Many high-caste Hindus objected to a new law in 1856 requiring new recruits to be available for service overseas in the growing Indian Ocean empire, for their religion prohibited ocean travel. The replacement of the standard military musket by the far more accurate Enfield rifle in 1857 also caused problems. Soldiers were ordered to use their teeth to tear open the ammunition cartridges, which were greased with animal fat. Hindus were offended by this order if the fat came from cattle, which they considered sacred. Muslims were offended if the fat came from pigs, which they considered unclean.

Although the cartridge-opening procedure was quickly changed, the initial discontent grew into rebellion by Hindu sepoys in May 1857. British troubles mushroomed when Muslim sepoys, peasants, and discontented elites joined in. The rebels asserted old traditions to challenge British authority: sepoy officers in Delhi proclaimed their loyalty to the Mughal emperor; others rallied behind the Maratha leader Nana Sahib. The rebellion was put down by March 1858, but it shook this piecemeal empire to its core.

Historians have attached different names and meanings to the events of 1857 and 1858. Concentrating on the technical fact that the uprising was an unlawful action by soldiers, nineteenth-century British historians labeled it the **"Sepoy Rebellion"** or the "Mutiny," and these names are still commonly used. Seeing in these events the beginnings of the later movement for independence, some modern Indian historians have termed it the "Revolution of 1857." In reality, it was much more than a simple mutiny, because it involved more than soldiers, but it was not yet a nationalist revolution, for the rebels' sense of a common Indian national identity was weak.

Sikh (seek)

Political Reform and Industrial Impact

Whatever it is called, the rebellion of 1857–1858 was a turning point in the history of modern India. In its wake, Indians gained a new centralized government, entered a period of rapid economic growth, and began to develop a new national consciousness.

The changes in government were immediate. In 1858, Britain eliminated the last traces of Mughal and EIC rule. In their place, a new secretary of state for India in London oversaw Indian policy, and a new governor-general in Delhi acted as the British monarch's viceroy on the spot. A proclamation by Queen Victoria in November 1858 guaranteed all Indians equal protection of the law and the freedom to practice their religions and social customs; it also assured Indian princes that so long as they were loyal to the queen, British India would respect their control of territories and "their rights, dignity and honour."[3]

A powerful and efficient bureaucracy controlled the Indian masses. Members of the elite **Indian Civil Service** (ICS), n tly graduates of Oxford and Cambridge Universities, held the senior administrative and judicial posts. Only a thousand men at the end of the nineteenth century, they visited the villages in their districts, heard lawsuits and complaints, and passed judgments. Beneath them were a far greater number of Indian officials and employees. Recruitment into the ICS was by open examination given only in England and thus inaccessible to most Indians. In 1870, only one Indian was a member of the ICS. Subsequent reforms led to fifty-seven Indian appointments by 1887, but there the process stalled.

A second transformation of India after 1857 resulted from involvement with industrial Britain. The government invested millions of pounds sterling in harbors, cities, irrigation canals, and other public works. British interests felled forests to make way for tea plantations, persuaded Indian farmers to grow cotton and jute for export, and created great irrigation systems to alleviate the famines that periodically decimated whole provinces. As a result, India's trade expanded rapidly.

Most of the exports were agricultural commodities for processing elsewhere: cotton fiber, opium,

Delhi Durbar, January 1, 1903   The parade of Indian princes on ornately decorated elephants and accompanied by retainers fostered their sense of belonging to the vast empire of India that British rule had created. The durbar was meant to evoke the glories of India's earlier empires, but many of the details and ceremonies were nineteenth-century creations.   (British Empire and Commonwealth Museum, Bristol, UK/The Bridgeman Art Library)

tea, silk, and sugar. In return, India imported manufactured goods from Britain, including the flood of machine-made cotton textiles that severely undercut Indian handloom weavers. The effects on individual Indians varied enormously. Some women found new jobs, though at very low pay, on plantations or in the growing cities, where prostitution flourished. Others struggled to hold families together or ran away from abusive husbands. Everywhere in India, poverty remained the norm.

The Indian government also promoted the introduction of new technologies into India not long after their appearance in Britain. Earlier in the century, there were steamboats on the rivers and a massive program of canal building for irrigation. Beginning in the 1840s, a railroad boom (paid for out of government revenues) gave India its first na-

tional transportation network, followed shortly by telegraph lines. Indeed, in 1870, India had the greatest rail network in Asia and the fourth largest in the world.

The freer movement of Indians and rapid urban growth promoted the spread of cholera°, a disease transmitted through water contaminated by human feces. In 1867, officials demonstrated the close connection between cholera and pilgrims who bathed in and drank from sacred pools and rivers. The installation of a new sewerage system (1865) and a filtered water supply (1869) in Calcutta dramatically reduced cholera deaths there. Similar measures in Bombay and Madras also led to great reductions, but most Indians lived in small

---

cholera (KAHL-uhr-uh)

Indian Railroad Station, 1866   British India built the largest network of railroads in Asia. People of every social class traveled by train.   (Eyre and Hobbs House Art Gallery)

villages, where famine and lack of sanitation kept cholera deaths high. Only after 1900 did sanitary improvements lower the death rate from cholera.

Rising Indian Nationalism

Both the successes and the failures of British rule stimulated the development of Indian nationalism. The failure of the rebellion of 1857 led some thoughtful Indians to argue that the only way to regain control of their destiny was to reduce their country's social and ethnic divisions.

Individuals such as Rammohun Roy (1772–1833) had promoted pan-Indian nationalism a generation earlier. A Western-educated Bengali from a Brahmin family, Roy was a successful ad-

ministrator for the EIC and a thoughtful student of comparative religion. His Brahmo Samaj° (Divine Society), founded in 1828, attracted Indians who sought to reconcile the values they found in the West with the ancient religious traditions of India. They backed the British outlawing of widow burning (*sati*°) in 1829 and of slavery in 1843 and sought to correct other abuses of women and female infanticide. Roy and his followers advocated reforming the caste system and urged a return to the founding principles set out in the Upanishads, ancient sacred writings of Hinduism.

Although Brahmo Samaj remained an influential movement, a growing number of Indian intellectuals based their nationalism on the secular

Brahmo Samaj (BRAH-moh suh-MAHJ   *sati* (suh-TEE)

values they absorbed in Western schools. European and American missionaries played a prominent role in the spread of Western education. In 1870, there were 790,000 Indians in over 24,000 elementary and secondary schools, and India's three universities (established in 1857) awarded 345 degrees.

Many of the new nationalists came from the Indian middle class. Hoping to increase their influence and improve their employment opportunities in the Indian government, they convened the first **Indian National Congress** in 1885. The members sought a larger role for Indians in the civil service and called for more money to be spent on alleviating the poverty of the Indian masses. The Indian National Congress effectively voiced the opinions of elite, Western-educated Indians, but it would need the support of the masses to challenge British rule.

BRITAIN'S EASTERN EMPIRE

In 1750 Britain's empire was centered on slave-based plantation and settler colonies in the Americas. A century later its main focus was on commercial networks and colonies in the East. In 1750 the French and Dutch were also serious contenders for global dominion. A century later they had been eclipsed by the British colossus that was straddling the world.

Several distinct changes facilitated the expansion and transformation of Britain's overseas empire. A string of military victories pushed aside other rivals for overseas trade and colonies; new policies favored free trade over mercantilism; and changes in shipbuilding techniques increased the speed and volume of maritime commerce. Linked to these changes were new European settlements in southern Africa, Australia, and New Zealand and the growth of a new long-distance trade in indentured labor.

Colonies and Commerce

As the story of Tipu Sultan told at the beginning of this chapter illustrates, France was still a serious rival for dominion in the Indian Ocean at the end of the eighteenth century. However, defeats in the wars of the French Revolu-

tion (see Chapter 19) ended Napoleon's dream of restoring French dominance overseas. The wars also dismantled much of the Netherlands' Indian Ocean empire. When French armies occupied the Netherlands, the Dutch ruler, who had fled to Britain in January 1795, authorized the British to take over Dutch possessions overseas in order to keep them out of French hands. During 1795 and 1796 British forces quickly occupied the Cape Colony at the tip of southern Africa, the strategic Dutch port of Malacca on the strait between the Indian Ocean and the South China Sea, and the island of Ceylon (modern Sri Lanka).

Then the British occupied Dutch Guiana and Trinidad in the southern Caribbean. In 1811 they even seized the island of Java, the center of the Netherlands' East Indian empire. British forces had also attacked French possessions, gaining control of the islands of Mauritius and Réunion in the southwestern Indian Ocean. At the end of the Napoleonic Wars in 1814, Britain returned Java to the Dutch and Réunion to the French but kept the Cape Colony, British Guiana (once part of Dutch Guiana), Trinidad, Ceylon, Malacca, and Mauritius.

The Cape Colony was valuable because of Cape Town's strategic importance as a supply station for ships making the long voyages between Britain and India. With the port city came some twenty thousand descendants of earlier Dutch and French settlers who occupied far-flung farms and ranches in its hinterland. Despite their European origins, these people thought of themselves as permanent residents of Africa and were beginning to refer to themselves as "Afrikaners" ("Africans" in their dialect of Dutch). British governors prohibited any expansion of the white settler frontier because such expansion invariably led to wars with indigenous Africans. This decision, along with the imposition of laws protecting African rights within Cape Colony (including the emancipation of slaves in 1834), alienated many Afrikaners.

Between 1836 and 1839 parties of Afrikaners embarked on a "Great Trek," leaving British-ruled Cape Colony for the fertile high *veld* (plateau) to the north that two decades of Zulu wars had depopulated. The Great Trek led to the foundation of three new settler colonies in southern Africa by 1850: the Afrikaners' Orange Free State and Transvaal on the high veld and the British colony of Na-

Great Trek Aided by African Servants The ox-drawn wagons of the Afrikaners struggled over the Drakensberg Mountains to the high plains in an effort to escape British control. (Liaison/Getty Images)

tal on the Indian Ocean coast. Although firearms enabled the settlers to win some important battles against the Zulu and other Africans, they were still a tiny minority surrounded by the populous and powerful independent African kingdoms that had grown up at the beginning of the century. A few thousand British settlers came to Natal and the Cape Colony by midcentury, but these colonies were important to Britain only as stopovers between Britain and British India.

Meanwhile, another strategic British outpost was being established in Southeast Asia. One prong of the advance was led by Thomas Stamford Raffles, who had governed Java during the period of British occupation from 1811 to 1814. After Java's return to the Dutch, Raffles helped the British East India Company establish a new free port at Singapore in 1824, on the site of a small Malay fishing village with a superb harbor. By attracting British

merchants and Chinese businessmen and laborers, Singapore soon became the center of trade and shipping between the Indian Ocean and China. Along with Malacca and other possessions on the strait, Singapore formed the "Straits Settlements," which British India administered until 1867.

Further British expansion in Malaya (now Malaysia) did not occur until after 1874, but it came more quickly in neighboring Burma. Burma had emerged as a powerful kingdom by 1750, with plans for expansion. In 1785 Burma tried to annex neighboring territories of Siam (now Thailand) to the east, but a coalition of Thai leaders thwarted Burmese advances by 1802. Burma next attacked Assam to the west, but this action led to war with British India, which was concerned for the security of its own frontier with Assam. After a two-year war, India annexed Assam in 1826 and occupied two coastal provinces of northern Burma. As rice and timber trade from these provinces grew important, the occupation became permanent, and in 1852 British India annexed the port of Rangoon and the rest of coastal Burma.

Imperial Policies and Shipping

Through such piecemeal acquisitions, by 1870 Britain had added several dozen colonies to the twenty-six colonies it had in 1792, after the loss of the thirteen in North America (see Chapter 19). Nevertheless, historians usually portray Britain in this period as a reluctant empire builder, its leaders unwilling to acquire new outposts that could prove difficult and expensive to administer. This apparent contradiction is resolved by the recognition that the underlying goal of most British imperial expansion during these decades was trade rather than territory. Most of the new colonies were meant to serve as ports in the growing network of shipping that encircled the globe or as centers of production and distribution for those networks.

This new commercial expansion was closely tied to the needs of Britain's growing industrial economy and reflected a new philosophy of overseas trade. Rather than rebuilding the closed, mercantilist network of trade with its colonies, Britain sought to trade freely with all parts of the world. Free trade was also a wise policy in light of the independence of so many former colonies in the Americas (see Chapter 19).

Whether colonized or not, more and more African, Asian, and Pacific lands were being drawn into the commercial networks created by British expansion and industrialization. As was pointed out earlier, uncolonized parts of West Africa became major exporters to Britain of vegetable oils for industrial and domestic use and of forest products for dyes and construction, while areas of eastern Africa free of European control exported ivory that ended up as piano keys and decorations in the elegant homes of the industrial middle class. From the far corners of the world came coffee, cocoa, and tea (along with sugar to sweeten them) for the tables of the new industrial classes in Britain and other parts of Europe, and indigo dyes and cotton fibers for their expanding textile factories.

In return, the factories of the industrialized nations supplied manufactured goods at very attractive prices. By the mid-nineteenth century a major part of their textile production was destined for overseas markets. Sales of cotton cloth to Africa increased 950 percent from the 1820s to the 1860s. British trade to India grew 350 percent between 1841 and 1870, while India's exports increased 400 percent. Trade with other regions also expanded rapidly. In most cases such trade benefited both sides, but there is no question that the industrial nations were the dominant partners.

A second impetus to global commercial expansion was the technological revolution in the construction of oceangoing ships under way in the nineteenth century. The middle decades of the century were the golden age of the sailing ship. Using iron to fasten timbers together permitted shipbuilders to construct much larger vessels. Merchant ships in the eighteenth century rarely exceeded 300 tons, but after 1850 swift American-built **clipper ships** of 2,000 tons were commonplace in the British merchant fleet. Huge canvas sails hung from tall masts made the streamlined clippers faster than earlier vessels. Ships from the East Indies or India had taken six months to reach Europe in the seventeenth century; after 1850 the new ships could complete the voyage in half that time.

This increase in size and speed lowered shipping costs and further stimulated maritime trade. The growth in size and numbers of ships increased the tonnage of British merchant shipping by 400 percent between 1778 and 1860. To extend the life of such ships in tropical lands, clippers intended for Eastern service generally were built of teak and other tropical hardwoods from new British colonies in South and Southeast Asia. Although tropical forests began to be cleared for rice and sugar plantations as well as for timbers, the effects on the environment and people of Southeast Asia came primarily after 1870.

Colonization of Australia and New Zealand

The development of new ships and shipping contributed to a third form of British rule in the once-remote South Pacific. Rather than rule indigenous populations, as they did in India, or set up commercial outposts, as they did in Singapore and Cape Town, British settlers displaced indigenous populations in the new colonies of Australia and New Zealand, just as they had done in North America.

Portuguese mariners had sighted the continent of Australia in the early seventeenth century, but it was too remote to be of much interest to Europeans. However, after the English adventurer Captain James Cook systematically explored New Zealand and the fertile eastern coast of Australia between 1769 and 1778, expanding shipping networks brought in growing numbers of visitors and settlers.

At the time of Cook's visits Australia was the home of about 650,000 hunting-and-gathering people, whose Melanesian° ancestors had settled there some forty thousand years earlier. The two islands of New Zealand, lying 1,000 miles (1,600 kilometers) southeast of Australia, were inhabited by about 250,000 Maori°, who practiced hunting, fishing, and simple forms of agriculture, which their Polynesian ancestors had introduced around 1200 C.E. Because of their long isolation from the rest of humanity, the populations of Australia and New Zealand were as vulnerable as the Amerindians had been to unfamiliar diseases introduced by new overseas contacts. In the 1890s only 93,000 aboriginal Australians and 42,000 Maori had survived the

Melanesian (mel-uh-NEE-zhuhn)   **Maori** (MOW-ree [*ow* as in *cow*])

exposure to Europeans. By then, British settler populations had come to outnumber and dominate the indigenous peoples.

The first permanent British settlers in Australia were 736 convicts, of whom 188 were women, sent into exile from British prisons in 1788. Over the next few decades, Australian penal colonies grew slowly and had only slight contact with the indigenous population, whom the British called "Aborigines." However, the discovery of gold in 1851 brought a flood of free European settlers (and some Chinese) and hastened the end of the penal colonies. When the gold rush subsided, government subsidies enabled tens of thousands of British settlers to settle "down under." Improved sailing ships made possible a voyage halfway around the world, although it still took more than three months to reach Australia from Britain. By 1860 Australia had a million immigrants, and the settler population doubled during the next fifteen years.

British settlers were drawn more slowly to New Zealand. Some of the first were temporary residents along the coast who slaughtered seals and exported seal pelts to Western countries to be made into men's felt hats. A single ship in 1806 took away sixty thousand sealskins. By the early 1820s overhunting had nearly exterminated the seal population. Special ships also hunted sperm whales extensively near New Zealand for their oil, used for lubrication, soap, and lamps; ambergris°, an ingredient in perfume; and bone, used in women's corsets (see Environment and Technology: Whaling). Military action that overcame Maori resistance, a brief gold rush, and the availability of faster ships and subsidized passages attracted more British immigrants after 1860. The colony especially courted women immigrants to offset the preponderance of single men. By the early 1880s the fertile agricultural lands of this most distant frontier of the British Empire had a settler population of 500,000.

Britain encouraged the settlers in Australia and New Zealand to become self-governing, following the 1867 model that had formed the giant Dominion of Canada out of the very diverse and thinly settled colonies of British North America. In 1901 a unified Australia emerged from the federation of six separate colonies. New Zealand became a self-governing dominion in 1907.

Britain's policies toward its settler colonies in Canada and the South Pacific reflected a desire to avoid the conflicts that had led to the American Revolution in the eighteenth century. By gradually turning over governing power to the colonies' inhabitants, Britain accomplished three things. It satisfied the settlers' desire for greater control over their own territories; it muted demands for independence; and it made the colonial governments responsible for most of their own expenses. Indigenous peoples were outvoted by the settlers or even excluded from voting.

North American patterns also shaped the indigenous peoples' fate. An 1897 Australian law segregated the remaining Aborigines onto reservations, where they lacked the rights of Australian citizenship. The requirement that voters had to be able to read and write English kept Maori from voting in early New Zealand elections, but four seats in the lower house of the legislature were reserved for Maori from 1867 on.

In other ways the new settler colonies were more progressive. Australia developed very powerful trade unions, which improved the welfare of skilled and semiskilled urban white male workers, promoted democratic values, and exercised considerable political clout. In New Zealand, where sheep raising was the main occupation, populist and progressive sentiments promoted the availability of land for the common person. Australia and New Zealand were also among the first states in the world to grant women the right to vote, beginning in 1894.

New Labor Migrations

Europeans were not the only people to transplant themselves overseas in the mid-nineteenth century. Between 1834 and 1870 many thousands of Indians, Chinese, and Africans responded to labor recruiters, especially to work overseas on sugar plantations. In the half-century after 1870 tens of thousands of Asians and Pacific Islanders made similar voyages.

In part these migrations were linked to the end of slavery. After their emancipation in British

---

ambergris (AM-ber-grees)

Whaling

The rapid expansion of whaling aptly illustrates the growing power of technology over nature in this period. Many contemporaries, like many people today, were sickened by the killing of the planet's largest living mammals. American novelist Herman Melville captured the conflicting sentiments in his epic whaling story, *Moby Dick* (1851). One of his characters enthusiastically explains why the grisly and dangerous business existed:

> But, though the world scorns us as whale hunters, yet does it unwittingly pay us the profoundest homage; yea, an all abounding adoration! for almost all the tapers, lamps, and candles that burn around the globe, burn, as before so many shrines, to our glory!

Melville's character overstates the degree to which whale oil dominated illumination and does not mention its many other industrial uses. Neither does he describe the commercial importance of whalebone (baleen). For a time its use in corsets allowed fashionable women to achieve the hourglass shape that fashion dictated. Whalebone's use for umbrella stays, carriage springs, fishing rods, suitcase frames, combs, brushes, and many other items made it the plastic of its day.

New manufacturing technologies went hand in hand with new hunting technologies. The revolution in ship design enabled whalers from Europe and North America to extend the hunt into the southern oceans off New Zealand. By the nineteenth century whaling ships were armed with guns that shot a steel harpoon armed with vicious barbs deep into the whale. In the 1840s explosive charges on harpoon heads ensured the whale's immediate death. Yet, as this engraving of an expedition off New Zealand shows, flinging small harpoons from rowboats in the open sea continued to be part of the dangerous work.

Another century of extensive hunting devastated many whale species before international agreements finally limited the killing of these giant sea creatures.

---

colonies in 1834, the freed men and women were no longer willing to put in the long hours they had been forced to work as slaves. When given full freedom of movement, many left the plantations. To compete successfully with sugar plantations in Cuba, Brazil, and the French Caribbean that were still using slave labor, British colonies had to recruit new laborers.

India's impoverished people seemed one obvious alternative. After planters on Mauritius successfully introduced Indian laborers, the Indian labor trade moved to the British Caribbean in 1838. In 1841 the British government also allowed Caribbean planters to recruit Africans whom British patrols had rescued from slave ships and liberated in Sierra Leone and elsewhere. By 1870 nearly 40,000 Africans had settled in British colonies, along with over 500,000 Indians and over 18,000 Chinese. After the French and Dutch abolished slavery in 1848, their colonies also recruited over 150,000 new laborers from Asia and Africa.

Slavery was not abolished in Cuba until 1886, but the rising cost of slaves led the burgeoning sugar plantations to recruit 138,000 new laborers from China between 1847 and 1873. Indentured labor recruits also became the mainstay of new sugar plantations in places that had never known slave labor. After 1850 American planters in Hawaii recruited labor from China and Japan; British planters in Natal recruited from India; and those in Queensland (in northeastern Australia) relied on laborers from neighboring South Pacific islands.

Larger, faster ships made transporting laborers halfway around the world affordable, though voyages from Asia to the Caribbean still took an average of three months. Despite close regulation and

South Pacific Whaling   One boat was swamped, but the hunters killed the huge whale.
(The Granger Collection, New York)

supervision of shipboard conditions, the crowded accommodations encouraged the spread of cholera and other contagious diseases that took many migrants' lives.

All of these laborers served under **contracts of indenture,** which bound them to work for a specified period (usually from five to seven years) in return for free passage to their overseas destination. They were paid a small salary and were provided with housing, clothing, and medical care. Indian indentured laborers also received the right to a free passage home if they worked a second five-year contract. British Caribbean colonies required forty women to be recruited for every hundred men as a way to promote family life. So many Indians chose to stay in Mauritius, Trinidad, British Guiana, and Fiji that they constituted a third or more of the total population of these colonies by the early twentieth century.

Although many early recruits from China and the Pacific Islands were kidnapped or otherwise coerced into leaving their homes, in most cases the new indentured migrants had much in common with contemporary emigrants from Europe (described in Chapter 20). Both groups chose to leave their homelands in hopes of improving their economic and social conditions. Both earned modest salaries. Many saved to bring money back when they returned home, or they used their earnings to buy land or to start a business in their new countries, where large numbers chose to remain. One major difference was that people recruited as indentured laborers were generally so much poorer than emigrants from Europe that they had to accept lower-paying jobs in less desirable areas because they could not pay their own way. However, it is also true that many European immigrants into distant places like Australia and New Zealand had their passages subsidized but did not have to sign a contract of indenture. This shows that racial and cultural preferences, not just economics, shaped the flow of labor into European colonies.

A person's decision to accept an indentured labor contract could also be shaped by political circumstances. In India disruption brought by British colonial policies and the suppression of the 1857 rebellion contributed significantly to people's desire to emigrate. Poverty, famine, and warfare had not been strangers in precolonial India. Nor were these causes of emigration absent in China and Japan.

The indentured labor trade reflected the unequal commercial and industrial power of the West, but it was not an entirely one-sided creation. The men and women who signed indentured contracts were trying to improve their lives by emigrating, and many succeeded. Whether for good or ill, more and more of the world's peoples saw their lives being influenced by the existence of Western colonies, Western ships, and Western markets.

CONCLUSION

What is the global significance of these complex political and economic changes in southern Asia, Africa, and the South Pacific? One perspective stresses the continuing exploitation of the weak by the strong, of African, Asian, and Pacific peoples by aggressive Europeans. In this view, the emergence of Britain as a dominant power in the Indian Ocean basin and South Pacific continued the European expansion that the Portuguese and the Spanish pioneered and the Dutch took over. Likewise, Britain's control over the densely populated lands of South and Southeast Asia and over the less populated lands of Australia and New Zealand can be seen as a continuation of the conquest and colonization of the Americas.

From another perspective what was most important about this period was not the political and military strength of the Europeans but their growing domination of the world's commerce, especially through long-distance ocean shipping. In this view, the British, like other Europeans, were drawn to Africa and southern Asia by a desire to obtain new materials.

However, Britain's commercial expansion in the nineteenth century was also the product of Easterners' demand for industrial manufactures. The growing exchanges could be mutually beneficial. African and Asian consumers found industrially produced goods far cheaper and sometimes better than the handicrafts they replaced or supplemented. Industrialization created new markets for African and Asian goods, as in the case of the vegetable-oil trade in West Africa or of cotton in Egypt and India. There were also negative impacts, as in the case of the weavers of India and the damage to species of seals and whales.

Europeans' military and commercial strength did not reduce Africa, Asia, and the Pacific to mere appendages of Europe. While the balance of power shifted in the Europeans' favor between 1750 and 1870, other cultures were still vibrant and local initiatives often dominant. Islamic reform movements and the rise of the Zulu nation had greater significance for their respective regions of Africa than did Western forces. Despite some ominous concessions to European power, Southeast Asians were still largely in control of their own destinies. Even in India, most people's lives and beliefs showed more continuity with the past than with the changes caused by British rule.

Finally, it must not be imagined that Asians and Africans were powerless in dealing with European expansion. The Indian princes who extracted concessions from the British in return for their cooperation and the Indians who rebelled against the raj both forced the system to accommodate their needs. Moreover, some Asians and Africans were beginning to use European education, technology, and methods to transform their own societies. Leaders in Egypt, India, and other lands, like those in Russia, the Ottoman Empire, and China—the subject of Chapter 22—were learning to challenge the power of the West on its own terms. In 1870 no one could say how long and how difficult that learning process would be, but Africans and Asians would continue to shape their own futures.

■ Key Terms

Zulu	nawab
Sokoto Caliphate	British raj
modernization	Sepoy Rebellion
Muhammad Ali	Indian Civil Service
"legitimate" trade	Indian National Congress
recaptives	clipper ship
sepoys	contract of indenture

■ Suggested Reading

Volumes 2 and 3 of *The Oxford History of the British Empire,* edited by William Roger Louis, (1998, 1999), are the most up-to-date global surveys of this period. Less Anglocentric in its interpretation is Immanuel Wallerstein's *The Modern World-System III: The Second Era of Great Expansion of the Capitalist World-Economy, 1730–1840s* (1989).

For more on African topics, see Roland Oliver and Anthony Atmore, *Africa Since 1800,* 4th ed. (1994); J. D. Omer-Cooper, *The Zulu Aftermath* (1966); Murray Last, *The Sokoto Caliphate* (1967); A. G. Hopkins, *An Economic History of West Africa* (1973); and Norman R. Bennett, *Arab Versus European: War and Diplomacy in Nineteenth Century East Central Africa* (1985).

Very readable introductions to India in this period are Sugata Bose and Ayeshia Jalal, *Modern South India* (1998); Burton Stein, *A History of India* (1998); and Stanley Wolpert, *A New History of India,* 6th ed. (1999). See also Daniel Headrick, *The Tentacles of Progress: Technology Transfer in the Age of Imperialism, 1850–1940* (1988).

A good introduction to the complexities of Southeast Asian history is D. R. SarDesai, *Southeast Asia: Past and Present,* 2nd ed. (1989). More detail can be found in the appropriate chapters of Nicholas Tarling, ed., *The Cambridge History of South East Asia,* 2 vols. (1992). The second and third volumes of *The Oxford History of Australia,* ed. Geoffrey Bolton (1992, 1988), deal with the period covered by this chapter. A very readable multicultural and gendered perspective is provided by *Images of Australia,* ed. Gillian Whitlock and David Carter (1992). *The Oxford Illustrated History of New Zealand,* ed. Keith Sinclair (1990), provides a wide-ranging introduction to that nation.

For summaries of recent scholarship on the indentured labor trade see David Northrup, *Indentured Labor in the Age of Imperialism, 1834-1922* (1995), and Robin Cohen, ed., *The Cambridge Survey of World Migration,* part 3, "Asian Indentured and Colonial Migration" (1995).

An outstanding analysis of British whaling is Gordon Jackson's *The British Whaling Trade* (1978). Edouard A. Stackpole's *Whales & Destiny: The Rivalry Between America, France, and Britain for Control of the Southern Whale Fishery, 1785-1825* (1972) is more anecdotal.

■ Notes

1. Quoted in P. J. Vatikiotis, *The History of Modern Egypt: From Muhammad Ali to Mubarak,* 4th ed. (Baltimore: Johns Hopkins University Press, 1991), 74.
2. David Eltis, "Precolonial Western Africa and the Atlantic Economy," in *Slavery and the Rise of the Atlantic Economy,* ed. Barbara Solow (New York: Cambridge University Press, 1991), table 1.
3. Quoted by Bernard S. Cohn, "Representing Authority in Victorian England," in *The Invention of Tradition,* ed. Eric Hobsbawm and Terence Ranger (Cambridge: Cambridge University Press, 1983), 165.

22 Land Empires in the Age of Imperialism, 1800–1870

CHAPTER OUTLINE

The Ottoman Empire

The Russian Empire

The Qing Empire

DIVERSITY AND DOMINANCE: The French Occupation of Egypt

When the emperor of the Qing° (the last empire to rule China) died in 1799, the imperial court received a shock. For decades officials had known that the emperor was indulging his handsome young favorite, Heshen°, allowing him extraordinary privileges and power. Senior bureaucrats hated Heshen, suspecting him of overseeing a widespread network of corruption. They believed he had been scheming to prolong the inconclusive wars against the native Miao° peoples of southwest China in the late 1700s. Glowing reports of successes against the rebels had poured into the capital, and enormous sums of government money had flowed to the battlefields. But there was no adequate accounting for the funds, and the war persisted.

After the emperor's death, Heshen's enemies ordered his arrest. When they searched his mansion, they discovered a magnificent hoard of silk, furs, porcelain, furniture, and gold and silver. His personal cash alone exceeded what remained in the imperial treasury. The new emperor ordered Heshen to commit suicide with a rope of gold silk. The government seized Heshen's fortune, but the financial damage could not be undone. The declining agricultural base could not replenish the state coffers, and much of the income that did flow in was squandered by an increasingly corrupt bureaucracy. In the 1800s the Qing Empire faced increasing challenges from Europe and the United States with an empty treasury, a stagnant economy, and a troubled society.

The Qing Empire's problems were not unique. They were common to all the land-based empires

Qing (ching)   Heshen (huh-shun)   Miao (mee-ow)

of Eurasia, where old and inefficient ways of governing put states at risk. The international climate was increasingly dominated by industrializing European economies drawing on the wealth of their overseas colonies. During the early 1800s rapid population growth and slow agricultural growth affected much of Eurasia. Earlier military expansion had stretched the resources of imperial treasuries (see Chapter 18), leaving the land-based empires vulnerable to European military pressure. Responses to this pressure varied, with reform and adaptation gaining headway in some lands and tradition being reasserted in others. In the long run, attempts to meet western Europe's economic and political demands produced financial indebtedness to France, Britain, and other Western powers.

This chapter contrasts the experiences of the Qing Empire with those of the Russian and Ottoman Empires. Whereas the Qing opted for resistance, the others made varying attempts to adapt and reform. Russia eventually became part of Europe and shared in many aspects of European culture, while the Ottomans and the Qing became subject to ever-greater imperialist pressure. These different responses raise the question of the role of culture in shaping western Europe's relations with the rest of the world in the nineteenth century.

As you read this chapter, ask yourself the following questions:

- Why did the Ottoman and Qing Empires find themselves on the defensive in their encounters with Europeans in the 1800s?

- By what strategies did the land-based empires try to adapt to nineteenth-century economic and political conditions?

- How did the Russian Empire maintain its status as both a European power and a great Asian land empire?

THE OTTOMAN EMPIRE

During the eighteenth century the central government of the Ottoman Empire lost much of its power to provincial governors, military commanders, ethnic leaders, and bandit chiefs. In several parts of the empire local officials and large landholders tried to increase their independence and divert imperial funds into their own coffers.

A kingdom in Arabia led by the Saud family, following the puritanical and fundamentalist religious views of an eighteenth-century leader named Muhammad ibn Abd al-Wahhab°, took control of the holy cities of Mecca and Medina and deprived the sultan of the honor of organizing the annual pilgrimage. In Egypt factions of mamluk slave-soldiers reemerged as political forces for the first time since the Ottoman conquest in 1517.

For the sultans, the outlook was bleak. The inefficient Janissary corps used the political power it enjoyed in Istanbul to force Sultan Selim III to abandon efforts to train a modern, European-style army at the end of the eighteenth century. This situation unexpectedly changed when France invaded Egypt.

Egypt and the Napoleonic Example, 1798–1840

Napoleon Bonaparte and an invasion force of 36,000 men and four hundred ships invaded Egypt in May 1798 (see Diversity and Dominance: The French Occupation of Egypt). The French quickly defeated the mamluk forces that for several decades had dominated the country under the loose jurisdiction of the Ottoman sultan in Istanbul. Fifteen months later, after being stopped by Ottoman land and British naval forces in an attempted invasion of Syria, Napoleon secretly left Cairo and returned to France. Three months later he seized power and made himself emperor.

Back in Egypt, his generals tried to administer a country that they only poorly understood. Cut off from France by British ships in the Mediterranean, they had little hope of remaining in power and

Muhammad ibn Abd al-Wahhab (Moo-HAH-muhd ib-uhn ab-dahl-wa HAHB)

agreed to withdraw in 1801. For the second time in three years, a collapse of military power produced a power vacuum in Egypt. The winner of the ensuing contest was **Muhammad Ali°**, the commander of a contingent of Albanian soldiers sent by the sultan to restore imperial control. By 1805 he had taken the place of the official Ottoman governor, and by 1811 he had dispossessed the mamluks of their lands and privileges.

Muhammad Ali's rise to power coincided with the meteoric career of Emperor Napoleon I. It is not surprising, therefore, that he adopted many French practices in rebuilding the Egyptian state. Militarily, he established special schools for training artillery and cavalry officers, army surgeons, military bandmasters, and others. The curricula of these schools featured European skills and sciences, and Muhammad Ali began to send promising officer trainees to France for education. In 1824 he started a gazette devoted to official affairs, the first newspaper in the Islamic world.

As discussed in Chapter 20, Muhammad Ali built all sorts of factories to outfit his new army. These did not prove efficient enough to survive, but they showed a determination to achieve independence and parity with the European powers.

In the 1830s Muhammad Ali's son Ibrahim invaded Syria and instituted some of the changes already under way in Egypt. The improved quality of the new Egyptian army had been proven during the Greek war of independence (see below), when Ibrahim had commanded an expeditionary force to help the sultan. In response, the sultan embarked on building his own new army in 1826. The two armies met when Ibrahim attacked northward into Anatolia in 1839 and defeated the army of his suzerain, the Ottoman sultan. The road to Istanbul seemed open until the European powers intervened and forced a withdrawal to the present-day border between Egypt and Israel.

Muhammad Ali remained Egypt's ruler, under the suzerainty of the sultan, until his death in 1849; and his family continued to rule the country until 1952. But his dream of making Egypt a mighty country capable of standing up to Europe faded. What survived was the example he had set for the sultans in Istanbul.

Ottoman Reform and the European Model, 1807–1853

At the end of the eighteenth century Sultan Selim° III (r. 1789–1807), a forward-looking ruler who stayed abreast of events in Europe, introduced reforms to create European-style military units, bring provincial governors under central government control, and standardize taxation. These reforms failed for political, more than economic, reasons.

The most violent and persistent opposition came from the **Janissary°** military corps (see Chapter 17). In the eighteenth century the Janissaries became a significant political force in Istanbul and in provincial capitals like Baghdad. At times, Janissary power produced military uprisings. In the Ottoman territory of **Serbia,** local residents intensely resented the control exercised by Janissary governors. The Orthodox Christians claimed that the Janissaries abused them. In response, Selim threatened to reassign the Janissaries to Istanbul. Suspecting that the sultan wanted to curb their political power, in 1805 the Janissaries revolted and massacred Christians in Serbia. Unable to reestablish central Ottoman rule over Serbia, the sultan had to rely on the ruler of Bosnia, another Balkan province, who joined his troops with the peasants of Serbia to suppress the Janissary uprising. The threat of Russian intervention prevented the Ottomans from disarming the victorious Serbians, so Serbia became effectively independent.

In the face of widespread rejection of his reforms, Selim suspended his program in 1806. Nevertheless, a massive military uprising occurred at Istanbul, and the sultan was deposed and imprisoned. Reform forces recaptured the capital, but not before Selim had been executed. Selim's cousin, Sultan Mahmud° II (r. 1808–1839), cautiously revived Selim's program, but he realized that reforms needed to be more systematic and imposed more forcefully. The effectiveness of radical reform in Muhammad Ali's Egypt drove this lesson home, as did the insurrection in Greece, during which the Egyptian military performed much better than the main Ottoman army.

Muhammad Ali (moo-HAM-mad AH-lee)

Selim (seh-LEEM)   **Janissary** (JAN-nih-say-ree)
Mahmud (MAH-mood)

C H R O N O L O G Y

	Ottoman Empire	Russian Empire	Qing Empire
1800			**1794–1804** White Lotus Rebellion
		1801–1825 Reign of Alexander I	
	1805–1849 Muhammad Ali governs Egypt		
	1808–1839 Rule of Mahmud II		
		1812 Napoleon's retreat from Moscow	
		1825 Decembrist revolt	
		1825–1855 Reign of Nicholas I	
	1826 Janissary corps dissolved		
	1829 Greek independence		
	1839 Abdul Mejid begins Tanzimat reforms		**1839–1842** Opium War
1850			**1850–1864** Taiping Rebellion
	1853–1856 Crimean War	**1853–1856** Crimean War	
		1855–1881 Reign of Alexander II	
			1856–1860 Arrow War
		1861 Emancipation of the serfs	
	1876 First constitution by an Islamic government		

DIVERSITY AND DOMINANCE

THE FRENCH OCCUPATION OF EGYPT

Napoleon's invasion of Egypt in 1798 strikingly illustrates the techniques of dominance employed by the French imperial power and the means of resistance available to noncombatant Egyptian intellectuals in reasserting their cultural diversity and independence. Abd al-Rahman al-Jabarti (1753–1826), from whose writings the first four passages are drawn, came from a family of ulama, or Muslim religious scholars. His three works concerning the French occupation, which lasted until 1801, provide the best Egyptian account of that period. The selections below start with the first half of Napoleon's first proclamation to the Egyptian people, which was published in Arabic at the time of the invasion and is quoted here from al-Jabarti's text.

In the Name of God the Compassionate the Merciful: There is no god but God. He has not begotten a son, and does not share in His Kingship.

On behalf of the French Republic, which is founded upon the principles of liberty and equality, the Commander-in-Chief of the French armies, the great head-general Bonaparte, hereby declares to all inhabitants of Egyptian lands that the Sanjaqid rulers of Egypt [i.e., the Mamluk commanders] have persisted far too long in their maltreatment and humiliation of the French nation and have unjustly subjected French merchants to all manner of abuse and extortion. The hour of their punishment has now come.

It is a great pity that this group of slave fighters [mamluks], caught in the mountains of Abkhazia and Georgia, have for such a long time perpetrated so much corruption in the fairest of all lands on the face of the globe. Now, the omnipotent Lord of the Universe has ordained their demise.

O people of Egypt, should they say to you that I have only come hither to defile your religion, this is but an utter lie that you must not believe. Say to my accusers that I have only come to rescue your rights from the hands of tyrants, and that I am a better servant of God—may He be praised and exalted—and that I revere His Prophet Muhammad and the grand Koran more than the group of slave fighters do.

Tell them also that all people stand equally before God and that reason, virtue, and knowledge comprise the only distinguishing qualities among them. Now, what do the group of slave fighters possess of reason, virtue, and knowledge that would distinguish them from the rest of the people and qualify them exclusively to benefit from everything that is desirable in this worldly life?

The most fertile of all agricultural lands, the prettiest concubines, the best horses, and most attractive residences, all are appropriated exclusively by them. If the land of Egypt was ever conferred upon this group of slave fighters exclusively, let them show us the document that God has written for them: of course, the Lord of the Universe acts with compassion and equity toward mankind. With His help—may He be Exalted—from this day on no Egyptian shall be excluded from high positions nor barred from acquiring high ranks, and men of reason, virtue and learning from among them will administer the affairs, and as a result the welfare of the entire Muslim community (*umma*) shall improve.

The following passages provide examples of al-Jabarti's line-by-line commentary on the proclamation and two examples of his more general comments on the French and on French rule.

Explanation of the wretched proclamation composed of incoherent words and vulgar phrases:

By saying, "in the Name of God the Compassionate the Merciful: There is no god but God. He has not begotten a son, and does not share in His Kingship" [the French] implicitly claim in three propositions that they concur with the three religions [Islam, Christianity, and Judaism] whereas in truth they falsify all three and indeed any other [viable] doctrine. They concur with the Muslims in opening [the statement] with the name of God and in rejecting His begetting a son or sharing in His Kingship. They differ from them in not professing the two essential Articles of Faith: refusing to recognize Prophet Muhammad, and rebuffing the essential teachings of Islam in word and deed. They concur with the Christians in most of what they say and do, but diverge over the question of Trinity, in their rejection of the vocation [of Christ], and furthermore in rebuffing their beliefs and rituals, killing the priests, and desecrating places of worship. They concur with the Jews in believing in one God, as the Jews also do not believe in the Trinity but hold on to anthropomorphism. [The French Republicans] do not share in the religious beliefs and practices of the Jews either. Apparently they do not follow any particular religion and do not adhere to a set of specific rituals: each of them fathoms a religion as it suits his own reason. The rest of the [people of France] are Christians but keep it hidden, and there are some real Jews among them as well. However, even those who may follow a religion, when they come to Egypt, they concur with the agents of the Republic in their insistence upon leading the Egyptians astray.

Their saying "On behalf of the French Republic, etc." implies that the proclamation comes from the Republic or their people directly, because unlike other nations they have no overlord or sovereign whom they unanimously appoint, and who has exclusive authority to speak on their behalf. It is now six years since they revolted against their sovereign and murdered him. Subsequently, the people agreed not to have a single ruler but rather to put the affairs of the government, provincial issues, legislation and administration, into the hands of men of discretion and reason among themselves. They chose and appointed men in a hierarchy: a head of the entire army followed in rank by generals and military commanders each in charge of groups of a thousand, two hundred, or ten men. They similarly appointed administrators and advisers by observing their essential equality and nonsupremacy of one over the others, in the same way that people are created equally in essence. This constitutes the foundation and touchstone of their system, and this is what "founded upon the principles of liberty and equality" means. The reference to "liberty" implies that unlike

the slaves and [the slave fighters ruling over Egypt] they are not anybody's slaves; the meaning of "equality" has already been explained.

[On that day the French] started to operate a new court bureau, which they named the Ad hoc Court (*mahkamat al-qadaya*). On this occasion they drafted a decree that included clauses framed in most unacceptable terms that sounded rather repellant to the ear. Six Copts and six Muslim merchants were appointed to the bureau, and the presiding judge and chief of the bureau was the Copt from Malta who used to work as secretary to Ayyub Bey, the notary (*daftardar*). Ad hoc cases involving commercial, civil, inheritance disputes, and other suits were referred to this bureau. [The French] formulated corrupt principles for this institution that were based on heresy, founded in tyranny, and rooted in all sorts of abominable unprecedented rulings (*bid'a al-sayyi'a*).

[The French] devastated the palace of Yusuf Salah al-Din including the cities where sovereigns and sultans held audiences, and they tore down strong foundations and demolished towering columns. They also destroyed mosques, meditation spots (*zawaya*), and shrines of martyrs (*mashahid*). They defaced the Grand Congregational Mosque, built by the venerable Muhammad b. Qalawan al-Malik al-Nasir: wrecked the pulpit, spoiled the mosque's courtyard, looted its lumber, undermined its columns, and razed the well-wrought iron enclosure inside of which the sultan used to pray.

*T*he final passage, which is not in any of al-Jabarti's chronicles, is the full text of an announcement distributed to Napoleon's thirty-six thousand troops on board ship as they headed for Egypt.

Soldiers,—You are about to undertake a conquest the effects of which on civilization and commerce are incalculable. The blow you are about to give to England will be the best aimed, and the most sensibly felt, she can receive until the time arrive when you can give her her death-blow.

We must make some fatiguing marches; we must fight several battles; we shall succeed in all we undertake. The destinies are with us. The Mameluke Beys, who favour exclusively English commerce, whose extortions oppress our merchants, and who tyrannise over the unfortunate inhabitants of the Nile, a few days after our arrival will no longer exist.

The people amongst whom we are going to live are Mahometans. The first article of their faith is this: "there is no God but God, and Mahomet is His prophet." Do not contradict them. Behave to them as you have behaved to the Jews—to the Italians. Pay respect to their muftis [jurists], and their Imaums [sic], as you did to the rabbis and the bishops. Extend to the ceremonies prescribed by the Koran and to the mosques the same toleration which you showed to the synagogues, to the religion of Moses and of Jesus Christ.

The Roman legions protected all religions. You will find here customs different from those of Europe. You must accommodate yourselves to them. The people amongst whom we are to mix differ from us in the treatment of women; but in all countries he who violates is a monster. Pillage enriches only a small number of men; it dishonours us; it destroys our resources; it converts into enemies the people whom it is our interest to have for friends.

The first town we shall come to was built by Alexander. At every step we shall meet with grand recollections, worthy of exciting the emulations of Frenchmen.
Bonaparte

QUESTIONS FOR ANALYSIS

1. Why are the reasons for invading Egypt given to the French soldiers different from those announced to the Egyptians?

2. How do Napoleon and al-Jabarti use religious feeling as a political tool?

3. What do texts like these suggest about the role culture plays in confrontations between imperial powers and imperialized peoples?

Source: First selection from *Abd al-Rahman al-Jabarti's History of Egypt,* ed. Thomas Phillipp and Moshe Perlmann (Stuttgart, 1994), translated by Hossein Kamaly. Second selection from Louis Antoine Fauvelet de Bourrienne, *Memoirs of Napoleon Bonaparte* (1843).

Greek independence in 1829 had dramatic international significance. A combination of Greek nationalist organizations and interlopers from Albania formed the independence movement. Europe's interest in the classical age of Greece and Rome led many Europeans to consider the Greeks' struggle for independence a campaign to recapture their classical glory from Muslim oppression. Some—including the "mad, bad and dangerous to know" English poet Lord Byron, who lost his life in the war—went to Greece to fight as volunteers. When the combined squadrons of the British, French, and Russian fleets, under orders to observe but not intervene in the war, made an unauthorized attack that sank the Ottoman fleet at the Battle of Navarino, Greek victory was assured (see Map 22.1).

Mahmud II concurred with the pro-Greek Europeans in viewing Ottoman military reversals in Greece as a sign of profound weakness. With popular outrage over the military setbacks strong, the sultan made his move in 1826. First he announced the creation of a new artillery unit, which he had

secretly been training. When the Janissaries rose in revolt, he ordered the new unit to bombard the Janissary barracks. The Janissary corps was officially dissolved.

Like Muhammad Ali, Mahmud felt he could not implement major changes without reducing the political power of the religious elite. He visualized restructuring the bureaucracy and the educational and legal systems, where ulama power was strongest. Before such strong measures could be undertaken, however, Ibrahim attacked from Syria in 1839. Battlefield defeat, the decision of the rebuilt Ottoman navy to switch sides and support Egypt, and the death of Mahmud, all in the same year, left the empire completely dependent on the European powers for survival.

Mahmud's reforming ideas received their widest expression in the **Tanzimat**° ("reorganization"), a series of reforms announced by his sixteen-year-old son and successor, Abdul Mejid°, in 1839 and

Tanzimat (TAHNZ-ee-MAT)   **Abdul Mejid** (ab-dul meh-JEED)

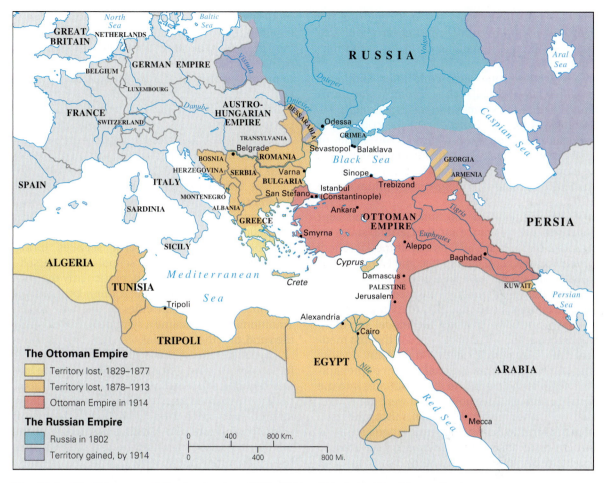

Map 22.1   The Ottoman and Russian Empires, 1829–1914   At its height the Ottoman Empire controlled most of the perimeter of the Mediterranean Sea. But in the 1800s Ottoman territory shrank as many countries gained their independence. The Black Sea, where the Turkish coast was vulnerable to assault, became a weak spot as Russian naval power grew. Russian challenges to the Ottomans at the eastern end of the Black Sea and to the Persians east and west of the Caspian aroused fears in Europe that Russia was trying to reach the Indian Ocean.

strongly endorsed by the European ambassadors. One proclamation called for public trials and equal protection under the law for all, whether Muslim, Christian, or Jew. It also guaranteed some rights of privacy, equalized the eligibility of men for conscription into the army (a practice copied from Egypt), and provided for a new, formalized method of tax collection that legally ended tax farming in the Ottoman Empire. It took many years and strenuous efforts by reforming bureaucrats, known

as the "men of the Tanzimat," to give substance to these reforms.

European observers praised the reforms for their noble principles and rejection of religious influence. Ottoman citizens were more divided; the Christians and Jews, for whom the Europeans showed the greatest concern, were generally more enthusiastic than the Muslims. Many historians see the Tanzimat as the dawn of modern thought and enlightened government in the

Middle East. Others point out that removing the religious elite from influence in government also removed the one remaining check on authoritarian rule.

Over time, one legal code after another—commercial, criminal, civil procedure—was introduced to take the place of the corresponding areas of religious legal jurisdiction. All the codes were modeled closely on those of Europe. The Shari'a, or Islamic law, gradually became restricted to matters of family law such as marriage and inheritance. As the Shari'a was displaced, job opportunities for the ulama shrank.

Like Muhammad Ali, Sultan Mahmud sent military cadets to France and the German states for training. In the 1830s an Ottoman imperial school of military sciences, later to become Istanbul University, was established. Instructors from western Europe taught chemistry, engineering, mathematics, and physics in addition to military history. Military education became the model for more general educational reforms. In 1838 the first medical school was established to train army doctors and surgeons. Later, a national system of preparatory schools was created to feed graduates into the military schools. The subjects that were taught and many of the teachers were foreign, raising the issue of whether Turkish should be a language of instruction. Because it was easier to import and use foreign textbooks than to write new ones in Turkish, French became the preferred language in all advanced professional and scientific training. In numerical terms, however, the great majority of students still learned to read and write in Quran schools down to the twentieth century.

In the capital city of Istanbul, the reforms stimulated the growth of a small but cosmopolitan milieu embracing European language and culture. The first Turkish newspaper, a government gazette modeled on that of Muhammad Ali, appeared in 1831. Other newspapers followed, many written in French. Travel to Europe—particularly to England and France—became popular among wealthy Turks. Interest in importing European military, industrial, and communications technology remained strong through the 1800s.

Changes in military practice had unforeseen cultural and social effects. Accepting the European notion that modern weapons and drill required modern military dress, beards were deemed unhygienic and, in artillery units, a fire hazard. Military headgear also became controversial. European military caps, which had leather bills on the front to protect against the glare of the sun, were not acceptable because they interfered with Muslim soldiers' touching their foreheads to the ground in prayer. The compromise was the brimless cap now called the *fez*, which was adopted by the military and then by Ottoman civil officials in the early years of Mahmud II's reign.

The empire's new orientation spread beyond the military. Government ministries that normally recruited from traditional bureaucratic families and relied on on-the-job training were gradually transformed into formal civil services hiring men educated in the new schools. Among self-consciously progressive men, particularly those in government service, European dress became the fashion in the Ottoman cities of the later 1800s. Traditional dress became a symbol of the religious, the rural, and the parochial.

Secularization of the legal code particularly affected non-Muslim Ottoman subjects. Islamic law had required non-Muslims to pay a special head tax that was sometimes explained as a substitute for military service. Under the Tanzimat, the tax was abolished and non-Muslims became liable for military service—unless they bought their way out by paying a new military exemption tax. The new law codes gave all male subjects equal access to the civil courts, while the operations of the Islamic law courts shrank. What enhanced the status of non-Muslims most, however, was the strong concern for their welfare consistently expressed by the European powers. The Ottoman Empire became a rich field of operation for Christian missionaries and European supporters of Jewish community life in the Muslim world.

The public rights and political participation granted during the Tanzimat applied specifically to men. Private life, including everything connected to marriage and divorce, remained within the sphere of religious law, and at no time was there a question of political participation or reformed education for women. Indeed, the reforms may have decreased the influence of women. The political changes ran parallel to economic changes that also narrowed women's opportunities.

After silver from the Americas began to flood the empire in the 1600s, workers were increasingly paid in cash rather than in goods, and businesses associated with banking and finance developed. But women were barred from the early industrial labor and the professions, and traditional "woman's work" such as weaving was increasingly mechanized and done by men.

Nevertheless, in the early 1800s women retained considerable power in the management and disposal of their own property, gained mostly through fixed shares of inheritance. After marriage a woman was often pressured to convert her landholdings to cash in order to transfer her personal wealth to her husband's family, with whom she and her husband would reside. However, this was not a requirement, since men were legally obligated to support their families single-handedly. Until the 1820s many wealthy women retained their say in the distribution of property through the creation of charitable trusts for their sons. Because these trusts were set up in the religious courts, they could be designed to conform to the wishes of family members. Then, in the 1820s and 1830s the secularizing reforms of Mahmud II, which did not always produce happy results, transferred jurisdiction over the charitable trusts from religious courts to the state and ended women's control over this form of property.

The Crimean War and Its Aftermath, 1853–1877

Since the reign of Peter the Great (r. 1689–1725) the Russian Empire had been attempting to expand southward at the Ottomans' expense (see "Russia and Asia," below). By 1815 Russia had pried the Georgian region of the Caucasus away from the Ottomans, and the threat of Russian intervention had prevented the Ottomans from crushing Serbian independence. When Muhammad Ali's Egyptian army invaded Syria in 1833, Russia signed a treaty in support of the Ottomans. In return, the sultan recognized Russia's claim to being the protector of all of the empire's Orthodox subjects. This set the stage for an obscure dispute that resulted in war.

Bowing to British and French pressure, the sultan named France Protector of the Holy Sepulchre in Jerusalem in 1852. Russia protested, but the sultan held firm. So Russia invaded Ottoman territories in what is today Romania, and Britain and France went to war as allies of the sultan. The real causes of the war went beyond church quarrels in Jerusalem and involved diplomatic maneuvering among European powers over whether the Ottoman Empire should continue to exist and, if not, who should take over its territory. The Eastern Question was the simple name given to this complex issue. Though the powers, including Russia, had agreed to save the empire in 1839, Britain subsequently became suspicious of Russian ambitions. Prominent anti-Russian politicians in Britain feared that Russia would threaten the British hold on India.

Between 1853 and 1856 the **Crimean° War** raged in Romania, on the Black Sea, and on the Crimean peninsula. Britain, France, and the Italian kingdom of Sardinia-Piedmont sided with the Ottomans. Austria mediated the outcome. Britain and France trapped the Russian fleet in the Black Sea, where its commanders decided to sink the ships to protect the approaches to Sevastopol, their main base in Crimea. An army largely made up of British and French troops landed and laid siege to the city. Official corruption and lack of railways hampered the Russians' attempts to supply their forces. On the Romanian front, the Ottomans resisted effectively. At Sevastopol, the Russians were outmatched militarily and suffered badly from disease. Tsar Nicholas died as defeat loomed, leaving his successor, Alexander II (r. 1855–1881), to sue for peace when Sevastopol finally fell three months later.

The Crimean War brought significant changes to all the combatants. The tsar and his government, already beset by demands for the reform of serfdom, education, and the military (discussed later), were further discredited. In Britain and France, the conflict was accompanied by massive propaganda campaigns. For the first time newspapers effectively mobilized public support for a war. British press accounts so glamorized British participation that the false impression has lingered that Ottoman troops played a negligible role in the conflict. At the time, however, British and French commanders noted the massive losses among Turkish troops in particular. The French press, dominant in Istanbul, promoted a sense of unity between Turkish and

---

Crimean (cry-ME-uhn)

Interior of the Ottoman Financial Bureau   This engraving from the eighteenth century depicts the governing style of the Ottoman Empire before the era of westernizing reforms. By the end of the Tanzimat period in 1876, government offices and the costumes of officials looked much more like those in contemporary European capitals.   (From Ignatius Mouradgea d'Ohsson, *Tableau General de l'Empire Ottoman,* large folio edition, Paris, 1787–1820, pl. 178, following p. 340)

French society that continued to influence many aspects of Turkish urban culture.

The larger significance of the Crimean War was that it marked the transition from traditional to modern warfare. All the combatants had previously prided themselves on the use of highly trained cavalry to smash through the front lines of infantry. Cavalry coexisted with firearms until the early 1800s, primarily because early rifles were awkward to load and not very accurate. Cavalry could attack during the intervals between volleys. Then in the 1830s and 1840s percussion caps that did away with pouring gunpowder into the barrel of a musket came into use. In Crimean War battles many cavalry units were destroyed by the rapid fire of rifles that loaded at the breech rather than down the barrel. That was the fate of the famed British

Light Brigade, which was sent to relieve an Ottoman unit surrounded by Russian troops.

After the Crimean War, the Ottoman Empire increased its involvement with European commerce. The Ottoman imperial bank was founded in 1840, and a few years later currency reform pegged the value of Ottoman gold coins to the British pound. Sweeping changes in the 1850s expedited the creation of banks, insurance companies, and legal firms throughout the empire. Bustling trade also encouraged a migration from country to city between about 1850 and 1880. Many of the major cities of the empire—Istanbul, Damascus, Beirut, Alexandria, Cairo—expanded. A small but influential urban professional class emerged, as did a considerable class of wage laborers. Other demographic shifts involved refugees from Poland and

Hungary, where rivalry between the European powers and the Russian Empire caused political tension and sporadic warfare, and from Georgia and other parts of the Caucasus, where Russian expansion forced many Muslims to emigrate (discussed later).

However, commercial vigor and urbanization could not make up for declining revenues and the chronic insolvency and corruption of the imperial government. From the conclusion of the Crimean War in 1856 on, the Ottoman government became heavily dependent on foreign loans. In return it lowered tariffs to favor European imports and allowed European banks to open in Ottoman cities. Europeans living in Istanbul and other commercial centers enjoyed **extraterritoriality,** the right to be subject to their own laws and exempt from Ottoman jurisdiction.

As the result of these measures, imported goods multiplied, but—apart from tobacco and the Turkish opium that American traders took to China to compete against British opium from India—Anatolia produced few exports. As foreign debt grew, so did inflationary trends that left urban populations in a precarious position. By contrast, Egyptian cotton exports soared during the American Civil War, when American cotton exports plummeted; but the profits benefited Muhammad Ali's descendants, who had become the hereditary governors of Egypt, rather than the Ottoman government. The Suez Canal, which was partly financed by cotton profits, opened in 1869, and Cairo was redesigned and beautified. Eventually overexpenditure on such projects plunged Egypt into the same debt crisis that plagued the empire as a whole.

The decline of Ottoman power and prosperity had a strong impact on a group of well-educated young urban men who aspired to wealth and influence. They doubted that the empire's rulers and the Tanzimat officials who worked for them would ever stand up to European domination. Though lacking a sophisticated organization, these **Young Ottomans** (sometimes called Young Turks, though that term properly applies to a later movement) promoted a mixture of liberal ideas derived from Europe, national pride in Ottoman independence, and modernist views of Islam. Prominent Young Ottomans helped draft a constitution that was promulgated in 1876 by a new and as yet untried sultan, Abdul Hamid II. This apparent triumph of liberal reform

was short-lived. With war against Russia again threatening in the Balkans in 1877, Abdul Hamid suspended the constitution and the parliament that had been elected that year. Though he ruthlessly opposed further political reforms, the Tanzimat programs of extending modern schooling, utilizing European military practices and advisers, and making the government bureaucracy more orderly continued during his reign.

THE RUSSIAN EMPIRE

In 1812, when Napoleon's march on Moscow ended in a disastrous retreat brought on more by what a later tsar called "Generals January and February" than by Russian military action, the European image of Russia changed. Just as Napoleon's withdrawal from Egypt led to Muhammad Ali briefly becoming a political power, so his withdrawal from Russia conferred status on Tsar Alexander I (r. 1801–1825). Conservative Europeans still saw Russia as alien, backward, and oppressive, but they acknowledged its immensity and potential and included the tsar in efforts to suppress revolutionary tendencies throughout Europe.

In several important respects Russia resembled the Ottoman Empire more than the conservative kingdoms of Europe whose autocratic practices it so staunchly supported. Socially dominated by nobles whose country estates were worked by unfree serfs, Russia had almost no middle class. Industry was still at the threshold of development by the standards of the rapidly industrializing European powers, though it was somewhat more dynamic than Ottoman industry. Like Egypt and the Ottoman Empire, Russia engaged in reforms from the top down under Alexander I, but when his conservative brother Nicholas I (r. 1825–1855) succeeded to the throne, iron discipline and suspicion of modern ideas took priority over reform.

Russia and Europe

In 1700 only three Russians out of a hundred lived in cities, two-thirds of them in Moscow alone. By the mid-1800s the town population had grown tenfold, though it still

Raising of the Alexander Monument in St. Petersburg The death of Alexander I in 1825 brought to power his conservative brother Nicholas I. Yet Alexander remained a heroic figure for his resistance to Napoleon. This monument in Winter Palace Square was erected in 1829. (Novosti Photo Library)

accounted for only 6 percent of the total because the territories of the tsars had grown greatly through wars and colonization (see Chapter 18). These figures demonstrate that, like the Ottoman Empire, Russia was an overwhelmingly agricultural land. However, it had poorer transportation than the Ottoman Empire, since many Ottoman cities were seaports. Both empires encompassed peoples speaking many different languages.

Well-engineered roads did not begin to appear until 1817, and steam navigation commenced on the Volga in 1843. Tsar Nicholas I built the first railroad from St. Petersburg, the Russian capital, to his summer palace in 1837. A few years later his commitment to strict discipline led him to insist that the trunk line from St. Petersburg to Moscow run in a perfectly straight line. American engineers, among them the father of the painter James McNeill Whistler, who learned to paint in St. Petersburg, oversaw the laying of track and built locomotive workshops. Industrialization projects depended heavily on foreign expertise. British engineers set up

the textile mills that gave woolens and cottons a prominent place among Russia's industries.

Until the late nineteenth century the Russian government's interest in industry was limited. An industrial revolution required educated and independent-minded artisans and entrepreneurs, but Nicholas feared the spread of literacy and modern education—especially anything smacking of liberalism, socialism, or revolution—beyond the minimum needed to train the officer corps and the bureaucracy. He preferred serfs to factory workers, and he paid for imported industrial goods with exports of grain and timber.

Like Egypt and the Ottoman Empire, Russia aspired to Western-style economic development. But when France and Britain entered the Crimean War, they faced a Russian army equipped with obsolete weapons and bogged down by lack of transportation. At a time when European engineers were making major breakthroughs in loading cannon through an opening at the breech end, muzzle-loading artillery remained the Russian standard.

Yet in some ways Russia bore a closer resemblance to other European countries than the Ottoman Empire did. From the point of view of the French and the British, the Cyrillic alphabet and the Russian Orthodox form of Christianity seemed foreign, but they were not nearly as foreign as the Arabic alphabet and the Muslim faith. Britain and France feared Russia as a rival for power in the east, but they increasingly accepted Tsar Nicholas's view of the Ottoman Empire as "the sick man of Europe," capable of surviving only so long as the European powers permitted.

From the Russian point of view, kinship with western Europe was of questionable value. Westernizers, like the men of the Tanzimat in the Ottoman Empire, put their trust in technical advances and governmental reform. Opposing them were intellectuals known as **Slavophiles,** who in some respects resembled the Young Ottomans and considered the Orthodox faith, the solidity of peasant life, and the tsar's absolute rule to be the proper bases of Russian civilization. After Russia's humiliation in the Crimea, the Slavophile tendency gave rise to **Pan-Slavism,** a militant political doctrine advocating unity of all the Slavic peoples, including those living under Austrian and Ottoman rule.

On the diplomatic front, the tsar's inclusion as a major European ruler contrasted sharply with the sultan's exclusion. However, this did not prevent a powerful sense of Russophobia from developing in the West. Britain in particular saw Russia as a threat to India and despised the subjection of the serfs, who gained their freedom from Tsar Alexander II only in 1861, twenty-seven years after the British had abolished slavery. The passions generated by the Crimean War and its outcome affected the relations of Russia, Europe, and the Ottoman Empire for the remainder of the nineteenth century.

Russia and Asia

The Russian drive to the east in the eighteenth century brought the tsar's empire to the Pacific Ocean and the frontiers of China (see Map 18.1) by century's end. In the nineteenth century Russian expansionism focused on the south. There the backwardness of the Russian military did not matter since the peoples they faced were even less industrialized and technologically advanced. In 1860 Russia established a military outpost on the Pacific coast that would eventually grow into the great naval port of Vladivostok, today Russia's most southerly city. In Central Asia the steppe lands of the Kazakh nomads came under Russian control early in the century, setting the stage for a confrontation with three Uzbek states farther south. They succumbed one by one, beginning in 1865, giving rise to the new province of Turkestan, with its capital at Tashkent in present-day Uzbekistan. In the region of the Caucasus Mountains, the third area of southward expansion, Russia first took over Christian Georgia (1786), Muslim Azerbaijan° (1801), and Christian Armenia (1813) before gobbling up the many small principalities in the heart of the mountains. Between 1829 and 1864 Dagestan, Chechnya°, Abkhazia°, and other regions that would one day gain political prominence after the breakup of the Soviet Union became parts of the Russian Empire.

The drive to the south intensified political friction with Russia's new neighbors: Qing China and Japan in the east, Iran on the Central Asian and Caucasus frontiers, and the Ottoman Empire at the eastern end of the Black Sea. In the latter two instances, Muslim refugees from the territories newly absorbed by Russia spread anti-Russian feelings, though some of them brought with them modern skills and ideas gained from exposure to Russian administration and education.

The Russian drive to the south added a new element to the Eastern Question. Many British statesmen and strategists reckoned that a warlike Russia would press on until it had conquered all the lands separating it from British India, a prospect that made them shudder, given India's enormous contribution to Britain's prosperity. The competition that ensued over which power would control southern Central Asia resulted in a standoff in Afghanistan, which became a buffer zone under the control of neither. In Iran, the standoff between the powers helped preserve the weak Qajar dynasty of shahs.

Cultural Trends

Unlike Egypt and the Ottoman Empire, which

Azerbaijan (ah-zer-by-JAHN)   **Chechnya** (CHECH-nee-yah)   **Abkhazia** (ab-KAH-zee-yah) began to send students to Europe for training only in the nineteenth century, Russia had been in cultural contact with western Europe since the time of Peter the Great (r. 1689–1725). Members of the Russian court knew Western languages, and the tsars employed officials and advisers from western countries. Peter had also enlisted the well-educated Ukrainian clerics who headed the Russian Orthodox Church to help spread a Western spirit of education. As a result, Alexander I's reforms met a more positive reception than those of Muhammad Ali and Mahmud II. However, his reforms promised more on paper than they brought about in practice. It took many years to develop a sufficient pool of trained bureaucrats to make the reforms effective.

Ironically, much of the opposition to Alexander's reforms came from well-established families that were not at all unfriendly to Western ideas. Their fear was that the new government bureaucrats, who often came from humbler social origins, would act as agents of imperial tyranny. This fear was realized during the conservative reign of Nicholas I in the same way that the Tanzimat-inspired bureaucracy of the Ottoman Empire served the despotic purposes of Sultan Abdul Hamid II after 1877. Individuals favoring more liberal reforms, including military officers who had served in western Europe, intellectuals who read Western political tracts, and members of Masonic lodges who exchanged views with Freemasons in the West, formed secret societies of opposition. Some placed their highest priority on freeing the serfs; others advocated a constitution and a republican form of government. When Alexander I died in December 1825, confusion over who was to succeed him encouraged a group of reform-minded army officers to try to take over the government and provoke an uprising. The so-called **Decembrist revolt** failed, and many of the participants were severely punished. These events ensured that the new tsar, Nicholas I, would pay little heed to calls for reform over the next thirty years.

The great powers meeting in Paris to settle the Crimean War in 1856 forced Russia to return land to the Ottomans in both Europe and Asia. This humiliation spurred Nicholas's son and successor, Alexander II (r. 1855–1881), to institute major new reforms to reinvigorate the country. The greatest of

his reforms was the emancipation of the serfs in 1861. He also authorized new joint-stock companies, projected a railroad network to tie the country together, and modernized the legal and administrative arms of government.

Earlier intellectual and cultural trends flourished under Alexander II. More and more people became involved in intellectual, artistic, and professional life. Most prominent intellectuals received some amount of instruction at Moscow University or some German university. Universities also appeared in provincial cities like Kharkov and Kazan. Student clubs, along with Masonic lodges, became places for discussing new ideas. As Russian scholars and scientists began to achieve recognition for their contributions to European thought, scholarly careers attracted young men from clerical families, who in turn helped stimulate reforms in religious education.

Just as the Tanzimat reforms of the Ottoman Empire preceded the emergence of the Young Ottomans as a new and assertive political and intellectual force in the second half of the nineteenth century, so the initially ineffective reforms of Alexander I set in motion cultural currents that would make Russia a dynamic center of intellectual, artistic, and political life under his nephew Alexander II. Thus Russia belonged to two different spheres of development. It entered the nineteenth century a recognized force in European politics, but in other ways it resembled the Ottoman Empire. Rulers in both empires instituted reforms, overcame opposition, and increased the power of their governments. These activities stimulated intellectual and political trends that would ultimately work against the absolute rule of tsar and sultan. Yet Russia would eventually develop much closer relations with western Europe and become an arena for every sort of European intellectual, artistic, and political tendency, while the Ottoman Empire would ultimately succumb to European imperialism.

THE QING EMPIRE

In 1800 the Qing Empire faced many problems, but no reform movement of the kind initiated by

Sultan Selim III emerged in China. The reasons are not difficult to understand. The Qing emperors had skillfully countered Russian strategic and diplomatic moves in the 1600s. Instead of having a Napoleon threatening them with invasion, they enjoyed the admiration of Jesuit priests, who likened them to enlightened philosopher-kings. In 1793, however, a British attempt to establish diplomatic and trade relations—the Macartney mission—turned European opinion against China (see Chapter 18).

China's most serious crises were domestic, not foreign: rebellions by displaced indigenous peoples and the poor, and protests against the injustice of the local magistrates. The Qing dealt with these problems in the usual way, by suppressing rebels and dismissing incompetent or untrustworthy officials. They paid little attention to the far-off Europeans and brushed aside the complaints from European merchants who chafed against the restrictions of the "Canton system" by which the Qing limited and controlled foreign trade.

Economic and Social Disorder, 1800–1839

Early Qing successes and territorial expansion sowed the seeds of the domestic and political chaos of the later period. The early emperors encouraged the recovery of farmland, the opening of previously uncultivated areas, and the restoration and expansion of the road and canal systems. These measures expanded the agricultural base and supported a doubling of the population between about 1650 and 1800. Enormous numbers of farmers, merchants, and day laborers migrated in search of less crowded conditions, and a permanent floating population of the unemployed and homeless emerged. By 1800 population strain had caused serious environmental damage in some parts of central and western China.

While farmers tried to cope with agricultural deterioration, other groups vented grievances against the government: minority peoples in central and southwestern China complained about being driven off their lands during the boom of the 1700s; Mongols resented appropriation of their grazing lands and the displacement of their traditional elites. In some regions, village vigilante or-

ganizations took over policing and governing functions from Qing officials who had lost control. Growing numbers of people mistrusted the government, suspecting that all officials were corrupt. The growing presence of foreign merchants and missionaries in Canton and in the Portuguese colony of Macao aggravated discontent in neighboring districts.

In some parts of China the Qing were hated as foreign conquerors and were suspected of sympathy with the Europeans. In 1794 the White Lotus Rebellion—partly inspired by a messianic ideology that predicted the restoration of the Chinese Ming dynasty and the coming of the Buddha—raged across central China and was not suppressed until 1804. It initiated a series of internal conflicts that continued through the 1800s. Ignited by deepening social instabilities, these movements were sometimes intensified by local ethnic conflicts and by unapproved religions. The ability of some village militias to defend themselves and attack others intensified the conflicts, though the same techniques proved useful to southern coastal populations attempting to fend off British invasion.

The Opium War and Its Aftermath, 1839–1850

Unlike the Ottomans, the Qing knew little about the enormous fortunes being made in the early 1800s by European and American merchants smuggling opium into China. They did not know that silver gained in this illegal trade was helping finance the industrial transformation of England and the United States. Only slowly did Qing officials become aware of British colonies in India that grew and exported opium, and of the major naval base at Singapore through which British opium reached East Asia.

In 1729 the first Qing law banning opium imports was promulgated. By 1800, however, opium smuggling had swelled the annual import level to as many as four thousand chests. Though British merchants had pioneered this profitable trade, Chinese merchants likewise profited from distributing the drugs. A price war in the early 1820s stemming from competition between British and American importers raised demand so sharply that as many as thirty thousand chests were being imported by the 1830s. Addiction spread to people at all levels of Qing society, including high-ranking officials. The Qing emperor and his officials debated whether to legalize and tax opium or to enforce the existing ban more strictly. Having decided to root out the use and importation of opium, in 1839 they sent a high official to Canton to deal with the matter.

Britain considered the ban on opium importation an intolerable limitation on trade, a direct threat to Britain's economic health, and a cause for war. British naval and marine forces arrived on the south China coast in late 1839. The **Opium War** (1839–1842) broke out when negotiations between the Qing official and British representatives reached a stalemate. The war exposed the fact that the traditional, hereditary soldiers of the Qing Empire—the **Bannermen**—were, like the Janissaries of the Ottoman Empire, hopelessly obsolete. As in the Crimean War, the British excelled at sea, where they deployed superior technology. British ships landed marines who pillaged coastal cities and then sailed to new destinations (see Map 22.2). The Qing had no imperial navy. Thus until they were able to engage the British in prolonged fighting on land, they were unable to defend themselves against British attacks. Even in the land engagements, Qing resources proved woefully inadequate. The British could quickly transport their forces by sea along the coast; Qing troops moved primarily on foot. Moving Qing reinforcements from central to eastern China took more than three months; and when the defense forces arrived, they were exhausted and basically without weapons.

The Bannermen used the few muskets the Qing had imported during the 1700s. The weapons were matchlocks, which required the soldiers to ignite the load of gunpowder in them by hand. Firing the weapons was dangerous, and the canisters of gunpowder that each musketeer carried on his belt were likely to explode if a fire broke out nearby—a frequent occurrence in encounters with British artillery. Most of the Bannermen, however, had no guns at all and fought with swords, knives, spears, and clubs. Soldiers under British command—many of them Indians—carried percussion-cap rifles, which were far quicker, safer, and more accurate than the matchlocks. In addition, the long-range

British artillery could be moved from place to place and proved deadly in the cities and villages of eastern China.

Qing commanders thought that British gunboats rode so low in the water that they could not sail up the Chinese rivers. So they evacuated the coastal areas to counter the British threat. But the British deployed new gunboats for shallow waters and moved without difficulty up the Yangzi River (see Chapter 20).

When the invaders approached Nanjing, the former Ming capital, the Qing decided to negotiate. In 1842 the terms of the **Treaty of Nanking** (the British name for Nanjing) dismantled the old Canton system. The number of **treaty ports**—cities opened to foreign residents—increased from one (Canton) to five (Canton, Xiamen, Fuzhou, Ningbo, and Shanghai°). The island of Hong Kong became a British colony, and British residents in China gained extraterritorial rights. The Qing government agreed to set a low tariff of 5 percent on imports and to pay Britain an indemnity of 21 million ounces of silver as a penalty for having started the war. A supplementary treaty the following year guaranteed **most-favored-nation status** to Britain: any privileges that China granted to another country would be automatically extended to Britain as well. This provision effectively prevented the colonization of China, because giving land to one country would have necessitated giving it to all.

With each round of treaties came a new round of privileges for foreigners. In 1860 a new treaty legalized their right to import opium. Later, French treaties established the rights of foreign missionaries to travel in the Chinese countryside and preach their religion. The number of treaty ports grew, too; by 1900 they numbered more than ninety.

The treaty system and the principle of extraterritoriality resulted in the colonization of small pockets of Qing territory, where foreign merchants lived at ease. Greater territorial losses resulted when outlying regions gained independence or were ceded to neighboring countries. Districts north and south of the Amur River in the northeast fell to Russia by treaty in 1858 and 1860; parts of

---

Shanghai (shahng-hie)

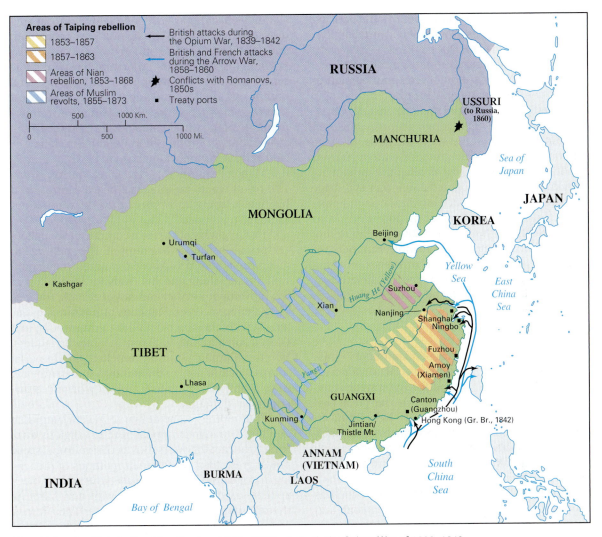

Map 22.2   Conflicts in the Qing Empire, 1839–1870   In both the Opium War of 1839–1842 and the Arrow War of 1856–1860, the seacoasts saw most of the action. Since the Qing had no imperial navy, the well-armed British ships encountered little resistance as they shelled the southern coasts. In inland conflicts, such as the Taiping Rebellion, the opposing armies were massive and slow moving. Battles on land were often prolonged attempts by one side to starve out the other side before making a major assault.

modern Kazakhstan and Kirgizstan in the northwest met the same fate in 1864. From 1865 onward the British gradually gained control of territories on China's Indian frontier. In the late 1800s France forced the court of Vietnam to end its tribute relationship to the Qing, while Britain encouraged Tibetan independence.

In Canton, Shanghai, and other coastal cities, Europeans and Americans maintained offices and factories that employed local Chinese as menial laborers. The foreigners built comfortable housing in zones where Chinese were not permitted to live, and they entertained themselves in exclusive restaurants and bars. Around the foreign establishments, gambling and prostitution offered employment to part of the local urban population.

Whether in town or in the countryside, Christian missionaries whose congregations sponsored hospitals, shelters, and soup kitchens or gave stipends to Chinese who attended church enjoyed a good reputation. But just as often the missionaries themselves were regarded as another evil. They seemed to subvert Confucian beliefs by condemning ancestor worship, pressuring poor families to put their children into orphanages, or fulminating against footbinding. The growing numbers of foreigners, and their growing privileges, became targets of resentment for a deeply dissatisfied, daily more impoverished, and increasingly militarized society.

The Taiping Rebellion, 1850–1864

The inflammatory mixture of social unhappiness and foreign intrusion exploded in the great civil war usually called the **Taiping° Rebellion.** In Guangxi, where the Taiping movement originated, entrenched social problems had been generating disorders for half a century. Agriculture in the region was unstable, and many people made their living from arduous and despised trades such as disposing of human waste, making charcoal, and mining. Ethnic divisions complicated economic distress. The lowliest trades frequently involved a minority group, the Hakkas, and tensions between them and the majority were rising. Problems may have been intensified by sharp fluctuations in the opium trade and reactions to the cultural and economic impact of the Europeans and Americans in Canton.

Hong Xiuquan°, the founder of the Taiping movement, experienced all of these influences. Hong came from a humble Hakka background. After years of study, he competed in the provincial

Confucian examinations, hoping for a post in government. He failed the examinations repeatedly, and it appears that he suffered a nervous breakdown in his late thirties. Afterward he spent some time in Canton, where he met both Chinese and American Protestant missionaries, who inspired him with their teachings. Hong had his own interpretation of the Christian message. He saw himself as the younger brother of Jesus, commissioned by God to found a new kingdom on earth and drive the Manchu conquerors, the Qing, out of China. The result would be universal peace. Hong called his new religious movement the "Heavenly Kingdom of Great Peace."

Hong quickly attracted a community of believers, primarily Hakkas like himself. They believed in the prophecy of dreams and claimed they could walk on air. Hong and his rivals for leadership in the movement went in and out of ecstatic trances. They denounced the Manchus as creatures of Satan. News of the sect reached the government, and Qing troops arrived to arrest the Taiping leaders. But the Taipings soundly repelled the imperial troops. Local loyalty to the Taipings spread quickly; their numbers multiplied; and they began to enlarge their domain.

The Taipings relied at first on Hakka sympathy and the charismatic appeal of their religious doctrine to attract followers. But as their numbers and power grew, they altered their methods of preaching and governing. They replaced the anti-Chinese appeals used to enlist Hakkas with anti-Manchu rhetoric designed to enlist Chinese. They forced captured villages to join their movement. Once people were absorbed, the Taipings strictly monitored their activities. They segregated men and women and organized them into work and military teams. Women were forbidden to bind their feet (the Hakkas had never practiced footbinding) and participated fully in farming and labor. Brigades of women soldiers took to the field against Qing forces.

As the movement grew, it began to move toward eastern and northern China (see Map 22.2). Panic preceded the Taipings. Villagers feared being forced into Taiping units, and Confucian elites recoiled in horror from the bizarre ideology of foreign gods, totalitarian rule, and walking, working,

Taiping (tie-PING)   **Hong Xiuquan** (hoong shee-OH-chew-an)

Nanjing Encircled For a decade the Taipings held the city of Nanjing as their capital. For years Qing and international troops attempted to break the Taiping hold. By the summer of 1864, Qing forces had built tunnels leading to the foundations of Nanjing's city walls and had planted explosives. The detonation of the explosives signaled the final Qing assault on the rebel capital. As shown here, the common people of the city, along with their starving livestock, were caught in the crossfire. Many of the Taiping leaders escaped the debacle at Nanjing, but nearly all were hunted down and executed. (Roger-Viollet/Getty Images)

warring women. But the huge numbers the Taipings were able to muster overwhelmed attempts at local defense. The tremendous growth in the number of Taiping followers required the movement to establish a permanent base. When the rebel army conquered Nanjing in 1853, the Taiping leaders decided to settle there and make it the capital of the new "Heavenly Kingdom of Great Peace."

Qing forces attempting to defend north China became more successful as problems of organization and growing numbers slowed Taiping momentum. Increasing Qing military success resulted mainly from the flexibility of the imperial military commanders in the face of an unprecedented challenge. In addition, the military commanders received strong backing from a group of civilian provincial governors who had studied the techniques developed by local militia forces for self-defense. Certain provincial governors combined their knowledge of civilian self-defense and local terrain with more efficient organization and the use of modern weaponry. The result was the formation of new military units, in which many of the Bannermen voluntarily served under civilian governors. The Qing court agreed to special taxes to fund the new armies and acknowledged the new combined leadership.

When the Taipings settled into Nanjing, the new Qing armies surrounded the city, hoping to starve out the rebels. The Taipings, however, had provisioned and fortified themselves well. They also had the services of several brilliant young military commanders, who mobilized enormous campaigns in nearby parts of eastern China, scavenging supplies and attempting to break the encirclement of Nanjing. For more than a decade the Taiping leadership remained ensconced at Nanjing, and the "Heavenly Kingdom" endured.

In 1856 Britain and France, freed from their preoccupation with the Crimean War, turned their attention to China. European and American missionaries had visited Nanjing, curious to see what their fellow Christians were up to. Their reports were discouraging. Hong Xiuquan and the other leaders appeared to lead lives of indulgence and abandon, and more than one missionary accused them of homosexual practices. Relieved of the possible accusation of quashing a pious Christian movement, the British and French surveyed the situation. Though the Taipings were not going to topple the Qing, rebellious Nian ("Bands") in northern China added a new threat in the 1850s. A series of simultaneous large insurrections might indeed destroy the empire. Moreover, since the Qing had not observed all the provisions of the treaties signed after the Opium War, Britain and France were now considering renewing war on the Qing themselves.

In 1856 the British and French launched a series of swift, brutal coastal attacks—a second opium war, called the Arrow War (1856–1860)—which culminated in a British and French invasion of Beijing and the sacking of the Summer Palace in 1860. A new round of treaties punished the Qing for not enacting all the provisions of the Treaty of Nanking. Having secured their principal objective,

the British and French forces then joined the Qing campaign against the Taipings. Attempts to coordinate the international forces were sometimes riotous and sometimes tragic, but the injection of European weaponry and money helped quell both the Taiping and the Nian rebellions during the 1860s.

The Taiping Rebellion ranks as the world's bloodiest civil war and the greatest armed conflict before the twentieth century. Estimates of deaths range from 20 million to 30 million. The loss of life came primarily from starvation and disease, for most engagements consisted of surrounding fortified cities and waiting until the enemy forces died, surrendered, or were so weakened that they could be easily defeated. Many sieges continued for months. Reports of people eating grass, leather, hemp, and human flesh were widespread. The dead were rarely buried properly, and epidemic disease was common.

The area of early Taiping fighting was close to the regions of southwest China in which bubonic plague had been lingering for centuries. When the rebellion was suppressed, many Taiping followers sought safety in the highlands of Laos and Vietnam, which soon showed infestation by plague. Within a few years the disease reached Hong Kong. From there it spread to Singapore, San Francisco, Calcutta, and London. In the late 1800s there was intense apprehension over the possibility of a worldwide outbreak, and Chinese immigrants were regarded as likely carriers. This fear became a contributing factor in the passage of discriminatory immigration bans on Chinese in the United States in 1882.

The Taiping Rebellion devastated the agricultural centers of China. Many of the most intensely cultivated regions of central and eastern China were depopulated. Some were still uninhabited decades later, and major portions of the country did not recover until the twentieth century.

Cities, too, were hard hit. Shanghai, a treaty port of modest size before the rebellion, saw its population multiplied many times by the arrival of refugees from war-blasted neighboring provinces. The city then endured months of siege by the Taipings. Major cultural centers in eastern China lost masterpieces of art and architecture; imperial libraries were burned or their collections exposed to the weather; and the printing blocks used to make books were destroyed. While the empire faced the mountainous challenge of dealing with the material and cultural destruction of the war, it also was burdened by a major ecological disaster in the north. The Yellow River changed course in 1855, destroying the southern part of impoverished Shandong province with flood and initiating decades of drought along the former riverbed in northern Shandong.

Decentralization at the End of the Qing Empire, 1864–1875

The Qing government emerged from the 1850s with no hope of achieving solvency. The corruption of the 1700s, attempts in the very early 1800s to restore waterworks and roads, and declining yields from land taxes had bankrupted the treasury. By 1850, before the Taiping Rebellion, Qing government expenditures were ten times revenues. The indemnities demanded by Europeans after the Opium and Arrow Wars compounded the problem. Vast stretches of formerly productive rice land were devastated, and the population was dispersed. Refugees pleaded for relief, and the imperial, volunteer, foreign, and mercenary troops that had suppressed the Taipings demanded unpaid wages.

Britain and France became active participants in the period of recovery that followed the rebellion. To ensure repayment of the debt to Britain, Robert Hart was installed as inspector-general of a newly created Imperial Maritime Customs Service. Britain and the Qing split the revenues he collected. Britons and Americans worked for the Qing government as advisers and ambassadors, attempting to smooth communications between the Qing, Europe, and the United States.

The real work of the recovery, however, was managed by provincial governors who had come to the forefront in the struggle against the Taipings. To prosecute the war, they had won the right to levy their own taxes, raise their own troops, and run their own bureaucracies. These special powers were not entirely canceled when the war ended. Chief among these governors was Zeng Guofan°, who oversaw programs to restore agriculture, commu-

nications, education, and publishing, as well as efforts to reform the military and industrialize armaments manufacture.

Like many provincial governors, Zeng preferred to look to the United States rather than to Britain for models and aid. He hired American advisers to run his weapons factories, shipyards, and military academies. He sponsored a daring program in which promising Chinese boys were sent to Hartford, Connecticut, a center of missionary activity, to learn English, science, mathematics, engineering, and history. They returned to China to assume some of the positions previously held by foreign advisers. Though Zeng was never an advocate of participation in public life by women, his Confucian convictions taught him that educated mothers were more than ever a necessity. He not only encouraged but also partly oversaw the advanced classical education of his own daughters. Zeng's death in 1872 deprived the empire of a major force for reform.

The period of recovery marked a fundamental structural change in the Qing Empire. Although the emperors after 1850 were ineffective rulers, a coalition of aristocrats supported the reform and recovery programs. Without their legitimization of the new powers of provincial governors like Zeng Guofan, the empire might have evaporated within a generation. A crucial member of this alliance was Cixi°, who was known as the "Empress Dowager" after the 1880s. Later observers, both Chinese and foreign, reviled her as a monster of corruption and arrogance. But in the 1860s and 1870s Cixi supported the provincial governors, some of whom became so powerful that they were managing Qing foreign policy as well as domestic affairs.

No longer a conquest regime dominated by a Manchu military caste and its Chinese civilian appointees, the empire came under the control of a group of reformist aristocrats and military men, independently powerful civilian governors, and a small number of foreign advisers. The Qing lacked strong, central, unified leadership and could not recover their powers of taxation, legislation, and military command once these had been granted to the provincial governors. From the 1860s forward, the Qing Empire disintegrated into a number of large

---

Zeng Guofan (zung gwoh-FAN)

Cixi (TSUH-shee)

Cixi's Allies   In the 1860s and 1870s, Cixi was a supporter of reform. In later years she was widely regarded as corrupt and self-centered and as an obstacle to reform. Her greatest allies were the court eunuchs. Introduced to palace life in early China as managers of the imperial harems, eunuchs became powerful political parties at court. The first Qing emperors refused to allow the eunuchs any political influence, but by Cixi's time the eunuchs once again were a political factor.   (Freer Gallery of Art and Arthur M. Sackler Gallery Archives. Smithsonian Institution, Washington, D.C. Photographer: Xunling, negative #SC-GR-261)

power zones in which provincial governors handed over leadership to their protégés in a pattern that the Qing court eventually could only ritually legitimate.

CONCLUSION

Most of the subjects of the Ottoman, Russian, and Qing rulers did not think of European pressure or competition as determining factors in their lives during the first half of the nineteenth century. They continued to live according to the social and economic institutions they inherited from previous generations. By the 1870s, however, the challenge of Europe had become widely recog-

nized. The Crimean War, where European allies achieved a hollow victory for the Ottomans and then pressured the sultan for more reforms, confirmed both Ottoman and Russian military weakness. The Opium War did the same for China. Though all three empires faced similar problems of reform and military rebuilding, Russia enjoyed a comparative advantage in being less appealing to rapacious European merchants and strategists concerned with protecting overseas empires.

The policies adopted by the three imperial governments responded both to traditional concerns and to European demands. The sultans gave first priority to strengthening the central government to prevent territorial losses that began when Serbia, Egypt, and Greece became fully or partially independent. The Qing emperors confronted population growth and agricultural decline that resulted in massive rebellions. The tsars focused on continued territorial expansion. However, each faced different European pressures. In China, the Europeans and Americans wanted trade rights. In the Ottoman Empire, Britain, France, and Russia wanted equality for Christians and freedom from naval and commercial competition in the eastern Mediterranean. In Russia, moral demands for the abolition of serfdom accompanied British determination to stop territorial advances in Asia that might threaten India.

Repeated crises in all three empires would eventually result in the fall of the Qing, Romanov, and Ottoman dynasties in the first two decades of the twentieth century, but in 1870 it was still unclear whether the traditional land empires of Asia would be capable of weathering the storm. One thing that had become clear, however, at least to European eyes, was that Russia was part of Europe, while the other two empires were fundamentally alien. This judgment was based partly on religion, partly on the enthusiasm of westernizing Russian artists and intellectuals for European cultural trends, and partly on the role Russia had played in defeating Napoleon at the beginning of the century, a role that brought the tsars into the highest councils of royal decision making in Europe.

■ Key Terms

Muhammad Ali	Pan-Slavism
Janissaries	Decembrist revolt
Serbia	Opium War
Tanzimat	Bannermen
Crimean War	Treaty of Nanking
extraterritoriality	treaty ports
Young Ottomans	most-favored-nation status
Slavophiles	Taiping Rebellion

■ Suggested Reading

For widely available general histories of the Ottoman Empire, see Stanford Shaw, *History of the Ottoman Empire and Modern Turkey* (1976–1977), and J. P. D. B. Kinross, *The Ottoman Centuries: The Rise and Fall of the Turkish Empire* (1977).

On the economy and society of the nineteenth-century Ottoman Empire, see Huri Islamoglu-Inan, ed., *The Ot-*

toman Empire and the World-Economy (1987); Resat Kasaba, *The Ottoman Empire and the World Economy: The Nineteenth Century* (1988); Sevket Pamuk, *The Ottoman Empire and European Capitalism, 1820–1913: Trade, Investment, and Production* (1987); Kemal H. Karpat, *Ottoman Population, 1830–1914: Demographic and Social Characteristics* (1985); and Carter V. Findley, *Bureaucratic Reform in the Ottoman Empire: The Sublime Porte, 1789–1922* (1980). On the reform program and the emergence of national concepts, see also Selim Deringil, *The Well-Protected Domains: Ideology and the Legitimation of Power in the Ottoman Empire, 1876–1909* (1998).

Marc Raeff, *Understanding Imperial Russia* (1984), sets nineteenth-century Russian developments in a broad context and challenges many standard ideas. Andreas Kappeler, *The Russian Multi-Ethnic Empire* (2001), and Mark Bassin, *Imperial Visions: Nationalist Imagination and Geographical Expansion in the Russian Far East, 1840–1865* (1999), address Russian expansion and the problems inherent in diversity of population. On economic matters see W. L. Blackwell, *The Beginnings of Russian Industrialization, 1800–1860* (1968). Daniel Field, *The End of Serfdom: Nobility and Bureaucracy in Russia, 1855–1861* (1976), addresses the primary problem besetting Russian society during this period. On the intellectual debates see M. Malia, *Alexander Herzen and the Birth of Russian Socialism* (1961), and Andrzej Walicki, *The Slavophile Controversy* (1975).

On the Qing Empire of the nineteenth century, see Pamela Kyle Crossley, *Orphan Warriors: Three Manchu Generations and the End of the Qing World* (1990), and for a more detailed political history see Mary C. Wright, *The Last Stand of Chinese Conservatism: The T'ung-chih Restoration, 1862–1874* (1971). There is a very large literature on both the Opium War and the Taiping Rebellion, including reprinted editions of contemporary observers. For general histories of the Opium War, see Peter Ward Fay, *The Opium War, 1840–1842: Barbarians in the Celestial Empire in the Early Part of the Nineteenth Century and the War by Which They Forced Her Gates Ajar* (1975); Christopher Hibbert, *The Dragon Wakes: China and the West, 1793–1911* (1970); and the classic study by Chang Hsin-pao, *Commissioner Lin and the Opium War* (1964). For a recent, more monographic study on Qing political thought in the period of the Opium War, see James M. Polachek, *The Inner Opium War* (1992). On the Taiping Rebellion, enduring sources are S. Y. Têng, *The Taiping Rebellion and the Western Powers: A Comprehensive Survey* (1971), and C. A. Curwen, *Taiping Rebel: The Deposition of Li Hsiu-ch'eng* (1976); see also Caleb Carr, *The Devil Soldier: The Story of Frederick Townsend Ward* (1992). The most recent study is Jonathan D. Spence, *God's Chinese Son: The Taiping Heavenly Kingdom of Hong Xiuquan* (1996)

State Power, the Census, and the Question of Identity

Between the American Revolution and the last decades of the nineteenth century, Europe and the Americas were transformed. The ancient power of kings and the authority of religion were eclipsed by muscular new ways of organizing political, economic, and intellectual life. The Western world was vastly different in 1870 than it had been a century earlier. One of the less heralded but enduringly significant changes was the huge expansion of government statistical services.

The rise of the nation-state was associated with the development of modern bureaucratic departments that depended on reliable statistics to measure the nation's achievements and discover its failures. The nation-state, whether democratic or not, mobilized resources on a previously unimaginable scale. Modern states were more powerful and wealthier, and they were also more ambitious and more intrusive. The growth of their power can be seen in the modernization of militaries, the commitment to internal improvements such as railroads, and the growth in state revenues. In recent years historians have begun to examine a less visible but equally important manifestation of growing state power: census taking.

Governments and religious authorities have counted people since early times. Our best estimates of the Amerindian population of the Western Hemisphere in 1500 rest almost entirely on what were little more than missionaries' guesses about the numbers of people they baptized. Spanish and Portuguese kings were eager to count native populations, since "indios" (adult male Amerindians) were subject to special labor obligations and tribute payments. So, from the mid-sixteenth century onward, imperial officials conducted regular censuses of Amerindians, adapting practices already in place in Europe.

The effort to measure and categorize populations was transformed in the last decades of the eighteenth century when the nature of European governments began to change. The Enlightenment belief that the scientific method could be applied to human society proved to be attractive both to political radicals, like the French Revolutionaries, and to

reforming monarchs like Maria Theresa of Austria. Enlightenment philosophers had argued that a science of government could remove the inefficiencies and irrationalities that had long subverted the human potential for prosperity and happiness. The French intellectual Condorcet wrote in 1782:

> Those sciences, created almost in our own days, the object of which is man himself, the direct goal of which is the happiness of man, will enjoy a progress no less sure than that of the physical sciences. . . . In meditating on the nature of the moral sciences [what we now call the social sciences], one cannot help seeing that, as they are based like the physical sciences on the observation of fact, they must follow the method, acquire a language equally exact and precise, attaining the same degree of certainty.[1]

As confidence in this new "science" grew, the term previously used to describe the collection of numbers about society, *political arithmetic*, was abandoned by governments and practitioners in favor of *statistics*, a term that clearly suggests its close ties to the "state." In the nineteenth century the new objectives set out by Condorcet and others led to both the formal university training of statisticians and the creation of government statistical services.

The ambitions of governments in this new era were great. Nation-states self-consciously sought to transform society, sponsoring economic development, education, and improvements in health and welfare. They depended on statistics to measure the effectiveness of their policies and, as a result, were interested in nearly everything. They counted taverns, urban buildings, births and deaths, and arrests and convictions. They also counted their populations with a thoroughness never before seen. As statistical reporting became more uniform across Europe and the Americas, governments could measure not only their own progress but also that of their neighbors and rivals.

The revolutionary governments of France modernized the census practices of the overthrown monarchy. They spent much more money, hired many more census takers, and devoted much more energy to training the staff that designed censuses and analyzed results. Great Britain set up an official census in 1801, but established a special administrative structure only in the 1830s. In the Western Hemisphere nearly every independent nation provided for "scientific" censuses. In the United States the federal constitution required that a census be taken every ten years. Latin American nations, often torn by civil war in the nineteenth century, took censuses less regularly, but even the poorest nations took censuses when they could. It was as if the census itself confirmed the existence of the government, demonstrating its modernity and seriousness.

Until recently, historians who relied on these documents in their research on economic performance, issues of race and ethnicity, family life, and fertility and mortality asked few questions about the politics of census design. What could be more objective than rows of numbers? But the advocates of statistics who managed census taking were uninhibited in advertising the usefulness of reliable numbers to the governments that employed them. At the 1860 International Statistical Congress held in London one speaker said, "I think the true meaning to be attached to 'statistics' is not every collection of figures, but figures collected with the sole purpose of applying the principles deduced from them to questions of importance to the state."[2] The desire to be useful meant that statistics could not be fully objective.

Subjectivity was an unavoidable problem with censuses. Censuses identified citizens and foreign residents by place of residence, sex, age, and family relationships within households as well as profession and literacy. These determinations were sometimes subjective. Modern scholars have demonstrated that census takers also often undercounted the poor and those living in rural areas.

Because census takers, as agents of nation-states, were determined to be useful, they were necessarily concerned with issues of nationality and, in the Americas, with race because these characteristics commonly determined political rights and citizenship. The assessment and recording of nationality and race would prove to be among the most politically problematic objectives of the new social sciences.

Nationality had not been a central question for traditional monarchies. For the emerging nation-state, nationality was central. A nation's strength was assumed to depend in large measure on the growth of its population, a standard that, once articulated, suggested that the growth of minority populations was dangerous. Who was French? Who was Austrian or Hungarian? European statisticians relied on both *language of use* and *mother tongue* as proxies for *nationality,* the first term being flexible enough to recognize the assimilation of minorities, the second suggesting a more permanent identity based on a person's original language. Both terms forced bilingual populations to simplify their more complex identities. Ethnic minorities, once identified, were sometimes subject to discrimination such as exclusion from military careers or from universities. In parts of Spanish America language was used as a proxy for *race.* Those who spoke Spanish were citizens in the full sense, even if they were indistinguishable from Amerindians in appearance. Those who spoke indigenous languages were "indios" and therefore subject to special taxes and labor obligations and effectively denied the right to vote.

Beyond providing a justification for continuing discrimination, census categories compressed and distorted the complexity and variety of human society to fit the preconceptions of bureaucrats and politicians. Large percentages of the residents of Mexico, Peru, and Bolivia, among other parts of the Americas, were descended from both Europeans and Amerindians and, in the Caribbean region, from Europeans and Africans. Census categories never adequately captured the complexities of these biological and cultural mixtures. We now know that the poor were often identified as "indios" or "blacks" and the better-off were often called something else, "Americanos," "criollos" (creoles), or even whites. Since this process flattened and streamlined the complexities of identity, censuses on their own are not reliable guides to the distribution of ethnicity and race in a population.

In Europe the issue of nationality proved similarly perplexing for census takers and similarly dangerous to those identified as minorities. Linguistic and ethnic minorities had always lived among the politically dominant majorities: Jewish and Polish minorities in areas controlled by German speakers, German speakers among the French, and Serbo-Croatian speakers among Hungarians, for example. The frontiers between these minority populations and their neighbors were always porous. Sexual unions and marriages were common, and two or more generations of a family often lived together in the same household, with the elder members speaking one language and the younger members another. Who was what? In a very real sense, nationality, like race in the Americas, was ultimately fixed by the census process, where the nation-state forced a limited array of politically utilitarian categories onto the rich diversity of ethnicity and culture.

Notes

1. Quoted in James C. Scott, *Seeing Like a State. How Certain Schemes to Improve the Human Condition Have Failed* (New Haven: Yale University Press, 1998), 91.
2. This discussion relies heavily on Eliza Johnson (now Ablovatski), "Counting and Categorizing: The Hungarian Gypsy Census of 1893" (M.A. Thesis, Columbia University, 1996), especially Chapter III. She quotes from the *Proceedings of the Sixth International Statistical Congress Held in London,* 1860, 379.

PART SEVEN

Global Diversity and Dominance, 1850–1949

CHAPTER 23
The New Power Balance, 1850–1900

CHAPTER 24
The New Imperialism, 1869–1914

CHAPTER 25
The Crisis of the Imperial Order, 1900–1929

CHAPTER 26
The Collapse of the Old Order, 1929–1949

CHAPTER 27
Striving for Independence: Africa, India, and Latin America, 1900–1949

In 1850, despite centuries of global contacts, the world still embraced a huge diversity of societies and cultures and of independent states. During the century that followed, much of the world came to be dominated by a few European nations, along with the United States and Japan.

Industrializing nations used their newfound power to dominate Africa, South and Southeast Asia, and the Pacific in a wave of conquest termed the New Imperialism. Domination went beyond military or economic measures as soldiers, administrators, missionaries, teachers, and merchants tried to promote their own cultures, business practices, and ways of life. They were partly successful, as the spread of Western religions, languages, clothing, and political ideas testifies.

By 1900, Europe had been largely at peace for almost a century. As memories of war faded, the rise of nationalism and the awesome power of modern armies and navies made national rivalries dangerously inflammable. Germany, a latecomer to national unity, found its imperial ambitions frustrated by the earlier conquests of France, Britain, and Russia. Mounting tensions between these powers led to the devastating Great War of 1914–1918. Far from settling issues, this war destabilized the victors as much as the vanquished. Russia and China erupted in revolution. The collapse of the Ottoman Empire led to the emergence of modern Turkey, while its Arab provinces were taken over by France and Britain. In the 1920s, the European powers struggled to maintain a precarious peace.

By the 1930s, the political and economic system crafted after the Great War fell apart. While the capitalist nations fell into a deep economic depression that their governments seemed helpless to stop, the Soviet Union industrialized at breakneck speed. Social disruption in Germany and Japan brought to power extremist leaders who sought to solve economic woes and political grievances by military conquest. Nationalism and industrial warfare assumed their most hideous forms in World War II, leading to the massacre of millions of innocent people and the destruction of countless cities.

World War II weakened European control of their overseas empires. Leaders of liberation movements in Asia, Latin America, and Africa adopted Western ideas of nationalism and communism as they sought to acquire the benefits of industrialization. India gained its independence in 1947. Two years later, Chinese communists led by Mao Zedong overthrew a government they viewed as subservient to the West. In Latin America, leaders turned to nationalist economic and social policies. Of all the once great powers, only the United States and the Soviet Union remained to compete for global dominance.

	1850	1870	1890
Americas		U.S. Civil War **1861–1865** British build railroads in Brazil and Argentina **1880s** •	Spanish-American War **1898** •
Europe	• **1851** Majority of British population living in cities • **1856** Transformation of steel and chemical industries begins	**1870–1914** Era of the New Imperialism • **1871** Unification of Germany, Italy	**1894–1906** Dreyfus affair in France
Africa	End of transatlantic slave trade **1867** •	• **1880s** West Africa conquered by France and Britain Berlin Africa Conference **1884–1885** Nigeria becomes British protectorate **1899** •	• **1896** Ethiopians defea Italian army at Adowa
Middle East	Suez Canal opens **1869** •	• **1882** British occupy Egypt • **1878** Ottoman Empire loses most of its European territories	• **1904** Young Turk reforms in Ottoman Empire
Asia and Oceania	Direct British rule in India **1858** •	• **1862** French conquer Indochina Meiji Restoration in Japan **1868** • First Indian National Congress **1885** • Russia conquers Central Asia **1884–1887**	Boxer Rebellion in China **1900** • Sino-Japanese War **1894** • **1904–1905** Russo-Japanese War

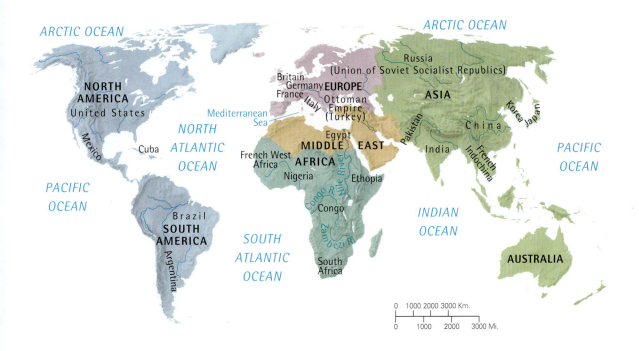

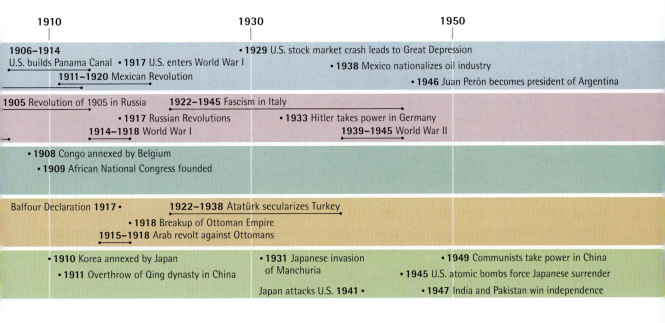

1910

1930

1950

1906–1914
U.S. builds Panama Canal • **1917** U.S. enters World War I   • **1929** U.S. stock market crash leads to Great Depression
    1911–1920 Mexican Revolution   • **1938** Mexico nationalizes oil industry
        • **1946** Juan Perón becomes president of Argentina

1905 Revolution of 1905 in Russia   **1922–1945** Fascism in Italy
    • **1917** Russian Revolutions   • **1933** Hitler takes power in Germany
    1914–1918 World War I   **1939–1945** World War II

• **1908** Congo annexed by Belgium
• **1909** African National Congress founded

Balfour Declaration **1917** •   **1922–1938** Atatürk secularizes Turkey
    • **1918** Breakup of Ottoman Empire
    1915–1918 Arab revolt against Ottomans

• **1910** Korea annexed by Japan   • **1931** Japanese invasion   • **1949** Communists take power in China
• **1911** Overthrow of Qing dynasty in China   of Manchuria   • **1945** U.S. atomic bombs force Japanese surrender
    Japan attacks U.S. **1941** •   • **1947** India and Pakistan win independence

23 The New Power Balance, 1850–1900

CHAPTER OUTLINE

New Technologies and the World Economy

Social Transformations

Nationalism and the Unification of Germany

The Great Powers of Europe, 1871–1900

New Great Powers: The United States and Japan

DIVERSITY AND DOMINANCE: Marx and Engels on Global Trade and the Bourgeoisie

On January 18, 1871, in the Hall of Mirrors of the palace of Versailles, King Wilhelm I of Prussia was proclaimed emperor of Germany before a crowd of officers and other German rulers. This ceremony marked the unification of many small German states into one nation. Off to one side stood Prussian chancellor Otto von Bismarck°, the man most responsible for the creation of a united Germany. A few years earlier, he had declared, "The great issues of the day will be decided not by speeches and votes of the majority—that was the great mistake of 1848 and 1849—but by iron and blood." Indeed it was "blood"—that is, victories on the battlefield—rather than popular participation that had led to the unification of Germany; among the digni-

taries in the Hall of Mirrors that day, only two or three were civilians. As for "iron," it meant not only weapons but, more important, the industries required to produce weapons. Thus, after 1871, nationalism, once a dream of revolutionaries and romantics, became ever more closely associated with military force and with industry.

This chapter deals with a small group of countries—Germany, France, Britain, Russia, the United States, and Japan—that we call "great powers." In the next chapter, which deals with the era of the "New Imperialism" (1869–1914), we will see how these nations used their power to conquer colonial empires in Asia and Africa and to control Latin America. Together, Chapters 23 and 24 describe an era in which a handful of wealthy industrialized nations—all but one of them of European culture—imposed on the

---

Otto von Bismarck (UTT-oh fun BIS-mark)

other peoples of the world a domination more powerful than any experienced before or since.

As you read this chapter, ask yourself the following questions:

- What new technologies and industries appeared between 1850 and 1900, and how did they affect the world economy?

- How did the societies of the industrial countries change during this period?

- Why do we call certain countries "great powers" but not others?

NEW TECHNOLOGIES AND THE WORLD ECONOMY

After 1850, industrialization took off in new directions. Germany and the United States surpassed Great Britain as the world's leading industrial powers by 1890. Small companies were overshadowed by large corporations owned by wealthy capitalists or (especially in Russia and Japan) by governments. New technologies based on advances in physics and chemistry revolutionized everyday life and transformed the world economy.

The Steel and Chemical Industries

Steel is a special form of iron, both hard and elastic. A series of inventions in the 1850s made steel the cheapest and most versatile metal ever known. As a result, world steel production rose from a half-million tons in 1870 to 28 million in 1900, of which the United States produced 10 million, Germany 8, and Britain 4.9. Steel became cheap and abundant enough to make rails, bridges, ships, and even "tin" cans meant to be used once and thrown away.

The new steel mills were hungry consumers of coal, iron ore, limestone, and other raw materials. They took up as much space as whole towns, belched smoke and particulates night and day, and left behind huge hills of slag and other waste products. Environmental degradation affected steel-producing regions such as the English Midlands, the German Ruhr, and parts of Pennsylvania.

The chemical industry followed a similar pattern. In the early nineteenth century, only soda, sulfuric acid, and chlorine bleach (used in the cotton industry) were manufactured on a large scale, especially in Britain. Then in 1856, the development of the first synthetic dye, aniline purple, from coal tar launched the mass production of organic chemicals—compounds containing carbon atoms. These bright, long-lasting colors delighted consumers but hurt tropical countries, such as India, that produced indigo, a blue vegetable dye.

Chemistry also made important advances in the manufacture of explosives. In 1866, the Swedish scientist Alfred Nobel found a way to turn nitroglycerin into a stable solid—dynamite. This and other new explosives were very useful in mining and the construction of railroads and canals. They also enabled the armies and navies of the great powers to arm themselves with increasingly accurate and powerful rifles and cannon.

The growing complexity of industrial chemistry made it one of the first fields where science and technology interacted on a daily basis. This development gave a great advantage to Germany, which had the most advanced engineering schools and scientific institutes of its time. By the end of the nineteenth century, Germany was the world's leading producer of dyes, drugs, synthetic fertilizers, ammonia, and nitrates used in making explosives.

Electricity

The third great innovation of the late nineteenth century was **electricity.** In the 1870s, inventors devised efficient generators that turned mechanical energy into electric current and opened the way to a host of new applications. Arc lamps lit up public squares, theaters, and stores. Then in 1879, **Thomas Edison** in the United States developed an incandescent lamp well suited to lighting small rooms and in 1882 created the world's first electrical distribution network, in New York City. By the turn of the century, electric lighting was rapidly replacing dim and smelly gas lamps in the cities of Europe and North America.

Other uses of electricity quickly appeared. Electric streetcars and, later, subways helped reduce the traffic jams that clogged large cities. Electric motors replaced steam engines and power belts, increasing productivity and improving workers' safety. As demand for electricity grew, engineers learned to use waterpower to produce electricity, and hydroelectric plants were built.

Electricity helped alleviate some environmental problems, since electric motors and lamps did not pollute the air. Power plants were built at a distance from cities. As electric trains and streetcars replaced horse-drawn trolleys and coal-burning locomotives, cities became noticeably cleaner and healthier. At the same time, electricity created a huge demand for copper, bringing Chile, Montana, and southern Africa into the world economy as never before.

Shipping and Telegraph Cables

At midcentury, a series of developments radically transformed ocean shipping. Iron and steel took the place of wood. Propellers replaced paddle wheels and sails. By the turn of the century, more efficient engines could convert the heat produced by burning a single sheet of paper into the power to move 1 ton over half a mile. The average size of freighters increased from 200 tons in 1850 to 7,500 tons in 1900. The Suez Canal, constructed in 1869, shortened the distance between Europe and Asia and triggered a massive switch from sail power to steam.

The world's fleet of merchant ships grew from 9 million to 35 million tons between 1850 and 1910, as passengers, mail, and perishable freight traveled on fast and reliable scheduled liners. To control their ships around the globe, shipping companies used a new medium of communications: **submarine telegraph cables** laid on the ocean floor linking the continents. Cables were laid across the Atlantic in 1866, and by the turn of the century, cables connected every country and almost every inhabited island.

Railroads

The fifty years after 1850 saw a tremendous expansion of the world's **railroad** networks. At the end of its Civil War in 1865, the United States already had 35,000 miles (over 56,000 kilometers) of track, three times as much as Britain, and still growing. Germany, France, Canada, Russia, and Japan also built large networks.

Railroads were not confined to industrialized nations, but were constructed around the world. The British built the fourth largest rail network in the world in India (see Chapter 21). Many old cities doubled in size to accommodate railroad stations, sidings, tracks, warehouses, and repair shops. In the countryside, railroads consumed vast amounts of land and timber for ties to hold the rails and for bridges. Throughout the world, they opened new land to agriculture, mining, and other uses.

World Trade and Finance

Thanks to the growing speed and falling cost of transportation between 1850 and 1913, world trade expanded tenfold, transforming the economies of different parts of the world in different ways. The capitalist economics of western Europe and North America grew more prosperous and diversified, despite deep depressions in which workers lost their jobs and investors their fortunes.

Long after German and American industries surpassed the British, Britain continued to dominate the flow of trade, finance, and information. In 1900, two-thirds of the world's submarine cables were British or passed through Britain. Over half of the world's shipping was British owned. Britain invested one-fourth of its national wealth overseas, much of it in the United States and Argentina.

Nonindustrial areas were more vulnerable to changes in price and demand than were the industrialized nations, for many of them produced raw materials that could be replaced by synthetic substitutes or alternative sources of supply. Nevertheless, until World War I, the value of exports from the tropical countries generally remained high.

SOCIAL TRANSFORMATIONS

The technological and economic changes of the late nineteenth century sparked profound social changes in the industrial nations. A fast-growing

C H R O N O L O G Y

	Europe	United States	East Asia
1850	**1851** Majority of British population living in cities		
			1853 Commodore Perry "opens" Japan
	1859 Charles Darwin, *On the Origin of Species*		
	1861 Emancipation of serfs (Russia)		
		1865 Civil War ends; economic expansion begins	
	1866 Alfred Nobel develops dynamite	**1865–1914** Surge of immigration from southern and eastern Europe	
	1867 Karl Marx, *Das Kapital*		**1868** Meiji Restoration begins modernization drive in Japan
	1871 Unification of Germany; unification of Italy		
1875		**1879** Thomas Edison develops incandescent lamp	
	1882 Married Women's Property Act (Britain)		
		1890s "Jim Crow" laws enforce segregation in southern states	
			1894 Sino-Japanese War
		1899 United States acquires Puerto Rico and the Philippines	
1900			**1900** Boxer uprising ended
			1904–1905 Russo-Japanese War
	1905 Revolution of 1905 (Russia)		
			1910 Japan annexes Korea

population swelled cities to unprecedented size, and millions of Europeans emigrated to the Americas. Workers spawned labor movements and new forms of radical policies, and women's lives were dramatically altered.

Population and Migrations

The population of Europe grew faster from 1850 to 1914 than ever before or since, almost doubling from 265 million to 468 million, despite mass migrations of Europeans to the United States, Canada, Australia, New Zealand, and Argentina. Between 1850 and 1900, on average, 400,000 Europeans migrated overseas every year; between 1900 and 1914, the flood rose to over 1 million a year. People of European ancestry rose from one-fifth to one-third in the world's population.

Much of the increase came from a drop in the death rate, as epidemics and starvation became less common. The Irish famine of 1847–1848 was the last peacetime famine in European history. North American wheat supplemented Europe's food. Year-round supplies of meat, fruit, vegetables, and oils improved the diet of European and North American city dwellers.

Urbanization and Social Structures

In 1851, Britain became the first nation to have a majority of its population living in towns and cities. By 1914, 80 percent of its population was urban, as were 60 percent of the German and 45 percent of the French populations. London grew from 2.7 million in 1850 to 6.6 million in 1900. New York reached 3.4 million by 1900, a fiftyfold increase in the century. In the English Midlands, in the German Ruhr, and around Tokyo Bay, towns fused into one another, filling in the fields and woods that once had separated them.

In early industrial cities, the poor crowded together in unsanitary tenements. New urban technologies transformed city life for most residents. Pipes brought in clean water and carried away sewage. First gas and then electric lighting made cities safer and more pleasant at night. By the end of the century, municipal governments provided police and fire departments, schools, parks, and other amenities unheard of a century earlier.

As sanitation improved, urban death rates fell below birthrates for the first time. Confident that their children would survive infancy, couples began to limit the number of children they had. To accommodate the growing population, planners laid out new cities, such as Chicago, on a rectangular grid, and middle-class families moved to new developments on the edges of cities. In Paris, older neighborhoods with narrow, crooked streets and rickety tenements were replaced with broad boulevards and modern apartment buildings. Brilliantly lit by gas and electricity, Paris became the "city of lights," a model for city planners from New Delhi to Buenos Aires. By 1900, electric streetcars and subways allowed working-class people to live miles from their workplaces.

In fast-growing cities such as London, New York, and Chicago, newcomers arrived so quickly that housing construction and municipal services could not keep up. Immigrants who saved their money to reunite their families could not afford costly municipal services. As a result, the poorest neighborhoods remained as overcrowded, unhealthy, and dangerous as they had been since the early decades of industrialization.

While urban environments improved in many ways, air quality worsened. Coal, burned to power steam engines and heat buildings, polluted the air, coating everything with a film of grimy dust. And the thousands of horses that pulled the carts and carriages covered the streets with their wastes, causing a terrible stench.

Labor Movements and Socialist Politics

Industrialization combined with the revolutionary ideas of the late eighteenth century to produce two kinds of movements—socialism and labor movements—calling for further changes. **Socialism** was an ideology developed by radical thinkers who questioned the sanctity of private property and argued in support of industrial workers against their employers. **Labor unions** were organizations formed by industrial workers to defend their interests in negotiations with employers. The socialist and labor movements were never identical. Most of the time they were allies; occasionally they were rivals.

Labor unions sought not only better wages but also improved working conditions and insurance against illness, accidents, disability, and old age. They grew slowly because strikes were illegal and hard to sustain. When laws were relaxed, British, German, and American labor grew rapidly.

By far the best-known socialist was **Karl Marx** (1818–1883), a German journalist who lived most of his life in England. The ideas he expressed succinctly in the *Communist Manifesto* (1848) and in great detail in *Das Kapital*° (1867) provided an intellectual framework for the growing dissatisfaction with raw industrial capitalism (see Diversity and Dominance: Marx and Engels on Global Trade and the Bourgeoisie). He argued that the capitalists unfairly extracted the "surplus value" of workers' labor—that is, the difference between workers' wages and the value of the goods they manufactured. The concentration of wealth in a few hands convinced Marx that class struggle between workers and owners was inevitable. But the International Working Man's Association Marx helped found in 1864 attracted more intellectuals than workers. Workers found other means of redressing their grievances, such as the vote and labor unions.

The nineteenth century saw a gradual extension of the right to vote throughout Europe and North America. Universal male suffrage became law in the United States in 1870, in France and Germany in 1871, in Britain in 1885, and in the rest of Europe soon after. With universal male suffrage, socialist politicians could expect to capture many seats in their nations' parliaments, because the newly enfranchised working class was so numerous. Democratic socialist parties sought to use voting power to gain concessions from government and eventually even to win elections.

teen or more hours a day, six and a half days a week, for little more than room and board. Their living quarters, usually in the attic or basement, contrasted with the luxurious quarters of their masters. Female servants were vulnerable to sexual abuse by their masters or their masters' sons.

Young women often preferred work in a factory to domestic service. Men worked in construction, iron and steel, heavy machinery, or on railroads; women worked in textiles and the clothing trades, two extensions of traditional women's household work. Most industrial countries passed legislation limiting the hours or forbidding the employment of women in the hardest and most dangerous occupations, such as mining and foundry work. Such legislation also reinforced gender divisions in industry, keeping women in low-paid, subordinate positions.

Married women with children were expected to stay home, even if their husbands did not make enough to support the family. In addition to the work of child rearing and housework, married women of the working class contributed to the family's income by taking in boarders, sewing, or weaving baskets. The hardest and worst-paid work was washing other people's clothes. Since electric lighting and indoor plumbing cost more than most working-class families could afford, even ordinary household duties like cooking and washing remained heavy burdens.

The poorest of the poor were orphans and single women with children. Unable to find jobs or support themselves at home, many turned to prostitution. The wealth of middle-class men made it easy for them to take advantage of the poverty of working-class women.

Working-Class Women and Men

Working-class women led lives of toil and pain, considerably harder than the lives of their menfolk. Although the worst abuses of child labor had been banned in most European countries by 1850, parents expected girls as young as ten to contribute to the household. Many became domestic servants, commonly working six-

The Victorian Age and Women's "Separate Sphere"

In English-speaking countries, the period from about 1850 to 1914 is known as the **Victorian Age.** The expression refers not only to the reign of Queen Victoria of England (r. 1837–1901) but also to rules of behavior and to an ideology surrounding the family and the relations between men and women. The Victorians contrasted the masculine ideals of strength and courage with the feminine virtues of beauty and kindness, and they idealized

Das Kapital (DUSS cop-ee-TALL)

DIVERSITY AND DOMINANCE

MARX AND ENGELS ON GLOBAL TRADE AND THE BOURGEOISIE

In 1848 the German philosophers Karl Marx (1818–1883) and Friedrich Engels (1820–1895), who were living in England at the time, published a small book called Manifesto of the Communist Party. *In it, they tried to explain why owners of manufactures and business—the "bourgeoisie"—had become the wealthiest and most powerful class of people in industrializing countries like Britain, and why urban and industrial workers—the "proletariat"—lived in poverty. In their view, the dominance of the European commercial and industrial bourgeoisie was in the process of destroying the diversity of human cultures, reducing all classes in Europe and all cultures to the status of proletarians selling their labor.*

In the Manifesto, *Marx and Engels did not limit themselves to publicizing social inequities. They also called for a social revolution in which the workers would overthrow the bourgeoisie and establish a new society without private property or government. Their* Manifesto *was soon translated into many languages and became the best-known expression of radical communist ideology.*

Whatever one may think of their call to revolution, Marx and Engels's analysis of class relations has had a lasting impact on social historians. Their ideas are especially interesting from the perspective of global history because of the way in which they connect the rise of the bourgeois with world trade and industrial technology. The following paragraphs explain these connections.

The history of all hitherto existing society is the history of class struggles.

Freeman and slave, patrician and plebeian, lord and serf, guild-master and journeyman, in a word, oppressor and oppressed, stood in constant opposition to one another, carried on an uninterrupted, now hidden, now open fight, a fight that each time ended, either in a revolutionary re-constitution of society at large, or in the common ruin of the contending classes.

In the earlier epochs of history, we find almost everywhere a complicated arrangement of society into various orders, a manifold gradation of social rank. In ancient Rome we have patricians, knights, plebeians, slaves; in the middle ages, feudal lords, vassals, guild-masters, journeymen, apprentices, serfs; in almost all of these classes, again, subordinate gradations.

The modern bourgeois society that has sprouted from the ruins of feudal society, has not done away with class antagonisms. It has but established new classes, new conditions of oppression, new forms of struggle in place of the old ones.

Our epoch, the epoch of the bourgeoisie, possesses, however, this distinctive feature; it has simplified the class antagonisms. Society as a whole is more and more splitting up into two great hostile camps, into two great classes directly facing each other: Bourgeoisie and Proletariat.

From the serfs of the middle ages sprang the chartered burghers of the earliest towns. From these burgesses the first elements of the bourgeoisie were developed.

The discovery of America, the rounding of the Cape, opened up fresh ground for the rising bourgeoisie. The East-Indian and Chinese markets, the colonization of America, trade with the colonies, the increase in the means of exchange and in commodities generally, gave to commerce, to navigation, to industry, an impulse never before known, and thereby, to the revolutionary element in the tottering feudal society, a rapid development.

The feudal system of industry, under which industrial production was monopolised by closed guilds, now no longer sufficed for the growing wants of the new markets. The manufacturing system took its place. The guild-masters were pushed on one side by the manufacturing middle-class; division of labour between the different corporate guilds vanished in the face of division of labour in each single workshop.

Meantime the markets kept ever growing, the demand, ever rising. Even manufacture no longer sufficed. Thereupon, steam and machinery revolutionised industrial production. The place of manufacture was taken by the giant, Modern Industry, the place of the industrial middle-class, by industrial millionaires, the leaders of whole industrial armies, the modern bourgeois.

Modern industry has established the world-market, for which the discovery of America paved the way. This market has given an immense importance to commerce, to navigation, to communication by land. This development has, in its turn, reacted on the extension of industry; and in proportion as industry, commerce, navigation, railways extended, in the same proportion the bourgeoisie developed, increased its capital, and pushed into the background every class handed down from the Middle Ages.

We see, therefore, how the modern bourgeoisie is itself the product of a long course of development, of a series of revolutions in the modes of production and of exchange. . . .

[T]he bourgeoisie has at last, since the establishment of Modern Industry and of the world-market, conquered for itself, in the modern representative State, exclusive political sway. The executive of the modern State is but a committee for managing the common affairs of the whole bourgeoisie.

The bourgeoisie, historically, has played a most revolutionary part. . . .

It has been the first to shew what man's activity can bring about. It has accomplished wonders far surpassing Egyptian pyramids, Roman aqueducts, and Gothic cathedrals; it has conducted expeditions that put in the shade all former Exoduses of nations and crusades.

The bourgeoisie cannot exist without constantly revolutionising the instruments of production, and thereby the relations of production, and with them the whole relations of society. Conservation of the old modes of production in unaltered form, was, on the contrary, the first condition of existence for all earlier industrial classes. Constant revolutionising of production, uninterrupted disturbance of all social conditions, everlasting uncertainty and agitation distinguish the bourgeois epoch from all earlier ones. All fixed, fast-frozen relations, with their train of ancient and venerable prejudices and opinions, are swept away, all new-formed ones become antiquated before they can ossify. All that is solid melts into air, all that is holy is profaned, and man is at last compelled to face with sober senses, his real conditions of life, and his relations with his kind.

The need of a constantly expanding market for its products chases the bourgeoisie over the whole surface of the globe. It must nestle everywhere, settle everywhere, establish connexions everywhere.

The bourgeoisie has through its exploitation of the world-market given a cosmopolitan character to production and consumption in every country. To the great chagrin of Re-actionists, it has drawn from under the feet of industry the national ground on which it stood. All old-fashioned national industries have been destroyed or are daily being destroyed. They are dislodged by new industries, whose introduction becomes a life or death question for all civilised nations, by industries that no longer work up indigenous raw material, but raw material drawn from the remotest zones; industries whose products are consumed, not only at home, but in every quarter of the globe. In place of the old wants, satisfied by the productions of the country, we find new wants, requiring for their satisfaction the products of distant lands and climes. In place of the old local and national seclusion and self-sufficiency, we have intercourse in every direction, universal interdependence of nations. And as in material, so also in intellectual production. The intellectual creations of individual nations become common property. National one-sidedness and narrow-mindedness become more and more impossible, and from the numerous national and local literatures there arises a world-literature.

The bourgeoisie, by the rapid improvement of all instruments of production, by the immensely facilitated means of communication, draws all, even the most barbarian, nations into civilisation. The cheap prices of its commodities are the heavy artillery with which it batters down all Chinese walls, with which it forces the barbarians' intensely obstinate hatred of foreigners to capitulate. It compels all nations, on pain of extinction, to adopt the bourgeois mode of production; it compels them to introduce what it calls civilisation into their midst, i.e., to become bourgeois themselves. In a word, it creates a world after its own image.

The bourgeoisie has subjected the country to the rule of the towns. It has created enormous cities, has greatly increased the urban population as compared with the rural, and has thus rescued a considerable part of the population from the idiocy of rural life. Just as it has made the country dependent on the towns, so it has made barbarian and semi-barbarian countries dependent on the civilised ones, nations of peasants on nations of bourgeois, the East on the West. . . .

The bourgeoisie, during its rule of scarce one hundred years, has created more massive and more colossal productive forces than have all preceding generations together. Subjection of Nature's forces to man, machinery, application of chemistry to industry and agriculture, steam-navigation, railways, electric telegraphs, clearing of whole continents for cultivation, canalization of rivers, whole populations conjured out of the ground—what earlier century had even a presentiment that such productive forces slumbered in the lap of social labour?

QUESTIONS FOR ANALYSIS

1. How did the growth of world trade since the European discovery of America affect relations between social classes in Europe?

2. What effect did the growth of trade and industry have on products, intellectual creations, and consumer tastes around the world?

3. Why does Marx think the bourgeoisie requires constant changes in technology and social relations? How well does that description fit the world you live in?

4. Can you think of recent examples of the Western bourgeoisie's creating "a world after its own image"?

Source: Karl Marx and Frederick Engels, *Manifesto of the Communist Party,* Authorized English Translation: Edited and Annotated by Frederick Engels (Chicago: Charles H. Kerr & Company, 1906), 12–20.

the home as a peaceful and loving refuge from the dog-eat-dog world of competitive capitalism.

Victorian morality claimed to be universal, yet it best fit the European upper- and middle-class family. Men and women were thought to belong in **"separate spheres."** Successful businessmen spent their time at work or relaxing in men's clubs. They put their wives in charge of rearing the children, running the household, and spending the family money to enhance the family's social status.

The most important duty of middle-class women was rearing children. Unlike the rich of previous eras, who handed their children over to wet nurses and tutors, Victorian mothers nursed their own babies and showered their children with love and attention. Even those who could afford nannies and governesses remained personally involved in their children's education. While boys were being prepared for the business world or the professions, girls were taught such skills as embroidery, drawing, and music, which offered no monetary reward or professional preparation but enhanced their social graces and marriage prospects.

Young women could work until they got married, but only in genteel occupations such as retail and office work. Jobs that required higher education, especially jobs in the professions, were closed to women. Until late in the century, few universities granted degrees to women. The first profession open to women was teaching, as more and more countries passed laws calling for universal compulsory education. Women were considered well suited to teaching young children and girls—an extension of the duties of Victorian mothers. Teaching, however, was judged suitable only for single women; married women were expected to stay home and take care of their own children.

Governments enforced legal discrimination against women. Until the end of the century, most European countries considered women minors for life—that is, subject to their fathers before marriage and to their husbands after. Even Britain,

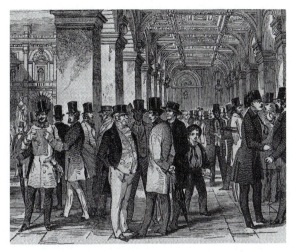

Separate Spheres in Great Britain   In the Victorian Age, men and women of the middle and upper classes led largely separate lives. In *Aunt Emily's Visit* (1845), we see women and children at home, tended by a servant. *The Royal Exchange*, meanwhile, was a place for men to transact business.   (Mary Evans Picture Library)

among the most progressive countries, did not give women the right to control their own property until 1882, with passage of the Married Women's Property Act.

Some middle-class women organized to fight prostitution, alcohol, and child labor. By the turn of the century, a few were challenging male domination of politics and the law. By 1914, women had won the right to vote in twelve states of the United States. British women did not vote until 1918.

NATIONALISM AND THE UNIFICATION OF GERMANY

The most influential idea of the nineteenth century was **nationalism.** The French revolutionaries had defined people, previously considered the subjects of a sovereign, as the citizens of a *nation*— a concept identified with a territory, the state that ruled it, and the culture of its people. Because the most widely spoken language in nineteenth-century Europe was German, the unification of most German-speaking people into a single state in 1871 had momentous consequences for the world.

National Identity Before 1871

The idea of redrawing the boundaries of states to accommodate linguistic, religious, or cultural differences was revolutionary. Language was usually the crucial element in creating a feeling of national unity, but language and citizenship seldom coincided. The fit between France and the French language was exceptional. The Italian- and German-speaking peoples were divided among many small states. Living in the Austrian Empire were peoples who spoke German, Czech, Slovak, Hungarian, Polish, and other languages. Even where people spoke a common language, they could be divided by religion or institutions. The Irish, though English speaking, were mostly Catholic, whereas the English were primarily Protestant.

Until the 1860s, nationalism was associated with **liberalism,** the revolutionary middle-class ideology emerging from the French Revolution (see Chapter 19) that asserted the sovereignty of the people and demanded constitutional government, a national parliament, and freedom of expression. The most famous nationalist of the early nineteenth century, Giuseppe Mazzini° (1805–1872), led

Giuseppe Mazzini (jew-SEP-pay mat-SEE-nee)

a failed liberal revolution of 1848 in Italy that sought to unify the Italian peninsula. Although the revolutions of 1848 failed except in France, their strength convinced conservative governments that they could not forever keep their citizens out of politics and that mass politics, if properly managed, could strengthen rather than weaken the state. A new generation of conservative political leaders learned how to preserve the social status quo through public education, universal military service, and colonial conquests, all of which built a sense of national unity.

The Unification of Germany

Some German nationalists wanted to unite all Germans under the Catholic Austrian throne. Others wanted to exclude Austria with its many non-Germanic peoples and unite all other German-speaking areas under Lutheran Prussia. The Prussian state had two advantages: (1) the newly developed industries of the Rhineland and (2) the first European army to make use of railroads, telegraphs, breechloading rifles, steel artillery, and other products of modern industry. The king of Prussia, Wilhelm I (r. 1861–1888), had entrusted the running of his government to his chancellor, the brilliant and authoritarian aristocrat **Otto von Bismarck** (1815–1898), who was determined to use Prussian military and German nationalism to advance the interests of the Prussian state.

In 1864, after a quick victory against Denmark, Bismarck set his sights on Austria, which surrendered in 1866. To everyone's surprise, Prussia took no Austrian territory. Instead, Prussia and some smaller states formed the North German Confederation, the nucleus of a future Germany. Then in 1870, Bismarck provoked a war with France. In this "Franco-Prussian War," German armies used their superior firepower and tactics to achieve a quick victory.

The spoils of victory included a large indemnity and two provinces of Alsace and Lorraine (see Map 23.1). To the Germans, this region was German because a majority of its inhabitants spoke German. To the French, it was French because it had been so when the nation of France was forged in the Revolution and because most of its inhabitants considered themselves French. These two conflicting definitions of nationalism kept enmity between France and Germany smoldering for decades.

Nationalism After 1871

The Franco-Prussian War changed the political climate of Europe. France became wholeheartedly liberal. The Italian peninsula became unified as the kingdom of Italy. Germany, Austria-Hungary (as the Austrian Empire had renamed itself in 1867), and Russia remained conservative.

All politicians tried to manipulate public opinion to bolster their governments. The spread of literacy allowed politicians and journalists to appeal to the emotions of the poor, diverting their anger from their employers to foreigners and their votes from socialist to nationalist parties.

In many countries, the dominant group used nationalism to justify the imposing of its language, religion, or customs on minority populations. The Russian Empire attempted to "Russify" its diverse ethnic populations. The Spanish government made the Spanish language compulsory in the schools, newspapers, and courts of its Basque- and Catalan-speaking provinces. Immigrants to the United States were expected to learn English.

Some people looked to science for support of political dominance. One of the most influential scientists of the century, and the one whose ideas were most widely cited and misinterpreted, was the English biologist **Charles Darwin** (1809–1882), who had spent years traveling through South America and the South Pacific studying plant and animal life. His famous book, *On the Origin of Species by Means of Natural Selection* (1859), argued that over hundreds of thousands of years, living beings had either evolved in the struggle for survival or become extinct. The philosopher Herbert Spencer (1820–1903) and others took up Darwin's ideas of "natural selection" and "survival of the fittest" and applied them to human society. Extreme Social Darwinists developed elaborate pseudo-scientific theories of racial differences, claiming that they were the result not of history but of biology.

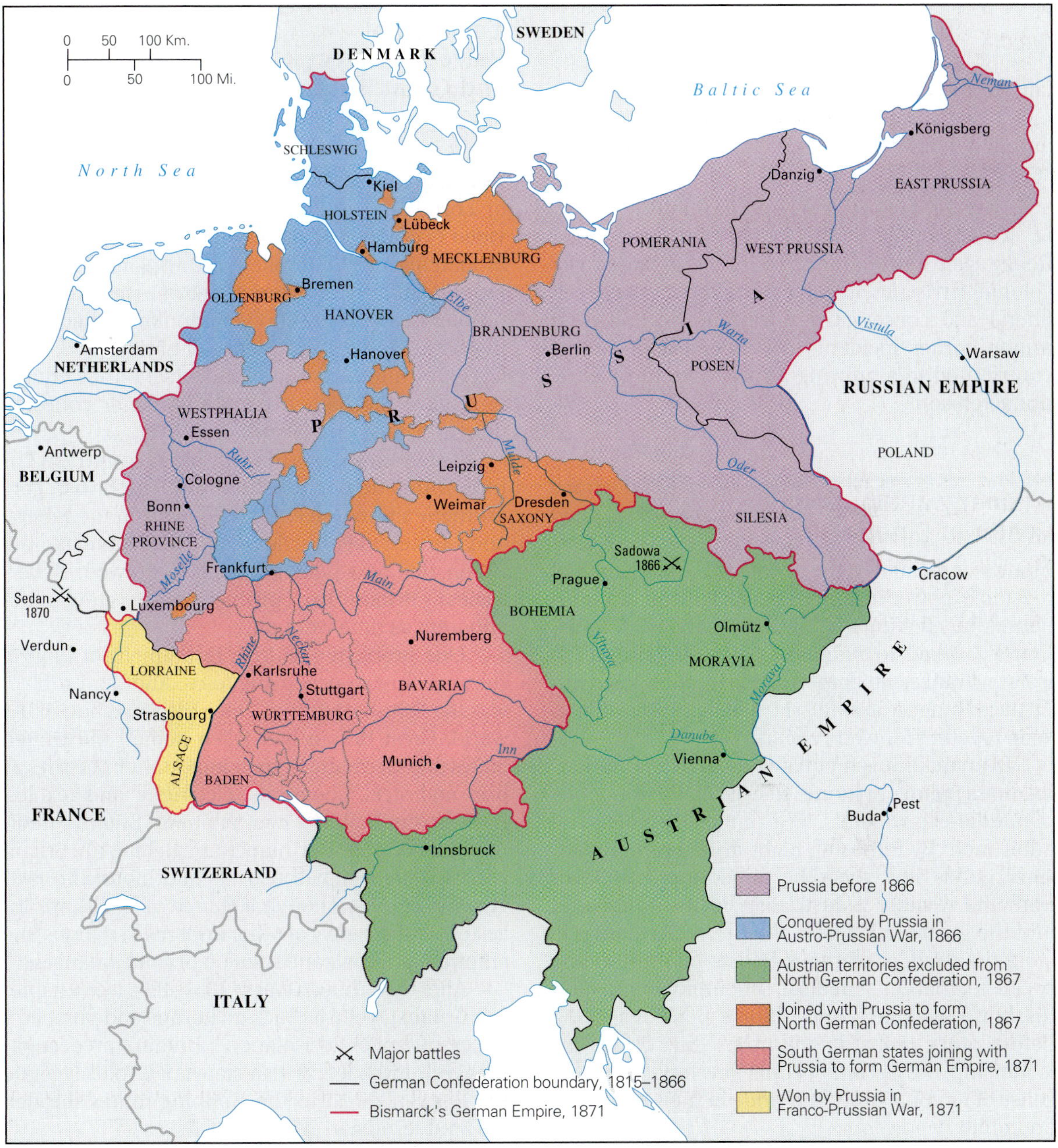
0 50 100 Km.
0 50 100 Mi.
DENMARK
SWEDEN
Baltic Sea
North Sea
SCHLESWIG
Kiel
HOLSTEIN
Lübeck
Hamburg
MECKLENBURG
Bremen
OLDENBURG
HANOVER
Hanover
Elbe
BRANDENBURG
Berlin
POMERANIA
WEST PRUSSIA
EAST PRUSSIA
Königsberg
Danzig
Neman
Vistula
Warta
POSEN
Warsaw
RUSSIAN EMPIRE
POLAND
Amsterdam
NETHERLANDS
WESTPHALIA
Essen
Ruhr
Antwerp
BELGIUM
Cologne
Bonn
RHINE PROVINCE
P R U S S I A
Leipzig
Mulde
Weimar
Dresden
SAXONY
Oder
SILESIA
Cracow
Moselle
Frankfurt
Main
Sadowa 1866
Prague
Sedan 1870
Luxembourg
BOHEMIA
Olmütz
Verdun
Nuremberg
Neckar
Rhine
Vltava
MORAVIA
LORRAINE
Karlsruhe
Stuttgart
BAVARIA
Morava
Nancy
Strasbourg
WÜRTTEMBURG
Danube
ALSACE
Inn
Vienna
BADEN
Munich
AUSTRIAN EMPIRE
FRANCE
Buda
Pest
Innsbruck
SWITZERLAND
ITALY
Prussia before 1866
Conquered by Prussia in Austro-Prussian War, 1866
Austrian territories excluded from North German Confederation, 1867
Joined with Prussia to form North German Confederation, 1867
South German states joining with Prussia to form German Empire, 1871
Won by Prussia in Franco-Prussian War, 1871
Major battles
German Confederation boundary, 1815–1866
Bismarck's German Empire, 1871

Map 23.1 The Unification of Germany, 1866–1871 Germany was united after a series of short, successful wars by the kingdom of Prussia against Austria in 1866 and against France in 1871.

THE GREAT POWERS OF EUROPE, 1871–1900

After 1871, politicians and journalists discovered how easily they could whip up popular frenzy against neighboring countries. Rivalries over colonial territories, ideological differences between liberal and conservative governments, and even minor border incidents or trade disagreements contributed to a growing atmosphere of international tension.

Germany at the Center of Europe

International relations revolved around a united Germany, because Germany was located in the center of Europe and had the most powerful army on the European continent. After creating a unified Germany in 1871, Bismarck worked to maintain peace in Europe. To isolate France, he forged a loose coalition with Austria-Hungary and Russia, which he was able to keep together for twenty years.

Bismarck proved equally adept at manipulating mass politics at home. To weaken the influence of middle-class liberals, he extended the vote to all adult men. By imposing high tariffs on manufactured goods and wheat, he gained the support of both the wealthy industrialists of the Rhineland and the great landowners of eastern Germany. He stole the thunder of the socialists by introducing social legislation—medical, unemployment, and disability insurance and old-age pensions—long before other industrial countries did. Under his leadership, the German people developed a strong sense of national unity and pride in their industrial and military power.

In 1888, Wilhelm I was succeeded by his grandson Wilhelm II (r. 1888–1918), who dismissed Chancellor Bismarck. Wilhelm II talked about his "global policy" and demanded that Germany, with the mightiest army and the largest industrial economy in Europe, have a colonial empire, "a place in the sun."

The Liberal Powers: France and Great Britain

France, once the dominant nation in Europe, had difficulty reconciling itself to being in second place. Its population and its army lagged far behind Germany's, and its industry was growing more slowly, thanks to the loss of the iron and coal mines of Lorraine. The French people were deeply divided over the very nature of the state: some were monarchists and Catholics; a growing number held republican and anticlerical views. Despite these problems, a long tradition of popular participation in politics and a strong sense of nationhood, reinforced by a fine system of universal public education, gave the French people a deeper cohesion than appeared on the surface.

Great Britain was the only other country in Europe with a democratic tradition. The British government alternated smoothly between the Liberal and Conservative Parties, and the income gap between rich and poor gradually narrowed. Nevertheless, Britain had problems that grew more apparent as time went on.

One problem was Irish resentment of English rule as a foreign occupying force. Another problem was the British economy. Once the workshop of the world, Great Britain had fallen behind the United States and Germany in such important industries as iron and steel, chemicals, electricity, and textiles. Even in shipbuilding and shipping, Britain's traditional specialties, Germany was catching up. Britain was also preoccupied with its enormous and fast-growing empire. Though a source of wealth for investors and the envy of other imperialist nations, the empire was a constant drain on Britain's finances.

After the Crimean War of 1853–1856 (see Chapter 22), Britain turned its back on Europe and pursued a policy of "splendid isolation." Britain's preoccupation with India led British statesmen to exaggerate the Russian threat to the shipping routes through the Mediterranean and Central Asia.

The Conservative Powers: Russia and Austria-Hungary

The forces of nationalism weakened rather than strengthened Russia and Austria-Hungary. The reason for this effect was that

The Doss House   Late-nineteenth-century cities showed more physical than social improvements. This painting by Makovsky of a street in St. Petersburg contrasts the broad avenue and impressive new buildings with the poverty of the crowd.   (The State Museum/St. Petersburg)

their populations were far more divided, socially and ethnically, than were the German, French, or British peoples.

Nationalism was most divisive in the Austrian Empire. The decision to rename itself the Austro-Hungarian Empire in 1867 appeased its Hungarian critics but alienated its Slavic-speaking minorities. The Austro-Hungarian Empire still thought of itself as a great power and attempted to dominate the Balkans. This strategy irritated Russia, which thought of itself as the protector of Slavic peoples everywhere, and it eventually led to war.

Russia was the most misunderstood country in Europe. Its enormous size and population led many Europeans to exaggerate its military potential, but Russia was weakened by national and so-

cial divisions. All in all, only 45 percent of the peoples of the tsarist empire spoke Russian.

To strengthen the bonds between the monarchy and the Russian people and promote industrialization by enlarging the labor pool, the moderate conservative Tsar Alexander II (r. 1855–1881) emancipated the peasants from serfdom in 1861. That measure, however, did not create a modern society but only turned serfs into communal farmers with few skills and little capital. Though technically "emancipated," the great majority of Russians had little education, few legal rights, and no say in their government. After Alexander's assassination in 1881, his successors Alexander III (r. 1881–1894) and Nicholas II (r. 1894–1917) opposed all forms of social change. Industrialization consisted largely of state-sponsored projects, such as railroads, iron foundries, and armament factories, and led to social unrest among urban workers. Wealthy landowning aristocrats continued to dominate the Russian court and administration and succeeded in blocking most reforms.

The weaknesses in Russia's society and government became glaringly obvious after Russia's defeat in the Russo-Japanese War of 1904–1905 (see below). The shock of defeat caused a popular uprising, the Revolution of 1905, that forced Tsar Nicholas II to grant a constitution and an elected Duma (parliament). But as soon as he was able to rebuild the army and the police, he reverted to the traditional despotism of his forefathers. Small groups of radical intellectuals, angered by the contrast between the wealth of the elite and the poverty of the common people, began plotting the violent overthrow of the tsarist autocracy.

NEW GREAT POWERS: THE UNITED STATES AND JAPAN

Europeans had come to regard their continent as the center of the universe and their states as the only great powers in the world. The rest of the world was either ignored or used as bargaining chips in the game of power politics. The late nineteenth century marked the high point of European power and arrogance, yet at that very moment, two nations outside Europe were becoming great powers. One of them, the United States, was inhabited mainly by people of European origin, and its rise to great-power status had been predicted early in the nineteenth century by astute observers like the French statesman Alexis de Tocqueville. The other one, Japan, seemed so distant and exotic in 1850 that no European had guessed it would join the ranks of the great powers.

The United States, 1865–1900

After the Civil War ended in 1865, the United States entered a period of vigorous growth. Hundreds of thousands of immigrants arrived every year, mainly from Russia, Italy, and central Europe, raising the population to 63 million in 1891. Although many settled on the newly opened lands west of the Mississippi, most of the migrants moved to the towns, which mushroomed into cities in a few years. In the process, the nation became an industrial giant. By 1900, the United States had overtaken Britain and Germany as the world's leading industrial power.

This explosive growth was accomplished with few government restrictions and much government help, such as free land for railroads and protective tariffs. In this atmosphere of unfettered free enterprise, the nation got rich fast, as did its upper and middle classes.

Expansion created many victims. First among them were the American Indians. When the railroads penetrated the west after the Civil War, they brought white colonists eager to start farming, ranching, or mining. The indigenous Indians whose lands they invaded fought back with great courage but were outnumbered and outgunned. In Canada, the government tried to protect the Indians from the whites. The United States Army, however, always sided with the settlers. The U.S. government had signed numerous treaties with the Indians but tore them up when settlers demanded land. After decades of warfare, massacres, and starvation, the government confined the remaining Indians to reservations on the poorest lands.

The U.S. government also abandoned African-Americans in 1877, after the end of Reconstruction, especially in the defeated southern states. Though freed from slavery in 1865, most of them became sharecroppers who were at the mercy of their landowners. In the 1890s, the southern states instituted "Jim Crow" laws segregating blacks in public transportation, jobs, and schools. Not only did southern judges apply harsh laws in a biased manner, but black Americans were also subject to the lawless violence of mobs, which lynched an average of fifty blacks a year until well into the twentieth century.

Racism also affected Asian immigrants, many of whom had come to the United States to build railroads in the western states. In 1882, the U.S. government barred the Chinese from immigrating by enacting the first of many racial exclusion laws.

Working-class whites benefited little from the booming economy. Economic depressions in

1873 and 1893 caused more distress in the United States than in Europe, because the United States had few labor laws and no unemployment compensation to soften the hardships. Police or the army repressed strikes and unions. The courts consistently supported employers against their employees, capital against labor, and business against government.

Working-class women bore the brunt of repressive labor practices because they earned less than men, had more responsibilities, and seldom were members of labor unions. As in Britain, activist middle-class women organized to demand female suffrage and to fight against alcohol, prostitution, and other social evils.

The booming economy and the waves of immigrants radically transformed the environment. Timber companies clear-cut large areas of Michigan, Wisconsin, and the Appalachian Mountains to provide lumber for railroad ties and frame houses, pulp for paper, and fuel for locomotives and iron foundries. Farmers cleared the forests and plowed the prairies. Buffalo, the dominant animals of the western territories, were massacred by the hundreds of thousands to starve out the Indians and clear the land for cattle. In the west, the government began massive irrigation projects. In the industrial northeast, iron foundries, steel mills, and steam engines caused severe local air pollution.

In spite of all the assaults, the North American continent was so huge that large parts of it remained unspoiled. A few especially beautiful areas were declared national parks, beginning with Yellowstone in Wyoming in 1872, thereby marking a new stage in Americans' attitude toward nature. Thanks to the efforts of naturalist John Muir and President Theodore Roosevelt (1901–1909), large parts of the western states were set aside as national forests.

Most citizens showed little interest in foreign affairs. Patriots tended to celebrate American freedom and democracy, the conquest of a huge continent, and the country's remarkable technological achievements. In this period, the inventor Thomas Edison was probably the most admired man in America.

The expansionism of the United States and its businesses did not stop at the borders but exerted a strong influence on Mexico and the Caribbean.

Naval officers, bankers, and politicians urged active intervention in the Western Hemisphere. In 1899, the United States defeated Spain, annexed Puerto Rico and the Philippines, and turned Cuba into an American protectorate (see Chapter 24). Long recognized as the leading power in the Americas, the United States found itself involved in Asian affairs as well. Nevertheless, although their country was fast becoming a global power, most Americans still preferred George Washington's policy of "no European entanglements."

The Crisis of the Tokugawa Shogunate

Japan's response to imperialist pressure differed entirely from China's. In the latter country, the **Empress Dowager Cixi°** (r. 1862–1908), who had once encouraged the construction of shipyards, arsenals, and telegraph lines, came to oppose railways and other foreign technologies that could carry foreign influences to the interior (see Chapter 22). Government officials secretly encouraged crowds to attack and destroy the intrusive devices. They were able to slow the foreign intrusion, but in doing so, they denied themselves the best means of defense against foreign pressure.

In Japan, which was very differently organized politically under the Tokugawa Shogunate (see Chapter 18), local lords called *daimyo* controlled their lands and populations with little interference from the shogunate and none at all from the emperor, whose political role was purely symbolic. Though the shoguns passed stringent laws against dealing with foreigners, many Japanese ignored them. The most flagrant violators were powerful lords in southern Japan who ran large and successful pirate or black-market operations. Though they took advantage of shogunal weakness, some lords recognized that a genuine foreign challenge, such as the one presaged by the appearance of Russian and British ships off the Japanese coast in 1792, might overwhelm them. The regional lords of Satsuma° and Choshu,° two large domains in southern Japan, responded by upgrading their armies, arsenals, and shipyards. Their remoteness from the

---

Cixi (TSUH-shee)   **Satsuma** (SAT-soo-mah)   **Choshu** (CHOE-shoo)

capital Edo (now Tokyo) along with their economic vigor and growing populations fostered a strong sense of local self-reliance.

In 1853 the American commodore Matthew C. Perry arrived off the coast of Japan with a fleet of steam-powered warships that the Japanese called "black ships." He demanded that Japan open its ports to trade and allow American ships to refuel and take on supplies during their voyages between China and California. He promised to return a year later to receive the Japanese answer.

Perry's demands sparked a crisis. After consultation with the provincial daimyo, the shogun's advisers advocated capitulation to Perry. They pointed to China's humiliating defeats in the Opium and Arrow Wars (see Chapter 22). The solution they proposed, the Treaty of Kanagawa,° resembled the unequal treaties between China and the Western powers. This spurred some angry provincial governors to encourage agitation against the Tokugawa regime and in favor of banning foreigners from Japan.

Political tensions between the shogunate and provincial leaders in Choshu, Satsuma, and elsewhere increased in the early 1860s. When British and French ships shelled the southwestern coasts in 1864 to protest the treatment of foreigners, provincial samurai exploded with anger against the treaty and the shogunate's inability to protect the country. Young, educated men who faced mediocre prospects under the rigid Tokugawa class system emerged as provincial leaders. In 1867 the Choshu leaders Yamagata Aritomo and Ito Hirobumi finally realized that they should stop warring with Satsuma and join forces to lead a rebellion against the shogunate.

The Meiji Restoration and the Modernization of Japan, 1868–1894

The civil war was intense but brief. In 1868 provincial rebels overthrew the Tokugawa Shogunate and declared the young emperor Mutsuhito° (r. 1868–1912) "restored." The new leaders called their regime the **"Meiji° Restoration,"** after Mutsuhito's reign name (*Meiji* means "enlightened rule"). Dedicated

to protecting their country from Western imperialism, the architects of the new regime visualized Japan's transformation into "a rich country with a strong army" and world-class industries. Though imposed from above, the Meiji Restoration changed Japan as profoundly as the French Revolution changed France.

In the Charter Oath issued in 1868, the young emperor included a prophetic sentence (written by his advisers): "Knowledge shall be sought throughout the world and thus shall be strengthened the foundation of the imperial polity." With the highest literacy rate in Asia, Japan was well prepared to learn and disseminate those foreign ideas, institutions, and techniques that could strengthen the nation, including a new educational system and a conscript army. Experimentation with industrial development and financing in the provinces in the earlier 1800s taught the government how to establish heavy industries through state financing without extensive foreign debt.

The Meiji leaders copied the government structure of imperial Germany. They modeled the new Japanese navy on the British and the army on the Prussian. They introduced Western-style postal and telegraph services, railroads and harbors, banking, clocks, and calendars. To learn the secrets of Western strength, they sent hundreds of students to Britain, Germany, and the United States. They even encouraged foreign clothing styles and pastimes.

Western technology was highly prized. The government opened vocational, technical, and agricultural schools and founded four imperial universities. Foreign experts gave advice on medicine, science, and engineering. At the newly created Imperial College of Engineering, an Englishman, William Ayrton, became the first professor of electrical engineering anywhere in the world. His students later went on to found major corporations and government research institutes.

State-owned factories turned out textiles and inexpensive consumer goods for sale abroad. The first Japanese industries, some dating to the early nineteenth century, exploited their workers ruthlessly, just as the first industries in Europe and America had done. Peasant families, squeezed by rising taxes and rents, sent their daughters to work in textile mills. In 1881, to pay off its debts, the government sold these enterprises to private investors,

---

Kanagawa (KAH-nah-GAH-wah) Mutsuhito (moo-tsoo-HE-toe) Meiji (MAY-gee)

Silk Factory in Japan   Silk manufacture, Japan's best-known industry, began to be mechanized in the 1870s. In this factory, as in most textile mills, the workers were women.   (The Metropolitan Museum of Art, gift of Lincoln Kirstein, 1959 [JP 3346]. Photograph by Otto E. Nelson. Photograph © 1986 The Metropolitan Museum of Art.)

mainly large *zaibatsu*°, or conglomerates. But individual technological innovation was also encouraged. Thus the carpenter Toyoda Sakichi founded the Toyoda Loom Works (now Toyota Motor Company) in 1906; ten years later he patented the world's most advanced automatic loom.

| The Birth of Japanese Imperialism, 1894–1905 | Japan's path to imperialism was laid out by **Yamagata Aritomo,** an influential Meiji leader. He believed that to be independent |

dependent Japan had to define a "sphere of influence" that included Korea, Manchuria, and part of China (see Map 23.2). If other countries controlled these areas, Japan would be at risk. To protect this

sphere of influence, Yamagata called for a vigorous program of military industrialization, culminating in the building of battleships.

Meanwhile, as Japan grew stronger, China weakened. In 1894 the two nations went to war over Japanese encroachments in Korea. The Sino-Japanese War, which lasted less than six months, forced China to evacuate Korea, cede Taiwan and the Liaodong° Peninsula, and pay a heavy indemnity. France, Germany, Britain, Russia, and the United States made Japan give up Liaodong in the name of the "territorial integrity" of China but in return forced China to grant them territorial and trade concessions, including ninety treaty ports.

In 1900 Chinese officials around the Empress Dowager Cixi encouraged a series of antiforeign riots known as the Boxer Uprising. European, American,

zaibatsu (zye-BOT-soo)

Liaodong (li-AH-oh-dong)

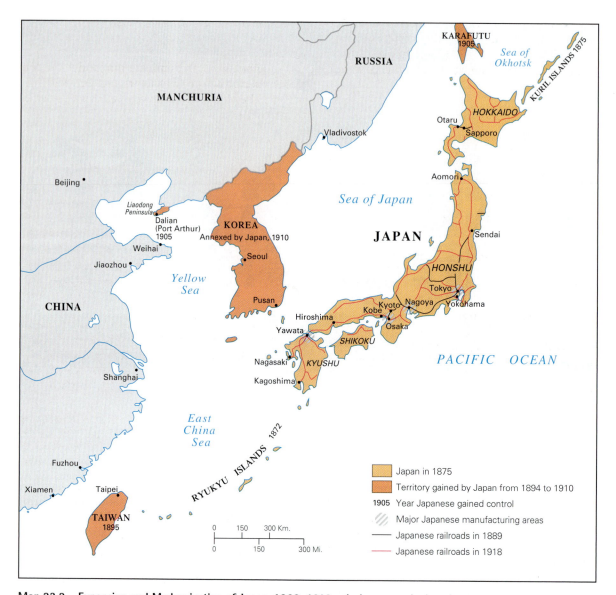

Map 23.2 Expansion and Modernization of Japan, 1868–1918 As Japan acquired modern industry, it followed the example of the European powers in seeking overseas colonies. Its colonial empire grew at the expense of its neighbors: Taiwan was taken from China in 1895; Karafutu (Sakhalin) from Russia in 1905; and all of Korea became a colony in 1910.

and Japanese military forces put down the riots and occupied Beijing. Emboldened by China's obvious weakness, Japan and Russia competed for possession of the mineral-rich Chinese province of Manchuria.

In 1905 Japan stunned the world by defeating Russia in the Russo-Japanese War. By the Treaty of Portsmouth that ended the war, Japan established a protectorate over Korea. In spite of Western attempts to restrict it to the role of junior partner,

Japan continued to increase its influence. It gained control of southern Manchuria, with its industries and railroads. In 1910 it finally annexed Korea, joining the ranks of the world's colonial powers.

CONCLUSION

After World War I broke out in 1914, many people, especially in Europe, looked back on the period from 1850 to 1914 as a golden age. For some, and in certain ways, it was. Industrialization was a powerful torrent changing Europe, North America, and East Asia. While other technologies like shipping and railroads increased their global reach, new ones—electricity, the steel and chemical industries, and the global telegraph network—contributed to the enrichment and empowerment of the industrial nations. Memories of the great scourges—famines, wars, and epidemics—faded. Clean water, electric lights, and railways began to improve the lives of city dwellers, even the poor. Goods from distant lands, even travel to other continents, came within the reach of millions.

European and American society seemed to be heading toward better organization and greater security. Municipal services made city life less dangerous and chaotic. Through labor unions, workers achieved some measure of recognition and security. By the turn of the century, liberal political reforms had taken hold in western Europe and the United States and seemed about to triumph in Russia as well. Morality and legislation aimed at providing security for women and families, though equality between the sexes was still beyond reach.

The framework for all these changes was the nation-state. The world economy, international politics, and even cultural and social issues revolved around a handful of countries—the great powers—that believed themselves in control of the destiny of the world. These included the most powerful European nations of the previous century, as well as two newcomers—the United States and Japan—that were to play important roles in the future. Seldom in history had there been such a concentration of wealth, power, and self-confidence.

The success of the great powers rested on their ability to extract resources from nature and from other societies, especially in Asia, Africa, and Latin America. In a global context, the counterpart of the rise of the great powers is the story of imperialism and colonialism. To complete our understanding of the period before 1914, let us turn now to the relations between the great powers and the rest of the world.

■ Key Terms

steel
electricity
Thomas Edison
submarine telegraph cables
railroads
socialism
labor union
Yamagata Aritomo
Karl Marx

Victorian Age
"separate spheres"
nationalism
liberalism
Otto von Bismarck
Charles Darwin
Empress Dowager Cixi
Meiji Restoration

■ Suggested Reading

More has been written on the great powers in the late nineteenth century than on any previous period in their histories. The following are some interesting recent works and a few classics.

Industrialization is the subject of Peter Stearns, *The Industrial Revolution in World History* (1993), and David Landes, *The Unbound Prometheus: Technological Change and Industrial Development in Western Europe from 1750 to the Present* (1969). Two interesting works on nationalism are E. J. Hobsbawm, *Nation and Nationalism Since 1780* (1990), and Benedict Anderson, *Imagined Communities: Reflections on the Origin and Spread of Nationalism* (1991).

Barrington Moore, *The Social Origins of Dictatorship and Democracy* (1966), is a classic essay on European society. On European women, see Renate Bridenthal, Susan Mosher Stuard, and Merry E. Wiesner, eds., *Becoming Visible: Women in European History,* 3d ed. (1998); Patricia Branca, *Silent Sisterhood: Middle-Class Women in the Victorian Home* (1975); Louise Tilly and Joan Scott, *Women, Work, and Family* (1987); and Theresa McBride, *The Domestic Revolution: The Modernization of Household Service in England and France, 1820–1920* (1976). The history of family life is told in Beatrice Gottlieb, *The Family in the Western World from the Black Death to the Industrial Age* (1993). Albert Lindemann, *A History of European Socialism* (1983), covers the labor movements as well.

There are many excellent histories of individual countries. On Germany in the nineteenth century, see David

Blackbourne, *The Long Nineteenth Century: A History of Germany, 1780–1918* (1998), and Gordon A. Craig, *Germany, 1866–1945* (1980). The standard works on Bismarck and the unification of Germany are Otto Pflanze, *Bismarck and the Development of Germany* (1990), and Lothar Gall, *Bismarck, the White Revolutionary* (1986). On Britain, see Donald Read, *The Age of Urban Democracy: England, 1868–1914* (1994), and David Thomson, *England in the Nineteenth Century, 1815–1914* (1978). On France, Eugen Weber, *Peasants into Frenchmen* (1976), and Roger Price, *A Social History of Nineteenth-Century France* (1987), are especially recommended. For Austria, see Alan Sked, *The Decline and Fall of the Habsburg Empire, 1815–1918* (1989). Two good introductions to Russian history are Hans Rogger, *Russia in the Age of Modernization and Revolution, 1881–1917* (1983), and Gregory L. Freeze, ed., *Russia: A History* (1997).

There are several interesting books on Japan, in particular Peter Duus, *The Rise of Modern Japan*, 2d ed. (1998), and Tessa Morris-Suzuki, *The Technological Transformation of Japan* (1994). Two fine books that cover the history of modern China are John King Fairbank, *The Great Chinese Revolution, 1800–1985* (1987), and Jonathan D. Spence, *The Search for Modern China* (1990).

The New Imperialism, 1869–1914

24

CHAPTER OUTLINE

The New Imperialism: Motives and Methods

The Scramble for Africa

Asia and Western Dominance

Imperialism in Latin America

The World Economy and the Global Environment

DIVERSITY AND DOMINANCE: Two Africans Recall the Arrival of the Europeans

I n 1869 Ismail°, the khedive° (ruler) of Egypt, invited all the Christian princes of Europe and all the Muslim princes of Asia and Africa—except the Ottoman sultan, his nominal overlord—to celebrate the inauguration of the greatest construction project of the century: the **Suez Canal.** Among the sixteen hundred dignitaries from the Middle East and Europe who assembled at Port Said° were Emperor Francis Joseph of Austria-Hungary and Empress Eugénie of France. A French journalist wrote:

> This multitude, coming from all parts of the world, presented the most varied and singular spectacle. All races were represented. . . . We saw, coming to attend this festival of civilization, men of the Orient wearing clothes of dazzling

colors, chiefs of African tribes wrapped in their great coats, Circassians in war costumes, officers of the British army of India with their shakos [hats] wrapped in muslin, Hungarian magnates wearing their national costumes.[1]

Ismail used the occasion to emphasize the harmony and cooperation between the peoples of Africa, Asia, and Europe and to show that Egypt was not only independent but was also an equal of the great powers. To bless the inauguration, Ismail had invited clergy of the Muslim, Orthodox, and Catholic faiths. A reporter noted: "The Khedive . . . wished to symbolize thereby the unity of men and their brotherhood before God, without distinction of religion; it was the first time that the Orient had seen such a meeting of faiths to celebrate and bless together a great event and a great work."[2]

Ismail (is-mah-EEL)   **khedive** (kuh-DEEV)   **Port Said** (port sah-EED)

The canal was a great success, but not in the way Ismail intended. Ships using it could travel between Europe and India in less than two weeks—much less time than the month or longer consumed by sailing around Africa and across the Indian Ocean. By lowering freight costs, the canal stimulated shipping and the construction of steamships, giving an advantage to nations that had heavy industry and a large maritime trade over land-based empires and countries with few merchant ships. Great Britain, which long opposed construction of the canal for fear that it might fall into enemy hands, benefited more than any other nation. France, which provided half the capital and most of the engineers, came in a distant second, for it had less trade with Asia than Britain did. Egypt, which contributed the other half of the money and most of the labor, was the loser. Instead of making Egypt powerful and independent, the Suez Canal provided the excuse for a British invasion and occupation of Egypt.

Far from inaugurating an era of harmony among the peoples of three continents and three faiths, the canal triggered a wave of European domination over Africa and Asia. Between 1869 and 1914 Germany, France, Britain, Russia, Japan, and the United States used industrial technology to impose their will on the nonindustrial parts of the world. Historians use the expression **New Imperialism** to describe this exercise of power.

As you read this chapter, ask yourself the following questions:

- What motivated the industrial nations to conquer new territories, and what means did they use?
- Why were some parts of the world annexed to the new empires, while others became economic dependencies of the great powers?
- How did the environment change in the lands subjected to the New Imperialism?

THE NEW IMPERIALISM: MOTIVES AND METHODS

The New Imperialism was characterized by an explosion of territorial conquests even more rapid than the Spanish conquests of the sixteenth century. Between 1869 and 1914, in a land grab of unprecedented speed, Europeans seized territories in Africa and Central Asia, and both Europeans and Americans took territories in Southeast Asia and the Pacific. Approximately 10 million square miles (26 million square kilometers) and 150 million people fell under the rule of Europe and the United States in this period.

The New Imperialism was more than a land grab. The imperial powers used economic and technological means to reorganize dependent regions and bring them into the world economy as suppliers of foodstuffs and raw materials and as consumers of industrial products. In Africa and other parts of the world, this was done by conquest and colonial administration. In the Latin American republics the same result was achieved indirectly. Even though they remained politically independent, they became economic dependencies of the United States and Europe.

What inspired Europeans and Americans to venture overseas and impose their will on other societies? There is no simple answer to this question. Economic, cultural, and political motives were involved in all cases.

Political Motives The great powers of the late nineteenth century, as well as less powerful countries like Italy, Portugal, and Belgium, were competitive and hypersensitive about their status. France, humiliated by its defeat by Prussia in 1871 (see Chapter 23), sought to reestablish its prestige through territorial acquisitions overseas. Great Britain, already in possession of the world's largest and richest empire, felt the need to protect India, its "jewel in the crown,"

C H R O N O L O G Y

	The Scramble for Africa	Asia and Western Dominance	Imperialism in Latin America
		1862–1895 French conquer Indochina	
		1865–1876 Russian forces advance into Central Asia	
	1869 Opening of the Suez Canal		
1870			**1870–1910** Railroad building boom; British companies in Argentina and Brazil; U.S. companies in Mexico
	1874 Warfare between the British and the Asante (Gold Coast)		
	1877–1879 Warfare between the British and the Xhosa and between the British and the Zulu (South Africa)		
		1878 United States obtains Pago Pago Harbor (Samoa)	
	1882 British forces occupy Egypt		
	1884–1885 Berlin Conference; Leopold II obtains Congo Free State		
		1885 Britain completes conquest of Burma	
		1887 United States obtains Pearl Harbor (Hawaii)	
1890		**1894–1895** China defeated in Sino-Japanese War	
		1895 France completes conquest of Indochina	**1895–1898** Cubans revolt against Spanish rule
	1896 Ethiopians defeat Italian army at Adowa; warfare between the British and the Asante		
	1898 Battle of Omdurman	**1898** United States annexes Hawaii and purchases Philippines from Spain	**1898** Spanish-American War; United States annexes Puerto Rico and Guam

(continued)

CHRONOLOGY *(continued)*

	The Scramble for Africa	Asia and Western Dominance	Imperialism in Latin America
	1899–1902 South African War between Afrikaners and the British	**1899–1902** U.S. forces conquer and occupy Philippines	
			1901 United States imposes Platt Amendment on Cuba
	1902 First Aswan Dam completed (Egypt)		
		1903 Russia completes Trans-Siberian Railway	**1903** United States backs secession of Panama from Colombia
		1904–1905 Russia defeated in Russo-Japanese War	**1904–1907, 1916** U.S. troops occupy Dominican Republic
			1904–1914 United States builds Panama Canal
1910	**1908** Belgium annexes Congo		
			1912 U.S. troops occupy Nicaragua and Honduras

by acquiring colonies in East Africa and Southeast Asia. German Chancellor Otto von Bismarck had little interest in acquiring colonies, but many Germans believed that a country as important as theirs deserved an overseas empire.

Political motives were not limited to statesmen in the capital cities. Colonial governors and political officers practiced their own diplomacy, often making a claim to a territory just to forestall some rival. Armies fighting frontier wars found it easier to defeat their neighbors than to make peace with them. In response to border skirmishes with neighboring states, colonial agents were likely to send in troops, take over their neighbors' territories, and then inform their home governments. Governments felt obligated to back up their men-on-the-spot in order not to lose face. The great powers of Europe acquired much of West Africa, Southeast Asia, and the Pacific islands in this manner.

Cultural Motives

The late nineteenth century saw a Christian revival in Europe and North America, as both Catholics and Protestants founded new missionary societies. Their purpose was not only religious—to convert nonbelievers, whom they regarded as "heathen"—but also cultural in a broader sense. They sought to export their own norms of "civilized" behavior: they were determined to abolish slavery in Africa and bring Western education, medicine, hygiene, monogamous marriage, and modest dress to all the world's peoples.

Opening the Suez Canal   When the canal opened in 1869, thousands of dignitaries and ordinary people gathered to watch the ships go by.   (Bildarchiv Preussischer Kulturbesitz/Art Resource, NY)

Many women joined missionary societies to become teachers and nurses, sometimes attaining positions of greater authority than they could hope to find at home. Their influence often helped soften the harshness of colonial rule—for example, by calling attention to issues of maternity and women's health. Mary Slessor, a British missionary who lived for forty years among the people of southeastern Nigeria, campaigned against slavery, human sacrifice, and the killing of twins and, generally, for women's rights. In India missionaries denounced the customs of child marriages and *sati* (the burning of widows on their husbands' funeral pyres). Such views often clashed with the customs of the people among whom they settled.

The sense of moral duty and cultural superiority was not limited to missionaries. Many Europeans and Americans equated technological innovations with "progress." They believed that Western technology proved the superiority of Western ideas, customs, and culture. While some concluded that non-Western peoples could achieve, through education, the same cultural level as Europeans and Americans, many others espoused racist ideas that relegated non-Europeans to a status of permanent inferiority. Racists assigned different stages of biological development to the world's various peoples based on physical appearance and ranked these races in a hierarchy that ranged from "civilized" at the highest level down through "semibarbarous," "barbarian," and finally, at the bottom, "savage." Caucasians—whites—were always at the top of this ranking. Such ideas were often presented as an excuse for permanent rule over Africans and Asians.

Imperialism first interested small groups of explorers, clergy, and businessmen but soon attracted people from other walks of life. Young men, finding few opportunities for adventure and glory at home in an era of peace, sought them overseas as the Spanish conquistadors had done over three centuries earlier. At first, European people and parliaments were indifferent or hostile to overseas adventures, but a few easy victories in the 1880s helped to overcome their reluctance. The United States was fully preoccupied with its westward expansion until the 1880s, but in the 1890s popular attention shifted to lands outside U.S. borders. Newspapers, which achieved wide readership in the second half of the nineteenth century, discovered that they could boost circulation with reports of wars and conquests. By the 1890s imperialism was a popular cause; it was the overseas extension of the nationalism propelling the power politics of the time.

Economic Motives

The industrialization of Europe and North America stimulated the demand for minerals—copper for electrical wiring, tin for canning, chrome and manganese for the steel industry, coal for steam engines, and, most of all, gold and diamonds. The demand for such industrial crops as cotton and rubber and for stimulants such as sugar, coffee, tea, and tobacco also grew. These products were found in the tropics, but never in sufficient quantities.

An economic depression lasting from the mid-1870s to the mid-1890s caused European merchants, manufacturers, and shippers to seek protection against foreign competition (see below). They argued that their respective countries needed secure sources of tropical raw materials and protected markets for their industries. Declining business opportunities at home prompted entrepreneurs and investors to look for profits from mines, plantations, and railroads in Asia, Africa, and Latin America. Since these investments were often extremely risky, businessmen sought the backing of their governments, preferably with soldiers.

The sudden increase in the power that industrial peoples could wield over nonindustrial peoples and over the forces of nature underlay the new imperialism as much as cultural and political factors. Indeed, technological advances explain

Pears Soap Is Best This advertisement appeared in the *Illustrated London News* in 1887. In identifying a brand of soap as "the formula for British conquest," it credited British manufactured products with the power to overawe spear-wielding indigenous warriors. (*Illustrated London News* Picture Library)

both the motives and the outcome of the New Imperialism.

The Tools of the Imperialists

To succeed, empire builders needed the means to achieve their objectives at a reasonable cost. The Industrial Revolution (see Chapter 20) provided these means. In the early part of the nineteenth century technological innovations began to tip the balance of power in favor of Europe.

Dominant at sea since about 1500, the Europeans increased their naval power still more with the introduction of steamships. The first steamer reached India in 1825; regular mail service followed in the 1830s. The long voyage around Africa was at first too costly for cargo steamers, for coal had to be shipped from England. The building of the Suez Canal and the development of increasingly efficient engines solved this problem and led to a boom in shipping to the Indian Ocean and East Asia. Whenever fighting broke out, passenger liners were requisitioned as troopships. This advantage in mobility was enhanced by the development of a global network of submarine telegraph cables connecting Europe with North America in the 1860s, with Latin America and Asia in the 1870s, with Africa in the 1880s, and finally across the Pacific in 1904.

Until the middle of the nineteenth century, western Europeans were much weaker on land than at sea. Thereafter, Europeans used gunboats with considerable success in China, Burma, Indochina, and the Congo Basin. Although gunboats opened the major river basins to European penetration, the invaders often found themselves hampered by other natural obstacles. *Falciparum* malaria, found only in Africa, was so deadly to Europeans that few explorers survived before the 1850s. In 1854 a British doctor discovered that the drug quinine, taken regularly during one's stay in Africa, could prevent the disease. This and a few sanitary precautions reduced the annual death rate among whites in West Africa from between 250 and 750 per thousand in the early nineteenth century to between 50 and 100 per thousand after 1850. This reduction was sufficient to open the continent to merchants, officials, and missionaries.

Muzzle-loading smoothbore muskets had been used in Europe, Asia, and the Americas since the late seventeenth century, and by the early nineteenth century they were also common in much of Africa. The development of new and much deadlier firearms in the 1860s and 1870s shifted the balance of power on land between Westerners and other peoples. One of these was the breechloading rifle: ten times faster to load and five or six times longer in range than a musket. By the 1870s all European and American armies had switched to these new rifles. The 1880s saw two more innovations, smokeless powder, which did not foul the gun or reveal the soldier's position, and repeating rifles, which could shoot fifteen rounds in fifteen seconds. Machine guns, which could fire eleven bullets per second, appeared a decade later.

In the course of the century Asians and Africans also acquired better firearms, mostly old weapons that European armies had discarded. As European firearms improved, however, the firepower gap widened, making colonial conquests easier than ever. By the 1880s and 1890s European-led forces of a few hundred could defeat non-European armies of thousands. Against the latest weapons, African and Asian soldiers armed with muskets or, in some cases, with spears did not stand a chance, no matter how numerous and courageous they were.

At the **Battle of Omdurman** in Sudan, on September 2, 1898, forty thousand Sudanese attacked an Anglo-Egyptian expedition that had come up the Nile on six steamers and four other boats. General Horatio Kitchener's troops had twenty machine guns and four artillery pieces; the Sudanese were equipped with muskets and spears. Within a few hours eleven thousand Sudanese and forty-eight British lay dead. Winston Churchill, the future British prime minister, witnessed the battle and called it

> the most signal triumph ever gained by the arms of science over barbarians. Within the space of five hours the strongest and best-armed savage army yet arrayed against a modern European Power had been destroyed and dispersed, with hardly any difficulty, comparatively small risk, and insignificant loss to the victors.[3]

Colonial Agents and Administration

Once colonial agents took over a territory, their home government expected them to cover their own costs and, if possible, return some profit to the home country. The system of administering and exploiting territories for the benefit of the home country is known as **colonialism.** In some places, such as along the West African coast or in Indochina, there was already a considerable trade that could be taxed. In other places profits could come only from investments and a thorough

The Battle of Omdurman In the late nineteenth century, most battles between European (or European-led) troops and African forces were one-sided encounters because of the disparity in the opponents' firearms and tactics. The Battle of Omdurman in Sudan in 1898 is a dramatic example. The forces of the Mahdi, some on horseback, were armed with spears and single-shot muskets. The British troops and their Egyptian allies, lined up in the foreground, used repeating rifles and machine guns able to shoot much farther than the Sudanese weapons. As a result, there were many Sudanese casualties but very few British or Egyptian. (The Art Archive)

reorganization of the indigenous societies. In applying modern scientific and industrial methods to their colonies, colonialists started the transformation of Asian and African societies and landscapes that has continued to our day.

Legal experts and academics emphasized the differences between various systems of colonial government and debated whether colonies eventually should be assimilated into the ruling nation, associated in a federation, or allowed to rule themselves. Colonies that were protectorates retained their traditional governments, even their monarchs, but had a European "resident" or "consul-general" to "advise" them. Other colonies were directly administered by a European governor. In fact, the impact of colonial rule depended much more on economic and social conditions than on narrow legal distinctions.

One important factor was the presence or absence of European settlers. In Canada, Australia, and New Zealand, whites were already in the majority by 1869, and their colonial "mother-country,"

Britain, encouraged them to elect parliaments and rule themselves. Where European settlers were numerous but still a minority of the population, as in Algeria and South Africa, settlers and the home country contested for control over the indigenous population. In colonies with few white settlers, the European governors ruled autocratically.

In the early years of the New Imperialism, colonial administrations consisted of a governor and his staff, a few troops to keep order, and a small number of tax collectors and magistrates. The cooperation of indigenous elites was essential to the maintenance of order. In most cases the colonial governors exercised power through traditional rulers willing to cooperate. Areas governed indirectly in this fashion were called "Princely States." In addition, colonial governments educated a few local youths for "modern" jobs as clerks, policemen, customs inspectors, and the like. These individuals came in time to rival the traditional rulers.

Western women seldom took part in the early stages of colonial expansion. Once peace was achieved and steamships and railroads made travel less difficult, however, colonial officials and settlers began bringing their wives to the colonies. By the 1880s the British Women's Emigration Association was recruiting single women to go out to the colonies to marry British settlers. As one of its founders, Ellen Joyce, explained, "The possibility of the settler marrying his own countrywoman is of imperial as well as family importance."

The arrival of white women in Asia and Africa increased racial segregation. Sylvia Leith-Ross, wife of a colonial officer in Nigeria, explained: "When you are alone, among thousands of unknown, unpredictable people, dazed by unaccustomed sights and sounds, bemused by strange ways of life and thought, you need to remember who you are, where you come from, what your standards are." Many colonial wives found themselves in command of numerous servants and expected to follow the complex etiquette of colonial entertainment in support of their husbands' official positions. Occasionally they found opportunities to exercise personal initiatives, usually charitable work involving indigenous women and children. However well meaning, their efforts were always subordinate to the work of men.

THE SCRAMBLE FOR AFRICA

Until the 1870s African history was largely shaped by internal forces and local initiatives (see Chapter 21). Outside Algeria and southern Africa, only a handful of Europeans had ever visited the interior of Africa, and European countries possessed only small enclaves on the coasts. As late as 1879 Africans ruled more than 90 percent of the continent. Then, within a decade, Africa was invaded and divided among the European powers in a movement often referred to as the **"scramble" for Africa** (see Map 24.1). This invasion affected all regions of the continent.

Egypt

Ironically, European involvement in Egypt resulted from Egypt's attempt to free itself from Ottoman Turkish rule. The khedives of Egypt, hereditary governors descended from Muhammad Ali (see Chapter 22), used profits from exporting cotton during the American Civil War to modernize their armed forces and build canals, harbors, railroads, and other public works. Their support for the Suez Canal project was part of this policy. Khedive Ismail even tried to make Egypt the center of an empire reaching south into Sudan and Ethiopia.

Once cotton prices returned to normal after 1865, the khedives supported their ambitions by borrowing from European creditors at high interest rates. By 1876 Egypt's foreign debt had risen to £100 million sterling. Interest payments alone consumed one-third of its foreign export earnings. To avoid bankruptcy the Egyptian government sold its shares in the Suez Canal to Great Britain and accepted four foreign "commissioners of the debt" to oversee its finances. French and British bankers, still not satisfied, lobbied their governments to secure the loans by stronger measures. In 1878 the two governments obliged Ismail to appoint a Frenchman as minister of public works and a Briton as minister of finance. When high taxes caused hardship and popular discontent, the French and British persuaded the Ottoman sultan to depose Ismail. This foreign intervention provoked a military uprising under Egyptian army colonel Arabi Pasha, which threatened the Suez Canal.

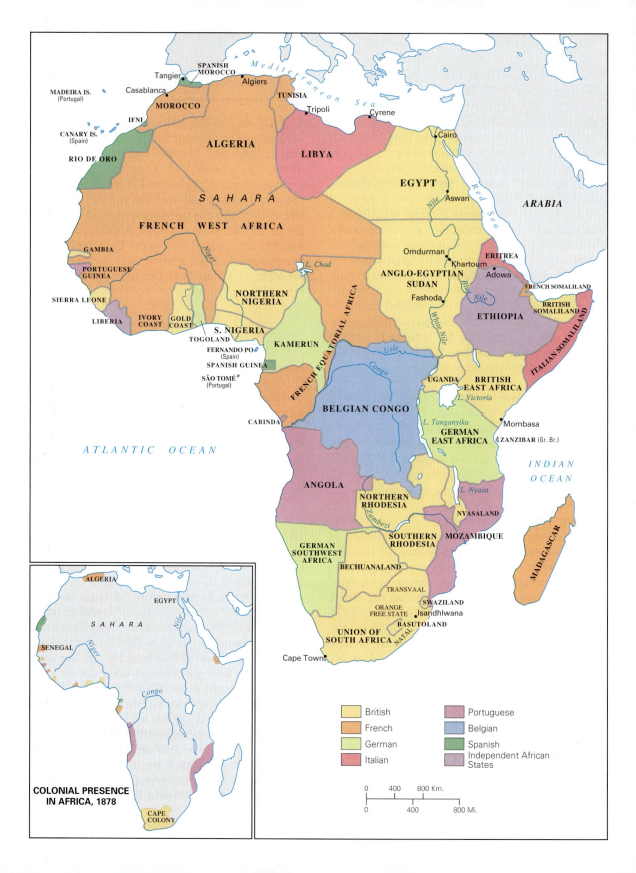

SPANISH MOROCCO
Tangier
Algiers
TUNISIA
Tripoli
Cyrene
MADEIRA IS.
(Portugal)
Casablanca
IFNI
MOROCCO
CANARY IS.
(Spain)
RIO DE ORO
ALGERIA
LIBYA
EGYPT
Cairo
Aswan
ARABIA
Mediterranean Sea

S A H A R A

FRENCH   WEST   AFRICA

Niger

GAMBIA
PORTUGUESE
GUINEA
SIERRA LEONE
LIBERIA
IVORY
COAST
GOLD
COAST
S. NIGERIA
TOGOLAND
FERNANDO PO
(Spain)
SPANISH GUINEA
SÃO TOMÉ
(Portugal)
NORTHERN
NIGERIA
L. Chad
KAMERUN
FRENCH EQUATORIAL AFRICA
ANGLO-EGYPTIAN
SUDAN
Omdurman
Khartoum
Fashoda
ERITREA
Adowa
FRENCH SOMALILAND
BRITISH
SOMALILAND
ETHIOPIA
ITALIAN SOMALILAND
Blue Nile
White Nile

CABINDA
Uele
Congo
BELGIAN CONGO
UGANDA
BRITISH
EAST
AFRICA
L. Victoria
L. Tanganyika
GERMAN
EAST AFRICA
Mombasa
ZANZIBAR (Gr. Br.)

ATLANTIC   OCEAN

*INDIAN
OCEAN*

ANGOLA
NORTHERN
RHODESIA
L. Nyasa
NYASALAND
GERMAN
SOUTHWEST
AFRICA
Zambezi
SOUTHERN
RHODESIA
MOZAMBIQUE
MADAGASCAR
BECHUANALAND
TRANSVAAL
ORANGE
FREE STATE
SWAZILAND
Isandhlwana
BASUTOLAND
NATAL
UNION OF
SOUTH AFRICA
Cape Town

ALGERIA
EGYPT
SAHARA
Nile
Niger
SENEGAL
Congo
CAPE
COLONY

**COLONIAL PRESENCE
IN AFRICA, 1878**

British
French
German
Italian
Portuguese
Belgian
Spanish
Independent African
States

0   400   800 Km.
0   400   800 Mi.

Map 24.1 Africa in 1878 and 1914 In 1878 the European colonial presence was limited to a few coastal enclaves, plus portions of Algeria and South Africa. By 1914, Europeans had taken over all of Africa except Ethiopia and Liberia.

Fearing for their investments, the British sent an army into Egypt in 1882. They intended to occupy Egypt for only a year or two. But theirs was a seaborne empire that depended on secure communications between Britain and India. So important was the Suez Canal to their maritime supremacy that they stayed for seventy years. During those years the British ruled Egypt "indirectly"—that is, they maintained the Egyptian government and the fiction of Egyptian sovereignty but retained real power in their own hands.

Eager to develop Egyptian agriculture, especially cotton production, the British brought in engineers and contractors to build the first dam across the Nile, at Aswan in upper Egypt. When completed in 1902, it was one of the largest dams in the world. It captured the annual Nile flood and released its waters throughout the year, allowing farmers to grow two, sometimes three, crops a year. This doubled the effective acreage compared with the basin system of irrigation practiced since the time of the pharaohs, in which the annual floodwaters of the Nile were retained by low dikes around the fields.

The economic development of Egypt by the British enriched a small elite of landowners and merchants, many of them foreigners. Egyptian peasants got little relief from the heavy taxes collected to pay for their country's crushing foreign debt and the expenses of the British army of occupation. Western ways that conflicted with the teachings of Islam—such as the drinking of alcohol and the relative freedom of women—offended Muslim religious leaders. Most Egyptians found British rule more onerous than that of the Ottomans. By the 1890s Egyptian politicians and intellectuals were demanding that the British leave, to no avail.

Western and Equatorial Africa

While the British were taking over Egypt, the French were planning to extend their empire into the interior of West Africa. Starting from the coast of Senegal, which had been in French hands for centuries, they hoped to build a railroad from the upper Senegal River to the upper Niger in order to open the interior to French merchants. This in turn led the French military to undertake the conquest of western Sudan.

Meanwhile, the actions of three individuals, rather than a government, brought about the occupation of the Congo Basin, an enormous forested region in the heart of equatorial Africa (see Map 24.1). In 1879 the American journalist **Henry Morton Stanley,** who had explored the area, persuaded King **Leopold II** of Belgium to invest his personal fortune in "opening up" equatorial Africa. With Leopold's money, Stanley returned to Africa from 1879 to 1884 to establish trading posts along the southern bank of the Congo River. At the same time, **Savorgnan de Brazza,** an Italian officer serving in the French army, obtained from an African ruler living on the opposite bank a treaty that placed the area under the "protection" of France.

These events sparked a flurry of diplomatic activity. German chancellor Bismarck called the **Berlin Conference** on Africa of 1884 and 1885. There the major powers agreed that henceforth "effective occupation" would replace the former trading relations between Africans and Europeans. This meant that every country with colonial ambitions had to send troops into Africa and participate in the division of the spoils. As a reward for triggering the "scramble" for Africa, Leopold II acquired a personal domain under the name "Congo Free State," while France and Portugal took most of the rest of equatorial Africa. In this manner, the European powers and King Leopold managed to divide Africa among themselves, at least on paper.

"Effective occupation" required many years of effort. In the interior of West Africa, Muslim rulers resisted the French invasion for up to thirty years. The French advance encouraged the Germans to stake claims to parts of the region and the British to move north from their coastal enclaves, until the entire region was occupied by Britain, France, and Germany.

Because West Africa had long had a flourishing trade, the new rulers took advantage of existing trade networks, taxing merchants and farmers, investing the profits in railroads and harbors, and paying dividends to European stockholders. In the Gold Coast (now Ghana) British trading companies bought the cocoa grown by African farmers at low prices and resold it for large profits. The interior of French West Africa lagged behind. Although the region could produce cotton, peanuts, and other crops, the difficulties of transportation limited its development before 1914.

Compared to West Africa, equatorial Africa had few inhabitants and little trade. Rather than try to govern these vast territories directly, authorities in the Congo Free State, the French Congo, and the Portuguese colonies of Angola and Mozambique granted huge pieces of land as concessions to private companies that thereby gained monopolies on natural resources and trade and the right to employ soldiers and impose taxes.

Freed from outside supervision, the companies forced the African inhabitants at gunpoint to produce cash crops and carry them, on their heads or backs, to the nearest railroad or navigable river. The worst abuses took place in the Congo Free State, where a rubber boom lasting from 1895 to 1905 made it profitable for private companies to coerce Africans to collect latex from vines that grew in the forests. One Congolese refugee told the British consul Roger Casement who investigated the atrocities:

> We begged the white men to leave us alone, saying we could get no more rubber, but the white men and their soldiers said: "Go. You are only beasts yourselves, you are only *nyama* (meat)." We tried, always going further into the forest, and when we failed and our rubber was short, the soldiers came to our towns and killed us. Many were shot, some had their ears cut off; others were tied up with ropes around their necks and bodies and taken away.[4]

After 1906 the British press began publicizing the horrors. The public outcry that followed, coinciding with the end of the rubber boom, convinced the Belgian government to take over Leopold's private empire in 1908.

Southern Africa

The history of southern Africa between 1869 and 1914 differs from that of the rest of the continent in attracting white settlers. **Afrikaners,** descendants of Dutch settlers on the Cape of Good Hope,

moved inland throughout the nineteenth century; British prospectors and settlers arrived later in the century; and, finally, Indians were brought over by the British and stayed.

Southern Africa attracted European settlers because of its good pastures and farmland and its phenomenal deposits of diamonds, gold, and copper, as well as coal and iron ore. This was the new El Dorado that imperialists had dreamed of since the heyday of the Spanish Empire in Peru and Mexico in the sixteenth century.

The discovery of diamonds at Kimberley in 1868 lured thousands of European prospectors as well as Africans looking for work. It also attracted the interest of Great Britain, colonial ruler of the Cape Colony, which annexed the diamond area in 1871, thereby angering the Afrikaners. Once in the interior, the British defeated the Xhosa° people in 1877 and 1878. Then in 1879 they confronted the Zulu, militarily the most powerful of the African peoples in the region.

The Zulu, led by their king Cetshwayo°, resented their encirclement by Afrikaners and British. A growing sense of nationalism and their proud military tradition led them into a war with the British in 1879. At first they held their own, defeating the British at Isandhlwana°, but a few months later they were defeated. Cetshwayo was captured and sent into exile, and the Zulu lands were given to white ranchers. Yet throughout those bitter times, the Zulu's sense of nationhood remained strong.

Relations between the British and the Afrikaners, already tense as a result of British encroachment, took a turn for the worse when gold was discovered in the Afrikaner republic of Transvaal° in 1886. In the gold rush that ensued, the British soon outnumbered the Afrikaners.

Britain's invasion of southern Africa was driven in part by the ambition of **Cecil Rhodes** (1853–1902), who once declared that he would "annex the stars" if he could. Rhodes made his fortune in the Kimberley diamond fields, founding De Beers Consolidated, a company that has dominated the world's diamond trade ever since. He

---

Xhosa (KOH-sah)   **Cetshwayo** (set-SHWAH-yo)
Isandhlwana (ee-sawn-dull-WAH-nuh)   **Transvaal** (trans-VAHL)

then turned to politics. He encouraged a concession company, the British South Africa Company, to push north into Central Africa, where he named two new colonies after himself: Southern Rhodesia (now Zimbabwe) and Northern Rhodesia (now Zambia). The Ndebele° and Shona peoples, who inhabited the region, resisted this invasion, but the machine guns of the British finally defeated them.

British attempts to annex the two Afrikaner republics, Transvaal and Orange Free State, and the inflow of English-speaking whites into the gold- and diamond-mining areas led to the South African War (also called the Boer War), which lasted from 1899 to 1902. At first the Afrikaners had the upper hand, for they were highly motivated, possessed modern rifles, and knew the land. In 1901, however, Great Britain brought in 450,000 troops and crushed the Afrikaner armies. Ironically, the Afrikaners' defeat in 1902 led to their ultimate victory. Wary of costly commitments overseas, the British government expected European settlers in Africa to manage their own affairs, as they were doing in Canada, Australia, and New Zealand. Thus, in 1910 the European settlers created the Union of South Africa, in which the Afrikaners eventually emerged as the ruling element.

Unlike Canada, Australia, and New Zealand, South Africa had a majority of indigenous inhabitants and substantial numbers of Indians and "Cape Coloureds" (people of mixed ancestry). Yet the Europeans were both numerous enough to demand self-rule and powerful enough to deny the vote and other civil rights to the majority. In 1913 the South African parliament passed the Natives Land Act, assigning Africans to reservations and forbidding them to own land elsewhere. This and other racial policies turned South Africa into a land of segregation, oppression, and bitter divisions.

Political and Social Consequences

Africa was home to a wide variety of indigenous societies, some of them long-established kingdoms with aristocracies or commercial towns dominated by a merchant class, others centered on agricultural villages without any outside government, and still others consisting of pastoral nomads organized along military lines. Not surprisingly, these societies responded in very different ways to the European invasion.

Some peoples welcomed the invaders as allies against local enemies. Once colonial rule was established, they sought work in government service or in European firms and sent their children to mission schools. In exchange, they were often the first to receive benefits such as clinics and roads.

Others, especially peoples with a pastoral or a warrior tradition, fought tenaciously. Examples abound, from the Zulu and Ndebele of southern Africa to the pastoral Herero° people of Southwest Africa (now Namibia), who rose up against German invaders in 1904; in repressing their uprising, the Germans exterminated two-thirds of them. In the Sahel, a belt of grasslands south of the Sahara, charismatic leaders rose up in the name of a purified Islam, gathered a following of warriors, and led them on part-religious, part empire-building campaigns called *jihads*. These leaders included Samori Toure in western Sudan (now Mali), Rabih in the Chad basin, and the Mahdi° in eastern Sudan. All of them eventually came into conflict with European-led military expeditions and were defeated.

Some commercial states with long histories of contact with Europeans also fought back. The kingdom of **Asante°** in Gold Coast rose up in 1874, 1896, and 1900 before it was finally overwhelmed. In the Niger Delta, the ancient city of Benin, rich with artistic treasures, resisted colonial control until 1897, when a British "punitive expedition" set it on fire and carted its works of art off to Europe.

One resistance movement succeeded, to the astonishment of Europeans and Africans alike. When **Menelik II** became emperor of Ethiopia in 1889 (see Chapter 21), his country was threatened by Sudanese Muslims to the west and by France and Italy, which controlled the Red Sea coast to the east. For many years, Ethiopia had been purchasing weapons. By the Treaty of Wichelle (1889), Italy agreed to sell more weapons to Ethiopia. Six years later, when Italians attempted to establish a protectorate over Ethiopia, they found the Ethiopians armed with thousands of rifles and even a few machine guns and artillery pieces. Although Italy sent

---

Ndebele (en-duh-BELL-ay)

Herero (hair-AIR-oh)   **Mahdi** (MAH-dee)   **Asante** (uh-SAWN-tay)

twenty thousand troops to attack Ethiopia, in 1896 they were defeated at Adowa° by a larger and better-trained Ethiopian army.

Most Africans neither joined nor fought the European invaders but tried to continue living as before. They found this increasingly difficult because colonial rule disrupted every traditional society. The presence of colonial officials meant that rights to land, commercial transactions, and legal disputes were handled very differently, and that traditional rulers lost all authority, except where Europeans used them as local administrators.

Changes in landholding were especially disruptive, for most Africans were farmers or herders for whom access to land was a necessity. In areas with a high population density, such as Egypt and West Africa, colonial rulers left peasants in place, encouraged them to grow cash crops, and collected taxes on the harvest. Elsewhere, the new rulers declared any land that was not farmed to be "waste" or "vacant" and gave it to private companies or to European planters and ranchers. In Kenya, Northern Rhodesia, and South Africa, Europeans found the land and climate to their liking, in contrast to other parts of Africa, where soldiers, officials, missionaries, or traders stayed only a few years. White settlers forced Africans to become squatters, sharecroppers, or ranch hands on land they had farmed for generations. In South Africa they forced many Africans off their lands and onto "reserves," much like the nomadic peoples of North America, Russia, and Australia.

The colonial rulers were even more interested in African labor than in the land. To get workers to take low-paid jobs on plantations, railroads, or other European enterprises, they imposed various taxes, such as the hut tax and the head tax. To pay the tax, Africans had little choice but to accept whatever work the Europeans offered. In the South African mines Africans were paid, on average, one-tenth as much as Europeans.

Some Africans migrated great distances to the cities and mining camps in search of a better life. Most migrant workers were men who left their wives and children behind in villages and on reserves, sometimes for years. Only occasionally did the authorities allow them to bring their families

and settle permanently. This caused great hardship for African women, who had to grow food for their families during the men's absences and care for sick and aged workers. Long separations between spouses also led to prostitution and the spread of sexually transmitted diseases.

Some African women welcomed colonial rule, for it brought an end to fighting and slave raiding, but others were led into captivity (see Diversity and Dominance: Two Africans Recall the Arrival of the Europeans). A few succeeded in becoming wealthy traders or owners of livestock. On the whole, however, African women benefited less than men from the economic changes that colonialism introduced. Whenever colonial rulers replaced communal property (traditional in most of Africa) with private property, property rights were assigned to the head of the household—that is, to the man. Almost all the jobs open to Africans, even those considered "women's work" in Europe, such as nursing and domestic service, were reserved for men.

Cultural Responses

More Africans came into contact with missionaries than with any other Europeans. Mission schools taught reading, writing, and arithmetic to village children. Boys learned crafts like carpentry and blacksmithing, while girls were taught domestic skills.

The first generation of Africans educated in mission schools also acquired Western ideas of justice and progress. Samuel Ajayi Crowther, a Yoruba rescued from slavery as a boy and educated in mission schools in Sierra Leone, went on to become an Anglican minister and, in 1864, the first African bishop. Crowther thought that Africa needed European assistance in achieving both spiritual and economic development:

> Africa has neither knowledge nor skill . . .
> to bring out her vast resources for her own
> improvement. . . . Therefore to claim Africa for
> the Africans alone, is to claim for her the right of
> a continued ignorance. . . . For it is certain, un-
> less help [comes] from without, a nation can
> never rise above its present state.[5]

After the first generation, many mission teachers were themselves African, the products of a mis-

---

Adowa (AH-do-ah)

sion education. They discovered that Christian ideals clashed with the reality of colonial exploitation. One convert wrote in 1911:

> There is too much failure among all Europeans in Nyasaland. The three combined bodies—Missionaries, Government and Companies or gainers of money—do form the same rule to look upon the native with mockery eyes. . . . If we had enough power to communicate ourselves to Europe, we would advise them not to call themselves Christendom, but Europeandom. Therefore the life of the three combined bodies is altogether too cheaty, too thefty, too mockery. Instead of "Give," they say "Take away from." There is too much breakage of God's pure law.[6]

Missionaries were not the only ones to bring religious change to Africa. In southern and Central Africa indigenous preachers adapted Christianity to African values and customs and founded new denominations known as "Ethiopian" churches.

Christianity proved successful in converting followers of traditional religions but made no inroads among Muslims. Instead, Islam, long predominant in northern and eastern Africa, spread southward as Muslim teachers established Quranic schools and founded Muslim brotherhoods. European colonialism unwittingly helped the diffusion of Islam. By building cities and increasing trade, colonial rule permitted Muslims to settle in new areas. As Islam—a universal religion untainted by colonialism—became increasingly relevant to Africans, the number of Muslims in sub-Saharan Africa probably doubled between 1869 and 1914.

ASIA AND WESTERN DOMINANCE

From 1869 to 1914 the pressure of the industrial powers was felt throughout Asia, the East Indies, and the Pacific islands (see Map 24.2). As trade with these regions grew in the late nineteenth century, so did their attractiveness to imperialists eager for economic benefits and national prestige.

By 1869 Britain already controlled most of India and Burma; Spain occupied the Philippines; and the Netherlands held large parts of the East Indies (now Indonesia). Between 1862 and 1895 France conquered Indochina (now Vietnam, Kampuchea, and Laos).

Central Asia

Farther north, Russia continued its colonial expansion, aided by the acquisition of modern rifles and artillery. Between 1865 and 1876 Russian forces advanced into Central Asia. Nomads like the Kazakhs, who lived east of the Caspian Sea, resisted; but soon Kazakhstan became home to 200,000 Russian settlers. Although the governments of Tsar Alexander II (r. 1855–1881) and Tsar Alexander III (r. 1881–1894) claimed not to interfere in indigenous customs, they declared communally owned grazing lands "waste" or "vacant" and turned them over to farmers from Russia. By the end of the century the nomads were fenced out and reduced to starvation. An eminent Russian jurist declared: "International rights cannot be taken into account when dealing with semibarbarous peoples."

South of the Kazakh steppe the fabled cities of Tashkent, Bukhara, and Samarkand served the caravan trade between China and the Middle East. By the 1860s and 1870s the Qing Empire was losing control over Central Asia, so it was fairly easy for Russian expeditions to conquer the indigenous peoples. Russia thereby acquired land suitable for cotton, along with a large Muslim population.

The Russians abolished slavery, built railroads to link the region with Europe, and planted hundreds of thousands of acres of cotton. Unlike the British in India, however, they did not attempt to change the customs, languages, or religious beliefs of their subjects.

Southeast Asia and Indonesia

Until the mid-nineteenth century, independent kingdoms ruled most of the Southeast Asian peninsula and the Indonesian archipelago. As in Africa, colonialism varied considerably from region to region. Burma (now Myanmar), nearest India, was gradually taken over by the British, the last piece being annexed in 1885. Indochina fell under French control bit by bit until it was finally subdued in 1895. Similarly, Malaya (now Malaysia) came under British rule in stages

파운드폭탄 4발 투하… 두 아들과 함께 사망

심진지 구축… 이틀째 시가戰

령이 대중 앞에 나타나거나 애국심
을 고취하는 노래만을 내보내면 방
송마저 중단됐다.

라크 전후
의에서는
영국 주도

DIVERSITY AND DOMINANCE

TWO AFRICANS RECALL THE ARRIVAL OF THE EUROPEANS

We know a great deal about the arrival of the Europeans into the interior of Africa from the perspective of the conquerors, but very little about how the events were experienced by Africans. Here are two accounts by African women, one from northern Nigeria whose land was occupied by the British, the other from the Congo Free State, a colony of King Leopold II of Belgium. They show not only how Africans experienced European colonial dominance, but also the great diversity of their experiences.

Baba of Karo, a Nigerian Woman, Remembers Her Childhood

When I was a maiden the Europeans first arrived. Ever since we were quite small the *malams* had been saying that the Europeans would come with a thing called a train, they would come with a thing called a motor-car, in them you would go and come back in a trice. They would stop wars, they would repair the world, they would stop oppression and lawlessness, we should live at peace with them. We used to go and sit quietly and listen to the prophecies. They would come, fine handsome people, they would not kill anyone, they would not oppress anyone, they would bring all their strange things. . . .

I remember when a European came to Karo on a horse, and some of his foot soldiers went into the town. Everyone came out to look at them, but in Zerewa they didn't see the European. Everyone at Karo ran away—"There's a European, there's a European!" He came from Zaria with a few black men, two on horses and four on foot. We were inside the town. Later on we heard that they were there in Zaria in crowds, clearing spaces and building houses. One of my younger "sisters" was at Karo, she was pregnant, and when she saw the European she ran away and shut the door.

At that time Yusufu was the king of Kano. He did not like the Europeans, he did not wish them, he would not sign their treaty. Then he say that perforce he would have to agree, so he did. We Habe wanted them to come, it was the Fulani who did not like it. When the Europeans came the Habe saw that if you worked for them they paid you for it, they didn't say, like the Fulani, "Commoner, give me this! Commoner, bring me that!" Yes, the Habe wanted them; they saw no harm in them. From Zaria they came to Rogo, they were building their big road to Kano City. They called out the people and said they were to come and make the road, if there were trees in the way they cut them down. The Europeans paid them with goods, they collected the villagers together and each man brought his large hoe. Money was not much use to them, so the Europeans paid them with food and other things.

The Europeans said that there were to be no more slaves; if someone said "Slave!" you could complain to the *alkali* who would punish the master who said it, the judge said, "That is what the Europeans have decreed." The first order said that any slave, if he was younger than you, was your younger brother, if he was older than you was your elder brother—they were all brothers of their master's family. No one used the word "slave" any more. When slavery was stopped, nothing much happened at our *rinji* except that some slaves whom we had bought in the market ran away. Our own father went to his farm and worked, he and his son took up their large hoes; they loaned out their spare farms. Tsoho our father and Kadiri my brother with whom I live now and Babambo worked, they farmed guineacorn and millet and groundnuts and everything; before this they had supervised the slaves' work—now they did their own. When the midday food was ready, the women of the compound would give us children the food, one of us drew water, and off we went to the farm to take the men their food at the foot of a tree; I was about eight or nine at that time, I think. . . .

In the old days if the chief liked the look of your daughter he would take her and put her in his house; you could do nothing about it. Now they don't do that.

Ilanga, a Congolese Woman, Recounts her Capture by Agents of the Congo Free State

Our village is called Waniendo, after our chief Niendo. . . . It is a large village near a small stream, and surrounded by large fields of *mohago* (cassava) and *muhindu* (maize) and other foods, for we all worked hard at our plantations, and always had plenty to eat. The men always worked in the fields clearing the ground, or went hunting. . . . We never had war in our country, and the men had not many arms except knives; but our chief Niendo had a gun, which he had bought long ago from another chief for forty-three beads, but he had no powder or caps, and only carried it when he went on a journey.

. . . we were all busy in the fields hoeing our plantations, for it was the rainy season, and the weeds sprang quickly up, when a runner came to the village saying that a large band of men was coming, that they all wore red caps and blue cloth, and carried guns and long knives, and that many white men were with them, the chief of whom was *Kibalanga* (Michaux). Niendo at once called all the chief men to his house, while the drums were beaten to summon the people to the village. A long consultation was held, and finally we were all told to go quietly to the fields and bring in ground-nuts, plantains, and cassava for the warriors who were coming, and goats and fowl for the white men. The women all went with baskets and filled them, and put them in the road, which was blocked up, so many were there. Niendo then commanded everyone to go and sit quietly in the houses until he gave other orders. This we did, everyone remaining quietly seated while Niendo went up the road with the head men to meet the white chief. We did not know what to think, for most of us feared that so many armed men coming boded evil; but Niendo thought that, by giving presents of much food, he would induce the strangers to pass on without harming us. And so it proved, for the soldiers took the baskets, and were then ordered by the white men to move off through the village. Many of the soldiers looked into the houses and shouted at us words we did not understand. We were glad when they were all gone, for we were much in fear of the white

men and the strange warriors, who are known to all the people as being great fighters, bringing war wherever they go. . . .

When the white men and their warriors had gone, we went again to our work, and were hoping that they would not return; but this they did in a very short time. As before, we brought in great heaps of food; but this time *Kibalanga* did not move away directly, but camped near our village, and his soldiers came and stole all our fowl and goats and tore up our cassava; but we did not mind as long as they did not harm us. The next morning it was reported that the white men were going away; but soon after the sun rose over the hill, a large band of soldiers came into the village, and we all went into the houses and sat down. We were not long seated when the soldiers came rushing in shouting, and threatening Niendo with their guns. They rushed into the houses and dragged the people out. Three or four came to our house and caught hold of me, also my husband Oleka and my sister Katinga. We were dragged into the road, and were tied together with cords about our necks, so that we could not escape. We were all crying, for now we knew that we were to be taken away to be slaves. The soldiers beat us with the iron sticks from their guns, and compelled us to march to the camp of *Kibalanga*, who ordered the women to be tied up separately, ten to each cord, and the men in the same way. When we were all collected—and there were many from other villages whom we now saw, and many from Waniendo—the soldiers brought baskets of food for us to carry, in some of which was smoked human flesh (*niama na nitu*).

We then set off marching very quickly. My sister Katinga had her baby in her arms, and was not compelled to carry a basket; but my husband Oleka was made to carry a goat. We marched until the afternoon, when we camped near a stream, where we were glad to drink, for we were much athirst. We had nothing to eat, for the soldiers would give us nothing, so we lay upon the ground, and at night went to sleep. The next day we continued the march, and when we camped at noon were given some maize and plantains, which were gathered near a village from which the people had run away. So it continued each day until the fifth day, when the soldiers took my sister's baby and threw it in the grass, leaving it to die, and made her carry some cooking pots which they found in the deserted village. On the sixth day we became very weak from lack of food and from constant marching and sleeping in the damp grass, and my husband, who marched behind us with the goat, could not stand up longer, and so he sat down beside the path and refused to walk more. The soldiers beat him, but still he refused to move. Then one of them struck him on the head with the end of his gun, and he fell upon the ground. One of the soldiers caught the goat, while two or three others stuck the long knives they put on the ends of their guns into my husband. I saw the blood spurt out, and then saw him no more, for we passed over the brow of a hill and he was out of sight. Many of the young men were killed the same way, and many babies thrown into the grass to die. A few escaped; but we were so well guarded that it was almost impossible.

After marching ten days we came to the great water (Lualaba) and were taken in canoes across to the white men's town at Nyangwe. Here we stayed for six or seven days, and were then put in canoes and sent down the river; . . . but on the way we could get nothing to eat, and were glad to rest here, where there are good houses and plenty of food; and we hope we will not be sent away.

QUESTIONS FOR ANALYSIS

1. How do Baba and Ilanga recall their existence before the Europeans came?

2. What did they expect when they first heard of the arrival of Europeans? Instead, what happened to them, their relatives, and their towns?

3. How do you explain the difference between these two accounts?

Source: From M. F. Smith, ed., *Baba of Karo: A Woman of the Muslim Hausa* (New York: Philosophical Library, 1955), 66–68; and Edgar Canisius, *A Campaign Amongst Cannibals* (London: R. A. Everett & Co., 1903), 250–256. Used by permission of the Philosophical Library.

during the 1870s and 1880s. By the early 1900s the Dutch had subdued northern Sumatra, the last part of the Dutch East Indies to be conquered. Only Siam (now Thailand) remained independent, although it lost several border provinces.

Despite their varied political histories, all these regions had features in common: fertile soil, constant warmth, and heavy rains along with a long tradition of intensive gardening, irrigation, and terracing. Where the population was sparse, Europeans imported landless laborers from China and India. The climate favored the transfer of commercially valuable plants from other parts of the world. Tobacco, cinchona° (an antimalarial drug), manioc (an edible root crop), maize (corn), and natural rubber came from the Americas; sugar from India; tea from China; and coffee and oil palms from Africa. By 1914 much of the world's supply of these valuable products—in the case of rubber, almost all—came from Southeast Asia and Indonesia.

Europe and North America formed the export market for most of these products. In exchange, the inhabitants of the region benefited from peace and a reliable food supply. As a result, their numbers increased at an unprecedented rate. For instance, the population of Java (an island the size of Pennsylvania) doubled from 16 million in 1870 to over 30 million in 1914.

Colonialism and population growth spurred many social changes. Agricultural and commercial peoples gradually moved into mountainous and forested areas, displacing groups that practiced hunting and gathering or shifting agriculture and had not experienced as much population growth. Javanese migrating to Borneo and Sumatra are but one example. Immigrants from China and India changed the ethnic composition and culture of every country in the region. Thus the population of the Malay Peninsula became one-third Malay, one-third Chinese, and one-third Indian.

As in Africa, European missionaries spread Christianity under the colonial umbrella. Islam, however, was much more successful in gaining new converts, for it had been established in the re-

---

cinchona (sin-CHO-nah)

Lim Nee Soon's Plantation   In British Malaya, pineapples and rubber trees were often cultivated together, because pineapples could be grown between the trees during the five or six years it took for the saplings to grow large enough to be tapped. Not all plantation owners were British. In this picture, Lim Nee Soon, known as the "Pineapple King," stands next to a truck that is taking pineapples to his canning factory.   (National Archives of Singapore)

gion for centuries and people did not consider it a religion imposed on them by foreigners.

Education and European ideas had an impact on the political perceptions in Southeast Asia and Indonesia, as did events in neighboring Asian countries: in India, where a nationalist movement arose in the 1880s; in China, where modernizers were undermining the authority of the Qing; and especially in Japan, whose rapid industrialization culminated in its brilliant victory over Russia in the Russo-Japanese War (1904–1905). A young Vietnamese writing soon after the Russo-Japanese War expressed the spirit of a rising generation:

> I, . . . an obscure student, having had occasion to study new books and new doctrines, have discovered in a recent history of Japan how they have been able to conquer the impotent Europeans. This is the reason why we have formed an organization. . . . We have selected from young

Annamites [Vietnamese] the most energetic, with great capacities for courage, and are sending them to Japan for study. . . . Several years have passed without the French being aware of the movement. . . . Our only aim is to prepare the population for the future.[7]

Hawaii and the Philippines, 1878–1902

By the 1890s the United States had a fast-growing population and industries that produced more manufactured goods than they could sell at home. Merchants and bankers began to look for export markets. The political mood was also expansionist, and many echoed the feelings of the naval strategist Alfred T. Mahan°: "Whether they will or

—————————————————————————

Mahan (mah-HAHN)

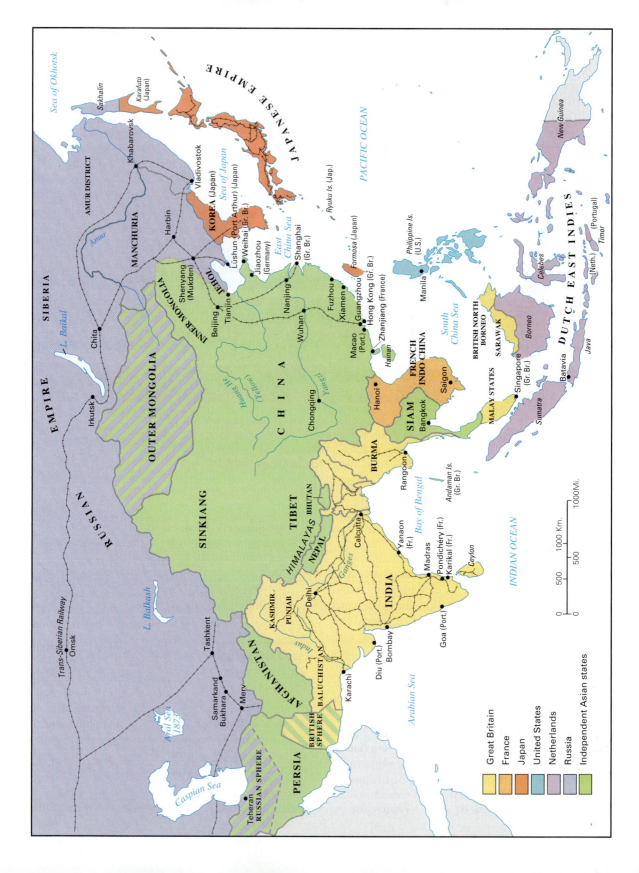

Map 24.2   Asia in 1914   By 1914, much of Asia was claimed by colonial powers. The southern rim, from the Pacific Gulf to the Pacific, was occupied by Great Britain, France, the Netherlands, and the United States. Central Asia had been incorporated into the Russian Empire. Japan, now industrialized, had joined the Western imperialist powers in expanding its territory and influence at the expense of China.

no, Americans must now begin to look outward. The growing production of the country requires it."

Some Americans had been looking outward for quite some time, especially across the Pacific to China and Japan. In 1878 the United States obtained the harbor of Pago Pago in Samoa as a coaling and naval station, and in 1887 it secured the use of Pearl Harbor in Hawaii for the same purpose. Six years later American settlers in Hawaii deposed Queen Liliuokalani (1838–1917) and offered the Hawaiian Islands to the United States. At the time President Grover Cleveland (1893–1897) was opposed to annexation, and the settlers had to content themselves with an informal protectorate. By 1898, however, the United States under President William McKinley (1897–1901) had become openly imperialistic, and it annexed Hawaii as a steppingstone to Asia. As the United States became ever more involved in Asian affairs, Hawaii's strategic location brought an inflow of U.S. military personnel, and its fertile land caused planters to import farm laborers from Japan, China, and the Philippines. These immigrants soon outnumbered the native Hawaiians.

While large parts of Asia were falling under colonial domination, the people of the Philippines were chafing under their Spanish rulers. The movement for independence began among young Filipinos studying in Europe. José Rizal, a young doctor working in Spain, was arrested and executed in 1896 for writing anti-Spanish and anticlerical novels. Thereafter, the center of resistance shifted to the Philippines, where **Emilio Aguinaldo,** leader of a secret society, rose in revolt and proclaimed a republic in 1899. The revolutionaries had a good chance of winning independence, for Spain had its hands full with a revolution in Cuba (see below).

Unfortunately for Aguinaldo and his followers, the United States went to war against Spain in April 1898 and quickly overcame Spanish forces in the Philippines and Cuba. President McKinley had not originally intended to acquire the Philippines; but after the Spanish defeat, he realized that a weakened Spain might lose the islands to another imperialist power. Japan, having recently defeated China in the Sino-Japanese War (1894–1895) and annexed Taiwan, was eager to expand. So was Germany, which had taken over parts of New Guinea and Samoa and several Pacific archipelagoes during the 1880s. To forestall them, McKinley purchased the Philippines from Spain for $20 million.

The Filipinos were not eager to trade one master for another. For a while, Aguinaldo cooperated with the Americans in the hope of achieving full independence. When his plan was rejected, he rose up again in 1899 and proclaimed the independence of his country. In spite of protests by anti-imperialists in the United States, the U.S. government decided that its global interests outweighed the interests of the Filipino people. In rebel areas, a U.S. army of occupation tortured prisoners, burned villages and crops, and forced the inhabitants into "reconcentration camps." Many American soldiers tended to look on Filipinos with the same racial contempt with which Europeans viewed their colonial subjects. By the end of the insurrection in 1902, the war had cost the lives of 5,000 Americans and 200,000 Filipinos.

After the insurrection ended, the United States attempted to soften its rule with public works and economic development projects. New buildings went up in the city of Manila; roads, harbors, and railroads were built; and the Philippine economy was tied ever more closely to that of the United States. In 1907 Filipinos were allowed to elect representatives to a legislative assembly, but ultimate authority remained in the hands of a governor appointed by the president of the United States. An American promise of independence made in 1916 was not fulfilled until thirty years later.

IMPERIALISM IN LATIN AMERICA

Nations in the Americas followed two divergent paths. In Canada and the United States manufacturing industries, powerful corporations, and wealthy financial institutions arose. By contrast,

Latin America and the Caribbean exported raw materials and imported manufactured goods. The poverty of their people, the preferences of their elites, and the pressures of the world economy made them increasingly dependent on the industrialized countries. Instead of suffering outright annexation by the colonial empires, they experienced manipulation by the industrial powers, including the United States, in a form of economic dependence called **free-trade imperialism.**

In the Western Hemisphere, therefore, the New Imperialism manifested itself not by a "scramble" for territories but in two other ways. In the larger republics of South America, the pressure was mostly financial and economic. In Central America and the Caribbean, it also included military intervention by the United States.

Railroads and the Imperialism of Free Trade

Latin America's economic potential was huge, for the region could produce many agricultural and mineral products in demand in the industrial countries. What was needed was a means of opening the interior to development. Railroads seemed the perfect answer.

Foreign merchants and bankers as well as Latin American landowners and politicians embraced the new technology. Starting in the 1870s almost every country in Latin America acquired railroads, usually connecting mines or agricultural regions with the nearest port rather than linking up the different parts of the interior. Since Latin America did not have any steel or mechanical industries, railroad equipment and building materi-

Railroads Penetrate South America   The late nineteenth century saw the construction of several railroad networks in South America, often through rugged and dangerous terrain. This photograph shows the opening of a bridge on the Transandine Railroad in Peru. Flags were raised in honor of American construction and British ownership of the railroad.   (Tony Morrison/South American Pictures)

als came from Britain or the United States. So did the money to build the networks, the engineers who designed and maintained them, and the managers who ran them.

Argentina, a rich source of wheat, beef, and hides, gained the longest and best-developed rail network south of the United States. By 1914, British firms owned 86 percent of the railroads in Argentina; 40 percent of the employees were British; and the official railroad language was English, not Spanish. Similar situations arose elsewhere throughout Latin America. The Argentine nationalist Juan Justo saw a parallel with Ireland:

> English capital has done what English armies could not do. Today our country is tributary to England . . . the gold that the English capitalists take out of Argentina or carry off in the form of products does us no more good than the Irish get from the revenues that the English lords take out of Ireland.[8]

The Irish, however, had little say in the matter because they were under British rule. But in Latin America the political elites encouraged foreign companies with generous concessions as the most rapid way to modernize their countries and enrich the property owners. In countries where the majority of the poor were Indians (as in Mexico and Peru) or of African origin (as in Brazil), they were neither consulted nor allowed to benefit from the railroad boom.

American Expansionism and the Spanish-American War, 1898

After 1865 Europeans used their financial power to penetrate Latin America. But they avoided territorial acquisitions for four reasons: (1) they were overextended in Africa and Asia; (2) there was no need, because the Latin American governments provided the political backing for their economic penetration; (3) Mexico's resistance to the French in the 1860s had shown that invasion would not be easy; and (4) the United States claimed to defend the entire Western Hemisphere against all outside intervention. This claim, made in the Monroe Doctrine (1823), did not prevent the United States itself from intervening in Latin American affairs.

The United States had long had interests in Cuba, the closest and richest of the Caribbean islands and a Spanish colony. American businesses had invested great sums of money in Cuba's sugar and tobacco industries, and tens of thousands of Cubans had migrated to the United States. In 1895 the Cuban nationalist José Martí started a revolution against Spanish rule. American newspapers thrilled readers with lurid stories of Spanish atrocities; businessmen worried about their investments; and politicians demanded that the U.S. government help liberate Cuba.

On February 15, 1898, the U.S. battleship *Maine* accidentally blew up in Havana harbor, killing 266 American sailors. The U.S. government immediately blamed Spain and issued an ultimatum that the Spanish evacuate Cuba. Spain agreed to the ultimatum, but the American press and Congress were eager for war, and President McKinley did not restrain them.

The Spanish-American War was over quickly. On May 1, 1898, U.S. warships destroyed the Spanish fleet at Manila in the Philippines. Two months later the United States Navy sank the Spanish Atlantic fleet off Santiago, Cuba. By mid-August Spain was suing for peace. U.S. secretary of state John Hay called it "a splendid little war." The United States purchased the Philippines from Spain but took over Puerto Rico and Guam as war booty. The two islands remain American possessions to this day. Cuba became an independent republic, subject, however, to intense interference by the United States.

American Intervention in the Caribbean and Central America, 1907–1914

The nations of the Caribbean and Central America were small and poor, and their governments were corrupt, unstable, and often bankrupt. They seemed to offer an open invitation to foreign interference. A government would borrow money to pay for railroads, harbors, electric power, and other symbols of modernity. When it could not repay the loan, the lending banks in Europe or the United States would ask for assistance from their home governments. To ward off European intervention, the United States sent in the marines on more than one occasion.

Presidents Theodore Roosevelt (1901–1909), William Taft (1909–1913), and Woodrow Wilson (1913–1921) felt impelled to intervene in the region, though they differed sharply on the proper policy the United States should follow toward the small nations to the south. Roosevelt encouraged regimes friendly to the United States, like Porfirian Mexico; Taft sought to influence them through loans from American banks; and the moralist Wilson tried to impose clean governments through military means.

Having "liberated" Cuba from Spain, the United States forced the Cuban government to accept the Platt Amendment in 1901. This gave the United States the "right to intervene" to maintain order on the island. The United States used this excuse to occupy Cuba militarily from 1906 to 1909, in 1912, and again from 1917 to 1922. In all but name Cuba became an American protectorate. U.S. troops also occupied the Dominican Republic from 1904 to 1907 and again in 1916, Nicaragua and Honduras in 1912, and Haiti in 1915. They brought sanitation and material progress but no political improvements.

The United States was especially forceful in Panama, which was a province of Colombia. Here the issue was not corruption or debts but the construction of a canal to speed shipping between the east and west coasts of the United States. In 1878 the Frenchman Ferdinand de Lesseps, builder of the Suez Canal, had obtained a concession from Colombia to construct a canal across the isthmus of Panama, which lay in Colombian territory. Financial scandals and yellow fever, however, doomed his project.

When the United States acquired Hawaii and the Philippines, it recognized the strategic value of a canal that would allow warships to move quickly between the Atlantic and Pacific Oceans. The main obstacle was Colombia, whose senate refused to give the United States a piece of its territory. In 1903 the U.S. government supported a Panamanian rebellion against Colombia and quickly recognized the independence of Panama. In exchange, it obtained the right to build a canal and to occupy a zone 5 miles (8 kilometers) wide on either side of it. Work began in 1904, and the **Panama Canal** opened on August 15, 1914.

THE WORLD ECONOMY AND THE GLOBAL ENVIRONMENT

The New Imperialists were not traditional conquerors or empire builders like the Spanish conquistadors. Their aim was not just to extend their power over new territories and peoples but also to control both natural resources and indigenous societies and put them efficiently to work. Both their goals and their methods were industrial. A railroad, for example, was an act of faith as well as a means of transportation. The imperialists expressed their belief in progress and their good intentions in the clichés of the time: "the conquest of nature," "the annihilation of time and space," "the taming of the wilderness," and "our civilizing mission."

Expansion of the World Economy

The Industrial Revolution vastly expanded the traditional demand for tropical products. Imports of foods and stimulants such as tea, coffee, and cocoa increased substantially during the nineteenth century. The trade in industrial raw materials, whether agricultural (cotton, jute for bags, and palm oil for soap and lubricants) or mineral (diamonds, gold, and copper), grew even faster. Wild forest products came only later to be cultivated: timber for buildings and railroad ties, cinchona bark, rubber for rainwear and tires, and gutta-percha° to insulate electric cables.

The growing needs of the industrial world could not be met by the traditional methods of production and transportation of the nonindustrial world. When the U.S. Civil War interrupted the export of cotton to England in the 1860s, the British turned to India, only to find that Indian cotton was ruined by exposure to rain and dust while being carted from interior regions to the harbors. To prevent such technological backwardness in the colonies from stifling the expansion of industry, the imperialists made every effort to bring those territories into the mainstream of the world market.

---

gutta-percha (gut-tah-PER-cha)

Transportation was key. The Suez and Panama Canals cut travel time and lowered freight costs dramatically. Steamships became more numerous, and as their size increased, deeper harbors were needed. As for railroads, India alone had 37,000 miles (nearly 60,000 kilometers) of track by 1915, almost as much as Germany or Russia. Railroads reached into the interior of Latin America, Canada, China, and Australia. In 1903 the Russians completed the Trans-Siberian Railway from Moscow to Vladivostok on the Pacific. Visionaries even made plans for railroads from Europe to India and from Egypt to South Africa.

Transformation of the Global Environment

The economic changes brought by Europeans and Americans altered environments around the world. The British, whose craving for tea could not be satisfied with the limited exports available from China, introduced tea into the warm, rainy hill country of Ceylon and northeastern India. In those areas and in Java thousands of square miles of tropical rain forests were felled to make way for tea plantations.

Economic botany and agricultural science were applied to every promising plant species. European botanists had long collected and classified exotic plants from around the world. In the nineteenth century they founded botanical gardens in Java, India, Mauritius°, Ceylon, Jamaica, and other tropical colonies. These gardens not only collected local plants but also exchanged plants with other gardens. They were especially active in systematically transferring commercially valuable plant species from one tropical region to another. Cinchona, tobacco, sugar, and other crops were introduced, improved, and vastly expanded in the colonies of Southeast Asia and Indonesia. Cocoa and coffee growing spread over large areas of Brazil and Africa; oil-palm plantations were established in Nigeria and the Congo Basin. Rubber originally came from the latex of *Hevea* trees growing wild in the Brazilian rain forest. Then, in the 1870s, British agents smuggled seedlings from Brazil to the Royal Botanic Gardens at Kew near London, and from there to the Botanic Garden of Singapore. These plants formed the nucleus of the enormous rubber economy of Southeast Asia.

Throughout the tropics forests and lands devoted to shifting slash-and-burn agriculture gave way to permanent farms and plantations. Even in areas not developed to export crops, growing populations put pressure on the land. In Java and India farmers felled trees to obtain arable land and firewood. They terraced hillsides, drained swamps, and dug wells.

Irrigation and water control transformed the dry parts of the tropics as well. In the 1830s British engineers in India had restored ancient canals that had fallen into disrepair. Their success led them to build new irrigation canals, turning thousands of previously barren acres into well-watered, densely populated farmland. The migration of European experts spread the newest techniques of irrigation engineering around the world. By the turn of the century irrigation projects were under way wherever rivers flowed through dry lands. In Egypt and Central Asia irrigation brought more acres under cultivation in one forty-year span than in all previous history.

Railroads had voracious appetites for land and resources. They cut into mountains, spanned rivers and canyons with trestles, and covered as much land with their freight yards as whole cities had needed in previous centuries. They also consumed vast quantities of iron, timber for ties, and coal or wood for fuel. Most important of all, railroads brought people and their cities, farms, and industries to areas previously occupied by small, scattered populations.

Prospectors looking for valuable minerals opened the earth to reveal its riches: gold in South Africa, Australia, and Canada; tin in Nigeria, Malaya, and Bolivia; copper in Chile and Central Africa; iron ore in northern India; and much else. Where mines were dug deep inside the earth, the dirt and rocks brought up with the ores formed huge mounds near mine entrances. Open mines dug to obtain ores lying close to the surface created a landscape of lunar craters, and runoff from the minerals poisoned the water for miles around. Refineries that processed the ores fouled the environment with slag heaps and more toxic runoff.

Mauritius (maw-REE-shuss)

The transformation of the land by human beings, a constant throughout history, accelerated sharply. Only the changes occurring since 1914 can compare with the transformation of the global environment that took place between 1869 and 1914.

CONCLUSION

The industrialization of the late nineteenth century increased the power of Europeans and North Americans over nature and over the peoples of other continents. They used their newfound power to conquer empires.

The opening of the Suez Canal in 1869 was the symbolic beginning of the New Imperialism. It stimulated shipping and trade between the industrial countries and the tropics, and it deepened the involvement of Europeans in the affairs of the Middle East, Africa, and Asia. From that year until 1914, not only the great powers but smaller countries too—even, in some cases, individual Europeans or Americans—had the power to decide the fate of whole countries. This was not just a matter of political will, but also of the gap that opened between European and American technologies and forms of organization and those available to Asians, Africans, and Latin Americans.

The result was in the most rapid conquest of territories in the history of the world. In less than half a century almost all of Africa and large parts of Asia and Oceania were added to the colonial empires, while Latin America, nominally independent, was turned into an economic colony of the industrial powers. In the process of developing the economic potential of their empires, the colonial powers transformed natural environments around the world.

The opening of the Panama Canal in August 1914 confirmed the new powers of the industrializing nations—but with a twist: it was the United States, a latecomer to the game of imperialism, that created the canal. In that same month, the other imperialist nations turned their weapons against one another and began a life-or-death struggle for supremacy in Europe. That conflict is the subject of the next chapter.

■ Key Terms

Suez Canal

New Imperialism

Battle of Omdurman

colonialism

"scramble" for Africa

Henry Morton Stanley

Leopold II

Savorgnan de Brazza

Berlin Conference

Afrikaners

Cecil Rhodes

Asante

Menelik II

Emilio Aguinaldo

free-trade imperialism

Panama Canal

■ Suggested Reading

Two good introductions to imperialism are D. K. Fieldhouse, *Colonialism, 1870–1945* (1981), and Scott B. Cook, *Colonial Encounters in the Age of High Imperialism* (1996). The debate on the theories of imperialism is presented in Roger Owen and Robert Sutcliffe, *Studies in the Theory of Imperialism* (1972), and in Winfried Baumgart, *Imperialism* (1982). The British Empire is the subject of Bernard Porter, *The Lion's Share: A Short History of British Imperialism, 1850–1970* (1976).

On Africa in this period, see Roland Oliver and Anthony Atmore, *Africa Since 1800*, new ed. (1994); Roland Oliver and G. N. Sanderson, eds., *From 1870 to 1905* (1985); A. D. Roberts, ed., *From 1905 to 1940* (1986), in *The Cambridge History of Africa*; and A. Adu Boahen, ed., *Africa Under Colonial Domination, 1880–1935* (1985), in *UNESCO General History of Africa*. The European conquest of Africa is recounted in Thomas Pakenham, *The Scramble for Africa* (1991); Bruce Vandervort, *Wars of Imperial Conquest in Africa, 1830–1914* (1998); and Ronald Robinson and John Gallagher, *Africa and the Victorians: The Climax of Imperialism* (1961). Adam Hochschild's *King Leopold's Ghost: A Story of Greed, Terror, and Heroism in Colonial Africa* (1998) is a very readable account of imperialism in the Belgian Congo. The classic novel about the impact of colonial rule on African society is Chinua Achebe's *Things Fall Apart* (1958).

Imperial rivalries in Asia are the subject of Akira Iriye, *Across the Pacific: An Inner History of American-East Asian Relations*, rev. ed. (1992); David Gillard, *The Struggle for Asia, 1828–1914: A Study in British and Russian Imperialism* (1977); and Peter Hopkirk, *The Great Game: The Struggle for Empire in Central Asia* (1994). On other aspects of imperialism in Asia, see Clifford Geertz, *Agricultural Involution: The Process of Ecological Change in Indonesia* (1963), especially chapters 4 and 5, and Stanley Karnow, *In Our Image: America's Empire in the Philippines* (1989).

On Latin America in this period, see David Bushnell and Neill Macauley, *The Emergence of Latin America in the Nineteenth Century* (1994). Free-trade imperialism is the subject of D. C. M. Platt, *Latin America and British Trade, 1806–1914* (1973). On American expansionism, see David Healy, *Drive to Hegemony: The United States in the Caribbean, 1898–1917* (1989), and Walter LaFeber, *The Panama Canal*, rev. ed. (1990).

On race relations in the colonial world, see Noel Mostert, *Frontiers: The Epic of South Africa's Creation and the Tragedy of the Xhosa People* (1992), and Robert Huttenback, *Racism and Empire: White Settlers and Colored Immigrants in the British Self-Governing Colonies, 1830–1910* (1976). Gender relations are the subject of Caroline Oliver, *Western Women in Colonial Africa* (1982), and Cheryl Walker, ed., *Women and Gender in Southern Africa to 1945* (1990). David Northrup's *Indentured Labor in the Age of Imperialism, 1834–1922* (1995) discusses migrations and labor. Franz Fanon, *The Wretched of the Earth* (1966), and Albert Memmi, *The Colonizer and the Colonized* (1967), examine colonialism from the point of view of the colonized.

The impact of technology on the New Imperialism is the subject of Daniel R. Headrick, *The Tools of Empire: Technology and European Imperialism in the Nineteenth Century* (1981) and *The Tentacles of Progress: Technology Transfer in the Age of Imperialism, 1850–1940* (1988), and Clarence B. Davis and Kenneth E. Wilburn, Jr., eds., *Railway Imperialism* (1991).

On the economic and demographic transformation of Africa and Asia, see Eric Wolf, *Europe and the People Without History* (1982), especially chapters 11 and 12. The impact on the environment is the subject of R. P. Tucker and J. F. Richards, *Deforestation and the Nineteenth-Century World Economy* (1983); Donal McCracken, *Gardens of Empire: Botanical Institutions of the Victorian British Empire* (1997); Lucile H. Brockway, *Science and Colonial Expansion: The Role of the British Royal Botanic Gardens* (1979); and David Arnold and Ramchandra Guha, eds., *Nature, Culture, Imperialism: Essays on the Environmental History of South Asia* (1995). In *Late Victorian Holocausts: El Niño Famines and the Making of the Third World* (2001), Mike Davis argues that imperialism exacerbated the social and demographic effects of famines.

■ Notes

1. *Journal Officiel* (November 29, 1869), quoted in Georges Douin, *Histoire du Règne du Khédive Ismaïl* (Rome: Reale Societá di Geografia d'Egitto, 1933), 453.
2. E. Desplaces in *Journal de l'Union des Deux Mers* (December 15, 1869), quoted in ibid., 453.
3. Winston Churchill, *The River War: An Account of the Reconquest of the Soudan* (New York: Charles Scribner's Sons, 1933), 300.
4. "Correspondence and Report from His Majesty's Consul at Boma respecting the Administration of the Independent State of the Congo," *British Parliamentary Papers, Accounts and Papers,* 1904 (Cd. 1933), lxii, 357.
5. Robert W. July, *A History of the Africa People,* 3d ed. (New York: Charles Scribner's Sons, 1980), 323.
6. George Shepperson and Thomas Price, *Independent African* (Edinburgh: University Press, 1958), 163–164, quoted in Roland Oliver and Anthony Atmore, *Africa Since 1800,* 4th ed. (Cambridge: Cambridge University Press, 1994), 150.
7. Thomas Edson Ennis, *French Policy and Development in Indochina* (Chicago: University of Chicago Press, 1936), 178, quoted in K. M. Panikkar, *Asia and Western Dominance* (New York: Collier, 1969), 167.
8. Quoted in Stanley J. Stein and Barbara H. Stein, *The Colonial Heritage of Latin America* (New York: Oxford University Press, 1970), 151.

25 The Crisis of the Imperial Order, 1900–1929

CHAPTER OUTLINE

Origins of the Crisis in Europe and the Middle East
The "Great War" and the Russian Revolutions
Peace and Dislocation in Europe
China and Japan: Contrasting Destinies
The New Middle East
Science, Culture, and Technology in the Industrialized World
ENVIRONMENT AND TECHNOLOGY: Cities Old and New

On June 28, 1914, Archduke Franz Ferdinand, heir to the throne of Austria-Hungary, was riding in an open carriage through Sarajevo, capital of the province of Bosnia-Herzegovina, which Austria had annexed six years before. When the carriage stopped momentarily, Gavrilo Princip, a member of a pro-Serbian conspiracy, fired his pistol twice, killing the archduke and his wife.

Those shots ignited a war that spread throughout Europe and then turned into a global war as the Ottoman Empire fought against Britain in the Middle East and Japan attacked German positions in China. France and Britain involved their empires in the war and brought Africans, Indians, Australians, and Canadians to Europe to fight and labor on the front lines. Finally, in 1917, the United States entered the fray.

The next three chapters tell a story of violence and hope. This chapter looks at the causes of war between the great powers; the consequences of that conflict in Europe, the Middle East, and Russia; and the upheavals in China and Japan. It also reviews the accelerating rate of technological change that made the first half of the twentieth century so violent and so hopeful. Entirely new technologies made war more dangerous yet allowed far more people to live healthier, more comfortable, and more interesting lives than ever before.

As you read this chapter, ask yourself the following questions:

- How did the First World War lead to revolution in Russia and the disintegration of other empires?

- What role did the war play in eroding European dominance in the world?

- Why did China and Japan follow such divergent paths in this period?

- How did European and North American society and technology change in the aftermath of the war?

ORIGINS OF THE CRISIS IN EUROPE AND THE MIDDLE EAST

When the twentieth century opened, the world seemed firmly under the control of the great powers (see Environment and Technology: Cities Old and New). Its first decade saw peace and economic growth in most of the world. New technologies—airplanes, automobiles, radio, and cinema—aroused much excitement. With their colonial conquests over, the great powers seemed matched and likely to maintain peace. The only international war of the period, the Russo-Japanese War (1904–1905), ended quickly with a decisive Japanese victory.

However, two major changes were undermining the apparent stability of the world. In Europe, tensions mounted as Germany challenged Britain at sea and France in Morocco. As the Ottoman Empire grew weaker, the resulting chaos in the Balkans gradually drew the European powers into its hostilities.

The Ottoman Empire and the Balkans

By 1900, economic, technological, and military decline had made the once-great Ottoman Empire the "sick man of Europe," and it was losing its outlying provinces. Between 1902 and 1913, Macedonia rebelled, Austria-Hungary annexed Bosnia, Crete merged with Greece, Italy conquered Libya, the Ottomans' last foothold in Africa, and Albania became independent. In 1912–1913, Serbia, Bulgaria, Romania, and Greece chased the Turks out of the Balkans, except for a small enclave around Constantinople.

The European powers meddled in the internal affairs of the Ottoman Empire. Russia and Austria-Hungary competed to become the protector of the Slavic peoples of the Balkans. France and Britain, posing as protectors of Christian minorities, controlled Ottoman finances, taxes, railroads, mines, and public utilities.

In reaction, Turks began to assert themselves against rebellious minorities and meddling foreigners. In 1909, the group known as the Young Turks overthrew the sultan and replaced him with his brother. The new regime began to reform the police, the bureaucracy, and the education system and hired a German general to modernize Turkey's armed forces. At the same time, it cracked down on Greek and Armenian minorities.

Nationalism, Alliances, and Military Strategy

Nationalism was deeply rooted in European culture. It united the citizens of France, Britain, and Germany behind their respective governments and gave them tremendous cohesion and strength of purpose. But nationalism could also be a dividing rather than a unifying force. In the large but fragile multinational Russian, Austro-Hungarian, and Ottoman Empires, ethnic and religious minorities, repressed for centuries, were stirring. The easy victories in the wars of the New Imperialism led some in power to believe that only war could heal the divisions in their societies.

What turned assassination of the Archduke Franz Ferdinand in a small town in the Balkans into a conflict involving all the great powers was the system of alliances that had grown up over the previous decades. At the center of Europe stood Germany, the most heavily industrialized country in Europe and yearning to dominate. Its army was the best trained and equipped, and its heavily armed battleships were challenging Great Britain's naval supremacy. Germany joined Austria-Hungary and Italy in the Triple Alliance in 1882. When in 1907 Britain, France, and Russia formed

Cities Old and New

Cities do not just grow larger; they change, sometimes radically, in response to culture and technology. The impact of cultural dominance and technological innovations on urban design is evident in these photographs of Cairo.

The European colonial presence was felt more strongly in cities than in the countryside. Cairo, the largest city in the Arab world before the British conquest, grew much larger after 1882. However, the construction of modern quarters for Europeans and wealthy Egyptians had little impact on the older quarters where most Cairenes lived. In the picture of the old quarter of Cairo in 1900 with its narrow streets and open stalls, men wear the burnoose and women cover their faces with a veil. The later picture, taken in 1904, shows Shepheard's Hotel, one of the most luxurious hotels in the world, built on a broad avenue in the city's modern quarter.

The picture at left reflects the traditional architecture of hot desert countries: narrow streets, thick whitewashed walls, small windows, and heavy doors, all designed to keep out the heat of the day and protect privacy. The picture below shows the ideas Europeans brought with them about how a city should look. The wide streets and high airy buildings with windows and balconies mimic the urban design of late-nineteenth-century Paris, London, and Rome.

Cairo—Modern and Traditional   The luxurious Shepheard's Hotel (below) was built in the European style on a broad avenue in the new quarter of Cairo. In stark contrast is the street (left) in the old quarter of the city: the street is narrow, the walls of the buildings are thick, and the windows small to protect the interiors from the heat of the sun.   (Billie Love Historical Collection)

C H R O N O L O G Y

	Europe and North America	Middle East	East Asia
1900			**1900** Boxer Rebellion in China
			1904–1905 Russo-Japanese War
	1907 British-French-Russian Entente		
1910		**1909** Young Turks overthrow Sultan Abdul Hamid	
			1911 Chinese revolutionaries led by Sun Yat-sen overthrow Qing dynasty
	1912-1913 Balkan Wars		
	1914 Assassination of Archduke Franz Ferdinand sparks World War I		
			1915 Japan presents Twenty-One Demands to China
	1916 Battles of Verdun and the Somme	**1916** Arab Revolt in Arabia	
	1917 Russian Revolutions; United States enters the war	**1917** Balfour Declaration	
	1918 Armistice ends World War I		
	1919 Treaty of Versailles		**1919** May Fourth Movement in China
1920	**1920** First commercial radio broadcast (United States)		
	1921 New Economic Policy in Russia		
		1922 Egypt nominally independent	
		1923 Mustafa Kemal proclaims Turkey a republic	
	1927 Charles Lindbergh flies alone across the Atlantic		**1927** Guomindang forces occupy Shanghai and expel Communists

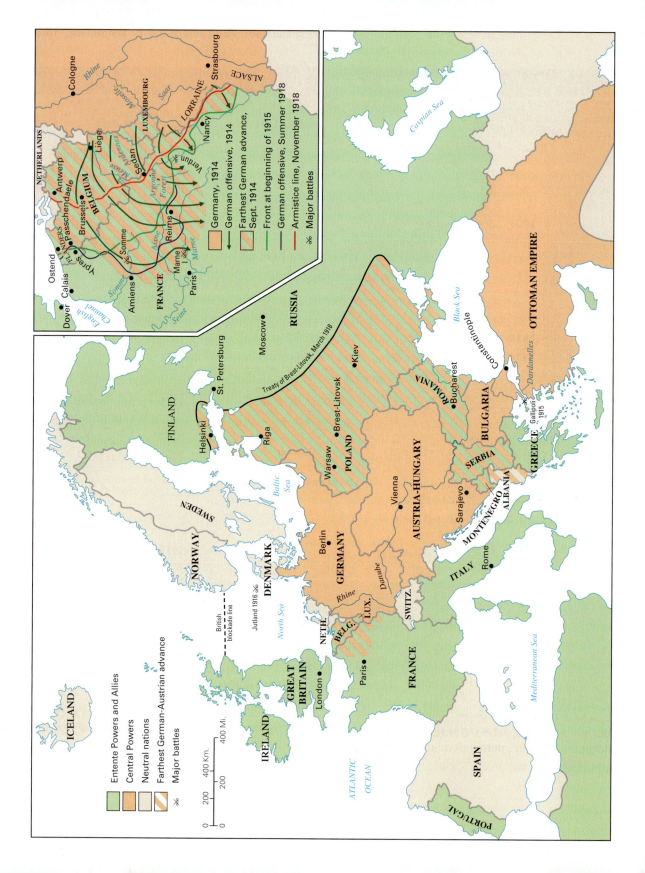

Cologne

Rhine

NETHERLANDS

Antwerp

LUXEMBOURG

Saar

Moselle

Strasbourg

ALSACE

LORRAINE

Nancy

Germany, 1914

German offensive, 1914

Farthest German advance,
Sept. 1914

Front at beginning of 1915

German offensive, Summer 1918

Armistice line, November 1918

Major battles

Liège

Sedan

Meuse

BELGIUM

Brussels

Argonne
Forest

Verdun

Ostend

Flanders

Passchendaele

Ypres

Somme

Aisne

Reims

Marne

Marne I

Calais

Dover

Amiens

FRANCE

Paris

Somme

Seine

English Channel

Caspian Sea

RUSSIA

Moscow

St. Petersburg

Treaty of Brest-Litovsk March 1918

Kiev

Brest-Litovsk

FINLAND

Helsinki

Riga

Warsaw

POLAND

Black Sea

Constantinople

Dardanelles

OTTOMAN EMPIRE

ROMANIA

Bucharest

BULGARIA

Gallipoli
1915

GREECE

SERBIA

Vienna

AUSTRIA-HUNGARY

Sarajevo

MONTENEGRO

ALBANIA

Baltic Sea

SWEDEN

NORWAY

DENMARK

Berlin

GERMANY

Danube

Rhine

North Sea

British
blockade line

Jutland 1916

NETH.

BELG.

LUX.

SWITZ.

ITALY

Rome

Mediterranean Sea

ICELAND

GREAT
BRITAIN

London

IRELAND

Paris

FRANCE

ATLANTIC
OCEAN

SPAIN

PORTUGAL

Entente Powers and Allies

Central Powers

Neutral nations

Farthest German-Austrian advance

Major battles

400 Mi.

200

400 Km.

200

0

0

Map 25.1   The First World War in Europe   Most of the fighting in World War I took place on two fronts. After an initial surge through Belgium into northern France, the German offensive bogged down for four years along the Western Front. To the east, the German armies conquered a large part of Russia during 1917 and early 1918. Despite spectacular victories in the east, Germany lost the war because its armies collapsed along the strategically important Western Front.

an Entente° ("understanding"), Europe was divided into two blocs of roughly equal power (see Map 25.1).

The alliance system was cursed by inflexible military planning. In the years before World War I, military planners in France and Germany had worked out elaborate railroad timetables to mobilize their respective armies in a few days. Other countries were less well prepared. Russia, a large country with an underdeveloped rail system, needed several weeks to mobilize its forces. Britain, with only a tiny volunteer army, had no mobilization plans. German generals, believing that the British would stay out of a future European war, made war plans to defeat France in a matter of days and then to transport their entire army by train across Germany to the Russian border before Russia could fully mobilize.

On July 28, 1914, emboldened by the backing of Germany, Austria-Hungary declared war on Serbia, triggering the mobilization plans of Russia, France, and Germany. On July 29, the Russian government ordered general mobilization to force Austria to back down. On August 1, France honored its treaty obligation to Russia and ordered general mobilization. Minutes later, Germany did the same. Because of the rigid railroad timetables, war was now automatic.

The German General Staff expected France to capitulate before the British could get involved. But on August 3, when German troops entered Belgium, Britain demanded their withdrawal. When Germany refused, Britain declared war on Germany.

Entente (on-TONT)

THE "GREAT WAR" AND THE RUSSIAN REVOLUTIONS

Throughout Europe, people greeted the outbreak of war with parades and hopes for a quick victory. The German sociologist Max Weber wrote: "This war, with all its ghastliness, is nevertheless grand and wonderful. It is worth experiencing." Very few imagined that their side might not win, and no one foresaw that everyone would lose. The effect of the war was especially devastating in Russia, for it destroyed the old society, introduced a radical new political system, and put professional revolutionaries in charge of Russia's industrialization.

Stalemate, 1914–1917

In 1914, the generals' carefully drawn-up plans went awry from the start. Believing that a spirited attack would always prevail, French generals hurled their troops, dressed in bright blue-and-red uniforms, against the well-defended German border and suffered a crushing defeat. By early September, the German armies held Belgium and northern France and were fast approaching Paris.

German victory seemed assured. But when Russia attacked, German troops needed for the final push into France were shifted to the Russian front. A gap opened between two German armies along the Marne River, into which France's last reserves moved. At the Battle of the Marne, the Germans were thrown back several miles.

During the next month, both sides spread out until they formed an unbroken line extending over 300 miles (some 500 kilometers) from the North Sea to the border of Switzerland. All along this **Western Front,** machine guns provided an almost impenetrable defense against advancing infantry but were useless for the offensive because they were too heavy for one man to carry and took too much time to set up. To escape the deadly streams of bullets, soldiers dug holes for themselves in the ground, connected the holes to form shallow trenches, and then dug communications trenches to the rear. Within weeks, the battlefields

Trench Warfare in World War I   German and Allied soldiers on the Western Front faced each other from elaborate networks of trenches. Attacking meant jumping out of the trenches and racing across a no man's land of mud and barbed wire. Here we see Princess Patricia's Canadian Light Infantry repelling a German attack near Ypres, in northern France, in March 1915, using machine guns, rifles, and hand grenades.   (Courtesy, The Princess Patricia's Canadian Light Infantry, Regimental Museum and Archives)

were scarred with lines of trenches several feet deep, their tops protected by sandbags and their floors covered with planks.

For four years, generals on each side again and again ordered their troops to attack. In battle after battle, thousands of young men on one side climbed out of their trenches, raced across the open fields, and were mowed down by enemy machine-gun fire. Poison gas added to the horror of battle.

The year 1916 saw the bloodiest and most futile battles of the war. The Germans attacked French forts at Verdun, losing 281,000 men and causing 315,000 French casualties. In retaliation, the British attacked the Germans at the Somme River and suffered 420,000 casualties—60,000 on the first day alone—while the Germans lost 450,000 and the French 200,000.

This was not warfare as it had ever been waged before; it was mass slaughter. Neither side could win, for the armies were stalemated by trenches and machine guns. During four years of the bloodiest fighting the world had ever seen, the Western Front moved no more than a few miles one way or another.

At sea, the war was just as inconclusive. As soon as the war broke out, the British cut the German overseas telegraph cables, blockaded the coasts of Germany and Austria-Hungary, and set out to capture or sink all enemy ships still at sea. The German High Seas Fleet, built at enormous cost, seldom left port. Only once, in May 1916, did it confront the British Grand Fleet. At the Battle of Jutland, off the coast of Denmark, the two fleets lost roughly equal numbers of ships, and the Germans escaped back to their harbors.

In early 1915, in retaliation for the British naval blockade, Germany announced a blockade of Britain by submarines. German submarines attacked every vessel they could. One attack sank the British ocean liner *Lusitania*, killing 1,198 people, 139 of them Americans. When the United States protested, Germany ceased its submarine campaign, hoping to keep America neutral.

The Home Front and the War Economy

The war economy transformed civilian life. In France and Britain, food rations were allocated according to need, improving nutrition among the poor. Unemployment vanished. Thousands of Africans, Indians, and Chinese were recruited for heavy labor in Europe. Employers hired women to fill jobs in steel mills, mines, and munitions plants vacated by men off to war. Women became streetcar drivers, mail carriers, and police or found work in government bureaucracies. Many joined auxiliary military services as doctors, nurses, mechanics, and ambulance drivers. These positions gave thousands of women a sense of participation and a taste of independence.

German civilians paid an especially high price because of the British naval blockade. The German chemical industry developed synthetic explosives and fuel, but synthetic food was not an option. Wheat flour disappeared, replaced first by rye, then by potatoes and turnips, then by acorns and chestnuts, and finally by sawdust. After the failure of the potato crop in 1916 came the "turnip winter," when people had to survive on 1,000 calories per day, half of the normal amount that an active adult needed. Women, children, and the elderly were especially hard hit.

During the war, the British and French overran all of Germany's African colonies except German East Africa, which remained undefeated until the end of the war (see Map 24.1). The war brought hardships to many African colonies, whose inhabitants faced heavy taxes, low prices for requisitioned export crops, and forced recruitment. Many Europeans stationed in Africa left to join the war, leaving large areas with little or no European presence. Over a million Africans served in the various armies, and perhaps three times that number were drafted as porters to carry army equipment. In some places, these impositions provoked African uprisings that lasted for years.

One country grew rich during the war: the United States, which for two and a half years stayed technically neutral while businesses engaging in war production did a roaring business supplying France and Britain. After the United States entered the war in 1917, civilians were exhorted to help the war effort by investing their savings in war bonds and growing food in backyard "victory gardens." Employment created by the war opened up jobs for women and African-Americans.

The Ottoman Empire at War

On August 2, 1914, the Turks signed a secret alliance with Germany. In November, they joined the fighting, hoping to gain land at Russia's expense. But the campaign in the Caucasus proved disastrous for both armies and for the civilian populations. Suspecting the Armenians of being pro-Russian, the Turks forced them to march from their homelands across the mountains in the winter. Hundreds of thousands of Armenians died of hunger and exposure, an omen of even ghastlier tragedies to come.

The Turks also closed the Dardanelles, the strait between the Mediterranean and Black Seas (see Map 25.1). When a British attempt to force open the Dardanelles failed, the British tried to subvert the Ottoman Empire from within by promising the emir (prince) of Mecca, Hussein ibn Ali, a kingdom of his own. In 1916, Hussein started an Arab revolt against the Turks. His son **Faisal**° led an Arab army into Palestine and Syria in support of the British advance from Egypt, thereby contributing to the Ottoman defeat.

Faisal (fie-SAHL)

The British made promises to Chaim Weizmann°, leader of the British Zionists, that a Jewish homeland in Palestine would be carved out of the Ottoman Empire and placed under British protection. In November, as British armies were advancing on Jerusalem, Foreign Secretary Sir Arthur Balfour wrote that "His Majesty's Government view with favor the establishment in Palestine of a national home for the Jewish people and will use their best endeavours to facilitate the achievement of that object, it being clearly understood that nothing shall be done which may prejudice the civil and religious rights of existing non-Jewish communities in Palestine." The British did not foresee that this statement, known as the **Balfour Declaration,** would lead to conflicts between Palestinians and Jewish settlers.

Double Revolution in Russia, 1917

At the beginning of the war, Russia had the largest army in the world, but its generals were incompetent, supplies were lacking, and soldiers were poorly trained and equipped. In August 1914, two Russian armies invaded eastern Germany but were thrown back. Several times the Russians defeated the Austro-Hungarian army, only to be defeated by the Germans. In 1916, after a string of defeats, the Russian army ran out of ammunition and other essential supplies. Soldiers were ordered into battle unarmed and told to pick up the rifles of fallen comrades.

With so many men in the army, railroads broke down for lack of fuel and parts, and crops rotted in the fields. Civilians faced shortages and widespread hunger. In the cities, food and fuel became scarce. During the bitterly cold winter of 1916–1917, factory workers and housewives had to line up in front of grocery stores before dawn to get something to eat. The court of Tsar° Nicholas II, however, remained as extravagant and corrupt as ever.

When food ran out in Petrograd, the capital, in early March 1917, housewives and women factory workers staged mass demonstrations. Soldiers mutinied and joined striking workers to form soviets (councils) to take over factories and barracks. A few

days later, the tsar abdicated, and leaders of the parliamentary parties formed a Provisional Government. Thus began what Russians called the "February Revolution" because their calendar was two weeks behind the one in use elsewhere.

Revolutionary groups came out of hiding. Most numerous were the Social Revolutionaries, who advocated the redistribution of land to the peasants. The Social Democrats, a Marxist party, were divided. The Mensheviks, who advocated electoral politics and reform in the tradition of European Socialists, had a large following among intellectuals and factory workers. The rival **Bolsheviks** were a small but tightly disciplined group dedicated to radical revolution. **Vladimir Lenin** (1870–1924), the Bolshevik leader, became a revolutionary in his teens when his older brother was executed for plotting to kill the tsar. His goal was to create a party that would lead the revolution rather than wait for it.

In early April 1917, the German government, hoping to destabilize Russia, allowed Lenin to travel from exile in Switzerland to Russia in a sealed railway car. As soon as he arrived in Petrograd, he announced his program: immediate peace, all power to the soviets, and transfers of land to the peasants and factories to the workers. This plan proved immensely popular among the soldiers and workers exhausted by the war.

When the Provisional Government ordered another offensive against the Germans a few months later, Russian soldiers began to desert by the hundreds of thousands, throwing away their rifles and walking back to their villages. The Bolsheviks, meanwhile, were gaining support among the workers of Petrograd and the soldiers and sailors stationed there. On November 6, 1917 (October 24 in the Russian calendar), they rose up and took over the city. This "October Revolution" overthrew the Provisional Government and arrested Mensheviks, Social Revolutionaries, and other rivals.

The Bolsheviks nationalized all private land and ordered the peasants to hand over their crops without compensation. The peasants, having seized their landlords' estates, resisted. In the cities, the Bolsheviks took over the factories and drafted the workers into compulsory labor brigades. To enforce his rule, Lenin created the Cheka, a secret police force with powers to arrest and execute op-

---

Chaim Weizmann (hi-um VITES-mun)   **tsar** (zahr)

ponents. The Bolsheviks also sued for peace with Germany and Austria-Hungary. By the Treaty of Brest-Litovsk, signed on March 3, 1918, Russia lost territories containing a third of its population and wealth.

The End of the War in Western Europe, 1917–1918

Like many other Americans, President **Woodrow Wilson** wanted to stay out of the European conflict. For nearly three years, he kept the United States neutral and tried to persuade the belligerents to compromise. But in late 1916, German leaders decided to starve the British into submission by using submarines to sink merchant ships carrying food supplies to Great Britain. The Germans knew that unrestricted submarine warfare was likely to bring the United States into the war, but they were willing to gamble that Britain and France would collapse before the United States could send enough troops to help them.

The submarine campaign resumed on February 1, 1917, but the German gamble failed. The British organized their merchant ships into convoys protected by destroyers, and on April 6, President Wilson asked the United States Congress to declare war on Germany.

On the Western Front, the two sides were so evenly matched in 1917 that the war seemed unlikely to end until one side or the other ran out of young men. Losing hope of winning, soldiers began to mutiny. In May 1917, before the arrival of U.S. forces, fifty-four of one hundred French divisions along the Western Front refused to attack. At Caporetto, Italian troops were so demoralized that 275,000 were taken prisoner.

Between March and August 1918, General Erich von Ludendorff launched a series of surprise attacks that broke through the front at several places and pushed to within 40 miles (64 kilometers) of Paris. But victory eluded him. Meanwhile, every month was bringing another 250,000 American troops to the front. In August, the Allies counterattacked, and the Germans began a retreat that could not be halted, for German soldiers, many of them sick with the flu, had lost the will to fight.

In late October, Ludendorff resigned, and sailors in the German fleet mutinied. Two weeks later,

Kaiser Wilhelm fled to Holland as a new German government signed an armistice. On November 11 at 11 A.M., the guns on the Western Front went silent.

PEACE AND DISLOCATION IN EUROPE

The Great War lasted four years. It took almost twice as long for Europe to recover. Millions of people had died or been disabled, political tensions lingered, and national economies remained depressed until the mid-1920s. The return of peace and prosperity in the late 1920s soon proved illusory.

The Impact of the War

The war left more dead and wounded and more physical destruction than any previous conflict. It is estimated that between 8 million and 10 million people died, almost all of them young men. Perhaps twice that many returned home wounded, gassed, or shell-shocked, many of them injured for life. In addition, the war created millions of refugees.

Many refugees found shelter in France, which welcomed 1.5 million people, but the preferred destination was the United States. About 800,000 immigrants succeeded in reaching it before U.S. immigration laws passed in 1921 and 1924 closed the door to eastern and southern Europeans. Canada, Australia, and New Zealand adopted similar restrictions on immigration. The Latin American republics welcomed European refugees, but their poverty discouraged potential immigrants.

One unexpected byproduct of the war was the great influenza epidemic of 1918–1919, which started among soldiers heading for the Western Front. This was no ordinary flu but a virulent strain that infected almost everyone on earth and killed one person in every forty. It caused the largest number of deaths in so short a time in the history of the world. Half a million Americans perished in the epidemic—five times as many as died in the war. Worldwide, some 30 million people died, 20 million in India alone.

The war also caused serious damage to the environment. No place on earth was ever so completely devastated as the scar across France and Belgium known as the Western Front. The fighting ravaged forests and demolished towns. The earth was gouged by trenches, pitted with craters, and littered with ammunition, broken weapons, chunks of concrete, and the bones of countless soldiers. After the war, it took a decade to clear away the debris and create military cemeteries with neat rows of crosses stretching for miles. The war also hastened the buildup of industry, with mines, factories, and railroad tracks.

The Peace Treaties

In early 1919, delegates of the victorious Allies met in Paris. The defeated powers were kept out until the treaties were ready for signing. Russia, in the throes of civil war, was not invited.

From the start, three men dominated the Paris Peace Conference: United States president Wilson, British prime minister David Lloyd George, and French premier Georges Clemenceau°. They ignored the Italians, who had joined the Allies in 1915, and paid even less attention to the delegates of smaller European nations. They rejected the Japanese proposal that all races be treated equally and ignored the call of the Pan-African Congress for attention to the concerns of African peoples around the world. They also ignored the ten thousand other delegates of various nationalities who did not represent sovereign states—the Arab leader Faisal, the Zionist Chaim Weizmann, and several Armenian delegations—who came to Paris to lobby for their causes.

Each man had his own agenda. Wilson wanted to apply the principle of self-determination, by which he meant creating nations that reflected European ethnic or linguistic divisions. He proposed a **League of Nations,** a world organization to safeguard the peace and foster international cooperation. His idealism clashed with the more hardheaded and self-serving nationalism of the Europeans. Lloyd George insisted that Germany pay a heavy indemnity. Clemenceau wanted Germany to give back Alsace and Lorraine, cede the industrial Saar region to France, and make the Rhineland a buffer state.

The result was a series of compromises that satisfied no one. The European powers formed a League of Nations, but the United States Congress, reflecting the isolationist feelings of the American people, refused to join. France recovered Alsace and Lorraine but was unable to detach the Rhineland and had to content itself with vague promises of British and American protection if Germany ever rebuilt its army. Britain acquired new territories in Africa and the Middle East but was greatly weakened by human losses and the disruption of its trade.

On June 28, 1919, the German delegates reluctantly signed the **Treaty of Versailles°.** Germany was forbidden to have an air force and was permitted only a token army and navy. It gave up large parts of its eastern territory to a newly reconstituted Poland. The Allies made Germany promise to pay reparations, but they did not set a figure or a period of time for payment. A "guilt clause," which was to rankle for years to come, obliged the Germans to accept "responsibility for causing all the loss and damage" of the war. The Treaty of Versailles left Germany humiliated but largely intact and potentially the most powerful nation in Europe. Establishing a peace neither of punishment nor of reconciliation, the treaty was one of the great failures in history.

In eastern Europe, the Allies created new national states in the lands lost by the old Russian, German, and Austro-Hungarian Empires. Austria and Hungary became separate states; Poland was resurrected after over a century; Czechoslovakia and Yugoslavia were created from parts of Austria-Hungary. These small nations all contained disaffected minorities and were safe only as long as Germany and Russia remained weak.

Russian Civil War and the New Economic Policy

Fighting continued in Russia for another three years after the end of the Great War. The Bolshevik Revolution had provoked Allied intervention, and, in December 1918, civil war broke out in Russia.

Georges Clemenceau (zhorzh cluh-mon-SO)

Versailles (vuhr-SIGH)

The Communists, as the Bolsheviks now called themselves, held central Russia, but all the surrounding provinces rose up against them. Counterrevolutionary armies led by former tsarist officers obtained weapons and supplies from the Allies. However, by 1921, the superior discipline of the Red Army, led by Leon Trotsky, gave the Communists victory over their enemies.

Gradually, the Communists reunited most of the rebellious provinces of the old Russian Empire. In 1920, Ukrainian Communists declared the independence of a Soviet republic of Ukraine; then, in 1922, this merged with Russia to create the Union of Soviet Socialist Republics (USSR), or Soviet Union. In 1920–1921, the Red Army reconquered the oil-rich Caucasus and reestablished Soviet control of Central Asia. In 1922, the new Soviet republics of Georgia, Armenia, and Azerbaijan joined the USSR.

Years of warfare, revolution, and mismanagement had ruined the Russian economy. Factories and railroads had shut down. Farmland had been devastated and livestock killed, causing hunger in the cities. Lenin decided to release the economy from party and government control. In March 1921, he announced the **New Economic Policy** (NEP), which allowed peasants to own land and sell their crops, private merchants to trade, and private workshops to produce goods and sell them on the free market. Only the biggest businesses, such as banks, railroads, and factories, remained under government ownership.

The relaxation of controls had an immediate effect. Production began to climb, and food and other goods became available. In the cities, food remained scarce because farmers used their crops to feed their livestock rather than sell them. But the NEP reflected no change in the goal of the Communist Party to create a modern industrial economy without private property, under party guidance. It merely provided breathing space—what Lenin called "one step back to advance two steps forward." This meant investing in heavy industry and electrification, moving farmers to the new industries, and providing food for the urban workers. In other words, it meant making the peasants, the great majority of the Soviet people, pay for the industrialization of Russia.

When Lenin died in January 1924, his associates jockeyed for power. Leon Trotsky, commander of the Red Army, had the support of many "Old Bolsheviks" who had joined the party before the Revolution, but Joseph Stalin, general secretary of the Communist Party, got the support of the majority and filled the party bureaucracy with individuals loyal to himself. In January 1929, he forced Trotsky to flee the country. Then, as absolute master of the party, he prepared to industrialize the Soviet Union at breakneck speed.

An Ephemeral Peace

The decade after the end of the war can be divided into two distinct periods: five years of painful recovery and readjustment (1919–1923), followed by six years of growing peace and prosperity (1924–1929). One of the big adjustments in many Western societies was granting political rights to women (see "Class and Gender" below). Changes in international politics and economics were more upsetting. In the first period, the German government had printed money recklessly to fund reparations payments, causing the most severe inflation the world had ever seen. As Germany teetered on the brink of civil war, radical nationalists called for revenge and tried to overthrow the government. Finally, the German government issued a new currency and promised to resume reparations payments, and the French agreed to withdraw their troops from the Ruhr.

Then in 1924, the vexed issue of reparations vanished as Germany borrowed money from New York banks to make its payments to France and Britain, which used the money to repay their wartime loans from the United States. This triangular flow of money stimulated the rapid recovery of the European economies. France began rebuilding its war-torn northern zone, Germany recovered from its hyperinflation and joined the League of Nations, and in the United States a boom began that was to last over five years.

While their economies flourished, governments grew more cautious and businesslike. Yet neither Germany nor the Soviet Union accepted its borders with the small nations that had arisen between them. In 1922, they signed a secret pact allowing the German army to conduct maneuvers in Russia (in violation of the Versailles treaty) in exchange for German help in building up Russian industry.

For a time, the League of Nations proved adept at resolving issues pertaining to health, labor relations, and postal and telegraph communications. But without U.S. participation, sanctions against states that violated League rules carried little weight.

CHINA AND JAPAN: CONTRASTING DESTINIES

China and Japan took different directions in the early twentieth century. Still in need of deep internal reform, giant China went through a revolution but soon collapsed into chaos. Japan's re-

The Bund, Shanghai Shanghai was the most important port and industrial city in China. This picture shows the Bund, or waterfront, where oceangoing ships docked and where Chinese and foreign merchants did business. Many of the people you see in the picture were stevedores, who loaded and unloaded ships, and drivers of rickshaws or man-powered taxis. (Corbis)

forms before 1900 had gained it industry and a powerful military, which it used to take advantage of China's weakness.

Revolution in China

China's population—about 400 million in 1900—was the largest of any country in the world and growing fast, but China's society and government were falling behind. Most Chinese worked incessantly, survived on a diet of grain and vegetables, and spent their lives in fear of floods, bandits, and tax collectors. Peasant plots averaged half as large as they had been two generations earlier. Landowners lived off the rents of their tenants. Officials, chosen through an elaborate examination system, enriched themselves from taxes and the government's monopolies on salt, iron, and other products. Wealthy merchants handled China's growing import-export trade in collaboration with foreign companies. The contrast between the squalor in which most urban residents lived and the luxury of the foreigners' enclaves in the treaty ports sharpened the resentment of educated Chinese.

In 1900, China's **Empress Dowager Cixi°,** who had seized power in a palace coup two years earlier, encouraged a secret society, the Righteous Fists, or Boxers, to rise up and expel all the foreigners from China. When the Boxers threatened the foreign legation in Beijing, an international force from the Western powers and Japan captured the city and forced China to pay a huge indemnity. Shocked by these events, many Chinese students became convinced that China needed a revolution to get rid of the Qing dynasty and modernize their country.

When Cixi died in 1908, the Revolutionary Alliance led by **Sun Yat-sen°** (Sun Zhongshan, 1867–1925) prepared to take over. Sun had spent much of his life in Japan, England, and the United States, plotting the overthrow of the Qing dynasty. His ideas, a mixture of nationalism, socialism, and Confucian philosophy, and his tenacious spirit attracted a large following. A revolutionary assembly elected Sun president of China in December 1911, and the last Qing ruler, the boy-emperor Puyi, abdicated

---

Cixi (TSUH-shee)   **Sun Yat-sen** (soon yot-SEN)

the throne. But Sun had no military forces at his command. To avoid a clash with the army, he resigned after a few weeks, and a new national assembly elected **Yuan Shikai°,** the most powerful of the regional generals, president of the new Chinese republic.

Yuan was an able military leader, but he had no political program. When Sun reorganized his followers into a political party called **Guomindang°** (National People's Party), Yuan quashed every attempt at creating a Western-style government and harassed Sun's followers. Victory in the first round of the struggle to create a new China went to the military.

Japan and World War I

Japan's population reached 60 million in 1925 and was increasing by a million a year. The crash program of industrialization begun in 1868 by the Meiji oligarchs (see Chapter 23) accelerated during the First World War, when Japan exported textiles, consumer goods, and munitions. In the war years, its economy grew four times as fast as western Europe's and eight times faster than China's. Blessed with a rainy climate and many fast-flowing rivers, Japan quickly expanded its hydroelectric capacity. By the mid-1930s, 89 percent of Japanese households had electric lights, compared with 44 percent of British households.

The main beneficiaries of prosperity were the *zaibatsu°,* four giant corporations—Mitsubishi, Sumitomo, Yasuda, and Mitsui—that controlled most of Japan's industry and commerce. Farmers, who constituted half of the population, remained poor; some, in desperation, sold their daughters to textile mills or into domestic service, where young women formed the bulk of the labor force. Labor unions were weak and repressed by the police.

The Japanese were quick to join the Allied side in World War I. They saw the war as a golden opportunity to advance their interests while the Europeans were occupied elsewhere. The war created an economic boom, as the Japanese suddenly found their products in greater demand than before.

The Japanese soon conquered the German colonies in the northern Pacific and on the coast of China, and then turned their attention to the rest of China. In 1915, Japan presented China with Twenty-One Demands, which would have turned it into a virtual protectorate. Britain and the United States persuaded Japan to soften the demands but could not prevent it from keeping the German coastal enclaves and extracting railroad and mining concessions at China's expense. Thus began a bitter struggle between the two countries that was to last for thirty years.

China in the 1920s

To many educated Chinese, the great powers' decision at the Paris Peace Conference to go along with Japan's seizure of the German enclaves in China was a cruel insult. On May 4, 1919, students demonstrated in front of the Forbidden City of Beijing. Despite a government ban, the May Fourth Movement spread to other parts of China. A new generation was growing up to challenge the old officials, the regional generals, and the foreigners.

China's regional generals—the warlords—still supported their armies through plunder and arbitrary taxation. They frightened off trade and investment in railroads, industry, and agricultural improvement. While neglecting the dikes and canals on which the livelihood of Chinese farmers depended, they fought one another and protected the gangsters who ran the opium trade. During the warlord era, China grew poorer, and only the treaty ports prospered.

Sun Yat-sen tried to make a comeback in Canton (Guangzhou) in the early 1920s. Though not a communist, he was impressed with the efficiency of Lenin's revolutionary tactics and let a Soviet adviser reorganize the Guomindang along Leninist lines. He also welcomed members of the newly created Chinese Communist Party into the Guomindang.

When Sun died in 1925, the leadership of his party passed to **Chiang Kai-shek°** (1886–1975). An officer and director of the military academy, Chiang trained several hundred young officers, who remained loyal to him thereafter. In 1927, he determined to crush the regional warlords. As his

---

Yuan Shikai (you-AHN she-KIE   **Guomindang** (gwo-min-dong)   *zaibatsu* (zie-BOT-soo)

Chiang Kai-shek (chang kie-shek)

army moved north from its base in Canton, he briefly formed an alliance with the Communists. Once his troops had occupied Shanghai, however, he allied himself with local gangsters to crush the labor unions and decimate the Communists, whom he considered a threat. He then defeated or co-opted most of the other warlords and established a dictatorship.

Chiang's government issued ambitious plans to build railroads, develop agriculture and industry, and modernize China from the top down. However, his followers were neither competent administrators like the Japanese officials of the Meiji Restoration nor ruthless modernizers like the Russian Bolsheviks. Instead, the government attracted thousands of opportunists whose goal was to "become an official and get rich" by taxing and plundering businesses. In the countryside, tax collectors and landowners squeezed the peasants ever harder. What little money reached the government went to the military. Twenty years after the fall of the Qing, China remained mired in poverty, subject to corrupt officials and the whims of nature.

THE NEW MIDDLE EAST

At the Paris Peace Conference, France, Britain, Italy, and Japan proposed to divide the territories of the Ottoman Empire among themselves, but their ambitions clashed with President Wilson's ideal of national self-determination. Turkish nationalists made modern Turkey a new independent country. The Arab-speaking territories of the old Ottoman Empire became part of the League of Nations' new **mandate system,** run by French and British administrations that were accountable to the League of Nations for "the material and moral well-being and the social progress of the inhabitants." In the midst of these territories, Zionists were encouraging Jewish immigration (see Map 25.2).

The Rise of Modern Turkey

At the end of the First World War, the Allied forces occupied the Ottoman Empire and made the sultan give up most of his lands. But they had to reckon with Mustafa Ke-

Mustafa Kemal Atatürk After World War I, Mustafa Kemal was determined to modernize Turkey on the Western model. Here he is shown wearing a European-style suit and teaching the Latin alphabet. (Stock Montage)

mal, a war hero who had formed a nationalist government in central Anatolia with the backing of fellow army officers. His armies reconquered Anatolia and the area around Constantinople in 1922 and expelled hundreds of thousands of Greeks. In response, the Greek government expelled all Muslims from Greece.

Map 25.2 Territorial Changes in the Middle East After World War I The defeat and dismemberment of the Ottoman Empire at the end of World War I resulted in an entirely new political map of the region. The Turkish Republic inherited Anatolia and a small piece of the Balkans, while the Ottoman Empire's Arab provinces were divided between France and Great Britain as "Class A Mandates." The French acquired Syria and Lebanon, and the British got Palestine (now Israel), Transjordan (now Jordan), and Iraq. Only Iran and Egypt remained as they had been.

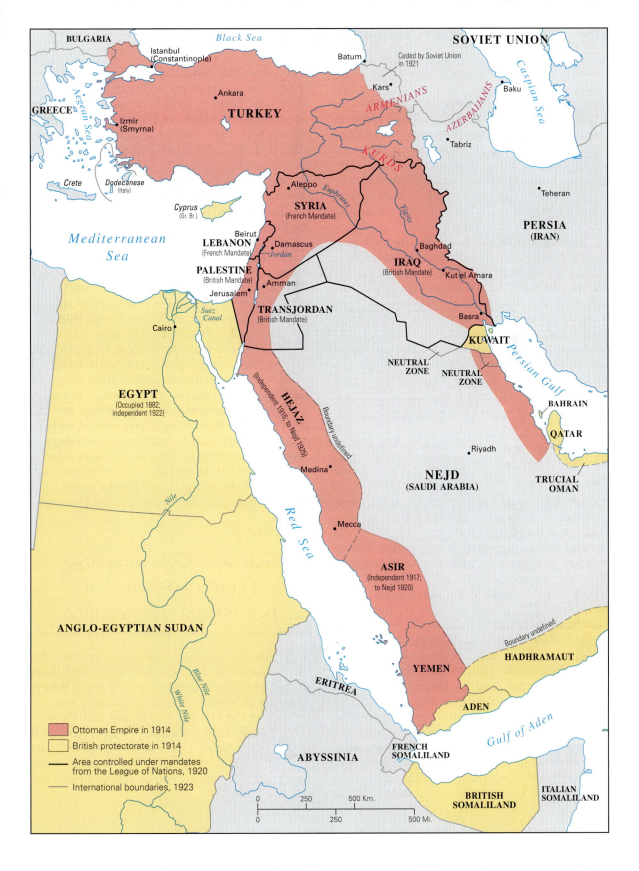

BULGARIA

Black Sea

SOVIET UNION

Istanbul
(Constantinople)

Batum

Ceded by Soviet Union
in 1921

Caspian Sea

GREECE

Aegean Sea

Ankara

TURKEY

Kars

ARMENIANS

Baku

AZERBAIJANIS

Izmir
(Smyrna)

KURDS

Tabriz

Teheran

Crete

Dodecanese
(Italy)

Cyprus
(Gr. Br.)

Aleppo

Euphrates

Tigris

SYRIA
(French Mandate)

PERSIA
(IRAN)

*Mediterranean
Sea*

Beirut

LEBANON
(French Mandate)

Damascus

Jordan

Baghdad

IRAQ
(British Mandate)

Kut el Amara

PALESTINE
(British Mandate)

Jerusalem

Amman

TRANSJORDAN
(British Mandate)

NEUTRAL
ZONE

Basra

NEUTRAL
ZONE

KUWAIT

Persian Gulf

Cairo

*Suez
Canal*

EGYPT
(Occupied 1882;
independent 1922)

BAHRAIN

QATAR

HEJAZ
(Independent 1916; to Nejd 1925)

Boundary undefined

Riyadh

NEJD
(SAUDI ARABIA)

TRUCIAL
OMAN

Medina

Nile

Red Sea

Mecca

ASIR
(Independent 1917;
to Nejd 1920)

ANGLO-EGYPTIAN SUDAN

Boundary undefined

HADHRAMAUT

Blue Nile

White Nile

ERITREA

YEMEN

ADEN

Ottoman Empire in 1914

British protectorate in 1914

Area controlled under mandates
from the League of Nations, 1920

International boundaries, 1923

ABYSSINIA

FRENCH
SOMALILAND

Gulf of Aden

BRITISH
SOMALILAND

ITALIAN
SOMALILAND

0   250   500 Km.

0   250   500 Mi.

As a war hero and proclaimed savior of his country, Kemal was able to impose wrenching changes on his people faster than any other reformer would have dared. An outspoken modernizer, he was eager to bring Turkey closer to Europe as quickly as possible. He abolished the sultanate, in 1923 declared Turkey a secular republic, and introduced European laws. In a radical break with Islamic tradition, he suppressed Muslim courts, schools, and religious orders and replaced the Arabic alphabet with the Latin alphabet.

Kemal attempted to Westernize the traditional Turkish family. Women received civil equality, including the right to vote and be elected to the national assembly. Kemal forbade polygamy and instituted civil marriage and divorce. He even changed people's clothing, strongly discouraging women from veiling their faces and ordering Turkish men to wear European brimmed hats instead of the fez. He ordered everyone to take a family name, choosing the name Atatürk ("father of the Turks") for himself.

Arab Lands and the Question of Palestine

Among the Arab people, the thinly disguised colonialism of the mandate system set off protests and rebellions. Arabs viewed the European presence not as "liberation" from Ottoman "oppression" but as foreign occupation.

The British attempted to control the Middle East with a mixture of bribery and intimidation. They helped Faisal, leader of the Arab Revolt, become king of Syria. When the French ousted him, the British made him king of Iraq. They used bombers to quell rural insurrections in Iraq. In 1931, they reached an agreement with King Faisal's government: official independence for Iraq in exchange for the right to keep two air bases, a military alliance, and an assured flow of petroleum. France, meanwhile, sent thousands of troops to Syria and Lebanon to crush nationalist uprisings.

In Egypt as in Iraq, the British substituted a phony independence for official colonialism. They declared Egypt independent in 1922 but reserved the right to station troops along the Suez Canal to secure their link with India in the event of war. Despite nationalist opposition, Britain was successful in keeping Egypt in limbo—neither independent nor a colony—thanks to an alliance with King Fuad (sultan 1917–1922; king 1922–1936) and conservative Egyptian politicians who feared both secular and religious radicalism.

As soon as Palestine became a British mandate in 1920, Jewish immigrants, encouraged by the Balfour Declaration of 1917, arrived to join the small community that had immigrated in the nineteenth century. Most settled in the cities, but some purchased land to establish *kibbutzim*, communal farms. Their goals were to become self-sufficient and reestablish their ties to the land of their ancestors. The purchases of land by Jewish agencies angered the indigenous Palestinians, especially tenant farmers who had been evicted to make room for settlers. In 1920–1921, riots erupted between Jews and Arabs. When far more Jewish immigrants arrived than they had anticipated, the British tried to limit immigration, thereby alienating the Jews without mollifying the Arabs. Increasingly, Jews arrived without papers, smuggled in by militant Zionist organizations. In the 1930s, the country was torn by strikes and guerrilla warfare that the British could not control. In the process, Britain earned the hatred of both sides and of much of the Arab world as well.

SCIENCE, CULTURE, AND TECHNOLOGY IN THE INDUSTRIALIZED WORLD

With the signing of the peace treaties, the countries that had fought for four years turned their efforts toward building a new future. Advances in science offered astonishing new insights into the mysteries of nature and the universe. New technologies, many of them pioneered in the United States, promised to change the daily lives of millions of people. At the same time, new cultural trends developed that had profound effects.

Class and Gender

After the war, class distinctions began to fade. Many European aristocrats had died on the battlefields, and with them went their class's long domination of the army, the diplomatic corps, and other elite sectors of society. The United States and Canada had never had as rigidly defined a class structure as European societies or as elaborate a set of traditions and manners. During the war, displays of wealth and privilege seemed unpatriotic. On both sides of the Atlantic, engineers, businessmen, lawyers, and other professionals rose to prominence, increasing the relative importance of the middle class.

The activities of governments had expanded during the war and continued to grow. Governments provided housing, highways, schools, public health facilities, broadcasting, and other services. This growth of government influence created a need for thousands more bureaucrats. Department stores, banks, insurance companies, and other businesses also increased the white-collar work force.

In contrast with the middle class, the working class did not expand. The introduction of new machines and new ways of organizing work, such as the automobile assembly line that Henry Ford devised, increased workers' productivity so that greater outputs could be achieved without a larger labor force.

Women's lives changed more rapidly in the 1920s than in any previous decade. Although the end of the war marked a retreat from wartime job opportunities, some women remained in the work force as wage earners and as salaried professionals. The young and wealthy enjoyed more personal freedoms than their mothers had before the war; they drove cars, played sports, traveled alone, and smoked in public. For others the upheavals of war brought more suffering than liberation. Millions of women had lost their fathers, brothers, sons, husbands, and fiancés in the war or in the great influenza epidemic. After the war the shortage of young men caused many single women to lead lives of loneliness and destitution.

In Europe and North America advocates of women's rights had been demanding the vote for women since the 1890s. New Zealand was the only nation to grant women the vote before the twentieth century. Women in Norway were the first to obtain it in Europe, in 1915. Russian women followed in 1917, and Canadians and Germans in 1918. Britain gave women over age thirty the vote in 1918 and later extended it to younger women. The Nineteenth Amendment to the U.S. Constitution granted suffrage to American women in 1920. Women in Turkey began voting in 1934. Most other countries did not allow women to vote until after 1945.

In dictatorships voting rights for women made no difference, and in democratic countries women tended to vote like their male relatives. In the British elections of 1918—the first to include women—they overwhelmingly voted for the Conservative Party. Everywhere, their influence on politics was less radical than feminists had hoped and conservatives had feared. Even when it did not alter politics and government, however, the right to vote was a potent symbol.

Women were active in many other areas besides the suffrage movement. On both sides of the Atlantic women participated in social reform movements to prevent mistreatment of women and children and of industrial workers. In the United States such reforms were championed by Progressives such as Jane Addams (1860–1935), who founded a settlement house in a poor neighborhood and received the Nobel Peace Prize in 1931. In Europe reformers were generally aligned with Socialist or Labour Parties.

Since 1874 the Women's Christian Temperance Union had campaigned against alcohol and taverns. In the early twentieth century the American Carrie Nation (1846–1911) became famous for destroying saloons and lecturing in the United States and Europe against the evils of liquor. As a result of this campaign, the Eighteenth Amendment imposed prohibition in the United States from 1919 until it was revoked by the Twenty-First Amendment fourteen years later.

Among the most controversial, and eventually most effective, of the reformers were those who advocated contraception, such as the American **Margaret Sanger** (1883–1966). Her campaign brought her into conflict with the authorities, who equated birth control with pornography. Finally, in 1923 she was able to found a birth control clinic in New York. In France, however, the government prohibited contraception and abortion in 1920 in an effort to increase the birthrate and make up for the loss of so many young men in the war. Only the Russian communists allowed abortion, for ideological reasons (see Diversity and Dominance: Women, Family Values, and the Russian Revolution in Chapter 26).

Revolution in the Sciences

For two hundred years, scientists, following in Isaac Newton's footsteps, had applied the same laws and equations to astronomical observations and to laboratory experiments. At the end of the nineteenth century, however, a revolution in physics undermined all the old certainties about nature. Physicists discovered that atoms, the building blocks of matter, are not indivisible but consist of far smaller subatomic particles. In 1900, the German physicist **Max Planck** (1858–1947) found that light and energy do not flow in a continuous stream but travel in small units, which he called *quanta*. These findings seemed strange enough, but what really undermined Newtonian physics was the general theory of relativity developed by **Albert Einstein** (1879–1955), another German physicist. In 1916, Einstein announced that not only is matter made of insubstantial particles, but also that time, space, and mass are not fixed but are relative to one another.

To nonscientists, it seemed as though theories expressed in arcane mathematical formulas were replacing truth and common sense. Far from being mere speculation, however, the new physics promised to unlock the secrets of matter and provide humans with plentiful—and potentially dangerous—new sources of energy.

The new social sciences were even more unsettling than the new physics, for they challenged Victorian morality, middle-class values, and notions of Western superiority. Sigmund Freud (1856–1939), a Viennese physician, developed a technique—psychoanalysis—to probe the minds of his patients. He found not only rationality but also hidden layers of emotion and desire repressed by social restraints. "The primitive, savage and evil impulses have not vanished from any individual, but continue their existence, although in a repressed state," he warned. Meanwhile, sociologists and anthropologists had begun the empirical study of

societies, both Western and non-Western. Before the war, the French sociologist Emile Durkheim (1858–1917) had come to the then-shocking conclusion that "there are no religions that are false. All are true in their own fashion."

If the words *primitive* and *savage* applied to Europeans as well as to other peoples, and if religions were all equally "true," then what remained of the superiority of Western civilization? Cultural relativism, as the new approach to human societies was called, was as unnerving as relativity in physics.

Wartime experiences helped call into question the West's faith in reason and progress. Some people accepted the new ideas with enthusiasm. Others condemned and rejected them, clinging to the sense of order and faith in progress that had energized European and American culture before the war.

The New Technologies of Modernity

Some Europeans and Americans viewed the new sciences with mixed feelings, but new technologies aroused almost universal excitement. In North America, even working-class people could afford some of the new products of scientific research, inventors' ingenuity, and industrial production. Mass consumption lagged in Europe, but science and technology were just as advanced, and public fascination with the latest inventions—the cult of the modern—was just as strong.

No other innovation attracted public interest as much as airplanes. In 1903, two young American mechanics, Wilbur and Orville Wright, built the first aircraft that was heavier than air and could be maneuvered in flight. From that moment on, wherever they appeared, airplanes fascinated people. During the war, the exploits of air aces relieved the tedium of news from the front. In the 1920s, aviation became a sport and a form of entertainment, and flying daredevils achieved extraordinary fame by pushing their planes to the very limit—and often beyond. Among the most celebrated pilots were three Americans: Amelia Earhart, the first woman to fly across the Atlantic Ocean; Richard Byrd, the first to fly over the North Pole, in 1926; and Charles Lindbergh, the first person to fly alone across the Atlantic, in 1927. The heroic age of flight lasted until the late 1930s, when aviation became a means of transportation.

Electricity's impact on home life was more sweeping. The first home use of electricity was for lighting, thanks to the economical and long-lasting tungsten bulb. Then, having persuaded people to wire their homes, electrical utilities joined manufacturers in advertising electric irons, fans, washing machines, hot plates, radios, and other electric appliances. After the war, radio moved from the battlefield into the home. The first commercial station began broadcasting in Pittsburgh in 1920. By 1930, hundreds of stations were broadcasting news, sports, soap operas, and advertising to 12 million homes in North America. In Europe, radio spread more slowly because governments reserved the airwaves for cultural and official programs and taxed radio owners to pay for the service.

Another medium that spread explosively in the 1920s was film. Motion pictures had begun in France in 1895 and flourished in Europe. In the United States, filmmaking started at almost the same time, but American filmmakers saw the medium's potential to entertain audiences rather than preserve outstanding theatrical performances. After World War I, filmmaking took root and flourished in Japan, India, Turkey, Egypt, and a suburb of Los Angeles, California, called Hollywood. American and European movie studios were both successful in exporting films, since silent movies presented no language problems. Then in 1927 the United States introduced the first "talking" motion picture, *The Jazz Singer,* which changed all the rules. The number of Americans who went to see their favorite stars in thrilling adventures and heart-breaking romances rose from 40 million in 1922 to 100 million in 1930, at a time when the population of the country was about 120 million. Europeans had the technology and the art but neither the wealth nor the huge market of the United States. Hollywood studios began the diffusion of American culture that has continued to this day.

Advances in medicine—some learned in the war—were another important and life-saving technology. Wounds were regularly disinfected, and x-ray machines helped diagnose fractures. After the war, cities built costly water supply and sewage treatment systems. By the 1920s, indoor plumbing and flush toilets were becoming common even in working-class neighborhoods. Interest in cleanliness altered private life. Soap and appliance manufacturers filled women's magazines with advertisements for products to help housewives keep their family's homes and clothing spotless and their meals fresh and wholesome. The decline in infant mortality and the improvements in general health and life expectancy in this period owe as much to the cult of cleanliness as to advances in medicine.

Technology and the Environment

Two new technologies—the skyscraper and the automobile—transformed the urban environment even more radically than the railroad had done in the nineteenth century. At the end of the nineteenth century, architects had begun to design ever-higher buildings using load-bearing steel frames and passenger elevators. Major corporations in Chicago and New York competed to build the most daring buildings in the world, such as New York's 55-story Woolworth Building (1912) and Chicago's 34-story Tribune Tower (1923). A building boom in the late 1920s produced dozens of skyscrapers, culminating with the 86-story, 1,239-foot (377-meter) Empire State Building in New York City, completed in 1932.

European cities restricted the height of buildings to protect their architectural heritage; Paris forbade buildings over 56 feet (17 meters) high. In innovative designs, however, European architects led the way. In the 1920s, the Swiss architect known as Le Corbusier° outlined a new approach to architecture that featured simplicity of form, absence of surface ornamentation, easy manufacture, and inexpensive materials. Among his influential designs were the main buildings of Chandigarh, the new capital of the Indian state of Punjab. Other architects—including the Finn Eero Saarinen, the Germans Ludwig Mies van der Rohe° and Walter Gropius, and the American Frank Lloyd Wright—advanced his lines of thought and added their own to create what became known as the International Style.

Le Corbusier (luh cor-booz-YEH) **Ludwig Mies van der Rohe** (LOOD-vig MEES fon der ROW-uh)

The Archetypal Automobile City   As Los Angeles grew from a modest town into a sprawling metropolis, broad avenues, parking lots, and garages were built to accommodate automobiles. By 1929, most families owned a car, and streetcar lines had closed for lack of passengers. This photograph shows a street in the downtown business district.   (South Pacific Collection/Los Angeles Public Library)

While central business districts were reaching for the sky, outlying areas were spreading far out into the countryside, thanks to the automobile. The assembly line pioneered by Henry Ford mass-produced vehicles in ever-greater volume and at falling prices. By 1929, the United States had one car for every five people, five-sixths of the world's automobiles. Far from being blamed for their exhaust emissions, automobiles were praised as the solution to urban pollution. As cars replaced carts and carriages, horses disappeared from city streets, as did tons of manure.

The most important environmental effect of automobiles was suburban sprawl. Middle-class families could now live in single-family homes too spread apart to be served by public transportation. By the late 1920s, paved roads rivaled rail networks both in length and in the surface they occupied. As middle- and working-class families bought cars, cities acquired rings of automobile suburbs. Los Angeles, the first true automobile city, consisted of suburbs spread over hundreds of square miles and linked together by broad avenues. In those sections of the city where streetcar lines went out of business, the automobile, at first a plaything for the wealthy, became a necessity for commuters. Many Americans saw Los Angeles as the portent of a glorious future when everyone would have a car;

only a few foresaw the congestion and pollution that would ensue.

Farmers began buying cars and light trucks, using them to transport produce as well as passengers. Governments obliged by building new roads and paving old ones to make automobile travel smoother and safer. In 1915, Ford introduced a gasoline-powered tractor, and by the mid-1920s, these versatile machines began replacing horses. Tractors hastened the end of agriculture as a family enterprise.

CONCLUSION

The Great War caused a major realignment among the nations of the world. France and Britain, the two leading colonial powers, emerged economically weakened despite their victory. The war brought defeat and humiliation to Germany but did not reduce its military or industrial potential. It destroyed the old regime and the aristocracy of Russia, leading to civil war and revolution from which the victorious powers sought to isolate themselves. Two other old empires—the Austro-Hungarian and the Ottoman—were divided into many smaller and weaker nations. For a while, the Middle East seemed ripe for a new wave of imperialism. But there and throughout Asia, the war unleashed revolutionary nationalist movements that challenged European influence.

Only two countries benefited from the war. Japan took advantage of the European conflict to develop its industries and press its demands on a China weakened by domestic turmoil and social unrest. The United States emerged as the most prosperous and potentially most powerful nation, restrained only by the isolationist sentiments expressed by many Americans.

Modern technology and industrial organization had long been praised in the name of "progress" for their ability to reduce toil and disease and improve living standards. The war showed that they possessed an equally awesome destructive potential. In the late 1920s, it seemed as though the victors in the Great War might restore the prewar prosperity and European dominance of the globe. But the spirit of the 1920s was an illusion—not real peace but the eye of a hurricane. The prosperity of the late 1920s in most industrial states also proved illusory.

■ Key Terms

Western Front	Empress Dowager Cixi
Faisal	Sun Yat-sen
Balfour Declaration	Yuan Shikai
Bolsheviks	Guomindang
Vladimir Lenin	mandate system
Woodrow Wilson	Margaret Sanger
League of Nations	Max Planck
Treaty of Versailles	Albert Einstein
New Economic Policy	

■ Suggested Reading

Bernadotte Schmitt and Harold C. Bedeler, *The World in the Crucible, 1914–1918* (1984), and John Keegan, *The First World War* (1999), are two engaging overviews of World War I. Imanuel Geiss, *July 1914: The Outbreak of the First World War* (1967), argues that Germany caused the conflict. Barbara Tuchman's *The Guns of August* (1962) and Alexander Solzhenitsyn's *August 1914* (1972) recount the first month of the war in detail. Keegan's *The Face of Battle* (1976) vividly describes the Battle of the Somme from the soldiers' perspective. On the technology of warfare, see William H. McNeill, *The Pursuit of Power: Technology, Armed Force, and Society* (1982), and John Ellis, *The Social History of the Machine Gun* (1975). The role of women and the home front is the subject of essays in Margaret Higonnet et al., eds., *Behind the Lines: Gender and the Two World Wars* (1987), and sections of Lynn Weiner, *From Working Girl to Working Mother* (1985). The definitive work on the flu epidemic is Alfred W. Crosby, *America's Forgotten Pandemic: The Influenza of 1918* (1989). Two famous novels about the war are Erich Maria Remarque's *All Quiet on the Western Front* (1928) and Robert Graves's *Goodbye to All That* (1929). The war in English literature is the subject of Paul Fussell, *The Great War and Modern Memory* (1975).

For the background to the Russian Revolution, read Theodore von Laue's *Why Lenin? Why Stalin?* 2d ed. (1971); but see also Richard Pipes, *The Russian Revolution* (1990), and Orlando Figes, *A People's Tragedy: The Russian Revolution, 1891–1924* (1996). The classic eyewitness account of the Revolution is John Reed's *Ten Days That Shook the World* (1919). On gender issues see Wendy Goldman, *Women, the State, and Revolution: Soviet Family Policy and Social Life, 1917–1936* (1993). The best-known novel about the Revolution and civil war is Boris Pasternak's *Doctor Zhivago* (1958).

John Maynard Keynes's *The Economic Consequences of the Peace* (1920) is a classic critique of the Paris Peace Conference. Arno Mayer's *Political Origins of the New Diplomacy, 1917–1918* (1959) analyzes the tensions and failures of great-power politics. The 1920s are discussed in Raymond Sontag's *A Broken World, 1919–1939* (1971).

The best recent book on Japan in the twentieth century is Daikichi Irokawa's *The Age of Hirohito: In Search of Modern Japan* (1995). See also Richard Storry, *A History of Modern Japan* (1982), and Tessa Morris-Suzuki, *The Technological Transformation of Japan* (1994). In the large and fast-growing literature on twentieth-century China, two general introductions are especially useful: John K. Fairbank, *The Great Chinese Revolution, 1800–1985* (1986), and Jonathan Spence, *The Search for Modern China* (1990). On the warlord and Guomindang periods, see Lucien Bianco, *Origins of the Chinese Revolution, 1915–1949* (1971).

On the war and its aftermath in the Middle East, see David Fromkin, *A Peace to End All Peace* (1989), and M. E. Yapp, *The Near East Since the First World War* (1991). Bernard Lewis, *The Emergence of Modern Turkey* (1968),

is a good introduction. On Africa in this period see A. Adu Boahen, ed., *Africa Under Colonial Domination, 1880–1935*, vol. 7 of the *UNESCO General History of Africa* (1985), and A. D. Roberts, ed., *Cambridge History of Africa*, vol. 7, *1905–1940* (1986).

The cultural transformation of Europe is captured in H. Stuart Hughes, *Consciousness and Society: The Reorientation of European Social Thought, 1890–1930* (1958). The towering intellectuals of that era are the subject of Peter Gay, *Freud: A Life for Our Time* (1988), and Abraham Pais, *Subtle Is the Lord: The Science and Life of Albert Einstein* (1982). Three books capture the enthusiastic popular response to technological innovations: David E. Nye, *Electrifying America: Social Meanings of a New Technology* (1990); Peter Fritzsche, *A Nation of Fliers: German Aviation and the Popular Imagination* (1992); and the sweeping overview by Thomas Hughes, *American Genesis: A Century of Invention and Technological Enthusiasm, 1870–1970* (1989). On the role of women in this period, see Ellen DuBois, *Woman Suffrage and Women's Rights* (1998); Sheila Rowbotham, *A Century of Women: The History of Women in Britain and the United States* (1997); and Renate Bridenthal, Claudia Koonz, and Susan Stuard, eds., *Becoming Visible: Women in European History* (1987).

The Collapse of the Old Order, 1929–1949

26

CHAPTER OUTLINE

Stalin's Revolution

The Depression

The Rise of Fascism

East Asia, 1931–1945

The Second World War

The Character of Warfare

DIVERSITY AND DOMINANCE: Women, Family Values, and the Russian Revolution

Before the First World War, the Italian futurist poets exalted violence as a noble and manly idea. Filippo Marinetti defined their creed in these words: "We want to glorify war, the world's only hygiene—militarism, deed, destroyer of anarchisms, the beautiful ideas that are death-bringing, and the subordination of women." His friend Gabriele d'Annunzio said: "If it is a crime to incite citizens to violence, I shall boast of this crime."

The war taught most survivors to abhor violence. During the 1920s, the world seemed to return to what United States president Warren Harding called "normalcy": prosperity in Europe and America, European colonialism in Asia and Africa, paternalistic U.S. domination of Latin America, and peace almost everywhere. But for a few, war and domination became a creed and a goal.

In 1929, the artificial normalcy of the 1920s began to come apart. The Great Depression caused governments to turn against one another in a desperate attempt to protect their people's livelihood. As the economic crisis spread around the world, businesses went bankrupt, prices fell, factories closed, and workers were laid off. Even wholly agricultural nations and colonies suffered as markets for their exports shriveled.

Some countries chose to solve their problems by violent means. When nations shut their doors to Japan's products, the Japanese military tried to save their country by conquering China. In Germany, the Depression reawakened resentments against the victors of the Great War; people who feared communism or blamed Jews for their troubles turned to Hitler and the Nazis, who promised to save their society by dominating others. In the Soviet Union, Stalin used energetic and murderous means to force his country into a communist version of the Industrial Revolution.

The result was war. The Second World War engulfed more lands and peoples and caused far more deaths and destruction than any previous conflict. At the end of it, much of Europe and East Asia lay in ruins, and millions of destitute refugees sought safety in other lands. The European colonial powers were either defeated or so weakened that they could no longer hold onto their empires when Asian and African peoples asserted their desire for independence.

As you read this chapter, ask yourself the following questions:

- How did the Soviet Union change under Stalin, and at what cost?

- What were the main causes of the Second World War?

- How was the war fought, and why did Japan and Germany lose?

STALIN'S REVOLUTION

After **Joseph Stalin** (1879–1953) achieved total mastery over the USSR in early 1929 (see Chapter 25), he led it through another revolution: an economic and social transformation that turned it into a great industrial and military power and intensified both admiration for and fear of communism throughout the world.

Five-Year Plans   Stalin's ambition to turn the USSR into an industrial nation was not intended initially to produce consumer goods for a mass market, much less en-

rich individuals as in Britain and the United States. Instead, his aim was to increase the power of the Communist Party domestically and the power of the Soviet Union in relation to other countries. By building up Russia's industry, Stalin was determined to prevent a repetition of the humiliating defeat Russia had suffered at the hands of Germany in 1917.

Stalin encouraged rapid industrialization through a series of **Five-Year Plans,** a system of centralized control copied from the German experience of World War I. The goal of the first five-year plan was to quintuple the output of electricity and double that of heavy industry: iron, steel, coal, and machinery. Beginning in October 1928, the Communist government created whole industries and cities from scratch, then recruited millions of peasants and trained them to work in the new factories and mines and offices. In every way except actual fighting, Stalin's Russia resembled a nation at war.

Rapid industrialization hastened environmental changes. Hydroelectric dams turned rivers into strings of reservoirs. Roads, canals, and railroad tracks cut the landscape. Forests and grassland were turned into farmland. From an environmental perspective, the outcome of the Five-Year Plans resembled the transformation that had occurred in the United States and Canada a few decades earlier.

Collectivization of Agriculture   Since the Soviet Union was still a predominantly agrarian country, the only way to pay for these massive investments, provide the labor, and feed the millions of new industrial workers was to squeeze the peasantry. Stalin therefore proceeded with the most radical social experiment conceived up to that time: the collectivization of agriculture.

Collectivization meant consolidating small private farms into vast collectives and making the farmers work together in commonly owned fields. Each collective was expected to supply the government with a fixed amount of food and distribute what was left among its members. Collectives were to become outdoor factories through the use of machinery and techniques of mass production. Collectivization was expected to bring the peasants once and for all under government control so they never again could withhold food supplies as

CHRONOLOGY

	Europe and North Africa	Asia and the Pacific
1930	**1931** Great Depression reaches Europe	**1931** Japanese forces occupy Manchuria
	1933 Hitler comes to power in Germany	
1935	**1936** Hitler invades the Rhineland	
		1937 Japanese troops invade China, conquer coastal provinces; Chiang Kai-shek flees to Sichuan
		1937–1938 Japanese troops take Nanjing
	1939 (Sept. 1) German forces invade Poland	
1940	**1940 (March–April)** German forces conquer Denmark, Norway, the Netherlands, and Belgium	
	1940 (May–June) German forces conquer France	
	1940 (June–Sept.) Battle of Britain	
	1941 (June 21) German forces invade USSR	**1941 (Dec. 7)** Japanese aircraft bomb Pearl Harbor
	1942–1943 Allies and Germany battle for control of North Africa; Soviet victory in Battle of Stalingrad (1943)	**1942 (Jan–March)** Japanese conquer Thailand, Philippines, Malaya
		1942 (June) United States Navy defeats Japan at Battle of Midway
	1943–1944 Red Army slowly pushes Wehrmacht back to Germany	
	1944 (June 6) D-day: U.S., British, and Canadian troops land in Normandy	
1945	**1945 (May 7)** Germany surrenders	**1945 (Aug. 6)** United States drops atomic bomb on Hiroshima
		1945 (Aug. 14) Japan surrenders
		1945–1949 Civil war in China
		1949 Communists defeat Guomindang; Mao proclaims People's Republic (Oct. 1)

they had done during the period of Lenin's New Economic Policy (see Chapter 25).

The government mounted a massive propaganda campaign to enlist the farmers' support. At first, all seemed to go well, but soon *kulaks*° ("fists"),

the better-off peasants, began to resist giving up all their property. When soldiers came to force them into collectives at gunpoint, the kulaks burned their own crops, smashed their own equipment, and slaughtered their own livestock. Within a few months, they slaughtered half of the Soviet Union's horses and cattle and two-thirds of its sheep and

---

kulaks (COO-lox)

goats. In retaliation, Stalin ruthlessly ordered the "liquidation of kulaks as a class" and incited the poor peasants to attack their wealthier neighbors. Over 8 million kulaks were arrested. Many were executed. The rest were sent to slave labor camps, where most starved to death.

The peasants who were left had been the least successful before collectivization and proved to be the least competent after. Many were sent to work in factories. The rest were forbidden to leave their farms. With half of their draft animals gone, they could not plant or harvest enough to meet the swelling demands of the cities. Yet government agents took whatever they could find, leaving little or nothing for the farmers themselves. After bad harvests in 1933 and 1934, a famine swept through the countryside, killing some 5 million people, about one in every twenty farmers.

Stalin's second Five-Year Plan, designed to run from 1933 to 1937, was originally intended to increase the output of consumer goods. But when the Nazis took over Germany in 1933 (see below), Stalin changed the plan to emphasize heavy industries that could produce armaments. Between 1927 and 1937, the Soviet output of metals and machines increased fourteen-fold while consumer goods became scarce and food was rationed. After a decade of Stalinism, the Soviet people were more poorly clothed, fed, and housed than they had been during the years of the New Economic Policy.

Terror and Opportunities

The 1930s brought both terror and new opportunities to the Soviet people. The forced pace of industrialization, the collectivization of agriculture, and the uprooting of millions of people could be accomplished only under duress. To prevent any possible resistance or rebellion, the NKVD, Stalin's secret police force, created a climate of suspicion and fear. The terror that pervaded the country was a reflection of Stalin's own paranoia, for he distrusted everyone and feared for his life.

First "Old Bolsheviks" and high officials were put on trial; then the terror spread steadily downward. The government regularly made demands on people that they could not meet, so everyone was guilty of breaking some regulation. People from all walks of life were arrested—sometimes on a mere suspicion or because of a false accusation by a jealous coworker or neighbor, sometimes for expressing a doubt or working too hard or not hard enough, sometimes for being related to someone previously arrested, sometimes for no reason at all. Millions of people were sentenced without a trial. At the height of the terror, some 8 million were sent to *gulags*° (labor camps), where perhaps a million died each year of exposure or malnutrition. To its victims, the terror seemed capricious and random.

Yet Stalin's regime received the support of many Soviet citizens. Suddenly, with so many people gone and new industries and cities being built everywhere, there were opportunities for those who remained, especially the poor and the young. Women entered careers and jobs previously closed to them, becoming steelworkers, physicians, and office managers; but they retained their household and child-rearing duties, receiving little help from men (see Diversity and Dominance: Women, Family Values, and the Russian Revolution). People who moved to the cities, worked enthusiastically, and asked no questions could hope to rise into the upper ranks of the Communist Party, the military, the government, or the professions, where the privileges and rewards were many.

Stalin's brutal methods helped the Soviet Union industrialize faster than any country had ever done. By the late 1930s, the USSR was the world's third largest industrial power, after the United States and Germany. To foreign observers, it seemed to be booming with construction projects, production increases, and labor shortages. Even anti-Communist observers admitted that only a planned economy subject to strict government control could avoid the Depression. To millions of Soviet citizens who took pride in the new strength of their country, and to many foreigners who contrasted conditions in the Soviet Union with the unemployment and despair in the West, Stalin's achievement seemed worth any price.

---

gulag (GOO-log)

THE DEPRESSION

O n October 24, 1929—"Black Thursday"—the New York stock market went into a dive. Within days, stocks lost half their value, and their value continued to fall for three years. Thousands of banks and businesses collapsed. Millions of workers lost their jobs. The stock market crash started the deepest and most widespread depression in history.

Economic Crisis

As consumers reduced their purchases, businesses cut production. General Motors, for example, saw its sales drop by half between 1929 and 1931. Companies laid off thousands of workers, throwing them onto public charity. Business and government agencies replaced their women workers with men, arguing that men had to support their families, whereas women worked only for "pin money." Jobless men deserted their families. As farm prices fell, small farmers went bankrupt and lost their land. By mid-1932, the American economy had fallen by half, and 25 percent of the work force was unemployed. Government spending on welfare and public works was unable to restore prosperity. Many observers thought the free-enterprise system would be replaced by bread lines, soup kitchens, men selling apples on street corners, and hoboes riding freight trains.

Frightened by the stock market collapse, the New York banks called in their loans to Germany and Austria. Without American money, Germany and Austria stopped paying reparations to France and Britain, which then could not repay their war loans to America. By 1931, the Depression had spread to Europe. Governments canceled both reparations payments and war loans, but it was too late to save the world economy.

In 1930, the U.S. government, hoping to protect domestic industries from foreign competition, imposed the highest import duty in American history. In retaliation, other countries raised their tariffs. As a result, global industrial production declined by 36 percent between 1929 and 1932, while world trade dropped by a breathtaking 62 percent.

Depression in Industrial Nations

This massive economic upheaval had profound political repercussions. In the United States, Franklin D. Roosevelt was elected president in 1932 on a "New Deal" platform of government programs to stimulate and revitalize the economy. British and French governments also intervened in their economies and escaped the worst of the Depression by making their colonial empires purchase their products. In the Soviet Union, the five-year plans continued to provide jobs and economic growth.

Nations that relied on exports to pay for imported food and fuel, in particular Japan and Germany, suffered much more. In Germany, unemployment reached 6 million by 1932, twice as high as in Britain. Half the German population lived in poverty. In Japan, the burden of the Depression fell on the farmers and fishermen, who saw their incomes drop sharply. Some, in desperation, revived the ancient practice of selling their daughters. As economic grievances worsened, radical politicians took over the governments in Germany and Japan, manipulated the economies, and turned their nations' military might to acquiring empires large enough to support a self-sufficient economy.

Depression in Nonindustrial Regions

The Depression affected Asia, Africa, and Latin America in different ways. A wall of new import duties protected India's infant industries from foreign competition; living standards stagnated but did not drop. The Depression added little to China's problems, except in coastal regions.

Countries that depended on exports were hard hit by the Depression. When automobile production dropped by half in the United States and Europe, so did imports of rubber, devastating the economies of Southeast Asia. When the Depression hit, American tourists vanished from Cuba's beaches and bars, and with them went Cuba's prosperity. The industrialization of Argentina and Brazil was set back a decade or more by the loss of their export markets. In response, military officers

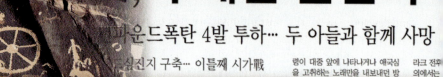

DIVERSITY AND DOMINANCE

WOMEN, FAMILY VALUES, AND THE RUSSIAN REVOLUTION

The Bolsheviks were of two minds on the subject of women. Following in the footsteps of Marx, Engels, and other revolutionaries, they were opposed to bourgeois morality and to the oppression of women, especially working-class women, under capitalism, with its attendant evils of prostitution, sexual abuse, and the division of labor. But what to put in its place?

Alexandra Kollontai was the most outspoken of the Bolsheviks on the subject of women's rights and the equality of the sexes. Before and during the Russian Revolution, she advocated the liberation of women, the replacement of housework by communal kitchens and laundries, and divorce on demand. Under social-ism, love, sex, and marriage would be entirely equal, reciprocal, and free of economic obligations. Child-bearing would be encouraged, but children would be raised communally, rather than individually by their fathers and mothers: "The worker mother . . . must re-member that there are henceforth only our children, those of the communist state, the common posses-sion of all workers."

In a lecture she gave at Sverdlov University in 1921, Kollontai declared:

. . . it is important to preserve not only the interests of the woman but also the life of the child, and this is to be done by giving the woman the opportunity to combine labour and maternity. Soviet power tries to create a situation where a woman does not have to cling to a man she has learned to loathe only be-cause she has nowhere else to go with her children, and where a woman alone does not have to fear her life and the life of her child. In the labour republic it is not the philanthropists with their humiliating char-ity but the workers and peasants, fellow-creators of the new society, who hasten to help the working woman and strive to lighten the burden of mother-hood. The woman who bears the trials and tribulations of reconstructing the economy on an equal footing with the man, and who participated in the civil war, has a right to demand that in this most important hour of her life, at the moment when she presents society with a new member, the labour republic, the collective, should take upon itself the job of caring for the future of the new citizen. . . .

I would like to say a few words about a question which is closely connected with the problem of mater-nity—the question of abortion, and Soviet Russia's at-titude toward it. On 20 November 1920 the labour republic issued a law abolishing the penalties that had been attached to abortion. What is the reason behind this new attitude? Russia after all suffers not from an overproduction of living labour but rather from a lack of it. Russia is thinly, not densely populated. Every unit of labour power is precious. Why then have we de-clared abortion to be no longer a criminal offence? Hypocrisy and bigotry are alien to proletarian politics. Abortion is a problem connected with the problem of maternity, and likewise derives from the insecure posi-tion of women (we are not speaking here of the bour-geois class, where abortion has other reasons—the reluctance to "divide" an inheritance, to suffer the slight-est discomfort, to spoil one's figure or miss a few months of the season, etc.).

Abortion exists and flourishes everywhere, and no laws or punitive measures have succeeded in rooting it out. A way round the law is always found. But "secret help" only cripples women; they become a burden on the labour government, and the size of the labour force is reduced. Abortion, when carried out under proper medical conditions, is less harmful and danger-ous, and the woman can get back to work quicker. So-viet power realizes that the need for abortion will only disappear on the one hand when Russia has a broad

624

and developed network of institutions protecting motherhood and providing social education, and on the other hand when women understand that *childbirth is a social obligation;* Soviet power has therefore allowed abortion to be performed openly and in clinical conditions.

Besides the large-scale development of motherhood protection, the task of labour Russia is to strengthen in women the healthy instinct of motherhood, to make motherhood and labour for the collective compatible and thus do away with the need for abortion. This is the approach of the labour republic to the question of abortion, which still faces women in the bourgeois countries in all its magnitude. In these countries women are exhausted by the dual burden of hired labour for capital and motherhood. In Soviet Russia the working woman and peasant woman are helping the Communist Party to build a new society and to undermine the old way of life that has enslaved women. As soon as woman is viewed as being essentially a labour unit, the key to the solution of the complex question of maternity can be found. In bourgeois society, where housework complements the system of capitalist economy and private property creates a stable basis for the isolated form of the family, there is no way out for the working woman. The emancipation of women can only be completed when a fundamental transformation of living is effected; and life-styles will change only with the fundamental transformation of all production and the establishment of a communist economy. The revolution in everyday life is unfolding before our very eyes, and in this process the liberation of women is being introduced in practice.

Fifteen years later Joseph Stalin reversed the Soviet policy on abortion.

The published draft of the law prohibiting abortion and providing material assistance to mothers has provoked a lively reaction throughout the country. It is being heatedly discussed by tens of millions of people and there is no doubt that it will serve as a further strengthening of the Soviet family. Parents' responsibility for the education of their children will be increased and a blow will be dealt at the lighthearted, negligent attitude toward marriage.

When we speak of strengthening the Soviet family, we are speaking precisely of the struggle against the survivals of a bourgeois attitude towards marriage, women, and children. So-called "free love" and all disorderly sex life are bourgeois through and through, and have nothing to do with either socialist principles or the ethics and standards of conduct of the Soviet citizens. Socialist doctrine shows this, and it is proved by life itself.

The elite of our country, the best of the Soviet youth, are as a rule also excellent family men who dearly love their children. And vice versa: the man who does not take marriage seriously, and abandons his children to the whims of fate, is usually also a bad worker and a poor member of society.

Fatherhood and motherhood have long been virtues in this country. This can be seen at first glance, without searching enquiry. Go through the parks and streets of Moscow or of any other town in the Soviet Union on a holiday, and you will see not a few young men walking with pink-cheeked, well-fed babies in their arms. . . .

It is impossible even to compare the present state of the family with that which obtained before the Soviet regime—so great has been the improvement towards greater stability and, above all, greater humanity and goodness. The single fact that millions of women have become economically independent and are no longer at the mercy of men's whims, speaks volumes. Compare, for instance, the modern woman collective farmer who sometimes earns more than her husband, with the pre-revolutionary peasant women who completely depended on her husband and was a slave in the household. Has not this fundamentally changed family relations, has it not rationalized and strengthened the family? The very motives for setting up a family, for getting married, have changed for the better, have been cleansed of atavistic and barbaric elements. Marriage has ceased to be matter of sell-and-buy. Nowadays a girl from a collective farm is not given away (or should we say "sold away"?) by her father, for now she is her own mistress, and no one can give her away. She will marry the man she loves. . . .

We alone have all the conditions under which a working woman can fulfill her duties as a citizen and as a mother responsible for the birth and early upbringing of her children.

A woman without children merits our pity, for she does not know the full joy of life. Our Soviet women, full-blooded citizens of the freest country in the world, have been given the bliss of motherhood. We must safeguard the family and raise and rear healthy Soviet heroes!

1. How does Kollontai expect women to be both workers and mothers without depending on a man? How would Soviet society make this possible?

2. Why does Alexandra Kollontai advocate the legalization of abortion in Soviet Russia? Does she view abortion as a permanent right or as a temporary necessity?

3. Why does Stalin characterize a "lighthearted, negligent attitude toward marriage" and "all disorderly sex life" as "bourgeois through and through"?

4. How does Stalin's image of the Soviet family differ from Kollontai's? Are his views a variation of her views, or the opposite?

5. Do the views of Kollontai and Stalin on the role of women represent a diversity of opinions within the Communist Party, or the dominance of one view over others?

Source: First selection from *Selected Writings of Alexandra Kollontai,* translated by Alix Holt (Lawrence Hill Books, 1978). Reprinted with permission. Second selection from Joseph Stalin, *Law on the Abolition of Legal Abortion* (1936).

seized power in several Latin American countries, consciously imitating dictatorships emerging in Europe.

Southern and Central Africa recovered from the Depression quickly, because falling prices made their gold and other minerals more valuable. But this mining boom benefited only a small number of mine owners and investors. For Africans, it was at best a mixed blessing, for mining offered jobs and cash wages to men, while women had to manage without them in the villages.

THE RISE OF FASCISM

The Depression sharpened the polarization of European society that had been under way for decades. Many underpaid or unemployed workers saw in the seeming collapse of the capitalist economy an opportunity as well as temporary suffering. They urged the establishment of a socialist society through the ballot box and strikes instead of the violent revolution that had torn Russia apart.

Frightened investors and factory owners, along with conservative elements in society such as the church and the military, feared the consequences of this political shift to the left. In the democracies of western Europe and North America, middle-income voters kept politics in balance.

But in some societies, the war and the Depression left people vulnerable to the appeals of ultranationalist politicians who became adept at using propaganda to appeal to people's fears. They promised to bring back full employment, stop the spread of communism, and achieve the territorial conquests that World War I had denied them.

Mussolini's Italy

The first country to seek radical answers was Italy. World War I, which had never been popular, left thousands of veterans who found neither pride in their victory nor jobs in the postwar economy. Unemployed veterans and violent youths banded together into *fasci di combattimento* (fighting units) to demand action and intimidate politicians. When socialist unions threatened to strike, factory and property owners hired gangs of these *fascisti* to defend them.

Benito Mussolini (1883–1945), a spellbinding orator, quickly became the leader of the **Fascist Party,** which glorified warfare and the Italian nation. By 1921, the party had 300,000 members, many of whom used violent methods to repress strikes, intimidate voters, and seize municipal governments. A year later, when the Fascists failed to win an election, Mussolini threatened to march on Rome if he was not appointed prime minister. The government gave in.

Mussolini proceeded to install Fascist Party members in all government jobs, crush all opposition parties, and jail anyone who criticized him. The party took over the press, public education, and youth activities and gave employers control over their workers. The Fascists lowered living standards but reduced unemployment and provided social security and public services. On the whole, they proved to be neither ruthless radicals nor competent administrators.

What Mussolini and the fascist movement really excelled at was publicity: bombastic speeches, spectacular parades, news bulletins full of praise for *Il Duce*° ("the leader"), and signs everywhere proclaiming "Il Duce is always right!" Mussolini's genius was to apply the techniques of modern mass communications and advertisement to political life. Billboards, movie footage, and radio news bulletins galvanized the masses in ways never before seen in peacetime. Although his rhetoric was filled with words like *war, violence,* and *struggle,* his foreign policy was cautious. But his techniques of whipping up public enthusiasm were not lost on other radicals. By the 1930s, fascist movements had appeared in most European countries, as well as in Latin America, China, and Japan.

Hitler the Orator   A masterful public speaker, Adolf Hitler often captivated mass audiences at Nazi Party rallies. (Roger-Viollet/Getty Images)

Hitler's Germany

Like Mussolini, **Adolf Hitler** (1889–1945) had served in World War I and looked back fondly on the clear lines of authority and the camaraderie he had experienced in battle. After the war, he too recreated that experience in a paramilitary group, the National Socialist German Workers' Party— **Nazis** for short. Hitler used his gifts as an orator to appeal to Germans disappointed at Germany's humiliation after the war and the hyperinflation of 1923. In 1924, he too led an uprising, but the attempted seizure of Munich was a failure. Germany was not yet ready to follow Italy's path.

The Depression changed that. While serving a jail sentence for the coup attempt, Hitler wrote *Mein Kampf*° (*My Struggle*), but when it was published in 1925, no one took the book or its author's extreme nationalist, racist, and anti-Jewish ideas seriously. Hitler believed that Germany should in-

Il Duce (eel DOO-chay)   *Mein Kampf* (mine compf)

corporate all German-speaking people, even those who lived in neighboring countries. He distinguished among a "master race" of Aryans (he meant Germans, Scandinavians, and Britons), a degenerate "Alpine" race of French and Italians, and an inferior race of Russian and eastern European Slavs, who, he believed, were fit only to be slaves of the master race. He reserved his most intense hatred for Jews, on whom he blamed every disaster that had befallen Germany, especially the defeat of 1918. He glorified violence, which would enable the "master race" to defeat and subjugate all others.

When the Depression hit, the Nazis gained supporters among the unemployed who believed Nazi promises of jobs for all and among property owners frightened by the growing popularity of Communists. In March 1933, as leader of the largest party in Germany, Hitler became chancellor.

Once in office, he quickly assumed dictatorial power, just as Mussolini had done. He expelled the Communist Party from the Reichstag° (parliament), intimidated it to give him dictatorial powers, and then put Nazis in charge of all government agencies, educational institutions, and professional organizations. He banned all other political parties and threw their leaders into concentration camps. The Nazis deprived Jews of their citizenship and civil rights, prohibited them from marrying "Aryans," ousted them from the professions, and confiscated their property. In August 1934, Hitler proclaimed himself *Führer*° ("leader") and called Germany the "Third Reich" (empire)—the third after the Holy Roman Empire and the German Empire of 1871 to 1918.

The Nazis' economic and social policies were spectacularly effective. The government undertook massive public works projects. Businesses got contracts to manufacture weapons for the armed forces. Women, who had entered the work force during and after World War I, were urged to return to *"Kinder, Kirche, Küche"* (children, church, kitchen), releasing jobs for men. By 1936, business was booming, unemployment was at its lowest level since the 1920s, and living standards were rising. Hitler's popularity soared because most Germans believed their economic well-being outweighed the loss of liberty.

The Road to War, 1933–1939

Hitler sought not prosperity or popularity, but conquest. As soon as he came to office, he began to build up the armed forces with conquest in mind. Meanwhile, he tested the reactions of the other powers through a series of surprise moves followed by protestations of peaceful intent.

In 1933, Hitler withdrew Germany from the League of Nations. France and Britain hesitated to retaliate by blockading or invading Germany. Two years later, he announced that Germany was going to introduce conscription, build up its army, and create an air force—in violation of the Versailles treaty. Instead of protesting, Britain signed a naval agreement with Germany. The message was clear: neither Britain nor France was willing to risk war by standing up to Germany. The United States, absorbed in its own domestic economic problems, had reverted to isolationism.

Emboldened by the weakness of the democracies, Italy in 1935 invaded Ethiopia, one of only two independent states in Africa and a member of the League of Nations. The League and the democracies protested but refused to close the Suez Canal to Italian ships or impose an oil embargo. The following year, when Hitler sent troops into the Rhineland on the borders of France and Belgium, the other powers merely protested.

By 1938, Hitler decided his rearmament plans were far enough advanced that he could escalate his demands. In March, Germany invaded and soon annexed Austria, with little protest from its German-speaking citizens. Then came the turn of Czechoslovakia. Hitler demanded autonomy for its German-speaking borderlands, then their annexation. At the Munich Conference of September 1938, the leaders of France, Britain, and Italy gave Hitler everything he wanted to keep him from starting a war. Once again, Hitler learned that aggression paid off and that the democracies always gave in.

The democracies' policy of "appeasement" ran counter to the European balance-of-power tradition for three reasons. The first was the deep-seated fear of war among all people who had lived through World War I. The second was fear of communism. The conservative politicians who ruled France and Britain were more afraid of Stalin than of Hitler, for Hitler claimed to respect Christianity and private property. Rather than revive the pre–World War I alliance of Britain, France, and Russia, they sold out the Czechs. The third cause was the very novelty of fascist tactics. Britain's prime minister, Neville Chamberlain, assumed that political leaders (other than the Bolsheviks) were honorable men and that an agreement was as valid as a business contract. Thus, when Hitler said he

---

Reichstag (RIKES-tog)   **Führer** (FEW-rer)

had "no further territorial demands," Chamberlain believed him.

After Munich, it was too late to stop Hitler, short of war. Germany and Italy were now united in an alliance called the Axis. In March 1939, Germany invaded what was left of Czechoslovakia. Belatedly realizing that Hitler could not be trusted, France and Britain sought Soviet help. Stalin, however, distrusted the "capitalists" as much as they distrusted him. Hitler, meanwhile, offered to divide Poland between Germany and the Soviet Union. On August 23, Stalin accepted. The Nazi-Soviet Pact freed Hitler from the fear of a two-front war and gave Stalin two more years of peace to build up his armies. One week later, on September 1, 1939, German forces swept into Poland across the Eastern Front. The war was on.

East Asia, 1931–1945

When the Depression ruined Japan's export trade, ultranationalists, including young army officers, resented their country's dependence on foreign trade. If only Japan had a colonial empire, they thought, it would not be beholden to the rest of the world. But Europeans and Americans had already taken most potential colonies in Asia. Japan had only Korea, Taiwan, and a railroad in Manchuria. Japanese nationalists saw China, with its vast population and resources, as the solution to their country's problems.

The Manchurian Incident of 1931

Meanwhile, the Guomindang° was becoming stronger in China and preparing to challenge the Japanese presence in Manchuria, a province rich in coal and iron ore. Junior officers in the Japanese army guarding the South Manchurian Railway, frustrated by the caution of their superiors, determined to take action. In September 1931, an explosion on a railroad track, probably staged, gave them an excuse to conquer the entire province. In Tokyo, weak civilian ministers acquiesced to the attack to avoid losing face

and shortly recognized the "independence" of Manchuria under the name *Manchukuo*°.

The U.S. government condemned the Japanese conquest. The League of Nations refused to recognize Manchukuo and urged the Japanese to remove their troops from China. Persuaded that the Western powers would not fight, Japan resigned from the League.

During the next few years, the Japanese built railways and heavy industries in Manchuria and northeastern China and sped up their rearmament. The government grew more authoritarian, jailing thousands of dissidents. On several occasions, superpatriotic junior officers who mutinied or assassinated leading political figures received mild punishments, and generals and admirals sympathetic to their views replaced more moderate civilian politicians.

The Chinese Communists and the Long March

Until the Japanese seized Manchuria, the Chinese government seemed to be consolidating its power and creating the conditions for a national recovery. The main challenge to the government of **Chiang Kai-shek**° came from the Chinese Communists, who were organizing industrial workers and who worked in alliance with the Nationalists until 1927, when Chiang Kai-shek arrested and executed Communists and labor leaders alike.

The few Communists who escaped the mass arrests fled to the remote mountains of Jiangxi°, in southeastern China. Among them was **Mao Zedong**° (1893–1976), a farmer's son who had left home to study philosophy. In the early 1920s, Mao discovered the works of Karl Marx, joined the Communist Party, and soon became one of its leaders. In Jiangxi, Mao began studying conditions among the peasants, in whom Communists had previously shown no interest. He planned to redistribute land from the wealthier to the poorer peasants, thereby gaining adherents for the coming struggle with the Guomindang army.

Mao's reliance on the peasantry was a radical departure from Marxist-Leninist ideology, which

---

Guomindang (gwo-min-dong)

Manchukuo (man-CHEW-coo-oh)   **Chiang Kai-shek** (chang kie-shek)   **Jiangxi** (jang-she)   **Mao Zedong** (ma-oh zay-dong)

stressed the backwardness of the peasants and pinned its hopes on industrial workers. Mao was also an advocate of women's equality. Before 1927, the Communists had organized the women who worked in Shanghai's textile mills, the most exploited of all Chinese workers. Later, in their mountain stronghold in Jiangxi, they organized women farmers, allowed divorce, and banned arranged marriages and footbinding.

The Guomindang army pursued the Communists into the mountains, building small forts throughout the countryside. Rather than risk direct confrontations, Mao responded with guerrilla warfare. Government troops often mistreated civilians, but Mao insisted that his soldiers help the peasants, pay a fair price for food and supplies, and treat women with respect. In spite of their good relations with the peasants of Jiangxi, the Communists decided to break out of the southern mountains and trek to Shaanxi°, an even more remote province in northwestern China. The so-called **Long March** took them 6,000 miles (nearly 9,700 kilometers) in one year, 17 miles (27 kilometers) a day over desolate mountains and through swamps and deserts, pursued by the army and bombed by Chiang's aircraft. Of the 100,000 Communists who left Jiangxi in October 1934, only 4,000 reached Shaanxi a year later.

The Sino-Japanese War, 1937–1945

On July 7, 1937, Japanese troops attacked Chinese forces near Beijing. As in 1931, the junior officers who ordered the attack quickly obtained the support of their commanders and then, reluctantly, of the government. By November, Japanese troops had seized Beijing, Tianjin, Shanghai, and other coastal cities, and the Japanese navy blockaded the entire coast of China.

Once again, the United States and the League of Nations denounced the Japanese atrocities. Yet the Western powers were too preoccupied with events in Europe and with their own economic problems to risk a military confrontation in Asia. When the Japanese sank a U.S. gunboat and shelled a British ship on the Yangzi River, the U.S. and

Shaanxi (SHAWN-she)

British governments responded only with righteous indignation and pious resolutions.

The large Chinese armies were poorly led and armed and lost every battle. Within a year, Japan controlled the coastal provinces of China and the lower Yangzi and Yellow River Valleys, China's richest and most populated regions, but the Chinese people continued to resist, either in the army or, increasingly, with the Communist guerrilla forces. Japan's periodic attempts to turn the tide by conquering one more piece of China only pushed Japan deeper into the quagmire.

Warfare between Chinese and Japanese was incredibly violent. In the winter of 1937–1938, Japanese troops took Nanjing, raped 20,000 women, killed 200,000 prisoners and civilians, and looted and burned the city. To slow them down, Chiang ordered the Yellow River dikes blasted open, causing a flood that destroyed 4,000 villages, killed 890,000 people, and made 12.5 million homeless. Two years later, when the Communists ordered a massive offensive, the Japanese retaliated with a "kill all, burn all, loot all" campaign, destroying hundreds of villages down to the last person, building, and farm animal.

The Chinese government, led by Chiang Kai-shek, escaped to the mountains of Sichuan in the center of the country. There he built up a huge army, both to fight Japan and to prepare for a future confrontation with the Communists. The army drafted over 3 million men, even though it had only a million rifles and could not provide food or clothing for all its soldiers. The Guomindang raised farmers' taxes, even when famine forced farmers to eat the bark of trees. Such taxes were not enough to support both a large army and the thousands of government officials and hangers-on who had fled to Sichuan. To avoid taxing its wealthy supporters, the government printed money, causing inflation, hoarding, and corruption.

From his capital of Yan'an in Shaanxi province, Mao also built up his army and formed a government. Unlike the Guomindang, the Communists listened to the grievances of the peasants, especially the poor, to whom they distributed land confiscated from wealthy landowners. Because they could present themselves as the only group in China that was serious about fighting the Japanese, the Communists obtained support and intelligence from farmers in Japanese-occupied territory.

THE SECOND WORLD WAR

The Second World War was much bigger and deadlier than the First in every way. It was fought around the world, from Norway to New Guinea, from Hawaii to Egypt, and on every ocean. It was a total war that showed how effectively industry, science, and nationalism could be channeled into mass destruction.

The War of Movement

Defensive maneuvers had dominated in World War I. In World War II, motorized weapons gave back the advantage to the offensive. Opposing forces moved fast, their victories hinging as much on the aggressive spirit of their commanders and the military intelligence they obtained as on numbers of troops or firepower.

The Wehrmacht°, or German armed forces, was the first to learn this lesson. It not only had tanks, trucks, and fighter planes but also had perfected their combined use in a tactic called *blitzkrieg*° (lightning war): fighter planes scattered enemy troops and disrupted communications, and tanks punctured the enemy's defenses and then, with the help of the infantry, encircled and captured enemy troops. At sea, the navies of both Japan and the United States had developed aircraft carriers that could launch planes against targets hundreds of miles away.

The very size and mobility of the opposing forces made the fighting far different from any the world had ever seen. Countries were conquered in a matter of days or weeks. The belligerents mobilized the economies of entire continents, squeezing them for every possible resource. They tried not only to defeat their enemies' armed forces but—by means of blockades, submarine attacks on shipping, and bombing raids on industrial areas—to damage the economies that supported those armed forces. They thought of civilians not as innocent bystanders but as legitimate targets and, later, as vermin to be exterminated.

War in Europe and North Africa

It took less than a month for the Wehrmacht to conquer Poland. Britain and France declared war on Germany but took no military action. Meanwhile, the Soviet Union invaded eastern Poland and the Baltic republics of Lithuania, Latvia, and Estonia. Although the Poles fought bravely, the Polish infantry and cavalry were no match for German or Russian tanks. During the winter of 1939–1940, Germany and the Western democracies faced each other in what soldiers called a "phony war" and watched as the Soviet Union attacked Finland, which resisted for many months.

In April 1940, Hitler went on the offensive again, conquering Denmark, Norway, the Netherlands, and Belgium in less than two months. In May, he attacked France. Although the French army had as many soldiers, tanks, and aircraft as the Wehrmacht, its morale was low, and it quickly collapsed. By the end of June, Hitler was master of all of Europe between Russia and Spain.

Germany still had to face one enemy: Britain. The British had no army to speak of, but they had other assets: the English Channel, the Royal Navy and Air Force, and a tough new prime minister, Winston Churchill. The Germans knew they could invade Britain only by gaining control of the airspace over the Channel, so they launched a massive air attack—the Battle of Britain—lasting from June through September. They failed, however, because the Royal Air Force had better fighters and used radar and code breaking to detect approaching German planes.

Frustrated, Hitler turned his attention eastward against the Soviet Union. Within five months, the Wehrmacht conquered the Baltic states, Ukraine, and half of European Russia; captured a million prisoners of war; and stood at the very gates of Moscow and Leningrad (now St. Petersburg). The USSR seemed on the verge of collapse when suddenly the weather turned cold, machines froze, and the fighting came to a halt. Like Napoleon, Hitler had ignored the environment of Russia at his peril.

The next spring, the Wehrmacht renewed its offensive. It surrounded Leningrad in a siege that was to cost a million lives. Leaving Moscow aside, it turned toward the Caucasus and its oil wells. In

Wehrmacht (VAIR-mokt)   *blitzkrieg* (BLITS-creeg)

German Dive-Bomber over Eastern Europe   In this painting, a German ME-100 fighter plane attacks a Soviet troop convoy on the Eastern Front.   (akg-images)

August, the Germans attacked **Stalingrad** (now Volgograd), the key to the Volga River and the supply of oil. For months, German and Soviet soldiers fought over every street and every house. When winter came, the Red Army counterattacked and encircled the city. In February 1943, the remnants of the German army in Stalingrad surrendered. Hitler had lost his greatest gamble (see Map 26.1).

From Europe, the war spread to Africa. During 1941, British forces conquered Italian East Africa and invaded Libya as well. The Italian rout in North Africa brought the Germans to their rescue. During 1942, the German army and the forces of the British Empire seesawed back and forth across the deserts of Libya and Egypt. Because the British could decode German messages and had more weapons and supplies, they were finally able to expel the Germans from Africa in May 1943.

War in Asia and the Pacific

The war presented Japan with the opportunity to take over European colonies in Southeast Asia, with their abundant oil, rubber, and other strategic materials. After Japanese forces occupied French Indochina in September 1940, the United States and Britain cut off shipments of steel, scrap iron, oil, and other products that Japan

Map 26.1   World War II in Europe and North Africa
In a series of quick and decisive campaigns from September 1939 to December 1941, German forces overran much of Europe and North Africa. There followed three years of bitter fighting as the Allies slowly pushed the Germans back. This map shows the maximum extent of Germany's conquests and alliances, as well as the key battles and the front lines at various times.

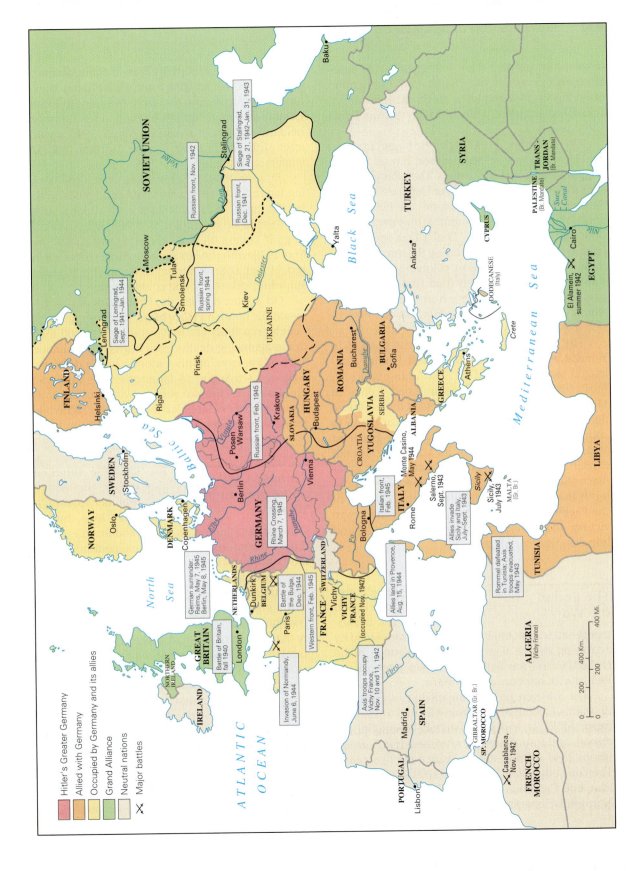

Hitler's Greater Germany
Allied with Germany
Occupied by Germany and its allies
Grand Alliance
Neutral nations
✕ **Major battles**

SOVIET UNION

Russian front, Nov. 1942

Siege of Stalingrad, Aug. 21, 1942–Jan. 31, 1943

Stalingrad

Russian front, Dec. 1941

Moscow

Tula

Smolensk

Russian front, spring 1944

Siege of Leningrad, Sept. 1941–Jan. 1944

Leningrad

Volga

Don

Dnieper

Baku

Yalta

Black Sea

TURKEY

SYRIA

TRANS-JORDAN (Br. Mandate)

PALESTINE (Br. Mandate)

Suez Canal

Nile

Cairo ✕ EGYPT

El Alamein, summer 1942

CYPRUS

Ankara

Mediterranean Sea

Kiev

UKRAINE

Pinsk

Bucharest

ROMANIA

BULGARIA

Sofia

Danube

GREECE

Athens

DODECANESE (Italy)

Crete

FINLAND

Helsinki

Riga

Baltic Sea

Warsaw

Posen

Kraków

Russian front, Feb. 1945

HUNGARY

SLOVAKIA

Budapest

Vienna

SERBIA

YUGOSLAVIA

CROATIA

ALBANIA

Monte Casino, May 1944 ✕

Italian front, Feb. 1945

ITALY

Rome

Salerno, Sept. 1943

Allies invade Sicily and Italy, July–Sept. 1943

Sicily ✕

Sicily, July 1943 ✕

MALTA (Gr. Br.)

LIBYA

SWEDEN

Stockholm

NORWAY

Oslo

DENMARK

Copenhagen

Elbe

Berlin

GERMANY

Rhine Crossing, March 7, 1945

Danube

Po

Bologna

German surrender: Reims, May 7, 1945 Berlin, May 8, 1945

NETHERLANDS

Dunkirk ✕

BELGIUM ✕

Battle of the Bulge, Dec. 1944

Paris ✕

Rhine

Western front, Feb. 1945

FRANCE

SWITZERLAND

Vichy

VICHY FRANCE

Allies land in Provence, Aug. 15, 1944

TUNISIA

Rommel defeated in Tunisia; Axis troops evacuated, May 1943

North Sea

GREAT BRITAIN

London

Battle of Britain, fall 1940

NORTHERN IRELAND

IRELAND

ATLANTIC OCEAN

Axis troops occupy Vichy France, Nov. 10 and 11, 1942

Invasion of Normandy, June 6, 1944

VICHY FRANCE (occupied Nov. 1942)

Ebro

SPAIN

Madrid

PORTUGAL

Lisbon

GIBRALTAR (Gr. Br.)

SP. MOROCCO

Casablanca, Nov. 1942 ✕

FRENCH MOROCCO

ALGERIA (Vichy France)

0   200   400 Km.

0   200   400 Mi.

desperately needed. This left Japan with three alternatives: accept the shame and humiliation of giving up its conquests, as the Americans insisted; face economic ruin; or widen the war. Japan chose war.

On December 7, 1941, Japanese planes bombed the U.S. naval base at **Pearl Harbor,** Hawaii, sinking or damaging scores of warships. Then, between December 1941 and March 1942, the Japanese bombed Singapore and occupied Thailand, the Philippines, and Malaya. Within a few months, they occupied all of Southeast Asia and the Dutch East Indies. The Japanese claimed to be liberating the inhabitants of these lands from European colonialism. But they soon began to confiscate food and raw materials and demand heavy labor from the inhabitants, whom they treated with contempt. Those who protested were brutally punished.

The entry of the United States into the war, in alliance with Britain and the Soviet Union, challenged Japan's dream of an East Asian empire. In April 1942, American planes bombed Tokyo. In May, the United States Navy defeated a Japanese fleet in the Coral Sea, ending Japanese plans to conquer Australia. A month later, at the **Battle of Midway,** Japan lost four of its six largest aircraft carriers. Japan did not have enough industry to replace them, for its war production was only one-tenth that of the United States. In the vastness of the Pacific Ocean, aircraft carriers held the key to victory, and without them, Japan faced a long and hopeless war (see Map 26.2).

The End of the War

Its new American ally also helped the Soviet Union capitalize on the advantage it had won in the Battle of Stalingrad. Aided by a growing stream of supplies from factories in the United States, the Red Army began pushing the Wehrmacht back toward Germany.

The Western powers, meanwhile, staged two invasions of Europe. Beginning in July 1943, they captured Sicily and invaded Italy. Mussolini resigned, and Italy signed an armistice, but German troops held off the Allied advance for two years. Then on D-day (June 6, 1944), 156,000 British, American, and Canadian troops landed on the coast of Normandy in western France. Within a week, the

Allies had more troops in France than Germany did. To meet this growing force, Hitler had to transfer part of the Wehrmacht from the Eastern Front. Despite advancing armies on three sides, Germany held out for almost a year. On May 7, 1945, a week after Hitler committed suicide, German military leaders surrendered.

By June 1944, U.S. bombers were also attacking Japan from newly captured island bases in the Pacific, and U.S. submarines were sinking larger numbers of Japanese merchant ships, gradually cutting off Japan's oil and other raw materials. After May 1945, with the Japanese air force grounded for lack of fuel, U.S. planes began destroying Japanese shipping, industries, and cities at will.

On August 6, 1945, the United States dropped an atomic bomb on **Hiroshima,** killing some 80,000 people in a flash and leaving about 120,000 more to die agonizing deaths from burns and radiation. Three days later, another atomic bomb destroyed Nagasaki. On August 14, Japan offered to surrender, and Emperor Hirohito gave the order to lay down arms. Two weeks later, Japanese leaders signed the terms of surrender. The war was officially over.

Chinese Civil War and Communist Victory

The Japanese surrender also meant the end of Japanese occupation of much of China, but instead of bringing peace, it marked an intensification of the contest between the Guomindang and the Communists. Guomindang forces started with many advantages: more troops and weapons, U.S. support, and control of China's cities. But their behavior eroded whatever popular support they had. They taxed the people they "liberated" more heavily than the Japanese had, looted businesses, confiscated supplies, and enriched themselves at the expense of the population. To pay its bills, Chiang's government printed money so fast that it soon lost all its value, ruining merchants and causing hoarding and shortages. In the countryside, the Guomindang's brutality alienated the peasants.

In contrast, the Communists' land reform programs had won them popular support, which was even more important than the heavy equipment brought by Guomindang soldiers, who began deserting by the thousands, and the Japanese equip-

Hiroshima After the Atomic Bomb   On August 6, 1945, an atomic bomb destroyed the city, killing over fifty thousand people. This photo shows the devastation of the city center, where only a few concrete buildings remained standing.   (Corbis)

ment seized by the Soviets in the last weeks of the war. By 1949, the Guomindang armies were collapsing everywhere, defeated more by their own greed and ineptness than by the Communists. As the Communists advanced, high-ranking members of the Guomindang fled to Taiwan, protected from the mainland by the United States Navy. On October 1, 1949, Mao Zedong announced the founding of the People's Republic of China.

THE CHARACTER OF WARFARE

The war left an enormous death toll. Recent estimates place the figure at close to 60 million deaths, six to eight times more than in World War I. Over half of the dead were civilian victims of massacres, famines, or bombs. The Soviet Union lost between 20 and 25 million people, more than any other country. China suffered 15 million deaths;

Poland lost some 6 million, of whom half were Jewish; the Jewish people lost another 3 million outside Poland. Over 4 million Germans and over 2 million Japanese died. In much of the world, almost every family mourned one or more of its members. In contrast, Great Britain lost 400,000 people, the United States 300,000.

One reason for the terrible toll in human lives and suffering was a change in moral values, as belligerents identified not just soldiers but entire peoples as enemies. Another reason for the devastation was the appearance of new technologies that carried destruction deep into enemy territory far beyond the traditional battlefields.

The War of Science

Scientists made many contributions to the technology of warfare. Chemists found ways to make synthetic rubber from coal or oil. Physicists perfected radar, which warned of

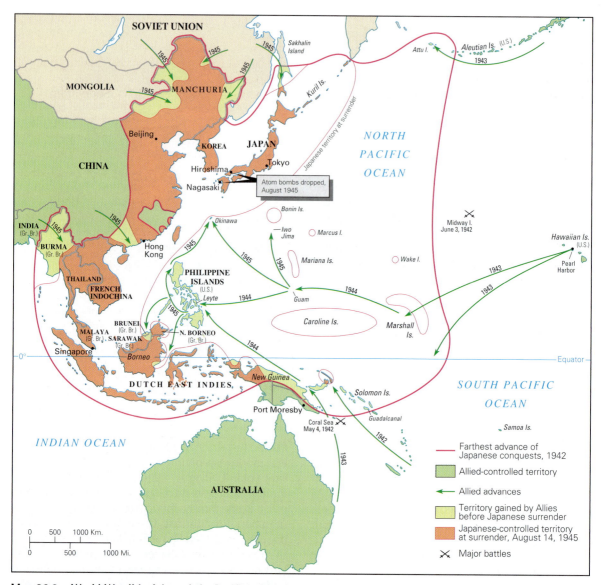

Map 26.2   World War II in Asia and the Pacific   After having conquered much of China between 1937 and 1941, Japanese forces launched a sudden attack on Southeast Asia, Indonesia, and the Pacific in late 1941 and early 1942. American forces slowly reconquered the Pacific islands and the Philippines until August 1945, when the atomic bombing of Hiroshima and Nagasaki forced Japan's surrender.

approaching enemy aircraft and submarines. Others broke enemy codes and developed antibiotics that saved the lives of countless wounded soldiers.

Aircraft development was especially striking.

As war approached, German, British, and Japanese aircraft manufacturers developed fast, maneuverable fighter planes. U.S. industry produced aircraft of every sort but was especially noted for its heavy bombers designed to fly in huge formations and drop tons of bombs on enemy cities. The Japanese developed the Mitsubishi "Zero" fighter plane—light, fast, and agile. Unable to produce heavy planes in large numbers, Germany responded with radically new designs, including the first jet fighters, low-flying buzz bombs, and fearful V-2 missiles.

In October 1939, President Roosevelt received a letter from physicist Albert Einstein, a Jewish refugee from Nazism, warning of the dangers of nuclear power. Fearing that Germany might develop a nuclear bomb first, Roosevelt placed the vast resources of the U.S. government at the disposal of physicists and engineers, both Americans and refugees from Europe. By 1945, they had built two atomic bombs, each one powerful enough to annihilate an entire city.

Bombing Raids

The Germans began the war from the air, but it was the British and Americans who excelled at large-scale urban bombardment. Since it was very hard to pinpoint individual buildings, especially at night, such raids were aimed at weakening the morale of the civilian population.

In May 1942, 1,000 British planes dropped incendiary bombs on Cologne, setting fire to most of the old city. Between July 24 and August 2, 1943, 3,330 British and Americans bombers set fire to Hamburg, killing 50,000 people. Later raids destroyed Berlin, Dresden, and other German cities. All in all, the bombing raids against Germany killed 600,000 people—more than half of them women and children—and injured 800,000. If the air strategists had hoped thereby to break the morale of the German people, they failed. The only effective bombing raids were those directed against oil depots and synthetic fuel plants; by early 1945, they had almost brought the German war effort to a standstill.

American bombing raids on Japanese cities were even more devastating than the fire-bombing of German cities, for Japanese cities were built of wood. In March 1945, a large raid set Tokyo ablaze, killing 80,000 people and leaving a million homeless. Five months later, single atomic bombs did something similar.

The Holocaust

The Nazis killed defenseless civilians on an even larger scale. Their murders were not the byproducts of some military goal but a calculated policy of extermination.

Their first targets were Jews. Soon after Hitler came to power, he deprived German Jews of their citizenship and legal rights. When eastern Europe fell under Nazi rule, the Nazis herded its large Jewish population into ghettos in the major cities, where many died of starvation and disease. Then, in early 1942, the Nazis decided to carry out Hitler's "final solution to the Jewish problem" by applying

U.S. Army Medics and Holocaust Victims At the end of World War II, Allied troops entered the Nazi concentration camps, where they found the bodies of thousands of victims of the Holocaust. In this picture, taken at Dachau in southern Germany, two U.S. Army medics are overseeing a truckload of corpses to be taken to a burial site. (Hulton Deutsch Collection/Corbis)

modern industrial methods to the slaughter of human beings. German companies built huge extermination camps in eastern Europe. Every day, trainloads of cattle cars arrived at the camps and disgorged thousands of captives and the corpses of those who had died of starvation or asphyxiation along the way. The strongest survivors were put to work and fed almost nothing until they died. Women, children, the elderly, and the sick were shoved into gas chambers and asphyxiated with poison gas. **Auschwitz,** the biggest camp, was a giant industrial complex designed to kill up to twelve thousand people a day. Most horrifying of all were the tortures inflicted on prisoners selected by Nazi doctors for "medical experiments." This mass extermination, now called the **Holocaust** ("burning"), claimed some 6 million Jewish lives.

Besides the Jews, the Nazis also killed 3 million Polish Catholics—especially professionals, army officers, and the educated—in an effort to reduce the Polish people to slavery. They also exterminated homosexuals, Jehovah's Witnesses, Gypsies, the disabled, and the mentally ill—all in the interests of "racial purity." Whenever a German was killed in an occupied country, the Nazis retaliated by burning a village with all its inhabitants. After the invasion of Russia, the Wehrmacht was given orders to execute all captured communists, government employees, and officers. They also worked millions of prisoners of war to death or let them die of starvation.

The Home Front

Rapid military movements and air power carried the war to people's homes in China, Japan, Southeast Asia, and Europe. Armies swept through the land, confiscating food, fuel, and anything else of value. Bombers and heavy artillery pounded cities into rubble, leaving only the skeletons of buildings, while survivors cowered in cellars. Air-raid sirens awakened people throughout the night. Millions fled their homes in terror. Of all the major belligerents, only Americans escaped such nightmares, and war production ended the deprivations of the Depression years.

The war demanded an enormous production effort from civilians. In the face of advancing Germans in 1941, the Soviets dismantled over fifteen hundred factories and rebuilt them in the Ural Mountains and Siberia, where workers soon turned out more tanks and artillery than the Axis. American factories produced an unending supply of ships, aircraft, trucks, tanks, and other materiel for the Allied effort. The Axis powers could not compete with this vast outpouring.

With so many men mobilized for war, women were responsible for much of this production. For example, 6 million women entered the American labor force during the war, 2.5 million of them in manufacturing jobs previously considered "men's work." Soviet women took over half of all industrial and three-quarters of all agricultural jobs. In the other belligerent countries, women also played a major role in the war effort, replacing men in fields, factories, and offices. The Nazis, in contrast, believed that German women should stay home and bear children, and they imported 7 million "guest workers"—a euphemism for war prisoners and captured foreigners.

War and the Environment

As in World War I, battles scarred the landscape, leaving behind spent ammunition and damaged equipment. Retreating armies flooded large areas of China and the Netherlands. The bombing of cities left ruins that remained visible for a generation or more. The main cause of environmental stress, however, was not the fighting but the economic development that sustained it.

As war industries boomed—the United States increased its industrial production fourfold during the war—so did the demand for raw materials. Mining companies opened new mines and towns in Central Africa to supply strategic minerals. Brazil, Argentina, and other Latin American countries deprived of manufactured imports began building their own steel mills, factories, and shipyards. In India, China, and Europe, timber felling accelerated far beyond forest regrowth.

We must keep the environmental effects of the war in perspective. From the vantage point of the present, the environmental impact of the war seems quite modest in comparison with the damage inflicted on the earth by the long consumer boom that began in the post–World War II years.

CONCLUSION

Between 1929 and 1949, the old global order—conservative, colonialist, and dominated by Great Britain and France—was shattered by the Depression, the politics of violence, and the most devastating war in history. Stalin transformed the Soviet Union into an industrial giant at enormous human cost. Reacting to the Depression, which weakened the Western democracies, Hitler in Germany and military leaders in Japan prepared for a war of conquest. Though Germany and Japan achieved stunning victories at first, their forces soon faltered in the face of the greater industrial production of the United States and the Soviet Union.

The war was so destructive and spread to so much of the globe because rapidly advancing technology was readily converted from civilian to military production. Machines that had made cars could also manufacture bombers or tanks. Engineers could design factories to kill people with maximum efficiency. The accelerating technology of missiles and nuclear bombs made the entire planet vulnerable to human destruction for the first time in history.

Into the power vacuum left by the collapse of Germany and Japan stepped the two superpowers: the United States and the USSR. When the war ended, U.S. soldiers were stationed in Australia, Japan, and western Europe, and the Red Army occupied all of eastern Europe and parts of northern China. Within months of their victory, these one-time allies became ideological enemies.

The global impact of World War II was drastic and almost immediate, because the war weakened the European colonial powers and because so much of the fighting took place in North Africa, Southeast Asia, and other colonial areas. Within fifteen years of the end of the war, almost every European colonial empire had disappeared. As the long era of European domination receded, Asians and Africans began reclaiming their independence.

■ Key Terms

Joseph Stalin

Five-Year Plans

Benito Mussolini

Fascist Party

Adolf Hitler

Nazis

Chiang Kai-shek

Mao Zedong

Long March

Stalingrad

Pearl Harbor

Battle of Midway

Hiroshima

Auschwitz

Holocaust

■ Suggested Reading

The literature on the period from 1929 to 1945 is enormous and growing fast. The following list is but a very summary introduction.

Charles Kindelberger's *The World in Depression, 1929–39* (1973) and Robert McElvaine's *The Great Depression: America, 1929–1941* (1984) provide a sophisticated economic analysis of the Depression. A. J. H. Latham's *The Depression and the Developing World, 1914–1939* (1981) gives a global perspective.

The best recent book on Japan in the twentieth century is Daikichi Irokawa's *The Age of Hirohito: In Search of Modern Japan* (1995). On Japanese expansion, see W. G. Beasley, *Japanese Imperialism, 1894–1945* (1987). The race to war is covered in Akira Iriye, *The Origins of the Second World War in Asia and the Pacific* (1987). Michael Barnhart, *Japan Prepares for Total War* (1987), is short and well written.

In the large and fast-growing literature on twentieth-century China, two general introductions are especially useful: John K. Fairbank, *The Great Chinese Revolution, 1800–1985* (1986), and Jonathan Spence, *The Search for Modern China* (1990). On the warlord and Guomindang periods, see Lucien Bianco, *Origins of the Chinese Revolution, 1915–1949* (1971). The Japanese invasion of China is the subject of Iris Chang, *The Rape of Nanking: The Forgotten Holocaust of World War II* (1997), and of James Hsiung and Steven Levine, eds., *China's Bitter Victory: The War with Japan, 1937–1945* (1992). Jung Chang, *Wild Swans: Three Daughters of China* (1991), is a fascinating account of women's experiences during the Revolution and the Mao era by the daughter of two Communist officials.

Among recent biographies of Stalin, see Dmitrii Volkogonov's *Stalin: Triumph and Tragedy* (1991) and Robert Tucker's *Stalin as Revolutionary, 1879–1929* (1973) and *Stalin in Power: The Revolution from Above, 1928–1941* (1990). On the transformation of the USSR, see Roy Medvedev's *Let History Judge: The Origins and Consequences of Stalinism* (1989) and Stephen Kotkin's *Magnetic Mountain: Stalinism as Civilization* (1995). Stalin's collectivization of agriculture is vividly portrayed in Robert Conquest's *Harvest of Sorrow* (1986); see also Sheila Fitzpatrick's *Stalin's Peasants: Resistance and Survival in the Russian Village After Collectivization* (1994). Conquest's

The Great Terror: A Reassessment (1990) describes the purges of the 1930s. Alexander Solzhenitsyn, a veteran of Stalin's prisons, explores them in a detailed history, *The Gulag Archipelago, 1918–1956* (3 vols., 1974–1978), and in a short, brilliant novel, *One Day in the Life of Ivan Denisovich* (1978).

Alexander De Grand provides an excellent interpretation of fascism in *Italian Fascism: Its Origins and Development,* 2d ed. (1989). William Shirer's *The Rise and Fall of the Third Reich* (1960) is a long but very dramatic eyewitness description of Nazi Germany by a journalist. The dictators are the subject of two fine biographies: Denis Mack Smith's *Mussolini* (1982) and Alan Bullock's *Hitler: A Study in Tyranny* (1965). See also A. J. P. Taylor's controversial classic, *The Origins of the Second World War* (1966) and Michael Burleigh's *Third Reich: A New History* (2000).

Two very detailed books on World War II are John Keegan, *The Second World War* (1990), and Gerhard Weinberg, *A World at Arms: A Global History of World War II* (1994). Particular aspects of the war in Europe are covered in Alexander Werth, *Russia at War, 1941–1945* (1965), and Conrad Crane, *Bombs, Cities, and Civilians* (1993). One of the most readable accounts of the war in Asia and the Pacific is Ronald Spector's *Eagle Against the Sun* (1988). Also

see Akira Iriye, *Power and Culture: The Japanese-American War, 1941–1945* (1981), and James Hsiung and Steven Levine, eds., *China's Bitter Victory: The War with Japan, 1937–1945* (1992).

The terror of life under Nazi rule is the subject of two powerful memoirs: Anne Frank's *The Diary of a Young Girl* (1953) and Eli Wiesel's *Night* (1960). On the Holocaust, see Lucy Dawidowicz, *The War Against the Jews, 1933–1945,* 2d ed. (1986); Leni Yahil, *The Holocaust: The Fate of European Jewry* (1990); and a controversial book by Daniel Goldhagen, *Hitler's Willing Executioners: Ordinary Germans and the Holocaust* (1996).

Among the many books that capture the scientific side of warfare, two are especially recommended: Richard Rhodes's long but fascinating *The Making of the Atomic Bomb* (1986) and F. H. Hinsley and Alan Stripp, eds., *Code Breakers* (1993).

Among the many books on the home front in the United States, the most vivid is Studs Terkel, *"The Good War": An Oral History of World War Two* (1984). Margaret Higonnet et al., eds., *Behind the Lines: Gender and the Two World Wars* (1987), discusses the role of women in the war.

Striving for Independence: Africa, India, and Latin America, 1900–1949

27

CHAPTER OUTLINE

Sub-Saharan Africa, 1900–1945

The Indian Independence Movement, 1905–1947

The Mexican Revolution, 1910–1940

Argentina and Brazil, 1900–1949

ENVIRONMENT AND TECHNOLOGY: Gandhi and Technology

Emiliano Zapata°, leader of a peasant rebellion in the Mexican Revolution, liked to be photographed on horseback, carrying a sword and a rifle and draped with bandoliers of bullets. Mahatma Gandhi°, who led the independence movement in India, preferred to be seen sitting at a spinning wheel, dressed in a *dhoti*°, the simple loincloth worn by Indian farmers. The images they liked to project and the methods they used could not have been more opposed. Yet their goals were similar: each wanted social justice and a better life for the poor in a country free of foreign domination.

The previous two chapters focused on a world convulsed by war and revolution. The world wars involved Europe, East Asia, the Middle East, and the United States, and they sparked violent revolutions in Russia and China. They accelerated the development of aviation, electronics, nuclear power, and other technologies. Although these momentous events dominate the history of the first half of the twentieth century, parts of the world that were little touched by war also underwent profound changes in this period, partly for internal reasons and partly because of the warfare and revolution in other parts of the world.

In this chapter we examine the changes that took place in sub-Saharan Africa, in India, and in

---

Zapata (sah-PAH-tah)   **Gandhi** (GAHN-dee)   *dhoti*
(DOE-tee)

three major countries of Latin America—Mexico, Brazil, and Argentina. These three regions represent three very distinct cultures, yet they had much in common. Africa and India were colonies of Europe, both politically and economically. Though politically independent, the Latin American republics were dependent on Europe and the United States for the sale of raw materials and commodities and for imports of manufactured goods, technology, and capital. In all three regions independence movements tried to wrest control from distant foreigners and improve the livelihood of their peoples. Their success was partial at best.

As you read this chapter, ask yourself the following questions:

- How did wars and revolutions in Europe and East Asia affect the countries of the Southern Hemisphere?

- Why did educated Indians and Africans want independence?

- What could Latin Americans do to achieve social justice and economic development? Were these two goals compatible?

SUB-SAHARAN AFRICA, 1900–1945

Of all the continents, Africa was the last to come under European rule (see Chapter 24). The first half of the twentieth century, the time when nationalist movements threatened European rule in Asia, was Africa's period of classic colonialism. After World War I Britain, France, Belgium, and South Africa divided Germany's African colonies among themselves. In the 1930s Italy invaded Ethiopia. The colonial empires reached their peak shortly before World War II.

Colonial Africa: Economic and Social Changes

Outside of Algeria, Kenya, and South Africa, few Europeans lived in Africa. In 1930 Nigeria, with a population of 20 million, was ruled by 386 British officials and by 8,000 policemen and military, of whom 150 were European. Yet even such a small presence stimulated deep social and economic changes.

Since the turn of the century the colonial powers had built railroads from coastal cities to mines and plantations in the interior in order to provide raw materials to the industrial world. The economic boom of the interwar years benefited few Africans. Colonial governments took lands that Africans owned communally and sold or leased them to European companies or, in eastern and southern Africa, to white settlers. Large European companies dominated wholesale commerce, while immigrants from various countries—Indians in East Africa, Greeks and Syrians in West Africa—handled much of the retail trade. Airplanes and automobiles were even more alien to the experience of Africans than railroads had been to an earlier generation.

Where land was divided into small farms, some Africans benefited from the boom. Farmers in the Gold Coast (now Ghana°) profited from the high price of cocoa, as did palm-oil producers in Nigeria and coffee growers in East Africa. In most of Africa women played a major role in the retail trades, selling pots and pans, cloth, food, and other items in the markets. Many maintained their economic independence and kept their household finances separate from those of their husbands, following a custom that predated the colonial period.

For many Africans, however, economic development meant working in European-owned mines and plantations, often under compulsion. Colonial governments were eager to develop the resources of the territories under their control but could not afford to pay high enough wages to attract workers. Instead, they used their police powers to force Africans to work under harsh conditions for little or no pay. In the 1920s, when the government of French Equatorial Africa decided to build a rail-

Ghana (GAH-nuh)

C H R O N O L O G Y

	Africa	India	Latin America
			1876–1910 Porfirio Díaz, dictator of Mexico
1900	**1900s** Railroads connect ports to the interior		
	1909 African National Congress founded	**1905** Viceroy Curzon splits Bengal; mass demonstrations	
		1906 Muslims found All-India Muslim League	
		1911 British transfer capital from Calcutta to Delhi	**1911–1919** Mexican Revolution; Emiliano Zapata and Pancho Villa against the Constitutionalists
			1917 New constitution proclaimed in Mexico
		1919 Amritsar Massacre	
1920	**1920s** J. E. Casely Hayford organizes political movement in British West Africa		
			1928 Plutarco Elías Calles founds Mexico's National Revolutionary Party
		1929 Gandhi leads March to the Sea	
		1930s Gandhi calls for independence; he is repeatedly arrested	
			1930–1945 Getulio Vargas, dictator of Brazil
			1934–1940 Lázaro Cárdenas, president of Mexico
			1938 Cárdenas nationalizes Mexican oil industry; Vargas proclaims Estado Novo in Brazil
	1939–1945 A million Africans serve in World War II	**1939** British bring India into World War II	
1940		**1940** Muhammad Ali Jinnah demands a separate nation for Muslims	

(continued)

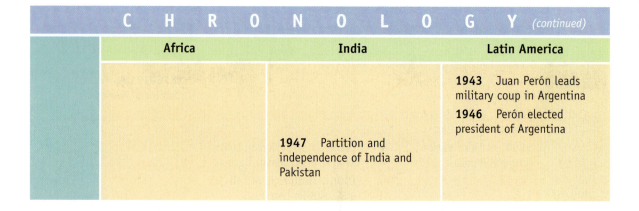

	Africa	India	Latin America
			1943 Juan Perón leads military coup in Argentina
			1946 Perón elected president of Argentina
		1947 Partition and independence of India and Pakistan	

road from Brazzaville to the Atlantic coast, a distance of 312 miles (502 kilometers), it drafted 127,000 men to carve a roadbed across mountains and through rain forests. Because of lack of food, clothing, and medical care, 20,000 of them died, an average of 64 deaths per mile of track.

Europeans prided themselves on bringing modern health care to Africa; yet before the 1930s there was too little of it to help the majority of Africans, and other aspects of colonialism actually worsened public health. Migrants to cities, mines, and plantations and soldiers moving from post to post spread syphilis, gonorrhea, tuberculosis, and malaria. Sleeping sickness and smallpox epidemics raged throughout Central Africa. In recruiting men to work, colonial governments depleted rural areas of farmers needed to plant and harvest crops. Forced requisitions of food to feed the workers left the remaining populations undernourished and vulnerable to diseases. Not until the 1930s did colonial governments realize the negative consequences of their labor policies and begin to invest in agricultural development and health care for Africans.

In 1900 Ibadan° in Nigeria was the only city in sub-Saharan Africa with more than 100,000 inhabitants; fifty years later, dozens of cities had reached that size, including Nairobi° in Kenya, Johannesburg in South Africa, Lagos in Nigeria, Accra in Gold Coast, and Dakar in Senegal. Africans migrated to cities because they offered hope of jobs and excitement and, for a few, the chance to become wealthy.

However, migrations damaged the family life of those involved, for almost all the migrants were men leaving women in the countryside to farm and raise children. Cities built during the colonial period reflected the colonialists' attitudes with racially segregated housing, clubs, restaurants, hospitals, and other institutions. Patterns of racial discrimination were most rigid in the white-settler colonies of eastern and southern Africa.

Religious and Political Changes

Traditional religious belief could not explain the dislocations that foreign rule, migrations, and sudden economic changes brought to the lives of Africans. Many therefore turned to one of the two universal religions, Christianity and Islam, for guidance.

Christianity was introduced into Africa by Western missionaries, except in Ethiopia, where it was indigenous. It was most successful in the coastal regions of West and South Africa, where the European influence was strongest. A major attraction of the Christian denominations was their mission schools, which taught both craft skills and basic literacy, providing access to employment as minor functionaries, teachers, and shopkeepers. These schools educated a new elite, many of whom learned not only skills and literacy but Western political ideas as well. Many Africans accepted Christianity enthusiastically, reading the suffering of their own peoples into the biblical stories of Moses

---

Ibadan (ee-BAH-dahn)   **Nairobi** (nie-ROE-bee)

Diamond Mining in Southern Africa   The discovery of diamonds in the Transvaal in 1867 attracted prospectors to the area around Kimberley. The first wave of prospectors consisted of individual "diggers," including a few Africans. By the late 1870s, surface deposits had been exhausted and further mining required complex and costly machinery. After 1889, one company, De Beers Consolidated, owned all the diamond mines. This photograph shows the entrance to a mineshaft and mine workers surrounded by heavy equipment.   (Royal Commonwealth Society. By permission of the Syndics of Cambridge University Library.)

and the parables of Jesus. The churches trained some of the brighter pupils to become catechists, teachers, and clergymen. A few rose to high positions, such as James Johnson, a Yoruba who became the Anglican bishop of the Niger Delta Pastorate. Independent Christian churches—known as "Ethiopian" churches—associated Christian beliefs with radical ideas of racial equality and participation in politics.

Islam spread inland from the East African coast and southward from the Sahel° toward the

West African coast, through the influence and example of Arab and African merchants. Islam also emphasized literacy—in Arabic through Quaranic schools rather than in a European language—and was less disruptive of traditional African customs such as polygamy.

In a few places, such as Dakar in Senegal and Cape Town in South Africa, small numbers of Africans could obtain secondary education. Even smaller numbers went on to college in Europe or America. Though few in number, they became the leaders of political movements. The contrast between the liberal ideas imparted by Western

Sahel (SAH-hel)

education and the realities of racial discrimination under colonial rule contributed to the rise of nationalism among educated Africans. In Senegal **Blaise Diagne**° agitated for African participation in politics and fair treatment in the French army. In the 1920s J. E. Casely Hayford began organizing a movement for greater autonomy in British West Africa. In South Africa Western-educated lawyers and journalists founded the **African National Congress** in 1912 to defend the interests of Africans. These nationalist movements were inspired by the ideas of Pan-Africanists from America such as W. E. B. Du Bois and Marcus Garvey, who advocated the unity of African peoples around the world, as well as by European ideas of liberty and nationhood. Before World War II, however, they were small and had little influence.

The Second World War (1939–1945) had a profound effect on the peoples of Africa, even those far removed from the theaters of war. The war brought hardships, such as increased forced labor, inflation, and requisitions of raw materials. Yet it also brought hope. During the campaign to oust the Italians from Ethiopia, Emperor **Haile Selassie**° (r. 1930–1974) led his own troops into Addis Ababa, his capital, and reclaimed his title. A million Africans served as soldiers and carriers in Burma, North Africa, and Europe, where many became aware of Africa's role in helping the Allied war effort. They listened to Allied propaganda in favor of European liberation movements and against Nazi racism, and they returned to their countries with new and radical ideas.

The early twentieth century was a relatively peaceful period for sub-Saharan Africa. But this peace—enforced by the European occupiers—masked profound changes that were to transform African life after the Second World War. The building of cities, railroads, and other enterprises brought Africa into the global economy, often at great human cost. Colonialism also brought changes to African culture and religion, hastening the spread of Christianity and Islam. And the foreign occupation awakened political ideas that inspired the next generation of Africans to demand independence (see Chapter 28).

Diagne (dee-AHN-yuh) **Haile Selassie** (HI-lee seh-LASS-ee)

THE INDIAN INDEPENDENCE MOVEMENT, 1905–1947

India was a colony of Great Britain from the late eighteenth to the mid-twentieth centuries. Under British rule the subcontinent acquired many of the trappings of Western-style economic development, such as railroads, harbors, modern cities, and cotton and steel mills, as well as an active and worldly middle class. The economic transformation of the region awakened in this educated middle class a sense of national dignity that demanded political fulfillment. In response, the British gradually granted India a limited amount of political autonomy while maintaining overall control. Religious and communal tensions among the Indian peoples were carefully papered over under British rule. Violent conflicts tore India apart after the withdrawal of the British in 1947.

The Land and the People

Much of India is fertile land, but it is vulnerable to the vagaries of nature, especially droughts caused by the periodic failure of the monsoons. When the rains failed from 1896 to 1900, 2 million people died of starvation.

Despite periodic famines the Indian population grew from 250 million in 1900 to 319 million in 1921 and 389 million in 1941. This growth created pressures in many areas. Landless young men converged on the cities, exceeding the number of jobs available in the slowly expanding industries. To produce timber for construction and railroad ties, and to clear land for tea and rubber plantations, government foresters cut down most of the tropical hardwood forests that had covered the subcontinent in the nineteenth century. In spite of deforestation and extensive irrigation, the amount of land available to peasant families shrank with each successive generation. Economic development—what the British called the "moral and material progress of India"—hardly benefited the average Indian.

Indians were divided into many classes. Peasants, always the great majority, paid rents to the landowner, interest to the village moneylender, and taxes to the government and had little left to improve their land or raise their standard of living. The government protected property owners, from village moneylenders all the way up to the maharajahs,° or ruling princes, who owned huge tracts of land. The cities were crowded with craftsmen, traders, and workers of all sorts, most very poor. Although the British had banned the burning of widows on their husbands' funeral pyres, in other respects women's lives changed little under British rule.

The peoples of India spoke many different languages: Hindi in the north, Tamil in the south, Bengali in the east, Gujerati around Bombay, Urdu in the northwest, and dozens of others. As a result of British rule and increasing trade and travel, English became, like Latin in medieval Europe, the common medium of communication of the Western-educated middle class. This new class of English-speaking government bureaucrats, professionals, and merchants was to play a leading role in the independence movement.

The majority of Indians practiced Hinduism and were subdivided into hundreds of castes, each affiliated with a particular occupation. Hinduism discouraged intermarriage and other social interactions among the castes and with people who were not Hindus. Muslims constituted one-quarter of the people of India but formed a majority in the northwest and in eastern Bengal. Muslim rulers had dominated northern and central India until they were displaced by the British in the eighteenth century. More reluctant than Hindus to learn English, Muslims felt discriminated against by both British and Hindus.

British Rule and Indian Nationalism

Colonial India was ruled by a viceroy appointed by the British government and administered by a few thousand members of the Indian Civil Service. These men, imbued with a sense of duty toward their subjects, formed one of the more honest (if not efficient) bureaucracies of all time. Drawn mostly from the English gentry, they liked to think of India as a land of lords and peasants. They believed it was their duty to protect the Indian people from the

maharajah (mah-huh-RAH-juh)

dangers of industrialization, while defending their own positions from Indian nationalists.

As Europeans they admired modern technology but tried to control its introduction into India so as to maximize the benefits to Britain and to themselves. For example, they encouraged railroads, harbors, telegraphs, and other communications technologies, as well as irrigation and plantations, because these increased India's foreign trade and strengthened British control. At the same time, they discouraged the cotton and steel industries and limited the training of Indian engineers, ostensibly to spare India the social upheavals that had accompanied the Industrial Revolution in Europe, while protecting British industry from Indian competition.

At the turn of the century the majority of Indians—especially the peasants, landowners, and princes—accepted British rule. But the Europeans' racist attitude toward dark-skinned people increasingly offended Indians who had learned English and absorbed English ideas of freedom and representative government, only to discover that thinly disguised racial quotas excluded them from the Indian Civil Service, the officer corps, and prestigious country clubs.

In 1885 a small group of English-speaking Hindu professionals founded a political organization called the **Indian National Congress.** For twenty years its members respectfully petitioned the government for access to the higher administrative positions and for a voice in official decisions, but they had little influence outside intellectual circles. Then, in 1905, Viceroy Lord Curzon divided the province of **Bengal** in two to improve the efficiency of its administration. This decision, made without consulting anyone, angered not only educated Indians, who saw it as a way to lessen their influence, but also millions of uneducated Hindu Bengalis, who suddenly found themselves outnumbered by Muslims in East Bengal. Soon Bengal was the scene of demonstrations, boycotts of British goods, and even incidents of violence against the British.

In 1906, while the Hindus of Bengal were protesting the partition of their province, Muslims, fearful of Hindu dominance elsewhere in India, founded the **All-India Muslim League.** Caught in an awkward situation, the government responded by granting Indians a limited franchise based on wealth. Muslims, however, were on average poorer than Hindus, for many poor and low-caste Hindus had converted to Islam to escape caste discrimination. Taking advantage of these religious divisions, the British instituted separate representation and different voting qualifications for Hindus and Muslims. Then, in 1911, the British transferred the capital of India from Calcutta to Delhi°, the former capital of the Mughal° emperors. These changes disturbed Indians of all classes and religions and raised their political consciousness. Politics, once primarily the concern of Westernized intellectuals, turned into two mass movements: one by Hindus and one by Muslims.

To maintain their commercial position and prevent social upheavals, the British resisted the idea that India could, or should, industrialize. Their geologists looked for minerals, such as coal or manganese, that British industry required. However, when the only Indian member of the Indian Geological Service, Pramatha Nath Bose, wanted to prospect for iron ore, he had to resign because the government wanted no part of an Indian steel industry that could compete with that of Britain. Bose joined forces with Jamsetji Tata, a Bombay textile magnate who decided to produce steel in spite of British opposition. With the help of German and American engineers and equipment, Tata's son Dorabji opened the first steel mill in India in 1911, in a town called Jamshedpur in honor of his father. Although it produced only a fraction of the steel that India required, Jamshedpur became a powerful symbol of Indian national pride. It prompted Indian nationalists to ask why a country that could produce its own steel needed foreigners to run its government.

During World War I Indians supported Britain enthusiastically; 1.2 million men volunteered for the army, and millions more voluntarily contributed money to the government. Many expected the British to reward their loyalty with political concessions. Others organized to demand concessions and a voice in the government. In 1917, in response to the agitation, the British government announced "the gradual development of self-governing institutions with a view to the progressive realization of responsible government in India

as an integral part of the British Empire." This sounded like a promise of self-government, but the timetable was so vague that nationalists denounced it as a devious maneuver to postpone India's independence.

In late 1918 and early 1919 a violent influenza epidemic broke out among soldiers in the war zone of northern France. Within a few months it spread to every country on earth and killed approximately 30 million people. India was especially hard hit; of the millions who died, two out of three were Indian. This dreadful toll increased the mounting political tensions. Leaders of the Indian National Congress declared that the British reform proposals were too little, too late.

On April 13, 1919, in the city of Amritsar in Punjab, General Reginald Dyer ordered his troops to fire into a peaceful crowd of some 10,000 demonstrators, killing at least 379 and wounding 1,200. Waves of angry demonstrations swept over India, but the government waited six months to appoint a committee to investigate the massacre. After General Dyer retired, the British House of Lords voted to approve his actions, and a fund was raised in appreciation of his services. Indians interpreted these gestures as showing British contempt for their colonial subjects. In the charged atmosphere of the time, the period of gradual accommodation between the British and the Indians came to a close.

Mahatma Gandhi and Militant Nonviolence

For the next twenty years India teetered on the edge of violent uprisings and harsh repression, possibly even war. That it did not succumb was due to **Mohandas K. Gandhi** (1869–1948), a man known to his followers as "Mahatma," the "great soul."

Gandhi began life with every advantage. His family was wealthy enough to send him to England for his education. After his studies he lived in South Africa and practiced law for the small Indian community there. During World War I he returned to India and was one of many Western-educated Hindu intellectuals who joined the Indian National Congress.

Gandhi had some unusual political ideas. Unlike many radical political thinkers of his time, he

Delhi (DEL-ee)   **Mughal** (MOO-guhl)

denounced the popular ideals of power, struggle, and combat. Instead, inspired by both Hindu and Christian concepts, he preached the saintly virtues of *ahimsa*° (nonviolence) and *satyagraha*° (the search for truth). He refused to countenance violence among his followers, and he called off several demonstrations when they turned violent.

Gandhi had an affinity for the poor that was unusual even among socialist politicians. In 1921 he gave up the Western-style suits worn by lawyers and the fine raiment of wealthy Indians and henceforth wore simple peasant garb: a length of homespun cloth below his waist and a shawl to cover his torso (see Environment and Technology: Gandhi and Technology). He spoke for the farmers and the outcasts, whom he called *harijan*°, "children of God." He attracted ever-larger numbers of followers among the poor and the illiterate, who soon began to revere him; and he transformed the cause of Indian independence from an elite movement of the educated into a mass movement with a quasi-religious aura.

Gandhi was a brilliant political tactician and a master of public relations gestures. In 1929, for instance, he led a few followers on an 80-mile (129-kilometer) walk, camped on a beach, and gathered salt from the sea in a blatant and well-publicized act of civil disregard for the government's monopoly on salt. But he discovered that unleashing the power of popular participation was one thing and controlling its direction was quite another. Within days of his "Walk to the Sea," demonstrations of support broke out all over India, in which the police killed a hundred demonstrators and arrested over sixty thousand.

Many times during the 1930s Gandhi threatened to fast "unto death," and several times he did come close to death, to protest the violence of both the police and his followers and to demand independence. He was repeatedly arrested and spent a total of six years in jail. But every arrest made him more popular. He became a cult figure not only in his own country but also in the Western media. He never won a battle or an election; instead, in the words of historian Percival Spear, he made the British "uncomfortable in their cherished field of

moral rectitude," and he gave Indians the feeling that theirs was the ethically superior cause.

India Moves Toward Independence

In the 1920s, slowly and reluctantly, the British began to give in to the pressure of the Indian National Congress and the Muslim League. They handed over control of "national" areas such as education, the economy, and public works. They also gradually admitted more Indians into the Civil Service and the officer corps.

India took its first tentative steps toward industrialization in the years before the First and then the Second World Wars. Indian politicians obtained the right to erect high tariff barriers against imports in order to protect India's infant industries from foreign, even British, competition. Behind these barriers, Indian entrepreneurs built plants to manufacture iron and steel, cement, paper, cotton and jute textiles, sugar, and other products. This early industrialization provided jobs, though not enough to improve the lives of the Indian peasants or urban poor. These manufactures, however, helped create a class of wealthy Indian businessmen. Far from being satisfied by the government's policies, they supported the Indian National Congress and its demands for independence. Though paying homage to Gandhi, they preferred his designated successor as leader of the Indian National Congress, **Jawaharlal Nehru**° (1889–1964). A highly educated nationalist and subtle thinker, Nehru, unlike Gandhi, looked forward to creating a modern industrial India.

Congress politicians won regional elections but continued to be excluded from the viceroy's cabinet, the true center of power. When World War II began in September 1939 Viceroy Lord Linlithgow declared war without consulting a single Indian. The Congress-dominated provincial governments resigned in protest and found that boycotting government office increased their popular support. When the British offered to give India its independence once the war ended, Gandhi called the offer a "postdated cheque on a failing bank" and demanded full independence immediately. His "Quit

---

ahimsa (uh-HIM-sah)   *satyagraha* (suh-TYAH-gruh-huh)
harijan (HAH-ree-jahn)

Nehru (NAY-roo)

Gandhi and Technology

In the twentieth century all political leaders but one embraced modern industrial technology. That one exception is Gandhi.

After deciding to wear only handmade cloth, Gandhi made a bonfire of imported factory-made cloth and began spending half an hour every day spinning yarn on a simple spinning wheel, a task he called a "sacrament." The spinning wheel became the symbol of his movement. Any Indian who wished to come before him had to dress in handwoven cloth.

Gandhi had several reasons for reviving this ancient craft. One was his revulsion against "the incessant search for material comforts," an evil to which he thought Europeans were "becoming slaves." Not only had materialism corrupted the people of the West, it had also caused massive unemployment in India. In particular, he blamed the impoverishment of the Indian people on the cotton industries of England and Japan, which had ruined the traditional cotton manufacturing by which India had once supplied all her own needs.

Gandhi looked back to a time before India became a colony of Britian, when "our women spun fine yarns in their own cottages, and supplemented the earnings of their husbands." The spinning wheel, he believed, was "presented to the nation for giving occupation to the millions who had, at least four months of the year, nothing to do." Not only would a return to the spinning wheel provide employment to millions of Indians, it would also become a symbol of "national consciousness and a contribution by every individual to a definite constructive national work."

Nevertheless, Gandhi was a shrewd politician who understood the usefulness of modern devices for mobilizing the masses and organizing his followers. He wore a watch and used the telephone and the printing press to keep in touch with his followers. When he traveled by train, he rode third class—but in a third-class railroad car of his own. His goal was the independence of his country, and he pursued it with every nonviolent means he could find.

Gandhi's ideas challenge us to rethink the purpose of technology. Was he opposed on principle to all modern devices? Was he an opportunist who used those devices that served his political ends and rejected those that did not? Or did he have a higher principle that accounts for his willingness to use the telephone and the railroad but not factory-made cloth?

Source: Quotations from Louis Fischer, *Gandhi: His Life and Message for the World* (New York: New American Library, 1954), 82–83.

Gandhi at the Spinning Wheel   Mahatma Gandhi chose the spinning wheel as his symbol because it represented the traditional activity of millions of rural Indians whose livelihoods were threatened by industrialization.   (Margaret Bourke-White, *LIFE Magazine* © Time Warner Inc.)

India" campaign aroused popular demonstrations against the British and provoked a wave of arrests, including his own. Nehru remarked: "I would fight Japan sword in hand, but I can only do so as a free man."

The Second World War divided the Indian people. Most Indian soldiers felt they were fighting to defend their country rather than to support the British Empire. As in World War I, Indians contributed heavily to the Allied war effort, supplying 2 million soldiers and enormous amounts of resources, especially the timber needed for emergency construction. A small number of Indians, however, were so anti-British that they joined the Japanese side.

India's subordination to British interests was vividly demonstrated in the famine of 1943 in Bengal. Unlike previous famines, this one was caused not by drought but by the Japanese conquest of Burma, which cut off supplies of Burmese rice that normally went to Bengal. Although food was available elsewhere in India, the British army had requisitioned the railroads to transport troops and equipment in preparation for a Japanese invasion. As a result, supplies ran short in Bengal and surrounding areas, while speculators hoarded whatever they could find. Some 2 million people starved to death before the army was ordered to supply food.

Partition and Independence

When the war ended, Britain's new Labour Party government prepared for Indian independence, but deep suspicions between Hindus and Muslims complicated the process. The break between the two communities had started in 1937, when the Indian National Congress won provincial elections and refused to share power with the Muslim League. In 1940 the leader of the League, **Muhammad Ali Jinnah°** (1876–1948), demanded what many Muslims had been dreaming of for years: a country of their own, to be called Pakistan (from "Punjab-Afghans-Kashmir-Sind" plus the Persian suffix -*stan* meaning "kingdom").

As independence approached, talks between Jinnah and Nehru broke down and battle lines were drawn. Violent rioting between Hindus and Muslims broke out in Bengal and Bihar. Gandhi's appeals for tolerance and cooperation fell on deaf ears. In despair, he retreated to his home near Ahmedabad. The British made frantic proposals to keep India united, but their authority was waning fast.

By early 1947 the Indian National Congress had accepted the idea of a partition of India into two states, one secular but dominated by Hindus, the other Muslim. In June Lord Mountbatten, the last viceroy, decided that independence must come immediately. On August 15 British India gave way to a new India and Pakistan. The Indian National Congress, led by Nehru, formed the first government of India; Jinnah and the Muslim League established a government for the provinces that made up Pakistan.

The rejoicing over independence was marred by violent outbreaks between Muslims and Hindus. In protest against the mounting chaos, Gandhi refused to attend the independence day celebration. Throughout the land, Muslim and Hindu neighbors turned on one another, and armed members of one faith hunted down people of the other faith. For centuries Hindus and Muslims had intermingled throughout most of India. Now, leaving most of their possessions behind, Hindus fled from predominantly Muslim areas, and Muslims fled from Hindu areas. Trainloads of desperate refugees of one faith were attacked and massacred by members of the other or were left stranded in the middle of deserts. Within a few months some 12 million people had abandoned their ancestral homes and a half-million lay dead. In January 1948 Gandhi died too, gunned down by an angry Hindu refugee.

After the sectarian massacres and flights of refugees, few Hindus remained in Pakistan, and Muslims were a minority in all but one state of India. That state was Kashmir, a strategically important region in the foothills of the Himalayas. India annexed Kashmir because the local maharajah was Hindu and because the state held the headwaters of the rivers that irrigated millions of acres of farmland in the northwestern part of the subcontinent. The majority of the inhabitants of Kashmir were Muslims, however, and would probably have joined Pakistan if they had been allowed to vote on the matter. The consequence of the partition and of Kashmir in particular was to turn India and Pakistan

Jinnah (jee-NAH)

The Partition of India   When India became independent, Muslims fled from Hindu regions, and Hindus fled from Muslims. Margaret Bourke-White photographed a long line of refugees, with their cows, carts, and belongings, trudging down a country road toward safety.   (Time Life Pictures/Getty Images)

into bitter enemies that have fought several wars in the past half-century.

THE MEXICAN REVOLUTION, 1910–1940

In the nineteenth century Latin America achieved independence from Spain and Portugal but did not industrialize. Throughout much of the century most Latin American republics suffered from ideological divisions, unstable governments, and violent upheavals. By trading their raw materials and agricultural products for foreign manufactured goods and capital investments, they became economically dependent on the wealthier countries to the north, especially on the United States and Great Britain. Their societies, far from fulfilling the promises of their independence, remained deeply split between wealthy landowners and desperately poor peasants.

Mexico, Brazil, and Argentina contained well over half of Latin America's land, population, and wealth, and their relations with other countries and their economies were quite similar. Mexico, however, underwent a traumatic social revolution, while Argentina and Brazil evolved more peacefully.

Mexico in 1910   Few countries in Latin America suffered as many foreign invasions and interventions as Mexico. A Mexican saying observed wryly: "Poor Mexico: so far from God, so close to the United States." In Mexico the chasm between rich and poor was so deep that only a revolution could move the country toward prosperity and democracy.

Mexico was the Latin American country most influenced by the Spanish during three centuries of colonial rule. After independence in 1821 it suffered from a half-century of political turmoil. At the beginning of the twentieth century Mexican society was divided into rich and poor and into persons of Spanish, Indian, and mixed ancestry. A few very wealthy families of Spanish origin, less than 1 percent of the population, owned 85 percent of Mexico's land, mostly in huge *haciendas* (estates). Closely tied to this elite were the handful of American and British companies that controlled most of Mexico's railroads, silver mines, plantations, and other productive enterprises. At the other end of the social scale were Indians, many of whom did not speak Spanish. *Mestizos°*, people of mixed Indian and European ancestry, were only slightly better off; most of them were peasants who worked on the haciendas or farmed small communal plots near their ancestral villages.

The urban middle class was small and had little political influence. Few professional and government positions were open to them, and foreigners owned most businesses. Industrial workers also were few in number; the only significant groups were textile workers in the port of Veracruz on the Gulf of Mexico and railroad workers spread throughout the country.

During the colonial period, the Spanish government had made halfhearted efforts to defend Indians and mestizos from the land-grabbing tactics of the haciendas. After independence in 1821 wealthy Mexican families and American companies used bribery and force to acquire millions of acres of good agricultural land from villages in southern Mexico. Peasants lost not only their fields but also their access to firewood and pasture for their animals. Sugar, cotton, and other commercial crops replaced corn and beans, and peasants had little choice but to work on haciendas. To survive, they had to buy food and other necessities on credit from the landowner's store; eventually, they fell permanently into debt. Sometimes whole communities were forced to relocate.

In the 1880s American investors purchased from the Mexican government dubious claims to more than 2.5 million acres (1 million hectares) traditionally held by the Yaqui people of Sonora, in northern Mexico. When the Yaqui resisted the expropriation of their lands, they were brutally repressed by the Mexican army.

Northern Mexicans had no peasant tradition of communal ownership, for the northern half of the country was too dry for farming, unlike the tropical and densely populated south. The north was a region of silver mines and cattle ranches, some of them enormous. It was thinly populated by cowboys and miners. The harshness of their lives and the vast inequities in the distribution of income made northern Mexicans as resentful as people in the south.

Despite many upheavals in Mexico in the nineteenth century, in 1910 the government seemed in control. For thirty-four years General Porfirio Díaz° (1830–1915) had ruled Mexico under the motto "Liberty, Order, Progress." To Díaz "liberty" meant freedom for rich hacienda owners and foreign investors to acquire more land. The government imposed "order" through rigged elections and a policy of *pan o palo* (bread or the stick)—that is, bribes for Díaz's supporters and summary justice for those who opposed him. "Progress" meant mainly the importing of foreign capital, machinery, and technicians to take advantage of Mexico's labor, soil, and natural resources.

During the Díaz years (1876–1910) Mexico City—with paved streets, streetcar lines, electric street lighting, and public parks—became a showplace, and new telegraph and railroad lines connected cities and towns throughout Mexico. But this material progress benefited only a handful of well-connected businessmen. The boom in railroads, agriculture, and mining at the turn of the century actually caused a decline in the average Mexican's standard of living.

Though a mestizo himself, Díaz discriminated against the nonwhite majority of Mexicans. He and his supporters tried to eradicate what they saw as Mexico's embarrassingly rustic traditions. On many middle- and upper-class tables French cuisine replaced traditional Mexican dishes. The wealthy replaced sombreros and ponchos with European garments. Though bullfighting and cockfighting remained popular, the well-to-do preferred horse racing and soccer. To the educated middle class—the only group with a strong sense of Mexican nationhood—this devaluation of Mexican culture became a symbol of the Díaz regime's failure to defend national interests against foreign influences.

---

mestizo (mess-TEE-zoh)

Díaz (DEE-as)

Revolution and Civil War, 1911–1920

Many Mexicans feared or anticipated a popular uprising after Díaz. Unlike the independence movement in India, the Mexican Revolution was not the work of one party with a well-defined ideology. Instead, it developed haphazardly, led by a series of ambitious but limited leaders, each representing a different segment of Mexican society.

The first was Francisco I. Madero (1873–1913), the son of a wealthy landowning and mining family, educated in the United States. When minor uprisings broke out in 1911, the government collapsed and Díaz fled into exile. The Madero presidency was welcomed by some, but it aroused opposition from peasant leaders like **Emiliano Zapata** (1879–1919). In 1913, after two years as president, Madero was overthrown and murdered by one of his former supporters, General Victoriano Huerta. Woodrow Wilson (1856–1924), president of the United States, showed his displeasure by sending the United States Marines to occupy Veracruz.

The inequities of Mexican society and foreign intervention in Mexico's affairs angered Mexico's middle class and industrial workers. They found leaders in Venustiano Carranza, a landowner, and in Alvaro Obregón°, a schoolteacher. Calling themselves Constitutionalists, Carranza and Obregón organized private armies and succeeded in overthrowing Huerta in 1914. By then, the revolution had spread to the countryside.

As early as 1911 Zapata, an Indian farmer, had led a revolt against the haciendas in the mountains of Morelos, south of Mexico City (see Map 27.1). His soldiers were peasants, some of them women, mounted on horseback and armed with pistols and rifles. For several years they periodically came down from the mountains, burned hacienda buildings, and returned land to the Indian villages to which it had once belonged.

Another leader appeared in Chihuahua, a northern state where seventeen individuals owned two-fifths of the land and 95 percent of the people had no land at all. Starting in 1913 **Francisco "Pancho" Villa** (ca. 1877–1923), a former ranch hand, mule driver, and bandit, organized an army of three thousand men, most of them cowboys. They

too seized land from the large haciendas, not to rebuild traditional communities as in southern Mexico but to create family ranches.

Zapata and Villa were part agrarian rebels, part social revolutionaries. They enjoyed tremendous popular support but could never rise above their regional and peasant origins and lead a national revolution. The Constitutionalists had fewer soldiers than Zapata and Villa; but they held the major cities, controlled the country's exports of oil, and used the proceeds of oil sales to buy modern weapons. Fighting continued for years, and gradually the Constitutionalists took over most of Mexico. In 1919 they defeated and killed Zapata; Villa was assassinated four years later. An estimated 2 million people lost their lives in the civil war, and much of Mexico lay in ruins.

During their struggle to win support against Zapata and Villa, the Constitutionalists adopted many of their rivals' agrarian reforms, such as restoring communal lands to the Indians of Morelos. The Constitutionalists also proposed social programs designed to appeal to workers and the middle class. The Constitution of 1917 promised universal suffrage and a one-term presidency; state-run education to free the poor from the hold of the Catholic Church; the end of debt peonage; restrictions on foreign ownership of property; and laws specifying minimum wages and maximum hours to protect laborers. Although these reforms were too costly to implement right away, they had important symbolic significance, for they enshrined the dignity of Mexicans and the equality of Indians, mestizos, and whites, as well as of peasants and city people.

The Revolution Institutionalized, 1920–1940

In the early 1920s, after a decade of violence that exhausted all classes, the Mexican Revolution lost momentum. Only in Morelos did peasants receive land, and President Obregón and his closest associates made all the important decisions. Nevertheless, the Revolution changed the social makeup of the governing class. For the first time in Mexico's history, representatives of rural communities, unionized workers, and public employees were admitted to the inner circle.

Obregón (oh-bray-GAWN)

Map 27.1   The Mexican Revolution   The Mexican Revolution began in two distinct regions of the country. One was the mountainous and densely populated area south of Mexico City, particularly Morelos, homeland of Emiliano Zapata. The other was the dry and thinly populated ranch country of the north, such as Chihuahua, home of Pancho Villa. The fighting that ensued crisscrossed the country along the main railroad lines, shown on the map.

In the arts the Mexican Revolution sparked a surge of creativity. The political murals of José Clemente Orozco and Diego Rivera and the paintings of Frida Kahlo focused on social themes, showing peasants, workers, and soldiers in scenes from the Revolution.

In 1928 Obregón was assassinated. His successor, Plutarco Elías Calles°, founded the National Revolutionary Party, or PNR (the abbreviation of its name in Spanish). The PNR was a forum where all the pressure groups and vested interests—labor, peasants, businessmen, landowners, the military, and others—worked out compromises. The estab-

lishment of the PNR gave the Mexican Revolution a second wind.

Lázaro Cárdenas°, chosen by Calles to be president in 1934, brought peasants' and workers' organizations into the party, renamed it the Mexican Revolutionary Party (PRM), and removed the generals from government positions. Then he set to work implementing the reforms promised in the Constitution of 1917. Cárdenas redistributed 44 million acres (17.6 million hectares) to peasant communes. He closed church-run schools, replacing them with government schools. He nationalized the railroads and numerous other businesses.

Calles (KAH-yace)

Lázaro Cárdenas (LAH-sah-roe KAHR-dih-nahs)

The Agitator, a Mural by Diegas Rivera Diego Rivera (1886–1957) was politically committed to the Mexican Revolution and widely admired as an artist. This mural, painted at the National Agricultural School at Chapingo near Mexico City, shows a political agitator addressing peasants and workers. With one hand, the speaker points to miners laboring in a silver mine; with the other, to a hammer and sickle. (Universidad Autonoma de Chapingo/ CENIDIAP-INBA)

Cárdenas's most dramatic move was the expropriation of foreign-owned oil companies. In the early 1920s Mexico was the world's leading producer of oil, but a handful of American and British companies exported almost all of it. In 1938 Cárdenas seized the foreign-owned oil industry, more as a matter of national pride than of economics. The oil companies expected the governments of the United States and Great Britain to come to their rescue, perhaps with military force. But Mexico and the United States chose to resolve the issue through negotiation, and Mexico retained control of its oil industry.

When Cárdenas's term ended in 1940, Mexico, like India, was still a land of poor farmers with a small industrial base. The Revolution had brought great changes, however. The political system was free of both chaos and dictatorships. A small group of wealthy people no longer monopolized land and other resources. The military was tamed; the Catholic Church no longer controlled education; and the nationalization of oil had demonstrated Mexico's independence from foreign corporations and military intervention.

The Mexican Revolution did not fulfill the democratic promise of Madero's campaign, for it brought to power a party that monopolized the government for eighty years. However, it allowed far more sectors of the population to participate in politics and made sure no president stayed in office more than six years. The Revolution also promised far-reaching social reforms, such as free education, higher wages and more security for workers, and the redistribution of land to the peasants. These long-delayed reforms began to be implemented during the Cárdenas administration. They fell short of the ideals expressed by the revolutionaries, but they laid the foundation for the later industrialization of Mexico.

ARGENTINA AND BRAZIL, 1900–1949

On the surface, Argentina and Brazil seem very different. Argentina is Spanish-speaking, temperate in climate, and populated almost exclusively by people of European origin. Brazil is tropical and Portuguese-speaking, and its inhabitants are of mixed European and African origin, with a substantial Indian minority. Yet in the twentieth century their economic, political, and technological experiences were remarkably similar.

The Transformation of Argentina

Most of Argentina consists of *pampas°*, flat, fertile land that is easy to till, much like the prairies of the midwestern United States and Canada. Throughout the nineteenth century Argentina's economy was based on two exports: the hides of longhorn creole cattle and the wool of merino sheep, which roamed the pampas in huge herds. Centuries earlier, Europeans had haphazardly introduced the animals and the grasses they ate. Natural selection had made the animals tough and hardy.

At the end of the nineteenth century railroads and refrigerator ships, which allowed the safe transportation of meat, changed not only the composition of Argentina's exports but also the way they were produced—in other words, the land itself. European consumers preferred the soft flesh of Lincoln sheep and Hereford cattle to the tough, sinewy meat of creole cattle and merino sheep. However, the valuable Lincolns and Herefords could not be allowed to roam and graze on the pampas; they were carefully bred and received a diet of alfalfa and oats. To safeguard them, the pampas had to be divided, plowed, cultivated, and fenced with barbed wire to keep out predators and other unwelcome animals. Once fenced, the land could be used to produce wheat as well as beef and mutton. Within a few years grasslands that had stretched to the horizon were transformed into farmland. Like the North American Midwest, the pampas became one of the world's great producers of wheat and meat.

Argentina's government represented the interests of the *oligarquía°*, a very small group of wealthy landowners. Members of this elite controlled enormous haciendas where they raised cattle and sheep and grew wheat for export. They also owned fine homes in Buenos Aires°, a city that was built to look like Paris. They traveled frequently to Europe and spent so lavishly that the French coined the superlative "rich as an Argentine." They showed little interest in any business other than farming, however, and were content to let foreign companies, mainly British, build Argentina's railroads, processing plants, and public utilities. In exchange for its agricultural exports Argentina imported almost all its manufactured goods from Europe and the United States. So important were British interests in the Argentinean economy that English, not Spanish, was used on the railroads, and the biggest department store in Buenos Aires was a branch of Harrods of London.

Brazil and Argentina, to 1929

Before the First World War Brazil produced most of the world's coffee and cacao, grown on vast estates, and natural rubber, gathered by Indians from rubber trees growing wild in the Amazon rain forest. Brazil's elite was made up of coffee and cacao planters and rubber exporters. Like their Argentinean counterparts, they spent their money lavishly, building palaces in Rio de Janeiro° and one of the world's most beautiful opera houses in Manaus°, deep in the Amazon. They had little interest in other forms of development; let British companies build railroads, harbors, and other infrastructure; and imported most manufactured goods. At the time this seemed to allow each country to do what it did best. If the British did not grow coffee, why should Brazil build locomotives?

Both Argentina and Brazil had small but outspoken middle classes that demanded a share in government and looked to Europe as a model. Beneath each middle class were the poor. In Argentina these were mainly Spanish and Italian immigrants who had ended up as landless farm laborers or workers in urban packing plants. In Brazil there was a large class of sharecroppers and plantation workers, many of them descendants of slaves.

Rubber exports collapsed after 1912, replaced by cheaper plantation rubber from Southeast Asia. The outbreak of war in 1914 put an end to imports from Europe as Britain and France focused all their

---

pampas (POM-pus) *oligarquía* (oh-lee-gar-KEE-ah)
Buenos Aires (BWAY-nihs AIR-eze)

Rio de Janeiro (REE-oh day zhuh-NAIR-oh)
Manaus (meh-NOWSE)

industries on war production and Germany was cut off entirely. The disruption of the old trade patterns weakened the landowning class. In Argentina the urban middle class obtained the secret ballot and universal male suffrage in 1916 and elected a liberal politician, **Hipólito Irigoyen°**, as president. To a certain extent, the United States replaced the European countries as suppliers of machinery and consumers of coffee. European immigrants built factories to manufacture textiles and household goods. Desperate for money to pay for the war, Great Britain sold many of its railroad, streetcar, and other companies to the governments of Argentina and Brazil.

In contrast to Mexico, the postwar years were a period of prosperity in South America. Trade with Europe resumed; prices for agricultural exports remained high; and both Argentina and Brazil used profits accumulated during the war to industrialize and improve their transportation systems and public utilities. Yet it was also a time of social turmoil, as workers and middle-class professionals demanded social reforms and a larger voice in politics. In Argentina students' and workers' demonstrations were brutally crushed. In Brazil junior officers rose up several times against the government, calling for universal suffrage, social reforms, and freedom for labor unions. Though they accomplished little, they laid the groundwork for later reformist movements. In neither country did the urban middle class take power away from the wealthy landowners. Instead, the two classes shared power at the expense of both the landless peasants and the urban workers.

Yet as Argentina and Brazil were moving forward, new technologies again left them dependent on the advanced industrial countries. Brazilians are justly proud that the first person to fly an airplane outside the United States was Alberto Santos-Dumont, a Brazilian. He did so in 1906 in France, where he lived most of his life and had access to engine manufacturers and technical assistance. Aviation reached Latin America after World War I, when European and American companies such as Aéropostale and Pan American Airways introduced airmail service between cities and linked Latin America with the United States and Europe.

Before and during World War I radio, then called "wireless telegraphy," was used not for broadcasting but for point-to-point communications. Transmitters powerful enough to send messages across oceans or continents were extraordinarily complex and expensive: their antennas covered many acres; they used as much electricity as a small town; and they cost tens of thousands of pounds sterling (millions of dollars in today's money).

Right after the war, the major powers scrambled to build powerful transmitters on every continent to compete with the telegraph cable companies and to take advantage of the boom in international business and news reporting. At the time, no Latin American country possessed the knowledge or funds to build its own transmitters. In 1919, therefore, President Irigoyen of Argentina granted a radio concession to a German firm. France and Britain protested this decision, and eventually four powerful radio companies—one British, one French, one German, and one American—formed a cartel to control all radio communications in Latin America. This cartel set up a national radio company in each Latin American republic, installing a prominent local politician as its president, but the cartel held all the stock and therefore received all the profits. Thus, even as Brazil and Argentina were taking over their railroads and older industries, the major industrial countries controlled the diffusion of the newer aviation and radio technologies.

The Depression and the Vargas Regime in Brazil

The Depression hit Latin America as hard as it hit Europe and the United States; in many ways, it marks a more important turning point for the region than either of the world wars. As long-term customers cut back their orders, the value of agricultural and mineral exports fell by two-thirds between 1929 and 1932. Argentina and Brazil could no longer afford to import manufactured goods. An imploding economy also undermined their shaky political systems. Like European countries, Argentina and Brazil veered toward authoritarian regimes that promised to solve their economic problems.

In 1930 **Getulio Vargas°** (1883–1954), a state governor, staged a coup and proclaimed himself president of Brazil. He proved to be a masterful

---

Hipólito Irigoyen (ee-POH-lee-toe ee-ree-GO-yen)

Getulio Vargas (jay-TOO-lee-oh VAR-gus)

politician. He wrote a new constitution that broadened the franchise and limited the president to one term. He raised import duties and promoted national firms and state-owned enterprises, culminating in the construction of the Volta Redonda steel mill in the 1930s. By 1936 industrial production had doubled, especially in textiles and small manufactures. Under his guidance, Brazil was on its way to becoming an industrial country. Vargas's policy, called **import-substitution industrialization,** became a model for other Latin American countries as they attempted to break away from neocolonial dependency.

The industrialization of Brazil brought all the familiar environmental consequences. Powerful new machines allowed the reopening of old mines and the digging of new ones. Cities grew as poor peasants looking for work arrived from the countryside. Around the older neighborhoods of Rio de Janeiro and São Paulo°, the poor turned steep hillsides and vacant lands into immense *favelas°* (slums) of makeshift shacks.

The countryside also was transformed. Scrubland was turned into pasture, and new acreage was planted in wheat, corn, and sugar cane. Even the Amazon rain forest—half of the land area of Brazil—was affected. In 1930 American industrialist Henry Ford invested $8 million to clear land along the Tapajós River and prepare it to become the site of the world's largest rubber plantation. Ford encountered opposition from Brazilian workers and politicians; the rubber trees proved vulnerable to diseases; and he had to abandon the project—but not before leaving 3 million acres (1.2 million hectares) denuded of trees. The ecological changes of the Vargas era, however, were but a tiny forerunner of the degradation of the Brazilian environment that was to take place later in the century.

Vargas instituted many reforms favorable to urban workers, such as labor unions, pension plans, and disability insurance, but he refused to take any measures that might help the millions of landless peasants or harm the interests of the great landowners. Although the Brazilian economy recovered from the Depression, the benefits of recovery were so unequally distributed that communist and fascist movements demanded even more radical changes.

In 1938, prohibited by his own constitution from being reelected, Vargas staged another coup, abolished the constitution, and instituted the Estado Novo°, or "New State," with himself as supreme leader. He abolished political parties, jailed opposition leaders, and turned Brazil into a fascist state. When the Second World War broke out, however, Vargas aligned Brazil with the United States and contributed troops and ships to the Allied war effort.

Despite his economic achievements, Vargas harmed Brazil. By running roughshod over laws, constitutions, and rights, he infected not only Brazil but all of South America with the temptations of political violence. It is ironic, but not surprising, that Vargas was overthrown in 1945 by a military coup.

Argentina After 1930

Economically, the Depression hurt Argentina almost as badly as it hurt Brazil. Politically, however, the consequences were delayed for many years. In 1930 General José Uriburu° overthrew the popularly elected President Irigoyen. The Uriburu government represented the large landowners and big business interests. For thirteen years the generals and the oligarquía ruled, doing nothing to lessen the poverty of the workers or the frustrations of the middle class. When World War II broke out, Argentina sympathized with the Axis but remained officially neutral.

In 1943 another military revolt flared, this one among junior officers angry at conservative politicians. It was led by Colonel **Juan Perón°** (1895–1974). The intentions of the rebels were clear:

> Civilians will never understand the greatness of our ideal; we shall therefore have to eliminate them from the government and give them the only mission which corresponds to them: work and obedience.[1]

Once in power the officers took over the highest positions in government and business and began to lavish money on military equipment and their own salaries. Their goal, inspired by Nazi victories, was nothing less than the conquest of South America.

As the war turned against the Nazis, the officers

São Paulo (sow PAL-oh)   *favela* (feh-VEL-luh)

Estado Novo (esh-TAH-doe NO-vo)   José Uriburu (hoe-SAY oo-ree-BOO-roo)   Juan Perón (hoo-AHN pair-OWN)

saw their popularity collapse. Perón, however, had other plans. Inspired by his charismatic wife **Eva Duarte Perón°** (1919–1952), he appealed to the urban workers. Eva Perón became the champion of the *descamisados*°, or "shirtless ones," and campaigned tirelessly for social benefits and for the cause of women and children. With his wife's help, Perón won the presidency in 1946 and created a populist dictatorship in imitation of the Vargas regime in Brazil.

Like Brazil, Argentina industrialized rapidly under state sponsorship. Perón spent lavishly on social welfare projects as well as on the military, depleting the capital that Argentina had earned during the war. Though a skillful demagogue who played off the army against the navy and both against the labor unions, Perón could not create a stable government out of the chaos of coups and conspiracies. He had to back down from a plan to make Eva his vice president. When she died in 1952, he lost his political skills (or perhaps they were hers), and soon thereafter he was overthrown in yet another military coup.

Mexico, Argentina, and Brazil: A Comparison

Until 1910 Mexico, Argentina, and Brazil shared a common history and similar cultures. In the first half of the twentieth century their economies followed parallel trajectories, based on unequal relations with the industrialized countries of Europe and North America. All three countries—indeed, all of Latin America—struggled with the failure of neocolonial economics to improve the lives of the middle class, let alone the peasants. And when the Depression hit, all three turned to state intervention and import-substitution industrialization. Like all industrializing countries, they did so by mining, farming, ranching, cutting down forests, and irrigating land, all at the expense of the natural environment.

Yet their political histories diverged radically. Mexico underwent a traumatic and profound social revolution. Argentina and Brazil, meanwhile, languished under conservative regimes devoted to the interests of wealthy landowners, sporadically interrupted by military coups and populist dema-

gogues. Mexicans, thanks to their experience of revolution, developed an acute sense of their national identity and civic pride in their history—pride largely missing in South America. Despite shortcomings, Mexico seriously committed itself to education, land reform, social justice, and political stability as national goals, not merely as the campaign platform of a populist dictator.

CONCLUSION

Sub-Saharan Africa, India, and Latin America lay outside the theaters of war that engulfed most of the Northern Hemisphere, but they were deeply affected by global events and by the demands of the industrial powers. Sub-Saharan Africa and India were still under colonial rule, and their political life revolved around the yearnings of their elites for political independence and their masses for social justice. Mexico, Argentina, and Brazil were politically independent, but their economies, like those of Africa and India, were closely tied to the economies of the industrial nations with which they traded. Their deeply polarized societies and the stresses caused by their dependence on the industrial countries clashed with the expectations of ever-larger numbers of their peoples.

In Mexico these stresses brought about a long and violent revolution, out of which Mexicans forged a lasting sense of national identity. Argentina and Brazil moved toward greater economic independence, but the price was social unrest, militarism, and dictatorship. In India the conflict between growing expectations and the reality of colonial rule produced both a movement for independence and an ethnic split that tore the nation apart. In sub-Saharan Africa demands for national self-determination and economic development were only beginning to be voiced by 1949 and did not come to fruition until the second half of the century.

Nationalism and the yearning for social justice were the two most powerful forces for change in the early twentieth century. These ideas originated in the industrialized countries but resonated in the independent countries of Latin America as well as in colonial regions such as the Indian subcontinent and sub-Saharan Africa. However, they did

---

Eva Duarte Perón (AY-vuy doo-AR-tay pair-OWN)
descamisados (des-cah-mee-SAH-dohs)

not always unite people against their colonial rulers or foreign oppressors; instead, they often divided them along social, ethnic, or religious lines. Western-educated elites looked to industrialization as a means of modernizing their country and ensuring their position in it, while peasants and urban workers supported nationalist and revolutionary movements in the hope of improving their lives. Often these goals were not compatible.

Key Terms

Blaise Diagne

African National Congress

Haile Selassie

Indian National Congress

Bengal

All-India Muslim League

Mohandas K. (Mahatma) Gandhi

Jawaharlal Nehru

Muhammad Ali Jinnah

Emiliano Zapata

Francisco "Pancho" Villa

Lázaro Cárdenas

Hipólito Irigoyen

Getulio Vargas

import-substitution industrialization

Juan Perón

Eva Duarte Perón

Suggested Reading

On Africa under colonial rule the classic overview is Melville Herskovits, *The Human Factor in Changing Africa* (1958). Two excellent general introductions are Roland Oliver and Anthony Atmore, *Africa Since 1800*, 4th ed. (1994), and A. E. Afigbo et al., *The Making of Modern Africa*, vol. 2, *The Twentieth Century* (1986). More detailed and challenging are *UNESCO General History of Africa*, vols. 7 and 8; *The Cambridge History of Africa*, vols. 7 and 8; and Adu Boahen, *African Perspectives on Colonialism* (1987). Outstanding novels about Africa in the colonial era include Chinua Achebe, *Arrow of God* (1964); Buchi Emecheta, *The Joys of Motherhood* (1980); and Peter Abraham, *Mine Boy* (1946).

For a general introduction to Indian history, see Sumit Sarkar, *Modern India, 1885–1947* (1983), and Percival Spear, *India: A Modern History*, rev. ed. (1972). On the in-

fluenza epidemic of 1918–1919 see Alfred W. Crosby, *America's Forgotten Pandemic: The Influenza of 1918* (1989). The Indian independence movement has received a great deal of attention. Judith M. Brown's most recent book on Gandhi is *Gandhi: Prisoner of Hope* (1989). *Gandhi's Truth: On the Origin of Militant Nonviolence* (1969) by noted psychoanalyst Erik Erikson is also recommended. Two collections of memoirs of the last decades of British rule are worth looking at: Charles Allen, ed., *Plain Tales of the Raj: Image of British India in the Twentieth Century* (1975), and Zareer Masani, ed., *Indian Tales of the Raj* (1988). The transition from colonialism to partition and independence is the subject of the very readable *Freedom at Midnight* (1975) by Larry Collins and Dominique Lapierre. The environment is discussed in M. Gadgil and R. Guha, *This Fissured Land: An Ecological History of India* (1993).

Thomas Skidmore and Peter Smith, *Modern Latin America*, 3d ed. (1992), offers the best brief introduction. Two fine general overviews of modern Mexican history are Enrique Krauze, *Mexico: Biography of Power: A History of Modern Mexico, 1810–1996* (1997), and Colin MacLachlan and William Beezley, *El Gran Pueblo: A History of Greater Mexico* (1994). On the Mexican Revolution, two recent books are essential: Alan Knight, *The Mexican Revolution*, 2 vols. (1986), and John M. Hart, *Revolutionary Mexico: The Coming and Process of the Mexican Revolution* (1987). But see also two classics by sympathetic Americans: Frank Tannenbaum, *Peace by Revolution: Mexico After 1910* (1933), and Robert E. Quirk, *The Mexican Revolution, 1914–1915* (1960). Mexico's most celebrated revolutionary is the subject of Manuel Machado, *Centaur of the North: Francisco Villa, the Mexican Revolution, and Northern Mexico* (1988). Mariano Azuela, *The Underdogs* (1988), is an interesting fictional account of this period. The standard work on Brazil is E. Bradford Burns, *A History of Brazil*, 3d ed. (1993). On the environmental history of Brazil, see Warren Dean, *Brazil and the Struggle for Rubber: A Study in Environmental History* (1987). The history of modern Argentina is ably treated in David Rock, *Argentina, 1517–1987: From Spanish Colonization to Alfonsín* (1987). Mark Jefferson, *Peopling the Argentine Pampas* (1971), and Jeremy Adelman, *Frontier Development: Land, Labour and Capital on the Wheatlands of Argentina and Canada, 1890–1914* (1994), describe the transformation of the Argentinean environment.

Notes

1. George Blanksten, *Perón's Argentina* (Chicago: University of Chicago Press, 1953), 37.

Famines and Politics

Nature is never reliable, and all living things periodically suffer from a catastrophic drop in food supplies. Human history is filled with tales of famines—times when crops failed, food supplies ran out, and people starved.

Natural famines India, dependent on the monsoon rains, has been particularly prone to such calamities, with famines striking two to four times a century, whenever the rains failed for several years in succession. Three times in the eighteenth century (1702–1704, 1769–1770, and 1790–1792) famines killed several million people in different parts of the subcontinent. The nineteenth century was worse, with famines in 1803–1804, 1837–1838, 1868–1870, and 1876–1878. The latter also afflicted northern China, causing between 9 and 13 million deaths from hunger and from the diseases of malnutrition. There were even incidents of cannibalism, as starving adults killed and ate starving children.

When a drought hit a region, it decimated not only the human population but also the animals they relied on to transport goods and plow the land. Likewise, droughts lowered the water levels in rivers and canals, so food could not be moved from one place to another.

Commercial famines That all changed in the nineteenth century. Railroads and steamships could transport foodstuffs across great distances in a matter of days or weeks, regardless of drought or heavy rains. Great Britain became dependent on imports of wheat from Russia and the American Midwest, and later of beef from Argentina. Yet famines were worse than ever, and the global death toll from starvation has been far higher since the mid-nineteenth century than it ever was in earlier times. Why?

Consider the Irish famine of 1845–1848. By the early nineteenth century the potato had become the main source of nutrition for the Irish people. Potatoes grew abundantly in the cool, moist climate of Ireland and produced more calories per acre than any other crop. Most of the Irish were poor tenant farmers, and potatoes had allowed their population to increase far more than wheat or rye could have.

In fall 1845 the blight turned the potatoes in the fields black, mushy, and inedible. The harvest was ruined the following year as well. It recovered slightly in 1847, but was bad again in 1848. Tens of thousands died of starvation, while hundreds of thousands died from the diseases that strike malnourished people, especially dysentery, typhus, and cholera. Travelers saw corpses rotting in their hovels or on the sides of roads. Altogether, a million or more people died, while another million managed to emigrate, reducing the population of Ireland by half.

Throughout those years, wheat grew in Ireland, but much of it was exported to England, where customers had money to pay for it. Like any other commodity, food cost money. The Irish farmers, poor even before the famines, were destitute and could not afford to buy the wheat. The British government, wedded to the ideology of laissez-faire, was convinced that interfering with the free market would only make things worse. Relief efforts were half-hearted at best; the official responsible for Irish affairs preferred to leave the situation to "the operation of natural causes."

The same held true in India, like Ireland a colony of Great Britain. The drought of 1876–1878 killed over 5 million Indians in the Deccan region, while British officials were helpless or indifferent. Part of the problem was transportation. In the 1870s only a few railway lines connected major cities. Most goods were still transported in bullock carts, but the bullocks also starved during the drought. Another obstacle was political. The idea that a government should be responsible for feeding the population was unthinkable at the time. And so, while millions were starving in the Deccan, the Punjab region was exporting wheat to Britain.

Over the next twenty years so-called famine railways were built in the regions historically most affected by the failures of the monsoon. When drought struck again at the end of the century, the railways were ready to transport food to areas that had previously been accessible only by bullock carts. However, the inhabitants of the affected regions had no money with which to buy what little food there was, and the government was still reluctant to interfere with free enterprise. Grain merchants bought all the stocks, hoarded them until the price rose, then used the railways to transport them out of the famine regions to regions where the harvests were better and people had more money.

In the twentieth century commercial famines have become rare, as governments have come to realize that they have a responsibility for food supplies not only for their own people, but for people in other countries as well. Yet commercial famines have not entirely disappeared. In 1974, when a catastrophic flood covered half of Bangladesh, the government was too disorganized to distribute its stocks of rice, while merchants bought what they could and exported it to India. Thousands died, and thousands more survived only because of belated shipments of food from donor countries.

Political famines To say that governments are responsible for food supplies does not mean that they exercise that responsibility for the good of the people. Some do, but in many instances food is used as a weapon. In the twentieth century global food supplies were always adequate for the population of the world, and transportation was seldom a problem. Yet the century witnessed the most murderous famines ever recorded.

War-induced famines were not new. In 1812, as the Russian army retreated, it practiced a "scorched-earth" policy of burning food stocks to prevent them from falling into the hands of Napoleon's army. In doing so, it also caused a famine among Russian peasants. Similar famines resulted from the destruction or requisitioning of crops in the Russian civil war of 1921–1922, the Japanese occupation of Indochina in 1942–1945, and the Biafran war in Nigeria in 1967–1969.

The Bengal famine of 1943 was also war-related. In 1942 the Japanese army had conquered Burma, a rich rice-producing colony. Food supplies in Bengal, which imported rice from Burma, dropped by 5 percent. As prices began to rise, merchants bought stocks of rice and held them in the hope that prices would continue to increase. Sharecroppers sold their stocks to pay off their debts to landlords and village moneylenders. Meanwhile,

the railroads that in peacetime would have carried food from other parts of India were fully occupied with military traffic. In October 1943, when a new viceroy, Lord Wavell, arrived in India and ordered the army to transport food to Bengal, food prices dropped to a level that the poor could afford. By then, however, between 1.5 and 2 million Bengalis had starved to death.

Worst of all were the famines that happened in peacetime as a result of the deliberate decisions of governments. The most famous of these political famines was caused by Stalin's collectivization of agriculture in 1932–1934. The Communist Party tried to force the peasants to give up their land and livestock and join collectives, where they could be made to work harder and provide food for the growing cities and industries. When they resisted, their crops were seized. Millions were sent to prison camps and millions of others died of starvation. Stalin chided the overly enthusiastic party members who had caused the famine for being "dizzy with success."

An even worse famine took place in China from 1958 to 1961 during the "Great Leap Forward" (see Chapter 28). Communist Party Chairman Mao Zedong decided to hasten the transformation of China into a communist state and industrial power by relying not on the expertise of economists and technocrats but on the enthusiasm of the masses. All farms were consolidated into huge communes. Peasants were mobilized to work on giant construction projects or to make steel out of household utensils and tools in backyard furnaces. The harvest of 1959 was poor, and later ones were even worse. The amount of grain per person declined from 452 pounds (205 kilograms) in 1957 to 340 pounds (154 kilograms) in 1961. Since the Central Statistical Bureau had been shut down, the central government was unaware of the shortages and demanded ever higher requisitions of food to feed the army and urban and industrial workers and to export to the Soviet Union to pay off China's debts. The amount of food left to the farmers was between one-fifth and one-half of their usual subsistence diet. From 1958 to 1961 20 to 30 million Chinese are estimated to have starved or died of the diseases of malnutrition in the most catastrophic famine in the history of the world. The leaders of the Communist Party either were unaware of its extent or, if they knew, did not dare mention it for fear of displeasing Mao, who denied its existence.

Nothing quite as horrible has happened since the Great Leap Forward. During the droughts in Africa in the 1970s and 1980s, most people in the affected regions received international food aid, but the governments of Ethiopia and Sudan either denied that their people were hungry or prevented food shipments from reaching drought victims in order to crush rebellions.

In the world today, natural disasters are as frequent as ever, and many countries are vulnerable to food shortages. No one now claims, as many did in the nineteenth century, that governments have no business providing free food to the starving. Though food is not equitably distributed, there is enough for all human beings now, and there will be enough for the foreseeable future. However, humanitarian feelings compete with other political agendas, and the specter of politically motivated famines still stalks the world.

PART EIGHT

Perils and Promises of a Global Community, 1945 to the Present

CHAPTER 28
The Cold War and Decolonization, 1945–1975

CHAPTER 29
Crisis, Realignment, and the Dawn of the
Post–Cold War World, 1975–1991

CHAPTER 30
Globalization at the Turn of the Millennium

The post–World War II decades brought promising changes to an increasingly interconnected world. Through the United Nations efforts were made to promote peace and international cooperation, and most countries agreed to human rights standards. Colonized peoples in Asia and Africa gained their independence, and expanding global trade offered the hope of economic growth.

However, these decades also saw major threats to peace, prosperity, and the environment. A Cold War between communist and anticommunist states disrupted dreams of a new era of peace and cooperation. The Iron Curtain divided Soviet-dominated eastern Europe from American-supported western Europe. Regional wars in Korea and Vietnam pitted the United States and its allies against communist regimes. Cold War rivalries sometimes provided a windfall of aid for new states but also intensified civil conflicts in Latin America, Africa, and elsewhere.

With the signing of nuclear arms limitation agreements in the 1970s tensions between the United States and the Soviet Union eased. In 1991 the Cold War finally ended with the collapse of the Soviet Union. As the sole remaining superpower, the United States had a unique capacity to act globally and a unique burden of suspicion of its motives.

Economic promises and perils also abounded in the post-war world. The wartime victors experienced rapid economic recovery, as did Germany and Japan, but in less developed lands prosperity came slowly or not at all. Global markets favored the industrialized nations. After 1975 a number of countries, including China, South Korea, Brazil, and Argentina, made dramatic strides in industrialization. But in less developed nations rapid population growth often offset economic gains. The divide between rich and poor nations widened.

Economic development meant new possibilities and perils for the environment. In the 1960s, the Green Revolution in agriculture greatly increased world food supplies, and in the 1990s genetic engineering produced plants that yielded more and resisted disease, drought, and insect damage better. But industrial growth accelerated the pollution of water and land. Atmospheric pollution increased exposure to harmful ultraviolet rays and led to increased global temperatures. Over-fishing and over-hunting imperiled many animal species, while thousands of acres of tropical forests were cut or burned for timber and farmland.

Finally, growing global interconnectedness held its own promises and perils. Many welcomed the emergence of English as the global language and the rapid spread of news, money, and ideas via the Internet. Others feared that Western material values and political and economic dominance posed a severe threat to cultural diversity around the world. A dangerous few reacted with violence.

	1950	1960	1970
Americas	• 1945 United Nations charter signed in San Francisco • 1946 International Monetary Fund and World Bank founded Cuban Revolution 1959 • • 1952 U.S. tests first hydrogen bomb	• 1962 Cuban missile crisis • 1964 Military takes power in Brazil Neil Armstrong walks on moon 1969 •	
Europe	1948–1952 Marshall Plan helps rebuild western Europe • 1949 NATO founded • 1955 Warsaw Pact formed Soviet troops crush revolt in Hungary 1956 • • 1957 Common Market founded	• 1961 Berlin Wall built Student uprising in France 1968 •	
Africa	• 1948 Apartheid becomes official in South Africa Ghana first British colony in Africa to win independence 1957 • • 1958 Guinea wins independence from France	• 1960 Nigeria, Congo, Somalia, Togo win independence • 1963 Kenya independent	
Middle East	• 1948 State of Israel founded; first Arab-Israeli War • 1956 Suez crisis 1954–1962 Algerian war for Independence		• 1967 Six Day Arab-Israeli War
Asia and Oceania	1951–1953 Korean War 1954–1975 Vietnam War • 1949 Indonesia wins independence from Netherlands	Cultural Revolution in China 1966–1969 Japan becomes world economic power 1970s •	

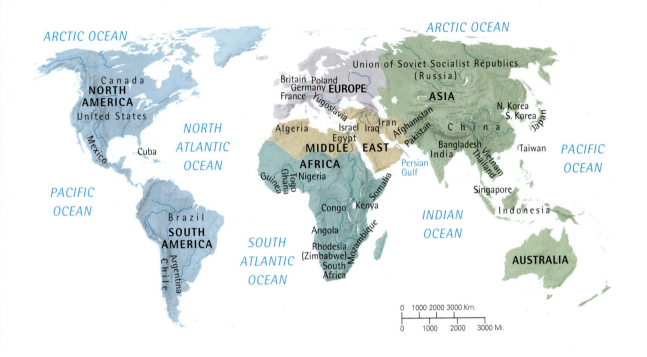

ARCTIC OCEAN

ARCTIC OCEAN

Canada
**NORTH
AMERICA**
United States

Union of Soviet Socialist Republics
(Russia)

Britain Poland
Germany **EUROPE**
France Yugoslavia

ASIA

N. Korea
S. Korea
Japan

*NORTH
ATLANTIC
OCEAN*

Mexico

Cuba

Algeria

Israel Iraq
Egypt
MIDDLE EAST

Iran
Afghanistan
Pakistan

C h i n a

Bangladesh
India

*PACIFIC
OCEAN*

Taiwan

*PACIFIC
OCEAN*

AFRICA

Persian
Gulf

Guinea
Togo
Ghana

Nigeria

Vietnam
Thailand

Singapore

B r a z i l
**SOUTH
AMERICA**

Congo

Kenya

Somalia

Indonesia

*INDIAN
OCEAN*

Argentina
Chile

*SOUTH
ATLANTIC
OCEAN*

Angola

Rhodesia
(Zimbabwe)
South
Africa

Mozambique

AUSTRALIA

0 1000 2000 3000 Km.

0   1000   2000   3000 Mi.

1980   **1990**   **2000**

• **1973** Military coup overthrows Allende in Chile

NAFTA agreement among
Canada, U.S., Mexico **1994** •

Terrorists attack New York,
Washington, D.C. **2001** •

• **1976** Military takes
power in Argentina

1983–1989 Democracy
restored in Brazil, Argentina, Chile

1994 Maya uprising
• in southern Mexico

• **1975** Helsinki Accords

Fall of communist regimes
in eastern Europe **1989** •

• **1991** End of USSR

Introduction of euro **1999** •

Solidarity union founded
in Poland **1980** •

Reunification of Germany **1990** •

1992–2000 Disintegration of Yugoslavia

• **1975** Angola and Mozambique win independence from Portugal

Democracy restored in Nigeria **1999** •

White domination of Rhodesia yields to
international pressure **1970–1980**

1994–1999 Nelson Mandela
president of South Africa

• **1973** October Arab-Israeli War leads
to oil embargo, price hikes

• **1979** Islamic Revolution overthrows shah of Iran

• **1991** Persian Gulf War

U.S., Britain invade, occupy Iraq **2003** •

1980–1988 Iran-Iraq War

U.S. invasion of Afghanistan **2001** •

• **1989** Chinese troops suppress Tiananmen Square protest

• **1980s** Taiwan, South Korea, Singapore industrialize

• **1971** Independence of Bangladesh

• **1979** USSR enters war in Afghanistan

Asian financial crisis starts in Thailand **1997** •

28 The Cold War and Decolonization, 1945–1975

CHAPTER OUTLINE

The Cold War

Decolonization and Nation Building

Beyond a Bipolar World

DIVERSITY AND DOMINANCE: Race and the Struggle for Justice in South Africa

In 1946, in a speech at Fulton, Missouri, Great Britain's wartime leader Winston Churchill declared that "an iron curtain has descended across the Continent [of Europe]. . . . I am convinced there is nothing they [the communists] so much admire as strength, and there is nothing for which they have less respect than weakness, especially military weakness." The phrase **"iron curtain"** became a watchword of the **Cold War,** the state of political tension and military rivalry that was then beginning between the United States and its allies and the Soviet Union and its allies.

In the early years of World War II, Churchill and President Franklin Roosevelt had looked forward to a postwar world of economic cooperation and restoration of sovereignty to peoples suffering Axis occupation and, above all, to a world where war and territorial conquest would not be tolerated. By the time Churchill delivered his "iron curtain" speech, however, Britain's electorate had voted him out of power, Harry S Truman had succeeded to the presidency after Roosevelt's death, and the Soviet Union was dominating eastern Europe and supporting communist movements in China, Iran, Turkey, Greece, and Korea. Although Soviet diplomats sat with their former allies in the newly founded United Nations Organization, confrontation rather than cooperation was the hallmark of relations between East and West.

The intensity of the Cold War sometimes obscured a postwar phenomenon of even greater importance. Western domination of Asia, Africa, and Latin America was largely ended, and the colonial empires of the New Imperialism were gradually dismantled. A new generation of national leaders sometimes skillfully played Cold

War antagonism to their own advantage. Their real business, however, was the difficult task of nation building.

Each land freeing itself from imperialism had its own specific history and conditions. After independence, some new nations sided openly with the United States and some with the Soviet Union. Others banded together in a posture of neutrality and spoke with one voice about their need for economic and technical assistance and the obligation of the wealthy nations to satisfy those needs.

The Cold War military rivalry stimulated extraordinary advances in weaponry and associated technologies, but many new nations struggled to educate their citizens, nurture industry, and escape the economic constraints imposed by their former imperialist masters. The environment suffered severe pressures, whether from oil exploration and transport to feed the growing economies of the wealthy nations or from deforestation in poor regions challenged by the need for cropland. Neither rich nor poor realized the costs associated with environmental change.

As you read this chapter, ask yourself the following questions:

- What impact did economic philosophy have on both the Cold War and the decolonization movement?

- How was a third world war averted?

- Was world domination by the superpowers good or bad for the rest of the world?

THE COLD WAR

The wartime alliance between the United States, Great Britain, and the Soviet Union had been an uneasy one. Fear of working-class revolution, which the Nazis had played on in their rise to power, was not confined to Germany. For more than a century political and economic leaders committed to free markets and untrammeled capital investment had loathed socialism in its several forms. After World War II, the iron curtain in Europe and communist insurgencies in China and elsewhere seemed to confirm the threat of worldwide revolution.

To protect themselves from the Soviet Union, which they perceived as the nerve center of world revolution and as a military power capable of launching a terrible new war, the United States and the countries of western Europe established the **North Atlantic Treaty Organization (NATO)** military alliance in 1949. Soviet leaders felt themselves surrounded by hostile forces just when they were trying to recover from the terrible losses sustained in the war. The distrust and suspicion between the two sides played out on a worldwide stage. The United Nations provided the venue for face-to-face debate.

The United Nations

In 1944, representatives from the United States, Great Britain, the Soviet Union, and China met and drafted specific charter proposals that finally bore fruit in the United Nations Charter, a treaty ratified on October 24, 1945. Like the League of Nations, the **United Nations** had two main bodies: the General Assembly, with representatives from all member states; and the Security Council, with five permanent members—China, France, Great Britain, the United States, and the Soviet Union—and seven rotating members. Various United Nations agencies focused on specialized international problems—for example, UNICEF (United Nations Children's Emergency Fund), FAO (Food and Agriculture Organization), and UNESCO (United Nations Educational, Scientific and Cultural Organization). The United Nations operated by majority vote, except that the five permanent members of the Security Council had veto power in that chamber.

All signatories to the United Nations Charter renounced war and territorial conquest. Nevertheless, peacekeeping, the sole preserve of the Security Council, became a vexing problem. The permanent members often exercised their veto to protect their friends and interests, though from time to time they authorized the United Nations to send observers or peacekeeping forces to monitor truces or agreements.

The decolonization of Africa and Asia greatly swelled the size of the General Assembly but not the Security Council. Many of the new nations looked to the United Nations for material assistance and access to a wider political world. While the vetoes of the Security Council's permanent members often stymied actions touching even indirectly on Cold War concerns, the General Assembly became an arena for expressing opinions on many issues involving decolonization, a movement that the Soviet Union strongly encouraged but the Western colonial powers resisted.

In the early years of the United Nations, General Assembly resolutions carried great weight. An example is a 1947 resolution that sought to divide Palestine into sovereign Jewish and Arab states. Gradually, though, the flood of new members produced a voting majority concerned more with poverty, racial discrimination, and the struggle against imperialism than with the Cold War. As a result, the Western powers increasingly disregarded the General Assembly, allowing the new nations of the world to have their say but not to act collectively.

Capitalism and Communism

In July 1944, with Allied victory a forgone conclusion, economic specialists representing over forty countries met at Bretton Woods, a New Hampshire resort, to devise a new international monetary system. The signatories eventually agreed to fix exchange rates. They also created the International Monetary Fund (IMF) to use currency reserves from member nations to finance temporary trade deficits and the **World Bank** to provide funds for reconstructing Europe and helping needy countries.

The Soviet Union attended the Bretton Woods Conference and signed the agreements, but by 1946, suspicion between the Soviet Union and the United States and Britain had deepened. While the rest of the world moved to a monetary system that relied for stability on most countries holding reserves of dollars and the United States holding reserves of gold, the Soviet Union established a closed monetary system for itself and the new communist regimes in eastern Europe. In the Western countries, supply and demand determined prices; in the Soviet command economy, government priorities and agencies allocated goods and set prices, irrespective of market forces.

Many leaders from the newly independent states preferred the Soviet Union's socialist example to the capitalism of their former colonizers. Thus, the relative success of economies patterned on Eastern or Western models became an element in the Cold War rivalry. Each side trumpeted economic successes measured by such things as industrial output, changes in per capita income, and productivity gains as evidence of its superiority.

During World War II, increased military spending and the draft brought full employment and high wages to the United States. With peace, the United States enjoyed prosperity and an international competitive advantage, while European economies were still heavily damaged from the war. To support European reconstruction, the U.S. **Marshall Plan** provided $12.5 billion to friendly countries between 1948 and 1952. By 1963, a resurgent European economy had doubled 1940 output.

Western European governments generally increased their role in economic management during this period. In Great Britain, the Labour Party government of the 1950s nationalized coal, steel, railroads, and health care. The French government nationalized public utilities; the auto, banking, and insurance industries; and parts of the mining industry.

In 1948, European governments also promoted economic cooperation and integration with the creation of the Organization of European Economic Cooperation (OEEC). After cooperative policies on coal and steel proved successful, some OEEC countries were ready to begin lowering tariffs to encourage the movement of goods and capital. In 1957, France, West Germany, Italy, the Netherlands, Belgium, and Luxembourg signed a treaty creating the European Economic Community, also known as the Common Market. The word "economic" was dropped from the group's title in 1967, making it simply the **European Community (EC).** By the 1970s, the EC nations had nearly over-

C H R O N O L O G Y

	Cold War	Decolonization
1945		
		1947 Partition of India
	1948–1949 Berlin airlift	
	1949 NATO formed	**1949** Dutch withdraw from Indonesia
	1950–1953 Korean War	
	1952 United States detonates first hydrogen bomb	
		1954 CIA intervention in Guatemala; defeat at Dienbienphu ends French hold on Vietnam
1955	**1955** Warsaw Pact concluded	**1955** Bandung Conference
	1956 Soviet Union suppresses Hungarian revolt	
	1957 Soviet Union launches first artificial satellite into earth orbit	**1957** Ghana becomes first British colony in Africa to gain independence
		1959 Fidel Castro leads revolution in Cuba
		1960 Shootings in Sharpeville intensify South African sturggle against apartheid; Nigeria becomes independent
	1961 East Germany builds Berlin Wall	
	1962 Cuban missile crisis	**1962** Algeria wins independence
1965		
		1971 Bangladesh secedes from Pakistan
1975	**1975** Helsinki Accords; end of Vietnam War	

taken the United States in industrial production. The economic alliance expanded after 1970, as Great Britain, Denmark, Greece, Ireland, Spain, Portugal, Finland, Sweden, and Austria joined.

Prosperity brought dramatic changes to European society. Average wages increased, unemployment fell, and social welfare benefits were expanded. Governments increased spending on health care, unemployment benefits, old-age pensions, public housing, and grants to poor families with children. The combination of economic growth and income redistribution raised living standards and fueled demand for consumer goods.

The Soviet experience provided a dramatic contrast. The economy of the Soviet Union was just as devastated at the end of the Second World War as those of western Europe. However, with enormous natural resources, a large population, and abundant energy at its disposal, Soviet recovery was rapid at first. Moreover, Soviet planners had made large investments in technical and scientific education, and the Soviet state had developed heavy industry in the 1930s and during the war years. But as the postwar period progressed, bureaucratic control of the economy grew less efficient. In the 1970s, the gap with the West widened. The Soviet economy failed to meet domestic demand for clothing, housing, food, automobiles, and consumer electronics. Agricultural inefficiency forced the Soviet Union to rely on food imports.

The socialist nations of eastern Europe were compelled to follow the Soviet economic model, although some national differences appeared. Poland and Hungary, for example, implemented agricultural collectivization more slowly than did Czechoslovakia. Significant growth occurred among the socialist economies, but the inefficiencies and failures that plagued the Soviet economy troubled them as well.

The United States and the Soviet Union competed in providing loans and grants and in supplying arms (at bargain prices) to countries willing to align with them politically. Thus, the relative success or failure of capitalism and communism in Europe and the United States was not necessarily the strongest consideration in other parts of the world when the time came to construct new national economies.

West Versus East in Europe and Korea

For Germany, Austria, and Japan, peace brought foreign military occupation and new governments that were initially controlled by the occupiers. When relations with the Western powers cooled at the end of the war, the Soviet Union sought to prevent the reappearance of hostile regimes on its borders. Initially, the Soviet Union seemed willing to accept governments in neighboring states that included a mix of parties as long as they were not hostile to local communist groups or to the Soviets. The nations of central and eastern Europe were deeply split by the legacies of the war, and many were willing to embrace the communists as a hedge against those who had supported fascism or cooperated with the Germans. As relations between the Soviets and the West worsened in the late 1940s, local communists, their strength augmented by Soviet military occupation, gained victories across eastern Europe. Western leaders saw the rapid emergence of communist regimes in Poland, Czechoslovakia, Hungary, Bulgaria, Romania, Yugoslavia, and Albania as a threat.

For the United States, the shift from viewing the Soviet Union as an ally against Germany to seeing it as a worldwide enemy took two years. In the waning days of World War II, the United States had seemed amenable to the Soviet desire for freer access to the Mediterranean through Turkish straits. But in July 1947, the **Truman Doctrine** offered military aid to help both Turkey and Greece resist Soviet military pressure and subversion. In 1951, Greece and Turkey were admitted to NATO. NATO's Soviet counterpart, the **Warsaw Pact,** emerged in 1955 in response to the Western powers' decision to allow West Germany to rearm within limits set by NATO.

The Soviet Union tested Western resolve in 1948–1949 by blockading the areas of Berlin occupied by British, French, and American forces, which were surrounded by Soviet-controlled East Germany. Airlifts of food and fuel defeated the blockade. In 1961, the East German government accentuated Germany's political division by building the Berlin Wall, as much to prevent its citizens from fleeing to the noncommunist western part of that city as to keep Westerners from entering East German territory. The West tested the East, in turn, by encouraging a rift between the Soviet Union and Yugoslavia. Western aid and encouragement resulted in Yugoslavia's signing a defensive treaty with Greece and Turkey (but not with NATO) and deciding against joining the Warsaw Pact.

Soviet power set clear limits on how far any eastern European country might stray from Soviet domination. In 1956, Soviet troops crushed an anti-Soviet revolt in Hungary. Czechoslovakia suffered Hungary's fate in 1968. The West, a passive onlooker, had no recourse but to acknowledge that the Soviet Union had the right to intervene in the domestic affairs of any Soviet-bloc nation whenever it wished.

A more explosive crisis erupted in Korea, where the Second World War had left Soviet troops in control north of the thirty-eighth parallel and American troops in control to the south. When no agreement could be reached on holding countrywide elections, communist North Korea and noncommunist South Korea became independent states in 1948. Two years later, North Korea invaded South Korea. The United Nations Security Council, in the absence of the Soviet delegation, voted to condemn the invasion and called on members of the United Nations to come to the defense of South Korea. The United States was the primary ally of South Korea. The People's Republic of China supported North Korea. The **Korean War** lasted until 1953, when the two sides eventually agreed to a truce along the thirty-eighth parallel, but no peace treaty was concluded.

Japan benefited from the Korean War in an unexpected way. Massive purchases of supplies by the United States and spending by American servicemen on leave provided a financial stimulus to the Japanese economy similar to the stimulus that Europe received from the Marshall Plan.

U.S. Defeat in Vietnam

A shooting war also developed in Vietnam. In 1954, United States president Dwight D. Eisenhower (1953–1961) and his foreign policy advisers decided not to aid France in its effort to sustain colonial rule in Vietnam, perceiving that the days of the European colonial empires were numbered. After winning independence, however, communist North Vietnam supported a guerrilla movement—the Viet Cong—against the noncommunist government of South Vietnam.

When John F. Kennedy became president (1961–1963), he and his advisers decided to support the South Vietnamese government of President Ngo Dinh Diem°. They realized that the Diem government was corrupt and unpopular, but they feared that a communist victory would encourage communist movements throughout Southeast Asia and alter the Cold War balance of power. Kennedy steadily increased the number of American military advisers from 685 to almost 16,000 while secretly encouraging the overthrow and execution of Diem in hopes of seeing a more popular and honest government come to power.

Lyndon Johnson, who became president (1963–1969) after Kennedy was assassinated, gained support from Congress for unlimited expansion of U.S. military deployment. By the end of 1966, 365,000 U.S. troops were engaged in the **Vietnam War.** Nothing the Americans tried, however, succeeded in stopping the Viet Cong guerrillas and their North Vietnamese allies. Diem's successors turned out to be just as corrupt and unpopular as he was, and the heroic nationalist image of North Vietnam's leader, Ho Chi Minh, evoked strong sympathies among many South Vietnamese.

In 1973, a treaty between North Vietnam and the United States ended U.S. involvement in the war and promised future elections. Two years later, in violation of the treaty, Viet Cong and North Vietnamese troops overran the South Vietnamese army and captured the southern capital of Saigon, renaming it Ho Chi Minh City. The two parts of Vietnam were reunited in a single state ruled from the north. The war was bloody and traumatic. The Vietnamese had over a million casualties. The deaths of fifty-eight thousand Americans overseas and the vigorous antiwar movement at home ensured that the United States would not easily be drawn into another shooting war.

The Vietnamese People at War   American and South Vietnamese troops burned many villages to deprive the enemy of civilian refuges. This policy undermined support for the South Vietnamese government in the countryside. (Dana Stone/stockphoto.com)

Diem (dee-EM)

The Race for Nuclear Supremacy

Fear of nuclear warfare affected strategic decisions in the Korean and Vietnam Wars. It also affected all other aspects of Cold War confrontation. The devastation of Hiroshima and Nagasaki by atomic weapons (see Chapter 26) had ushered in a new era. Nuclear weapons fed into a logic of total war that was already reaching a peak in Nazi genocide and terror bombing and in massive Allied air raids on large cities. After the Soviet Union exploded its first nuclear device in 1949, fears of a worldwide holocaust grew. Fears increased when the United States exploded a far more powerful weapon, the hydrogen bomb, in 1952 and the Soviet Union followed suit less than a year later. The possibility of the theft of nuclear secrets by Soviet spies fostered paranoia in the United States, and the conviction that the nuclear superpowers were willing to use their terrible weapons if their vital interests were threatened spread despair around the world.

In 1954, President Eisenhower warned Soviet leaders against attacking western Europe. In response to such an attack, he said, the United States would reduce the Soviet Union to "a smoking, radiating ruin at the end of two hours." A few years later, the Soviet leader Nikita Khrushchev° offered an equally stark promise: "We will bury you." His reference was to economic competition, but the image produced in Americans was of literal burial.

Everyone's worst fears seemed about to be realized in the **Cuban missile crisis** of 1962. When the Soviet Union deployed nuclear-tipped missiles in Cuba in response to the U.S. installation of similar missiles in Turkey, the world held its breath. Confronted by unyielding diplomatic pressure and military threats from President Kennedy, Khrushchev backed down and pulled the missiles from Cuba. Subsequently, the United States removed its missiles from Turkey.

Arms limitation also saw progress. In 1963, Great Britain, the United States, and the Soviet Union agreed to ban the testing of nuclear weapons in the atmosphere, in space, and under water, thus reducing the environmental danger of radioactive fallout. In 1968, the United States and the Soviet Union together proposed a world treaty against further proliferation of nuclear weapons. It was signed by 137 countries. Not until 1972, however, did the two superpowers truly recognize the futility of squandering their wealth on ever-larger missile forces.

In Europe, the Soviet-American arms race outran the economic ability of atomic powers France and Britain to keep pace. Instead, the European states sought to relax tensions. Between 1972 and 1975, the Conference on Security and Cooperation in Europe (CSCE) brought delegates from thirty-seven European states, the United States, and Canada to Helsinki. The goal of the Soviet Union was to gain European acceptance of the political boundaries of the Warsaw Pact nations. The **Helsinki Accords** affirmed that no boundaries should be changed by military force. It also contained formal (but nonbinding) declarations calling for economic, social, and governmental contacts across the iron curtain, and for cooperation in humanitarian fields, a provision that paved the way for dialogue about human rights.

Space exploration was another offshoot of the nuclear arms race. The contest to build larger and more accurate missiles for delivery of warheads prompted the superpowers to prove their skills in rocketry by launching space satellites. The Soviet Union placed a small *Sputnik* satellite into orbit around the earth in October 1957. The United States responded with its own satellite three months later. The space race was on, a contest in which accomplishments in space were understood to signify equivalent achievements in the military sphere. *Sputnik* administered a deep shock to American pride and confidence, but in 1969 two Americans, Neil A. Armstrong and Edwin E. "Buzz" Aldrin, became the first humans to walk on the moon.

Despite rhetorical Cold War saber-rattling by Soviet and American leaders, the threat of nuclear war forced a measure of restraint on the superpower adversaries. Because fighting each other directly would have risked escalation to the level of nuclear exchange, they carefully avoided crises that might provoke such confrontations.

Khrushchev (KROOSH-chef)

DECOLONIZATION AND NATION BUILDING

Whereas the losing countries in World War I were stripped of colonies, it was primarily countries on the winning side in World War II that ended up losing their colonies (see Map 28.1).

Circumstances differed profoundly from place to place. In some Asian countries, where colonial rule was of long standing, newly independent states found themselves in possession of viable industries, communications networks, and education systems. In other countries, notably in Africa, decolonization gave birth to nations facing dire economic problems and internal disunity. In Latin America, where political independence already had been achieved, the quest was for freedom from foreign economic domination, particularly by the United States.

New Nations in Southern Asia

Newly independent India and Pakistan were strikingly dissimilar. Muslim Pakistan defined itself according to religion and quickly fell under the control of military leaders. Though 90 percent Hindu, the much larger republic of India, led by Prime Minister Jawaharlal Nehru, was secular. It inherited most of the considerable industrial and educational resources the British had developed, along with the larger share of trained civil servants and military officers.

The decision of the Hindu ruler of the northwestern state of Jammu and Kashmir to join India without consulting his overwhelmingly Muslim subjects led to a war between India and Pakistan in 1947 that ended with an uneasy truce, only to resume briefly in 1965. Though Kashmir remains a flashpoint of patriotic feeling, the two countries managed to avoid further warfare.

Despite recurrent predictions that multilingual India might break up into a number of linguistically homogeneous states, most Indians recognized that unity benefited everyone; and the country pursued a generally democratic and socialist line of development. Pakistan, in contrast, did break up. In

1971, its Bengali-speaking eastern section seceded to become the independent country of Bangladesh.

Elsewhere in the region, nationalist movements won independence as well. Britain granted independence to Burma (now Myanmar°) in 1948 and established the Malay Federation that same year. (Singapore, once a member of the federation, became an independent city-state itself in 1965.) In 1946, the United States kept its promise of postwar independence for the Philippine Islands but retained close economic ties and leases on military bases. In the Dutch East Indies, Sukarno (1901–1970) had cooperated with the Japanese occupation in hopes that the Dutch would never return. After a military confrontation, Dutch withdrawal was finally negotiated in 1949, and Sukarno went on to become the dictator of his resource-rich but underdeveloped nation of Indonesia.

In all these cases, communist insurgents plagued the departing colonial powers and the newly formed governments. The most important postwar communist movement arose in the part of Southeast Asia known as French Indochina. There, Ho Chi Minh° (1890–1969), who had spent several years in France during World War I, played the pivotal role. After training in Moscow, he returned to Vietnam to found the Indochina Communist Party in 1930.

Ho Chi Minh's nationalist coalition, then called the Viet Minh, fought the French with help from the People's Republic of China. After a brutal struggle, the French stronghold of Dienbienphu° fell in 1954, marking the doom of France's colonial enterprise. Ho's Viet Minh government took over in the north, and a noncommunist nationalist government ruled in the south. As already described, fighting between North and South Vietnam eventually became a major Cold War conflict (see "U.S. Defeat in Vietnam" above).

The Struggle for Independence in Africa

In the quarter-century between 1955 and 1980, African nationalists succeeded in ending European colonial rule. Mostly they gained their

---

Myanmar (myahn-MAH)   **Ho Chi Minh** (hoe chee min)
Dienbienphu (dyen-byen-phu)

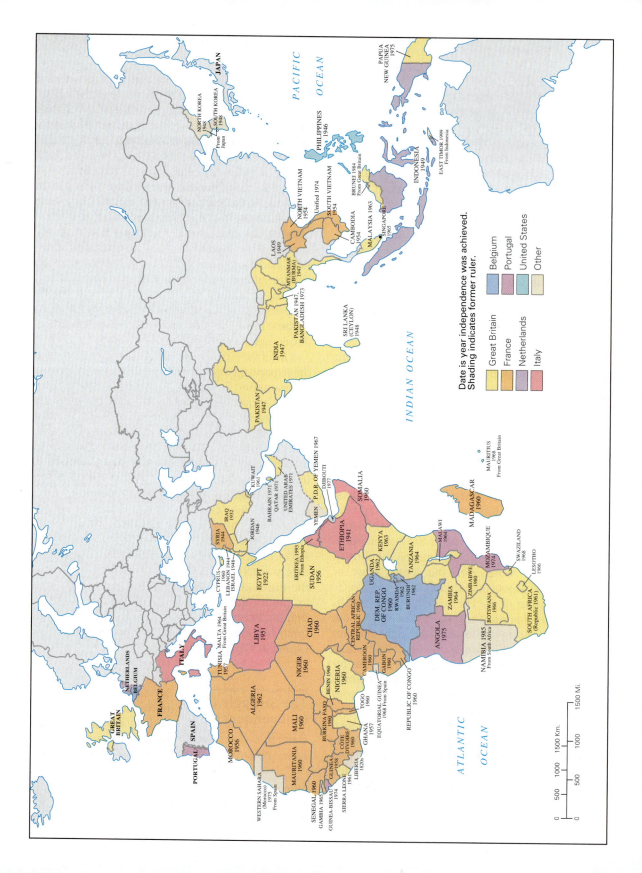

PACIFIC OCEAN

JAPAN

NORTH KOREA 1948
SOUTH KOREA 1948
From Japan

PAPUA NEW GUINEA 1975

PHILIPPINES 1946

BRUNEI 1984
From Great Britain

EAST TIMOR 1999
From Indonesia

INDONESIA 1949

NORTH VIETNAM 1954

SOUTH VIETNAM 1954

Unified 1974

CAMBODIA 1954

MALAYSIA 1963

SINGAPORE 1965

LAOS 1949

MYANMAR (BURMA) 1947

PAKISTAN 1947
BANGLADESH 1973

SRI LANKA (CEYLON) 1948

INDIA 1947

PAKISTAN 1947

INDIAN OCEAN

MAURITIUS 1968
From Great Britain

KUWAIT 1961

BAHRAIN 1971

QATAR 1971

UNITED ARAB EMIRATES 1971

P.D.R. OF YEMEN 1967

DJIBOUTI 1977

SOMALIA 1960

MADAGASCAR 1960

IRAQ 1932

JORDAN 1946

SYRIA 1944

CYPRUS 1960

LEBANON 1944

ISRAEL 1948

YEMEN

ETHIOPIA 1941

ERITREA 1993
From Ethiopia

KENYA 1963

UGANDA 1962

TANZANIA 1964

MALAWI 1964

MOZAMBIQUE 1974

SWAZILAND 1968

LESOTHO 1966

EGYPT 1922

SUDAN 1956

DEM. REP. OF CONGO 1960

RWANDA 1962

BURUNDI 1962

ZAMBIA 1964

ZIMBABWE 1980

BOTSWANA 1966

SOUTH AFRICA (Republic 1961)

MALTA 1964
From Great Britain

ITALY

TUNISIA 1957

LIBYA 1951

CHAD 1960

CENTRAL AFRICAN REPUBLIC 1960

CAMEROON 1960

GABON 1960

ANGOLA 1975

NAMIBIA 1985
From South Africa

NETHERLANDS

BELGIUM

GREAT BRITAIN

FRANCE

SPAIN

PORTUGAL

MOROCCO 1956

ALGERIA 1962

NIGER 1960

MALI 1960

NIGERIA 1960

BENIN 1960

BURKINA FASO 1960

TOGO 1960

GHANA 1957

EQUATORIAL GUINEA 1968 From Spain

REPUBLIC OF CONGO 1960

MAURITANIA 1960

SENEGAL 1960

GAMBIA 1965

GUINEA-BISSAU 1974

GUINEA 1958

SIERRA LEONE 1961

LIBERIA 1820s

CÔTE D'IVOIRE 1960

WESTERN SAHARA (Morocco) 1975
From Spain

ATLANTIC OCEAN

Date is year independence was achieved.
Shading indicates former ruler.

Great Britain

France

Netherlands

Italy

Belgium

Portugal

United States

Other

0   500   1000   1500 Mi.

0   500   1000   1500 Km.

Map 28.1   Decolonization, 1947–1999   Notice that independence came a decade or so earlier in South and Southeast Asia than in Africa. Numerous countries that gained independence after World War II in the Caribbean, in South and Central America, and in the Pacific are not shown.

independence peacefully, but where European settlers were numerous, violence became the norm.

Algeria rebelled in 1954. The French government was as determined to hold on to Algeria as it had been to keep Vietnam. Ten percent of the Algerian population was European, and Algeria's economy was strongly oriented toward France. Both sides pursued the revolt with great brutality. When the Algerians finally won independence in 1962, the flood of angry colonists returning to France undermined the Algerian economy because very few Arabs had received technical training or acquired management experience.

None of the independence movements in sub-Saharan Africa matched the Algerian struggle in scale. Some of the politicians who led the nationalist movements had devoted their lives to ridding their homelands of foreign occupation. An example is Kwame Nkrumah° (1909–1972), who in 1957 became prime minister of Ghana (formerly the Gold Coast), the first British colony in Africa to achieve independence. Only a few hundred Ghanaian children of Nkrumah's generation had graduated each year from the seven-year elementary schools, and he was one of only a handful who made it through teacher training college. After graduation, he spent a decade reading philosophy and theology in the United States and absorbing ideas about black pride and independence then being propounded by black leaders W. E. B. Du Bois and Marcus Garvey.

After a brief stay in Britain, Nkrumah returned in 1947 to the Gold Coast to work for independence. The time was right. Great Britain had already freed its Asian colonies, and Nkrumah quickly united the people of Ghana behind him. Independence thus came without war or protracted bloodshed. Nkrumah turned out to be more effective internationally as a spokesman for colonized peoples than

he was at home as an administrator. In 1966, a group of army officers ousted him.

Jomo Kenyatta (ca. 1894–1978) traveled a more difficult road in Kenya, where a substantial number of European coffee planters strengthened Britain's desire to retain control. A movement the settlers called Mau Mau, formed mostly by the Kikuyu° people, became active in 1952. As violence between settlers and movement fighters escalated, British troops hunted down the leaders and resettled the Kikuyu. The British charged Kenyatta with being a Mau Mau leader and held him in prison and then in internal exile for eight years during a declared state of emergency. They released him in 1961, and negotiations with the British to write a constitution for an independent Kenya followed. In 1964, Kenyatta was elected the first president of the Republic of Kenya. He proved to be an effective, though autocratic, ruler.

In contrast, African leaders in the French colonies of sub-Saharan Africa were slow to call for independence. They visualized change in terms of promises of greater political and civil rights made in 1944 by the Free French movement of General Charles de Gaulle at a conference in Brazzaville. This Brazzaville Conference also had promised to expand French education at the village level, to improve health services, and to open more lower-level administrative positions to Africans, but the word *independence* was never mentioned.

African politicians also realized that some French colonies—such as Ivory Coast with its coffee and cacao exports, fishing, and hardwood forests—had good economic prospects and others, such as land-locked, desert Niger, did not. As a Malagasy politician said in 1958, "When I let my heart talk, I am a partisan of total and immediate independence [for Madagascar]; when I make my reason speak, I realize that it is impossible." Ultimately, however, the heart prevailed everywhere. Guinea, under the dynamic leadership of Sékou Touré°, led the way in 1958. By the time Nigeria, the most populous West African state, achieved independence from Great Britain in 1960, the leaders of many former French colonies in West Africa could attend the celebrations as independent heads of state.

Kwame Nkrumah (KWAH-mee nn-KROO-muh)

Kikuyu (kih-KOO-you)   **Sékou Touré** (SAY-koo too-RAY)

European settlers fought hard to hold on in southern Africa. The African struggle against Portuguese rule in Angola and Mozambique dragged on until frustrated Portuguese military commanders overthrew the government of Portugal in 1974 and granted the African colonies independence the following year. After a ten-year fight, European settlers in the British colony of Southern Rhodesia ceded power in 1980 to the African majority, who renamed the country Zimbabwe. The change had been swift; a century after the "scramble" for Africa began, European colonial rule in Africa had ended.

Only South Africa and neighboring Southwest Africa remained in the hands of European minorities. After World War II, the white minority government had reconstructed South Africa along extreme racial separation, or *apartheid*°. The cities, the best jobs, and most of the land were reserved for Europeans. Africans and others classified as "nonwhites" were subjected to strict limitations on place of residence, right to travel, and access to jobs and public facilities.

The African National Congress (ANC), formed in 1912, led the fight against apartheid and in favor of a nonracial society. After police fired on demonstrators in the African town of Sharpeville in 1960, an African lawyer named Nelson Mandela (b. 1918) organized guerrilla resistance by the ANC. Mandela was sentenced to life in prison in 1964, and the government outlawed the ANC and other opposition organizations. For a time, things were quiet, but in 1976 young students reignited the bloody and prolonged struggle that would force an end to apartheid (see Diversity and Dominance: Race and the Struggle for Justice in South Africa).

The Quest for Economic Freedom in Latin America

In Latin America, the postwar decades saw continuing struggles over foreign ownership and social inequality. American and European companies dominated Chile's copper, Cuba's sugar and resort hotels, Colombia's coffee, Guatemala's bananas, and the communications networks of several countries. Even in a country like Mexico, where the ruling Institutional

Revolutionary Party, or PRI, was officially committed to revolutionary independence and economic development, a yawning gulf between rich and poor, urban and rural, persisted. According to one estimate from the mid-1960s, not more than 300 foreign and 800 Mexican companies dominated the country, and some 2,000 families made up the industrial-financial elite. At the other end of the economic scale were peasants and the 14 percent of the population classified as Indian.

Jacobo Arbenz Guzmán, elected president of Guatemala in 1951, was typical of Latin American leaders who tried to confront the power of foreign interests. His expropriation of large estates angered the United Fruit Company, a U.S. corporation that dominated banana exports and held vast tracts of land in reserve. Reacting to reports that Arbenz was becoming friendly toward communism, the United States Central Intelligence Agency (CIA) prompted a takeover by the Guatemalan military in 1954. CIA intervention removed Arbenz from the scene; it also condemned Guatemala to decades of governmental instability and growing violence between leftist and rightist elements in society.

In Cuba, U.S. companies owned 40 percent of raw sugar production, 23 percent of nonsugar industry, 90 percent of telephone and electrical services, and 50 percent of public service railways. The needs of the U.S. economy largely determined Cuban foreign trade and held back development. Profits went north to the United States or to a small class of wealthy Cubans, many of foreign origin. Cuba's ruler during that period, Fulgencio Batista, became a symbol of corruption, repression, and foreign economic domination.

In 1959, a popular rebellion forced Batista to flee the country. Fidel Castro, the lawyer leader of the rebels, his brother Raoul Castro, and Ernesto "Che" Guevara°, who was the main theorist of communist revolution in Latin America, created a new regime. Within a year, Fidel Castro's government had redistributed land, lowered urban rents, and raised wages, effectively transferring 15 percent of the national income from rich to poor. Within twenty-two months, the Castro government seized almost all U.S. property in Cuba and most Cuban corporations. This action resulted in a

---

apartheid (uh-PART-hate)

Che Guevara (chay guh-VAHR-uh)

blockade by the United States, the flight of middle-class and technically trained Cubans, a drop in foreign investment, and the beginning of chronic food shortages.

Little evidence supports the view that Castro undertook his revolution to install a communist government. But at that time, the East-West rivalry of the Cold War was increasingly influencing international politics, and Castro soon turned to the Soviet Union for economic aid. In doing so, he unwittingly committed his nation to economic stagnation and dependence on a foreign power as damaging as the previous relationship with the United States had been.

In April 1961, some fifteen hundred Cuban exiles, whom the CIA had trained for a year in Guatemala, landed at the Bay of Pigs in an effort to overthrow Castro. The Cuban army defeated the attempted invasion in a matter of days, partly because the new U.S. president, John F. Kennedy, decided not to provide all the air support that the plan originally called for. The failure of the Bay of Pigs invasion tarnished the reputation of the United States and the CIA and provoked Castro into declaring that he and his revolution were and always had been Marxist-Leninist.

Challenges of Nation Building

Decolonization occurred on a vast scale. Fifty-one nations signed the United Nations Charter in the closing months of 1945. During the United Nations' first decade twenty-five new members joined, a third of them upon gaining independence. During the next decade forty-six more new members were admitted, nearly all of them former colonial territories.

Each of these nations had to organize and institute some form of government. Comparatively few were able to do so without experiencing coups, rewritten constitutions, or regional rebellions. Leaders did not always agree on the form independence should take. In the absence of established constitutional traditions, leaders frequently tried to impose their own visions by force. Most of the new nations, while trying to establish political stability, also faced severe economic challenges, including foreign ownership and operation of key resources and the need to build infrastructure.

Overdependence on world demand for raw materials and on imported manufactured goods persisted in many places long after independence.

Because the achievement of political and economic goals called for educated and skilled personnel, education was another common concern in newly emerging nations. Addressing that concern required more than building and staffing schools. In some countries, leaders had to decide which language to teach and how to inculcate a sense of national unity in students from different—and sometimes historically antagonistic—ethnic, religious, and linguistic groups. Another problem was how to provide satisfying jobs for new graduates, many of whom had high expectations because of their education.

Only rarely were the new nations able to surmount these hurdles. Even the most economically and educationally successful, such as South Korea, suffered from tendencies toward authoritarian rule. Costa Rica, a country with a remarkably stable parliamentary regime from 1949 onward and a literacy rate of 90 percent, remained heavily dependent on world prices for agricultural commodities and on importation of manufactured goods.

BEYOND A BIPOLAR WORLD

Although the East-West superpower rivalry dominated world affairs, newly independent states had concerns that were primarily domestic and regional. The challenge they faced was to find a way to pursue their ends within the bipolar structure of the Cold War—and possibly to take advantage of the East-West rivalry. In short, the superpowers dominated the world but did not control it. And as time progressed, they dominated it less and less.

The Third World

As one of the most successful leaders of the decolonization movement, Indonesia's President Sukarno was an appropriate figure to host a meeting in 1955 of twenty-nine African and Asian countries at Bandung, Indonesia. The conferees proclaimed solidarity among all peoples fighting

DIVERSITY AND DOMINANCE

RACE AND THE STRUGGLE FOR JUSTICE IN SOUTH AFRICA

One of South Africa's martyrs in the struggle against apartheid was Steve Biko (1946–1977), a thinker and activist especially concerned with building pride among Africans and asserting the importance of African cultures. Biko was one of the founders of the Black Consciousness Movement, focusing on the ways in which white settlers had stripped Africans of their freedom. As a result of his activism, he was restricted to his hometown in 1973. Between 1975 and 1977 he was arrested and interrogated four times by the police. After his arrest in August 1977 he was severely beaten while in custody. He died days later without having received medical care. His death caused worldwide outrage. The following is an excerpt from a 1970 essay by Biko.

But these are not the people we are concerned with [those who support apartheid]. We are concerned with that curious bunch of nonconformists who explain their participation in negative terms: that bunch of do-gooders that goes under all sorts of names—liberals, leftists etc. These are the people who argue that they are not responsible for white racism and the country's "inhumanity to the black man." These are the people who claim that they too feel the oppression just as acutely as the blacks and therefore should be jointly involved in the black man's struggle for a place under the sun. In short, these are the people who say that they have black souls wrapped up in white skins.

The role of the white liberal in the black man's history in South Africa is a curious one. Very few black organisations were not under white direction. True to their image, the white liberals always knew what was good for the blacks and told them so. The wonder of it all is that the black people have believed in them for so long. It was only at the end of the 50s

that the blacks started demanding to be their own guardians.

Nowhere is the arrogance of the liberal ideology demonstrated so well as in their insistence that the problems of the country can only be solved by a bilateral approach involving both black and white. This has, by and large, come to be taken in all seriousness as the modus operandi in South Africa by all those who claim they would like a change in the status quo. Hence the multiracial political organisations and parties and the "nonracial" student organisations, all of which insist on integration not only as an end goal but also as a means.

The integration they talk about is first of all artificial in that it is a response to conscious manoeuvre rather than to the dictates of the inner soul. In other words the people forming the integrated complex have been extracted from various segregated societies with their inbuilt complexes of superiority and inferiority and these continue to manifest themselves even in the "nonracial" setup of the integrated complex. As a result the integration so achieved is a one-way course, with the whites doing all the talking and the blacks the listening. Let me hasten to say that I am not claiming that segregation is necessarily the natural order; however, given the facts of the situation where a group experiences privilege at the expense of others, then it becomes obvious that a hastily arranged integration cannot be the solution to the problem. It is rather like expecting the slave to work together with the slave-master's son to remove all the conditions leading to the former's enslavement.

Secondly, this type of integration as a means is almost always unproductive. The participants waste lots of time in an internal sort of mudslinging designed to prove that A is more of a liberal than B. In other words the lack of common ground for solid identification is all the time manifested in internal strifes [sic] inside the group.

It will not sound anachronistic to anybody genuinely interested in real integration to learn that blacks are asserting themselves in a society where they are being treated as perpetual under-16s. One does not need to plan for or actively encourage real integration. Once the various groups within a given community have asserted themselves to the point that mutual respect has to be shown then you have the ingredients for a true and meaningful integration. At the heart of true integration is the provision for each man, each group to rise and attain the envisioned self. Each group must be able to attain its style of existence without encroaching on or being thwarted by another. Out of this mutual respect for each other and complete freedom of self-determination there will obviously arise a genuine fusion of the life-styles of the various groups. This is true integration.

From this it becomes clear that as long as blacks are suffering from [an] inferiority complex—a result of 300 years of deliberate oppression, denigration and derision—they will be useless as co-architects of a normal society where man is nothing else but man for his own sake. Hence what is necessary as a prelude to anything else that may come is a very strong grass-roots build-up of black consciousness such that blacks can learn to assert themselves and stake their rightful claim.

Thus in adopting the line of a nonracial approach, the liberals are playing their old game. They are claiming a "monopoly on intelligence and moral judgement" and setting the pattern and pace for the realisation of the black man's aspirations. They want to remain in good books with both the black and white worlds. They want to shy away from all forms of "extremisms," condemning "white supremacy" as being just as bad as "Black Power!" They vacillate between the two worlds, verbalising all the complaints of the blacks beautifully while skilfully extracting what suits them from the exclusive pool of white privileges. But ask them for a moment to give a concrete meaningful programme that they intend adopting, then you will see on whose side they really are. Their protests are directed at and appeal to white conscience, everything they do is directed at finally convincing the white electorate that the black man is also a man and that at some future date he should be given a place at the white man's table.

In the following selection Anglican bishop Desmond Tutu (b. 1931) expressed his personal anguish at the death of Steve Biko. He summarized Biko's contributions to the struggle for justice in South Africa. Tutu won the Noble Peace Prize in 1984 and was named archbishop in 1988. From 1995 to 1998 he chaired the Truth and Reconciliation Commission, which investigated atrocities in South Africa during the years of apartheid. He stated that his objective was to create "a democratic and just society without racial divisions."

When we heard the news "Steve Biko is dead" we were struck numb with disbelief. No, it can't be true! No, it must be a horrible nightmare, and we will awake and find that really it is different—that Steve is alive even if it be in detention. But no, dear friends, he is dead and we are still numb with grief, and groan with anguish "Oh God, where are you? Oh God, do you really care—how can you let this happen to us?"

It all seems such a senseless waste of a wonderfully gifted person, struck down in the bloom of youth, a youthful bloom that some wanted to see blighted. What can be the purpose of such wanton destruction? God, do you really love us? What must we do which we have not done, what must we say which we have not said a thousand times over, oh, for so many years—that all we want is what belongs to all God's children, what belongs as an inalienable right—a place in the sun in our own beloved mother country. Oh God, how long can we go on? How long can we go on appealing for a more just ordering of society where we all, black and white together, count not because of some accident of birth or a biological irrelevance—where all of us black and white count because we are human persons, human persons created in your own image.

God called Steve Biko to be his servant in South Africa—to speak up on behalf of God, declaring what the will of this God must be in a situation such as ours, a situation of evil, injustice, oppression and exploitation. God called him to be the founder father of the Black Consciousness Movement against which we have had tirades and fulminations. It is a movement by which God, through Steve, sought to awaken in the Black person a sense of his intrinsic value and worth as a child of God, not needing to apologise for his existential condition as a black person, calling on blacks to glorify and praise God that he had created them black. Steve, with his brilliant mind that always saw to the

681

heart of things, realised that until blacks asserted their humanity and their personhood, there was not the remotest chance for reconciliation in South Africa. For true reconciliation is a deeply personal matter. It can happen only between persons who assert their own personhood, and who acknowledge and respect that of others. You don't get reconciled to your dog, do you? Steve knew and believed fervently that being pro-black was not the same thing as being anti-white. The Black Consciousness Movement is not a "hate white movement," despite all you may have heard to the contrary. He had a far too profound respect for persons as persons, to want to deal with them under ready-made, shopsoiled [sic] categories.

All who met him had this tremendous sense of a warm-hearted man, and as a notable acquaintance of his told me, a man who was utterly indestructible, of massive intellect and yet reticent; quite unshakeable in his commitment to principle and to radical change in South Africa by peaceful means; a man of real reconciliation, truly an instrument of God's peace, unshakeable in his commitment to the liberation of all South Africans, black and white, striving for a more just and more open South Africa.

QUESTIONS FOR ANALYSIS

1. What are Steve Biko's charges against white liberals in South Africa?

2. What was the proper role for whites in the anti-apartheid movement according to Biko?

3. How does Bishop Tutu's eulogy differ from the political spirit and point of view expressed in Biko's 1970 essay?

4. According to Bishop Tutu, what were Biko's strongest characteristics? Were these characteristics demonstrated in Biko's essay?

Source: First selection from Steve Biko, *I Write What I Like,* ed. by Aelred Stubbs (Harper & Row, 1972). Reprinted with the permission of Bowerdean Publishing Co., Ltd.; second selection from *Crying in the Wilderness: The Struggle for Justice in South Africa,* ed. John Webster (William B. Eerdmans Publishing Co., 1982). Reprinted by permission of the Continuum International Publishing Group.

against colonial rule. The Bandung Conference marked the beginning of an effort by the many new, poor, mostly non-European nations emerging from colonialism to gain more weight in world affairs by banding together. The terms **nonaligned nations** and **Third World,** which became commonplace in the following years, signaled these countries' collective stance toward the rival sides in the Cold War. If the West, led by the United States, and the East, led by the Soviet Union, represented two worlds locked in mortal struggle, the Third World consisted of everyone else.

Leaders of the so-called Third World countries preferred the label *nonaligned,* which signified freedom from membership on either side. However, because the Soviet Union supported national liberation movements and the nonaligned movement included communist countries such as China and Yugoslavia, many Western leaders did not take the term *nonaligned* seriously. They saw Sukarno, Nehru, Nkrumah, and Egypt's Gamal Abd al-Nasir° as stalking horses for a communist takeover of the world. This may also have been the hope of some Soviet leaders, who were quick to offer some of these countries military and financial aid.

For the movement's leaders, however, nonalignment was a means to extract money and support from one or both superpowers. By flirting with the Soviet Union, the United States, or the People's Republic of China, a country could get military and economic aid.

Some skillful nonaligned leaders were able to gain from both sides. Nasir, who ruled Egypt from 1952 to 1970, and his successor, Anwar al-Sadat°, played the game well. The United States offered to build a dam at Aswan°, on the Nile River, to increase Egypt's electrical generating and irrigation capacity. When Egypt turned to the Soviet Union for arms, the United States reneged on the dam project in 1956. The Soviet Union then picked it up and in the 1960s brought it to conclusion. In 1956, Israel, Great Britain, and France conspired to invade Egypt. Their objective was to overthrow Nasir, regain the Suez Canal (he had recently nationalized it), and secure Israel from any Egyptian threat. The invasion succeeded militarily,

Gamal Abd al-Nasir (gah-MAHL AHB-d al-NAH-suhr)

al-Sadat (al-seh-DAT)   **Aswan** (AS-wahn)

Bandung Conference, 1955   India's Jawaharlal Nehru (in white hat) was a central figure at the conference held in Indonesia to promote solidarity among nonaligned developing nations. The nonalignment movement failed to achieve the influence that Nehru, Egypt's Nasir, and Indonesia's Sukarno sought.   (Wide World Photos)

but both the United States and the Soviet Union pressured the invaders to withdraw, thus saving Nasir's government. In 1972, Sadat evicted his Soviet military advisers but a year later used his Soviet weapons to attack Israel. After he lost that war, he announced his faith in the power of the United States to solve Egypt's political and economic problems.

Numerous other countries adopted similar balancing strategies. In each case, local leaders were trying to develop their nation's economy and assert or preserve their nation's interests. Manipulating the superpowers was simply a means toward those ends and implied very little about true ideological orientation.

Japan and China

No other countries took better advantage of the opportunities presented by the superpowers' preoccupation than did Japan and China. Japan signed a peace treaty with most of its former enemies in 1951 and regained independence from American occupation the following year. Renouncing militarism and its imperialist past, Japan remained on the sidelines throughout the Korean War. Its new constitution, written under American supervision in 1946, allowed only a limited self-defense force, banned the deployment of Japanese troops abroad, and gave the vote to women.

The Japanese turned their talents and energies to rebuilding their industries and engaging in world commerce. By isolating Japan from most world political issues, the Cold War provided an exceptionally favorable environment for Japan to develop its economic strength.

Three industries that took advantage of government aid and the newest technologies paved the way for Japan's emergence as an economic superpower after 1975. Projects producing 60 million kilowatts of electricity were completed between 1951 and 1970, almost a third through dams on Japan's many rivers. Between 1960 and 1970, steel production more than quadrupled, reaching 15.7 percent of the total capacity of countries outside the Soviet bloc. The shipbuilding industry produced six times as much tonnage in 1970 as in 1960, almost half of the new tonnage produced outside the Soviet bloc.

While Japan benefited from being outside the Cold War, China was deeply involved in Cold War politics. When Mao Zedong° and the communists

Mao Zedong (maow dzuh-dong)

defeated the nationalists in 1949 and established the People's Republic of China (PRC), their main ally and source of arms was the Soviet Union. By 1956, however, the PRC and the Soviet Union were beginning to diverge politically, partly in reaction to the Soviet rejection of Stalinism and partly because of China's reluctance to be cast forever in the role of student. Mao had his own notions of communism, focusing strongly on the peasantry, whom the Soviets ignored in favor of the industrial working class.

Mao's Great Leap Forward in 1958 was supposed to vault China into the ranks of world industrial powers by maximizing the use of labor in small-scale, village-level industries. The policy failed but demonstrated Mao's willingness to carry out massive economic and social projects of his own devising.

In 1966, Mao instituted another radical nationwide program, the **Cultural Revolution.** He ordered the mass mobilization of Chinese youth into Red Guard units. His goal was to kindle revolutionary fervor in a new generation and to ward off the stagnation and bureaucratization he saw in the Soviet Union. Red Guard units criticized and purged teachers, party officials, and intellectuals for "bourgeois values." Internal party conflict continued until 1971, when Mao admitted that attacks on individuals had gotten out of hand. Meanwhile, small-scale industrialization resulted in record levels of agricultural and industrial production. The last years of the Cultural Revolution were dominated by radicals led by Mao's wife, Jiang Qing°, who focused on restrictions on artistic and intellectual activity.

In the meantime, the rift between the PRC and the Soviet Union had opened so wide that United States President Richard Nixon (1969–1974), by reputation a staunch anticommunist, dropped objections to the PRC's joining the United Nations. In 1971, the PRC occupied China's permanent seat on the Security Council, displacing the Chinese nationalist government on Taiwan. The following year, Nixon visited Beijing, making dramatically clear the new cooperation between the People's Republic of China and the United States.

Jiang Qing (jyahn ching)

The Middle East

Independence had come gradually to the Arab countries of the Middle East. Britain granted Syria and Lebanon independence after World War II. Other Arab countries—Iraq, Egypt, Jordan—enjoyed nominal independence during the interwar period but remained under indirect British control until the 1950s.

Overshadowing all Arab politics, however, was the struggle with the new state of Israel. British policy on Palestine between the wars oscillated between favoring Zionist Jewish immigrants and the indigenous Palestinian Arabs. After the war, under intense pressure to resettle European Jewish refugees, Britain turned the Palestine problem over to the United Nations. In November 1947, the General Assembly voted in favor of partitioning Palestine into two states, one Jewish and one Arab. The Jewish community made plans to declare independence while the Palestinians, who felt the proposed land division was unfair, reacted in horror and took up arms. When Israel declared its independence in May 1948, neighboring Arab countries sent armies to help the Palestinians crush the newborn state.

Israel, however, prevailed on all fronts. Some 700,000 Palestinians became refugees. They found shelter in United Nations refugee camps in Jordan, Syria, Lebanon, and the Gaza Strip (a bit of coastal land on the Egyptian-Israeli border). The right of these refugees to return home remains a focal point of Arab politics. In 1967, Israel responded to threatening military moves by Egypt's Nasir by preemptively attacking Egyptian and Syrian air bases. In six days, Israel won a smashing victory. Israel won control of Jerusalem, previously split with Jordan, the West Bank, the Gaza Strip, the strategic Golan Heights in southern Syria, and the entire Sinai Peninsula (see Map 28.2). Acquiring all of Jerusalem satisfied Jews' deep longing to return to their holiest city, but Palestinians continued to

Map 28.2 Middle East Oil and the Arab–Israeli Conflict, 1947–1973 Oil resources were long controlled by private European and American companies. In the 1960s most countries, guided by OPEC, negotiated agreements for sharing control, eventually leading to national ownership. This set the stage for the use of oil as a weapon in the 1973 Arab-Israeli war and for subsequent price increases.

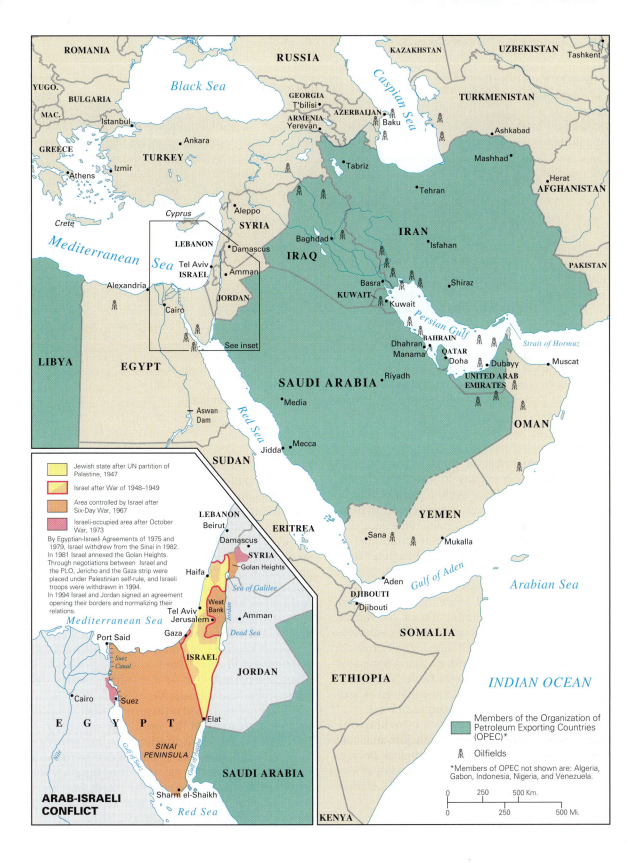

ROMANIA

Black Sea

RUSSIA

KAZAKHSTAN

UZBEKISTAN

•Tashkent

YUGO.

BULGARIA

MAC.

•Istanbul

GEORGIA
T'bilisi•

AZERBAIJAN
•Baku

Caspian
Sea

TURKMENISTAN

•Ashkabad

GREECE

•Ankara

ARMENIA
Yerevan•

•Mashhad

•Herat

•Izmir

TURKEY

•Tabriz

AFGHANISTAN

Athens•

Crete

•Aleppo

SYRIA

Cyprus

•Damascus
LEBANON

Mediterranean

Tel Aviv•
ISRAEL

•Amman

Baghdad•

•Tehran

IRAN

•Isfahan

PAKISTAN

Sea

IRAQ

Basra•

•Shiraz

Alexandria•

JORDAN

KUWAIT

•Kuwait

Cairo•

See inset

LIBYA

EGYPT

•Aswan
Dam

Red Sea

SAUDI ARABIA

•Media

Persian Gulf
Dhahran•
Manama•

BAHRAIN
QATAR
•Doha

•Dubayy

Strait of Hormuz

•Muscat

UNITED ARAB
EMIRATES

•Riyadh

OMAN

SUDAN

Jidda•

•Mecca

YEMEN

Arabian Sea

Sana•

•Mukalla

DJIBOUTI

Djibouti•

•Aden

Gulf of Aden

SOMALIA

ETHIOPIA

INDIAN OCEAN

KENYA

ARAB-ISRAELI
CONFLICT

Jewish state after UN partition of
Palastine, 1947

Israel after War of 1948–1949

Area controlled by Israel after
Six-Day War, 1967

Israeli-occupied area after October
War, 1973

By Egyptian-Israeli Agreements of 1975 and
1979, Israel withdrew from the Sinai in 1982.
In 1981 Israel annexed the Golan Heights.
Through negotiations between Israel and
the PLO, Jericho and the Gaza strip were
placed under Palestinian self-rule, and Israeli
troops were withdrawn in 1994.
In 1994 Israel and Jordan signed an agreement
opening their borders and normalizing their
relations.

LEBANON
Beirut•

ERITREA

Damascus•

SYRIA

Golan Heights

Haifa•

Sea of Galilee

Mediterranean Sea

West
Bank

Tel Aviv•
Jerusalem•

•Amman

Port Said•

Gaza•

Dead Sea

Jordan

ISRAEL

JORDAN

Suez
Canal

•Cairo

Suez•

E G Y P T

Nile

SINAI
PENINSULA

Gulf of Suez

Gulf of Aqaba

•Elat

SAUDI ARABIA

Sharm el-Shaikh•

Red Sea

Members of the Organization of
Petroleum Exporting Countries
(OPEC)*

Oilfields

*Members of OPEC not shown are: Algeria,
Gabon, Indonesia, Nigeria, and Venezuela.

0   250   500 Km.

0   250   500 Mi.

Oil Crisis at the Gas Station   Dislocations in the oil industry caused by OPEC price increases that began in 1974 produced long lines at gas pumps and local shortages. The crisis brought Middle East politics home to consumers and created a negative stereotype of "oil sheikhs."   (Keza/Gamma)

regard Jerusalem as their destined capital, and Muslims in many countries protested Israeli control of the Dome of the Rock, a revered Islamic shrine located in the city. These acquisitions resulted in a new wave of Palestinian refugees.

The rival claims to Palestine continued to plague Middle Eastern politics. The Palestine Liberation Organization (PLO), headed by Yasir Arafat°, waged guerrilla war against Israel, frequently engaging in acts of terrorism. The militarized Israelis were able to blunt or absorb these attacks and launch counterstrikes that likewise involved assassinations and bombings. Though the United States proved a firm friend of Israel and the Soviet Union armed the Arab states, neither superpower saw the struggle between Zionism and Palestinian nationalism as a vital concern—until oil became a political issue.

The phenomenal concentration of oil wealth in the Persian Gulf states—Iran, Iraq, Kuwait, Saudi Arabia, Qatar, Bahrain, and the United Arab Emirates—was not fully realized until after World War II when demand for oil rose sharply as civilian

economies recovered. As a world oversupply diminished in the face of rising demand, oil-producing states in 1960 formed the **Organization of Petroleum Exporting Countries (OPEC)** to promote their collective interest in higher revenues.

Oil politics and the Arab-Israeli conflict intersected in October 1973. A surprise Egyptian attack across the Suez Canal threw the Israelis into temporary disarray. Within days, the war turned in Israel's favor, and an Egyptian army was trapped at the canal's southern end. The United States then arranged a cease-fire and the disengagement of forces. But before that could happen, the Arab oil-producing countries voted to embargo oil shipments to the United States and the Netherlands as punishment for their support of Israel.

The implications of oil as an economic weapon profoundly disturbed the worldwide oil industry. Prices rose—along with feelings of insecurity. In 1974, OPEC responded to the turmoil in the oil market by quadrupling prices, setting the stage for massive transfers of wealth to the producing countries and provoking a feeling of crisis throughout the consuming countries.

Arafat (AR-uh-fat)

The Emergence of Environmental Concerns

Skyrocketing oil prices focused new attention on natural resource issues. Before the mid-1960s, only a few people noticed that untested technologies and all-out drives for industrial productivity were rapidly degrading the environment. The superpowers were particularly negligent of the environmental impact of pesticide and herbicide use, automobile exhaust, industrial waste disposal, and radiation hazards.

New youth activism focused awareness on environmental problems. In 1968, a wave of student unrest swept many parts of the world. Earth Day was first celebrated in 1970, the year in which the United States established its Environmental Protection Agency.

After 1974, making gasoline engines and home heating systems more efficient and lowering highway speed limits to conserve fuel became matters of national debate in the United States while poorer countries struggled to find the money to import oil. A widely read 1972 study, *The Limits of Growth,* forecast a need to cut back on consumption of natural resources in the twenty-first century. Thus, as the most dangerous moments of the Cold War seemed to be passing, ecological and environmental problems of worldwide impact vied with the superpower rivalry and Third World nation building for public attention.

CONCLUSION

The Cold War and the decolonization movement seemed to arise as logical extensions of World War II. The question of who would control the parts of Europe and Asia liberated from Axis occupation led to Churchill's notion of an iron curtain dividing East and West. The war exhaustion of the European imperialist powers encouraged Asian and African peoples to seek independence and embark on building their own nations.

Intellectuals often framed their understanding of the period in terms of a philosophical struggle between capitalism and socialism dating back to the nineteenth century. But for leaders facing the challenge of governing new nations and creating viable economies, ideology became intertwined with questions of how to profit from the Cold War rivalry between the United States and the Soviet Union.

Historians do not all agree on the year 1975 as the end of the postwar era. The end of the Vietnam War, the beginning of the world oil crisis, and the signing of the Helsinki Accords that brought a measure of agreement among Europeans on both sides of the iron curtain were pivotal events for some countries. But the number of independent countries in the world had grown enormously, and each was in the process of working out its own particular problems. What marks the mid-1970s as the end of an era, therefore, is not a single event so much as the emergence of new concerns. Young people with no memories of World War II were less concerned with the Cold War and the specter of nuclear annihilation than with newly recognized threats to the world environment and with making their own way in the world. In the wealthier nations, this meant taking advantage of economic growth and increasing technological sophistication. In the developing world, it meant seeking the education and employment needed for playing active roles in the drama of nation building.

■ Key Terms

iron curtain
Cold War
North Atlantic Treaty Organization (NATO)
United Nations
World Bank
Marshall Plan
European Community (EC)
Truman Doctrine
Warsaw Pact
Korean War
Vietnam War
Cuban missile crisis
Helsinki Accords
nonaligned nations
Third World
Cultural Revolution (China)
Organization of Petroleum Exporting Countries (OPEC)

■ Suggested Reading

The period since 1945 has been particularly rich in memoirs by government leaders. Some that are particularly relevant to the Cold War and decolonization are Dean Acheson (U.S. secretary of state under Truman), *Present at the Creation* (1969); Nikita Khrushchev, *Khrushchev Remembers* (1970); and Anthony Eden (British prime minister), *Full Circle* (1960).

Geoffrey Barraclough, *An Introduction to Contemporary History* (1964), is a remarkable early effort at understanding the broad sweep of history during this period. See also David Reynolds, *One World Divisible: A Global History Since 1945* (2000).

Scholarship on the origins of the Cold War is extensive and includes Akira Iriye, *The Cold War in Asia: A Historical Introduction* (1974); Bruce Kuniholm, *The Origins of the Cold War in the Middle East* (1980); Madelaine Kalb, *The Congo Cables: The Cold War in Africa—From Eisenhower to Kennedy* (1982); and Michael J. Hogan, *A Cross of Iron: Harry S Truman and the Origins of the National Security State* (1998). For a recent reconsideration of earlier historical viewpoints, see Melvyn P. Leffler and David S. Painter, eds., *Origins of the Cold War: An International History* (1994).

Good general histories of the Cold War include Martin Walker, *The Cold War: A History* (1993), and Walter Lafeber, *America, Russia, and the Cold War, 1945–1992* (1993). The latter emphasizes how the Cold War eroded American democratic values. For a look at the Cold War from the Soviet perspective, see William Taubman, *Stalin's America Policy* (1981); for the American perspective, see John Lewis Gaddis, *Strategies of Containment: A Critical Appraisal of Postwar American National Security Policy* (1982). The Cuban missile crisis is well covered in Graham Allison, *Essence of Decision: Explaining the Cuban Missile Crisis* (1971), and Michael Beschloss, *The Crisis Years: Kennedy and Khrushchev, 1960–1963* (1991). Also see Aleksandr Fursenko and Timothy Naftali, *"One Hell of a Gamble": Khrushchev, Castro, and Kennedy, 1958–1964: The Secret History of the Cuban Missile Crisis* (1997); and the more recent John L. Gaddis, *We Now Know: Rethinking Cold War History* (1997); Mark Mazower, *Dark Continent* (1999); and William Hitchcock, *The Struggle for Europe: The Turbulent History of a Divided Continent 1945–2002* (2003).

The nuclear arms race and the associated Soviet–U.S. competition in space are well covered by McGeorge Bundy, *Danger and Survival: Choices About the Bomb in the First Fifty Years* (1988), and Walter MacDougall, *The Heavens and the Earth: A Political History of the Space Age* (1985). Among the many novels illustrating the alarming impact of the arms race on the general public are Philip Wylie, *Tomorrow!* (1954), and Nevil Shute, *On the Beach* (1970). At a technical and philosophical level, Herman Kahn's *On Thermonuclear War* (1961) had a similar effect.

The end of the European empires is broadly treated by D. K. Fieldhouse, *The Colonial Empires* (1982); a broad view is provided by D. A. Low, *The Egalitarian Moment: Asia and Africa, 1950–1980* (1996); for the British Empire in particular, see Brian Lapping, *End of Empire* (1985). For a critical view of American policies toward the decolonized world, see Gabriel Kolko, *Confronting the Third World: United States Foreign Policy, 1945–1980* (1988).

Books on some of the specific episodes of decolonization treated in this chapter include the following: on Algeria, Alistaire Horne, *A Savage War of Peace: Algeria, 1954–1962* (1987); on Africa, H. S. Wilson, *African Decolonization* (1994), and Frederick Cooper, *Decolonization and African Society: The Labor Question in French and British Africa* (1996); on Cuba, Hugh Thomas, *Cuba: The Pursuit of Freedom* (1971); on the Suez crisis of 1956, Keith Kyle, *Suez 1956* (1991); on Britain's role in the Middle East over the period of the birth of Israel, William Roger Louis, *The British Empire in the Middle East, 1945–1951* (1984); on Vietnam, George Herring, *America's Longest War: The United States and Vietnam, 1950–1975* (1986), and Stanley Karnow, *Vietnam: A History* (1991); and on Latin America, Thomas E. Skidmore and Peter H. Smith, *Modern Latin America*, 5th ed. (2001).

The special cases of Japan and China in this period are covered by Takafusa Nakamura, *A History of Showa Japan, 1926–1989* (1998); John Dower, *Embracing Defeat: Japan in the Wake of World War II* (1999); Marius B. Jansen, *Japan and China: From War to Peace, 1894–1972* (1975); and Maurice Meisner, *Mao's China and After: A History of the People's Republic* (1986). On the consequences of the Great Leap Forward, see Jasper Becker, *Hungry Ghosts* (1998); and on the Cultural Revolution, see Lynn T. White, *Policies of Chaos: The Organizational Causes of Violence in China's Cultural Revolution* (1989). John Merrill, *Korea: The Peninsular Origins of the War* (1989), presents the Korean War as a civil and revolutionary conflict as well as an episode of the Cold War. Among the hundreds of books on the Arab-Israeli conflict, Charles D. Smith, *Palestine and the Arab-Israel Conflict* (1992), and Trevor N. Dupuy, *Elusive Victory: The Arab-Israeli Wars, 1947–1974* (1978), stand out.

Crisis, Realignment, and the Dawn of the Post–Cold War World, 1975–1991

29

CHAPTER OUTLINE

Postcolonial Crises and Asian Economic Expansion, 1975–1991

The End of the Bipolar World, 1989–1991

The Challenge of Population Growth

Unequal Development and the Movement of Peoples

Technological and Environmental Change

DIVERSITY AND DOMINANCE: **The Struggle for Women's Rights in an Era of Global Political and Economic Change**

On Thursday, July 22, 1993, police officers in Rio de Janeiro's banking district attempted to arrest a young boy caught sniffing glue. In the resulting scuffle, one police officer was injured by stones thrown by a group of homeless children who lived in nearby streets and parks. Late the following night, hooded vigilantes in two cars fired hundreds of shots at a group of these children sleeping on the steps of a church. The attackers, later identified as off-duty police officers, killed five children there and two more in a park.

At that time, more than 350,000 abandoned children lived in Rio's streets and parks and resorted to begging, selling drugs, stealing, and prostitution to survive. In 1993 alone, death squads and drug dealers killed more than four hundred of them. Few people sympathized with the victims. One person living near the scene of the July shootings said, "Those street kids are bandits, and bandits have to die. They are a rotten branch that has to be pruned."[1]

At the end of the twentieth century, the brutality of those children's lives was an increasingly common feature of life in the developing world, where rapid population growth was outstripping economic resources. Similar problems of violence, poverty, and social breakdown could be found in most developing nations.

In wealthy industrialized nations as well, politicians and social reformers worried about the effects of unemployment, family breakdown, substance abuse, and homelessness. As had been true during the eighteenth-century Industrial Revolution (see Chapter 20), dramatic economic growth, increased global economic integration, and rapid technological progress in the post–World War II period coincided with growing social dislocation and inequality. Among the most important events of the period were the emergence of new industrial powers in Asia and the precipitous demise of the Soviet Union and its socialist allies.

New challenges also appeared in the form of world population growth and large-scale migrations. Population grew most rapidly in the world's poorest nations, worsening social and economic problems and undermining fragile political institutions. In the industrialized nations, the arrival of large numbers of culturally and linguistically distinct immigrants fueled economic growth but also led to the appearance of anti-immigrant political movements and, in some cases, violent ethnic conflict.

As you read this chapter, ask yourself the following questions:

- How did the Cold War affect politics in Latin America and the Middle East in the 1970s and 1980s?

- What forces led to the collapse of the Soviet Union?

- What is the relationship between the rate of population growth and the wealth of nations?

- How has technological change affected the global environment in the recent past?

POSTCOLONIAL CRISES AND ASIAN ECONOMIC EXPANSION, 1975–1991

Between 1975 and 1991, wars and revolutions provoked by a potent mix of ideology, nationalism, ethnic hatred, and religious fervor spread death and destruction through many of the world's least developed regions. Although often tied to earlier colonialism and foreign intervention, each conflict reflected a specific set of historical experiences. In many cases, conflicts provoked by local and regional causes tended to become more deadly and long lasting because the United States and the Soviet Union intervened. Conflicts in which the rival superpowers financed and armed competing factions or parties were called **proxy wars.**

Local and regional conflicts and proxy wars were not universal. During this same period, Japan gained a position among the world's leading industrial powers, while a small number of other Asian economies quickly entered the ranks of industrial and commercial powers. By the early 1990s, the collapse of the Soviet system in eastern Europe had ended the Cold War. As former socialist nations opened their markets to foreign investment and competition, economic transformation was often accompanied by wrenching social change. Other challenges facing the late twentieth century included growing inequalities among nations and within nations, rapid population expansion, and degradation of the environment.

Revolutions, Repression, and Democratic Reform in Latin America

After the Cuban Revolution, Fidel Castro sought to end the domination of the United States and uplift the Cuban masses by changing the economy in fundamental ways. Both objectives led to confrontation with the United States. The Cuban Revolution was the first revolution in the Western Hemisphere to nationalize foreign investment, redistribute the wealth of the elite, and forge an alliance with the

C H R O N O L O G Y

	The Americas	Middle East	Asia	Eastern Europe
1970	**1964** Military takeover in Brazil			
	1970 Salvador Allende elected president of Chile			
	1973 Allende overthrown			
			1975 Vietnam war ends	
	1976 Military takeover in Argentina			
			1978 China opens its economy	
	1979 Sandinistas overthrow Anastasio Somoza in Nicaragua	**1979** Islamic Revolution over-throws shah of Iran		**1979** USSR sends troops to Afghanistan
1980		**1980–1988** Iran-Iraq War		
	1983–1990 Democracy returns in Argentina, Brazil, and Chile			
				1985 Mikhail Gorbachev becomes Soviet head of state
			1986 Average Japanese income overtakes income in United States	
			1989 Tiananmen Square confrontation	**1989** USSR with-draws troops from Afghanistan; Berlin Wall falls
				1989–1991 End of communism in eastern Europe
1990	**1990** Sandinistas defeated in elections in Nicaragua	**1990** Iraq invades Kuwait		**1990** Reunifica-tion of Germany
		1991 Persian Gulf War		

Soviet Union. The fact that a communist government could come to power and thwart efforts by the United States to overthrow it energized the revolutionary left throughout Latin America (see Chapter 28). Unable to overthrow Castro and fearful that revolution would spread across Latin America, the United States mobilized its political and military allies in Latin America to defeat communism at all costs.

Brazil was the first to experience the full effects of the conservative reaction to the Cuban Revolution. Claiming that Brazil's civilian political leaders could not protect the nation from communist subversion, the army overthrew the democratically elected government in 1964. The military suspended the constitution, outlawed all existing political parties, and exiled former presidents and opposition leaders. Death squads—illegal paramilitary organizations sanctioned by the government—detained, tortured, and executed thousands of citizens. The dictatorship also undertook an ambitious economic program that promoted industrialization through import substitution, using tax and tariff policies to compel foreign-owned companies to increase investment in manufacturing.

Elements of this "Brazilian Solution" were imposed across much of Latin America in the 1970s and early 1980s. In 1970, Chile's new president, **Salvador Allende°**, undertook an ambitious program of socialist reforms to redistribute wealth from the elite and middle classes to the poor. He also nationalized most of Chile's heavy industry and mines, including the American-owned copper companies that dominated the Chilean economy. From the beginning of Allende's presidency, the administration of United States President Richard Nixon (1969–1973) worked in Chile to organize opposition to Allende's reforms. After Chile's economy weakened, Allende was overthrown in 1973 by a military uprising led by General Augusto Pinochet° and supported by the United States. President Allende and thousands of Chileans died in this uprising, and thousands of others were illegally seized, tortured, and imprisoned without trial. Once in power, Pinochet rolled back Allende's reforms, reduced state participation in the economy, and en-

couraged foreign investment. In 1976, Argentina followed Brazil and Chile into military dictatorship. During the next seven years, the military fought what it called the **Dirty War** against terrorism. More than nine thousand Argentines lost their lives, and thousands of others endured arrest, terrible tortures, and the loss of property.

The flow of U.S. arms to regimes with the worst human rights records stopped during the four-year term of United States president Jimmy Carter (1977–1980). Carter championed human rights in the hemisphere and sought to placate Latin American resentment for past U.S. interventions by renegotiating the Panama Canal treaty and agreeing to the reestablishment of Panamanian sovereignty in the Canal Zone at the end of 1999. He also tried, but failed, to find some common ground with the **Sandinistas°**, a revolutionary movement in Nicaragua that overthrew the corrupt dictatorship of Anastasio Somoza in 1979. The Sandinistas received significant political and financial support from Cuba and, once in power, sought to imitate the command economies of Cuba and the Soviet Union. The Nicaraguan Revolution nationalized properties owned by members of the Nicaraguan elite and U.S. citizens.

In 1981, Ronald Reagan became president and replaced Carter's policy of conciliation with efforts at reversing the results of the Nicaraguan Revolution and defeating a revolutionary movement in neighboring El Salvador. His options, however, were limited by the U.S. Congress, which feared that Central America might become another Vietnam. The Reagan administration sought to roll back the Nicaraguan Revolution through punitive economic measures and support for the anti-Sandinista Contras (counterrevolutionaries), using both legal and illegal funds.

The Contras were unable to defeat the Sandinistas, but they did gain a bloody stalemate by the end of the 1980s. Confident that they were supported by the majority of Nicaraguans and assured that the U.S. Congress was close to cutting off aid to the Contras, the Sandinistas called for free elections in 1990. But they had miscalculated and lost the election. Exhausted by more than a decade of violence, a majority of Nicaraguan voters rejected

---

Salvador Allende (sal-vah-DOR ah-YEHN-day) **Augusto Pinochet** (ah-GOOS-toh pin-oh-CHET)

Sandinistas (sahn-din-EES-tahs)

the Sandinistas and elected a middle-of-the-road coalition led by Violeta Chamorro°.

The military dictatorships established in Brazil, Chile, and Argentina all came to an end between 1983 and 1990. In each case, reports of kidnappings, tortures, and corruption by military governments undermined public support. In Argentina, the military junta foolishly decided in 1982 to seize the Falkland Islands—the Argentines called them the "Malvinas." The Argentine junta had helped President Reagan support the Contras in Nicaragua and believed he would keep Britain's prime minister, Margaret Thatcher, from taking military action. When the Argentine garrison in the Falklands surrendered, military rule in Argentina itself collapsed.

In Chile and Brazil, the military dictatorships ended without the drama of foreign war. Despite significant economic growth under Pinochet, Chileans resented the violence and corruption of the military. In 1988, Pinochet called a plebiscite to extend his authority, but the majority vote went against him. Brazil's military initiated a gradual transition to civilian rule in 1985. By 1991, nearly 95 percent of Latin America's population lived under civilian rule.

In 1991 most Latin American countries were also dominated by the United States and were reducing the economic role of the state. However, after 1994 new political movements have been demanding more government participation in the economy (see Diversity and Dominance: The Struggle for Women's Rights in an Era of Global Political and Economic Change).

Islamic Revolutions in Iran and Afghanistan

The Middle East was another region where the superpowers were involved in local revolutions. The United States was motivated to act in support of Israel and to protect access to petroleum from the region. The Soviet Union wished to prevent the spread of radical Islamic movements across the border into its own Muslim regions.

The Iranian Revolution of 1979 proved enormously frustrating to the United States. In 1953,

covert intervention by the United States Central Intelligence Agency (CIA) helped Shah Muhammad Reza Pahlavi° retain his throne in the face of a movement to usurp royal power. Even when he finally nationalized the foreign-owned oil industry, the shah continued to enjoy special American support. As oil revenues increased following the price increases of the 1970s, the United States encouraged the shah to spend his nation's growing wealth on equipping the Iranian army with advanced American weaponry. By the 1970s, there was mounting popular resentment against the shah's dependence on the United States, the ballooning wealth of the elite families that supported him, and the inefficiency, malfeasance, and corruption of his government, which led to mass opposition.

Ayatollah Ruhollah Khomeini°, a Shi'ite° philosopher-cleric who had spent most of his eighty-plus years in religious and academic pursuits, became the voice and symbolic leader of the opposition. Massive street demonstrations and crippling strikes forced the shah to flee Iran and ended the monarchy in 1979. In the Islamic Republic of Iran, which replaced the monarchy, Ayatollah Khomeini was supreme arbiter of disputes and guarantor of religious legitimacy. Elections were held, but monarchists, communists, and other groups opposed to the idea of an Islamic Republic were barred from running for office. Shi'ite clerics with little training for government service emerged in many of the highest posts, and stringent measures were taken to replace Western styles and culture with Islamic norms. Universities were temporarily closed, and their faculties were purged of secularists and monarchists. Women were compelled to wear modest Islamic garments outside the house, and semi-official vigilante committees policed public morals.

The United States under President Carter had criticized the shah's repressive regime, but the overthrow of a long-standing ally and the creation of the Islamic Republic were blows to American prestige. Khomeini saw the United States as a "Great Satan" opposed to Islam, and he helped to foster Islamic revolutionary movements elsewhere, which threatened the interests of both the United

---

Violeta Chamorro (vee-oh-LET-ah cha-MOR-roe)

Reza Pahlavi (REH-zah PAH-lah-vee)   **Ayatollah Ruhollah Khomeini** (eye-uh-TOLL-uh ROOH-ol-LAH ko-MAY-nee)   **Shi'ite** (SHE-ite)

DIVERSITY AND DOMINANCE

THE STRUGGLE FOR WOMEN'S RIGHTS IN AN ERA OF GLOBAL POLITICAL AND ECONOMIC CHANGE

The struggle for women's rights is one of the most important social movements of the twentieth century. Although fundamental similarities in objectives can be identified across cultural and political boundaries, women in less-developed nations are forced to recognize that their objectives and strategies must take into account international inequalities in power and wealth. In this section Gladys Acosta, a militant Peruvian feminist, discusses the appropriate agenda for this struggle in the era after the fall of the Soviet Union and the rise of neo-liberalism.

Neo-liberalism is the term used in Latin America to identify the free-market economic policies advocated by the United States. Among its chief characteristics are an end to the protection of local industries, a reduction in government social welfare policies, a reduction in public-sector employment, a commitment to paying debts to international creditors, and the removal of impediments to foreign investment. Many Latin Americans believe neo-liberalism is a new form of imperialism.

No one can abstain from the debate about the great historical systems of our time. Not even those of us who are trying to change the complex web of human relationships from a feminist perspective. Everywhere people are talking about the end of ideologies. But before we can grasp the significance of current events and their consequences, we need to pinpoint our various doubts and blank spots. Capitalism is the main pivot of our lives because we were born under its influence. It [has] hegemony. . . .

Gender, the main distinction between all people, is ignored in most philosophical, political or economic discussions. The reason for this lies partly in the low level of women's participation, but not entirely, because women are not always aware of the system of submission and repression to which we are subjected against

our will. We need to find something which unites women in a gender-specific manner. That doesn't mean sweeping under the carpet all the differences between us, like social position, culture or age. . . .

Neo-Liberalism in Action

For those of us who live under the influence of the capitalist system, the situation is different. When I talk of neo-liberalism, I mean austerity measures, foreign debts, and increased liberties for all those who have the power of money at their disposal and the power of repression over those who make demands. We have now reached a new form of capitalist accumulation. The world's economic system is in a state of change and capital has become more concentrated and centralised. I would not go as far as to say countries don't exist anymore but national identities do certainly play a different role now. It is important to understand the dynamics because otherwise historical responsibilities are obscured and we no longer know whom we're fighting against. If we look at the bare face of neo-liberalism from a woman's point of view, we cannot fail to notice its murderous consequences. To create a more humane society we must continue to reject neo-liberalism here and now in the hope of being able to change the dead present into a living future. Under neo-liberalism there is a breathtaking circulation of commodities, but also an exchange of ideas, illusions and dreams. At the moment we're experiencing capitalism's greatest ideological offensive. It's all business: everything is bought and sold and everything has its price.

The Consequences of Neo-Liberal Politics

We women play an important role in this ever-more internationalized economy because we represent, as ever, a particularly exploitable workforce. A number of studies have revealed the existence of subcontractor chains

694

who work for transnational companies "informally" and mainly employ women. Basically we are dealing with a kind of integration into the world market which often uses our own homes as its outlet. Obviously, this work is badly paid and completely unprotected and has to be done without any of those social rights which were formerly achieved by trade union struggles. The most important thing for us is to keep hold of just one thread of the enterprise so we can show how the commodities make their way to their final destination. As it advances worldwide, this capitalism also encourages the expansion of certain kinds of tourism. A visible increase in prostitution is part of this, whereby women from poor countries are smuggled into large, internationally-operated rings which exploit them. The reports of Filipina women traded on the West German market send shivers down our spines. . . . What kind of freedom are you talking about there?

How the Adoption of Austerity Measures Affects Women's Lives

It is obvious that foreign debt is one of the most inhuman forms of exploitation in our countries when one considers the ratio between work necessary for workers' needs and work producing profit for employers. The experts have already explained how the prevailing exchange and investment structures have created international finance systems which keep whole populations in inhuman conditions. Although many people might think it crazy, the development model of the global economy has a marked relation to gender. As long as prices were slapped on some luxury consumer items there weren't any serious problems; but now the snares have been set around basic commodities. Women in every household are suffering every day as a result of impoverished economies and those who are most exposed to the effects of foreign debt are women.

When it comes to shopping, caring for sick children or the impossibility of meeting their schooling costs, the illusion of "leaving poverty behind" evaporates. Yet the problem is not only of an economic nature because under such circumstances the constant tension leads to grave, often lasting exhaustion. The psychosocial damage is alarming. The situation is ready to explode, so to speak. . . . The adoption of austerity measures means a curtailment of the state's commitment to social services with a direct effect on women. Daily life becomes hell for them. The lack of even minimal state welfare presents women (and obviously children too) with crushing working days. There is a constant expenditure of human energy without any hope of rest! No relaxation, no breaks. . . . And if we consider what happens within the family, we notice that women keep the smallest portion of the meagre family income. They give everything to their children or those adults who bring home a pay packet. As a result malnutrition among women is increasing at an alarming rate and their frequent pregnancies represent a superhuman physical achievement.

Women's valiant achievements in defending life and survival are not acknowledged by society. The efforts of women's organisations, whether it be communal kitchens, the glass-of-milk committees [milk distribution among the poor] or health services don't get the appropriate social esteem. The social value of women cannot be calculated. Perhaps in years to come the fate of millions of women who sacrifice everything to support the children and youth of Peru and other countries in Latin America will be acknowledged. We should not ignore the fact that violence of every form . . . goes hand-in-hand with the difficult situation I have described.[1] It's nothing new for women because the open wounds of sexual violence, abuse at home and the contempt of this *machista* culture, have always featured in our lives and our mothers' lives. The challenge is to prevent these from also affecting our future generations.

And the Future?

The neo-liberal offensive is international and demands international opposition strategies combined with political proposals by new social forces which address women's problems. We want to change estimations of our worth and achieve society's acknowledgement of what has been belittled until now as "women's affairs." Such important decisions as the right to the termination of unwanted pregnancies can no longer be ignored on the political stage. We want our place in the political decision-making process; we want to have a say in all problems which concern the Peruvian people and the

[1] In the last Report of the Comisaria de mujeres in Lima (the only one in the country at present) 4,800 rapes were filed for 1990, of which 4,200 went to trial. The police commissioner, in reading the document, personally acknowledged the alarming social problem which is posed by the violence of men who are connected to their victims in some way and which, indeed, persists throughout all levels of society.

whole world. We want to be informed so as not to be deceived by those who are used to practising politics for a flock of sheep. This road will be difficult but at least we shall regain the strengths of socialism and create social alternatives which are aimed at changing the destructive technological order as well as eliminating the international division of labour and the sexual hierarchy inherent within it. In so doing we shall try to create democratic structures which include the people in the decision-making process. The barriers thrown up by formal representative structures must be overcome urgently. A new democracy should be founded as the basic prerequisite for the society of the future.

QUESTIONS FOR ANALYSIS

1. What is neo-liberalism?
2. According to Acosta, how does global economic integration fostered by neo-liberalism affect the lives of women as workers?
3. Acosta claims that indebtedness to foreign lenders leads to austerity measures. How does this impact families in poor countries?
4. What does Acosta advocate?

Source: Gaby Küppers, ed., *Compañeras. Voices from the Latin American Women's Movement* (London: Latin American Bureau, 1994), 167–172.

States and Israel. In November 1979, Iranian radicals seized the U.S. embassy in Tehran and then held fifty-two diplomats hostage for 444 days. Americans felt humiliated by their inability to do anything, particularly after the failure of a military rescue attempt. In the fall of 1980, shortly after negotiations for the release of the hostages began, **Saddam Husayn°**, the ruler of neighboring Iraq, invaded Iran to topple the Islamic Republic. His own dictatorial rule rested on a secular Arab nationalist philosophy and long-standing friendship with the Soviet Union, which had provided him with advanced weaponry. He feared that the fervor of Iran's revolutionary Shi'ite leaders would infect his own country's Shi'ite majority and threaten his power. The war pitted American weapons in the hands of the Iranians against Soviet weapons in the hands of the Iraqis, but the superpowers avoided overt involvement during eight years of bloodshed. Covertly, however, the Reagan administration sent arms via Israel to Iran, hoping to gain the release of other American hostages held by radical Islamic groups in Lebanon and to help finance the Contra war against the Sandinista government of Nicaragua. When this deal came to the light in 1986, the resulting political scandal intensified American hostility toward Iran. Openly tilting toward Iraq, President Reagan sent the United States Navy to the Persian Gulf, ostensibly to protect nonbelligerent shipping. The move helped persuade Iran to accept a cease-fire in 1988.

Saddam Husayn (sah-DAHM who-SANE)

While the United States faced anguish and frustration in Iran, the Soviet Union found itself facing even more serious problems in neighboring Afghanistan. Since World War II, the Soviet Union had succeeded in staying out of shooting wars by using proxies to challenge the United States. But in 1979, the Soviet Union sent its army to Afghanistan to bolster communist rule against a hodgepodge of local, religiously inspired guerrilla bands that had taken control of much of the countryside.

With the United States, Saudi Arabia, and Pakistan paying, equipping, and training the Afghan rebels, the Soviet Union found itself in the same kind of unwinnable war the United States had stumbled into in Vietnam. Unable to justify the continuing drain on manpower, morale, and economic resources and facing widespread domestic discontent over the war, Soviet leaders finally withdrew their troops in 1989. The Afghan communists held on for another three years. But once rebel groups took control of the entire country, they began to fight among themselves over who should rule.

Asian Transformation

Japan has few mineral resources and is dependent on oil imports, but the Japanese economy weathered the oil price shocks of the 1970s better than did the economies of Europe and the United States. In fact, Japan experienced a faster rate of economic growth in the 1970s and 1980s than did any other major developed economy, growing at about 10 percent a year. Average income also increased rapidly, overtaking that of the United States in 1986.

There are some major differences between the Japanese industrial model and that of the United States. During the American occupation, Japanese industrial conglomerates, *zaibatsu* (see Chapter 25), were broken up. Although ownership of major industries became less concentrated as a result, new industrial alliances appeared. There are now six major **keiretsu°** that each include firms in industry, commerce, construction, and a major bank tied together in an interlocking ownership structure. There are also minor keiretsu dominated by a major corporation, like Toyota, and including its major suppliers. These combinations of companies have close relationships with government. Government assistance in the form of tariffs and import regulations inhibiting foreign competition was crucial in the early stages of the development of Japan's automobile and semiconductor industries, among others.

Through the 1970s and 1980s, Japanese success at exporting manufactured goods produced huge trade surpluses with other nations, prompting the United States and the European Community to try to pry open the Japanese market through tough negotiating. These efforts had only limited success. In 1990, Japan enjoyed a trade surplus with the rest of the world that was twice as large as in 1985. Many experts assumed that the competitive advantages that Japan enjoyed in the 1980s would propel Japan past the United States as the world's preeminent industrial economy. But the Japanese economy began to stall at the end of the decade.

The Japanese model of close cooperation between government and industry was imitated by a small number of other Asian states. The most important of them was South Korea, which overcame the devastation of the Korean War in little more than a decade through a combination of inexpensive labor, strong technical education, and substantial domestic capital reserves. Despite large defense expenditures, South Korea developed heavy industries such as steel and shipbuilding, as well as consumer industries such as automobiles and consumer electronics. Japanese investment and

Muslim Women Mourning the Death of Ayatollah Khomeini in 1989   An Islamic revolution overthrew the shah of Iran in 1979. Ayatollah Khomeini sought to lead Iran away from the influences of Western culture and challenged the power of the United States in the Persian Gulf.   (Alexandra Avakian/Woodfin Camp & Associates)

technology transfers accelerated this process. Hyundai was typical of the four giant corporations that accounted for nearly half of South Korea's gross domestic product (GDP) in manufacturing products ranging from supertankers and cars to electronics and housing.

Taiwan, Hong Kong, and Singapore also developed modern industrial and commercial economies so rapidly that these three nations and South Korea were often referred to as the **Asian Tigers.** All shared many characteristics that helped explain their rapid industrialization. All had disciplined and hard-working labor forces, and all invested heavily in education. For example, as early as 1980, Korea had as many engineering graduates as Germany, Britain, and Sweden combined. All had high

keiretsu (kay-REHT-soo)

Dry Docks Owned by Korea's Hyundai Corporation Korea's rapid industrialization symbolizes Pacific Rim economic growth. (Paul Chesley/Getty Images)

rates of personal saving that allowed them to fund investment in new technology generously. In 1987, the saving rates in Taiwan and South Korea were three times higher than in the United States. All emphasized outward-looking export strategies. And, like Japan, all of these dynamic Pacific Rim economies benefited from government sponsorship and protection. All were beneficiaries of the extraordinary expansion in world trade and international communication that permitted technology to be disseminated more rapidly than at any other time in the past. As a result, newly industrializing nations began with current technologies.

In China after Mao Zedong's death in 1976, the communist leadership introduced a comprehensive economic reform that allowed more individual initiative and permitted individuals to accumulate wealth. Beginning in 1978, the Communist Party in Sichuan province freed more than six thousand firms to compete for business outside the state planning process. The results were remarkable. Under China's leader, **Deng Xiaoping°,** these reforms were expanded across the nation. China also began to permit foreign investment for the first time since the communists came to power in 1949. Between 1978 and the end of the 1990s, foreign investors committed more than $180 billion to the Chinese economy, and McDonald's, Coca-Cola, Airbus, and other foreign companies opened for business. But more than 100 million workers were still employed in state-owned enterprises, and most foreign-owned companies were segregated in special economic zones. The result was a dual industrial sector—one modern and efficient and

Deng Xiaoping (dung show-ping)

connected to international markets, the other dominated by government and directed by political decisions.

In the countryside, Deng Xiaoping permitted the contracting of land to individuals and families, who were free to consume or sell whatever they produced. By 1984, 93 percent of China's agricultural land was in effect in private hands and producing for the market, tripling agricultural output.

Perhaps the best measure of the success of Deng's reforms is that between 1980 and 1993, China's per capita output more than doubled, averaging more than 8 percent growth per year in comparison with the world average of slightly more than 1 percent and Japan's average of 3.3 percent. This growth was overwhelmingly the result of exports to the developed nations of the West, especially the United States. Nevertheless, per capita measures of wealth indicated that China remained a poor nation. China's per capita GDP was roughly the same as Mexico's—about $3,600 per year. By comparison, Taiwan had a per capita GDP of $14,700.

Deng Xiaoping's strategy of balancing change and continuity helped China avoid some of the social costs and political consequences experienced by Russia and other European socialist countries that abruptly plunged into capitalism and democracy. As Chinese officials put it, China was "changing a big earthquake into a thousand tremors." The nation's leadership faced a major challenge in 1989. Responding to mass movements in favor of democracy across the globe and to inflation, Chinese students and intellectuals, many of whom had studied outside China, led a series of protests demanding more democracy and an end to inflation and corruption. This movement culminated in a massive occupation of **Tiananmen Square**° by protestors, in the heart of Beijing. After weeks of standoff, tanks pushed into the square, killing hundreds, perhaps thousands. Many more were arrested. Although the Communist Party survived this challenge, it was not clear whether rapid economic growth, increasing inequality, high levels of unemployment, and massive migration from the countryside to the cities could occur without triggering a political transformation.

THE END OF THE BIPOLAR WORLD, 1989–1991

F ew in 1980 predicted the startling collapse of the Soviet Union and the socialist nations of the Warsaw Pact. The once-independent nations and ethnic groups that had been brought within the Soviet Union and the eastern European nations seemed securely transformed by the experiences and institutions of communism. By 1990, however, nationalism was resurgent, and communism was nearly finished.

Crisis in the Soviet Union

Under United States president Ronald Reagan and the Soviet Union's general secretary, Leonid Brezhnev°, the rhetoric of the Cold War remained intense. Massive new U.S. investments in armaments, including a space-based missile protection system that never became operational, placed heavy burdens on the Soviet economy, which was unable to absorb the cost of developing similar weapons. Soviet economic problems were systemic. Obsolete industrial plants and centralized planning stifled initiative and responsiveness to market demand. Government bureaucrats and Communist Party favorites received special privileges, including permission to shop in stores that stocked Western goods, but the average citizen faced long lines and waiting lists for goods. Soviet citizens contrasted their lot with the free and prosperous life of the West depicted in the increasingly accessible Western media. The arbitrariness of the bureaucracy, the cynical manipulation of information, and deprivations created a generalized crisis in morale.

Despite the unpopularity of the war in Afghanistan and growing discontent, Brezhnev refused to modify his rigid and unsuccessful policies. But he was unable to contain an underground current of protest. Self-published underground writings by critics of the regime circulated widely despite government efforts to suppress them. The physicist Andrei Sakharov and his wife, Yelena

---

Tiananmen (tee-yehn-ahn-men)

Leonid Brezhnev (leh-oh-NEED BREZ-nef)

Bonner, protested the nuclear arms race and human rights violations and were condemned to banishment within the country. Some Jewish dissidents spoke out against anti-Semitism, but many more left for Israel or the United States.

By the time **Mikhail Gorbachev°** took up the reins of the Soviet government in 1985, war weariness, economic decay, and vocal protest had reached critical levels. Casting aside Brezhnev's hard line, Gorbachev authorized major reforms in an attempt to stave off total collapse. His policy of political openness (*glasnost*) permitted criticism of the government and the Communist Party. His policy of *perestroika°* ("restructuring") was an attempt to address long-suppressed economic problems by moving away from central state planning and toward a more open economic system. In 1989, he ended the war in Afghanistan, which had cost many lives and much money.

The Collapse of the Socialist Bloc

Events in eastern Europe were very important in forcing change on the Soviet Union. In 1980, protests by Polish shipyard workers in the city of Gdansk led to the formation of **Solidarity,** a labor union that soon enrolled 9 million members. The Roman Catholic Church in Poland, strengthened by the elevation of a Pole, Karol Wojtyla°, to the papacy as John Paul II in 1978, gave strong moral support to the protest movement. As Gorbachev loosened political controls in the Soviet Union after 1985, communist leaders elsewhere lost confidence in Soviet resolve, and critics and reformers in Poland and throughout the rest of eastern Europe were emboldened (see Map 29.1).

Beleaguered Warsaw Pact governments vacillated between relaxation of control and the suppression of dissent. As the Catholic clergy in Poland had supported Solidarity, Protestant and Orthodox religious leaders aided the rise of opposition groups elsewhere. This combination of nationalism and religion provided a powerful base for opponents of the communist regimes. Threatened by these forces, communist governments sought to

Gorbachev (GORE-beh-CHOF)   *perestroika* (per-ih-STROY-kuh)   **Karol Wojtyla** (KAH-rol voy-TIL-ah)

The Fall of the Berlin Wall   The Berlin Wall was the most important symbol of the Cold War. Constructed to keep residents of East Germany from fleeing to the West and defended by armed guards and barbed wire, for many in the West it was the public face of communism. As the Soviet system fell apart, the residents of East and West Berlin broke down sections of the wall. Here young people straddle the wall, signaling the end of an era.   (Bossu Regis/ Corbis Sygma)

quiet the opposition by seeking solutions to their severe economic problems. They turned to the West for trade and financial assistance and opened their nations to travelers, ideas, styles, and money from Western countries, all of which accelerated the demand for change.

By the end of 1989, communist governments across eastern Europe had fallen. The dismantling of the Berlin Wall, the symbol of a divided Europe and the bipolar world, vividly represented this transformation. In Poland, Hungary, Czechoslovakia, and

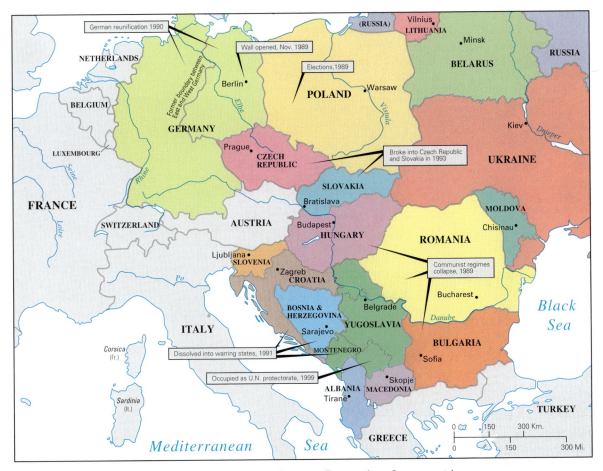

German reunification 1990

Wall opened, Nov. 1989

Elections, 1989

Broke into Czech Republic
and Slovakia in 1993

Communist regimes
collapse, 1989

Dissolved into warring states, 1991

Occupied as U.N. protectorate, 1999

Former boundary between
East and West Germany

NETHERLANDS

BELGIUM

LUXEMBOURG

FRANCE

SWITZERLAND

(RUSSIA)

Vilnius
LITHUANIA

Minsk

RUSSIA

BELARUS

Berlin

GERMANY

Warsaw

POLAND

Prague
CZECH
REPUBLIC

SLOVAKIA

Bratislava

AUSTRIA

Budapest
HUNGARY

Ljubljana
SLOVENIA

Zagreb
CROATIA

ITALY

BOSNIA &
HERZEGOVINA

Sarajevo

MONTENEGRO

Kiev

Dnieper

UKRAINE

MOLDOVA

Chisinau

ROMANIA

Bucharest

Belgrade

YUGOSLAVIA

Danube

BULGARIA

Sofia

Black
Sea

Corsica
(Fr.)

Sardinia
(It.)

Skopje

ALBANIA MACEDONIA
Tirane

GREECE

TURKEY

Elbe

Vistula

Rhine

Seine

Loire

Po

Mediterranean   Sea

0   150   300 Km.

0   150   300 Mi.

Map 29.1   The End of Soviet Domination in Eastern Europe   The creation of new countries
out of Yugoslavia and Czechoslovakia and the reunification of Germany marked the most complicated changes of national borders since World War I. The Czech Republic and Slovakia separated
peacefully, but Slovenia, Croatia, Macedonia, and Bosnia and Herzegovina achieved independence
only after bitter fighting.

Bulgaria, communist leaders decided that change
was inevitable and initiated political reforms. When
Romanian dictator Nicolae Ceausescu° refused to
surrender power, he provoked a rebellion that ended
with his arrest and execution. The comprehensive-
ness of these changes became clear in 1990, when
Solidarity leader Lech Walesa° was elected president
of Poland and dissident playwright Vaclav Havel°

was elected president of Czechoslovakia. That same
year, East and West Germany were reunited, and the
eastern Baltic states of Lithuania, Estonia, and Latvia
declared their independence from the Soviet Union.

The end of the Soviet Union came suddenly in
1991 (see Map 29.2). Gorbachev's efforts to transform the Soviet system could not keep up with the
tide of change sweeping through the region. After
communist hardliners botched a poorly conceived
coup against Gorbachev, disgust with communism boiled over. Boris Yeltsin, the president of the
Russian Republic and long-time member of the

Nicolae Ceausescu (neh-koh-LIE chow-SHES-koo)   **Lech
Walesa** (leck wah-LEN-suh)   **Vaclav Havel** (vah-SLAV
hah-VEL)

Map 29.2   The End of the Soviet Union   When Communist hardliners failed to overthrow Gorbachev in 1991, popular anti-Communist sentiment swept the Soviet Union. Following Boris Yeltsin's lead in Russia, the republics that constituted the Soviet Union declared their independence.

Communist Party, led popular resistance to the coup in Moscow and emerged as the most powerful leader in the country. Russia, the largest republic in the Soviet Union, was effectively taking the place of the disintegrating USSR. In September 1991, the Congress of People's Deputies voted to dissolve the union. Mikhail Gorbachev went into retirement.

The ethnic and religious passions that fueled the breakup of the Soviet Union soon challenged the survival of Yugoslavia and Czechoslovakia. The dismemberment of Yugoslavia began with declarations of independence in Slovenia and Croatia in 1991. A year later, Czechoslovakia peacefully divided into the Czech Republic and Slovakia.

The Persian Gulf War, 1990–1991

The breakup of the Soviet Union and the end of the Cold War did not bring an end to international conflict. The Persian Gulf War began when Iraq's ruler, Saddam Husayn, invaded Kuwait in August 1990. Husayn had failed to get Kuwait's royal family to reduce the size of Iraq's debt to the oil-rich nation. He was also eager to gain control of Kuwait's oil fields. Husayn believed that the smaller and militarily weaker nation could be quickly defeated and suspected, as a result of a conversation with an American diplomat, that the United States would not react.

Saudi Arabia, a key regional ally of the United States and a major oil producer, felt threatened by Iraq's action and helped draw the United States into the conflict. Soon the United States and its allies had concentrated an imposing military force of 500,000 in the region. With his intention to use force endorsed by the United Nations and with many Islamic nations supporting military action, President George Bush ordered an attack in early 1991. Iraq proved incapable of countering the sophisticated weaponry of the coalition. The missiles and bombs of the United States destroyed not only military targets but also "relegated [Iraq] to a pre-industrial age," reported the United Nations after the war. Although Iraq's military defeat was comprehensive, Husain remained in power, and the country was not occupied. Husain, in fact, crushed an uprising in the months following this defeat. In the wake of this event, the United States and its key allies imposed "no fly" zones that denied Iraq's military aircraft access to the northern and southern regions of the country.

In the United States, the results of the war were interpreted to mean that the U.S. military defeat in the Vietnam War could be forgotten and that U.S. military capability was unrivaled. Unable to deter military action by the U.S.-led coalition or to meaningfully influence the diplomacy that surrounded the war, Russia had been of little use to its former ally Iraq, and its impotence was clear.

THE CHALLENGE OF POPULATION GROWTH

For most of human history, population growth was viewed as beneficial, and human beings were seen as a source of wealth. Since the late eighteenth century, however, population growth has been viewed with increasing alarm. Some feared that food supplies could not keep up with population growth. Others foresaw class and ethnic struggle as numbers overwhelmed resources. By the second half of the twentieth century, population growth was increasingly seen as a threat to the environment.

Demographic Transition

World population exploded in the twentieth century (see Table 29.1). Unlike population growth in the eighteenth and nineteenth centuries, when much of the increase occurred in the wealthiest nations, population growth at the end of the twentieth century was overwhelmingly in the poorest nations. Fertility rates had dropped in most developing nations but remained much higher than rates in the industrialized nations. At the same time, improvements in hygiene and medical treatment caused mortality rates to fall. The result was rapid population growth. At current rates of growth, the world population still increases by a number equal to the total population of the United States every three years.

Educated Europeans of the nineteenth century had been ambivalent about the rapid increase in human population. Some saw it as a blessing that would promote economic well-being. Others warned that the seemingly relentless increase would bring disaster. Best known of these pessimists was the English cleric **Thomas Malthus,** who in 1798 argued convincingly that unchecked population growth would outstrip food production. When Malthus looked at Europe's future, he used a prejudiced image of China's huge population to terrify his European readers.

The generation that came of age in the years immediately following World War II inherited a world in which the views of Malthus were casually dismissed. Industrial and agricultural productivity had multiplied supplies of food and other necessities. Cultural changes associated with expanded female employment, older age at marriage, and more effective family planning had combined to slow the rate of population increase. And by the late 1960s, Europe and other industrial societies had made what was called the **demographic transition** to lower fertility rates (average number of births per woman) and reduce mortality. The number of births in the developed nations was just adequate for the maintenance of current population levels. Thus, many experts argued that the population growth then occurring in developing nations was a short-term phenomenon that would be ended by the combination of economic and social changes that had altered European patterns.

Table 29.1   Population for World and Major Areas, 1750–2050

Population Size (Millions)

Major Area	1750	1800	1850	1900	1950	1995	(estimated) 2050
World	791	978	1,262	1,650	2,521	5,666	8,909
Africa	106	107	111	133	221	697	1,766
Asia	502	635	809	947	1,402	3,437	5,268
Europe	163	203	276	408	547	728	628
Latin America and the Caribbean	16	24	38	74	167	480	809
North America	2	7	26	82	172	297	392
Oceania	2	2	2	6	13	28	46

Percentage Distribution

Major Area	1750	1800	1850	1900	1950	1995	(estimated) 2050
World	100	100	100	100	100	100	100
Africa	13.4	10.9	8.8	8.1	8.8	12	19.8
Asia	63.5	64.9	64.1	57.4	55.6	61	59.1
Europe	20.6	20.8	21.9	24.7	21.7	13	7.0
Latin America and the Caribbean	2.0	2.5	3.0	4.5	6.6	8	9.1
North America	0.3	0.7	2.1	5.0	6.8	5	4.4
Oceania	0.3	0.2	0.2	0.4	0.5	1	0.5

Source: J. D. Durand, "Historical Estimates of World Population: An Evaluation" (Philadelphia: University of Pennsylvania, Population Studies Center, 1974, mimeographed); United Nations, *The Determinants and Consequences of Population Trends*, vol. 1 (New York: United Nations, 1973); United Nations, *World Population Prospects as Assessed in 1963* (New York: United Nations, 1966); United Nations, *World Population Prospects: The 1998 Revision* (New York: United Nations, forthcoming); United Nations Population Division, Department of Economic and Social Affairs, http://www.popin.org/pop1998/4.htm.

When the demographic transition failed to occur in the Third World by the late 1970s, the issue of population growth had become politicized. The leaders of some developing nations actively promoted large families, arguing that larger populations would increase national power. Industrialized, mostly white, nations raised concerns about rapid population growth in Asia, Africa, and Latin America. Populist political leaders in those regions asked whether these concerns were not fundamentally racist.

However, once the economic shocks of the 1970s and 1980s revealed the vulnerability of developing economies, governments in the developing world jettisoned pronatalist policies. In the 1970s, Mexico's government had encouraged high fertility, and population growth in Mexico rose to 3 percent per year. By the 1980s, Mexico started to promote birth control, and the annual population growth rate fell to 2.3 percent.

The Industrialized Nations

In much of Europe and Japan at the beginning of the twenty-first century, fertility levels are so low that population will fall unless immigration increases. In Japan, women have an average of 1.39 children; in Italy, the number is 1.2. Sweden provides cash payments, tax incentives, and job leaves to families with children, but the average number of births there fell to 1.4 in recent years. The low fertility found in mature industrial nations is tied to higher levels of female education and employment, the material values of consumer culture, and access to contraception and abortion. Educated women now defer marriage and child rearing until they are established in careers.

As fertility has declined in the industrialized nations of western Europe, life expectancy has improved because of more abundant food, improved hygiene, and better medical care. Italy, for example, soon will have more than twenty adults fifty years old or over for each five-year-old child. Japan faces an even more drastic aging of its population. This demographic transformation presents a challenge very different from the one foreseen by Malthus. These nations generally offer a broad array of social services, including retirement income, medical services, and housing supplements for the elderly. As the number of retirees increases relative to the number of people who are employed, the costs of these services may become unsustainable.

In contrast, in Russia and some former socialist nations, life expectancy and birthrates have both fallen. Life expectancy for Russian men is now only fifty-seven years, down almost ten years since 1980. In the Czech Republic, Hungary, and Poland, life expectancy is improving in response to improved economic conditions, but most of the rest of eastern Europe follows the Russian pattern of declining life expectancy. High unemployment, low incomes, food shortages, and the dismantling of the social welfare system of the communist era have all contributed to this decline.

The Developing Nations

Population pyramids generated by demographers clearly illustrate the profound transformation in human reproductive patterns and life expectancy in the years since World War II. Figure 29.1 shows the 2001 age distributions in Pakistan, South Korea, and Sweden—nations at three different stages of economic development. Sweden is a mature industrial nation. South Korea is a rapidly industrializing nation that has surpassed many European nations in both industrial output and per capita wealth. Pakistan is a poor, traditional Muslim nation with rudimentary industrialization, low educational levels, and little effective family planning.

These demographic changes are transforming the global balance of population. At current rates, 95 percent of all future population growth will be in developing nations (see Table 29.1). A comparison between Europe and Africa illustrates these changes. In 1950, Europe had twice the population of Africa. By 1985, Africa had drawn even. According to projections, by 2025 Africa's population will be three times larger than Europe's.

As the 1990s ended, the populations of Latin America and Asia also were expanding dramatically, but at rates slower than those in sub-Saharan Africa and the Muslim world. In Asia, the populations of India and China continued to grow despite government efforts to reduce family size. In China, efforts

Figure 29.1 Age Structure Comparison: Islamic Nation (Pakistan), Non-Islamic Developing Nation (South Korea), and Developed Nation (Sweden), 2001. *Source:* U.S. Bureau of the Census, *International Database*, 2001.

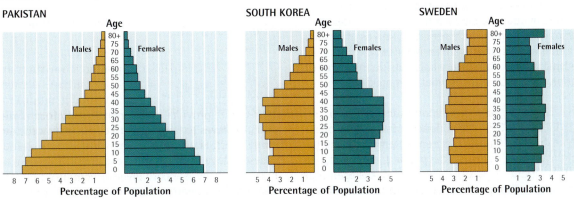

to enforce a limit of one child per family led to large-scale female infanticide as rural families sought to produce male heirs. India's policies of forced sterilization created widespread outrage and led to the electoral defeat of the ruling Congress Party. Yet both countries achieved some successes. Between 1960 and 1982, India's birthrate fell from 48 to 34 per thousand, while China's rate declined even more sharply—from 39 to 19. Still, by 2025, China and India will each have some 1.5 billion people.

UNEQUAL DEVELOPMENT AND THE MOVEMENT OF PEOPLES

Two characteristics of the postwar world should now be clear. First, despite decades of experimentation with state-directed economic development, most nations that were poor in 1960 were as poor or poorer at the end of the 1990s. The only exceptions were a few rapidly developing Asian industrial nations and an equally small number of oil-exporting nations. Second, world population increased to startlingly high levels, and most of the increase was in the poorest nations.

The combination of intractable poverty and growing population generated a surge in international immigration, both legal and illegal. Few other issues stirred more controversy. Even moderate voices sometimes framed the discussion of immigration as a competition among peoples. One commentator summarized his analysis this way: "As the better-off families of the northern hemisphere individually decide that having only one or at the most two children is sufficient, they may not recognize that they are in a small way vacating future space (that is, jobs, parts of inner cities, shares of population, shares of market preferences) to faster-growing ethnic groups both inside and outside their boundaries. But that, in fact, is what they are doing."[2]

The Problem of Growing Inequality

Since 1945, global economic productivity has expanded more rapidly than at any other time in the past. Faster, cheaper communications and transportation have combined with improvements in industrial and agricultural technologies to create levels of material abundance that would have amazed those who experienced the first Industrial Revolution (see Chapter 20). Despite this remarkable economic expansion and growing market integration, the majority of the world's population remains in poverty. The industrialized nations of the Northern Hemisphere now enjoy a larger share of the world's wealth than they did a century ago. As a result, the gap between rich and poor nations has grown much wider. The thousands of homeless street children who live among the gleaming glass and steel towers of Rio's banking district can be seen as a metaphor for the social consequences of postwar economic development.

Wealth inequality within nations also grew. In the United States, for example, the South and Southwest grew richer in the past three decades relative to the older industrial regions of the Midwest. Regional inequalities also appeared in developing nations. Generally, capital cities such as Buenos Aires, in Argentina, and Lagos, in Nigeria, attracted large numbers of migrants from rural areas because they offered more opportunities, even if those opportunities could not compare to the ones available in developed nations.

Even in the industrialized world, people were divided into haves and have-nots. During the presidency of Ronald Reagan (1981–1989), wealth inequality in the United States reached its highest level since the 1929 stock market crash. Some scholars estimated that the wealthiest 1 percent of households in the United States controlled more than 30 percent of the nation's total wealth. Even in Europe, where tax and inheritance laws redistributed wealth, unemployment, homelessness, and substandard housing were increasingly common.

Internal Migration: The Growth of Cities

Migration from rural areas to urban centers in developing nations increased threefold from 1925 to 1950. After that, the pace accelerated (see Table 29.2). Shantytowns sprawling around major cities in developing nations are commonly seen as signs of social breakdown and economic failure. Nevertheless, even in the shantytowns city life was

Table 29.2   The World's Largest Metropolitan Areas (Population of 10 Million or More)

City	1950	City	1975	City	2000	City	2015
1 New York	12.3	1 Tokyo	19.8	1 Tokyo	26.4	1 Tokyo	26.4
		1 New York	15.9	2 Mexico City	18.1	2 Bombay	26.1
		3 Shanghai	11.4	3 Bombay	18.1	3 Lagos	23.2
		4 Mexico City	11.2	4 Sao Paulo	17.8	4 Dhaka	21.1
		5 Sao Paulo	10.0	5 New York	16.6	5 Sao Paulo	20.4
				6 Lagos	13.4	6 Karachi	19.2
				7 Los Angeles	13.1	7 Mexico City	19.2
				8 Calcutta	12.9	8 New York	17.4
				9 Shanghai	12.9	9 Jakarta	17.3
				10 Buenos Aires	12.6	10 Calcutta	17.3
				11 Dhaka	12.3	11 Delhi	16.8
				12 Karachi	11.8	12 Metro Manila	14.8
				13 Delhi	11.7	13 Shanghai	14.6
				14 Jakarta	11.0	14 Los Angeles	14.1
				15 Osaka	11.0	15 Buenos Aires	14.1
				16 Metro Manila	10.9	16 Cairo	13.8
				17 Beijing	10.8	17 Istanbul	12.5
				18 Rio de Janeiro	10.6	18 Beijing	12.3
				19 Cairo	10.6	19 Rio de Janeiro	11.9
						20 Osaka	11.0
						21 Tianjin	10.7
						22 Hyderabad	10.5
						23 Bangkok	10.1

Source: International Migration Report 2002, United Nations, Department of Economic and Social Affairs, Population Division, "World Urbanization Prospects: The 1999 Revision," p. 6. Reprinted by permission of United States Publications.

generally better than life in the countryside. A World Bank study estimated that three out of four migrants to cities made economic gains. Residents of cities in sub-Saharan Africa, for example, were six times more likely than rural residents to have safe water. An unskilled migrant from the depressed northeast of Brazil could triple his or her income by moving to Rio de Janeiro.

As the scale of rural-to-urban migration grew, these benefits proved more elusive, however. In many West African cities, basic services were crumbling under the pressure of rapid population growth. In 1990 in Mexico City, one of the world's largest cities, more than thirty thousand people lived in garbage dumps, where they scavenged for food and clothing. Worsening conditions and the threat of crime and political instability led many governments to try to slow migration to cities and, in some cases, to return people to the countryside. Indonesia, for example, has relocated more than half a million urban residents since 1969. Despite some successes with slowing the rate of internal migration, nearly every poor nation still faces the challenge of rapidly growing cities.

Global Migration   Each year, hundreds of thousands of men and women leave the developing world to emigrate to industrialized nations. After 1960, this movement increased in scale, and ethnic and racial tensions in the host nations worsened. By the 1990s, levels of immigration posed daunting social and cultural challenges for both host nations and immigrants.

When an expanding European economy first confronted labor shortages in the 1960s, many European nations actively promoted guest worker programs and other inducements to immigration. However, attitudes toward immigrants changed as the size of the immigrant population grew and as European economies slowed in the 1980s. Facing higher levels of unemployment, native-born workers saw immigrants as competitors willing to work for lower wages and less likely to support unions.

Because immigrants generally are young adults and commonly retain the positive attitudes toward early marriage and large families dominant in their native cultures, immigrant communities in Europe and the United States tended to have fertility rates higher than the rates of the host populations. In Germany in 1975, for example, immigrants made up about 7 percent of the population but accounted for nearly 15 percent of all births. Although the fertility of the Hispanic population in the United States is lower than the rates in Mexico and other Latin American nations, Hispanic groups will contribute well over 20 percent of all population growth in the United States during the next twenty-five years.

As the Muslim population in Europe and the Asian and Latin American populations in the United States expand in the twenty-first century, cultural conflicts will test definitions of citizenship and nationality. The United States will have some advantages in meeting these challenges because of long experience with immigration and relatively open access to citizenship. Yet in the 1990s, the United States was moving slowly in the direction of European efforts to restrict immigration and defend a culturally conservative definition of nationality.

TECHNOLOGICAL AND ENVIRONMENTAL CHANGE

Technological innovation powered the economic expansion that began after World War II by increasing productivity and disseminating human creativity. Because most of the economic benefits were concentrated in the advanced industrialized nations, technology increased the power of those nations relative to the developing world. Even within developed nations, postwar technological innovations did not benefit all classes, industries, and regions equally.

The multiplication of farms and factories intensified environmental threats. Loss of rain forest, soil erosion, global warming, pollution of air and water, and extinction of species imperiled human societies. Environmental protection measures, like the acquisition of new technology, progressed furthest in societies with the most economic resources.

New Technologies and the World Economy

Nuclear energy, jet engines, radar, and tape recording were among the many World War II developments that later had an impact on consumers' lives. When applied to industry, new technology increased productivity, reduced labor requirements, and improved the flow of information. As the Western economies recovered from the war and incomes rose, consumers purchased new products that reduced their workloads or provided entertainment.

Improvements in existing technologies accounted for much of the developed world's productivity increases during the 1950s and 1960s. Larger and faster trucks, trains, and airplanes cut transportation costs. Both capitalist and socialist governments expanded highway systems, improved railroad track, and constructed airports and nuclear power plants.

No other technology had greater significance in this period than the computer. Only large corporations, governments, and universities could afford the first computers. But by the mid-1980s, desktop computers had replaced typewriters in most of the developed world's offices, and technological advances continued. Each new generation of computers was faster and more powerful than the one before.

Computers also altered manufacturing. Small dedicated computers were used to control and monitor machinery in some industries. European and Japanese companies were the first to introduce such robots into the factory. The United States introduced robots more slowly because it enjoys lower labor costs.

The transnational corporation became the primary agent of these technological changes. In the post–World War II years, many companies with multinational ownership and management invested in and marketed products throughout the world. International trade agreements and open markets furthered the process.

As transnational manufacturers, agricultural conglomerates, and financial giants became wealthier and more powerful, they increasingly escaped the controls imposed by national governments. If labor costs were too high in Japan, antipollution measures too intrusive in the United States, or taxes too high in Great Britain, transnational companies relocated—or threatened to do so. Governments in the developing world were often hard-pressed to control the actions of these powerful enterprises. As a result, the worst abuses of labor or of the environment usually occurred in poor nations.

Conserving and Sharing Resources

In the 1960s, environmental activists and political leaders began warning about the devastating environmental consequences of population growth, industrialization, and the expansion of agriculture onto marginal lands. Assaults on rain forests and redwoods, the disappearance of species, and the poisoning of streams and rivers raised public consciousness. Environmental damage occurred in the advanced industrial economies and in the poorest of the developing nations. Perhaps the worst environmental record was achieved in the former Soviet Union, where industrial and nuclear wastes were often dumped with little concern for environmental consequences. The accumulated effect of scientific studies and public debate led to national and international efforts to slow, if not undo, damage to the environment.

The expanding global population required increasing quantities of food, housing, energy, and other resources as the twentieth century ended. In the developed world, the consumer-driven economic expansion of the post–World War II years became an obstacle to addressing environmental problems. How could the United States, Germany, or Japan change consumption patterns to protect the environment without endangering corporate profits, wages, and employment levels?

Many developing countries saw exploitation of their environmental resources and industrialization as the solution to their rapidly growing populations. The results were predictable: erosion and pollution.

Responding to Environmental Threats

Despite the gravity of environmental threats, there were many successful efforts to preserve and protect the environment. The Clean Air Act, the Clean Water Act, and the Endangered Species Act were passed in the United States in the 1970s as part of an environmental effort that included the nations of the European Community and Japan. Environmental awareness spread by means of the media and grassroots political movements, and most nations in the developed world enforced strict antipollution laws and sponsored massive recycling efforts. Many also encouraged resource conservation by rewarding energy-efficient factories and the manufacturers of fuel-efficient cars and by promoting the use of alternative energy sources such as solar and wind power.

These efforts produced significant results. In western Europe and the United States, air quality improved dramatically. In the United States, smog levels were down nearly a third from 1970 to 2000 even though the number of automobiles increased more than 80 percent. Emissions of lead and sulfur dioxide were down as well. The Great Lakes, Long Island Sound, and Chesapeake Bay were all much cleaner at the end of the century than they had been in 1970. The rivers of North America and Europe also improved. Still, more than thirty thousand deaths each year in the United States are attributed to exposure to pesticides and other chemicals.

New technologies made much of this improvement possible. Pollution controls on automobiles, planes, and factory smokestacks reduced harmful emissions. Similar progress was made in the chemical industry. Scientists identified the chemicals that threaten the ozone layer, and the phase-out of their use in new appliances and cars began.

Clearly the desire to preserve the natural environment was growing around the world. In the developed nations, continued political organization and enhanced awareness of environmental issues seemed likely to lead to step-by-step improvements in environmental policy. In the developing world and most of the former Soviet bloc, however, population pressures and weak governments were major obstacles to effective environmental policies. In China, for example, respiratory disease caused by pollution was the leading cause of death. Thus, it was likely that the industrialized nations would have to fund global improvements, and the cost was likely to be high.

CONCLUSION

The world was profoundly altered between 1975 and 1991. The Cold War dominated international relations to the end of the 1980s. Every conflict threatened to provoke a confrontation between the nuclear-armed superpowers, for both the United States and the Soviet Union feared that every conflict and every regime change represented a potential threat to their strategic interests. As a result, the superpowers were drawn into a succession of civil wars and revolutions. The costs in lives and property were terrible, the gains small. As defense costs escalated, the Soviet system crumbled. By 1991, the Soviet Union and the socialist Warsaw Pact had disappeared, transforming the international stage.

Latin America was pulled into the violence of the late Cold War period and paid a terrible price. The 1970s and 1980s witnessed a frontal assault on democratic institutions, a denial of human rights, and economic decline. This was the period of death squads and Dirty War. With the end of the Cold War, peace returned there, and democracy began to replace dictatorship.

In the Persian Gulf, the end of the Cold War did not lead to peace. Iran and Iraq have experienced deep cycles of political turmoil, war, and foreign threats since the late 1970s.

The world also was altered by economic growth and integration, by population growth and movement, and by technological and environmental change. Led by the postwar recovery of the industrial powers and the remarkable economic expansion of Japan and the Asian Tigers, the world economy grew dramatically. The development and application of new technology contributed significantly to this process. International markets were more open and integrated than at any other time. The new wealth and exciting technologies of the postwar era were not shared equally, however.

Population growth in the developing world was one reason for this divided experience. Unable to find adequate employment or, in many cases, bare subsistence, people in developing nations migrated across borders hoping to improve their lives. These movements often provided valuable labor in the factories and farms of the developed world, but they also provoked cultural, racial, and ethnic tension. Problems of inequality, population growth, and international migration would continue to challenge the global community in the coming decades.

Technology seemed to offer some hope for meeting these challenges. Engineering, financial services, education, and other professions developed an international character thanks to the communications revolution. Ambitious and talented people in the developing world could now fully participate in global intellectual and economic life. However, most people working in the developing world remained disconnected from this liberating technology by poverty. Technology also bolstered efforts to protect the environment, providing the means to clean auto and factory emissions, even while it helped produce much of the world's pollution. Technology has been intertwined with human culture since the beginning of human history. Our ability to control and direct its use will determine the future.

■ Key Terms

proxy wars

Salvador Allende

Dirty War

Sandinistas

Ayatollah Ruhollah Khomeini

neo-liberalism

Saddam Husayn

keiretsu

Asian Tigers

Deng Xiaoping

Tiananmen Square

Mikhail Gorbachev

perestroika

Solidarity

Thomas Malthus

demographic transition

■ Suggested Reading

Among the works devoted to postwar economic performance are W. L. M. Adriaasen and J. G. Waardensburg, eds., *A Dual World Economy: Forty Years of Development Experience* (1989); P. Krugman, *The Age of Diminished Expectations: U.S. Economic Policy in the 1990s* (1990); B. J. McCormick, *The World Economy: Patterns of Growth and Change* (1988); and H. van der Wee, *Prosperity and Upheaval: The World Economy, 1945–1980* (1986).

For Latin America, Thomas E. Skidmore and Peter H. Smith, *Modern Latin America,* 4th ed. (1996), provides an excellent general introduction to the period 1975 to 1991.

For the Pacific Rim, see Jonathan Spence, *The Search for Modern China* (1990); Edwin O. Reischauer, *The Japanese* (1988); H. Patrick and H. Rosovsky, *Asia's New Giant: How the Japanese Economy Works* (1976); and Staffan B. Linder, *Pacific Century: Economic and Political Consequences of Asian-Pacific Dynamism* (1986).

Focused examinations of the Soviet bloc are provided in K. Dawisha, *Eastern Europe, Gorbachev and Reform: The Great Challenge* (1988); Barbara Engel and Christine Worobec, eds., *Russia's Women: Accommodation, Resistance, Transformation* (1990); David Remnick, *Lenin's Tomb: The Last Days of the Soviet Empire* (1993); and Charles Maier, *Dissolution: The Crisis of Communism and the End of East Germany* (1997).

The story of the Iranian Revolution and the early days of the Islamic Republic of Iran is well told by Shaul Bakhash, *The Reign of the Ayatollahs: Iran and the Iranian Revolution* (1990). Barnet Rubin, *The Fragmentation of Afghanistan* (1995), provides excellent coverage of the struggle between Soviet forces and the Muslim resistance in that country.

A number of studies examine the special problems faced by women in the postwar period. See, for example, Elisabeth Croll, *Feminism and Socialism in China* (1978); J. Ginat, *Women in Muslim Rural Society: Status and Role in Family and Community* (1982); June Hahner, *Women in Latin America* (1976); P. Hudson, *Third World Women Speak Out* (1979); A. de Souza, *Women in Contemporary India and South Asia* (1980); and M. Wolf, *Revolution Postponed: Women in Contemporary China* (1985).

For general discussions of economic, demographic, and environmental problems facing the world, see R. N. Gwynne, *New Horizons? Third World Industrialization in an International Framework* (1990); P. R. Ehrlich and A. E. Ehrlich, *The Population Explosion* (1990); Paul M. Kennedy, *Preparing for the Twenty-First Century* (1993); and J. L. Simon, *Population Matters: People, Resources, Environment and Immigration* (1990).

For issues associated with technological and environmental change, see M. Feshbach and A. Friendly, *Ecocide in the U.S.S.R.* (1992); John Bellamy Foster, *Economic History of the Environment* (1994); S. Hecht and A. Cockburn, *The Fate of the Forest: Developers, Destroyers, and Defenders of the Amazon* (1989); K. Marton, *Multinationals, Technology, and Industrialization: Implications and Impact in Third World Countries* (1986); S. P. Huntington, *The Third Wave: Demoralization in the Late Twentieth Century* (1993); L. Solomon, *Multinational Corporations and the Emerging World Order* (1978); and B. L. Turner II et al., eds., *The Earth as Transformed by Human Action: Global and Regional Changes in the Biosphere over the Past 300 Years* (1990).

■ Notes

1. *New York Times,* July 24, 1993, 1.
2. Paul Kennedy, *Preparing for the Twenty-First Century* (New York: Random House, 1993), 45.

30 Globalization at the Turn of the Millennium

CHAPTER OUTLINE

Global Political Economies

Trends and Visions

Global Culture

ENVIRONMENT AND TECHNOLOGY: Global Warming

The workday began normally at the World Trade Center in lower Manhattan on the morning of September 11, 2001. The 50,000 people who work there were making their way to the two 110-story towers, as were some 140,000 others who visit on a typical day. Suddenly, at 8:46 A.M., an American Airlines Boeing 767 with 92 people on board, traveling at a speed of 470 miles per hour (756 kilometers per hour), crashed into floors 94 to 98 of the north tower, igniting the 10,000 gallons (38,000 liters) of fuel in its tanks. Just before 9:03 A.M. a United Airlines flight with 65 people on board and a similar fuel load hit floors 78 to 84 of the south tower.

As the burning jet fuel engulfed the collision areas, the buildings' surviving occupants struggled through smoke-filled corridors and down dozens of flights of stairs. Many of those trapped above the crash sites used cell phones to say good-bye to loved ones. Rather than endure the flames and fumes, a few jumped to their deaths.

Just before 10 o'clock, temperatures that had risen to 2,300° Fahrenheit (1,260° Celsius) caused the steel girders in the impacted area of the south tower to give way. The collapsing upper floors crushed the floors underneath one by one, engulfing lower Manhattan in a dense cloud of dust. Twenty-eight minutes later the north tower pancaked in a similar manner. Miraculously, most of the buildings' occupants had escaped before the towers collapsed. Besides the people on the planes, nearly 2,600 lost their lives, including some 200 police officers and firefighters helping in the evacuation.

That same morning another American Airlines jet crashed into the Pentagon, killing all 64 people on board and 125 others inside the military complex near Washington, D.C. Passengers

Lower Manhattan, March 11, 2002 Six months after the terrorist attacks, beams of light commemorated the destroyed twin towers of the World Trade Center and those who perished in them.

on a fourth plane managed to overpower their hijackers, and the plane crashed in rural Pennsylvania, killing all 45 on board.

The four planes had been hijacked by teams of Middle Eastern men who slit the throats of service and flight personnel and seized control. Of the nineteen hijackers, fifteen were from Saudi Arabia. All had links to an extremist Islamic organization, al Qaeda° (the base or foundation), supported by a rich Saudi named Usama bin Laden°, who was incensed with American political, military, and cultural influence in the Middle East. The men were educated and well traveled, had lived in the United States, and

spoke English. Some had trained as pilots so that they could fly the hijacked aircraft.

The hijackers left few records of their personal motives, but the acts spoke for themselves. The Pentagon was the headquarters of the American military, the most technologically sophisticated and powerful fighting force the world had even seen. The fourth plane was probably meant to hit the Capitol or the White House, the legislative and executive centers of the world's only superpower. The Twin Towers may have been targeted because they were the tallest buildings in New York, but they were not just American targets. The World Trade Center housed 430 companies involved in international commerce and finance. Among the dead were people from more than half the countries in the world. New York was the site

---

al Qaeda (el KAW eh duh)   **Usama bin Laden** (oo-SAH-mah bin LAH-din)

of the attack, but the World Trade Center was a powerful symbol of the international economy.

The events of September 11 (9/11) can be understood on many levels. The hijackers and their supporters saw themselves as engaged in a holy struggle against economic, political, and military institutions they believed to be evil. They believed so deeply in their mission that they were willing to give their lives for it and to take as many other lives as they could. People directly affected and political leaders around the world tended to describe the attacks as evil acts against innocent victims.

To understand why the nineteen attackers were heroes to some and terrorists to others, one needs to explore the historical context of global changes at the turn of the millennium and the ideological tensions they have generated. While domestic and localized issues in Muslim countries provide part of the explanation, another part is unique prominence of the United States in every major aspect of global integration, which elicits sharply divergent views in the rest of the world's peoples.

As you read this chapter, ask yourself the following questions:

- What are the main benefits and dangers of growing political, economic, and cultural integration?

- What roles do religious beliefs and secular ideologies play in the contemporary world?

- How has technology contributed to the process of global interaction?

GLOBAL POLITICAL ECONOMIES

At the turn of the millennium growing trade and travel and new technologies were bringing all parts of the world into closer economic, political, and cultural contact. The collapse of the Soviet Union had ended the colonial era, and au-

tonomous national states (numbering about two hundred) had become an almost universal norm. Yet many world leaders had become convinced of the need to balance national autonomy with international agreements and associations in areas of trade and markets.

The Spread of Democracy

Democratic institutions spread widely in the last decades of the twentieth century. In 2003, 140 countries regularly held elections and people in 125 had access to free (or partly free) presses.[1] The appeal of democracy has been that elections provide a peaceful way of settling differences among a country's social classes, cultural groups, and regions. Democracies also tend to encourage political moderation.

In eastern Europe, the Czech Republic, Poland, Romania, and most other formerly communist-ruled states adopted democratic institutions. In the Russian Federation and neighboring Ukraine and Belarus, democratic institutions experienced a shakier start, while the former Soviet republics of Central Asia and the Caucasus mostly continued to experience authoritarian rule and rigged elections.

Since 1991 democracy, sometimes accompanied by significant shifts in the political balance, has become almost universal in South and Central America. In 2000 Mexican voters elected a reformist president with a centrist agenda, Vincente Fox, ending the half-century rule of the corrupt Institutional Revolutionary Party (PRI). In 2002 leftist Workers' Party candidate Luiz Inácio Lula da Silva° won the presidency of Brazil by appealing to nationalism and popular discontent with the economy.

In Asia, the death of long-time Chinese Communist leader Deng Xiaoping in 1997 ushered in a period of somewhat greater freedom of expression, but democracy seemed a long way off despite a booming economy. India saw a major political shift in 1998 when the Bharatiya Janata Party (BJP) ended four decades of Congress Party rule. The BJP success came through blatant appeals to Hindu nationalism, the condoning of violence against India's

---

Luiz Inácio Lula da Silva (loo-EES ee-NAH-see-oh LOO-lah dah SEAL-vah)

C H R O N O L O G Y

	Politics	Economics and Society
1991		**1991** Mercosur free trade association formed
	1992 Yugoslavia disintegrates—Croatia and Slovenia become independent states	
	1992–1995 Bosnia crisis	
	1994 Nelson Mandela elected president of South Africa; Tutsi massacred in Rwanda	**1994** North Atlantic Free Trade Agreement adopted
1995		**1995** World Trade Organization founded; United Nations women's conference in China
	1997 Hong Kong reunited with China	**1997** Asian financial crisis begins
	1998 Terrorists bomb U.S. embassies in Kenya and Tanzania; India and Pakistan test atomic bombs	
	1999 East Timor secedes from Indonesia (officially independent 2002)	**1999** Nobel Peace Prize to Doctors Without Borders
2000	**2001** Terrorists destroy the World Trade Center and damage the Pentagon on September 11; The United States invades Afghanistan and overthrows Taliban regime	**2001** Start of global recession
		2002 Euro the only currency in twelve European countries
	2003 United States and Britain invade and occupy Iraq	
	2004 Presidential election in Afghanistan	

Muslims, and opposition to the social and economic progress of the Untouchables (those traditionally confined to the dirtiest jobs). In 2004, the Congress Party regained control of the government.

In sub-Saharan Africa, democracy had mixed results. Many elected leaders used their offices to enrich themselves and limit their opponents, while other countries experienced military coups and conflicts over resources such as diamonds. Southern Africa, however, has seen democratic progress and a decline in armed conflicts since 1991. A key change came in South Africa in 1994, when long-time political prisoner Nelson Mandela and his African National Congress (ANC) won the first national elections in which the African majority could participate equally. Also hopeful has been the return to democracy in Nigeria, Africa's most populous state. In 1999, after a succession of military governments, Nigerians elected President Olusegun Obasanjo° (a former coup leader), and a 2003 vote renewed his term, despite serious voting irregularities.

Democracy is as exceptional in the Middle East as it is in much of Africa. Some once-democratic states such as Algeria have manipulated elections because those in power fear the rising power of Islamic militants. On the other hand, in Turkey, the most democratic Muslim-majority state in the

---

Olusegun Obasanjo (oh-LOO-say-goon oh-bah-SAHN-joh)

region, a once-strident Islamist party won a parliamentary majority in 2002 by moderating its tone and politics. A presidential election in Afghanistan in 2004 and plans for elections in Iraq may mark a move toward more democratic rule in these countries.

As examples later in the chapter will indicate, the growth (or decline) of democracy has only partly been due to internal changes in individual countries. Two international factors have also played important roles: the changed politics of the post–Cold War era and the demands of global economic forces.

Global Politics

Modern nation-states have considerable autonomy under international law. Other nations may intervene in a state's affairs only when seriously threatened or when the state is engaging in extreme human rights abuses. Although necessary to protect smaller, weaker countries from the imperial bullying that was once common, this autonomy greatly complicates international policing and peacekeeping efforts.

After the Cold War ended, the United Nations struggled to reclaim its roles as defender of human rights and peacekeeper. This was especially noticeable under the leadership of Kofi Annan, who became United Nations secretary general in 1997. The members of the United Nations Security Council often had difficulty agreeing on a course of action. Individual countries often acted alone or with their neighbors to resolve conflicts in nearby countries, whether through peaceful negotiation or military intervention. As the lone superpower, the United States was in a unique position to use its economic power and military might to defend its national interests and promote the general good. However, interventions also brought charges of American imperialism.

There were some notable peacemaking successes. The United Nations, South Africa, and other countries helped end the long civil war in Mozambique in 1992 and struggled to do the same in Angola, where peace shakily returned in 2002. Nigeria, the major military power in West Africa, helped end fighting in Sierra Leone in 1998, and again in 2003 in Liberia, which had become the

world's poorest country as the result of warlords and embezzlement.

However, the international community sometimes had great difficulty in agreeing on when and how to stop civil conflicts and human rights abuses. In 1991 Yugoslavia, which had existed since 1920, dissolved into a morass of warring ethnic and religious groups. Slovenia and Croatia, the heavily Roman Catholic western provinces, became independent states in 1992 after brief struggles with federal Yugoslav forces. Reflecting centuries of Muslim, Catholic, and Orthodox competition in the Balkans, the people of the province of Bosnia and Herzegovina were religiously mixed—40 percent Muslim, 30 percent Serbian Orthodox, and 18 percent Catholic. The murderous three-sided fighting that broke out with the declaration of Bosnian national independence in 1992 gave rise to **ethnic cleansing,** an effort by one racial, ethnic, or religious group to eliminate the people and culture of a different group. In this case, the Orthodox Serbs attempted to rid the state of Muslims.

At first, no European power acted to stop the growing tragedy in the Balkans. Finally, after much indecision—and extensive television coverage of atrocities and wanton destruction—the United States made a cautious intervention and eventually brokered a tentative settlement in 1995. In 1999 vicious new fighting and ethnic cleansing broke out in the southernmost Yugoslavian province of Kosovo, the ancient homeland of the Serbs, which had become predominantly Muslim and Albanian. When NATO's warnings went unheeded in Kosovo, the United States, with aid from Britain and France, launched an aerial war against Serbia. Suffering few casualties themselves, the NATO allies damaged military and infrastructure targets in Serbia and forced the withdrawal of Serbian forces from Kosovo. A trial of former Serbian president Slobodan Milosevic° at a special tribunal in the Hague on charges of crimes against humanity began in 2002 but was often delayed by his ill health.

Another tragedy unfolded in 1994, when political leaders in the Central African nation of Rwanda incited Hutu people to massacre their Tutsi neighbors. The major powers avoided characterizing the

---

Slobodan Milosevic (SLOH-boh-duhn mee-LOH-seh-vitch)

slaughter as genocide because an international agreement mandated intervention to stop genocide. Only after some 750,000 people were dead and millions of refugees had fled into neighboring states did the United States and other powers intervene. Belatedly, the United Nations set up a tribunal to try those responsible for the genocide. In 1998 violence spread from Rwanda to neighboring Congo, where growing opposition and ill health had forced President Joseph Mobutu from office after over three decades of dictatorial misrule. Various peacemaking attempts failed to restore order. By mid-2003 more than 3 million Congolese had died from disease, malnutrition, and injuries related to the fighting.

Fear that intervention could result in long and costly commitments was one reason the major powers were reluctant to intervene. Nor was it easy to distinguish conflicts that would benefit from forceful intervention from those that might better be resolved by diplomatic pressure. Many conflicts reflected deep-seated differences that were difficult to resolve. Tamil-speaking Hindus in Sri Lanka have waged a merciless guerrilla struggle against the dominant Sinhalese-speaking Buddhists for decades. Militant Hindus and Muslims in South Asia continue a violent struggle over the territories of the state of Kashmir, which was divided between India and Pakistan at their independence in 1947. Sometimes it took decades of international pressure to bring a conflict to an end, as was the case in East Timor (a mostly Catholic former Portuguese colony that Indonesia had annexed in 1975), whose people voted to separate from Muslim Indonesia in 1999 and gained full independence in 2002.

Arms Control and Terrorism

In addition to agreements on collective action against genocide and other crimes against humanity (see below), international treaties govern **weapons of mass destruction.** Nuclear, biological, and chemical devices pose especially serious dangers to global security because they can kill large numbers of people quickly.

For a time after international agreements were signed in the 1960s and 1970s (see Chapter 28), considerable progress was made in restricting the testing and spread of nuclear weapons and reduc-

ing their numbers. When the Soviet Union broke up, Russia alone retained a nuclear arsenal, but disposing of raw materials for nuclear weapons remained a problem in several successor states. Meanwhile, China resumed nuclear weapons tests in 1992.

Anxiety over nuclear proliferation increased in 1998 when India and Pakistan openly tested nuclear bombs and missile delivery systems, acts that raised the stakes in any future conflict between them. Although North Korea was a signatory of the nuclear nonproliferation treaty, it secretly continued nuclear weapons programs. Iran too pursued nuclear research while denying any intention of producing weapons, a practice that Israel had engaged in in the 1970s when it was developing its undeclared nuclear arsenal.

Chemical and biological weapons are difficult to detect and can easily be produced in seemingly ordinary chemical and pharmaceutical plants. As part of the settlement of the 1991 Persian Gulf War, United Nations inspectors in Iraq uncovered and destroyed extensive stocks of chemical munitions and plants for producing nerve gas and lethal germs. In 1997, however, the government of Saddam Husain, while pursuing an effective disarmament program, refused to allow United Nations weapons inspectors access to suspected weapons sites.

Weapons of mass destruction in the hands of terrorists constituted a growing fear. Terrorists believe that horrendous acts of violence can provoke harsh reprisals that will win them sympathy or cause the regimes they oppose to lose legitimacy. **Terrorism** has a long history, but much recent concern has focused on the network of terrorist organizations created by **Usama bin Laden,** a wealthy Saudi. Though his own family disowned him and Saudi Arabia stripped him of his citizenship, his anti-American stance and patronage attracted followers throughout the Islamic world. In 1992 bin Laden established himself in Sudan, where he invested in many projects. Suspecting that a pharmaceutical plant near the Sudanese capital Khartoum was being used for making chemical weapons, President Clinton had it destroyed by rockets in 1998, but no evidence of weapons production was found.

After being expelled from Sudan in 1996, bin Laden went to Afghanistan, where he had close ties with the Taliban, a fundamentalist Islamic organization that had taken control of most of that country in 1995. Bin Laden's agents bombed the American embassies in Kenya and Tanzania in 1998 as well as the destroyer USS *Cole,* which was making a port call in Yemen in 2000, before turning to targets in the United States itself. In response to the terrorist attacks of September 2001 and the subsequent panic caused by an unknown terrorist mailing spores of anthrax, a lethal disease, the U.S. government adopted a more aggressive policy against terrorism and weapons of mass destruction. In December 2001, American and other NATO forces joined with Afghan opposition groups to overthrow the Taliban-supported regime in Afghanistan, an act that President Bush declared to be the first step in a much larger "war on terrorism."

The issue of when military intervention is justified became the focus of international debate after President Bush pushed for extension of the war on terrorism against the brutal regime of Saddam Husayn in Iraq. Strong opposition to unilateral action came from America's NATO allies France and Germany, as well as from Russia and China. German chancellor Gerhard Schröder won a close election in September 2002 by campaigning against American imperialism. Faced with this opposition, the Bush administration changed tactics. In November 2002 it persuaded the United Nations Security Council to order the return of United Nations weapons inspectors to Iraq and require the Iraqi government to specify what weapons of mass destruction it still possessed.

When the new United Nations inspectors in Iraq failed to find any evidence of banned weapons, which the Iraqis had already destroyed, the split widened between those nations wanting to continue inspections and those, led by the United States and Britain, wanting to intervene militarily. Abandoning efforts to gain Security Council authorization, an American-led "coalition of the willing" invaded Iraq in March 2003.

By the time the new Persian Gulf war began, the overwhelming international sympathy the United States had received after September 11 had evaporated. Public disapproval ran well over 80 percent in Russia and in NATO allies France, Germany, and Turkey (whose parliament voted not to allow American troops to attack Iraq from Turkish soil). Public opinion in most of the Muslim world was almost unanimously against the intervention. Even in Britain and Poland, which sent troops to Iraq, most people disapproved of the war.

Driving Saddam's regime from power took only six weeks. But postwar Iraqi looters and saboteurs did immense damage to utility plants, oil well equipment, and government offices. Moreover, the arsenals of banned weapons that the Bush administration had used to justify the war were never found.

In May the Security Council authorized the American and British occupation of Iraq and lifted the sanctions on petroleum exports that had been imposed on the old regime. But American efforts to secure a larger United Nations role in rebuilding Iraq faced resistance from other world powers, who insisted on curbing American control. Meanwhile, a growing insurgency featuring daily ambushes, kidnappings, and car bombings prevented the establishment of security.

Most Iraqis welcomed the end of Saddam's rule and applauded his capture, but they were also eager for American occupiers to leave. They criticized the slow pace of restoring electricity and water to the cities and the lack of law and order. They had scant faith in the American-nominated Iraqi Governing Council, and only slightly more in the provisional government led by Ayad Allawi that took power at the end of June 2003. As in Afghanistan, reestablishing political and civil order in Iraq would be a long and costly process.

The Global Economy

From 1991 to 2000 the world experienced a rapid expansion in manufacturing and trade that tied the world ever more tightly together. Manufactured products were increasingly likely to be the product of materials and labor from many countries. Overall, the already developed economies increased their wealth the most, but the fastest rates of growth were in developing countries and in economies making a transition from communism. Net private capital flows to developing nations rose almost sevenfold between 1990 and 2000. This was not foreign aid. Investors

"All the News
That's Fit to Print"

The New York Times

New England Edition
Boston: Windy, some clearing late.
High 37. Mainly clear, brisk. Low 28.
Tomorrow, partly sunny and not as
cold, much lighter winds. High 42.
Weather map appears on Page D12.

VOL. CLIII .... No. 52,698   Copyright © 2003 The New York Times   MONDAY, DECEMBER 15, 2003   ONE DOLLAR

HUSSEIN CAUGHT IN MAKESHIFT HIDE-OUT; BUSH SAYS 'DARK ERA' FOR IRAQIS IS OVER

BETRAYED BY CLAN

Breakthrough Capped
a Renewed Effort to
Ferret Out Leads

By ERIC SCHMITT

BAGHDAD, Iraq, Dec. 14 — The
hunt for Saddam Hussein ended late
Saturday with information from a
member of his tribal clan.

Seizing Mr. Hussein, a man who
one senior general said had 20 to 30
hide-outs and moved as often as every three to four hours, had become a
maddening challenge. Eleven previous times in the last several months,
a brigade combat team from the
Army's Fourth Infantry Division
thought it had a bead on Mr. Hussein
and began raids to kill or capture
him, only to come up empty, sometimes missing its man by only a
matter of hours, military officials
here said.

But at 8:26 p.m. Saturday, less
than 11 hours after receiving the
decisive tip, 600 American soldiers
and Special Operations forces
backed by tanks, artillery and
Apache helicopter gunships surrounded two farmhouses, and near
one of them found Mr. Hussein hiding
alone at the bottom of an eight-foot
hole.

He surrendered without a shot.

"He was just caught like a rat,"
Maj. Gen. Raymond T. Odierno, the
commander of the Fourth Infantry
Division, told reporters at his headquarters in Tikrit on Sunday. "He
could have been hiding in a hundred
different places, a thousand different
places like this all around Iraq. It
just takes finding the right person
who will give you a good idea where
he might be."

In recent weeks, American officials had started a new effort to draw
up a list of people likely to be hiding
Mr. Hussein, including bodyguards,
former palace functionaries, tribal

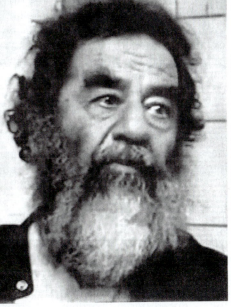

Arrest by U.S. Soldiers — President Still Cautious

By SUSAN SACHS

BAGHDAD, Iraq, Dec. 14 — Saddam Hussein, once the all-powerful
leader of Iraq, was arrested without
a fight on Saturday night by American soldiers who found him crouching in an eight-foot hole at an isolated
farm near Tikrit, haggard, dirty and
disoriented after eluding capture for
nearly nine months.

News of Mr. Hussein's arrest, announced Sunday after being kept secret for 18 hours, electrified Iraq and
much of the world, sending joyous
Iraqis into the streets with the first
real catharsis of liberation since the
invasion toppled him in April.

For the Bush administration,
which has been struggling to stabilize Iraq, the capture of Mr. Hussein
was the most triumphal moment
since American forces ousted him.

"In the history of Iraq, a dark and
painful era is over," President Bush
said in a televised noontime address
from Washington. "A hopeful day
has arrived. All Iraqis can now come
together and reject violence and
build a new Iraq." But Mr. Bush was
careful to couch his message with
caution that Iraq remains violent
and dangerous.

American officials said Mr. Hussein was being held in Iraq, but they
would not disclose the exact location.
They said he had been unresistant in
medical tests and other procedures
but was not cooperating with interro-
gators on substantive matters.

American-appointed Iraqi leaders
said he would eventually face a war
crimes trial, but it was unclear when.

President Bush, in a brief televised speech yesterday. Page A16.

Maj. Gen. Raymond T. Odierno,
commander of the Fourth Infantry
Division, which captured Mr. Hussein with a force of 600 soldiers, said
he was armed with only a pistol and
had surrendered without firing a
shot. Two AK-47 rifles and $750,000 in
American cash were found nearby.

It was an ignominious ending for
Mr. Hussein, 66, who survived American attempts to kill him during the
invasion and had eluded capture apparently by moving from one dingy
hide-out to another.

Whether his arrest will undermine
the insurgency against the American-led forces in Iraq is unclear.
Hours after his capture but before it
was announced publicly, a car bomb
killed at least 17 people in a town
west of Baghdad. [Page A12.]

Even in hiding, Mr. Hussein had

Continued on Page A12

In the Streets, a Shadow Lifts

By JOHN F. BURNS

Capture of Saddam in Iraq   Acting on a tip from Iraqi sources, American troops captured Saddam
Husayn in December 2003. The bearded former dictator of Iraq was discovered in a small underground "spider hole" about ten miles southeast of the city of Tikrit.   (©New York Times. Reprinted with
permission.)

put their funds in countries whose political stability, legal systems, level of education, and labor
costs promised the most profitable returns.

The greatest single beneficiary was China.
While officially espousing communism, the Chinese
government took major steps to open its economy
to freer trade and investment. Newly opened markets in eastern Europe and the former Soviet Union
also received significant private investment. Stimulated by foreign investment, the Latin American nations of Brazil, Argentina, and Mexico experienced
great economic growth. Investors put much less
money into the shaky economies and political sys-

tems of sub-Saharan Africa, except for countries
with significant petroleum resources.

Electronic transfers via the Internet made it possible to invest capital quickly; but when conditions
became unfavorable, funds could be withdrawn
just as fast. When investors lost faith in Thailand in
1997 and shifted their funds out, the country's currency and stock values plummeted. Political corruption and unrest in Indonesia brought on a
similar capital flight the next year, and the widening Asian collapse eventually triggered a serious recession in Japan, business failures in South Korea,
and a slowing of economic growth in China.

Government intervention sometimes helped. When Mexico's economy stumbled badly in 1995, U.S. loan guarantees helped it recover rapidly, and by 2001 Mexico had the largest economy in Latin America. However, when Argentina had to abandon its attempt to link its currency to the U.S. dollar in 2001, the value of the Argentine peso plummeted.

Although the largest economies were better able to weather tough times, they were not immune to economic downturns. The extraordinary economic and stock market boom of the 1990s cooled in 2000 and plunged deeper into recession in the wake of the September 11 attacks. The rate of growth in world trade fell from 13 percent in 2000 to only 1 percent in 2001.

The economic boom of the 1990s did little to change historic disparities in regional economic size and in per capita income. The gigantic U.S. economy continued to be larger than the economies of the next five countries combined— Japan, Germany, Great Britain, China (including Hong Kong), and France. In 2002 one person in six lived in a country whose per capita income was over $20,000, while four of every six lived in countries with per capita incomes of under $2,000. Some sixty countries grew poorer in the 1990s, but there were some remarkable overall improvements in the length and quality of life. The average lifespan grew by ten years in three decades. Infant mortality fell by 40 percent and adult illiteracy by 50 percent.

Managing the Global Economy

To promote economic growth and reduce their vulnerabilities, many countries joined with their neighbors in free-trade zones and regional trade associations (see Map 30.1). The granddaddy of these is the European Union (EU), most of whose members replaced their coins and bills with a new common currency (the Euro) in 2002. Ten new members from eastern Europe and the Mediterranean were admitted in May 2004. Turkey, Bulgaria, and Romania were hoping to join. Despite the EU's expansion, the North American Free Trade Agreement (NAFTA), which eliminated tariffs among the United States, Canada, and Mexico in 1994, governed the world's largest free-trade zone. A South American free-trade zone, Mer-

Map 30.1   Regional Trade Associations, 2004   International trade and development are major concerns of governments in developed and developing countries. NAFTA, Mercosur, and the EU are free-trade areas. The other associations promote trade and development.

cosur, created by Argentina, Brazil, Paraguay, and Uruguay in 1991, is the world's third largest trading group. In 2002 Mercosur decided to allow the free movement of people within its area and gave equal employment rights to the citizens of all member states. President Bush promoted a Free Trade Area of the Americas, which would include all the democracies of the Western Hemisphere. Chile was the first to sign on. Other free-trade associations operate in West Africa, southern Africa, Southeast Asia, Central America, the Pacific Basin, and the Caribbean.

Because of the inequalities and downturns that are intrinsic to capitalism, the global economic bodies that try to manage world trade and finance find it hard to convince poorer nations that they are not concerned only with the welfare of richer countries. In 1995 the world's major trading powers established the **World Trade Organization (WTO)** to replace earlier collective efforts to negotiate tariffs and trading rules. The WTO encourages reduced trading barriers and enforces international trade agreements. Despite the membership of some 150 nations, the WTO has many critics, as became evident in Seattle in 1999, when street demonstrations, partly organized by American labor unions fearful of foreign competition, forced the organization to suspend a meeting. Moreover, the seven richest nations plus Russia form the Group of Eight (G-8), whose annual meetings have an enormous impact on international trade and politics and also attract a variety of protestors.

Countries in economic trouble have little choice but to turn to the international financial agencies for funds to keep things from getting worse. The International Monetary Fund (IMF) and World Bank make their assistance conditional on internal economic reforms that are often politically unpopular, such as terminating government subsidies for basic foodstuffs, cutting social programs, and liberalizing investment. Although the bitter pill of economic reform may be good in the

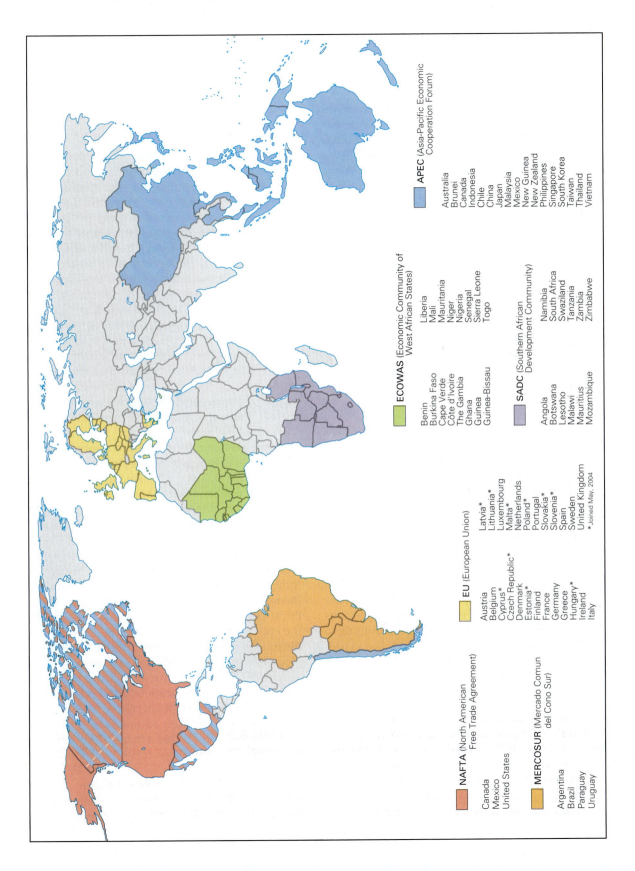

APEC (Asia-Pacific Economic Cooperation Forum)

Australia
Brunei
Canada
Indonesia
Chile
China
Japan
Malaysia
Mexico
New Guinea
New Zealand
Philippines
Singapore
South Korea
Taiwan
Thailand
Vietnam

ECOWAS (Economic Community of West African States)

Benin
Burkina Faso
Cape Verde
Côte d'Ivoire
The Gambia
Ghana
Guinea
Guinea-Bissau
Liberia
Mali
Mauritania
Niger
Nigeria
Senegal
Sierra Leone
Togo

SADC (Southern African Development Community)

Angola
Botswana
Lesotho
Malawi
Mauritius
Mozambique
Namibia
South Africa
Swaziland
Tanzania
Zambia
Zimbabwe

EU (European Union)

Austria
Belgium
Cyprus*
Czech Republic*
Denmark
Estonia*
Finland
France
Germany
Greece
Hungary*
Ireland
Italy
Latvia*
Lithuania*
Luxembourg
Malta*
Netherlands
Poland*
Portugal
Slovakia*
Slovenia*
Spain
Sweden
United Kingdom
*Joined May, 2004

NAFTA (North American Free Trade Agreement)

Canada
Mexico
United States

MERCOSUR (Mercado Comun del Cono Sur)

Argentina
Brazil
Paraguay
Uruguay

long run, it also fuels criticism of the international economic system.

The emphasis on free trade led to changes in the term of government-to-government aid programs. During the Cold War countries had often gained funds for economic development by allying themselves with one of the superpowers. In the decade after the Cold War ended, however, foreign economic aid to poor nations fell by a third. On an African tour in 2000 President Clinton told African countries that the days of large handouts were over and that they would have to rely on their own efforts to expand their economies.

In the face of rising criticism at home and protests at international meetings, world leaders in the 2000s have pledged to increase attention to the problem of economic backwardness, especially in Africa. At a Millennium Summit in September 2000 the states of the United Nations agreed to make sustainable development and the elimination of world poverty their highest priorities. A 2002 United Nations meeting in Monterrey, Mexico, called for special commitments to Africa.

Freer trade has also put pressure on developed countries to change domestic aid programs. Though agriculture occupies a small part of the work force in Europe and the United States, agricultural interests are politically powerful. Government subsidies have led to vast overproduction of some products. Some of this surplus food is distributed as famine relief, but critics point out that subsidies to farmers in developed countries actually hurt farmers in poor countries, who cannot compete with the artificially low prices that subsidies produce. A WTO meeting collapsed in 2003 when richer countries refused to meet the demands of delegates from poorer states to reduce agricultural subsidies.

TRENDS AND VISIONS

As people around the world faced the opportunities and problems of **globalization,** they tried to make sense of these changes in terms of their own cultures and beliefs. With 6 billion people, the world is big enough to include a variety of different approaches, from intensely religious or local visions to broad secular views that champion a new universal value system. In some cases, however, conflicting visions have fed violence.

A New Age?

In 1999 Thomas L. Friedman, a veteran Middle East and international reporter and columnist for the *New York Times*, published a penetrating analysis of the state of the planet. "The world is ten years old," proclaimed the opening essay of *The Lexus and the Olive Tree*. Friedman argued that the political and economic changes associated with the collapse of the Soviet Empire and the technological advances (computers, satellite and fiber-optic communications, and the Internet) that had made possible a huge drop in telecommunications costs had ushered in a new age of political and economic globalization. In his view, global capitalism and American power and values characterized this new era of history, which held the promise (but not the certainty) of increased prosperity, peace, democracy, environmental protection, and human rights.

In Friedman's analysis, the Lexus, a splendidly engineered Japanese luxury car produced for a global market on a computer-run assembly line of mechanical robots, symbolizes global progress and prosperity, as well as the international cooperation needed to achieve them. A Middle Eastern symbol, the olive tree, stands for the communal values of family, ethnicity, and religion that give people's lives stability, depth, and meaning.

Was Friedman too optimistic in seeing the dawning of an age of great promise? Many who thought so cited *The Clash of Civilizations and the Remaking of the World Order,* in which Harvard political scientist Samuel P. Huntington argues that the end of the Cold War left the world divided into distinct regional civilizations. For Huntington, religious and cultural differences are more likely to shape the future than are globalizing economic, political, and communication forces. It is impossible to predict whether global clashes or global convergence are more likely to dominate the future. Recent trends seem to point in both directions.

Militant Islam

While the year 2000 excited anticipations of the end of the world among certain Christian groups, some people in other faiths also interpreted contemporary events from deeply religious perspectives. In the Jewish calendar a millennial change (the year 6000) will not arrive until 2240 C.E., but many on the religious right in Israel interpret the struggle of modern Israel to survive and prosper in terms of the biblical accounts of the Israelites' conquests more than four thousand years ago. Some Christian believers have gone to Israel to support Jewish settlers' efforts to reclaim the lands of the ancient Jewish kingdoms. For Muslims the year 1400 coincided with the Iranian Revolution of 1979. Since that time publications dealing with the end of the world have become common among certain groups, just as they have in some Christian circles. But the issues that concern most Muslims arise from the real circumstances in which they find themselves. While moderate views on how to cope with economic stagnation and autocratic rule predominate, extreme and intolerant groups have been able to recruit supporters among those who feel politically frustrated or distressed by what they see as foreign cultural practices eroding their tradition. Since becoming independent in the 1950s, some Middle Eastern states have earned great wealth from petroleum exports, but per capita income in Muslim-majority countries in 2002 averaged half as much as in the world as a whole. No Muslim state is a major industrial or geopolitical power. The spread of mass media has also fed discontent by making ordinary Muslims more aware of the political difficulties and violence facing fellow Muslims in places like Chechnya, Iraq, Kashmir, and the occupied territories of the West Bank and Gaza.

Because American aid and support have helped Israel acquire the most powerful military force in the Middle East, much Islamic hatred and opposition has been directed against the United States. Many Muslims also denounce American support for unpopular and undemocratic governments in Muslim-majority countries like Egypt and Saudi Arabia. Although most Muslims admire American technological and cultural achievements, a 2002 poll by the Pew Research Center for the People and the Press found that the majority of Egyptians, Jordanians, and Pakistanis held a "very unfavorable" opinion of the United States, a negative appraisal that has only deepened with the prolongation of the American occupation of Iraq.

This view of the world order has many roots, but it reflects an ideological vision of Muslims under attack that is widely published in the media in Muslim states and promoted by a few Muslim leaders who use religious ideas to justify violent actions. From this perspective the Palestinian suicide bombers in Israel appear as martyrs and heroes rather than terrorists. Such a vision explains why some Muslims celebrated when the Twin Towers collapsed in New York.

Universal Rights and Values

At the same time that religiously based visions of society and government have gained support in various faith communities, efforts to promote adherence to universal standards of human rights have also gained wider acceptance. The modern human rights movement grew out of the secular statements of the French Declaration of the Rights of Man (1789) and the U.S. Constitution (1788) and Bill of Rights (1791). Over the next century, the logic of universal rights moved Westerners to undertake international campaigns to end slave trading and slavery throughout the world and to secure equal legal rights (and eventually voting rights) for women. (As the millennium began, the cause of animal rights was gaining increasing support in Europe and North America.)

International organizations in the twentieth century secured agreement on labor standards, the rules of war, and the rights of refugees. The pinnacle of these efforts was the **Universal Declaration of Human Rights,** passed by the United Nations General Assembly in 1948, which proclaimed itself "a common standard of achievement for all peoples and nations." Its thirty articles condemned slavery, torture, cruel and inhuman punishment, and arbitrary arrest, detention, and exile. The Declaration called for freedom of movement, assembly, and thought. It asserted rights to life, liberty, and security of person; to impartial public trials; and to education, employment, and leisure. The principle of equality was most fully articulated in Article 2:

> Everyone is entitled to all the rights and freedoms set forth in this Declaration, without distinction of any kind, such as race, color, sex, language, religion, or political or other opinion,

national or social origin, property, birth or other status.[2]

This passage reflected an international consensus against racism and imperialism and a growing acceptance of the importance of social and economic equality. Most newly independent countries joining the United Nations willingly signed the Declaration because it implicitly condemned European colonial regimes.

The idea of universal human rights has not gone unchallenged. Some have asked whether a set of principles whose origins were so clearly Western could be called universal. Others have been uneasy with the idea of subordinating the traditional values of their culture or religion to a broader philosophical standard. Despite these objections, important gains have been made in implementing these standards.

Besides the official actions of the United Nations and individual states, individual human rights activists, often working through international philanthropic bodies known as **nongovernmental organizations (NGOs),** have been important forces for promoting human rights. Amnesty International, founded in 1961 and numbering a million members in 162 countries by the 1990s, concentrates on gaining the freedom of people who have been tortured or imprisoned without trial and campaigns against summary execution by government death squads or other gross violations of rights. Arguing that no right is more fundamental than the right to life, other NGOs have devoted themselves to famine relief, refugee assistance, and health care around the world. Médecins Sans Frontières (Doctors Without Borders), founded in 1971, was awarded the Nobel Peace Prize for 1999 for the medical assistance it offered in scores of crisis situations.

The rising tendency to see health care as a human right has made a new disease, acquired immune deficiency syndrome (AIDS), the focus of particular attention because its incidence and high mortality rate are closely associated with poverty, and treatments are very expensive. Over 40 million people worldwide are infected with the HIV retrovirus that causes AIDS. Of them, 70 percent live in sub-Saharan Africa (see Figure 30.1). The number of sick and dying is already large enough in some parts of Africa to pose a significant risk to the pro-

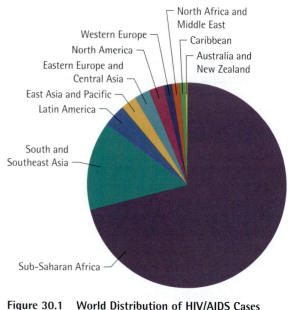

Figure 30.1 World Distribution of HIV/AIDS Cases (2001 estimates) *Source:* United Nations AIDS and World Health Organization, *Report on the Global HIV/AIDS Epidemic* (June 2000).

duction of food, the care of the young and elderly, and the staffing of schools. Because sexual promiscuity among young men serving in the armed forces has made them especially likely to be infected, death and incapacitation from AIDS have significantly imperiled military preparedness in parts of Africa. Great international efforts are being made to provide drugs at a lower cost so that more Africans can be treated. Because the disease is not contagious except by very intimate contact, education is a more cost-effective way of stemming the spread of AIDS. In Uganda, South Africa, and Ethiopia, for example, education campaigns have reduced the incidence of new HIV infections in targeted groups. An inexpensive drug has also been successful in cutting the transmission of the infection from mother to infant during childbirth.

Other international agreements have made genocide a crime and have promoted environmental protection of the seas, of Antarctica, and of the atmosphere. The United States and a few other nations were greatly concerned that such treaties would unduly limit their sovereignty or threaten their national interests. For this reason the U.S. Congress delayed ratifying the 1949 convention on genocide until 1986. More recently the United States drew widespread international criticism for demanding exemption for Americans from the jurisdiction of the International Criminal Court, created in 2002 to try international criminals, and for withdrawing in 2001 from the 1997 Kyoto Protocol requiring industrial nations to sharply reduce emissions of pollutants that damage the atmosphere (see Environment and Technology: Global Warming). To many nations it seemed as if Americans, with the world's greatest industrial economy, were trying to exempt themselves from standards that they wanted to impose on other nations.

Women's Rights

The women's rights movement, which began on both sides of the North Atlantic in the nineteenth century, became an important human rights issue in the twentieth century. Rights for women became accepted in Western countries and were enshrined in the constitutions of many nations newly freed from colonial rule. A series of international conferences on the status of women sponsored by the Division for the Advancement of Women of the United Nations have shown the international importance of women's rights at the end of the twentieth century. The first meeting, held in Nairobi, Kenya, in 1985, attracted seventeen thousand women from all over the world. The delegates focused on equal access to education and jobs and on quality-of-life matters such as ending sexual exploitation and gaining control of reproduction. A second conference in Beijing in 1995 also examined a variety of women's issues and perspectives, in some cases to the discomfort of the Chinese government. The Beijing conference recognized the advances that had been made in the status of women and called for efforts to remove remaining obstacles to equality, including those caused by poverty.

Besides highlighting the similarity of the problems women faced around the world, the conferences also revealed great variety in the views and concerns of women. Feminists from the West, who had been accustomed to dictating the agenda and who had pushed for the liberation of women in other parts of the world, sometimes found themselves accused of having narrow concerns and condescending attitudes. Some non-Western women complained about Western feminists' endorsement of sexual liberation and about the deterioration of family life in the West. They found Western feminists' concern with matters such as comfortable clothing misplaced and trivial compared to the issues of poverty and disease.

Other cultures came in for their share of criticism. Western women and many secular leaders in Muslim countries protested Islam's requirement that a woman cover her head and wear loose-fitting garments to conceal the shape of her body, practices enforced by law in countries such as Iran and Saudi Arabia. Nevertheless, many outspoken Muslim women voluntarily donned concealing garments as expressions of personal belief, statements of resistance to secular dictatorship, or defense against coarse male behavior. Much Western criticism focused on the African custom of circumcising girls, a form of genital mutilation that can cause chronic infections or permanently impair sexual enjoyment. While not denying the problems this practice can lead to, many African women saw deteriorating economic conditions, rape, and AIDS as more important issues.

The conferences were more important for the attention they focused on women's issues than for the solutions they generated. The search for a universally accepted women's rights agenda proved elusive because of local concerns and strong disagreement on abortion and other issues. Nevertheless, increases in women's education, access to employment, political participation, and control of fertility augured well for the eventual achievement of gender equality.

Such efforts raised the prominence of human rights as a global concern and put pressure on governments to consider human rights when making foreign policy decisions. Skeptics observed, however, that a Western country could successfully prod a non-Western country to improve its human rights performance—for example, by granting women

Global Warming

Until the 1980s environmental alarms focused mainly on localized episodes of air and water pollution, exposure to toxic substances, waste management, and the disappearance of wilderness. The development of increasingly powerful computers and complex models of ecological interactions in the 1990s, however, made people aware of the global scope of certain environmental problems.

Many scientists and policymakers came to perceive global warming, the slow increase of the temperature of the earth's lower atmosphere, as an environmental threat requiring preventive action on an international scale. The warming is caused by a layer of atmospheric gases (carbon dioxide, methane, nitrous oxide, and ozone) that allow solar radiation to reach earth and warm it, but keep infrared energy (heat) from radiating from earth's surface into space. Called the *greenhouse effect*, this process normally keeps the earth's temperature at a level suitable for life. However, increases in greenhouse-gas emissions—particularly from the burning of fossil fuels in industry and transportation—have added to this insulating atmospheric layer.

Recent events have confirmed predictions of global temperature increases and melting glaciers and icecaps. Globally, the five warmest years on record were 1995,

1997, 1998, 2001, and 2002. Record heat hit northern Europe in the summer of 2003. Greenland glaciers and Arctic Ocean sea ice melted at record rates during 2002, and a huge section of the Antarctic ice shelf broke up and floated away. Andean glaciers are shrinking so fast they could disappear in a decade, imperiling water supplies for drinking, irrigation, and hydroelectric production. Drought has affected much of the United States in recent years, and in 2002 Australia experienced the "Big Dry," its worst drought in a century.

Despite this evidence, governments of the industrialized countries that produce the most greenhouse gasses have been slow to adopt measures stringent enough to reduce emissions because of the negative effects they believe this could have on their economies. There is also fear that it may be already too late to reverse global warming. The pledges that representatives from 178 countries made at the first Earth Summit in Rio de Janeiro in 1992 to limit their *increase* in greenhouse-gas production have so far been ineffective. Fearing limits on gas emissions could cripple their plans for industrial and economic expansion, many nations hesitated to sign the 1997 Kyoto Protocol, the first international agreement to impose penalties on countries that failed to cut greenhouse-gas

---

more equal access to education and careers—but that reverse criticism of a Western country often fell on deaf ears—for example, condemnation of the death penalty in the United States. For such critics the human rights movement was not an effort to make the world more humane but another form of Western cultural imperialism, a club with which to beat former colonial societies into submission. Still, support for universal rights has grown, especially because increasing globalization has made common standards of behavior more important.

GLOBAL CULTURE

Along with the human rights movement, other kinds of cultural globalization were also proceeding rapidly at the turn of the millennium. A global language, a global educational system, and global forms of artistic expression have all come into being. Trade, travel, and migration have made a common culture necessary. Electronic communications that were once confined to members of a jet-setting elite have enabled global cultural

emissions. It was a major environmental victory when Japan added its signature in March 2001, but to the consternation of many world leaders President George W. Bush has rejected the agreement. The war on terrorism also appears to have made the environment a lower American priority. Until the destructive effects of global warming, such as the inundation of coastal regions and large cities by rising sea levels, match the destruction of terrorists, the political focus is unlikely to shift.

Flooding in Bangladesh Typhoon-driven floods submerge the low-lying farmlands of Bangladesh with tragic regularity. Any significant rise in the sea level will make parts of the country nearly uninhabitable. (D. Aubert/Sygma)

influences to move deeper into many societies, and a sort of global popular culture has also emerged. These changes have angered some and delighted others.

The Media and the Message

Although cultural influences from every continent travel around the world, the fact that the most pervasive elements of global culture have their origins in the West raises concerns in many quarters about **cultural imperialism.** Critics complain that entertainment conglomerates are flooding the world's movie theaters and television screens with Western tastes and styles and that manufacturers are flooding world markets with Western goods—both relying on sophisticated advertising techniques that promote consumption and cultural conformity. In this view, global marketing is an especially insidious effort not only to overwhelm the world with a single Western outlook shaped by capitalist ideology, but also to suppress or devalue traditional cultures and alternative ideologies. As the leader of the capitalist world, the United States is seen as the primary culprit.

727

But in truth, technology plays a more central role than ideology in spreading Western culture. Moreover, even though imperialist forces old and new shape choices, strongly democratic forces are also at work as people around the world make their selections in the cultural marketplace. Thus, a diversity of voices is more characteristic of cultural globalization than the cultural imperialism thesis maintains.

The pace of cultural globalization began to quicken during the economic recovery after World War II. The Hollywood films and American jazz recordings that had become popular in Europe and parts of Asia continued to spread. But the birth of electronic technology opened contacts with large numbers of people who could never have afforded to go to a movie or buy a record.

The first step was the development of cheap transistor radios that could run for months on a couple of small batteries. Perfected by American scientists at Bell Telephone Laboratories in 1948, solid-state electronic transistors replaced power-hungry and less reliable electron tubes in radios and a wide array of other devices. Just as tube radios had spread in Europe and America in the decades before the war, small portable transistor radios, most made in Japan and elsewhere in Asia, spread rapidly in parts of the world where homes lacked electricity.

Because the transistor radios sold in Asia and Africa were designed to receive shortwave broadcasts, they brought people in remote villages the news, views, and music that American, European, Soviet, and Chinese transmitters beamed to the world. For the first time in history, the whole world could learn of major political and cultural events simultaneously. Although such broadcasts came in local and regional languages, many were in English. Electronic audiotape and CD players added to the diversity of music available to individuals everywhere. Television, made possible by the invention of an electron scanning gun in 1928, became widely available to consumers in Western countries in the 1950s. In poorer parts of the world TVs were not common until the 1980s and 1990s, after mass production and cheap transistors made sets more affordable and reliable.

Outside the United States, television broadcasting was usually a government monopoly at first, following the pattern of telegraph and postal service and radio broadcasting. Governments expected news reports and other programming to disseminate a unified national viewpoint. These government monopolies eroded as the high cost of television production opened up global markets for rebroadcasts of American soap operas, adventure series, and situation comedies. By the 1990s a global network of satellites brought privately owned television broadcasting to even remote areas of the world, and the VCR (videocassette recorder) brought an even greater variety of programs to people everywhere. British programs found a secondary market in the United States, Canada, Australia, and other countries. As a result of wider circulation of programming, people often became familiar with different dialects of English and other languages. People in Portugal, for example, who in the 1960s had found it difficult to understand Brazilian Portuguese, have become avid fans of Brazilian soap operas. Immigrants from Albania and North Africa often arrive in Italy with a command of Italian learned from Italian stations whose signals they could pick up at home.

Further internationalization of culture resulted from satellite transmission of TV signals. Specializing in rock music videos aimed at a youth audience, MTV (Music Television) became an international enterprise offering special editions in different parts of the world. Music videos shown in Uzbekistan°, for example, often featured Russian bands, and Chinese groups appeared in MTV programs shown in Singapore. CNN (Cable News Network) expanded its international market after becoming the most-viewed and informative news source during the 1991 Persian Gulf War, when it broadcast live from Baghdad. Despite CNN's fundamentally American view of the news, its round-the-clock coverage and global resources began to supplant other commercial and government news programming as the best source of information about rapidly developing events. By the new millennium global satellite networks (Fox, Sky) assembled by Rupert Murdock and new regional networks competed for viewers.

The Internet, a linkage of academic, government, and business computer networks developed

---

Uzbekistan (ooz-BEK-ih-STAN)

in the 1960s, became a major cultural phenomenon. Personal computers proliferated in the 1980s, and with the establishment of the easy-to-use graphic interface of the World Wide Web in 1994, the number of Internet users skyrocketed. Myriad new companies formed to exploit "e-commerce," the commercial dimension of the Internet. In the new century many college students spent less time studying conventional books and scholarly resources than they spent exploring the Web for information and entertainment.

As has happened so often throughout history, technological developments have had unanticipated consequences. Although the new telecommunications and entertainment technologies derived disproportionately from American invention, industry, and cultural creativity, Japan and other East Asian nations came to dominate the manufacture and refinement of computer devices. In the 1990s Japan introduced digital television broadcasting at about the time that disks containing digitized movies and computer programs with movie-like action became increasingly available. In the early 2000s digital cameras, DVD players, and new generations of cell phones became popular, providing opportunities for companies in a variety of developing countries to capture a corner of the market. In contrast to these rapid changes in technology, Western, especially American, cultural domination of the content of the Web has changed more slowly, but people around the world can adapt the medium to their own purposes.

The Spread of Pop Culture

New technologies changed perceptions of culture as well as its distribution around the world and among different social classes. For most of history, popular culture was folk culture, highly localized ways of dress, food, music, and expression. Only the educated and urban few had access to the riches of a broader "great tradition," such as Confucianism in East Asia or Western culture in Europe and the Americas. The schools of modern nation-states promoted national values and beliefs, as well as tastes in painting, literature, and art. Governments also promoted a common language or dialect and frequently suppressed local traditions and languages. In a more democratic way, the transistor helped break down barriers and create a global popular culture that transcended regional great traditions and national cultures.

Initially, the content of **global pop culture** was heavily American. Singer Michael Jackson was almost as well known to the youth of Dar-es-Salaam (Tanzania) and Bangkok (Thailand) as to American fans. Basketball star Michael Jordan became a worldwide celebrity, heavily promoted by Nike, McDonald's, and television. American television programs such as *Wheel of Fortune* and *Friends* acquired immense followings and inspired local imitations. In the late twentieth century American movies, which had long had great popular appeal, substantially increased their share of world markets. In the 1990s the vast majority of the most popular films in Europe were American made. Many Europeans complained loudly about this American cultural imperialism—and then bought tickets to see the latest Hollywood spectacular.

As with music and fast food, companies spent heavily to promote profitable overseas markets, but the United States did not have a lock on global pop culture. Latin American soap operas, *telenovelas,* have a vast following in the Americas, eastern Europe, and elsewhere. Bombay, India, long the largest producer of films in the world, is now making more films for an international audience, rather than just for the home market. Bruce Lee popularized kung fu (Chinese martial arts) movies. A sophisticated kung fu film, *Crouching Tiger, Hidden Dragon* by Hong Kong–born director Ang Lee, was very popular in the United States and won four Academy Awards for 2000, including one for the best foreign-language film.

In the post–World War II decades American, European, and Japanese companies sought international markets for their products. In the 1970s and 1980s American brand names like Levi's, Coca-Cola, Marlboro, Gillette, McDonald's, and Kentucky Fried Chicken were global phenomena. But in time Asian names—Hitachi, Sony, Sanyo, and Mitsubishi—were blazoned in neon and on giant video screens on the sides of skyscrapers, along with European brands such as Nestlé, Mercedes, Pirelli, and Benetton. The location of manufacturing plants overseas and the acquisition of corporate operations by foreign buyers rendered such global firms as transnational as the products they sell.

The content of international pop culture does not have to remain any more monolithic than the typical McDonald's lunch, which consists of a meat patty named for a German city, potatoes prepared in a French manner, and a soft drink named after the South American coca leaves and West African kola that were its original ingredients. Popular music also became increasingly international. Latin American styles extended their appeal beyond the Americas. The hybrid rhythms known as Afropop spread around Africa and found fans in Europe and the Americas.

The Emerging Global Elite Culture

While the globalization of popular culture has been criticized, cultural links across national and ethnic boundaries at a more elite level have generated little controversy. The end of the Cold War reopened intellectual and cultural contacts between former adversaries, making possible such things as Russian-American collaboration on space missions and extensive business contacts among former rivals. The English language, modern science, and higher education became the key elements of this **global elite culture.**

The emergence of English as the first global language depended on developments that had been building for centuries. The British Empire introduced the language to far-flung colonies. When the last parts of the empire gained independence after World War II, most former colonies chose to continue using English as an official language because it provided national unity and a link to the outside world that the dozens or hundreds of local languages could not. After independence, representatives of former British colonies formed the Commonwealth on the basis of their shared language and commercial ties. Newly independent countries that made a local language official for nationalist reasons often found the decision counterproductive. Indian nationalists had pushed for Hindi to be India's official language, but they found that students taught in Hindi were unable to compete internationally because of poor knowledge of English. Sri Lanka, which had made Sinhala its official language in 1956, reversed itself after local reporters revealed in 1989 that prominent officials were sending their children to English-medium private schools.

The use of English as a second language was greatly stimulated by the importance of the United States in postwar world affairs. Individuals recognized the importance of mastering English for successful business, diplomatic, and military careers. After the collapse of Soviet domination, students in eastern Europe flocked to study English instead of Russian. Ninety percent of students in Cambodia (a former French colony) choose to study English, even though a Canadian agency offers a sizeable cash bonus if they will study French. In the 1990s China made the study of English as a second language nearly universal from junior high school onwards, but it also forced an English-medium school in Hong Kong to teach most subjects in Chinese.

English has become the language of choice for most international academic conferences, business meetings, and diplomatic gatherings. International organizations that provide equal status to many languages, such as the United Nations and the European Union, tend to conduct all informal committee meetings in English. English has even replaced Latin as the working language for international consultations in the Catholic Church. In cities throughout the world, signs and notices are now posted in the local language and English.

The utility of English as a global language is also evident in the emergence of an international literature in English. The trend has been evident for decades in former British colonies in Africa, where most writers use English to reach both a national audience and an international one. Wole Soyinka, the first sub-Saharan African to win the Nobel Prize in literature for 1986, wrote in English, the national language of Nigeria, rather than his native Yoruba. When Arundhati Roy won the prestigious Booker Prize in 1997 for *The God of Small Things,* a novel set in her native state of Kerala in southwest India, she was part of an English-language literary tradition that has been growing in India for a century. V. S. Naipaul of Trinidad, winner of the Nobel Prize in literature for 2001, is a good example of the way global migration has fostered the use of English. Naipaul's ancestors had emigrated from India in the nineteenth century.

World literature remains highly diverse in form and language, but science and technology have become standardized components of global culture. Though imperialism helped spread the Western disciplines of biology, chemistry, and physics around the world, their popularity continued to expand even after imperial systems ended because they worked so much better than other approaches to the natural world. Their truth was universal even if plants and animals continue to be classified in Latin and the less common elements are called by names originally derived from Latin and Greek. Global manufacturing could not function without a common system of applied science. Because of their scientific basis, Western medicine and drugs are increasingly accepted as the best treatments, even though many cultures also use traditional remedies.

The third pillar of global elite culture is the university. The structure and curricula of modern universities are nearly indistinguishable around the world, permitting students today to cross national boundaries as freely as students in the medieval Latin West or the Muslim world. Instruction in the pure sciences varies little from place to place, and standardization is nearly as common in social science and in applied sciences such as engineering and medicine. There may be more diversity in the humanities, but professors and students around the world pay attention to the latest literary theories and topics of historical interest.

While university subjects are taught in many languages, instruction in English is spreading rapidly. Because discoveries are often first published in English, advanced students in science, business, and international relations need to know that language to keep up with the latest developments. The global mobility of professors and students also promotes classroom instruction in the most global language. Many courses in the Netherlands and in Scandinavian countries have long been offered in English, and elsewhere in Europe offering more courses in English was the obvious way to facilitate the EU's efforts to encourage students to study outside their countries of origin. When South Africa ended the apartheid educational systems that had required people to study in their own languages, most students chose to study in English.

Because global elite culture is so deeply rooted in years of training, complex institutions, and practical utility, it is less subject to fads and commercial promotion than is global pop culture. Because such elite culture is confined to a distinct minority in most places, it poses little threat to national and folk cultures and, therefore, is much less controversial.

Enduring Cultural Diversity

Although protestors regularly denounce the "Americanization" of the world, a closer look suggests that cultural globalization is more complex and multifaceted. Just as English has largely spread as a second language, so global culture is primarily a second culture that dominates some contexts but does not displace other traditions. From this perspective, American music, fast food, and fashions are more likely to add to a society's options than to displace local culture.

Japan first demonstrated that a country with a non-Western culture could perform at a high industrial level. Individuality was less valued in Japan than the ability of each person to fit into a group, whether as an employee, a member of an athletic team, or a student in a class. Moreover, the Japanese considered it unmannerly to directly contradict, correct, or refuse the request of another person. From a Western point of view, these Japanese customs seemed to discourage individual initiative and personality development and to preserve traditional hierarchies. Japanese women, for example, even though they often worked outside the home, responded only slowly to the American and European feminist advocacy of equality in economic and social relations. However, the Japanese approach to social relations was well suited to an industrial economy. The efficiency, pride in workmanship, and group solidarity of Japanese workers, supported by closely coordinated government and corporate policies, played a major role in transforming Japan from a defeated nation with a demolished industrial base in 1945 to an economic power by the 1980s.

Japan's success in the modern industrial world called into question the older assumption that successful industrialization required the adoption of Western culture. As awareness of the economic impact of Japanese culture and society began to spread, it became apparent that Taiwan and South Korea, along with Singapore and Hong Kong (a British colony before being reunited with China in 1997), were developing dynamic industrial economies of their own. Other countries seem likely to follow this model.

This does not mean that the world's culture diversity is secure. Every decade a number of languages cease to be spoken, usually as the result of the spread of national languages. Many religious practices are also disappearing in the face of the successful expansion of Islam, Christianity, and other religions, although secular values also play a role. Televised national ceremonies or performances for tourists may prevent folk customs and costumes from dying out, but they also tend to standardize rituals that once had many local variations. Whereas it was possible to recognize the nationality of people from their clothing and grooming a century ago, today most urban men dress the same the world over, although women's clothing shows much greater variety.

CONCLUSION

Have we entered a golden age, or is the world descending into a fiery abyss? The future is unknowable, but the study of history suggests that neither extreme is likely. Golden ages and dark ages are rare, and our understanding of our own time is easily swayed by hopes, fears, and other emotions. If the exuberant optimism of the 1990s now seems excessive, the pessimism of the early 2000s may in time seem equally far off the mark.

What is undeniable is that the turn of the millennium has been a time of important global changes. The iron curtain that had divided Europe since the end of the Second World War fell, taking with it the tensions and risks of the Cold War. The great Soviet Empire broke up, while dozens of countries joined new economic coalitions. The bastions of communism embraced capitalism with

varying degrees of enthusiasm. As trading barriers tumbled, world trade surged, creating new wealth and new inequalities in its distribution.

Aided by new electronic marvels, individuals communicate around the planet and interact across cultural barriers in ways never before imagined. News of disasters and human rights violations bring more rapid responses than ever before. Culturally, the English language, higher education, and science form a viable global culture for the elite.

History teaches that change is always uneven. The rate of change in global telecommunications and international economic institutions is notably faster than in international political institutions. The nation-state remains supreme. The structure of the United Nations has changed little since its founding six decades earlier. States resist limits on their autonomy, and the more powerful ones take unilateral actions, whether supported or opposed by international public opinion. Never before has one state, the United States, stood so far above the rest.

Rather than giving ground to globalization, many older ideas and values continue to be strong. The less powerful adapt slowly, dig in their heals to resist change, or raise voices and fists against it. Protests have forced new attention on global poverty, disease, exploitation, and environmental damage that globalization causes or fails to relieve. Adjustments have been made, but on the whole change on these fronts has come slowly.

In many places religious fundamentalism, ethnic nationalism, and social conservatism have seemed to reach new levels of intensity. In some quarters globalization has fomented and fostered violent responses, contributing to some degree to the "war on terrorism" led by the United States. The resulting clashes have raised concerns and inspired apocalyptic visions. Adjusting to the new age of globalization will be neither quick nor easy.

■ Key Terms

ethnic cleansing

weapons of mass destruction

terrorism

Usama bin Laden

World Trade Organization (WTO)

globalization
Universal Declaration of Human Rights
nongovernmental organizations (NGOs)
cultural imperialism
global pop culture
global elite culture

■ Suggested Reading

Among those attempting to describe the world at the turn of the millennium are Benjamin R. Barber, *Jihad vs. McWorld: How Globalism and Tribalism are Reshaping the World* (1995); Thomas L. Friedman, *The Lexus and the Olive Tree* (1999); Samuel P. Huntington, *The Clash of Civilizations and the Remaking of the World Order* (1996); and Paul Kennedy, *Preparing for the Twenty-First Century* (1993).

Recent studies of American military policies and the widening split with Europe include Dana Priest, *The Mission: Waging War and Keeping Peace with America's Military* (2003); Robert Kaplan, *Of Paradise and Power: America and Europe in the New World Order* (2002); Charles A. Kulpchan, *The End of the American Era: U.S. Foreign Policy and the Geopolitics of the Twenty-First Century* (2002); and Joseph S. Nye, Jr., *The Paradox of American Power: Why the World's Only Superpower Can't Go It Alone* (2002).

Mike Moore, a former director-general of the WTO, provides an insider's view of the global economy in *A World Without Walls: Freedom, Development, Free Trade and Global Governance* (2003). Amy Chua, *World on Fire: How Exporting Free Market Democracy Breeds Ethnic Hatred and Global Instability* (2003), offers a quite different perspective.

Gilles Kepel, *The Revenge of God: The Resurgence of Islam, Christianity and Judaism in the Modern World* (1994), Philip Jenkins, *The Next Christendom: The Coming of Global Christianity* (2002), and Bernard Lewis, *What Went Wrong? The Clash Between Islam and Modernity in the Middle East* (2003), deal with recent religious-political movements. Eugen Weber, *Apocalypses: Prophesies, Cults, and Millennial Beliefs Through the Ages* (1999), provides a deeper historical perspective. The Bosnian crisis is well covered in Susan L. Woodward, *Balkan Tragedy: Chaos and Dissolution After the Cold War* (1995). Other world crises involving international intervention are treated in William J. Durch, ed., *UN Peacekeeping, American Policy, and the Uncivil Wars of the 1990s* (1996). Terrorism is well covered by Bruce Hoffman, *Inside Terrorism* (1998).

Standard reviews of human rights include Thomas Buergenthal et al., *International Human Rights in a Nutshell,* 3d ed. (2002); Carol Devine and Carol Rae Hansen, *Human Rights: The Essential Reference* (1999); and Jack Donnelly, *International Human Rights,* 2d ed. (1998). Ronald Inglehart and Pippa Norris, *Rising Tide: Gender Equality and Cultural Change Around the World* (2003), surveys the condition of women.

The interrelationships between high culture and popular culture during the twentieth century are treated from different perspectives in Arjun Appadurai, *Modernity at Large: Cultural Dimensions of Globalization* (1996); Peter L. Berger and Samuel Huntington, eds., *Many Globalizations: Cultural Diversity in the Contemporary World* (2002); Tyler Cowen, *Creative Destruction: How Globalization Is Changing the World's Cultures* (2002); and Diana Crane, Nobuko Kawashima, and Kenichi Kawasaka, eds., *Global Culture: Media, Arts, Policy, and Globalization* (2002). Two very readable books by James B. Twitchell detail the rise of popular culture in the United States and present various reactions to this phenomenon: *Carnival Culture: The Trashing of Taste in America* (1992) and *Adcult USA: The Triumph of Advertising in American Culture* (1996). Walter LaFeber, *Michael Jordan and the New Global Capitalism* (1999), explores the relationship between a sports star and global marketing.

Some personal accounts of cultural change are Philippe Wamba, *Kinship: A Family's Journey in Africa and America* (1999); William Dalrymple, *The Age of Kali: Indian Travels and Encounters* (1998); V. S. Naipaul, *Beyond Belief: Islamic Excursions among the Converted Peoples* (1997); Fergal Keane, *A Season of Blood: A Rwandan Journey* (1995); Nelson Mandela, *Long Walk to Freedom* (1994); and Mark Mathabane, *African Women: Three Generations* (1994).

On global English see David Crystal, *English as a Global Language* (1997); Alistaire Pennycock, *The Cultural Politics of English as an International Language* (1994); and Robert Phillipson, *Linguistic Imperialism* (1992).

■ Notes

1. "Liberty's Great Advance," *The Economist,* June 28–July 4, 2003, pp. 5–6.
2. "Universal Declaration of Human Rights," in *Twenty-five Human Rights Documents* (New York: Center for the Study of Human Rights, Columbia University, 1994), 6.

Glossary

The glossary for *The Earth and Its Peoples,* 3/e Brief is for the complete text, Chapters 1 through 30.

Abbasid Caliphate   Descendants of the Prophet Muhammad's uncle, al-Abbas, the Abbasids overthrew the **Umayyad Caliphate** and ruled an Islamic empire from their capital in Baghdad (founded 762) from 750 to 1258.   (*p. 187*)

abolitionists   Men and women who agitated for a complete end to slavery. Abolitionist pressure ended the British transatlantic slave trade in 1808 and slavery in British colonies in 1834. In the United States the activities of abolitionists were one factor leading to the Civil War (1861–1865).   (*p. 475*)

Acheh Sultanate   Muslim kingdom in northern Sumatra. Main center of Islamic expansion in Southeast Asia in the early seventeenth century, it declined after the Dutch seized **Malacca** from Portugal in 1641.   (*p. 427*)

Aden   Port city in the modern south Arabian country of Yemen. It has been a major trading center in the Indian Ocean since ancient times.   (*p. 309*)

African National Congress   An organization dedicated to obtaining equal voting and civil rights for black inhabitants of South Africa. Founded in 1912 as the South African Native National Congress, it changed its name in 1923. Though it was banned and its leaders were jailed for many years, it eventually helped bring majority rule to South Africa.   (*p. 646*)

Afrikaners   South Africans descended from Dutch and French settlers of the seventeenth century. Their Great Trek founded new settler colonies in the nineteenth century. Though a minority among South Africans, they held political power after 1910, imposing a system of racial segregation called apartheid after 1949.   (*p. 580*)

Agricultural Revolution(s) (ancient)   The change from food gathering to food production that occurred between ca. 8000 and 2000 B.C.E. Also known as the Neolithic Revolution.   (*p. 8*)

agricultural revolution (eighteenth century)   The transformation of farming that resulted in the eighteenth century from the spread of new crops, improvements in cultivation techniques and livestock breeding, and the consolidation of small holdings into large farms from which tenants and sharecroppers were forcibly expelled.   (*p. 481*)

Aguinaldo, Emilio (1869–1964)   Leader of the Filipino independence movement against Spain (1895–1898). He proclaimed the independence of the Philippines in 1899, but his movement was crushed and he was captured by the United States Army in 1901.   (*p. 589*)

Akbar (1542–1605)   Most illustrious sultan of the Mughal Empire in India (r. 1556–1605). He expanded the empire and pursued a policy of conciliation with Hindus.   (*p. 425*)

Akhenaten   Egyptian pharaoh (r. 1353–1335 B.C.E.). He built a new capital at Amarna, fostered a new style of naturalistic art, and created a religious revolution by imposing worship of the sun-disk. The Amarna letters, largely from his reign, preserve official correspondence with subjects and neighbors.   (*p. 66*)

Alexander (356–323 B.C.E.)   King of Macedonia in northern Greece. Between 334 and 323 B.C.E. he conquered the Persian Empire, reached the Indus Valley, founded many Greek-style cities, and spread Greek culture across the Middle East. Later known as Alexander the Great.   (*p. 113*)

Alexandria   City on the Mediterranean coast of Egypt founded by Alexander. It became the capital of the Hellenistic kingdom of the **Ptolemies.** It contained the famous Library and the Museum—a center for leading scientific and literary figures. Its merchants engaged in trade with areas bordering the Mediterranean and the Indian Ocean.   (*p. 114*)

Allende, Salvador (1908–1973)   Socialist politician elected president of Chile in 1970 and overthrown by the military in 1973. He died during the military attack.   (*p. 692*)

All-India Muslim League   Political organization founded in India in 1906 to defend the interests of India's Muslim minority. Led by Muhammad Ali Jinnah, it attempted to negotiate with the **Indian National Congress.** In 1940, the League began demanding a separate state for Muslims, to be called Pakistan. (See also **Jinnah, Muhammad Ali.**)   (*p. 647*)

amulet   Small charm meant to protect the bearer from evil. Found frequently in archaeological excavations in Mesopotamia and Egypt, amulets reflect the religious practices of the common people.   (*p. 19*)

Amur River   This river valley was a contested frontier between northern China and eastern Russia until the settlement arranged in Treaty of Nerchinsk (1689).   (*p. 442*)

Anasazi   Important culture of what is now the Southwest United States (700–1200 C.E.). Centered on Chaco Canyon in New Mexico and Mesa Verde in Colorado, the Anasazi culture built multistory residences and worshiped in subterranean buildings called kivas.   (*p. 254*)

aqueduct A conduit, either elevated or underground, using gravity to carry water from a source to a location—usually a city—that needed it. The Romans built many aqueducts in a period of substantial urbanization. (*p. 139*)

Arawak Amerindian peoples who inhabited the Greater Antilles of the Caribbean at the time of Columbus. (*p. 342*)

Armenia One of the earliest Christian kingdoms, situated in eastern Anatolia and the western Caucasus and occupied by speakers of the Armenian language. (*p. 172*)

Asante African kingdom on the **Gold Coast** that expanded rapidly after 1680. Asante participated in the Atlantic economy, trading gold, slaves, and ivory. It resisted British imperial ambitions for a quarter century before being absorbed into Britain's Gold Coast colony in 1902. (*p. 581*)

Ashikaga Shogunate (1338–1573) The second of Japan's military governments headed by a shogun (a military ruler). Sometimes called the Muromachi Shogunate. (*p. 293*)

Ashoka Third ruler of the **Mauryan Empire** in India (r. 270–232 B.C.E.). He converted to Buddhism and broadcast his precepts on inscribed stones and pillars, the earliest surviving Indian writing. (*p. 124*)

Ashurbanipal The sixth century B.C.E. Assyrian ruler who assembled a large collection of writings drawn from the ancient literary, religious, and scientific traditions of Mesopotamia. The many tablets unearthed by archaeologists constitute one of the most important sources of present-day knowledge of the long literary tradition of Mesopotamia. (*p. 75*)

Asian Tigers Collective name for South Korea, Taiwan, Hong Kong, and Singapore—nations that became economic powers in the 1970s and 1980s. (*p. 697*)

Atahualpa (1502?–1533) Last ruling Inca emperor of Peru. He was executed by the Spanish. (*p. 356*)

Atlantic system The network of trading links after 1500 that moved goods, wealth, people, and cultures around the Atlantic Ocean Basin. (*p. 388*)

Augustus (63 B.C.E.–14 C.E.) Honorific name of Octavian, founder of the **Roman Principate,** the military dictatorship that replaced the failing rule of the **Roman Senate.** After defeating all rivals, between 31 B.C.E. and 14 C.E. he laid the groundwork for several centuries of stability and prosperity in the Roman Empire. (*p. 136*)

Auschwitz Nazi extermination camp in Poland, the largest center of mass murder during the **Holocaust.** Close to a million Jews, Gypsies, Communists, and others were killed there. (*p. 638*)

ayllu Andean lineage group or kin-based community. (*p. 256*)

Aztecs Also known as Mexica, the Aztecs created a powerful empire in central Mexico (1325–1521 C.E.). They forced defeated peoples to provide goods and labor as a tax. (*p. 251*)

Babylon The largest and most important city in Mesopotamia. It achieved particular eminence as the capital of the Amorite king **Hammurabi** in the eighteenth century B.C.E. and the Neo-Babylonian king Nebuchadnezzar in the sixth century B.C.E. (*p. 13*)

balance of power The policy in international relations by which, beginning in the eighteenth century, the major European states acted together to prevent any one of them from becoming too powerful. (*p. 382*)

Balfour Declaration Statement issued by Britain's Foreign Secretary Arthur Balfour in 1917 favoring the establishment of a Jewish national homeland in Palestine. (*p. 604*)

Bannermen Hereditary military servants of the **Qing Empire,** in large part descendants of peoples of various origins who had fought for the founders of the empire. (*p. 534*)

Bantu Collective name of a large group of sub-Saharan African languages and of the peoples speaking these languages. (*p. 169*)

Batavia Fort established ca. 1619 as headquarters of Dutch East India Company operations in Indonesia; today the city of Jakarta. (*p. 430*)

Battle of Midway U.S. naval victory over the Japanese fleet in June 1942, in which the Japanese lost four of their best aircraft carriers. It marked a turning point in World War II. (*p. 634*)

Battle of Omdurman British victory over the Mahdi in the Sudan in 1898. General Kitchener led a mixed force of British and Egyptian troops armed with rapid-firing rifles and machine guns. (*p. 575*)

Beijing China's northern capital, first used as an imperial capital in 906 and now the capital of the People's Republic of China. (*p. 282*)

Bengal Region of northeastern India. It was the first part of India to be conquered by the British in the eighteenth century and remained the political and economic center of British India throughout the nineteenth century. The 1905 split of the province into predominantly Hindu West Bengal and predominantly Muslim East Bengal (now Bangladesh) sparked anti-British riots. (*p. 647*)

Berlin Conference (1884–1885) Conference that German chancellor Otto von Bismarck called to set rules for the partition of Africa. It led to the creation of the Congo Free State under King **Leopold II** of Belgium. (See also **Bismarck, Otto von.**) (*p. 579*)

Bhagavad-Gita The most important work of Indian sacred literature, a dialogue between the great warrior Arjuna and the god Krishna on duty and the fate of the spirit. (*p. 125*)

bin Laden, Usama Saudi-born Muslim extremist who funded the al Qaeda organization that was responsible for several terrorist attacks, including those on the World Trade Center and the Pentagon in 2001. (*p. 717*)

Bismarck, Otto von (1815–1898) Chancellor (prime minister) of Prussia from 1862 until 1871, when he became chancellor of Germany. A conservative nationalist, he led Prussia to victory against Austria (1866) and France (1870) and was responsible for the creation of the German Empire in 1871. (*p. 558*)

Black Death An outbreak of **bubonic plague** that spread across Asia, North Africa, and Europe in the mid-fourteenth century, carrying off vast numbers of persons. (*p. 318*)

Bolívar, Simón (1783–1830) The most important military leader in the struggle for independence in South America. Born in Venezuela, he led military forces there and in Colombia, Ecuador, Peru, and Bolivia. (*p. 471*)

Bolsheviks Radical Marxist political party founded by Vladimir Lenin in 1903. Under Lenin's leadership, the Bolsheviks seized power in November 1917 during the Russian Revolution. (See also **Lenin, Vladimir.**) (*p. 604*)

Bonaparte, Napoleon. See **Napoleon I.**

bourgeoisie In early modern Europe, the class of well-off town dwellers whose wealth came from manufacturing, finance, commerce, and allied professions. (*p. 373*)

Brazza, Savorgnan de (1852–1905) Franco-Italian explorer sent by the French government to claim part of equatorial Africa for France. Founded Brazzaville, capital of the French Congo, in 1880. (*p. 579*)

British raj The rule over much of South Asia between 1765 and 1947 by the East India Company and then by a British government. (*p. 506*)

bubonic plague A bacterial disease of fleas that can be transmitted by flea bites to rodents and humans; humans in late stages of the illness can spread the bacteria by coughing. Because of its very high mortality rate and the difficulty of preventing its spread, major outbreaks have created crises in many parts of the world. (See also **Black Death.**) (*pp. 228, 275*)

Buddha (563–483 B.C.E.) An Indian prince named Siddhartha Gautama, who renounced his wealth and social position. After becoming "enlightened" (the meaning of *Buddha*) he enunciated the principles of Buddhism. This doctrine evolved and spread throughout India and to Southeast, East, and Central Asia. (See also **Mahayana Buddhism, Theravada Buddhism.**) (*p. 120*)

Byzantine Empire Historians' name for the eastern portion of the Roman Empire from the fourth century onward, taken from "Byzantion," an early name for Constantinople, the Byzantine capital city. The empire fell to the Ottomans in 1453. (See also **Ottoman Empire.**) (*p. 203*)

caliphate Office established in succession to the Prophet Muhammad, to rule the Islamic empire; also the name of that empire. (See also **Abbasid Caliphate; Sokoto Caliphate; Umayyad Caliphate.**) (*p. 185*)

capitalism The economic system of large financial institutions—banks, stock exchanges, investment companies—that first developed in early modern Europe. *Commercial capitalism,* the trading system of the early modern economy, is often distinguished from *industrial capitalism,* the system based on machine production. (*p. 403*)

caravel A small, highly maneuverable three-masted ship used by the Portuguese and Spanish in the exploration of the Atlantic. (*p. 343*)

Cárdenas, Lázaro (1895–1970) President of Mexico (1934–1940). He brought major changes to Mexican life by distributing millions of acres of land to the peasants, bringing representatives of workers and farmers into the inner circles of politics, and nationalizing the oil industry. (*p. 655*)

Carthage City located in present-day Tunisia, founded by **Phoenicians** ca. 800 B.C.E. It became a major commercial center and naval power in the western Mediterranean until defeated by Rome in the third century B.C.E. (*p. 82*)

Catholic Reformation Religious reform movement within the Latin Christian Church, begun in response to the **Protestant Reformation.** It clarified Catholic theology and reformed clerical training and discipline. (*p. 369*)

Celts Peoples sharing a common language and culture that originated in central Europe in the first half of the first millennium B.C.E.. After 500 B.C.E. they spread as far as Anatolia in the east, Spain and the British Isles in the west, and later were overtaken by Roman conquest and Germanic invasions. Their descendants survive on the western fringe of Europe (Brittany, Wales, Scotland, Ireland). (*p. 50*)

Champa rice Quick-maturing rice that can allow two harvests in one growing season. Originally introduced into Champa from India, it was later sent to China as a tribute gift by the Champa state. (See also **tributary system.**) (*p. 242*)

Chang'an City in the Wei Valley in eastern China. It became the capital of the Qin and early Han Empires. Its main features were imitated in the cities and towns that sprang up throughout the Han Empire. (*p. 147*)

Charlemagne (742–814) King of the Franks (r. 768–814); emperor (r. 800–814). Through a series of military conquests he established the Carolingian Empire, which encompassed all of Gaul and parts of Germany and Italy. Though illiterate himself, he sponsored a brief intellectual revival. (*p. 202*)

chartered companies Groups of private investors who paid an annual fee to France and England in exchange for a monopoly over trade to the West Indies colonies.   (*p. 403*)

Chavín   The first major urban civilization in South America (900–250 B.C.E.). Its capital, Chavín de Huántar, was located high in the Andes Mountains of Peru. Chavín became politically and economically dominant in a densely populated region that included two distinct ecological zones, the Peruvian coastal plain and the Andean foothills.   (*p. 56*)

Chiang Kai-shek   (1886–1975) Chinese military and political leader. Succeeded Sun Yat-sen as head of the **Guomindang** in 1925; headed the Chinese government from 1928 to 1948; fought against the Chinese Communists and Japanese invaders. After 1949 he headed the Chinese Nationalist government in Taiwan.   (*p. 629*)

chiefdom   Form of political organization with rule by a hereditary leader who held power over a collection of villages and towns. Less powerful than kingdoms and empires, chiefdoms were based on gift giving and commercial links.   (*p. 255*)

Chimú   Powerful Peruvian civilization based on conquest. Located in the region earlier dominated by **Moche.** Conquered by **Inca** in 1465.   (*p. 258*)

chinampas   Raised fields constructed along lake shores in Mesoamerica to increase agricultural yields.   (*p. 246*)

city-state   A small independent state consisting of an urban center and the surrounding agricultural territory. A characteristic political form in early Mesopotamia, Archaic and Classical Greece, Phoenicia, and early Italy. (See also **polis.**)   (*p. 15*)

civilization   An ambiguous term often used to denote more complex societies but sometimes used by anthropologists to describe any group of people sharing a set of cultural traits.   (*p. 5*)

Cixi, Empress Dowager (1835–1908)   Empress of China and mother of Emperor Guangxi. She put her son under house arrest, supported antiforeign movements, and resisted reforms of the Chinese government and armed forces.   (*p. 608*)

clipper ship   Large, fast, streamlined sailing vessel, often American built, of the mid-to-late nineteenth century rigged with vast canvas sails hung from tall masts.   (*p. 512*)

Cold War (1945–1991)   The ideological struggle between communism (Soviet Union) and capitalism (United States) for world influence. The Soviet Union and the United States came to the brink of actual war during the **Cuban missile crisis** but never attacked one another. The Cold War came to an end when the Soviet Union dissolved in 1991. (See also **North Atlantic Treaty Organization; Warsaw Pact.**)   (*p. 668*)

colonialism   Policy by which a nation administers a foreign territory and develops its resources for the benefit of the colonial power.   (*p. 575*)

Columbian Exchange   The exchange of plants, animals, diseases, and technologies between the Americas and the rest of the world following Columbus's voyages.   (*p. 407*)

Columbus, Christopher (1451–1506)   Genoese mariner who in the service of Spain led expeditions across the Atlantic, reestablishing contact between the peoples of the Americas and the Old World and opening the way to Spanish conquest and colonization.   (*p. 345*)

Confucius   Western name for the Chinese philosopher Kongzi (551–479 B.C.E.). His doctrine of duty and public service had a great influence on subsequent Chinese thought and served as a code of conduct for government officials.   (*p. 44*)

Congress of Vienna (1814–1815)   Meeting of representatives of European monarchs called to reestablish the old order after the defeat of **Napoleon I.**   (*p. 469*)

conquistadors   Early-sixteenth-century Spanish adventurers who conquered Mexico, Central America, and Peru. (See **Cortés, Hernán; Pizarro, Francisco.**)   (*p. 354*)

Constantine (285–337 C.E.)   Roman emperor (r. 312–337). After reuniting the Roman Empire, he moved the capital to Constantinople and made Christianity a favored religion.   (*p. 141*)

Constitutional Convention   Meeting in 1787 of the elected representatives of the thirteen original states to write the Constitution of the United States.   (*p. 465*)

contract of indenture   A voluntary agreement binding a person to work for a specified period of years in return for free passage to an overseas destination. Before 1800 most **indentured servants** were Europeans; after 1800 most indentured laborers were Asians.   (*p. 515*)

Cortés, Hernán (1485–1547)   Spanish explorer and conquistador who led the conquest of Aztec Mexico in 1519–1521 for Spain.   (*p. 354*)

Cossacks   Peoples of the Russian Empire who lived outside the farming villages, often as herders, mercenaries, or outlaws. Cossacks led the conquest of Siberia in the sixteenth and seventeenth centuries.   (*p. 442*)

Council of the Indies   The institution responsible for supervising Spain's colonies in the Americas from 1524 to the early eighteenth century, when it lost all but judicial responsibilities.   (*p. 388*)

creole   In colonial Spanish America, term used to describe someone of European descent born in the New World. Elsewhere in the Americas, the term is used to describe all nonnative peoples.   (*p. 392*)

Crimean War (1853–1856)   Conflict between the Russian and Ottoman Empires fought primarily in the Crimean Peninsula. To prevent Russian expansion, Britain and France sent troops to support the Ottomans.   (*p. 527*)

Crusades (1096–1291) Armed pilgrimages to the Holy Land by Christians determined to recover Jerusalem from Muslim rule. The Crusades brought an end to western Europe's centuries of intellectual and cultural isolation. (*p. 220*)

Crystal Palace Building erected in Hyde Park, London, for the Great Exhibition of 1851. Made of iron and glass, like a gigantic greenhouse, it was a symbol of the industrial age. (*p. 487*)

Cuban missile crisis (1962) Brink-of-war confrontation between the United States and the Soviet Union over the latter's placement of nuclear-armed missiles in Cuba. (*p. 674*)

cultural imperialism Domination of one culture over another by a deliberate policy or by economic or technological superiority. (*p. 727*)

Cultural Revolution (China) (1966–1969) Campaign in China ordered by **Mao Zedong** to purge the Communist Party of his opponents and instill revolutionary values in the younger generation. (*p. 684*)

culture Socially transmitted patterns of action and expression. *Material culture* refers to physical objects, such as dwellings, clothing, tools, and crafts. Culture also includes arts, beliefs, knowledge, and technology. (*p. 5*)

cuneiform A system of writing in which wedge-shaped symbols represented words or syllables. It originated in Mesopotamia and was used initially for Sumerian and Akkadian but later was adapted to represent other languages of western Asia. Because so many symbols had to be learned, literacy was confined to a relatively small group of administrators and **scribes.** (*p. 19*)

Cyrus (600–530 B.C.E.) Founder of the Achaemenid Persian Empire. Between 550 and 530 B.C.E. he conquered Media, Lydia, and Babylon. Revered in the traditions of both Iran and the subject peoples, he employed Persians and Medes in his administration and respected the institutions and beliefs of subject peoples. (*p. 96*)

czar See **tsar.**

daimyo Literally, great name(s). Japanese warlords and great landowners, whose armed **samurai** gave them control of the Japanese islands from the eighth to the later nineteenth century. Under the **Tokugawa Shogunate** they were subordinated to the imperial government. (*p. 433*)

Daoism Chinese school of thought, originating in the Warring States Period with Laozi (604–531 B.C.E.). Daoism offered an alternative to the Confucian emphasis on hierarchy and duty. Daoists believe that the world is always changing and is devoid of absolute morality or meaning. They accept the world as they find it, avoid futile struggles, and deviate as little as possible from the *Dao*, or "path" of nature. (See also **Confucius.**) (*p. 44*)

Darius I (ca. 558–486 B.C.E.) Third ruler of the Persian Empire (r. 521–486 B.C.E.). He crushed the widespread initial resistance to his rule and gave all major government posts to Persians rather than to Medes. He established a system of provinces and tribute, began construction of Persepolis, and expanded Persian control in the east (Pakistan) and west (northern Greece). (*p. 96*)

Darwin, Charles (1809–1882) With Alfred Russell Wallace (1823–1913) he developed the theory of evolution through natural selection. Their work was first made known simultaneously in 1858. (*p. 558*)

Decembrist revolt Abortive attempt by army officers to take control of the Russian government upon the death of Tsar Alexander I in 1825. (*p. 532*)

Declaration of the Rights of Man (1789) Statement of fundamental political rights adopted by the French **National Assembly** at the beginning of the French Revolution. (*p. 466*)

deforestation The removal of trees faster than forests can replace themselves. (*p. 375*)

Delhi Sultanate (1206–1526) Centralized Indian empire of varying extent, created by Muslim invaders. (*p. 299*)

democracy A system of government in which all "citizens" (however defined) have equal political and legal rights, privileges, and protections, as in the Greek city-state of Athens in the fifth and fourth centuries B.C.E. (*p. 106*)

demographic transition A change in the rates of population growth. Before the transition, both birthrates and death rates are high, resulting in a slowly growing population; then the death rate drops but the birthrate remains high, causing a population explosion; finally the birthrate drops and the population growth slows down. This transition took place in Europe in the late nineteenth and early twentieth centuries, in North America and East Asia in the mid-twentieth, and, most recently, in Latin America and South Asia. (*p. 703*)

Deng Xiaoping (1904–1997) Communist Party leader who forced Chinese economic reforms after the death of **Mao Zedong.** (*p. 698*)

dhow Ship of small to moderate size used in the western Indian Ocean, traditionally with a triangular sail and a sewn timber hull. (*p. 307*)

Diagne, Blaise (1872–1934) Senegalese political leader. He was the first African elected to the French National Assembly. During World War I, in exchange for promises to give French citizenship to Senegalese, he helped recruit Africans to serve in the French army. After the war, he led a movement to abolish forced labor in Africa. (*p. 646*)

Dias, Bartolomeu (1450?–1500) Portuguese explorer who in 1488 led the first expedition to sail around the southern tip of Africa from the Atlantic and sight the Indian Ocean. (*p. 345*)

Diaspora   A Greek word meaning "dispersal," used to describe the communities of a given ethnic group living outside their homeland. Jews, for example, spread from Israel to western Asia and Mediterranean lands in antiquity and today can be found throughout the world.   (*p. 79*)

Dirty War   War waged by the Argentine military (1976–1983) against leftist groups. Characterized by the use of illegal imprisonment, torture, and executions by the military.   (*p. 692*)

divination   Techniques for ascertaining the future or the will of the gods by interpreting natural phenomena such as, in early China, the cracks on oracle bones or, in ancient Greece, the flight of birds through sectors of the sky.   (*p. 42*)

division of labor   A manufacturing technique that breaks down a craft into many simple and repetitive tasks that can be performed by unskilled workers. Pioneered in the pottery works of Josiah Wedgwood and in other eighteenth-century factories, it greatly increased the productivity of labor and lowered the cost of manufactured goods. (See also **Wedgwood, Josiah.**)   (*p. 485*)

driver   A privileged male slave whose job was to ensure that a slave gang did its work on a plantation.   (*p. 402*)

Druids   The class of religious experts who conducted rituals and preserved sacred lore among some ancient Celtic peoples. They provided education, mediated disputes between kinship groups, and were suppressed by the Romans as a potential focus of opposition to Roman rule. (See also **Celts.**)   (*p. 51*)

Dutch West India Company (1621–1794)   Trading company chartered by the Dutch government to conduct its merchants' trade in the Americas and Africa.   (*p. 403*)

Edison, Thomas (1847–1931)   American inventor best known for inventing the electric light bulb, acoustic recording on wax cylinders, and motion pictures.   (*p. 549*)

Einstein, Albert (1879–1955)   German physicist who developed the theory of relativity, which states that time, space, and mass are relative to each other and not fixed.   (*p. 614*)

electricity   A form of energy used in telegraphy from the 1840s on and for lighting, industrial motors, and railroads beginning in the 1880s.   (*p. 549*)

electric telegraph   A device for rapid, long-distance transmission of information over an electric wire. It was introduced in England and North America in the 1830s and 1840s and replaced telegraph systems that utilized visual signals such as semaphores. (See also **submarine telegraph cables.**)   (*p. 489*)

encomienda   A grant of authority over a population of Amerindians in the Spanish colonies. It provided the grant holder with a supply of cheap labor and periodic payments of goods by the Amerindians. It obliged the grant holder to Christianize the Amerindians.   (*p. 392*)

English Civil War (1642–1648)   A conflict over royal versus parliamentary rights, caused by King Charles I's arrest of his parliamentary critics and ending with his execution. Its outcome checked the growth of royal absolutism and, with the Glorious Revolution of 1688 and the English Bill of Rights of 1689, ensured that England would be a constitutional monarchy.   (*p. 381*)

Enlightenment   A philosophical movement in eighteenth-century Europe that fostered the belief that one could reform society by discovering rational laws that governed social behavior and were just as scientific as the laws of physics.   (*pp. 372, 461*)

equites   In ancient Italy, prosperous landowners second in wealth and status to the senatorial aristocracy. The Roman emperors allied with this group to counterbalance the influence of the old aristocracy and used the *equites* to staff the imperial civil service.   (*p. 136*)

Estates General   France's traditional national assembly with representatives of the three estates, or classes, in French society: the clergy, nobility, and commoners. The calling of the Estates General in 1789 led to the French Revolution.   (*p. 466*)

Ethiopia   East African highland nation lying east of the Nile River. (See also **Menelik II; Selassie, Haile.**)   (*p. 172*)

ethnic cleansing   Effort to eradicate a people and its culture by means of mass killing and the destruction of historical buildings and cultural materials. Ethnic cleansing was used by both sides in the conflicts that accompanied the disintegration of Yugoslavia in the 1990s.   (*p. 716*)

European Community (EC)   An organization promoting economic unity in Europe formed in 1967 by consolidation of earlier, more limited, agreements. Replaced by the European Union (EU) in 1993.   (*p. 670*)

extraterritoriality   The right of foreign residents in a country to live under the laws of their native country and disregard the laws of the host country. In the nineteenth and early twentieth centuries, European and American nationals living in certain areas of Chinese and Ottoman cities were granted this right.   (*p. 529*)

Faisal I (1885–1933)   Arab prince, leader of the Arab Revolt in World War I. The British made him king of Iraq in 1921, and he reigned under British protection until 1933.   (*p. 603*)

Fascist Party   Italian political party created by Benito Mussolini during World War I. It emphasized aggressive nationalism and was Mussolini's instrument for the creation of a dictatorship in Italy from 1922 to 1943. (See also **Mussolini, Benito.**)   (*p. 626*)

fief In medieval Europe, land granted in return for a sworn oath to provide specified military service. (*p. 210*)

First Temple A monumental sanctuary built in Jerusalem by King Solomon in the tenth century B.C.E. to be the religious center for the Israelite god Yahweh. The Temple priesthood conducted sacrifices, received a tithe or percentage of agricultural revenues, and became economically and politically powerful. The First Temple was destroyed by the Babylonians in 587 B.C.E., rebuilt on a modest scale in the late sixth century B.C.E., and replaced by King Herod's Second Temple in the late first century B.C.E. (destroyed by the Romans in 70 C.E.) (*p. 78*)

Five-Year Plans Plans that Joseph Stalin introduced to industrialize the Soviet Union rapidly, beginning in 1928. They set goals for the output of steel, electricity, machinery, and most other products and were enforced by the police powers of the state. They succeeded in making the Soviet Union a major industrial power before World War II. (See also **Stalin, Joseph.**) (*p. 620*)

foragers People who support themselves by hunting wild animals and gathering wild edible plants and insects. (*p. 6*)

free-trade imperialism Economic dominance of a weaker country by a more powerful one, while maintaining the legal independence of the weaker state. In the late nineteenth century, free-trade imperialism characterized the relations between the Latin American republics, on the one hand, and Great Britain and the United States, on the other. (*p. 590*)

Gama, Vasco da (1460?–1524) Portuguese explorer. In 1497–1498 he led the first naval expedition from Europe to sail to India, opening an important commercial sea route. (*p. 345*)

Gandhi, Mohandas K. (Mahatma) (1869–1948) Leader of the Indian independence movement and advocate of nonviolent resistance. After being educated as a lawyer in England, he returned to India and became leader of the **Indian National Congress** in 1920. He appealed to the poor, led nonviolent demonstrations against British colonial rule, and was jailed many times. Soon after independence he was assassinated for attempting to stop Hindu-Muslim rioting. (*p. 648*)

Genghis Khan (ca. 1167–1227) The title of Temüjin when he ruled the Mongols (1206–1227). It means the "oceanic" or "universal" leader. Genghis Khan was the founder of the Mongol Empire. (*p. 270*)

gens de couleur Free men and women of color in Haiti. They sought greater political rights and later supported the Haitian Revolution. (See also **L'Ouverture, Toussaint.**) (*p. 469*)

gentry In China, the class of prosperous families, next in wealth below the rural aristocrats, from which the emperors drew their administrative personnel. Respected for their education and expertise, these officials became a privileged group and made the government more efficient and responsive than in the past. The term *gentry* also denotes the class of landholding families in England and France below the aristocracy. (*pp. 148, 374*)

Ghana First known kingdom in sub-Saharan West Africa between the sixth and thirteenth centuries C.E. Also the modern West African country once known as the Gold Coast. (*p. 189*)

global elite culture At the beginning of the twenty-first century, the attitudes and outlook of well-educated, prosperous, Western-oriented people around the world, largely expressed in European languages, especially English. (*p. 730*)

global pop culture Popular cultural practices and institutions that have been adopted internationally, such as music, the Internet, television, food, and fashion. (*p. 729*)

globalization The economic, political, and cultural integration and interaction of all parts of the world brought about by increasing trade, travel, and technology. (*p. 722*)

Gold Coast (Africa) Region of the Atlantic coast of West Africa occupied by modern Ghana; named for its gold exports to Europe from the 1470s onward. (*p. 345*)

Golden Horde Mongol khanate founded by Genghis Khan's grandson Batu. It was based in southern Russia and quickly adopted both the Turkic language and Islam. Also known as the Kipchak Horde. (*p. 276*)

Gorbachev, Mikhail (b. 1931) Head of the Soviet Union from 1985 to 1991. His liberalization effort improved relations with the West, but he lost power after his reforms led to the collapse of communist governments in eastern Europe. (*p. 700*)

Gothic cathedrals Large churches originating in twelfth-century France; built in an architectural style featuring pointed arches, tall vaults and spires, flying buttresses, and large stained-glass windows. (*p. 325*)

Grand Canal The 1,100-mile (1,700-kilometer) waterway linking the Yellow and the Yangzi Rivers. It was begun in the **Han** period and completed during the Sui Empire. (*p. 225*)

Great Circuit The network of Atlantic Ocean trade routes between Europe, Africa, and the Americas that underlay the Atlantic system (*p. 404*)

"great traditions" Historians' term for a literate, well-institutionalized complex of religious and social beliefs and practices adhered to by diverse societies over a broad geographical area. (See also **"small traditions."**) (*p. 168*)

Great Western Schism A division in the Latin (Western) Christian Church between 1378 and 1415, when rival claimants to the papacy existed in Rome and Avignon. (*p. 333*)

Great Zimbabwe City, now in ruins (in the modern African country of Zimbabwe), whose many stone structures were built between about 1250 and 1450, when it was a trading center and the capital of a large state. (*p. 307*)

guild In medieval Europe, an association of men (rarely women), such as merchants, artisans, or professors, who worked in a particular trade and banded together to promote their economic and political interests. Guilds were also important in other societies, such as the Ottoman and Safavid Empires. (*p. 324*)

Gujarat Region of western India famous for trade and manufacturing; the inhabitants are called Gujarati. (*p. 305*)

gunpowder A mixture of saltpeter, sulfur, and charcoal, in various proportions. The formula, brought to China in the 400s or 500s, was first used to make fumigators to keep away insect pests and evil spirits. In later centuries it was used to make explosives and grenades and to propel cannonballs, shot, and bullets. (*p. 235*)

Guomindang Nationalist political party founded on democratic principles by **Sun Yat-sen** in 1912. After 1925, the party was headed by **Chiang Kai-shek,** who turned it into an increasingly authoritarian movement. (*p. 609*)

Gupta Empire (320–550 C.E.) A powerful Indian state based, like its Mauryan predecessor, on a capital at Pataliputra in the Ganges Valley. It controlled most of the Indian subcontinent through a combination of military force and its prestige as a center of sophisticated culture. (See also **theater-state.**) (*p. 125*)

Habsburg A powerful European family that provided many Holy Roman Emperors, founded the Austrian (later Austro-Hungarian) Empire, and ruled sixteenth- and seventeenth-century Spain. (*p. 379*)

hadith A tradition relating the words or deeds of the Prophet Muhammad; next to the **Quran,** the most important basis for Islamic law. (*p. 194*)

Hammurabi Amorite ruler of **Babylon** (r. 1792–1750 B.C.E.). He conquered many city-states in southern and northern Mesopotamia and is best known for a code of laws, inscribed on a black stone pillar, illustrating the principles to be used in legal cases. (*p. 16*)

Han A term used to designate (1) the ethnic Chinese people who originated in the Yellow River Valley and spread throughout regions of China suitable for agriculture and (2) the dynasty of emperors who ruled from 206 B.C.E. to 220 C.E. (*p. 146*)

Hanseatic League An economic and defensive alliance of the free towns in northern Germany, founded about 1241 and most powerful in the fourteenth century. (*p. 322*)

Harappa Site of one of the great cities of the Indus Valley civilization of the third millennium B.C.E. It was located on the northwest frontier of the zone of cultivation (in modern Pakistan), and may have been a center for the acquisition of raw materials, such as metals and precious stones, from Afghanistan and Iran. (*p. 31*)

Hatshepsut Queen of Egypt (r. 1473–1458 B.C.E.). She dispatched a naval expedition down the Red Sea to Punt (possibly northeast Sudan or Eretria), the faraway source of myrrh. There is evidence of opposition to a woman as ruler, and after her death her name and image were frequently defaced. (*p. 66*)

Hebrew Bible A collection of sacred books containing diverse materials concerning the origins, experiences, beliefs, and practices of the Israelites. Most of the extant text was compiled by members of the priestly class in the fifth century B.C.E. and reflects the concerns and views of this group. (*p. 76*)

Hellenistic Age Historians' term for the era, usually dated 323–30 B.C.E., in which Greek culture spread across western Asia and northeastern Africa after the conquests of **Alexander** the Great. The period ended with the fall of the last major Hellenistic kingdom to Rome, but Greek cultural influence persisted until the spread of Islam in the seventh century C.E. (*p. 114*)

Helsinki Accords (1975) Political and human rights agreement signed in Helsinki, Finland, by the Soviet Union and western European countries. (*p. 674*)

Henry the Navigator (1394–1460) Portuguese prince who promoted the study of navigation and directed voyages of exploration down the western coast of Africa. (*p. 343*)

Herodotus (ca. 485–425 B.C.E.) Heir to the technique of *historia*—"investigation"—developed by Greeks in the late Archaic period. He came from a Greek community in Anatolia and traveled extensively, collecting information in western Asia and the Mediterranean lands. He traced the antecedents of and chronicled the **Persian Wars** between the Greek city-states and the Persian Empire, thus originating the Western tradition of historical writing. (*p. 107*)

Hidalgo y Costilla, Miguel (1753–1811) Mexican priest who led the first stage of the Mexican independence war in 1810. He was captured and executed in 1811. (*p. 473*)

Hidden Imam Last in a series of twelve descendants of Muhammad's son-in-law Ali, whom **Shi'ites** consider divinely appointed leaders of the Muslim community. In occlusion since ca. 873, he is expected to return as a messiah at the end of time. (*p. 421*)

hieroglyphics A system of writing in which pictorial symbols represented sounds, syllables, or concepts. It was used for official and monumental inscriptions in ancient Egypt. Because of the long period of study required to master this system, literacy in hieroglyphics was confined to a relatively small group of **scribes** and administrators. Cursive symbol-forms were developed for rapid composition on other media, such as **papyrus.** *(p. 27)*

Hinduism A general term for a wide variety of beliefs and ritual practices that have developed in the Indian subcontinent since antiquity. Hinduism has roots in ancient Vedic, Buddhist, and south Indian religious concepts and practices. It spread along the trade routes to Southeast Asia. *(p. 121)*

Hiroshima City in Japan, the first to be destroyed by an atomic bomb, on August 6, 1945. The bombing hastened the end of World War II. *(p. 634)*

history The study of past events and changes in the development, transmission, and transformation of cultural practices. *(p. 6)*

Hitler, Adolf (1889–1945) Born in Austria, Hitler became a radical German nationalist during World War I. He led the National Socialist German Workers' Party—the **Nazis**—in the 1920s and became dictator of Germany in 1933. He led Europe into World War II. *(p. 627)*

Hittites A people from central Anatolia who established an empire in Anatolia and Syria in the Late Bronze Age. With wealth from the trade in metals and military power based on chariot forces, the Hittites vied with New Kingdom Egypt for control of Syria-Palestine before falling to unidentified attackers ca. 1200 B.C.E. (See also **Ramesses II.**) *(p. 64)*

Holocaust Nazis' program during World War II to kill people they considered undesirable. Some 6 million Jews perished during the Holocaust, along with millions of Poles, Gypsies, Communists, Socialists, and others. *(p. 638)*

Holocene The geological era since the end of the Great Ice Age about 11,000 years ago. *(p. 10)*

Holy Roman Empire Loose federation of mostly German states and principalities, headed by an emperor elected by the princes. It lasted from 962 to 1806. *(pp. 212, 379)*

hoplite A heavily armored Greek infantryman of the Archaic and Classical periods who fought in the close-packed phalanx formation. Hoplite armies—militias composed of middle- and upper-class citizens supplying their own equipment—were for centuries superior to all other military forces. *(p. 105)*

horse collar Harnessing method that increased the efficiency of horses by shifting the point of traction from the animal's neck to the shoulders; its adoption favors the spread of horse-drawn plows and vehicles. *(p. 218)*

House of Burgesses Elected assembly in colonial Virginia, created in 1618. *(p. 397)*

humanists (Renaissance) European scholars, writers, and teachers associated with the study of the humanities (grammar, rhetoric, poetry, history, languages, and moral philosophy), influential in the fifteenth century and later. *(p. 329)*

Hundred Years War (1337–1453) Series of campaigns over control of the throne of France, involving English and French royal families and French noble families. *(p. 333)*

Husayn, Saddam (b. 1937) President of Iraq from 1979 until overthrown by an American-led invasion in 2003. Waged war on Iran from 1980 to 1988. His invasion of Kuwait in 1990 was repulsed in the Persian Gulf War in 1991. *(p. 696)*

Ibn Battuta (1304–1369) Moroccan Muslim scholar, the most widely traveled individual of his time. He wrote a detailed account of his visits to Islamic lands from China to Spain and the western Sudan. *(p. 296)*

Il-khan A "secondary" or "peripheral" khan based in Persia. The Il-khans' khanate was founded by Hülegü, a grandson of **Genghis Khan,** and was based at Tabriz in modern Azerbaijan. It controlled much of Iran and Iraq. *(p. 276)*

import-substitution industrialization An economic system aimed at building a country's industry by restricting foreign trade. It was especially popular in Latin American countries such as Mexico, Argentina, and Brazil in the mid-twentieth century. It proved successful for a time but could not keep up with technological advances in Europe and North America. *(p. 659)*

Inca Largest and most powerful Andean empire. Controlled the Pacific coast of South America from Ecuador to Chile from its capital of Cuzco. *(p. 259)*

indentured servant A migrant to British colonies in the Americas who paid for passage by agreeing to work for a set term ranging from four to seven years. *(p. 397)*

Indian Civil Service The elite professional class of officials who administered the government of British India. Originally composed exclusively of well-educated British men, it gradually added qualified Indians. *(p. 507)*

Indian National Congress A movement and political party founded in 1885 to demand greater Indian participation in government. Its membership was middle class, and its demands were modest until World War I. Led after 1920 by Mohandas K. Gandhi, it appealed increasingly to the poor, and it organized mass protests demanding self-government and independence. (See also **Gandhi, Mohandas K.**) *(pp. 510, 647)*

Indian Ocean Maritime System In premodern times, a network of seaports, trade routes, and maritime culture linking countries on the rim of the Indian Ocean from Africa to Indonesia. *(p. 159)*

indulgence   The forgiveness of the punishment due for past sins, granted by the Catholic Church authorities as a reward for a pious act. Martin Luther's protest against the sale of indulgences is often seen as touching off the **Protestant Reformation.**   *(p. 366)*

Industrial Revolution   The transformation of the economy, the environment, and living conditions, occurring first in England in the eighteenth century, that resulted from the use of steam engines, the mechanization of manufacturing in factories, and innovations in transportation and communication.   *(p. 480)*

investiture controversy   Dispute between the popes and the Holy Roman Emperors over who held ultimate authority over bishops in imperial lands.   *(p. 212)*

Irigoyen, Hipólito (1850–1933)   Argentine politician, president of Argentina from 1916 to 1922 and 1928 to 1930. The first president elected by universal male suffrage, he began his presidency as a reformer, but later became conservative.   *(p. 658)*

Iron Age   Historians' term for the period during which iron was the primary metal for tools and weapons. The advent of iron technology began at different times in different parts of the world.   *(p. 62)*

iron curtain   Winston Churchill's term for the Cold War division between the Soviet-dominated East and the U.S.-dominated West.   *(p. 668)*

Iroquois Confederacy   An alliance of five northeastern Amerindian peoples (six after 1722) that made decisions on military and diplomatic issues through a council of representatives. Allied first with the Dutch and later with the English, the Confederacy dominated the area from western New England to the Great Lakes.   *(p. 398)*

Islam   Religion expounded by the Prophet Muhammad (570–632 C.E.) on the basis of his reception of divine revelations, which were collected after his death into the **Quran.** In the tradition of Judaism and Christianity, and sharing much of their lore, Islam calls on all people to recognize one creator god—Allah—who rewards or punishes believers after death according to how they led their lives. (See also **hadith.**)   *(p. 184)*

Israel   In antiquity, the land between the eastern shore of the Mediterranean and the Jordan River, occupied by the Israelites from the early second millennium B.C.E. The modern state of Israel was founded in 1948.   *(p. 76)*

Janissaries   Infantry, originally of slave origin, armed with firearms and constituting the elite of the Ottoman army from the fifteenth century until the corps was abolished in 1826.   *(pp. 415, 520)*

jati.   See *varna.*

Jesus (ca. 5 B.C.E.–34 C.E.)   A Jew from Galilee in northern Israel who sought to reform Jewish beliefs and practices. He was executed as a revolutionary by the Romans. Hailed as the Messiah and son of God by his followers, he became the central figure in Christianity, a belief system that developed in the centuries after his death.   *(p. 138)*

Jinnah, Muhammad Ali (1876–1948)   Indian Muslim politician who founded the state of Pakistan. A lawyer by training, he joined the **All-India Muslim League** in 1913. As leader of the League from the 1920s on, he negotiated with the British and the **Indian National Congress** for Muslim participation in Indian politics. From 1940 on, he led the movement for the independence of India's Muslims in a separate state of Pakistan, founded in 1947.   *(p. 651)*

joint-stock company   A business, often backed by a government charter, that sold shares to individuals to raise money for its trading enterprises and to spread the risks (and profits) among many investors.   *(p. 374)*

junk   A very large flatbottom sailing ship produced in the **Tang, Ming,** and **Song Empires,** specially designed for long-distance commercial travel.   *(p. 234)*

Kamakura Shogunate   The first of Japan's decentralized military governments. (1185–1333).   *(p. 241)*

kamikaze   The "divine wind," which the Japanese credited with blowing Mongol invaders away from their shores in 1281.   *(p. 292)*

Kangxi (1654–1722)   Qing emperor (r. 1662–1722). He oversaw the greatest expansion of the **Qing Empire.**   *(p. 440)*

karma   In Indian tradition, the residue of deeds performed in past and present lives that adheres to a "spirit" and determines what form it will assume in its next life cycle. The doctrines of karma and reincarnation were used by the elite in ancient India to encourage people to accept their social position and do their duty.   *(p. 119)*

keiretsu   Alliances of corporations and banks that dominate the Japanese economy.   *(p. 697)*

khipu   System of knotted colored cords used by preliterate Andean peoples to transmit information.   *(p. 256)*

Khomeini, Ayatollah Ruhollah (1900?–1989)   Shi'ite philosopher and cleric who led the overthrow of the shah of Iran in 1979 and created an Islamic republic.   *(p. 693)*

Khubilai Khan (1215–1294)   Last of the Mongol Great Khans (r. 1260–1294) and founder of the **Yuan Empire.** Original architect of the Forbidden City.   *(p. 282)*

Kievan Russia   State established at Kiev in Ukraine ca. 879 by Scandinavian adventurers asserting authority over a mostly Slavic farming population.   *(p. 203)*

Korean War (1950–1953)   Conflict that began with North Korea's invasion of South Korea and came to involve the United Nations (primarily the United States) allying with South Korea and the People's Republic of China allying with North Korea.   *(p. 672)*

Koryo Korean kingdom founded in 918 and destroyed by a Mongol invasion in 1259. (*p. 239*)

Kush An Egyptian name for Nubia, the region alongside the Nile River south of Egypt, where an indigenous kingdom with its own distinctive institutions and cultural traditions arose beginning in the early second millennium B.C.E. It was deeply influenced by Egyptian culture and at times under the control of Egypt, which coveted its rich deposits of gold and luxury products from sub-Saharan Africa carried up the Nile corridor. (*p. 49*)

labor union An organization of workers in a particular industry or trade, created to defend the interests of members through strikes or negotiations with employers. (*p. 552*)

laissez faire The idea that government should refrain from interfering in economic affairs. The classic exposition of laissez-faire principles is Adam Smith's *Wealth of Nations* (1776). (*p. 493*)

lama In Tibetan Buddhism, a teacher. (*p. 282*)

Las Casas, Bartolomé de (1474–1566) First bishop of Chiapas, in southern Mexico. He devoted most of his life to protecting Amerindian peoples from exploitation. His major achievement was the New Laws of 1542, which limited the ability of Spanish settlers to compel Amerindians to labor for them. (See also **encomienda**.) (*p. 391*)

Latin West Historians' name for the territories of Europe that adhered to the Latin rite of Christianity and used the Latin language for intellectual exchange in the period ca. 1000–1500. (*p. 317*)

League of Nations International organization founded in 1919 to promote world peace and cooperation but greatly weakened by the refusal of the United States to join. It proved ineffectual in stopping aggression by Italy, Japan, and Germany in the 1930s, and it was superseded by the **United Nations** in 1945. (*p. 606*)

Legalism In China, a political philosophy that emphasized the unruliness of human nature and justified state coercion and control. The **Qin** ruling class invoked it to validate the authoritarian nature of their regime and its profligate expenditure of subjects' lives and labor. It was superseded in the **Han** era by a more benevolent Confucian doctrine of governmental moderation. (*p. 44*)

"legitimate" trade Exports from Africa in the nineteenth century that did not include the newly outlawed slave trade. (*p. 503*)

Lenin, Vladimir (1870–1924) Leader of the Bolshevik (later Communist) Party. He lived in exile in Switzerland until 1917, then returned to Russia to lead the Bolsheviks to victory during the Russian Revolution and the civil war that followed. (*p. 604*)

Leopold II (1835–1909) King of Belgium (r. 1865–1909). He was active in encouraging the exploration of Central Africa and became the ruler of the Congo Free State (to 1908). (*p. 579*)

liberalism A political ideology that emphasizes the civil rights of citizens, representative government, and the protection of private property. This ideology, derived from the **Enlightenment,** was especially popular among the property-owning middle classes of Europe and North America. (*p. 559*)

Linear B A set of syllabic symbols, derived from the writing system of **Minoan** Crete, used in the Mycenaean palaces of the Late Bronze Age to write an early form of Greek. It was used primarily for palace records, and the surviving Linear B tablets provide substantial information about the economic organization of Mycenaean society and tantalizing clues about political, social, and religious institutions. (*p. 70*)

Li Shimin (599–649) One of the founders of the **Tang Empire** and its second emperor (r. 626–649). He led the expansion of the empire into Central Asia. (*p. 225*)

Little Ice Age A century-long period of cool climate that began in the 1590s. Its ill effects on agriculture in northern Europe were notable. (*p. 375*)

llama A hoofed animal indigenous to the Andes Mountains in South America. It was the only domesticated beast of burden in the Americas before the arrival of Europeans. It provided meat and wool. The use of llamas to transport goods made possible specialized production and trade among people living in different ecological zones and fostered the integration of these zones by **Chavín** and later Andean states. (*p. 57*)

loess A fine, light silt deposited by wind and water. It constitutes the fertile soil of the Yellow River Valley in northern China. Because loess soil is not compacted, it can be worked with a simple digging stick, but it leaves the region vulnerable to devastating earthquakes. (*p. 40*)

Long March (1934–1935) The 6,000-mile (9,600-kilometer) flight of Chinese Communists from southeastern to northwestern China. The Communists, led by **Mao Zedong,** were pursued by the Chinese army under orders from **Chiang Kai-shek.** The four thousand survivors of the march formed the nucleus of a revived Communist movement that defeated the **Guomindang** after World War II. (*p. 630*)

L'Ouverture, Toussaint (1743–1803) Leader of the Haitian Revolution. He freed the slaves and gained effective independence for Haiti despite military interventions by the British and French. (*p. 471*)

ma'at Egyptian term for the concept of divinely created and maintained order in the universe. Reflecting the ancient Egyptians' belief in an essentially beneficent world, the divine ruler was the earthly guarantor of this order. (See also **pyramid**.) (*p. 26*)

Macartney mission (1792–1793)   The unsuccessful attempt by the British Empire to establish diplomatic relations with the **Qing Empire.**   (*p. 444*)

Magellan, Ferdinand (1480?–1521)   Portuguese navigator who led the Spanish expedition of 1519–1522 that was the first to sail around the world.   (*p. 348*)

Mahabharata   A vast epic chronicling the events leading up to a cataclysmic battle between related kinship groups in early India. It includes the Bhagavad-Gita, the most important work of Indian sacred literature.   (*p. 125*)

Mahayana Buddhism   "Great Vehicle" branch of Buddhism followed in China, Japan, and Central Asia. The focus is on reverence for **Buddha** and for bodhisattvas, enlightened persons who have postponed nirvana to help others attain enlightenment.   (*p. 121*)

Malacca   Port city in the modern Southeast Asian country of Malaysia, founded about 1400 as a trading center on the Strait of Malacca. Also spelled Melaka.   (*p. 311*)

Mali   Empire created by indigenous Muslims in western Sudan of West Africa from the thirteenth to fifteenth century. It was famous for its role in the trans-Saharan gold trade. (See also **Mansa Kankan Musa** and **Timbuktu.**)   (*p. 300*)

Malthus, Thomas (1766–1834)   Eighteenth-century English intellectual who warned that population growth threatened future generations because, in his view, population growth would always outstrip increases in agricultural production.   (*p. 703*)

mamluks   Under the Islamic system of military slavery, Turkic military slaves who formed an important part of the armed forces of the **Abbasid Caliphate** of the ninth and tenth centuries. Mamluks eventually founded their own state, ruling Egypt and Syria (1250–1517).   (*p. 188*)

Manchu   Federation of Northeast Asian peoples who founded the **Qing Empire.**   (*p. 432*)

Mandate of Heaven   Chinese religious and political ideology developed by the **Zhou,** according to which it was the prerogative of Heaven, the chief deity, to grant power to the ruler of China and to take away that power if the ruler failed to conduct himself justly and in the best interests of his subjects.   (*p. 43*)

mandate system   Allocation of former German colonies and Ottoman possessions to the victorious powers after World War I, to be administered under League of Nations supervision.   (*p. 610*)

manor   In medieval Europe, a large, self-sufficient landholding consisting of the lord's residence (manor house), outbuildings, peasant village, and surrounding land.   (*p. 209*)

mansabs   In India, grants of land given in return for service by rulers of the **Mughal Empire.**   (*p. 425*)

Mansa Kankan Musa   Ruler of Mali (r. 1312–1337). His pilgrimage through Egypt to **Mecca** in 1324–1325 established the empire's reputation for wealth in the Mediterranean world.   (*p. 301*)

Mao Zedong (1893–1976)   Leader of the Chinese Communist Party (1927–1976). He led the Communists on the **Long March** (1934–1935) and rebuilt the Communist Party and Red Army during the Japanese occupation of China (1937–1945). After World War II, he led the Communists to victory over the **Guomindang.** He ordered the **Cultural Revolution** in 1966.   (*p. 629*)

maroon   A slave who ran away from his or her master. Often a member of a community of runaway slaves in the West Indies and South America.   (*p. 402*)

Marshall Plan   U. S. program to support the reconstruction of western Europe after World War II. By 1961 more than $20 billion in economic aid had been dispersed. (*p. 670*)

Marx, Karl (1818–1883)   German journalist and philosopher, founder of the Marxist branch of **socialism.** He is known for two books: *The Communist Manifesto* (1848) and *Das Kapital* (Vols. I–III, 1867–1894).   (*p. 553*)

mass deportation   The forcible removal and relocation of large numbers of people or entire populations. The mass deportations practiced by the Assyrian and Persian Empires were meant as a terrifying warning of the consequences of rebellion. They also brought skilled and unskilled labor to the imperial center.   (*p. 74*)

mass production   The manufacture of many identical products by the division of labor into many small repetitive tasks. This method was introduced into the manufacture of pottery by Josiah Wedgwood and into the spinning of cotton thread by Richard Arkwright. (See also **Industrial Revolution; Wedgwood, Josiah.**)   (*p. 484*)

Mauryan Empire   The first state to unify most of the Indian subcontinent. It was founded by Chandragupta Maurya in 324 B.C.E. and survived until 184 B.C.E. From its capital at Pataliputra in the Ganges Valley it grew wealthy from taxes on agriculture, iron mining, and control of trade routes. (See also **Ashoka.**)   (*p. 123*)

Maya   Mesoamerican civilization concentrated in Mexico's Yucatán Peninsula and in Guatemala and Honduras but never unified into a single empire. Major contributions were in mathematics, astronomy, and development of the calendar.   (*p. 246*)

Mecca   City in western Arabia; birthplace of the Prophet **Muhammad,** and ritual center of the Islamic religion.   (*p. 182*)

mechanization   The application of machinery to manufacturing and other activities. Among the first processes to be mechanized were the spinning of cotton thread and the weaving of cloth in late-eighteenth- and early-nineteenth-century England.   (*p. 486*)

medieval   Literally "middle age," a term that historians of Europe use for the period ca. 500 to ca. 1500, signifying its intermediate point between Greco-Roman antiquity and the Renaissance.   (*p. 203*)

Medina   City in western Arabia to which the Prophet Muhammad and his followers emigrated in 622 to escape persecution in Mecca.   (*p. 184*)

megaliths   Structures and complexes of very large stones constructed for ceremonial and religious purposes in **Neolithic** times.   (*p. 11*)

Meiji Restoration   The political program that followed the destruction of the **Tokugawa Shogunate** in 1868, in which a collection of young leaders set Japan on the path of centralization, industrialization, and imperialism. (See also **Yamagata Aritomo**.)   (*p. 564*)

Memphis   The capital of Old Kingdom Egypt, near the head of the Nile Delta. Early rulers were interred in the nearby **pyramids**.   (*p. 27*)

Menelik II (1844–1911)   Emperor of Ethiopia (r. 1889–1911). He enlarged Ethiopia to its present dimensions and defeated an Italian invasion at Adowa (1896).   (*p. 581*)

mercantilism   European government policies of the sixteenth, seventeenth, and eighteenth centuries designed to promote overseas trade between a country and its colonies and accumulate precious metals by requiring colonies to trade only with their motherland country. The British system was defined by the Navigation Acts, the French system by laws known as the *Exclusif.*   (*p. 403*)

Meroë   Capital of a flourishing kingdom in southern Nubia from the fourth century B.C.E. to the fourth century C.E. In this period Nubian culture shows more independence from Egypt and the influence of sub-Saharan Africa.   (*p. 49*)

Middle Passage   The part of the **Great Circuit** involving the transportation of enslaved Africans across the Atlantic to the Americas.   (*p. 404*)

Ming Empire (1368–1644)   Empire based in China that Zhu Yuanzhang established after the overthrow of the **Yuan Empire.** The Ming emperor **Yongle** sponsored additions to the Forbidden City and the voyages of **Zheng He.** The later years of the Ming saw a slowdown in technological development and economic decline.   (*pp. 285, 438*)

Minoan   Prosperous civilization on the Aegean island of Crete in the second millennium B.C.E. The Minoans engaged in far-flung commerce around the Mediterranean and exerted powerful cultural influences on the early Greeks.   (*p. 69*)

mit'a   Andean labor system based on shared obligations to help kinsmen and work on behalf of the ruler and religious organizations.   (*p. 257*)

Moche   Civilization of north coast of Peru (200–700 C.E.). An important Andean civilization that built extensive irrigation networks as well as impressive urban centers dominated by brick temples.   (*p. 257*)

Moctezuma II (1466?–1520)   Last Aztec emperor, overthrown by the Spanish conquistador Hernán Cortés.   (*p. 355*)

modernization   The process of reforming political, military, economic, social, and cultural traditions in imitation of the early success of Western societies, often with regard for accommodating local traditions in non-Western societies.   (*p. 500*)

Mohenjo-Daro   Largest of the cities of the Indus Valley civilization. It was centrally located in the extensive floodplain of the Indus River in contemporary Pakistan. Little is known about the political institutions of Indus Valley communities, but the large-scale of construction at Mohenjo-Daro, the orderly grid of streets, and the standardization of building materials are evidence of central planning.   (*p. 32*)

moksha   The Hindu concept of the spirit's "liberation" from the endless cycle of rebirths. There are various avenues—such as physical discipline, meditation, and acts of devotion to the gods—by which the spirit can distance itself from desire for the things of this world and be merged with the divine force that animates the universe.   (*p. 120*)

monasticism   Living in a religious community apart from secular society and adhering to a rule stipulating chastity, obedience, and poverty. It was a prominent element of medieval Christianity and Buddhism. Monasteries were the primary centers of learning and literacy in medieval Europe.   (*p. 213*)

Mongols   A people of this name is mentioned as early as the records of the **Tang Empire,** living as nomads in northern Eurasia. After 1206 they established an enormous empire under **Genghis Khan,** linking western and eastern Eurasia.   (*p. 270*)

monotheism   Belief in the existence of a single divine entity. Some scholars cite the devotion of the Egyptian pharaoh **Akhenaten** to Aten (sun-disk) and his suppression of traditional gods as the earliest instance. The Israelite worship of Yahweh developed into an exclusive belief in one god, and this concept passed into Christianity and Islam.   (*p. 79*)

monsoon   Seasonal winds in the Indian Ocean caused by the differences in temperature between the rapidly heating and cooling landmasses of Africa and Asia and the slowly changing ocean waters. These strong and predictable winds have long been ridden across the open sea by sailors, and the large amounts of rainfall that they deposit on parts of India, Southeast Asia, and China allow for the cultivation of several crops a year.   (*pp. 117, 297*)

most-favored-nation status   A clause in a commercial treaty that awards to any later signatories all the privileges previously granted to the original signatories.   (*p. 534*)

movable type Type in which each individual character is cast on a separate piece of metal. It replaced wood-block printing, allowing for the arrangement of individual letters and other characters on a page, rather than requiring the carving of entire pages at a time. It may have been invented in Korea in the thirteenth century. (See also **printing press.**) (*p. 239*)

Mughal Empire Muslim state (1526–1857) exercising dominion over most of India in the sixteenth and seventeenth centuries. (*p. 425*)

Muhammad (570–632 C.E.) Arab prophet; founder of religion of Islam. (*p. 182*)

Muhammad Ali (1769–1849) Leader of Egyptian modernization in the early nineteenth century. He ruled Egypt as an Ottoman governor, but had imperial ambitions. His descendants ruled Egypt until overthrown in 1952. (*pp. 500, 520*)

mummy A body preserved by chemical processes or special natural circumstances, often in the belief that the deceased will need it again in the afterlife. In ancient Egypt the bodies of people who could afford mummification underwent a complex process of removing organs, filling body cavities, dehydrating the corpse with natron, and then wrapping the body with linen bandages and enclosing it in a wooden sarcophagus. (*p. 30*)

Muscovy Russian principality that emerged gradually during the era of Mongol domination. The Muscovite dynasty ruled without interruption from 1276 to 1598. (*p. 446*)

Muslim An adherent of the Islamic religion; a person who "submits" (in Arabic, *Islam* means "submission") to the will of God. (*p. 184*)

Mussolini, Benito (1883–1945) Fascist dictator of Italy (1922–1943). He led Italy to conquer Ethiopia (1935), joined Germany in the Axis pact (1936), and allied Italy with Germany in World War II. He was overthrown in 1943 when the Allies invaded Italy. (*p. 626*)

Mycenae Site of a fortified palace complex in southern Greece that controlled a Late Bronze Age kingdom. In Homer's epic poems Mycenae was the base of King Agamemnon, who commanded the Greeks besieging Troy. Contemporary archaeologists call the complex Greek society of the second millennium B.C.E. "Mycenaean." (*p. 70*)

Napoleon I (1769–1832) Overthrew French Directory in 1799 and became emperor of the French in 1804. Failed to defeat Great Britain and abdicated in 1814. Returned to power briefly in 1815 but was defeated and died in exile. (*p. 468*)

Nasir al-Din Tusi (1201–1274) Persian mathematician and cosmologist whose academy near Tabriz provided the model for the movement of the planets that helped to inspire the Copernican model of the solar system. (*p. 278*)

National Assembly French Revolutionary assembly (1789–1791). Called first as the Estates General, the three estates came together and demanded radical change. It passed the **Declaration of the Rights of Man** in 1789. (*p. 466*)

nationalism A political ideology that stresses people's membership in a nation—a community defined by a common culture and history as well as by territory. In the late eighteenth and early nineteenth centuries, nationalism was a force for unity in western Europe. In the late nineteenth century it hastened the disintegration of the Austro-Hungarian and Ottoman Empires. In the twentieth century it provided the ideological foundation for scores of independent countries emerging from **colonialism.** (*p. 557*)

nawab A Muslim prince allied to British India; technically, a semi-autonomous deputy of the Mughal emperor. (*p. 504*)

Nazis German political party joined by Adolf Hitler, emphasizing nationalism, racism, and war. When Hitler became chancellor of Germany in 1933, the Nazis became the only legal party and an instrument of Hitler's absolute rule. The party's formal name was National Socialist German Workers' Party. (See also **Hitler, Adolf.**) (*p. 627*)

Nehru, Jawaharlal (1889–1964) Indian statesman. He succeeded Mohandas K. Gandhi as leader of the **Indian National Congress.** He negotiated the end of British colonial rule in India and became India's first prime minister (1947–1964). (*p. 649*)

Neo-Assyrian Empire An empire extending from western Iran to Syria-Palestine, conquered by the Assyrians of northern Mesopotamia between the tenth and seventh centuries B.C.E. They used force and terror and exploited the wealth and labor of their subjects. They also preserved and continued the cultural and scientific developments of Mesopotamian civilization. (*p. 72*)

Neo-Babylonian kingdom Under the Chaldaeans (nomadic kinship groups that settled in southern Mesopotamia in the early first millennium B.C.E.), **Babylon** again became a major political and cultural center in the seventh and sixth centuries B.C.E. After participating in the destruction of Assyrian power, the monarchs Nabopolassar and Nebuchadnezzar took over the southern portion of the Assyrian domains. By destroying the **First Temple** in Jerusalem and deporting part of the population, they initiated the **Diaspora** of the Jews. (*p. 86*)

neo-liberalism The term used in Latin America and other developing regions to describe free-market policies that include reducing tariff protection for local industries; the sale of public-sector industries, like national airlines and public utilities, to private investors or foreign corporations; and the reduction of social welfare policies and public-sector employment. (*p. 714*)

Neolithic The period of the Stone Age associated with the ancient **Agricultural Revolution(s).** It follows the **Paleolithic** period. *(p. 6)*

Nevskii, Alexander (1220–1263) Prince of Novgorod (r. 1236–1263). He submitted to the invading Mongols in 1240 and received recognition as the leader of the Russian princes under the **Golden Horde.** *(p. 280)*

New Economic Policy Policy proclaimed by Vladimir Lenin in 1921 to encourage the revival of the Soviet economy by allowing small private enterprises. Joseph Stalin ended the N.E.P. in 1928 and replaced it with a series of **Five-Year Plans.** (See also **Lenin, Vladimir.**) *(p. 607)*

New France French colony in North America, with a capital in Quebec, founded 1608. New France fell to the British in 1763. *(p. 398)*

New Imperialism Historians' term for the late-nineteenth- and early-twentieth-century wave of conquests by European powers, the United States, and Japan, which were followed by the development and exploitation of the newly conquered territories for the benefit of the colonial powers. *(p. 570)*

new monarchies Historians' term for the monarchies in France, England, and Spain from 1450 to 1600. The centralization of royal power was increasing within more or less fixed territorial limits. *(p. 334)*

nomadism A way of life, forced by a scarcity of resources, in which groups of people continually migrate to find pastures and water. *(p. 271)*

nonaligned nations Developing countries that announced their neutrality in the **Cold War.** *(p. 682)*

nongovernmental organizations (NGOs) Nonprofit international organizations devoted to investigating human rights abuses and providing humanitarian relief. Two NGOs won the Nobel Peace Prize in the 1990s: International Campaign to Ban Landmines (1997) and Doctors Without Borders (1999). *(p. 724)*

North Atlantic Treaty Organization (NATO) Organization formed in 1949 as a military alliance of western European and North American states against the Soviet Union and its east European allies. (See also **Warsaw Pact.**) *(p. 669)*

Olmec The first Mesoamerican civilization. Between ca. 1200 and 400 B.C.E., the Olmec people of central Mexico created a vibrant civilization that included intensive agriculture, wide-ranging trade, ceremonial centers, and monumental construction. The Olmec had great cultural influence on later Mesoamerican societies, passing on artistic styles, religious imagery, sophisticated astronomical observation for the construction of calendars, and a ritual ball game. *(p. 54)*

Oman Arab state based in Musqat, the main port in the southwest region of the Arabian peninsula. Oman succeeded Portugal as a power in the western Indian Ocean in the eighteenth century. *(p. 429)*

Opium War (1839–1842) War between Britain and the **Qing Empire** that was, in the British view, occasioned by the Qing government's refusal to permit the importation of opium into its territories. The victorious British imposed the one-sided **Treaty of Nanking** on China. *(p. 534)*

Organization of Petroleum Exporting Countries (OPEC) Organization formed in 1960 by oil-producing states to promote their collective interest in generating revenue from oil. *(p. 686)*

Ottoman Empire Islamic state founded by Osman in northwestern Anatolia ca. 1300. After the fall of the **Byzantine Empire,** the Ottoman Empire was based at Istanbul (formerly Constantinople) from 1453 to 1922. It encompassed lands in the Middle East, North Africa, the Caucasus, and eastern Europe. *(pp. 282, 412)*

Paleolithic The period of the Stone Age associated with the **evolution** of humans. It predates the **Neolithic** period. *(p. 6)*

Pan-Slavism Movement among Russian intellectuals in the second half of the nineteenth century to identify culturally and politically with the Slavic peoples of eastern Europe. *(p. 531)*

Panama Canal Ship canal cut across the isthmus of Panama by United States Army engineers; it opened in 1914. It greatly shortened the sea voyage between the east and west coasts of North America. The United States turned the canal over to Panama on January 1, 2000. *(p. 592)*

papacy The central administration of the Roman Catholic Church, of which the pope is the head. *(pp. 211, 365)*

papyrus A reed that grows along the banks of the Nile River in Egypt. From it was produced a coarse, paper-like writing medium used by the Egyptians and many other peoples in the ancient Mediterranean and Middle East. *(p. 27)*

Parthians Iranian ruling dynasty between ca. 250 B.C.E. and 226 C.E. *(p. 155)*

patron/client relationship In ancient Rome, a fundamental social relationship in which the patron—a wealthy and powerful individual—provided legal and economic protection and assistance to clients, men of lesser status and means, and in return the clients supported the political careers and economic interests of their patron. *(p. 133)*

Paul (ca. 5–65 C.E.) A Jew from the Greek city of Tarsus in Anatolia, he initially persecuted the followers of Jesus but, after receiving a revelation on the road to Syrian Damascus, became a Christian. Taking advantage of his Hellenized background and Roman citizenship, he traveled throughout Syria-Palestine, Anatolia, and Greece, preaching the new religion and establishing churches. Finding his greatest success among pagans ("gentiles"), he began the process by which Christianity separated from Judaism.   (*p. 138*)

pax romana   Literally, "Roman peace," it connoted the stability and prosperity that Roman rule brought to the lands of the Roman Empire in the first two centuries C.E. The movement of people and trade goods along Roman roads and safe seas allowed for the spread of cultural practices, technologies, and religious ideas.   (*p. 137*)

Pearl Harbor   Naval base in Hawaii attacked by Japanese aircraft on December 7, 1941. The sinking of much of the U.S. Pacific Fleet brought the United States into World War II.   (*p. 634*)

Peloponnesian War   A protracted (431–404 B.C.E.) and costly conflict between the Athenian and Spartan alliance systems that convulsed most of the Greek world. The war was largely a consequence of Athenian imperialism. Possession of a naval empire allowed Athens to fight a war of attrition. Ultimately, Sparta prevailed because of Athenian errors and Persian financial support.   (*p. 113*)

perestroika   Policy of "openness" that was the centerpiece of Mikhail Gorbachev's efforts to liberalize communism in the Soviet Union. (See also **Gorbachev, Mikhail.**)   (*p. 700*)

Pericles (ca. 495–429 B.C.E.)   Aristocratic leader who guided the Athenian state through the transformation to full participatory democracy for all male citizens, supervised construction of the Acropolis, and pursued a policy of imperial expansion that led to the **Peloponnesian War.** He formulated a strategy of attrition but died from the plague early in the war.   (*p. 109*)

Perón, Eva Duarte (1919–1952)   Wife of **Juan Perón** and champion of the poor in Argentina. She was a gifted speaker and popular political leader who campaigned to improve the life of the urban poor by founding schools and hospitals and providing other social benefits.   (*p. 660*)

Perón, Juan (1895–1974)   President of Argentina (1946–1955, 1973–1974). As a military officer, he championed the rights of labor. Aided by his wife **Eva Duarte Perón,** he was elected president in 1946. He built up Argentinean industry, became very popular among the urban poor, but harmed the economy.   (*p. 659*)

Persepolis   A complex of palaces, reception halls, and treasury buildings erected by the Persian kings **Darius I** and Xerxes in the Persian homeland. It is believed that the New Year's festival was celebrated here, as well as the coronations, weddings, and funerals of the Persian kings, who were buried in cliff-tombs nearby.   (*p. 99*)

Persian Wars   Conflicts between Greek city-states and the Persian Empire, ranging from the Ionian Revolt (499–494 B.C.E.) through Darius's punitive expedition

that failed at Marathon (490 B.C.E.) and the defeat of Xerxes' massive invasion of Greece by the Spartan-led Hellenic League (480–479 B.C.E.). This first major setback for Persian arms launched the Greeks into their period of greatest cultural productivity. **Herodotus** chronicled these events in the first "history" in the Western tradition.   (*p. 109*)

Peter the Great (1672–1725)   Russian tsar (r. 1689–1725). He enthusiastically introduced Western languages and technologies to the Russian elite, moving the capital from Moscow to the new city of St. Petersburg.   (*p. 449*)

pharaoh   The central figure in the ancient Egyptian state. Believed to be an earthly manifestation of the gods, he used his absolute power to maintain the safety and prosperity of Egypt.   (*p. 26*)

Phoenicians   Semitic-speaking Canaanites living on the coast of modern Lebanon and Syria in the first millennium B.C.E. From major cities such as Tyre and Sidon, Phoenician merchants and sailors explored the Mediterranean, engaged in widespread commerce, and founded **Carthage** and other colonies in the western Mediterranean.   (*p. 80*)

pilgrimage   Journey to a sacred shrine by Christians seeking to show their piety, fulfill vows, or gain absolution for sins. Other religions also have pilgrimage traditions, such as the Muslim pilgrimage to **Mecca** and the pilgrimages made by early Chinese Buddhists to India in search of sacred Buddhist writings.   (*p. 220*)

Pilgrims   Group of English Protestant dissenters who established Plymouth Colony in Massachusetts in 1620 to seek religious freedom after having lived briefly in the Netherlands.   (*p. 397*)

Pizarro, Francisco (1478?–1541)   Spanish explorer who led the conquest of the **Inca** Empire of Peru in 1531–1533.   (*p. 355*)

Planck, Max (1858–1947)   German physicist who developed quantum theory and was awarded the Nobel Prize for physics in 1918.   (*p. 614*)

polis   The Greek term for a **city-state,** an urban center and the agricultural territory under its control. It was the characteristic form of political organization in southern and central Greece in the Archaic and Classical periods. Of the hundreds of city-states in the Mediterranean and Black Sea regions settled by Greeks, some were oligarchic, others democratic, depending on the powers delegated to the Council and the Assembly.   (*p. 105*)

positivism   A philosophy developed by the French count of Saint-Simon. Positivists believed that social and economic problems could be solved by the application of the scientific method, leading to continuous progress. Their ideas became popular in France and Latin America in the nineteenth century.   (*p. 493*)

Potosí   Located in Bolivia, one of the richest silver mining centers and most populous cities in colonial Spanish America.   (*p. 391*)

printing press   A mechanical device for transferring text or graphics from a woodblock or type to paper using ink. Presses using movable type first appeared in Europe in about 1450. See also **movable type.**   (*p. 330*)

Protestant Reformation   Religious reform movement within the Latin Christian Church beginning in 1519. It resulted in the "protesters" forming several new Christian denominations, including the Lutheran and Reformed Churches and the Church of England.   (*p. 366*)

proxy wars   During the **Cold War,** local or regional wars in which the superpowers armed, trained, and financed the combatants.   (*p. 690*)

Ptolemies   The Macedonian dynasty, descended from one of Alexander the Great's officers, that ruled Egypt for three centuries (323–30 B.C.E.). From their magnificent capital at Alexandria on the Mediterranean coast, the Ptolemies largely took over the system created by Egyptian pharaohs to extract the wealth of the land, rewarding Greeks and Hellenized non-Greeks serving in the military and administration.   (*p. 114*)

Puritans   English Protestant dissenters who believed that God predestined souls to heaven or hell before birth. They founded Massachusetts Bay Colony in 1629.   (*p. 397*)

pyramid   A large, triangular stone monument, used in Egypt and Nubia as a burial place for the king. The largest pyramids, erected during the Old Kingdom near **Memphis** with stone tools and compulsory labor, reflect the Egyptian belief that the proper and spectacular burial of the divine ruler would guarantee the continued prosperity of the land. (See also **ma'at.**)   (*p. 27*)

Qin   A people and state in the Wei Valley of eastern China that conquered rival states and created the first Chinese empire (221–206 B.C.E.). The Qin ruler, Shi Huangdi, standardized many features of Chinese society and ruthlessly marshaled subjects for military and construction projects, engendering hostility that led to the fall of his dynasty shortly after his death. The Qin framework was largely taken over by the succeeding **Han** Empire.   (*p. 144*)

Qing Empire   Empire established in China by Manchus who overthrew the **Ming Empire** in 1644. At various times the Qing also controlled Manchuria, Mongolia, Turkestan, and Tibet. The last Qing emperor was overthrown in 1911.   (*p. 440*)

Quran   Book composed of divine revelations made to the Prophet Muhammad between ca. 610 and his death in 632; the sacred text of the religion of **Islam.**   (*p. 185*)

railroads   Networks of iron (later steel) rails on which steam (later electric or diesel) locomotives pulled long trains at high speeds. The first railroads were built in England in the 1830s. Their success caused a railroad-building boom throughout the world that lasted well into the twentieth century.   (*p. 550*)

Rajputs   Members of a mainly Hindu warrior caste from northwest India. The Mughal emperors drew most of their Hindu officials from this caste, and **Akbar** married a Rajput princess.   (*p. 425*)

Ramesses II   A long-lived ruler of New Kingdom Egypt (r. 1290–1224 B.C.E.). He reached an accommodation with the **Hittites** of Anatolia after a standoff in battle at Kadesh in Syria. He built on a grand scale throughout Egypt.   (*p. 68*)

Rashid al-Din (d.1318)   Adviser to the **Il-khan** ruler Ghazan, who converted to Islam on Rashid's advice.   (*p. 278*)

recaptives   Africans rescued by Britain's Royal Navy from the illegal slave trade of the nineteenth century and restored to free status.   (*p. 503*)

reconquest of Iberia   Beginning in the eleventh century, military campaigns by various Iberian Christian states to recapture territory taken by Muslims. In 1492 the last Muslim ruler was defeated, and Spain and Portugal emerged as united kingdoms.   (*p. 334*)

Renaissance (European)   A period of intense artistic and intellectual activity, said to be a "rebirth" of Greco-Roman culture. Usually divided into an Italian Renaissance, from roughly the mid-fourteenth to mid-fifteenth century, and a Northern (trans-Alpine) Renaissance, from roughly the early fifteenth to early seventeenth century.   (*pp. 325, 364*)

Revolutions of 1848   Democratic and nationalist revolutions that swept across Europe. The monarchy in France was overthrown. In Germany, Austria, Italy, and Hungary the revolutions failed.   (*p. 469*)

Rhodes, Cecil (1853–1902)   British entrepreneur and politician involved in the expansion of the British Empire from South Africa into Central Africa. The colonies of Southern Rhodesia (now Zimbabwe) and Northern Rhodesia (now Zambia) were named after him.   (*p. 580*)

Romanization   The process by which the Latin language and Roman culture became dominant in the western provinces of the Roman Empire. The Roman government did not actively seek to Romanize the subject peoples, but indigenous peoples in the provinces often chose to Romanize because of the political and economic advantages that it brought, as well as the allure of Roman success.   (*p. 137*)

Roman Principate   A term used to characterize Roman government in the first three centuries C.E., based on the ambiguous title *princeps* ("first citizen") adopted by Augustus to conceal his military dictatorship.   (*p. 136*)

Roman Republic The period from 507 to 31 B.C.E., during which Rome was largely governed by the aristocratic **Roman Senate.** (*p. 131*)

Roman Senate A council whose members were the heads of wealthy, landowning families. Originally an advisory body to the early kings, in the era of the **Roman Republic** the Senate effectively governed the Roman state and the growing empire. Under Senate leadership, Rome conquered an empire of unprecedented extent in the lands surrounding the Mediterranean Sea. In the first century B.C.E. quarrels among powerful and ambitious senators and failure to address social and economic problems led to civil wars and the emergence of the rule of the emperors. (*p. 131*)

sacrifice A gift given to a deity, often with the aim of creating a relationship, gaining favor, and obligating the god to provide some benefit to the sacrificer, sometimes in order to sustain the deity and thereby guarantee the continuing vitality of the natural world. The object devoted to the deity could be as simple as a cup of wine poured on the ground, a live animal slain on the altar, or, in the most extreme case, the ritual killing of a human being. (*p. 106*)

Safavid Empire Iranian kingdom (1502–1722) established by Ismail Safavi, who declared Iran a Shi'ite state. (*p. 420*)

Sahel Belt south of the Sahara; literally "coastland" in Arabic. (*p. 167*)

samurai Literally "those who serve," the hereditary military elite of the **Tokugawa Shogunate.** (*p. 433*)

Sandinistas Members of a leftist coalition that overthrew the Nicaraguan dictatorship of Anastasia Somoza in 1979 and attempted to install a socialist economy. The United States financed armed opposition by the Contras. The Sandinistas lost national elections in 1990. (*p. 692*)

Sanger, Margaret (1883–1966) American nurse and author; pioneer in the movement for family planning; organized conferences and established birth control clinics. (*p. 613*)

Sasanid Empire Iranian empire, established ca. 226, with a capital in Ctesiphon, Mesopotamia. The Sasanid emperors established **Zoroastrianism** as the state religion. Islamic Arab armies overthrew the empire ca. 640. (*p. 156*)

satrap The governor of a province in the Achaemenid Persian Empire, often a relative of the king. He was responsible for protection of the province and for forwarding tribute to the central administration. Satraps in outlying provinces enjoyed considerable autonomy. (*p. 99*)

savanna Tropical or subtropical grassland, either treeless or with occasional clumps of trees. Most extensive in **sub-Saharan Africa** but also present in South America. (*p. 167*)

schism A formal split within a religious community. See **Great Western Schism.** (*p. 204*)

scholasticism A philosophical and theological system, associated with Thomas Aquinas, devised to reconcile Aristotelian philosophy and Roman Catholic theology in the thirteenth century. (*p. 329*)

Scientific Revolution The intellectual movement in Europe, initially associated with planetary motion and other aspects of physics, that by the seventeenth century had laid the groundwork for modern science. (*p. 370*)

"scramble" for Africa Sudden wave of conquests in Africa by European powers in the 1880s and 1890s. Britain obtained most of eastern Africa, France most of northwestern Africa. Other countries (Germany, Belgium, Portugal, Italy, and Spain) acquired lesser amounts. (*p. 577*)

scribe In the governments of many ancient societies, a professional position reserved for men who had undergone the lengthy training required to be able to read and write using **cuneiforms, hieroglyphics,** or other early, cumbersome writing systems. (*p. 18*)

seasoning An often difficult period of adjustment to new climates, disease environments, and work routines, such as that experienced by slaves newly arrived in the Americas. (*p. 402*)

Selassie, Haile (1892–1975) Emperor of Ethiopia (r. 1930–1974) and symbol of African independence. He fought the Italian invasion of his country in 1935 and regained his throne during World War II, when British forces expelled the Italians. He ruled **Ethiopia** as a traditional autocracy until he was overthrown in 1974. (*p. 646*)

Semitic Family of related languages long spoken across parts of western Asia and northern Africa. In antiquity these languages included Hebrew, Aramaic, and Phoenician. The most widespread modern member of the Semitic family is Arabic. (*p. 14*)

"separate spheres" Nineteenth-century idea in Western societies that men and women, especially of the middle class, should have clearly differentiated roles in society: women as wives, mothers, and homemakers; men as breadwinners and participants in business and politics. (*p. 556*)

sepoy A soldier in South Asia, especially in the service of the British. (*p. 504*)

Sepoy Rebellion The revolt of Indian soldiers in 1857 against certain practices that violated religious customs; also known as the Sepoy Mutiny. (*p. 507*)

Serbia The Ottoman province in the Balkans that rose up against **Janissary** control in the early 1800s. After World War II the central province of Yugoslavia. Serb leaders struggled to maintain dominance as the Yugoslav federation dissolved in the 1990s. (*p. 520*)

serf In medieval Europe, an agricultural laborer legally bound to a lord's property and obligated to perform set services for the lord. In Russia some serfs worked as artisans and in factories; serfdom was not abolished there until 1861. (*pp. 209, 447*)

shaft graves A term used for the burial sites of elite members of Mycenaean Greek society in the mid-second millennium B.C.E. At the bottom of deep shafts lined with stone slabs, the bodies were laid out along with gold and bronze jewelry, implements, weapons, and masks. (*p. 70*)

Shah Abbas I (r. 1587–1629) The fifth and most renowned ruler of the **Safavid** dynasty in Iran. Abbas moved the royal capital to Isfahan in 1598. (*p. 421*)

shamanism The practice of identifying special individuals (shamans) who will interact with spirits for the benefit of the community. Characteristic of the Korean kingdoms of the early medieval period and of early societies of Central Asia. (*p. 239*)

Shang The dominant people in the earliest Chinese dynasty for which we have written records (ca. 1750–1027 B.C.E.). Ancestor worship, divination by means of oracle bones, and the use of bronze vessels for ritual purposes were major elements of Shang culture. (*p. 41*)

Shi Huangdi Founder of the short-lived **Qin** dynasty and creator of the Chinese Empire (r. 221–210 B.C.E.). He is remembered for his ruthless conquests of rival states, standardization of practices, and forcible organization of labor for military and engineering tasks. His tomb, with its army of life-size terracotta soldiers, has been partially excavated. (*p. 144*)

Shi'ites Muslims belonging to the branch of Islam believing that God vests leadership of the community in a descendant of Muhammad's son-in-law Ali. Shi'ism is the state religion of Iran. (See also **Sunnis.**) (*pp. 180, 421*)

Siberia The extreme northeastern sector of Asia, including the Kamchatka Peninsula and the present Russian coast of the Arctic Ocean, the Bering Strait, and the Sea of Okhotsk. (*p. 446*)

Silk Road Caravan routes connecting China and the Middle East across Central Asia and Iran. (*p. 155*)

Slavophiles Russian intellectuals in the early nineteenth century who favored resisting western European influences and taking pride in the traditional peasant values and institutions of the Slavic people. (*p. 531*)

"small traditions" Historians' term for a localized, usually nonliterate, set of customs and beliefs adhered to by a single society, often in conjunction with a **"great tradition."** (*p. 168*)

socialism A political ideology that originated in Europe in the 1830s. Socialists advocated government protection of workers from exploitation by property owners and government ownership of industries. This ideology led to the founding of socialist or labor parties throughout Europe in the second half of the nineteenth century. (See also **Marx, Karl.**) (*p. 552*)

Socrates Athenian philosopher (ca. 470–399 B.C.E.) who shifted the emphasis of philosophical investigation from questions of natural science to ethics and human behavior. He attracted young disciples from elite families but made enemies by revealing the ignorance and pretensions of others, culminating in his trial and execution by the Athenian state. (*p. 111*)

Sokoto Caliphate A large Muslim state founded in 1809 in what is now northern Nigeria. (*p. 500*)

Solidarity Polish trade union created in 1980 to protest working conditions and political repression. It began the nationalist opposition to communist rule that led in 1989 to the fall of communism in eastern Europe. (*p. 700*)

Song Empire Empire in central and southern China (960–1126) while the Liao people controlled the north. Empire in southern China (1127–1279; the "Southern Song") while the Jin people controlled the north. Distinguished for its advances in technology, medicine, astronomy, and mathematics. (*p. 232*)

Stalin, Joseph (1879–1953) Bolshevik revolutionary, head of the Soviet Communist Party after 1924, and dictator of the Soviet Union from 1929 to 1953. He led the Soviet Union with an iron fist, using **Five-Year Plans** to increase industrial production and terror to crush all opposition. (*p. 620*)

Stalingrad City in Russia, site of a Red Army victory over the German army in 1942–1943. The Battle of Stalingrad was the turning point in the war between Germany and the Soviet Union. Today Volgograd. (*p. 632*)

Stanley, Henry Morton (1841–1904) British-American explorer of Africa, famous for his expeditions in search of Dr. David Livingstone. Stanley helped King **Leopold II** establish the Congo Free State. (*p. 579*)

steam engine A machine that turns the energy released by burning fuel into motion. Thomas Newcomen built the first crude but workable steam engine in 1712. **James Watt** vastly improved his device in the 1760s and 1770s. Steam power was later applied to moving machinery in factories and to powering ships and locomotives. (*p. 487*)

steel A form of iron that is both durable and flexible. It was first mass-produced in the 1860s and quickly became the most widely used metal in construction, machinery, and railroad equipment. (*p. 549*)

steppes Treeless plains, especially the high, flat expanses of northern Eurasia, which usually have little rain and are covered with coarse grass. They are good lands for nomads and their herds. Living on the steppes promoted the breeding of horses and the development of military skills that were essential to the rise of the Mongol Empire. (*p. 167*)

stirrup   Device for securing a horseman's feet, enabling him to wield weapons more effectively. First evidence of the use of stirrups was among the Kushan people of northern Afghanistan in approximately the first century C.E.   (*p. 159*)

stock exchange   A place where shares in a company or business enterprise are bought and sold.   (*p. 374*)

Stone Age   The historical period characterized by the production of tools from stone and other nonmetallic substances. It was followed in some places by the Bronze Age and more generally by the Iron Age.   (*p. 6*)

submarine telegraph cables   Insulated copper cables laid along the bottom of a sea or ocean for telegraphic communication. The first short cable was laid across the English Channel in 1851; the first successful transatlantic cable was laid in 1866. (See also **electric telegraph**.)   (*p. 550*)

sub-Saharan Africa   Portion of the African continent lying south of the Sahara.   (*p. 167*)

Suez Canal   Ship canal dug across the isthmus of Suez in Egypt, designed by Ferdinand de Lesseps. It opened to shipping in 1869 and shortened the sea voyage between Europe and Asia. Its strategic importance led to the British conquest of Egypt in 1882.   (*p. 569*)

Suleiman the Magnificent (1494–1566)   The most illustrious sultan of the **Ottoman Empire** (r. 1520–1566); also known as Suleiman Kanuni, "The Lawgiver." He significantly expanded the empire in the Balkans and eastern Mediterranean.   (*p. 415*)

Sumerians   The people who dominated southern Mesopotamia through the end of the third millennium B.C.E. They were responsible for the creation of many fundamental elements of Mesopotamian culture—such as irrigation technology, **cuneiform**, and religious conceptions—taken over by their **Semitic** successors.   (*p. 14*)

Sunnis   Muslims belonging to branch of Islam believing that the community should select its own leadership. The majority religion in most Islamic countries. (See also **Shi'ites**.)   (*p. 180*)

Sun Yat-sen (1867–1925)   Chinese nationalist revolutionary, founder and leader of the **Guomindang** until his death. He attempted to create a liberal democratic political movement in China but was thwarted by military leaders.   (*p. 608*)

Swahili   Bantu language with Arabic loanwords spoken in coastal regions of East Africa.   (*p. 430*)

Swahili Coast   East African shores of the Indian Ocean between the Horn of Africa and the Zambezi River; from the Arabic *sawahil*, meaning "shores."   (*p. 307*)

Taiping Rebellion (1850–1864)   The most destructive civil war before the twentieth century. A Christian-inspired rural rebellion threatened to topple the **Qing Empire**.   (*p. 536*)

Tamil kingdoms   The kingdoms of southern India, inhabited primarily by speakers of Dravidian languages, which developed in partial isolation, and somewhat differently, from the Aryan north. They produced epics, poetry, and performance arts. Elements of Tamil religious beliefs were merged into the Hindu synthesis.   (*p. 125*)

Tang Empire   Empire unifying China and part of Central Asia, founded 618 and ended 907. The Tang emperors presided over a magnificent court at their capital, Chang'an.   (*p. 225*)

Tanzimat   "Restructuring" reforms by the nineteenth-century Ottoman rulers, intended to move civil law away from the control of religious elites and make the military and the bureaucracy more efficient.   (*p. 524*)

Tenochtitlan   Capital of the Aztec Empire, located on an island in Lake Texcoco. Its population was about 150,000 on the eve of Spanish conquest. Mexico City was constructed on its ruins.   (*p. 252*)

Teotihuacan   A powerful **city-state** in central Mexico (100 B.C.E.–750 C.E.). Its population was about 150,000 at its peak in 600.   (*p. 245*)

terrorism   Political belief that extreme and seemingly random violence will destabilize a government and permit the terrorists to gain political advantage. Though an old technique, terrorism gained prominence in the late twentieth century with the growth of worldwide mass media that, through their news coverage, amplified public fears of terrorist acts.   (*p. 717*)

theater-state   Historians' term for a state that acquires prestige and power by developing attractive cultural forms and staging elaborate public ceremonies (as well as redistributing valuable resources) to attract and bind subjects to the center. Examples include the **Gupta Empire** in India and **Srivijaya** in Southeast Asia.   (*p. 125*)

Thebes   Capital city of Egypt and home of the ruling dynasties during the Middle and New Kingdoms. Amon, patron deity of Thebes, became one of the chief gods of Egypt. Monarchs were buried across the river in the Valley of the Kings.   (*p. 27*)

Theravada Buddhism   "Way of the Elders" branch of Buddhism followed in Sri Lanka and much of Southeast Asia. Theravada remains close to the original principles set forth by the **Buddha**; it downplays the importance of gods and emphasizes austerity and the individual's search for enlightenment.   (*p. 121*)

third-century crisis   Historians' term for the political, military, and economic turmoil that beset the Roman Empire during much of the third century C.E.: frequent changes of ruler, civil wars, barbarian invasions, decline of urban centers, and near-destruction of long-distance commerce and the monetary economy. After 284 C.E. Diocletian restored order by making fundamental changes.   (*p. 139*)

Third World Term applied to a group of developing countries who professed nonalignment during the **Cold War.** (*p. 682*)

three-field system A rotational system for agriculture in which one field grows grain, one grows legumes, and one lies fallow. It gradually replaced two-field system in medieval Europe. (*p. 317*)

Tiananmen Square Site in Beijing where Chinese students and workers gathered to demand greater political openness in 1989. The demonstration was crushed by Chinese military with great loss of life. (*p. 699*)

Timbuktu City on the Niger River in the modern country of Mali. It was founded by the Tuareg as a seasonal camp sometime after 1000. As part of the **Mali** empire, Timbuktu became a major terminus of the trans-Saharan trade and a center of Islamic learning. (*p. 312*)

Timur (1336–1405) Member of a prominent family of the Mongols' Jagadai Khanate, Timur through conquest gained control over much of Central Asia and Iran. He consolidated the status of Sunni Islam as orthodox, and his descendants, the Timurids, maintained his empire for nearly a century and founded the **Mughal Empire** in India. (*p. 277*)

Tiwanaku Name of capital city and empire centered on the region near Lake Titicaca in modern Bolivia (375–1000 C.E.). (*p. 258*)

Tokugawa Shogunate (1603–1868) The last of the three shogunates of Japan. (*p. 434*)

Toltecs Powerful postclassic empire in central Mexico (900–1156 C.E.). It influenced much of Mesoamerica. Aztecs claimed ties to this earlier civilization. (*p. 251*)

trans-Saharan caravan routes Trading network linking North Africa with **sub-Saharan Africa** across the Sahara. (*p. 165*)

Treaty of Nanking (1842) The treaty that concluded the **Opium War.** It awarded Britain a large indemnity from the **Qing Empire,** denied the Qing government tariff control over some of its own borders, opened additional ports of residence to Britons, and ceded the island of Hong Kong to Britain. (*p. 534*)

Treaty of Versailles (1919) The treaty imposed on Germany by France, Great Britain, the United States, and other Allied Powers after World War I. It demanded that Germany dismantle its military and give up some lands to Poland. It was resented by many Germans. (*p. 606*)

treaty ports Cities opened to foreign residents as a result of the forced treaties between the **Qing Empire** and foreign signatories. In the treaty ports, foreigners enjoyed **extraterritoriality.** (*p. 534*)

tributary system A system in which, from the time of the **Han** Empire, countries in East and Southeast Asia not under the direct control of empires based in China nevertheless enrolled as tributary states, ac-knowledging the superiority of the emperors in China in exchange for trading rights or strategic alliances. (*p. 228*)

tribute system A system in which defeated peoples were forced to pay a tax in the form of goods and labor. This forced transfer of food, cloth, and other goods subsidized the development of large cities. An important component of the Aztec and Inca economies. (*p. 253*)

trireme Greek and Phoenician warship of the fifth and fourth centuries B.C.E. It was sleek and light, powered by 170 oars arranged in three vertical tiers. Manned by skilled sailors, it was capable of short bursts of speed and complex maneuvers. (*p. 110*)

tropical rain forest High-precipitation forest zones of the Americas, Africa, and Asia lying between the Tropic of Cancer and the Tropic of Capricorn. (*p. 167*)

tropics Equatorial region between the Tropic of Cancer and the Tropic of Capricorn. It is characterized by generally warm or hot temperatures year-round, though much variation exists due to altitude and other factors. Temperate zones north and south of the tropics generally have a winter season. (*p. 297*)

Truman Doctrine Foreign policy initiated by U.S. president Harry Truman in 1947. It offered military aid to help Turkey and Greece resist Soviet military pressure and subversion. (*p. 672*)

tsar (czar) From Latin *caesar,* this Russian title for a monarch was first used in reference to a Russian ruler by Ivan III (r. 1462–1505). (*pp. 381, 446*)

tyrant The term the Greeks used to describe someone who seized and held power in violation of the normal procedures and traditions of the community. Tyrants appeared in many Greek **city-states** in the seventh and sixth centuries B.C.E., often taking advantage of the disaffection of the emerging middle class and, by weakening the old elite, unwittingly contributing to the evolution of **democracy.** (*p. 106*)

Uighurs A group of Turkic-speakers who controlled their own centralized empire from 744 to 840 in Mongolia and Central Asia. (*p. 232*)

ulama Muslim religious scholars. From the ninth century onward, the primary interpreters of Islamic law and the social core of Muslim urban societies. (*p. 191*)

Umayyad Caliphate First hereditary dynasty of Muslim caliphs (661 to 750). From their capital at Damascus, the Umayyads ruled an empire that extended from Spain to India. Overthrown by the **Abbasid Caliphate.** (*p. 186*)

umma The community of all Muslims. A major innovation against the background of seventh-century Arabia, where traditionally kinship rather than faith had determined membership in a community. (*p. 184*)

United Nations   International organization founded in 1945 to promote world peace and cooperation. It replaced the **League of Nations.**   (*p. 669*)

Universal Declaration of Human Rights   A 1948 United Nations covenant binding signatory nations to the observance of specified rights.   (*p. 723*)

universities   Degree-granting institutions of higher learning. Those that appeared in Latin West from about 1200 onward became the model of all modern universities.   (*p. 528*)

Ural Mountains   This north-south range separates Siberia from the rest of Russia. It is commonly considered the boundary between the continents of Europe and Asia.   (*p. 446*)

Urdu   A Persian-influenced literary form of Hindi written in Arabic characters and used as a literary language since the 1300s.   (*p. 312*)

utopian socialism   A philosophy introduced by the Frenchman Charles Fourier in the early nineteenth century. Utopian socialists hoped to create humane alternatives to industrial capitalism by building self-sustaining communities whose inhabitants would work cooperatively. (See also **socialism.**)   (*p. 493*)

Vargas, Getulio (1883–1954)   Dictator of Brazil from 1930 to 1945 and from 1951 to 1954. Defeated in the presidential election of 1930, he overthrew the government and created a dictatorship that emphasized industrialization and helped the urban poor but did little to alleviate the problems of the peasants.   (*p. 658*)

varna/jati   Two categories of social identity of great importance in Indian history. *Varna* are the four major social divisions: the *Brahmin* priest class, the *Kshatriya* warrior/administrator class, the *Vaishya* merchant/farmer class, and the *Shudra* laborer class. Within the system of *varna* are many *jati,* regional groups of people who have a common occupational sphere, and who marry, eat, and generally interact with other members of their group.   (*p. 119*)

vassal   In medieval Europe, a sworn supporter of a king or lord committed to rendering specified military service to that king or lord.   (*p. 210*)

Vedas   Early Indian sacred "knowledge"—the literal meaning of the term—long preserved and communicated orally by Brahmin priests and eventually written down. These religious texts, including the thousand poetic hymns to various deities contained in the Rig Veda, are our main source of information about the Vedic period (ca. 1500–500 B.C.E.).   (*p. 119*)

Versailles   The huge palace built for French King Louis XIV south of Paris in the town of the same name. The palace symbolized the preeminence of French power and architecture in Europe and the triumph of royal authority over the French nobility.   (*p. 382*)

Victorian Age   The reign of Queen Victoria of Great Britain (r. 1837–1901). The term is also used to describe late-nineteenth-century society, with its rigid moral standards and sharply differentiated roles for men and women and for middle-class and working-class people. (See also **"separate spheres."**)   (*p. 553*)

Vietnam War   (1954–1975) Conflict pitting North Vietnam and South Vietnamese communist guerrillas against the South Vietnamese government, aided after 1961 by the United States.   (*p. 673*)

Villa, Francisco "Pancho" (1877–1923)   A popular leader during the Mexican Revolution. An outlaw in his youth, when the revolution started, he formed a cavalry army in the north of Mexico and fought for the rights of the landless in collaboration with **Emiliano Zapata.** He was assassinated in 1923.   (*p. 654*)

Wari   Andean civilization culturally linked to **Tiwanaku,** perhaps beginning as a colony of Tiwanaku.   (*p. 258*)

Warsaw Pact   The 1955 treaty binding the Soviet Union and countries of eastern Europe in an alliance against the **North Atlantic Treaty Organization.**   (*p. 672*)

Washington, George (1732–1799)   Military commander of the American Revolution. He was the first elected president of the United States (1789–1799).   (*p. 464*)

water wheel   A mechanism that harnesses the energy in flowing water to grind grain or to power machinery. It was used in many parts of the world but was especially common in Europe from 1200 to 1900.   (*p. 321*)

Watt, James (1736–1819)   Scot who invented the condenser and other improvements that made the **steam engine** a practical source of power for industry and transportation. The watt, an electrical measurement, is named after him.   (*p. 487*)

weapons of mass destruction   Nuclear, chemical, and biological devices that are capable of injuring and killing large numbers of people.   (*p. 727*)

Wedgwood, Josiah (1730–1795)   English industrialist whose pottery works were the first to produce fine-quality pottery by industrial methods.   (*p. 484*)

Western Front   A line of trenches and fortifications in World War I that stretched without a break from Switzerland to the North Sea. Scene of most of the fighting between Germany, on the one hand, and France and Britain, on the other.   (*p. 601*)

Wilson, Woodrow (1856–1924)   President of the United States (1913–1921) and the leading figure at the Paris Peace Conference of 1919. He was unable to persuade the U.S. Congress to ratify the **Treaty of Versailles** or join the **League of Nations.**   (*p. 605*)

witch-hunt   The pursuit of people suspected of witchcraft, especially in northern Europe in the late sixteenth and seventeenth centuries.   (*p. 369*)

Women's Rights Convention   An 1848 gathering of women angered by their exclusion from an international antislavery meeting. They met at Seneca Falls, New York, to discuss women's rights.   *(p. 477)*

World Bank   A specialized agency of the United Nations that makes loans to countries for economic development, trade promotion, and debt consolidation. Its formal name is the International Bank for Reconstruction and Development.   *(p. 670)*

World Trade Organization (WTO)   An international body established in 1995 to foster and bring order to international trade.   *(p. 720)*

Xiongnu   A confederation of nomadic peoples living beyond the northwest frontier of ancient China. Chinese rulers tried a variety of defenses and stratagems to ward off these "barbarians," as they called them, and finally succeeded in dispersing the Xiongnu in the first century C.E.   *(p. 150)*

Yamagata Aritomo (1838–1922)   One of the leaders of the **Meiji Restoration.**   *(p. 565)*

Yi (1392–1910)   The Yi dynasty ruled Korea from the fall of the **Koryo** kingdom to the colonization of Korea by Japan.   *(p. 290)*

yin/yang   In Chinese belief, complementary factors that help to maintain the equilibrium of the world. Yin is associated with feminine, dark, and passive qualities; yang with masculine, light, and active qualities.   *(p. 45)*

Yongle   Reign of Zhu Di (1360–1424), the third emperor of the **Ming Empire** (r. 1403–1424). He sponsored further work on the Forbidden City, a huge encyclopedia project, the expeditions of **Zheng He,** and the reopening of China's borders to trade and travel.   *(p. 285)*

Young Ottomans   Movement of young intellectuals to institute liberal reforms and build a feeling of national identity in the Ottoman Empire in the second half of the nineteenth century.   *(p. 529)*

Yuan Empire (1271–1368)   Empire created in China and Siberia by **Khubilai Khan.**   *(p. 272)*

Yuan Shikai (1859–1916)   Chinese general and first president of the Chinese Republic (1912–1916). He stood in the way of the democratic movement led by **Sun Yat-sen.**   *(p. 609)*

Zapata, Emiliano (1879–1919)   Revolutionary and leader of peasants in the Mexican Revolution. He mobilized landless peasants in south-central Mexico in an attempt to seize and divide the lands of the wealthy landowners. Though successful for a time, he was ultimately defeated and assassinated.   *(p. 654)*

Zen   The Japanese word for a branch of **Mahayana Buddhism** based on highly disciplined meditation. It is known in Sanskrit as *dhyana*, in Chinese as *chan*, and in Korean as *son*.   *(p. 236)*

Zheng He (1371–1433)   An imperial eunuch and Muslim, entrusted by the Ming emperor **Yongle** with a series of state voyages that took his gigantic ships through the Indian Ocean, from Southeast Asia to Africa.   *(pp. 285, 340)*

Zhou   The people and dynasty that took over the dominant position in north China from the **Shang** and created the concept of the **Mandate of Heaven** to justify their rule. The Zhou era, particularly the vigorous early period (1027–771 B.C.E.), was remembered in Chinese tradition as a time of prosperity and benevolent rule. In the later Zhou period (771–221 B.C.E.), centralized control broke down, and warfare among many small states became frequent.   *(p. 43)*

ziggurat   A massive pyramidal stepped tower made of mudbricks. It is associated with religious complexes in ancient Mesopotamian cities, but its function is unknown.   *(p. 19)*

Zoroastrianism   A religion originating in ancient Iran with the prophet Zoroaster. It centered on a single benevolent deity—Ahuramazda—who engaged in a twelve-thousand-year struggle with demonic forces before prevailing and restoring a pristine world. Emphasizing truth-telling, purity, and reverence for nature, the religion demanded that humans choose sides in the struggle between good and evil. Those whose good conduct indicated their support for Ahuramazda would be rewarded in the afterlife. Others would be punished. The religion of the Achaemenid and Sasanid Persians, Zoroastrianism may have spread within their realms and influenced Judaism, Christianity, and other faiths.   *(p. 101)*

Zulu   A people of modern South Africa whom King Shaka united in 1818.   *(p. 499)*

Index

Abbas I, Shah, 421, 422, 424

Abbasid Caliphate, 192, 199; literature of, 187–188; political fragmentation of, 188–189 *and map*; Mongols and, 272, 276

Abbas (uncle of prophet Muhammad), 187

Abbots, 212, 213, 215. *See also* Monasteries

Abd al-Rahman III, 191

Abdul Hamid II, Sultan, 529, 532

Abdul Mejid, Sultan, 524–525

Abolitionists, 572. *See also* Slave trade, African, end of; in Americas, 475–477; in Cuba, 475, 476–477, 514; in Dutch colonies, 514; in French colonies, 460, 471, 514; Great Britain and, 476, 503; in Venezuela, 471

Abortion, 613–614; in Soviet Union, 624–626

Abraham (Ibrahim), 76, 182, 184

Abu Bakr, 182, 185, 186, 195, 296

Abu Dulaf al-Khazraji, 196, 246

Academy of Athens, 111

Achaean League, 116

Achaeans, 71, 72. *See also* Greece, ancient

Achaemenids, 96, 157. *See also* Persian Empire

Acheh Sultanate, 427, 429, 430

Acosta, Gladys, 694–696

Acropolis, in Athens, 105, 109

Addams, Jane, 613

Aden, 309–310, 313, 353, 354, 415

Adena people, 255

Administration. *See also* Bureaucracy; Civil service; Government; Mesopotamian, 16, 17; ancient Egypt, 27–28; early China, 43; Assyrian Empire, 74–75; Carthage, 84; Persian Empire, 99–100; Hellenistic era, 114; Gupta India, 125; Roman Empire, 135, 136, 137, 139, 151; Han China, 146, 148, 151; Islamic caliphate, 187; Andean, 256, 261, 263; Mongol, 278; Delhi India, 305; Ottoman, 417; colonial Americas, 462, 471; and empire, 451, 575–577, 582

Adowa, Battle of (1896), 582

Aedisius, 172–173

Aegean Sea region, 68–72

Aeschylus, 111

Afghanistan (Afghans), 68, 277, 303, 424, 426, 441, 531, 716; Bactria, 117, 121; Kushan, 159, 170; Soviet war in, 693, 696, 699, 700; Taliban regime in, 171 *(illus.)*, 717–718

Afonso I (Kongo), 349–352

Africa, tropical: *See also* Mali; Sub-Saharan Africa; chronology (1200–1500), 299; environment, 297

Africa (Africans). *See also* East Africa; North Africa; Southern Africa; Sub-Saharan Africa; West Africa; *and specific countries and peoples;* foragers in, 6; agricultural revolution in, 20; climatic zones of, 164

(map); trans-Saharan trade and caravan routes in, 164 *(map);* Pygmy people in, 298; (1200–1500), 302 *(map);* gold trade of, 343, 348; ivory trade, 161, 349 *and illus.;* Portuguese exploration of, 343–345, 346 *(map),* 349–352, 429; Atlantic system and, 405–407; New World foods in, 409; Christianity in, 349, 500, 503; chronology (1795–1889), 501; in nineteenth century, 502 *(map);* "legitimate" trade in, 503; new states in, 499–500, 502 *(map);* European imperialism in, 500, 502 *(map),* 503, 570, 577–583, 603; in British colonies, 513, 514; Christian missionaries in, 582–583; chronology (1869–1908), 571–572; World War I and, 603; World War II and, 632, 646; mining boom in, 626, 638; decolonization of, 670; population growth in, 704 *(illus.),* 705; development aid to, 722; HIV/AIDS in, 724 *and illus.;* women's issues in, 725; Afropop music, 730

African-Americans: *See also* Slaves (slavery), African; as abolitionists, 475; after Civil War, 478, 562; World War I and, 603

African languages, 393, 402, 430, 431

African National Congress, 646, 678, 715

African slaves. *See* Slaves (slavery), African

African slave trade. *See* Slave trade, African

Afrikaners, 510–511 *and illus.,* 580, 581

Afterlife, belief in: Stone Age, 7; ancient Egyptian, 26, 29–30, 34; Chinese, 144; Kushite, 49; Celtic, 53; Muslim, 182; mystery cults and, 139; Moche, 258, 260; of Mound-building cultures, 255

Agamemnon (Mycenae), 70, 71

Agitator, The (Rivera), 656 *(illus.)*

Agriculture, 58–59. *See also* Farmers; Irrigation; Landowners; Peasants; Plows; Rural societies; *and specific crops;* Neolithic, 8–10, 13; swidden (shifting cultivation), 8, 246, 298; Mesopotamia, 14, 15; ancient Egypt, 25; and cities, in early civilizations, 32; early China, 40–41, 148; Assyrian Empire, 97; India, 9, 32, 190, 298; Olmec, 57; Celts, 73; Chavín, 77; Greece, 8, 18, 104, 105, 106; Roman Empire, 150; Southeast Asia, 20; imperial China, 142, 150, 236, 287; Silk Road Trade and, 212; Islam, 192; Spain, 191; tropical Africa, 20, 168; medieval Europe, 209, 218; Mesoamerican, 245, 246, 251, 253; Andean, 256, 257, 258–259; Il-khanate, 277; Korea, 290; North American desert, 254; Japan, 293; tropical, 298; sugar plantations, 228, 345, 349; climate change and, 375; Russian, 447; Columbian exchange, 407, 408–409; Ottoman, 417; Chinese, 439, 445, 533, 538, 699; Industrial Revolution and, 481–482; British India, 506, 507; irrigation for, 500,

507, 508, 579, 586, 593, 646; tropical, 593; global environment and, 592; mechanization of, 617; Soviet collectivization of, 620–622, 663, 672; Green Revolution in, 666; government subsidies to, 722

Aguinaldo, Emilio, 589

Ahmadabad, 311

Ahmed III, Sultan, 420

Ahmose (Egypt), 66

Ahuramazda, 101, 102–103

AIDS (Acquired Immune Deficiency Syndrome), 724 *and illus.*

Ain Jalut, Battle of (1260), 192, 274

Aircraft (aviation): invention of, 614–615; World War II, 631, 632 *(illus.),* 634, 636–637; in Latin America, 658; September 11 attacks (2001), 702–703

Aircraft carriers, 631, 634

Air pollution, 490, 616, 617, 709–710

A'isha, 185, 195

Ajanta, cave temples at, 126 *(illus.)*

Akbar (India), 354, 425, 426

Akhenaten (Amenhotep IV, Egypt), 66–67

Akkad (Akkadian Empire), 16, 22, 23 *(illus.),* 85

Akkadian language, 14–15, 22, 65, 76

Aksum, 172 *and illus.*

Al-Andalus (Islamic Spain), 190, 220

Alaska, Russians in, 446, 450

Ala-ud-din Khalji, Sultan, 305, 313

Al-Bakri, 221

Albania (Albanians), 597, 672, 716

Alchemists, 224, 288

Aldrin, Edwin E. "Buzz," 674

Alexander III (Russia), 561, 583

Alexander II (Russia), 527, 583; freeing of the serfs by, 531, 532, 562

Alexander I (Russia), 529, 530 *(illus.),* 532

Alexander the Great, 113–114, 127; in Punjab, 123–124; Mausoleum of (Alexandria), 116

Alexandria, 113, 114, 137, 220; Christianity in, 172, 173, 194; Library of, 116; patriarch of, 173, 194, 352

Alexius Comnenus, 204, 206, 220

Algeria, 166, 190, 238, 241, 715; France and, 457, 500, 677

Al-Hajj Ahmed, 312

Ali, Caliph, 180–181, 183, 185, 186, 190

Ali (Muhammad's son-in-law), 421

Ali-Quli Jubbadar, 422 *(illus.)*

Al-Jabarti, Abd al-Rahman, 522–524

Al-Kashi, Ghiyas al-Din Jamshid, 279

Allah (Islamic god), 182, 184, 185, 199

Allawi, Ayad, 718

Allende, Salvador, 692

Alliances: early modern Europe, 382–383, 468; World War I, 597, 600 *(map),* 601, 605, 606–607

Allies, World War II, 633 *(map)*, 634, 636 *(map)*, 659, 669, 670. *See also* Axis (World War II)

Alpacas. *See* Llamas and alpacas

Alphabet: Ugarit cuneiform, 65; Phoenician, 80, 104, 176; Greek, 104–105, 175; Armenian, 172; Cyrillic, 206, 216; Tibetan, 232; Arabic, 312; Latin, 610 *(illus.)*, 612

Al Qaeda (Islamic organization), 713

Alsace and Lorraine, 558, 560, 606

Al-Umari, 342

Amarna, 67

Amenhotep IV (Akhenaten, Egypt), 66–67

American Revolution, 462–465; 513; France and, 464, 466, 478; frontiers and taxes, 462; military course of, 464; republican institutions in, 464–465

American system of manufactures, 487. *See also* United States, Industrial Revolution in

Americas, colonial. *See* Brazil, colonial; British North America; Latin America, colonial

Americas, the (New World; Western Hemisphere). *See also* Andean civilizations; Caribbean region; Central America; Latin America; Mesoamerica; North America; agriculture in, 20; animal domestication in, 21; migrations to, 53; chronology, 57; and Eastern Hemisphere compared, 59; Iberian conquest of, 354–356; small pox in, 355 *and illus.*, 356; new foods from, 408–409; abolition of slavery in, 475–477; chronology (1754–1804), 463; Enlightenment ideas in, 462; European immigrants in, 393, 409, 487, 494–495, 562; women's rights and social justice in, 477–478; race and nationality in, 543

Amerindians (native peoples), 244, 372, 562. *See also* Andean civilization; Mesoamerica; *and specific peoples;* hunting of, 10; Northern peoples, 247, 254–256; maritime exploration by, 338; Spanish conquest and, 354–356; Pacific voyages of, 338; disease and death among, 354, 355 *and illus.*, 356, 361, 387; in Caribbean, 354, 356; traveling in France, 376–377; Christianity and, 399; fur trade and, 398–399 *and illus.*; in colonial Latin America, 387, 388, 391, 392, 393; *mestizos* (mixed race), 393 *(illus.)*, 394–395, 653; horses of, 408; in colonial North America, 397, 398–399; labor of, 391, 542, 543; American Revolution and, 462; hunting by, 399, 408, 563; census of, 542, 543; in Mexico, 473, 591, 653, 678

Amnesty International, 724

Amon, 29, 30, 49, 50, 66

Amorites, 16

Amritsar (India) Massacre (1919), 648

Amsterdam, 373, 374 *and illus.*

Amur River, 442, 447, 534

Anahita, 184 *(illus.)*

Anasazi, 254–255

Anatolia (modern Turkey), 96, 172, 225, 417, 520, 610. *See also* Hittites; Ionia; Turkic

(Turkish) peoples; Çatal Hüyük, 11, 13; in Late Bronze Age, 62, 64, 65 *(map)*, 68, 73; Greeks in, 71–72, 113, 114; Lydian kingdom, 107, 109, 170; Christianity in, 138, 139; Crusades and, 220; Mongols and, 281

Ancestor worship, 11, 134 *(illus.)*, 443. *See also* Confucianism; in early China, 42, 44, 45, 58–59; in imperial China, 142, 143, 148

Andean civilizations (Andean region), 256–263, 256 *(map)*; chronology (3500–500 B.C.E.), 39; Chavín, 54 *(map)*, 56–58, 82 *(illus.)*, 83; Chimú, 257, 258; chronology (200–1525), 247; clans (ayllus) in, 256–257, 260–261; cultural response to environment of, 256–257, 258; Inca, 256 *(map)*, 259–263, 355–356; Moche, 257–258, 260, 261 *(illus.)*, 262; Tiwanaku, 258–259; Wari, 258, 259

Angkor, 299

Anglicanism (Church of England), 368 *(map)*, 380, 381, 503; in Africa, 582, 645

Anglo-Dutch Wars (1653–1658), 383, 403

Angola, 406–407, 409, 580, 678, 716

Angra Mainyu, 101

Animals: *See also* Camels; Cattle; Horses; Hunting; Llamas and alpacas; domestication of, 8, 9–10, 89–90, 170; ritual sacrifice of, 18, 19, 106, 144

An Lushan rebellion (755–763), 229, 231

Anna Comnena, 206

Annan, Kofi, 716

Anne of Brittany, 334

Antigone (Sophocles), 112

Antigonids, 114, 115–116 *and map*

Antioch, 114, 137, 172, 194; and Crusades, 192, 220, 222

Apartheid, in South Africa, 678, 680, 731

Apollo, 105, 106, 108 *(illus.)*

Appeasement of Nazi Germany, 628–629

Aqueducts, 139, 140 *(illus.)*, 146

Arab empires. *See* Caliphates (Arab Caliphates); Sasanid Empire (Iran) *and specific empire*

Arabia (Arabian Peninsula), 161, 177, 185, 429, 519, 603. *See also* Arabs; Yemen; before Muhammad, 181–182; pastoralism in, 181, 298; Indian Ocean trade and, 307, 309–310

Arabian Nights, The, 188, 238

Arabic language, 187, 189, 296, 307, 312; and conversion to Islam, 188, 191, 266

Arabic script, 421

Arabic numerals, 126

Arab Rebellion (1916), 612

Arabs: *See also* Arabia; Islam; Middle East; Muslim(s); Indian Ocean trade and, 159; Sasanid Empire and, 186, 187; Berber revolts against, 189; as traders, 189, 427, 504; Jewish hostilities, 612, 684–686 *and map*

Arafat, Yasir, 686

Aragon, 335, 343

Aramaic language, 14, 76, 266

Arawak people, 342, 354

Arches, 325; Roman use of, 139, 140 *(illus.)*

Archilochus, 107

Architecture. *See also* Construction materials and techniques; Housing; *and specific building types (e.g: church buildings; mosques; pyramids; temples);* Chavín, 56, 57; Byzantine, 206 *and illus.*; Japanese, 241; Maya, 247, 249 *(illus.)*; Toltec, 251; Anasazi, 254–255; Chinese in Beijing, 285; Egyptian, 48; Islamic, 311–312; Russian, under Peter the Great, 449, 450; in Cairo, 598 *and illus.*; International style, 615

Ardashir, 157

Argentina, 665; British investment in, 476–477; *and illus.*, 550, 591, 657; immigration to, 476, 552, 656, 658; livestock in, 408, 591, 657; manufacturing in, 638; railroads in, 591, 657; Depression of 1930s in, 623, 659; after 1930, 659–660; and Brazil compared, 656–657, 658, 660; military rule in (1976–1992), 693; economic growth in, 719; trade agreement and, 720, 721 *(map)*

Arimoto, Yamagata, 565

Aristocracy (nobility). *See also* Elite class; Landowners; ancient Egyptian, 27 *(illus.)*; early Chinese, 41, 44; Assyrian, 73; Carthaginian, 84; Greek, 106, 109; imperial China, 144, 148, 150, 226, 228, 283; Roman Empire, 134, 137, 150–151; Sasanid, 184 *(illus.)*; Byzantine, 204; medieval Europe, 208, 209, 212; Mesoamerican, 244, 246, 249; Andean, 257, 262; Aztec, 252, 253; Japanese, 241, 242, 291, 292–293; Mongol, 277, 283; late medieval Europe, 317, 334; European bourgeoisie and, 374–375; and monarchy, in Europe, 379; taxation of, in Europe, 383, 385; French Revolution and, 465, 466, 467, 469; Qing China, 441, 444, 539; Russian (boyars), 447, 450, 529, 562

Aristophanes, 111, 112

Aristotle, 187, 191, 221, 328, 329, 370, 371

Aritomo, Yamagata, 564

Arjuna, 122, 125

Armed forces. *See also* Cavalry; Infantry; Military, the; Navy; Warrior class, *and specific wars;* chariots and, 40; Assyrian Empire, 73–74; Carthaginian, 84; Persian Empire, 96; Greek hoplites, 105, 106, 107, 110, 113; Gupta India, 124; Chinese, 145 *(illus.)*, 225, 234–235; Roman, 139; Arab Muslim, 185, 186–187, 204, 209; medieval Europe, 281; Aztec, 251, 252 *(illus.)*; Mongol, 281; Delhi sultanate, 306; Spanish conquistadors, 354–356; early modern Europe, 382, 383; Ottoman, 415 (*See also* Janissaries); Safavid, 424; China, 432, 534, 537–538; French Revolution, 467, 468; American Revolution, 464; Russian modernization, 450, 451, 530; Blacks in U.S. Civil War, 475–476; Latin American independence and, 472; Egypt, 520; Ethiopia, 500; British India, 504, 506–507; Crimean War and, 528, 530; Japan, 564, 630; New Imperialism and, 572, 575, 581, 585–586; World War I, 597, 600; World War I, 601–602 *and illus.*, 604, 605; Guomindang (China), 609–610, 630; Mexican civil war, 654; Nazi Wehrmacht, 628, 629, 631–632,

634, 638; Soviet Red Army, 607, 632; Vietnam, 673

Armenians, 172, 374, 606, 607; in Safavid Iran, 422, 424; Ottomans and, 531, 597, 603

Armillary sphere, 234, 235 (illus.), 278, 279 (illus.), 284

Armor, body, 225, 232, 235; European knights, 210, 221, 331, 333; conquistadors, 354, 356

Armstrong, Neil A., 674

Arrow War (1856–1860), 535 (map), 538

Art and artists. See also Paintings and specific artist; ancient Egyptian, 48 (illus.); Cretan frescoes, 69, 70 (illus.) in; rock art, 4, 165–166 and illus., 168; Aztec, 252 (illus.); Renaissance, 330–331; London tenements, 491 (illus.); Mexican Revolution and, 655, 656, (illus.)

Arthashastra (Kautilya), 124

Articles of Confederation (United States), 465

Artillery, 333, 530, 534, 581. See also Cannon

Artisans (craftspeople), 492. See also specific crafts; Mesopotamian, 15; Neolithic, 14, 24; Kushite, 49; Olmec, 55; Assyrian, 75; Indian, 124; tanning/leather working, 119, 301, 310; Chinese, 156; Tiwanaku, 259; Inca, 262; Kievan Russian, 272; European guilds, 324, 328; African, 349 (illus.); apprenticeship and, 378; slaves as, 402; in Safavid Iran, 422; Ottoman glassmakers, 416 (illus.); East Asian, 434, 436 and illus.

Aryas, 119, 120, 121

Asante kingdom, 406, 581

Ashikaga shogunate (Japan), 293

Ashoka (India), 124, 171

Ashurbanipal, library of, 75

Ashur (god), 64, 73

Asia (Asians): See also Central Asia; East Asia; East Indies; Southeast Asia; agriculture in, 20; trade and communication routes, 210 (map); tropical, chronology (1206–1500), 299; as immigrant laborers, 494, 513–516, 562, 708; chronology (1862–1905), 571–572; New Imperialism in, 571–572, 583, 586–587, 589 (map); chronology (1931–1949), 621; World War II in, 632, 634, 636 (map); decolonization of, 669; chronology (1975–1989), 691; economic expansion in (1970s–1990s), 690, 696–699; population in (1730–2050), 704 (illus.); financial collapse in (1998), 719; trade agreement in (APEC), 721 (map); global pop culture and, 729

Askia Muhammad, 313

Assam, 511. See also Vietnam (Vietnamese)

Assassins (Shi'ite sect), 278

Assembly: in Athens, 109; in Carthage, 84; in Rome, 131

Assembly-line manufacture, 439, 613, 616

Assembly of Notables (France), 460, 466

Assyrian Empire (Neo-Assyrian Empire), 49, 81; administration, 74–75; chronology, 63–64; conquests of, 73–74, 80; decline and fall of, 85–87, 96; god and king in, 73, 75; language of, 64, 72–75, 76; mass deporta-

tion in, 74; military in, 73–74, 75; society and culture, 75

Astarte, 79, 81

Astrolabe, 234, 278, 343

Astronomy, 440; Mesopotamian, 24; Assyrian, 75; Chinese, 233–234, 235 (illus.), 283, 294; Copernican, 370–371; Inca, 262; Islamic, 195, 278–279, 284

Aswan Dam (Egypt), 579, 682

Atahualpa (Inca), 356

Aten (sun-god), 66–67

Athens, 105, 107, 108–109, 116. See also Greece, ancient; democracy in, 109, 111; navy of, 110; Peloponnesian War and, 113

Atlantic Ocean: See also Columbus, Christopher

Atlantic Ocean, exploration of (before 1500), 339, 341–342

Atlantic trading system, 348, 388, 403–409. See also Slave trade, African; Africa and, 405–407; capitalism and mercantilism, 403–404; Columbian exchange, 407–409; Great Circuit and Middle Passage, 404–405

Atman (self), 119, 121

Atomic bombs: See also Nuclear arms; dropped on Japan (1945), 634, 635 (illus.), 636 (map), 637, 674

Atoms, pre-Socratic theory of, 107

Augustus (Octavian), 133, 136, 139, 148, 151

Aurangzeb, Sultan, 426

Auschwitz death camp, 638

Australia, 10, 430, 457, 581; aboriginal peoples of, 512, 513; immigration to, 513, 516, 552, 576, 605; drought in, 726

Austria-Hungary (1867–1918), 596; language and nationalism in, 557, 561; as conservative power, 558, 560–561; World War I and, 597, 601, 604, 605; end of, 606, 617

Austria (to 1867 and 1918 to present), 321, 382, 671; Habsburgs of, 379; French Revolution and, 467; Napoleonic France and, 468, 469; after World War I, 606; World War I debts of, 623; German annexation of (1938), 628

Authoritarianism (dictatorship): See also Fascism; populist, 468; in Japan, 629; in Latin America, 623, 626, 658–660, 692–693; in South Korea, 679; in former Soviet bloc, 714

Automobiles, 613, 616–617 and illus., 623, 697; air pollution and, 616, 617, 709

Avicenna (Ibn Sina), 221, 328, 329

Avignon, papacy in, 333

Axis (World War II), 629, 633 (map)

Ayllus (Andean clans), 256–257, 260–261

Ayrton, William, 564

Azerbaijan, 277, 531, 607

Azores, 342, 343, 344, 392

Aztecs (Aztec civilization), 248 (map), 251–254, 388, 393; aristocracy, 252, 253; and Inca compared, 262–263; tribute system, 252, 253, 254, 262, 263, 355; warriors in, 252 and illus.; Spanish conquest of, 354–355

Baal, 79, 85

Baba of Karo, 584–585

Babur (India), 425

Babylon, 16, 18, 19; Assyria and, 64, 73, 74, 86

Babylonia, 16, 64. See also Mesopotamia; Creation Myth, 13–14, 18, 19, 20–22; Neo-Babylonian kingdom and, 86, 96

Bactria, 117, 121

Baghdad, 191, 303, 728; and Abbasid caliphate, 187, 188, 192; Ottomans and, 420, 421, 520

Bahamas, 342, 354

Bahmani Empire (India), 304 (map), 305

Balance of power: in early modern Europe, 362, 382–383, 385; Congress of Vienna and, 469; industrialization and, 574–575; before World War II, 628; Cold War, 673

Balboa, Vasco Núñez de, 348, 356

Balfour, Sir Arthur, 604

Balfour Declaration (1917), 604, 612

Balkans: See also specific states; Ottoman Empire and, 412–413, 415, 416, 417, 529; Austria-Hungary and, 561; crisis in (1912–1913), 597; breakup of Yugoslavia, 701 (map), 702; ethnic cleansing in, 716

Balkh, 274, 277

Ball games, Mesoamerican, 249 (illus.), 254, 255

Baltic states. See also Estonia; Latvia; Lithuania; Soviet invasion of, 631; independence of, 701

Bananas, 161, 168, 298, 313, 407, 678

Bandung Conference (1955), 679, 682–683

Bangladesh, 675; flooding in, 663, 727 (illus.)

Banks, 483, 493, 607, 623; in medieval Europe, 324–325, 331; Dutch, 373, 385; Ottoman, 527, 528 and illus., 529

Bannerman (China), 534, 538

Bantu language, 164 (map), 169–170, 173, 430

Banu Sasan, 196

Barbarians: See also Nomadic peoples; Greeks and, 105, 112; imperial China and, 224, 230

Barley, 8, 13, 14, 104, 208

Barter (barter economy): Mesopotamia, 17; Roman Empire, 140; medieval Europe, 208; Aztec, 253

Basra, 161, 194

Bastille, storming of, 466, 467 (illus.)

Batista, Fulgencio, 678

Batu, Khan, 272, 275, 279, 281

Bayeaux Tapestry, 211, 218

Bay of Pigs invasion (1961, Cuba), 679

Beer, 10, 313, 373, 375

Beijing, 272, 282–283, 290, 538, 684; Forbidden City complex in, 283, 285, 287, 609; Manchus and, 432–433, 434, 440; Jesuits in, 440, 443 (illus.); Boxer Uprising (1900), 566, 608; Japanese seizure of (1937), 630; Tiananmen massacre (1989), 699

Beijing Women's Conference in (1995), 725

Belgium, 631, 670. See also Flanders; industrialization in, 482; cities in, 490; railroads in, 488; colonies of, 570, 578 (map), 579, 584, 676 (map); World War I and, 601, 606

Bell Telephone Laboratories, 728
Benedictine monasteries, 213, 215
Benedict of Nursia, 213
Bengal, 305, 312, 426, 504–505, 507, 647; famine in, 651, 663
Benin, 349 *and illus.*, 581
Bentham, Jeremy, 493
Berbers, 84, 162, 188, 300; invasion of Spain by, 186, 191, 209; revolts against Arab rule, 189
Bering, Vitus, 450
Berlin: bombing of, 637; airlift to, 672
Berlin Conference (1884–1885), 579
Berlin Wall, 672; dismantling of, 700 *and photo*
Bhagavad-Gita, 122–123, 125
Bharatiya Janata Party (India, BJP), 714
Biafra, 406, 663
Bible, the, 329, 371; Hebrew, 5, 77, 78, 79, 99; Muslim view of, 184, 185; Gutenberg, 330; Luther and, 366; in vernacular, 369
Biko, Steve, 680–682
Bill of Rights (England, 1668), 381
Bill of Rights (United States,1791), 464, 723
Bin, Laden, Usama, 713, 717–718
Bindusara, 124
Biological weapons, 717, 718
Birmingham Lunar Society, 480, 486
Birth control (family planning), 703, 704, 705–706; abortion, 613–614, 624–626
Birthrates (fertility rates), 552; (1970s–1990s), 703, 704–705, 708
Bishops, 139, 157, 173, 379–380; appointment (investiture) of, 212–213; councils of, 157, 211; African, 503, 582, 645
Bismarck, Otto von, 560; German unification and, 548, 558; imperialism and, 572, 579
Black Consciousness Movement, 681
Black Death, 317, 318, 320, 335, 359, 538. *See also* Bubonic plague
"Black Hole of Calcutta," 504
Black Sea region: colonies in, 322; Russia and, 449, 525 *(map)*; Crimean War (1853–1856), 527
Boccacio, Giovanni, 329, 330
Bodhisattvas, 121, 171 *(illus.)*, 172, 226, 231, 233
Boer war (1899–1902), 581
Bolívar, Simón, 471–472
Bolivia, 392; independence of, 471, 472
Bolshevik Revolution (October Revolution, Russia), 604–605, 606
Bolsheviks, 606–607, 622, 624. *See also* Communist Party, Soviet Union
Bombay, film industry in, 729
Bombay Presidency, 506
Bombs and bombing (explosives): *See also* Nuclear weapons; Weapons and military technology; Taiping Rebellion, 537; dynamite, 549; hand grenades, 602 *(illus.)*; World War II, 631, 632 *(illus.)*, 634, 637, 674; Persian Gulf War, 703; terrorist, 718
Bonaparte, Joseph, 471
Boniface VIII, Pope, 333
Bonner, Yelena, 699–700

Book of the Dead, Egyptian, 30
Books. *See* Libraries; Literature
Borneo, 427, 586
Bornu, 301, 302 *(map)*, 313
Borobudur temple complex, 160 *(illus.)*
Bose, Pramatha Nath, 648
Bosnia, 520, 597; and Herzegovina, 596, 716
Boston, colonial, 397, 462, 464 *(illus.)*
Boulton, Matthew, 480, 485, 487
Bourbon dynasty, 380 *and illus.*, 381, 382
Bourgeoisie, 373–375, 378, 379; French Revolution and, 465; Marx on, 554–556
Bourke-White, Margaret, 650, 652 *(photos)*
Bows and arrows (archers): Mesopotamian, 40; Hyksos, 66; Assyrian, 73; mounted warriors and, 159, 209; in chariots, 68; crossbows, 149, 225, 303, 331, 333, 340; English longbow, 333; flaming arrows, 235, 274, 288 *and illus.*; Malinke, 301; Mongol, 274; Amerindian, 255; Ottoman, 415
Boxer Uprising (1900, China), 565–566, 608
Boyle, Robert, 371
Bo Zhuyi, 231
Brahe, Tycho, 371
Brahmin class (Brahmin priests), 123, 127, 176; Vedic Age, 119, 120; Muslim elite and, 305
Brahmo Samaj (Divine Society), 509
Brazil, 348, 408, 471, 638, 665. *See also* Brazil, colonial; independence of, 472–473; abolition of slavery in, 475, 476, 478; coffee in, 492, 593, 657; rubber in, 593, 657, 659; Vargas regime in, 658–659; Argentina compared to, 656–657, 658, 660; Depression (1930s), 623, 658–659; military rule in, 692, 693; economic growth in, 719; populist leadership in, 714; Portugal and, 728; trade agreement and, 720, 721 *(map)*
Brazil, colonial, 348, 390 *(map)*, 403, 472; chronology (1540–1777), 389; sugar plantations in, 391, 392, 409, 514, *and illus.*; slaves and slave trade in, 388, 392, 400 *and illus.* 404, 406, 503, 514, 657
Brazza, Savorgnan de, 579
Brazzaville Conference (1944), 677
Brest-Litovsk, Treaty of (1918), 605
Bretton Woods Conference (1946), 670–671
Brezhnev, Leonid, 699, 700
Britain: *See also* England; Great Britain; Celts in, 51, 53; Romans in, 133; medieval, 208, 211
Britain, Battle of (1940), 631
British East India Company (EIC), 444, 462, 511; in India, 496, 498, 504–506, 507
British Empire (British colonies) 510–516, 560, 583. *See also* British North America; Great Britain; India, under British rule; *and specific colonies;* Caribbean colonies, 399–400, 401–402, 514, 515; African colonies, 510–511, 578 *(map)*, 579–581; trade and, 482, 495, 511–512; Australia and New Zealand, 457, 512–513, 514, 516; chronology (1763–1877), 501; in Asia, 588 *(map)*; policies and shipping, 511–512; labor migrations to, 513–516; New Imperialism and, 570, 574 *(illus.)*, 575, 576

(illus.), 577, 583; decolonization of, 676 *(map)*, 677, 678; English language and, 730
British Navy, 462, 468, 482, 498; end of slave trade and, 476, 503; Japan and, 564; Ottoman Empire and, 519, 524; Qing China and, 534, 535 *(map)*; in World War I, 602–603; in World War II, 631
British North America, 387, 396–398, 401. *See also* American Revolution; Canada; chronology (1607–1763), 389; Middle Atlantic, 398; New England, 397; South, 396–397; immigrants to, 409
British South Africa Company, 581
British Women's Emigration Association, 577
Bronze, 1–2; in Middle East, 23; in Indus Valley civilizations, 32, 33 *(illus.)*; in early China, 41, 42 *and illus.*, 43, 58, 148; iron's advantages over, 62, 92, 173; in Aegean Sea region, 71; in imperial China, 235, 287
Bronze Age. *See* Late Bronze Age
Bruges, 219, 322
Brunei Sultanate, 287, 427
Brutus (the Liberator), 131
Bubonic plague, 204, 281, 320; in Asia, 228, 237, 275–276, 284; in Crimea, 276, 280; Black Death in Europe, 317, 318, 320, 335, 359, 538
Buddha (Siddhartha Gautama), 120–121, 122, 126 *(illus.)*, 533
Buddhism (Buddhists), 124, 152, 157, 717; *bodhisattvas,* 121, 171 *(illus.)*, 172, 226, 231, 233; Central Asians and, 159; in East Asia, 177, 241; enlightenment *(nirvana)* in, 120–121, 171–172, 230; Mahayana, 121, 123, 172, 225–226, 232, 241; missionaries, 171; monasteries, 121, 127, 226, 229–230, 231, 312; Mongols and, 276, 282; Muslims in India and, 312; nuns, 185, 191, 230; pilgrims, 126, 127, 171, 232, 266; in Song China, 233, 236, 238, 242; spread of, 158 *(map),* 171–172; Theravada, 121, 171, 185, 226; Zen (Chan, Son), 236, 290, 293; in Japan, 437; Tibetan, 439–440
Buenos Aires, 472, 476–477, 657, 706
Buffalo hunters, Amerindian, 408, 563
Bukhara, 154, 156, 189, 232
Bulgaria, 597, 672, 701, 720
Bureaucracy (bureaucrats): *See also* Administration; Civil Service; ancient Ur, 16; ancient Egypt, 27, 28; Mycenaean Greece, 71; imperial China, 236, 239; Inca, 261, 263; colonial Latin America, 391; Qing China, 518; Ottoman, 416, 524–526, 528 *(illus.)*, 529; British India, 507, 647; Russian, 532; census and, 542–543; expansion of, after World War I, 613; Soviet Russia, 607, 671, 699
Burials (burial practices), 94. *See also* Tombs; Neolithic, 11; Egyptian, 23, 43; Kushite, 49; Celtic, 53; Mycenaean, 70; Carthaginian, 85; Chinese, 145 *(illus.)*; Russian, 218; northern Amerindian, 255, 256; Chimú, 258; Maya and Moche compared, 260–261 *and illus.*
Burma (Myanmar), 511, 583, 646, 675; Japanese occupation of, 651, 663

Bush, George H. W., 703
Bush, George W., 718, 720, 727
Business (companies). *See also* Capitalism;
    Corporations; Industries; Monopoly;
    Trade; government and, 383; joint-stock,
    374 *and illus.*, 429, 431, 483, 532; slave
    trade and, 403, 405, 406; chartered, 403,
    493; Great Depression and, 623; Japanese
    (*zaibatsu*), 434, 565, 609, 697
Buyid family, 188, 191
Byblos, 80, 81
Byrd, Richard, 614
Byron, Lord (George Gordon Noel), 524
Byzantine Empire (Byzantium), 203–206,
    219, 220; Nestorian Christians and, 157;
    challenges to, 203–204; *culture of*, 206;
    Kievan Russia and, 177, 217 *(map)*; society
    and urban life, 204–206; end of, 267, 282,
    413
Byzantium, 141, 177, 216, 281. *See also*
    Constantinople; Istanbul

Cabral, Pedro Alvares, 345, 348
Cahokia, 255–256
Cairo, 190, 192, 500, 529, 598 *(illus.)*
Cakchiquel of Guatemala, 387
Calcutta, under British rule, 504, 505, 506,
    648
Calendars: Egyptian, 31; Olmec, 56; Chi-
    nese, 233–234, 235 *(illus.)*; Maya, 249–
    250; Mongol, 278, 283, 285; Korean, 290;
    Gregorian, 371; Qing China, 440, 442
Calicut, 310, 341, 353, 354. *See also* Calcutta
Caliphates (Arab Caliphates), 186–192;
    Abbasid, 187–189 *and map*, 192, 199, 272;
    decline of, 191–192; Fatimid, 189 *(map)*,
    190, 191, 192; Umayyad, 186, 187, 189
    (map), 190–191
Calixtus II, Pope, 267
Calles, Plutarco Elías, 655
Calvin, John, 366
Calvinism, 366, 368 *(map)*, 379, 380
Cambay, 310, 311
Cambodia, 299–300, 730
Cambridge University, 328
Cambyses (Kambujiya), 96
Camel, Battle of the (656), 185, 195
Camels: domestication of, 68, 90, 167;
    caravan trade and, 166–167, 181–182
Canaan (Canaanites), 77, 79, 80. *See also*
    Phoenicia
Canada, 562, 589, 674; French fur trade in,
    387, 389, 398–399 *and illus.*; British
    (Dominion of), 513; railroads in, 550;
    immigration to, 552, 576, 605; indepen-
    dence of, 581; women's rights in, 477, 613;
    in World Wars, 602 *(illus.)*, 634; and
    NAFTA, 720, 721 *(map)*
Canals, 412. *See also* Irrigation; Suez Canal;
    in Egypt, 31; in China, 142, 145, 147 *and
    illus.*, 149, 225, 227, 228, 445, 533; in
    Europe, 374; in Russia, 450; in Britain, 482,
    485, 490; Industrial Revolution and, 482,
    485, 487, 490; in United States, 487;
    Panama, 592, 593, 594, 692
Canary Islands, 344, 347

Candace (Nubia), 50
Cannon, 294, 325, 334, 364, 382, 424, 431,
    549; in China and Korea, 287, 288; on
    warships, 340; conquistador, 356;
    Ottoman, 412, 413; artillery, 333, 530,
    534, 581
Canoes: of Southeast Asian peoples, 214;
    Polynesian, 338, 341 *(illus.)*
Canons (canon law), 211, 212
Canterbury Tales (Chaucer), 321, 324, 329
Canton (Guangzhou), 227, 228, 535, 536, 609
Canton trading system, 444–445, 533, 534
Cape Colony (South Africa), 510–511,
    580–581
Cape Verde, 344, 345, 392
Capitalism, 407, 556. *See also* Free trade; and
    mercantilism, 403–404; laissez faire, 493,
    494, 497, 662; global, 550; Marx's view of,
    553; Communism and, 669, 671–672, 673
Caracalla (Rome), 138
Caracol, 244
Caramansa, 348–349
Caravan trade and routes, 282. *See also* Silk
    Road; Trans-Saharan trade and caravan
    routes; Arab camels and, 181–182; cities
    and, 212, 234, 289; Mali, 301; Yemen and,
    233
Caravel (ship), 343, 344 *(illus.)*
Cárdenas, Lázaro, 655–656
Caribbean region (West Indies), 390 *(map)*.
    See also specific island; agriculture in, 9;
    Arawak voyages in, 342; Spanish conquest
    of, 354, 356; disease in, 354, 355, 356, 387;
    chronology (1500–1680), 389; French
    colonies in, 399, 400, 404, 462, 514; sugar
    plantations in, 399–402, 409, 492; slavery
    in, 399–402, 404, 492, 514; Indian immi-
    grants in, 494, 514, 515; United States'
    intervention in (1904–1914), 563, 591–592;
    population in (1730–2050), 704 *(illus.)*
Carib people, 342
Carpet manufacture, in Iran, 424
Carrió de la Vandera, Alonso, 394
Carter, Jimmy, 692, 693
Carthage (Carthaginians), 61, 82–85, 151;
    trading empire of, 82–84; war and religion
    in, 84–85; wars with Rome, 85, 135, 137
Casement, Roger, 580
Cassava, 354, 409
Castile, 335, 343
Castro, Fidel, 678–679, 690, 692
Çatal Hüyük, 11, 13
Catapults, 113, 134, 143; Mongol, 274, 288,
    291
Catherine of Aragon, 379
Catherine the Great (Russia), 450–451, 453
Catholic Church (Catholicism), 365–366,
    369. *See also* Jesuits; Papacy; Protestant
    Reformation and, 365–366, 368 *(map)*,
    369; European monarchies and, 379–380,
    381; Inquisition of, 371, 379; in colonial
    Latin America, 391, 393; in China, 452;
    French Revolution and, 465, 467, 468; in
    Africa, 503; in Mexico, 654, 656; in Poland,
    452, 638, 700; in Yugoslavia, 716; English
    used in, 730

Cattle (cattle herders), 27. *See also* Livestock;
    domestication of, 9, 10, 89, 90, 219; of
    pastoralists, 21; in Mesopotamia, 31, 37;
    oxen and plows, 8, 14, 90, 119, 318; Saha-
    ran peoples and, 165–166 *and illus.*, 298
Caucasus region, 527, 529, 531; Soviet Union
    and, 607, 631, 714
Cavalry (horsemen): *See also* Horses;
    Knights; Assyrian, 73, 95; Macedonian,
    113; Chinese, 149, 150, 340; stirrups and,
    209–210; Mongolian, 274, 291; Conquista-
    dor, 354, 355, 356; Ottoman Turk, 415, 416;
    Safavid Iran, 420; Crimean War and, 528;
    Polish, 631
Cave paintings: Saharan rock art, 4, 165–166
    (illus.), 168; Buddhist, 126 *(illus.)*, 230
    (illus.)
Ceausescu, Nicolae, 701
Celtic peoples, 50–53, 318. *See also* Ireland;
    Scotland; Wales; chronology, 39; Druid
    priests of, 51, 53, 176; languages of, 50;
    religion of, 52–53; Roman conquest, 51, 52,
    53, 135; society of, 51–52; spread of, 50–51
Census, 78, 142, 542–544. *See also*
    Population
Central America, 720. *See also specific
    country*; United States' interventions in,
    591–592, 692–693
Central Asia, 288, 570, 593. *See also specific
    country and people*; and Silk Road, 154,
    155, 156, 159; Chinese trade with, 160;
    chronology (711–1036 C.E.), 183; Mamluk
    slaves from, 188; chronology (552–850
    C.E.), 227; stirrup invented in, 209, 210; in
    Mongols in, 192, 271–272, 277, 306; Tang
    China and, 225, 226, 228, 229 *and illus.*,
    231–232; chronology (1219–1453 C.E.),
    273–274; Turkic peoples of, 412, 424, 447;
    Qing China and, 440, 441 *(map)*; Russia
    and, 446, 531, 583, 588 *(map)*; Soviet
    Union and, 607, 714
Central Intelligence Agency (CIA), 678; Bay
    of Pigs invasion (1961) and, 679; Iran and,
    693
Centralization: *See* Authoritarianism (dicta-
    torship); Communist Party; European
    Community; Fascism; Monarchy
Ceramics: *See also* Pottery; Chinese porce-
    lain, 229, 275, 289; Hohokam, 254; mass
    production of, 235; Wari, 259; Dutch, 373
Cernunnos, 52 *and illus.*
Cerro Blanco, 257
Cetshwayo (Zulu), 580
Ceuta, 335, 343
Ceylon. *See* Sri Lanka (Ceylon)
Chaco Canyon culture, 254–255
Chaldean dynasty (Neo-Babylonia), 86, 96
Chamberlain, Neville, 628–629
Chamorro, Violeta, 693
Champa, 242, 274, 293. *See also* Vietnam
Champlain, Samuel de, 398
Chan Chan, 258
Chandra Gupta, 125
Chandragupta Maurya, 123–124
Chang'an, 142, 147, 151, 154; as Tang capi-
    tal, 225, 226, 227–228, 241

Chan (Zen) Buddhism, 226, 290, 293
Charcoal, 321; and ironmaking, 375, 486
Chariots, 68, 166, 219–220, 232; used in warfare, 23, 43, 66, 159
Charlemagne (Charles, King of the Franks), 202, 209, 212, 213
Charles I (England), 380–381
Charles Martel, 207
Charleston, colonial, 397
Charles V (Holy Roman Emperor), 379, 383
Charles VII (France), 334
Charles X (France), 469
Charter Oath (Japan,1868), 564
Chartist movement (England), 494
Chaucer, Geoffrey, 321, 324, 329
Chavín civilization, 54 (map), 56–58, 82 (illus.), 83
Chavín de Huantar, 56–57
Chechnya, 531, 723
Chemical industry, 549, 603, 635, 709
Chemical weapons (poison gas), 602, 638, 717
Chemistry, in ancient Egypt, 30
Cheras, 125
Chiang Kai-shek (Jiang Jieshi), 609–610, 629, 630; Chinese civil war and, 634–635
Chicago, 488, 552, 615
Chiefdoms: Celtic, 51; Mound builders, 255
Child labor, 481, 489, 492, 494, 553
Children. See also Education; Family; Schools; in Mesopotamia, 18; Carthaginian sacrifice of, 85; Greek infanticide, 112; education of, 378; Industrial Revolution and, 481, 489, 492, 494; decline in mortality of, 552; Victorian Age, 556; and Soviet system, 624; Rio de Janiero homeless, 689, 706
Chile, 720; colonial, 390 (map); independence of, 472; women's rights in, 477–478; copper mining in, 550; military rule in, 692, 693
Chimú, 257, 258
China, early, 5, 12 (map), 38–45; agriculture, 9, 40–41; ancestor worship, 42, 44, 45, 58–59; bronze, 41, 42 and illus., 43, 58; burial practices, 42; chronology, 39; divination, 42 (illus.), 43; elites of, 41, 43, 44; geography and resources, 38, 40–41; government and administration, 43, 44; monarchy, 41, 42, 43; political thought, 45; religion, 42, 43, 44; Shang period, 38, 40 (map) 41–43; slavery in, 45; women and family, 45; Zhou period, 38, 40 (map), 43–45
China, imperial, 142. See also Han Empire; Ming Empire; Qing Empire; Song Empire; Tang Empire and individual emperors; aristocracy in, 144, 148, 150, 226, 228, 283; Warring States period, 40 (map), 44, 141, 145, 148; Indian Ocean trade and, 159, 160, 161, 307; Silk Road and, 143 (map), 146, 149, 154; Buddhist pilgrims from, 171, 266; expansion of, 142, 143 (map), 146–147, 225, 226 (map); gentry in, 148, 236, 237, 238, 283; chronology (220–1279 c.e.), 227; nomadic peoples and, 142, 143, 150, 229, 233; population growth in, 142, 149,
151, 236, 284, 287, 317; science and technology of, 148–149, 224–225, 285, 287–288; Southern Song Empire, 233, 234 (map), 272, 283; Sui Empire, 224, 225; Tanggut Empire, 232, 272, 283; taxation in, 226, 230, 237, 284, 285; urban centers in, 147, 149, 151, 228–229, 236–237, 238 (illus.); writing system of, 240; Liao (Khitan) in, 233, 234, 239, 240; Mongol domination (Yuan Empire), 271, 272, 283–285, 287, 288, 289, 359; Portuguese and, 353; slavery in, 313; Yuan Empire, 272, 282–285, 288, 289; Indian Ocean exploration by (Zheng He), 268, 285–287 and map, 339, 340–341 and map; Malacca and, 311; Portuguese in (See Macao); chronology (1517–1796), 435; climate changes in, 455; population in, 359, 360 (illus.), 445, 451, 533, 703; agriculture in, 439, 445, 533; Dutch trade with, 436; footbinding of women in, 536, 630; Jesuit missionaries in, 376, 440, 442–443 and illus.; Korea and, 565; porcelain production by, 436, 439; opium trade in, 506, 507, 529, 533–534, 609; Zeng Guofan and, 539; France and, 534, 535 and map, 538, 539, 565; Heavenly Kingdom of Great Peace, 536–537, 538; revolution and war in (1900–1918), 608–609; warlords in, 609–610; Guomindang in, 609
China, Japan and, 226 (map), 232; invasion of Korea (1582) and, 433–434, 440; Boxer Uprising (1900), 565–566, 608; war between (1894–1895), 565, 589; Twenty-One Demands (1915), 609; Manchuria and, 629; war between (1937–1945), 630
China, People's Republic of, 665. See also Communist Party (China); Mao Zedong; civil war in (1945–1949), 634–635; famine in (1958–1961), 663–664; Great Leap Forward in, 663–664; Cold War and, 669, 672, 682, 683–684; United Nations and, 669; Taiwan and, 684; economic reform in, 698–699; foreign investment in, 698–699, 719; economic boom in, 714; family-planning in, 705–706; nuclear weapons testing by, 717; pollution and health in, 710; and U.S. invasion of Iraq (2003), 718; English in, 730; Hong Kong and, 730, 732
Chinampas (floating gardens), 246, 259
Chinese immigrants, 515, 516, 603; in Southeast Asia, 440; in Caribbean sugar plantations, 513, 514; to United States, 494, 538, 562; to Hawaii, 589
Chinese language, 41, 240, 284; script, 433
Chocolate, 253, 404, 407, 409, 444
Chola kingdom, 125
Cholera, 490, 508–509, 515
Christian Church. See also Ethiopian Christianity; Orthodox Christianity; Papacy; Byzantine Empire and, 141, 203; condemnation of usury by, 325; conversion of Slavs, 206, 211, 222, 281; European monarchies and, 334; investiture controversy, 212; medieval Europe (300–800), 211–215;
monasticism, 203, 208, 211, 213, 215; politics and, 212–213; schisms in, 204, 333
Christianity (Christians), 141. See also Bible, the; Christian Church; Crusades and specific churches, cults, denominations, and sects; rise of, 138–139, 152; Zoroastrianism and, 101, 157; Nestorian, 157, 159, 225; spread of, 172–173; Islamic Spain and, 191; origins of Islam and, 184, 185, 188; pilgrims, 213, 220, 221; and Holy Roman Empire, 202; monasteries, 203, 208, 211, 213, 215, 378, 380; spread of, 226–227, 257 (map), 266; Sasanid Empire and, 232–233; Muslim rivalry with, 316; persecution of Jews by, 326–328; theology and, 329; in colonial Americas, 347; Portuguese promotion of, in Africa, 343, 344, 349–352; Reformation and, 365–366, 369; in China, 443, 451; in Japan, 452; Ethiopian, 352, 500, 583, 644, 645; in Ottoman Empire, 525; and Islam, in Africa, 523, 583; in Israel, 722–723
Christian missionaries, 159, 177. See also Jesuits (Society of Jesus); Orthodox in Russia, 216; Slavs and, 206, 211, 215; in Ethiopia, 172–173; in Latin America, 391, 393; in Africa, 349–350, 500, 503; in China, 440, 443; Orthodox in Siberia, 447, 452; in Japan, 436–437; in Ottoman Empire, 526; in China, 534, 536, 538; in East Indies, 586; in India, 506; New Imperialism and, 572–573; in colonial Africa, 582–583, 644–645, 646
Chu nom writing, 240
Church buildings: Byzantine, 205–206 and illus., 216, 218; Ethiopian, 312; Gothic cathedrals, 325; monastic, 215; organs in, 214 and illus.; St. Peter's Basilica, 331
Churchill, Winston, 575, 631, 668, 687
Church of England. See Anglicanism
Cities and towns (urban areas). See also City-states; Urbanization; and specific cities and towns; Neolithic, 11, 13; Mesopotamian, 15, 17; Indus Valley, 32, 33; early China, 41, 43; Mesoamerican, 55; Assyrian, 75; Carthage, 83–84; Hellenistic, 113, 114; Egyptian, 28; Roman Empire, 135, 136–137, 151; imperial China, 147, 149, 151, 228–229, 236–237, 238 (illus.); Islamic, 194–195; along caravan routes, 234; Byzantine, 205–206; medieval Europe, 218, 219; Mesomerican, 252, 253–254; Kievan Russia, 272; Mongol seige of, 274; Gujarati, 310; late medieval Europe, 321–325; Indian Ocean trade and, 353; European bourgeoisie and, 373; colonial Latin America, 394–396; Ming China, 439; Ottoman and Iranian compared, 421–424; industrialization and, 488, 490, 491 (illus.); Ottoman Empire, 528; Chinese treaty ports, 534, 535–536, 565, 608, 609; railroads and, 550; automobile and, 616–617 and illus.; modern architecture in, 615; World War II bombing of, 634, 635 (illus.), 637, 638; colonial Africa, 644; global growth of, 706–707

Citizenship: Greek, 116; Roman, 135, 138; and nationality, 543, 557, 708; denied to German Jews, 628, 637

City-states: Mesopotamian, 15, 16, 17; Olmec, 55; Phoenician, 61, 74, 78, 80, 81–82; Greek (polis), 104–106, 110, 113, 116, 141; Islamic, 185; Arab, in North Africa, 190, 220; Maya, 244, 245, 247; Hausa, in Africa, 301, 302 (map), 500; East African, 307–309; northern Italy, 342–343 (See also Florence; Genoa; Venice); Malacca, 311, 312, 353, 415, 431, 511

Civil Code of 1804 (France), 468

Civilization(s): See also Andean civilizations; India; Islam; Mesopotamia, and specific civilizations; characteristics of, 5; river valley, 12 (map); Minoan, 62, 68–70, 86; Mycenean, 62, 70–72, 86; Olmec, 39, 53–56, 58, 245

Civil law, 259, 268. See also Laws (legal codes)

Civil service. See also Administration; Bureaucracy; Roman and Han Chinese compared, 151, 152; Song China, 236; Ottoman, 526; Indian, 507, 647, 649, 675

Civil wars: Roman, 136; Islamic caliphate, 180, 185; Inca, 262; Japan (late 1500s), 433; English (1642), 380–381; United States (1861–1865), 475–476, 500, 529, 592; Russian (1918–1921), 606–607; Mexican (1910–1920), 654; Argentine (1976–1983), 692; Chinese (1945–1949), 634–635, 683–684; African, 716

Cixi (China), 539, 540 (illus.), 563, 565, 608

Clans: Neolithic Age, 11; early China, 45; Chavín, 57; Aztec, 251, 252, 253; Andean ayllu, 256–257, 260–261

Clash of Civilizations and the Remaking of the World Order, The (Huntington), 722

Claudius (Rome), 133

Cleanliness, cult of, 615. See also Sanitation

Clemenceau, Georges, 606

Cleopatra (Egypt), 115

Clergy. See Priests (clergy)

Cleveland, Grover, 589

Climate and weather (climate change). See also Monsoons; Natural disasters; Rainfall; adoption of agriculture and, 8, 10; Saharan, 8, 10, 26, 169; Indus Valley and, 33, 34; Mediterranean, 101, 131; Moche region, 258; Korean science of, 290; tropical, 297–298; and population, to 1500, 359; Little Ice Age, 375, 439, 455; global warming, 666, 726–727

Clinton, William, 717, 722

Clocks: Chinese, 233–234, 235 (illus.); Korean, 290

Clothing: See also Textiles; Stone Age, 6; Roman, 83, 138; Chinese silk, 228; Aztec warrior, 252 (illus.); Mongol elites, 275; Russian westernization, 450; Ottoman reforms, 526, 528 (illus.); Turkish westernization, 610 (illus.), 612; for Islamic women, 725; global culture and, 732

CNN (Cable News Network), 728

Cnossos, 69, 70

Coal mining, 375, 488 (illus.), 492; and iron industry, 482 (map), 486; pollution from, 552

Coca, 57, 257

Cocoa (cacao), 253, 512, 580, 582, 593, 657

Codex Mendoza, 252 (illus.)

Coeur, Jacques, 334

Coffee, 404, 407, 417, 419, 430, 444, 512; in Brazil, 492, 593, 657; in East Africa, 642; New Imperialism and, 586, 592

Coins (coinage): invention of, 17, 92, 106, 170; in India, 127; devalued Roman, 140; gold, 187, 189, 190, 219, 344, 528; Islamic, 187, 189, 190, 195, 215, 219; imperial China, 283, 287; copper, 283, 439; silver, 187, 219

Coke, for ironmaking, 375, 486

Colbert, Jean Baptiste, 374, 375, 385

Cold War (Bipolar world; 1946–1991), 668–674. See also Superpowers; arms race in, 674; capitalism versus communism and, 670–672, 679; China and, 669, 672, 682, 683–684; chronology (1945–1975), 671; decolonization and (1947–1990), 668–669; Eastern Europe and, 671, 672, 699, 700–701; end of (1989–1991), 665, 690, 699–703; environment and, 669, 687; Japan and, 673, 683; Korean War and, 672–673; Middle East and, 684–686 and map; nonaligned nations and, 679, 682–683; Soviet Union crisis, 699–700; United Nations and, 668, 669–670; Vietnam War and, 673–674; collapse of Soviet bloc and 700–702 and map

Collectivized agriculture, in Soviet bloc, 620–622, 663, 672

Colleges. See Universities and colleges

Colombia, 592; independence of, 472

Colonies (colonization). See also British Empire; Decolonialization; Dutch colonies; Expansion; French colonies; Imperialism; Latin America, colonial New Imperialism and specific colonies and colonial powers; Phoenician, in Mediterranean, 80, 81 (map), 85, 86, 161; Greek, 105, 106, 161, (map); Black sea area, 322; European, in Indian Ocean states, 428 (map); European, in Asia, 588 (map)

Columbian exchange, 407–409

Columbus, Christopher, 268, 345, 346 and illus., 348; first Atlantic crossing of, 335, 347 (illus.), 354

Comanche people, 399, 408

Commercial and Political Atlas, The, 485

Communication, 706. See also Language(s); Telegraph; Writing; in ancient Egypt, 27–28; horses and, 68; in Assyrian Empire, 74; roads and, 91; in Asia (300 B.C.E.–1100 C.E.), 210 (map); across Indian Ocean, 218; in imperial China, 226, 227–228, 233, 282, 441; radio, 615, 627, 658, 728, 729; technological revolution in, 710; telecommunication, 722; digital, 729; global culture and, 726–729; Internet, 719, 728–729; television, 727, 728, 729

Communism: and appeasement of Nazi Germany and, 628; in Vietnam, 673, 675;

Cold War rivalry with capitalism, 669, 671–672, 673; in Cuba, 674, 690–691; in Afghanistan, 696; and collapse of Soviet-bloc, 700–701 (map)

Communist Manifesto (Marx and Engels), 553, 554

Communist Party (China), 609–610. See also China, People's Republic of; Mao Zedong; Long March (1934–1935) and, 629–630; civil war (1945–1949) and victory of, 634–635, 683–684; famine and, 663; Deng Xiaoping's reform of, 698–699

Communist Party (Soviet Union), 607, 622, 699. See also Soviet Union; famine and, 663; Gorbachev's perestroika and, 700, 701; fall of (1990), 700–702 and map

Companies. See Business (companies)

Company Men (India), 504–506

Compass, 234, 308, 343, 364

Computers, 708; Internet and, 719, 728–729

Concentration camps, 637–638 and illus.

Concordat of 1801 (France), 468

Concordat of Worms (1122), 212

Condorcet, Marie-Jean-Antoine, 542

Confederacy of Corinth, 113

Conference on Security and Cooperation in Europe (CSCE), 674

Confucianism, 46–47; in East Asia (other than China), 433, 437; fathers and, 44, 45, 143; gentry class and, 148; in Han China, 142–143, 146, 148, 151; in Liao Empire, 233; in Ming China, 285, 287; Neo-Confucianism and, 230, 236, 290; in Qing China, 442 (illus.), 443, 452, 536, 539; in Tang China, 227, 230; in East Asia (other than China), 177, 233, 238, 239, 241, 293; Mongols and, 282, 283; women and, 237

Confucius (Kongzi), 44, 142–143

Congo, 717. See also Kongo

Congo, Belgian, 580

Congo Free State, 579, 580; Europeans in, 584, 585–586

Congo River, 503, 593

Congress of People's Deputies (Soviet Union), 702

Congress of Vienna (1814–1815), 469

Congress Party (India), 714–715

Congress (United States), 475, 605, 692, 725

Conquistadors, 354–356, 392

Conservatism, 469; great powers of Europe, 558, 560–562; and fascism, 626

Conservative Party (Great Britain), 560, 613

Constantine (Rome), 141

Constantinople, 141, 205, 267, 282, 322. See also Istanbul; and Crusades, 220, 221, 222; patriarchs of, 204, 211, 216; Russia and, 216, 280, 281, 446, 449; Ottoman siege of, 413, 446

Constitutional Convention (1787, United States), 465

Constitutionalists (Mexico), 654

Constitutions, 679; French, 467, 469, 557; Haitian, 460; Mexican, 654, 655; Ottoman Empire, 529; Russian, 562; United States, 464–465, 476, 543, 613, 723; Brazilian, 659; Japanese, 683

Construction and building techniques, 385–386. *See also* Architecture; Engineering; Housing, *and specific buildings;* in Mesopotamia, 19, 23; in ancient Egypt, 27, 30, 31; in Harappa, 32; in China, 41, 43, 142; Olmec, 55; concrete (cement), 139, 146; Roman, 139, 140 *(illus.)*, 146; Mayan, 248; medieval churches, 210 *(illus.)*; Andean, 259, 262; Great Zimbabwe, 307–308, 309 *(illus.)*; Gothic cathedrals, 325; British in Argentina, 476–477 *and illus.*; Industrial Revolution and, 487

Consumer electronics, 697

Continental Congress, 464

Contra War (Nicaragua), 692, 696

Cook, James, 512

Cooke, William, 489

Copernicus, Nicholas, 278, 370–371

Copper, 550, 580, 692; African trade in, 169, 300, 301; American, 258; and Bronze Age cultures, 2, 23, 26, 32, 42–43, 62, 68, 71; coinage, 283, 439; Hungarian, 325

Córdoba (Argentina), 395

Cordoba (Spain), 191, 198

Corn. *See* Maize (corn)

Cornwallis, Charles, 464

Corporations, 549. *See also* Business; tax farming in Yuan China, 283; universities as, 328; foreign, in Mexico, 653, 656, 678; Japanese *zaibatsu*, 565, 609, 697; South Korean, 697, 698 *(illus.)*; transnational, 695, 709, 730

Corpus Juris Civilis (Body of Civil Law), 213

Cort, Henry, 486

Cortés, Hernán, 253, 354–355

Cosmopolitanism: in Middle East, 62–68; in Islamic caliphate, 187; in Tang China, 227; in Malacca, 311, 353; Ottoman, 416, 424

Cossacks, 412, 447

Costa Rica, 679

Cotton (cotton industry), 83. *See also* Spinning; Textiles; Islamic, 195; Andean, 257; Aztec, 253; Chinese, 228, 284, 287; Korean, 290; African, 301; Gujarati, 310; Caribbean, 354; slavery and, 492; Egyptian, 495, 500, 529, 577, 579; in Britain, 482 *(map)*, 484, 486, 494, 512; Indian, 404, 425, 486, 496, 506, 507–508, 592, 650; in United States, 475, 486, 490, 492, 529, 592; mechanization of, 486, 496, 508; Russian, 583; women in, 492

Cotton gin, 486

Council of bishops, 157, 211

Council of Clermont (1095), 220

Council of the Indies, 388

Council of Trent (1545), 366, 369

Crafts and craftspeople. *See* Artisans (craftspeople)

Creation myths: West African, 5; Babylonian, 13–14, 18, 19, 20–22; Egyptian, 25; Indian, 119

Credit, 237, 437. *See also* Banks

Creoles (mixed race), 471, 473, 543; in colonial Latin America, 392, 393

Crete, 322, 597; Minoan civilization, 62, 68–70

Crimea, 446; plague in, 276, 280

Crimean War (1853–1856), 527–529, 530, 531, 532, 540; modernization of warfare in, 528

Croatia, 206, 702

Cromwell, Oliver, 381

Crossbows, 303, 331, 333. *See also* Bows and arrows (archers); Chinese, 149, 225, 340

Crowther, Samuel Adjai, 503, 582

Crusades (crusaders), 178, 220–222, 276; First (1096–1099), 192, 220–221; Second (1147–1149), 221; Third (1189–1192), 222; Fourth (1202–1204), 221, 322

Cruzado (gold coin), 344

Crystal Palace (London), 487

Cuba, 503, 623. *See also* Castro, Fidel; Cuban Revolution; abolition of slavery in, 475, 476–477, 514; sugar production in, 514, 591; United States and, 563, 589, 591, 592, 674; communism in, 674, 690–691

Cuban missile crisis (1962), 674

Cuban Revolution (1959), 678–679

Cults: *See also* Ancestor worship; Gods and goddesses; Shrines; Neolithic goddess, 13; Mesopotamian, 15; fertility, 17, 52, 106, 122, 144; mystery, 139; Aztec, 254

Cultural imperialism, 726, 727–728, 729. *See also* Westernization (Western culture)

Cultural relativism, 614

Cultural Revolution (China, 1966), 684

Culture. *See also* Art and artists; Civilization(s); Literature; Oral culture; Poets and poetry; Society; *and specific cultures;* Stone Age, 5–6, 7; African, 168–169; great traditions and small traditions, 168, 173; exchange, in Mongolia Empire, 271; Russian, 531–532; New Imperialism and, 572–574; global, 726–732; Hollywood films and, 615, 727; popular, 729–730, 731; English language and, 730–731, 732; Japanese, 731–732

Cuneiform writing, 16, 19, 22, 65, 100, 104–105

Currency: *See also* Coins; copper bars as, 300; Ottoman crisis and reform, 416, 528; paper, 237, 277, 280, 283, 439, 467; launch of Euro, 720; crisis in, 719–720

Curzon, Lord George Nathaniel, 647

Cuzco, 259, 261–262, 356

Cylinder seal, Mesopotamian, 23 *(illus.)*

Cyril, 206

Cyrillic alphabet, 206, 216, 531

Cyrus (Kurush), 96, 109

Czechoslovakia, 606, 700; Nazi Germany and, 628, 629; Soviet domination of, 672; division of (1992), 701 *(map)*, 702

Czech Republic, 701 *(map)*, 702, 705, 714

Dachau concentration camp, 637 *(illus.)*

Daedalus, 69

Da Gama, Christopher, 352

Da Gama, Vasco, 298, 344 *(illus.)*, 345, 346 *(map)*, 352, 353

Dagur peoples, 442

Daimyo (warlords), 433, 434, 437, 451, 563

Dai Viet, 241–242. *See also* Vietnam

Dakar (Senegal), 644, 645

Dalai Lama, 439–440

Damascus, 187, 192, 194

Dams, 299, 321; Aswan (Egypt), 579, 682; hydroelectric, 550, 620, 682; in Japan, 609, 683

D'Annunzio, Gabriele, 619

Dante Alighieri, 329, 330

Danube Valley, agriculture in, 8

Daoism, 44–45, 148, 283; in Tang China, 224, 225, 231

Darby, Abraham, 486

Darby, Abraham, III, 487

Dardanelles Strait, 603

Darius I (Persia), 94, 96, 98, 100; as lawgiver, 99; religious views of, 102–104; war with Greece and, 109–110

Darius III (Persia), 113, 114

Darwin, Charles, 558

Darwin, Erasmus, 480

Dasas, 119

Date Masamune, 437

Davar, Cowasjee Nanabhoy, 496

David (Israel), 78

Da Vinci, Leonardo, 331

D-Day (World War II, 1944), 634

Death squads, 724; in Latin America, 692, 710

De Beers Consolidated, 580, 645 *(illus.)*

Deborah the Judge, 79

Debt. *See also* Foreign debt: Spain (sixteenth century), 383; Japanese samurai, 437; to Western powers, 519

Debt slavery: in Mesopotamia, 17; in Egypt, 29; in Greece, 106, 109

Decameron (Boccaccio), 330

Deccan plateau, 117, 126, 298, 305, 662

Decembrist revolt (Russia), 532

Declaration of Independence (1776, United States), 464, 466, 471, 475

Declaration of the Rights of Man (1789, France), 466, 471, 723

Decolonization, 669, 675–683. *See also* Independence; Nationalism; in Africa, 675–678 *and map*, 680–682; chronology (1947–1971), 671; in Latin America, 678–679; in Middle East, 684; in Southern Asia, 675; Third World, 679, 682–683 *and illus.*

Deforestation, 362, 401, 669; in Africa, 309; in China, 287, 445; in Europe, 321, 375, 490; tropical forests, 593, 646, 659, 666; in Americas, 490; in World War II, 638

De Gaulle, Charles, 677

Deir el-Bahri, mortuary temple at, 66, 67 *(illus.)*

De Lesseps, Ferdinand, 592

Delhi, 507, 648

Delhi sultanate (India), 277, 300, 303–306, 304 *(map)*; Gujarat and, 305, 310; slavery in, 313; water-control systems in, 299; women in, 304–305, 313

Delian League, 110

Delphi, oracle of Apollo at, 105, 106

Democracy: in Greece, 106, 109, 110; in colonial Virginia, 397; Revolutions of 1848 and, 469; in Latin America, 471; in Great

Britain and France, 560; in China, 699; in India, 714–715; globalization and, 714–716

Deng Xiaoping, 698–699, 714

Denmark, 208, 558, 631, 671

Deportations, mass, 74, 124

Depression (economic): *See also* Great Depression; in Ming China, 439; French Revolution and, 466; (1870s–1890s), 550, 562–563, 574

Developing nations (Third World), 709, 729. *See also* Nonindustrial world; deforestation in, 669; in Cold War, 679, 682–683; social problems in, 690; environmental damage in, 709; foreign investment in, 718–719; immigrants from, 690, 707–708, 710; population growth in, 690, 703, 704, 705–706, 710; rural-to-urban migration in, 706–707

Devi, 121, 122

Dhows (ships), 307, 308 *and illus.*, 353

Diagne, Blaise, 646

Diamond mining, African, 580, 645 *(illus.)*, 715

Dias, Bartholomeu, 345, 346 *(map)*

Diaspora, Jewish, 79, 86

Díaz, Porfirio, 653

Dictatorship. *See* Authoritarianism (dictatorship)

Dido, 61, 84

Diem, Ngo Dinh, 673

Diocletian (Rome), 141

Directory (France), 468

Dirty War (Argentina, 1976–1983), 692

Disease. *See also* Bubonic plague; Epidemics; Malaria; Medicine (physicians); Small pox; in Neolithic Age, 10; Amerindians and, 354, 355 *and illus.*, 356, 387; dysentery, 405, 490, 662; measles, 387; influenza, 276, 387, 605, 613, 648; slaves and, 402, 405; yellow fever, 387, 471, 472 *(illus.)*, 592; industrialization and, 490; cholera, 490, 508–509, 515, 662; native peoples and, 512; in colonial Africa, 582, 644; famine and, 662; and warfare, 538, 605; HIV/AIDS, 724 *and illus.*

Diu, 353, 354

Divination, 18–19; in China, 42 *and illus.*, 43, 144

Divine Comedy (Dante), 329

Divine kingship: in Babylonia, 20; in ancient Egypt, 26–27, 29–30, 34, 66–67; Chinese Mandate of Heaven, 43, 59, 148, 152

Division of labor, 485, 555

Divorce, 379, 526, 612, 630. *See also* Marriage; in ancient civilizations, 18, 29; in Islam, 195

Djoser (Egypt), 27

Doctors. *See* Medicine (physicians)

Doctors without Borders, 724

Domestication: *See also specific animals and plants*; of animals, 8, 9–10, 14, 89–90, 170, 298; of plants, 8–9, 14, 89, 298

Domestic servants, 378, 492, 497, 553

Dominican order, 328, 329, 443

Dominican Republic, 592. *See also* Hispaniola

Doré, Gustav, 491 *(illus.)*

Dos Pilas, 244

Doss House, The (Makovsky), 561 *(illus.)*

Douglass, Frederick, 475

Drama: Greek, 111; Gupta theatre-state, 125–126

Dravidian language, 32, 119, 121

Drought, 40, 258, 646, 726. *See also* Rainfall; in Africa, 407, 429, 664; famine and, 662, 664

Druids (Celtic priests), 51, 53

Du Bois, W. E. B., 646, 677

Duma (Russian parliament), 562

Dunhuang, Buddhist cave painting at, 230 *(illus.)*

Dupleix, Joseph François, 426–427

Durbars (pageants) in India, 508 *(illus.)*

Durkheim, Emile, 614

Dushan, Stephen, 281–282

Dutch, the. *See* Netherlands (the Dutch)

Dutch colonies, 588 *(map)*, 636 *(map)*, 676 *(map)*. *See also* Dutch East Indies; Dutch Guiana, 403, 510; Cape Colony (South Africa), 510–511, 580–581; abolition of slavery in, 514

Dutch East India Company (VOC), 374 *and illus.*, 403, 430, 436; in China, 440, 444

Dutch East Indies, 430, 583, 588 *(map)*. *See also* Indonesia; World War II and, 634, 636 *(map)*; nationalist movement in, 675

Dutch studies (Japan), 437

Dutch West India Company, 374, 400, 403, 405

Dyer, Reginald, 648

Dysentery, 405, 490, 662

Ea, 21, 23 *(illus.)*

Earhart, Amelia, 614

Earth Mother, 11

Earthquakes, 258; in Lisbon (1755), 369

Earth Summit (Rio de Janeiro, 1992), 726

East Africa. *See also* Swahili Coast; *specific countries*; Kikuyu people, 11; trading city-states in, 307–309; Portuguese in, 352, 429–430; ivory trade in, 429, 504, 512; Muslims in, 301, 427, 429–430; coffee in, 642

East Asia, 231. *See also* Southeast Asia *and specific countries*; origins of cooking in, 6; bubonic plague in, 228; Buddhism in, 177; emergence of, 232–243; writing systems of, 240 *and illus.*; centralization in (1200–1500), 289–293; European trade with, 440; chronology (1853–1910), 551; Indian Ocean trade and, 575; chronology (1900–1927), 599; events in (1931–1945), 629–631; Chinese Communists in, 629–630; Sino-Japanese War (1937–1945), 630; Pacific Rim economies of, 696–699

Eastern Europe, 605, 705, 719. *See also* Europe; Slavs *and specific countries*; chronology (634–1204), 205; World War II bombing in, 632 *(illus.)*; Nazi Holocaust in, 637–638; chronology in (1979–1990), 691; Cold War and, 648, 665, 672, 674; fall of communism in, 699, 700–701 *and map*; democracy in, 714; English in, 730

Eastern Zhou era, 43

East Germany, 672. *See also* Germany

East India Company, British (EIC), 444, 462, 511; in India, 496, 498, 504–506, 507

East India Company, Dutch (VOC), 374 *and illus.*, 403, 430, 436; in China, 440, 444

East Indies (maritime Southeast Asia), 338, 583. *See also* Indian Ocean states; Southeast Asia; Portuguese expedition to, 337; spice trade in, 348; Muslim traders in, 427; Chinese immigration to, 440; Dutch, 430, 583, 588 *(map)*, 634, 636 *(map)*, 675 (*See also* Indonesia)

East Timor, independence of, 717

Ebla, 22

Ebu's-Su'ud, 418

Ecological crisis: *See also* Deforestation; Environment, the; and introduction of agriculture, 10; in Indus Valley, 33

Economic crisis: *See also* Depression; Great Depression; Inflation; Safavid Iran, 424; Ming China, 439; French Revolution, 465–466; German (1923), 607; Soviet Union, 699

Economic growth: European industrialization and, 374, 550; in Japan, 434, 437; in Revolutionary era, 461; statistics and, 542; in British India, 496, 506, 507, 646; in World War II, 638; in United States, 607, 670; in Africa, 643; in Europe, 671; in Japan, 603, 609, 673, 683, 690, 696–697, 731; in China (1980s–1990s), 714; in East Asia, 696–699; in Hong Kong, 697, 732; in Singapore, 697, 732; in South Korea, 697–698 *and illus.*, 732; in Taiwan, 697, 698, 699, 732

Economics (economic theories). *See also* Capitalism; Free trade; graphmaking and, 484–485 *(illus.)*; laissez faire, 493, 494; Lenin's N.E.P., 607; Marx's, 553, 554–556; Cold War ideology and, 670–672; neo-liberalism and women's rights, 694–696; chronology (1994–2002), 715

Economy (economic factors). *See also* Business; Global economy; Industrialization; Taxation; Trade; Sumerian, 22; ancient Egypt, 27; barter, 17, 140, 208, 253; Roman Empire, 140, 141; medieval Europe, 209–211, 218; imperial China, 236–238, 242, 283, 285; Russia, under Mongols, 280–281; Spanish decline, 383; government role in, 383, 385; Ottoman, 417; British, 495; British India, 506; Qing China, 518; New Imperialism and, 574, 590; World War I, 603; Soviet Union, 607; Cuban, 623, 679; German, 628; World War II, 638; Brazilian, 719

Ecuador, 262; independence of, 472

Edessa, 192

Edict of Nantes (1598), 379

Edison, Thomas, 549, 563

Education (educational institutions). *See also* Literacy; Schools; Universities and colleges; Academy of Plato, 111; Confucianism and, 143; Chinese academies, 236; of women, in East Asia, 237, 242;

Education (*cont.*)
Islamic madrasas, 199, 250, 328; early modern Europe, 378; Ottoman, 415, 526; British India, 510; Egyptian military, 520; Russia, 532; Qing China, 539; Victorian Age, 556; France, 560; New Imperialism and, 572–573, 577, 582–583, 587; nationalism and, 648, 679; of African leaders, 644–646; of women, 378, 477–478, 539, 704, 725–726; secular, in Mexico, 654, 656; South Korea, 697; disease and, 724; global English culture and, 731
Edward II (England), 333
Edward III (England), 333, 334
Egypt, ancient, 5, 12 *(map)*, 24–31; chronology, 7; administration, 27–28; Assyria and, 73, 110; climate in, 26; Creation Myth, 25; divine kingship in, 26–27, 29–30, 34, 66–67; river boat, 25 *(illus.)*; people, 28–29; trade, 27, 28; geography of, 24–25; religion, 29–30; foreign policy, 28; hieroglyphs, 27, 49, 66, 104–105; Hyksos in, 65–66, 77, 86; chronology (2040–671 B.C.E.), 63–64; Israelites in, 77; Middle Kingdom, 48, 62, 65, 66; New Kingdom, 49, 65–68, 86, 111; Nubia and, 25, 28, 45, 48–50, 66, 72, 168; Nubian dynasty (800 B.C.E.–350 C.E.), 69–70; Old Kingdom, 45, 169; pigs in, 170
Egypt (Egyptians), 354, 540, 575, 684. *See also* Egypt, ancient; Mamluk Sultanate (Egypt); Suez Canal; Ptolemaic, 114–115 *and map*, 116–117; Rome and, 136, 137, 208; Islamic conquest of, 186, 190 *and illus.*, 192; industrialization in, 481, 495; under Muhammad Ali, 495, 498, 520, 527, 529; Napoleon's invasion of, 498, 500, 519–520, 522–524; Cairo, 500, 529, 598 *and illus.*; cotton production in, 495, 500, 529, 577, 579; irrigation in, 593; British and, 577, 579, 598, 612; Aswan Dam in, 579, 682; in World War II, 632; under Nasir, 682–683 *and illus.*; Israeli-Arab wars and, 686
Egyptian Book of the Dead, 30
Einstein, Albert, 614, 637
Eisenhower, Dwight D., 673, 674
Ekwesh, 72. *See also* Greece
Elam, 64, 73, 74, 85
Elamites, 15, 16, 65, 86, 100
Eleanor of Aquitaine, 221–222
Electricity, 549–550; telegraph and, 489; hydroelectric dams for, 550, 609, 620, 682, 683; for lighting, 549, 552, 615
Elephants, 425 *(illus.)*, 508 *(illus.)*; ivory trade, 71, 161, 349 *(illus.)*, 429, 504, 512
Elite class. *See also* Aristocracy; Landowners; Warrior class; Mesopotamian, 17; in ancient Egypt, 29, 30, 49; scribes as, 2, 18, 22, 27, 105; early China, 42, 45; Celtic, 51, 53, 58; Olmec, 53, 55, 56, 58; Assyrian, 75; and ideologies of power, 59; Persian satraps, 99; Roman and Han China compared, 151; and Silk Road trade, 155; Islamic caliphate, 187; oral culture and literacy, 176; and Confucianism in China, 229–230, 231, 233, 236; Korean, 239;

Andean, 257–258; Maya burials, 260, 261 *(illus.)*; Mesoamerican, 244, 245, 246, 249, 251; Mound-builder burials, 255, 256; Muslim in India, 305, 312; in colonial Latin America, 388, 391, 393; Russian, 450; urban, in China, 439, 440; Haitian, 460, 469, 471; Japanese, 437–438; Latin American, 476; Ottoman, 524; indigenous colonial, 577; British India, 506–507; Argentine, 657; domination of, 613; Iranian, 693; global culture and, 730–731
Elmina (St. George of the Mine), 349, 403
El Salvador, 692
Emancipation Proclamation (United States), 476
Emperors. *See* Monarchy, *and specific emperors*
Empires. *See* Colonies; Expansion; Imperialism; New Imperialism, *and specific empires and emperors*
Empire State Building (New York City), 615
Enclosure movement (England), 481
Endangered Species Act (United States), 709
Engels, Friedrich, 553, 554–556, 624
Engineering. *See also* Construction materials and techniques; Assyrian, 73; Roman, 139, 140 *(illus.)*, 146; Chinese, 142, 146–147 *and illus.*, 234, 235 *(illus.)*, 237; Persian (Il-khanate), 284; Gothic cathedrals, 325; Industrial Revolution, 490–491; in Japan, 564; in British India, 647, 648
England. *See also* British Empire; Great Britain; Neolithic megaliths in, 11, 13; Norman conquest of, 208, 211, 220; peasants of, 209, 320; population growth (1086–1200), 218; Henry II's conflict with church and, 212–213; wool trade of, 219, 320, 322, 323, 334, 484; Hundred Years War in, 331, 333–334; Magna Carta in, 333; dynasties in, 380 *(illus.)*; Civil War in (1642), 381; iron industry in, 375, 382; education of women in, 378; merchant fleet of, 383; religion and state in, 379–381; society in, 372–373, 374; Dutch wars with (1653–1658), 383, 403; Mughal India and, 426; slave trade and, 403, 404, 405, 406; trade with Iran, 411; graph-making in, 484–485 *and illus.*; Irish immigration to, 494
English language, 557, 558, 591, 647, 657; as global second language, 666, 728, 730–731
Enkidu, 4, 18
Enlightenment, the, 372, 451, 484, 542; Revolutionary era and, 461–462, 471, 475
Enlightenment *(nirvana)*, 120–121, 171–172, 230
Entente (France, Great Britain, and Russia), 597
Environmental Protection Agency (U.S.), 687
Environment (environmental stress). *See also* Climate and weather; Deforestation; Ecological crisis; Natural disasters; in Indus Valley civilization, 33, 34; of Americas, 53; in sub-Saharan Africa, 167–168; Maya and, 250; Andean response to, 256–257, 258; tropical, 297–298; medieval

industry and, 321; mining, 391–392; sugar plantation, 401; Qing China, 445; slave trade and, 407; soil erosion, 401, 490; industrialization, 490–491; steel mills, 549; global threats, 593–594; World Wars and, 606, 638; Soviet industrialization, 620; Cold War, 669, 674; population growth and, 709; Brazil, 659; preservation of, 687, 708, 709; technology and, 708, 709–710; global warming and, 726–727
Epic of Gilgamesh, 4, 16, 34
Epidemics. *See also* Bubonic plague; Disease; Small pox; slave trade and, 405; in China, 439; industrialization and, 490; influenza (1918–1919), 605, 613, 648; HIV/AIDS, 724 *and illus.*
Equites (Roman elites), 136, 148
Erasmus of Rotterdam, 330
Ericsson, Leif, 342
Estado Novo (New State, Brazil), 659
Estates General (France), 334, 381, 466, 469
Esther (biblical), 99
Estonia, 701; Soviet invasion of, 631
Ethiopia, 313, 431, 502 *(map)*, 646, 724; modernization in, 500; famine and drought in, 664; Italian invasions of, 581–582, 628, 642
Ethiopian Christianity, 172–173, 301, 310, 500, 583, 644, 645; churches, 312; Portugal and, 352
Ethnic cleansing, 716–717. *See also* Genocide
Ethnicity: and race in colonial Americas, 393 *(illus.)*, 394–396; and nationalism, 558, 597; and race, 543–544
Etruscans, 81 *(map)*, 131
Eunuchs: *See also* Zheng He; in imperial China, 229, 540 *(illus.)*; as slaves, 313
Eurasia, Mongol domains in (1330), 267, 275 *(map)*; *See also* Mongolian Empire
Euro (currency), 720
Europe (1500–1730), 364–385; in 1720, 384 *(map)*; bourgeoisie in, 373–375, 378; chronology, 367; culture and ideas in, 372; debt and taxes in, 383, 385; Holy Roman Empire in, 379, 382; Little Ice Age in (1590s), 455; mapmaking in, 376–377 *and illus.*; peasants and laborers, 375–377; political innovation in, 378–385; religious reformation in, 365–366, 368 *(map)*; scientific revolution in, 370–372; social and economic life, 372–378; religious policies, 379–380; state development in, 379; war and diplomacy in, 382–383; witch hunts and tradition in, 369–370 *and illus.*; women and family in, 377–378
Europe, great powers of: (1720), 384 *(map)*; (1871–1900), 548, 560–562, 565, 567; (1900–1913), 596–597
European Community (EC), 670–671, 697, 709
European immigrants: to Americas, 393, 409, 487, 494, 562; in Argentina, 476, 658; colonialism and, 515–516, 570, 576–577; as indentured servants, 397, 399, 400–401; in

Ottoman Empire, 525, 526, 529; in South Africa, 510–511, 582; in Africa, 584–586, 642, 677; post–World War I, 613

European Union (EU), 720, 721 *(map)*; English language in, 730, 731

Europe (Europeans). *See also* Eastern Europe; European immigrants; Industrial nations; Latin West; Medieval Europe; Roman Empire; Western Europe; *and specific countries, and empires;* adoption of agriculture in, 8, 11; Celtic peoples of, 50–53; population of (1000–1200), 274; Mongols and, 322; famine in (1315–1317), 318, 359; in 1453, 333 *(map)*; climate and population in, 359–360; Atlantic economy, 404, 406, 407; China trade of, 438–439, 440, 443–445, 533; Indian Ocean trade of, 431; Japan and, 434, 436–437; Revolutionary era, 463; Napoleonic, 470 *(map)*; industrialization in, 481, 483–484 (*See also* Industrial Revolution); trading companies of, 504; Greek independence and, 524; India and, 504; nationality and census in, 543–544; Ottoman reforms and, 525, 526, 529; Russia and, 529–531; Qing China and, 519, 533, 541; domination of, 548–549; nationalism in, 557–558; population of, 552; possessions in Asia and Pacific, 570, 588 *(map)*; chronology (1851–1905), 551; gunboat diplomacy of, 575; chronology (1904–1927), 599; radio in, 615; World War I in, 600 *(map)*; fascism in, 626, 627; Great Depression in, 623; World War II in, 631–632, 633 *(map)*; chronology (1930–1945), 621; Bretton Woods Conference (1944), 670–671; Cold War and, 674; demographic transition in, 703; guest workers in, 708; inequality in, 706; population of, 704 *(illus.)*, 705; heat waves in, 726; global culture and, 729

Evenk peoples, 442

Exchange, medium of: *See also* Barter; Trade; coinage as, 106, 170; silver as, 17, 75, 97

Exchange networks, 222, 227. *See also* Indian Ocean maritime system; Silk Road; Trans-Saharan trade and caravan routes; (300 B.C.E.–1100 C.E.), 209

Exclusif (France), 403–404

Expansion (expansionism). *See also* Colonies; Globalization; Imperialism; Maritime Expansion; New Imperialism; *and specific empires and emperors;* Egyptian, 49, 66; Assyrian, 73–75, 85; Indian, 123–127; Roman, 132 *(map)*, 135–136; Chinese imperial, 142, 143 *(map)*, 146–147, 225, 226 *(map)*; Islamic, 186–187, 189 *(map)*; Andean cultures, 259, 262; Mongol (1215–1283), 272, 274, 294; Delhi sultanate, 303–304; maritime, 338–342; Iberian, 342–348; Ottoman, 342, 361, 412–413, 415; Qing China, 440, 441 *(map)*, 451, 533; Russian Empire (1500–1800), 445–446, 448 *(map)*, 451, 525 *(map)*, 531; British India, 511; United States, 562, 563,

587, 589, 591; Western European, 457–458; Japan (1868–1918), 565–567; Nazi Germany, 631–632 *and map*

Exploration (expeditions). *See also* Portuguese exploration; *and specific explorers;* Carthaginian, 84; Persian, 98; Chinese, 155–156; Zheng He, 268, 285–287 *and map,* 339, 340–341 *and map,* 344 *(illus.)*; Spanish maritime, 337, 342, 343, 345–348, 354–356; by Europeans in Africa, 500, 503; in outer space, 674

Extraterritoriality, 529, 534. *See also* Treaty ports

Ezana, 172–173

Factory Act of 1833 (Britain), 494

Fagan, Brian, 455

Faisal (Iraq), 603, 606, 612

Falkland Islands (Malvinas) war, 693

Family. *See also* Ancestor worship; Children; Clans; Divorce; Fathers; Kinship groups; Marriage; Women; Neolithic Age, 11; in Mesopotamia, 18; in ancient Israel, 78; in China, 142, 143, 150, 151; Roman, 133, 150; and Indian Ocean trade, 165; in Byzantine Empire, 204; Maya, 249; in China, 237, 283; Nomadic, 271; in Europe, 377–378; Ottoman, 527; Victorian Age, 553, 556; Stalin on, 625; Turkish westernization and, 612; African colonial, 644; globalization and, 715

Family planning. *See* Birth control

Famine, 722; in Europe (1315–1319), 318, 359, 455; in China, 439, 630, 662, 663–664; in Ireland (1847–1848), 494, 552, 662; warfare and, 603, 663; in Russia and Soviet Union, 622, 663; in India, 646, 651, 662, 663; politics and, 662–664

Farmers. *See also* Agriculture; Peasants; Rural societies; Neolithic, 8, 10–11; Mesopotamian, 14; Greek, 104, 105, 106; Roman, 15, 131, 136, 137; Chinese, 150, 151, 156; Sasanid Iran, 157; Byzantine, 205; medieval Europe, 209, 317, 318; Maya, 246; Chinese, 236, 284; Delhi India, 299; Kievan Russia, 272; Ottoman, 417; Chinese, 439, 445, 609, 663; *kibbutzim,* in Palestine, 612; tractors and, 617; Great Depression and, 623; Ghanaian, 642

Fascism, 626–629, 659. *See also* Nazi Germany

Fathers. *See also* Family; Men; Patriarchy; in early human society, 13; Confucianism and, 44, 45, 143

Fatima (daughter of Muhammad), 185, 195

Fatimid caliphate, 189 *(map)*, 190, 191, 192

Fatwas (Islamic decrees), 418–420

Faud (Egypt), 612

Faxian, 126, 171

Feng shui (cosmic order), 41, 43, 144

Ferdinand (Spain), 335, 345

Ferdinand VI (Spain), 471

Ferghana, 156

Fertility cults: Neolithic, 17; Celtic, 52; Greek, 106; Hindu, 122; Chinese, 144

Fertility rates (1970s–1990s), 703, 704–705, 708

Festivals: Babylon, 19, 20–22; Egypt, 28, 30; Celtic, 52; Persia, 100; Greece, 109, 111, 112; India, 178, 508 *(illus.)*; Islam, 180–181; Zulu, 500

Feudalism (feudal law), 209, 213

Fief (land grant), 210–211

Fiji, 338, 515

Film (motion pictures), 615, 727, 728, 729

Finance. *See* Coinage; Currency; Economic factors; Fiscal crisis; Foreign debt; Inflation; Taxation

Financial institutions: *See also* Banks; British, 482; Ottoman, 528 *(illus.)*; world trade and, 550

Financial markets (stock exchanges), 374, 493, 720; crash of (1929), 623

Finland (Finns), 215, 281, 455, 631, 671

Finney, Ben, 338

Firearms (guns), 287, 288, 333, 334, 349. *See also* Cannon; Rifles; Gunpowder; Weapons and military technology; Conquistador, 356; Amerindians and, 399; muskets, 417, 507, 528, 534, 575; British colonies, 511; Ottoman, 415, 416, 417; Safavid Iran, 424; Japanese, 434; African trade in, 406, 499, 504; interchangeable parts for, 487; machine guns, 575, 576 *(illus.)*, 581, 601, 602

Firuz Shah, 305, 313

Fiscal crises: *See also* Depression; Economic crisis; French Revolution and, 465–466

Fishing (fishermen), 10, 298

Five-Year Plans (Soviet Union), 620, 622, 623

Flanders (Flemish): artists of, 330, 331; textile trade in, 219, 322, 323–324 *and illus.*

Floods (flooding), 5, 539; Nile River, 5, 8, 25–26, 31, 34; in Mesopotamia, 14; Indus River, 31; in China, 40, 41, 284; Niger River, 299; in China, 445, 630, 638; in Bangladesh, 663, 727 *(illus.)*

Florence, 219, 323, 329, 330; banking in, 324–325, 331

Folk cultures (traditional customs): pork prohibition, 79, 170; trading networks and, 155, 159, 167; as small traditions, 168, 173, 200; Germanic, 202, 208, 213; witchcraft and, 369–370 *and illus.*; Mexican, 653; global culture and, 727, 731–732

Food crops: *See also* Agriculture; *specific foods;* Silk Road trade and, 156; Columbian exchange, 407–409; from Africa to New World, 408; from Americas to Old World, 362, 375, 408–409, 445, 552; production, and population growth, 703

Food (diet; nutrition): *See also* Famine; *and specific foods;* Stone Age, 6; domestication of animals for, 9–10; Indian Ocean trade and, 161; prohibition on eating pork, 79, 170; of medieval Europe, 208; Amerindian, 253, 354; women's role in preparation of, 6, 313; and climate change, 359, 376; shortages in

Food (*cont.*)
colonial Africa, 644; World War I shortages, 603, 604; prison camp shortages, 622, 638; scarcity in Soviet Union, 607, 620–621, 622

Footbinding in China, 238, 239 (*illus.*), 536, 630

Foragers (hunting and food-gathering peoples). *See also* Hunting; dwellings of, 6; present-day, 6; agricultural revolution and, 8–11; Saharan, 219–220

Forbidden City (Beijing), 283, 285, 287, 609

Ford, Henry, 613, 616, 617, 659

Foreign debt (international loans): British war, 462, 484 (*illus.*); French war, 466; Eurasian, 519; Ottoman, 529; Chinese, 539, 663; Egyptian, 577–578; Central American, 591, 592; German, after World War I, 607, 623; Latin American, 694; neo-liberalism and, 695

Foreign investment: in Argentina, 476–477 *and illus.*; in China, 698–699, 719; in Cuba, 690; in developing countries, 718–719; in Latin America, 678, 692

Forests, 246–247. *See also* Deforestation; Russian, 375; North American, 563; products of, 592; tropical, 167, 297, 300, 512, 593, 646, 659, 666

Fortifications: ancient Indian, 32; Celtic, 51; Mycenaean, 70, 72; Assyrian, 73; Chinese, 44, 143 (*map*), 145, 147; medieval Europe, 209; Teotihuacan, 246; against Mongols, 287, 292; Kremlin, 280 (*illus.*)

"Forty-Seven Ronin" incident (Japan), 438 *and illus.*

Forum, in Rome, 131, 134

Four Corners region, Amerindians in, 254–255

Fourier, Charles, 493–494

Fox, Vincente, 714

France, 493, 510. *See also* French colonies; French Revolution; cave paintings in, 5, 7; Celts in, 51, 53; as Gaul, 51, 135, 137, 208; Muslim threat to, 209; population growth (1086–1200), 218; peasants of, 209, 320; medieval fairs in, 322–323; watermills in, 321, 322 (*illus.*); monarchy and war in, 333–334; print shop in (1537), 331 (*illus.*); canals, 374, 490; dynasties, 379, 380 (*illus.*); aristocracy, 374–375; peasant revolts, 377; religion and state, 381–382; tax reforms, 385; trading companies, 403–404; war with Britain (1756–1763), 399, 461; American Revolution and, 464; Haitian Revolution and, 471, 472 (*illus.*); Revolution of 1848, 469; graph-making, 484; industrialization, 482; railroads, 489, 550; steamships, 487; Mexico and, 473 (*illus.*); slavery and, 460, 469, 471, 514; Mughal India and, 426–427, 504, 505–506; invasion of Egypt by, 498, 519–520, 522–524; in Crimean War, 527–528, 530; Russia and, 530–531; Qing China and, 534, 535 *and map*, 538, 539, 565; census, 542; language and nation, 557; war with Prussia (1870–1871), 558; as great power, 560; British rivalry with, 564, 658; Ot-

toman Empire and, 597; in World War I, 597, 600–602 *and illus.*, 603, 605; birth control in, 613–614; World War I peace and, 606, 607, 617; Depression of 1930s, 623; appeasement of Germany by, 628; in World War II, 631, 633 (*map*), 634; Middle East and, 612; Suez Canal and, 577, 682–683; nationalization, 670; United Nations and, 669; Serbia and, 716; Iraq invasion and, 718

Franciscan order, 328, 329, 443

Francis I (France), 379

Franco-Prussian War (1870–1871), 558

Frankincense, 161, 181

Franz Ferdinand, assassination of, 596, 597

Franz Josef (Austria), 569

Frederick Barbarossa (Holy Roman Emperor), 276

Frederick II (Holy Roman Emperor), 281

Free trade (free market), 562, 623, 663, 720; as British policy, 495, 511–512; imperialism and, 590–591; women's rights and, 694–696; China and, 719

French and Indian War (1756–1763), 399, 461

French colonies, 623. *See also* French Indochina, 570, 676 (*map*); in North America, 387, 389, 398–399, 409; abolition of slavery in, 469, 471; Algeria, 457, 500, 677; in Africa, 578 (*map*), 579, 580, 581, 642, 644; in West Indies, 399, 400, 404, 462, 514 (*See also* Haiti)

French Indochina, 583, 588 (*map*), 632; independence of, 673, 675, 676 (*map*); Vietnam, 535, 673, 675

French language, 526, 557

French Revolution, 460, 465–469, 503, 510, 542; protest leading to, 466; radical reforms of, 467–468, 557–558; reaction to, and dictatorship, 468; retrenchment and reform, 469; society and fiscal crisis, 465–466; war against Austria and Prussia, 469

French West Indies, 399, 400, 404. *See also* Haiti (St. Domingue); migration to, 462, 514

Freud, Sigmund, 614

Friedman, Thomas L., 722

Frumentius, 172–173

Fuggers of Augsburg, 325

Fujiwara family, 241, 242

Fulani people, 298, 312, 584

Fulton, Robert, 487

Fur trade (furs): colonial North America, 387, 398–399 *and illus.*, 409; Russia, 446, 450

Fustat, 190 *and illus.*, 194. *See also* Cairo

Gabriel (Jibra'il), 182

Gaius Marius, 136

Galdan (Mongolia), 440, 442, 446

Galilee, 76

Galilei, Marie Celeste, 378

Galileo Galilei, 371

Gandhi, Mohandas K. (Mahatma), 641; assassination of, 651; nonviolence and, 648–649; technology and, 650 *and illus.*

Ganges River, 123

Garvey, Marcus, 646, 677

Gaugamela, Battle at (331 B.C.E.), 113

Gaul (ancient France), 51, 135, 137, 208

Ge Hong, 224

Gender differences. *See also* Men; Women. *See also* Women; in Stone Age, 6, 8; in early China, 45; Andean civilizations, 257; Islam and, 313–314 *and illus.*; in late medieval Europe, 377–378; in Victorian Age, 553, 556–557 *and illus.*; after World War I, 613–614

Genghis Khan (Temüjin), 267, 270, 272, 294

Genoa, 219, 275, 322, 354; sea routes of, 342, 343

Genocide, 716–717, 724–725. *See also* Holocaust

Gentry, Chinese, 148, 236, 237, 238, 283

George III (England), 444–445

Georgia (Caucasus), 527, 529, 531, 607

Germanic peoples, 209, 318; Celts in, 51, 53; Roman Empire and, 138, 139, 150; custom and law of, 202, 206, 208, 212, 213; kingdoms of, 207 (*map*), 222; and Slavic Christianity, 215, 281

Germany (Germans), 613. *See also* Nazi Germany; Prussia; in colonial North America, 398; Lutheranism and, 366; nationalism in, 379; ethnic minorities in, 543; railroads in, 489, 550; as great power, 560; industry in, 549, 603; male suffrage in, 553; Ruhr district, 490, 549; unification of (1866–1871), 548, 557–560; African colonies of, 578 (*map*), 579, 581, 603, 642; colonies of, 570, 589, 609; before World War I, 597; World War I and, 545, 600 (*map*), 601–603, 604–605; Ottoman modernization and, 597; World War I peace and, 605, 606, 617; economic crisis in (1923), 607; Great Depression in, 619–620, 623, 627–628; Nazis in (*See* Nazi Germany); radio cartel and, 658; in World War II, 631–632, 633 (*map*), 634, 635, 637, 639; Cold War division of, 670, 672; reunification of (1990), 701 *and map*; environmental awareness in, 709; immigration to, 708; invasion of Iraq and, 718

Ghadir al-Khumm, 180, 181, 185

Ghana (Gold Coast), 189–190, 428, 642, 644; gold trade in, 300, 301, 406; Portuguese trade and, 345, 348; Asante kingdom in, 406, 581; European imperialism in, 579–580; independence of, 677

Ghazan, Il-khan, 276–277, 278

Ghent, 219, 322

Gilgamesh, 4, 16, 34

Giotto, 330

Giza, pyramids at, 27

Glacial period. *See* Ice Age

Glassmakers, Ottoman, 416 (*illus.*)

Global climate, 359; Little Ice Age (1590s), 375, 439, 455; warming of, 666, 726–727

Global culture, 722, 726–732; and American imperialism, 726, 727–728, 729; diversity in, 731–732; English language and, 730–

731, 732; media and, 727–729; pop culture and, 729–730

Global economy (world economy), 718–722. *See also* Globalization; technology and (1850–1900), 549–550; Marx on, 553, 554–556; expansion of, 570, 592–593, 706; free market and, 590, 694–696; Great Depression and, 623; raw materials for, 570, 574, 592; Africa and, 646; China and, 439, 719; current problems of, 718–720; new technologies and, 708–709; management of, 720, 722

Global environment, 593–594

Global inequality, 690, 706

Globalization, 722–732. *See also* Global economy; arms control and terrorism, 717–718; culture and, 726–732; democracy and, 714–716; global warming, 726–727; Islam and, 722–723; New Age of, 722; politics of, 716–717; trade associations, 709, 714, 720, 721 *(illus.)*; universal rights and, 723–725; women's rights, 725–726

Global warming, 10, 359, 666, 726–727

Glorious Revolution of 1668 (England), 381

Goa, 353, 354, 415, 430

Go-Daigo (Japan), 293

God of Small Things, The (Roy), 730

Gods and goddesses (deities). *See also* Divine kingship; Religion(s); Shrines; Sun-gods; Supernatural, the; Temples; *and specific deities:* Sky, 11, 18, 106; Neolithic, 11, 13; Mesopotamia, 13–14, 16, 18, 20–21, 23 *(illus.)*; ancient Egypt, 26, 29–30, 49, 50; early China, 42, 43, 44, 144; Nubian, 49, 50; Celtic, 52; jaguar, 56, 57, 82 *(illus.)*, 83; Assyrian Empire, 73; Israelite, 76, 77, 78, 79; Phoenician, 81; Carthaginian, 85; Persian Empire, 101, 102–103; Hindu, 23, 121–123, 125; Vedic, 119, 120; Greek, 108 *and illus.*, 135, 139; Roman, 134–135, 139; Buddhist, 123, 226; Inca, 261; Islamic, 182, 184, 195, 199; polytheism, 182, 211, 218; Mesoamerican, 245, 251, 254; Mongol, 271; monotheism, 66, 79, 139, 152; Semitic, 32, 233

Gold Coast. *See* Ghana (Gold Coast)

Golden Horde (Kipchak Khanate), 272, 275 *(map)*, 279–281, 445–446; rivalry with Il-Khans, 276, 282, 294

Gold (gold trade), 122 *(illus.)*; Nubian, 26, 28, 45, 48 *and illus.*, 49; Andean, 57, 258, 262; coins, 187, 189, 190, 219, 344, 528; East African, 307, 308; West African, 189, 300, 301, 303 *(illus.)*; from colonial Americas, 253, 354, 355, 356, 383, 391, 392; African, 343, 348, 404, 406, 429; in Australia, 513; in South Africa, 580, 581, 626

Gomes, Fernão, 345

Good and evil, in Zoroastrianism, 101, 159

Gorbachev, Mikhail, 700, 701–702

Gothic cathedrals, 325

Government: *See also* Administration; Bureaucracy; Constitutions; Monarchy; Political systems; Political thought; Mesopotamia, 15; Akkad, 16, 69; ancient Egypt, 27–28; early China, 43, 44; Myce-

naean Greece, 71; Assyrian Empire, 74–75; Carthage, 83, 84; Persian Empire, 99–100; classic era Greece, 109; Indian, 124; Roman Republic, 131, 133, 135, 138; Han China, 142, 148; Byzantine Empire, 204; Islam, 237, 238, 239; Song China, 235, 236, 237; Uighur, 232; Il-khanate, 277, 278; Europe, 334; colonial Americas, 388, 391, 397; economic management by, 374, 383, 385, 439, 493; Qing China, 441, 539–540; Ottoman, 417; in United States, 464–465; British industrialization and, 482; laissez faire economics and, 493; British colonial, 506, 513; Egyptian, under French occupation, 523; Ottoman reforms, 529; power of, and census, 542–543; Russian reform of, 532; Central American, 591; Bolshevik Revolutionary, 604–605; Great Depression and, 622, 623; in industrialized world, 613; and industry, in East Asia, 697, 698; and rural-to-urban migration, 707; economic intervention by, 720; transnational corporations and, 709; communications monopolies, 728; global pop culture and, 729

Granada, 335, 343, 345, 356

Grand Canal (China), 147, 225, 227, 228

Grand National Consolidated Trade Union, 494

Grapes, 104, 156

Graphmaking, 484–485 *and illus.*

Great Britain, 671. *See also* British Empire; British Navy; Qing Empire (China), Britain and; England; India, British rule in; war with French (1756–1763), 399, 461; American Revolution and, 462, 464 *and illus.*; and Greek independence, 469; Napoleonic France and, 468, 470 *(map)*; free trade in, 495; abolition of slavery in, 476; Ireland and, 382, 557, 560, 591, 662; Argentina and, 476–477 *and illus.*, 550, 591, 657, 658; Canada and, 513, 581; Crimean War and, 527, 528, 530; Russia and, 530–531; census in, 543; steel production in, 549; urbanization in, 552; women's rights in, 556–557, 613; as great power, 560; financial power of, 550; male suffrage in, 550; Suez Canal and, 577, 579, 682–683; Egypt and, 577–578, 579, 598, 603, 612; African independence and, 677, 678; Middle East and, 604, 612; Ottomans and, 597, 603–604; Russia and, 530; Latin America and, 672; World War I and, 597, 601, 602–603, 605; World War I peace and, 606, 617; Great Depression in, 623; Nazi Germany and, 628–629; World War II and, 631, 632, 633 *(map)*, 634, 635, 637, 669; Brazil and, 658; Mexico and, 656; Cold War and, 670, 674; Falklands War and, 693; Serbia and, 716; Iraq invasion (2003) and, 718, 723

Great Britain, Industrial Revolution in (1760–1851): child labor in, 481, 494; enclosure movement in, 481; graphmaking, 484–485 *and illus.*; iron industry in, 484 *(illus.)*, 486–487; laissez faire, 493; population and cities, 481, 482, 490;

pottery industry, 484–486; protests and reforms, 494; railroads in, 482, 488, 494, 550, *(map)*; social changes, 492; socialism in, 494; steam engines, 485, 487, 488 *(illus.)*; telegraph in, 489; tenements, 490, 492 *(illus.)*; textile industry in, 482 *(map)*, 484, 486, 494

Great Depression (1930s): in Argentina and Brazil, 623, 626, 658; in Germany, 619–620, 623, 627–628; in industrial nations, 545, 623; in Japan, 623, 629; in nonindustrial regions, 623, 626; in Soviet Union, 622

Great Lakes (North America), 399, 487, 709

Great Leap Forward (China), 663–664, 684

Great Northern War (1680–1701), 382, 450

Great Plaza at Tikal, 249 *(illus.)*

Great powers: *See also* New Imperialism; of Europe (1720), 384 *(map)*; of Europe (1871–1900), 548, 560–562, 565, 567; Japan as (1868–1900), 563–567; United States as (1865–1900), 562–563, 565, 567; Asian colonial possessions of (1914), 588 *(map)*; of Europe (1900–1913), 596–597

Great Trek, 502 *(map)*, 510, 511 *(illus.)*

Great Wall (China), 44, 143 *(map)*, 145

Great Western Schism (1378–1415), 333

Great Western (steamship), 488, 489 *(illus.)*

Greco-Roman traditions, 203, 283, 365, 370, 524. *See also* Hellenistic Age; revival of, 325, 328, 329–330

Greece, ancient, 104–114, 138, 156. *See also* Athens; Hellenistic Age; agriculture, 8, 18, 104, 105, 106; alphabet and writing systems, 104–105, 175; Archaic period, 104–110; astrolabe of, 234; chronology, 97; city states (polis), 104–106, 110, 113, 116, 141; Classical period, 110, 139, 176; colonies of, 105, 106, 161, *(map)*; Dark Age, 72, 104; geography and resources, 101, 104; hoplites in, 105, 106, 107, 110, 113; Indian Ocean trade of, 160, 162–163; inequality in, 111–112; intellectual life in, 106–107, 111, 176, 221; medicine of, 232; and Minoans, 69; Mycenaean, 62, 70–72, 86; oral culture and literacy, 105, 111, 175–176; Persians and, 95, 99, 101, 109–110, 113; Phoenicians and, 80, 85, 104; population growth in, 105; pottery, 71, 92, 108 *(illus.)*; religion, 106, 108 *(illus.)*; Sparta, 107–108, 110, 112, 113, 116; trade, 106; women, 112

Greece (Greeks), 597, 671, 672; Ottoman Turks and, 412; independence of, 469, 520, 524, 540; Muslims expelled from, 610

Greek language, 70, 72, 117, 176, 731

Greek philosophy, 107, 111, 221

Greenhouse effect, 726–727

Greenland, 208, 342

Green Revolution, 666

Gregory I, Pope, 214, 326

Gregory VII, Pope, 212, 215

Gregory X, Pope, 326

Gregory XIII, Pope, 371

Gropius, Walter, 615

Guangzhou. *See* Canton (Guangzhou)

Guatemala, 387, 678

Guerrilla warfare: in Middle East, 612; in China, 630; in Vietnam, 673; in South Africa, 678; in Afghanistan, 696; of Palestinians, 686; in Sri Lanka, 717

Guevara, Ernesto "Che," 678

Guianas, 402–403, 415, 515

Guilds, 324, 328, 422

Gujarat, 305, 310, 353, 354, 415, 427

Gulags (Russian/Soviet prison camps), 446, 633

Gundestrup cauldron, 52 *(illus.)*

Gunpowder, 235, 287, 290, 294, 412, 451, 534, 575; invention of, 288; in Europe, 333, 343

Guns. *See* Firearms (guns)

Guomindang (China), 609; civil war and defeat of, 634–635; Communists and, 629, 630

Gupta Empire (India), 118 *(map)*, 120, 122 *(illus.)*, 125–127

Gutenberg, Johann, 330

Güyük, Great Khan, 272

Guzmán, Jacobo, 678

Habsburg dynasty, 379, 380 *(illus.)*

Hadith, 194, 195

Hagia Sophia (Constantinople), 206

Haiti (St. Domingue), 401, 592; slave rebellion in, 460–461, 471, 472 *(illus.)*; revolution in (1789–1804), 469, 471, 503

Hakka people, 536

Hakra River, 31

Halevi, Judah, 191

Hammurabi, 16, 17, 64

Han Empire (China), 141–152, 143 *(map)*; administration of, 146–148; chronology (206 B.C.E.–220 C.E.), 133; Daoism in, 148; decline, 150; emperors, 148, 151–152; gentry, 144, 148; nomadic peoples and, 142, 143, 150; Qin origins of, 45, 141–142, 143 *(map)*, 144–146; resources and population, 142, 149, 151; Roman Empire compared to, 130, 142, 145, 150–152; Silk Road and, 143 *(map)*, 146, 149; taxation, 142, 148; technology and trade, 148–149

Han'gul (Korean writing), 240, 290, 291 *(illus.)*

Hangzhou, 237

Hanno, 84

Hanoverian dynasty, 380 *(illus.)*

Hanseatic League, 322, 331

Harappa, 31–32

Harding, Warren, 619

Haremhab (Egypt), 67

Harkhuf, 37, 38

Harness, 149 *and illus.*, 218–219

Hart, Robert, 539

Harun al-Rashd, 188

Hasan (son of caliph Ali), 186

Hatshepsut (Egypt), 66

Hattusha, 64, 71, 72

Hausa city-states (Africa), 301, 302 *(map)*, 500

Havel, Vaclav, 701

Hawaii, 338, 514, 587, 592; Pearl Harbor, 589, 634

Hay, John, 591

Hayford, J. E. Casely, 646

Heaven (god), 42, 43, 44, 148, 151, 271

Heavenly Kingdom of Great Peace (Chinese religious movement), 536–537, 538

Hebrew Bible (Old Testament), 5, 76, 78, 79, 99

Hebrew language, 14, 76, 191

Hebrews. *See* Israel, ancient

Heian period (Japan), 240. *See also* Kyoto (Heian)

Helena (Ethiopia), 352

Hellenistic Age (Hellenization), 94, 105; Alexandria, 115–116, 117; Antigonid dynasty, 114, 115–116 *and map*; belief systems in, 139; cameo, 116 *(illus.)*; culture in, 116–117; Ptolemaic Egypt, 114–115 *and map*, 116–117; Roman wars with Hellenistic kingdoms, 135; Seleucids, 114, 115 *(map)*, 155, 156

Helots, 107–108

Helsinki Accords, 674, 687

Henry II (England), 212–213, 222

Henry IV (France), 379

Henry IV (Holy Roman Emperor), 212

Henry of Navarre (France), 379

Henry the Navigator, 343, 344

Henry V (Holy Roman Emperor), 212

Henry VIII (England), 379–380, 382

Herero people, 581

Heresy, 157, 379

Herodotus, 94, 103, 107, 160

Heshen, 518

Heyerdahl, Thor, 338

Hidalgo y Costilla, Miguel, 473, 475

Hidden Imam, 421

Hideyoshi, 433

Hierarchy, in China, 44, 45, 46, 151, 283. *See also* Confucianism; Social classes

Hieroglyphics, 27, 49, 66, 104–105, 250

Hildebrand (Pope Gregory VII), 212

Hinduism (Hindus): *See also* India (Indian civilization); merchants, 310; pilgrimages, 123; rise of, 121–123; and sati (widow burning), 127, 313; Southeast Asia and, 312; temples, 122 *(illus.)*, 127, 311; Delhi sultanate and, 304, 305

Hindu-Muslim relations, 507, 714–715, 717; in Mughal India, 424, 425–426; Indian independence and, 647–648, 649, 651, 652 *(illus.)*

Hippalus, 160

Hiram (Tyre), 78, 81

Hirobumi, Ito, 564

Hirohito (Japan), 634

Hiroshima, atomic bombing of, 634, 635 *(illus.)*, 636 *(map)*, 674

Hispanics: *See also* Latin America; Spain *and specific country*; in United States, 708

Hispaniola, 354, 355, 356, 402. *See also* Dominican Republic; Haiti (St. Dominigue)

History (historians): culture and, 6; Greek, 107

Hitler, Adolf, 627–629, 631, 632, 634, 639. *See also* Nazi Germany; Jews and, 620, 627, 628, 637–638

Hittites, 68, 71, 72, 86, 224; iron working of, 62, 64–65, 169

Ho Chi Minh, 673, 675

Hohokam peoples, 254

Hokulea (canoe), 338

Hollywood films, 615, 727, 728

Holocaust, 637–638 *and illus.*

Holocene epoch, 10

Holy Land, Crusades to, 220–222

Holy Roman Empire, 202, 212, 222, 379, 382

Homer, 70, 71, 80, 106, 107, 175

Homosexuality: bisexuality in ancient Greece, 112–113; male, in Islam, 198, 423

Honduras, 592

Hong Kong, 534, 697, 730, 732

Hong Xiuquan, 536, 538

Hopewell culture, 255

Hoplites (hoplite tactics), 105, 106, 107, 110, 113

Hormuz, 353, 415

Horse-drawn vehicles, 149 *(illus.)*. *See also* chariots

Horses. *See also* Cavalry; domestication of, 90; harness for, 149 *and illus.*, 218–219; used in warfare, 23, 44, 150, 209–210, 232; stirrups for, 159, 209–210, 225; conquistador, 354, 355, 356; Amerindians and, 399; in Americas, 408; Afghan, 441; urban pollution and, 552, 616

Horton, James Africanus, 503

Horus, 26, 29

Hospitallers, 243

House of Burgesses (Virginia), 397

Housing (dwellings). *See also* Architecture; Stone Age, 6; Celtic, 51; in Rome, 137; imperial China, 147, 236; of Central Asian nomads, 159; Chaco Canyon culture, 254–255; in Teotihuacan, 246; in late medieval Europe, 317, 318 *(illus.)*; Industrial Revolution, 481, 490, 491 *(illus.)*; nineteenth century tenements, 552; for Brazilian poor, 659

Huan (China), 130

Huang Chao rebellion, 231

Huang Dao Po, 284

Huang He River. *See* Yellow (Huang He) River

Huayna Capac, 262

Huerta, Victoriano, 654

Huitzilopochtli (sun-god), 254

Hülegü, Il-khan, 275, 276, 278

Humanism: Greek, 107; European, 329–330

Human rights, 674, 700, 716, 723–725; and death penalty, 726; United Nations Declaration of, 665, 723–724; violations in Latin America, 692, 710

Hundred Years War (1337–1453), 331, 333–334

Hungary, 529, 543, 606, 672, 700, 705; mining in, 321, 325; Mongols and, 281

Huns, 257, 260; Gupta Empire and, 193

Hunting. *See also* Foragers (hunting and food-gathering peoples); Fur trade: in Stone Age, 6, 7; at Çatal Hüyük, 13; by Amerindians, 10, 399, 408, 563; of seals and whales, 513, 514–515 *and illus.*

Huntington, Samuel P., 722

Husayn, Saddam, 696, 702–703; and invasion of Iraq (2003), 717, 718, 719 (photo)

Husayn (Shi'ite martyr), 180, 181, 186, 421

Hussein ibn Ali, 603

Hutu-Tutsi rivalry, in Rwanda, 716–717

Hydraulic works (water engineering): See also Watermills; in ancient Rome, 139, 140 (illus.), 146; in China, 142, 146–147 and illus.; in Moche civilization, 257

Hydroelectric dams, 550, 609, 620, 682, 683

Hyksos, 65–66, 77, 86

Hyundai corporation, 697, 698 (illus.)

Iberian expansion (1400–1550), 342–348. See also Portuguese exploration; Spanish exploration, 337, 342, 343, 345–348, 354–356

Iberian peninsula: See also Portugal; Spain; Muslims in, 261, 343; unification of, 334–335

Ibn Abd al-Wahhab, Muhammad, 519

Ibn al-Arabi, 191

Ibn al-Haytham, 195

Ibn Battuta, Muhammad ibn Abdullah, 296, 297, 298, 309; in Delhi, 299, 305, 313; in Mali, 300, 301, 307, 311, 313

Ibn Hazm, 191

Ibn Khaldun, 278

Ibn Rushd (Averoës), 191

Ibn Sina (Avicenna), 221, 328, 329

Ibn Tufayl, 191

Ibn Tughluq, Muhammad, Sultan, 305, 313

Ibn Tulun, Mosque of, 190 and illus.

Ibrahim (Egypt), 520, 524

Ice Age, 5, 6, 10, 169. See also Stone Age

Ice Age, Little (1590s), 375, 439, 455

Iceland, 208, 342

Ideas, spread of, 170–173. See also Intellectual life; Political ideology; Buddhism, 171–172; Christianity, 172–173; and material evidence, 170

Ignatius of Loyola, 369

Iliad (Homer), 70, 71, 106, 175

Il-khanate (Iran), 272, 275 (map), 276–278, 284; rivalry with Golden Horde, 276, 282, 294

Iltutmish, Sultan, 303, 304

Immigrants (immigration). See also Chinese immigrants; European immigrants; Indian immigrants; Migration; Hellenistic Greeks, 114, 115 (map), 116–117; Etruscans, 131; Irish, 492, 494, 662; to Americas, 397, 476, 494, 552; acculturation and, 494–495; Asian, 494, 513, 562, 708; in Hawaii, 589; to Australia and New Zealand, 513, 516, 552, 576, 605; to Caribbean, 494, 514; to United States, 494, 538, 552, 558, 562, 605; Jews to Palestine, 604, 610, 612; World War I refugees, 605; to industrialized nations, 706, 710; English language and, 730–731

Imperialism. See also Colonies; Expansion; New Imperialism; and specific empires; in Africa, 500, 502 (map), 503; Japanese, 565–567; in Latin America, 589–592; cultural, 726, 727–728, 729; science and, 731

Import duties, 495, 623, 697. See also Tariffs

Import substitution, in China, 228

Import-substitution industrialization, 659, 660, 692

Inca (Inca Empire), 259–263; and Aztecs compared, 262–263; bureaucracy, 261, 263; civil war (1525), 262; roads, 256 (map), 260–261, 355; Spanish conquest of, 355–356, 388, 393

Incense trade, 161, 181

Indentured laborers, 514–516

Indentured servants, 397, 399, 400–401

Independence (independence movements). See also Decolonization (1947–1990); Dutch, 383; American Revolution and, 464; Latin American, 471–475 and map, 642; Haitian, 460, 469, 471; Serbian, 520, 527, 540; Greek, 469, 520, 524, 540; Philippine, 589; in sub-Saharan Africa, 642–646, 677; Vietnamese, 674; Indian, 646–652; in Soviet bloc, 700–702; in East Timor, 717

India, 369. See also Delhi Sultanate; India, ancient; Mughal Empire (India); India, under British rule; Indian immigrants; Gujarat, 305, 310, 353, 354; literacy in, 312; Chinese in, 341; Portuguese in, 353–354; cotton textiles, 427, 486; British trade, 498; deforestation, 593; ivory trade, 504; independence movement, 646–652; Pakistan and, 651–652, 717; democracy in, 675; Hindu-Muslim strife, 651, 652 (illus.); Kashmir and, 651, 675, 717; war with Pakistan, 675; birth control, 704, 705; English language in, 730

India, ancient: domestic cattle in, 9; chronology (1500 B.C.E.–647 C.E.), 97–98; agriculture in, 9, 32, 190, 298; Arya-Dasa rivalry and conflict in, 119; class in, 119, 120; epic literature of, 120, 125; geography of, 117; Greco-Bactrian kingdom in, 117, 121; Gupta Empire, 118 (map), 120, 122 (illus.), 125–127; Islam (Muslims) in, 186; diversity in, 122; Vedic Age, 118–120; as subcontinent, 117–118; mathematics in, 126; Mauryan Empire, 118 (map), 123–124, 171; political fragmentation in, 124–125; Sanskrit writing in, 119, 120, 125; science and technology in, 125; trade and, 124, 125, 127, 159, 161; women in, 120, 127; China and, 126, 226, 232, 266; Tibet and, 232; chronology (1206–1398), 299; gold trade in, 300; water-control systems in, 299

India, independence movement in (1905–1945), 646–652; chronology, 643; Gandhi and, 648–649, 650 and illus., 651; Muslim League and, 647, 649, 651; Nehru and, 649, 651; partition (1947), 644, 651–652 and illus., (map); World War II and famine in, 646, 651, 662, 663

India, religion in. See also Hinduism; Islam (Islamic civilization), in India; Jainism, 120, 124, 127, 311; origins of Buddhism in, 120–121; Vedic religion, 119–120, 121, 127

India, under British rule, 504–510, 516, 570, 583; (1687–1805), 505 (map); bureaucracy in, 507, 510; ceremonials, 508 (illus.); cholera, 490, 508–509; chronology (1756–1885), 501; company men, 504–506; cotton textiles, 496, 506, 507–508, 592; expansion, 511; industrialization, 481, 496, 507–508, 648, 649; tea production, 506, 507; irrigation, 507, 593; nationalism (1828–1900), 507, 509–510, 587, 647–648; opium trade, 506, 507, 529, 533; political reform, 507; traditions, 507, 509; railroads, 496, 508, 509 (illus.), 550, 588 (map), 593; raj and rebellion, 506–507; Russian threat, 531, 560; trade, 506, 507–508, 512; famine in, 646, 651; influenza in (1918–1919), 605, 648; women in, 508, 509, 573

Indian Civil Service (ICS), 507, 647, 649

Indian immigrants, 513–515, 516, 586, 603; in Caribbean, 494, 514, 515, 730–731

Indian National Congress, 510, 647, 648, 649, 651

Indian Ocean states. See also East Indies and specific states; Zheng He's travels in, 268, 285–287 and map, 339, 340–341 (map); Portuguese in, 345, 353–354; European colonies in, 588 (map)

Indian Ocean trade, 158 (map), 159–163, 300, 306–311; chronology (1st century C.E.), 157; impact of, 161, 165; origins of contact, 161; Periplus of the Erythraean Sea and, 162–163; Champa and, 242; China and, 229, 234; Africa and, 307–309; Arabia and, 309–310; empires and, 304 (map); India and, 310–311; monsoons and, 118, 160, 161, 297, 306–307, 309; Southeast Asia and, 306, 307, 311; ships in, 307, 308 and illus.; Portuguese and, 348, 361, 415, 430; Dutch in, 373, 374, 403, 430; Muslims and, 340, 427, 429–430; European domination, 417, 428 (map), 431; Chinese and, 440; Suez Canal and, 575

Indigo, 397, 512

Individual (individual rights). See also Citizenship; Human rights; Rights; Voting rights; Chinese Daoism and, 44–45; in ancient Greece, 106–107; Buddhism and, 121; Rome and Han China compared, 151; Enlightenment view of, 461; Declaration of Independence (US) and, 464; in France, 466, 468, 469; citizenship and, 543, 628, 637

Indochina. See also Burma; Cambodia; Southeast Asia; Thailand; Vietnam; French in, 583, 588 (map), 632, 673, 675; Japanese occupation of, 632, 663; independence of, 673, 675, 676 (map)

Indo-European languages, 23, 32, 50, 70, 95, 127. See also specific language; in India, 118, 119

Indonesia, 160 (illus.), 161, 415, 707, 719. See also Dutch East Indies; Java; Indian Ocean trade and, 165; New Imperialism in, 583, 586–587; independence of, 675; East Timor and, 717

Industrialization. See also Industrial nations; Industrial Revolution; in British India, 481, 496, 507–508, 648, 649; in

Industrialization (*cont.*)
Egypt, 495, 520; in Europe, 481; in Japan, 564–565, 587; nationalism and, 548, 558; nonindustrial world and, 495–496, 550; in Russia, 529, 530, 561–562; in Brazil and Argentina, 658, 665; in Soviet Union, 545, 607, 620, 622; working women and, 553; import-substitution, 659, 660, 692; in Japan, 683, 731–732; in Asia, 697–699 *and illus.*, 732; environmental effects of, 709; Western culture and, 731–732

Industrial nations (developed world), 612–617. *See also* Industrialization; Industrial Revolution; domination of, 548–549, 660; New Imperialism of, 545, 570, 574, 583, 590, 592; overseas trade of, 495, 512, 519, 660; social transformations (1850–1900), 550, 552–557; women's separate sphere in, 553, 556–557 *and illus.*; technology in (1850–1900), 549–550; labor movements, 552–553; urbanization in, 552; scientific revolution in, 614; technology in, 614–617, 708; class and gender in, 613–614; Depression (1930s), 623; environment in, 615–617, 709; immigration to, 552, 690, 707–708, 710; population in, 552, 703, 704–705; Chinese trade with, 699; agricultural subsidies in, 722; global warming and, 726; pollution agreements by, 725; Group of Eight (G-8), 720

Industrial Revolution (1760–1851), 457, 480–497. *See also* Great Britain, Industrial Revolution in; United States, Industrial Revolution in; agriculture and, 481–482; causes of, 481–484; social change in, 482, 492–493; chronology, 483; cities in, 490, 491 *(illus.)*; continental Europe, 482–484; division of labor, 485; impact of, 489–493; inventiveness in, 480; iron industry, 484–487; mass production, 484–486; cotton industry, 486; migrations, 482, 490, 494–495; new economic and political ideas in, 493–495; in nonindustrial world, 495–496; population growth, 490; railroads, 488–489; rural areas, 490–491; steam engines, 487–488; technology of, 484–489, 574; telegraph, 489; women in, 492; labor conditions in, 491–492

Industrial robots, 708, 722

Industries. *See also* Industrialization; Iron industry; Manufactured goods; Porcelain; Steel industry; Textile industry; chemical, 549, 603, 635, 709; tobacco in colonial Mexico, 408 *(illus.)*; World War II boom, 638; robots for, 708, 722

Indus Valley civilization, 5, 12 *(map)*, 31–34; bronze statue, 33 *(illus.)*; chronology, 7; environmental stress in, 33, 34; material culture of, 31–32; transformation of, 34

Inequality: *See also* Gender differences; Social classes; in classical Greece, 111–112; in Roman society, 134; global, 690, 706

Infanticide, in ancient Greece, 112

Infantry. *See also* Armed forces; chariots and, 40; Greek hoplites, 105, 106, 107, 110,

113; Chinese, 225, 340; Ottoman, 413; Crimean War and, 528; World War I, 601, 602 *(illus.)*

Inflation: Roman Empire, 141; Song China, 237; 16th century Europe, 383; Ottoman, 416; Safavid Iran, 424; Ming China, 439; Germany, 607; Guomindang China, 630, 634

Influenza, 276, 387, 605, 613, 648

Inheritance: in Egypt, 28, 29; in ancient China, 45, 144–145; in Celtic society, 52; in ancient Israel, 78; by women, 29, 191, 195, 237; Chimú dynasty and, 258

Inquisition, 371, 379

Institutes of the Christian Religion (Calvin), 366

Institutional Revolutionary Party (Mexico, PRI), 678, 714

Intellectual life (intellectuals): *See also* Culture(s); Ideas; Philosophy; Political thought; Science(s); in ancient Greece, 106–107, 111, 176, 221; in Muslim Spain, 191; Enlightenment, 372, 461–462; Slavophiles, 531, 532, 562; and socialism, 553

Interchangeable-parts manufacturing, 487

International Criminal Court (the Hague), 725

International Monetary Fund (IMF), 670, 720

International Statistical Congress (1860), 543

International Style in architecture, 615

International Working Man's Association, 553

Internet, the (World Wide Web), 719, 728–729

Investments: *See also* Foreign investment; in European industry, 483

Ionian Revolt, 109

Iran, 95, 119–120, 122. *See also* Il-khanate (Iran); Parthia; Persian Empire; Safavid Empire (Iran); Medes, 86, 96; geography and resources, 120, 122; chronology (711–1036 C.E.), 183; Sasanids in, 156–157, 181, 184, 186, 187; Silk Road trade and, 156 *(illus.)*, 157; taboo on eating pork, 170; Abbasid Caliphate and, 187, 188; Samanid dynasty in, 189, 191; political fragmentation in, 192; urbanization in, 194; madrasas colleges in, 199; Sufism in, 199; and Tibet, 232; conversion to Islam in, 186, 187, 265–266 *and illus.*; Mongol Il-khanate in, 272, 275 *(map)*, 276–278, 284; European merchants in, 411, 412; Mughal India and, 426; Qajar dynasty in, 531; oil wealth of, 685 *(map)*, 686; Islamic Revolution (1979), 693, 696, 697 *(illus.)*, 723; nuclear weapons research by, 717; women's rights in, 725

Iraq, 188, 192, 684, 696. *See also* Mesopotamia; after World War I, 611 *(map)*, 612; cities in, 194, 242, 245; oil wealth of, 612, 685 *(map)*, 686, 718; Persian Gulf War (1990–1991) and, 702–703; invasion of (2003), 718, 723

Ireland (Irish), 254, 333, 375, 492, 671; Celts in, 51, 52, 53, 72; monks, 203, 213; Great

Britain and, 382, 494, 557, 560, 591, 662; famine in (1847–1848), 494, 552, 662

Irigoyen, Hipólito, 658, 659

Iron curtain, 665, 668, 669, 674, 687. *See also* Cold War; Warsaw Pact

Iron industry and tools, 61. *See also* Steel industry; early China, 44; Meroë, 50, 169; advantages over bronze, 62, 92, 173; Assyrian, 73; Hittite, 62, 64–65, 169; India, 119; imperial China, 149; in sub-Saharan Africa, 169, 170, 173, 300; in Song China, 235, 236; Turkic, 272; stirrups, 159, 209–210, 225; late medieval Europe, 321; British, 375, 382, 482 *(map)*, 486–487; deforestation and, 375, 486; Industrial Revolution and, 482 *(illus.)*, 486–487

Iroquois Confederacy, 398, 399

Irrigation, 1, 579, 586, 593, 646; Mesopotamia, 14, 15, 19, 22; ancient Egypt, 25; Persian Empire, 95–96; Mesoamerica, 55, 246; Spain, 191; for rice cultivation, 241; India, 118, 299; Anasazi, 254, 255; Andean region, 256, 257, 258; in tropics, 299–300; and cotton, 500, 507, 508

Isabella (Spain), 335, 345

Isfahan, 421–424

Isis, 29, 50, 139

Islamic law (Shar'ia), 187, 193–194, 423, 429; in Mughal India, 426; in Ottoman Empire, 416, 418–420, 526

Islamic Revolution (Iran,1979), 693, 696, 697 *(illus.)*, 723

Islam (Islamic civilization), 180–200. *See also* Mosques; Muhammad (prophet); Muslim(s); Islamic law (Shar'ia); Shi'ite Islam; origins of, 181–186; Arab Caliphate and, 186–192; assault on (1050–1258), 191–193; Byzantine Empire and, 204; China and, 228; chronology (570–1260 C.E.), 183; cities and, 194–195; civil war in, 180, 185; conquests of (634–711), 177, 186–187; converts to, 188, 190, 191, 192, 193, 194, 265–266; Crusades and, 192, 220–221; Five Pillars of, 185, 193; in Ghana, 189–190; in India, 186 (*See also* Delhi sultanate; Mughal Empire); revolts against, 187, 188, 189; women and, 18, 195–198 *and illus.*; Kharijite sect, 186, 187, 189; political fragmentation, 188–191; Quran, 185, 187, 193–194, 195, 301, 312; recentering of, 198–199; slavery and, 188, 198; Sufism, 199, 305, 426, 429; Sunni tradition, 180–181, 191, 310, 421; Mongolian Empire and (1260–1500), 272, 276–279; scholars (ulama), 191, 193 *(illus.)*, 194, 198–199, 522–524, 526; science of, 195, 278–279, 284; conversion to, 265–266 *and illus.*, 312; in Mali, 300–301, 302 *(map)*; Gujarat and, 305; Indian Ocean trade and, 340; printing technology and, 365; *fatwas* (decrees), 418–420; pilgrims, 425, 519; African trade and, 430; in Russia, 447; in West Africa, 500, 516; *jihad* (holy war), 500, 581; slaves in, 504; Egypt and, 522–524; in East Indies, 586–587; Wahhabism, 519; spread of, in Africa, 583, 644,

645, 646; women in, 579, 612, 613, 693, 697 *(illus.),* 725; in Iran, 693; Persian Gulf War and, 703; September 11 (2001) attacks and, 713–714; in Afghanistan, 717–718; militancy of: 715–716, 722–723

Ismail, Shah, 421

Ismail (Egypt), 500, 569–570, 577

Israel, 717, 723; Suez Canal crisis (1956), 682–683; Arab conflict, 684–686 *and map*

Israel, ancient, 75–79, 85; diaspora, 79, 86; in Egypt, 77; geography and resources, 75–76; monarchy in, 78–79; origins and early history, 76–78; taboo on eating pork, 79, 170; women in, 78–79; Christianity in, 138–139

Istanbul, 420, 519, 526, 527–528. *See also* Constantinople; and Isfahan compared, 421–424; mosque in, 423 *(illus.);* Janissary power in, 520

Italy (Italian peninsula), 570, 670; Roman Republic in, 131, 135; medieval, 208; trading cities in, 219, 321, 322, 331, 342; Renaissance artists in, 330–331; maize in, 375; stock exchanges in, 374; city-states of, 342–343; immigrants from, 562, 657; unification of, 557–558; conquest of Libya by, 597; in World War I, 597, 605; invasion of Ethiopia by, 581–582, 628, 642; Mussolini's fascism in, 626–627; World War II and, 632, 633 *(map),* 634; decolonization of, 676 *(map);* aging demographic in, 704, 705; immigration to, 728

Iturbide, Augustín de, 475

Ituri Forest people, 6

Ivan III (Russia), 281

Ivan IV (Ivan the Terrible; Russia), 412

Ivory Coast (Côte d'Ivoire), 677

Ivory trade, 71, 161, 349 *(illus.),* 429, 504, 512

Izmir (Smyrna), 417

Jacquerie revolt (1358), 320

Jagadai Khanate, 272, 275 *(map),* 276, 294

Jaguar deity, 56, 57, 82 *(illus.),* 83

Jahiz, 196

Jainism, 120, 124, 127, 311

Jamaica, sugar plantations on, 401–402

James I (England), 380

James II (England), 381

Jamestown, Virginia, 396

Jamshedpur, 648

Janissaries, 415–416, 417, 519; Mahmud II's defeat of, 524; uprisings by, 420, 520, 524

Japan (Japanese), 225, 362. *See also* China, Japan; chronology (645–1185), 227; early history of, 239, 241; Fujiwara era, 241, 242; Kamakura Shogunate, 241, 291, 293; plague in, 228; Buddhism in, 241, 293; women in, 242; written language of, 240, 242; Ashikaga Shogunate, 293; Mongol attack on, 273, 274, 290–292 *and illus.,* 294; steel swords of, 287, 292; trade, 293; chronology (1543–1792), 435; climate changes in, 455; civil war in, 433; reunification of, 433–438; Korea and, 433–434, 440, 452; elite decline and social crisis in, 437–438, 563–564; foreigners and, 452,

563–564; Tokugawa shogunate, 434–438, 451, 452, 563–564; chronology (1853–1910), 551; immigrants from, 516, 589; Meiji Restoration and modernization of, 564–565; birth of imperialism in (1894–1905), 565–567, 570; Korea and, 565, 566–567, 629; railroads in, 566 *(map);* silk industry in, 565 *(illus.);* expansion of, 588 *(map),* 629; war with Russia (1904–1905), 562, 566, 587, 597; as great power (1868–1900), 563–567; industrialization in, 564–565, 587, 609; World War I and, 609, 617; Great Depression in, 623, 629; ultranationalism in, 628; World War II and, 632, 634, 635 *(illus.),* 636–637 *and map;* occupation of Burma by, 651, 663; Korean War and, 673, 683; booming economy and trade of, 673, 683, 690, 696–697, 731; low fertility in, 704; aging population in, 705; environmental awareness in, 709; industrial robots in, 708; recession in, 719; development model of, 731–732

Jati (Indian castes), 341, 506, 509, 646–647, 648. *See also* Brahmin class; origins of, 119, 120

Java, 274, 311, 430, 510, 511; temple complex in, 126 *(illus.);* population in, 586, 593

Jazz Singer, The (film), 615

Jenkinson, Anthony, 411

Jericho, 11, 13

Jerusalem, 79, 138, 172, 194, 281, 527, 604; Temple in, 78, 81; Crusades to, 192, 220–221; Israeli control of, 684, 686

Jesuits (Society of Jesus), 427. *See also* Ricci, Matteo; in North America, 399; Reformation and, 369; in Japan, 437; in China, 440, 442–443 *and illus.,* 452, 533

Jesus (Christ), 138, 157, 185, 366

Jewelry, 32, 258, 310; amulets, 19, 30

Jews, 99, 117, 310. *See also* Israel; Judaism; diaspora of, 79, 86; rules and strictures of, 79, 170; and Christianity, 138–139, 266; in Alexandria, 147; Jesus and, 162; Roman rule and, 162–163; in Spain, 191; in Sasanid Iran, 157, 232; Muslim view of, 185, 198; Ethiopian, 227; as merchants, 311, 334; as moneylenders, 325; as scholars, 191, 328; as mapmakers, 303 *(illus.),* 343; persecution of, 324, 326–328; expelled from Iberia, 324, 335, 373, 383; Egyptian, 523; in Germany, 373, 543; Ottoman, 525, 526; in Palestine (1930s), 604, 610, 612; Nazi Germany and, 620, 627, 628; Holocaust and, 635, 637–638; Soviet, 700

Jiang Jieshi. *See* Chiang Kaishek

Jiang Qing, 684

Jiangxi region (China), 629, 630

Jihad (Muslim holy war), 500, 581

Jim Crow laws (United States), 562

Jin Empire (China), 233, 234 *(map),* 239; Mongols and, 272, 283

Jingdezhen, 289, 436, 439

Jinnah, Muhammad Ali, 651

Joan of Arc, 333–334

João III (Portugal), 350

John (England), 222, 333

John Paul II, Pope, 700

Johnson, James, 645

Johnson, Lyndon, 673

John VI (Portugal), 472

Joint-stock companies, 374 *and illus.,* 429, 431, 483, 532

Jordan, 684, 723

Joseph (biblical), 77

Joyce, Ellen, 577

Juan, Jorge, 394

Juarez, Benito, 473 *(illus.)*

Judah, 79, 85

Judaism, 97. *See also* Israel; Jews; Zoroastrianism and, 128; Christianity and, 162–163; Islam and, 184; Vladimir I's rejection of, 216

Julius Caesar, 51, 135, 136

Jungle, 297. *See also* Forests, tropical

Junks (ships), 234, 307, 340, 343, 344 *(illus.)*

Junta Central (Spain), 471

Jupiter (god), 134

Jurchens, 233, 235. *See also* Jin Empire (China)

Justinian (Byzantium), 204, 206

Justo, Juan, 591

Jutland, Battle of (1916), 603

Juvaini, 277–278

Ka' ba, 182, 184, 185

Kaffa, black death in, 276, 318

Kahlo, Frida, 655

Kaifeng (Song capital), 233, 235 *(illus.),* 238 *(illus.)*

Kalahari Desert people, 6

Kamakura Shogunate (Japan), 241, 291, 293

Kamikaze, 292

Kamose (Egypt), 66

Kanagawa, Treaty of (1854), 564

Kanem-Bornu, 301, 302 *(map)*

Kangxi (China), 440–443 *and illus.,* 452

Kanishka, 171

Kapital (Marx), 553

Karakorum, 272

Kashmir, 651, 675, 717, 723

Kassites, 15, 64

Kautilya, 124

Kazakhs (Kazakhstan), 531, 535, 583

Keiretsu (Japanese corporate alliances), 697

Kemal Atatürk, Mustafa, 610 *and illus.,* 612

Kennedy, John F., 673; Cuba and, 674, 679

Kenya, 429, 644, 718; independence of, 677

Kenyatta, Jomo, 677

Kepler, Johannes, 371

Keraits, 270

Khadija, 182, 195

Khajuraho, Hindu temple at, 122 *(illus.)*

Khanates. *See* Golden Horde; Il-khanate (Iran); Jagadai khanate; Yuan Empire (China)

Khans, 275 *(map). See also* Mongolian Empire, *and specific khan*

Kharijites (Islamic sect), 186, 187, 189

Khazar Turks, 215

Khefren, pyramid of, 27

Khipus, 256, 262

Khitan people (Liao Empire), 233, 234, 240

Khoisan peoples, 223

Khomeini, Ayatollah Ruhollah, 693, 697 (illus.)

Khrushchev, Nikita, 674

Khubilai, Great Khan, 272, 275, 278, 283, 284; invasion of Japan by, 274, 291–292; Marco Polo and, 282, 322

Khufu, Great Pyramid of, 27

Khurusan, 187

Kievan Russia, 177, 203, 215–218, 222; rise of, 215–216; society and culture, 215, 218

Kikuyu people, 11, 677

Kilwa, 307

Kimberley diamond fields, 580, 645 (illus.)

Kingship. See Monarchy (kingship, emperors)

King's Peace (387 B.C.E.), 113

Kinship groups: See also Clans; Lineages; Neolithic Age, 11; Celtic, 58; and Greek colonies, 105

Kipchak khanate. See Golden Horde khanate

Kitchener, Lord Horatio, 575

Kivas, 254, 255

Knights, 210, 318, 331, 333. See also Conquistadors; Warriors; Crusades and, 192, 220–221 and illus.; Portuguese, 334, 335, 343

Knights of the Hospital of St. John, 243, 415

Knights Templar, 243, 344

Kollantai, Alexandra, 624–625

Kongjo, 232

Kongo, slave trade in, 349–352. See also Congo

Kon Tiki (raft), 338

Korea (Koreans), 225, 287, 289–290. See also South Korea; plague in, 228; han'gul writing system, 240, 290, 291 (illus.); chronology (1258–1392), 273–274; printing technology in, 239, 289, 290, 291 (illus.); Song China and, 232, 238; Yuan China and, 288, 289; climate change in, 455; China and, 565; Japan and, 433–434, 440, 452, 565, 566–567, 629; North, 672, 717

Korean War (1950–1953), 665, 672–673, 674, 683, 697

Koryo, 239, 290. See also Korea

Kosovo, Battle of (1389), 282, 412–413

Kosovo crisis (1999), 716

Kremer, Gerhard (Mercator), 376–377 (map)

Kremlin, 280 (illus.)

Krishna, 122, 125

Kshatriya class (India), 119, 120

Kush, 25, 49. See also Nubia

Kushan people, 159, 170

Kuwait, 686, 702

Kyoto (Heian), 240, 241, 434

Kyoto Protocol (1997), 725, 726–727

Labor (labor force): See also Labor unions; Slaves; Working class; Egyptian, 27, 28; Chavín civilization, 57; Assyrian, 74 (illus.), 75; Persian Empire, 95–96; Roman, 141; in China, 168; Teotihuacan, 245–246; Andean (mit'a), 257, 259, 260–261, 263, 392; Spanish colonial (encomienda), 354, 391, 392; child labor, 481, 489, 492, 494,

553; division of, 485, 555; indentured, 397, 399, 400–401, 514–516; African colonial, 582, 642, 644, 645 (illus.); Asian immigrant, 494, 513–516, 562, 708; Japanese occupation and, 634; shortages in Europe, 708; robot technology and, 708, 722

Labor unions (trade unions), 695, 708, 720; in Australia, 513; in late nineteenth century, 494, 495, 552–553; in United States, 563; Polish Solidarity, 700, 701

Labour Party (Great Britain), 651, 670

Laissez faire economics, 493, 494, 497. See also Free trade; famine and, 662

Lalibela (Ethiopia), 312

Lamas (Tibetan priests), 282, 439–440

Land grants, 75, 192; medieval fiefs, 210–211

Landowners (landownership): Mesopotamian, 17; in early China, 45; in Assyria, 75; in Persian Empire, 99; in Greece, 106; in Roman Republic and Empire, 131, 136, 137, 141, 148, 150–151; in imperial China, 144, 148, 150–151, 236; in medieval Europe, 204, 209, 219; tax farming and, 277; English, 320; in late medieval Europe, 317, 318; European gentry, 374–375; indentured Europeans, 401; Amerindians, 462, 473; imperial China, 439; Ottoman, 416, 419, 527; Russian serfs, 447, 449; Safavid Iran, 420; colonial Latin America, 471; English enclosure movement, 481; French Revolution, 466; Indian mansabs, 425, 426; British India, 506, 646, 647; colonial Africa, 582, 678; Russia, 583, 604; Jewish kibbutzim, 612; Argentine oligarquía, 657, 659; Brazil, 658, 659; Mexico, 653, 654

Land reform: in China, 629, 630, 634, 699; in Cuba and Guatemala, 678; in Mexico, 655, 656

Language(s). See also English language; Writing; and specific languages; Indo-European, 23, 32, 95, 181, 182; Semitic, 14–15, 16, 22, 28, 76; Akkadian, 14–15, 22, 65, 126; Celtic, 58; Arabic, 187, 188, 189, 191, 266, 296, 307, 312; Babylonian, 64; Egyptian hieroglyphs, 27, 49, 66, 104–105; Germanic, 261; Sanskrit, 119, 120, 125; Latin, 137–138, 191, 260, 328, 330, 731; Malayo-Polynesian, 340; Mandarin Chinese, 284; Slavic, 215, 216, 280; African, 168, 169–170, 307, 393, 402, 430, 431; and religious conversion, 266; in India, 312, 426, 647; Malayo-Polynesian, 340; Os-manli, 416; vernacular, 330; Russian, 452, 531, 561; Safavid Iran, 421; and immigrants to Americas, 495; French, 526, 557; in India, 647; nationalism and, 543–544, 557, 558, 679

Laozi, 44

Las Casas, Bartolomé de, 391

Lascaux, France, cave paintings in, 5

Late Bronze Age (2200–500 B.C.E.), 62–72. See also China, early; in Aegean region, 68–72; fall of civilizations of, 85–87; in Middle East, 62–68

Lateen sails, 160, 308, 343, 347

Latin alphabet, 610 (illus.), 612

Latin America. See also Americas, the; Central America; Latin America, colonial; and specific countries; independence, 471–475, 474 (map), 642; immigration to, 494; women's rights in, 477; chronology (1870–1912), 571–572; imperialism in, 589–592, 594; military coups in, 623, 626, 659, 660; Depression of 1930s in, 623, 626; development in, 638; economic dependence of, 652, 659; radio cartel in, 658; chronology (1876–1946), 643–644; revolutionary movements in (1950s–1960s), 678–679, 690; chronology (1964–1990), 691; communists in, 678–679, 692; foreign investment in, 678, 692; United States and, 678–679, 690, 692–693, 696; military coups and dictatorships in (1960s–1970s), 692–693, 710; population growth in, 708; population in (1730–2050), 704 (illus.); music from, 730; soap operas from, 729

Latin America, colonial, 388–396, 390 (map). See also Brazil, colonial; and specific colony; chronology (1518–1620), 389; economy in, 391–392; gold and silver from, 356, 383, 391–392, 404, 439; livestock in, 408; Mexico, 388, 391, 408 (illus.), 473, 475; North America compared to, 396; Peru, 390 (map), 391, 392; race and ethnicity in, 393 (illus.), 394–396; society in, 388, 392–393; state and church in, 388, 391, 393

Latin language, 137–138, 191, 328, 330, 731

Latin West (Europe 1200–1500), 316–335; Black Death in, 317, 318, 320; cathedrals in, 325; chronology, 319–320; culture in, 319; humanism and printers in, 329–330; Hundred Years War (1337–1453) and, 331, 333–334; Iberian unification in, 334–335; mines and mills in, 320–321; monarchy and nobles, 331; peasant revolts in, 320; persecution of Jews in, 326–328; Renaissance artists, 330–331; rural life, 317–318, 320; technology and environment in, 319, 324; universities in, 328–329; urban revival in, 316, 321–325

Latvia, 701; Soviet invasion of, 631

La Venta (Olmec center), 55

Laws (legal codes). See also Islamic law (Shar'ia); Code of Hammurabi, 16, 17; Persian Empire, 99; Indian, 127; Roman, 203, 213, 222; Vietnamese, 293; Spanish colonial, 391; mercantilist, 403–404; Enlightenment ideas and, 461; Napoleonic Code (France), 468; British factory, 494; Ottoman reforms, 525–527; and gender division in industry, 553; German social, 560; Jim Crow (United States), 562; environmental protection, 709

League of Nations, 606, 607, 608, 669; German departure from, 628; Japanese departure from, 629; mandate system and, 610; Sino-Japanese War (1937–1945) and, 630

Leather working (tanneries), 119, 301, 310, 321

Lebanon, 611 *(map)*, 612, 684, 696
Le Corbusier (Charles-Edouard Jeanneret), 615
Lee, Ang, 729
Lee, Bruce, 729. *See also under* Li
Legalism (China), 44, 45, 144, 146, 151, 152
Legislative Assembly (France), 467, 468
Leith-Ross, Sylvia, 577
Lenin, Vladimir I., 604, 607
Leningrad, seige of, 631. *See also* St. Petersburg
Leo III, Pope, 202
Leopold II (Belgium), 579, 580, 584
Leo X, Pope, 366–367
Lepanto, Battle of (1571), 416
Le Roy, Loys, 364–365
Lexus and the Olive Tree, The (Friedman), 722
Liao (Khitan), 233, 234, 239, 240
Liberalism, 557–558
Liberia, 503, 716
Libraries: in Assyrian Empire, 75; in Alexandria, 116; in Timbuktu, 312; Vatican, 330; Jesuit in Beijing, 443 *(illus.)*
Libya, 219, 597, 632
Life expectancy: in nineteenth-century England, 490; for industrialized nations, 705
Lighting, electric, 549, 552, 615
Liliuokalani (Hawaii), 569
Limbourg brothers, 318 *(illus.)*
Limits of Growth, The, 687
Lim Nee Soon, 587 *(illus.)*
Lincoln, Abraham, 476
Lindbergh, Charles, 614–615
Lineages: *See also* Clans; Patriarchy; Neolithic, 11; Matrilineage, 11, 50; Maya, 249
Linear B (Mycenaean tablets), 70–71, 72
Linlithgow, Lord, 649
Li Qingzhao, 237
Lisbon, earthquake in (1755), 369
Li Shimin, 225, 231, 232
Literacy, 92, 208. *See also* Education; Schools; in Mesopotamia, 22; in ancient Egypt, 44; transition from orality to, 175–176; monasteries and, 213; and Confucianism, 239; in Inner Asia, 289; in Korea, 290, 291 *(illus.)*; of European women, 378; Muslim, 301, 312; nationalism and, 558; in Japan, 564; in Africa, 644, 645
Literature. *See also* Libraries; Poets and poetry; Printing; Writing; in ancient Egypt, 27, 30; Indian, 120, 122–123, 125; Tamil, 125; Abbasid Caliphate and, 187–188; Persian, 189; Japanese, 240, 241, 242; Chinese, 289; of late medieval Europe, 329–330; Safavid (Iran) poetry, 421; Jesuits and, 443 *(illus.)*; in English, 730–731
Lithuania, 281, 332 *(map)*, 631; Poland-Lithuania, 446, 447; independence of, 701
Liu Bang (China), 146
Livestock, 391. *See also* Cattle; Pastoralism; in Argentina, 408, 591, 657; in Britain, 481; and Soviet collectivization, 621–622
Livingstone, David, 500, 503
Li Zicheng, 432–433, 440
Llamas and alpacas, 9, 57, 83, 257, 259, 262

Lloyd George, David, 606
Loans. *See* Foreign debt (international loans)
Locke, John, 382, 461, 464
London, 543; growth of (1680), 373; Crystal Palace, 487; growth of (1850–1914), 490, 552; tenements in, 491 *(illus.)*
Long March (China), 629–630
Longshan complex, 41
Looms, power, 486, 492, 565. *See also* Weaving
Lorraine. *See* Alsace and Lorraine
Los Angeles, automobiles in, 616 *and illus.*
Louisiana, 399, 486
Louis Napoleon (France), 469
Louis Philippe (France), 469
Louis the Pious, 208
Louis VII (France), 221–222
Louis XIII (France), 379
Louis XIV (France), 379, 381 *(illus.)*, 382, 465
Louis XVI (France), 460, 466, 468
Lowell, Francis Cabot, 492
Ludendorff, Erich von, 605
Lugal (big man), 15–16
Lula da Silva, Luiz Inácio, 714
Luo Guanzhong, 289
Luoyang (Chinese capital), 43, 142, 147
Lusitania (ocean liner), 603
Luther, Martin, 366, 371, 379
Lutheranism, 366, 368 *(map)*, 378–379
Lydia, 107, 109, 170
Lysistrata (Aristophanes), 112

Ma'at (order of the universe), 26
Macao, 353, 430, 440, 533
Macartney, George, 444–445
McDonald's restaurants, 729, 730
Macedonia, 113–114, 597; Antigonid dynasty in, 115–116 *and map*
Machine guns, 575, 576 *(illus.)*, 581, 601, 602
McKinley, William, 589, 591
Madagascar, 160 *(illus.)*, 161, 340, 677
Madeira, 342, 343
Madero, Francisco I., 654, 656
Madras, 426, 504, 506, 508
Madrasa (Islamic college), 199, 250, 328
Magellan, Ferdinand, 337, 346 *(map)*, 348
Magic Canal, 145, 147 *and illus.*
Magi (Persian priests), 96
Magna Carta (1215), 333
Mahabharata, 120, 125
Mahan, Alfred T., 587
Mahavira, 120
Mahayana Buddhism, 121, 123, 172, 241; in China, 225–226; in Tibet, 232
Mahdi, 576 *(illus.)*, 581
Mahmud II, Sultan, 520, 524, 526
Ma Huan, 310
Maimonides, 191
Maine (battleship), 591
Maize (corn), 9, 57, 255, 257, 262, 586; in Africa, 409; in Caribbean, 354; in Europe, 375, 408, 481
Majapahit Empire, 304 *(map)*, 311
Makovsky, 561 *(illus.)*
Malabar Coast, 306, 310–311, 353, 354

Malacca, 311, 312, 353, 415, 431, 511
Malacca, Strait of, 307, 310, 311
Malaria, 236, 387, 644; quinine and, 442, 557; slaves and, 402, 405
Malawi (Nyasaland), 583
Malaya (Malay Peninsula), 311, 338, 415, 431, 511, 634; Indian Ocean trade and, 159, 165; British in, 583, 587 *(illus.)*; Chinese immigrants in, 586
Malay Federation, 675
Malayo-Indonesians, travels of, 340 *and map*
Malayo-Polynesian languages, 340
Malaysia, 583. *See also* Malaya
Malcomb, John, 464 *(illus.)*
Mali, 166, 176, 199; Islamic empire of, 300–301, 302 *(map)*, 303, 313; as Western Sudan, 303 *(map)*, 581
Malindi, 352, 429
Malinke people, 301
Malta, 80, 416
Malthus, Thomas, 703, 705
Malvinas (Falkland Islands), 693
Mamluks (Turkic people), 188, 191, 281; Mongols and, 192, 274, 276, 278
Mamluk Sultanate (Egypt), 192, 274, 276, 281, 522, 523–524; Ottoman rule in, 352, 354, 412, 415, 420, 495, 519
Manchuria, 432, 434, 452; Japan and (Manchukuo), 565, 566, 567, 629
Manchurian Incident (1931), 629
Manchus, 434, 452, 536. *See also* Qing Empire; and end of Ming Empire, 432–433, 439–440
Mandate of Heaven (China), 43, 59, 148, 152, 241
Mandate system, 610, 611 *(map)*, 612
Mandela, Nelson, 678, 715
Manetho, 26
Manichaeism, 159
Manioc, 9, 55
Manors (estates), 209, 211
Mansa Kankan Musa, 301, 303 *(illus.)*, 342
Mansa Muhammad, 342
Mansa Suleiman, 301
Manuel (Portugal), 353
Manufactured goods (manufacturing). *See also* Industrialization; Industrial Revolution; Mass production *and specific manufactures;* Mesopotamian, 15; Roman Empire, 137, 167; trans-Sahara trade, 189; medieval Europe, 219; Gujarati, 310; late medieval Europe, 323, 324; Atlantic trade, 404; Carpet making, in Iran, 424; Chinese wallpaper, 444; interchangeable parts for, 487; American foreign markets, 587, 652, 657; British foreign markets, 508, 512, 516, 574 *(illus.)*, 652; import of, in Latin America, 590, 652, 657; in India, 649; by women in wartime, 638; dependence on imported, 679; foreign investment in, 692; consumer goods, 708; computers and, 708; global expansion in, 718; science and, 731
Manuzio, Aldo, 330
Manzikert, Battle of (1071), 191, 220
Maori people, 512, 513

Mao Zedong, 546, 629–630, 635, 683–684; death of, 698; and Great Leap Forward, 663–664, 684

Mapmaking, 303 *(illus.)*, 343; Jesuit in China, 336, 442; Mercator and, 376–377 *(illus.)*

Maquet, Jacques, 169

Marcus Aurelius Antoninus, 130

Marduk, 13–14, 18, 19, 20–21

Maria Theresa (Austria), 542

Marie Antoinette (France), 467

Marinetti, Filippo, 619

Maritime expansion (to 1550): before 1450, 338–342; Americas and, 354–356; Atlantic Ocean, 341–342; chronology, 339; East Africa, 352; Iberian (1400–1550), 342–348; Indian Ocean, 340–341, 353–354; Pacific Ocean, 338; Portuguese voyages, 343–344; Spanish voyages, 337, 345–348; West Africa and, 348–352

Markets. *See also* Merchants; Trade; Greek agora, 105; Aztec, 253; late medieval fairs, 322–323; in colonial Brazil, 400 *(illus.)*; African slave, 406; and African women, 642; global culture, 729–730

Marne, Battle of (1914), 601

Maroons (runaway slaves), 402–403

Marquesas Islands, 338

Marriage: *See also* Polygamy; Neolithic, 11; Mesopotamia, 15, 18; China, 45; Celtic, 52; Egypt, 29; Greece, 112; India, 127; divorce and, 18, 29, 195; Rome, 134; imperial China, 144, 150; Islam, 195; Kievan Russia, 218; Israel, 78; Mongol, 271, 290; religious conversion and, 266; Aztec, 314; India, 305, 313; late medieval Europe, 324; European monarchies, 211, 333, 334, 335; in early modern Europe, 377–378, 379; Hindu-Muslim, 426; Ottoman, 417, 526, 527; and class in Britain, 482; and nationality, 544; Victorian Age, 556–557; and divorce, 379, 526, 612, 630; and abortion, in Soviet Union, 625; in China, 630; and family planning, 703

Married Women's Property Act (Britain), 557

Mars (god), 134, 135

Marshall Plan for Europe, 670, 673

Martí, José, 591

Martin, P.-D., 381 *(illus.)*

Marx, Karl, 553, 554–556, 624, 629

Mary (mother of Jesus), 157, 391

Mary of Burgundy, 334

Massachusetts, colonial, 397, 462

Mass deportations, 74, 124

Mass media, 699, 723. *See also* Motion pictures; Newspapers; Radio; Television

Mass production. *See also* Industrial Revolution; in Song China, 235, 236; assembly-line, 439, 613, 616; of British pottery, 484–486; division of labor in, 485, 555; interchangeable parts for, 487; Japanese porcelain, 434, 436 *and illus.*; Soviet agriculture and, 620; of transistor radios, 728

Mathematics: Mesopotamian, 23–24; Egyptian, 31; fractions, 233; Indian, 126; invention of zero, 126, 250; Islamic, 195;

Chinese, 233, 234, 235 *(illus.)*, 294; Maya, 249, 250; Mongol Il-khanate, 278, 279, 284; value for pi (π), 279; and graphmaking, 484–485 *and illus.*; European revolution in, 370–371; and new physics, 614

Matrilineality, 11, 50, 249

Mauritius, 510, 514, 515

Mauryan Empire (India), 118 *(map)*, 123–125, 170

Maximilian (Mexico), 473 *(illus.)*

Maya (Maya civilization), 246–250, 251, 262, 391; architecture of, 247, 249 *(illus.)*; calendar, 249–250; city-states, 244, 245, 247; elite burials, 260, 261 *(illus.)*; writing system, 249, 250 *(illus.)*

May Fourth Movement (China), 609

Mazzini, Guiseppe, 557–558

Mecca, 182, 184, 185, 603; pilgrimage to, 194, 199, 342, 425, 519

Mechanization, cotton industry, 486, 496, 508

Medes, 86, 96

Medici, Cosimo de', 331

Medici, Lorenzo de', 331

Medici family, 324–325, 365

Medicine (physicians): *See also* Disease; Egyptian, 30; Assyrian, 75; Indian, 125; Chinese, 156, 283; Greek, 232; Islamic, 195; Muslim, 221; European, in Africa, 351; Jesuit in China, 442, 443; women and, 477–478; Ottoman reforms, 526; cleanliness and, 615; antibiotics, World War II, 636; health care in Africa, 644, 724; Doctors without Borders, 724; Western *vs.* traditional, 731

Medieval Europe (300–1200), 203, 206–214; chronology (634–1204), 205; self-sufficient economy of, 208–209; society in, 209–211; insecurity in, 207–208; Christian church in, 211–214; monarchy in, 202, 208, 211, 212–213; revival of (1000–1200), 218–219; cities and trade in, 219; technology in, 218–219

Medina, 184, 186

Mediterranean Sea and region. *See also specific civilizations, peoples and countries;* Minoan and Mycenaean trade, 71; chronology (2000–330 B.C.E.), 63–64; Phoenicians in, 80, 81 *(map)*, 85, 86; Carthaginian trade, 84; climate, 101, 131; Roman expansion into, 135; Indian Ocean trade compared to, 160–161; European trading cities and, 208, 219, 220, 321, 322, 342–343; Ottoman trade in, 415, 417

Meenakshi Temple, India, 306 *(illus.)*

Megaliths, 11, 13

Mehmed II, Sultan, 282, 413

Meiji Restoration (Japan), 564–565

Mein Kampf (Hitler), 627

Melanesia (Melanesians), 338, 512

Melville, Herman, 514

Memphis (Egypt), 27, 29, 49

Men: *See also* Family; Gender differences; Marriage; Patriarchy; Women; as Ice Age hunters, 6; in Kikuyu legends, 11; in Mesopotamia, 18; in ancient Israel, 78; as

fathers, 13, 44, 45, 143; in India, 123; Roman *paterfamilias*, 133, 134; sexuality and, 112–113, 198, 213, 423; Muslim, 195, 198

Menelik (Ethiopia), 500, 581

Menes (Egypt), 26

Mengzi (Mencius), 44, 144

Mensheviks, 604. *See also* Bolsheviks

Mercantilism, 403–404. *See also* Capitalism

Mercator (Gerhard Kremer), 376–377 *(map)*

Merchants (merchant class). *See also* Markets; Trade; Mesopotamia, 17; Indus Valley, 33; Assyria, 64, 75; Olmec, 55; Crete, 71; Phoenicia, 81; Carthage, 84; India, 124, 310; China, 147, 150, 151, 237; medieval Italy, 220; Persian Gulf, 234; Uighur, 232; Aztec, 253; Mongolian Empire and, 275, 277; Yuan China, 282, 283–284; Chinese in Southeast Asia, 285; tropical trade routes and, 297; Indian Ocean trade and, 307; Jewish, 311, 334; late medieval Europe, 323, 324; Muslim, 309–310, 311, 340, 342, 353, 422, 427; Portuguese, in Africa, 349; taxes on, 353, 354; European, 353–354, 372, 373–374, 407; North American, 397, 462; African, 406, 407; British India, 496; foreign, in Moscow, 449; Japan, 434, 437–438; European in China, 439, 440, 444, 608 *and illus.*

Mercosur (Mercado Comun del Cono Sur), 721

Merneptah (Egypt), 72

Meroë, 49–50, 169

Mesoamerica, 244–254. *See also* Maya; agriculture in, 9; ball games, 249 *(illus.)*, 254, 255; chronology (3500–400 B.C.E.), 39; Olmec, 53–56, 245; chronology (100–1502), 247; classic era, 245–250; Northern cultures and, 255; post-classic era, 250–254; Teotihuacan, 245–246, 250, 251; Aztecs, 248 *(map)*, 251–254, 262–263, 354–355, 388, 393

Mesopotamia (Mesopotamian civilization), 4–5, 12 *(map)*, 13–24. *See also* Babylonia; Iraq; Sumerians; chronology, 7; geographical features of, 14; religion and myths of, 13–14, 18–19, 20–22, 34; society, 17–18; technology and science, 19, 22–24; trade, 17; cities and kingship in, 15–17; cylinder seals, 23 *(illus.)*; divination in, 18–19; and Egypt compared, 25, 27, 34; in Late Bronze Age, 62, 64–65, 85–86; Assyrian Empire and, 72, 75; Persian Empire and, 96, 99; Manichaeism in, 159; Silk Road trade and, 156, 157; population decline in, 192; Indian Ocean trade and, 214, 215

Metals (metallurgy). *See also* Bronze; Coins; Copper; Gold; Iron industry and tools; Mining; Silver; Steel; Tin; Neolithic, 13; Indus Valley, 32; Kushite, 49; Chavín, 57; Late Bronze Age, 88; China, 57, 173; Iran, 122; Inca, 262; Japan, 287; sub-Saharan Africa, 300

Methodius, 206

Metternich, Klemens von, 469

Mexican Revolution (1910–1940), 641, 652–656; civil war (1911–1920), 654; institutionalized (1920–1940), 654–656; social conditions for, 652–653

Mexican Revolutionary Party (PRM), 655

Mexico City, 653, 707; colonial, 388, 408 (illus.)

Mexico (Mexicans), 245, 355, 471. See also Aztecs; Mesoamerica; Valley of, 248 (map), 251; colonial, 391; Amerindians in, 473, 591, 653, 678; Catholic Church in, 473 (illus.), 654, 656; independence of, 473, 475; United States and, 563, 592; civil war in, 654–656; constitutionalism in, 654, 655; railroads in, 653, 655 (map); Brazil and Argentina compared to, 652, 660; nationalism in, 653; population growth in, 704, 708; under Institutional Revolutionary Party, 678, 714; democratic reform in, 714; economic swings in, 719, 720; and free trade, 720, 721 (map)

Miao peoples, 518

Michelangelo, 331

Middle class, 613. See also Bourgeoisie; Mesopotamian, 27; Egyptian, 28; Greek, 106, 109; Roman, 134, 151; Chinese goods and, 443; Revolutions of 1848 and, 469; French Revolution, 557; women and domesticity, 493, 497, 556; liberalism and, 557; urbanization and, 552, 616; Victorian Age, 556–557 and illus.; Indian nationalism, 646, 647; in Brazil and Argentina, 657, 658, 659; in Mexico, 653

Middle East. See also Arabs; Islam; Mesopotamia; and specific countries, cultures, empires, and regions; agriculture in, 8; domestication of animals in, 9, 89; Late Bronze Age cosmopolitanism in, 62, 64–65 and map; and Silk Road, 154; chronology (1219–1453), 273–274; Mongols in, 277, 278; Timur's conquests in, 274; Chinese trade with, 284; chronology (1909–1923), 599; after World War I, 610–612; Arab-Israel conflict in, 684–686 and map; chronology (1979–1991), 691; Islamic militants in, 715–716

Middle Passage, 404–405

Midway, Battle of (1942), 634, 636 (map)

Mies van der Rohe, Ludwig, 615

Migrations (population movements). See also Immigrants; Nomadic peoples; to Americas, 53; Celts in Europe, 50–51; Bronze Age, 65–66, 72; Jewish diaspora, 79, 86; of Hellenistic Greeks, 114, 115 (map), 116–117; mass deportations, 74, 124; in Roman Empire, 138, 139; in sub-Saharan Africa, 167, 168, 169–170, 173; from Southeast Asia to Madagascar, 160 (illus.), 161; by converts to Islam, 194–195; Industrial Revolution and, 482, 490, 494–495; rural-to-urban, in Africa, 582, 644, 707; and India-Pakistan partition, 651, 652 (illus.); rural-to-urban, 376, 528, 706–707; to industrialized countries, 690, 707–708

Militant nonviolence, Gandhi and, 648–649

Military. See also Armed forces; Navy; Warfare; Weapons and military technol-

ogy; Assyrian, 73–74, 75; Israelite, 78; Carthaginian, 84–85; Spartan, 108; Roman, 135, 138; Arab, 188; medieval Europe, 207, 210–211, 212; imperial China, 150, 225, 231, 234–235; Teotihuacan, 246; Inca, 261; Zulu, 499 and illus.; and Eurasian expansion, 519; Ottoman, 520, 524, 526; Egypt, 520; Qing China, 534, 536–538 and illus., 609; Russian, 531; Japan, 619, 629; China (Red Guard), 684; rule of, in Latin America, 623, 659, 660, 692–693; in Africa, 715

Military slaves, 188, 192, 313, 387, 424. See also Janissaries

Millennium Summit (2000), 722

Mills: in China, 149; in late medieval Europe, 320–321, 322 (illus.), 324

Milosevic, Slobodan, 716

Mines Act of 1842 (Britain), 494

Ming Empire (China), 267, 285–289, 438–440; achievements of, 289; Mongol foundation of, 284, 285–287; naval expeditions by, 285–287 and map, 339, 340–341, 344 (illus.); technology and population of, 287–288; Vietnam and, 293; end of, 432, 439–440, 452

Mining (minerals). See also Coal mining; and specific metals; central Europe, 321; tropical, 300; environment and, 391–392, 593; in colonial Latin America, 391–392; Industrial Revolution and, 487; New Imperialism and, 574, 592; in Africa, 626, 638; in Mexico, 656 (illus.); in British India, 648; in Africa, 580, 582, 626, 645 (illus.), 715

Minoan civilization, 62, 68–70, 86

Minos (Crete), 69

Minotaur, 69

Minyak people, 232

Missionaries. See Christian missionaries; Jesuits

Mississipian culture, 255–256

Mithra (sun god), 101, 139

Mitsui companies, 434

Mobutu, Joseph, 717

Moby Dick (Melville), 514

Moche, 257–258, 262; burials in, 260, 261 (illus.)

Mocteczuma II (Aztec), 253, 355

Modernization (modernity): See also Industrialization; Westernization; British in Argentina, 476–477 and illus.; in Egypt and Ethiopia, 500; of warfare, 528; of Turkey, 610 (illus.), 612; cult of, 614

Mogadishu, 296

Mohenjo-Daro, 32, 33 (illus.)

Moksha (liberation), 120, 123

Moluccas (Spice Islands), 348, 353

Mombasa, 429, 431

Monarchy (kingship, emperors). See also Divine kingship; and specific monarchs and emperors; Sumeria, 15–16; Babylonia, 38–39; ancient Egypt, 26–27, 29–30, 34; early China, 41, 42, 43; Olmec, 55; Nubia, 49, 50; Assyrian Empire, 73, 75; Israel, 78–79; Persian Empire, 99, 100 (illus.) 102–104;

India, 123–124, 125; Roman Empire, 136, 138, 139, 141, 151–152; Han China, 141, 151; sub-Saharan Africa, 168–169; medieval Europe, 202, 208, 211; imperial China, 228; Christian church and, 212–213; Japan, 241; Maya, 248; Africa, 300–301, 349–352; Aztec, 253; Inca, 261; Kongo, 349–352; late medieval Europe, 323, 331, 333–335; European dynasties, 380 (illus.); European trade and, 374; European nationalism and, 379; royal absolutism, 382; French Revolution and, 466–467, 468, 469; in Russia, 449–450 and illus., 453, 561; Congress of Vienna and, 469; Enlightenment and, 461–462; Brazil, 472–473; Iran, 693

Monasteries (monasticism): Buddhist, 121, 127, 226, 229–230, 231; Christian, 203, 208, 211, 213, 215, 378, 380

Monetary system. See also Banks; Coins; Currency; Rome, 141; in Song China, 237; in Il-khanate (Iran), 278; capitalist vs. communist, 670–672

Mongolian Empire (Mongols), 270–294, 322. See also specific Khanates; chronology (1206–1433), 273–274; conquests of (1215–1283), 267, 272, 274; culture and science in, 277–279; invasion of Japan by, 274, 290–292 and illus., 294; Islam and (1260–1500), 272, 276–279; Mamluks and, 192, 274, 276, 278; nomadic way of life and, 271–272; plague and disease in, 275–276; rise of (1200–1260), 270–277; rulers of (1206–1260), 274 (illus.); threats to China by, 287, 288, 359; trade in, 274–275, 306; Vietnam and, 274, 285, 289, 293; Yuan Empire (China), 272, 282–285, 288, 289

Mongols (Mongolia), 192, 233, 359, 421; China and, 439, 533; Galdan in, 440, 442, 446

Monopolies, government, 728

Monopoly, trading: Egyptian, 27; Carthaginian, 84; Song China, 235, 237; royal, 345, 349; royal, 345, 349, 403; in colonial Americas, 392; Indian Ocean, 353, 354, 430; chartered companies for, 403; Portuguese, 345, 349, 403, 580; Alaskan fur, 450; African colonial, 579–580

Monotheism: Akhenaten and, 66; in Israel, 79; Christianity and, 139, 152

Monroe Doctrine, 591. See also Expansion, United States

Monsoons (seasonal winds), 31, 299; and China, 38, 40 (map), 143 (map); and India, 117, 119; Indian Ocean trade and, 118, 160, 161, 297, 307, 309

Morelos, José, 475

Morocco, 190, 335; Portuguese invasion of, 343

Moro Wars (Philippines), 427

Morse, Samuel, 489

Moscow, 281, 445–446, 449, 532, 631; Kremlin in, 280 and illus.

Moses, 77, 78

Mosques, 194; Ibn Tulun, 190 and illus.; in Canton, 228; in Delhi sultanate, 303, 305;

Mosques (*cont.*)
    in Africa, 301, 311; Gujarati, 311–312; in
    Istanbul, 423 *(illus.)*; in Iran, 421
Most-favored nation status, 534
Motion pictures (film), 615, 727, 728, 729
Mound-building cultures, North America,
    255–256
Mountbatten, Lord, 651
Mount Huanyaputina, 455
Moveable type, for printing, 236, 239, 330
Mozambique, 429, 430, 580, 678, 716
Mozambique Channel, 161
MTV (Music Television), 728
Mu'awiya, 185–186
Mughal Empire (India), 277, 414 *(map)*, 424–
    427; chronology (1526–1739), 413; Hindu-
    Muslim coexistence in, 424, 425–426;
    Portuguese and, 353–354, 425; regional
    challenges to, 426–427; British challenge
    to, 504, 505 *(map)*
Muhammad Ali (Egypt), 498, 529; modern-
    ization and reforms of, 495, 500, 520
Muhammad (prophet), 180, 193, 194, 427;
    death of, 185; revelations of, 182, 184
Muir, John, 563
Mummification, in Egypt, 30, 49
Munich Conference (1938), 628–629
Murasaki Shikibu, 240, 242
Murdock, Rupert, 728
Muscovy, 411, 446. *See also* Moscow
Music: Silk Road trade and, 156 *(illus.)*; in
    sub-Saharan Africa, 168; slave girls in
    Baghdad, 196–197; Byzantine, 206; cathe-
    dral organs, 214 *and illus.*; European
    troubadours, 220; global culture and,
    728, 730
Muslim Empires, (1520–1656), 414 *(map)*.
    See also Ottoman Empire; Mughal Empire
    (India); Safavid Empire (Iran)
Muslim League, All-India, 647, 649, 651
Muslims (Muslim countries), 170, 177, 184.
    See also Arabs; Islam; Hindu-Muslim
    relations; Mosques; Byzantium conquered
    by, 204; in Spain, 208; and Crusades, 192,
    220–222; in Ghana, 221, 222; hospitality of,
    296; pilgrims, 185, 194, 199, 301, 342;
    Christian rivalry with, 316, 352; driven
    from Iberian peninsula, 334–335, 343, 345,
    383; traders, 310, 311, 340, 342, 353, 422;
    astronomy of, 370; in Africa, 352, 429, 579,
    581; in East Indies, 427; and Russia, 531,
    583; expelled from Greece, 610; in Pak-
    istan, 675; in former Yugoslavia, 716;
    Iranian Revolution and, 723; women's
    rights in, 612, 613, 725
Mussolini, Benito, 626–627, 628, 634
Mutsuhito (Japan), 564
Myanmar. *See* Burma (Myanmar)
Mycenaean civilization, 62, 70–72, 86;
    linear B tablets, 70–71, 72
Myrrh (incense), 66, 161, 181
Mysore, 498, 506
Mystery cults, 139

Nabopolassar, 86
Nadir Shah, 426

NAFTA (North American Free Trade Agree-
    ment), 720, 721 *(map)*
Nagasaki, 437; bombing of (1945), 634, 674
Naipaul, V.S., 730–731
Nairobi (Kenya), 644, 725
Namibia (Southwest Africa), 581
Nanjing (Nanking), 285, 537 *and illus.*, 538,
    630
Nanking, Treaty of (1842), 534, 538
Napata, 49
Napoleon Bonaparte, 468–469, 472 *(illus.)*;
    defeat of, 468, 510; Europe of (1810), 470
    (map); invasion of Egypt by, 498, 500, 519–
    520, 522–524; invasion of Portugal and
    Spain by, 471, 478; invasion of Russia by,
    468, 529, 530 *(illus.)*, 541, 663
Napoleonic Civil Code, 468
Napoleonic Wars, 470 *(map)*
Napoleon III (Louis Napoleon), 469
Naqsh-i Rustam, 100, 103
Nara, 241
Naranjo, 244
Narmer (Egypt), 26
Nasir, Gamil Abd al-, 682–683 *and illus.*
Nasir al-Din Tusi, 278
Natal, 510, 514
Nation, Carrie, 613
National Assembly (France), 466, 467
National Convention (France), 468, 471
Nationalism (self-determination), 513, 606,
    660. *See also* Decolonization; Indepen-
    dence; Revolutionary era (1775–1848), 457,
    469; census and, 542–544; European, 557–
    558; Indian, 507, 509–510, 587, 647–648;
    Austria-Hungary, 557, 560–561; German,
    379, 548, 557, 558–560, 607; language and,
    543–544, 557, 558, 679; Italian, 557–558;
    imperialism and, 574; Zulu, 580; World
    War I, 545, 597, 606, 617; Arab, 610, 612,
    696; mandate system and, 610, 611 *(map)*,
    612; fascism and, 546, 626; Japanese
    ultranationalism, 629; Mexican, 653;
    African, 675; Brazilian, 714; Eastern
    European, 700; Hindu, 714
Nationality: census and, 543–544; citizen-
    ship and, 543, 557, 708
Nationalization (expropriation): in France
    and Great Britain, 670; in Cuba, 690; in
    Iran, 693; in Latin America, 655–656, 678,
    692; in Russia, 604
National liberation, 546, 682. *See also*
    Decolonization; Independence
National parks (North America), 563
National Revolutionary Party (Mexico),
    655
National Socialist German Workers' Party
    (Nazis), 627. *See also* Nazi Germany
Natives Land Act (South Africa, 1913), 581
NATO (North Atlantic Treaty Organization),
    669, 672, 716, 718
Natural disasters, 33. *See also* Floods;
    earthquakes, 258, 369
Nature. *See* Ecological crisis; Environ-
    ment, the
Navajo people, 408
Navigation Acts (Great Britain), 403

Navigation (navigational instruments). *See
    also* Navy; Sailing; Ships and shipping;
    astrolabe, 343; astrolabe for, 234, 278, 343;
    compass for, 234, 308, 343, 364; Polyne-
    sian, 338; Viking, 341; Portuguese, 343;
    British manufacture of, 482
Navy (warships). *See also* British Navy;
    Pirates; Minoan, 69 *(illus.)*; Carthaginian,
    84; Athenian, 110, 113; Korean, 290;
    Mongol, 292 *(illus.)*; Portuguese, 352, 353–
    354; English, 382; timber for, 375; Japa-
    nese, 451, 565, 630; Korean, 433; Ottoman,
    413, 415, 416, 524; Panama Canal and, 592;
    Russian, 449, 450, 451, 525, 527; Spanish-
    American War (1898), 591; steam-powered
    (gunboats), 495, 534, 564, 575; submarine
    warfare, 603, 605, 631, 634; World War I,
    602–603, 605; United States, 564, 634, 635,
    696, 718; World War II, 631, 634; aircraft
    carriers, 631, 634
Nawab, 504, 505
Nazi Germany, 620, 627–629, 669. *See also*
    Germany, in World War II; Argentina and,
    659; economic and social policies, 628,
    638; Jews and, 620, 627, 628, 637–638; pact
    with Soviets (1939), 629
Ndebele people, 581
Nebuchadnezzar, 79, 86, 101, 110
Nefertiti (Egypt), 67
Nehru, Jawaharlal, 649, 651, 675, 682, 683
    (illus.)
Nemesis (gunboat), 495
Neo-Assyrian Empire. *See* Assyrian Empire
Neo-Babylonian kingdom (Chaldean
    dynasty), 86, 96
Neo-Confucianism, 230, 236, 290. *See also*
    Confucianism
Neoliberalism, women's rights and, 694–695
Neolithic Age (New Stone Age): agricultural
    revolution in, 8–11; culture, 6; dwellings
    of, 11; life in communities of, 10–11, 13; in
    China, 41
Nerchinsk, Treaty of (1669), 442, 446
Nestorian Christians, 157, 159, 225
Netherlands, the (the Dutch; Holland), 323
    (illus.), 670, 686. *See also* Dutch colonies;
    East India Company (Dutch, VOC); bour-
    geoisie in, 373, 374; independence of, 383;
    mapmaking by, 377 *and illus.*; poverty in,
    376; wars with England (1653–1658), 383,
    403; in North America, 398, 399; slave
    trade and, 401, 405; West India Company,
    374, 400, 403, 405; China trade and, 444;
    Atlantic trade and, 403, 404; Japan and,
    436 *and illus*, 437; Mughal India and, 504;
    German invasion of, 631; English in, 731
Nevskii, Alexander, 280, 281
Newcomen, Thomas, 487, 488 *(illus.)*
New Deal (United States), 623
New England, 397, 462; industry in, 486, 492
Newfoundland, 208, 342
New Guinea, 338, 589
New Imperialism (1869–1914), 545, 548,
    569–595; in Africa, 571–572, 577–583, 584–
    586; in Asia, 571–572, 583, 588 *(map)*;
    chronology, 571–572; colonial administra-

tion, 575–577; cultural motives, 572–574; economic motives, 574; global environment and, 593–595; in Hawaii and Philippines, 587, 589; in Latin America, 571–572, 589–592; political motives, 570, 572; possessions of great powers, 588 *(map)*; in Southeast Asia, 583, 586–587; weapons and technology, 576 *(illus.)*; world economy and, 592–593

New Lanark, 494

New Laws of 1542 (Spain), 391

Newspapers, 520, 526; Crimean War and, 527; imperialism and, 574, 591

Newton, Isaac, 371, 614

New Year's Festival, Babylonian, 19, 20–22

New York City, 488, 549, 707; colonial, 398; growth of, 552; skyscrapers in, 615; terrorist attacks in (2001), 712–714

New Zealand, 338, 430, 457, 581, 613; immigration to, 513, 516, 552, 576, 605; Maori in, 512, 513; whaling in, 513, 514

Nicaragua, 592; Sandinistas in, 692–693, 696

Nicholas I (Russia), 527, 529, 530, 532

Nicholas IV, Pope, 276

Nicholas V, Pope, 330

Niger, 166, 169

Niger Delta, 503, 581

Nigeria, 170, 573, 593, 644, 730; women in, 584–585; British in, 642; independence of, 677; civil war in, 663; democracy in, 715

Niger River, 299, 301

Nile River: floods, 5, 8, 25–26, 31, 34; geography of, 24–25; in Nubia, 48

Nile Valley, 8, 224

Niña (ship), 345, 347

Nineveh, 74 *(illus.)*, 75

Nippur, 18

Nirvana, 120–121, 171–172, 226, 230

Nishapur, 194

Nixon, Richard, 684, 692

Nizam al-Mulk, 426

Nkrumah, Kwame, 677, 682

Nobel, Alfred, 549

Nomadic peoples. *See also* Mongolian Empire; Turkic peoples; *and specific peoples;* Ur and, 16; early China and, 44; Egypt and, 28; Meroë and, 50; Israelites and, 76; imperial China and, 142, 143, 150, 229, 233; Silk Road and, 155, 156, 159; Islamic conquests and, 237; Kievan Russia and, 270–271

Nongovernmental organizations (NGOs), 724

Nonindustrial world: *See also* Developing nations; industrialization and, 550; domination of, 570, 574; Great Depression and, 623, 626

Norman conquest (1066), 208, 211, 220

North Africa, 188. *See also specific country;* Phoenicians in, 80, 81 *(map)*, 219; Carthage in, 61, 82–85; domestication of animals in, 89, 167; Muslim ports in, 190, 219; Portuguese in, 335, 343; Portuguese in, 343; World War II in, 621, 632, 633 *(map)*, 646

North America, 550. *See also* British North America; Canada; Mexico; United States; Vikings in, 342; Amerindians in, 247, 254–256, 398–399 *and illus.*, 408, 462; French and Indian War, 399, 461; domination of, 495; modern technology in, 614–615; population (1730–2050), 704 *(illus.)*; environment in, 709

North American Free Trade Agreement (NAFTA), 720, 721 *(map)*

North Atlantic Treaty Organization (NATO), 669, 672, 716, 718

Northeast Asia, chronology (668–1125), 227

Northern Rhodesia (Zambia), 581

North Korea, 672, 717. *See also* Korea

North River (steamboat), 487

North Vietnam, 673, 675. *See also* Vietnam

Norway, 208, 613, 631

Novgorod, 216, 280

Nubia (Nubians), 37, 58; chronology (4500–300 B.C.E.), 39; Egypt and, 48–50, 66, 69–70, 72, 168; gold trade, 26, 28, 45, 48 *(illus.)*, 49; Meroitic, 49–50; Christianity in, 173, 227, 301

Nuclear arms (nuclear weapons): atomic bombing of Japan, 634, 635 *(illus.)*, 636 *(map)*, 637, 674; treaties limiting, 665, 674, 717

Nuclear power, 637, 708; waste from, 709, 717

Number systems, 23–24, 126

Nuns, 127, 213, 230. *See also* Monasteries

Nur al-Din ibn Zangi, 192

Obregón, Alvaro, 654, 655

Observatories: *See also* Astronomy; in imperial China, 233–234, 235 *(illus.)*, 284, 285, 294; Il-khanate Iran, 278–279, 284; Korean, 290

Odyssey (Homer), 70, 106, 175

Ögödei, Great Khan, 272, 273, 275

Ohio River Valley, 399, 487; Amerindians in, 254, 255

Oil crisis (1974), 686 *and illus.*

Oil (oil industry), 719, 723; Arab-Israel conflict and, 685 *(map)*, 686; in Iran, 685 *(map)*, 686, 693; in Iraq, 612, 685 *(map)*, 686, 718; in Kuwait, 702; in Mexico, 656; World War II and, 631–632, 634, 637

Old Stone Age (Paleolithic Age), 6, 169

Old Testament (Hebrew Bible), 5, 76, 78, 79, 99. *See also* Bible, the

Oligarchy: Japan, 437–438; Argentina, 657, 659

Olmec civilization, 53–56, 54 *(map)*, 245; chronology of, 39; elites in, 53, 55, 56, 58

Olusegun Obasanjo, 715

Oman, Sultanate of, 504

Omar Khayyam, 278

Omdurman, Battle of (1898), 575, 576 *(illus.)*

Onin War (1477), 293

On the Origin of Species (Darwin), 558

Opium trade, 506, 507, 529, 533–534, 609

Opium War (1839–1842), 533–536, 540

Oracles: Greek, 105, 106; Shang China, 42 *(illus.)*

Oral culture (orality): Stone Age, 7; ancient Israel, 77; Greek, 105, 111; and literacy, 175–176

Orange Free State, 510, 581

Order of Christ, 344

Organization of European Economic Cooperation (OEEC), 670

Organization of Petroleum Exporting Countries (OPEC), 685 *(map)*, 686 *and illus.*

Orozco, José Clemente, 473 *(illus.)*, 655

Orthodox Christianity, 204, 206; Russian, 177, 216, 218, 222, 280, 281, 446, 449, 450, 452, 531, 532; Serbian, 520, 527, 716

Osman, 412, 429

Osmanli language, 416

Ottoman Empire, 267, 277, 282, 412–420, 451, 519–529. *See also* Istanbul; Janissaries; Turkey; Portugal and, 352, 353; chronology (1500–1710), 413; crisis in (1585–1650), 416–417; economy (1650–1730), 417, 420; Egypt and, 412, 415, 420, 495, 498, 519–520; expansion of, 342, 361, 412–413, 415; Greek independence and, 469, 520, 524; Holy Roman Empire and, 379; trade, 411; institutions of, 415–416; Islam and, 416, 418–420, 524, 525–526, 529; legal codes in, 525–527; navy of, 413, 415, 416, 524; chronology (1805–1876), 521; Russia and, 412, 449, 469, 520, 524, 529, 531; (1829–1914), 525 *(map)*; European model for, 457–458, 520, 524–527, 528 *(illus.)*, 597; Tanzimat reforms, 524–526, 527, 532; Crimean War and (1853–1856), 527–529, 540; Balkan crisis and, 597; World War I and, 603–604; division of, after World War I, 545, 610, 611 *(map)*, 617

Owen, Robert, 494

Oxen and plows, 8, 14, 90, 119, 318

Oxford University, 328, 329

Pacific Islanders, 514, 515

Pacific Ocean (Oceania), 583. *See also specific island;* chronology, 339; Polynesian exploration of, 268, 338, 340 *(map)*, 341 *(illus.)*; Magellan's crossing of, 337, 348; colonial possessions in, 589; whaling in, 513, 514–515 *and illus.*; World War II in, 632, 634, 636 *(map)*; population (1730–2050), 704 *(illus.)*

Pacific Rim economies, 696–699. *See also* East Asia; *specific countries*

Pahlavi, Muhammad Reza, Shah, 693

Paintings. *See also* Art and artists; Egyptian tomb, 29; Nubian tomb, 48 *(illus.)*; Buddhist, 230 *(illus.)*; cave, 4, 126 *(illus.)*, 165–166 *(illus.)*, 168, 230 *(illus.)*; frescoes, 69 *(illus.)*, 70, 330, 331; Song China, 238 *(illus.)*; Iran miniatures, 278; of French peasants, 318 *(illus.)*; Renaissance, 330–331; of Versailles, 381 *(illus.)*; colonial Spanish, 393 *(illus.)*; Safavid Iran, 422 *(illus.)* 423; Mughal India, 425 *(illus.)*, 426; of St. Petersburg, 561 *(illus.)*; Mexican, 473 *(illus.)*, 655, 656 *(illus.)*

Pakistan, 696, 717, 723; Bangladesh and, 675; partition of 1947 and, 651–652 (illus.); age distribution in, 705 (illus)

Paleolithic (Old Stone Age), 6, 169

Palestine Liberation Organization (PLO), 686

Palestine (Palestinians), 220, 603. See also Syria-Palestine; Jewish homeland in, 604, 612; partitioning of (1947), 670; Israeli-Arab conflict, 684–686; terrorism and, 686, 723

Palm oil, 167, 170, 499, 503, 512, 516, 593, 642

Pan-African Congress, 606, 646

Panama, 356; United States and, 592, 692

Panama Canal, 592, 593, 594, 692

Pandyas, 125

Panini, 125

Pan o palo policy (Mexico), 653

Papacy (popes), 208, 211. See also individual popes; monarchies and, 212–213; schisms and, 204, 333; Holy Roman Emperors and, 202, 212, 281; Crusades and, 220; and forced conversions, 326; Peter's pence (collection), 324; treaty negotiation by, 347–348; and Protestant Reformation, 365–366, 369; Henry VIII's challenge to, 379–380

Paper currency, 439, 467. See also Currency; in China, 237, 283; Mongol, 277, 280

Papermaking, 44, 173, 187; Egyptian papyrus, 26, 27, 80; in India, 312; in late medieval Europe, 324

Paraguay, 720, 721 (map)

Paris, 373, 375, 615; University of, 328, 329; watermills in, 321, 322 (illus.); French Revolution and, 467, 468; Parlement of, 465; Revolution in (1848), 469; as "City of Lights," 552

Paris Peace Conference (1919), 606, 610

Parliament (Britain), 321, 334, 380–381, 486; American Revolution and, 462; Chartism and, 494

Parsees, 128. See also Zoroastrianism

Parthenon, 133 (illus.), 139

Parthia (Parthians), 114, 117, 144 (map), 172; and Rome, 139; Sasanid Empire, 156–157; Silk Road and, 155, 156

Parvati, 122, 187

Pastoralism (pastoralists), 10, 11. See also Cattle; early Israelites, 76; Arab, 181, 298; in sub-Saharan Africa, 168; in tropics, 298; Inca, 259–260; Islam and, 312

Pataliputra (modern Patna), 124, 125

Paterfamilias, 133, 134

Patriarch of Alexandria, 173, 194, 352

Patriarch of Constantinople, 204, 211, 216

Patriarch of Serbia, 282

Patriarchy: in China, 45; in Persia, 96; in India, 119; in Rome, 133, 134, 150

Patrilineal societies, 11; Maya, 249

Patron/client ties, Roman, 133–134

Paul, 138–139, 162

Pavia, 219

Pax deorum, 134, 155

Pax romana, 137, 161

Peace of Augsburg (1555), 379

Pearl Harbor, 589; Japanese attack (1941), 634

Peasants (peasantry). See also Farmers; Rural societies; Serfs; Mesopotamia, 17, 72; Middle East, 62; Egypt, 28–29, 115; Greece, 106; Rome, 136, 141; China, 145, 150; medieval Europe, 208–209; revolts by, 320, 377, 417; France, 318 (illus.); European, 375–377; and industrialization, 481; Egyptian, 495; French Revolution and, 465, 466; Indian, 496, 506, 646; Japanese, 564; Serbian, 520; African colonial, 582; Mexican, 653, 654, 655, 656; Soviet Russian, 604, 607, 620–622, 663; Brazilian, 659; Chinese Communists and, 610, 629, 630, 663; Latin American, 652

Pedro I (Brazil), 472

Peloponnesian League, 108

Peloponnesian War (431–404 B.C.E.), 113

Penates (household gods), 134, 155

Penn, William, 398

Pennsylvania, 487, 549; colonial, 398

Pentagon, attack on (2001), 702–703

Pepi II (Egypt), 37

Perestroika (Soviet reform), 700, 701

Pericles (Greece), 109, 111, 113

Periplus of the Erythraean Sea, The, 162–163

Perón, Eva Duarte, 660

Perón, Juan, 659–660

Perry, Matthew C., 564

Persepolis (Parsa), 99, 100 (illus.), 103

Persia, 525. See also Iran; languages of, 421

Persian Empire, 94, 95–101, 159; chronology, 97–98; geography and resources, 95–96; monarchy and, 100, 102–104; organization and ideology of, 98–101; rise of, 96, 98; rivalry with Greeks, 95, 99, 101, 109–110, 113; Alexander the Great and, 113–114

Persian Gulf (Persian Gulf states), 29, 31, 161, 353, 686, 696. See also specific countries; Indian Ocean trade and, 214, 215; ships in, 234

Persian Gulf War (1990–1991), 702–703, 717, 728

Persian language, 37, 189, 312

Persian literature, 240

Peru: Chavín civilization of, 82 (illus.), 83; colonial, 390 (map), 391, 392; independence of, 472; railroad in, 590 (illus.)

Peter's pence, 324

Peter the Great (Russia), 449–450 and illus., 527; westernization of: 449–450, 453, 532

Petrarch, Francesco, 329, 330

Petroleum industry. See Oil (oil industry)

Pharoahs (Egypt), 26, 77. See also Egypt, ancient

Philadelphia, 488; colonial, 398, 464

Philip II (Macedonia), 113

Philip II (Spain), 379, 383

Philippine Islands, 337, 348, 675; Spanish and, 427, 429, 440, 583; United States and, 563, 587, 589, 592; World War II in, 634, 636 (map)

Philip the Fair (France), 333

Philistines, 72, 76, 78

Philosophy. See also Confucianism; Ideas; Political ideology; Daoism, 44–45, 148, 224, 225, 231, 283; Greek, 107, 111, 221; Jewish, in Spain, 191, 328; positivism, 493–494

Phoenicia (Phoenicians), 80–82, 160. See also Carthage; alphabet, 80, 104, 176; Canaanites and, 77, 79, 80; city-states, 61, 74, 78, 80, 81–82; colonies of, 80, 81 (map), 85, 86, 161; Greeks and, 80, 104; language, 14, 76, 80; in North Africa, 169; textile dyes of, 83

Physicians. See Medicine

Physics, 371, 614, 637

Piccolomini, Aenius Sylvius, 316

Pilgrim, Islamic, 425, 519

Pilgrimages (pilgrims): Buddhist, 126, 127, 171, 232, 266; Christian, 213, 220, 221; Hindu, 123; Muslim, 185, 194, 199, 301, 342, 425, 519; Teotihuacan, 246

Pilgrims (Protestant sect), 397

Pi (π, mathematical symbol), 279

Pinochet, Augusto, 692, 693

Pirates: Mycenaean Greek, 70, 71; East Asian, 287, 289, 290, 293, 311, 437, 440, 451, 452, 563

Pisistratus, 109

Pizarro, Francisco, 355–356

Planck, Max, 614

Plantations: See also Sugar plantations; clove, 504; indigo, 397, 512; pineapple, 587 (illus.); slavery and, 475

Plantocracy (gens de couleur), 460, 469, 471

Plato, 107, 111, 176, 328

Platt Amendment (United States), 592

Playfair, William, 484–485 and illus.

Plows, 9, 90; in central Europe, 8; in Mesopotamia, 14; in ancient India, 119; Byzantine, 205; in China, 236; in medieval Europe, 218–219, 318

Plutarch, 85

Poets and poetry: See also Literature; Egyptian, 29; Greek, 106, 107, 175; Arabic, 196; Chinese, 154, 231, 237; troubadours, 222; Il-khanate, 278; Persian, 421; Italian, 619

Poison gas (chemical weapons), 602, 638, 717

Poland-Lithuania, 446, 447

Poland (Polish), 219, 281, 528, 543, 705, 718; Christianity of, 206, 215; Russia and, 450, 452; independence of, 606; Nazi invasion of, 629, 631; World War II casualties, 635, 638; Catholicism of, 452, 638; Soviet model and, 672; fall of communism in, 700, 701; democracy in, 714

Political systems and institutions: See also Administration; Democracy; Government; Monarchy; and specific institutions; Mesopotamian, 18; Indus Valley civilizations, 34; Chavín, 56; Olmec, 55; Mycenaean, 71; colonial, 397; Aztec, 251, 252; Tang China, 231; Inca, 261; Christian Church and, 267–268; Japan, 434

Political thought (ideology). See also Confucianism; Legalism in China, 44, 45, 144; of Persian Empire, 99; Han China and Rome compared, 151–152; Locke and, 382, 461, 464; Chinese, 444; Enlightenment and, 461–462; Industrial Revolution and, 493–495; socialism, 493–494, 553; Darwinism and, 558; Western, in Africa, 644, 646; Gandhi's nonviolence, 648–649

Politics. *See also specific political parties and movements;* European innovation in, 378–385; revolutionary era, 462; New Imperialism and, 570–572; famine and, 662–664; women's rights and, 613, 694–696; chronology (1992–2004), 715; environmental concern and, 709; global, 716–717; population growth and, 704

Pollution, 549, 552, 563, 709–710, 725; industry and, 321, 490; automobiles and, 616, 617, 709

Polo, Marco, 233, 275 *(map)*, 282, 308, 322

Polo (game), in China, 229 *and illus.*

Polygamy, 18, 68, 99, 195, 218, 253

Polynesians, 512; Pacific exploration by, 268, 338, 340 *(map)*, 341 *(illus.)*

Polytheism, 182, 211, 218

Ponce de León, Juan, 354

Pontius Pilate, 138

Pope, Alexander, 371

Popes. *See* Papacy *and specific popes*

Popular culture, 729–730

Population movements. *See* Migration(s)

Population (population growth): adoption of agriculture and, 10, 11; ancient Egypt, 28–29; ancient Greece, 105, 109; census, 78, 142; China, 59, 142, 149, 151; medieval Europe, 218, 219; Mesoamerican, 245–246, 250, 251, 253; imperial China, 284, 287, 317; South Asia, 298; late medieval Europe, 317, 318; and climate (to 1500), 359; Great Britain, 481; imperial China, 359, 445, 451, 533, 538, 539; industrialized Europe, 493; Russia, 452, 529; census and, 542–544; United States, 587, 708; East Indies, 586; British India, 646; environment and, 709; demographic transition and, 703–704; developing nations, 690, 705–706, 710; industrialized nations, 704–705; world (1730–2050), 704 *(illus.)*

Porcelain: *See also* Pottery; Chinese, 229, 275, 289, 436, 439; mass-produced, 434, 436 *(illus.)*, 484–485

Pork, custom and dietary rules on, 79, 170

Portsmouth, Treaty of (1905), 566

Portugal (Portuguese), 570, 671, 728. *See also* Portuguese exploration; African slave trade and, 344, 345, 349–352, 405, 406; African trade of, 302 *(map)*, 348–352; in China, 436, 440; in East Africa, 429–430; Hormuz and, 353, 415; Indian Ocean trade and, 348, 353–354, 361, 415, 430; monopoly trade of, 345, 349, 403, 580; Muslims driven from, 334–335, 343; Napoleon's invasion of, 471, 478

Portuguese colonies. *See also* Brazil, colonial: in Africa, 578 *(map)*, 579, 580; in China, 353, 354 (*See also* Macao); and decolonization, 676 *(map)*, 678

Portuguese exploration, 337, 342, 348; in Africa, 344, 346 *(map)*, 349–350, 351–352, 429; in Atlantic, before 1500, 343–345; Henry the Navigator and, 343, 344

Positivism, 493

Potatoes, 57, 257, 362, 375, 408, 481, 603

Potato famine (Ireland,1845–1848), 494, 552, 662

Potosí, silver mines in, 391

Pottery. *See also* Ceramics; Porcelain, Chinese; Mesopotamian, 23; Greek, 71, 104, 108 *(illus.)*, 109; Chinese, 41, 156 *(illus.)*, 161; Teotihuacan, 246; Anasazi, 254; Hohokam, 254; Wari, 259; mass production of, 434, 436 *and illus.*, 484–486

Poverty (the poor). *See also* Peasants; in Roman Empire, 136, 137; in Tang China, 287; in medieval Europe, 317, 325; American foods and, 375; in Europe, 376–377; French Revolution and, 465; of factory workers, 492; diseases of, and housing for, 490; laissez faire and, 493; nationalism and, 558; in Tsarist Russia, 561 *(illus.)*, 562; of women, 553, 725; Amerindian, 591; in China, 610; in Great Depression, 623; in India, 508, 510, 641, 647, 649; in Mexico, 641, 678; in Brazil, 659; women and, 695; world trends in, 706; in developing nations, 710

Po Zhuyi, 154, 209

Prakrits language, 125

Price controls: in Japan, 437; in Rome, 141; in Delhi, 305

Price war: Chinese opium trade, 533; Arab oil embargo (1974), 686 *and illus.*

Priestley, Joseph, 480

Priests (clergy). *See also* Bishops; Papacy; Religion(s); Mesopotamian, 15, 16, 18–19, 24; ancient Egyptian, 66–67; Celtic Druids, 51, 53, 176; Andean, 58; Assyrian, 73; Israelite, 78; Magi, in Iran, 96; Indian Brahmin, 119, 120, 123, 127, 176, 305; Greek, 106; Roman, 134; Christian, 139, 211, 212–213, 215; Japanese Christian, 437; European monks, 203, 213, 215; Kievan Russia, 216, 218; Mesoamerican, 246; Tibetan lamas, 282, 439–440; colonial Latin America, 391, 473 *(illus.)*; French Revolution and, 465, 467; fall of Communism and, 700

Primogeniture, in China, 144–145

Princip, Gavrilo, 596

Printing technology, 364, 365; in China, 236; in Korea, 239, 289, 290, 291 *(illus.)*., 433; in late medieval Europe, 330, 331 *(illus.)*; moveable type, 236, 239, 290, 291 *(illus.)*, 330; woodblock, 236, 239, 289, 290, 330, 438 *(illus.)*; Dutch, 373; Luther and, 366

Proclamation of 1763 (Great Britain), 462

Progress, 372; technology and, 614, 617, 653

Prohibition (United States), 613

Prostitution, 376, 378, 508, 536, 553, 582, 695

Protest. *See* Student protest

Protestant Reformation, 365–366, 368 *(map)*, 372, 379; Luther and, 366, 371, 379

Proxy wars, by superpowers, 682–683, 686, 690, 696. *See also* Cold War era

Prussia, 318, 322, 382, 450, 489, 548, 558, 564; French Revolution and, 467, 468, 469

Psychoanalysis, 614

Ptolemies, 114–115 *and map)*, 116–117

Pueblo Bonito, 254–255

Puerto Madero, 476–477 *and illus.*

Puerto Rico, 354, 476, 563, 591

Puja (service), 187

Punjab, 31, 124

Punt, 66, 86

Puritans (Protestant sect), 380, 381, 397

Pygmy people, 298

Pylos, 71

Pyramids: Egyptian, 27, 30, 31, 49; Maya, 247, 249 *(illus.)*; Teotihuacan, 245; Chimú, 258

Pythagoras, 370

Qianlong (China), 440, 444, 450, 453

Qin Empire (China), 45, 141–142, 143 *(map)*, 144–146, 152, 239; and Shi Huangdi, 142, 144, 145 *(illus.)*, 146

Qing Empire (China), *See also* Qing Empire, Britain and; 441 *(map)*, 457–458, 462, 532–540, 587; chronology (1644–1796), 435; Confucianism in, 442 *(illus.)*, 443, 452, 536; Emperor Kangxi, 440–443 *and illus.*, 452; rise of, 438, 439–440; European trade and, 438–439, 440, 444, 519, 533, 541; Russia and, 442, 446, 451–452, 531, 534–535, 583; missionaries in, 440, 442–443 *and illus.*, 452, 533, 534, 536, 538; chronology (1794–1860), 521; economic and social disorder in, 518, 533; decentralization at end of, 458, 539–540, 608–609; Taiping Rebellion, 535 *(map)*, 536–539

Qing Empire (China), Britain and: *See also* Hong Kong; gunboat diplomacy, 495, 534; McCartney mission, 444–445, 533; Opium War (1839–1842), 533–536, 540; Arrow War (1856–1860), 535 *(map)*, 538; Treaty of Nanking (1842), 534

Quebec, colonial, 398, 399

Quebec Act of 1774 (Britain), 462

Quetzalcoatl, 245, 251, 355

Quinine and malaria, 442, 575

"Quit India" campaign, 649, 651

Quito, colonial, 394–395

Quran, 185, 187, 193–194, 195, 301, 312

Quraysh, 182, 185

Racism (racial discrimination): in colonial Americas, 393 *(illus.)*, 394–396; in Americas, 478, 562; slavery and, 400, 471; census and, 543–544; in Philippines, 589; New Imperialism and, 573, 577; in Nazi Germany, 627; in colonial Africa, 581, 644, 646; in British India, 647; apartheid in South Africa, 678, 680–682, 731

Radio, 615, 627, 658, 728, 729

Raffles, Thomas Stamford, 511

Railroads: in Asia (1914), 588 *(map)*; in Britain, 482 *(map)*, 488, 491 *(illus.)*, 550; canal systems and, 490–491; in United

Railroads (*cont.*)
    States, 488, 562; in Egypt, 500; in Europe, 488–489; in India, 496, 508, 509 *(illus.),* 550, 588 *(map),* 593, 651, 663; in Japan, 566 *(map),* 588 *(map);* in Mexico, 653, 655 *and map;* in Russia, 530, 532, 550, 562, 588 *(map);* 593; streetcars and subways, 550, 552; environmental and, 490–491; in Latin America, 590–591 *(photo);* Manchurian, 629; World War I mobilization and, 601; in Africa, 642–643, 644; in Argentina, 591, 657; famine and, 662, 663
Rainfall: *See also* Drought. *See also* Droughts; Monsoons; in Africa, 455–456; and early agriculture, 8; tropical regions, 297
Rama, 120, 122, 125
Ramayana, 120, 125
Ramesses (Egypt), 67, 68, 72
Rashid al-Din, 278
Raw materials (resources), 549, 550, 652. *See also* Metals; Mining; *and specific raw materials;* in Mesopotamia, 17; in Egypt, 26; in Indus Valley, 33; in ancient Greece, 101, 104; world economy and, 570, 574, 592, 679; World War II and, 634, 638; of colonial Africa, 642, 646; conservation of, 709
Raziya, Sultana, 304–305
Reagan, Ronald, 692, 696, 699, 706
Rebellions (revolts): *See also under* Revolution; peasant, 377, 417; slave, 402, 460–461, 471, 472 *(illus.);* Islamic, 187, 188, 189; An Lushan (China), 229, 231; Arab (1916), 612; in Ottoman Empire, 417, 420, 520, 524; in China, 432, 518, 533, 566, 608; European peasant, 320; in Philippines, 589; Russia, 532; Sepoy (India), 507; Taiping (1850–1864), 535 *(map),* 536–539; in Romania, 701
Red Army (Soviet Union), 607, 632, 634, 672
Red Guard (China), 684
Red Sea trade, 172, 307, 310, 313, 353, 415
Reforms: *See also* Land reform; of Akhenaten, 66–67; Roman empire, 139; of Gregory VII, 212, 215; Taika, in Japan, 241; Protestant, in Europe, 365–366, 369, 372; Enlightenment, 372, 461–462; French Revolution, 467; industrialization and, 494; modernization in Egypt, 500; democratic, in Europe, 469, 560; Islamic, in West Africa, 500, 516; British India, 506; Russia, 449–450, 529, 532; Ottoman, 416, 457–458, 520, 524–527, 528 *(illus.),* 529, 597; economic, in China, 539, 540 *(illus.);* New Deal (U.S.), 623; Brazil, 659; Guatemala, 678; Mexican Revolution and, 654, 655, 656; socialist, in Chile, 692; economic, in China, 698–699; Soviet *perestroika,* 700, 701
Reign of Terror (1793–1794, France), 468
Reincarnation, 53, 119–120, 125
Religion, 614. *See also* Afterlife, belief in; Buddhism; Christianity; Confucianism; Creation myths; Cults; Gods and goddesses; Hinduism; Islam; Judaism; Priests; Sacrifice; Salvation; Shamans; Shrines; Supernatural, the; Temples; *and specific religions;* Neolithic, 11; Çatal Hüyük, 13;

Mesopotamian, 18–19; ancient Egyptian, 29–30; Olmec, 56; Chavín, 57; monotheistic, 66, 79, 139, 152; Assyrian, 73; Persian, 101; ancient Greek, 106, 108 *(illus.),* 135; Chinese (*See* Confucianism); Daoism, 44–45, 148, 224, 225, 231, 283; Silk Road trade and, 157–159 *and map;* paganism, 139; Sasanid Iran, 157, 159; Shinto, in Japan, 241; Aztec, 254; Zoroastrianism, 101, 157, 172, 184 *(illus.),* 198; scientific challenge to, 371–372; Maya, 391; Caribbean plantations, 402; Mughal, 426; Russian, 452; and nationality, 557; Heavenly Kingdom of Great Peace (China), 536–537, 538; colonial Africa, 644–645; Eastern European nationalism and, 700; secularism and, 732
Religions, in India, 118–121. *See also* Hinduism; Buddhism, 120–121, 123, 124, 312; Jainism, 120, 124, 127, 311; Vedic religion, 119–120, 121, 127
Religious conversion, 265–266; Islam, 188, 190, 191, 192, 193, 194
Religious orders, 328, 344. *See also* Jesuits
Renaissance, 325, 329, 330–331, 342, 364
Renfrew, Colin, 11
Re (sun-god), 26, 29, 30, 46
Revolutionary era (1730–1850), 460–478; abolition of slavery in, 457, 475–476; economic and social liberation in, 475–478; Enlightenment and old order, 461–462; equal rights for women and blacks, 477–478; in France, 465–468; Haitian Revolution (1789–1804), 460, 469, 471, 472 *(illus.);* in Latin America, 471–475; Napoleonic France, 468, 470 *(map);* nationalism in, 457, 469; in North America, 462–465; Conservative retrenchment in, 469
Revolution in Iran (1979), 693
Revolution of 1857 (India), 506–507
Revolution of 1905 (Russia), 562
Revolutions of 1848 (Europe), 469
Rhetoric, 111
Rhineland, 558, 606, 628
Rhodes, Cecil, 580–581
Ricci, Matteo, 372, 376, 440, 443 *(illus.)*
Rice and rice cultivation, 238, 298; domestication of, 9; in China, 40–41, 236; in Vietnam, 241, 242, 293; in North America, 397; in Japan, 434, 437; in India, 663
Richard I (the Lion-Hearted, England), 222
Rifles, 446, 549, 576 *(illus.),* 581, 602 *(illus.).* *See also* Firearms; breech-loading, 528, 575; Enfield, 507; percussion-cap, 528, 534
Rights: *See also* Human rights; Individual; Voting rights; Women's rights; and British colonialism, 507, 510; Napoleonic France, 507; and Ottoman reforms, 525
Rig Veda, 120
Rio Azul, Maya burial at, 260, 261 *(illus.)*
Rio de Janeiro, 657, 707; colonial, 400 *(illus.);* slums of, 659; Earth Summit in (1992), 726; homeless children in, 689, 706
Rivera, Diego, 655, 656 *(illus.)*
Rivers: *See also* Flooding; *and specific rivers;* early civilizations and, 28; shifts in the

courses of, 51; of sub-Saharan Africa, 222, 223
River Valley civilizations, 1, 5, 12 *(map),* 91. *See also* Egypt, ancient; Indus Valley civilization; Mesopotamia
Rizal, José, 589
Roads, 91; in ancient Egypt, 31; in Persian Empire, 99; in Roman Empire, 139, 145, 151; in imperial China, 143, 145, 149, 151; Industrial Revolution and, 485, 490; in Japan, 293, 434; in China, 533; Inca, 256 *(map),* 260–261, 355; in Russia, 530; automobile and, 616–617
Robot technology, 708, 722
Rock art, in Sahara, 4, 165–166 *and illus.,* 168. *See also* Cave paintings
Romance of the Three Kingdoms, 289
Roman Empire (27 B.C.E.– 476 C.E.), 132 *(map),* 208. *See also* Greco-Roman traditions; *and individual emperors;* Celts and, 51, 52, 53, 135; Christianity and, 138–139; chronology, 153; economy, 140, 141; Germanic peoples and, 138, 139, 150; Han China compared to, 130, 142, 145, 150–152; Principate in, 136, 152; slavery in, 136, 137; technology, 139–140; third century crisis in, 139; trade, 137, 140; trans-Saharan trade and, 167, 168; as urban empire, 136–138; water engineering in, 139, 140 *(illus.);* decline and collapse of, 139–141, 167
Romania, 133, 527, 597, 672, 720; democracy in, 714; overthrow of Ceausescu in, 701
Romanization, 137–138. *See also* Greco-Roman tradition
Roman law, 203, 213, 222
Romanov, Mikhail, 447
Romanov dynasty (Russia), 447, 541
Roman Republic (507 B.C.E.–31 C.E.), 133–136; Carthage and, 85; chronology, 133; expansion of, 135; failure of, 136, 152; government of, 131; slavery in, 133; society, 133–134
Rome (city), 151, 260. *See also* Papacy; founding of, 131; expansion of, 135; grain imported by, 137; Renaissance buildings in, 331
Romulus, 131
Roosevelt, Franklin D., 623, 637, 668
Roosevelt, Theodore, 563, 592
Rosetta Stone, 27
Rousseau, Jean-Jacques, 461, 464
Roy, Arundhati, 730
Roy, Rammohun, 509
Royal African Company (RAC), 403, 405, 406
Royal Botanic Gardens (Kew), 593
Royal trade monopoly, 345, 349, 403
Rubber, 586, 587 *(illus.),* 593, 623, 657, 659; synthetic, 635
Ruhr district (Germany), 490, 549, 552, 607
Rural societies (rural areas). *See also* Farmers; Peasants; Villages; in Roman Empire, 137; in tropical Africa and Asia, 314; in late medieval Europe, 317–318 *and illus.,* 376; in Ottoman Empire, 417; industrialization and, 490–491

Russia: Kievan, 177, 203, 215–218, 222; chronology (1221–1505), 273–274; Mongols and, 272, 279–281

Russian Federation (former Soviet Union), 714, 717, 719, 720; life expectancy in, 705; and Soviet collapse (1991), 701–702 *and map*; and U.S. invasion of Iraq (2003), 718

Russian language, 452, 531, 561

Russian Orthodox Church, 218, 222, 280, 449, 450, 531, 532; Byzantium and, 177, 206, 216, 281; Siberian missions of, 447, 452

Russian Revolutions (1914–1918), 604–605; women and family values in, 624–626

Russia (Russian Empire), 445–453, 458, 540, 570, 613. *See also* Russian Federation; Serfs, in Russia; Soviet Union (USSR); British India and, 531, 560; society and politics, 446–447, 449; war with Sweden (1680–1701), 382, 447, 450; chronology (1547–1799), 435; Crimean War and, 527–529, 531; cultural trends, 531–532; emigration from, 562, 583; Europe and, 411, 519, 529–531, 541; expansion of, 445–446, 448 *(map)*, 525 *(map)*; forest resources of, 375; as great power, 558, 560–562; industrialization in, 529, 530, 561–562; Napoleon's invasion of, 468, 529, 530 *(illus.)*, 541, 663; Ottoman Empire and, 412, 449, 469, 520, 524, 529, 531; chronology (1801–1861), 521; Peter the Great and westernization of, 449–450 *and illus.*, 453, 527, 532; Qing China and, 442, 446, 451–452, 531, 534–535, 583; railroads in, 530, 532, 550, 562, 588 *(map)*, 593; Central Asia and, 531, 583, 588 *(map)*; Balkans and, 529, 561, 597; double Revolution in, 604–605; civil war in, 606–607, 663; World War I and, 597, 600, 601, 604, 617

Russo-Japanese War (1904–1905), 562, 566, 587, 597

Rwanda, Hutu-Tutsi genocide in, 716–717

Saarinen, Eero, 615

Sacrifice, 59; Celtic, 51; Chinese, 42, 79; Kushite, 68; animal, 18, 19, 106, 144; child, in Carthage, 85; Greek, 106, 108 *(illus.)*; Vedic, 120; Roman, 134; Mesoamerican, 245, 248, 251, 254, 355; Hopewell, 255; Andean, 258, 261, 262

Sadat, Anwar, 683

Safavid Empire (Iran), 415 *(map)*, 420–424, 446; chronology (1502–1747), 413; economic crisis and collapse of, 424; Isfahan and Istanbul compared, 421–424; Ottomans and, 416, 417; Shi'ite Islam in, 419, 421

Sahara region, 297. *See also* Trans-Saharan trade and caravan routes; agriculture in, 8; animal domestication in, 89; climate change in, 8, 10, 26, 169; early cultures of, 42; pastoralism in, 10, 165, 298; rock art in, 165–166 *and illus.*, 168

Sahel region, 167, 189

Sailing (seafaring): *See also* Navigation; Ships and shipbuilding; Indian Ocean trade and, 213–215

St. Domingue. *See* Haiti (St. Domingue)

St. Peter's Basilica (Rome), 365

St. Petersburg, 450, 530, 561 *(illus.)*

Saint George of the Mine (Elmina), 349, 403

Saint-Simon, Claude Henri de Rouvray, 382, 493

Sakharov, Andrei, 699–700

Saladin (Salah-al-Din), 192, 222

Salt trade, 167, 189, 308

Salvation: Zoroastrianism and, 101; Buddhism and, 120, 236, 285; Christianity and, 204

Samanid dynasty (Iran), 189, 191

Samarkand, 232, 277, 278; observatory in, 279; and Silk Road, 154, 156

Samarra, 188

Samori Toure, 581

Samuel (Israel), 78

Samurai warriors, 241, 433, 437, 438, 564

Sandanistas (Nicaragua), 692–693, 696

Sanger, Margaret, 613

Sanitation: and disease, 228, 237, 575; and sewerage, 490, 508–509, 552, 615

San Lorenzo, 55

Sanskrit language, 119, 120, 125, 266

Santos-Dumont, Alberto, 658

São Tomé, 345, 349, 350, 392

Saqqara, pyramid at, 27

Sardinia, 80, 81 *(map)*, 84, 135, 527

Sargon, 16

Sasanid Empire (Iran), 156–157, 181, 184 *(illus.)*; Islam and, 186, 187

Satellites, 674, 728

Sati (widow burning), 127, 313, 509, 573, 647

Satraps (Persian Empire), 99

Saudi Arabia, 696, 702–703, 717, 723; oil wealth of, 685 *(map)*, 686; women in, 725

Savanna (grasslands), 167, 168

Savannah (steamship), 488

Scandanavia, 208, 209, 219, 366, 375, 731. *See also* Denmark; Finland; Norway; Sweden; Vikings

Schism, 121, 204, 333

Schlieman, Heinrich, 70

Scholars, Islamic (ulama), 191, 193 *(illus.)*, 194, 198–199

Scholasticism, in Europe, 329

Schools. *See also* Education; Literacy; Islamic madrasas, 199, 250, 328; Islamic, in Africa, 301, 312; in European cities, 378; women and, 378; in Egypt, 520; Ottoman military, 526; Islamic (Quranic), 526, 583, 645; German engineering, 549; English in, 731; in Africa, 582–583, 644–645; national culture in, 729

Schröder, Gerhard, 718

Science(s). *See also* Astronomy; Chemistry Mathematics; Technology; Mesopotamian, 23–24, 37, 39–40; Indian, 125, 190; Islamic, 195, 278–279, 284; Chinese, 224–225, 285; Korean, 290; physics, 371, 614, 637; revolution in, 370–372, 461, 614; of graphs, 484–485 *and illus.*; statistical, 542–543; and political dominance, 558; World War II, 635–637; global culture and, 731

Scotland (Scots), 53, 207, 334, 380, 382

Scribes, 1, 27, 105; Mesopotamian, 18, 22; Mycenaean Greek, 71; Mayan, 250 *(illus.)*; monastic, 213

Script: *See also* Writing (written language); ancient Egyptian, 44; Linear B (clay tablets), 70–71; Japanese syllabic, 242; Khitan, 240; Sogdian, 232, 289; Arabic, 307

Scythians, 98, 163

Second Treatise on Civil Government (Locke), 382

Security Council, United Nations, 669–670, 672, 684, 718; peacekeeping and, 669, 716

Sékou Touré, 677

Selassie, Haile, 646

Seleucids, 114, 115 *(map)*, 155, 156

Selim I, Sultan, 415

Selim II, Sultan, 418

Selim III, Sultan, 519, 520

Seljuks, 191, 192, 204, 220, 278, 282

Semites (Semitic peoples), 14, 77, 85, 99; in Egypt, 65–66; languages, 14–15, 16, 22, 28, 76; religion and deities of, 15, 18, 182

Senate: Carthaginian, 84, 85; Roman, 131, 133, 136

Senegal, 190, 579, 644, 645, 646

Sennacherib, palace of, 74 *(illus.)*

Separate spheres, for men and women, 553, 556–557 *and illus.. See also* Gender differences

Sepoys (India), 504; rebellion of, 506–507

September 11 (2001) terrorist attacks, 712–714 *and photo*, 718

Serbia, 281–282, 412–413, 601; Ottoman Empire and, 520, 527, 597; independence of, 520, 527, 540, 596; NATO bombing of, 716

Serbian Orthodox Church, 520, 527, 716

Serfs (serfdom), 209, 320; in Russia, 446, 447, 449, 452; freeing of, 458, 531, 532, 562

Seth, 29, 170

Seven Years War (1756–1763), 399, 461, 505

Sexuality. *See also* Prostitution; bisexuality in Greece, 112–113; male homosexuality in Islam, 198, 423; monastic celibacy, 213; rape and sexual abuse, 553, 696; and AIDS crisis, 724 *and illus.*; women's liberation and, 725

Shaka (Zulu), 499–500

Shamans (shamanism): Olmec, 56; in early China, 45; Korean, 239; Mongol, 271, 276

Shamash, 18, 23 *(illus.)*

Shandong (China), 539

Shanghai, 535, 538, 608 *(photo)*, 630

Shang period (China), 38, 40 *(map)*, 41–43, 58, 141; divination in, 42 *and illus.*; monarchy and administration in, 41–42

Shar'ia. *See* Islamic law (Shar'ia)

Shawabtis, 30, 48

Sheba, Israelite trade with, 78, 310

Shifting (swidden) cultivation, 8, 246, 298

Shi Huangdi (China), 142, 144, 146; tomb of, 145 *(illus.)*

Shi'ite Islam, 187, 190, 276, 415 *(map)*, 419, 421, 693; Abbasid Caliphate and, 186, 188; Assassin sect, 278; rivalry with Sunnis, 180–181, 191, 277, 310

Shinto religion, 241
Ships and shipping (merchant marine), 214.
    See also Navigation; Navy; Pirates; Sailing;
    Steamships; Egyptian, 25 (illus.), 31;
    Celtic, 51; Minoan and Mycenaean, 69
    (illus.), 71; Carthaginian, 8; Greek, 104;
    Indian Ocean, 118, 160–161 and illus., 306;
    lateen sails, 160, 308, 343, 347; Viking, 208;
    Chinese junks, 228, 234, 307, 340, 343, 344
    (illus.); Indian dhows, 307, 308 and illus.,
    353; Italian, 322; Polynesian, 338, 341
    (illus.); Portuguese caravels, 343, 344
    (illus.), 353; Dutch, 373; European, 422;
    slave trade, 404–405, 503; Argentine, 476–
    477 and illus., 657; British, 510, 511, 512,
    560; Japanese, 634, 683; whaling, 514–515
    and illus.; Korean, 697, 698 (illus.)
Shiva, 121, 122 and illus.
Shoguns (Japanese warriors), 291, 434, 563
Shona people, 581
Shrines: Neolithic, 13; Muslim, 182, 184,
    199; in Spain, 220
Shudra class (India), 119
Siberia, 446; Orthodox missionaries in, 447,
    452
Sicily, 80, 81 (map), 328, 634; Rome and, 135,
    137; Normans in, 208, 220
Siddhartha Gautama. See Buddha
Siege weapons and tactics, 23, 139. See also
    Fortifications; Weapons and military
    technology; Mesopotamian, 23; Assyrian,
    73–74; Macedonian, 113; catapults, 113,
    134, 143, 274, 288, 291; Kitan, 233; Mon-
    gol, 274, 288, 291
Sierra Leone, 345, 503, 514, 582
Sijilmasa, 189, 220, 221
Sikhism (Sikhs), 507
Silk Road: chronology (247 B.C.E.–400 C.E.),
    157; impact of, 159; imperial China and,
    143 (map), 146, 149, 154; India and, 127;
    origins and operations, 155–156; Sasanid
    Empire and, 156–157; Mongol diversion
    of, 192, 271
Silk (silk industry and trade): in China, 41,
    149, 228, 229, 275; Chinese, 439; Japanese,
    565 (illus.); Safavid Iran, 424
Silla (Korea), 226 (map), 239
Silver, 25, 34; Anatolian, 64, 68; British in
    China, 444, 533; as medium of exchange,
    17, 75, 97; Celtic, 52 (illus.); coinage, 187,
    219; from colonial Americas, 258, 356, 383,
    391–392, 404, 416, 424, 439, 527, 656
    (illus.); Sasanid Iran, 157, 184 (illus.); and
    inflation, 383, 416, 424, 439
Sinai Peninsula, 684, 685 (map)
Sind, 186
Sin (deity), 18, 36
Singapore, 511, 533, 593; independence of,
    675; Japanese in, 634; economy of, 697,
    732
Sinhalese, in Sri Lanka, 299, 717
Sino-Japanese War (1894–1895), 565, 589
Sino-Japanese War (1937–1945), 630
Sioux people, 399, 408
Sirius (star), 31
Sirius (steamship), 488, 489 (illus.)

Sky gods, 11, 18, 106
Skyscrapers, 615
Slave rebellions, 402, 460–461, 471, 472
    (illus.)
Slave soldiery, 188, 192, 313, 387, 424. See
    also Janissaries
Slaves (slavery). See also Abolitionists; Slaves
    (slavery), African; in Mesopotamia, 17; in
    ancient Egypt, 29; in Assyria, 73; in Israel,
    78; in Carthage, 84; in Roman Republic
    and Empire, 133, 136, 137; in China, 41,
    145, 313; Islamic, 188, 195, 196–197, 198; in
    Greece, 106, 109, 112; Indian Shudras, 119;
    in medieval Europe, 203; Mongol, 271; in
    Delhi sultanate, 312–313; in Arabia, 309–
    310; and serfdom compared, 447, 449; on
    sugar plantations, 392, 399–402, 492, 514;
    freedom for, 510 (See also Abolitionists)
Slaves (slavery), African, 313, 344, 345, 349–
    352; in Brazil, 392, 400 and illus., 657;
    freedom for, 402, 503, 584; in Haiti, 469,
    471, 472 (illus.); in Latin America, 388,
    395; in North America, 397, 398; punish-
    ment for, 402, 405; runaway, 393, 402–403;
    on sugar plantations, 392, 399–402; US
    Constitution and, 465, 476
Slave trade, African, 502 (map); Portuguese
    and, 344, 350, 351–352, 405; Europe and,
    375; sugar plantations and, 392, 400; in
    colonial Americas, 375, 393; disease and
    death in, 402, 405; Dutch and, 401, 405;
    Atlantic system, 403, 404–407; Middle
    Passage, 404–405; prisoners of war, 400,
    406, 407; Eastern Africa, 429; Islam and,
    500, 504; Great Britain and, 476, 503, 504;
    Sokoto Caliphate and, 500; trans-Saharan,
    502 (map); end of, 475, 476, 492, 503, 504,
    584
Slavic languages, 215, 216, 280
Slavophiles, 531, 532, 562
Slavs (Slavic peoples), 204, 412, 531, 561,
    597, 627. See also specific countries; and
    Christianity, 177, 206, 211, 222, 281
Slessor, Mary, 573
Slovakia, 701 (map), 702
Slovenia, 702
Small pox, 224, 276, 405, 644; Amerindians
    and, 355 and illus., 356, 387
Smith, Adam, 493
Smoking Squirrel, 244, 249
Social classes (social stratification). See also
    Jati (Indian castes); specific class; Meso-
    potamia, 17–18; China, 44, 45, 46; Egypt,
    28–29; Celt, 51–52; Chavín, 58; Persia, 96;
    Athens, 109; Rome, 137; Africa, 168–169;
    imperial China, 237, 283; Islam, 312–313;
    Europe (1500–1730), 372–378; colonial
    Americas, 388, 392–393, 397; slave planta-
    tion, 401–402; pre-revolutionary France,
    465–466; Industrial Revolution and, 482,
    492–493; and gender, in industrial world,
    553, 613–614; Mexican, 652–653
Social Contract, The (Rousseau), 461
Social Darwinism, 558
Socialism, 552–553, 560, 604, 669; in Chile,
    692; utopian, 493–494

Society (societal conditions). See also Social
    classes; and specific societies; Stone Age, 6;
    Mesopotamian, 17–18; Celtic, 51–52; Islam
    and, 184; Byzantine Empire, 204–205;
    Kievan Russia, 215; in tropical Islamic
    Empires, 311–314; black death and, 318,
    320; in industrialized nations, 550, 552–
    557; labor movements, 552–553; Nazi
    Germany, 628; socialism and, 553; popula-
    tion and migrations, 552, 586; in colonial
    Africa, 642, 644; in Argentina, 660; global
    inequality, 690; Victorian women, 553,
    556–557
Socrates, 107, 111, 176
Sogdiana (Sogdians), 154, 209; language of,
    184 (illus.); script of, 232, 289
Soil depletion, 40, 401, 490
Sokoto Caliphate, 500
Solidarity (Polish labor union), 700, 701
Solomon (Israel), 78, 81, 310
Solon, 109
Somalia (Somalis), 161, 215, 298, 312
Somme, Battle of (1916), 602
Somoza, Anastasio, 692
Song Empire (China), 232–243, 234 (map),
    288; Buddhism in, 233, 236, 238, 242;
    clocks in, 233–234, 235 (illus.); economy
    and society in, 236–238, 242; industries of,
    233–235, 236; Liao and Jin challenge to,
    233, 239; science of, 224–225; Southern
    Song, 233, 234 (map), 272, 283; Vietnam
    (Annam) and, 241, 293
Songhai Empire, 313
Soninke people, 190
Sophists, 111, 176
Sophocles, 111, 112
South Africa, 550, 577, 724; Zulu of, 499–500,
    510, 511, 580, 581; Afrikaners in (Cape
    Colony), 510–511 and illus., 580, 581;
    diamond mining in, 580, 645 (illus.), 715;
    landownership in, 581; gold in, 580, 581,
    626; schools in, 644, 645, 731; African
    National Congress in, 646, 678, 715;
    democracy in, 715; racial justice in, 678,
    680–682, 731; trade agreement (SADC),
    720, 721 (map)
South America: See also Americas; Andean
    region; Latin America; and specific coun-
    tries; agriculture in, 9; European expedi-
    tions to (1420–1542), 346 (map); Iberian
    claims to, 345, 347; Spanish conquest of,
    356
South Carolina, colonial, 397
South China Sea, 31, 159, 307
Southeast Asia, 720. See also East Asia; East
    Indies; Indochina; South Asia; and specific
    countries and cultures; British colonies in,
    511; migrations to Madagascar from, 160
    (illus.), 161; pork consumption in, 170;
    navigation in, 234; China and, 285;
    chronology (1283–1500), 273–274; agri-
    culture in, 298; farming in, 300; water
    control systems in, 299–300; empires and
    maritime trade in, 304 (map); Indian
    Ocean trade and, 306, 307, 311; Islam in,
    427, 429; Chinese immigration to, 440;

New Imperialism in, 583, 586–587; Japanese conquest of, 632, 634, 636 (map); rubber in, 586, 587 (illus.), 593, 623, 657; communism threat in, 673

Southern Song Empire (China), 233, 234 (map); Mongols and, 272, 283

South Korea, 665, 672, 679, 705 (illus.), 719. See also Korea; economic growth in, 697–698 (illus.), 732

South Vietnam, 673, 675. See also Vietnam

Southwestern desert cultures, North America, 254–255

Soviet Union (Union of Soviet Socialist Republics, USSR). See also Russia; collectivization of agriculture in, 620–622; Communist Party in, 607, 620; European distrust of, 628; famine in, 622, 663; five-year plans in, 620, 622, 623; industrialization in, 545, 607, 620, 638; New Economic Policy in, 607, 622; pact with Germany (1922), 607; pact with Germany (1939), 629; in World War II, 631–632, 633 (map), 634, 635, 638; United Nations and, 669, 670

Soviet Union, Cold War era, 668–674. See also Cold War; China and, 669; Cuba and, 692; Eastern Europe and, 648, 672, 699, 700–701 (map); economy of, 670, 671–672; environmental damage in, 709, 710; Korean War, 672; perestroika policy in, 700–702; rivalry with United States in, 668, 669, 674, 679, 682–683, 690; war in Afghanistan, 693, 696, 699; break up of, 690, 702, 710, 714, 722

Soylinka, Wole, 730

Space exploration, 674

Spain, 321, 476, 670. See also under Spanish; Celtiberian culture of, 51, 53; Phoenicia and, 80, 81 (map); Carthage and, 84; Roman, 135, 140 (illus.); agriculture in, 191; Jews in, 191; Caliphate in, 186, 187, 189 (map), 190–191; Visigoths in, 207 and map; Muslims in, 198 (illus.), 207, 208; maritime exploration by, 337, 342, 343, 345–348; unification of, 334–335; Inquisition in, 371, 379; Jews expelled from, 324, 335, 373, 383; dynasties in, 380 (illus.); economic decline in, 373; Netherlands and, 373, 383; Louisiana and, 399; Asian trade, 436, 440; Napoleon's invasion of, 471, 478

Spanish-American War (1898–1899), 563, 589, 591

Spanish colonies, 354–356, 462, 578 (map). See also Latin America, colonial; Philippines, 427, 429, 440, 583

Spanish language, 558

Sparta, 107–108, 110, 112, 113, 116

Spear, Percival, 649

Spencer, Herbert, 558

Spice trade, 161, 219, 348, 427, 430; Portuguese and, 353, 354

Spinning, 323 (illus.), 486, 650 and illus. See also Textiles; Weaving; in Muslim India, 313, 314 (illus.)

Spring and Autumn Period (China), 44

Sputnik (satellite), 674

Sri Lanka (Ceylon), 117, 305, 506, 510, 593, 730; Buddhism in, 171; Sinhalese in, 299, 717

Stalin, Joseph, 607, 620, 622, 639, 684; on abortion, 625–626; Germany and, 628, 629

Stalingrad, Battle of (1942–1943), 632, 634

Stamp Act of 1765, 462

Stanley, Henry Morton, 503, 579

Starry Messenger, The (Galileo), 371

Statistics: census and, 542–543; graphmaking and, 484–485 and illus.

Steam engines, 485, 486, 487–488 and illus., 496 and illus.

Steamships, 487–488, 489 (illus.), 490, 508, 530, 550; freight costs and, 593; gunboats, 495, 534, 564, 575

Steel industry (steel weapons and tools): China, 44, 149, 235, 287, 296; conquistador, 355, 356; Japan, 287, 292, 434, 683; United States, 549; Brazil, 659; India, 648

Steppes, 167, 168, 271

Stirrups, 159, 209–210, 225

Stock exchanges, 374, 493, 720

Stock market crash (1929), 623

Stone Age, 6, 169. See also Neolithic Age

Stonehenge, 11, 13

Stone tools, 5, 6, 8, 13, 27, 246

Strasbourg, 325, 327

Strikes: in Ming China, 439; legalization of, 553; Russian Revolution, 604; fascist response to, 626; and Islamic Revolution in Iran, 693

Strogonov family, 446, 447

Stuart dynasty, 380 and illus., 381

Student protests: and apartheid in South Africa, 678; in China, 608, 609, 699; Earth Day, 687

Submarine telegraph cable, 489, 550, 575

Submarine warfare, 603, 605, 631, 634

Sub-Saharan Africa, 167–170, 719. See also Africa, tropical; and specific countries; cattle in, 9; Nubia and, 28, 45, 48, 49–50, 58; cultural characteristics of, 168–169; geography of, 167–168; iron and Bantu migrations in, 169–170, 173; European expeditions in, 500, 503; trade links to, 167, 178, 302 (map); agriculture in, 298; camels in, 221; Islam and literacy in, 178, 312; rainfall in, 455–456; European trade and, 407, 579, 580; new states in, 499–500; Islam (Muslims) in, 579, 581, 583; economic and social change, 642, 644; independence in, 642–646, 677; religious and political change in, 644–646; cities in, 707; democracy in, 715; AIDS in, 724 and illus..

Sudan, 430, 579, 581, 717; Islamic empires in, 300–301, 303 (illus.); Battle of Ondurman in, 575, 576 (illus.); famine in, 664

Suez Canal, 529, 550, 612, 628; New Imperialism and, 577, 579, 592, 593; opening of (1869), 569–570, 573 (illus.), 594; Arab-Israeli tensions and, 682

Sufism, 199, 305, 426, 429

Sugar plantations, 228, 345, 349; in Africa (São Tomé), 345, 349, 350, 392; in Barbados, 399–400; in colonial Brazil, 391, 392, 400; slave labor for, 392, 399–402; technology and environment for, 401–403; in West Indies, 399–402, 409, 462; in Cuba, 514, 591, 678; Asian laborers on, 513–516

Sugar trade, 373, 404, 407, 482

Sui Empire (China), 224, 225

Sukarno, 675, 682, 683 (illus.)

Suleiman the Magnificent, Sultan, 415

Sultans, 191, 192. See also specific sultan

Sulu Empire (Philippines), 427

Sumanguru (Mali), 301

Sumatra, 286, 311, 415, 427, 430, 583, 586

Sumerian language, 16, 22

Sumerians, 4–5, 14–15, 16, 85, 161. See also Mesopotamia; religion of, 18

Summa Theologica (Aquinas), 326, 329

Sundiata, 301

Sun-gods: Re, 26, 29, 30, 46; Aten, 66–67; Mithra, 101, 139; Aztec, 254; Inca, 355

Sunni Islam, 415 (map), 421; rivalry with Shi'ites, 180–181, 191, 277, 310

Sun Yat-sen (Sun Zhongshan), 608–609

Supernatural, belief in. See also Religion(s); Celtic, 53; Chinese, 45, 144; Mayan, 248

Superpowers, 674, 679, 687, 722. See also Cold War; Soviet Union; United States; proxy wars of, 682–683, 686, 690, 696

Surinam (Dutch Guiana), 402–403

Susa, 74, 99

Su Song, 233–234, 235 (illus.)

Swahili Coast, 307, 313, 341, 353, 429, 504; Islam in, 311, 312

Swahili language, 307, 431

Sweden (Swedes), 398, 446, 671; Varangians, 208, 215–216; war with Russia (1680–1701), 382, 447, 450; population in, 704, 705 (illus.)

Swidden (shifting) agriculture, 8, 246, 298

Syria, 192, 194, 208, 220, 519; Arab caliphate in, 186, 209; independence of, 684; Ottomans and, 412, 415, 603; Egypt and, 520, 524, 527; after World War I, 611 (map), 612

Syria-Palestine region, 22, 79, 138. See also Phoenicia; Late Bronze Age, 63–64, 66, 68, 72, 73

Tacky (slave), 402

Taft, William, 592

Tahert, 189

Tahiti, 338

Taika reforms (Japan), 241

Taiping Rebellion (1850–1864), 535 (map), 536–539

Taiwan, 440, 635; Japan and, 565, 577, 589, 629, (map); Chinese nationalists on, 684; economic growth in, 697, 698, 699, 732

Takrur (Mali), 301

Talas River, Battle of (751), 226 (map), 231, 232

Tale of Genji (Shikibu), 240, 242

Tale of the Heike, 241

Taliban (Afghanistan), 171 (illus.), 717–718

Tamil kingdoms, 125

Tang Empire (China), 177, 224, 225–232, 226 (map), 242; Buddhism and, 225–226, 229–231 and illus., 238; Central Asia and, 229, 231–232; end of, 231; integration of, 228–229; Korea and, 239; reaction and repression in, 229–231; Song Empire and, 233; transport and trade in, 227–228; Vietnam (Annam) and, 241, 242, 293; Wu Zhao as emperor, 230–231

Tanggut Empire (China), 232, 272, 283

Tanzania, 718

Tanzimat reforms (Ottoman Empire), 524–526, 528 (illus.), 529, 532

Tariffs, 495, 649. See also Trade; lowering of, 526, 529, 534; and United States, 562, 623; and European Community, 670; Japanese, 697

Tarquinus Superbus, 131

Tarragona (Spain) Roman aqueduct in, 140 (illus.)

Tasman, Abel, 430

Tasmania, 430

Tata, Jamsetji and Dorabji, 648

Taxation (taxes): in ancient Egypt, 27, 29; in Persian Empire, 99; in India, 124; in Han China, 142, 148, 152; in Roman Empire, 135, 137, 138, 140, 152; in Islamic caliphate, 187, 188, 192; in imperial China, 226, 230, 237; in Kievan Russia, 218, 281; Yuan (Mongol) China, 267, 284, 285; in Delhi sultanate, 304, 305; of English wool trade, 323; by French monarchy, 334; by Portuguese, 353, 354; peasant revolts against, 377; in France, 382, 385; in England, 380; Safavid Iran, 424; Ottoman Empire, 416, 417, 525, 526; American Revolution and, 462; French Revolution and, 465, 466; in British India, 506; on colonial trade, 575, 580; in colonial Africa, 579, 582, 603; in China, 609, 610, 630, 634

Tax farming, 277, 283, 385, 417, 431, 525

Teachers, women as, 478, 556, 573

Tea trade, 228, 404, 407, 444, 462, 482, 492, 512; in British India, 506, 507, 593; in Ceylon, 506, 593; New Imperialism and, 586, 592

Technology: See also Construction and building techniques; Engineering; Manufacturing; Science; Ships and shipping; Technology, Industrial Revolution and; Weapons and military technology; Mesopotamian, 19, 22–24; defined, 37; Indian, 31, 125; Egyptian, 66; Roman, 139; imperial China, 148–149, 287–288; medieval European, 218–219, 319; Islamic, 195; Japanese, 293; of early modern Europe, 364; colonial sugar plantation, 401; Jesuit, in China, 440, 443 and illus.; whaling, 514; global economy and (1850–1900), 549–550; British India, 647; early twentieth century, 596, 597, 614–617; New Imperialism and, 574–575; Japan, 564, 565; progress and, 614, 617, 653; Gandhi's rejection of, 650 and illus.; environmental change and, 708, 709–710; globalization and, 708–709, 722; computers, 708, 728–729

Technology, Industrial Revolution and, 482, 496. See also Railroads; chronology (1759–1851), 483; division of labor, 485; graph-making, 484–485 and illus.; iron industry, 486–487; mass production and, 484–486; mechanization in cotton industry, 486, 496, 508; steam engine, 487–488; telegraph, 489

Tehuacán Valley, Mexico, agriculture in, 9

Telegraph, 508, 603, 653, 658; submarine, 489, 550, 575

Television, 727, 728, 729

Temples: Mesopotamian, 15, 16, 17, 18–19; in Jerusalem, 78, 81; Egyptian, 66, 67 (illus.); Greek, 109, 111; Indian, 122 (illus.), 123, 127, 306 (illus.), 311; Japanese, 241; Buddhist, 160 (illus.); Mesoamerican, 247, 248; Inca, 262

Ten Commandments, 77

Tenochtitlan, 252, 253, 262, 355

Teotihuacan, 245–246, 250, 251

Terror: in Assyrian Empire, 74; in Stalinist Russia, 622; Palestinian Arab, 686, 723; in Latin America, 692; September 11 (2001) attacks, 712–714; Bin Laden and, 713, 717–718; United States' war on (2001–), 718, 727, 732

Teutonic Knights, 281, 318

Téwodros II (Ethiopia), 500

Texas, 408, 486

Textiles (textile industry). See also Cotton; Silk; Wool trade; African, 301; Chavín, 57, 82 (illus.), 83; Gujarati, 310; Mycenaean Greek, 71; Tang China, 227; Dutch, 373; Indian, 404; power looms, 486, 492, 565; African trade and, 404, 406, 499, 512; as women's work, 82–83, 258, 262, 376, 477, 492, 564, 565 (illus.), 630; British, 483, 530; late medieval Europe, 322, 323–324 and illus.; Russian, 530; Japanese, 564, 609

Thailand (Siam), 196, 311, 511, 634, 719

Thatcher, Margaret, 693

Theater-state, Gupta Empire as, 125–126

Thebes (Egypt), 27, 29, 49, 145; in Late Bronze Age, 66, 67, 74, 85

Theology, 329, 366. See also Religion

Thera, paintings from, 69 (illus.)

Theravada Buddhism, 121, 171, 185, 226

Thermopylae, Battle at, 138

Thesmophoria festival, 112, 142

Third Dynasty of Ur, 16

Third Estate (France), 465, 466

Third Reich, 628. See also Nazi Germany

Third World. See Developing nations; Nonindustrial world; and specific countries

Thirty Years War (1618–1648), 382

Thomas à Becket, 212–213

Thomas Aquinas, 317, 326, 329

Thrace, 98

Three-field system, 317–318

Thucydides, 108

Tiamat, 13–14, 20–21

Tiananmen Square massacre (1989), 699

Tibet (Tibetans), 228, 229, 232, 535; Buddhism in, 282, 439–440

Tiglathpileser (Assyria), 73

Tigris-Euphrates Valley, 5, 14, 34. See also Mesopotamia

Tigris River, 5, 29, 34

Tikal, 244; Great Plaza at, 249 (illus.)

Timbuktu, 301, 312

Timekeeping. See Calendars; Clocks

Timur, Il-khan (Tamerlane), 277, 278, 282, 305

Timurids, 277, 278, 282

Tin, 17, 84; for bronze, 2, 23, 32, 42–43, 62, 68, 71; Celtic trade in, 51–52

Tipu, Sultan, 498, 505, 510

Tiwanaku, 258–259

Tlaloc, 254

Tlatelolco, 252, 253

Tobacco, 354, 406, 586, 591; in Caribbean, 399, 400; in colonial Americas, 373, 397, 408 (illus.); in Middle East, 417, 422 (illus.)

Tokugawa Ieyasu, 434

Tokugawa shogunate (Japan), 434–438, 451, 452, 564; porcelain in, 434, 436 and illus..

Tokyo (Edo), 434, 437; population growth in, 552, 564, 707; bombing of (World War II), 634, 637

Toledo, Spain, 191, 328, 334

Tombs: See also Burials (burial practices); in ancient Egypt, 26–27, 29, 30, 66, 67 (illus.); Nubian, 48 (illus.); Mycenaean, 70; in Persepolis, 100; in ancient China, 42, 144, 145 (illus.)

Topiltzin, 251

Tordesillas, Treaty of (1494), 346 (map), 347–348, 429

Totalitarianism, in ancient China, 144, 145 (illus.) See also Authoritarianism

Toussaint L'Ouverture, François, 460, 471

Toyota Motor Company, 565, 697

Trade associations, 709, 714, 720, 721 (illus.)

Trade routes. See also Caravan trade and routes; Exploration (expeditions); Indian Ocean trade; Silk Road; Trade; Trans-Saharan trade and caravan routes; Aegean Sea, 62; Andean (Chavín), 57; Western Asia, 64; in Late Bronze Age, 72, 73; in India, 124, 125; Russian, 279

Trade (trading). See also Barter; Free trade; Merchants; Monopoly, Ships and shipping; Tariffs; Trade, with Africa and specific commodities; long distance, 2, 13, 92; Mesopotamian, 17, 19; ancient Egyptian, 27, 28, 66; Indus Valley civilization, 32, 33; Nubian, 37, 48, 58; early Chinese, 43; Celtic Europe, 51–52; Mesoamerican, 53, 55; Chavín, 57; Late Bronze Age, 68, 86; Minoan and Mycenaean, 69, 70, 71, 72; Assyrian Empire, 75; Israelite, 78; Phoenician, 81; Carthaginian, 84, 85; Greek, 106; Indian, 124, 125; Roman Empire, 137, 140; Han Chinese, 149; Islamic, 195; spice, 161, 219, 353, 354; Russian, 216, 218; Teotihuacan, 246; Aztec, 253; Northern Amerindian, 255; Andean, 259, 261; Mongol, 272, 274–275, 294; Chinese, 228–229, 283, 289; Islam and, 312; Japanese, 293; medieval Europe, 322–324; Italian cities, 342;

Dutch, 373–374; Anglo-Dutch rivalry in, 383; colonial Americas, 388, 397, 398–399, 462; English with Iran, 411; Ottoman, 417; European with Japan, 434, 436, 437; Russian expansion of, 450; Mughal India, 425; Industrial Revolution and, 481, 483; laissez faire and, 493; British Empire, 482, 495, 511–512; colonial, 575; British India, 506, 507–508; industrialized nations, 495, 512, 519, 660; Opium War and, 533–536; in tropical products, 550, 592; Great Depression and, 623; European with Latin America, 658; Japanese, 697; global, 623, 718; regional associations, 709, 714, 720, 721 *(map)*; e-commerce, 729

Trade (trading), with Africa. See also Gold (gold trade); Palm oil; Slave trade, African: ivory trade, 349 *(illus.)*, 429, 504, 512; West African, 348–349; Sub-Saharan with Europe, 407, 579, 580; legitimate trade, 503; nineteenth century, 502 *(map)*

Trade (trading) networks. See Atlantic trading system; Indian Ocean trade

Trading companies: See also specific companies; British, in Africa, 579; European, in China, 440, 444; European, in India, 504

Trading monopolies. See Monopoly, trading

Traditions. See also Folk cultures; Greco-Roman traditions; great and small, 168, 173, 200; in British India, 506, 507, 509; Mexican, 653

Trajan (Rome), 133

Transnational corporations, 695, 709, 729–730

Transportation. See also Aircraft; Automobiles; Canals; Railroads; Roads; Ships and shipping; llamas for, in Andean region, 57; in Late Bronze Age, 68; in imperial China, 228; Industrial Revolution and, 482, 487–489, 490–491; in Russia, 530; streetcars and subways, 550, 552; global economy and, 593; and famine, 662; twentieth century, 706, 708

Trans-Saharan trade and caravan routes, 298, 301; chronology (500 B.C.E.–300 C.E.), 157; early cultures and, 165–167; salt trade, 167, 189; sub-Saharan Africa and, 164 *(map)*, 167, 178

Trans-Siberian Railway, 588 *(map)*, 593

Transvaal, 581, 645 *(illus.)*

Travel (travelers). See also Exploration; Pilgrimages; Roads; Ships and shipping; Trade routes; Transportation; by Egyptians, 48; in Persian Empire, 99; African, 296 (See also Ibn Battuta, Muhammad ibn Abdullah); to and in China, 209 *(illus.)*, 310; Marco Polo, 233, 275 *(map)*, 282, 308, 310, 322; Silk Road, 209, 211–212; spread of Buddhism and, 191, 225

Treaty ports, in China, 534, 535–536, 565, 608, 609. See also Hong Kong; Macao; Shanghai

Trench warfare, World War I, 602 *(illus.)*

Trent, Council of (1545), 366, 369

Tres Zapotes (Olmec center), 55

Tributary systems: Persian Empire, 123; Gupta India, 125; Chinese, 173–174, 226 *(map)*, 228, 242, 286, 293, 433; Aztec, 252, 253, 254, 262, 263, 355; Mongol, 271, 274

Trinidad, 510, 515, 730–731

Trinidad (ship), 337

Triremes (ships), 110

Tropical forests, 167, 297, 300, 512; clearing of, 593, 646, 659, 666

Tropics (tropical lands and peoples), 297–314. See also Africa, tropical; Sub-Saharan Africa; South Asia; Southeast Asia; *and specific countries;* Maya and, 246; architecture, learning and religion in, 311–312; environment of, 297–298; gender distinctions in, 312–314; human ecosystems in, 298; and Indian Ocean trade, 306–311; Islamic empires in, 300–306; mineral resources in, 300; social and cultural change (1200–1500), 311–314; water systems in, 299–300; exports of, 550, 592; botany of, 593

Trotsky, Leon, 607

Troy (Anatolia), 71–72

Truce of God, 220

Truman, Harry S, 668

Truman Doctrine (1947), 672

Trung sisters, 242

Tsar, 281, 446. See also specific tsar

Tuareg people, 166, 298, 301

Tudor dynasty (England), 380 *(illus.)*

Tughril Beg, 191

Tula, 251

Tunisia, 186, 219. See also Carthage; Islamic caliphate, in 190, 191, 198

Turkey, 672, 715–716, 718. See also Anatolia; Ottoman Empire; rise of modern, 610–612 *and map;* women's rights in, 612, 613, European Union and, 720

Turkic (Turkish) peoples, 215, 284. See also Mamluks; Mamluk Sultanate; Uzbeks; Xiongnu, 150; and Silk Road, 159; Central Asian, 412, 424, 447; Crimean, 446; iron-working by, 272; Keraits, 270; Seljuks, 191, 192, 204, 220, 278, 282; and Tang China, 225, 231–232; Uighurs, 229, 231, 240, 278; in Delhi sultanate, 303, 305

Tutankhamun (Egypt), 67

Tutu, Desmond, 681–682

Twenty-One Demands (Japan), 609

Tyler, Wat, 320

Tyre, 61, 74, 78, 80, 81; purple dyes of, 83, 204

Ugarit, 65, 68, 72

Uighurs, 229, 231, 240, 278

Ukraine, 447, 607, 631, 714; Mongols and, 279, 280

Ulama (Islamic scholars), 191, 193, 194, 198–199

Ulloa, Antonio de, 394

Ulugh Beg, 278–279

Umma (Islam), 184–186, 188, 191, 198, 199

Ummayad caliphate, 186, 187, 189 *(map)*, 190–191

Union of South Africa, 581. See also South Africa

Union of Soviet Socialist Republics (USSR). *See* Soviet Union

United Fruit Company, 678

United Nations (UN), 731, 732; Arab-Israeli conflict and, 684; Charter of, 669, 679; Cold War and, 668, 669–670; General Assembly, 669, 670, 723; human rights declarations of, 665, 723, 725; Millennium Summit (2000), 722; Persian Gulf War and, 703; Security Council, 669–670, 672, 684, 716, 718; peacekeeping efforts of, 669–670, 672, 716, 717; weapons inspection in Iraq, 717, 718

United Provinces of the Río de la Plata, 472

USS Cole (destroyer), 718

United States. *See also* American Revolution; United States, Cold War era; United States, Industrial Revolution in; slavery debate in, 475, 503; civil war (1861–1865) in, 475–476, 500, 529; abolition of slavery in, 476; racism in, 478, 538; Qing China and, 538, 539; technology and development in, 550, 560; male suffrage in, 553; chronology (1865–1899), 551; women's rights in, 477, 557, 613; steel production in, 549; census in, 543; as great power, 562–563, 565, 567; immigrants and English in, 558; national parks in, 563; Mexico and, 563, 592; imperialism of, 570, 574, 588 *(map)*, 594; Hawaii and Philippines and, 587, 589; war with Spain (1898–1899), 563, 589, 591; Central America and Caribbean and, 590, 591–592, 692; World War I and, 603, 605, 606, 607; technology in, 612; automobiles in, 613, 616–617 *and illus.;* filmmaking in, 615; isolationism in, after World War I, 617, 628; Great Depression in, 623; Japanese and, 629, 630, 632, 634; in World War II, 634, 635, 636–637 *and illus.,* 638; Latin America and, 659, 672; Mexico and, 655 *(map)* 656; manufactured goods of, 657; Philippine independence and, 675, 676 *(map)*; low savings rate in, 698; Persian Gulf War (1990–1991), 702–703, 717; wealth inequality in, 706; environmental awareness in, 709; Hispanics in, 708; invasion of Iraq by, 717–718; economic growth in, 720; Serbia and, 716; war on terrorism of, 718, 727, 732; Muslim militancy and, 723; and NAFTA, 720, 721 *(map)*; English language in, 730; cultural imperialism of, 726, 727–728, 729

United States, Cold War era (1946–1991), 668–674; economic growth in, 670; Japan and, 673, 697; Korean War and, 672–673, 674; monetary policy, 670; nuclear arms race, 674; rivalry with Soviet Union, 668, 669, 674, 679, 690, 710; United Nations and, 669, 672; Vietnam War and, 673–674; oil crisis (1974), 686; China and, 684, 698–699; interventions in Latin America, 678–679, 690, 692–693, 696; Iranian Revolution and, 693, 696

United States, Industrial Revolution in (1760–1851): cotton industry in, 486, 490, 492; steamships in, 487; telegraph in, 489;

United States (cont.)
railroads in, 488, 550, 562; rural areas in, 490; manufacturing innovation, 487
Universal Declaration of Human Rights, 723–724
Universities and colleges, 148, 328–329; in British India, 510; in Japan, 564; in Russia, 532; statistical science and, 542; women in, 556; Iranian Revolution and, 693; English in, 731
Upanishads, 120, 121, 509
Ur, Third Dynasty of, 16
Urartu, 73, 85, 86, 96
Urban II, Pope, 220
Urbanization: See also Cities and towns; Migration, rural-to-urban; in Mesopotamia, 17; in Indus Valley, 32, 33; Olmec, 56; Islamic, 194–195; industrialization and, 481, 552, 556; in Ottoman Empire, 528–529
Urdu language, 312, 426
Uriburu, José, 659
Uruguay, 408, 477, 720, 721 (map)
Uruk, 4, 16
Usuman dan Fodio, 500
Uthman, 185
Utilitarianism, 493
Utopian socialism, 493–494
Uzbeks (Uzbekistan), 424, 531, 728

Vaishya class (India), 119, 126
Vallon Pont-d'Arc, France, cave paintings, 7
Valois dynasty, 379, 380 (illus.)
Van Eyck, Jan, 330
Varangians (Swedes), 208, 215–216
Vargas, Getulio, 658–659
Varna system, in India, 119, 341
Vassals and lords, 209, 210–211, 212, 331
Vatican library, 330. See also Papacy (popes)
Vatsyayana, 194
Vedas, 119
Vedic Age (India), 118–120
Vedic religion (Vedism), 119–120, 121, 127
Venezuela, independence of, 471–472
Venice, 219, 322, 324, 354, 415; Muslim alliance with, 342; printing in, 330
Verdun, Battle of (1916), 602
Verdun, Treaty of (843), 208
Versailles, Treaty of (1919), 606, 628
Versailles Palace, 381 (illus.), 382, 466, 548
Vespucci, Amerigo, 346 (map), 347
Victoria (England), 507, 553
Victorian Age, 553, 556–557, 614
Victoria (ship), 337
Vienna, 379, 415; Congress of (1814), 469
Vietnam (Annam), 238, 511, 535, 538, 587, 675; China and, 226 (map), 241–242, 293; Chu nom writing on, 274, 285, 289, 293; Mongol attack on, 274, 285, 289, 293; rice in, 241, 242
Vietnam War, 665, 673–674, 703
Vikings, 208, 209, 341–342, 359
Villa, Francisco "Pancho," 654, 655 (map)
Villages: Neolithic, 11, 13; Mesopotamian, 15; ancient Egyptian, 26, 28; medieval Europe, 209; Chinese industry in, 284

Vinland, 208, 342
Virginia, colonial, 396–397, 399
Vishnu, 121–122, 125
Visigoths, 207, 250, 251 (map)
Vjayanagar Empire (India), 304 (map), 305
Vladimir I (Russia), 216
Volga River, 215, 216
Volta, Alessandro, 489
Voltaire, 372, 444, 461–462
Voting rights (suffrage), 494; Europe, 469, 553; for Blacks, 478; Amerindian, 543; British colonies, 513, 647–648; Germany, 553, 560; Mexico, 654; for women, 513, 573, 607, 612, 613, 683; Argentina, 658

Wac-Chanil-Ahau, 244, 249
Walesa, Lech, 701
Wales (Welsh), 207, 333, 412; Celts in, 52, 53
Wang Ziyuan, 158–159
Warfare. See also Civil wars; Cold War; Guerrilla wars; World Wars; Mesopotamia, 16; Carthage, 85; among Greek city-states, 113; civil, 136, 180, 185, 262; Roman Republic and, 135; in imperial China, 225, 232; in medieval Europe, 209–210; Maya, 248; Tibetans and, 232; Aztec and Toltec, 251, 252 and illus.; Mongol invasion of Japan, 273, 274, 290–292 and illus., 294; in late medieval Europe, 382, 383, 403, 450; prisoners of, as slaves, 400, 406, 407; Napoleonic, 470 (map); disease and, 538, 605; Islamic jihad, 500, 581; modernization of, 528; Russo-Japanese, 562, 566, 587, 597; in South Africa, 581; Spanish-American (1898), 563, 589, 591; trench, World War I, 601–602 and illus.; Nazi Blitzkrieg, 631; famine and, 603, 663; French-Algerian, 677; India-Pakistan, 675; superpower proxy wars, 682–683, 686, 690, 696; Falkland Islands, 693; in Middle East, 684–686, 696, 702–703, 717; Nicaraguan, 692, 696; Soviet, in Afghanistan, 693, 696, 699, 700
Wari, 258, 259
War of the Spanish Succession (1681–1694), 382
War on Terrorism (2001–), 718, 727, 732
Warring States Period (China), 40 (map), 44, 141, 145, 148
Warrior class. See also Knights; early Chinese, 41; Celtic, 51, 58; Iranian, 96, 157; Indian Kshatriyas, 119, 120; Indian rajputs, 425; Japanese, 241, 291, 433, 434, 437, 438, 451, 563–564; Aztec, 252 and illus.; Moche burials, 258, 260, 261 (illus.); Ottoman (See Janissaries); Russian Cossacks, 412, 447; Russian (druzhina), 215, 216; Vikings, 208, 209, 341–342, 359
Warsaw Pact, 672, 674. See also Iron Curtain; collapse of, 699, 700–701 and map, 710
Wars of Religion (1562–1598), 379, 381
Washington, George, 464
Water control systems. See also Dams; Irrigation; Chinese, 142, 146–147 and illus.; Roman, 139, 140 (illus.), 146;

Mesoamerican, 248 and illus., 253; Moche, 257; French, 322 (illus.)
Water Margin, 289
Watermills: in China, 149; in France, 321, 322 (illus.); in late medieval Europe, 320–321, 324
Water wheels, for Chinese clock, 233–234, 235 (illus.)
Watt, James, 480, 485, 487, 488
Wavell, Lord (Archibald Percival), 663
Wealth: Industrial Revolution, 481; concentration of, 553; global inequality in, 690, 706; redistribution of, 678, 690, 692
Wealth of Nations, The (Smith), 493
Weapons and military technology: See also Bombs and bombing; Bows and arrows; Cannon; Firearms; Fortifications; Nuclear arms; Rifles; Siege weapons; Warfare; Mesopotamian, 23; early China, 42, 43, 58; Assyrian, 73–74; chariots as, 23, 43, 66, 159; imperial China, 149, 225, 235, 287, 288, 340; body armor, 210, 221 (illus.), 225, 232, 235, 331, 333, 354, 356; stirrups, 159, 209–210, 225; explosives, 235, 287, 288, 292; gunpowder, 235, 287, 288, 290, 294, 333, 343; Korean, 360; Mongol, 274, 288, 291; early modern Europe, 382; gunpowder, 412, 451, 534, 575; Iberian conquistador, 354, 355, 356; Ottoman, 413, 415, 416, 526; Zulu, 499 (illus.); industry and, 548; Russian, 449, 450, 530; transition to modern warfare, 528; for whale hunting, 514; New Imperialism and, 575, 576 (illus.); Qing China, 534, 537 (illus.), 538; steel swords, 287, 292, 355, 356; Ethiopian, 500, 581; machine guns, 575, 576 (illus.), 581, 601, 602 and illus.; hand grenades, 602 (illus.); poison gas, 602, 638, 717; Soviet industry, 622; World War I, 602, 638; World War II, 628, 631, 635–637, 639; Cold War, 669, 674, 699; United States' arms trade, 682, 692, 693; Persian Gulf War, 703
Weapons of mass destruction, 717–718. See also Nuclear arms (nuclear weapons)
Weather. See Climate and weather; Rainfall
Weaving (textiles). See also Spinning; Textiles; Chavín, 57, 82 (illus.), 83; Chinese, 287; in medieval Europe, 211, 322, 323 (illus.); in Muslim India, 313; Navajo, 408; industrialization and, 486, 496, 508, 527, 565; women and, 82, 83, 211, 258, 323 (illus.)
Webb, James L. A., Jr., 455
Weber, Max, 601
Wedgwood, Josiah, 480, 484–486
Wehrmacht (Nazi German army), 628, 629, 631–632, 634, 638
Wei River Valley, 43, 141, 144, 147
Weizmann, Chaim, 604, 606
West Africa, 169. See also Mali and specific country; agriculture in, 9, 20, 300; Carthaginians in, 84; gold in, 189, 190, 300, 303 (illus.); Europe and, 348–352; Islam in, 301–302 and map, 303, 500, 516; slave trade and, 406, 503; vegetable oil

trade in, 503, 512, 516; new states in, 500, 502 *(map)*; sanitation and disease in, 575; New Imperialism and, 579–580; independence of, 677; mission schools in, 644; urban growth in, 707; ECOWAS trade agreement, 720, 721 *(map)*

Western Asia: *See also* Middle East; in Late Bronze Age, 63–65; Tang China and, 228

Western Europe, 451. *See also* Europe; *and specific countries;* telegraph in, 489; deforestation in, 490; domination of, 495, 519; economic growth in, 550, 670–671; Marshall Plan for, 670; NATO and, 669; arms race and, 674; aging population in, 705

Westernization (Western culture): *See also* Industrialization; Modernization; in Russia, 449–451, 453, 532; in West Africa, 503; in British India, 506, 510; in Turkey, 610 *(illus.)*, 612; industrialization and, 731–732

Western Zhou era (China), 43

West Germany, 670, 672. *See also* Germany; reunification and, 701 *(map)*

West India Company, Dutch, 374, 400, 403, 405

West Indies. *See* Caribbean region (West Indies)

Whaling, 513, 514–515 *and illus.*

Wheat, 40, 167, 208, 298, 375, 407, 495, 552, 657, 662; domestication of, 8, 9 *(illus.)*, 13

Wheatstone, Charles, 489

Whistler, James McNeill, 530

White Horde (khanate), 279

White Lotus Rebellion (1794–1804), 533

Whitney, Eli, 486

Wichelle, Treaty of (1889), 581

Wilhelm I (Germany), 548, 558, 560

Wilhelm II (Germany), 560, 605

Williams, Eric, 400

William the Conqueror, 208, 211

William the Pious, 215

Wilson, Woodrow, 592, 605; League of Nations and, 606, 610; Mexico and, 654

Witch-hunts, 365, 369–370 *and illus.*, 372

Women. *See also* Birth control; Family; Gender differences; Marriage; Men; Polygamy; Women's rights; Ice Age, 6; Neolithic Age, 8, 13; in Mesopotamia, 18; in ancient Egypt, 29, 34; in early China, 45; Nubian royalty, 49, 50; and fertility cults, 17, 52, 106, 122, 144; Celtic, 52; Minoan, 70; in ancient Israel, 78–79; textile production and, 82–83; in Persian Empire, 100; in ancient Greece, 112; Confucianism and, 144; Indian, 120, 127; Roman, 134; and Indian Ocean trade, 165; matrilineal societies, 11, 50, 249; inheritance and, 29, 191, 195, 237; Byzantine, 204, 206; footbinding in China and, 238, 239 *(illus.)*; European nobility, 210 *(illus.)*, 211; in Islam, 18, 195–198 *and illus.*, 266; as slaves, 196–197; as nuns, 127, 213, 230; as shamans, in Japan, 239; in imperial China, 229 *(illus.)*, 230–231, 237–238, 239 *(illus.)*;

Maya, 249; Vietnamese, 242, 293; Anasazi, 255; Andean, 257; Mongol, 271; textile production by, 258, 262; Delhi sultanate (India), 304–305; in late medieval Europe, 317, 318 *and illus.*, 324; spinning by, 313, 314 *(illus.)*; colonial Latin America, 393 *(illus.)*, 400 *(illus.)*; European families and, 377–378; prostitutes, 376, 378; slave, 402; as Acheh rulers, 429; witches, 369–370 *and illus.*; Ottoman and Iranian compared, 422–423; Revolutionary era, 466, 468, 471; domesticity of, 493, 497; factory work, 492, 494, 497; abolitionist, 475, 478; colonial Australia, 513; education of, 378, 477–478, 539; teachers, 478, 556, 573; textile manufacture by, 376, 477, 492; British India, 508, 509, 573, 647; Ottoman, 526–527; Taiping Rebellion and, 536–537; prostitutes, 508, 536, 553; separate sphere of, 553, 556–557 *and illus.*; working-class, 492, 553, 556, 564, 565 *(illus.)*; colonialism and, 513, 573, 577; colonial Africa, 577, 582, 642; textile manufacture by, 564, 565 *(illus.)*, 609, 630; African, and Europeans, 584–586; in World Wars, 603, 613, 638; Islamic, 579, 612, 613; poverty of, 553, 725; in Great Depression, 623; in Russian Revolution, 622, 624–626; Nazi German, 638; Chinese Communism, 630; widow burning (sati), 127, 313, 509, 573, 647; Islamic, 693, 697 *(illus.)*, 725; birth control and, 704–705, 725–726; European fertility rates and, 703, 704–705; education of, 704, 725–726; feminism and, 725, 731

Women's Christian Temperance Movement, 613

Women's Convention (Beijing, 1995), 725

Women's rights, 573, 607, 723, 725–726; in Americas, 477–478; property and inheritance, 237, 293, 377, 527, 557, 582; in Britain, 556–557, 613; voting rights, 477, 513, 557, 612, 613, 683; in United States, 477, 557, 613; neo-liberalism and, 694–696; United Nations declaration on, 725

Women's Rights Convention (1848), 477

Woodblock printing, 236, 239, 330, 438 *(illus.)*

Wool trade, 91, 275; Mycenaean Greek, 71; Andean, 257, 260, 262; English, 219, 320, 322, 323, 334, 484; Navajo, 408

Worker's Party (Brazil), 714

Working class: *See also* Labor; Labor unions; China, 439; and French Revolution, 466, 468, 469; and Industrial Revolution, 481, 491–492; housing for, 490, 491 *(illus.)*; socialism and unions, 493–494, 552–553; women, 478, 492, 553, 556, 564, 565 *(illus.)*; and depressions, 550, 562–563; and Russian Revolution, 604; and automobile, 616; industrialized world, 613, 614, 615; Argentine, 659, 660; Mexican, 653

World Bank, 720

World economy. *See* Global economy

World Trade Center attack (2001), 712–714 *and illus.*

World Trade Organization (WTO), 720, 722

World War I (1914–1918), 545, 596–608. *See also specific battles and combatants;* alliances in, 597, 600 *(map)*, 601, 605, 606–607; origins of, 596–597; stalemate (1914–1917), 601–603; in Europe, 600 *(map)*; homefront and economy, 603; impact of, 605–606, 619; Indian soldiers in, 648, 651; military strategy in, 597, 601; aircraft in, 614; casualties in, 602, 603, 605, 606; Ottoman Empire and, 603–604; peace treaties after, 606; Russian Revolutions and, 604–605; Western (battle) front, 601–602 *and illus.*, 605, 606

World War II (1939–1945), 620, 631–639. *See also specific battles and combatants;* Africa and, 632, 646; aircraft in, 631, 632 *(illus.)*, 634, 636–637; alliances in, 629, 633 *(map)*, 634, 636 *(map)*, 659, 669, 670; in Asia and the Pacific, 632, 634, 636 *(map)*; bombing in, 632 *(illus.)*, 634, 635 *(illus.)*, 637; China and, 634–635; deaths in, 546, 635, 637–638; environment and homefront in, 638; in Europe and North Africa, 631–632, 633 *(map)*; Japan in, 632, 634, 635 *(illus.)*, 636–637 *and map*; science of, 635–637, 708; as war of movement, 631

World Wide Web (Internet), 719, 728–729

Worms, Concordat of (1122), 212

Wright, Frank Lloyd, 615

Wright, Orville and Wilbur, 614

Writing (written language), 92. *See also* Literature; Literacy; Scribes; Script; Indian, 32, 120; Chinese, 41, 239, 300; cuneiform, 16, 19, 22, 65, 100, 104–105; Mycenaean Linear B tablets, 70–71, 72; Phoenician, 80, 104; Greek, 104–105; hieroglyphics, 27, 49, 66, 104–105, 250; Cyrillic, 206, 216; East Asian, 239, 240 *and illus.*; Kitan, 240; Korean, 240, 290, 291 *(illus.)*; Mayan, 249, 250 *(illus.)*; Urdu, 312

Wu (China), 43, 146, 156

Wulstan, 214

Wu Sangui, 432

Wu Zhao, 230–231

Xavier, Francis, 436–437

Xenophanes, 107

Xerxes (Ahasuerus), 99, 100, 103, 110

Xhosa people, 580

Xia dynasty (China), 41

Xiongnu, 150

Yahweh, 77, 78, 79

Yamato (Japan), 241

Yams, 9, 37, 161, 168, 298

Yang Guifei, 231, 290, 292

Yangzi River, 38, 282, 534

Yangzi River Valley, 142, 144, 146, 225

Yaqui people, 653

Yazdigird III, Shah, 186

Yazid, Caliph, 186

Yellow fever, 387, 471, 472 *(illus.)*, 592

Yellow River (Huang He), 5, 38, 142; flooding of, 40 *and map*, 284, 539, 630
Yellowstone national park, 563
Yeltsin, Boris, 701–702
Yemen, 172, 173, 191, 310, 417, 718
Yi dynasty (Korea), 290, 433–434
Yin and yang concept, 45
Yohannes IV (Ethiopia), 500
Yongle (China), 285, 287
Yosef, 310
Young Ottomans (Young Turks), 529, 532, 597
Ypres, 219, 322, 323 *(illus.)*, 602 *(illus.)*
Yuan Empire (China), 282–285; Beijing as capital of, 272, 282–283, 285; cultural and scientific exchange in, 284; fall of, 284–285; Korea and, 288, 289
Yuan Shikai, 609

Yugoslavia, 672, 682; formation of, after World War I, 606; breakup of, 701 *(map)*, 702; ethnic cleansing in, 716
Yunnan, plague in, 275–276

Zaibatsu (Japanese conglomerates), 565, 609, 697
Zambesi River, 300
Zambia (Northern Rhodesia), 581
Zamorin, 310
Zamzam, 182
Zanzibar, 504
Zapata, Emiliano, 641, 654, 655 *(map)*
Zeila, 310, 313
Zen (Chan) Buddhism, 236, 290, 293
Zeng Guofan, 539
Zero, invention of, 126, 250
Zeus, 106, 135

Zhang Jian, 155–156, 160
Zhang Zeduan, 238 *(illus.)*, *(illus.)*
Zheng He, travels of, 268, 285–287 *and map*, 339, 340–341 *and map*, 344 *(illus.)*
Zhou dynasty (China), 38, 43–45, 58, 59. *See also* Warring States Period (China); Daoism and Confucianism in, 44–45; kingship in, 43
Zhu Xi, 296
Zhu Yuanzhang, 284, 285
Ziggurat, 19, 23
Zimbabwe, 224, 307–308, 309 *(illus.)*, 581, 678
Zionism, 606, 610, 612, 684. *See also* Israel
Zoroaster (Zarathrustra), 101
Zoroastrianism, 101, 157, 172, 184 *(illus.)*, 198
Zulu, 499–500 *and illus.*, 510, 511, 516, 580, 581